YALE LAW LIBRARY SERIES IN
LEGAL HISTORY AND REFERENCE

MARRIAGE
EQUALITY

FROM OUTLAWS TO IN-LAWS

William N. Eskridge Jr.
Christopher R. Riano

Yale UNIVERSITY PRESS   NEW HAVEN AND LONDON

Published with support from the Lillian Goldman Law
Library, Yale Law School.

Yale University Press books may be purchased in quantity
for educational, business, or promotional use. For
information, please e-mail sales.press@yale.edu
(U.S. office) or sales@yaleup.co.uk (U.K. office).

Set in Scala type by Westchester Publishing Services.
Printed in the United States of America.

Library of Congress Control Number: 2020935693
ISBN 978-0-300-22181-7 (hardcover: alk. paper)

A catalogue record for this book is available from the
British Library.

This paper meets the requirements of ANSI/NISO
Z39.48-1992 (Permanence of Paper).

10 9 8 7 6 5 4 3 2 1

To Elizabeth Eskridge, Lois van Beers, Ben van Eskridge,
and Mei van Eskridge
—W.N.E., Jr.

To Dr. William G. Gorman and Mrs. Edna E. Gorman,
Mr. Robert M. Riano, and Dr. Matthew M. Krumholtz
—C.R.R.

Contents

Abbreviations and Glossary of Terms

ACLU American Civil Liberties Union, a national organization with
thousands of affiliated attorneys who litigate to protect First Amendment
and other rights. Its Women's Rights Project (WRP) persuaded the
Supreme Court to treat sex as a quasi-suspect classification for equal
protection purposes. Its Lesbian and Gay Rights Project (now called the
Lesbian Gay Bisexual Transgender and HIV Project), established in 1986,
was centrally involved in the marriage debate.

ACT-UP AIDS Coalition to Unleash Power, founded in 1987 by Larry
Kramer to empower persons with AIDS to demand more responsive
health care policies from the government and private institutions.

ADF Alliance Defense Fund or (after 2012) Alliance Defending Freedom,
a national organization with thousands of affiliated attorneys who litigate
to defend religious freedom, pro-life views, and traditional family values.
Founded in 1993 by Focus on the Family and other Christian advocacy
groups.

AFA American Family Association, founded as the National Federation for
Decency in 1977 (renamed AFA in 1988) by Rev. Donald Wildmon as a
network of Christian radio stations and other media outlets.

AIDS Acquired immune deficiency syndrome, a breakdown of the body's
immune system, associated with infection by the human immunodeficiency virus (HIV).

ARLINGTON GROUP A coalition of traditional values organizations
established in 2003, with its initial goal support for the FMA.

ART Assisted reproductive technology, such as assisted insemination,
in vitro fertilization, and surrogacy.

BYU Brigham Young University, the flagship educational institution for the Church of Jesus Christ of Latter-day Saints.

CAP Center for Arizona Policy, a traditionalist political and lobbying organization in Phoenix.

CCF Campaign for California Families, founded by Randy Thomasson, to support Proposition 22 in 2000 and to head off efforts by California LGBT groups to expand the definition of marriage.

CCV Citizens for Community Values, founded in 1983 to combat pornography and other affronts to traditional morality in Cincinnati. CCV was the prime mover behind DOMA.

CFV Colorado Family Values, created in 1991 to develop and support Amendment 2 to the Colorado Constitution.

CHURCH OF JESUS CHRIST Short form for Church of Jesus Christ of Latter-day Saints. Before 2018, this church was often referred to as the *LDS Church* and its members as *Mormons,* but the Church in 2018 announced that these short forms were inconsistent with its core identification with Christ. We have sometimes used the earlier terms where our sources (including the Church itself) used them.

CLOSET Secrecy or denial about a feature core to a person's identity because one fears social disapproval. In the late 1960s, "coming out of the closet" was a term popularized by the gay community for the process of becoming open about one's sexual (and, later, gender) identity.

CWA Concerned Women for America, founded by Beverly LeHaye in 1979 to support traditional family values and pro-life policies.

DOMA Defense of Marriage Act of 1996. Section 2 authorized states to refuse to recognize out-of-state marriages between persons of the same sex. Section 3 defined *marriage* and *spouse* everywhere in federal statutory and regulatory law to exclude same-sex marriages, even if legally valid.

ENDA Employment Non-Discrimination Act, introduced as a bill in 1995 and in subsequent Congresses. If enacted, ENDA would have barred employment discrimination because of sexual orientation. In 2007, the ENDA bill was revised to include gender identity discrimination. After 2015, the LGBTQ rights movement dropped ENDA and pressed for a broader Equality Act.

ERA Equal Rights Amendment, passed by Congress and referred to the states for ratification in 1972. An effective campaign by STOP ERA prevented the ERA from securing ratification by the necessary thirty-eight states by 1982, when the (once-extended) deadline for ratification expired. Most states have passed ERA amendments to their constitutions.

EVANGELICALS Christians who hew closely to what they consider the strict lessons of Scripture and who enthusiastically share the Good News with others and with their communities. Broadly understood, Evangelicals would include most Baptists as well as Pentecostals, Mennonites, Southern Methodists, and members of the Church of God, Lutheran Church—Missouri Synod, and the Presbyterian Church in America, among others. Most independent megachurches consider themselves Evangelical. See NEA.

FMA Federal Marriage Amendment, a proposal advanced in 2002 and subsequent years to amend the US Constitution to bar same-sex marriage and to prevent courts from requiring that marital benefits be extended to unmarried couples. Starting in 2005, the proposals were called the Marriage Protection Amendment.

FRC Family Research Council, created in 1983 as a spin-off from Focus on the Family. Working out of Washington, DC, FRC engages in public education and lobbying from a conservative Christian family values perspective.

FRI Family Research Institute, located in Colorado Springs and operated by Paul Cameron, a discredited social scientist.

GAY Term used to self-identify by people attracted to persons of the same sex in the 1960s and afterward but sometimes still used as a general term for gender as well as sexual minorities, similar to *LGBTQ*.

GAYOCRACY Leaders of the political and legal movement seeking rights and benefits for LGBTQ+ persons. The gayocracy includes prominent movement lawyers and organizational officials, their academic allies, funders, and even celebrities. (Robert Raben originated this term.)

GLAAD Founded in 1985 as the Gay and Lesbian Anti-Defamation League, and soon renamed the Gay & Lesbian Alliance Against Defamation. Since 2013, GLAAD is the official name, no longer just its acronym.

GLAD Gay & Lesbian Advocates & Defenders, a Boston-based gay rights advocacy organization founded in 1979, now renamed GLBTQ Advocates & Defenders. GLAD lawyers were partners in all of the New England marriage cases as well as in subsequent challenges to DOMA.

GLF Gay Liberation Front, a radical organization created within weeks of the June 1969 Stonewall riots. Local GLFs were associated with marriage litigation in Louisville and Seattle.

H F T Hawai'i's Future Today, a coalition of Mormons, Catholics, and Evangelicals organized in 1997 to stop gay marriage in the state.

H I V Human immunodeficiency virus, which disables white blood cells needed for the body's immune system and is associated with AIDS.

H O M O S E X U A L Term popularized by nineteenth-century sexologists to identify people attracted to persons of the same sex. By the late 1960s, such persons preferred *gay,* their own term. By the 1990s, the "homosexual agenda" was a snide term used by traditionalists and considered offensive by the gay or LGBT community.

H R C Human Rights Campaign, founded by Steve Endean in 1977 as the Human Rights Campaign Fund and renamed HRC in 1984.

J U N I O R - DOMA State law or constitutional amendment barring the state from issuing or recognizing marriages between persons of the same sex. See DOMA.

J U N I O R - RFRA State law or constitutional amendment assuring religious persons (sometimes defined to include corporations) protection against government policies burdening their free exercise. See RFRA.

L A M B D A O R L A M B D A L E G A L Lambda Legal Defense and Education Fund, Inc., founded in 1973 to litigate the rights of gay people and, later, the rights of people with AIDS and transgender and intersex persons. Lambda was the key organization in challenges to consensual sodomy laws and one of several key organizations in the marriage equality campaign.

L D S The Church of Jesus Christ of Latter-day Saints. In 2018, the Church requested that this abbreviation be discontinued, as it detracted from its focus on Jesus Christ (rather than a focus on the followers).

L G B T Lesbian, gay, bisexual, transgender. Collective term for sexual and gender minorities in the 1990s and afterward.

L G B T Q Lesbian, gay, bisexual, transgender, queer. Collective term for sexual and gender minorities in the 2010s. Even more inclusive are *LGBTQ+* or *LGBTQI,* which includes *intersex.*

L G B T Q T A S K F O R C E See NGLTF.

L I B E R T Y C O U N S E L Christian values litigation organization founded in 1989 by Mathew and Anita Staver. Associated with Liberty University, founded by Rev. Jerry Falwell.

L L E G O Latino/a Lesbian & Gay Organization, founded 1987 and later renamed National Latino/a Lesbian, Gay, Bisexual, and Transgender Organization.

L M F Love Makes a Family, founded in 1999 to serve as an umbrella group to seek adoption, relationship, and marriage rights for sexual and gender minorities in Connecticut.

M C C Metropolitan Community Church, established as a gay-friendly denomination in 1968 by Rev. Troy Perry and now counting several thousand congregations across the country. In chapters 8 and 9, MCC is the Massachusetts Catholic Conference, which sought to override *Goodridge*.

M F I Massachusetts Family Institute, a traditional values organization that led the charge to override *Goodridge*.

M O R M O N S *Latter-day Saints* is now the preferred term for members of this church, but the Church itself used the term *Mormon* during most of the period covered by this volume. See Church of Jesus Christ.

M P A Marriage Protection Amendment. See FMA.

N A A C P National Association for the Advancement of Colored People. Founded in 1909 by W. E. B. DuBois, Ida Wells, and other civil rights activists, the NAACP engaged in political and legal challenges against apartheid. The NAACP contributed critically to marriage equality and was a bridge to other civil rights organizations.

N C L R National Center for Lesbian Rights. Founded in 1977 by Donna Hitchens and other lesbian activists, the Lesbian Rights Project was the first LGBTQ+ rights organization founded by women. NCLR was the key organization in the California state marriage litigation and a key organization in the national campaign for marriage equality.

N E A National Association of Evangelicals, founded in 1942 to represent Evangelical Christians. Today, its membership includes more than forty-five thousand churches across forty denominations.

N G L T F National Gay and Lesbian Task Force, founded in 1973 to provide grassroots support for lesbian and gay rights. Renamed LGBTQ Task Force in 2012. See Task Force.

N O N B I N A R Y (O R G E N D E R Q U E E R) Term describing a spectrum of gender identities that are not exclusively masculine or feminine— identities that are outside the gender binary.

P - F L A G Parents and Friends of Lesbians and Gays, founded in 1973. There are P-FLAG chapters in all fifty states.

R F R A Religious Freedom Restoration Act of 1993. RFRA was enacted by Congress to protect religious persons against undue burdens on their religious free exercise even under laws or measures of general application and not aimed at their suppression. See Junior-RFRA.

SBC Southern Baptist Convention, the largest Protestant denomination in the United States.

SJC The Massachusetts Supreme Judicial Court, its highest court, whose judgment in *Goodridge* delivered the first legal marriage licenses for same-sex couples in American history.

SOGI LAW Law prohibiting discrimination because of sexual orientation and gender identity.

SUPER-DOMA State or federal law or constitutional amendment barring the government from issuing or recognizing marriages between persons of the same sex *and* from extending marital benefits or rights to unmarried couples, almost always with a focus on same-sex couples. (Josh Friedes originated this term.)

TASK FORCE NGLTF or, today, LGBTQ Task Force. In chapter 7, *task force* refers to the Vermont Freedom to Marry Task Force.

TIP Take It to the People, founded in 2000 to demand a constitutional referendum on the gay marriage issue in Vermont.

TRANSGENDER Term used to describe a person whose gender identity does not match up with her/his/their sex assigned at birth.

TVC Traditional Values Coalition, founded in 1981 by Rev. Louis Sheldon in California to advocate Christian values in politics and law.

UCC United Church of Christ, the modern name for Congregationalists.

WRP Women's Rights Project, created in 1972 by the ACLU to focus on constitutional litigation aimed at sex-based discriminations. Ruth Bader Ginsburg led the WRP between 1972 and 1979.

Prelude · A Family Vacation

It was just missing a head-on crash that persuaded April DeBoer and Jayne Rowse to get serious about legally protecting their children. In the winter of 2011, they were on their way home from a weekend trip to Castaway Bay, an indoor water park in Sandusky, Ohio, with two-year-old Nolan and one-year-old Ryanne and Jacob in the back seats, driving their minivan down a two-lane highway. A pickup truck with a heavy trailer pulled out from the oncoming lane to pass someone. It was snowing hard and the driver did not see the oncoming minivan—and he had no time to get back into his own lane. April and Jayne just caught a glimpse of his white baseball cap, his panicked face, and the large industrial washer and dryer on his trailer as he swerved off the road at the last moment, barely missing their side mirror and coming to rest in a snowy cornfield.[1]

The two mothers were badly shaken. Back home in Hazel Park, Michigan, they came to terms with the fact that they had more at risk than most parents. If either of them died, whether through an accident or from illness—Jayne had already lost two sisters to heart disease—their children would not only suffer the loss of a parent; they might be separated from each other as well.

April and Jayne had met in 1999 but did not start dating until several years later. In 2006, when April was working in the neonatal ICU at Hutzel Women's Hospital in Detroit and Jayne was at Henry Ford Hospital, they moved in together, and then held a commitment ceremony in February 2007. April's parents, Wendy and Ken DeBoer, were pleased to attend, but Jayne's family stayed in Indiana. Although April and Jayne considered themselves married for all practical purposes, the state of Michigan did not. In 1998, the Michigan legislature had passed a law refusing to recognize same-sex marriages, and in

Jayne Rowse and April DeBoer. (Photo courtesy of Jayne
Rowse and April DeBoer.)

2004 Michigan voters amended the state constitution to bar recognition of
same-sex marriages or "similar unions."

The state did not, however, prohibit lesbians from raising children. Jayne
formally adopted their first child, Nolan, in November 2009; April adopted
Ryanne in April 2011, and Jayne adopted Jacob in October 2011. Jayne and April
rearranged their lives around the three children—all of whom needed parental attention, and one of whom, Jacob, needed a great deal of medical treatment
and therapy because of maternal drug use during his gestation. They juggled
their work schedules, including working during the night, so that at least one
mother would be home at all times. They bought a new home, a two-story
craftsman-style house in Hazel Park whose three bedrooms would accommodate the five of them comfortably, for the time being. April's mother Wendy
DeBoer signed on to do a lot of the housework and babysitting. The children
in the first years of their lives had the advantage of two parents and a grandparent who were utterly devoted to their flourishing.

But the near-accident in 2011 left Jayne and April deeply rattled. If the truck
had hit them head-on, neither mother would have survived. One or more of
the children would have been injured as well. April's Lutheran mom and dad
were supportive of her family, but Jayne's Catholic family was not: If Jayne died,
could they take Nolan and Jacob away from their surviving mother and sister?

The prospect filled the nurses with despair. Once they returned home—sticking to the interstate the rest of the way—April and Jayne resolved to call a lawyer to help them plan for potential tragedies. Searching the internet, they discovered that Dana Nessel, a lawyer in Detroit, had represented Renee Harmon, a lesbian parent denied visitation with children she had helped raise. They called Nessel immediately.[2]

Over the phone, Nessel explained that Michigan law did not allow two women to jointly adopt children. From her own experience in joint parenting with another woman, she knew how the law could make a bad breakup much worse for lesbian co-parents. April and Jayne wondered whether they could protect their family through guardianship agreements that would assure the surviving mother or grandmother (Wendy) rights to raise the children. Dana cautioned that Michigan judges might not respect such agreements. There was a real possibility that if Jayne were to die, the family might be broken up.

This news was tremendously disconcerting to the nurses. Was this the law everywhere in the United States? Not at all, Dana assured them. Many states recognized lesbian co-parenting through what is called "second-parent adoption." Indiana sanctioned second-parent adoptions, although Ohio (like Michigan) did not. Unfortunately, Jayne and April could not easily move to another state. They had excellent jobs, Jacob's therapists and doctors were local, and their individual adoptions of Ryanne and Jacob had not yet been finalized. For the time being they were stuck in Michigan, living with the knowledge that if their children lost one mother, the state could take them away from the other.

Dana Nessel had a suggestion. Why not challenge Michigan's discrimination against lesbian co-parents? Leapfrog the conservative state judges, and bring a constitutional challenge in federal court? Dana was strongly motivated to change what she considered an unjust family law regime in Michigan. She asked her colleague Carole Stanyar, an experienced trial attorney who had been married and had raised several children before coming out as a lesbian, to assist her on the case.

April DeBoer was reluctant to be a plaintiff in such a lawsuit because she was not completely out of the closet at work. She worried that if she did come out, her supervisor and maybe her coworkers would create problems for her. As lesbians who had inched out of the closet themselves, Dana and Carole understood her concerns, but Dana calmed them immediately. She had worked as a prosecutor under Mike Duggan, who in 2011 was the head of the Detroit Medical Center, which included Hutzel Women's Hospital. She called Duggan, who assured her that DeBoer's job was safe.

With the nurses on board, Dana called her old Wayne State constitutional law professor, Bob Sedler, to ask him to work on the case. Bob suggested something more ambitious. Why not challenge Michigan's exclusion of lesbian and gay couples from marriage itself? Five states were giving marriage licenses to same-sex couples, two because of state constitutional lawsuits. In 2010, a federal judge had ordered California to resume issuance of marriage licenses to same-sex couples; the order was on appeal to the liberal Ninth Circuit. That summer, New York's legislature was expected to pass a marriage equality statute. This is an exciting issue, Bob Sedler advised, and one we can win.

Not with us! the nurses answered. A marriage lawsuit would make their case about the adults, and Jayne and April adamantly wanted to keep the focus on the needs of the children. As mothers themselves, Carole and Dana understood immediately—and they were relieved not to ask for marriage, because that would require a larger investment of money, experts, and time. Representing the nurses pro bono, they were better able to handle the more limited case.

On January 23, 2012, Carole Stanyar and Dana Nessel filed a lawsuit in the United States District Court for the Eastern District of Michigan, *DeBoer and Rowse v. Snyder* (the defendant was Michigan governor Rick Snyder). The nurses and their children asked the court to require Michigan to allow lesbian partners to enjoy joint parental rights over children they were raising together. The state already allowed a heterosexual stepparent to enjoy joint rights to his or her spouse's children, they said; extend the same rights to us.

The nurses' lawsuit started a process that ended up in front of the US Supreme Court, whose judges surprised the nation and changed it forever.

1 • Coming Out of the Constitutional Closet

Every home needs closets, but the closet is a terrible place to call your home. For two generations of gay Americans, the central moment in their lives was the day they came out of the sexual closet. In the early 1970s, political activism and lawsuits began to bring gay Americans, and ultimately same-sex marriage, out of the constitutional closet.

Norman, Oklahoma, twenty miles south of Oklahoma City, serves as the site of the football-crazed University of Oklahoma and dozens of Baptist churches. Born in 1942, James Michael McConnell grew up in Norman in a classic postwar family: Mother and Daddy were married for life and raised five kids in a house with a picket fence. But Mike knew there was something different about him; he figured out early on that he was homosexual. In Norman this was nothing to brag about, but he was not ashamed of his feelings. Working as a cashier in his father's barbershop, Mike developed crushes on the engineering and ROTC students who regularly needed their crew cuts updated. When he became a student at the university, he met and fell in love with another student; their intense relationship dissolved after four years. Devastated, Mike returned to college, where he secured a degree in library science.[1]

Richard John Baker, also born in 1942, came from Chicago and was the last of ten children. By his sixth birthday he had accepted the loss of both parents and spent the rest of his childhood in a Catholic boarding school. Living in an all-boys dormitory, Jack was able to act on his early homosexual feelings. In 1965, while serving four years in the US Air Force, he completed his college degree in industrial engineering. His military career was cut short because of an advance he made to another airman as well as the discovery of homoerotic

5

Jack Baker and Michael McConnell. (Photo courtesy of the
LOOK Magazine Photograph Collection, Library of Congress,
Prints & Photographs Division.)

letters he had exchanged with other gay airmen. In 1966, Jack moved to Oklahoma City for graduate school.

Like 99 percent of America then, Oklahoma did not tolerate homosexuality. It was a felony for two men or two women to engage in sexual activity. Known homosexuals could lose their professional licenses, their jobs, and their standing in polite society. For that reason, homosexuals carried on a masquerade to pass as straight or made sure their socializing remained *in the closet*, the term that became popular in the late 1960s. Although the more flamboyant Mike McConnell was out of the closet to his family and many friends, the conventionally masculine Jack Baker wore a straight-pretending mask within his extended family, in the air force, at school, and in his workplaces.[2]

The regime of the closet fostered an underground homosexual subculture in Norman. Among its stars was McConnell, nicknamed the Masked Mother for his maternal solicitude of his many friends and his impish, campy defiance of the closet. Mike was not feeling very impish, however, after his breakup with his first serious boyfriend. To cheer him up, Mike's buddy Cruz Moreno Sanchez pestered him into attending a small barn party on Halloween 1966. Because police and neighbors were likely to close down permanent establishments catering to homosexuals, much of their socializing had to be improvised. And what better place to assemble, toss back some drinks, and find a date for the evening than a barn—a large sheltered interior on a private farm, isolated from prying neighbors and the police. That night, Mike met Jack Baker.

For Jack, it was love at first sight: the blue-eyed, animated library science student with the incandescent smile and the alluring cleft on his chin was a beautiful find. Mike recalls that Jack "stood about six feet tall, lean body, arms that rippled with muscle. His facial features could have been chiseled onto a Greek statue," reminding him of television celebrity Rick Nelson. He worried that Jack's severe crew cut and taciturn demeanor might be masking a police decoy, but "when he flashed his movie star smile at me, I forgot to breathe." That night, Mike and Jack retired to Joe Clem's house and did their part for the sexual revolution; they casually dated after that.[3]

To celebrate Jack's twenty-fifth birthday, March 10, 1967, the boys went to Oklahoma City to see a play, *Two for the Seesaw*, and then returned to Jack's apartment. There, the engineer proposed: "I think we should become lovers," which meant living together full-time. Mike said, "Okay. But I want to get married. Mother and Daddy always told me that I'm as good as anybody else. And the man that I marry had better agree. If other couples have the right to marry, so do we." Taken aback, Jack hesitated, then flashed his charismatic smile, "Well, I guess I'm going to have to figure out how we can do that, then."[4]

About the same time in 1967, Wendy Brown, a cute seventeen-year-old high school student in Grosse Pointe, Michigan, found her life changing in some of the same ways Mike and Jack's lives were changing. Through friends, she met Kenneth DeBoer, a ruggedly handsome eighteen-year-old who caught her fancy. Wendy became pregnant, and they got married during her senior year. A son was born shortly after she graduated from high school (her daughter, April, followed four years later). Any embarrassment from Wendy's premarital pregnancy was forgotten after the marriage. Mike McConnell's dream was that any social disapproval for sex between two men would also be forgotten if those two men could get married.

In September 1969, Jack enrolled as one of 275 law students at the University of Minnesota. In his class there were 253 white men, nineteen white women, two black men, and one black woman. At the end of his first semester, library research revealed that the Minnesota family code's definition of marriage was not clearly gendered: "Marriage, so far as its validity in law is concerned, is a civil contract, to which the consent of the *parties*, capable in law of contracting, is essential." The statute did not say that only an adult male and adult female could marry, and Jack reasoned that what is not explicitly prohibited is permitted. Mike was living in Kansas City, and that night Jack called him long distance (a luxury they rarely indulged) with the exciting news:

"There's no regulation in Minnesota that prohibits marriage between two consenting men. So that means we can get married. It's as simple as pie."[5]

It would turn out to be not quite so simple. But Baker and McConnell, along with lesbian and gay couples in other states, took the idea of same-sex marriage out of its constitutional closet and started the nation on a legal roller coaster that lasted almost half a century.

Coming Out of the Closet

Millions of men and women throughout American history who were attracted to persons of the same sex either denied their feelings altogether or expressed them discreetly. In the 1960s, however, this regime of the closet came under fire. The Stonewall riots in New York City in June 1969, when lesbians, gay men, and drag queens humiliated the New York City police in several nights of rioting, are considered the galvanizing moment, but Stonewall was not the first time sexual minorities fought back. One early skirmish occurred in Norman, Oklahoma.[6]

The weekend after Baker and McConnell's catalytic barn party was the occasion for the big annual social event for Norman's gay community: the All Saints' Ball. The ball was held on November 5 at the Star Brite Studios, on the university's south campus. After dancing to Martha and the Vandellas and the Mamas and the Papas, the partiers were rousted by the local police. A rowdy group of proud homosexuals protested the raid and taunted the police. Surprised and angered, the officers arrested as many as they could lay their billy clubs on. Jack went to jail and emerged an angry rebel. McConnell was impressed that his dashing Prince Charming was "one of the louder voices." "I'm sure the police never intended to turn us into crusaders or activists by raiding a harmless dance, but that was one of the lasting effects of that evening." For decades, homosexuals had meekly accepted their degraded status and cowed before police harassment—but many were now pushing back.[7]

This was a rambunctious generation, not afraid to protest forcefully and defiantly against discrimination and war. Millions of young women agreed with Betty Friedan's complaint in *The Feminine Mystique:* "I want something more than my husband and my children and my home." Increasing numbers of women wanted their own identities and opportunities to grow and fulfill their potential as human beings, independent of their families. The idea was more general: for a new generation, the proper constitutional baseline was not traditional attitudes but equal opportunities and treatment for everyone. An

emerging gay rights movement questioned the apartheid of the closet, the regime under which homosexuals were best unseen and not heard. Like
women's liberation, gay liberation was associated with the sexual revolution
of the 1960s. Baby boomers not only believed that sexual satisfaction and expression were important to human happiness and flourishing, they said so
openly and loudly. Key to these new attitudes and practices were women's
sexual, reproductive, and marital choices. The birth control pill and safer
abortion methods enabled more women to have careers and postpone marriage
and childbearing. Women's increasing independence and assertiveness inspired gay men like Baker and McConnell to be unashamed of their own unconventional sexuality. The couple, now living in Minnesota, dedicated their
recent memoir to Mike's mother, Vera McConnell, and to Jack's grandmother,
Margaret Danek.[8]

In the 1960s, Dr. Franklin Kameny and the Mattachine Society of Washington had developed a constitutional vision of homophile rights, grounded
on the maxim "Gay is Good" (not just tolerable). Discrimination against this
minority was no more defensible than discrimination against Jews and African Americans. Kameny and a handful of other brave homosexual women and
men brought gay rights out of the constitutional closet. In August 1968, Mc-
Connell and Baker drove to a homophile conference in Kansas City just to meet
Kameny. Advising them on strategy to remedy Jack's unfair treatment by the
armed forces, Kameny gave them a lesson in activism: homophobia, not homosexuality, was the problem, and the way to deal with homophobia was to confront it openly, aggressively, and loudly with the facts of gay life.[9]

People of the same sex had long lived together in close, often sexual, unions.
Jack's proposal to Mike was in that tradition—the boys would be best friends
and sexual partners for the foreseeable future—but Mike turned it into a political plan. By insisting on a marriage proposal, he was committing them to
a highly public act: coming out as a gay couple and boldly asserting that
homosexual relations could serve as the foundation of civil or even religious
marriage.[10]

McConnell's counterproposal departed from earlier homophile thinking. In
the 1950s, most homosexuals married persons of the opposite sex, and even
the few who could have imagined same-sex marriage found it a "dubious proposition." Writing in One, an early homophile magazine, the pseudonymous
E. B. Saunders cautioned in 1953 that most homosexuals would not want to
get married, because the institution, designed and well suited for straight
couples wanting to raise children, did not fit the needs of most homosexuals.

"Rebels such as we demand freedom!" By the 1960s, however, more homosexuals were open to the idea. "Marriage is not anybody's 'convention.' It is a way of living and is equally good for homosexuals and heterosexuals," wrote Randy Lloyd in a 1963 issue of *One*. He claimed that "married homophiles regard our way of life as much, much superior" to the hedonistic lifestyle others followed and that such marriages, which undermined stereotypes of homosexuals as predatory and promiscuous, were the path toward social acceptance. "It seems to me that when a society finally accepts homophiles as a minority with minority rights, it is going first of all to accept the married homophiles."[11]

Some gay men and lesbians wanted long-term committed relationships, and a few wanted to raise children as well. For many post-1969 activists, including Mike and Jack, gay liberation meant something more than equal treatment and expanded choice (such as the option to marry). It meant transformation of the status quo, not assimilation into it. Radical feminists, including many lesbian feminists, associated demands for sexual freedom and reproductive choice with resistance to the larger constraining ideology that underwrote women's unequal status.

Kate Millett's 1969 book *Sexual Politics* defended the sexual revolution and its pro-choice program in broader terms. "A sexual revolution would bring the institution of patriarchy to an end, abolishing the ideology of male supremacy and the traditional socialization by which it is upheld," meaning the insistence on well-defined gender traits and roles and the valorization of those considered masculine. Millett's argument linked women's liberation with gay liberation. Adrienne Rich went so far as to say that "compulsory heterosexuality" was foundational to patriarchy. One of the gay marriage prophets of the 1960s was Daisy De Jesus, a gregarious Puerto Rican lesbian feminist in New York City. At the Broadway Central, an East Village bar, two of her lesbian friends mused about how wonderful it would be to get married—and Daisy volunteered to officiate, right on the spot. For several years, she conducted lesbian and gay weddings in the lobby of the hotel next door. The weddings were not lawful marriages but were symbolic protests against the illegality of lesbian relationships.[12]

This feminist argument exposed several institutions to fundamental critique. Patriarchy was the parent of many features of marriage, including the coverture rules that once prevented wives from contracting or owning property in their own names, as well as the link between marriage and procreation, in which wives traditionally raised as well as bore marital children. Martha Shelley, a founder of the Gay Liberation Front (GLF) within weeks of Stone-

wall, reflected the views of many other radicals: marriage was inevitably patriarchal and therefore irrelevant to women's and gay liberation. Later, in 1974,
Daisy De Jesus helped found Salsa Soul Sisters, Third World Women, a collective for women of color seeking alternatives to traditional gender roles, including butch-femme understandings of lesbian relationships. Seeking to free
women from traditional sex roles, gender stereotypes, and shame about female
sexuality, Salsa Soul Sisters made no demand for government recognition of
lesbian relationships as marriages.[13]

Other liberated gay people were not prepared to discard marriage. Many
were religious or spiritual and felt a hunger for God-sanctioned marriage. For
example, in *Christ and the Homosexual* (1960), United Church of Christ pastor Robert Wood urged Christian churches to celebrate marriages between
committed homosexuals. A more famous pioneer was Troy Perry, a southern
Pentecostal lay minister with thick black hair that cascaded over long bushy
sideburns. His passion, eloquence, and intensity made him the perfect Evangelical pastor—until he discovered homophile pornography and started to have
sex with men. When his church discovered he was involved with a male pa-
rishioner, Perry's career as a Pentecostal preacher and his marriage to a pastor's daughter both ended. In despair, he tried to commit suicide. When he
woke up in the hospital, he believed that God had spoken to him: "'I love you,
and you are my son.' God talked to me; I didn't believe God would ever talk to
me again. I knew beyond a shadow of a doubt that I was a gay man and a homosexual, and that was okay." Because God brought him back from death's
precipice, he concluded, God must love him as a homosexual. Prayer brought
Troy Perry to the same place as Frank Kameny: Gay is Good.[14]

Unwelcome in traditional religions, Praise-the-Lord homosexuals needed to
create their own church. On October 6, 1968, Reverend Perry held the first
service of the Metropolitan Community Church (MCC) of Los Angeles. Worship
for the first few months was in the living room of his one-story white frame
house in Huntington Park. Nine friends and three visitors attended the first
service, but more worshippers showed up each subsequent week. A male Latino
couple asked Perry if he would perform their wedding ceremony. Lord yes, he
told the couple, we want to do all the things churches normally do, and that
includes weddings. In December 1968, Perry officiated at their "holy union."
California did not recognize the union, but MCC did, and they thought God did,
too. In the next four years, as MCC grew out of Perry's home and into a traditional
church building—complete with stained glass windows and an altar—the
pastor performed more than 150 lesbian and gay holy unions or weddings.[15]

In March 1970, Reverend Perry celebrated the holy union of Neva Heckman and Judith Bellew, both members of MCC. The gay press described it as the first ceremony in American history that was explicitly conceived as a step toward legal recognition of same-sex marriages. Perry describes them as "a butch-femme couple. It was obvious to me that Neva was the butch," the more masculine partner. Judy had a "baby face" and was conventionally feminine. "Neva wore a pantsuit (white blouse with blue pants) and Judy wore a white blouse and blue skirt. Besides the two of them, there was a female couple with them who acted as their witnesses. Al Gordon, the attorney, was there as well as a reporter from *The Advocate*," a gay magazine. Perry treated the occasion as a genuine wedding. "I modified the wedding ceremony from the Episcopal Church book of common prayer, and used that especially for small weddings." Gordon later filed the couple's lawsuit against the government, based upon the claim that the discrimination against them violated state statutory and constitutional law. The trial court dismissed the case without a published opinion.[16]

There was an interesting twist for half of this landmark couple. Around 1972 Neva Heckman entered the sex-change program at the Stanford University Medical Center and transitioned from female to male, taking the name Jason Heckman. Nevada, where Neva was born, changed the birth certificate to reflect the new name and sex. In the Stanford program, Neva met Gary Paul Townsend, a surgical technician who was transitioning from male to female. Gary changed his name to Tonnea Vance, but California authorities would not change his birth certificate. Jason and Tonnea fell in love; after their respective transitions, they lived together in San Jose. "We've both been raised in a very moral atmosphere," Tonnea told the local newspaper. "Even living together out of wedlock is not right to us. We are very much in love." Because Jason knew that California would not license a same-sex couple, they applied for a marriage license as a different-sex couple. Genetically, they were of different sexes; their post-transition bodies were different sexes, and their gender identification was different. But because their birth certificates indicated they were both male, the authorities would not license the couple.[17]

In short, the first lawsuit seeking marriage rights for same-sex couples was filed by a transgender person (Neva Heckman) who sought to marry a partner of the same sex (Judith Bellew) and who later sought to marry another transgender person (Tonnea Vance) who had transitioned to the opposite sex. Earlier same-sex couples had secured marriage licenses because they presented as different-sex couples, and at least some of those marriages were satisfying to both partners. Other marriages involving transgender persons were annulled because courts found them same-sex and therefore void. In 1976, a New Jersey court upheld the validity of a marriage between a postoperative male-to-female transgender person and a cisgender man. No out-of-the-closet same-sex romantic couple had exchanged public vows, with hope that they would secure open legal recognition, until Judy Bellew and Neva Heckman did it in 1970. At the time, the same issue was arising all over the country.[18]

The First Gay Marriage Celebrities

Jack Baker arrived at the University of Minnesota five months after the Heckman-Bellew wedding and three months after two former students created a group reaching out to sexual minorities, called Fight Repression of Sexual Expression (FREE). Jack was elected FREE's first president, upon an agenda of "full equality" for gay people, an agenda that made some members nervous. Unlike its founders, Jack was completely out of the closet and courted the press as a proud (and mediagenic) gay man.[19]

Armed with his marriage research, Jack urged Mike to leave Kansas City and join him in Minneapolis no later than May 1970, when they could celebrate Mike's birthday by getting married. In March, Mike received an offer to work in the cataloging department at the University of Minnesota, and his new boss assured him that his sexual orientation posed no difficulty. Mike told his parents that he planned to marry Jack; his parents wondered why he would stir the pot when their relationship was already perfect, but were acquiescent. Jack wrote each of his siblings, all but one of whom (sister Judy) ignored his letter. FREE issued a news release announcing the marriage and urging that "any relationship that promotes honesty, self-respect, mutual growth and understanding for two people and which harms no other person should be accepted by the law."[20]

On May 18, 1970, Jack and Mike dressed in white shirts, matching striped ties, and their best dark suits. In their memoirs, Mike described themselves as "mirror images of two young men with fine prospects." The couple arrived at the Hennepin County Courthouse at 3:00 p.m. accompanied by reporters, cameras, and several members of FREE. They filled out the application for a marriage license and paid the ten-dollar fee. The clerk was Minnesota-nice polite, while the office workers stared and tittered.[21]

On May 22, Hennepin County district attorney George Scott advised the clerk that Minnesota law did not authorize same-sex marriages. Several provisions of the state marriage law were gendered. For state residents, a marriage license had to be issued in the county where the woman lived, suggesting that male-male marriages were not within the statutory purview. The state marriage law prohibited incestuous marriages in terms that were gendered and also required that "the parties shall declare in the presence of [an authorized officiant] and the attending witnesses that they take each other as husband and wife." Such provisions were not a coincidence, he reasoned, since the term *marriage* itself was intrinsically gendered. "To permit two males to marry would result in an undermining and destruction of the entire legal concept of our family structure in all areas of law." Based on Scott's legal opinion, County Clerk Gerald Nelson rejected the marriage license application.[22]

"Jack and I certainly believed that our love for each other was momentous," Mike wrote, "but neither of us would have claimed the extraordinary power to destroy our society's entire family structure by merely saying 'I do.'" Jack felt that the county had flagrantly violated what he considered the clear terms of the marriage statute—but he and Mike were even more surprised when the university's board of regents voided Mike's contract, because his "personal conduct," as reported in the media, was "not consistent with the best interest of the University." One of the regents said that hiring a gay marriage advocate "would enrage ninety percent of the people in the state." The Minnesota Civil Liberties Union (MCLU) offered to represent Mike in a federal lawsuit to overturn the decision.[23]

The couple found it hard to secure legal representation for their marriage suit. Although the Minnesota Law School's legal aid clinic had been developing statutory and constitutional arguments for the case, Dean William Lockhart vetoed any further involvement by the clinic because he was asking the legislature to fund a new law school building. The national ACLU declined to get involved, but MCLU's Matt Stark helped raise money to finance the lawsuit and provided an affiliated attorney, Mike Wetherbee (who was also Baker and McConnell's housemate), to be lead counsel, working with Jack, who was still a law student. Wetherbee later became the first openly gay staff attorney at an ACLU affiliate.[24]

On October 29, 1970, Wetherbee filed a writ of mandamus in state court, seeking to require the clerk to issue a marriage license. His and Baker's supporting memorandum of November 12 argued that the marriage statute on its face allowed two adult men to marry one another and that the county's refusal denied the couple several federal constitutional rights:

• Freedom from cruel and unusual punishment protected by the Eighth Amendment;

- Fundamental rights to marry and to secure personal privacy, retained by the people under the Ninth Amendment and affirmatively protected by the due process clause of the Fourteenth Amendment; and
- Equality rights not to be discriminated against based upon gender, an arbitrary classification under the Fourteenth Amendment's equal protection clause.

The Eighth Amendment argument was not well-founded in constitutional doctrine, but the Fourteenth Amendment arguments would be accepted by dozens of federal judges almost half a century later. Wetherbee and Baker relied on *Loving v. Virginia* (1967), in which the US Supreme Court had invalidated laws barring interracial marriages, both because they used a race-based classification to entrench white supremacy (a denial of equal protection) and because they deprived different-race couples of their fundamental right to marry without good justification (an unlawful denial of liberty). They argued that Minnesota was using a gender-based classification to entrench heterosexual supremacy (a violation of equal protection) and was denying the couple the same fundamental right to marry that Virginia denied the Lovings (an unlawful denial of liberty). Although Wetherbee was an inexperienced lawyer and Baker still a law student, their November 12 memorandum was an insightful statement of constitutional principle. Its gender discrimination claim was especially prescient: the US Supreme Court would not strike down a sex-based classification on constitutional grounds until 1971.[25]

On November 18, 1970, Judge Stanley Kane rejected the statutory arguments, agreeing with the county that marriage between two men was inconsistent with "the entire legal concept of our family structure in all areas of law." He dismissed the constitutional arguments because Wetherbee had not notified the Minnesota attorney general, as required by statute, and for that reason the judge refused to hear five expert witnesses who had been assembled to testify about the facts of homosexuality and about religious, policy, and moral arguments supporting civil marriage for gay and lesbian couples. The young lawyers filed a new petition on December 10, arguing that the county was denying them their fundamental right to marry and was discriminating against them on the basis of two illegitimate classifications, sex and (a new claim) sexual orientation. In an opinion issued January 11, 1971, Judge Tom Bergin found no constitutional problem with the county's position. Wetherbee immediately filed an appeal to the Minnesota Supreme Court.[26]

On the heels of the legal setbacks came a public relations coup. Two weeks after Judge Bergin's decision, *LOOK* magazine published a special issue titled *The American Family,* including an article on "The Homosexual Couple," Jack and Mike, whose cover photo charmed the nation and opened this chapter. The men, looking over their left shoulders at the camera, seem as though they have been interrupted during a quiet moment together outdoors. Their smiles are relaxed and inviting—not the faces of radical bomb-throwers but the boys next door, familiar and nonthreatening. Indeed, *LOOK* depicted Jack and Mike as a normal churchgoing married couple: they had organized their house together, with handmade furniture and an office for Jack; they socialized on weekends and went to dances at the student union; and they attended Catholic mass every Sunday at the university's Newman Chapel. The article closed with a sermon describing Christ's openness to all of God's children. In front of the congregation, Jack asked the priest whether Christ would be open to a loving, committed same-sex couple. "The priest hesitated a long moment and finally answered: 'Yes, in my opinion Christ would be open.'" With a circulation of 6.5 million, *LOOK* gave gay marriage huge exposure and made Baker and McConnell national celebrities. In April, Baker became the first openly gay person in American history to be elected president of a university student body.[27]

On September 21, 1971, Wetherbee argued their case before the Minnesota Supreme Court. Asking not a single question, the judges were an impassive stone wall. Justice L. Fallon Kelly swiveled his seat so that he literally turned his back on counsel. The court unanimously rejected the statutory and constitutional claims in a brusque opinion that traced marriage back to Adam and Eve. Even though it contained some gender-neutral language, the court ruled, the occasional gendered references in the marriage law showed that legislators did not intend to change the traditional definition of marriage. Nor did this statutory rule conflict with the Fourteenth Amendment. Marriage as a fundamental right rested upon procreation and the special biological bonds it created among husband, wife, and child. Nor did the state exclusion violate equal protection. Unless the state was deploying a suspect classification like race, it was allowed a great deal of leeway to draw lines that were not perfectly symmetrical with the core policy justifications.[28]

As deflating as these setbacks were, the couple was determined to press their case to the US Supreme Court. On February 11, 1972, Wetherbee and MCLU filed a jurisdictional statement supporting an appeal of right to the nation's highest court. Their central claim was that the state was denying two gay men a fundamental right to marry, with all the legal rights and duties associated with it, for reasons that were arbitrary, whether that reason was the sex of the partners or their sexual orientation. The appellants (Baker and McConnell) challenged the state to explain why all the benefits and duties of marriage were routinely extended to childless different-sex couples but not to same-sex couples, some of whom were raising children from prior different-sex relationships or marriages. "There is nothing in the nature of single-sex marriages that precludes procreation [or adoption] and child rearing." Religion-based morality was not a sufficient justification for the exclusion. It was thus a core violation of both the due process clause and the equal protection clause of the Fourteenth Amendment, much like the different-race marriage bans overturned in *Loving.* As in *Loving,* the two constitutional doctrines "tend to merge."[29]

Hennepin County responded that states have wide discretion in structuring their family law regimes: "What we are confronted with in this case . . . must be considered an attack upon the very foundation itself of the institution of marriage and family as we know it today and as it has been since the beginning of recorded history." In October 1972, the justices unanimously voted to dismiss the Baker and McConnell appeal "for want of a substantial federal question," which meant that not a single justice believed there was a significant or plausible claim under the Fourteenth Amendment. As a disposition on the federal constitutional merits, *Baker v. Nelson* was binding on all American judges.[30]

Marriage Lawsuits in Kentucky, Wisconsin, and Washington

Despite the disappointing results at every stage of *Baker v. Nelson,* Reverend Perry and other MCC ministers kept performing holy union and marriage ceremonies, and other couples kept filing right-to-marry lawsuits. The first major same-sex marriage lawsuit was actually brought by publicity-seeking attorneys on behalf of two lesbians they recruited for the case in Kentucky. Other suits followed. They all failed.

MARJORIE JONES AND TRACY KNIGHT

After talking with Jack Baker about his marriage license application, Stuart Lyon and David Kaplan, lawyers in Louisville, Kentucky, wanted to beat him to the courthouse. In the cloistered world of the Louisville bar, they were considered oddballs: loud Yankees who represented unconventional clients. One of Kaplan's clients was Marjorie Jones, who agreed to help him and the community by applying with the woman she was in love with, Tracy Knight. (Both names are pseudonyms.)[31]

Thirty-nine-year-old Margie Jones was a churchgoing blonde with a bouffant hairdo. She had been married twice and had three children—a nineteen-year-old son serving in the marine corps, an eighteen-year-old daughter, and a fifteen-year-old son living with her. Her second husband, a race car driver, beat her and forced her to have sex with a woman; after these experiences, Margie figured out that heterosexual marriage was not for her. When the husband landed in jail for raping a girl, she divorced him and fled to Louisville. There, she settled into the lesbian community and opened up a series of businesses, most prominently the L-A-M Reducing Salon. Located in a fringe section of the city, the salon offered diet advice, hairstyling, massages, and perhaps erotic services. At a gay club called the Downtowner, Jones met Tracy Knight, who performed in drag on weekends as Elvis Presley and Tom Jones. A sandal-wearing hippie, Tracy was then in her early twenties. On the evenings when she was not working as a male impersonator, she was a go-go dancer and server at a local nightclub. She also worked in some capacity at Jones's salon.[32]

Jones and Knight were intense lovers. Although Jones described Knight as "flighty," historian Catherine Fosl thinks they were a committed couple, with a streak of social activism. "We [asked for marriage] to help get a gay liberation movement started," Jones recalled, and "to make people begin to realize that we are human beings the same as [they] are." Indeed, the Minnesota couple's well-publicized application inspired them; "we couldn't let the boys get ahead of us." Knight was a fighter, and even the less feisty Jones was determined to stir things up. This most unconventional couple certainly caused a commotion when they applied for a marriage license. "I saw the clerks literally drop their pens and go into shock," one observer recalled. "Snickers, gasps, and guffaws sounded from the crowd of more conventional brides- and grooms-to-be." An old-fashioned southerner, County Clerk James Hallahan politely accepted the application and submitted it to the thirty-one-year-old Jefferson County attorney, J. Bruce Miller, for a legal evaluation.[33]

Miller and his assistant Boyce Martin (later a federal appellate judge) were educated at the toniest colleges and law schools in the region—Miller at Vanderbilt for college and law school, Martin at Davidson for college and Virginia for law school. They saw themselves as representing the postapartheid New South. In their report to Hallahan, they wrote that marriage exclusion was not discrimination because homosexual unions were grounded on sexual activities that were "against public policy and contrary to nature." The Jones-Knight household offered nothing but "the pure pursuit of hedonistic and sexual pleasure."[34]

On July 9, 1970, the day after Miller delivered his opinion, thirteen lesbians and seven gay men met in Lynn Pfuhl's apartment to form the Louisville Gay Liberation Front. Like FREE in Minnesota, this group was formed to urge gay people to come out of their closets and to challenge prejudices and stereotypes. Gay is good; what was bad was stigmatizing decent people. The next day, Jones and Knight filed suit—more than three months ahead of Baker and McConnell. Unlike the Minnesota plaintiffs, the Kentucky plaintiffs and their counsel could not attract the support of the Kentucky Civil Liberties Union, whose attorneys feared that "any lawyer who takes [the case] is going to be suspected of being queer." Like Baker and McConnell, the Kentucky plaintiffs argued that denying marriage licenses to same-sex couples violated both their constitutional right to marry and the equal protection of the laws. In the autumn, while awaiting trial, Jones and Knight had a private marriage ceremony at The Living Room, an underground gay bar in Lexington, attended by friends, other GLF members, and Jones's supportive family.[35]

Shortly after their wedding, a Kentucky court oversaw the nation's first gay marriage trial. The presiding officer was Jefferson County judge Lyndon Schmid, a traditionalist who a few years earlier had terminated a white mother's parental rights because she married a black man. (In light of his own reading of the Bible and the Constitution, he found *Loving* irrelevant.) Schmid started the day by expelling Tracy Knight from the courtroom because he found her attire, a beige silk pantsuit, "offensive to the court. She is a woman, and she will dress as a woman." When Knight returned wearing a green dress, the judge expressed interest in her shapely legs. Before starting the two-hour evidentiary hearing, Schmid called the lawyers to the bench. "He looked down at us," recalls Miller, and asked, "Which of the two is the he-she, and which one's the she-she?" Miller recalls he "literally broke out laughing. I couldn't believe a judge was saying this."[36]

Plaintiffs' counsel called four witnesses. The first was an anthropologist, Ed Segal, who testified that woman-woman marriage was common in Africa. Judge Schmid dismissed this (accurate) statement as irrelevant to an understanding of American marriage traditions. Sandor Klein, a psychologist, testified that Jones and Knight were mentally normal women who simply did not feel heterosexual attraction to men. Jones recalls telling Klein in her evaluation interview "that I just had had enough with men and abuse and I just didn't want any more abuse and I never got that with a woman. And I said I just had

had enough of it, and he says, 'Well, I can understand that,' because I told him about getting hit in the head by my husband with a tripod."[37]

Knight testified that marriage would give her emotional and financial security, and Jones testified that it would provide a better household for her children. The ebullient Knight was much more expansive in her testimony, partly because Jones was cowed by Miller's statements to the press that he intended to take away her children. Miller's view was that "they can do whatever they want to do, but to drag a couple of kids into it is outrageous. I mean, I could accept the fact that they were doing what they were doing, [but] they ought to not involve children, and I remember that really set me off. I remember I blew my gasket about that." Frightened that she might lose her family, Jones briefly sent her two younger kids to stay with friends.[38]

On February 19, 1971, Judge Schmid dismissed the complaint and summarily rejected the statutory and constitutional claims, writing: "There is no reason why we should condone and abet a spirit of what is accepted as perverted lust." Two-and-one-half years later, the Kentucky court of appeals affirmed the ruling. Citing several dictionary definitions of *marriage*, the court found that Jones and Knight were "prevented from marrying, not by the statutes of Kentucky or the refusal of the Jefferson County Clerk to issue them a license, but rather by their own incapability of entering into a marriage as that term is defined." With a perfunctory reference to *Baker v. Nelson*, the court opined that "no constitutional issue is involved."[39]

DONNA BURKETT AND MANONIA EVANS

The first marriage lawsuit in federal court was brought by an African American lesbian couple. Donna Burkett and Manonia Evans met at The Castaways, a gay bar in Milwaukee, Wisconsin. There was instant chemistry. *Jet* magazine described Donna: "Although her facial features are sharp and rugged, the harshness of her manner gives way in conversation to the demureness of a woman." Born in 1946, Donna had known she was attracted to girls since the age of eight or nine. She had been on her own since she was sixteen, graduating from high school, working in a series of blue-collar jobs, and serving in the army. "I joined the Army to see the world, but they fooled me: I got to see Alabama," where she was appalled by the "out and out blatant" racism. As quickly as possible, she returned to Milwaukee, where she became involved in the Gay People's Union (GPU), which was trying to do for gays what the NAACP was doing for blacks.[40]

Born in 1950 and then attending the University of Wisconsin, Manonia was taller, thinner, and smashingly attractive. *Jet* considered her the more feminine partner: she had softer features, brilliant white teeth and a warm smile, and an ambitious beehive hairstyle. While Donna liked to wear slacks, men's shirts, a jacket, and a porkpie hat, Manonia preferred fashionable, well-cut dresses. She attracted a lot of male attention, including a marriage proposal, but was more interested in activism. As a university student, Manonia protested unfair treatment of women and people of color, and she joined Donna at GPU meetings.[41]

Donna describes her family as "down to earth," while Manonia's family were "higher echelon people." Manonia's father, Dr. Charles Evans, was for half a century the pastor of the Midwest Church of Christ in Milwaukee; he was also an important figure in local politics. Manonia suggested, in the summer of 1971, that she and Donna get married. Encouraged by discussions with GPU colleagues, their decision to get married was as much political as personal. Donna believed that the government had "no business telling me who I could marry and who I could not marry. I thought their business was trying to run the country, not trying to run me. Not my personal life." Manonia believed that "adults should be allowed to do what they want so long as it was not hurting anyone else."[42]

As they steeled themselves for the big step of applying for a marriage license, each woman felt her family needed to know beforehand. "Once you state your case, people just have to accept you or not," Donna said. Family members were not surprised that she was a lesbian, as she had always been a "blue jeans and undershirts" kind of girl and had not dated boys. But they were quite surprised that Donna wanted to marry another woman. Out of maternal loyalty, her mom showed immediate support; her aunts and grandmother disapproved. In contrast, the Evans family could not believe that Manonia was a lesbian, and everyone was hostile to the marriage plan. According to Donna, Dr. Evans took Manonia back to his house and locked her in a room for a week. Although Mrs. Evans took pity and released her daughter, she also strongly disapproved and refused to speak with her. Manonia's three sisters were "barely tolerant" of the idea, and her brother, away at college, was not told about it.[43]

On October 1, 1971, Burkett and Evans applied for a marriage license. They were an attractive match in their large sunglasses and complementing black-and-white outfits. Milwaukee county clerk Thomas Zablocki refused even to accept their application. Through their thirty-one-year-old attorney, James Wood, the women filed a class action lawsuit in the US District Court for the

Eastern District of Wisconsin, seeking a judicial declaration that the county's refusal to issue licenses to same-sex couples violated the Fourteenth Amendment. "The law should protect us and help us the way it does any two straight people who love each other and want to live together," Burkett said. "That's our civil rights."[44]

On Christmas Day 1971, with their lawsuit pending, Burkett and Evans were married in a ceremony at Jefferson Hall officiated by the Reverend Joseph Feldhausen, a gay Russian Orthodox priest presiding over the mostly gay congregation of Milwaukee's St. Nicholas Church. The 250 friends and family members attending the service included most of Burkett's extended family but no one from Evans's side. Burkett wore a black Edwardian tuxedo; Evans wore a white floor-length gown with lace sleeves, a flowered scalloped cap, and an extended train. But district judge Myron Gordon dismissed the couple's lawsuit after their attorney failed to submit a brief responding to Zablocki's motion to dismiss the case. The couple did not know about the hearing and learned the fate of their case by reading about it in the newspaper.[45]

The relationship did not long survive the lawsuit. "I didn't have a problem with my family," Donna explained. "Not at all. Not until we decided to get married and then the stuff was in the paper. Her family were the ones who really came between us." According to Donna, Dr. Evans said "he'd rather his daughter marry a drug dealer, a dope head, a drunk, a wife beater, anybody but another woman." Manonia says she left the relationship on her own in 1972. A few years later, her father presided over her wedding to Robert Horn, with whom she had two sons and a daughter. They divorced in 1981. For the last three decades, Manonia has been happily married to Tyrone Nathan Glass. She enjoyed a career as a resource and budget manager for the Veterans Administration and other agencies, during which she strenuously objected to the lower wages paid to women. Today, she is retired and working on an advanced degree.[46]

JOHN SINGER/FAYGELE BEN MIRIAM AND PAUL BARWICK

Like other cities in the 1970s, Seattle saw hip young gays establish activist organizations emphasizing gay pride and open confrontation against discriminatory practices and institutions. Two activists, companions in a gay commune, were the community's representatives in challenging traditional marriage.

John Singer (1944–2000) was an anti-war, pro–civil rights activist who drove from his native New York to Seattle in a van proudly displaying stickers announcing "Gay Power" and "Faggots Against Fascism." His friends described him as "acute, intelligent, acrid, sometimes rabid, decidedly and markedly pro-feminist, and angry. Pissed off." Singer helped establish Seattle's Gay Liberation Front and organized its first gay pride weekend. In 1972, he changed his name to Faygele ben Miriam; the new name combined an anti-gay slur (faygele or fag) with a last name that identified him with his mother, a radical feminist who had been quick to accept him as a gay man. Singer's best buddy in the collective was Paul Barwick (born 1946), a burly former military police officer who was inching out of the closet; he was the manager of Seattle's first Gay Community Center. Inspired by a visit to the state by Baker and McConnell, activists were persuaded that they should stir things up by demanding marriage recognition in King County. Singer and Barwick felt secure enough in their jobs to serve as the test plaintiffs, although they were casual sexual partners and not a committed couple. Indeed, they believed that marital monogamy was an "oppressive institution."[47]

Accompanied by others in the gay community as well as a press battery, on September 21, 1971, Barwick and Singer went to the office of the King County auditor and asked for a marriage license application. "Singer wore a pin-striped suit and tie; Barwick, a fitted t-shirt with the word 'GAY' emblazoned across the front." The office could not accept their application, even though they met the age and other requirements set forth in the new marriage law. County auditor Lloyd Hara felt the law excluded same-sex couples—an interpretation that pained him. "As a person of color, I've always been concerned about discrimination against anyone," he recalled years later. "I thought it was wrong then and I still firmly feel the same way." The couple were happy to file a lawsuit. After the Washington Civil Liberties Union declined, Robert Welden, a gay lawyer, brought the case to his progressive rights-protecting law firm, where openly straight Michael Withey represented the couple. Ironically, Christopher Bayley, who defended the statute, was a reform prosecutor who was a closeted homosexual.[48]

Withey and his colleagues made most of the same arguments that had been made in the earlier cases, including claims that the gender-neutral marriage law already included same-sex couples and that their exclusion violated federal and state constitutional rights to marriage and equal protection. They emphasized the sex discrimination argument, because the Washington Constitution included an ERA explicitly barring discrimination because of sex.

The lawyers also argued that, like sex and gender, sexual orientation should be a suspect classification, because the disadvantaged class (homosexuals) were politically powerless and subject to pervasive discrimination based upon myths and stereotypes grounded upon their more-or-less immutable trait. King County Superior Court judge Frank Roberts summarily rejected these arguments and dismissed the case on August 9, 1972.[49]

Michael Withey's "Brandeis brief" on appeal is a landmark in the history of the marriage debate. Bringing to bear a wealth of social science and historical information (in the tradition of Louis Brandeis), Withey explained why homosexual marriages were not destructive of society (as the county assumed) but instead fit snugly with the purposes of civil marriage. Under Washington law, marriage was a matter of choice: two people who wanted to commit to one another for life could get married, and the state would support their relationship. There was no requirement that the couple have children, and sterile or elderly couples got married in the state every day. Conversely, gay people could adopt children in Washington: Why not allow them to form a committed household, for the benefit of the kids? Withey linked the plaintiffs' claim that denying same-sex couples marriage licenses was sex discrimination with King County's morality argument. Why were gay people so disparaged? "A fixation on gender has created the concept that men *must* act differently from women." As a social convention, gender roles varied from person to person and did not always correlate with biological sex. The irrationality of this form of sex discrimination was illustrated by the widely accepted myths about same-sex attraction. Contrary to sex-based stereotypes, homosexuality was not a mental illness, was not something that people either chose or could easily change, and could be the source of happiness and flourishing.[50]

Affirming the trial judge's order, the Washington court of appeals relied on the inherently gendered nature of marriage to deny both the statutory and the constitutional claims. "Appellants are not being denied entry into the marriage relationship because of their sex; rather, they are being denied entry into the marriage relationship because of the recognized definition of that relationship as one which may be entered into only by two persons who are members of the opposite sex." It was not "discrimination," the court suggested, unless similar unions were being treated differently. Thus, *Loving* was distinguishable from this case: given the procreative purpose of civil marriage, the interracial straight couple was not materially different from single-race male-female couples. Because race (unlike sex) was not fundamental to marriage, the court in *Loving* found an invidious discrimination. On October 10, 1974, the Washington Supreme Court declined to certify an appeal. So ended the last major marriage case of the 1970s.[51]

What the Marriage Plaintiffs Were Trying to Accomplish

JOINING AND REDEFINING MARRIAGE

Baker and McConnell were in love and remain so to this day. Burkett and Evans, despite the brevity of their relationship, cared deeply for each other. Knight and Jones convincingly testified about their devotion to one another. All three couples had happy wedding ceremonies that were meaningful to them and to the surrounding community. The same was true of the hundreds of wedding ceremonies conducted by Reverend Perry during this period. Baby boomers grew up in a culture where one's wedding day was supposed to be a high point of one's life. Many gay and lesbian boomers loved the choreography of weddings and wanted to participate in the culture of marriage. Others did not, including Barwick and Singer/ben Miriam, who believed in free love, were not interested in a lifetime commitment, and did not want a wedding ceremony. De Jesus, who had playfully conducted lesbian weddings in the late 1960s, joined her Salsa Soul Sisters in rejecting marriage in the 1970s.

The marriage plaintiffs and their lawyers knew that their lawsuits were asking judges to expand society's understanding of civil marriage. They believed their participation would change marriage for the better, making it less gendered and less associated with the patriarchal tradition whereby the male husband had formal authority over a female, childbearing wife. Like feminists such as Millett, gay liberationists such as Burkett, Singer, and McConnell believed that traditional marriage tended to oppress wives. Old-fashioned weddings started with the bride's father "giving her away" to the groom, as though she were the father's property until he voluntarily relinquished her to be the property of the husband. A legacy of the common law coverture era, this cultural tradition had ongoing consequences for women's lives. Dr. Evans not only withheld his consent from his daughter's marriage to Burkett but apparently pressured her into an unhappy marriage to her first husband. Jones recalls that her husband was "abusive to me, beat me up all the time. And I just had an awful rough life with him. And the only way I could get away from him, he was arrested on a rape charge [and] was in jail."

While he was in jail, Jones and the kids fled. "He had no idea where I was, because he'd kill me. He beat me up and he took a tripod and beat me in the head with it, and I passed out."[52]

The plaintiffs and their gay liberation supporters articulated a vision of marriage that was not tied to the conjugal understanding of marriage asserted by counsel defending their exclusion. They understood marriage as companionate, reflecting mutual love, sexual attraction, and commitment to support one another—the consent-based or mutual-commitment understanding of marriage. "Procreation cannot be the only standard used to legally recognize a significant love relationship," said Baker. "We feel it's the relationship, i.e., love and concern, that is important—not procreation. Any relationship that promotes honesty, self-respect, mutual growth and understanding for two people and which harms no other person should be accepted by the law." Singer and Barwick's brief said this: "Any relationship that encourages mutual growth, understanding and maturity between the two *people* involved and which hurts no other person has got to be beneficial, not only to the couple involved, but to the society at large."[53]

Although Singer and Barwick were the most unconventional of the early marriage plaintiffs, their legal documents presented gay people as basically just like straight people. But Withey's brief on appeal was also a thoroughly feminist challenge to conventional thinking about marriage. By separating marriage from conjugality and gender from sex, Withey sought to recast the institution in terms of mutuality and choice rather than biology and tradition. Indeed, at the same time he was representing Singer and Barwick on appeal, Withey was representing Sandy Schuster and Madeleine Isaacson in a pathbreaking trial where a conservative judge upheld their primary custody of their children, against anti-lesbian claims by their former husbands. Similarly, McConnell and Baker explained that their goal was to compel a "re-examination and re-evaluation of the institution of marriage," or (more dramatically) to "turn the whole institution upside down." Notice that the vision of marriage held by the lesbian and gay couples reflected the direction in which the institution was already headed. Like Cassandra in Greek mythology, they were prophets whose predictions were not believed.[54]

The reexamination McConnell and Baker advocated was a rejection of the gender roles culturally associated with being a spouse. All of the couples fielded such questions as "Who will be the wife in the relationship? Who will be the husband?" They answered: it doesn't work that way in lesbian and gay relationships, which involve gender equals and require a greater degree of mutuality. Said Singer: "We don't believe in role playing. We're two people," each worthy of complete respect and autonomy. At trial, Knight testified that she and Jones were a "butch-femme" couple (she was the butch) in the bedroom, but that did not carry over into their everyday affairs. "There really are no roles. We're both women and we do not take a man's stand either in our social or sexual affairs. . . . The only real identity that a woman plays in a lesbian role is that of a woman who loves a woman." *Jet* magazine depicted Burkett and Evans as a butch-femme couple, but Evans told the reporter that they, too, did not follow rigid gender roles. On the steps of the Hennepin County courthouse, Baker said this: "The nice thing about gay relationships is you both come into it as two equal human beings and then negotiate among yourselves as to how your relationship will be structured."[55]

COMMUNITY ORGANIZING AND STEAM-PIPE POLITICS

Weddings and marriage litigation were one way that lesbian and gay communities organized themselves as a political force and secured media attention to their demands for equal treatment. The Louisville Gay Liberation Front, for example, was formed only after Jones and Knight brought their lawsuit. The marriage issue energized FREE at the University of Minnesota despite its members' range of views about the matter. Seattle's Gay Liberation Front found it hard enough just "to get people to say the word 'gay,'" as Barwick put it. Before his lawsuit, there was zero media coverage of gay events—but gay marriages were "so freaky they *had* to cover it," added ben Miriam. "It was an incredible consciousness-raising tool."[56]

Baker and McConnell epitomized the new leaders. They wanted to get married for romance and commitment, but they also saw their case as a "good way to get the heterosexual majority to sit up and take notice of the gay movement." Baker called the effort "steam-pipe politics." "That's how you get people to pay attention. When the pipe hisses and sizzles the public is reacting to a hot issue. Then you keep the pressure on. You try to cause a backlash. If enough pressure builds, the pipe will crack." To the present day, he and McConnell adamantly believe that any person of good will who focuses on the gay marriage issue and talks to lesbian and gay couples will find it in his or her heart to support marriage equality.[57]

In some cities, leadership on marriage-related issues was assumed by Gay Activists Alliance (GAA) groups. These groups were less radical and were dominated by white men, which is a reason Salsa Soul Sisters broke off from GAA in 1974 and pursued an agenda focused on lesbians of color. GAA groups were confrontational and media savvy. In New York's Greenwich Village, for instance, Robert Clement, pastor of the Church of the Beloved Disciple, conducted "holy unions" of gay and lesbian couples in 1970–71. City clerk Herman Katz threatened legal action against the church and its minister— which provoked a GAA *zap*. On June 4, 1971, several dozen activists paraded into the clerk's office, where they set up coffee urns and handed out slices of wedding cake. When one brave bureaucrat told them they had no right to be in these offices, a protester retorted, "Our rights as gay people have been slandered by a public official!" The protesters entered Katz's (empty) office, with shouts of "Bigot! Bigot! Bigot!" When the police showed up, they were offered cake as well, and the protesters left peacefully. A month later, Troy Perry presided at the gay wedding of Clement and his partner, John Noble, at the Performing Garage in SoHo, with not a peep from the clerk's office. Four years later, the Washington, DC, GAA would rally the community around a marriage bill proposed by an ally on the DC council.[58]

INCLUSIVE CITIZENSHIP

For most of the twentieth century, the morals-enforcing regulatory state cut its teeth on sexual and gender minorities—human beings who were officially denigrated as enemies of the people under the labels "inverts," "degenerates," and "sexual perverts." In earlier decades, Donna Burkett and Manonia Evans might have been committed to a mental health facility as "psychopaths," Mike McConnell would have been blacklisted from any employment, Jack Baker might have been denied a license to practice law, Paul Barwick and John Singer would have been put in jail, and Margie Jones would have lost her children. All of these persons were American citizens who were treated as objects of governmental concern, and the management of sexual and gender minorities, as well as any women who did not conform to the gender role of wife, was a central mechanism by which the modern regulatory state took shape.[59]

The plaintiff couples in the gay marriage cases were angry about the second-class citizenship reflected in the state's vilification or dismissal of their relationships. Just as civil rights lawyers argued that laws against different-race relationships were the last bastion of apartheid, so the marriage plaintiffs and their lawyers argued that the exclusion of gay couples from civil marriage was the last bastion of patriarchy and the deepest denial of equal citizenship for gay people. *Dred Scott v. Sanford* (1857) was the best citation for this idea. In *Dred Scott*, the US Supreme Court held that persons of African descent could never be citizens of any state. In support, Chief Justice Taney cited America's then-traditional definition of marriage as racially pure, evidence that Africans were a "subordinate and inferior class of beings" incapable of citizenship. Because "intermarriages between white persons and negroes or mulattoes were regarded as unnatural and immoral, and punished as crimes, not only in the parties, but in the person who joined them in marriage," Taney deduced that a "stigma, of the deepest degradation, was fixed upon the whole race." The Fourteenth Amendment repudiated *Dred Scott*'s citizenship holding and, implicitly, its denigration of African Americans. *Dred Scott* illustrated the strong connection between citizenship and marriage—a point that some civil rights advocates extended to lesbian and gay people. All forms of discrimination were inexorably linked.[60]

We should note that most lesbian and gay activists did not believe that marriage was the best vehicle for advancing gay people's equal citizenship and an inclusive Constitution. According to Baker, many gay men, including Kameny, initially rejected marriage as a goal because of its requirement of sexual fidelity. "Don't roll back the sexual revolution," they cautioned. In his experience, most lesbian activists objected to marriage because of its history as a bulwark of male privilege, domination, and violence. Seattle's lesbian community distanced themselves from Singer and Barwick's litigation, and the older, closeted gay men in the Dorian Society were appalled by it. Conversely, a Minnesota contemporary of Baker and McConnell who later founded the Human Rights Campaign Fund, Steve Endean, felt that marriage was too ambitious a goal and that the movement needed to focus on repealing consensual sodomy laws and securing laws barring discrimination based on sexual orientation.[61]

The Wedding Heard 'Round the World

"You know," Jack Baker said to Mike McConnell one evening in 1971, "adoption gives you about 90 percent of the benefits of marriage." Mike didn't see the point: "I've already got a mother and daddy, and I happen to like them just fine." Jack responded: "But what about me? I'm just a poor orphan boy. Won't you take me under your wing?" Mike still didn't get it.[62]

"Well, let's say one of us was in a bad wreck and ended up in a coma in the hospital. If we were next of kin, they would have to consult us about any major medical decisions for each other." Or if one partner died, the other would control the estate, even if there were no will. This scenario did interest Mike, who still found it odd that he could adopt Jack as his son, because they were both thirty years old.

In fact, Minnesota law allowed one adult to adopt another. By 1971, gay men or lesbians were using adult adoption to form a legal relationship with some of the decision-making and inheritance rights of marriage. The most famous gay couple in America were the author Christopher Isherwood and artist Don Bachardy. To assure Don control over the house they shared and his estate after he died, Christopher, who was thirty years older, adopted Don as his son. Civil rights icon Bayard Rustin adopted his partner, Walter Naegle, for the same reason. (After Rustin died, in 1987, Naegle turned their apartment into a shrine for his partner.) Jack was proposing the same idea.

On this issue, the Minnesota Law School's legal aid clinic was available to help. Danny Berenberg, an eager student assistant, asked Jack whether he wanted to change his name as part of the process. At dinner that night, Jack suggested that he change his name to Pat—the same name as Mike's sister Patricia. "And if you changed your name to a gender-free name, like Pat . . . and if we applied for a marriage license with your new name, how would the clerk of the court know whether you were a guy or a girl?" Bingo. With their marriage case looking like a long shot, Jack and Mike hatched this backup plan.

Step one was for Mike to petition Hennepin County to adopt Jack and for Jack to change his name to Pat Lyn McConnell. The judge ran the couple through all sorts of procedural hoops before, reluctantly, following the plain letter of the law to grant the adoption, including the name change, on August 3, 1971. The next day, "Pat" and Mike moved in with some friends in Mankato, in Blue Earth County, some seventy-five miles southwest of Minneapolis. After establishing temporary residency there, Mike on August 9 applied for a marriage license for Michael McConnell and Pat McConnell.

Blue Earth county clerk Audrey Connor and her staff were completely fooled. "Of course, Pat can be either male or female," Connor recalls with no ill will, and the person taking the application had no idea "Pat Lyn" was a man. So the clerk's office processed the application and issued the marriage license on August 16 as well as a public announcement that caught the attention of the newspapers in Minneapolis and St. Paul. The jig was up, and the grooms needed to scramble quickly if they wanted to marry before the Blue Earth license was revoked or nullified because of the unexpected publicity.

The wedding was set for 9:15 p.m. on Friday, September 3, 1971. Neither Jack's sister Judy in Chicago nor Mike's parents and siblings in Oklahoma could make it to Minnesota on such short notice. Buddy Paul Hagen, the photographer for Jack's successful campaign for student body president, agreed to host the ceremony and to provide refreshments in his one-bedroom apartment in south Minneapolis. Other friends helped with invitations, marriage vows, and unconventional outfits (matching white bell-bottom pantsuits with pointy collars). Terry Vanderplas, whom Mike had dated before Jack, created unique eighteen-karat gold bands to serve as wedding rings. Through an artful scroll design, when the rings are held side by side, they spell "Jack Loves Mike"; when flipped, they spell "Mike Loves Jack."[63]

Equally unconventional was the presiding official, the Reverend Roger Lynn, sporting shoulder-length blond hair, an Abe Lincoln beard, and a double-breasted jacket over bell-bottom slacks and black boots. Conducted on a sweltering day largely without air conditioning, the ceremony took seven sweat-soaked minutes. After the spouses exchanged vows, they performed a dramatic kiss, and the dozen or so guests applauded.

It was not quite happily ever after.

Start with the Methodist minister. Trained in religion and psychology, Roger Lynn believed in a humane Christianity open to sexual and gender minorities. A high school friend had been bullied into suicide, which led Roger to work with Mike on a gay community project. But performing the ceremony, Roger says, "I came in touch with my own homophobia." He had a "viscerally negative reaction" to the grooms' kiss at the end. But he remained "basically positive, because my core belief is that we're judged not by whom we can't love but by whom we love."[64]

After the service, Lynn recalls, "there was just a huge uproar. All the papers got the word, and I started getting phone calls" as well as hate mail. Methodist bishop Paul Washburn condemned Lynn's participation in an illegal marriage, and his Model Cities contract was tentatively canceled. Hennepin County attorney George Scott commenced criminal proceedings against the pastor for marriage fraud, though the grand jury rejected an indictment on March 27, 1972. Unhappily, the nation's most celebrated gay marriage undermined Lynn's own marriage. His wife, he says, did not like the severely negative publicity or "the nontraditional path" his ministry was taking toward a social Gospel supporting the dispossessed and socially marginalized. (He remarried in 1988.) But "I've never regretted it," he said. "It defined who I am."[65]

The same could be said for Jack Baker and Mike McConnell. Their path toward legal marriage that Jack promised Mike in 1967 helped define who they were: visionary, determined, stubborn, and resilient. On the other hand, the government's response to their Blue Earth marriage license helped define the values held by the state of Minnesota. Even in a decade when women were marrying later than before and refusing the fruits of conjugality through birth control and abortions, public officials reaffirmed that they considered conjugality central to marriage. They refused to entertain the possibility of nonprocreative same-sex marriages. After the September 3 wedding, Jack and Mike returned the signed marriage certificate to Blue Earth County to be entered as a lawful marriage. Upon advice of the county attorney, Audrey Connor never recorded the marriage of "Pat" and Mike.

This was the beginning of a decade of frustration for the couple. Every time Baker and McConnell asked the government to recognize a gay-inclusive view of citizenship and marriage, officials stuck to the traditional understanding. They were a couple marked for discrimination:

- The Minnesota Bar Association required an extra personal interview before Baker could take the bar exam, which he failed twice. Allegedly, the chief justice tried to disqualify Baker on moral grounds. (He was ultimately certified on May 1, 1974.)
- McConnell lost his job at the University of Minnesota, and on October 18, 1971, he lost his First Amendment case. The federal appeals court depicted the librarian as "seeking to foist tacit approval of this socially repugnant concept [gay marriage] upon his employer."
- While unemployed, McConnell cofounded a community center, "Gay House." Because its goal was serving people with a "homosexual lifestyle," the IRS's Exempt Organizations Branch in June 1973 concluded that Gay House was not entitled to tax exemption as a "charitable institution."
- In 1974, after Baker joined the bar and McConnell found a job with the Hennepin County Library System, the couple applied to adopt a child through Children's Home Society (CHS), Catholic Welfare Services, and Lutheran Social Service. All three agencies expressed a preference for placing children with intact husband-wife households, and CHS told them that their "affectional preferences" disqualified them.
- Also in 1974, Baker asked the Veterans Administration (VA) to provide statutory benefits to McConnell as a "dependent spouse." The VA repeatedly turned down the request.

The federal and state governments were just as stubborn in defense of traditional marriage as Baker and McConnell were in support of marriage equality.[66]

By the end of the decade, the Minnesota couple had been rebuffed at almost every turn in their quest for government recognition of their marriage. They were left with a license obtained under mistaken assumptions and a happy wedding—but no legally recognized marriage. To be sure, they were not the first openly gay or lesbian couple to apply for a marriage license, not the first to file a lawsuit, and not the first to secure a marriage license under mistaken pretenses. Yet theirs was (as they titled their recent memoir) the "wedding heard 'round the world." They had put gay marriage on the national media's radar. Once the door to the constitutional closet was cracked open, even fleetingly, it was never going to close.

2 • Opening Pandora's Box

In the wake of Jack Baker and Mike McConnell's application for a marriage license, state representative Thomas Ticen introduced legislation amending the Minnesota family code to confirm that civil marriage can only be between one man and one woman. In a televised debate with Baker on January 30, 1971, Ticen disclaimed any intent "to interfere with your personal rights. I just don't think the state should be put into the position of blessing your relationship, that's all. It's foreign to the whole idea of marriage." Baker begged to differ: "As long as the state blesses the marriages of impotent men or infertile women—for companionship—as long as it permits couples in their seventies to marry, long past the age where they can produce children, seeking to wed only for companionship—then why should not the state offer these same legal benefits to couples of the same sex, who also marry for companionship?"

Ticen answered: "It would open Pandora's box."[1]

This was an apt metaphor. In 1971, people feared that fundamentally redefining marriage to include lesbian and gay couples would have all sorts of unpredictable, perhaps disastrous consequences. Anything involving sexuality, especially "deviant" sexuality, was hard to predict or control. Many who had fought a world war and were tensely living through a Cold War defending American civilization against existential foreign threats saw the events of the 1960s—civil rights, the anti-war movement, and the sexual revolution—as an equally dangerous internal threat. By the early 1970s, more than anything else, they wanted the upheavals to stop. Minnesota's clerks, district attorneys, and judges made sure that Baker and his partner were not able to unleash the forces that might sweep away marriage and, they feared, the stable social order it upheld. Four years later and nine hundred miles away, however, Pandora did open the box. She was a willowy, brown-eyed, thirty-one-year-old county clerk in Boulder, Colorado, named Clela Rorex.[2]

Clela Rorex had grown up in Steamboat Springs, Colorado. Her father was the Routt county clerk for three decades, and she worked for him during her high school and college summers. After earning a master's degree in public administration at the University of Colorado, Rorex settled in Boulder, the small, charming city housing the university against the backdrop of the imposing Rocky Mountains. She was a strong feminist, inspired by such works as Kate Millett's *Sexual Politics,* and a leader in the local chapter of the National Organization of Women. Her car's license plate read "MS 1." Like increasing numbers of baby boomers, she was a single mother raising her eight-year-old son, Scott.

In 1974, Rorex attended a meeting of the local Democrats, where they discussed an electoral opportunity. The incumbent county clerk, a Republican, was retiring, and that party had nominated a female candidate. The Democrats hoped to win the office and thought their chances would improve if they nominated a man. Rorex found this an outrageous display of sexism, and her consciousness-raising group urged her to upset her party's plan. She ran a grassroots campaign featuring origami-decorated brochures and the slogan, "People are more than their Social Security Numbers." She vowed to open up the voting process to university students, whom the Twenty-Fourth Amendment had just granted the right to vote. She swept the primary, won the general election, and took office in January 1975. County Clerk Rorex immediately started registering students, even setting up registration tables at a liquor store near the campus.

She had been on the job just three months when two men—Dave McCord and Dave Zamora—applied for a marriage license. Casually dressed in light jackets, their shaggy hair essentially uncombed, the Daves looked like typical Colorado marriage license applicants, except that they were a gay couple. Small-town boys, the Daves had moved to Colorado Springs and met several years earlier in a gay bar. How did they end up applying for a marriage license in Boulder? Well, "a marriage tickled our fancies," McCord told us. "We also saw it as a way to push our gay lifestyle against the social norms of the day." Also, McCord was going through bankruptcy and had been advised that marriage would assure him and Zamora of the state's homestead exemption for the house they shared. They could not get a marriage license in Colorado Springs, but a helpful clerk told them they might have better luck in Boulder, which had passed a homosexual rights ordinance in 1973.[3]

So the Daves made the hour-and-a-half drive from Colorado Springs to Boulder. They filled out the application. Rorex, still a novice, did not know what to make of it, so she asked Assistant District Attorney William Wise what the law required and what it allowed. As in Minnesota and Kentucky, Colorado's general marriage provisions were gender-neutral. Wise advised her that there was no statutory law prohibiting the issuance of a license, probably because the situation simply had not been contemplated in the past by the legislature. The law explicitly barred marriages between close blood relations (incest) or with someone already legally married (bigamy), but it said nothing about the sex of the partners. Because the marriage statute did not "specify" an exclusion for same-sex couples, Wise opined that "if you want to go ahead and issue a license, you'd be within your legal right to do so. It's your decision." Rorex considered her options for a couple of days and then contacted the Daves to return to her office to collect their marriage license.[4]

"I can't tell you how naive I was," she now recalls. "I was pretty young, 31, and I hadn't had a lot of exposure to many other places, and certainly not to the gay and lesbian community." (She had never met an openly gay person until the Daves.) "Here were two people who were asking for a legal right. I was an active feminist at the time. We were asking for legal rights. To me, there just wasn't any difference. The very core of me said I'm not the person to discriminate if people of the same sex want to get married. If other people were seeking equal rights, then why not all people? If the law did not prohibit me issuing same-sex marriage licenses, then I truly felt that I should do so."[5]

The Boulder county clerk was unaware of the fierce public debate over marriage licenses for gay and lesbian couples then going on in Minneapolis and elsewhere. Nor had she heard about the hostile reaction to the clerk in Maricopa County, Arizona, who issued a marriage license to two black men in January 1975. Because Arizona law did not specifically ban same-sex marriages, the clerk gave the couple a marriage license. They immediately held a marriage ceremony and returned the signed license for the clerk to record—but following a firestorm of media attention and public revulsion, the clerk's office refused to record the marriage. According to local sources, alarmed citizens picketed the couple's house, and one zealot broke in to their home and threatened them with a butcher knife. Dunned with objections and an admonishment by the Maricopa county attorney, the clerk's office charged the couple with "filing false documents." In April, the Arizona House of Representatives passed a measure prohibiting marriage between individuals of the same sex; the legislature would enact the measure in 1980.[6]

So on March 26, 1975, Boulder county clerk Clela Rorex issued a marriage license to Dave McCord and Dave Zamora, who returned to Colorado Springs and got married the next day; the license was signed by the officiant and returned to Rorex's office, which recorded a valid civil marriage. Boulder County's March 26 license was the first time in American history that a clerk had knowingly issued an official marriage license to an openly lesbian or gay couple that was used in a marriage which was later officially recorded. To Rorex's utter astonishment, the community responded hysterically—and the public's reaction helps us to understand why the marriage plaintiffs in Kentucky, Minnesota, Wisconsin, and Washington were rebuffed by county clerks, judges, and legislators. In 1975, Americans had never heard of "homosexual marriage," and the prospect alarmed almost everyone who seriously contemplated it. If accepted, homosexual marriage would, by some accounts, unleash unrestrained sexual license, inviting God's judgment as well as social decline. The intensity of the responses was exacerbated by the perception that it was a modern Eve who opened Boulder's version of Pandora's box.[7]

Colorado Closes Pandora's Box

As soon as she issued the license to the male couple, Rorex faced a barrage of criticism. Citizens, the media, and all levels of government responded as though innumerable demons and miseries had been released into the community. The *Daily Camera*, Boulder's newspaper, ran an editorial lamenting her action. "What average, normal American family would choose residence here on the basis of this type of conduct and the reflection it gives? The unsavory publicity about Boulder and the damaging effects on its reputation do not reflect the true character of our community. The deviates, weirdos, drones and revolutionaries are in the rank of the minority."[8]

"I honestly did not anticipate the degree of hate," Rorex recalls. "It was threats—people needed to kill me for doing this, and that kind of stuff." She was denounced in the press, on listener call-in radio programs, and from the pulpits of churches. Her eight-year-old son would sometimes pick up the phone when people called. "If he answered, they'd spiel their hatred to him," sometimes referring to her as a lesbian. People lamented that granting a marriage license to a single gay couple would bring ruin to society. "They said [Boulder] was going to become a mecca of gay people and it was going to destroy property values." The controversy "cost me any relationship I ever had with my brother. He didn't like me much already because I was a feminist, but this was the frosting on the cake. I lost friends, too. It was pretty much a nightmare."[9]

Boulder was not quite the bastion of progressive politics that the clerk in Colorado Springs had supposed. Boulder had long been a sleepy, conservative Republican town, with an academic edge. As Denver boomed after World War II, young professionals, university students, artists, and, by the 1960s, a lot of hippies had moved into Boulder. Although the city's demography and politics were changing, Old Boulder and its traditional values still dominated. In 1973, when Penfield Tate II, Boulder's first black mayor, sponsored a local ordinance barring discrimination on the basis of "sexual preference," a public hearing drew an overflow crowd of angry residents to city council chambers. One woman said that if the ordinance passed, Boulder would become a "sex deviate mecca" and would have to be renamed "Lesbian Homoville." Responding to strong public opposition, the city council subjected the ordinance to a referendum, held on May 7, 1974; it was overwhelmingly vetoed. Later, the voters removed a gay council member from office, and Mayor Tate was defeated for reelection. Boulder has not had a black mayor since then.[10]

Like the 1974 gay rights referendum, the marriage license controversy provided Old Boulder traditionalists with a way to express their pent-up resentment against the pot smokers, feminists, homosexuals, hippies, students, and other so-called freaky outsiders who were taking over their charming city. As a newcomer, Rorex did not fully appreciate these entrenched attitudes. What surprised and dismayed her the most, however, was her abandonment by supposed allies. Democratic Party leaders shunned her for associating the party with homosexual marriage. No one from the University of Colorado stepped forward to defend her. A spokesman for Gay Lib Boulder, which had sponsored the anti-discrimination ordinance, told the *Daily Camera* that there would not be "any great rush of gays to the county clerk's office," because they tend to be "wary of marriage." Only the dozen or so members of Rorex's feminist consciousness-raising group and her county clerk staff stood by her against the criticism and ridicule. Her chief deputy clerk, Dave Fisher (also straight), provided needed support in the face of relentless attacks.[11]

"But I kept issuing licenses," Rorex says, as new gay and lesbian couples trickled into her office (in this pre-Internet era). On April 7, 1974, almost two weeks after the Daves received their licenses, she issued a license to Susan Paula Mele and Sheila Harriet Sernovitz. Susan had come to Boulder in 1974 as a student at the University of Colorado's law school, where she met Sheila. Like Rorex, both women were thoughtful feminists. Neither romanticized

marriage, nor were they deeply in love—but they strongly believed that lesbian and gay couples ought to have the same marriage rights as straight
couples. Their application was a political act.

The third application came from Boulder's deputy county clerk Neil Patrick
Prince, who had done some friendly lobbying to support the Daves. On April 11,
he received his license to marry Chauncey Hagan, and they married the next
day at the Boulder Unitarian Church. Rorex had not realized that her colleague
was gay until he applied for the license. On the same day, Boulder County issued a marriage license to Terry Paul Guillen and Davey Keith Hough, who
had traveled from Laramie, Wyoming. They were married that day at the gay-
friendly Metropolitan Community Church in Denver.[12]

The experience was not without its lighter moments. On April 15, Rorex was
at the office, "looking out my window, and this horse trailer drives up and some
media vans. This cowboy gets out." Roswell "Ros" Howard was a grizzled character, a retired man who spent most of his waking hours in local saloons and
bars. "All of a sudden it just dawned on me: He was gonna ask for a marriage
license for his horse," Rorex says. "My deputy and I were flipping through the
marriage code like crazy, you know, 'What are we gonna do?' So the cowboy
comes in and asked for a marriage license, and I started taking information.
I ask him his name and Dolly's name—Dolly was the horse. And I said, 'And
how old is Dolly?' He said, 'Eight.' And I put my pen down, calm as could be,
and said, 'Well, I'm sorry, but that's too young without parental approval.'" The
aborted marriage of Dolly the horse made national headlines and was lampooned in Johnny Carson's opening monologue on *The Tonight Show*.[13]

Among Carson's audience were a gay couple in Los Angeles, California—
Anthony Sullivan, a blond Australian immigrant, and Richard Adams, his Filipino American partner. They had first met in a Los Angeles gay bar and had
been together since May 1971. "This is the first place in the world where I felt
completely happy," Tony recalls. He felt that Richard's family, especially his
siblings, loved and cared for him in ways his Australian family did not. When
he came out to his parents in Sydney, his mother wanted to have him loboto-
mized. He came to America to escape his relatives. When they heard about
the Boulder County licenses from Johnny Carson, Richard, Tony and a few
friends flew to Colorado on April 21. They hoped that their marriage would let
Tony secure a green card and allow him to remain in this country and ultimately become a citizen.[14]

On the same day that Sullivan and Adams received their marriage licenses,
so did Annice Joan Ritchie and Violet Garcia, a lesbian couple living outside

Denver. Violet was twenty years old and working on a degree to teach preschool children, and twenty-five-year-old Annice was the breadwinner, working as a supervisor at a warehouse. They were a discreet butch-femme couple: Violet had brown hair down to her shoulders and a feminine hippie vibe, while Annice sported short hair and rode a motorcycle. "There is no better way to see the Rocky Mountains than on a motorcycle," she told your less adventurous authors. Violet and Annice loved each other and wanted to have children together. Right after they received their license on April 21, they were married at Red Rocks, in the foothills outside of Denver, with five other couples as witnesses and celebrants.[15]

Those April 21 licenses were the last ones. At the request of outraged citizens and legislators, Colorado attorney general J.D. MacFarlane issued an opinion on April 24, interpreting state family law as not authorizing marriage licenses to same-sex couples. Although the opinion did not formally require Rorex to stop issuing licenses, she did so after consultation with Wise. She told the *Colorado Daily* that the issue was "definitely not" resolved—even if, for the time being, the state legislature was "too chicken to touch the issue."[16]

Shortly afterward, the District of Columbia went through a similar marriage panic. In early 1975, during the District's first years of self-government, Council Member Arrington Dixon introduced a comprehensive family law reform bill. Its main innovation was no-fault divorce, but it also defined marriage as a union "between two persons." The dashing legislator stated that his bill was "structured to protect the individual rights of all citizens in the District as well as address the specific concerns and interests of the gay community." In July, the Catholic archdiocese labeled the Dixon Bill a "public scandal" and an "abomination." On September 23, about 150 Baptist and Evangelical ministers and parishioners assembled at the district building to petition the council to reject legislation legalizing gambling, marijuana, and "marriages between homosexuals." Black Evangelical preachers denounced the bill, and on December 22, 1975, Dixon announced that he was dropping the gay marriage provision.[17]

Why America Was Not Yet Ready for Gay Marriage

Apart from Clela Rorex, no county clerk, district attorney, or state or federal judge believed lesbian and gay couples were eligible for civil marriage—even when the defining provisions were gender-neutral and federal courts were recognizing a fundamental right to marry. Why was same-sex marriage overwhelmingly rejected? The short answer is that almost everyone found the basic idea incomprehensible.

In 1970, a large majority of Americans, gay and straight alike, had never heard of or imagined homosexual marriage. Wendy DeBoer and her husband, Ken, for instance, were Michigan baby boomers who had played their part in the sexual revolution, but they had conventional views about who could get married. Wendy remembers being surprised to see interracial couples—and she does not recall knowing lesbian or gay couples. When we talked with her in 2018, she vaguely recalled a newspaper article about homosexuals who staged a marriage ceremony in Detroit, and she went downtown once to see a public gathering of homosexuals, but only out of curiosity. When April was born, in 1971, Wendy would never have guessed that she would be a lesbian as an adult. Wendy wanted grandchildren—she now has eight, and also eight great-grandchildren—but she could not have imagined that April would raise children with another woman.[18]

No American state had ever recognized same-sex relationships as marriages, and all of them at least implicitly tied marriage to conjugality. State family law presumed that a child born within a marriage was the husband's biological offspring, a long-standing rule that assumed the procreative potential of marital unions. As historian Sally Goldfarb puts it, "Heterosexual intercourse is technically not a prerequisite for all marriages," but "marriage law creates a regulatory regime in which the performance of heterosexual intercourse is necessary to safeguard the legal integrity of marriages." Legal novelty was the main reason officials rejected same-sex marriage in California, Minnesota, Kentucky, Wisconsin, Washington, Arizona, Colorado, and the District of Columbia between 1970 and 1975.[19]

Indeed, a gendered, conjugal understanding of marriage was philosophically central to Western beliefs about the flourishing of society. Starting with Jean-Jacques Rousseau and continuing with Georg Hegel and John Stuart Mill, social philosophers maintained that because familial affections formed the foundation from which bonds to fellow citizens could grow, citizens could learn to love their country only through "the small fatherland" of the family. Children would learn virtuous behavior through the model of their parents' love and respect for one another; in turn, husbands' tendencies toward selfishness and tyranny in the household would be tempered by their affection for their wives and concern for their (biological) children's welfare. As Mill put it, the family functioned as a "school for sympathy, tenderness, and loving forgetfulness of self." For Rousseau, it was "the good son, the good husband, and the good father that make the good citizen."[20]

American folk culture had thoroughly absorbed this gendered understanding of citizenship. In one of the letters McConnell and Baker received after the 1971 *LOOK* article, an anonymous heterosexual woman explained to them: "The love of the two partners for each other is very strong and involves giving themselves completely to another. This love and giving is so strong it produces a new person who is part of both partners—the complete act of love." In contrast, "homosexual love involves self-gratification and self-satisfaction while expressing oneself to another person through sexual stimulation techniques. Therefore, the same laws should not apply. There is always the possibility of children in a marriage and the property distribution should protect those who cannot defend themselves. I have a one week-old baby boy now, plus poor health. I would hate to be left high and dry now." We could imagine Wendy DeBoer writing a letter like that in 1971. This is why one critic of the Rorex licenses appealed to all Boulder Christians to rally together and again proclaim that "homosexual marriage, or marriage motivated by financial gain, is harmful to the individual and the society."[21]

For these reasons, very few Americans would have considered *Loving v. Virginia* relevant to same-sex marriage applications. Although the US Supreme Court's decision introduced novelty into Virginia's family law, laws against interracial marriage were far from universal. Thirty-three states and the District of Columbia recognized different-race marriages in 1967, whereas not a single state recognized same-sex marriages in 1971. When Virginia defended its discriminatory law based upon tradition and the timeless nature of marriage, its attorneys were simply fabricating history. In contrast, American law and Western culture defined marriage as conjugal relations between one man and one woman long before there was any concept of homosexuality. Many non-Western cultures recognized same-sex relationships as marriages, but usually as unions involving gender-bending partners and not as marriages between homosexuals.[22]

Minnesota senator (later vice president) Walter Mondale spoke for many liberals when he wrote to his constituent Jack Baker that he believed there should be no government discrimination against homosexuals. But he found it "difficult to understand or accept the idea of marriage between people of the same sex. In human and religious terms, to me marriage has always involved the special and sacred relationship between husband and wife in the formation of a family and for the raising of children." As Mondale saw it, the gendered necessity of marriage was linked to its central purpose, procreation resulting from male-female intercourse. For that reason, the broad-minded Mondale could not see this as a civil rights issue.[23]

AMERICAN RELIGION AND CONJUGAL MARRIAGE

Clela Rorex attributes most of the negative reaction to her marriage licenses to religious attitudes. "A local paper said that I was creating a Sodom and Gomorrah. . . . I had entire church congregations in the area writing letters to me—mostly based on biblical references." Most churchgoing Boulder County residents were either Catholic or mainstream Protestant (Methodist, Presbyterian, Episcopal, Lutheran), with a small number of Evangelical churches and some Latter-day Saints. All of these traditions powerfully reinforced the understanding of marriage as conjugal and limited to one man and one woman.[24]

The story of Sodom and Gomorrah (Genesis 19:1–29) is a Christian variation on the Pandora's box parable, in which private sexualized activity traversing moral boundaries led to public disaster. Some Christians read the Genesis account as a condemnation of sodomy, consistent with the Levitical condemnation of men "who lie with mankind" (Leviticus 20:13). By comparison, the story of Adam and Eve in the Garden of Eden, an even stronger parallel to Pandora's box, offers an Old Testament foundation for the Christian view of conjugal unity: "A man shall leave his father and his mother, and shall cleave unto his wife; and they shall be one flesh" (Genesis 2:24). The Catholic, Southern Baptist, and Methodist Churches—the three largest denominations in the United States—read Genesis and Ephesians 5:25 ("Husbands, love your wives, as Christ also loved the church") as confirmation that God created marriage as a conjugal union between one man and one woman. Any effort to open up marriage beyond God's plan would have the same disastrous effects as Eve's taking the apple or Pandora's opening the box.[25]

Rorex's religious supporters responded that ancient biblical teachings had to be read in light of modern realities. "How many people," asked a columnist in the *Colorado Daily*, "really take every teaching explained in the Bible for face value and proceed to do just that? Our modern society is a different one than that existing 2000 years ago and must regulate itself differently." Minority faith traditions—the Congregationalists, the Unitarians, the Quakers, and Reformed Jews—were open to lesbian and gay unions, and five of the six gay weddings based on the Boulder licenses were performed by ministers. But most Christians and Jews hewed to the traditional understanding of Scripture.[26]

For most religious Americans, Rorex's actions, like the marriage applications in other states, would have represented an existential moral crisis.
The argument most commonly put forward in newspaper op-eds about the
issue was that acceptance of same-sex marriage signaled a disastrous end of
society's commitment to any kind of moral truth. "We are adrift on the sea of
moral relativism. Why not marry your horse? On what grounds can we question sadomasochism or any other sexual practice?" A concerned Evangelical
lamented the "absence of a standard for moral behavior" and predicted that
Rorex's actions marked the beginning of an all-out cultural war against the
traditional vision of marriage. "Eventually marriage will be forbidden," he
wrote, "and the world will be as perverted as Sodom was."[27]

Boulder traditionalists feared that, by grounding marriage in nonprocreative
sex, the state would be sending the message that marriage need not be ordered
toward procreation and responsible child-rearing. They believed Rorex had
acted under the assumption that the "quest for personal pleasure leaves no time
for the burden of children." A devout Boulder resident argued that the foundation of marriage was a couple's commitment to each other, and its true end
was the flourishing of the couple's children. "Don't believe two confused members of the same sex can do as well for a child." If popular culture absorbed a
vision of marriage as primarily intended to fulfill the spouses' emotional desires, it would be difficult for the church to explain why any marriage should
be bound to the forms conducive to stable child-rearing. Formerly selfless marriage would decay into solipsism, and children would suffer.[28]

For those Christians hewing to a conjugal understanding of marriage, the
stakes were a lot higher in 1975 than they had been ten or even five years earlier,
because the traditional Christian vision of marriage was increasingly at odds
with legal requirements and with social practice, especially in student-packed
Boulder. In virtually every state, family law in 1970 supported traditional marriage with many carrot-and-stick incentives. Conjugal marriage earned several hundred state benefits; divorce required a showing of fault; nonprocreative
sodomy was a crime, as was sex outside of marriage (punishable as fornication or adultery). This close connection between traditional Christian morality and law, however, was rapidly unwinding, with Colorado at the forefront.
By 1975, Colorado and twenty-four other states had decriminalized fornication,
or conjugal sex by two unmarried persons; Colorado and twenty-eight other
states had decriminalized sexual cohabitation. Many of those states (but not
Colorado) also decriminalized adultery. Colorado and fourteen other states had
decriminalized sodomy for consenting adults (seven other states decriminal-

ized it only for different-sex couples). Forty-two states, including Colorado, had passed laws allowing no-fault divorce.[29]

Federal constitutional law reflected the same evolution. In *Eisenstadt v. Baird* (1972), for example, the US Supreme Court extended the right to purchase and use contraceptives to unmarried individuals and couples. And *Roe v. Wade* (1973) famously protected the right of an unmarried woman to have an abortion under most circumstances. The Supreme Court declined to extend the right of sexual privacy to homosexual relations, and the leading faith traditions rallied around anti-sodomy reasoning as a fortress from which they hoped to roll back the availability of abortion and contraception.[30]

Traditionalist religion pushed back. The Catholic Church, for instance, responded to the sexual revolution in the declaration *Persona humana* (1975). The declaration reaffirmed that "sensuality-based" sins against the body are the worst of all sins, because the body is the temple of the Holy Spirit and fornication degrades God's temple as a well as the sinner. Chastity has a positive value: the chaste body assures a pure mind that is most open to the Lord and the teachings of His Church. "Love must find its safeguard in the stability of marriage, if sexual intercourse is truly to respond to the requirements of its own finality and to those of human dignity. These requirements call for a conjugal contract [for the exclusive union of the man and the woman] sanctioned and guaranteed by society." Based on this eternal norm, the Vatican disapproved of sexual cohabitation, sex outside of marriage, and nonprocreative sexual activities—all examples of sex for pleasure. From a perspective where sex must be justified by something larger than pleasure, homosexual acts were the worst, and so *Persona humana* considered them "intrinsically disordered."[31]

In the Catholic tradition, conjugal marriage is a sacrament, a covenant between husband and wife, the permanence and complementarity of which mirror the permanent union that binds Christ to the Church (Ephesians 5:25). The interaction among the spouses' mutual promises, the Church's blessing, and the marital consummation is an intrinsic human good, "a full communion of persons: a communion of will by mutual covenantal agreement, and of organism by the generative act they share in." The marriage of two men might be considered the appropriation of a sacramental institution by sodomites. As the Reverend Warren Heidgen, the priest at Boulder's Sacred Heart of Jesus Church, explained, "Marriage is a sacred institution entered into by a man and woman. [Rorex's] decision does not recognize either the sacred or legal aspects of marriage and constitutes gross mockery of this special relationship which was instituted by God and reaffirmed by man." To conflate marriage with an amorous relationship between two gay men or women was, he believed, "a grave injustice."[32]

There were dissenters within the Church who sought to absolve homosexuality of moral condemnation. Father John McNeill, SJ, argued that traditional Catholic teaching on homosexuality was "based in a questionable interpretation of Scripture, prejudice and blind adherence to purely human traditions falsely interpreted as laws of nature and of God." In contrast, Father Charles Curran accepted homosexual relations as sinful but mediated that moral stance with an acceptance of gay people as God's children, whom God loved and admonished the faithful to respect as dignified human beings. Throughout the 1970s, the pages of the *Denver Catholic Register* carried heated debates among traditionalists, mediationists, and revisionists, as each group wrestled with how to square the Church's long-standing moral teachings with changing social attitudes toward homosexuality, gender roles, and marriage.[33]

Most Catholics rejected the mediationist and revisionist arguments. A Colorado layperson worried that, if homosexuality were morally wrong, then relaxing civil and criminal penalties discouraging homosexuality was not charitable but malicious: it represented a callous disregard for the well-being of one's fellow citizens under the misleading banner of tolerance. "We love the homosexual but hate their SIN," he explained. "To allow the Church to defend the SIN of homosexuality and the abnormal sex acts is going to destroy the Church." Rather than reforming the Church to keep pace with changing social mores, it was imperative that the Church offer a coherent alternative to the moral confusion of the 1970s. "My only hope and prayer is that more Christians will have understanding towards the homosexual and at the same time become more concerned with Spiritual Reform rather than Social Reform and not give in to the liberal sex attitudes of some of our peers."[34]

Reflecting the views of thoughtful Evangelicals, *Christianity Today* largely ignored homosexuality in the 1950s, but after 1965 it increasingly focused on gay people and couples as alarming challenges to a Christian society. In 1977, the Southern Baptist Convention (SBC) Resolution on Homosexuality warned that "a campaign is being waged to secure legal, social, and religious acceptance for homosexuality and deviant moral behavior at the expense of personal dignity." This "radical scheme to subvert the sacred pattern of marriage in America" would, if successful, "necessarily have devastating consequences for family life in general and our children in particular."[35]

Responding to fears of Pandora's box most aggressively, Evangelicals created political and cultural institutions meant to put the lid back on public homosexuality. Among the most influential of these were Dr. James Dobson's Focus on the Family (established in 1977); Rev. Donald Wildmon's American Family Association (1977); Rev. Jerry Falwell's Moral Majority (1979); and Beverly LeHaye's Concerned Women for America (1979). Jim Dobson emerged as the leading figure. The son, grandson, and great-grandson of Church of the Nazarene pastors, he started his career as an associate professor of clinical psychology and pediatrics. Witnessing firsthand the effects of the sexual revolution on the family, he launched a parental-advice radio show in 1977 that soon reached millions of listeners. Dobson counseled parents in a folksy, avuncular manner that his audience found wise and reassuring. One premise of his advice was that children needed a mother and a father who were married and that working wives should place their household and child-rearing duties ahead of their careers. Focus on the Family was strongly committed to conjugal marriage as the only moral family structure.[36]

STOP ERA AND REAFFIRM TRADITIONAL GENDER ROLES

"My feminist beliefs were 100 percent of the reason I issued those licenses," Clela Rorex says today. "How can I say no to equal rights for someone else when I was asking for equal rights as a woman?" Rorex was part of the second wave of the American women's rights movement, which mobilized large numbers of women to support equal treatment in the workplace and by the state. Starting in 1964, Congress enacted a series of laws barring sex discrimination, and on March 22, 1972, it voted by overwhelming margins to submit the Equal Rights Amendment (ERA) to the states for ratification as an addition to the US Constitution. Hawai'i ratified the ERA the same day. Within a year, thirty state legislatures had ratified it (Colorado was number thirteen); only eight more were needed to add it to the Constitution.[37]

The leading academic opponent of the ERA was Harvard law professor Paul Freund. An owlish, soft-spoken giant of constitutional scholarship, Freund was the first to notice the implications of *Loving v. Virginia* for the ERA. In 1970, he told Congress that "if the law must be as undiscriminating concerning sex as it is toward race, it would follow that laws outlawing wedlock between members of the same sex would be as invalid as laws forbidding miscegenation." In other words, if it is discrimination on account of *race* for the state to deny marriage by a white woman to a black man, surely it is discrimination on account of *sex* (the ERA language) for the state to deny marriage by the same woman to another woman. In each case, the regulatory variable—the item whose change creates a different legal result (marriage versus no marriage)— was a suspect classification under the Fourteenth Amendment (race) or the ERA (sex). Freund was not seeking to disrespect homosexual couples and their unions, for his argument was consistent with his long-standing opposition to the ERA, whose broad rule threatened to open what he considered extravagant constitutional claims. Ironically, he enjoyed a discreet Boston marriage with his Harvard colleague, Ernest Brown. The two had shared a home since the 1940s.[38]

A Barry Goldwater Republican from suburban Illinois, a devout Catholic, and a wife and mother of six, Phyllis Schlafly led a conservative feminist crusade against the ERA. Dressed in smart business suits and coifed with an elaborate, unyielding beehive, she was an organizational genius, creating a network of activists and housewives under the umbrella of STOP ERA. Pointing to her support of laws and policies that benefited women, especially women who were married and raising children, Schlafly did not dispute that women ought to be full and equal citizens. But equality did not require defiance of nature, nor ought it undermine marriage and family. Situating herself as the feminist heir to Jean-Jacques Rousseau, she maintained that relaxing gender roles would undermine the capacity of the marital family to incubate the next generation in the virtues of fidelity and responsibility. STOP ERA echoed Freund's view that the ERA would require recognition of homosexual marriages. ERA supporters such as senate sponsor Birch Bayh ran away from this charge as fast as Boulder liberals ran from Clela Rorex.[39]

Some of the religious citizens scandalized by Rorex's marriage licenses asked "how far Colorado's ERA influenced the clerk who so misguidedly issued the license." This correspondent noted that "no less an authority than the *Yale Law Journal* (Jan., 1973) has said that 'the stringent requirements of the proposed [Federal] Equal Rights Amendment argue strongly for granting marriage licenses to homosexual couples.'" Representing Boulder's League of Housewives, which had formed to oppose the ERA, Mary San Filippo wrote that the "legal opinion" justifying Rorex's licenses "was based upon Colorado's adoption of the Equal Rights Amendment." Many of the women who objected to the Boulder marriage licenses were grassroots opponents of the ERA. One was Hilma Skinner, a Boulder housewife who had led the movement to recall the Boulder officials sponsoring the 1973 anti-discrimination ordinance. Deeming the marriage licenses "an abomination to the Supreme Ruler," she called for Rorex's recall as well. Like Schlafly, Skinner and other critics understood both the ERA and the marriage licenses in sexual terms. Just as Eve took the apple and Pandora opened the box, modern feminists demanded freedoms that would unleash the demons of sexual license onto society.[40]

The Freund argument against the ERA inspired mobilization from STOP ERA's most effective political ally: the Church of Jesus Christ of Latter-day Saints. Viewing God as a Holy Mother conjoined with a Holy Father, Mormon cosmology understands all human beings to have a gendered preexistence, either male or female, and a destiny on earth that requires marrying and pro-creating with someone of the (eternally) opposite sex. Under the first presidency of Spencer Kimball (1973–1985), homosexuality became a minor obsession of the Church. Its leadership declared homosexuality a sickness that needed to be cured through electroshock, counseling, or a proper conjugal marriage; the unrepentant homosexual should be separated from the faith community. In 1974, Gordon Hinckley, the head of the Church's public affairs committee, persuaded the Church's leadership to oppose the ERA as a challenge to the gendered family. Specifically, "passage of the ERA could extend legal protection to same-sex lesbian and homosexual marriages, giving legal sanction to the rearing of children in such homes." The marriages themselves were inconsistent with their natural gender roles and with God's plan for the human race; even worse, children raised in such households would be mighty confused about their God-wired gender identities.[41]

The Church mobilized just before January 1975, when the Utah legislature was poised to debate and pass the ERA. Within days after the Church announced its opposition, the ERA's main legislative sponsor withdrew his support, and the measure failed. With only a handful of states needed to add the ERA to the US Constitution, the Latter-day Saints committed resources and networks to other battleground jurisdictions, including Nevada, where Mormon mobilization was critical in a 1977 referendum against the ERA. In Virginia and Missouri, a similar mobilization played a supporting role to the same effect. Mormon opposition contributed to the defeat of the ERA, which secured only one state (Indiana) after 1975 and permanently lapsed in 1982.[42]

HOMOPHOBIA AND GENDER DEVIANCE

As Rorex discovered, people's reactions to homosexual marriage were often hysterical and sometimes near-violent. We saw this in the previous chapter: Manonia Evans was allegedly threatened by her father, Mike McConnell lost the university library job he had been offered, Marjorie Jones was told her children could be taken away, and John Singer/Faygele ben Miriam lost his job with the Equal Employment Opportunity Commission, the agency that enforces federal workplace anti-discrimination laws. Many Americans felt deeply threatened by gay marriage and lashed out wildly. Why?

Homosexuality and sodomy generated feelings of disgust among many Americans. One Boulder Evangelical decried Rorex's same-sex marriage licenses as the end of public morals, no better than giving marriage licenses to "man-animal couples." Treating gay people as subhuman, sexualized animals was not uncommon. An alumnus of the University of Minnesota wrote to Baker and McConnell: "Wolves of the homosecual [sic] sort should be castrated so they would not ruin another person. Fairies belong in mental institutions. The animals do not indulge in the foul procedures homos do." Another letter denied that McConnell and his "girl friend buddy" were discernibly "HUMAN" and closed: "We ask you baboons to get out [of the state] as fast as you can, before there is a tar and feathering."[43]

This visceral response owed much to hysteria about the larger sexual revolution. One can read the Pandora's box fable as a warning that satisfying one's sexual curiosity can unleash demons upon oneself and the world. Because homosexual relations could not be associated with procreation, they were naked exemplars of sex for pleasure alone, a phenomenon many Americans found disturbing. If we are sexual creatures, how are we different from wild animals? Homosexuals also bore some of the anger generated by feminism and its critique of traditional gender roles. Americans repelled by women's liberation were often even more deeply repelled by gay people.

The line between homophobia and anti-gay stereotyping is often thin. Many Americans who were not hateful simply did not believe there were many committed homosexual couples. Few Americans knew an open homosexual, and fewer still knew committed couples like Baker and McConnell. So what was the big deal? And what Americans thought they knew about homosexuals did not suggest that they were prime candidates for marriage. In part because of a decades-long government campaign of misinformation, Americans believed homosexuals were hedonistic, selfish, and predatory—traits that were antithetical to those found in a self-giving marriage and altruistic family. Many Americans assumed that most gay people were sexual sociopaths, and even those with more benign views thought of gays as eternal adolescents, flitting from bed to bed, seeking love but incapable of the deep love that accompanies marriage, procreation, and children. In a still-popular metaphor, Americans viewed homosexuals as sex addicts. Like the alcoholic who is consumed by addiction to the bottle, the homosexual is consumed by addiction to the pleasures of Sodom. But as Mike Withey's appellate brief in the Washington marriage case documented, these stereotypes never rested upon scientific or sociological evidence.[44]

Except for Baker's long-term relationship with McConnell, however, none of the unions described in chapter 1 proved to be lasting. Did the six couples who secured their Boulder County marriage licenses in 1975 fare any better?

What Happened to the Six Couples?

Although Tony Sullivan and Richard Adams were happy to be married, the ceremony drew negative reactions from Richard's relatives in the Philippines, and even more from Tony's family in Australia. Tony's mother wrote him, "Perversion is bad enough, but public display *never*. It is finished." Those were the last words he heard from her before she died. The US Immigration and Naturalization Service (INS) responded even more harshly. Rejecting his application for a green card based on the Colorado marriage, the INS sent Tony a letter that concluded: "You have failed to establish that a bona fide marital relationship can exist between two faggots." When Tony opened the letter, he could not believe what he was reading; he asked the postman to confirm the disrespectful language.[45]

Represented by David Brown, an ACLU-affiliated private attorney, Adams and Sullivan took the INS to court. Given the hostile public culture and federal judges' deference to immigration authorities, this was an uphill battle. In *Adams v. Howerton* (1982), the US Court of Appeals for the Ninth Circuit rejected their petition to have their Colorado marriage recognized by the INS. Citing *Baker v. Nelson,* Judge Clifford Wallace wrote that the couple's marriage was unlikely to be valid under Colorado law and that Sullivan was certainly not a "spouse" for purposes of federal immigration law. The primary immigration statute barred persons with a "psychopathic personality" from even entering the country, language the US Supreme Court applied to all homosexuals and bisexuals. Sullivan had also petitioned the agency to exercise its discretion to allow him to remain in the country in light of statutory hardship. He maintained that severance of his relation with Adams would cause him and his spouse personal anguish and hurt and that deportation to Australia would cause him undue hardship because homosexuals were not accepted in that society.[46]

After the INS denied his hardship petition, Sullivan brought another fed-eral lawsuit. On September 30, 1985, Ninth Circuit judge Anthony Kennedy delivered a judicious but unsympathetic opinion, deferring to the INS's find-ings and to the Ninth Circuit's previous determination that Sullivan and Ad-ams did not constitute a recognized family. Judge Harry Pregerson dissented on the ground that the INS had read Sullivan's petition so ungenerously that it was an abuse of discretion. The agency, he wrote, "gave no recognition to the strain Sullivan would experience if he were forced to separate from the per-son with whom he has lived and shared a close relationship for the past twelve years. This failure to recognize Sullivan's emotional hardship is particularly troublesome because he and Adams have lived together as a family."[47]

Following the Kennedy decision, Sullivan and Adams left the country, but in October 1986 they sneaked back across the border at Tijuana, Mexico. In Los Angeles, they resided in what they dubbed the "undocumented closet." Tony suffered two heart attacks, and Richard, a heavy smoker, had a stroke in 2008. In March 2009, in a moment of rebellion, Sullivan and Adams came out of the undocumented closet to speak to a gay rights rally in Los Angeles. Tony believes that the INS knew he was in California but left him alone, partly out of embarrassment at the "two faggots" letter. Tony and Richard were a de-voted couple until Richard died from cancer in December 2012. In his final year of life, Richard found in Tony not only a caregiver who helped him through the ravages of cancer and its treatment but also a cheerful companion. In sick-ness and in health.

Susan Mele earned her juris doctor in 1977 and joined the Colorado bar. As she progressed professionally, her relationship with Sheila Sernovitz deterio-rated, in part because the two women wanted different things from marriage. Susan wanted to bear and raise children, while Sheila did not. In 1977, the two women separated. Wanting to have the marriage annulled, Susan slipped the uncontested divorce into the routine docket of the Denver trial court. In 1987, in the middle of a successful career as a lawyer, Susan married David Furt-ney, and they raised a family in Boulder. Now divorced, she lives in Longmont, Colorado. Sheila Sernovitz moved to the San Francisco Bay area, where she met her long-term partner, Virginia Woodward. In 2004 and 2008, Sheila and Virginia were married and changed their names to Sheila and Virginia Burgos-Law. Together, they operated an assisted-living facility for the elderly in Moss Beach, California. After selling their business, they are now retired.

The marriage of Neil Patrick Prince (Rorex's deputy) and Chauncey Hagan lasted only a little longer than Susan and Sheila's. Both apparently died young:

Neil in 1987, Chauncey in 2004. Married the same day as Neil and Chauncey, Terry Paul Guillen and Davey Keith Hough, from Wyoming, also did not last as a couple. We are informed that Terry moved to San Francisco, where he died in 1992, only thirty-eight years old. As of 2018, Davey lives in Jackson, Wyoming, with his spouse Robbin Oberheu.

Annice Joan Ritchie and Violet Garcia had a family. Working with the University of Colorado's medical center, Violet became pregnant by artificial insemination and bore twin boys in 1978. But in 1979 they broke up as a couple, and Violet moved to California with her sons. Although she was the boys' co-parent for more than a year, Annice had no legal connection with them. In the 1980s, Violet secured a divorce in the California courts; she still lives in California. Annice met her longtime partner in 1981, and they have retired and live in Orlando, Florida.

The saddest story was that of Dave McCord and Dave Zamora, who received the first marriage licenses. By his account, McCord broke up with Zamora because of the latter's drinking and promiscuity. Upon McCord's petition to nullify the union, a Colorado Springs judge found there was no legal status to annul. In 1994, Zamora reportedly committed suicide in Colorado Springs, at age forty-six. In the meantime, McCord had joined the Church of Jesus Christ. He says he found peace of mind through the Church and today identifies as a Latter-day Saint. But he confessed to us: "I have never been able to settle the conflicts between my faith and my, at worst, homosexuality, and at best, bi-sexuality."[48]

McCord moved to Arizona, where he participated in religious group-counseling sessions to deal with what his church calls "same-gender affection." He also became a foster parent. One of his counseling colleagues reported that McCord described having fantasies of sex with boys, triggering a state evaluation of his fitness. The examining doctor raised questions about his suitability as an adoptive parent in January 1983, and several months later McCord agreed to termination of his care for a boy he was fostering. In 1983, he married Barbara Rabe; their marriage was (by his account) sealed in the Mormon temple in Mesa, Arizona. Upon marriage, McCord became the stepfather of Rabe's three developmentally disabled children. As a married man, he applied to add a foster son to their family. The psychologist evaluating him knew of his past relationships but concluded that "McCord continues to show improvement in his life circumstances. His marriage is viewed as a strength in terms of his ability to parent successfully." The agency placed an emotionally troubled boy with the family, and a local newspaper published an article praising the couple for their care for disabled children.[49]

In 1984, McCord secured a high school teaching position in Mesa, where he was a popular and energetic teacher—often offering to tutor students after hours and even in their homes. Barbara and Dave separated in mid-1985, and in 1986 Rabe filed a lawsuit against McCord for sexually molesting her three children. She won a $6.3 million award in 1988, just after McCord had been hired to teach at South Mountain High, an inner-city magnet school in Phoenix. The school knew nothing of this settlement or of the child abuse investigations. McCord married a second time, again to a woman who worked with disabled children, and again in a marriage sealed within a Mormon temple.

On January 7, 1991, Dave McCord was arrested on forty-nine counts of sexual contact with minors. He was convicted of sex crimes a year later and sentenced to life in prison. As of January 2020, more than a quarter-century later, he remains in the Florence Correctional Facility in Florence, Arizona. His second wife died in 2014. McCord believes he will reunite with her in the Celestial Kingdom. The Church's position is that his crimes against children nullified his marriage and ended his relationship with his longtime faith community.[50]

From a traditionalist perspective, the failure of five of the six Boulder County marriages was to be expected. If homosexual marriages rested on a pro-choice, individualistic philosophy, they were elevating sexual attraction and companionship over permanent conjugal commitment as the basis for family. When the sex got boring or the spouses' individual goals diverged, the reason for the marriage ended. In 1975, an overwhelming majority of religious Americans believed that the ties that bind couples in traditional marriages simply could not be replicated in homosexual marriages. The couples themselves would respond that their decisions were immature (like those of many straight couples) and that society made it doubly difficult for their unions to last.

Dave McCord's story represents a sobering lesson for all sides of the debate. He molested untold numbers of boys, including his stepsons and many of his students. Evangelical pastors viewed men like him as the kind of sexual predator who would be turned loose on society by tolerance of homosexual behavior. Did Rorex's act of validating his marriage to Zamora release McCord and his demons onto unsuspecting children and their parents? We don't see how.

If anything, it seems to us that gay marriage was McCord's last hope, because it was an effort to have a mature relationship with a consenting adult. (If Zamora committed suicide, his marriage to McCord may have been his last hope as well.) To the extent that marriage released McCord's demons, it was his sealed marriage to his first wife. Legal, church-sanctioned marriage was the perfect cover for a child molester raising four children with his legal wife. Marriage, parenting, and religion helped shield this confirmed pedophile against suspicion. And the protections of the closet may also have helped intimidate McCord's victims into guilt-induced silence: Who would believe them?

A tragic lesson of the first recorded same-sex marriage in the United States is that the threat posed by sexual demons may be greatest when Pandora's box is bolted tightly shut.

3 • Trojan Horses

The Trojan horse of Greek mythology was a giant wooden stallion left by the Greeks when they pretended to lift their siege of Troy. Greek soldiers were hiding inside its hollow belly. The Trojans voluntarily brought an enemy through the city gates that would destroy Troy from within.

Phyllis Schlafly argued that the ERA was a Trojan horse. It looked constitutionally just (who could oppose equal treatment?), but if actually imported into the text of the US Constitution, it would prove a corrosive principle that would destroy American society. Abortion, working mothers, and homosexual marriages would be smuggled into the body politic, with catastrophic results.[1]

The Trojan horse metaphor had long been applied to homosexuals. During the Cold War, paranoid politicians charged that homosexuals were a Fifth Column, disloyal Americans working from their hiding places to undermine its moral fiber. The gay-suffocating closet was thus seen as straight-threatening as well: it concealed sexualized citizens whose contagion could infect the entire society. Once lesbians and gay men came out of the closet and insisted on constitutional rights, even more Americans came to consider them Trojan horses: they were demanding to participate in familiar American institutions like marriage, but many suspected their aim was to undermine those institutions. Some skeptics still consider gay marriage "a Trojan horse movement."[2]

In September 1982, the Centers for Disease Control and Prevention recognized a new disorder affecting men who had sex with other men: acquired immune deficiency syndrome, or AIDS. A few years later, AIDS was shown to be caused by the human immunodeficiency virus (HIV), a retrovirus that enters white blood cells and destroys them from within. With their immune systems compromised, the infected victims became susceptible to a variety of rare and terrifying diseases; they also became vectors for transmitting HIV to others. The mechanisms for sexual transmission, called "Trojan horse leukocytes," were contained in the semen of HIV-infected partners; if those leukocytes penetrated tears in the skin during sex, the uninfected partner could acquire the disease as well. The association of homosexual intercourse with AIDS suggested to the Reverend Jerry Falwell and other Americans that gay and bisexual men were Trojan horses who had brought a dangerous disease into American society.[3]

As the media publicized AIDS and its link to men having sex with men, public disapproval of homosexual conduct soared. A December 1985 Gallup poll reported that one-third of Americans had a more negative view of homosexuals because of AIDS—very bad numbers revealed seven months before the US Supreme Court ruled in *Bowers v. Hardwick* (1986) that it was constitutional for a state to make "homosexual sodomy" in the home between consenting adults a felony subject to a mandatory one-to-twenty-year prison sentence. Already reeling from AIDS, gay people were devastated by the *Bowers* decision. Because of the nonconjugal (i.e., nonmarital) nature of their sexual activities, lesbians, gay men, and bisexuals were presumptive criminals in half of America; and in 1987 an estimated 78 percent of the country believed that homosexual relations were always morally wrong. By the end of that year, over forty thousand Americans were dead from complications associated with AIDS, and the annual fatalities were climbing rapidly.[4]

The lesbian and gay lawyers who were aware of the same-sex marriage cases in the 1970s felt that *Bowers* snuffed out hopes for a constitutional right to marry. As Abby Rubenfeld, the former legal director of Lambda Legal Defense and Education Fund (Lambda), put it, "We cannot concentrate on things like spousal benefits until we put considerable resources into ridding ourselves of sodomy laws" through grassroots organizing, public education, and political engagement. Lawyers focused on trying to meet the short-term needs of their clients and the families they were forming. On the other hand, the major constitutional defeat galvanized the social movement: AIDS and *Bowers* together invigorated the gay rights movement and motivated discussion of a new family law concept, domestic partnership, and then a fresh look at the marriage issue.[5]

AIDS and a Politically Energized Community

"What we showed the world in the caretaking part of HIV was our full humanity. And so you saw the world say, Wow!" recalls Tim Sweeney, Lambda's executive director (1981–1986). "It was men doing end of life care. Men don't do end of life care pretty much anywhere in society, so when you saw men having to do it, men doing it well and lovingly and dedicating their whole being to it, I think that really made people think, 'Well, you know what? There's a moral center there that I respect. In fact, I even admire it. In fact, I'm not even sure I could do that like you just did it.'" Some gay and bisexual men deserted their partners, many others were careless or impatient caregivers, but many, some who were themselves HIV-positive, revealed that gay relationships could engender the same kind of selfless, till-death-do-us-part devotion as traditional marriages. This was a revelation to many in the gay community as much as to mainstream society.[6]

From the beginning of the AIDS epidemic, lawyers were involved. Symptoms like facial lesions and dramatic weight loss not only suggested that young men had AIDS but outed them as gay or bisexual. The death of movie star Rock Hudson from AIDS-related complications in 1985 was such a double outing. Employer and business discrimination against people with AIDS sometimes occurred because of their sexual orientation, sometimes because of their disease, and often because of both. Another set of problems emerged when hospitals denied caregivers access to their loved ones and refused to allow them to make medical decisions for partners suffering from AIDS-related dementia. Other tragedies followed an AIDS victim's death. Unless he had a will, his next of kin would be his blood family, not his caregiver, who usually had no legal relationship to the deceased. If the next of kin disapproved of the relationship, the partner might be excluded from the funeral, evicted from their shared apartment, and deprived of keepsakes and remembrances of his loved one. As the decade wore on, more gay and bisexual men (as well as Americans infected through blood transfusions, needle sharing, or heterosexual transmission) were affected by these problems.[7]

Dozens of lawyers struggled to meet the legal needs of the AIDS population. For example, in Los Angeles, John Duran and three other HIV-positive lawyers established a law firm devoted to AIDS clients in 1987. They represented ACT UP members arrested for their confrontational protests, people with AIDS who needed wills and medical powers of attorney to empower their caregiving lovers, HIV-positive men subject to discrimination, and surviving partners seeking basic rights to shared housing and goods. Lawyers like Duran did most of the individual representation but were joined by lawyers affiliated with advocacy and policy groups. Lambda did much of the legal work in New York City that Duran was doing in Los Angeles. In 1986, when ACLU activist Tom Stoddard became Lambda's executive director, one-quarter of its caseload was AIDS-related; by the end of 1988 it was one-half. Working with the Lambda board of directors, cochaired for most of this period by Carol Buell and David Hollander, Stoddard's primary mission was to raise enough money to expand Lambda's staff to meet the escalating needs of those with AIDS and the lesbian and gay community. AIDS and the rise in homophobia were motivators for donors. Between 1986 and 1992, the staff grew from six to twenty-two, while cumulative AIDS deaths grew fifteen-fold, from 12,529 to 194,476.[8]

Before taking the helm at Lambda, Stoddard said this: "The general public seems to feel that being gay is an individual existence that precludes family life. In fact, it often involves being part of a family in every possible sense: as a spouse, as a parent, as a child. Society needs to foster greater stability in gay relationships." Many in the gay and lesbian community disagreed about the need for greater stability, but every year in which AIDS deaths increased brought new converts to the idea. When Stoddard refined the proposal in a 1988 opinion piece arguing that gay marriage ought to be legalized, he added: "In an increasingly loveless world, those who wish to commit themselves to a relationship founded upon devotion should be encouraged, not scorned. Government has no legitimate interest in how that love is expressed." He believed that we are not complete human beings until we have committed ourselves fully and altruistically to a beloved.[9]

Stoddard's challenge coincided with a revival of the idea that civil marriage should be available to lesbian and gay couples. ACT UP founder Larry Kramer saw marriage as a response to AIDS: "Had we been allowed to marry, we would never have felt the obligation to be promiscuous." Pro-marriage advocacy also came from a new generation of conservative gay public intellectuals—Oxford-educated Andrew Sullivan, critic and essayist Bruce Bawer, and columnist Jonathan Rauch—as well as AIDS activists like Gabriel Rotello. As Sullivan put it in 1989, "Gay marriage also places more responsibilities upon gays." In light of AIDS, marriage would "qualify as a genuine health measure. Those conservatives who deplore promiscuity among some homosexuals should be among the first to support it." Sullivan himself would later reveal that he was HIV-positive.[10]

Stoddard supported civil marriage as an option for lesbian and gay couples for standard civil libertarian reasons: every citizen of the polity should presumptively have the same legal rights and duties as every other citizen. A dashing young lawyer from Illinois, he was an old-fashioned romantic liberal and a law school protégé of NYU professor Norman Dorsen, the ACLU president from 1976 to 1991. Annie Leibovitz photographed Stoddard teaching a sexual orientation and the law class at NYU and asked him to write something on the chalkboard. He wrote his favorite quotation from Martin Luther King Jr.: "The arc of the moral universe is long, but it bends towards justice." Asking Stoddard to lean to one side with his right arm extended, Leibovitz chose an angle from which his torso and arm formed two curves, suggesting visually that he himself was part of the arc.[11]

A new generation of gay liberals agreed with Stoddard, including Evan Wolfson. Raised in the Squirrel Hill neighborhood of Pittsburgh, Wolfson had sublimated his sexual feelings for men during his high school and college years but enjoyed a sexual awakening with young Togolese men as a Peace Corps volunteer between 1978 and 1980. He was impressed that his sexual partners had no language to express any sexual identity other than husband in a conjugal union. "What that taught me as a 21-year-old was, who you are is profoundly influenced by the choices your society gives you, and even the language your society gives you." At Harvard Law School (1980–1983), he gradually came out of the closet as a gay man and was inspired to write, for his senior paper, a constitutional analysis that reflected "the importance of claiming this language of marriage" for gay people. Marriage for gay people was socially important, because "it's the language of family, of inclusion, of self-sacrifice, of connection. And by claiming that language, we would be claiming an engine of transformation that would help nongay people better understand who we are." In 1989, Wolfson (after years as a volunteer cooperating counsel) became a staff attorney at Lambda to work on AIDS cases, which confirmed his view that gay people needed the commitment language offered by marriage.[12]

Another legacy of AIDS was that it brought lesbians and gay men together for a common cause—helping those with the disease and combatting the public health crisis—after a decade of separate agendas. At the same time that more gay men were forming committed caregiving relationships with adult partners, more lesbians were raising children they adopted or had borne through artificial reproductive techniques with sperm donors. Many lesbians wanted to raise those children with their female partners. Because the law did not provide a structure for supporting such families or resolving disputes, they became interested in the idea of marriage. At the 1987 March on Washington for Lesbian and Gay Rights, for example, Robin Tyler orchestrated a mass wedding in which hundreds of lesbian and gay couples were married by the Reverend Troy Perry, who had never given up on marriage. Other lesbian feminists, however, had a different response to Tom Stoddard's challenge.

An important voice was that of Paula Ettelbrick, who like Stoddard and Wolfson had been raised in the Midwest and brought a stubborn optimism to her work. (Her favorite movie as a child was *The Sound of Music*.) A feminist social worker and labor activist, she joined Lambda and became its legal director in 1988. Ettelbrick had a clear vision of the central challenge: as the county clerks had said in the 1970s, society understood marriage as conjugal—a social fact that limited this institution as a model for lesbian and gay families. "The problem in this area is not so much that lesbian and gay couples cannot marry. Rather, it is that all of the legal and social benefits and privileges constructed for families are available only to those families joined by marriage or biology." She believed the gay-liberal strategy of focusing on marriage for homosexual couples would not have liberal consequences for most gay people. Religious fundamentalists saw *gay* marriage as an effort to undermine a citadel of heterosexuality, but progressives saw gay *marriage* as a move that would undermine the sexual and gender liberty that was the special legacy of Stonewall. Queer theorists and activists like Urvashi Vaid, Michael Warner, and Kendall Thomas attacked Kramer and Sullivan for their advocacy of marriage, and Sullivan additionally for his denigration of anti-discrimination laws. In 1995, Sullivan published his argument for gay marriage in a book titled *Virtually*

A gathering of early members of the Lambda Legal team, 1990 (*left to right*): staff attorneys Evan Wolfson and Sandra Lowe; former legal director Roslyn Richter; former cochair of the board Judith Turkel; cochair of the board Carole Buell; Legal Director Paula Ettelbrick; and former executive director Tim Sweeney.

Normal, which called forth a counter-volume by Warner in 1999, *The Trouble with Normal.*[13]

Sexually liberated gays were not the only group excluded from the gay-liberal vision; Ettelbrick feared that poor and black gays had family needs not met by marriage. Between 1970 and 1990, the decline in the marriage rate was much steeper for Americans of color and for persons who never went to college. The rise in the divorce rate was also much smaller for well-to-do, college-educated white couples. Unless lesbians and gay men were immune from these trends, the gay-liberal goal of securing access to marriage would not address the needs of a growing segment of the lesbian and gay community. By the 1990s, AIDS itself was becoming ghettoized in communities of color.[14]

Ettelbrick posed this question: Rather than joining the morally freighted institution of marriage, why not expand the idea of family and extend state benefits beyond marriage? Straight cohabiting couples were already claiming family-based benefits. Why shouldn't lesbian and gay partners do the same thing? Shouldn't the state support bonds of mutuality rather than obstruct or even criminalize socially beneficial relationships? Such a move would require new institutions of family law, and that became her life project—just as freedom to marry became Wolfson's.

Domestic Partnership in California

One of the new family law institutions Ettelbrick had in mind was domestic partnership. Both the idea and the name came from gay activist Tom Brougham. In 1979, he had unsuccessfully petitioned his employer, the city of Berkeley, California, to provide his partner, Barry Warren, the same fringe benefits that spouses of straight employees had. The letter he wrote to the city contained the first use of the term *domestic partner.* "We were looking for something quasi-legal sounding and that was nonsexual," he later recalled. "We wanted to emphasize the everyday living and sharing of people. What was important was that we were a household. We were taking care of each other every day, doing all the normal family things together—that's where 'domestic' comes in."[15]

SAN FRANCISCO'S 1982 DOMESTIC PARTNERSHIP BILL

In 1981, Brougham pitched his domestic partnership idea at a community meeting with San Francisco supervisor Harry Britt, the openly gay successor to martyred supervisor Harvey Milk, and Matt Coles, a young gay activist-lawyer in San Francisco. People liked the idea but not the name. "It sounded like a home cleaning service," Coles remarked, but no one had a better suggestion. In early 1982, Coles drafted a domestic partnership bill, which Britt then sponsored. The key drafting decisions were to create a registry, so that couples could have formal recognition that would render their relationships more visible and would make it easier for private employers or other third parties to grant benefits, and to make the new status available to everyone—different-sex as well as same-sex couples. The Coles-Britt bill defined domestic partners as "two individuals" who "reside together," "share the common necessaries of life," and "declare that they are each other's sole domestic partners." Drawn from judicial decisions articulating marital rights, the "common necessaries of life" language was important to insurance carriers, who did not want to offer domestic partnership coverage without assurances that this new status would entail a marriage-like level of commitment. Coles included a provision requiring the city to accord domestic partners the same legal treatment it gave married spouses, a general commitment with the details to be filled in later.[16]

Without fanfare, the board of supervisors passed the domestic partnership bill by a vote of 8-3 on November 22, 1982—a move that turned out to be more controversial than expected. The leading critic was John Quinn, the Catholic archbishop of San Francisco (1977–1995). A steel-gray-haired prelate with a broad smile and a generous spirit, Quinn was committed to a pastoral mission that included AIDS victims. At the beginning of the epidemic, he transformed the convent across the street from the Cathedral of St. Mary of the Assumption into a hospice for AIDS victims, and Catholic Charities offered housing and assistance. He made sure the Church of the Most Holy Redeemer, in the Castro neighborhood, was staffed with priests and assistants who were gay- and AIDS-friendly and committed to a welcoming church experience. When Pope John Paul II visited San Francisco's Mission Dolores Basilica in September 1987, Archbishop Quinn included one hundred parishioners and two priests suffering from AIDS-related diseases. A few months later, the US Catholic Conference released a statement titled *The Many Faces of AIDS*. Quinn was a key player in the production of this document, which expressed support for all persons with AIDS and opposed any form of discrimination.[17]

In October 2016, just months before he died, we asked Quinn about his overall philosophy. "The Church wants to accompany people where they are," he told us, "to help them and not judge or condemn them—to encourage them." The Church's mission is to bring people into election, to be redeemed by the sacrifice of the Lord Jesus. "The Way of the Church has to be accompanying people toward election, not condemning and abandoning them." Consistent with that philosophy, Archbishop Quinn had posed no objection in 1978 when the San Francisco Board of Supervisors adopted an ordinance (drafted by Coles for Supervisor Milk) prohibiting discrimination based on sexual orientation. But he did object, on behalf of the Church, to the domestic partnership ordinance. Why?[18]

Notwithstanding his pastoral liberality, Quinn believed the Church could not sacrifice doctrinal tradition. In *The Many Faces of AIDS*, for example, he and the other bishops held to the norm of conjugal marriage as the only acceptable situs for sexual expression and opposed "safe sex" as a solution to the epidemic. This admonition went against medical authority but was grounded in the Church's understanding of Scripture. The same thinking was at work in the Church's response to domestic partnership. In a December 1982 letter to Mayor Dianne Feinstein, Quinn wrote that "to reduce the sacred covenant of marriage and family by inference or analogy to a 'domestic partnership' is offensive to reasonable persons and injurious to our legal, cultural, moral, and societal heritage." The Britt-Coles measure was a Trojan horse, a seemingly innocuous new institution that would eat away at conjugal marriage from within the law and undermine the Christian foundations of society. The Catholic Church was not alone: most Evangelicals also opposed the bill on the grounds that it was too much like marriage—as did Rabbi Robert Kirschner of Congregation Emanu-El, Mayor Feinstein's synagogue. As Coles later put it, "the core religious opposition understood the ordinance, in some ways, better than some of the supporters. This was not about health insurance, not about giving benefits, it was about getting society to see gay people and heterosexual couples differently. It was about showing the public that there were couples with important intimate, supportive relationships that didn't see themselves through marriage." The measure would also refute the common view that gay people "are incapable of any kind of emotional depth."[19]

Claiming that the Britt-Coles bill was an open-ended blank check with unpredictable applications, Mayor Feinstein vetoed it. Few observers thought that was the only reason for the veto. Surely, the religious opposition was important, but Mayor Feinstein may have also been spooked by Pandora's box concerns. The day after she vetoed the bill, she told gay leaders, "Women would not be able to get men to marry them" if everyone could be a domestic partner instead. Many feminists had supported no-fault divorce as a pro-choice measure, but easy, unilateral divorce had left millions of women destitute. Was it in women's interests to create another institution that might enable straight men to escape marital responsibilities? Whatever Feinstein's reasons for the veto, it stuck. Although the board had passed the bill by a veto-proof vote of 8-3, supervisor Louise Renne would not vote to override the mayor, which would have produced a 7-4 vote falling short of two-thirds.[20]

SAN FRANCISCO'S DOMESTIC
PARTNERSHIP REFERENDA

In 1983, Brougham and his friends formed the East Bay Lesbian & Gay Democratic Club, whose candidates won control of the Berkeley City Council in 1984. Based upon a report of the Domestic Partner Task Force, headed by Leland Traiman, Berkeley adopted a domestic partnership ordinance that was copied from the 1982 Coles-Britt proposal. The ordinance established a registry and gave all couples—different sex as well as same sex—rights to hospital visitation and, for city employees, sickness and bereavement leaves as well as the promise of health and dental insurance for domestic partners. Because insurers were reluctant to cover domestic partners in the AIDS era, medical insurance benefits were not added until January 1987. Following the Berkeley script of grassroots organizing, and with tepid opposition from churches that did not want to seem uncharitable to a suffering minority, similar domestic partnership benefit policies were adopted for municipal or county employees in West Hollywood (1985), Santa Cruz (1986), Laguna Beach (1990), San Mateo County (1992), Marin County (1993), Oakland (1995), Los Angeles City County (1995) and City (1998), and Alameda County (1996).[21]

Gay and AIDS activists followed a similar process in each of these jurisdictions: (a) document the incidence of same-sex couples who were committed to one another and economically interdependent; (b) invoke the equal protection principle that similar things need to be treated the same; and (c) reassure municipal budget hawks that domestic partnership would be narrowly defined to approximate marriage. Often after enactment, health insurance companies had to be persuaded to offer spousal insurance for domestic partners. "To gain support for non-marital rights and benefits," Doug NeJaime writes, "advocates cast same-sex relationships as marriage-like and built domestic partnership in reference to marriage, thus reinscribing—rather than resisting—the centrality of marriage." At the same time, however, "this non-marital advocacy contributed to an ascendant model of marriage characterized by adult romantic affiliation, mutual emotional support, and economic interdependence—a model of marriage capable of including same-sex couples."[22]

Having learned from the earlier setback, Matt Coles remained determined to bring domestic partnership to San Francisco, and he and his allies revised the 1982 bill to present it as an anti-discrimination measure and sought to dilute the perceived marriage similarities. The board of supervisors unanimously passed the revised domestic partnership bill on May 22, 1989, and Mayor Art Agnos (Feinstein's successor) signed it. In a letter sent to Agnos the next day, Quinn objected that the new ordinance still "equates domestic partnerships with marriage," which his faith community interpreted as "a serious blow to our society's commitment to marriage and family life." The new law raised concerns in other faith communities, too. Evangelical pastors, Catholic lay leaders, and a rabbi met with Agnos to share their fears that domestic partnership threatened the definition of marriage. When the mayor dismissed their concerns, the group organized a popular referendum to challenge the ordinance before it could be implemented.[23]

Two leaders emerged to sponsor the referendum: Rabbi Leib Feldman and Presbyterian pastor Chuck McIlhenny. (McIlhenny was already a controversial figure because he had fired his church's gay organist; he prevailed in a lawsuit brought by the organist.) The alliance of the pastor and the rabbi was fraught from the beginning, though. Feldman was a political strategist intent on turning back the perceived assault on marriage, while McIlhenny wanted the campaign to recruit souls for Christ. Quinn kept his distance, but his priests supported the referendum.[24]

AIDS experts portrayed the ordinance as a vital piece of public health policy that could help limit the number of sexual partners in the gay community and reduce the spread of the disease. Affected citizens shared heartbreaking stories of being denied basic rights to help their dying partners. Religious opponents felt the heat personally. Archdiocesan official George Wesolek lamented: "Anyone who holds traditional moral values regarding sexuality and family life is now, by definition, considered a bigot." McIlhenny's church brought food to an AIDS food bank, but when the recipients linked the donations to the pastor, the food was turned away.[25]

The referendum campaign was disorganized but generated grassroots enthusiasm across religious denominations. Referendum opponents recruited a rainbow coalition of progressive groups and public officials but did not inspire grassroots enthusiasm. Mayor Agnos did the progressives no favors by linking the domestic partnership referendum with an unpopular referendum to determine whether the city would pay for a new baseball stadium. San Francisco suffered a terrible earthquake a few weeks before the election. Had God cast an early vote? Perhaps: the rabbi, the pastor, and the archbishop won an upset victory when the ordinance was rejected 50.4 percent to 49.5 percent. The victory was propelled by Catholic and Evangelical voters, including black Evangelicals. McIlhenny and Quinn believed their triumph was not driven by homophobia. Another proposition on the same ballot, for the city to continue AIDS programs, won with 81 percent of the vote. Said a McIlhenny ally: "We were written off as a bunch of right-wing, fundamentalist crazies, but we're just traditional families. This is a victory of gray power over gay power."[26]

Matt Coles and his allies did not give up. The board of supervisors placed a more modest measure on the November 1990 ballot as Proposition K: "Shall two unmarried, unrelated people over the age of 18 who live together and agree to be jointly responsible for their basic living expenses be allowed to formally establish their relationship as a 'domestic partnership'?" The gay and lesbian community was better organized this time. The cochairs of the Campaign for Prop K, Jean Harris and Melinda Paras, orchestrated a grassroots effort that included most social groups in the city, including the Chinese American neighborhoods that had voted overwhelmingly against domestic partnership in 1989. There was a specific outreach to people of color: Dr. Amos Brown, pastor of the Third Baptist Church and an opponent in 1989, lent his support this time, as did other civil rights progressives. (Ironically, there was pushback by at least one gay leader in the mayor's office who erroneously claimed that domestic partnership would cost people with AIDS their social security disability benefits.) The Harvey Milk Club and the Alice B. Toklas Club—the leading gay and lesbian political groups, respectively—invested heavily in the effort, as did neighborhood activists, who went door-to-door to stir participation in the Castro and other gay neighborhoods. Harris and Paras also worked with a broader coalition, including the American Association of Retired Persons, which saw domestic partnership as an intermediate form of family recognition useful for older couples who did not want to marry because one person would lose Medicaid or other benefits.[27]

As before, the archdiocese opposed the ordinance. Father Wesolek thought it reflected "a real clash of values between those who would want to legitimize a non-traditional life-style and those who felt there was a need, in a public arena specifically, to protect and support traditional family arrangement and style." The Catholic Church worried that the proposal would give legal sanction to "very impermanent relationships," including relationships of convenience, which prominent Catholics argued were more like friendships than marriage. Still, there was less parish-level involvement than before, and Protestant skeptics seemed less invested this time around. Pastor McIlhenny told us that his tiny band of ministers was exhausted from the last campaign, and some feared a further backlash against them.[28]

Proposition K won by a relative landslide, 54 to 46 percent. This was the first time in American history that a popular referendum ratified a measure recognizing lesbian and gay relationships of any sort. In addition to the proposal's modest scope, a critical reason for the victory was that the 1990 local elections energized the lesbian and gay community. Voters turned out in great numbers to vote for governor and for local lesbian and gay candidates. In a lavender sweep, Roberta Achtenberg and Carole Migden were elected to the board of supervisors, Tommy Ammiano to the board of education, and Donna Hitchens to the superior court. Mayor Agnos signed the new domestic partnership law on January 14, 1991, so that the first couples would register on Valentine's Day. Matt Coles was at city hall that day: "When I watched the first couple come down that set of steps, it looked like the wedding day, the reception, and the prom all rolled into one." Altogether, 251 couples registered: 149 gay male couples, 87 lesbian couples, 15 straight couples. The first year saw 1,085 registrations.[29]

Also reflecting the views of Britt and Brougham, Coles understood domestic partnership to be a recognition of family diversity and a big move toward family law pluralism, where partnership would be a legal alternative to marriage, with many rights and benefits but not as many duties and responsibilities. Seeking to create an institution that would appeal to both lesbian and gay couples and to the insurance industry, "the idea was that it was a way of creating government recognition of a committed relationship—who gets into the hospital, jail, takes sick leave—without buying into the 'single unit' idea of marriage with the full measure of marital property" and mutual responsibilities. Founded by Hitchens in 1977, with Achtenberg as its first executive director, the Lesbian Rights Project (later renamed the National Center for Lesbian Rights) was deeply engaged with the idea of a family law pluralism.[30]

The Archdiocese of San Francisco was hardly in favor of new institutions of relationship recognition, but its strong opposition to domestic partnership owed more to the Trojan horse concern that domestic partnership would be "one of the strategic moves" toward same-sex marriage, as Father Wesolek expressed it. "I think that's what they're really looking at and they're looking for on a state-wide basis and to change the law which would recognize two persons, rather than a man and a woman." The lesbian and gay male couples who registered that day saw things more as Wesolek did than as Coles did.[31]

Diane Whitacre interviewed forty-one of the same-sex couples who registered on Valentine's Day: How would they like the law to evolve? One of the lesbian couples said they'd like to see marriage wither away, replaced with contract-based rights and duties. All of the other couples wanted more— the rights and benefits of marriage, co-parenting rights, and social respect. As Anita put it: "I want to be treated just like every other married person." David: "This is a separate and unequal status." His partner, Hugh: "I think we should get married and I've proposed and we would if we could." Jane: "I prefer that the domestic partnership law didn't exist and we could get married if we wanted to." Wally: "I would like to see it change on a national level, mandated by the Supreme Court as equal rights for same-sex couples."[32]

Both opponents and beneficiaries viewed domestic partnership as a Trojan horse, filled with lesbian and gay couples hoping someday to invade the sacred institution of marriage itself. The beneficiaries saw domestic partnership as a gift to the sagging institution of marriage, while the critics thought it would leave the institution in ruins.

EXPANDING DOMESTIC PARTNERSHIP

Domestic partnership was a popular measure for lesbian and gay activist and legal groups to champion for a number of reasons. People with AIDS and many gay men were enthusiastic about the support it gave to caregiving relationships. Some lesbians were enthusiastic because their relationships were often situses of child-rearing. More lesbians were choosing to have children through artificial insemination, and these decisions were increasingly made by the mother and her partner as a family. Although hospitals and sperm banks discriminated against unmarried women, lesbian insemination networks sprouted all over the country, and by 1990 there was a veritable lesbian baby boom. Smaller numbers of gay men were becoming biological fathers through the same technology, with the cooperation of female (often lesbian) surrogate mothers. And more lesbian and gay couples were adopting children than ever before, despite ongoing state discrimination. As more partnered lesbians and gay men began raising children, their demand for employer-based family health insurance coverage became more intense. Domestic partnership found support from feminists and queers critical of marriage as well as from religious and conservative gay and lesbian couples who yearned for marriage or marriage-lite.[33]

An important reason for its popularity was that domestic partnership could be granted by counties and cities, where open lesbians and gay men were concentrated and politically significant. State-level responses were more difficult to sell to legislatures, which included small-town and rural representatives who assumed no gay people lived in their districts. As the San Francisco experience revealed, domestic partnership proposals made local officials nervous everywhere, but a determined grassroots, political, and legal effort promised success. Domestic partnership benefits for government employees were adopted in Seattle, Washington (1989, 1990); Palm Beach, Florida (1992); Ann Arbor, Michigan (1992); Multnomah County, Oregon (1993); Travis County, Texas (1993); and Burlington, Vermont (1993). Registries similar to the San Francisco model were created in Ithaca, New York (1990); New York City (1990); Ann Arbor, Michigan (1991); Minneapolis (1991); the District of Columbia (1992); Atlanta (1993); Boston (1997); Philadelphia (1998); and Denver (1999). Each ordinance had an interesting story. The Madison, Wisconsin, "alternative families" ordinance, for example, was developed in 1983–1985 by a task force chaired by Barbara Cox and Duane Kolterman. As adopted in 1990, registration entitled family members to hospital and jail visitation and zoning allowances; subsequently, the University of Wisconsin and Madison extended health care benefits to employees for their partners.[34]

In New York City, the key breakthrough was led by schoolteachers. Representing the Gay Teachers Association in a lawsuit seeking health insurance benefits for the domestic partners of unmarried school teachers, Paula Ettelbrick argued that the committed relationships of these educators were indistinguishable from a state-sanctioned marriage in all substantive respects. After the trial judge refused to dismiss the complaint, Mayor David Dinkins used executive orders to create a domestic partnership registry, with visitation benefits. He then settled the schoolteachers' case and committed the city to provide all municipal employees with health and other insurance for their partners. In 1998, after Ettelbrick assembled a large coalition in support of the measure, the council and Mayor Rudy Giuliani adopted an ordinance confirming the registration system, extending all spousal benefits to domestic partners of all municipal employees, and requiring all city agencies to treat partners the same as spouses.[35]

At the same time that cities and counties were creating domestic partnership benefits for government employees, the private sector was doing the same. Like local governments, for-profit firms were initially discouraged by the cost of AIDS treatment and the reluctance of health insurers to cover domestic partners. As early as 1981, the *Village Voice* gave health insurance and other spousal benefits to designated lesbian and gay partners, and progressive non-profits like Lambda and the ACLU followed. In 1991, Lotus Development Corp., a Massachusetts software company, became the first Fortune 1000 company to offer health, dental, and medical insurance to the "spousal equivalents" of its lesbian and gay employees. In 1992, Apple began extending spousal benefits to its employees' domestic partners. Apple's process was replicated in company after company: internal pressure from lesbian or gay executives (such as Apple's litigation counsel Elizabeth Birch) and employees put domestic partnership on the corporate agenda, board members and executives figured out that the measure was not going to cost a lot of money and would improve employee morale as well as attract lesbian and gay customers, and very little pushback developed. By January 1997, at least 287 employers were offering spousal benefits to domestic partners.[36]

A Broader Understanding of Family

In the shadow of AIDS caregiving relationships and amid the lesbian baby boom, the domestic partnership movement engendered a broader conversation: Who makes a family? Family diversity task forces tackled this question in Los Angeles, Madison, San Francisco, and Washington, DC. The report of the San Francisco task force, written by Roberta Achtenberg, offered a broad definition of family as "a unit of interdependent and interacting persons, related together over time by strong social and emotional bonds and/or by ties of marriage, birth, and adoption, whose central purpose is to create, maintain, and promote the social, mental, physical and emotional development and well-being of each of its members." As these task forces sought a broader sociological understanding, movement lawyers were pressing the same points in litigation.[37]

In 1989, Paula Ettelbrick created the Lambda Family Relationships Project, "to stress the growing importance of our work on lesbian and gay family issues." The same year, Lambda filed an important amicus brief in *Braschi v. Stahl Associates* (1990). New York hairstylist Leslie Blanchard had died of AIDS in September 1986, survived by his partner and caregiver, Miguel Braschi. Blanchard's landlord sought to evict Braschi from the couple's rent-stabilized apartment, but Braschi argued he should be allowed to stay because he was a family member protected by state law. The ACLU's Nan Hunter and Bill Rubenstein took Braschi's case to the New York Court of Appeals.[38]

Ettelbrick's amicus brief started with the observation that Braschi and Blanchard lived a life much "like any married couple," in a mutually meaningful relationship. Her brief documented the importance of nonmarital cohabitation generally:

- *Gay and lesbian couples.* There were as many as 2.5 million gay male couples and 2 million lesbian couples in the United States. One-third of the lesbian couples were raising children within their households.
- *Straight cohabiting couples.* There were as many as 1.8 million cohabiting straight couples—4 percent of all straight couples in 1981, up threefold from 1970, and expected to double by 1990.
- *AIDS and homelessness.* Thousands of New Yorkers had become homeless because landlords were evicting people with AIDS or their surviving partners; Lambda represented dozens of plaintiffs suing landlords for this reason.

Although the estimated number of lesbian and gay couples was probably too high, Ettelbrick's brief provided a vision of family law that included cohabiting relationships and extended legal benefits and rights to the partners. The ACLU's merits brief developed legal grounds supporting a broad interpretation of statutory families based on previous appellate decisions recognizing nontraditional families, the purpose of the rent-control law, and New York City's ordinance barring discrimination based on sexual orientation. New York City's corporation counsel Peter Zimroth filed an amicus brief documenting the intersection of the AIDS epidemic and the city's housing shortage and argued that a narrow interpretation of family would undermine the statute's purpose of providing stable housing for residents and their loved ones.[39]

Because the chief judge did not participate, the court that heard the case consisted of six judges, all appointed by Democratic governor Mario Cuomo: Judith Kaye and Fritz Alexander, the most liberal judges; Joseph Bellacosa and Vito Titone, devout Catholics; and Richard Simons and Stewart Hancock Jr., more conservative. Within the court, Braschi's champion was Judge Titone, a traditionalist from Staten Island whose son Matthew was gay. Mark the social context. Because of AIDS and the lesbian baby boom, as well as the outrage against *Bowers,* more lesbian, gay, and bisexual Americans were out of the closet with their family and friends than ever before. Empathy with known gay people made straight officials think twice before approving discrimination against an increasingly sympathetic minority.[40]

To avoid a looming deadlock of three votes for Braschi versus three votes against, Judge Titone worked to tailor his arguments to better persuade Judge Bellacosa that he should join in finding that Braschi had an equitable right to his shared home, without mention of his sexuality. After several drafts, Judge Titone won over his fellow devout Catholic jurist based on that appeal to a belief in fundamental fairness. When the opinion was issued, Judges Kaye and Alexander joined Judge Titone's plurality opinion, which concluded that the term *family* "should not be rigidly restricted" to married couples. In the context of housing, it should realistically include "two adult lifetime partners whose relationship is long term and characterized by an emotional and financial commitment and interdependence. This view comports both with our society's traditional concept of 'family' and with the expectations of individuals who live in such nuclear units." The plurality recognized Braschi as Blanchard's "life partner" and described their life together as intertwined, just like a married couple's. Concurring only in the judgment, Judge Bellacosa also interpreted the statute generously to protect Braschi's right to stay in his "shared home," but he left unmentioned the homosexual nature of his relationship with the "tenant-in-chief." The two dissenting judges would have ruled that the statutory purpose was to assure orderly and predictable succession of Blanchard's property rights to remain in the apartment and that *family* should be tied to state rules of intestacy and succession. These would include blood relatives and spouses but not "roommates" like Braschi.[41]

Most of the judges and virtually all of the court personnel "felt this was the right thing to do, we didn't see it as groundbreaking at the time—on the contrary it was just the New York way that we believed that 'family' was defined." Surely a reasonable legislator would balk at the proposition "that someone's grandmother could randomly come in from California, be considered family, and by law would then be able to keep the apartment, but someone like Miguel could not." Their view of the case as unremarkable proved mistaken. *Braschi* made front-page news and was intensely discussed in the national media, including a vigorous debate between Pat Buchanan and Michael Kinsley on CNN's *Crossfire*. Miguel Braschi did not enjoy his legal victory for long, as he died in 1990 from complications associated with AIDS.[42]

Lambda and the ACLU saw the decision as a gateway precedent. In the Minnesota case of *In re Guardianship of Kowalski* (1990), for example, Ettelbrick argued that cohabiting families like Blanchard and Braschi were overtaking the traditional nuclear family. In 1987, one-third of American women aged nineteen to forty-four had sexually cohabited at some point in their lives, a figure

that zoomed up to 45 percent by 1995. After Sharon Kowalski was incapacitated by an auto accident, the Minnesota Court of Appeals ruled that her
caregiver-partner must be her guardian, over the objections of Sharon's blood
family.[43]

Another important doctrine for what Ettelbrick called "a lesbian conscious
family law" was second-parent adoption—where a lesbian adopted the biological child of her partner, giving the child two legal mothers. Family law normally required the biological parent to give up all rights and relations with the
child upon adoption, with an exception for "stepparent adoptions" by the wedded spouse of the parent. Because the norm for parent-child law was the "best
interests of the child," the conjugal marriage anchor was amenable to adapta-
tion when two women were raising the child in a family environment. In the
1980s, dozens of lesbian couples persuaded trial judges from Alaska to New
York to allow second-parent adoptions, especially if children's service agencies
did not object. From the beginning, Ettelbrick was central to the network of
attorneys bringing these petitions, and she filed Lambda briefs on appeal in
New Mexico and Vermont, the latter resulting in the leading case endorsing
second-parent adoptions. Beatrice Dohrn, Ettelbrick's successor as Lambda's
legal director, represented a lesbian couple in *In re Jacob* (1995), New York's
landmark ruling recognizing second-parent adoptions for straight, gay, and lesbian cohabiting couples.[44]

The Marriage Debate Within the Gayocracy

In 1989, Evan Wolfson drafted a Family Bill of Rights, explicitly recognizing the "diversity of cultures within American society" and the "many kinds
of living arrangements sharing the values properly associated with family." Rejecting traditional formalities, the Lambda document argued that the understanding of *family* ought to focus on "the level of emotional and financial
commitment, the manner in which the family members have conducted their
everyday lives and held themselves out to society and friends, the reliance
placed upon one another for daily family services, the longevity of the family
relationship," and similar agreements or actions. Based upon the American
traditions of "individual freedom in shaping one's own destiny" and pluralism and diversity in interpersonal relationships, the Family Bill of Rights asserted both that same-sex couples ought to be allowed to marry and that
married and cohabiting couples "should be entitled to equal treatment in allocation of government and employee benefits, ability to raise children, and

access to protections afforded in criminal and civil law." Never published, this document offered a radical agenda for family law. From a traditional values perspective, it was a double Trojan horse, undermining marriage both by ending the conjugality requirement and by subsidizing nonmarital, cohabiting relationships with the same benefits long allotted only to married couples.[45]

Although the defender of marriage as a goal for the lesbian and gay rights movement, Tom Stoddard was not sure he wanted marriage recognition for himself, as he had never been head over heels in love. Every summer, Lambda held a fundraiser at a magnificent modernist house in the Pines section of Fire Island. By 1988, Lambda's Fire Island fundraiser had become a must-be-seen-at event for wealthy gays, and Stoddard was the host of a gala that would generate much of Lambda's annual budget. The August 13, 1988, event started with cocktails on the deck facing the bay, as the sun was setting. One of the guests was Walter Rieman, an associate at the tony New York law firm of Paul, Weiss, Rifkind, Wharton & Garrison.

Something about Walter caught Tom's eye. Maybe it was the young lawyer's thin, angular face, his thick, dark hair and eyebrows, his mahogany-colored eyes, and his lean runner's physique, or maybe it was Walter's keen intellect and the suggestion that he knew more than he let on. They struck up a conversation, and Tom invited Walter to sit with him at dinner. The two spent the evening absorbed in conversation as they downloaded each other's life stories. After the event closed, they walked back and forth across the island before spending the night at Tom's place.[46]

"He took my breath away—he was smart, he was kind, he was extremely attentive," Walter recalls. "Most of the time we were together, on the thirteenth of the month, Tom would send me flowers." Not every month, lest the gesture lose its capacity to surprise and delight. Often, living together cures a couple of romantic illusions, but for Walter and Tom, exposure to personal quirks and moods deepened rather than disrupted their affection for one another. During the spring of his relationship with Walter, Tom asked Paula whether they should publish the thoughts about marriage that they had exchanged during Lambda meetings. Their short articles, which appeared side by side in the fall 1989 issue of *OUT/LOOK* and have been reprinted many times, are best read as a conversation.[47]

Ettelbrick's article, "Since When Is Marriage a Path to Liberation," laid down the gauntlet: "Marriage runs contrary to two of the primary goals of the lesbian and gay movement: the affirmation of gay identity and culture and the validation of many forms of relationships." As to the former, "justice for gay men and lesbians will be achieved only when we are accepted and supported in this society *despite* our difference from the dominant culture and the choices we make regarding our relationships." What is inherently distinctive about lesbians and gay men is that they violate the gender roles dictated by the central marital trope of conjugality. In seeking the right to marry, gay rights lawyers would be forced to claim that there is no material difference between straight married couples and gay or lesbian couples. "We end up mimicking all that is bad about the institution of marriage in our effort to appear the same as straight couples."[48]

In "Why Gay People Should Seek the Right to Marry," Stoddard conceded that he "personally found marriage in its present state rather unattractive." In a draft of his article, he specifically mentioned Rieman as someone he loved but did not want to marry. (He deleted that line, lest it mislead readers regarding his deep love for his partner.) But expanding marriage to include lesbian and gay couples "would necessarily transform it into something new," providing a mechanism "through which the institution divests itself of the sexist trappings of the past." Note that the two pieces, when read side by side, confirmed Archbishop Quinn's worst fears, that gay marriage would transform marriage into a nongendered institution (Stoddard) disconnected from its traditions and from its core of conjugality (Ettelbrick). Conversely, Ettelbrick maintained that marriage rights would be a reverse Trojan horse, in which the Greeks hiding inside would not conquer Troy but would be assimilated by it.

Ettelbrick lamented that even as it normalized some gay relationships, gay marriage would deepen the exclusion of nonmarital relationships, especially those involving "more marginal members of the lesbian and gay community (women, people of color, working class and poor)." Stoddard thought this would be an improvement over their current circumstances, in which the culture generally denigrated lesbian and gay Americans and considered all their relationships "less significant, less valuable." For gay people to have the *right to marry*, whether exercised or not, would benefit the entire community. Ettelbrick responded: "If the laws change tomorrow and lesbians and gay men were allowed to marry, where would we find the incentive to continue the progressive movement we have started that is pushing for societal and legal recognition of all kinds of family relationships? To create other options and alternatives?"

The Ettelbrick-Stoddard debate reflected discussions that were already occurring at the semiannual Litigators' Roundtables, where gay rights lawyers shared information and planned overall strategies. In the early 1990s, participants like Kate Kendell, Tim Sweeney, and Nancy Polikoff agreed with Ettelbrick's approach of expanding the law's understanding of family, while Evan Wolfson was like a dog with a bone on the centrality of marriage. He found support from Barbara Cox, William Eskridge, and Nan Hunter. The ACLU's Matt Coles felt that "neither the legal nor the political groundwork had really been laid." James Esseks recalls, "it was still not clear when we were going to get rid of sodomy laws. So marriage just seemed much further distant."[49]

Two lawsuits brought the issue into sharper focus. In December 1990, Craig Dean and Patrick Gill sued the District of Columbia for a marriage license. A recent Georgetown law graduate, Dean represented himself and Gill, ultimately with the assistance of Eskridge and GAYLAW (Gay & Lesbian Lawyers of Washington). In 1991, three Hawai'i couples who had been denied marriage licenses asked the mainland litigation groups to represent them. Through a mutual friend, Evan Wolfson contacted Ninia Baehr, one of the Hawai'i plaintiffs, and brought the case to the attention of Lambda. Ettelbrick, his boss, was as unenthusiastic as Wolfson was excited. Stoddard, although he supported marriage as a goal, believed that both cases were premature. Most of the Litigators' Roundtable agreed. The Hawai'i plaintiffs found a local lawyer, who filed a state marriage equality lawsuit on May 1, 1991.[50]

Marriage Comes to Lambda Legal

Around September 1989, after years of procrastination, Tom Stoddard tested positive for HIV. Some HIV-negative boyfriends in Walter's situation would have eased out of a new relationship, but Walter was committed for better or for worse. Tom developed AIDS, which undermined his ability to work. In 1992, he suggested to his board of directors that he should retire.

One reason Stoddard felt not up to the job was that Lambda was engaged in a take-no-prisoners civil war. Evan Wolfson kept insisting that Lambda join the Hawai'i marriage litigation. Paula Ettelbrick was opposed to any involvement beyond filing amicus briefs. As Wolfson recalls, "It was a hugely contentious, quarrelsome time. Lambda was in real disarray, partly over marriage, but partly over just personalities and growing pains." Ettelbrick recalled that she and Wolfson could not even have a conversation without his condescending and constantly interrupting her, which infuriated her. She felt disrespected because she did not have a law degree from an elite school like Harvard (Wolfson) or NYU (Stoddard).[51]

Lambda's board of directors was aware of this conflict but treasured both advocates—Wolfson as a visionary and Ettelbrick as a brilliant fighter for community needs. Stoddard sadly believed that tackling the marriage issue in the 1990s was a likely train wreck. He agreed with Matt Coles that it would require a longer campaign of public education and building of alliances and electoral clout before civil recognition of gay and lesbian marriages would be realistic. You don't move from being outlaws to in-laws overnight. The Lambda board agreed that the organization would stay out of both the Hawai'i and District of Columbia lawsuits but were okay with filing amicus briefs. Feeling certain that the Hawai'i lawsuit would itself be a gigantic moment for public education, Wolfson interpreted this directive to allow him to work with the plaintiffs' lawyer, Dan Foley, behind the scenes. Ettelbrick and Stoddard did not interpret the directive so liberally. Frustrated by the internal bickering and by the perceived insubordination, Stoddard fired Wolfson.[52]

Wolfson called his friend Richard Socarides, a member of Lambda's board. Like other members, Socarides was uncertain whether marriage was the best goal for the movement, but the payoff was potentially huge. To remain on the cutting edge, as Lambda aspired to do, they needed visionaries like Wolfson. Socarides called John Duran and other buddies on the board, and that rump group of board members pressed Stoddard to reconsider. An enervated lame duck, he agreed to rescind his decision. Wolfson stayed. The women on the board learned about the mini-coup after the fact. Later in 1992, Ettelbrick announced she was leaving Lambda. Stoddard retired as planned. His successor as executive director was Kevin Cathcart, and Beatrice Dohrn replaced Ettelbrick as legal director. Both supported Wolfson's marriage initiative and freed him to participate in the Hawai'i case.

After Stoddard and Ettelbrick left Lambda, each found deeper personal satisfaction, consistent with his and her core commitments. A few years after she relocated at Empire Pride, Paula became a committed partner to Lambda staff attorney Suzanne Goldberg. In March 1997, Suzanne gave birth to Adam Ettelbrick, and in September 1999 to Julia Ettelbrick. From Suzanne's side, each child would be raised Jewish but would bear the last name of his and her other mother. Enabled to be joint parents by the New York Court of Appeals' recognition of second-parent adoption in 1995, Paula and Suzanne raised the children as exactly the sort of nonmarital family Paula had championed. When they broke up in 2005, they remained close friends and cooperative co-parents. Each committed to new female partners, and the four women socialized and went on family vacations together.

In 1993, Stoddard assumed the leadership of the Campaign for Military Service, a frustrating effort to hold President Clinton to his promise to end the military exclusion of gay people. With the president's support, Congress enacted a statutory exclusion in August 1993. The same month, as a present for Tom's fifth anniversary with Walter, Annie Leibovitz did a haunting photograph of the couple. Dressed in a leather jacket and seated, Tom peered languidly into the camera with a wan smile and tired eyes, looking older than his forty-five years. With his arms wrapped around his partner and a wide toothy smile, Walter was a youthful, handsome thirty-seven. "The picture got me thinking about appearances," Tom later recalled, "the importance of declaring our commitment before people we love." What has my life meant? With the clarity that fatal illness often brings, he observed that "our movement is based on a very simple notion, the right to love. It's also based, I think, upon a somewhat broader, more demanding notion: the duty to love." He did not feel a strong duty to procreate, but by the twilight of his life he was proud to have found Walter and to have jointly created a marvelous relationship.[53]

He wanted to die a spouse, partly to assert the equality of gay people, partly to fulfill his joyous duty to love. In November, Tom went to Tiffany's and purchased a $600 gift certificate for matching wedding rings. That night, he asked Walter to marry him. Before Tom popped this most unexpected question, Walter had professed indifference to the idea—but once asked, he was thrilled. The wedding was on December 4, 1993, the twentieth anniversary of Tom's coming out as gay. They arranged the nuptials as a dinner-and-drinks gathering of about seventy friends and relatives, including Tom's brother and Walter's brother and two sisters, in Tribeca at Chanterelle, their favorite restaurant. At a dramatic moment, the two grooms appeared in an open space between two tables, both wearing dignified gray suits, Walter sporting a red tie. Facing each other, with no intermediary, they spoke their vows: "I commit to you my life and my love for the rest of our days." They exchanged their matching gold wedding bands. And closed with the ceremonial wedding kiss—not too passionate, but heartfelt.

Tom's illness hovered over the marriage ceremony. As he put it, "The subtext of so many straight weddings is about expanding possibility, for gay men with AIDS it has more to do with closure. The relationship has that precious quality of something that's going away." For the next few years, Tom stayed active in the politics of sexuality and AIDS. In 1996, a promising new therapy, consisting of a cocktail of different protease inhibitors, became available, and Tom started it immediately. The treatment contributed to the first decline in AIDS-related deaths since the advent of the disease. In 1996, 42,155 people died from AIDS, down from the 48,979 in 1995.[54]

Tom felt well enough to journey with Walter to France in 1996, but when they returned home, his body gave out. Opportunistic infections ran amok, and he suffered multiple organ failures. He was unable to take nourishment except intravenously. At Thanksgiving 1996, Tom went into the hospital for more than a month. Walter took a leave from Paul, Weiss to be his full-time caregiver, staying with him in the hospital all day and sometimes all night. This was the worst period of Walter's life. He brought Tom home on New Year's Eve. Every day it became more difficult for Tom to take nourishment, and he died on February 13, 1997. He was one of 28,688 Americans who died that year of AIDS-related illnesses.

Evan Wolfson and Paula Ettelbrick continued to champion rights for lesbian and gay persons and couples and eventually put ill feelings behind them. A longtime partner at Paul, Weiss, Walter has spent much of his career doing legal work associated with AIDS, a plague that continues to claim the lives of Americans. One was Tom's brother John, who succumbed in 2010. The next year, on October 7, Paula died of ovarian cancer. Like Tom's, her voice still resonates.

4 • Aloha, Same-Sex Marriage

As explained in Hawai'i state law, "Aloha is more than a word of greeting or farewell or a salutation. Aloha means mutual regard and affection and extends warmth in caring with no obligation in return. Aloha is the essence of relationships in which each person is important to every other person for collective existence." As the nation's most ethnically diverse state, Hawai'i boasts the nation's highest level of racial intermarriage.[1]

Born in 1960, Genora Dancel exemplifies the state's heritage. Her father was of Spanish, Italian, Filipino, and Chinese ancestry; her mother was a mix of native Hawai'ian and Japanese backgrounds. She has enjoyed a career as a broadcast engineer—and a passion for motorcycles and cars. In the past twenty years, Genora has changed very little from the raven-haired young woman with a broad smile and easy laugh who epitomized the aloha spirit—and who was gay. Ironically, her homosexuality was not a welcome topic in the aloha culture, which valued harmony and was ambivalent about sexuality, reflecting the importance of Christian missionaries in the state's history. Genora was not open about her sexuality with her acquaintances and her coworkers at the KHNL (Fox) television station in Honolulu or at the PBS station, KHET.[2]

Also working at KHET was C.J. Baehr, a former schoolteacher whose daughter, Ninia, was a feminist historian with a master's degree in women's studies. After living in New York City, she was also an out-of-the-closet lesbian. Her mother mentioned to her how wonderful her colleague Genora was and told Genora that her daughter, Ninia, was thinking of buying a cycle and traveling cross-country. They should talk. Ninia dropped by the station in early June 1990, wearing a long-sleeved shirt and jeans. Genora was nervous about

Ninia Baehr and Genora Dancel. (Photo by Angela Wade.)

meeting this out lesbian, but even the most clueless coworkers saw sparks fly when the women met. Ninia was immediately smitten, and Genora wondered whether her frustrating search for a soul mate was over. That night, Genora called, and the two women talked for hours.[3]

On their first date, Genora drove them to the top of Mount Tantalus in her Porsche 928. Towering above the city lights of Honolulu, they became a romantic couple. In September, when Genora was on the mainland doing technical training, she and Ninia spoke every day, and one evening Genora said, "When I get back you'll know that I love you. Will you marry me?" Stunned, Ninia immediately answered "yes." Genora bought an engagement ring, a gold band studded with three rubies and two diamonds. The fiancées were excited to be engaged but had no plans to marry, as the state did not recognize same-sex marriages, and Genora was still not out at work. In 1991, the two women moved in together, in a one-bedroom apartment in Lanikai Beach, outside Honolulu. The open floor plan of the living area culminated in a large kitchen whose picture window gave them a view of the beach and the two Mokulua Islands, dark mounds set off by blue-green sea water that sparkled in the morning sun.[4]

In late 1990, Genora rushed Ninia to the emergency room to treat a bad ear infection. Because Ninia had no health insurance, she incurred medical expenses that the couple could ill afford. KHET did not let employees add non-spouses to their employer-provided health insurance policies. Vaguely aware that some mainland cities had created domestic partnership registries, Ninia called the Gay Community Center to see if Honolulu had any such law. Long-time activist Bill Woods answered the telephone and told her she was out of luck under current law—but he was thinking about putting together a marriage lawsuit: Would she and her partner be interested?

Bill Woods was a brash mainlander whom the discreet Honolulu lesbian and gay community considered too pushy. Yet he successfully lobbied for laws prohibiting discrimination because of sexual orientation. Woods was determined to bring the marriage issue out of its constitutional closet, through an impact lawsuit that would attract media attention. Baehr and Dancel were ideal plaintiffs because they were articulate, mediagenic, and nonthreatening. Neither, however, felt she was in a position to join such an ambitious effort. Both women were working two jobs, and Genora was one of the few women working at KHNL, which was affiliated with Fox, the conservative television network. Might the publicity cost her that job?

Other couples were considering the proposed lawsuit. Forty-two-year-old Antoinette Pregil and Tammy Rodrigues, thirty-eight, had met at a school dance in 1972. They dated until 1975, went their separate ways, and reconnected in 1979. As a fairly open lesbian couple, they had been raising Toni Pregil's biological daughter, Leina'ala, who had just graduated from Pearl City High School. Tammy did not worry about losing her job as a federal worker; a bill collector, Toni did fear reprisals but was ready to stand up for equal treatment. With strong encouragement from Leina'ala, the two moms told Bill Woods to include them in the marriage lawsuit.[5]

Another couple expressing interest were Joe Melillo, forty-two years old, and Patrick Lagon, thirty-three. Joe was an outspoken mainlander, having grown up in an Italian household in New Jersey. Beefy and balding, he often wore a bushy Fu Manchu mustache. He had met the shorter, quieter Pat Lagon at a disco dance lesson in 1977, and they had been a couple since then. In 1990, they owned a house together in the Honolulu suburbs, near Pearl Harbor. Described as "relaxed, warm and a touch campy," they had interests ranging from the silk-screening company they jointly owned, to "catering (Joe was a professional chef) to art (Pat was a talented stylist in ink and watercolor) to designing and sewing costumes for Waikiki Beach hotel shows, arranging flowers and fashioning leis from the bounty of the blooming trees gracing their house." They sought legal marriage because they wanted to adopt a child.[6]

Woods envisioned a lawsuit that would feature a rainbow coalition of education, vocation, and ethnicity reflective of Hawai'i itself: a Western European woman (Baehr); a Hawai'ian, Asian, and European woman (Dancel); a Portuguese Latina woman (Rodrigues); a Filipina woman (Pregil); an Italian man (Melillo); and a Filipino Hawai'ian man (Lagon). On December 16, 1990, Woods called Dancel at work and pressed her for a decision that day. After a hurried consultation at KHNL, Ninia and Genora joined the lawsuit.

At nine o'clock the next morning, the three couples entered the vital records division in downtown Honolulu and applied for marriage licenses. Walking past reporters and cameramen, they made a colorful cast of plaintiffs: Melillo wore a Panama hat and blue Hawai'ian floral shirt; Baehr looked chic in a black jacket and a geometric-pattern design skirt; Dancel was still hoping for some anonymity by wearing computer glasses and a smart jacket and pants. The clerk, Irene Takeda, appeared ready to give them licenses, but her boss told the couples he would have to secure legal advice. On December 27, the attorney general advised him that state law did not permit licenses for same-sex couples, and the health department formally denied the applications on April 12, 1991.[7]

Meanwhile, Woods was searching for an attorney to represent the couples in a lawsuit. He was turned down by Lambda Legal and other mainland litigation organizations, whose leaders believed a marriage lawsuit premature. This conclusion was reinforced when the local ACLU, at the request of Nan Hunter (the founding director of the ACLU's Lesbian and Gay Rights Project), discovered that many in the local gay community were hostile to the lawsuit. Woods then brought the case to Dan Foley, a former legal director of the ACLU of Hawai'i who had his own civil rights firm. He was the perfect lawyer for such a case. Dan was happily married and raising two sons with his wife, Carlyn Tani (an official at the famed Punahou School)—but he had grown up in San Francisco and had known gay people all his life, including a beloved gay uncle and his discreet partner. In college, he had written a thesis titled "The Sexual Minority," which argued that homosexuals were much like everyone else, but they and their culture were skewed by social stigma.[8]

As a lawyer, Foley enthusiastically pitched for social underdogs. In 1985, he had successfully represented the organizers of the Miss Molokai beauty pageant, which featured transgender contestants vying for the crown. He had represented people with AIDS, and in 1990 he was representing Hare Krishnas who had been prevented from selling religious T-shirts in public places. A mellow attorney with a Vandyke beard, Foley was somewhat surprised to hear that lesbian and gay couples even wanted to get married—but he thought the couples should have their day in court. Jewish by birth, Catholic by upbringing, Foley was a practicing Buddhist who struck his clients as one of the kindest, calmest, wisest persons they had ever met. In early 1991, he met with Woods and the three couples and agreed to represent them, but he warned that it would be an uphill battle. Because the US Supreme Court had ruled in *Bowers v. Hardwick* (1986) that "homosexual sodomy" could constitutionally be a felony, Foley believed there were no credible federal constitutional arguments against the statutory exclusion. But it might violate the Hawai'i Constitution, which explicitly recognized a privacy right and a broad antidiscrimination rule, including a state equal rights amendment.[9]

On May 1, 1991, Dan Foley filed the complaint in *Baehr et al. v. Lewin* (the head of the department of health, the agency in charge of marriage licenses). Like marriage plaintiffs in the 1970s, the complainants asserted that their exclusion from civil marriage violated their right to sexual privacy, denied them their fundamental right to marry, and discriminated against them on the basis of a constitutionally arbitrary trait, their sexual orientation. The complaint attracted little support. When Foley met with representatives of the lesbian and gay community, he learned that most of those present were opposed to or even angry about the lawsuit. It brought unwanted attention to the mostly closeted Honolulu gayocracy.

On October 1, 1991, Judge Robert Klein dismissed the *Baehr* complaint, ruling that Hawai'i's limitation of marriage to one man and one woman "is obviously designed to promote the general welfare interests of the community by sanctioning traditional man-woman family units and procreation." This finding satisfied the constitutional requirement that every legal distinction plausibly rest upon a legitimate public interest, and Klein rejected Foley's efforts to impose a tougher form of judicial scrutiny. For example, Foley argued that sexual orientation was a suspect classification because the 1978 Hawai'i Constitutional Convention agreed that it was covered by the existing equal protection language—but the judge ruled that sexual orientation was unlike race and other classifications named in the constitution. Plaintiffs had failed to refute the commonly held belief that sexual orientation is a lifestyle choice, unlike race. Klein also found that gay people, unlike blacks in the 1950s, were not politically powerless.[10]

Foley promptly appealed the loss to the Hawai'i Supreme Court. Given the title of this chapter, the reader may suspect that the state supreme court did not follow the lead of earlier state courts. The court did, indeed, surprise everyone, including the plaintiffs' counsel—but the judges, in turn, were taken aback by the public reactions to their disposition of Dan Foley's appeal. Aloha, constitutional theater!

The Hawai'i Supreme Court's Constitutional Surprise

As constituted in October 1991, the Hawai'i Supreme Court would have affirmed Judge Klein's judgment. Four of the five justices were men in their sixties who were part of the liberal, multiethnic Democratic Party coalition that had dominated Hawai'ian politics since 1962: Chief Justice Herman Lum and Associate Justices Yoshimi Hayashi, Frank Padgett, and James Wakatsuki. The only dissent might have come from fifty-one-year-old justice Ronald Moon. But in the next eighteen months, the first three older justices retired and Wakatsuki died. Governor John Waihee, the first Native Hawai'ian governor, replaced the old guard with young progressives: Moon became chief justice, and Robert Klein (forty-five years old), Steven Levinson (forty-six), Paula Nakayama (thirty-nine), and Mario Ramil (forty-six) had been sworn in as justices by April 1993.[11]

When the court heard the *Baehr* oral argument in October 1992, however, Dan Foley and Deputy Attorney General Sonia Faust faced only a slightly younger court than they would have faced in 1991: Moon, Levinson, and Hayashi (sitting by designation for Wakatsuki) as well as two intermediate court judges designated to sit for this case, James Burns and Walter Meheula Heen. Heen sat for Klein, disqualified from hearing an appeal of his own judgment, and Burns sat for Lum, who recused himself. Ethnically and religiously, this was a more diverse state supreme court panel than any that had ever decided a landmark case in the United States.

The oral argument was marked by this irony: just as in the earlier Washington marriage case (*Singer v. Hara* [1974]), the lawyer for the lesbian and gay couples was a straight person who had never contemplated the possibility of marriage between two women, while the lawyer for the state was a quasi-closeted homosexual who probably regretted that the state did not value lesbian relationships. Foley urged the court to find that the state constitutional right to privacy protected "homosexual sodomy" and, correlatively, the right of homosexuals to marry. The justices listened politely—but became engaged when Foley turned to his argument that homosexuals were a protected class under the state equal protection clause. Federal precedents suggested that judges ought to give strict scrutiny to discrimination against a class (1) that has been subject to pervasive discrimination, (2) that is politically powerless, and (3) whose characteristic trait is not one that a rational decision-maker would consider and (4) is immutable. He argued that homosexuals met all of these requirements.[12]

In a confident, gravelly voice, Sonia Faust opened with the fact that no judge had ever seriously entertained the proposition that the state was required to issue marriage licenses to same-sex couples. Leaning forward, wispy-haired James Burns interrupted her: "They want you not to discriminate against them." The state will give a marriage license to a man asking to marry a woman, he said, but not to a man asking to marry a man. Why isn't that discrimination? Faust responded: "That is permissible discrimination." Steve Levinson asked: "Why is that permissible? Doesn't that conclusion rest upon some factual assumptions, such as the assumption that homosexuals are not a suspect class? Plaintiffs have raised factual issues: Don't they preclude judgment on the pleadings?" Having raised that very point before Klein, Faust conceded that the lower court had erroneously relied on facts not in evidence but insisted the error was "absolutely harmless in this case."

In the conference after argument, Levinson suggested that Klein's reliance on facts not offered as evidence was enough to justify vacating the lower court's order; Moon and Burns agreed. But the justices could not send the case back to the lower court without instructions about what kind of facts a hearing or trial might develop. Levinson felt the couples had a fundamental right to marry that the state could deny only by showing that their exclusion was needed to advance a compelling public interest. But no one else agreed. Burns, a devout Catholic and the son of Hawai'i governor John Burns (1963–1975), was reluctant to constitutionalize an understanding of marriage so discordant with religious as well as legal traditions, and other justices shared his caution. Moon felt that the traditions anchoring the constitutional right to marry were not applicable to lesbian and gay relationships. Of Native Hawai'ian ancestry, Walter Meheula Heen was aware of the *mahu* tradition. *Mahus* were biological men who presented themselves as women and often married or formed relationships with men. This native tradition had been suppressed by the missionaries and by Hawai'i's eagerness to integrate its culture with that of the mainland. Heen ignored that tradition and, after the conference, remarked to his colleagues, "I know the *Ali'i* [the elites] had their little boys." In his only

contribution to the discussion, Yoshimi Hayashi declared: "I'm a traditionalist kind of guy. I'm with *him*," pointing to Heen.[13]

Levinson followed up on Burns's suggestion and Faust's admission that the
exclusion of same-sex couples was a discrimination. As amended through the
Constitutional Convention of 1978, the Hawai'i Constitution contained a broad
anti-discrimination rule: "no person" can be "denied the equal protection of
the laws, nor be denied the enjoyment of the person's civil rights or be discriminated against in the exercise thereof because of race, religion, sex or ancestry." Invoking this language, Foley had argued that sexual orientation was
a suspect classification, but the complaint had not alleged that the six plaintiffs were gay. Levinson believed that there was a simpler argument inspired
by Burns's questions: on its face, the state marriage statute literally discriminated on the basis of sex. A woman could marry a man but could not marry a
woman. The classification whose change created a different legal result was
sex—in the same way that race had been the key classification in *Loving v.
Virginia* (1967), in which the US Supreme Court struck down laws against
different-race marriage. If the exclusion were a form of sex discrimination,
then the state had a high burden of persuasion. Moon was open to this argument. *Loving* was a precedent that resonated with him because of his personal
encounters with prejudice against interracial dating when he had been a student on the mainland. Potentially relevant was that his beloved niece was a
lesbian, and so he could see the lawsuit through the lens of civil rights.[14]

Although this sex discrimination argument for gay marriage had been made
earlier, in the Minnesota and Washington marriage cases, Dan Foley did not
make that argument; nor did the amicus briefs filed by Lambda and the ACLU
in either the Hawai'i or District of Columbia marriage cases. The brief for the
plaintiff couple in *Dean v. District of Columbia* made the constitutional right
to marry argument as well as a sexual orientation discrimination argument
but did not make a sex discrimination argument, either. In short, no one was
making the sex discrimination claim anymore—until Burns suggested it at
oral argument and Levinson pressed it in the *Baehr* conference.[15]

At conference, Burns understood the constitutional meaning of *sex* to include all aspects of a person's gender and sexual identity that are "biologically
fated." If sexual orientation were biologically fated, he reasoned, it would be
unfair for the state to deny gay people equal rights, and that was the best reason to read the state ERA's understanding of *sex* broadly. The US Supreme
Court, for example, had ruled that states could not punish nonmarital children
for their parents' extramarital conduct, which the children did not control.

None of his colleagues agreed with Burns, largely because they did not think the trial court could make headway on an issue of unresolved scientific debate. But his analysis meant that there were three votes to reverse the lower court's judgment dismissing the complaint, against two votes to affirm.[16]

The supreme court released its ruling on May 5, 1993. Speaking for himself and Chief Justice Moon, Justice Levinson's plurality opinion rejected Foley's privacy argument, for he read the precedents recognizing the fundamental right to marry as "rooted in the traditions and collective conscience of our people," which suggested male-female unions only. But Levinson accepted an equal protection claim that Foley had not advanced. Denying same-sex couples marriage licenses because of the sex of one partner is discrimination because of sex. Thus, if Genora Dancel had asked to marry Joe Melillo, Hawai'i would have given these two homosexuals a marriage license—but it refused to do so for Dancel and Ninia Baehr, for no other reason than Genora's sex or that of her proposed spouse. Because sex was a "suspect classification" (like race) under the state constitution, Levinson ruled that the marriage discrimination "is presumed to be unconstitutional" and the state needs to show that the discrimination "is justified by compelling state interests" and "is narrowly drawn to avoid unnecessary abridgments of the applicant couples' constitutional rights."[17]

Judge Burns concurred in the result, on the basis of his view that there needed to be a trial to determine whether, like other features of "sex," sexual orientation is "biologically fated." Because Burns's vote was necessary for a 3-2 majority disposition, the attorney general sought a clarification: Does the trial court have to determine the biologically fated issue or just the compelling state interest issue? Or both? On May 27, the supreme court responded. With Paula Nakayama having replaced Yoshimi Hayashi (whose commission expired when he turned seventy), she joined Ron Moon and Steve Levinson in a mandate that the trial court must apply strict scrutiny to the state's justifications.[18]

Within Hawai'i's collegial judiciary, steeped in the aloha tradition of harmony, the reaction to the supreme court's decision in *Baehr v. Lewin* was unprecedented. Justice Hayashi insisted that his original dissenting vote be noted in the official report of the disposition. Former chief justice William Richardson (1966–1982) publicly rebuked the court. As the first judicial decision to give any recognition to the statutory or constitutional arguments for gay marriage, *Baehr* caused a sensation on the mainland as well. Thousands of lesbian and gay persons and couples began to think seriously about gay marriage for the first time. Other Americans were alarmed.

Baehr helped motivate Lambda to create its Marriage Project, which freed Evan Wolfson of almost all other litigation responsibilities so he could formally join Dan Foley as cocounsel in *Baehr v. Lewin*. Wolfson had already been strategizing with Foley on the case and had written Lambda's amicus brief, but some of the plaintiffs wondered why they needed mainland representation; they loved their current lawyer. As Foley explained to his clients, a trial on the merits would require expert witnesses and significant court costs that they could not afford. Lambda was offering to bear those costs and find the best experts the mainland had to offer. The plaintiffs welcomed Lambda into the case.[19]

Wolfson was thinking several steps ahead. The state would surely lose the trial. Because Hawai'i did not limit marriage licenses to in-state couples, lesbian and gay couples from all over the country could fly to Hawai'i, get legally married, and then return home to insist on local recognition of their Hawai'i marriages. Heading up a project organized by Wolfson and Mary Bonauto, Barbara Cox was charting the rules each state followed as to whether it would recognize valid out-of-state marriages for couples to whom the state would not itself have given marriage licenses. She reported that almost all the states would recognize marriages valid in the state of their celebration (i.e., Hawai'i)— *unless* recognition would violate a fundamental state policy. Wolfson maintained that the full faith and credit clause of the US Constitution would require even these states to recognize valid Hawai'i marriages.[20]

At the same time, Wolfson was assembling a National Freedom to Marry Coalition of around twenty pro-gay advocacy and litigation groups "to coordinate an education and political organizing campaign to win and keep the right to marry in the face of a likely backlash to a court decision in Hawaii." He felt the time was ripe for a national conversation: as the media's association of AIDS with homosexuality had receded and examples of out-of-the-closet lesbian and gay Americans (including couples) had exploded, public opinion in the 1990s shifted toward tolerance of gay people and acceptance of rights for them. Openly gay officials were proliferating, and Governor Bill Clinton won the presidency in 1992 after promising to end the exclusion of gay citizens from the armed forces. Based upon polling by the Human Rights Campaign (HRC) and discussions among the associated organizations, the coalition's message was that "marriage is a personal choice and a basic human right" and was "best understood as a relationship of emotional and financial interdependence between two people who make a legal and public commitment to that effect."[21]

Religious skeptics of same-sex marriages were thinking nationally as well. On February 1, 1994, the First Presidency (President Howard Hunter and Counselors Gordon Hinckley and Thomas Monson) of the Church of Jesus Christ of Latter-day Saints issued a statement reaffirming their view that "marriage between a man and a woman is ordained of God to fulfill the eternal destiny of His children. We encourage members to appeal to legislators, judges, and other government officials to preserve the purposes and sanctity of marriage between a man and a woman, and to reject all efforts to give legal authorization or other official approval or support to marriages between persons of the same gender." The Southern Baptist Convention and the US Conference of Catholic Bishops issued statements to the same effect.[22]

Within Hawai'i, the most vocal critic was Mike Gabbard, a lean, tanned, charismatic member of an offshoot of the Hare Krishna faith tradition; he usually wore a lei around his neck and a bright floral Hawai'i print shirt, sometimes with a sports jacket. Gabbard and his wife were committed to traditional family values and homeschooled their five children to avoid corrupting influences. (One of those children, Tulsi Gabbard, ran for president in 2019–2020.) His genial demeanor contrasted with his hard-edged words about gay people. "One morning I woke up to a world in which an unnatural, unhealthy, immoral activity, which was taking thousands of lives [through AIDS], was being portrayed in the media as moral, natural, healthy and normal." From Gabbard's perspective, *Baehr* was a calamitous decision, for it opened the door to state approval and social normalization of homosexual relationships that he considered immoral, sick, and harmful to children.[23]

Here Come the Latter-day Saints . . .

The Hawai'i legislature was overwhelmingly controlled by the Democrats. They had a 23-2 majority in the senate, 44-7 in the house of representatives. Most members, in both chambers, did not welcome *Baehr v. Lewin*. The key player on the house side was chairman Terrance Tom of the judiciary committee, which had jurisdiction over constitutional issues. Legally blind, Tom was the first lawyer in the nation to take (and pass) the bar examination in Braille. Normally an ACLU ally, he privately assured his law school classmate Dan Foley that he would approach the issue with an open mind. Terry asked Dan whether he was homosexual, and on being told he wasn't, asked: "Why are you doing this case, then? You have children!" Dan had two young boys. Terry then asked: "Are your boys gay?" The unflappable civil rights lawyer

responded: Who knows? It did not bother him that his kids might ultimately be gay, an attitude that confounded his old friend. Terry Tom found
homosexual marriage incomprehensible and scary in ways that Dan Foley
did not.[24]

The Hawai'i senate was more supportive. The president of the senate, Norman Mizuguchi, was a liberal, ACLU Democrat who was not inclined to go
along with a policy he saw as discriminatory. The same could be said of senate judiciary committee chair Reynaldo Graulty, a Catholic Filipino American
and a progressive friend of Foley's. Even more liberal was Senator Matt Matsunaga, who also served on the judiciary committee and was the leading legislative defender of *Baehr*. Because only half of the senators faced the voters in
most election cycles, Mizuguchi, Graulty, Matsunaga, and their colleagues felt
the heat generated by *Baehr* less intensely than their house colleagues, who
faced elections every two years.

Not wanting to give the Republicans an opening, the Democratic leadership
agreed to proceed cautiously. In 1994, the Hawai'i legislature passed an Act
Relating to Marriage, sponsored by Tom. Section 1 declared that the *Baehr* decision "effaces the recognized tradition of marriage in this State and, in so
doing, impermissibly negates the constitutionally mandated role of the legislature as a co-equal, coordinate branch of government." Section 2 added a provision to the family code reaffirming the traditional definition of marriage as
between one man and one woman. Section 6 created a Commission on Sexual Orientation and the Law, with commissioners to be named by the governor, the house speaker, the senate president, the Catholic Church, and the
Church of Jesus Christ. Notwithstanding the legislative ire reflected in sections 1 and 2, neither chamber acted on proposals to enshrine that rule in the
Hawai'i Constitution.[25]

THE PARTICIPATION OF LATTER-DAY SAINTS
IN *BAEHR V. LEWIN*

On April 16, 1994, Brigham Young University professor Lynn Wardle was
on an academic panel with Evan Wolfson, who boasted that once *Baehr* was
decided in the plaintiffs' favor after trial, gay marriages would immediately
go nationwide, as couples would fly to Hawai'i and return home legally married. Wardle alerted the leadership of the Church of Jesus Christ of Latter-day
Saints that "homosexual and lesbian marriage" might spread faster than anyone expected. The Council of the First Presidency and the Quorum of the

Twelve Apostles (the governing body for the Church) planned an aggressive response.[26]

Church counsel in February 1995 filed a motion to intervene as a party defendant in *Baehr*—the first time a religious group had participated in a same-sex marriage case. The stated rationale was the fear that religious marriage officiants would be required to perform same-sex marriages. In its supporting memorandum, the Church identified public interests that it would press to justify the traditional definition of marriage:

- Same-sex couples lack the parenting skills of heterosexual couples, and some of their children thus "will be condemned to a higher incidence of some social maladies such as substance abuse, poverty, and violence. Children will also suffer from sexual identity problems because they lack a traditional family role model."
- The state has a strong interest in fostering procreation, which "will be severely undermined by the recognition of same-sex marriages."
- The current family law regime holds up conjugal marriage as the ethical gold standard for relationships—a standard that would be diluted if marriage were redefined.

"We do not see this as a civil-rights issue," the Mormons asserted. "We see it as a protection of traditional marriage."[27]

Attorney General Margery Bronster opposed the Church's participation, in part because her office feared that it would insist upon witnesses who would make sectarian arguments inconsistent with Hawai'i's tradition of pluralism and anti-discrimination. At the March 15 hearing, the state and the plaintiffs both opposed the motion, arguing that the Church would transform the case into a "referendum of unspecified scope on the morality and religious stature of homosexuality." In addition, Hawai'i law already guaranteed religious organizations the freedom to conduct only marriage ceremonies consistent with their faith traditions. Judge Herbert Shimabukuro denied the motion for this reason, and his ruling was affirmed by the Hawai'i Supreme Court.[28]

In September 1995, while the Church's appeal to the Hawai'i Supreme Court was pending, Gordon Hinckley, the Church's new president, issued "The Family: A Proclamation to the World" on behalf of the First Presidency and the Quorum. The proclamation defined marriage as having been ordained by God as a holy union between a man and a woman. It was grounded upon the Church's belief that all human beings have an eternal gender and that holy, conjugal marriage is a perfect wedding of the two sexes, with each playing a different role in the family: the husband as the primary breadwinner, the wife as the primary caregiver. One of the drafters of the proclamation later recalled: "We could see the people of the world wanting to define the family in ways contrary to God's eternal plan for the happiness of His children. . . . Gender is being confused, and gender roles are being repudiated. Same-gender marriage is being promoted in direct opposition to one of God's primary purposes." Recall that Hinckley, as chair of the Church's public affairs committee, had spearheaded the Church's efforts to stop the ERA, based in part on the belief that prohibiting sex discrimination would entail recognition of same-sex marriages. Because Hawai'i's constitution contained an ERA, *Baehr*'s logic was precisely what the Church had predicted would happen if the national ERA were ratified.[29]

The primary objection to the sex discrimination argument for gay marriage was its lack of symmetry: the classification, sex, did not match up with the disadvantaged class, lesbians and gay men. But the Church opposed "homosexual and lesbian marriage" because it violated eternal gender roles, denied the need for men and women to progress together toward eternal life, and deprived a child of the unique benefits of being raised by a father and a mother. As presented in the proclamation, the traditional definition of marriage was rooted in strong gender roles, not homophobia. From the feminist perspective that informed the ERA, the lesson was clear: If one reason for limiting marriage to different-sex couples is to entrench traditional gender roles, women will be the class most strongly affected. Although the *Baehr* justices were not inspired by Mormon cosmology, their sex discrimination argument for same-sex marriage was a tighter fit with *Loving* once it was understood in the light of that worldview.[30]

HAWAI'I'S FUTURE TODAY

Soon after the proclamation, the church leadership launched an effort to head off homosexual and lesbian marriage, under the command of Elder Loren Dunn, president of the Church's North American West Area. Ironically, Elder Dunn had been appointed to a leadership position because the leading candidate had been seen in the presence of a suspected homosexual. The white-haired Dunn (now deceased) had the appearance of a stern, tight-lipped bank president and commanded the same kind of respect. Over the next three years, he would devote more time and effort than anyone else to stopping gay marriage in Hawai'i.[31]

On October 19, Dunn met in Hawai'i with lobbyist Linda Rosehill, business-man Jack Hoag, Father Marc Alexander of the Roman Catholic Church, and representatives of a lobbying firm. Later that day, he met with Francis DiLorenzo, the bishop of Honolulu, who confirmed that the Catholics would take the leading position in an alliance to stop gay marriage that would be fi-nanced by the Church of Jesus Christ. The campaign would be run by an organization called Hawai'i's Future Today (HFT), with Hoag and Alexander as the initial cochairs. Dunn brought prominent Mormons to Hawai'i: Rich-ard Wirthlin to conduct opinion polls, Arthur Andersen to provide orga-nizational and financial advice, and Lynn Wardle to provide legal advice and drafting. To finance these efforts, he secured an immediate grant of $50,000 from Salt Lake City.[32]

HFT's mission was to place a constitutional amendment on the ballot, so that voters could override a likely constitutional judgment. According to Dunn, "This is a hard road to take but a sitting justice of the supreme court has sug-gested it." Placing a constitutional amendment on the ballot would require either a two-thirds supermajority vote in both chambers or majority votes in successive legislatures. Because the Democrats would want something for their gay and lesbian constituents, the religious coalition might have to accept some compromise—but it could not include marriage-like public registration and benefits. Dunn was open to Wardle's suggestion that humanitarian reasons could justify hospital visitation, estate planning, and perhaps state employee benefits for what he termed lesbian and gay "co-dependents."[33]

In December 1995, Dunn reported that everyone of consequence was talk-ing with the coalition—including House Speaker Joe Souki, Terry Tom, Rey Graulty (who was noncommittal), two commission members, Attorney Gen-eral Bronster, and "a member of the State Supreme Court who favors our po-sition but will be excused because of earlier involvement." (That would have been Justice Klein. Although he had been raised as a Mormon, Klein denies any conversations with HFT or the Church.) As pollster Wirthlin found, the Church of Jesus Christ was not viewed favorably in the state—a finding that reinforced Hinckley's insistence that the Catholics should take center stage and that HFT should emphasize "family values," not religious values, in its lobby-ing and public presentations. Wirthlin also reported that three-quarters of vot-ers thought the marriage issue should be decided by them and not by judges.[34]

On December 5, 1995, the Commission on Sexual Orientation issued its re-port. Led by chairman Thomas Gill, the 5-2 majority recommended that the legislature amend the marriage law to include same-sex couples or, failing that, pass a domestic partnership law granting all the legal benefits and duties of marriage to same-sex domestic partners. All of the commissioners nominated by Governor Waihee and President Mizuguchi joined the majority report. In lengthy dissenting views, the two commissioners nominated by Speaker Souki argued that either of these proposed reforms would undermine marriage and introduce AIDS and other diseases into Hawai'i families. Lynn Wardle suggested edits to the dissenters but was not able to dissuade them from extreme claims that "homosexuality is a psychological pathology" and that "evidence of widespread health problems in the homosexual community appears as robust as is that against smoking."[35]

The bitterly divided commission reflected a fraying of the aloha spirit. This was the primary reason the lead plaintiff couple, Baehr and Dancel, had fled Hawai'i and relocated in Baltimore, Maryland. The hate mail and negative publicity had been bad enough, but they also felt hostility to them from the lesbian and gay community, which felt excluded from Bill Woods's initiatives. Both women described the experience as more suffocating than the closet had been.[36]

THE 1996 SESSION OF THE LEGISLATURE

Confident of unwavering support from Terry Tom and Joe Souki in the house of representatives and armed with a promise of more money from Salt Lake City, HFT turned up the pressure on the senate. It warned Rey Graulty and other senators that it would support primary opponents if they didn't go along with a constitutional amendment. Also, HFT's lobbyists were pressuring senators one-on-one and drumming up grassroots input and editorials arguing that this was a family definition, and not a civil rights, issue. Described as a "Cuomo-type" who was a devout Catholic in his private life but willing to see public issues through a civil rights lens, Graulty bottled up the amendment in committee, which instead reported a comprehensive domestic partnership bill on February 25. The Graulty measure was unacceptable to the Church of Jesus Christ. Elder Dallin Oaks from the Quorum of the Twelve suggested that Dunn oppose any sexualized institution mimicking marriage, but the Church might support legislation giving rights to social partners, such as power of attorney, hospital visitation, insurance, and pension benefits.[37]

With the advice and support of HFT, the house judiciary committee ignored the domestic partnership proposal and, instead, reported a proposed constitutional amendment, drafted by Wardle: "Marriage shall be defined in the State of Hawai'i as the legal association reserved exclusively for the lawful union of a man and a woman." On March 5, the senate passed the domestic partnership bill by a 14-11 vote and sent it to the house. Within hours, the house passed the constitutional amendment by 37-14 and sent it to the senate. The two chambers had voted themselves into a deadlock.[38]

Later that month, the Church provided $100,000 to HFT, which used some of it to step up its public relations and lobbying efforts. With this boost, HFT's senate allies were able to append a statutory marriage amendment to an unrelated house bill. In conference to resolve differences between the two chambers, Senator Richard Matsuura proposed a compromise: "A provision in a statute which provides for the issuance of marriage licenses solely to couples of the opposite sex shall be interpreted as consistent with all of the rights protected by this Constitution: provided that governmental benefits and obligations will be allocated to all on an equal basis." Terry Tom and the house conferees rejected this proposal. Thwarted by the stalemate, HFT's lobbyists tried one final play. On the last night of the legislative session, nine senators moved to lift the constitutional amendment out of the judiciary committee for immediate consideration on the senate floor. When it was brought to a vote, however, President Mizuguchi and his allies succeeded in defeating the proposal, 10-15. End of session.[39]

It was clear to HFT that Senators Mizuguchi and (especially) Graulty were the main obstacles—and they were up for reelection. Dunn reported: "Jack Hoag was invited to a private meeting with prominent Democrats who are trying to unseat Graulty and they have a viable candidate. Jack tells me with Graulty gone, the amendment will pass next session. Our people know who to vote for but not enough are registered. Does the First Presidency letter preclude use of our chapels in a general drive for voter registration? What about the school as a location?" The Latter-day Saints were not alone. Mike Gabbard's political action committee, Alliance for Traditional Marriage—Hawai'i (ATM), spent the summer raising money and recruiting volunteers to oust Graulty, Mizuguchi, and other foot-draggers on marriage.[40]

The Hawai'i Marriage Trial

While HFT and ATM were organizing politically, Foley and Wolfson were preparing for the upcoming trial in *Baehr v. Miike* (as it was renamed when Lawrence Miike succeeded John Lewin as head of the health department). The case was assigned to Judge Kevin Chang, whose attention to detail, focus on facts over politics, respectful treatment of counsel and witnesses, and poker-faced demeanor were legendary. He was ideal for a case that raised such intense emotions. Police were posted all around the courthouse, and metal detectors screened everyone entering Judge Chang's tiny fourth-floor courtroom. The state's witnesses were registered in a hotel under false names and driven to the courthouse each day by a police escort. On the second day of the trial there was a bomb scare, and the witnesses were sent back to the hotel.[41]

In his opening statement, on September 10, 1996, Deputy Attorney General Rick Eichor argued that the state had a compelling interest "to pursue the optimal development of children, to unite children with their mothers and fathers, and to have mothers and fathers take responsibility for their children." The state's religious allies thought Eichor was slighting the strongest justification: conjugal marriage as the only natural and moral understanding of the institution. Additionally, they maintained that a redefinition of marriage would generate untold ills for society and would undermine families by bringing the homosexual Trojan horse into the polis.[42]

When Eichor had taken over the case the previous June, his predecessor had done no preparatory work, so Eichor spent all summer figuring out what kind of case to present and what witnesses to offer. Mormon and Catholic leaders suggested morality-inspired witnesses supporting traditional marriage, but Bronster, Eichor, and Deputy Attorney General Larry Goya believed they should meet the compelling-interest test only with secular third-party harms. Given the Hawai'i tradition of tolerance and its 1991 anti-discrimination law, they were not going to denigrate lesbian and gay people or their families—and they felt that most of the witnesses suggested by the religious groups had invoked anti-gay stereotypes in their publications or public comments. Eichor telephoned dozens of recognized experts on child psychology and marriage sociology, but almost all turned him down because they did not want to publicly oppose gay rights.[43]

Nonetheless, he assembled an impressive witness list, and his first witness was gold-plated: Dr. Kyle Pruett, a renowned child psychologist associated with the Yale Child Study Center. In a decade-long longitudinal study of parenting, Pruett had found that children raised by different-sex couples are advantaged by their contrasting parental styles: mothers are usually more comforting and enabling, and fathers are more challenging and physical. Having both caregiving styles helps inculcate different capacities in the child. Because biological parents tend to bond over the process leading up to the birth of their children and to provide complementary parental styles, Pruett further testified that intact mom-dad families are the "optimum" or "least burdened" environment for child-rearing. "In terms of probabilities, same-sex marriages are more likely to provide a more burdened nurturing domain." Eichor hoped this testimony would show that Hawai'i's compelling interest in the welfare of children justified its limitation of marriage to different-sex couples.[44]

In demeanor and expertise, Pruett was a model witness. The only problem was that he did not entirely agree with the state's theory. In his clinical practice, he had worked with lesbian couples raising children and found that they were capable parents. In fact, they illustrated his theory, as one of the lesbians would typically be the more challenging parent, and the other would be more comforting. Gendered parenting styles, in other words, were not inevitably linked to biological sex. Not only were lesbian couples good parents, but their children would be better off if their parents could get married. Pruett told us that the state's attorneys were fully aware of his views. On cross-examination, he testified that lesbian and gay couples can be just as effective parents as straight couples and that same-sex couples should be allowed to adopt and raise children.[45]

After the bomb scare, the second day of trial was equally educational. David Eggebeen, an associate professor of sociology at Penn State, testified as an expert on family demography. He described the changes that had occurred in partnering, childbearing, and labor-force behavior in the United States between 1966 and 1996:

- Many more women were working outside the home than ever before, including mothers with children under six.
- Women were cohabiting rather than marrying at increasing rates. One in four Hawai'i couples was cohabiting rather than married.
- Women were having children outside of marriage at increasing rates. In Hawai'i, 10 percent of births were outside of marriage in 1970, climbing to 26 percent by 1990.
- The median age of marriage for women had risen and the birth rate had fallen.
- The annual divorce rate in the US population had increased.

Although the state was not emphasizing the argument that same-sex marriage would contribute to the decline of marriage, this testimony would have been the starting point for such an argument. Eggebeen, however, did not explain how recognizing same-sex marriages would exacerbate the trends he identified.

He did testify that the biological mom-dad-kids family is a much better environment for children than cohabiting families or even stepparent families, because the nonbiological parent will not be as invested in the child. His primary evidence for this proposition was the fairy tale *Cinderella*, in which the stepmother favors her shiftless biological daughters over her hardworking stepdaughter. Although listening impassively behind his owlish glasses, Judge Chang did an internal eye roll over the Cinderella evidence. On cross-examination, Eggebeen conceded that single parents, adoptive parents, lesbian mothers, gay fathers, and same-sex couples can create stable family environments and raise healthy and well-adjusted children. Like Pruett, he affirmed that children raised in lesbian and gay households would benefit from the social and material benefits of marriage for their parents.[46]

At the end of the state's case on September 13, Mike Gabbard was very impressed—with the plaintiffs' counsel Evan Wolfson, whose cross-examinations turned the state's experts into witnesses for his side. "My concern is how weak the state's case is and [Wolfson] keeps exposing it," Gabbard lamented. David Coolidge, head of the Marriage Project at Catholic University, found the trial "a distressing experience, despite the well-intentioned efforts of Deputy Attorney General Eichor. Virtually all the passion was on one side—worsened by the fact that Eichor, a low-key lawyer originally from Kansas, gambled that a laid-back approach would win points with the judge. A state hesitant to make an openly moral argument found itself pitted against lawyers, including Lambda's top national litigator on marriage issues, ready to press their claims with all the passionate moral intensity of a children's crusade."[47]

The plaintiffs' counsel opened their case with Dr. Pepper Schwartz, a sociologist who testified that the primary quality of parenting is not parenting structure or biology but the nurturing relationship between parent and child. Child psychologist Charlotte Patterson testified that she had studied fifty-five lesbian and twenty-five straight families and that the parents' sexual orientation was not a good predictor of a child's well-being and adjustment. The best predictor of good adjustment was whether the children enjoyed a harmonious family environment. Two other medical experts, David Brodzinsky of Rutgers University and Robert Bidwell of the University of Hawai'i Medical School, agreed that the primary quality of good parenting is not biology or a particular family structure but the nurturing relationship between parent and child. When Brodzinsky was testifying that stepparents and adoptive parents can raise children just as well as biological parents, Dan Foley noticed that

Judge Chang was leaning forward and listening intensely. The judge and his wife were the parents of an adopted son.

Like Wolfson, Eichor conducted impressive cross-examinations. The deputy attorney general faulted Patterson's study as unscientific because it was heavily populated with well-educated lesbians with high incomes, a demographic biased to produce good results. Also, the study accepted as fact the self-reporting of parents about how well their kids were doing. Neither her nor Schwartz's study was based on a random sample of the population, a fundamental problem made worse by the small sample size of the studies. Such studies might suggest that lesbian and gay parents were capable of good parenting, but they did not demonstrate that this performance was typical. Schwartz conceded that a random sample would have been better and that there is a "biological advantage" between natural parents and their children—but insisted that it didn't mean nonbiological parents (like the Changs) were necessarily "less intense or less committed to the child."

On September 20, the tenth day of the trial, counsel presented closing arguments to Judge Chang. "Marriage means more than love," said Rick Eichor. It is "the institution favored for raising children," and that distinctive feature justifies the state in limiting it to different-sex, potentially procreating couples. Allowing one alternative lifestyle—gay marriage—would open up Pandora's box to others, such as polygamy or incest. These arguments saddened the plaintiff couples—Pat Lagon and Joe Melillo and Tammy Rodrigues and Toni Pregil—who sat right behind Foley and Wolfson for parts of the trial. Rodrigues commented, "It's hard for me to understand what the state is saying because we've raised a child. Our daughter is perfect. She's living proof." Leina'ala Pregil was a star high school and college student; she graduated from the University of Hawai'i School of Law in 2006.[48]

As Judge Chang was studying the record and the post-trial briefs, Professor Coolidge lamented that the state had fallen into a trap laid by the plaintiffs' lawyers. Afraid of being labeled "homophobic," the state declined to make its strongest arguments, based upon tradition and morality, and had relied instead on inconclusive social science. "Marriage is not simply a pragmatic institution created by the state to accomplish some instrumental purpose. It is a unique sexual community that binds together the two sexes into a full image of humanity, and carries on the human project from generation to generation." This criticism was not fair to the attorney general's office, because the strict scrutiny standard demanded by the supreme court could only be met by pragmatic evidence, not by Coolidge's morals-based reasoning. But he was astute to question whether rights-based constitutional litigation was the best forum for resolving the moral and policy issues surrounding the definition of marriage.[49]

On December 3, 1996, Judge Chang ruled that Hawai'i had not met its burden under *Baehr v. Lewin*. The state had "failed to establish a causal link between allowing same-sex marriage and adverse effects upon the optimal development of children." Conversely, the court found "that the single most important factor in the development of a happy, healthy and well-adjusted child is the nurturing relationship between parent and child"; that "gay and lesbian parents and same-sex couples have the potential to raise children that are happy, healthy and well adjusted"; and that "gay and lesbian parents and same-sex couples can be as fit and loving parents, as non-gay men and women and different sex couples." Contrary to the state's argument, "if same-sex marriage is allowed, the children being raised by gay or lesbian parents and same-sex couples may be assisted, because they may obtain certain protections and benefits that come with or become available as a result of marriage." Accordingly, the judge ruled that the sex discrimination violated the Hawai'i Constitution. He was not the first judge to say that same-sex marriage bars were unconstitutional. In the District of Columbia marriage case, Judge John Ferren of the court of appeals had found that the District's exclusion violated the fundamental right to marry and was unconstitutional sexual orientation discrimination. Because the other two judges on the panel rejected these arguments, the court of appeals in January 1995 upheld the same-sex marriage exclusion in *Dean v. District of Columbia*.[50]

For two of the named plaintiffs, the victory was bittersweet. Five thousand miles away in Baltimore, Ninia Baehr and Genora Dancel were not only distancing themselves from the marriage case but were drifting apart as a couple. Raising money for litigation expenses, constant interviews with the press, and negative comments from other gay people diverted them from deepening their relationship. Ninia, who took the negative publicity very personally, thinks the pressure from the litigation drove them apart. Genora thinks it was more a matter of each woman sorting through her evolving emotional needs. In February 1997, Ninia and Genora separated as a couple but remained plaintiffs in *Baehr v. Miike*.[51]

The 1997 Legislative Session

As the marriage trial was proceeding, Hawai'i politics was churning around the same issue. In the 1996 election, ATM and HFT raised money and enthusiasm for challengers to senators and representatives who dragged their feet on a constitutional amendment. HRC in Washington, DC, and the Equality Fund in Hawai'i raised money to support the same incumbents. Once Gabbard learned which incumbents HRC was supporting, he knew for sure whom his group needed to target—and the top of the hit list was Senator Graulty. During the *Baehr* trial, Rey Graulty told Dan Foley that "this trial is killing me" with the voters in his district. The Democratic Party primary was held on September 21, the day after the trial ended.[52]

Senator Graulty was routed in the primary by a newcomer who pledged to support a marriage amendment. Senate President Mizuguchi barely beat his primary challenger. On the other hand, supporters of same-sex marriage succeeded in defeating Senator Milton Holt, the traditional marriage leader in the senate, and they almost knocked off Representative Terry Tom, who won his primary by eighty-seven votes. In November, Republicans critical of gay marriage picked up four house seats—moving from seven to eleven representatives. When the legislature reconvened in January 1997, Mizuguchi managed to secure another term as senate president, and Senators Matt Matsunaga and Avery Chumbley were named chairs of the senate judiciary committee. But Matsunaga warned Foley: "I cannot stop this."[53]

On January 22, 1997, Chief Justice Moon spoke to the legislative session with a report on the judiciary: "When deciding cases, judges often apply common law, statutory law, or constitutional law to new facts and circumstances. In so doing, we do not intend to usurp the legislative function. However, under our system of checks and balances, if we stray into legislative prerogative, the legislature has the ability to cure the trespass." He seemed to be signaling that the supreme court would not decide the appeal in *Baehr* until legislators had an opportunity to vote on a constitutional amendment. Two days later, Elder Dunn reflected, "We won't have to worry about the Hawai'i Supreme Court second guessing the Legislature on passing this legislation." As before, he was well-informed: none of the justices was prepared to grant Foley and Wolfson's motion to lift the stay imposed by Judge Chang or to decide the *Baehr* appeal until the political dust had settled. As he suggested to legislators, Moon felt that any early decision in *Baehr* would disrespect the democratic process and would create friction with legislators whose support was needed to fund the judiciary. Levinson and Nakayama worried that couples receiving marriage licenses would be emotionally wounded if the voters then abrogated their marriages.[54]

On January 24, HFT (Catholics and Latter-day Saints) and ATM (Krishnas and Evangelicals) sponsored a rally in support of the existing marriage law.

More than five thousand people peacefully but vocally petitioned the legislature to pass a constitutional amendment. Bishop DiLorenzo directed Catholic parishes to read a letter from the pulpit admonishing the faithful to "make it absolutely clear to [the senators] that we want true marriage protected and supported." HFT volunteers, lobbyists, and allies worked the legislature around the clock, meeting with almost every member. They provided committee testimony from family law experts Coolidge and Wardle, polling data strongly supporting traditional marriage, constituent letters and petitions, and drafting advice to their legislative allies.[55]

In January, the house passed H.B. 117, a proposed constitutional amendment allowing the legislature to limit the definition of marriage, and H.B. 118, which would create a new relationship category, *reciprocal beneficiaries,* who could receive rights to hospital visitation, inheritance, and wrongful death of their partners. Wardle was the primary drafter, and his draft of H.B. 118 reflected the views of Elder Oaks, noted above. On February 5, the senate passed a different constitutional amendment, empowering the legislature to act only through measures that did not "deprive any person of civil rights on the basis of sex," and a reciprocal beneficiaries bill that offered many more family-based benefits for same-sex couples. Matsunaga sponsored these proposals. Each chamber appointed members to a conference committee to reconcile the bills.[56]

On February 24, the *Honolulu Star-Bulletin* reported that voters disapproved of same-sex marriages by a wide margin, 70 to 20 percent. Even domestic partnerships were disfavored, 55 to 42 percent. Despite public opinion, the senate and house remained at an impasse through March. The deadlock was broken when the Church of Jesus Christ gave HFT the go-ahead to propose a compromise, to be drafted by Wardle and Coolidge. On April 5, Terry Tom offered the senators a modest constitutional amendment, allowing the legislature to limit marriage and its benefits to opposite-sex couples. And he accepted most of the new benefits for reciprocal beneficiaries. On Tuesday, April 8, the senators countered with a narrower amendment and a broader list of benefits for reciprocal beneficiaries. The next day, the house offered this: "The legislature shall have the power to reserve marriage to opposite-sex couples." A last-minute ad campaign by HRC and the ACLU did not prevent the conferees from reaching a deal.[57]

On April 21, the senate passed the reciprocal beneficiaries bill (H.B. 118) by a vote of 22-3. Eight days later, the house passed it by a vote of 38-10. The final version included concessions from both sides. The house agreed to allow many of the benefits added by the senate to remain in the statute, including health benefits. On the other hand, the senate agreed to a two-year cap on health benefits for public employees and agreed to limit the costs of reciprocal beneficiary-related health benefits for private employers. The senate also agreed to delete provisions treating reciprocal beneficiaries as a quasi-marital unit for purposes of joint property rights and income tax liability. From the perspective of the Catholics and Mormons, it was most important that the final bill use the antiseptic term "reciprocal beneficiaries" and that it disengage this term from a sexual relationship by opening up the institution to related persons who no one felt could get married, such as siblings or parents and children. Although HFT did not approve of the many rights included in H.B. 118, Dunn concluded that these concessions were a small price to pay for the constitutional amendment, and "we believe that what has occurred will set back the opposition's movement significantly, both in Hawai'i and nationally." Wardle worried that H.B. 118 created a registration system that could be expanded. It was, he wrote, "more than just the camel's nose [inside the tent]; it is the camel's nose, head, and neck," which could eventually provide "mandatory private sector equivalent benefits, and even more extensive public benefits." Governor Cayetano declined to either sign or veto the Reciprocal Beneficiaries Act, and it became law without his signature.[58]

As for the marriage amendment, the text itself was unchanged from that proposed by the house on April 9: "The legislature shall have the power to reserve marriage to opposite-sex couples." On April 29, the senate passed H.B. 118, 24-0, and the house followed, 44-6. That was more than the two-thirds vote required to place the proposed amendment immediately on the ballot without going through a second vote in the next legislative session.[59]

On July 8, the reciprocal beneficiaries law went into effect. Although this was the first statewide recognition of rights for lesbian and gay couples, it generated a ho-hum reaction from the lesbian and gay community. Because reciprocal beneficiaries could be different-sex and could be blood relatives, it presented itself more as a "best friends" or "caregiver" law than a "till death do us part" relationship law. The most significant benefit the law promised—workplace health insurance—disappeared almost immediately: in August 1997, Attorney General Bronster interpreted the law's health insurance guarantee to apply only to insurance companies, not to health maintenance organizations or mutual benefit societies, thus excluding most of the workforce. In 1999, the Hawai'i legislature defunded the program for state employees. Between July 1997 and May 2001, there were only 571 registered beneficiary couples.

The 1998 Marriage Amendment Referendum

The summer after the legislature's vote, Gordon Hinckley's First Presidency approved full engagement of church resources for the 1998 referendum on the constitutional amendment. Jack Hoag and HFT teamed up with Mike Gabbard and ATM to form a new political action organization, Save Traditional Marriage—'98 (STM'98). Its strategy was to present itself as a "moderate community coalition," sympathetic to gay people—unlike the Hawai'i Christian Coalition and the Hawai'i Family Forum, which still claimed that homosexuals were child molesters despised by God. STM'98 argued that same-sex marriage would undermine the family, jeopardize interstate recognition of Hawai'i marriages, and compel schools to teach that gay marriages are as legitimate as straight marriages.[60]

Opposing the amendment was Protect Our Constitution (POC), headed by Jackie Young, a former vice-speaker of the Hawai'i house. The media campaign was funded and managed by HRC, whose communications director, David Smith, camped out in Hawai'i for most of 1998. Smith recruited the state's top polling firm, its premier ad agency, and Joe Napolitan, a cigar-puffing political consultant with decades of experience. Based upon polls and focus groups suggesting that people in the Aloha State were proud of their tradition of pluralist inclusion, HRC's strategy was to frame the referendum as a question of whether "discrimination" should be included in the Hawai'i Constitution. Basically, the campaign tried to change the subject, away from gay marriage and toward toleration, privacy, and even abortion. Today, gay people lose their rights; tomorrow, women needing abortions or family planning?[61]

The "no" campaign was endorsed by a number of labor unions and many civic and civil rights groups as well as the leading newspapers. On the other hand, both Governor Cayetano and his GOP challenger, Maui mayor Linda Lingle, endorsed the marriage amendment. Cayetano's supporters launched a whisper campaign that the twice-divorced Lingle was a lesbian. Still, opponents hoped for support among racial and ethnic minorities, based on the message: "Never before have we amended our constitution here in Hawai'i, a land of aloha, to specifically discriminate against one group of people. What if that group were you?" Evangelical pastor Jon Honold objected: "They're saying that if I vote this way, I'm not a good American. I can still vote yes and be a good citizen."[62]

The amendment received strong support from the Church of Jesus Christ, the Catholic Church, and the Christian Coalition, while clerics from the Lutheran, Methodist, and UCC churches spoke against it. STM'98 ran television ads in September and October. The first ad featured a boy, played by Linda Rosehill's eight-year-old son, reading from a book called *Daddy's Wedding*. The camera zoomed in to show a picture of two men kissing as they get married. "If you don't think homosexual marriage will affect you, how do you think it will affect your children?" Another ad started with a man and a woman in wedding attire running toward each other on a beach, in romantic slow motion. Their faces were filled with joy as they closed in on one another—but the man ran past the woman and into the arms of another man. These ads were controversial. UCC pastor Joan Ishibashi scoffed that "using the child for their purposes is a very subtle way to hit the triggers of intolerance."[63]

In August 1998, a complaint to the state Campaign Spending Commission changed the campaign's funding dynamics. Bill Woods accused amendment supporters of violating the $1,000 limit on individual campaign contributions. Attorney General Bronster advised the commission that the campaign spending limit was unconstitutional. By October 1998, STM'98 had raised $845,224 and POC had raised $1,145,388, mostly from HRC. But it was the Latter-day Saints' $600,000 donation that captured the media's attention.[64]

The political climate grew more acrimonious during the last weeks of the campaign. ATM sponsored a thirty-second television spot featuring Mike Gabbard and his entire family testifying that you should not be able to marry *anyone* you want, like your daughter (Tulsi, who spoke out in the ad), or your sister, or your dog (said one of the Gabbard sons). "Don't open the door to *weird marriages*," the silver-haired patriarch concluded. "Don't let homosexuals force their values on the people of Hawai'i." The Christian Coalition printed two hundred thousand voter guides for distribution in churches the weekend before the election; the guides warned of the bad consequences homosexual marriage would carry for families and children. The Christian Coalition also suggested repealing the state's anti-discrimination laws, drawing a sharp rebuke from Speaker Joe Souki, who supported both traditional marriage and laws barring discrimination against gay people.[65]

On November 3, 1998, the voters overwhelmingly ratified the amendment, 69 percent to 29 percent (2 percent of the ballots were spoiled or left blank). Although HRC raised and invested $1.7 million on the opposition campaign, the Hawai'i amendment won by about the same margin as a similar one in libertarian Alaska, where there had been virtually no spending by gay rights supporters. Contrary to the earlier, poll-based optimism, public opinion was more deeply resistant to gay marriage and more susceptible to emotional appeals to anti-gay stereotypes than expected.[66]

Despite the vote, Foley and Wolfson urged the Hawai'i Supreme Court to affirm Judge Chang's judgment, on the grounds that the legislature needed to take fresh action in light of the constitutional amendment's authorization. Alternatively, they asked the court to require the state to provide their clients with the hundreds of legal benefits and duties of marriage—if not marriage, at least comprehensive domestic partnership. The Hawai'i Supreme Court unanimously rejected both suggestions. Not wanting to make a big deal of the court's action, Chief Justice Moon and Justices Levinson and Nakayama signed a per curiam unpublished summary disposition vacating the lower court's judgment and reaffirming the *Baehr* reasoning that discrimination based on the sex of one's romantic partners was suspect under the state constitution. This disposition irked Justice Mario Ramil, who wrote a concurring opinion denouncing the original disposition. As he told his colleagues, "I owe it to my sons." They should not be exposed to state endorsement of rights for gay people.

Lessons from the Hawai'i Marriage Litigation

The Hawai'i marriage debate ended with a disappointing defeat for supporters of lesbian and gay marriages and a thumping victory for its faith-based critics. The win was bittersweet for Ben Cayetano, who was reelected by the smallest margin (50-49 percent) in the state's history; Terry Tom, who was defeated in his race to ascend to the senate; and Joe Souki, who was ousted as speaker in a 1999 coup by finance committee chairman Calvin Say. But some larger themes emerged in Hawai'i that would inform the marriage debate for the next twenty years.

A TOLERANT SOCIETY AND NO GAY MARRIAGE

Why did Hawai'i—a politically liberal, ethnically diverse state that was the first to ratify the ERA and one of the first to repeal consensual sodomy laws and enact sexual orientation anti-discrimination laws—reject same-sex marriage? Some gay rights advocates attributed the defeat to homophobia: irrational prejudice against and hysterical fear of homosexuals. A more nuanced explanation invokes the old distinction between toleration and acceptance. STM'98, consistent with the aloha spirit, argued that the state ought to tolerate and not persecute lesbian and gay relationships. But "there's a drastic difference between being tolerant and legalizing something like same-sex marriage," said Linda Rosehill. "Legalizing it would say: 'This is acceptable, normal, and OK to teach about in school.'" This is why the ad depicting her son's reading *Daddy's Wedding* as a school homework assignment was so powerful: parents did not like the consequences, for their children, of a society where the "homosexual lifestyle" was endorsed by the state and socially accepted. The reluctance of LGBT couples to come out of the closet suggested an even more conservative Don't Ask, Don't Tell approach.[67]

The Hawai'i marriage case also partook of a larger moral debate over what marriage fundamentally means in modern society. Many faith traditions viewed it as social and communitarian as well as a divine command. For them, the unitive feature of marriage as a society of love and commitment could not be separated from its procreative feature as a dedication to the future of humankind. What makes marriage special is its social and psychological wedding of two individuals into the unity that is the married couple—the very thing that modern constitutional rights discourse would undermine through the marriage campaign's focus on individual freedom of choice. Ron Moon felt that courts were not the right forum for recasting this communitarian ideal. But he and Steve Levinson and Paula Nakayama were performing the traditional judicial role when, on remanding the case back to the lower court, they required the state to justify discrimination against a minority group. Critics complained that the sex discrimination argument in effect put marriage and its communitarian ideal on trial anyway.[68]

RELIGION AND NORMALIZATION

In the Hawai'i marriage case, the Latter-day Saints and the Catholics claimed that recognizing marriage rights for gay people would mean a loss of liberty for religious people. The reason was that gay marriage would represent a *normalization* of homosexuality, and their faith traditions considered that normalization a moral calamity. For one thing, it would further erode traditional rules of sexual behavior and gender presentation that those traditions considered morally essential for a good society. This is why traditionalist critics of same-sex marriage employed slippery-slope arguments. In their minds, they were not equating homosexuality with bestiality, though that sounded like the message to gay people. Their point was that if society abandoned tradition, faith, and a social-communitarian understanding of the family as the foundation of marriage, and instead rooted the institution in individual choice, then there would be no limiting principle in defining marriage and no essential core to its meaning. This would open the door to state recognition of adult incestuous or plural relationships as marriages. Even if liberal principles, such as the ability to consent or the preservation of equality, might bar certain marital permutations, faith traditions would have responded that gay marriage would be the moment communitarian arguments completely lost traction in the constitutional sphere. They feared that a social and legal understanding of marriage as primarily a vehicle for facilitating romantic relationship choices would undermine a duty-based institution oriented toward family life and the welfare of children.

Moreover, normalization of homosexuality would inhibit shaming or even reverse its valence. In a tolerant society, there could still be a sense of shame about homosexuality—but in a society where gay people were completely accepted, shame would shift to those who did not accept them. In 1996, Jim Woodall, of the Concerned Women for America, objected to the normalization of same-sex marriage in a family values video. As an example, he cited the January 18, 1996, episode of the situation comedy *Friends*. Carol and Susan, two beautiful lesbians, planned a wedding, which caused anguish for Carol's former husband, Ross, a mopey straight paleontologist. Carol's blood family decided to stay away because they did not approve of homosexual marriages, and Carol wondered whether she should proceed with the ceremony. Setting aside his earlier reservations, Ross encouraged her and agreed to fill in for her father as the family member who walked her down the aisle. For Woodall, the moral lesson suggested by *Friends* was not just that lesbian marriages were good and normal but also that the attitude of Carol's family was bad and abnormal. To rub in the lesson, the minister officiating the television wedding was Candace Gingrich, the lesbian-activist sister of US House of Representatives Speaker Newt Gingrich, who had compared homosexuality to alcoholism. The implication was that lesbian Candace was the nice Christian Gingrich, while the adulterous gay-bashing Newt was the Gingrich who stole Christmas.[69]

The Hawai'i legislators and judges supporting same-sex marriage relied heavily on its analogy to *Loving v. Virginia*. For traditionalists, it was of utmost importance to dislocate *Loving* from homosexual marriage. In a 1998 symposium paper, David Coolidge cautioned that gay rights advocates (including one of this book's authors, who had been Coolidge's professor) were seeking to assume the honorable mantle of civil rights activism "while simultaneously painting one's opponents as the Bull Connor of the 1990s." (Connor was an infamous Alabama police officer who brutally suppressed peaceful civil rights demonstrators in the mid-1960s.) Coolidge thought the analogy was "a subtle way of telling people that they are no different than a bunch of Jim Crow racists, and ought to be ashamed of themselves—so ashamed that they should get out of the way and leave the *definition of marriage* to the courts." This would tend to silence expression of traditional beliefs regarding marriage, family, gender, and sexuality; delegitimize faith communities that uphold such beliefs; and (eventually) bring religious institutions into direct conflict with the modern civil rights regime.[70]

POPULAR OPINION AND POLITICAL MOBILIZATION

For critics of same-sex marriage, Hawai'i was a warning that judges and liberal legislators would be susceptible to equality arguments—but their ace in the hole was public opinion. Officials' support for gay marriage collapsed in the face of strong public resistance: the senate folded after the 1996 election results, Governor Cayetano bowed to public opinion to win reelection in 1998, and the Hawai'i Supreme Court declined to risk its legitimacy in 1999.

Supporters of same-sex marriage took away a similar lesson from *Baehr* and from *Dean*, the District of Columbia marriage case that concluded in 1995: Tom Stoddard and Nan Hunter were right to believe that even liberal jurisdictions were not ready for gay marriage in the 1990s and that judges could not deliver marriage rights in the face of strong public opposition. Dan Foley understood how hard it was to protect unpopular minorities through the courts alone, and when opponents were as well organized and well funded as the Church of Jesus Christ, the task was much harder. As Abby Rubenfeld and Matt Coles had been saying for years, something as important as marriage would not be won without a comprehensive political campaign of grassroots mobilization, public education, and recruitment of allies. Evan Wolfson acted on that insight when he created the Freedom to Marry Coalition in 1994–1995.[71]

Although *Baehr* ended with a fizzle, its aspirations had echoes all over the country. The Hawai'i litigation helped motivate Tom Stoddard to propose marriage to his life partner, Walter Rieman. Thousands of lesbian and gay couples across the country had similar conversations and packed their bags to go to Hawai'i as soon as marriage became legal there. The moment never came, but spiritually their bags remained packed.

On the other hand, most gay people in America were not tempted to fly to Hawai'i, because they were still in the closet. Like many lesbians before her, April DeBoer married a man in 1992. After she and her husband separated later in the decade, April moved in with a girlfriend but remained discreet about her romantic life. Her parents, preoccupied with constant drama in her brother Ken's family, found it completely natural that a single woman would have a female roommate. Looking back on it, her mother, Wendy, thinks it was obvious that the roommate was a lover: the apartment had just one bedroom. She calls this her "blond moment." Although April dated and hung out with other women, she was focused on finding a career path. In 1999, she entered nursing school. She would not have wanted to fly to Hawai'i.[72]

We opened this chapter with the standard salutation in Hawai'i, "Aloha, Same-Sex Marriage." Aloha means goodbye as well as hello. Goodbye, for how long? David Coolidge and Lynn Wardle hoped it was forever. Their 1998 triumph seemed confirmed in 2002, when Hawai'i voters elected gay marriage critics Linda Lingle as governor and Duke Aiona as lieutenant governor; they were reelected in 2006 with 62 percent of the vote. A broader national alliance of traditional family values people and institutions was working on legislation to reaffirm traditional marriage and discourage recognition of gay marriage.

Others believed the goodbye was far from final. The day after the November 1998 election, the Freedom to Marry Coalition met to discuss plan B: what to do after a crushing loss in Hawai'i. Almost all the leading gay rights organizations agreed that, once conservative opponents focused their attention on gay marriage and started making claims that could not be ignored without harm to lesbian and gay rights generally, their side must commit itself to marriage equality. It would be central to their agenda going forward—and most of the lawyers agreed that the biggest mistake made in Hawai'i and the District of Columbia was that the lawsuits were not preceded by a full-on political campaign, including grassroots efforts to generate support within the lesbian and gay community, public education through the media and get-to-know-you appearances by gay representatives, and recruitment of mainstream allies, including businesses, labor organizations, and religious leaders. And it was not enough that the lawyers and the political advocacy groups (like the National Gay and Lesbian Task Force and HRC) were working together on a cobbled-together campaign, as they had been since 1995. Collectively, leaders such as Mary Bonauto, Evan Wolfson, Matt Coles, Nan Hunter, and others believed that national public opinion had to be changed *and* that the freedom to marry needed to secure a beachhead in one pioneer jurisdiction and to head off the expected backlash. The leaders did not realize how strong the backlash was going to be.[73]

5 • Defense of Marriage

The best defense is a good offense. For many Americans in 1993, marriage was an institution under attack—and the most serious assault was same-sex marriage. Phil Burress, an anti-pornography activist from Cincinnati, was the Paul Revere who alerted the countryside to counterattack in defense of traditional marriage.

Born on a farm in Hamilton County, Ohio, in 1942, Phil Burress is a towering man with a gentle, fleshy face and a sociable smile that belies a tough-as-nails will. Together with a calm demeanor in the face of conflict, these features made him a successful negotiator on behalf of unionized truck drivers. But Phil was living what he calls a double life because, starting at age fourteen, he was addicted to hard-core pornography. His obsession with pornography consumed his waking hours, destroyed his first marriage, and left him fighting for any time he could spend with his three daughters, who had drifted away from him.

His life drastically changed on September 6, 1980.[1]

Phil had come to hear his new son-in-law preach at the Church of God in Loveland, Ohio. As he bowed his head for prayer at the end of the service, he became overwhelmed with God's presence and felt a transcendent spiritual joy. Time stood still. When he opened his eyes, the preacher was standing right in front of him, asking Phil Burress to come forward and accept the Lord as his Savior. He did, and shed purgative tears for half an hour. After that day, he dedicated his life to opposing pornography and the unbridled carnality that it stimulated. He apologized to his daughters and made peace with his former wives. He found a crusading home in the Cincinnati-based Citizens for Community Values (CCV).

Phil Burress

More a doer than a talker, Phil brought concerned citizens together to fig-ure out practical steps to close down pornography stores in Cincinnati. He knew how to run a meeting: set forth clear goals that everyone agreed upon, let people talk, decide on a plan of action, and then see who would do what for that plan. When tempers flared, Phil would stand up—all six feet two inches of him—and boom, "Don't you just hate it when you interrupt someone and they keep talking?" Calm would descend. In 1991, Burress became the full-time CCV president. That same year, the Cincinnati City Council enacted an ordinance barring sexual orientation discrimination by the municipal govern-ment. In November 1992, the council adopted a broader ordinance, making it illegal for private employers, landlords, and public accommodations to discrim-inate because of sexual orientation.[2]

Like many other Evangelicals, Burress believed that open homosexuals should be treated with respect but that their sexual and gender choices should not be encouraged. In 1990, CCV had led a successful campaign to shut down the local municipal art gallery's plans to display the photographs of Robert Mapplethorpe, some of which depicted homosexual acts and eroticized minors. For twenty-five years, Burress had been a consumer of pornography, and he had chosen to end that obsession. Just as government should not tell employ-ers or hotels they cannot discriminate against people addicted to porn, Burress believed, it also should not dictate to employers, landlords, and hotels that they cannot discriminate against open homosexuals who continue to make what he considered bad choices.

Traditionalists throughout the nation were homing in on the same issue. Colorado for Family Values (CFV) collected enough signatures to place a con-stitutional amendment on the November 1992 ballot to overturn municipal and administrative directives that protected gay people against discrimination. Amendment 2 would prevent state and local governments from adopting any rule or policy "whereby homosexual, lesbian or bisexual orientation, conduct, practices or relationships shall constitute or otherwise be the basis of . . . any minority status, quota preferences, protected status or claim of discrimina-tion." CFV and Focus on the Family, which had moved to Colorado Springs in 1991, argued that Amendment 2 was needed to protect ordinary people against aggressive homosexuals. "You'll lose your freedom of speech and conscience to object to homosexual behavior. Your church or business may be forced to hire gays. If you are a landlord, you will be compelled to rent to gays. . . . If you are a day care center, you will be forced to employ homosexuals and lesbians."[3]

CFV and Focus on the Family also maintained that homosexuals did not deserve the protections of anti-discrimination laws. Protections for gay people were special rights, unlike the equal rights justly accorded to racial minori-ties. Amendment 2 supporters distributed a twenty-minute video, *The Gay Agenda*, which depicted homosexuals as lewd and predatory, in contrast to the honorable civil rights leaders of yesteryear. Although most public officials op-posed the measure and the Catholic archbishop of Denver remained neutral, Colorado voters endorsed Amendment 2 by a decisive 53-47 percent. In April 1993, Lou Sheldon's Traditional Values Coalition (TVC) released a video titled *Equal Rights, Not Special Rights,* arguing that special rights for gay people would erode civil rights for black people.[4]

As part of the traditional values network, Phil Burress was familiar with CFV and Amendment 2. To override the Cincinnati ordinance, he formed Equal Rights Not Special Rights (ERNSR), which gathered enough signatures to place a local initiative, Issue 3, on the November 1993 ballot. Issue 3 sought to amend the municipal constitution to bar the city or its agencies from adopt-ing any "rule or policy which provides that homosexual, lesbian, or bisexual orientation, status, conduct, or relationship constitutes, entitles, or otherwise provides a person with the basis to have any claim of minority or protected status, quota preference or other preferential treatment." The similarity to Amendment 2 was no coincidence. The same man, Robert Skolrood, had drafted both.

To clinch the special rights trope, Burress sought support from Cincinnati's Black Baptist Ministers Association. He approached the Reverend Kazava (K.Z.) Smith, pastor of the Corinthian Baptist Church in Cincinnati and the president of the association. We need your support, Burress said, to "Take Back Cincinnati" (the ERNSR slogan). A charismatic and learned preacher with an incandescent smile, Reverend Smith demurred at first, knowing he was being enlisted because of his race, but he actually did agree with Burress's cause. As Smith put it to us, Christians should have compassion for gay people, notwithstanding their flaws, but compassion does not justify extra protections under the city's anti-discrimination law, any more than any other category of sinners should be protected as a class. He found it "insulting" that gay people were appropriating the rhetoric and terms of the civil rights struggle. "I have never met a black person who believes gays have suffered anything like the way blacks have." Yet (a statement that surprised us), "God loves homosexuality. . . . As Christians, we all wrestle with something. We all see ourselves as Dr. Jekyll, but we all have some Mr. Hyde inside as well." The church must welcome all who seek its guidance—but it cannot support lesbian and gay romantic couples. Reverend Smith was not moved by the argument that gay people are born that way. "All of us have been born the wrong way. All of us need to be born again." Note an interesting parallel. Being born again is a transformative experience in which the sinner's acceptance of Christ as one's Savior liberates one to live a life consistent with God's Will. For a gay person, coming out is a transformative experience in which acceptance of one's homosexuality liberates one to live a life consistent with one's nature.[5]

The dedicated pastor and the born-again union negotiator made a dynamite political alliance, and in November 1993, Cincinnati voters ratified Issue 3 by a 62-38 percent margin. Reverend Smith went back to saving souls and ministering to his flock. Phil Burress became a mini-celebrity within the Focus on the Family network. And it was through that network that Burress met Mike Gabbard, the chief foe of marriage equality in Hawai'i. In spring 1994, Burress and Gabbard attended a conference sponsored by Focus on the Family in Glen Eyrie Castle, Colorado. The consensus of the meeting was that traditional family values groups should aggressively mold public opinion at the grassroots and cultural levels, not through big federal efforts. The messaging should be secular rather than sectarian, and pro-family rather than anti-homosexual. Family values advocates should avoid "overt appeals to biblical authority" and should never say that "homosexuality is an abomination to God." Instead, the message should be "why heterosexuality is best for America." Phil Burress translated that message into the "defense of marriage" against appropriation by lesbian and gay couples. To this day, he is surprised at how much trouble he stirred up for those seeking to "redefine marriage."[6]

Full Faith and Credit and the Memphis Accords

Participating in *Baehr v. Lewin,* Evan Wolfson of Lambda Legal provided a link between the local case and a national network. In a framework memorandum dated November 7, 1994, Wolfson asserted that once Hawai'i recognized same-sex marriages, lesbian and gay couples from all over the country could fly there, get married, and require their home states to recognize those marriages. Most states recognize all marriages validly performed in another state. A marriage between first cousins celebrated under the laws of State A will normally be recognized by State B, even if State B would not issue a marriage license to such a couple. As a matter of their own practice, most states follow this celebration rule—but not if recognizing the out-of-state marriage would violate an important public policy. Thus, state legislatures could trump the celebration rule by barring such interstate recognition on public policy grounds, and even without legislation, courts might also recognize a public policy exception.[7]

Wolfson's memorandum argued that Article IV of the US Constitution *requires* states to follow the celebration rule for marriages. Article IV says that states must give "Full Faith and Credit" to the "public Acts, Records, and judicial Proceedings of every other State." The US Supreme Court had held that each state must honor valid judgments (including divorce judgments) entered by another state's court, but it had not required states to follow the public laws adopted or licenses issued by other states. Wolfson's response was that the Supreme Court had never explicitly rejected his interpretation and that marriage created a res (Latin for *thing*) or status that was the functional equivalent of a judgment. No leading choice-of-law scholar agreed with this analysis, and the leading scholar repeatedly advised him that the Supreme Court would reject it.[8]

The celebration rule was the cornerstone of a national network that Wolfson assembled in 1995. He and his Lambda colleagues proposed that once

Hawai'i started issuing marriage licenses, gay rights groups in every state should help couples fly to Hawai'i, get married, and then demand that their home states and their employers recognize those marriages as legal. By June 1995 there was a nationwide steering committee consisting of forty-two leaders of gay and lesbian organizations nationwide. The National Freedom to Marry Coalition went public in October. For the next three years, strategizing around the marriage issue occurred in periodic meetings of the marriage coalition as well as at the semiannual Litigators' Roundtable.[9]

Earlier in 1995, Wolfson's memorandum found its way into the halls of Congress—where it gained all the notoriety of Pandora's box. In July, Oklahoma representative Ernest Istook circulated a letter to his colleagues headed "Preserving the Future of Our Families." Istook had earlier sponsored appropriations riders barring the District of Columbia from spending money to implement its 1992 domestic partnership law. His July letter expressed alarm that other states might recognize Hawai'i's lesbian and gay marriages—either because of their own choice-of-law rules or because of Lambda's reading of the full faith and credit clause. The small cadre of lesbian and gay staffers on Capitol Hill worried that Istook's letter would launch a new round of anti-gay bills in Congress. In the 1994 elections, the Democrats had lost the US House of Representatives for the first time since 1952. Most pundits attributed the losses to President and Mrs. Clinton's bungled health care plan or to Speaker Newt Gingrich's Contract with America, but the Christian Coalition had played a critical role in at least thirty House races. Although Gingrich had several gay friends, he went along with anti-gay measures, and others on the leadership team expressed prejudice. Majority Leader Richard Armey referred to openly gay representative Barney Frank as Barney Fag in a taped press briefing.[10]

For the Human Rights Campaign (HRC), the Republican majority and prospect of Hawai'i marriages were a double whammy. Executive Director Elizabeth Birch (1996–2005) feared that these twin developments would set back its lobbying for lesbian and gay rights for years. HRC arranged an informational meeting between Wolfson and gay congressional staffers, including most of the following: Mark Agrast (working for Representative Studds), Mike Iskowitz (Senator Kennedy), Jim Jones (Senator Kerry), Marcia Kuntz and Robert Raben (Representative Frank), and Tim Westmoreland (Representative Waxman). The staffers warned that if Hawai'i started handing out marriage licenses to same-sex couples, Congress would pass something in response—either a statute or a proposed constitutional amendment. Even more than the 1993 law excluding gay people from military service, "this would be a steamroller." Wolfson was not persuaded: he thought that once Hawai'i began issuing marriage licenses to lesbian and gay couples, normal politics would become irrelevant. Not at all, thought the staffers. Representative Frank labeled this a "serious strategic misjudgment."[11]

In December 1995, Mike Gabbard called his friend Phil Burress: "Are you not concerned about what's going on in Hawai'i with same-sex marriage?" Burress told us he thought it was a joke, but Gabbard insisted this was a real possibility. Burress responded: "How does that affect us" in Ohio? Gabbard: "Because of full faith and credit. If you don't do something about it, and we lose here, all the other forty-nine states are going to have to accept same-sex marriage, if this goes down in Hawai'i."[12]

We've got to do something about this, Burress decided. As a union negotiator, he had formed a philosophy that informed his new career as a family values organizer: "Run toward the gun fire. Assess the lay of the land. Strike first." The lay of the land was full of risks, but public opinion was on his side. After consulting colleagues in the traditional family values network, he proposed a conference of the worker bees, the doers, from the leading organizations in Memphis on January 18, 1996. (Many of these folks were planning to be in Memphis for a presidential fundraiser.) Burress secured meeting space in the basement of a Baptist church.[13]

The twenty-plus participants represented most of the leading organizations that would be interested in a national campaign to defend traditional marriage. Here is a partial list:

- Robert Knight, Family Research Council (FRC)
- Jim Woodall, Concerned Women for America (CWA)
- Lou Sheldon, TVC
- Mike Gabbard, Alliance for Traditional Marriage in Hawai'i
- Will Perkins and Kevin Tebedo, CFV
- Bill Horn, The Report, a traditional values newsletter
- Phil Burress, CCV
- Buddy Smith and Vickie Bowman, American Family Association (AFA)

The consensus was that homosexual marriage was an issue these groups should make a priority ("Run into the fire"). Traditional family values supporters needed to get out in front of the issue before Hawai'i started issuing licenses ("Strike first").

After about nine hours of discussion, the group agreed on a three-pronged plan of action, which we call the Memphis Accords. First, Mike Gabbard and his allies would fight for a constitutional amendment in Hawai'i to nullify any judicial effort to recognize gay marriage. Second, Bob Knight and FRC would take the lead in drafting federal legislation to protect states against having to recognize homosexual marriages. Third, FRC, CCV, and Focus would work with their allied family policy councils (then in thirty-eight states) to develop state laws defining marriage as one man and one woman and barring recognition of homosexual marriages entered into elsewhere. Their goals were to defend traditional marriage against a new liberalizing threat, to reaffirm the nation's moral commitment to traditional marriage, and to energize a network of local activists who would remake American politics. The Memphis Accords would frame the marriage debate for the next eight years.[14]

The Defense of Marriage Act

Bill Horn suggested that the coalition make its national debut with a rally the next month in Iowa, right before the Republican presidential caucuses, which were dominated by Evangelicals. Televised from the First Federated Church in Des Moines, the rally was a kickoff for a National Campaign to Protect Marriage. C-SPAN identified the sponsoring organizations as the Christian Coalition, The Report, AFA, TVC, CWA, and Phyllis Schlafly's Eagle Forum. The campaign's centerpiece was a Marriage Protection Resolution: "Resolved, the State should not legitimize homosexual relationships by legalizing same-sex 'marriage' but should continue to reserve the special sanction of civil marriage for one man and one woman as husband and wife." All but one of the GOP presidential candidates signed onto it.[15]

The opening prayer for the February 10, 1996, rally apologized to God for the country's "moral pluralism" and toleration of "perversion." Mike Gabbard, the third speaker, called for immediate action to stop homosexual activists seeking to destroy traditional marriage. "If we as a nation legalize homosexual marriage, we will be opening a Pandora's box that will be impossible to close," opening the way for incest, polygamy, and other "aberrant sexual behaviors." Legislatures needed to act, because the full faith and credit clause would force other states to recognize homosexual marriages entered in Hawai'i. Schools would have to teach children that homosexual marriage is the equivalent of heterosexual marriage, and parents would lose control of their children's moral education. Like alcoholics and drug addicts, homosexuals should be helped and not persecuted, but the state should do all that it can to discourage their "destructive lifestyle." Presidential candidates Alan Keyes, Pat Buchanan, and Phil Gramm saw this as an important moment in the larger "culture war." The closing prayer feared that gay marriages were an "attack that is on our society."[16]

Bill Horn's video *The Ultimate Target*, released the same day, sounded the same themes. It warned of the "legal nightmare" that would ensue if Hawai'i started issuing marriage licenses to lesbian and gay couples and judges forced other states to recognize them. Most of the speakers shown on the video talked about normalization. "If you sanction same-sex marriage, you immediately criminalize all those people who disagree with it," Bob Knight explained. CWA's Peggy Young Nance worried that the gay agenda would soon dominate the media, squeezing out "alternative voices." Several speakers emphasized how the hedonistic homosexual philosophy eliminated all sexual boundaries and led to promiscuity. Even when homosexuals were raising children, they were destroying America's moral fiber, because they were denying those children their right to a mom and a dad.[17]

The Des Moines rally got a lot of media attention and was an explosive kick-off for the national campaign, which Burress coordinated from the CCV offices. In early 1996, the campaign established local contacts in all fifty states who could press marriage protection laws, drafted through local groups allied with and supported by FRC from Washington. By March, FRC had developed talking points for the "defense of marriage," based upon the claim that marriage for "homosexual couples" would "impose" their family norms on the rest of the country, which "would turn the civil rights laws into a battering ram" against tradition-minded parents, employers, and churches. "The more homosexuality is encouraged, the more damage will be wreaked among individuals, families, and society."[18]

THE DEFENSE OF MARRIAGE ACT

Bob Knight and other advocates drafted a Defense of Marriage Act (DOMA) that could be introduced into Congress. At some point, the drafters expanded the bill beyond Burress's original concern with the full faith and credit clause. The draft that Knight shopped around with members of Congress apparently included a provision ensuring that federal statutes and regulations never include lesbian and gay marriages or spouses, even if valid under state law. Although Congress had enacted laws regulating interstate recognition of orders and judgments, it had never combined a broad exclusion of a minority group from federal substantive law with state nonrecognition rules.

Majority Leader Robert Dole (together with Majority Whip Don Nickles) agreed to sponsor DOMA in the Senate, but the obvious sponsor in the House was not interested: Representative Henry Hyde, chairman of the House Judiciary Committee. One admiring Democrat told us, "It was beneath him." Like Speaker Gingrich, however, Hyde would not stand in the way of legislation that his own church, party, and likely presidential candidate supported. Freshman representative Bob Barr (R-Georgia) agreed to act as primary sponsor. A Georgetown law graduate and former US attorney, Barr was ambitious and aggressive. Like the Speaker, he was on his third marriage, having divorced twice. Like Hyde, he was a libertarian. On gay rights issues, he was laser-focused on urgent religious liberty concerns. For drafting advice, Barr immediately turned to a fellow Southern Baptist, Florida representative Charles Canady, the chair of the subcommittee on constitutional amendments of the House Judiciary Committee.[19]

Canady and his subcommittee counsel, Bill McGrath, revised Knight's draft legislation. McGrath's revision—which would be enacted by Congress without change—was immaculately drafted, spare, and sweeping. Section 1 introduced the bill's title, the Defense of Marriage Act. Section 2 invoked Congress's Article IV authority to assure states that the full faith and credit clause would not require them to recognize same-sex marriages validly entered in another state. Section 3 directed that "spouse" and "marriage" in federal statutes and regulations could never be applied to same-sex marriages.[20]

Why, given the jurisdiction of Canady's subcommittee, was this not a constitutional amendment? The Campaign to Protect Marriage demanded immediate action, not the long, frustrating process of a constitutional amendment. They and their congressional allies believed that a statutory DOMA would sail through Congress, while a constitutional DOMA might be held up or even defeated in the Senate, where the popular Flag Desecration Amendment lost by a handful of votes year after year. From the perspective of the Republican Congress, a big bonus was that the statutory DOMA would force President Clinton (a Democrat) to decide whether to sign or veto it, meaning he would have to choose between his lesbian and gay supporters and the conservative southern voters he was courting in his presidential campaign against likely opponent Bob Dole. Although DOMA was partly a Dole Campaign Rehabilitation Act (as HRC's Elizabeth Birch dubbed it), the bill enjoyed wide bipartisan support.[21]

CONGRESS AND THE WHITE HOUSE DELIBERATE
THE DEFENSE OF MARRIAGE

On May 7, Representative Barr introduced DOMA in the House, and the next day, Senators Dole and Nickles introduced the same bill in the Senate. Earlier in the year, the Clinton White House had leaned toward the view that the definition of marriage was best left to the states, but that stance was overtaken by strategizing in connection with the president's campaign for reelection. "We were having political strategy meetings once a week," every Wednesday night about 8:00 p.m., recalls White House press secretary Mike McCurry. "The President and Vice President Gore were always there, and very often Tipper Gore and Hillary Clinton were there. And then there were all the senior staff people, all the people from the Democratic National Committee, and the people from the reelection campaign," especially campaign manager Dick Morris, pollsters Mark Penn and Doug Schoen, and media advisers Bob Squier and Bill Knapp. Earlier in the afternoon, the president sometimes met with Morris and McCurry; Morris also met regularly with the first lady. Against likely GOP nominee Bob Dole and Independent Ross Perot, Bill Clinton had a comfortable lead, largely owing to the booming economy, but the campaign team was taking nothing for granted. In the wake of the Democrats' staggering losses in the 1994 off-year elections, 1996 saw the president "fashion the most comprehensive melding of politics and domestic policy ever in a White House."[22]

Morris was the Clintons' longtime political adviser, and his trademark strategic advice was to *triangulate,* to embrace popular conservative policies while endorsing popular liberal ones and, ideally, to pair the two kinds of political appeals on the same issue. Pollsters told the campaign that about 60 percent of the public opposed gay marriage, and even more opposed interstate recognition of potential Hawai'i gay marriages—but voters also disapproved of job discrimination against qualified gay persons. Accordingly, triangulation would suggest that the president support DOMA but pair it with support for the proposed Employment Nondiscrimination Act (ENDA), which would bar anti-gay job discrimination.[23]

Morris urged an immediate presidential endorsement of DOMA, but was countered by Elizabeth Birch, who personally confronted President Clinton and Vice President Gore with HRC's claim that DOMA was blatantly unconstitutional. HRC persuaded Gore, and Clinton was reportedly "ambivalent" about throwing this supportive minority group under the bus once again, as he had done in 1993, when he endorsed a ban on gays in the military. According to both Morris and McCurry, Hillary Clinton showed no ambivalence in siding with Morris. McCurry's recollection is that as soon as DOMA appeared to be heading toward enactment, there was a consensus that the president should promise to sign it. Although McCurry, George Stephanopoulos, and Gore thought DOMA was "noxious," that judgment did not carry much weight in the executive branch's strategizing.[24]

Most of the White House governance staff were not privy to campaign discussions. Among those out of the loop were members of the domestic policy council as well as Marsha Scott, the liaison between the White House and the lesbian and gay community. In March and April, Scott told skeptical representatives of the gay community that the administration had their backs—just as Morris was sharpening the knife for insertion into said backs. Scott and her successor, Richard Socarides, urged the president to take a progressive stand on this issue, but Associate Attorney General John Schmidt immediately trumped them: "Given the president's opposition to same sex marriage, it would seem to me to make sense to make clear as quickly as possible that, in light of that opposition, he supports enactment of the proposed statute." On May 10, White House counsel Jack Quinn torpedoed Birch's view that DOMA was unconstitutional. To the contrary, "there would not be a substantive basis" to oppose DOMA, and Quinn recommended that Clinton "sign this legislation if it is enacted." The president did not immediately left-check any of the options (Agree, Disagree, Discuss) at the end of Quinn's memo—but we think that by May 10, the die was cast.[25]

At a press briefing on May 13, McCurry stated that the president opposed "gay marriage." When asked why, he mumbled something about Clinton's support for traditional families. Unknown to McCurry, the marriage-defending chief executive was in the middle of a secret extramarital affair with a twenty-two-year-old White House intern, Monica Lewinsky. By her account, the president had sex with her at least nine times between 1995 and 1997.

THE MAY 15 HEARING

A week after DOMA was introduced, Canady's constitutional amendments subcommittee held a hearing. Although invited to participate, the Department of Justice (DOJ) instead sent a short letter: "The Department of Justice believes that [DOMA] would be sustained as constitutional, and that there are no legal issues raised by [DOMA] that necessitate an appearance by a representative of the Department." The department's letter blindsided HRC and humiliated Birch during her testimony against the bill.[26]

Canady also introduced into the record a new memorandum written by Evan Wolfson, reiterating his constitutional claim that mainland states would have to recognize valid same-sex marriages. Flying in from Hawai'i, Terrence Tom told the subcommittee that the Hawai'i legislature was still deadlocked over his proposed constitutional amendment. Gay marriages were a real possibility—meaning that Wolfson's scenario might be mere months away from becoming reality. Legislators pretended to be alarmed at this possibility. Lynn Wardle explained how DOMA was a moderate response to Wolfson's scenario.[27]

Elizabeth Birch made an important substantive point: "The real issue is what does a nation do with its lesbian and gay sons and daughters?" The majority's answer seemed to be that they should be unseen and not heard. Closing the federal government's eyes to even the prospect of lesbian and gay marriages seemed to endorse the regime of the closet. Ironically, several of the Republicans directly involved in committee deliberations were homosexuals leading double lives or were heterosexuals dealing with the discovery of a gay relative.[28]

The Supreme Court's Bombshell

Recall Colorado's Amendment 2, which barred all organs of the state government from adopting any rule or policy "whereby homosexual, lesbian or bisexual orientation, conduct, practices or relationships shall constitute or otherwise be the basis of . . . any minority status, quota preferences, protected status or claim of discrimination." Lambda and the ACLU challenged this new state constitutional rule as a violation of the equal protection clause of the Fourteenth Amendment. They argued that it denied gay people a fundamental right to participate in the ordinary political process as well as denying them the equal protection of the law. Rex Lee and Carter Phillips, representing Colorado, argued that Amendment 2 served neutral public purposes: (1) conserving scarce enforcement resources for state and local anti-discrimination laws by focusing them on the groups most in need of protection (i.e., blacks and women); (2) protecting religious liberty and the freedom of traditionalist landlords, employers, and schools to exclude homosexuals as needed to serve their moral codes; and (3) creating uniformity of anti-discrimination rules within the state and heading off the "factionalism" accompanying the "divisive" issue of homosexuality.[29]

Matt Coles, the new head of the ACLU's Lesbian & Gay Rights Project, and Lambda's Suzanne Goldberg responded that Amendment 2's sweeping exclusion of gay people did not advance any of those policies and went well beyond what any of them required. For example, because few complaints under municipal anti-discrimination ordinances were brought by gay people, Amendment 2 did almost nothing to conserve scarce resources, and because the scope of the exclusion seemed to bar gay people from objecting to government action that harmed them, the amendment went far beyond resource conservation. The exclusion was so broad that it could only have been driven by antipathy to gay people.[30]

Vigorously contesting this argument was an amicus brief filed by Robert Bork, Michael Carvin, and Bill McGrath, representing Phil Burress's CCV, the group sponsoring Cincinnati's copycat amendment. Amendment 2, they argued, was a neutral law responding to local measures "that prohibited state residents from acting on their sincerely held moral and religious beliefs that homosexuality—unlike, for example, race, ethnicity, or gender—is a morally relevant characteristic. Amendment 2 respects the right of all Colorado residents to accord to homosexuality such significance as they believe it warrants." Reflecting Burress's philosophy, the brief maintained that Amendment 2 should be understood as pro-family, not anti-gay.[31]

For the first time in a gay rights case, the American Bar Association (ABA) filed an amicus brief with the US Supreme Court. The municipal ordinances barred employment discrimination because of sexual orientation. After Amendment 2, gay people could not invoke these legal protections—but straight people still could, because the amendment preempted those ordinances only insofar as they protected sexual minorities. Under Amendment 2, a barbershop in Boulder could refuse to hire a gay hair stylist, but a gay bookstore could not discriminate against a straight job applicant. Amendment 2 thus transformed laws meant to protect a minority into laws that created new discriminations against that minority—a first in American history. If the amendment's purpose was to conserve enforcement resources, it was absurd that it left in place protections for straight people. The ABA brief also argued that the plain meaning of Amendment 2 would bar gay people, and only gay people, from seeking *any* redress from a government official or agency for *any* discriminatory treatment, however outrageous. A scholars' brief filed by Professor Laurence Tribe and four other constitutional law professors made a similar point. Both briefs argued that this was a core violation of the Fourteenth Amendment's equal protection clause.[32]

At oral argument on October 10, 1995, Colorado solicitor general Tim Tym-kovich maintained that Amendment 2 did nothing more than preempt local ordinances and did not really authorize discrimination against homosexuals—but this response was at odds with the amendment's broad text and was undermined by religious amicus briefs, which maintained that the goal of Amendment 2 was to allow "discrimination" by religious institutions. The free exercise clause protects the right of churches to discriminate, but Amendment 2 expanded this right to "parachurch organizations," private employers, hotels and restaurants, and government officials.[33]

Robert Skolrood had done his clients a disservice by writing the amendment so broadly; one wonders if he was, subconsciously, a double agent, as he was reportedly picking up men for sexual encounters outside of his marriage during his career as a family values activist. In its official ballot materials, CFV did Amendment 2 no favors with its assertions about predatory and diseased homosexuals and the fantastic claim that the average lesbian lived only to her mid-forties. Yet the coalition sponsoring Amendment 2 saw it as a *moderate* assertion of their deeply held values. Kevin Tebedo had (according to a disapproving CFV pragmatist) "wanted to write moral laws condemning homosexuality as a sin, waging what amounted to a Biblical *jihad.*" In 1992, religious and conservative groups in Oregon had sponsored Measure 9, which would have amended the state constitution to bar state and local governments from using resources "to promote, encourage or facilitate homosexuality, pedophilia, sadism or masochism." The measure lost, 56.5 percent to 43.5 percent, suggesting the electoral wisdom of Amendment 2.[34]

When the challenge reached the US Supreme Court, it prompted an unusual amount of informal conversations among the justices. Stephen Breyer raised concerns about the measure's breadth with his colleagues, especially his ally Sandra Day O'Connor. Amendment 2 seemed to say that if police ignored violence against gay people, the state could provide no remedy. It could even be read to bar the police department from instructing officers not to look the other way when gay people are assaulted, for such admonitions would constitute a "rule or policy" whereby "homosexual, lesbian or bisexual orientation" would "be the basis of . . . any protected status or claim of discrimination." At oral argument, Breyer, O'Connor, and other justices peppered Colorado's counsel Tymkovich with service-denying hypotheticals. If lower-level officials refused to serve or protect gay citizens, Amendment 2 seemed to prohibit their bosses from instructing them not to discriminate in the provision of basic services, like fire and police protection.[35]

At the court's conference, Chief Justice William Rehnquist, a judicial conservative, said he did not favor equal protection review of state morals legislation. More importantly, he believed the burdens anti-discrimination laws placed on private businesses and persons were increased, and their efficacy diluted, when legislators added new protected classes to those laws. The senior associate justice, John Paul Stevens, viewed Amendment 2 as an "excessive" response to the claimed problems and said it encouraged discrimination against an unpopular minority. Like Rehnquist, her old friend from Stanford Law School, O'Connor thought laws disadvantaging homosexuals did not merit "strict scrutiny"—the usually fatal level of close examination required in evaluating laws that disadvantage racial minorities—but like Stevens and her friend Breyer, she could not go along with a sweeping constitutional "carve out" that specifically targeted gay people.[36]

Antonin Scalia spoke most forcefully. He entertained no doubts about the state's authority to regulate morals, and in public appearances he argued that if the state could make murder a crime, it ought to be able to make homosexual sodomy a crime, too, as the court had held in *Bowers v. Hardwick* (1986). Colorado had repealed its consensual sodomy law in 1972, and Amendment 2 reflected a tolerant middle ground. If Colorado could put these people in jail for a felony, why could it not deny them the special rights enjoyed by traditionally protected groups (like blacks) under anti-discrimination laws? Scalia added that Amendment 2 advanced another rational policy: Colorado was signaling to its youth that homosexuals (even partnered ones) were bad role models. Finally, he rejected the broad reading of the amendment. Though normally an advocate of following plain meaning, here he insisted that his colleagues were reading Amendment 2 "literally" rather than "reasonably." Understanding CFV better than his colleagues, Scalia was sure Amendment 2's purpose was to preempt anti-discrimination ordinances, not to deny homosexuals the ordinary legal protections enjoyed by all.

Within the gayocracy, the conventional wisdom has been that decision makers with friends or family who are openly gay will, on average, be more sympathetic to equal treatment for that minority. Antonin Scalia knew a few gay people but often would not admit it. Such deliberate obliviousness would contribute to his willingness to uphold the gay-bashing policy of Amendment 2. But John Paul Stevens told us that he could not recall knowing any gay people in 1986, when he dissented in *Bowers*. Neither he nor O'Connor had gay friends in 1996, when they cast their votes in *Romer*. In the *Bowers* conference, Stevens had shocked his colleagues by confessing that he was ignorant and prejudiced on the matter of homosexuality and that he considered it a problem he needed to overcome. So the conventional wisdom does not explain his and O'Connor's votes—nor those of the affable Bill Rehnquist, who lived in northern Virginia next door to a gay couple, and whose family worshipped at the gay-friendly Redeemer Lutheran Church in McLean, where they were friends with openly gay representative Steve Gunderson and his partner.[37]

A complicated example of the contact-with-gays wisdom, Anthony Kennedy would play a central role in the future of gay rights. Raised in the Land Park neighborhood of Sacramento, California, Kennedy was an Irish Catholic who lived in a happy cultural bubble, insulated from the turbulence roiling American society. Not until he entered military service, in 1961, does he even remember hearing about people reputed to be homosexuals. When he took over his father's Sacramento law practice in 1965, he and his wife, Mary, settled just blocks from his parents' house, which they occupied after his mother died.[38]

In Sacramento, Kennedy's mentor was Gordon Schaber, a gentle-spirited man with a round, owlish face dominated by large eyeglasses. He was a baron of the Sacramento bar, a judge, and for many decades the dean of the McGeorge School of Law at University of the Pacific. The consummate networker, Schaber transformed McGeorge from an unaccredited night school into a powerhouse whose graduates now dominate the California judiciary. He appointed Kennedy to teach constitutional law at McGeorge every year between 1965 and 1988, when he was named to the Supreme Court. Even after he joined the court, Kennedy taught almost every summer in McGeorge's program in Salzburg, Austria. Gordon Schaber never married and was apparently a closeted gay man, as Mary and Tony Kennedy assumed but never discussed with their friend. "It was just not the sort of thing you talked about," they told us. According to Tony, Gordon's sexual orientation "was irrelevant."[39]

On November 10, 1992, McGeorge celebrated Dean Schaber's retirement and his sixty-fifth birthday. In a show-stopping testimonial, Tony Kennedy warmly reminisced how Gordon had led the Sacramento bar to adjust to the social changes of the 1960s, including the integration of people of color and women into the practice of law. Gordon was a contracts professor, and Tony praised him as a person who always behaved as though agreements and promises carried with them "an implied covenant of good faith and fair dealing. Gordon *always* gave more than he bargained for." That practice bespoke a larger philosophy of life: "Each of us ha[s] a compact with our fellow citizens, and for Gordon, he has a covenant with all of humanity."[40]

Justice Kennedy cast his vote in *Romer* three years later. "Each of us has a compact with our fellow citizens" to treat them with equal dignity, he had said at the tribute, and this was why he thought Amendment 2 unconstitutional. At oral argument, he had stumped Tymkovich by asking whether the Supreme Court had ever seen a measure like Amendment 2, which saddled a unique set of disabilities upon a minority group not applicable to any other group. As the ABA and scholars' amicus briefs argued, excluding a group in order to signal social disapproval was not a permissible objective of government. It was a violation of the covenant of good faith and fair dealing implicit in the social contract.

That he and his wife knew discreet gay people as friends and neighbors in Sacramento freed Kennedy to think about them as normal citizens who were entitled to the dignified treatment suggested by Roman Catholic philosophy and required by the Constitution, our social contract. Just as important as knowing gay people or respecting the Catholic tradition of dignity was Kennedy's attraction to a particular theory of constitutionalism, that of Friedrich von Hayek. When we asked him about Hayek's influence, Kennedy enthusiastically recalled attending Hayek's lectures in London; they were probably based on his 1955 Cairo Lectures, the basis of *The Constitution of Liberty* (1960). Hayek's rule-of-law constitutionalism probably crystallized the assumptions Kennedy brought with him from Sacramento.[41]

Hayek's view was that societies flourish through "spontaneous ordering," the accumulated wisdom of millions of decisions rationally made by individual citizens advancing their personal goals. Free markets and custom-based freedoms are examples of accumulated wisdom. A successful polity is one where its citizens understand that government is limited in its ability to interfere with the market and customary liberties; central planning and rent-seeking by interest groups are toxic. For Hayek, a judge's role is to ensure that "laws must be general, equal, and certain" so that legislators are limited and all citizens can make decisions based upon well-known precepts applicable to everyone. Constitutionalism protects individual liberty—the same liberty that enables spontaneous ordering—as its goal. The rules and liberty protections "must be the same for all," and any "differentiation which [law] makes must not be aimed at benefitting particular people." Amendment 2 was a deep violation of Hayek's equality principle, which finds expression in the Fourteenth Amendment's equal protection clause.[42]

Also voting to invalidate Amendment 2 were David Souter, a New Hampshire libertarian appointed by President Bush (1990), and two former law professors, Breyer and Ruth Bader Ginsburg, the constitutional feminist litigator from Columbia Law, named to the court by President Clinton (1993). They were unmoved by Scalia's invocation of *Bowers,* which Souter and Ginsburg (as well as Kennedy) thought was a toxic precedent, because it branded gay people as an outlaw class subject to arbitrary treatment by state actors. Clarence Thomas, a conservative appointed by President Bush (1991), felt that consensual sodomy laws were a bad idea but followed Scalia and his fans in the Federalist Society in thinking them not unconstitutional. As the senior justice in the majority, Stevens assigned the task of writing the court's opinion to Kennedy, a Reagan Republican and a devout Catholic who would be an unexpected messenger for equal treatment of gay people.

Characteristically, Kennedy opened his opinion with a dramatic flair: "One century ago, the first Justice Harlan admonished this Court that the Constitution 'neither knows nor tolerates classes among citizens.'" The line came from Harlan's dissent in *Plessy v. Ferguson,* the decision upholding state-imposed racial segregation. "Unheeded then, those words now are understood to state a commitment to the law's neutrality where the rights of persons are at stake." Rejecting the state's claim that it was only voiding special rights given homosexuals, Kennedy ruled that so-called special rights were merely "protections taken for granted by most people either because they already have them or do not need them; these are protections against exclusion from an almost limitless number of transactions and endeavors that constitute ordinary civic life in a free society." Further, "it is a fair, if not necessary, inference from the broad language of the amendment that it deprives gays and lesbians even of the protection of general laws and policies that prohibit arbitrary discrimination in governmental and private settings."[43]

At this point, Kennedy had several doctrinal options for evaluating this Hayekian anomaly, such as the scholars' claim that the amendment was a per se violation of the equal protection clause or the application of heightened scrutiny because sexual orientation was a suspect classification. Instead, he followed the situation-specific approach the ACLU, Lambda, and the ABA had urged: Amendment 2 was invalid because the disadvantages it imposed upon gay people went well beyond what might be needed to advance the asserted goals of the measure, such as conservation of enforcement resources. "Its sheer breadth is so discontinuous with the reasons offered for it that the amendment seems inexplicable by anything but animus toward the class it affects." Channeling Hayek: "Central both to the idea of the rule of law and to our own Constitution's guarantee of equal protection is the principle that government and each of its parts remain open on impartial terms to all who seek its assistance." Amendment 2 was ultimately a status-based law aimed at a class of citizens and having no apparent connection to the public interest. Such laws violate the equal protection command that "a bare . . . desire to harm a politically unpopular group cannot constitute a *legitimate* government interest."[44]

Writing also for Rehnquist and Thomas, Scalia opened his dissenting opinion with his own rhetorical flourish: "The Court has mistaken a *Kulturkampf* for a fit of spite. The constitutional amendment before us here is not the manifestation of a 'bare . . . desire to harm' homosexuals, but is rather a modest attempt by seemingly tolerant Coloradans to preserve traditional sexual mores against the efforts of a politically powerful minority to revise those mores through use of the laws." Echoing the Amendment 2 ballot materials and the Bork-Carvin-McGrath brief, Scalia depicted homosexuals as a wealthy, somewhat greedy group seeking special rights that tolerant Coloradans were entitled to curtail. He concluded with his best legal argument: the court's holding was starkly inconsistent with the holding in *Bowers,* which ruled that anti-homosexual sentiment was a rational basis for a law that punished private homosexual sodomy between consenting adults with at least a year of prison time. Kennedy's opinion did not even mention *Bowers.*[45]

The court handed down its decision in *Romer v. Evans* on May 20, 1996—almost exactly one hundred years after Harlan's *Plessy* dissent. (*Plessy* was handed down on May 18, 1896. Exactly one hundred years later, May 18, 1996, was a Saturday, when the court conducted no business.) Constitutional lawyers and, especially, the gay legal community were electrified by the disposition and reasoning. As HRC's lobbyists insisted to the White House and Congress, DOMA was as unprecedented as Amendment 2 had been, and its exclusion in section 3 was sweeping. Like Amendment 2, DOMA sought to "withdraw[] from homosexuals, but no others, specific legal protection from the injuries caused by discrimination, and it forbids reinstatement of these laws and policies." Was it in constitutional trouble?

The Clinton administration purported to think it was not. The day after *Romer* was handed down, Walter Dellinger, assistant attorney general for the Office of Legal Counsel, faxed the White House counsel an analysis minimizing the ruling's significance. President Clinton confirmed his support for the bill based upon section 2's authorization for states to refuse recognition to valid out-of-state marriages between persons of the same sex—but his staff had to remind him that the vulnerable provision was section 3, because it excluded legally married lesbian and gay couples from more than one thousand statutory and regulatory rights and duties associated with marriage. The National Gay and Lesbian Task Force wrote to the president the same day "to express our deep disappointment, and dismay," at his support for DOMA. "What the legislation does do is to draw a circle around gays, lesbians, and bisexuals and state that our families do not deserve recognition." Clinton grumbled that he did not get sufficient credit for what he considered his strong record of support for gay rights. (Remembering his 1993 betrayal on the gays-in-the-military issue, some progressives had a different view about how "strong" his record was.)[46]

The House Judiciary Committee was not as dismissive of the ruling as the Clinton administration. Its staff felt that *Romer* raised constitutional questions about DOMA section 3 but that *Romer* could be read to allow a statute that re-affirmed the nation's long-standing definition of marriage. When the Canady subcommittee met to mark up the DOMA bill on May 30, the chairman produced a fresh letter from the Department of Justice stating that its constitutional analysis had not changed in light of *Romer*. Nonetheless, *Romer* made some DOMA boosters nervous. Amherst professor Hadley Arkes, who had testified in favor of DOMA on May 15, warned that homosexual activists and their academic allies (Eskridge of Georgetown and Tribe of Harvard) were already claiming that DOMA and other targeted exclusions of lesbian and gay people and couples would be constitutionally vulnerable under a *Romer*-type equal protection analysis.[47]

Consistent with DOJ's stance, judges initially read *Romer* cautiously. For example, even DOJ expected *Romer* to have supported Alphonse Gerhardstein's constitutional challenge to Phil Burress's Issue 3, which added Amendment 2's language to the Cincinnati Charter. Nonetheless, the Sixth Circuit upheld Issue 3. When the Supreme Court declined to review the decision, it seemed to signal that *Romer* was no Magna Carta for gay rights. In February 1998, voters in Maine revoked local and state rules barring sexual orientation discrimination in a referendum whose wording openly denigrated gay people as immoral, predatory, and a threat to children. After the Sixth Circuit's narrow view of *Romer*, gay rights organizations declined to challenge this referendum.[48]

Although *Romer* did reveal the Supreme Court's increasingly skeptical view of *Bowers*, its Hayekian reasoning did not suggest that same-sex marriage was on the constitutional horizon. Although sodomy laws were falling to state constitutional challenges even in conservative jurisdictions like Kentucky and Georgia, no state recognized marriage equality. Hayek's logic of the market—an efficient aggregation of millions of individual decisions—applied to long-standing custom, and almost any Burkean would have said that the one-man, one-woman understanding of marriage was socially entrenched, consistent with DOMA. Even gay marriage supporter Jonathan Rauch conceded the force of tradition: "You can't mess with the [custom-based] formula without causing unforeseen consequences, possibly including the implosion of marriage itself." Rauch felt that the Hayekian defense of marriage ought to yield to the great unfairness of excluding lesbian and gay couples, but no respectable federal judge was prepared to go that far in 1996.[49]

DOMA Becomes Law

Neither the Supreme Court's views on gay rights nor the president's—whatever they actually were—had any significant effect on Congress's consideration of DOMA and ENDA. The dominant factor was public opinion. Between 1973 and 1991, pollsters consistently found two-thirds or more respondents saying that sexual relations between two persons of the same sex is "always wrong"; that number dipped to 56 percent by 1996, but it was still a decisive majority. Although polls in the 1990s reported that Americans disapproved of gay marriage by 2-to-1 margins, they found increasing public support for the anti-discrimination norm. In 1997, four-fifths of the country thought gay people should have equal job rights, and eleven states and two hundred municipalities had adopted laws barring sexual orientation discrimination by 2000. The polls varied by region: residents of the Northeast, the Pacific Rim, and the Great Lakes area were gay tolerant, while those in the South and the Great Plains were least accepting. The votes cast by members of Congress generally followed those regional differences.[50]

HOUSE DOMA DEBATE

On July 9, 1996, the House Judiciary Committee reported DOMA to the full House. The Republican majority voted down several amendments proposed by liberal skeptics—including Patricia Schroeder's (D-Colorado) provocative proposal that the federal definition of marriage in DOMA section 3 should also limit marriage to "monogamous" or "non-adulterous" relationships (rejected 9-20) and her alternative proposal that the definition exclude unions where either spouse had previously been divorced under a no-fault regime (rejected 3-22). Barney Frank (D-Massachusetts) proposed deleting section 3 (rejected

13-19) and adding recognition for nontraditional marriages legalized by state legislatures or voter initiatives (rejected 8-14).

As explained in the committee's report, section 2 was needed to head off Lambda's aggressive reading of the full faith and credit clause. Section 3 was needed to reaffirm conjugal marriage as the means of "responsible procreation and child-rearing" and to "reflect and honor a collective moral judgment and to express moral disapproval of homosexuality." DOMA as a whole would prevent the government from delivering a "stamp of approval on a union that many people think is immoral" and would advance government interests in democratic self-governance and preserving scarce resources. Through the House Rules Committee, Speaker Gingrich controlled the schedule for the full House, and he kept DOMA on the fast track. The House adopted the rule expediting DOMA's consideration by a vote of 290-133—a surprisingly large number of dissenters. Many Democrats and some Republicans would rather have kept DOMA off the legislative agenda.[51]

The House debate on July 11–12 replicated the earlier deliberations. Barr and Canady wielded the Wolfson memoranda like Jedi lightsabers to answer the taunt that no one really thought Ohio would have to recognize Hawai'ian same-sex marriages. Frank and other opponents framed DOMA as a sweeping discrimination against lesbian and gay couples, but the sponsors defended it as reaffirming "our collective moral understanding—as experienced in the law— of the essential nature of the family—the fundamental building block of society." Canady said: "Should the law express its neutrality between homosexual and heterosexual relationships? Should we tell the children of America that we as a society believe there is no moral difference between homosexual relationships and heterosexual relationships?" Added Barr: "The very foundations of our society are in danger of being burned. The flames of hedonism, the flames of narcissism, the flames of self-centered morality are licking at the very foundation of our society: the family unit." The committee's staff realized that such language was venturing into animus territory that raised *Romer* issues. They cringed as others crossed the line, supporting the measure because of their constituents' "very profound beliefs that homosexuality is wrong." Bob Dornan (R-California) objected to even discussing homosexuals having marriage rights. What's next? In a few years, "we are going to be discussing pedophilia."[52]

Most of the debate on July 12 pertained to Frank's amendments to delete section 3 and to give full faith and credit to some nonmarital unions. John Lewis (D-Georgia), a legendary civil rights leader, described the bill as resting upon "fear" and "prejudice." Steve Gunderson (R-Wisconsin) observed that DOMA's process revealed it as a "mean, political-wedge issue at the expense of the gay and lesbian community," at odds with *Romer*. "The debate fails to recognize the painful reality thrown on so many innocent people who happen to be in long-term relationships outside of marriage." He spoke of his partner of thirteen years and of a mutual friend who lost his longtime partner to AIDS. The hospital allowed him to visit his dying partner, but the funeral home would not let him sign documents or make arrangements for his loved one's funeral.[53]

Few votes, if any, were changed by the floor debate. The House rejected the Frank amendments—by voice vote against his proposal to delete section 3 and by 103-311 against recognizing nontraditional unions. DOMA passed, 342–67, with 224 Republicans and 118 Democrats voting for it. Voting against DOMA were sixty-five Democrats, mostly from coastal states, plus Bernie Sanders (Independent-Vermont), plus Gunderson, the only Republican dissenter.[54]

THE SENATE DEBATE

Because the Senate has no rules committee and no limitation on debate unless agreed to by unanimous consent or cloture (requiring sixty votes), it has traditionally been the chamber that delays, kills, or significantly changes controversial legislation. In this case, however, Michael Iskowitz (Senator Kennedy's committee staffer focused on gay rights and AIDS issues) reportedly came up with the idea of pairing ENDA and DOMA. If the Republicans agreed to bring ENDA to a vote, the Democrats would not filibuster DOMA. Elizabeth Birch and HRC welcomed this opportunity to debate ENDA, because they believed that job opportunities and other "kitchen table issues" were of greatest importance to the lives of lesbian and gay persons. A favorable Senate ENDA vote would advance that goal immeasurably. The pairing also offered the White House an opportunity to triangulate. President Clinton's support for both traditional marriage and anti-discrimination legislation closely paralleled public opinion and might help him defeat former majority leader Dole, who had left the Senate to focus on his presidential campaign.[55]

On September 10, 1996, the Senate voted on both DOMA and ENDA. Under the unanimous consent agreement negotiated between the party leaders, the DOMA debate was respectful, partly because the outcome was not in doubt. Senators Ted Kennedy and Barbara Boxer (D-California) led the opposition, arguing that DOMA addressed no genuine social or legal problem and was mainly an unconstitutional exercise in "scapegoating." Majority Whip Don Nickles quarterbacked the defense of DOMA, but without the derogatory rhetoric of his House counterparts. Speaking with his flat Oklahoma twang, Nickles emphasized that DOMA protected the right of each state to make its own decision about what family law regime met the needs and preferences of its people. Section 3 was needed to assure that federal law continued to support traditional marriage as a matter of the best policy for the country. Notable supporters of the law included leading Democrats such as Bill Bradley, a New Jersey liberal, and Robert Byrd of West Virginia, a former majority leader. Byrd spent much of this time reading into the congressional record passages from Eskridge's 1996 book, *The Case for Same-Sex Marriage,* including the prediction that "efforts to head it off will only be successful in the short term." He did not seem to appreciate the irony.[56]

After the brief debate, the Senate passed the bill, 85-14, with all of the Republican and all but fourteen Democratic senators voting for it.[57]

The Senate immediately turned to discussion of ENDA, sponsored by Senators Kennedy (D-Massachusetts), Lieberman (D-Connecticut), and Jeffords (R-Vermont). Senator Nickles, as the floor manager for the GOP opposition, emphasized that ENDA would force many religious employers into a position of "promoting homosexuality as a lifestyle." "If this bill becomes a law," argued Senator Dan Coats (R-Indiana), "it would give a federal stamp of approval to activities [homosexual sodomy] that are still illegal in many states." Although seven Republicans voted for ENDA, Nickles held forty-five of his own party and picked up five Democrats. Campaigning in Pennsylvania, Vice President Gore was prepared to helicopter into the Senate to break a 50-50 tie, but David Pryor (D-Arkansas), an ENDA supporter, was absent to be at the bedside of his ailing son, future senator and ENDA supporter Mark Pryor. The final tally was 49-50, a painful loss for HRC.[58]

Because the Senate passed the House bill without amendments, DOMA went to President Clinton's desk for signature or veto. No one expected him to veto it, for reasons recalled by Richard Socarides: "Inside the White House, there was a genuine belief that if the President vetoed the Defense of Marriage Act, his reelection could be in jeopardy. There was a heated debate about whether this was a realistic assessment, but it became clear that the President's chief political advisers were not willing to take any chances. Some in the White

House pointed out that DOMA, once enacted, would have no immediate practical effect on anyone—there were no state-sanctioned same-sex marriages then for the federal government to ignore. I remember a Presidential adviser saying that he was not about to risk a second term on a veto, however noble, that wouldn't change a single thing nor make a single person's life better."[59]

There would be no veto, but neither would there be a Rose Garden celebration. When Clinton returned to the White House after a West Coast trip in the wee hours of September 21, he sheepishly slipped the signed legislation under the office door of Chief of Staff Leon Panetta, with instructions to put out a signing statement (dated the day before). In a classic bit of triangulation, the statement emphasized that the president had "long opposed governmental recognition of same-gender marriages" but that DOMA "should not be understood to provide an excuse for discrimination on the basis of sexual orientation," which would "violate the principle of equal protection under the law and have no place in American society."[60]

Recently, both Bill and Hillary Clinton have claimed that DOMA was signed in order to "defuse a movement to enact a constitutional amendment" enshrining one-man, one-woman marriage in the US Constitution. Elizabeth Birch considers this claim specious, because a constitutional amendment, which does not require presidential approval, would not have served the Republicans as a wedge issue. Neither Phil Burress nor his allies in Congress had plans for such an amendment, because it would take too long to pass it and the odds were long even for more popular measures. When Hillary Clinton floated the constitutional amendment story during her presidential campaigns in 2007–2008 and 2015–2016, even top campaign officials such as Jake Sullivan could not find any support for it.[61]

On the other hand, Mike McCurry reports that the topic was mentioned in the private presidential campaign meetings. "If we don't pass this legislation and provide some kind of federal protection for traditional marriage, there will be a grassroots effort at the state level to pass a constitutional amendment. That's the argument that finally Clinton succumbed to. I thought it was a bit of an artificial argument. I think maybe Bill Clinton thought it was a bit artificial." This account by an honest insider lends only a little support to the Clintons' current posthoc justification, however. Supporting DOMA, which was certain to pass even if Clinton had vetoed it, would not have forestalled a constitutional amendment if it had served the purposes of the Evangelicals and their GOP allies, as the White House well understood. In fact, the Clintons' default on DOMA only encouraged traditional values supporters to seek bigger prophylactics against redefining marriage. If Republicans would support their cause and the Democrats would roll over, why not kill the idea of homosexual marriage permanently? The idea of a constitutional amendment was seriously percolating within a year after DOMA was passed, and by 1998 there was an organized movement to write DOMA into the Constitution. Birch got it right.[62]

For the Clinton reelection team, the DOMA wedge was probably the last obstacle to an easy triumph against Dole's sagging campaign. But Clinton wanted to win big and even reclaim the South. Internal polling revealed that the issues most likely to persuade fence-sitting southerners to vote for him were cultural values like marriage and family. The president suggested a DOMA ad that could be aired on Christian radio stations in southern states. When Vice President Gore and senior adviser George Stephanopoulos tried to dissuade him, Clinton allegedly threw a tantrum and insisted on a family-values commercial. The following radio ad ran in early October: "President Clinton wants a complete ban on late term abortions except when the mother's life is in danger or faces severe health risks, such as the inability to have another child. The President signed the Defense of Marriage Act, supports curfews and school uniforms to teach our children discipline." The day the ad aired, Birch, among others, called the White House and threatened to denounce the Clinton-Gore campaign to HRC's 1.5 million members. Chief of Staff Harold Ickes agreed to pull the ad—but only if Birch did not take credit for the retreat. She remained discreet. Lesbian and gay organizations overwhelmingly supported Clinton against Dole, who had been a DOMA sponsor.[63]

On November 5, Bill Clinton, the triangulator-in-chief, won reelection with 49 percent of the vote, compared with 41 percent for Bob Dole and 9 percent for Ross Perot. Clinton carried thirty-one states, including four states in the South (Florida, Louisiana, Arkansas, and Tennessee). But his big win had no coattails: the Republicans lost only three seats in the House and gained two in the Senate. In his second term, Clinton sought to redeem the disappointing gay rights record of his first term. By 2001, he had appointed 150 lesbian and gay officials and the first openly gay ambassador (James Hormel). After dogged nudging from Socarides, Clinton signed an executive order officially barring sexual orientation discrimination in federal employment, a move supported by 70 percent of the electorate. If not exactly a profile in courage, Executive Order 13,087 was at least an exercise in productive triangulation.[64]

The First DOMA Case

The first appellate case where DOMA played an important role came a few years after the statute was passed; the appeal involved a vivacious Latina hairdresser with cascades of thick curly hair, Christie Lee Cavazos. A native of San Antonio, Texas, Christie moved to Kentucky, where she met Jonathan Mark Littleton. In 1989, they were legally married in Pikeville, Kentucky. They returned to San Antonio, where Christie opened a beauty salon and Jonathan worked as a window washer. After almost seven years of happy marriage, Jonathan entered a period of health difficulties and died in July 1996. His widow believed his death was the result of medical malpractice and brought suit, as the spousal survivor, against Dr. Mark Prange.

At a deposition in the malpractice case, the doctor's attorneys asked Christie whether she had ever been known by any other name. She answered, truthfully, that she had been christened Lee Cavazos Jr. Although biologically male at birth, her gender identity, from age four onward, was female. In 1975, she entered the University of Texas's Health and Science Center, whose medical experts diagnosed her as "transsexual," meaning a person whose psychological gender identity is different from her biological sex. She underwent reconstructive surgery to align her anatomy with her gender identity and had her name legally changed to Christie Lee Cavazos; she also secured a new state-issued identity card that gave her sex as "F." Kentucky accepted Christie's Texas identification card as proof that she was the bride in her and Mark Littleton's marriage license application. They consummated their Kentucky marriage with penile-vaginal intercourse on their honeymoon.[65]

Armed with this information, the doctor's attorneys argued that Christie had no standing to sue as the surviving spouse, because her marriage to Mark Littleton had never been valid. Was Texas not bound, by its own precedents, to give full faith and credit to the Kentucky marriage? Like most states, Texas recognized marriages that were valid in their place of celebration (Kentucky), but in *Littleton v. Prange* the Texas courts rejected that claim as a matter of state law and federal law—namely, DOMA. Section 2 of DOMA freed the state of any duty to recognize a same-sex marriage, and section 3 reaffirmed the norm that marriage had to be one man, one woman.[66]

Christie's attorneys argued that DOMA was not relevant because her marriage was a union of one man (Mark) and one woman (Christie). Her official state identification was female, and in 1998 (while the litigation was proceeding) she changed her birth certificate to the same effect. Anatomically, she was female; her dominant hormone was estrogen. Texas and the IRS treated her and Mark as a heterosexual married couple. In his opinion for the court of appeals, Chief Justice Phil Hardberger confessed uncertainty and then punted: leave the matter to the Texas legislature. Justice Karen Angelini agreed but reserved judgment on how Texas would treat intersex persons, those who were born with ambiguous markers of sex and gender. Justice Alma Lopez objected that sex and gender are not always finally determined at birth—which is the reason Texas allowed birth certificates to be updated, as Christie had done in 1998. The 2-1 court affirmed the lower court's judgment that Christie was not a lawful spouse.[67]

So the first reported DOMA case was an intersection of the conjugal understanding of marriage and equality rights of gender minorities. After Christie lost on appeal, Phyllis Frye of Houston, the most famous transgender lawyer in America, and another transgender attorney, Alyson Dodi Meiselman, filed a petition for rehearing with the Texas court and then a petition for a writ of certiorari (review) with the US Supreme Court. Frye and Meiselman objected to the lower court's refusal to recognize the Kentucky marriage and to its retroactive application of DOMA to a marriage entered seven years earlier. This line of argument did not attract the justices' attention; they refused to hear Christie's appeal, and so the lower courts' judgments dismissing her case were left in place. But Frye and Meiselman's Supreme Court petition raised fundamental issues of American public law.

To begin with, their petition insisted on an inquiry into what *marriage* is. Frye and Meiselman argued: "Marriage is an economic partnership, or a civil contract between parties, and procreation is not a requirement." Phil Burress would have responded that marriage was grounded in conjugal intercourse—but Frye had a response: How is Christie's marriage to Mark, consummated by penile-vaginal intercourse, different from the marriage of a male-female couple who are sterile? In *Turner v. Safley* (1987), the Supreme Court had held that convicted prisoners had a constitutional right to marry. Some of the prisoners were in jail for life, and Missouri, where the case arose, did not allow conjugal visits—yet the court recognized their right to marry because of the emotional, social, and financial benefits of civil marriage. Christie and Mark enjoyed exactly the same benefits and consummated their marriage with penile-vaginal intercourse—and were law-abiding citizens. Did they not enjoy at least as many civil rights as convicted murderers?[68]

Frye and Meiselman's petition also asked the court to consider the question, "Who is a woman?" Hardberger's holding that Christie was a man was inconsistent with biology (she had a vagina and secondary gender traits of women), with culture (she and her friends and family understood her as a woman), and with all the official legal documents, including her birth certificate. Was Hardberger reduced to saying that you have to have XX chromosomes to be a woman? But Christie had never been tested for chromosomal makeup. And how about intersex persons, many of whom had unusual chromosomal patterns (XXY, X, XXYY)? Were they precluded from marrying anyone? To the extent that the conjugal understanding of marriage rested upon natural law, the attorneys demonstrated that it was at odds with nature itself.

Another meta-theme saturating Frye and Meiselman's brief was the emerging tension between the lesbian, gay, and bisexual rights movement and increasingly visible transgender, queer, and nonbinary communities. (Nonbinary persons reject rigid or stable gender identifications.) Phyllis Frye had organized the International Conference on Transgender Law & Employment Policy, which met annually from 1992 to 1997 and was instrumental in creating a network of transgender lawyers, activists, and bloggers. The concept of gender identity as an anti-discrimination category was popularized by this network. In April 1993, the March on Washington for Lesbian, Gay, and Bi[sexual] Equal Rights and Liberation had signaled an evolution of gay rights thinking to include bisexual as well as homosexual persons—but in a speech at the march, Frye insisted that the liberation movement must include transgender persons— and hence should rebrand itself as a movement for lesbian, gay, bisexual, and transgender (LGBT) rights.[69]

Inspired by Phyllis Frye and the burgeoning transgender rights movement, our 1996 book, *The Case for Same-Sex Marriage,* made the sex discrimination argument for gay marriage in part by invoking the experiences of intersex and transgender persons. Our 1997 *Sexuality, Gender, and the Law* casebook with Nan Hunter drew upon these same experiences to argue that issues of identity based on sex (man or woman) and gender (feminine or masculine) inherently mobilized concerns of sexuality, and that sexuality was an incoherent concept without reference to sex and gender. Conceptually, our casebook sought to integrate the overlapping concerns of gaylaw, trans law, and feminism. In short, the July 2000 petition in *Littleton v. Prange* was an important moment in both the LGBT social movement and the marriage conversation. Ironically, the ruling also confirmed the legality of Phyllis Frye's own marriage to her second wife, Trish. A former Eagle Scout and decorated Army lieutenant, Phyllis was chromosomally male and Trish female, so their marriage was validated by *Littleton.*[70]

Christie Lee Littleton ultimately settled her malpractice lawsuit with Dr. Prange, allegedly for a seven-figure amount, and got married a second time, to Pierre van de Putte. In 2009, the Texas legislature amended the state marriage law to recognize the chosen sex of transgender persons for purposes of a marriage license if such persons could produce a court order relating to their "name change or [their] sex change." Christie van de Putte died in 2014, the same year the Texas Court of Appeals ruled that the 2009 law overrode *Littleton v. Prange*.[71]

Junior-DOMAs

Roughly a dozen states had responded to the early marriage lawsuits with statutes explicitly limiting marriage *licensing* to the union of one man and one woman, but few of these laws addressed *recognition* of same-sex marriages licensed in another state. As noted, the conventional wisdom among choice-of-law scholars was that State A would ordinarily recognize marriages validly entered in State B—unless such recognition would violate an important public policy of State A. If traditional marriage supporters wanted to entrench this result in state law, they had a straightforward solution: pass a statute setting forth the legislature's understanding that one-man, one-woman marriage was an important public policy barring recognition of out-of-state marriages between persons of the same sex. We call such laws junior-DOMAs.[72]

The first junior-DOMA was the product of the same-gender marriage advisory committee of the Church of Jesus Christ of Latter-day Saints. The committee included some of the heaviest hitters in the Mormon network—Arthur Anderson, Marlin Jensen, Loren Dunn, Lance Wickman, Richard Wirthlin, and Lynn Wardle. A family law expert teaching at BYU Law, Wardle drafted a bill that sailed through the Utah legislature in March 1995: "A marriage solemnized in any other country, state, or territory, if valid where solemnized, is valid here, unless it is a marriage . . . that would be prohibited and declared void in this state." The law specifically referenced Utah's 1975 law barring marriages between persons of the same sex.[73]

Junior-DOMAs did not take off until after the January 1996 Memphis Accords. Coordinated by FRC and Burress's CCV, state family research councils all over the country worked with lawyers affiliated with the Alliance Defense Fund to draft and lobby for simple legislation that would reaffirm traditional, conjugal marriage and prohibit recognition of same-sex marriage as a matter of the state's commanding family law policy. Copies of Bill Horn's video, *The*

Ultimate Target, and other materials were provided to the state family councils. Within three years after Utah enacted its statute, twenty-nine other states had followed.[74]

Although his home state of Ohio did not adopt a junior-DOMA until 2004, Phil Burress had stacked up many accomplishments. By 2000, Cincinnati was virtually free of pornography and lewd shops. DOMA was a landmark statute that seemed to entrench traditional, conjugal marriage as the universal legal as well as cultural norm for our society. Most of the states had adopted junior-DOMAs. Every three months, he and other key players continued to meet in Washington, DC, to discuss strategies for preserving traditional marriage. The "DC Group" continues to this day.

Burress's biggest legacy, however, is that he brought together thinkers and activists to create a defense-of-marriage philosophy that was an advance over the gay-bashing rhetoric of Amendment 2. Conjugal marriage, by this way of thinking, was special in our culture in ways that friendship and sexual cohabitation were not: procreative consummation entailed in religious and civil marriage was the perfect union of sexual joy, interpersonal commitment, and propagation of the human race. Conjugal marriage respected and built upon the different gender roles of men and woman; the sexes complement one another productively in cementing the relationship, procreating children, and raising those children with gender-differentiated role models. Traditional marriage has been good for America, and something so beneficial should not be tampered with—an argument that religious thinkers, conservative Hayekians, and some political liberals found persuasive. Homosexual marriage, according to Burress and his allies, was not just another pro-choice liberalization of marriage—it was a "counterfeit marriage" that devalued the real thing.[75]

In 1998, Phil Burress married Vickie Bowman, an AFA activist whom he had worked with on the marriage issue. Their extended family—Phil's four daughters and Vickie's two children, together with grandchildren—has been the crowning joy of a life devoted to marriage and sexual morality. Vickie is, like her husband, a sly jokester. We asked her to describe Phil, and the first word she used was *thrifty.* Could she provide an example? Well, every time he leaves the house, he unscrews the light in the refrigerator. We recited that anecdote in a public address, and Phil was quick to point out that we had been pranked by his wife. (Hint: When you close the refrigerator door, what happens to the light?)

6 • A Place at the Table

On television, Sheila Kuehl portrayed brainy, pig-tailed Zelda Gilroy on *The Many Loves of Dobie Gillis,* an offbeat comedy that ran from 1959 to 1963. Zelda was a nerdy tomboy who chased, mentored, and consoled girl-crazy Dobie, affably portrayed by Dwayne Hickman, and his beatnik buddy, Maynard G. Krebs, the role that gave Bob Denver his start in television. Sheila was so good that CBS in 1962 ordered a spin-off, *Zelda.* The show's comic edge came from the funny encounters between cute but clueless boys and a go-getting girl who was smarter than they were. On the cusp of second-wave feminism, *Zelda* was a daring show for a network whose big hit that year was *The Beverly Hillbillies.* A *Zelda* pilot was filmed and presented to the CBS president, who vetoed the series because he found the main character "a little too butch."[1]

Even at twenty-one, Sheila was savvy enough to suspect that CBS knew her career-killing secret. She had fallen in love with a female camp counselor in the summer of 1959 and had spent her years on *Dobie* lying about pretend boyfriends. She believes "lavender menace" rumors dogged her waning acting career after she finished her last season with *Dobie.* Although she had been acting since the age of eight, she turned to other pursuits in the 1970s—first as a professor and administrator at UCLA and then as a student at Harvard Law School, where she won the Ames Moot Court competition and graduated with honors in 1978. An ABA committee named her one of the top five law students in the country.[2]

In the 1980s, Kuehl practiced law and was involved in local politics. Her legal reform work took her to Sacramento, where legislators had the power to change the law in ways that could help or hurt gay people. Because a state constitutional amendment imposed six-year term limits on members of the California

Assembly, seats opened up frequently, and she was elected to the assembly in 1994, becoming the first openly lesbian or gay California legislator. When she showed up in Sacramento in December 1994, she was shocked. The Republicans controlled the assembly, and some of them spoke about homosexuals as though they were from another planet. A gregarious person with a megawatt smile, Kuehl made friends with them. Everyone remembered Zelda with fondness, and she proved to be a hard worker and a serious, earnest policy advocate who did not personalize disagreements.

In *A Place at the Table* (1993), Bruce Bawer had urged Americans to embrace the great mass of emerging lesbian and gay citizens who shared their values and wanted nothing more than a voice in government decisions affecting their lives. The book was published just as gay people were realizing they had no guarantee of such a voice within the Clinton administration. "I realized we needed to be at the table" in Sacramento, Kuehl recalls. It would not come overnight, as she learned when she proposed a bill against bullying in schools: Republican assembly members belittled it as promoting pedophilia, bestiality, and necrophilia. "This is a community that has been invisible, and the major problem we're having these days is that it just isn't invisible anymore," Kuehl calmly told her skeptical colleagues.[3]

In a special election in March 1996, the voters added a second lesbian to the assembly: Carole Migden from San Francisco. She was a lean, brassy New Yorker with curly blond hair and chestnut eyes who had moved to San Francisco with her boyfriend in the 1970s. She married the boyfriend and then divorced him at the same time that she came out as a lesbian. The AIDS crisis and an encounter with Harvey Milk inspired her to become an activist for gay and lesbian causes and ultimately to enter politics. Between 1991 and 1996, Migden served on the San Francisco Board of Supervisors. "I had a lipstick in one hand and a bayonet in the other," she recalls. "Any time I was on TV, any time I had a platform, I wanted them to know I was queer. I thought they liked me and it would help." Kuehl felt that doubling the number of lesbians in the assembly made homosexuality more normal.[4]

As chair of the appropriations committee, through which all bills had to pass, and as a prodigious fundraiser for her allies, Migden garnered tremendous influence in the assembly. Between 1996 and 2000, she and Kuehl were tag-team legislators, pushing each other's bills and reminding their colleagues that gays were people and not monsters. They got the anti-bullying bill reported from committee and debated on the floor in 1997 and 1999. Kuehl pleaded with her colleagues to protect schoolchildren against violence: "There is a horror involved in knowing that you will be the target of discrimination." Traditionalists warned that the bill would foist a depraved homosexual lifestyle onto innocent children. Migden responded: "Look at me, look at Sheila: Are we depraved?" Dressed in a pink designer suit and crisp white blouse, Migden epitomized stylish femininity. "It isn't about whether you approve or disapprove of lesbian and gay life," she said. "We've existed since the beginning of time, and we'll continue to exist long after many of us have deposed from this chamber. It is a fact of life."[5]

The next year, Sheila Kuehl ran for an open seat in the California Senate (whose members were limited to two four-year terms). Jackie Goldberg was elected to the assembly from a Los Angeles district. A longtime schoolteacher, Goldberg was a gentle, maternal woman who had led the Los Angeles School Board to adopt aggressive AIDS education programs and a rule barring sexual orientation discrimination against teachers and staff. San Diego's Christine Kehoe also joined the assembly in 2000, after several decades of community service. It is no coincidence that the first four open LGBT legislators in California were women who had been civil rights activists in the 1960s. Many of that generation's male leaders had been felled by AIDS; in addition, Migden thinks that "as women, we were less threatening."[6]

Kehoe suggested that the four lesbian legislators form an LGBT caucus, and they decided to meet over dinners together. Because Goldberg was the only one of the four who could cook a decent meal, she and her partner, Sharon Stricker, hosted most of the caucus meetings at their house in a modest, integrated Sacramento neighborhood. Every week or two during the legislative sessions, the women met at the dinner table to talk about legislative priorities and plan strategy. Their ideas changed the face of California law and politics and pioneered a legislative rather than judicial approach to creating legal frameworks for lesbian and gay relationships.[7]

By 1999, much of the "homosexual agenda" had already been enacted. In 1976, Assembly Speaker Willie Brown orchestrated the enactment of criminal law reform that relieved gay people of outlaw status. Between 1977 and 1999, California law moved to bar sexual orientation discrimination in employment, housing, public accommodations, and education. Kuehl authored a 1997 law that added sexual orientation to the list of categories protected by hate crime laws. Her anti-bullying bill was finally enacted in 1999.[8]

In the late 1990s, Kuehl and Migden believed the next area they should target was discrimination against lesbian and gay families. Kuehl had enjoyed two lengthy relationships with women, and Migden had been in a committed

Christine Kehoe, Jackie Goldberg, Carole Migden, and Sheila
Kuehl share a laugh during a grueling legislative floor session.
(Photo courtesy of Senator Carole Migden [retired].)

relationship since 1985 with the lawyer Cristina Arguedas. Also in long-term
committed relationships when they came to the legislature in 2000, Kehoe
and Goldberg agreed that family recognition should be a top priority. No one
was thinking that gay marriage would soon come to California—but the LGBT
caucus felt that legislators needed to become aware of the hundreds of thousands of lesbian and gay couples, who should not be the objects of state exclusion. Even after setbacks like DOMA, decent treatment for gay families was
an idea whose time had come in California.

At the same time that lesbians were entering the legislature, five key lawyers
were coming into influential posts in California's LGBT organizations. Jon
Davidson left a Los Angeles law firm to head up the ACLU of Southern California in 1988 and then joined Lambda Legal's Los Angeles office in 1995,
followed by Jenny Pizer in 1996. (Davidson would be Lambda's legal director
from 2004 to 2017.) Kate Kendell became legal director of the National Center
for Lesbian Rights (NCLR) in 1994 and executive director in 1996, when
Shannon Minter succeeded her as legal director. After working for the ACLU
of Northern California (1987–1995), Matt Coles became the director of the
ACLU's National Lesbian & Gay Rights Project in 1995. Over a generation,
these lawyers—two gay men who survived the sweep of AIDS, two lesbians,
and one person who would transition from female to male in the middle of
the decade (Minter)—led the fight to remake gaylaw in California. The LGBT

caucus in the legislature would rely on them for legal drafting, constitutional advice, and strategic thinking about their ambitious agenda for relationship recognition.

The caucus had formidable opponents. The most famous was William (Pete) Knight, who had been elected to the assembly from Palmdale in 1992 after a three-decade career as a colonel in the US Air Force. He was best known as the test pilot who in 1968 flew the X-15 rocket research aircraft at 4,520 MPH (Mach 6.7), establishing a world speed record in a fixed-wing aircraft. He subsequently logged over six thousand hours as a pilot in the Vietnam War. The much-decorated Colonel Knight was a short, weather-beaten, modest man whose proudest achievement was his family. He and his wife, Helena Stone Knight, raised three sons within the Catholic Church. Though not a great debater like Sheila Kuehl nor an aggressive strategist like Carole Migden, Pete Knight quietly opposed every gay rights bill Kuehl or Migden introduced. He said he was fine with giving lesbian and gay Californians a place at the table—but he opposed proposals that he thought would turn the table topsyturvy. There was a personal history behind his view that gays should be quietly tolerated but not publicly encouraged. Knight's younger brother was gay or bisexual and had died from complications associated with AIDS. Shortly before that, Knight learned that his son David was also gay and was in a committed relationship with another man. "It is hard to deal with," he told the press, with libertarian stoicism. "But if it's one of your children, you accept it. It's his life."[9]

Senator Knight's legal adviser was Andy Pugno, who had interned with Knight while he was a student at the McGeorge School of Law and then became the office's chief of staff in 1997. Also a devout Catholic and loyal family man, Pugno was perfectly in sync with his boss and was almost his and Helena's fourth son. The California Conference of Catholic Bishops was a strong ally on any issue involving morality, and Pugno also relied on the Church of Jesus Christ of Latter-day Saints—especially BYU professor Lynn Wardle, who had been the Church's legal representative in the Hawai'i marriage campaign, as well as in the national network of traditional family values supporters. California's most prominent Evangelical group was the Reverend Lou Sheldon's Traditional Values Coalition (TVC). Although its anti-gay messaging was too shrill for Knight and Pugno, TVC was an important ally on morals-based legislation.

With diverse gay and religious communities, California was an important location for the post-DOMA marriage debate. The debate was framed by the state's popular lawmaking process: by gathering voter signatures, Californians could put initiatives on the ballot that would by simple majority votes add either statutes (which required signatures from 6 percent of the vote in the last gubernatorial election) or constitutional amendments (8 percent). Knight and Pugno believed that if judges required same-sex marriage, the voters would override them. This was their trump card, a political fact that influenced the strategic choices made by Kuehl and her allies. Their initial question was whether to focus their efforts on domestic partnerships rather than marriage— and to understand that choice, we need to return to San Francisco after the domestic partnership ordinance was passed by the voters in 1990.[10]

San Francisco's Equal Benefits Ordinance

After the election of 1990, the influence of the lesbian and gay community was entrenched in San Francisco, and that was most apparent in private companies' treatment of domestic partnerships. By 1996, as many as five hundred companies nationwide had recognized these partnerships, including Bay Area firms such as Apple and Levi Strauss. Irked that the anti-gay Salvation Army took municipal funds for providing meals for people with AIDS, Geoff Kors and Jeff Sheehy, the legislation committee chair and president, respectively, of the Harvey Milk Lesbian/Gay/Bisexual Democratic Club, proposed an equal benefits measure that would require businesses having contracts with San Francisco to provide health insurance and other benefits to the partners of their lesbian and gay employees. Kors brought the bill to his boss, lesbian supervisor Leslie Katz. Kors and Sheehy built support among private groups and within the board of supervisors. In October 1996, the board passed it without dissent, and the Equal Benefits Ordinance was signed into law by Mayor Willie Brown in early November.[11]

On December 20, San Francisco archbishop William Levada petitioned the mayor and the board for an exemption for Catholic Charities, which received almost half of its $13 million budget from the city. The board wrote back saying it would grant no exemptions. In February, Catholic Charities was scheduled to open Leland House, a home for people with AIDS that had been the capstone of Archbishop Jack Quinn's AIDS ministry. Would the new domestic partnership ordinance imperil Leland House? On February 3, Archbishop Levada held a press conference on the steps of St. Mary's Cathedral, lamenting the absence of universal health coverage. "I am in favor of increasing benefits, especially health coverage, for anyone." Later in the week, he reported that he and municipal officials had "a cordial meeting and worked out some language that would be an alternative means of compliance with the city ordinance. Basically, it means that employees could designate *any legally domiciled member* of their household (to receive benefits) and that would be in compliance with the ordinance. For me, it was a useful solution. I think it's also useful for the city and for framing the question generally." The compromise covered domestic partners and many others, consistent with the Church's support for broad health care.[12]

The board of supervisors was amenable to the archbishop's constructive solution, but they played hardball with the Salvation Army, which lost its municipal contract. At a press conference, Supervisor Katz announced that other providers—notably AIDS Hospice and Meals on Wheels—were prepared to take up the slack. The deft strategic vision of Geoff Kors undergirded the city's tough stance: any business that wanted contracts with San Francisco needed to adopt a plan for domestic partnership benefits for lesbian and gay employees. His strategy faced its greatest test with United Airlines, which would lose its lease at the San Francisco Airport (SFO) unless it adopted such a policy. United with Pride, an association of the airline's gay managers and workers, had been lobbying for domestic partner benefits; the American Flight Association had also made them a priority. There was also pressure from the company's marketing staff, engaged in outreach to LGBT passengers, who allegedly spent $17 billion a year on travel.[13]

Despite these pressures, United held firm to its policy, and the Air Transport Association of America (ATA), representing the major carriers operating out of SFO, brought its claim to federal court. The ATA lawsuit had strong legal arguments: that the municipal effort to alter employer benefit policies was preempted by the Employee Retirement Income Security Act of 1974 (ERISA), a 1974 federal statute comprehensively regulating pensions, and that it was an unconstitutional interference with interstate commerce. Kors had written the ordinance in anticipation of these claims, and the city argued that it was not "regulating" the airlines but was only exercising its freedom, as a "market participant," to choose whom it would do business with. The preemption and constitutional doctrines were thus irrelevant. Soon after the lawsuit was filed, Sheehy formed Equal Benefits Advocates, which organized a boycott of United Airlines. In July 1997, dozens of protesters picketed United's downtown ticket office, some of them dressed as Tinky Winky, a purple character in the children's cartoon "Teletubbies" who had been attacked by the Reverend Pat Robertson (a secret sponsor of the ATA lawsuit) as a perverting plant, seeking to lure children into the homosexual "lifestyle."[14]

In her ruling, Judge Claudia Wilken split the baby, refusing to invalidate the ordinance but limiting its impact. She accepted the "market participant" argument to allow San Francisco to condition a contract on benefits for workers at SFO, but she ruled that it did not permit the city to insist that United adopt a domestic partnership policy for its entire system. As for the ERISA argument, the judge ruled that some benefits "such as moving expenses, memberships and membership discounts, and travel benefits, are not governed by ERISA at all," and so their regulation was not preempted. The court also held that the city could regulate non-pension benefits that were not offered through an ERISA plan, such as family and medical leave and bereavement leave. But what the city could not regulate, the court concluded, were benefits that were covered by ERISA and offered through an ERISA plan—including health insurance and pension benefits.[15]

The ATA appealed the part of Judge Wilken's ruling that went against the airlines. Soon after the ruling, HRC endorsed a nationwide consumer boycott of United, with gay people cutting up their frequent-flyer cards and blocking the doors of airline offices. On July 30, 1999, after the Ninth Circuit refused to stay the effect of the Equal Benefits Ordinance, United announced that it would offer a comprehensive fringe benefits package (health insurance, pension survivors' benefits, bereavement leaves, and travel privileges and discounts) to the domestic partners of persons who could not marry. This went well beyond Judge Wilken's remedy, as did United's announcement that the domestic partnership policy would ultimately apply to all ninety-seven thousand employees. On August 5, American Airlines announced that it was adopting a domestic partnership policy, and U.S. Airways followed the next day. Continental fell into line a few months later, but Delta did not do so until 2003, when Atlanta (its hub) created a domestic partnership registry. The Big Three automobile manufacturers and the United Automobile Workers (UAW) made a similar announcement—without the drama of a lawsuit—on June 8, 2000, covering 465,000 employees. The move was a result of collective bargaining pressure from the UAW, plus the Equal Benefits Ordinance, plus consumer pressure and diminishing fears of religion-based boycotts.[16]

As the airline and automaker examples dramatically illustrate, San Francisco's Equal Benefits Ordinance had a galvanizing effect on businesses throughout the state and nationally. In January 1997, HRC promulgated a list of 287 employers who were providing domestic partnership benefits to their lesbian and gay employees and often to their straight employees as well. A year later, after the San Francisco ordinance was in full effect, that number was over 1,500, a 600 percent increase that HRC attributed to the ordinance. In 2002, the city claimed that the ordinance had led more than 4,500 employers to begin offering equal benefits; almost all of the companies opted to change their policies nationwide and to offer equal benefits, including health and pension benefits, in all areas. But as the airline and automaker examples illustrate, the ordinance was most effective in combination with other factors: the recognized purchasing power of LGBT consumers and their perceived loyalty to first-mover companies; workers and managers coming out as LGBT or gay-allied and organizing within companies; and union pressure at the bargaining table.[17]

Nicole Raeburn demonstrates that there was also a domino effect facilitated by internet networking among lesbian and gay employees and by advocacy groups like the Task Force and HRC. By listing the ever-expanding array of institutions offering domestic partnership benefits for employees, HRC's Work Net induced further adoptions by companies worried that failing to follow the trend could mark them as anti-gay. Since 2002, Work Net has reported companies' Workplace Equality Scores, in which domestic partnership policies weigh heavily.[18]

By the 1990s the concept of domestic partnership, pioneered by the California cities, was attracting support from big business as well as civil rights organizations across the country. Even as gay rights lawyers were working on state constitutional lawsuits in Hawai'i, Vermont, and Massachusetts, activists in California were working to establish a statewide domestic partnership registry from which they hoped to build a structure similar to, and perhaps ultimately including, marriage for lesbian and gay couples.

State Domestic Partnership and Junior-DOMA Bills

Given political successes in San Francisco and Los Angeles, some LGBT activists wanted to file a state constitutional challenge to the California Family Code's limitation of marriage to one man and one woman. Lambda and the ACLU warned that any such lawsuit would almost certainly be unsuccessful. The state judiciary was still emerging from shock after liberal chief justice Rose Bird and Justice Cruz Reynoso lost their retention votes in 1986. They were replaced by justices named by conservative GOP governor George Deukmejian; he and his Republican successor, Pete Wilson, remade the court in the 1990s. Under Chief Justice Ron George, a Wilson protégé, the California Supreme Court was considered right of center. But even if a same-sex marriage lawsuit succeeded in court, the voters would almost certainly override the decision through a DOMA-type initiative. Worse, a state supreme court win might trigger a campaign to amend the US Constitution, creating a Super-DOMA that would preempt municipal domestic partnership ordinances and render employee domestic partner benefits unenforceable. With the gayocracy issuing stern doomsday warnings, California couples avoided constitutional lawsuits in the late 1990s. Instead, Lambda, NCLR, and the ACLU worked with California legislators to advance legislation recognizing domestic partnership on the one hand and, on the other hand, to oppose legislation entrenching the one-man, one-woman definition of marriage.[19]

The first serious statewide domestic partnership bill was Assembly Bill (A.B.) 2810, introduced in February 1994 by Assembly Member Richard Katz (D-Sylmar). The bill would have allowed cohabiting straight, lesbian, and gay couples living in an "intimate and committed relationship of mutual caring" to register as domestic partners and enjoy the same conservatorship and hospital visitation rights as married couples. At the time there were more than four hundred thousand unmarried couples living together in California (93 percent straight, 7 percent gay or lesbian), and Katz argued that the state ought to give them basic protections. Recalling the opposition to domestic partnership in San Francisco, critics of Katz's bill claimed that it would create the equivalent of gay marriage. Both chambers passed it, but on September 11, Governor Wilson vetoed it for that reason.[20]

Katz continued to introduce domestic partnership bills, as did Kuehl in 1996, but Republican control of the assembly doomed those measures. In 1996, Assembly Member Knight sponsored a bill to bar recognition of out-of-state same-sex marriages. Knight was concerned that "forced government sanctioning of same-sex marriages will lead to a public school curriculum that equates homosexual and traditional marriages as equally acceptable." His press release opined that "the economic and legal benefits extended to married couples are society's way of regulating and legally binding personal relationships that appear to be capable of creating children. A mother-father couple is the healthiest environment in which a child can grow up, and this environment is fostered with benefits that encourage[] couples to be married before procreating." This is the earliest public expression by a legislator of the faith-based understanding of marriage as a vehicle for responsible procreation or of concern that state recognition of lesbian and gay relationships would send the wrong message to schoolchildren.[21]

In committee hearings, Lambda's Jon Davidson argued that the Knight bill was an unconstitutional abridgment of gay people's fundamental right to marry and their equality rights as enforced by *Romer v. Evans* (1996). Recall, from the last chapter, that *Romer* invalidated a Colorado constitutional amendment that excluded gay, lesbian, and bisexual persons from state and local legal protections. Lambda, the ACLU, and NCLR maintained that the Knight bill would do the same thing. Professor Wardle responded that *Romer* might require the state to *tolerate* gay people and same-sex relationships—but it did not require the state to give their relationships a preferred status, as domestic partnership would do. For that reason, Knight was shocked when the senate judiciary committee amended his bill to create a domestic partnership registry, entitling couples to health and conservators benefits. The amendment was a poison pill that motivated Knight to disavow his junior-DOMA the month before President Clinton signed the national DOMA into law.[22]

The 1996 elections that sent Pete Knight to the state senate went badly for California Republicans: they lost their slender majority in the assembly, and the Democrats padded their majority in the senate. Modeled on the 1994 Katz bill, Carole Migden introduced A.B. 1059, designed to create a statewide domestic partnership registry open to straight, lesbian, and gay couples and to recognize just a few rights, namely, the right to be with your domestic partner in the hospital and a nondiscrimination duty for health insurers. "This bill responds to reality. It responds to families the way they are today," Migden told reporters. "They're not as traditional as they once were." To her LGBT allies, she said: "You've got to start somewhere." Once you establish the domestic partnership structure, you can add rights and benefits to it later.[23]

Kuehl praises Migden as someone who was able to find a way to persuade almost anyone that it was in her or his interest to support her bills. Assembly Bill 1059 drew support from small businesses, senior citizens' organizations, labor unions, civil rights leaders, and many religious leaders. Some expected opponents remained on the sidelines. Ned Dolejsi, the new executive director of the California Conference of Bishops, was persuaded to see A.B. 1059 as a health insurance measure—an extension of the policy Archbishop Levada had created in 1996. Because Migden knew exactly how far she could press public policy and still secure majority votes in both chambers (including several GOP legislators), her bill sailed through both chambers in August 1998. Governor Wilson, however, vetoed it in September. Although claiming that domestic partner health benefit coverage would expose employers to excessive costs and fraudulent declarations, Wilson was mainly concerned with the stamp of approval the measure would place on straight as well as gay cohabiting relationships.[24]

Carole Migden's Statewide Domestic Partnership Law

In November 1998, Democrat Gray Davis was elected governor, and the Democrats added to their majorities in both legislative chambers. On December 7, Migden introduced A.B. 26, which proposed a statewide domestic partnership registry, available to any two unmarried "adults who have chosen to share one another's lives in an intimate and committed relationship of mutual caring." Registered partners would enjoy hospital visitation rights, would have conservatorship authority for one another, and, for municipal and state employees, would be able to receive health insurance and other benefits. The stakes were high: most observers believed that this time, domestic partnership would actually pass into law.

There was ambiguity on the LGBT side as to the bill's purpose. Many activists and supporters viewed A.B. 26 as what we call "equality practice"—what Migden called the "camel's nose under the tent," a starting point for complete marriage equality. But Matt Coles understood it as a move toward family law pluralism—a "world in which marriage would be open to everyone, and something that provided a less highly defined but still significant safety net—like domestic partnership—would also be available to everyone." Lambda's Jon Davidson and Jenny Pizer (who advised Migden and helped draft the bill) tended to see A.B. 26 as both a path toward marriage equality and a new family institution that could address the day-to-day problems faced by lesbian and gay couples. Assembly Bill 26 addressed the needs of people with AIDS by including intestate succession and guardianship as well as health insurance rights. These benefits led the California Catholic Conference and many businesses to oppose the bill. It passed the assembly, 41-38, in April 1999, but the senate trimmed the property rights in the original bill. As Migden explained to us, a bill's author always needs to include policy ballast that can be given up to satisfy foot-dragging legislators. But how much would she be willing to give up?[25]

Like previous bills, A.B. 26 would have made registration and benefits available to different-sex as well as same-sex couples. When he was lieutenant governor, Gray Davis had cast the deciding vote on the California Board of Regents to expand spousal benefits within the University of California system to the domestic partners of lesbian and gay employees. That was a politically gutsy move, but the governor told Migden that he was not willing to sign a domestic partnership bill that also covered straight couples, because including them would make domestic partnerships "too marriage." In the summer of 1999, Migden had to decide whether to call the governor's bluff.[26]

She met privately with Davis and his deputy chief of staff, Susan Kennedy (also an out lesbian), who warned her that legislative enactment of A.B. 26 was endangered by the bill's inclusion of couples who could choose to get married. Given the Catholic Church's opposition, several moderate Democratic legislators were reluctant to support the bill in its current form. Migden and her aide Alan LoFaso had devised a backup plan for the meeting. I *might* be willing to give up the inclusion of all different-sex adult couples, she told the governor—but not older couples where at least one partner is age sixty-two or higher. Including them was very important to seniors' groups, and Dolejsi's concerns might be mollified if the man-woman couples were those who would not be procreating. A deal was reached, and the senate voted 22-14 for the amended A.B. 26 on September 9. The amended bill went back to the assembly, which approved it at 12:01 a.m. on September 10. Governor Davis signed it into law on October 2.[27]

The compromise needed to keep the governor and his allies on board would have important consequences. It indelibly associated domestic partnership with lesbian and gay couples. As amended, A.B. 26 was still a first step toward gay marriage—but it was a step away from creating an institution that could rival marriage, with fewer benefits but also easier to exit. In the same year, the French Parliament created such an institution, open to all couples: *pacte civil de solidarité* (PaCS). Because the PaCS offered most marital benefits but was much easier to dissolve, it became a popular alternative for both gay and straight couples. (Same-sex couples can now marry in France, yet there has been no significant push to repeal the PaCS law.) The French parallel suggests that the bishops and the legislators with majority Catholic constituencies had a deep understanding of the implications of an inclusive domestic partnership regime—and that for legislative sponsors, the first-step-to-marriage rationale was dominant.[28]

At San Francisco's gay pride celebration the year after A.B. 26, Migden presided over a public ceremony in which dozens of lesbian and gay couples, armed with their domestic partnership registrations, committed themselves to one another for life. Implicitly acknowledging that domestic partnerships had little legal punch, she promised: "Every year, I pledge to you, we'll make it bigger and bigger, and then we'll get married in the real kind of way." Goldberg described the 1999 law as a "beachhead." Like social security, which started out as a modest benefit program and grew into a safety net for tens of millions, domestic partnership would grow into marriage or its equivalent. These assurances led fourteen thousand Californians to sign up for domestic partnership in its first year of operation.[29]

Pete Knight's Junior-DOMA Initiative

After Pete Knight's junior-DOMA was left for dead in the California legis-lature, the Church of Jesus Christ of Latter-day Saints made plans for a mar-riage initiative in California "along the same lines we organized in Hawai'i." With the approval of the First Presidency, Loren Dunn and Richard Wirthlin met with Ned Dolejsi and Oakland bishop Stephen Cummins, who headed the California Catholic Conference. The conference would support a marriage ini-tiative, especially if the Mormons took the lead, as they had in Hawai'i. In 1997, they and TVC formed an ecumenical Defense of Marriage Leadership Group to work with Knight and Pugno. If the California legislature would not protect traditional marriage, California voters would do so, if given an opportunity.[30]

The leadership group worked with political consultant Gary Lawrence, an-other Latter-day Saint. Based on focus group reactions to different wording, Lawrence determined that a simple declarative sentence worked best: "Only marriage between one man and one woman is valid or recognized in Califor-nia." In June 1997, this language was submitted to the California attorney gen-eral, who had 45 days to prepare the initiative petition, and then the sponsors would have 150 days to gather the almost seven hundred thousand signatures needed to qualify for the ballot in 1998.[31]

The proposal was not pursued in 1997, because of uncertainty within the holy alliance. Elders Marlin Jensen and Loren Dunn recommended that the Church of Jesus Christ commit resources to the effort. "The California homo-sexual and lesbian communities are well-organized and well-financed and can be vindictive," they wrote to the Church's public affairs committee—but the committee suddenly became noncommittal. Catholic enthusiasm depended upon the Mormons taking the lead. Meanwhile, Andy Pugno was wondering whether his coalition of the faithful ought to press for a constitu-tional initiative—a move that would have been much more expensive because it would need signatures from at least 8 percent of the voters in the 1994 gov-ernor's race, as opposed to 6 percent for statutory initiatives. By the end of 1997, moreover, marriage equality seemed unlikely in Hawai'i. With no state recognizing same-sex marriage, Pugno feared that a constitutional initiative would be seen as anti-homosexual overkill.[32]

Remarkably, some "traditionalists" worried that recognizing only "marriage between one man and one woman" might be interpreted to restrict the rights of straight men who wanted to marry a second or third time. It was one thing to exclude lesbian couples from marriage but quite another to inconvenience straight people who were divorced or widowed. The no-remarriage interpretation struck Wardle as highly implausible, but Pugno accommodated those concerns by changing the language to this: "Only marriage between a man and a woman is valid or recognized in California." On March 2, 1998, he filed this new language with the secretary of state, and the attorney general approved it on April 22. With the help of professional signature-gathering firms and churches, the proponents filed 677,512 signatures on September 21, many more than needed to secure a vote on Proposition 22 for March 2, 2000. The proponents of Proposition 22 were off and running—while opponents did not even have their first meeting until December 5, 1998.[33]

MORMONS MOBILIZE FOR PROPOSITION 22

Also in December 1998, the leadership of the Church of Jesus Christ decided to "participate in the coalition supporting the California initiative." Andy Pugno's Protect Marriage committee welcomed the Latter-day Saints into the coalition and Richard Wirthlin onto its executive committee, which also included Dolejsi and Knight. In May 1999, a letter from church authorities was read to congregations, soliciting support for Proposition 22: "Marriage between a man and a woman is ordained of God, and is essential to His eternal plan. It is imperative for us to give our best effort to preserve what our Father in Heaven has put in place."[34]

Also in May, the church leadership sent a letter to all California stake presidents, who were asked to encourage their members to mail contributions to the Glendale address of Protect Marriage. (A *stake* is a cluster of five or more Mormon congregations, or *wards*.) The letter suggested starting with big asks from the most affluent members. In June 1999, stakes were assessed specific amounts of money to raise for this effort, and the Salt Lake City headquarters sent individual letters to 740,000 Californians, urging them to contribute money and time to Proposition 22. That summer, Yes on 22 raised between three and four million dollars—almost all of it from Latter-day Saints and Catholic archdioceses.[35]

In September, the Church sent packets of materials to all 160 California stake presidents, along with videos telling how to get members organized to support the initiative. Each ward (congregation) was supposed to have a "Knight coordinator," who was in charge of the dozens of volunteers called to work on Proposition 22; the ward coordinators reported to a stake coordinator. Each stake was expected to attract fifty or more volunteers to walk the streets, contacting neighbors, plying them with fact sheets and friendly arguments for Proposition 22, and collecting voter information and emails that were then given to the Protect Marriage committee. In January 2000, stake presidents and bishops were directed to call emergency stake meetings to drum up money and volunteers for the March vote.[36]

NO ON KNIGHT

On February 1, 1999, opponents of Proposition 22 formed a No on Knight steering committee, with Mike Marshall as its campaign director. In April 1999, Lake Snell, its polling firm, reported that most voters believed there were committed lesbian and gay couples who should enjoy hospital visitation and other rights but did not support marriage. "Voters' biggest fears about same-sex marriage are values-based and relate to declining moral standards, explaining homosexuality to children, and damaging religious marriage." The focus groups also revealed that many voters felt threatened by lesbian and gay "flaunting," especially public kissing. The firm recommended a focus on personal stories of couples whose lack of legal status had caused them terrible problems; emphasis on these couples' "depth of commitment," just like that of happily married couples; and no public displays of affection in the campaign.[37]

The message for No on Knight was "Unfair, Divisive, and Intrusive." The opponents attracted endorsements from dozens of prominent Californians, such as Los Angeles district attorney Gil Garcetti and Assembly Speaker Antonio Villaraigosa, who signed the official No on 22 ballot statements. Opponents worked the press very effectively. For example, David Knight, the sponsor's estranged gay son, denounced his father's initiative as unhinged in an October 14 *Los Angeles Times* opinion piece. In November, No on Knight persuaded Attorney General Bill Lockyer to reject the proponents' title for Proposition 22, "Definition of Marriage," and substitute the more negative "Limit on Marriage."[38]

One legacy of DOMA and No on Knight was a new name for the same-sex marriage movement. On February 12, 1998, National Marriage Day, Connie Ress, Cathy Marino-Thomas, and other activists had launched Equality Through Marriage—renamed Marriage Equality New York in August. Its mission was to secure legally recognized civil marriage equality for all, without regard to sexual orientation or gender identity, at the state and federal level through grassroots organizing, education, action, and partnerships. In 1999, Molly McKay, Davina Kotulski, and J.J. Carusone founded Marriage Equality

California to generate grassroots opposition to Proposition 22. On Valentine's Day 2000, when dozens of same-sex couples appeared at the Beverly Hills courthouse seeking marriage licenses, Molly McKay wore her trademark wedding dress. The protest was peaceful, but no one was issued a license.[39]

PROPOSITION 22'S GRAND FINALE

Reflecting its financial advantage, Yes on 22 began Spanish-language ads on January 20, 2000, with English ads going up February 7. The theme of the campaign and its ads was "protect marriage." Don't experiment with this treasured but embattled institution. Most of the ads were rather bland, but one featured a black schoolteacher who asked parents what they wanted their children exposed to. "I've dedicated my life to their education . . . and teaching them the principles to shape their lives. That's why parents and teachers like me all across California are voting Yes on 22." Would schools not be forced to support gay marriage if judges forced it on the state? Although teachers' unions found the ad misleading, it was effective with parents and showed up in leaflets and radio ads as well.

The No on Knight ads started February 14, 2000, and featured attacks on the sponsor. One early ad said: "Pete Knight, the California politician behind Prop 22, may not like it that his son is gay. But he shouldn't make us vote on his private problem." Another showed a photo montage of parents and their kids: "What if your child, or the child of someone you know, turns out to be gay? Do you still want the best for them?" Another ad featured a fictional Jeff Davis, who explained: "Most people don't support gay marriage, but we do support keeping government out of people's private lives." Some gay groups found this depiction "a shockingly sympathetic image of a homophobe."[40]

On February 29, No on Knight aired its most hard-hitting ad: "Prop 22 won't save a single marriage, but it will hurt gay people. That's what it's intended to do." The ad showed followers of pastor Fred Phelps at the funeral of gay-bashing victim Matthew Shepard. They were holding signs, "God hates fags," and "Fags burn in Hell." Mike Marshall defended the inflammatory ad: "When people vote yes, they are going to hurt someone they know who is gay or lesbian." Andy Pugno and the Yes on 22 campaign viewed it and the attack-Pete-Knight pieces as hateful and ineffective.[41]

On the morning of February 25, thirty-two-year-old Stuart Matis, a saintly Mormon consumed with guilt over being gay, fatally shot himself on the steps of the stake center in Los Altos, California. In his suicide note, he wrote that the "Knight Initiative will certainly save no family. It is codified hatred." Within two weeks, two other young gay Mormons—Clay Witmer and Brian Thompson—cited Proposition 22 in their own suicide notes. They did not slow the Church's efforts, however. Thousands of Latter-day Saints blanketed neighborhoods with home visits, fact sheets, and arguments that gay marriage would corrupt children and undermine families. On March 3, Elder Richard Wirthlin sent an email to all Proposition 22 area coordinators, challenging each stake to call twenty thousand voters by the Monday before the election.[42]

On March 7, Proposition 22 won, 61.4 percent to 38.6 percent, sweeping all areas of the state. Most Californians started out agreeing with Senator Knight, and the No on Knight campaign had neither the money nor the volunteer base to compete with the Yes on 22 juggernaut. Although the LGBT community surprised itself by raising more than $6.3 million, it was dwarfed by the $11 million raised by Yes on 22. Importantly, Yes on 22 had a simple, positive, powerful message: protect marriage; don't rock the boat. No on Knight's mantra of "divisive, intrusive, unfair" was complicated, negative, and weak. It especially failed to persuade female voters. The overwhelming electoral victory for Proposition 22 reflected the facts that LGBT Californians had a place at the table, but the table was still set according to the overall plan laid out by more tradition-minded Californians.[43]

On April 4, Lorri Jean, the manager of the Los Angeles Gay & Lesbian Center, called a meeting of grassroots activists, the California Alliance for Pride and Equality (CAPE), and gay rights organizations to figure out lessons for future campaigns that might be derived from this defeat. First and most important, the marriage equality movement needed to develop the infrastructure and funding to support an ongoing campaign to change the hearts and minds of the general population. A community organizer, Jean pointed to the successful efforts to defeat anti-gay initiatives in Oregon. LGBT groups there had developed extensive voter files, enhanced in each successive campaign, and "a permanent, community-based infrastructure (Basic Rights Oregon) which is staffed year-round rather than simply being mobilized whenever a new anti-gay initiative is introduced."[44]

Second, morally neutral messaging was not persuading undecided voters. For marriage equality to win at the polls, straight people had to be persuaded that there were committed lesbian and gay couples with families like theirs, who were suffering unjustly from being denied the right to marry. Third, the marriage movement needed to be more inclusive in its outreach and genuinely diverse in its leadership. This lesson was hard to implement, but a new generation of leaders assumed command of the marriage movement. None was more important than Geoff Kors, the director of CAPE. Under his leadership, CAPE morphed into Equality California, whose focus would be on educating the public about the lives and relationships of gay people in order to secure marriage equality in the state.[45]

Carole Migden's 2001 Domestic Partnership Amendments

The November 2000 election, eight months after Proposition 22, promoted Sheila Kuehl to the senate and added Jackie Goldberg and Chris Kehoe to the assembly. The Democrats increased their majorities to 26-14 in the senate and 50-30 in the assembly. Kuehl and Migden had given lesbians and gay men a place at the table in California politics; now the table in the legislature was filling up with lesbians and in 2002 would add a few gay men. The lesbian legislators had a unified agenda on family law: they wanted to add new legal rights and benefits to the 1999 domestic partnership law. Migden compared the process to a Christmas tree: the 1999 statute created the tree, with just a couple of ornaments, and the goal was to adorn the tree with additional rights and benefits.

Alan LoFaso, Migden's chief of staff, secluded himself in the law library for several months in 2000 to catalog all the statutes that contained spousal rights, benefits, or duties and worked with litigation groups to learn which benefits and rights were most important to the LGBT community. Private groups offered valuable suggestions. NCLR's Kate Kendell made second-parent adoption her special mission: state judges were granting lesbians parental rights to their partners' children, but it would be great if the issue did not have to be litigated case by case. Lambda's Jenny Pizer had represented a lesbian who lost a case for the wrongful death of her partner, so the right to sue was added to the bill. As always, Migden pruned the Christmas tree down to make sure it would have majority support in both chambers. Her prime directive after 1999 was that *every* domestic partnership bill had to pass the legislature; failure to secure majority votes was not an option. Let the lawyers worry about Proposition 22.[46]

On December 4, 2000, Migden introduced A.B. 25, a measure that would significantly liberalize the 1999 domestic partnership law. The definition of *domestic partner* would be expanded to include opposite-sex couples where only one person was over age 62 (previously, both had to be that age), and new rights and benefits would be added:

- a right for employers to purchase coverage from insurers for domestic partners of employees, as they did for other dependents;
- equal treatment for domestic partners receiving employer health insurance or seeking unemployment or disability benefits;
- survivors' benefits, including continued health coverage (with surviving children also included);
- the same family- and sick-leave rights as were accorded married couples;
- the right to make medical decisions on behalf of their partners incapable of giving informed consent;
- the right to be appointed a conservator, the same as spouses;
- inheritance rights if a partner dies without a will, and the right to be appointed administrator of a deceased partner's estate;
- authorization for a partner to recover damages for infliction of emotional distress and wrongful death, the same as spouses; and
- second-parent adoption by each partner of the other's children, just like stepparent adoption for married couples.

Governor Davis told Migden he would veto a law with inheritance rights—again, "too marriagy"—and so that was dropped without much fanfare. Migden knew she would have to break some ornaments to get the Christmas tree properly decorated.[47]

Because there were now three lesbians in the assembly and Migden was chair of the appropriations committee, which had to pass on all legislation involving public spending, the author and sponsors were playing a strong hand. But even with their dwindling numbers, Republican opposition was just as fierce as it had been in 1999. Although both were experienced in politics, Goldberg and Kehoe were astounded at the rhetoric of opponents. One Republican: "These kind of relationships in the eyes of my God that I worship are an abomination." This left Goldberg literally speechless for a few minutes. When she composed herself, she reminded the legislator that "this is my life" and that she had loved the same woman for twenty-two years. "There is no definition of family that does not include my family." Surely, some Republicans were ashamed that their party was a haven for bigoted statements, but it was ultimately public opinion that diminished GOP gay bashing.[48]

The lesbian colleagues offered contrasting styles in response to strident opposition. Warm and friendly Jackie Goldberg proved to be an aggressive questioner. At one hearing, a tight-lipped witness in a white shirt and pale gray suit who favored traditional marriage praised its capacity to cement committed relationships. Leaning forward, Goldberg asked whether he considered that many men carry on adulterous affairs, yet still get all the benefits and rights of marriage. Well, that's an "unfortunate situation," replied the witness. "What kind of commitment are you making," Goldberg continued, "when you are having a series of affairs behind the back of your partner? I'd call that a bad one." The witness looked bewildered that a woman would back him into a corner like that—and that a homosexual would assume a position of moral superiority.[49]

Chris Kehoe's dignified demeanor complemented that of her colleagues. Another GOP witness was Scott Lively, who handed out copies of *Homosexuality in the Nazi Party* (1995) to support his claim that evil things happen to a country that "embraces the homosexual alternative." He ignored the Nazis' policy of brutal murder and torture of gay people. Standing to the right of the seated witness, Migden looked like she wanted to throttle him, but Kehoe had the microphone. She held up the book. "It's difficult to understand how a simple fairness issue could engender such ridiculous hostility," she said in the gentle, sad manner of a disappointed parent. Later, she pointed out that she and her partner were about to celebrate their sixteenth anniversary as a committed couple, one of the happiest achievements in her life. "It's time for us to move forward on this."[50]

One witness opposed A.B. 25 because it "advances the most dangerous lifestyle in America." He was probably referring to AIDS, but he noticed the lesbian legislators and added: "For lesbians it's not as bad, but it's far worse than smoking or driving without seat belts." This was a head-scratcher. The assembly passed A.B. 25 by a lopsided vote of 42-28, which meant that a few Republicans were ashamed to vote no.[51]

In the senate, the California Catholic Conference came out against the bill, saying it would "expand benefits to domestic partners in such a way as to further blur the lines between those associations and marriage." Because a child ought never be treated as property, "adoption of a child can never be an entitlement." The Catholic opposition was relatively moderate, compared with more contentious opposition from Evangelical groups like the Committee on Moral Authority, TVC, and individual churches and pastors. On the other side, CAPE and various progressive organizations applied the lessons of Proposition 22: relationship rights needed to be backed up by a political campaign. "For the first time in California's history," reported the ACLU of Southern California, "there were more letters, phone calls, e-mails, and faxes in support of an LGBT civil rights bill than in opposition."[52]

Governor Davis signed A.B. 25 into law on October 14. Domestic partnerships were beginning to look a lot like families. The next February, Assembly

Member Paul Koretz (D-Beverly Hills) introduced a bill to establish civil unions in California, similar to the 2000 Vermont law discussed in the next chapter. The four lesbian legislators cosponsored the bill, which would have left domestic partnerships in place and added a new institution for lesbian and gay couples, with all the legal benefits of marriage but not the name. Civil union proposals were considered in both 2001 and 2002 but never came to a vote, as the LGBT caucus instead chose to push for big expansions to the domestic partnership law.[53]

In 1999, the LGBT caucus and the governor had agreed that they would hold off on major relationship legislation in election years—but in 2002, the caucus added several new rights to the domestic partner tree. Right after the sponsors agreed to drop inheritance rights from A.B. 25, the terrorist attacks of September 11, 2001, brought the issue into sharp relief. Californian Keith Bradkowski lost his domestic partner, Jeff Collman, a flight attendant who died on the first airplane that crashed into the World Trade Center. Because they were not married, Keith was cut out of his inheritance and struggled for months to persuade the 9/11 commission that he was Jeff's legitimate survivor. Lambda's Jenny Pizer was Keith's lawyer, and they launched a crusade to change the law. Assembly Member Fred Keeley (D-Santa Cruz) took up Pizer's crusade as the sponsor of A.B. 2216, to add inheritance rights to the domestic partnership law. With Bradkowski and Pizer both testifying before assembly and senate committees and CAPE drumming up grassroots support, A.B. 2216 was in a compelling political position. Although it was no less "marriagy" in 2002 than it had been months earlier, Governor Davis said not a word in opposition, nor did the Catholic Conference.[54]

Also in 2002, Sheila Kuehl sponsored S.B. 1161, which expanded the domestic partnership law to grant six weeks of paid family leave to employees caring for a sick partner. Four other bills, mostly sponsored by straight Democratic legislators, also added new rights and benefits to the domestic partnership law that year. Governor Davis was reelected by a decisive but modest margin, and the California legislature remained overwhelmingly Democratic. Carole Migden was term-limited out of her assembly seat, replaced by openly gay Mark Leno, and new assembly member John Laird joined the LGBT caucus as well.[55]

Jackie Goldberg's 2003 Domestic Partnership Law

During and after the 2002 legislative session, the lesbian legislators discussed various paths toward relationship recognition. Let's take the simple approach, they decided over a home-cooked meal at Goldberg's house. Why not just give domestic partners *all* of the legal rights and benefits of spouse-hood and marriage? They started to explore their options. For starters, if they went for the whole ball of wax, what would they call it? By then, Vermont had *civil unions,* the term used in the Koretz bill, but the caucus favored sticking with the term everyone already knew, *domestic partnership.* CAPE and the legal groups liked the idea, because comprehensive domestic partnership would be easier to defend against the inevitable lawsuit challenging it as inconsistent with Proposition 22.[56]

Lambda's Jon Davidson and Jenny Pizer drafted the proposed Domestic Partner Rights and Responsibilities Act of 2003, which would provide that do-mestic partners "shall have the same rights, protections, and benefits, and shall be subject to the same responsibilities, obligations, and duties under law . . . as are granted to and imposed upon spouses." To be sure, the law would not create complete parity: DOMA cordoned off more than 1,100 federal ben-efits and duties; spousal rights and duties created by initiative-based statutes like Proposition 22 could not be modified by legislation; and the bill created an easy exit for domestic partners without kids and with a partnership dura-tion of less than five years. While they were working on this bill, Davidson and Pizer were heading off plans for a premature constitutional lawsuit seeking marriage equality.[57]

On January 28, 2003, Goldberg introduced the proposed Rights and Respon-sibilities Act as A.B. 205. Her cosponsors were Assembly Members Kehoe, Koretz, Laird, and Leno as well as Senator Kuehl. The rollout and subsequent hearings were dominated by stories reflecting problems confronted by some of the more than one hundred thousand households headed by same-sex part-ners, many of whom were raising children. "There is simply no good reason," explained Goldberg, "to deny these additional rights and duties to registered, committed domestic partners and their children." Equality California and other groups generated public enthusiasm for the measure that surpassed all previous efforts.[58]

This ambitious bill was strongly opposed by the California Catholic Con-ference, Concerned Women for America, the Campaign for California Fami-lies, TVC, and other faith-based organizations. These critics argued that it was precisely the kind of effort to redefine marriage that Proposition 22 was sup-posed to block. The Catholic Conference announced that while it had not op-posed some earlier domestic partnership bills because they were "based on compassion for certain needs of individuals in long term relationships," A.B.

205 "moves beyond those needs to appropriate a battery of rights for which there can be no justification other than to include same-sex unions in the social and contractual arrangements reserved for marriages." TVC's Lou Sheldon condemned the legislation because it "would sanction into law policies that lie contrary to nature." Claiming that almost all homosexuals were promiscuous, Sheldon worried that the legislation would undermine public health and that "school curricula will be forced to reflect the new definition of 'marriage' and 'family.' All health and sex education classes will have to expand to include discussions of homosexuality."[59]

The Republican caucus also opposed A.B. 205, and no Republican legislator would vote for the bill. Though there were only thirty-two Republicans in the assembly, many rural and Latino Democrats would have preferred not to vote, as they feared voter backlash. Proposition 22 had won large majorities in Latino communities. But Geoff Kors and Equality California were prepared to play hardball and were not inclined to let these legislators off the hook. Any legislator who "passed" would be counted as a "no" vote, and her or his equality score would suffer. At least one legislator, Assembly Member Hannah-Beth Jackson, sought to hide behind a claimed veto by the governor; Kors called the governor's office, which denied that Gray Davis had ever given her that impression, and Jackson promised her support.[60]

On June 4, 2003, the assembly debated and voted on A.B. 205. The presiding officer was Christine Kehoe, and Jackie Goldberg presented the case for the bill. "I believe that there are some of you who will never accept me and my family for who we are. I want your acceptance, but I don't need it. I do need equal protection under the law." After a short debate, Kehoe called the vote. The electronic board lit up almost immediately with 39 yes and 29 no votes. Long seconds ticked by. Goldberg believed she had forty-one votes—and in the closing seconds Assembly Members Joe Canciamilla of Contra Costa County and Manny Diaz of San Jose lit up with yes votes. (We were told that Simón Salinas, who did not vote, would have come through if his vote had been needed.)[61]

As before, Governor Davis dragged his feet, his reluctance heightened by a recall election scheduled for October 7, 2003. The governor was in trouble over soaring utility bills, not domestic partnership, and his 2002 reelection campaign was being interpreted as a dishonest cover-up of the state's fiscal problems. Nervous about the recall, he once again declared the community property and spousal support duties "too marriagy" and asked Goldberg to drop them. She was not willing to do that, and Lambda in early July gave her ammunition to resist. California practice was to award spousal support upon marital breakups quite sparingly and for limited periods of time, but this regime should be preferred to a palimony one, where awards were more unpredictable but sometimes much more lavish (and therefore unfair). Lambda's case files were full of examples of lesbian and gay couples who broke up and left the dependent partner destitute after he or she had sacrificed for home and children. Because custodial parents often needed child support payments to maintain their household after a split, lack of partner support had hurt children. Armed with legal research and rigorous policy analysis, Goldberg called the governor's bluff. A deal was worked out, whereby the community property and spousal support obligations would remain in the bill, but she would drop her demand that domestic partners be allowed to file joint tax returns with the state. Even after the deal, it was not completely clear whether the governor would sign the bill.[62]

Gray Davis in August 2003 was a desperate politician. The polls were showing that he would not survive the recall. He needed every angle he could play, and Kors knew that he could not afford to lose the LGBT vote. On the morning of Saturday, August 16, Kors tipped off the Davis campaign that Equality California's board of directors was meeting that afternoon to decide whether to endorse anyone in the upcoming recall and governorship race. The suggestion was that EQCA would not endorse Davis unless he made a public announcement in favor of A.B. 205. Within hours, the governor endorsed the bill.[63]

On August 28, A.B. 205, as amended to reflect the deal with the governor, passed the senate, 23-14, and the assembly concurred with the senate's amendments, 41-33, on September 3. Simón Salinas, who had not voted on June 4, provided the forty-first vote this time. Supporting the bill were not only civil rights organizations and the LGBT caucus but labor unions, the state teachers' and public employees' retirement systems, and state health, human services, consumer, and finance agencies. Governor Davis signed it into law on September 19 at the San Francisco Gay & Lesbian Center—but was turned out of office three weeks later. On the same day, Republican movie star Arnold Schwarzenegger was elected to replace him.[64]

The 2003 amendments took effect on January 1, 2005, in order to give current domestic partners an opportunity to opt out if they did not want the new rights and responsibilities. The effect was major, increasing the number of legal rights and duties from fifteen to the hundreds enjoyed by married spouses (with the notable exception of tax filing). Starting in 2004, when Carole Migden entered the senate, the California legislature chipped away each year at the state law differences between domestic partnership and marriage. At the same time, Senator Knight and the Proposition 22 Legal Defense and Education Fund sued in state court to overturn A.B. 205 as inconsistent with Proposition 22. By creating the substantive equivalent of marriage, the legislature had contravened the decision made by the people in March 2000. Knight put together an advisory committee, with representatives from Catholic, Evangelical, and Mormon faiths, to plan a voter initiative to entrench the one-man, one-woman definition of marriage in the state constitution.[65]

In May 2004, Pete Knight died of leukemia. Stoic to the end of his life, he never reconciled with his son David. Kate Kendell, who knew both men, told us that David is the son every military hero would dream of having—tall, athletic, handsome, smart, loyal, patriotic. It was an American tragedy, she feels, that these two outstanding men were separated by the son's homosexuality. In any event, Knight's widow, Gail, and his protégé Andy Pugno succeeded him as leaders of the traditional family values organization seeking to override comprehensive domestic partnership and marriage equality.

By September 2003, the legislating lesbians had achieved almost all of their immediate goals. But the struggle to win comprehensive domestic partnership and omnibus anti-discrimination protections had persuaded them that marriage was the ultimate goal. Sheila Kuehl told us why marriage was so important to sexual and gender minorities as well as other marginalized groups. Marriage is "a usual thing" in American society; it is a shared tradition and vocabulary, a common aspiration, and an institution with religious as well as legal consequences. "It is very important for a group that has been ostracized in society to do the usual thing."[66]

7 • Equality Practice

Susan Bellemare and Susan Hamilton of Waterbury, Vermont, had been committed partners for ten years when Hamilton delivered a healthy little boy, whom they named Collin. On May 15, 1989, Bellemare was driving the family in their blue Toyota Camry on a two-lane back road when a speeding truck hit them head-on. Hamilton died at the hospital, and Bellemare suffered a fractured hip and patella and bruises to her heart and lungs. Miraculously, fourteen-month-old Collin escaped with just a broken rib, as he had been strapped in his kid seat in the back. While Bellemare was recovering, Collin's grandparents, Philip and Elsa Hamilton, secured a court order giving them temporary custody.[1]

Susan Murray, a young lawyer in the Middlebury office of Langrock, Sperry & Wool, read about the tragedy and offered to help a fellow lesbian with her legal problem. In July 1989, Chittenden County (Vermont) probate judge John Cain awarded temporary guardianship to Bellemare and "asked that the sheriff take the boy from the grandmother's arms and hand him over to Ms. Bellemare. There wasn't a dry eye in the courtroom as the sheriff complied with Judge Cain's order." Murray negotiated an agreement assuring the Hamiltons of visitation rights each month and during holidays, so that Collin would enjoy a relationship with his grandparents. Over time, the Hamiltons grew comfortable spending time at Bellemare's house.[2]

The Case of the Three Susans made Murray the go-to family planning counsel for Vermont's lesbian community. California judges were granting petitions for second-parent adoptions, whereby a lesbian could adopt the biological child of her partner without affecting the partner's parental rights. Murray and Paula Ettelbrick filed amicus briefs that helped persuade the Vermont Supreme

Court to authorize second-parent adoptions under the state's family law. Writing for a unanimous Vermont Supreme Court in *In re B.L.V.B.* (1993) was Justice Denise Johnson, a former civil rights attorney and the first woman to serve on the court. In light of the social science evidence, the best-interests-of-the-child purpose of adoption law supported the petition, as did a constitutional equality norm. "To deny the children of same-sex partners," she wrote, "the security of a legally recognized relationship with their *second parent* serves no legitimate state interest."[3]

Susan Murray emerged as a role model to other lesbian lawyers, including Beth Robinson, who joined the Langrock firm in 1993. Susan described her new protégée as "a small and incredible bundle of energy" with an "exquisite legal mind" honed at the University of Chicago Law School. The same year, both lawyers were electrified when *Baehr v. Lewin* suggested the possibility of marrying their partners, Kym (for Beth) and Karen (for Susan) in Hawai'i. Robinson was impressed with Justice Steven Levinson's argument that denying marriage licenses to same-sex couples was questionable sex discrimination comparable to the ban on interracial marriage struck down in *Loving v. Virginia* (1967). Most attorneys found the conclusion puzzling, because they believed sex discrimination jurisprudence protected only women, not gay men. A student of feminist law professors Catherine MacKinnon and Robin West, Robinson understood the analogy perfectly: sex discrimination laws protect everybody, not just women, from pigeonholing based upon gender stereotypes such as the notion that women are not interested in careers outside the home. Lesbians and gay men suffer from these stereotypes, most deeply the notion that women's natural sex role is to bear children as a result of impregnation by men. As opponents of the ERA had recognized in the 1970s, bars to same-sex marriage were vulnerable to a strong sex discrimination jurisprudence.[4]

In December 1993, the Vermont Coalition for Lesbian and Gay Rights (VCLGR) hosted its first annual Queer Town Meeting, a gathering for activists and the community. The keynote luncheon featured Ettelbrick, who impressed the audience with her argument that marriage should not be a primary goal of the gay rights movement. Nonetheless, at the November 1994 Queer Town Meeting, Murray found more grassroots interest in same-sex marriage. She still thought no action should be taken without stronger community support; indeed, she had declined to represent a lesbian couple (Pasha and Penny) mistakenly given a marriage license but whose marriage was not recorded by the town clerk. The next month, Murray and Robinson joined attorneys from all over New England at the offices of Gay and Lesbian Advocates and Defend-

Beth Robinson, Mary Bonauto, and Susan Murray at a
celebration July 1, 2000, the first day civil unions were
legalized in Vermont. (Photo by Kym Boyman.)

ers (GLAD) of Boston. Mary Bonauto, GLAD's chief litigator, asked whether
there should be a second marriage lawsuit, parallel to the one then going on
in Hawai'i. "There were people at the table who thought this was a folly, even
reckless," Bonauto recalls. "Beth and Susan clearly said, there is a path forward in Vermont." This once-conservative bastion had been liberalized by
an influx of urban emigrants, called flatlanders by the "woodchucks" who
had long family histories in the state. Its political culture was increasingly
gay friendly, with the enactment of a state hate crime law in 1990 and an
anti-discrimination law in 1992, topped off by *B.L.V.B.* in 1993. Importantly,
Vermont's constitution was hard to change: any proposed amendment had to
be passed by two successive sessions of the legislature and then ratified by a
majority of voters.[5]

When they returned to Vermont, the two women continued to discuss the
possibility of lesbian and gay marriages, often strategizing at the dining room
table in Beth and Kym's rustic house outside of Ferrisburgh, with a picture-
window view of the Adirondack Mountains. While they appreciated Ettelbrick's
concerns, the women's experiences also suggested a deeper value of a marriage
lawsuit, as the VCLGR board recognized in February 1995. So long as lesbians and gay men were viewed as pleasure-seeking hedonists uninterested in
the self-giving attitude presumed necessary for marriage and family, they

would not be taken seriously. Married lesbian and gay couples raising children, like Hamilton and Bellemare, would refute those stereotypes and change public opinion about all gay persons.

At the same time that Murray and Robinson were dreaming about lesbian and gay marriages in Vermont, the same possibility was a nightmare for the Reverend Craig Bensen, who since 1976 had been the pastor of the Cambridge United Church in tiny Cambridge, Vermont, located at the foot of the Green Mountains. Cambridge United was affiliated with the gay-friendly United Church of Christ (UCC), the modern incarnation of the Congregationalist Church, but its pastor and parishioners were Scripture-based adherents to traditional views about sexuality, gender, and marriage. A short, affable man with a cherubic, white-bearded face, Craig Bensen looks like one of Santa's elves, but he has the sharp mind of a Nino Scalia and shares the late judge's love of history, tradition, and the original meaning of sacred texts. Craig and his wife, Deb, had been closely following the marriage issue for decades. Starting in the early 1970s, the UCC had adopted a series of resolutions endorsing recognition of nonmarital families, domestic partnerships for lesbian and gay couples, and, finally, "equal marriage rights for same gender couples." Reverend Bensen opposed these resolutions, and in 1997 his church separated from the UCC for theological reasons. In 2005, the UCC's general synod would formally endorse marriage as a sacrament available to lesbian and gay couples.[6]

In 1986, a proposal to add an ERA to the Vermont Constitution had been on the November ballot. The Bensens were among the many religious fundamentalists who joined Phyllis Schlafly's campaign against the ERA. As she had done in the 1970s, Schlafly argued that the ERA was anti-family because it would entrench *Roe v. Wade* and open the door to homosexual marriages. Although early polls suggested strong support for the ERA, it narrowly failed in November (49–51 percent). Apparently the marriage issue was a decisive reason for the defeat, and Bensen sounded the same alarm as *Baehr* was being litigated in Hawai'i throughout the 1990s. In 1996, he sponsored a Vermont Republican Party resolution endorsing DOMA.[7]

The Bensens estimate that only 40 percent of Vermonters are churchgoing Christians; about a quarter of the churched population is Evangelical Protestant, a quarter is mainline Protestant, and half is Roman Catholic. Bishop Kenneth Angell of the Diocese of Burlington zealously followed the Vatican's long-standing theology of the family, which had been reaffirmed in a 1986 "Letter on the Pastoral Care of Homosexual Persons." Because "homosexual activity is not a complementary union, able to transmit life," such intimacy "thwarts the call to a life of that form of self-giving which the Gospel says is the essence of Christian living. This does not mean that homosexual persons are not often generous and giving of themselves; but when they engage in homosexual activity they confirm within themselves a disordered sexual inclination which is essentially self-indulgent." Based upon a similar reading of Scripture, Craig and Deb Bensen described gay marriage to us as a "counterfeit covenant." Marriage is the "gold standard" for religious families, and if the government dilutes marriage with a bronze copy, its action devalues all marriages. Indeed, for them, homosexual marriage is currency consisting of "fool's gold." If enough counterfeit coins are circulated, the whole currency system will collapse.[8]

Murray and Robinson did not understand the emotional depth of the religious opposition to redefining marriage. In turn, the Bensens and Angell did not appreciate the depth of Murray's and Robinson's committed relationships with their partners and underestimated the political wisdom of their grassroots campaign for marriage. This mutual misunderstanding was guaranteed to produce a bitter debate. Yet the debate took turns no one anticipated. Both sides would be astounded and dismayed by the actions of the Vermont Supreme Court and legislature. Traditionalists, frustrated by both bodies, adopted the rallying cry "Take It to the People." Like Pete Knight in California, Craig Bensen would insist that something as fundamental as the definition of marriage should be resolved only by a direct vote of the people. Murray and Robinson maintained it would not be a fair vote unless judges opened the door to same-sex marriage first and then let the people decide whether it was a good idea. Neither side would get exactly what it wanted, but the people of Vermont would have ample opportunities to debate the issue.

Vermont Marriage Lawsuit

Notwithstanding the backlash illustrated by DOMA, the mid-1990s reflected a swiftly improving political climate for gay people, in large part because of their increasing visibility. Before 1990, only a quarter of the country knew of a close acquaintance who was gay, and half believed they knew no one. By 2000, three-quarters of the country knew of a gay friend, relative, or coworker; 56 percent described the gay person as a close acquaintance or friend. That year, Parents and Friends of Lesbians and Gays had five hundred chapters and more than eighty thousand members. In 1997, Ellen DeGeneres popped out of the closet on the cover of *Newsweek* at the same time her television character came out. The NBC sitcom *Will and Grace,* about the friendship between a gay man and a straight woman, debuted the next year. Lesbians and gay men were no longer strangers in America.[9]

If those lesbians and gay men wanted to get married, they'd be joining an institution that had changed markedly from marriage in the early 1970s. Expanding upon *Loving,* the US Supreme Court had guaranteed deadbeat dads and even prisoners the right to marry as a fundamental civil right. Enforcing a constitutional presumption against sex-based discriminations, the court had also, in the 1970s, swept away state laws giving husbands power over their wives. States were repealing marital rape exemptions. Family planning rights were constitutionally entrenched—so marriage no longer meant compulsory motherhood—and state deregulation of consensual sex crimes meant that marriage no longer enjoyed a monopoly on sexual activities and child-rearing. Not only was family law drifting away from the old, natural law idea of conjugality, but different-sex marriages were looking increasingly like lesbian and gay relationships, a phenomenon we explore in chapter 24.

THE FREEDOM TO MARRY TASK FORCE

While the Hawai'i (1991–1999) and Washington, DC (1991–1995), marriage cases had been brought by same-sex couples to enforce abstract rights without broad consultation within local lesbian and gay communities, Murray and Robinson were determined that any Vermont marriage case would proceed only if it met the needs and had the approval of the community and only if there was political support to resist a proposed constitutional amendment in the event of a court victory.[10]

Initially, however, Murray was focused on stirring up grassroots support for the *B.L.V.B.* decision authorizing second-parent adoption. In 1994, as the Vermont legislature was working on a comprehensive revision of the state's outdated adoption code, Representative Leon Graves proposed that the new code prohibit second-parent adoptions. Lesbian families and their allies rallied in district after district, and in a 1995 letter to legislators, Graves withdrew his proposal after heart-to-heart talks with lesbian parents. The Adoption Act of 1996 explicitly codified second-parent adoption.[11]

The political energy devoted to saving second-parent adoption carried over to the issue of marriage. At the October 1995 Queer Town Meeting in Montpelier, Murray, Robinson, and Amelia Craig, GLAD's executive director, shared their excitement about marriage with some seventy-five interested Vermonters. In November, the same three women and other key organizers founded the Vermont Freedom to Marry Task Force. All summer, representatives of the task force talked with interested partners at county fairs. Joe Watson built them a booth where they could display snapshots of lesbian and gay couples such as Lois Farnham and Holly Puterbaugh. Holly, a math professor, and Lois, a nurse, were a deacon and lay leader in the United Church of Milton; had cared for fifteen foster children over the years and adopted thirteen-year-old Kimberly Farnham in 1994; operated the Red Shovel Christmas tree business; and maintained close relationships with many family members, whose children considered them a couple. Holly, short, rotund and energetic, and Lois, taller, grayer, and quieter, were committed partners in every aspect of their lives— exactly the sort of couple who could be plaintiffs in a lawsuit.

The task force also participated in Burlington's gay pride parade. Many observers were curious about marriage signs in a gay parade. Peter Harrigan, a professor of theatre and drama, was one of the curious observers. He and Stan Baker, a developmental and expressive therapist, wanted their relationship to be recognized by the state. A bona fide woodchuck, whose ancestor Remember Baker was one of Ethan Allan's Green Mountain Boys, Stan had been married to a woman until 1993 and wanted the same social recognition for his relationship with Peter. Peter and Stan were Episcopalians, worshipping at the gay-affirming Cathedral Church of St. Paul, where Peter is now a deacon. Stan narrated the 1996 task force video *The Freedom to Marry: A Green Mountain View.*[12]

In 1996, young field organizer Marty Rouse worked with progressives to flip five state senate seats from conservative Republicans to liberal Democrats in the November election. The Vermont Senate went from eighteen Republicans and twelve Democrats to seventeen Democrats and thirteen Republicans. Rouse believes that this election reflected a tipping point in Vermont public opinion, proving that pro-gay legislators can win elections. Also optimistic was GLAD attorney Mary Bonauto, who had been working closely with the Vermonters on the legal as well as community-organizing issues. Bonauto had also been talking up Vermont as a promising second front in the emerging national marriage debate. There was strong interest in Vermont among the organizations that were partners in the National Freedom to Marry Coalition described in the previous chapter.[13]

In December 1996, Bonauto and Craig drove to Ferrisburgh. Sitting at the same dining room table where Robinson and Murray had been strategizing, the four women made a deal: Murray and Robinson would bring a marriage lawsuit in Vermont, and GLAD would be what Beth later called "cocounsel for life." Together, they would search for plaintiff couples who were scandal-free, articulate, and unafraid of media attention; research all possible state statutory and constitutional arguments; solicit experts and amicus allies for the litigation and political allies to oppose a junior-DOMA or state constitutional DOMA; and work with the attorney general's office to minimize the emotional fireworks surrounding the issue. The GLAD representatives assured the Vermont lawyers that the national organizations would not interfere with their management of the litigation. In the tradition of the Green Mountain Boys, Vermonters did not like outside interference.[14]

Plaintiff couples were not hard to find. Lois and Holly were already on board. In February 1997, Stacy Jolles and Nina Beck, also from Burlington in Chittenden County, expressed interest in joining. They had met in California and celebrated their relationship in a marriage ceremony in March 1992. Feminist concerns about joining a traditionally patriarchal institution gave them pause, but after Nina gave birth to their son Noah in 1995, they wanted the social validation and the public announcement of their family that civil marriage would bring. Daughters of Holocaust survivors, both women were martial arts experts and fighters for their ideals. When Peter Harrigan and Stan Baker joined in April, the lawyers felt they had an excellent collection of plaintiff couples.[15]

THE LAWSUIT

Before filing the lawsuit, Murray and Robinson met with more state officials, including Governor Howard Dean, Attorney General Jeffrey Amestoy, and key legislators. Nervous about the political implications, Dean suggested a more indirect approach: Why not find one or two friendly clerks who could be persuaded to issue licenses to these couples? The executive branch could make sure that state agencies respected the licenses, and then after a few years—after Dean had left office—the state could concede the validity of the marriages. The task force did not want to sneak gay marriage through the back door and proceeded with its own plan. In January 1997, the governor nominated Amestoy to be chief justice of the Vermont Supreme Court. By naming a pragmatic Republican to a court dominated by liberal Democrats appointed by Governor Madeleine Kunin, Governor Dean not only scored points for bipartisanship but made it less likely that the court would hand down a political bombshell in the marriage case.[16]

The three couples unsuccessfully applied for marriage licenses in Chittenden County. On July 22, Murray, Robinson, and Bonauto filed their constitutional marriage lawsuit, *Baker v. State of Vermont*. As Robinson put it at the press conference, the plaintiff couples "want to marry each other for the same reasons many people want to marry each other. They love each other, they want to make a public legal commitment to one another, and their lives are already intermingled emotionally, spiritually, and financially." She was flanked by two of the couples. Missing were Stacy and Nina, who were at the hospital where Noah was being treated for congenital heart failure. He would die on August 29. Nina and Stacy continued as plaintiffs to honor his memory.

The plaintiffs' counsel maintained that their exclusion from marriage violated the common benefits clause of the Vermont Constitution:

> The government is, or ought to be, instituted for the common benefit, protection, and security of the people, nation, or community, and not for the particular emolument or advantage of any single person, family, or set of persons, who are only part of that community. . . .

Because same-sex couples were also "part of the community," the clause's ordinary meaning suggested that civil marriage ought to be available to them. In their merits brief, Robinson, Murray, and Bonauto argued that there was no "common benefit" (or neutral policy) justifying the exclusion of the plaintiff couples. As lawyers had argued in the 1970s, they also claimed lesbian and gay couples were denied a fundamental right to marry (*Loving*) and were discriminated against solely because of their sex or sexual orientation, both suspect classifications.[17]

Attorney General William Sorrell responded that the fundamental right to marry rested in its procreative foundation and that the plaintiffs were barred from marrying not because of any discrimination but because of the definition of marriage itself. The state suggested that altering the definition of marriage "would open a Pandora's box of issues that should not be dealt with by the courts," including the desirability of same-sex role models for children, the recognition of Vermont marriages by other states, and the possible destabilization of marriage as an institution. When she dismissed the lawsuit on December 17, 1997, Judge Linda Levitt accepted the state's interest in "furthering the link between procreation and child rearing." The lawyers filed an immediate appeal.[18]

TAKE IT TO THE PEOPLE

At the same time the Freedom to Marry Task Force was drumming up interest in a constitutional marriage lawsuit, Reverend Bensen was drumming up interest in preventing judges from having the last word. By early 1998, he had assembled a coalition of Vermonters supporting traditional marriage under an umbrella organization called Take It to the People (TIP). Bishop Angell and his staff were immediate allies; others included the Latter-day Saints, the Vermont Christian School Association, various Baptist and Congregational pastors and lay leaders, the Knights of Columbus, Evangelical and Catholic pro-life activists, and thousands of Scot-Presbyterians in the northern counties.[19]

Bensen's central concern was that same-sex marriage would undermine a building block of civilization, with disastrous effects, especially for children. He saw same-sex marriage through the lens of family and tradition, not through the lens of civil rights. "Civil rights talk," he told *Mother Jones*, "is political cover for politicians who don't want to listen to what people have to say." Like the Bensens, a lot of the TIPsters were woodchucks who felt their way of life was under siege by flatlanders and the hedonistic culture they brought with them. Take It to the People objected that important decisions were being made in Montpelier without being submitted to the democratic process epitomized by the New England town meeting. A recent example involved the Vermont Supreme Court's decision in *Brigham v. State* (1997) to invalidate the state's method for apportioning funds for public schools. To meet the court's mandate, the legislature passed a statewide property tax. That raised many Vermonters' taxes and reminded them that important decisions were made in Montpelier, no longer in their towns. In November 1998, Governor Dean was reelected with a smaller margin than in previous races, and the Democrats lost twelve house seats. The woodchucks were pushing back.[20]

The Vermont Supreme Court Decision in *Baker v. State*

On appeal, the plaintiffs' lawyers had to decide which argument to emphasize. Their initial inclination was the sex discrimination argument that had delivered strict scrutiny in *Baehr*—but that argument bombed at a practice moot hosted by lawyers in Burlington. Returning to Beth's dining room table, they agreed to focus on a California precedent instead. At oral argument, on November 18, 1998, Robinson opened with the California Supreme Court's 1948 decision in *Perez v. Lippold*, which had struck down that state's different-race marriage exclusion. Both *Perez* and *Baker* involved the right to marry; in each case it was denied to a couple for an invidious reason (race in one case, sex and sexual orientation in the other); in neither case was the discrimination justified by anything other than tradition and prejudice. By taking a risk to advance a noble principle two decades before *Loving*, the California Supreme Court had assured itself an inspiring place in the history books. Robinson dared the Vermont Supreme Court to do the same.[21]

Several justices expressed reservations about going as far as *Perez*. John Dooley asked: "What if [the state] gave [plaintiff couples] all of the individual bundle of rights but was unwilling to call it marriage? Would that be sufficient in your view?" (The previous month, France had legalized *pactes civils*, which invested most of the rights and benefits of marriage in a new civil institution open to same-sex couples.) Robinson insisted that the "status of marriage is in and of itself a value, a benefit," and criticized such a solution as equivalent to separate but equal. Is it imaginable, she asked, that the *Perez* or *Loving* courts would have been satisfied with a law reserving marriage for same-race couples and creating domestic partnership for different-race couples? James Morse: "So the label is everything? If the legislature just said we are just changing the label and calling marriage domestic partnership instead of marriage, but you get all the bundle of rights that marriage has, then it couldn't do that?" Robinson answered, "Probably not." She was struggling to explain that the plaintiffs were seeking the dignity and social respectability of marriage, rich with cultural associations. They wanted marriage, not a euphemism.[22]

The state's lawyers, Eve Jacobs-Carnahan and Timothy Tomasi, argued that the analogy to *Perez* and *Loving* was inapt. As Jeff Amestoy suggested in his questions, laws against interracial marriage changed the definition of marriage in order to maintain "white supremacy," a goal at war with the Reconstruction amendments. So the plaintiffs in *Perez* and *Loving* were restoring the traditional definition. The *Baker* plaintiffs, by contrast, were asking the court to change the long-standing definition of marriage in a fundamental way. The state stopped short of the position taken by amicus briefs submitted by TIP and its Catholic allies. Those briefs urged the justices to accept, as a matter of natural law, the view that only male-female procreative intercourse can create the human flourishing and altruism that have made marriage the cornerstone of American society, religion, and governance.

What was the public purpose for excluding committed lesbian and gay couples from civil marriage? Disappointing the faith-based amici, the state's lawyers abandoned the arguments that the exclusion could be justified by traditional morality or that husband-wife marriage was optimal for child-rearing. Instead, they argued that because marriage had long been associated with procreation, expanding the definition would send a socially disruptive message to younger Vermonters that procreation was no longer central to the institution. Marilyn Skoglund and Denise Johnson were skeptical. Why didn't the state exclude straight couples who were infertile? Why single out lesbian and gay couples? Jacobs-Carnahan responded that unless there was a fundamental right or a suspect classification, the court was obliged to give legislators leeway to adopt laws that were underinclusive.[23]

In rebuttal, Robinson noted there was a lot more public support for same-sex marriage in 1998 than for different-race marriage in 1948 (*Perez*) or even 1967 (*Loving*), and young people were especially favorable. The Vermont legislature had explicitly recognized gay families and equal rights in the workplace, public accommodations, schools, and adoption. "Against this backdrop, we're confident that fifty years from now our grandchildren will look back at this case and wonder what the big deal was. What were they so afraid of?"

By random assignment, Jeff Amestoy had the opinion and led the discussion at conference. The unfairness of entirely excluding lesbian and gay couples from marriage rights struck him as unconstitutional—but he did not accept the *Perez* analogy. Anything we write, he assumed, would frame a subsequent constitutional debate. We don't want to frame it as a referendum on whether gay people should receive the same constitutional solicitude as racial minorities. The debate needs to be framed as whether the "common benefit" is served by excluding committed couples from a supportive state family law. John Dooley and Denise Johnson countered that the court should apply heightened scrutiny, either because the sex (Johnson) or sexual orientation (Dooley) classification was suspect. Unless the court applied heightened scrutiny because of the civil rights nature of the case, how could the justices discourage common benefit challenges to regular economic and fiscal legislation?[24]

Ultimately, all five jurists found a constitutional violation. Normally, the remedy would be an injunction requiring clerks to issue marriage licenses to same-sex couples. But because the issue was so controversial, Amestoy suggested that the court retain jurisdiction and, essentially, remand the issue to the political process to determine how to rectify the inequality. Vividly recalling the 1986 ERA referendum, where he had been on the losing end of the vote, Amestoy felt this was not an issue on which the court should insist on having the final word. Morse and Dooley had raised the possibility during oral argument and were inclined to agree. They were among the justices who had decided *Brigham*, the school funding case, and were aware that many Vermonters already viewed the court with suspicion. Skoglund, even more cautious than her colleagues, also agreed.

Consider this analogy. In *Brown v. Board of Education* (1954), the US Supreme Court ruled that public school segregation violated the equal protection clause. The remedy came a year later, in *Brown II*, which remanded all the cases to the trial courts, to give school districts opportunities to come up with desegregation plans "with all deliberate speed." Why not separate the right from the remedy here as well? Johnson took away the opposite lesson from *Brown*. Anything short of full marriage rights for lesbian and gay couples would be separate but equal, the regime that *Brown I* had declared unconstitutional. Moreover, there was no guarantee that the legislature would even honor the equal part. Well, Amestoy responded, that's why we're retaining jurisdiction.

On December 20, 1999, the Vermont Supreme Court delivered its judgment in *Baker v. State*, unanimously invalidating the plaintiffs' exclusion as a violation of the common benefits clause. Chief Justice Amestoy's opinion for the court examined the government justifications for the exclusion in light of "(1) the significance of the benefits and protections of the challenged law; (2) whether the omission of members of the community from the benefits and protections of the challenged law promotes the government's stated goals; and (3) whether the classification is significantly underinclusive or overinclusive." Concurring, Justice Dooley objected that this was a novel standard of review. We agree with Amestoy. The common benefits clause said nothing about levels of scrutiny, and so his framework fit the constitutional language and its inclusionary purpose. It also reflected the approach advanced by the greatest equal protection lawyer of the twentieth century—Thurgood Marshall. Justice Marshall's earlier synthesis of equal protection doctrine anticipated the *Baker* framework of a sliding scale that considers the harm to particular persons or social groups, the fishiness of the classification, and the strength of the government's justifications.[25]

This approach provided a workable framework for examining questionable state policies that were outside the purview of race. The state's main argument was that traditional one-man, one-woman marriage was justified by the public interest in linking procreation to marriage. But given the fishiness of sexual orientation as a classification and the hundreds of state benefits denied the plaintiff couples, the majority demanded a tighter fit between the state interest and the exclusion. On the one hand, using sexual orientation as the regulatory classification was overinclusive, because it excluded couples (like Beck and Jolles) who actually did procreate within their relationship. On the other hand, it was underinclusive, because it allowed marriage to older couples, contraceptive couples, and sterile couples, who were not going to procreate. As a matter of public policy, was it essential that civil marriages be sealed by pro-creative intercourse?

The state and its amici had also invoked, as a rational basis for the exclu-sion, a threat of destabilization of marriage if gay people could enter the insti-tution. While such an argument could not be a ground for upholding the exclusion, the *Baker* majority ruled, it was "not altogether irrelevant." Because a "sudden change in the marriage laws" could have "disruptive and unfore-seen consequences," the majority held that the exclusion should remain in ef-fect "for a reasonable period of time to enable the Legislature to consider and . enact implementing legislation" correcting the discrimination, either by "amending the marriage law or creating a new institution for equal recogni-tion of lesbian and gay relationships." Johnson dissented from this remedy. Constitutional rights are not negotiable, she wrote, and the remand to the leg-islature left open the possibility of a separate but equal legal regime for a mi-nority group that had been unfairly discriminated against.[26]

At a press conference that afternoon, Stan Baker recalls, the plaintiffs were "amazingly moved by some of the writing" in the opinions. "Amestoy's words were beautiful," said Holly Puterbaugh and Lois Farnham. But all six were dis-appointed that the court did not require the state to issue them marriage li-censes. As Stacy Jolles put it, "We got on the bus but are still being made to ride at the back of the bus." Nina Beck felt that their disappointment should be set against "the fact that this is so much more than anyone else [among lesbian and gay people] has had in the United States before." Despite winning the biggest case of her life and assuring that the fruits of her and Susan Murray's advocacy would be celebrated for decades to come, Beth Robinson's immediate reaction was that December 20 was "the worst day of my profes-sional career."[27]

Surprisingly, the initial response by faith-based groups was muted, perhaps because they were also expecting the court to require marriage equality. Bishop Angell lauded the court's decision not to require same-sex marriage, but he rejected domestic partnership as a "basic threat to the sanctity of marriage." TIP praised the court for leaving traditional marriage intact and took no im-mediate position on domestic partnership. Reflecting on the decision years later, Reverend Bensen saw both wisdom and cowardice in Amestoy's "crafty" ruling.[28]

After polling his colleagues, the Democrats' leader in the lower chamber of the Vermont legislature reported that domestic partnership was the only al-ternative that would align with both the Vermont Supreme Court and public opinion. Governor Dean agreed, as did many conservatives. Republican senator Vincent Illuzzi, TIP's ally, prepared a domestic partnership bill with all "the same opportunities, rights and responsibilities" as marriage. But an opinion poll found that 52 percent of Vermonters disagreed with the court's ruling that lesbian and gay couples must be given the same benefits and duties as straight married couples; nearly half favored a constitutional amendment to override the decision.[29]

Back to the Legislature: Investigate, Then Deliberate

As Amestoy had hoped, legislators responded to *Baker* as a problem they needed to solve. Governor Dean promptly met with House Speaker Michael Obuchowski, Senate President Peter Shumlin, and Tom Little and Dick Sears, chairs of the house and senate judiciary committees, respectively. The consensus of the meeting was that Little's committee should start the ball rolling; if the house passed a reasonable response to *Baker*, the senate and governor would go along.[30]

Nothing in his career had prepared Tom Little for this moment. Married and the father of five, he had been a successful lawyer in Burlington. Like two of the plaintiffs, he was a lay leader in the gay-friendly Episcopal Church— but he did not know any lesbians and gay men who wanted to get married. Avuncular and low-key, he was the classic example of the thoughtful, public-spirited legislator: Mr. Smith Goes to Montpelier. He imposed on his committee of five Democrats, five Republicans, and one Progressive six weeks of hard labor. Although a Republican, Little had a warm relationship with Democrats Bill Lippert, the openly gay vice-chair of the committee, and Diane Carmolli, a fifty-nine-year-old mother of seven and a Sunday school teacher at the Immaculate Heart of Mary Church.

In a framing memorandum, Little accepted *Baker*'s premise that gay and lesbian couples should have the same rights and benefits as married couples. The legislators' task was to implement this constitutional principle and "build consensus and avoid divisiveness within the General Assembly and throughout the state." He urged his colleagues to approach the issue the same way a jury does: each person should keep her or his mind open, listen to the evidence on both sides, and exchange individual judgments as part of a deliberative process that would yield proposed legislation. For more than six weeks, the committee heard from gay Vermonters and their families, religious leaders, and expert witnesses on all sides of the marriage debate.[31]

On January 11, Robinson and Murray, the opening witnesses, made a strong case for a marriage statute, not only for reasons of dignity but also because domestic partnerships would not be recognized in other states. This would leave Vermont gays with an institution that was "separate but unequal." The next day, the committee heard from the Diocese of Burlington, whose representative offered a diplomatic statement from Bishop Angell. Homosexuals, like everyone else, he said, are "gifts from God, deserving of love and respect," but homosexual marriage is "objectively wrong," along the lines suggested by the 1986 Vatican missive. Because it was a step toward marriage, domestic partnership was also the wrong solution. "If civil rights are being denied, the matter needs to be addressed in some manner that does not derogate the sanctity and time-honored place of marriage and the family in our society." This message, however, was diluted by notes sent by priests and nuns to Carmolli and other Catholic legislators, urging them to support domestic partnership rights for committed couples.[32]

Yale history professor Nancy Cott explained to the committee how dramatically marriage has evolved in the last two centuries. The biggest changes had been the disengagement of civil marriage from religion and the liberation of wives from the common law regime of coverture, whereby the married woman lost the right to own property or make contracts in her own name. In defiance of claims that they were redefining marriage and harming children, states had slowly abandoned coverture and liberalized divorce law. These changes shifted the purpose of civil marriage away from procreation and child-rearing and toward the goal of spousal satisfaction. Other witnesses observed that California, Hawai'i, and several European countries had already extended some marriage-based rights to lesbian and gay couples. The Netherlands was expected to pass a same-sex marriage statute later in 2000.[33]

On January 25, the senate and house judiciary committees held a joint public hearing. Both TIP and the Vermont Freedom to Marry Task Force turned out their supporters, and an estimated 1,200 Vermonters braved a blizzard to fill the capitol. A hundred testified. Many were lesbians and gay men in committed relationships; others were their parents, relatives, and friends; yet others were strong critics, mostly from a faith-based perspective. Impressed at the display of civic activism, the committees held another joint hearing on February 1, drawing as many as 1,800 participants. Interested observers could also attend the house judiciary committee's investigative hearings, held in a small conference room on the second floor of the state house. The most notable presence was Randall Terry, the pro-life activist who founded Operation Rescue.

Sporting a black fedora and cape, Terry and his associates (dubbed the God Squad) roamed the halls, haranguing Bill Lippert while mobbing and jostling female legislators. Reverend Bensen and Bishop Angell were appalled by the God Squad's hateful rhetoric, crude behavior, and nasty remarks about TIP. Some traditionalists were disturbed that Terry was divorcing his wife of nineteen years in order to marry his twenty-five-year-old assistant.[34]

On February 9, the eleven committee members met in a large first-floor conference room to discuss the options. Tom Little opened the discussion by saying there was no such thing as "traditional marriage," because the institution had changed radically over the last hundred years. The goal of the law was to assure that "our families ought to have a common set of legal protections and benefits," and this assurance should, as a constitutional matter, apply equally to lesbian and gay families. In his view, "a civil rights or legal benefits act is the right thing for the people of Vermont now, and not an expansion of the marriage laws." In making this point, the chair was bowing to tradition and the deeply held feelings of many Catholics and Evangelicals who had spoken at the public hearings, written to their newspapers, and rallied in front of the capitol.[35]

Little's respectful, personal approach set the tone for the entire meeting. Murray thought most of the members had been persuaded that lesbian and gay families deserved full marriage recognition—but only Democrats Bill Lippert and Bill MacKinnon and Progressive Steve Hingtgen supported expanding the marriage law. The other seven members, some of them close to tears, agreed to something other than marriage: Republicans John Edwards, Cathy Voyer, Mike Kainen, and Judy Livingston and Democrats Mike Vinton, Alice Nitka, and Diane Carmolli. Little suggested, however, that the committee come up with a better term than *domestic partnership*. At the January 25 public hearing, Donna Lescoe had said: "I strongly oppose any attempt to construct any type of separate but equal system, whatever you call it, [like] domestic partnership. I've always disliked that term; it makes me feel like the domestic help."[36]

Various people have claimed credit for the term the committee ultimately adopted: civil unions. During the fact-gathering process, Vermont lawyer John Newman had described for the committee the *pacte civil de solidarité* created by the French Parliament in 1999. The term *pacte civil* might be translated as a "civil accord," the term favored by Judy Livingston, or "civil union," the term Cathy Voyer used in the committee discussion. So long as it provided equal benefits and responsibilities, Voyer supported "a *civil union* package at this time, because we have to be realistic in what can happen within this building and in our society." On March 2, the committee voted to report H. 847 to the house. The bill created two new institutions: civil unions for same-sex couples, which carried the same procedures, legal benefits, and obligations as different-sex marriage; and reciprocal beneficiaries, much like the Hawai'i compromise, available to family caregivers.[37]

Steve Kimball and Keith Ellis, the Freedom to Marry Task Force's lobbyists, had warned that marriage equality was politically impossible. Marriage advocates feared, however, that if they acquiesced in civil unions from the beginning, the legislature would offer an even weaker compromise. That strategy had run its course, and the task force now faced a choice. On the one hand, they could oppose the civil unions bill, which would end any legislative initiative in 2000. Once the legislature failed to act, the task force could ask for marriage recognition from the supreme court, which had retained jurisdiction. On the other hand, they could support the civil unions bill, which would probably satisfy the mandate in *Baker* but would put off the marriage quest for a number of years. Complicating the calculus, they did not know whether the Vermont House would pass the civil unions bill.

The task force called a meeting in Kimball's Montpelier office. All six plaintiffs were there, as were key volunteers, some allies, the lobbyists, and the attorneys (including Mary Bonauto)—about thirty people altogether. Should we support the civil unions bill? The plaintiffs were divided, but most of the activists wanted to insist on marriage. Robert Dostas, one of the marriage allies, spoke up cheerfully in favor of civil unions. Privately, Beth groaned, but Susan halfway agreed with Bob. Several days later, Robinson and Murray hosted a conference call among the participants. They recommended going with the civil unions bill, because it would be the most comprehensive family law regime for lesbian and gay families in world history; it was the product of hard work by allies like Tom Little and had bipartisan support; and the odds of securing marriage from the Vermont Supreme Court were uncertain.[38]

The Civil Unions Bill in the Vermont House

Fifty town hall meetings considered the issue on March 7. Thirty-eight rejected any recognition for lesbian and gay relationships, eleven voted in favor of domestic partnership or civil unions, one town had a tie vote, and zero voted in favor of marriage. Even more ominous were hundreds of letters written to the state's newspapers. The writers were overwhelmingly hostile to lesbian and gay people, let alone recognition of their relationships. Homosexuality was "sick," "a perversion no less than pedophilia and bestiality," "depravity," "moral filth," "sinful," an "abomination," and "unnatural, immoral, and unhealthy."[39]

On March 15, when the Vermont House commenced debate, no one knew exactly how the votes would line up. Although H. 847 already provided that civil unions were separate from marriage, Representative Bruce Hyde wanted to add this language: "Marriage means the legally recognized union between one man and one woman." In an anguished meeting with the task force, committee members argued that adding "half a DOMA" was essential to pulling in undecided representatives. The new language had no new legal effect—*Baker* had already held that Vermont family law limited marriage to one man and one woman—and was critical to seeing the bill advance. Susan Murray acquiesced. Beth Robinson was not at the meeting but gagged when she heard about the concession.[40]

TIP's lobbyist Bill Shouldice was working closely with Republican representative Margaret Flory, a devout Catholic from the Northeast Kingdom, to develop a fallback proposal that they claimed would satisfy the *Baker* mandate. Most of the March 15 session involved discussion of the Flory amendment, which would have created, instead of a civil union, a *domestic unit*. This would allow same-sex couples and caregivers who were legally barred from marriage to form contractual relationships that entitled their participants to a few legal rights, such as hospital visitation and power of attorney in the event of incapacitation. Flory said her amendment sought "to take sexual activity out of the equation." If these contractual relationships included those between an aunt and her nephew, citizens would be less likely to understand the state as sanctioning gay and lesbian sexuality. This was a pitch that the Catholic Church could live with, as it had done with reciprocal beneficiaries in Hawai'i.[41]

Tom Little opposed the Flory amendment because he thought it would not meet the *Baker* mandate, and he asked his committee vice-chair, Bill Lippert, to speak on the issue. An ambivalent supporter of H. 847, Lippert started: "I think it's important to put a face on this. I've had the privilege of developing a deep, devoted, loving, caring relationship with another man." He paused, as he often did, to collect his thoughts, and the entire chamber held its breath. Recalling the admonitions about sin, disease, and predation rained upon legislators, he said, "I am here to tell you that gay and lesbian couples deserve not only rights, they deserve to be celebrated. Our lives in the midst of historic prejudice and historic discrimination are to my view, in some ways, miracles." His voice was cracking, and others were overcome with emotion. "We are not a threat to your communities. We are, in fact, an asset. We deserve to be welcomed because we are your neighbors. We are your friends. Indeed, we are your family." Please, he asked, "don't tell me what a committed relationship is and isn't. I've watched my gay brothers care for each other. There is no love and no commitment greater than what I've seen and what I've known." He tearfully asked the chamber to support civil unions and not domestic units.[42]

As his colleagues applauded, Bob Kinsey jumped out of his seat to say he had just heard the greatest speech on the floor in thirty years. Although a staunch conservative, Kinsey voted against the Flory amendment, as did most of his GOP colleagues. It failed, 29-118. Also failing, on a bipartisan vote of 22-125, was an amendment proposed by Progressive members to expand the definition of marriage to include same-sex couples.[43]

At a few points in the debate, one could hear legislators "quacking." After he learned of the committee's endorsement of civil unions rather than marriage, Shouldice had originated the "duck argument." If it looks like a duck, walks like a duck, and quacks like a duck—it's a duck. Civil unions look like marriage, carry the same rights as marriage, and sound like marriage—they are marriage. TIP gave every legislator a yellow duck key chain; rather than make speeches, some legislators just quacked. The most zealous opponent of H. 847 was Republican representative Nancy Sheltra, who did a lot more than quack. In a lengthy speech, she argued that civil unions would promote "teaching of homosexuality" in the public schools, "taxpayer-funded homosexual activism," and homosexual "reeducation programs and hate speech regulations." Normalizing lesbian and gay relationships would discourage officials from saying that straight relationships are better than gay ones. Answering Sheltra, GOP representative Mary Mazzariello stood up for her two lesbian daughters: they are good, normal people, she said, and we "need to allow them the same sorrows, joys, and responsibilities of married couples."[44]

At the end of the day, the house voted 79-68 to send H. 847 to a third and final reading the next day. On March 16, the house passed the bill, 76-69. Voting in favor were fourteen Republicans, fifty-seven Democrats, four Progressives, and one Independent; voting against were fifty Republicans and nineteen Democrats. Female legislators voted 35-9 in favor; male legislators voted 41-60 against. Some of the yes votes were swayed by Lippert's speech, others had lesbian or gay children or close relatives, some felt sympathy for the couples they encountered or learned about, and several were won over by the half-DOMA language. The no votes reflected fears about how the legislation would affect traditional marriage and, probably most important, intense pressure from constituents. Some yes voters realized that "this decision may cost some of us our political careers," as Republican Marion Milne put it. One of the no votes came from Bill MacKinnon, who considered the committee's bill a constitutionally deficient separate-but-equal measure.

The Civil Unions Bill in the Vermont Senate

After the house vote, the stakes and acrimony escalated. Focus on the Family, fearing that other states would recognize civil unions, warned: "We cannot allow Vermont to decide the fate of marriage for the rest of this country." Focus's nationwide alert urged defenders of marriage to call Governor Dean, Senator Sears, and their colleagues, and it provided their office and home phone numbers. So did TIP's ad in the *Burlington Free Press*. Dick Sears reported many abusive calls and messages to his home telephone. "This *Is* Marriage's Eleventh Hour," another TIP ad warned. Readers were told to stop "homosexual marriage" by urging their senator to vote against the house bill and to support a constitutional amendment taking the issue away from the judges. On March 30, TIP-allied Rev. D. A. Stertzbach mailed a plea to thousands of Vermont voters to send postcards or letters to "derail this homosexual powergrab."[45]

Under heavy fire, Senator Sears and Senate President Shumlin reportedly got cold feet. A messy debate in the senate might defeat the measure or, worse, cost the Democrats control of the chamber in November 2000. Sears and Shumlin hoped that their pragmatic governor would help them lower the temperature of this overheated debate. Could the matter be postponed? Governor Dean reportedly blew his stack at the suggestion, his neck and face turning beet red. He lectured them: "Every once in a while you have an opportunity to change history and do the right thing. And that's what we're going to do."[46]

Kicking off two weeks of senate committee hearings on March 22, Nina Beck discussed her commitment to her partner, Stacy Jolles, and the painful story of their son Noah's suffering and death from congenital heart failure. "We survived that loss because of the strength of the bond between us and in no small part because of the vows we exchanged eight years ago," when they held a wedding ceremony in California. The senators could see the bond for themselves, as Stacy and their second son, Seth, sat right behind Nina, the mother softly crying, Seth basking in the crowd's attention. "Civil marriage can strengthen the fabric of our society as it protects and nurtures the bonds between a couple and a family," Beck concluded. The senators were virtually speechless.[47]

In his senate testimony on March 29, Bishop Angell declared holy war. "Do not let the court or anybody else push you around," he insisted. "You have no duty, moral or constitutional, to weaken the institution of marriage." On the basis of the duck argument, the bishop opposed civil unions and advocated a constitutional amendment limiting marriage to one man, one woman. The Diocese of Burlington was paying the salary and expenses for Dick Shouldice, who was gathering support for an amendment to override *Baker* entirely. Bishop Angell personally called and met with Catholic senators and implored them to stop civil unions and support the constitutional amendment.

Dick Sears keenly wanted to win over a respected Republican—like Rutland senator John Bloomer, also a member of the judiciary committee. On April 10, Sears presented an alternative version of H. 847 to the committee. He proposed three big changes designed to woo Bloomer: to restore the less romantic *domestic partnership* as the name for the new institution, to push back the effective date of the new law, and to bar people who lived out of state from applying for domestic partnerships in Vermont if such arrangements were illegal in their home states. The Freedom to Marry Task Force adamantly opposed these changes because they would make a disappointing bill even more discriminatory.[48]

The next day, Sears and seven other legislators traveled to a public question-and-answer session at the Bellows Free Academy in St. Albans, in far northwestern Vermont. The event attracted close to five hundred very angry Vermonters, who booed and shouted down the legislators. Bill Lippert watched with increasing fear as one speaker after another denounced "deviants" and "child abuse." John Edwards, who represented St. Albans, knew many in the audience but said he barely recognized them: they had turned from neighbors into a mob. Senators Dick Sears and Ann Cummings came away appalled at the level of hatred—and determined to pass the law without the April 10 concessions. On a straight party vote, 4-2, the judiciary committee sent the civil unions bill to the floor for debate.[49]

On April 18, the Vermont Senate started its deliberations, with three different proposals to amend the state constitution. (Proposals to amend the Vermont Constitution must start in the senate.) Surprisingly, the senators fell into a debate over constitutional interpretation. Reflecting TIP's views, Vince Illuzzi denounced *Baker*'s dynamic interpretation of the common benefits clause and maintained that the only legitimate approach would be to implement its original meaning. In 1777, when it was ratified, the clause admonished the government against granting special privileges to cronies of state officials; no one would have imagined that it would be applied to protect modern social groups such as gay people. Senator Mike McCormack, invoking *Brown*, responded that an original-meaning approach would leave us with a dead constitution, unresponsive to changing times. The constitution exists "for the purpose of protecting minorities from the majority." Dick Sears added an anecdote: "A man named Curtis lived in Putney, Vermont, most of his adult life. He was a man of color in an overwhelmingly white state." Curtis asked the senator what his colleagues were planning to do to the Vermont Constitution. "Why do you ask?" inquired the senator. Curtis replied, "I just wonder whether I'm next."[50]

The senate rejected all three constitutional amendments to entrench traditional marriage; Illuzzi's amendment, which would have overridden *Baker*, lost on a 9-21 bipartisan vote. On the civil unions bill itself, Sears emphasized that if the legislature rejected it, the state would be in violation of the *Baker* mandate, and the Vermont Supreme Court might impose marriage instead. One senator asked: "If this bill is passed, would it have a tendency to increase homosexuality?" Believing sexual orientation was not a matter of choice, Sears dismissed the idea but did not dispute the further suggestion that the bill would "have the effect of making homosexuality or same-sex marriage more acceptable in our society."

House Bill 847 had brought homosexuality out of the closet for many Vermonters. Ever the diplomat, John Bloomer felt that his friends were moving too fast on the issue, but he appreciated that they focused his attention on the humanity of gay people. He had a two-year-old son. If the kid turns out to be gay, he said, he would love him just as much and would bless a committed relationship. James Leddy read a letter from Helena Blair, a seventy-eight-year-old Roman Catholic mother of eight children, one of whom was gay. Blair wrote: "What were we to do—understand instantly or cast him aside? Accept him in a patronizing way or continue to love him unconditionally?" The answer was obvious: "God blessed us with eight children, and my God made no mistake when He created homosexuals and when He gave us our gay son."

Jean Ankeny recounted her journey, starting with her attendance at an early meeting of Freedom to Marry. She supported marriage for lesbian and gay couples but agreed that civil unions were an acceptable compromise. This is the least we can do, she suggested. In her gay-affirming faith community, a same-sex couple was raising an adopted child and a foster child in a loving household. "Please think about the children," she urged her colleagues. Would they not be better off if their parents' union could be recognized by the state? Her own marriage of twenty-eight years was not threatened by this couple, who exemplified the fidelity, forgiveness, commitment, and hard work that are the core of marriage.

The intensity of the opposition—reflected in the hard-hitting TIP ads, the abrasive messages left on legislators' home answering machines, the St. Albans ambush, and the antics of Randall Terry—backfired with some senators. Ben Ptashnik recalled that many of his relatives had died in Buchenwald, the Nazi concentration camp. People forget, he said, that the Nazis targeted gay people as well as Jews, deeming all of them subhuman. Some constituent letters against H. 847 used hateful language of dehumanization that reminded him of anti-Semitism. On the other side, Vince Illuzzi and Julius Canns complained that they were unfairly assailed as bigots because they would not rush to change state law. Canns found the charge particularly offensive because he was partly Native American and was certain that race-based discrimination was much more invidious than discrimination against homosexuals.

On April 19, the Senate voted 19-11 for H. 847. All seventeen Democrats and two Republicans (Helen Riehle and Peter Brownell) supported the measure; eleven Republicans opposed it. All ten women in the Senate voted for the bill; the men voted 9-11 against it. Most of the senators from the northern part of the state voted no. The notable exception was Mark McDonald, from the Northeast Kingdom, a schoolteacher who had been given a pass by the leadership to vote no. But a constituent asked him, "What are you going to tell your students about such a vote?" He could not return to the classroom without a good reason; having none, he voted yes. On April 25, the house voted in favor of the senate-revised bill, 79-68. In a low-key lunchtime ceremony the next day, Governor Dean signed the Vermont Civil Unions Law, which would take effect on July 1, 2000.[51]

The six *Baker* plaintiffs had attended at least some of the hearings and debates, and all of them were present when the house passed the bill on April 25. Holly Puterbaugh's initial reaction to the civil union idea had been "Yech," but on reflection she saw it as a "brilliant compromise." Lois Farnham, Nina Beck, and Stacy Jolles each independently told us that they strongly preferred the term *civil union* over *domestic partnership*. Peter Harrigan and Stan Baker were disappointed when the house judiciary committee opted for civil unions rather than same-sex marriage, but they were the first pair of plaintiffs to come out in favor of the compromise when the task force was deliberating in late February. All three couples were joined in civil unions by the end of 2001, as were 622 other Vermont couples and 2,954 couples who came to Vermont from out of state. One of those couples was Mary Bonauto and Jennifer Wriggins, who were joined in civil union, with their families as witnesses, in July 2001.[52]

Take Back Vermont?

The civil unions law was the "place at the table" moment for Vermont's lesbian and gay community. Vermonters learned a lot about the humanity of some of their neighbors and relatives. Gay and lesbian advocates had emerged as a political force, especially in the Democratic Party, where Bill Lippert had established himself as a major player. On the other hand, many Vermonters resented the fact that the supreme court had forced them to talk about sexuality, let alone homosexuality. Many were angry about the law—and their reactions illustrated the famous backlash effect that political scientists have noted when judges enforce constitutional norms in an unwelcoming political environment.[53]

Deb and Craig Bensen explained to us the difference between two kinds of anger. *Hot anger* is fleeting. The person feels insulted, has a rush of emotion, and then eventually calms down. *Cold anger* does not go away. The person feels betrayed and disrespected at a deeper, more permanent level and resents the affront to her or his loved ones, deep community, and very essence. Cold anger can be tribal when a group sees rejection as an existential threat. A lot of traditionalist Vermonters felt cold anger in the summer of 2000. It seemed to them that the Montpelier crowd viewed them as a bunch of prejudiced yahoos and were shoving homosexual marriage down their throats (recall the duck argument) knowing it was not only bad for marriage but a sacrilege. A retired Navy man who was raising sheep and homeschooling his kids on a farm near Topsham, Tom Wilson felt that cold anger. Based upon FRC materials, he put together a packet that purported to expose the "homosexual agenda" to force gay-is-good propaganda upon schoolchildren. He introduced these materials at a town hall meeting in Topsham, where they were warmly received, and they spread to other town meetings in the Northeast Kingdom.[54]

Dick Lambert, a dairy farmer, had a bad case of cold anger. He created two-by-four signs with the words "Take Back Vermont"—meaning, take it back from the flatlanders and the homosexuals. When he took them to state fairs, people snapped them up to display on their lawns. Soon the dairy farmer was printing and selling hundreds of signs. "Civil unions are like the straw that broke the camel's back," said Ken Paronto, a retired machine shop owner. He had Take Back Vermont stickers on all four of his vehicles and a sign hanging from a tree in front of his house. By the end of the summer, the signs and bumper stickers were all over the state. In July, Steve Cable and Craig Bensen organized a rally on the lawn of the state capitol to protest civil unions with the rallying cry, "Remember in November—Take Back Vermont." They invoked AIDS, child molestation, and drug use as the consequences of homosexuality unleashed.[55]

The voters' cold anger drew political blood in September 2000, when five pro–civil union lawmakers—including John Edwards, Marion Milne, and Bob Kinsey—lost in Republican primaries. For governor, the Republicans nominated Ruth Dwyer, who adopted the slogan Take Back Vermont. At a candidates debate in September, Governor Dean defended the civil unions law against attacks from both the right (Dwyer argued that it was too close to marriage) and the left (Progressive Anthony Pollina favored marriage equality). Polls indicated that no candidate enjoyed support from a majority of the electorate.[56]

The November election results offered something for everyone. Republicans swept the house races and would control ninety-five seats in the next session (with sixty-eight Democrats). Although losing Mark MacDonald, the Democrats kept the senate, 16-14, and reelected Governor Dean, with a bigger majority than he had enjoyed two years earlier against Dwyer. Ironically, the biggest winner was Senator Jim Jeffords, a pro–civil union Republican who ran against an openly gay Democrat. He won a smashing reelection and then, on May 23, 2001, left the Republican Party to caucus with the Democrats. With his departure, the GOP lost control of the US Senate, 49-50-1.

As in California, the advance of relationship rights in Vermont was dominated by legislators and grassroots politics, but in Vermont, judges played a key role, not only forcing marriage onto the legislative agenda but setting an equality baseline. Nonetheless, both states ended up in essentially the same place, with new institutions providing the legal benefits and rights of marriage but not the name. In 2002, Congress passed the Mychal Judge Police and Fire Chaplains Public Safety Officers Benefits Act, which provided $250,000 in compensation to the designated beneficiaries of police officers, firefighters, and others who died in response to 9/11. Notwithstanding DOMA, Peggy Neff, whose partner, Sheila Hein, had died at the Pentagon in January 2003, became the first lesbian to be treated as a survivor under federal law.

Susan Murray, Beth Robinson, and Mary Bonauto had hoped for more. Should they have settled for civil unions in early March 2000? As a political matter, if the task force had renounced the civil unions bill, they would have alienated allies who had invested huge amounts of energy and political capital and would have emboldened their adversaries. On the other hand, if the Vermont legislature had adopted something like Peg Flory's "domestic unit" bill or had gridlocked entirely, the Vermont Supreme Court, according to the justices we interviewed, would have required the state to issue marriage licenses. Leaving the legislature to gridlock would probably have secured marriage equality—but at the price of making a constitutional backlash more likely.

Thoughtful critics of the civil unions compromise have assailed it as separate and unequal because *civil unions* did not carry the social meaning associated with marriage and would not be recognized as marriages in other jurisdictions. The plaintiff couples and most of the activists saw themselves as bold civil rights pioneers. But the civil unions law only gave them the right to sit in the back of the family law bus. Given the worthiness of their lives and their families, this was a severe harm to their dignity. Why shouldn't they, like Rosa Parks, refuse to sit in the back of the bus? Well, suggested Peter Harrigan and Susan Murray, the civil unions bill at least got us on the bus! If we rejected civil unions, we would not be on the bus at all, and we would have angered the bus driver who tried to let us on. The analogy to separate but equal, they argued, was also unfair. In the race context, separate but equal was an apology for white withholding of rights from people of color. In the civil unions context, separate but equal was a substantial advance in rights for lesbian and gay couples.[57]

In 2001, gay and lesbian couples were in the back of the family law bus, but the same process that brought them civil unions might bring them to the front. If the task force was right, that lesbian and gay families were worthy, civil unions would let Vermonters see that worthiness in action. As more lesbian and gay families came out of the closet by joining in civil unions, more neighbors would understand their families, and the democratic process would, sooner or later, deliver full equality.

The civil unions law is best understood as *equality practice,* a provisional movement toward complete integration into the body politic, with an opportunity for feedback, discussion, and further advancement. In California, equality practice was the progressive strategy for getting to marriage, in large part because lesbian and gay rights groups were cowed by the ease of amending statutes and the constitution through the initiative process, as happened with Proposition 22 in 2000. In Europe and Canada, the path toward marriage equality at the turn of the millennium was precisely the path Vermont was following: small steps toward equal treatment of lesbian and gay citizens, through hate crime and anti-discrimination laws, followed by recognition of lesbian and gay partnerships through legislation, with marriage equality likely in the near future. Indeed, marriage came to the Netherlands in 2000–2001, then Belgium, then Canada and Spain in 2005, all after the same kind of equality practice that Vermont embarked on.[58]

So equality practice has the virtue of necessity. In a representative democracy, the views of We the People cannot be ignored; reformers need to work with skeptics and undecided neighbors to persuade them, over time, of the justice of their proposals. Equality practice also bears the virtue of legitimacy: in a constitutional democracy, major social changes are more legitimately adopted through the legislative process, with opportunity for citizen input and voter retribution. Does equality practice also have the virtue of managing backlash? Beth Robinson thinks not. If the Vermont Supreme Court (on which she now sits) had been bold enough to insist on full marriage equality in 1999, she believes the backlash would have been swift, severe, and short-lived.[59]

That hypothesis would be tested three years later, in Massachusetts.

8 · The Cinderella Moment

Most modern romances have a Cinderella moment, the moment when two soul mates can see their futures in each other.

April DeBoer had her Cinderella moment in 1999, when she was separated from her husband and met Jayne Rowse. Jayne was openly lesbian, but April was still mostly in the closet. Upon a chance introduction, the attraction April felt to Jayne was instantaneous. Seven years older and very handsome, Jayne had a butch energy that April found mesmerizing. They put off a relationship to focus on nursing school, but each felt they would be together for the rest of their lives, perhaps after a winding trail. Such a Cinderella moment can happen with social movements, when it becomes clear that the movement's point of view and popular opinion are fated to be wed. For marriage equality, that moment came on November 18, 2003.

Standing around five feet off the ground, slender and cheerfully blue-eyed, Mary Bonauto headed the team of rebels that was, collectively, responsible for marriage equality's Cinderella moment.[1]

The roots of Mary's leadership are in Newburgh, New York, where she was born in 1961 and raised in a close-knit household. Family and faith, along with discipline and hard work, tempered with plenty of love, were the defining values of that family. Starting in her early teens, she knew that something about her did not fit with the rest of her family—and it was not just that she was the only daughter, outnumbered by three brothers. As a sophomore at Hamilton College, a private liberal arts school in upstate New York, her confused feelings came into sharp focus: she was a lesbian. At first, this discovery left Mary distraught and alone. Feeling like you are the only homosexual in your circle of friends and family has inspired many

suicide attempts, but Mary found an emotional resilience that led her to figure a way forward.

Upon reflection, she was the same person she had always been, and so if
she had value and integrity before her discovery, none of that should change—
whatever society might say otherwise. Mary drew additional strength from
the small feminist community at Hamilton, a school that had become coedu-
cational only a year before she arrived as a freshman. Her study of feminist
theory and history, mostly under the direction of comparative literature professor Nancy Rabinowitz, taught her about the instability of cultural consensus. Practices taken for granted for generations—that women gave up the
rights to make contracts or own property when they married, or that pregnant
women could not be schoolteachers—could become indefensible in a historical instant. The same process could work for gay people. Being a student at
Hamilton also taught Mary many positive things. She says she received a
first-rate education and also learned about the incredible power of cultural
prejudice. By her senior year, she was ready to engage social prejudice directly.
"I should not have to put up with this nonsense. Nor should anyone else."

A family trip to the nation's capital (featuring the Lincoln Memorial) when
Mary was thirteen had inspired an interest in law. By the time she graduated
from Hamilton in 1983, she could imagine herself fighting for decent people
like herself and her expanding circle of gay friends. She chose Northeastern
School of Law because it was in Boston, where she already knew people, and
because it integrated clinical and experiential learning at every stage of instruction. Northeastern was also one of the most gay-friendly law schools in a gay-
fearing era. Between work-study jobs and a paying internship for Ward & Lund,
a private firm with gay clients, Mary earned tuition money and acquired legal
skills and experience. After graduating in 1987, she joined a socially minded
law firm in Portland, Maine. As one of three out attorneys in Maine and as
cooperating counsel with the local ACLU, she gained experience representing
gay persons and people with AIDS in all matters of life and death. Like social
justice lawyers before her, Mary had to improvise and stretch the law to help
nudge judges and officials to do the right thing for people unjustly treated. In
1989, she read an advertisement for an attorney position in the region's leading gay advocacy group.

John Ward had founded Gay & Lesbian Advocates & Defenders (GLAD) of
Boston in 1978. It provided legal advice and representation to gay persons and
people with AIDS—but its work expanded after the Massachusetts General
Court (legislature) enacted the Massachusetts Gay and Lesbian Civil Rights Law

in 1989. Adopted after a seventeen-year campaign spearheaded by Arline Isaacson, the director of the Gay and Lesbian Political Caucus, the 1989 statute prohibited discrimination against lesbian and gay persons in employment, housing, public accommodations, and services. The campaign to secure these valuable legal protections energized the small lesbian and gay community and encouraged a steady stream of lesbians and gay men to ease out of the closet at work and in their neighborhoods. With more rights and more gays willing to claim them came more legal work. Mary was GLAD's fifth employee and the second full-time attorney.[2]

When she joined GLAD, Mary was already interested in the marriage question. She had studied the feminist history of marriage and believed that the institution was constantly in flux. If it had been deeply patriarchal before 1900, it was less so in the twentieth century and would be even less so in the new millennium. In her first week on the job, a couple from western Massachusetts inquired about filing a marriage lawsuit. Overwhelmed by incidents of police harassment and claims under the new anti-discrimination law, and also doubtful that such a lawsuit could succeed, Mary reluctantly turned them away—but she and her colleagues did not neglect lesbian and gay families.

In 1980, John Ward had helped persuade the Massachusetts Supreme Judicial Court (SJC) to rule that sexual orientation cannot be the basis for denying custody or visitation rights to children. Subsequently, GLAD represented Don Babets and David Jean, a gay couple in Roxbury whose two fostered sons were taken away by Governor Michael Dukakis's administration. In 1990, the commonwealth settled the case and revoked guidelines that designated gay and lesbian couples as the least preferred situs for placing children in need. In two cases decided in 1993, including one brought by GLAD, the SJC interpreted the state family code to allow second-parent adoption. Justice John Greaney's opinion in *Adoption of Tammy* was responsive to GLAD's close textual analysis and the public need to serve the best interests of children whom the Department of Social Services believed would benefit from two-parent households. Consistent with church doctrine, the court's three practicing Catholic justices dissented.[3]

GLAD was also providing legal advice for other forms of family recognition, including a grievance filed in 1991 against Cambridge to compel it to provide its employees with bereavement leaves for their domestic partners. The organization played a key role, alongside Council Member Alice Wolf, when Cambridge adopted a domestic partnership registry and benefits in September 1992. The same year, Governor William Weld issued an executive order extending some domestic partnership benefits (such as bereavement leave) to same-sex partners of senior state employees. This move triggered an array of private companies and universities to do the same. On October 9, 1992, the Massachusetts Catholic Conference (MCC) objected to domestic partnership benefits on the ground that they treated friendship relationships too much like marriages, which were limited to conjugal unions.[4]

The Hawai'i Supreme Court's surprising decision in *Baehr v. Lewin* (1993) was a game changer. Mary believed this opportunity could not be squandered. And, of course, she had long wanted to marry her partner, Jennifer Wriggins, a feminist attorney who would join the faculty of the University of Maine School of Law in 1996. *Baehr* generated a great deal of lesbian and gay interest in a state constitutional lawsuit in Massachusetts. Although Mary Bonauto would be the primary architect of that lawsuit, it was a collective effort with many leaders, including the ACLU's Norma Shapiro, Sue Hyde of the National Gay and Lesbian Task Force, Gary Buseck and other GLAD lawyers, grassroots activists like Valerie Fein-Zachary and Josh Friedes, and religious leaders such as the Reverend Kim Harvie. Massachusetts freedom-to-marry advocates were determined not to follow the approaches that failed in Hawai'i and earlier top-down campaigns. Like the campaign Beth Robinson, Susan Murray, and GLAD had pioneered in Vermont, this would be a bottom-up campaign for marriage equality.

GLAD's grassroots constitutionalism posited that an enormous amount of on-the-ground educational and political work had to be done before a lawsuit could even be filed. The lesbian and gay community needed to understand the stakes of exclusion, the merits of arguments for inclusion, and the need to speak up. If there was sufficient interest in marriage, the community needed to form institutions to discuss strategies and goals, train speakers and lobbyists, promulgate educational materials, and develop a website and efficient forms of internet communication and education. Supporters had to find and develop allies from all segments of society and government—including the legislature.

Article 48 provided that the Massachusetts Constitution could be amended if two successive sessions of the legislature, sitting as a convention that combined the house and senate, voted for a proposal and then a majority of the voters ratified it in the next regular election. Alternatively, if voters equaling 3 percent of the electorate in the last gubernatorial election signed a petition for a constitutional proposal, only a quarter of the legislators (in constitutional conventions in two successive years) had to support the proposal for it to go to the voters. One lesson of the Hawai'i and Vermont marriage campaigns was that a court victory would not last long without legislative, executive, and political backup. Taking that lesson further than GLAD did, Arline Isaacson favored an incremental approach that started with and built upon a domestic partnership statute, the approach being followed in California. Isaacson feared that an early marriage lawsuit would cost the caucus friendly legislators, as had occurred in both Hawai'i and Vermont.[5]

Although grassroots constitutionalism was the result of a sobering learning curve from the previous lawsuits, it was also, we think, molded by feminist theory. The women who developed the grassroots strategy for constitutional litigation in Vermont, Massachusetts, and Connecticut—Beth Robinson and Susan Murray, Mary Bonauto and Sue Hyde and Norma Shapiro, Anne Stanback and Charlotte Kinlock—were informed by important feminist precepts. First, their thinking went, the personal is political: we must persuade people with the stories of our lives and how they productively connect with our blood relatives, our chosen families, our neighbors, our churches, our children's schools, and our public officials. Second, marriage should be conceptualized not as a hard, absolute right but as a purposive institution that meets the legitimate needs of lesbian and gay families. We must emphasize marriage's concrete benefits that help the entire family, not abstractions such as freedom and equality. Third, supporters should share their stories and arguments with a wide array of social and economic groups—unions, churches, women's groups, bar associations, child welfare organizations—and with the press and other organs influencing public opinion. Between 1997 and 2001, Bonauto and other leaders spent thousands of hours on the road and with the media. GLAD also favored legislative hearings on the issue, but the caucus feared backlash, and so legislators were educated through quiet, off-the-record conversations.[6]

Baehr also stimulated grassroots constitutionalism from the Roman Catholic Church, the Evangelical community, and the Massachusetts Family Institute, a policy group affiliated with Family Research Council. They would work together to battle GLAD's marriage agenda and to reaffirm what they considered traditional marriage. Their leader was Cardinal Bernard Francis Law, the archbishop of Boston, who led the MCC to oppose domestic partnerships, civil unions, and marriages for gay people. The cardinal's signature gesture was to spread his arms and lift up his palms—imploring sinners to abandon their misguided ways and admonishing politicians to provide no approval or encouragement to homosexual relationships. Following the Vatican's lead, Cardinal Law considered homosexuality "an intrinsic moral evil." The Church was a powerful voice among legislators, two-thirds of whom were Catholic. Traditionally, a phone call from the archbishop could veto legislative proposals the Church opposed, such as the death penalty bill in 1997. But its influence was waning. In 1999, for example, Cardinal Law's personal intervention with Catholic governor Paul Cellucci could not block the promotion of then-justice Margaret Marshall, a social liberal, to be chief justice of the SJC.[7]

GLAD's campaign for lesbian and gay marriage generated an interconnected set of political and constitutional debates. One can imagine these evolving debates as a journey story for the commonwealth of Massachusetts, as it changed from a political community dominated by Catholic communitarian and family values, in which sexual and gender minorities were barely tolerated, to one that epitomized a broader pluralism and a less gendered vision of marriage and family. The political actors who drove this journey were disproportionately female, black, gay, and lesbian. The opposition was almost exclusively older Irish or Italian Catholic men who headed traditional families.

When you ask them about their families, most of those older guys describe a Cinderella moment when they fell in love with their future wives. The Cinderella moment for the marriage equality movement would be a decision by the SJC, but its consummation, as in the fairy tale, would be delayed by dramatic circumstances that we shall explore in the next chapter. The court's decision stirred up a wide range of emotions. While GLAD celebrated Cinderella, the Catholic Church and the Evangelical community recoiled at Pandora.

Freedom to Marry Coalition of Massachusetts

In 1997, Sue Hyde and Mary Bonauto formed Boston Freedom to Marry, later renamed the Freedom to Marry Coalition of Massachusetts (FMCM). Other early members of this tiny band of activists included Valerie and Jackie Fein-Zachary, a lesbian couple who appeared every year in their wedding dresses in an FMCM car in Boston's pride parade; Robert DeBenedictis and Don Picard, computer gurus who managed the coalition's website and much of its publicity; and Josh Friedes, the parent of many inventive grassroots and political strategies. Working closely with GLAD, FMCM generated grassroots interest in the marriage issue.[8]

The primary political forum for the marriage debate would be the Massachusetts State House. Completed in 1798, the State House is a colonnaded red brick building with a splendid gold-plated dome rising above the summit of Beacon Hill, overlooking Boston Common. The governor's office, the cabinet meeting room, and the house and senate chambers are all found there. The most important lobbyist roaming the halls of the State House during the marriage debates was Gerry D'Avolio, representing the Catholic bishops, and his priority was to press for a Massachusetts junior-DOMA. Between 1997 and 1999, Representative John Rogers, a handsome young Catholic Democrat from Norfolk, introduced a series of bills providing that "a purported marriage contracted between persons of the same sex shall be neither valid nor recognized in the Commonwealth." Rogers was one of the "Conserva-Dems" who ran the house. Like many other junior-DOMA supporters, he was apparently not hostile to gay people. For example, he sponsored the Adoption Act of 1999, which liberalized the state adoption laws and left *Adoption of Tammy* in place, implicitly confirming the practice of second-parent adoption.[9]

Opposing Rogers and D'Avolio was Arline Isaacson. Immaculately coifed and attired, often with her trademark pearls, Arline could flirt with the most sexist Catholic Conserva-Dem one minute and trade f-bombs the next. After decades of experience as a lobbyist for teachers, unions, and gay people, Isaacson knew the rules of the general court better than anyone else except the parliamentarian, who was her constant tutor. Gay people had a voice in the legislature, which Isaacson and her caucus cochair Gary Daffin could use to stop anti-gay legislation. But they did not believe that the Conserva-Dems would go so far as to support a civil unions or marriage law.

As Isaacson explained to us, the caucus learned some valuable lessons from the campaign to enact the 1989 state anti-discrimination law. First, a successful campaign needs to mobilize its base, even if it is small, to make political actors know that they exist, what they want, and that they are not going away. Make your case in person, and provide human faces as context for policies you support or oppose. Second, expect strong pushback that employs traditional stereotypes of gay people as hedonistic, sterile, predatory, promiscuous, and (for all these reasons) the antithesis of family. Don't take the attacks personally and don't respond with incendiary behavior—like chaining yourself to a State House stairway, as some protesters did in the 1980s. Third, don't remind politicians about what homosexuals do in the bedroom. Isaacson understood the criticism that she was advocating a "gays are just like straights" message, and she took heat in the community for it. Her answer was: What do we want from politics? Do we want to use it to express our disparaged identity and our emotions? If so, misbehave all you want. But if we want to use politics to accomplish legal reform that helps us keep our jobs, protect our families, and earn more social respect, the community needs to persuade the majority to support those measures, or at least acquiesce in them.

A general lesson the gay rights lobbyists drew from their experience with the legislature was to emphasize commonalities, not differences, between gay and straight people. An effective tactic was to rely on third-party allies who could attest that gay people were normal, decent human beings who were your relatives, neighbors, coworkers, and friends. The caucus and ACLU deployed this lesson to head off opposition bills and initiatives. It was (and remains) much easier in the general court for a minority to kill a bill than for a majority to pass it. But defeating junior-DOMA proposals did not significantly advance the positive case for marriage that GLAD favored as the movement's immediate goal.[10]

Josh Friedes orchestrated the creation of a Religious Coalition for the Freedom to Marry. Although half of Massachusetts's population was Catholic, the other half was dominated by gay-friendly denominations—the Episcopal Church, the United Church of Christ, the Unitarian Universalist Church, Reform Judaism, and the Society of Friends. Friedes's religious coalition drew from clergy in these faith traditions to offer readings of Scripture that provided moral support for social and legal recognition of committed lesbian and gay unions. Ministers, rabbis, and lay leaders wrote op-eds, preached inclusion from the pulpit, and engaged in public events to send a message that there was not a monolithic religion-based viewpoint about marriage and family.[11]

Because gay people were a small and partially closeted minority, it was important that its leaders work together. FMCM, GLAD, the National Gay and Lesbian Task Force, the Gay and Lesbian Political Caucus, and other organizations formed a "Group of Groups," an umbrella organization supporting political efforts to back up marriage litigation. In 2000, Friedes left his job to become FMCM's first full-time staffer and played the leading role in the grassroots effort. This was a vocation he was born to do well. With his effervescent personality and graying beard, he looked like a Jewish gay uncle. His mantra was that lesbian and gay people and couples needed to share true accounts of their lives, their meaningful relationships, and the struggles they and their families encountered. Drawing from materials promulgated by Basic Rights Oregon and the Vermont marriage campaign in the 1990s, Friedes developed a "Speakers Training Manual" for representatives of Freedom to Marry who traveled all over the state to talk with citizens in community centers, rotary clubs, churches and synagogues, town squares, and informal dinners at people's homes. Robert DeBenedictis and Don Picard created an interactive website that enabled FMCM user-members to link directly with their legislators and send them their stories. The website also provided information on the hundreds of rights and benefits linked to civil marriage, an extensive regime that surprised most couples.

In 2001, Representative Rogers again introduced a proposal to define marriage as the union of a man and a woman, but H. 3375 included a new, second sentence: "Any other relationship shall not be recognized as a marriage, or its legal equivalent, or receive the benefits exclusive to marriage in the Commonwealth." Friedes dubbed the new bill a "Super-DOMA," an expanded defense of marriage proposal that also barred civil unions and other marriage equivalents. Activists assembled a coalition of nongay groups to join the caucus and GLAD in opposition to this bill: NOW, ACLU Massachusetts, the Massachusetts AFL-CIO and specific unions like SEIU (representing public employees), the Women's Bar Association, and of course the rapidly expanding Religious Coalition for the Freedom to Marry. Importantly, the legislature boasted a number of openly gay and lesbian legislators, including Senator Cheryl Jacques and Representatives Jarrett Barrios and Liz Malia. Former representative Patrick Guerriero was Acting Governor Jane Swift's openly gay deputy chief of staff. As in California, lesbian and gay representation in the legislature was essential to having a place at the table where political decisions were made and deals worked out.[12]

FMCM flexed its grassroots muscles on March 29, 2001, when the house judiciary committee held a public hearing on H. 3375. Hundreds of gay marriage supporters showed up, and more than one hundred presented testimony. Speakers were urged to humanize their remarks with stories showing how gay and lesbian couples were worthy families with the same needs as heterosexual couples, how the Rogers bill would deny those families needed protections that traditional families take for granted, and how the bill would hurt children being raised by same-sex couples, as well as their parents, friends, and other relatives. Like the junior-DOMAs proposed in 1999 and 2000, the 2001 Super-DOMA proposal died without a vote in either the house or the senate. Grassroots constitutionalism revealed itself to be a powerful weapon in the emerging political struggle between lesbian and gay rights advocates and defenders of traditional conjugal marriage. The first victory went to the gays, but traditional values supporters had not yet begun to fight.

The Marriage Lawsuit and the Constitutional Convention

In 1999, Mary Bonauto and GLAD executive director Gary Buseck told Josh Friedes that they intended to file a constitutional lawsuit seeking full marriage rights for lesbian and gay couples. They made the decision only after much deliberation and expressions of support within the lesbian and gay community. The lesson that GLAD, FMCM, and the Group of Groups drew from the Hawai'i and Vermont lawsuits was that good constitutional arguments were insufficient. A marriage lawsuit should not be brought until the lesbian and gay community was behind it, and the hearts and minds of the general public were evolving as they learned about lesbian and gay families.[13]

Researching every corner of state constitutional law, GLAD's attorneys discovered that the SJC had repeatedly ruled that the Massachusetts Constitution's individual rights guarantees went beyond what was required by the analogous protections of the US Constitution. Moreover, the seven justices of the SJC looked like a potentially favorable forum for the marriage coalition's arguments. Liberal Democratic governor Michael Dukakis had appointed John Greaney, the senior jurist and the author of the court's opinion in the second-parent adoption case. Two of the justices had been appointed by liberal GOP governor Bill Weld: Margaret Marshall, a South African lawyer who had risen to be president of the Boston Bar Association and then general counsel to Harvard University, and Roderick Ireland, a longtime lower-court judge and the first African American to serve on the SJC. In 2001, they were joined by four justices appointed by moderate-conservative GOP governor Paul Cellucci (who in 1999 promoted Marshall to be chief justice): Francis Spina, Judith Cowin, Martha Sosman, and Robert Cordy, all former prosecutors or (in Sosman's case) a lawyer for the civil side of the US Department of Justice.

Long regarded as one of the great state supreme courts, the SJC was populated with graduates from the nation's toniest law schools, all of whom had extensive experience in state government and had been either trial judges or leaders of the bar, or both. The court was more diverse than it had ever been, with three female justices, one justice of color, and a variety of religious backgrounds. (In the twentieth century, most justices had been Irish or Italian Catholic men.) This was a bench that would be open to GLAD's claims, but it was far from clear that four justices would dare to be the first court in world history to require same-sex marriage as a constitutional necessity. Equally up for grabs would be the legislative reaction to an SJC decision favoring lesbian and gay couples. Most of the legislators in the general court were Catholic Conserva-Dems.

GLAD'S STATE CONSTITUTIONAL
MARRIAGE LAWSUIT

Once GLAD decided to bring a constitutional lawsuit, Bonauto launched a systematic search for plaintiff couples. Expanding upon the process by which the Vermont plaintiffs were recruited, she wanted couples who reflected the demographic and geographic diversity of the commonwealth and who would be effective ambassadors for their message. They wanted to know from each couple: How did they meet and commit? Why do they want or need marriage and not some other legal protection? What kinds of problems did they face because they were not legally married? How did it affect their children? What stresses did they encounter as a couple? "Their job as plaintiffs was simply to be themselves," Bonauto said. "We knew they would have to explain, again and again, why they had taken the extraordinary step of becoming plaintiffs in a case challenging the government's marriage discrimination." Before she had finished the selection process, however, GLAD's timetable was accelerated by grassroots constitutionalism from their adversaries.[14]

In 2000, Catholic publishers J. Edward and Sarah McVay Pawlick recruited Bryan Paul Rudnick and James Couture, two Brandeis University seniors, to establish the Massachusetts Citizens Alliance as a lobbying group to protect traditional marriage and, soon after that, the Massachusetts Citizens for Marriage (MCM) to press for an initiative to amend the state constitution. GLAD had anticipated that there might be a protection-of-marriage amendment—and the best hope for defeating it, according to Bonauto, was "shining a light (through a lawsuit) on the lives of the real people affected and the bedrock American principles of fairness and equality." After giving a heads-up to Matt Coles and other national gay rights litigators, Bonauto believed the time for launching the marriage lawsuit had arrived.[15]

On April 11, 2001, GLAD filed the complaint in *Goodridge v. Department of Public Health*. Counsel for the plaintiffs were Mary Bonauto, Jennifer Levi, Gary Buseck, Ben Klein, and Karen Loewy. Reflecting GLAD's grassroots constitutionalism, the bulk of the complaint was the stories of the seven plaintiff couples and the needless difficulties they faced because they could not get married. The legal relief part of the complaint, alleging that the Declaration of Rights in the Massachusetts Constitution guaranteed same-sex couples the right to marry the person they loved, was almost perfunctory. By filing early, GLAD hoped that it would secure marriage rights from the SJC by 2003 or 2004, before a proposed constitutional amendment would go to the voters.[16]

The lead plaintiffs, who supplied the first name in the caption, were Hillary and Julie Goodridge, a Boston professional couple in their forties who had been together for thirteen years. To signify their lifetime together, they had a commitment ceremony and had changed their last names to Goodridge, the maiden name of one of Julie's grandmothers. In 1995, Julie bore a child, Annie, whom they raised within the relationship. "When their daughter was born," the complaint read, "she breathed in fluid and was sent to neonatal intensive care. Julie had a difficult caesarian and was in recovery for several hours. Even with a health care proxy, Hillary had difficulty gaining access to Julie and their newborn daughter at the hospital." What triggered their immediate desire to get married came when seven-year-old Annie told her mothers about how much her friends' married parents loved each other. "How about Mommy and Ma," quizzed Hillary. Her heart stopped when Annie replied: "If you really loved each other you'd get married."[17]

So the Goodridges were determined to seal their love with civil marriage. Equally motivated were a diverse array of six other couples:

- David Wilson and Rob Compton, business executives in their fifties, an interracial couple since 1997, both previously married with children.
- Mike Horgan and Ed Balmelli, an Irish couple since 1994, both raised as Catholics but active in the Old South Church, a UCC church in Boston, and both closely connected with their extended families.
- Maureen Brodoff and Ellen Wade, a lawyer couple since 1981 who were raising their daughter in Newton, with Ellen as the second parent under *Tammy*. Ellen was combatting breast cancer.
- Linda Davies and Gloria Bailey, a couple since 1971 who were partners in a psychotherapy practice in Orleans. Linda was immobilized after a bilateral hip replacement operation, and Gloria was her caregiver.
- Gary Chalmers and Richard Linnell, a teacher-nurse couple since 1988, living in Northridge, taking care of Rich's elderly mother and their adopted daughter.
- Gina Smith and Heidi Norton, an interracial couple living in Northampton. Heidi bore two sons (Avery and Quinn), and Gina became a legal parent through second-parent adoption. They later took the same last name: Nortonsmith.

Because the complaint sought "the freedom to join in civil marriage with the person [you] love," MCC sounded the alarm that the lawsuit was "as radical an attack on the institution of marriage as one could imagine. A freedom so broadly fashioned, if sanctioned by the courts, would force the state to issue marriage licenses to *anyone* who professes to love *anyone,* or any two or three for that matter, notwithstanding the particular make-up of the couples filing the lawsuit."[18]

THE SUPER-DOMA CONSTITUTIONAL INITIATIVE

On July 31, MCM announced it would begin the petition process to entrench the following understanding of marriage and marital rights in the state constitution:

> Only the union of one man and one woman shall be valid or recognized as a marriage in Massachusetts. Any other relationship shall not be recognized as a marriage or its legal equivalent, nor shall it receive the benefits or incidents exclusive to marriage from the Commonwealth, its agencies, departments, authorities, commissions, offices, officials and political subdivisions.

This proposed Super-DOMA would have thwarted GLAD's constitutional claims and would have barred statutory civil unions, but it had to run the legislative gauntlet in two successive sessions. It encountered some immediate snags.[19]

Acting Governor Jane Swift, a Republican, called the constitutional amendment "totally unnecessary." Although opposed to gay marriage (a stance that brought a public rebuke from her gay stepson), Swift issued an executive order extending a limited set of domestic partnership benefits to all lesbian and gay state employees. MCM criticized the action: "Any expansion of domestic partnership benefits is a slippery slope, creating a Trojan horse for gay marriage." Rudnick and the Pawlicks criticized Swift again in September when she agreed to a union contract extending domestic partnership benefits (including health insurance) to 8,500 state social workers.[20]

On September 5, Attorney General Tom Reilly certified the Protection of Marriage Amendment—which started a three-month period for MCM to gather 57,100 signatures needed to send the proposed Super-DOMA to the legislature for a constitutional convention (Con Con). MCM brought in Ballot Access Company, which was already collecting signatures for two other ballot measures in the state. According to freedom-to-marry supporters, the collectors bundled signatures, telling voters that they were signing the initiative against horse slaughtering and then slipping the marriage initiative into the mix. MCM

Mary Bonauto and Jennifer Wriggins

gathered more than 110,000 signatures. After the attorney general certified the initiative amendment on December 20, freedom-to-marry supporter Amy Hunt published the signatures on the internet, and hundreds of citizens responded that their signatures had been fraudulently procured. The press reported the alleged signature fraud with gusto. Rudnick resigned from MCM in February 2002. The constitutional initiative was allowed to proceed, but was tarnished by this scandal.[21]

In the meantime, Mary Bonauto was adding to her own journey story. She watched much of the drama from the sidelines, having given birth to twin daughters in December. Mary and Jenny had in 1998 bought a white frame house in Portland, just blocks from the University of Maine School of Law, where Jenny taught. It was a perfect neighborhood to raise kids. The couple had in 2001 joined in a Vermont civil union, with the full support of their relatives. Although Mary never allowed *Goodridge* to be about her own circumstances, her growing family only intensified her determination to prevail in the case.

The Pawlicks' constitutional initiative threatened to derail the marriage campaign. As few as fifty of the two hundred legislators who would participate in the Con Con supported marriage for lesbian and gay couples. Because opponents of expanding marriage needed only fifty votes to send the constitutional initiative to the next round of deliberations, there seemed no way to prevent the initiative from succeeding in 2002 and again in 2003. That would place it on the ballot in November 2004. GLAD believed that if there were legally married lesbian and gay spouses in 2004, voters would reconsider their opposition, and the ballot initiative might fail. But that was the minority view; most pundits believed the Super-DOMA would secure the needed majority.

2002 CONSTITUTIONAL CONVENTION

Once the signatures had been certified, the MCM ballot initiative qualified for a state constitutional convention—where it had a surprisingly rocky reception. With the governorship up for grabs in 2002, Arline Isaacson used the lesbian and gay community's small leverage to obtain an early advantage. Running for governor with support from the Gay and Lesbian Political Caucus and some gay donors, Senate President Tom Birmingham agreed to refer the initiative to Harriette Chandler's joint committee on public service rather than the judiciary committee. Senator Chandler worked with the caucus and GLAD to orchestrate a favorable public hearing on the petition, held on April 10 in Gardner Auditorium at the State House. Hundreds of citizens, organized by MassEquality (the new umbrella organization superseding the Group of Groups) and FMCM, showed up to support marriage for gay couples and to protest the apparently fraudulent process of signature gathering. The hearing itself focused on the serious arguments: Do gay people form relationships? Raise children within those relationships? What is the purpose of marriage? The most dramatic moment came when Attorney General Tom Reilly (another possible gubernatorial candidate) testified that the proposed amendment "sweeps broadly to deprive the children and dependents of same-sex relationships as less worthy of our protection, less worthy of our gratitude when their parents or partners are killed in service to us, and less worthy of our empathy in time of personal hardship and loss." Opponents of the initiative told their stories of tangible hardships, while most of the supporters relied on religious doctrine and abstract fears about the social consequences of same-sex marriage.[22]

With assistance from the caucus, Senator Chandler wrote a majority report that strongly criticized the amendment. A measure that barred a segment of society from enjoying the rights and privileges accorded to others was, the committee concluded, discrimination. Also, concerns about the manner in which signatures were gathered for this ballot initiative called into question the fairness and legitimacy of the process. Isaacson visited every member of the committee and persuaded skeptical Republicans to abstain, meaning there would be no minority report to frame the issue for the Pawlicks.[23]

Earlier grassroots work paid off, with an outpouring of constituent opposition to the initiative. Josh Friedes and his FMCM colleagues assembled a massive book of letters to legislators: "Families formed by same-sex couples face the same challenges as their heterosexual peers—raising children, aging, death and serious illness, family economic security, buying property and obtaining insurance together, dissolution of relationships—but same-sex couples face these challenges without legal protections." The centerpiece of the book was the stories of 108 lesbian and gay couples, all with the same message: We want to legally marry the person we love, and marriage for us is about long-term commitment. We also need the partner benefits that married couples take for granted, especially hospital visitation and decision making in emergencies, health insurance that includes partners, and inheritance rights. Twenty-three letters came from lesbian and gay parents worried about the message a constitutional amendment would send to their children. One mother wrote that her son was taught in school that *family* consists of mom, dad, and kids. What are we, then? "We're just a collection of people," responded the child. Senator Cheryl Jacques distributed a copy of the book to each legislator.[24]

The Con Con met in the mahogany-paneled house chamber on the third floor of the State House to consider H. 4840, the proposed constitutional amendment. Behind the speaker's podium are a set of murals by Albert Herter, "Milestones on the Road to Freedom." Although the senators were guests of the house, the presiding officer of the Con Con was the president of the senate, Tom Birmingham. He gaveled the Con Con to order on May 1, but thirty seconds later recessed it to June 19. He repeated the process in June, recessing until July 17. During the second recess, he charged Cheryl Jacques with counting votes. She identified three distinct voting blocs: (1) traditional marriage conservatives, (2) liberals comfortable with gay marriage, and (3) legislators asserting they were in favor of marriage themselves but believed that the people deserved a right to directly vote on the issue. Block 1 was the largest, and blocks 1 and 3 were a big majority of the Con Con. Given that the initiative needed only a quarter of the legislators to pass, there was no way to prevail on a merits vote.[25]

Isaacson's recommendation was that the presiding officer entertain a final motion to recess to the last day of the legislative session, December 31, 2002, when almost no legislators would be in the State House. Plan B was to entertain a motion to adjourn, thus closing the legislative session for the year. This was less promising because Acting Governor Swift could recall the legislators, who might feel obliged to consider the amendment. Majority Leader Salvatore DiMasi, Isaacson's macho Italian-Catholic buddy, agreed to coordinate the caucus's strategy. He and Isaacson rounded up more than twenty representatives who would whip their colleagues to support a recess vote; some of the whips were opposed to marriage rights but agreed with DiMasi and Isaacson that the issue was best set aside for another day.[26]

Right before the July 17 session of the Con Con was to open, Isaacson and the whips were meeting over noshes in DiMasi's opulent office. They were confident of victory—until Jacques dropped by to inform them that the senate president had decided to accept a motion to adjourn, not the recess idea that they had been working on. An adjournment would leave them vulnerable to a call from the acting governor to reconvene. After much swearing and carrying on by legislators, DiMasi and Isaacson managed to calm them down, aided by large doses of coffee and cannoli.

When President Birmingham gaveled the July 17 Con Con to order, he entertained an immediate motion to adjourn from Senate Minority Leader Brian Lees, a moderate Republican who was Birmingham's friend. The motion caught the Super-DOMA supporters by surprise. As the clerk began the roll-call vote on adjournment, Jacques noticed that, by luck, seven of the first nine names voted yes. "The alphabet worked strongly in our favor." Knowing that her colleagues sometimes voted like sheep, Jacques relaxed. DiMasi and Isaacson's whips did their job. The motion passed 137-53, effectively killing the constitutional initiative.[27]

Why did the motion to adjourn receive such overwhelming support? The conventional wisdom, which we share, is that legislators, faced with a proposal that was far too broad, on an issue that was not really ripe for constitutional action, were more than happy to avoid a substantive vote. Because the amendment was a political hot potato, any vote a legislator took on the Super-DOMA would alienate many constituents, which is not a path toward reelection. Friedes believes that legislators were also moved by the journey stories: Why should they go out of their way to impose real harm on those families? Some of the families included their legislative colleagues. Isaacson thinks the unfair process of signature gathering created space for twenty to thirty legislators to support a procedural dodge. Because there were so many signatures that legislators personally knew must be fraudulent, they believed that the Super-DOMA came to them after a tainted process. Why encourage this?

Sotto voce, everyone agreed that another factor was critical. Father John Geoghan was indicted in 2001 for sexual abuse of boys under his supervision as parish priest as far back as the 1980s. In January 2002, the *Boston Globe* began running its Pulitzer Prize–winning "Spotlight" series about sexual abuse of children by Geoghan and other priests in the Boston archdiocese. Cardinal Law piously expressed shock at this misconduct—but the *Globe* also reported that the cardinal and his predecessor early on knew the details of what Geoghan had done to parish boys. Ultimately, 250 priests were accused of child abuse in the archdiocese, which had covered up their crimes and relocated many of the priests to new parishes, where they committed new offenses. Just as the Super-DOMA battle was engaged, in mid-2002, the Church was dealing with recriminations that by December would lead to Cardinal Law's resignation as archbishop. He went into exile at the Vatican, narrowly avoiding indictment for obstruction of justice. The ongoing scandal severely undercut the Church's moral authority: Catholic legislators who were utterly loyal to guidance from the bishops before 2002 became more open to other viewpoints.[28]

Whatever the reasons for the adjournment, the Pawlicks were furious, and they had constitutional cause to feel aggrieved. Article 48 of the Massachusetts Constitution governed the process by which the general court was supposed to consider initiative amendments. It said that "if the two houses . . . fail to continue [the joint session, or Con Con] *until final action has been taken upon all amendments pending,* the governor shall call such joint session or continuance thereof." The Pawlicks petitioned Swift to call the legislature back into session. She sought an advisory opinion from the SJC, which told her that she could call the adjourned Con Con back into session but declined to say whether Article 48 required her to do so. The acting governor declined to exercise that authority. With the legislature adjourned for the year, the proposed constitutional amendment was officially dead after December 31.[29]

Meanwhile, voters went to the polls that autumn. Tom Birmingham, who had stood up for gay marriage at the Con Con, came in a disappointing third in the Democratic primary for governor. Jane Swift was nudged out of the Republican primary by handsome multimillionaire Mitt Romney. In the general election, state treasurer Shannon O'Brien supported gay marriage as well as abortion rights for minors, and those issues probably tipped the election to Romney, who ran a gaffe-filled campaign but prevailed, 50 percent to 45 percent.

The *Goodridge* Decision

The Suffolk County trial judge dismissed the *Goodridge* complaint on May 7, 2002, and GLAD not only filed an appeal but successfully petitioned the SJC to skip the intermediate appellate court. Its constitutional arguments strongly resembled those made in the Vermont marriage case. The SJC should, GLAD argued, subject the exclusion of same-sex couples to strict scrutiny because (1) the exclusion denied those couples their fundamental right to marry, and denied that right based upon suspect classifications, namely, (2) sex and/or (3) sexual orientation. Nonetheless, GLAD's appeals brief led with the argument that the marriage exclusion did not even rest upon a rational basis, namely, that the discrimination did not plausibly advance a valid public policy. The SJC had struck down discriminations lacking a rational basis in a number of cases, and in 1978 had announced that it would recognize "a continuum of constitutional vulnerability determined at every point by the competing values involved." (This was similar to the constitutional sliding scale adopted by the Vermont Supreme Court in *Baker.*) Because the state was withholding hundreds of rights and benefits from committed couples on the basis of either their sexual orientation or the sex of their partners (fishy classifications), GLAD maintained that the commonwealth did not meet its burden of showing how the discrimination actually contributed to good public policy.[30]

Attorney General Reilly argued that the fundamental definition of marriage was one man, one woman, because only that union could be consummated by procreative intercourse. GLAD's demonstration that civil marriage had evolved over the decades was not on point, he claimed, because coverture rules and laws against interracial unions were not essential features of marriage. Conjugality was central; coverture and race were not. If the court agreed with this view of the definitional feature of marriage, the commonwealth would avoid strict scrutiny, because the fundamental right to marry would be limited to procreative couples. And there would be no discrimination if couples failing to meet the essential requirement for marriage were not included. The attorney general argued that defining marriage in the traditional way served the public interest because it channeled procreative intercourse into a domesticating institution and because it encouraged the sexual unions that created families in which children were reared by their biological mothers and fathers, which was the best environment for them. Religious groups—including the MCC, the Knights of Columbus, Focus on the Family, and the Massachusetts Family Institute—submitted amicus briefs strongly reinforcing the definitional and purposive features of the defense of marriage argument. They also pressed a normalization argument: if the justices recognized the liberty of homosexuals to marry, they would deny religious persons and institutions the liberty to disapprove of such relationships.

Anticipating the commonwealth's arguments, Mary Bonauto had assembled eleven amicus briefs to provide a larger context. Closest to her heart was the brief from Yale professor Nancy Cott and twenty-four other historians, cataloging the many ways civil marriage had evolved to meet changes in American society. What had been stable about civil marriage, the historians argued, had not been any requirement of procreation but its foundation upon mutual consent and, increasingly, the equal status of both spouses. Given the historians' choice-based understanding of the institution, it was not such a big step to allow two women to marry—and in their view not a fundamental redefinition at all. Equally important was an amicus brief documenting the social-science consensus that lesbian and gay persons formed serious committed relationships that filled the same emotional needs that marriage did for straight persons, and that children raised by lesbian and gay parents fared as well as children raised by straight parents. This consensus was reflected in resolutions from the American Psychological Association (1995), the National Association of Social Workers (1987, 1997), and the American Academy of Pediatrics (2002).[31]

That GLAD was offering a powerhouse case for equal marriage rights made House Speaker Thomas Finneran, a Conserva-Dem, nervous. He dispatched Representatives John Rogers and Gino O'Flaherty to propose a deal. If the *Goodridge* plaintiffs would drop or stay their appeal, conservative legislators would support legislation providing lesbian and gay couples with hospital visitation, bereavement leaves, inheritance rights, and a few other benefits. The virtue of a domestic partnership–lite statute was that it would give lesbian and gay couples immediate rights in a law that would likely prove durable because of the legislative and religious buy-in. As a lawyer zealously representing her clients, Bonauto could hardly recommend that the couples accept such a separate but grossly unequal solution. Also, GLAD's marriage coalition was dedicated to a campaign for full marriage rights; even if they lost in court, the grassroots and public education work would propel the community and the commonwealth closer to marriage equality.[32]

GLAD's persistence in the litigation was buoyed by a private 2003 poll. Although most of the respondents took a dim view of whether lesbian and gay families were good for society, 53 percent viewed marriage as primarily about commitment and responsibilities to the partner you love, and only 10 percent saw it as primarily about bearing and raising children. Respondents were okay with gay marriage by a surprising 59-35 percent margin. Although half believed the electorate should decide the issue and only a quarter thought the

SJC should resolve it, 64 percent said they would agree or strongly agree with an SJC decision finding a constitutional right to marriage for lesbian and gay couples. The respondents disfavored a constitutional amendment limiting marriage to one man and one woman (44-54 percent) and much more strongly opposed a Super-DOMA prohibiting civil unions and comprehensive domestic partnerships (26-72). Large majorities agreed that same-sex couples wanted to marry for the same reasons different-sex couples wanted to marry, that it was discrimination not to recognize such marriages, and that kids raised by same-sex couples would be better off if their parents could marry. On the other hand, most agreed with the commonwealth's argument that children were better served by a mom-and-dad household than by a mom-and-mom household (53-43).[33]

The most likely votes for marriage equality on the SJC were John Greaney, Rick Ireland, and Margie Marshall. Greaney, a liberal who had authored *Adoption of Tammy*, saw marriage as the next step. If the commonwealth recognized co-parenting rights for lesbian partners because it was in the best interests of the children they were raising as a family, wouldn't those children also be better off if their parents were legally joined to one another through marriage? Ireland had been a twenty-three-year-old newlywed in 1967, when the US Supreme Court invalidated southern states' bans on interracial marriage in *Loving*. His wife, Alice, had a black father and white mother, so the decision had personal meaning that helped him sympathize with the lesbian and gay couples before him in *Goodridge*. He also knew that Virginians had invoked the Bible to defend their ban on interracial marriage, and that context fortified his view that such discrimination had to be evaluated against the equality norm and needed to be justified by tangible, public-regarding reasons.[34]

Marshall, the commonwealth's first female chief justice, had grown up in South Africa and was an admirer of the South African Supreme Court's post-apartheid equality jurisprudence, which had strongly favored gay rights. (That court would require marriage recognition in 2005.) Emily Bazelon recounts a story Marshall liked to tell:

> "The very first case heard by the Massachusetts Supreme Judicial Court involved slavery," she said. "A man by the name of Quock Walker came to the court in 1780." Walker was a slave who had run away to work for a neighbor. When his master recaptured him and beat him, he sued for assault. To win his case and hold the master accountable, Walker had to convince the court to declare him free. "He said, 'Look, it says here in

your state declaration of rights: All men are created equal,'" Marshall said. "So the question for the court was: What are you going to do with slavery in 1780? 'Excuse me, Judge, it says equal.'" Marshall was miming Quock Walker by pointing to her palm as if the words were written there. "Judge Cushing said, 'You have curly hair and thick lips, but you look like a man to me.'" Marshall paused and her voice shook a bit. "Do I think that was a political decision? I think it was a *constitutional* decision."

Although Cushing's SJC did not abolish slavery on the spot, Marshall found his bold enforcement of the equality principle appealing, and her graduate study at the Yale Law School had only encouraged this heroic concept of judging. She had little experience with gay rights issues before 2002–2003, but GLAD and its amici provided her with a rich education, including points of similarity between their case and that of Quock Walker. Like the South African Supreme Court, Margie Marshall was open to making a big move.[35]

Bob Cordy and Francis Spina were not. From his days as a star on the undefeated 1970 Dartmouth football squad through a distinguished career in private practice and public service, Cordy was an indefatigable team player and decidedly not a boat-rocker. A graduate of Harvard Law School, he was steeped in the school's conservative legal process tradition: the role of judges is to adjudicate narrow disputes and to leave larger policy issues to the political branches. By seeking a redefinition of marriage, *Goodridge* plaintiffs were asking the SJC to make a big policy adjustment decision that should be left to the legislature. Cordy might have joined a decision like *Baker*, requiring equal treatment while leaving the remedy to the legislature, but neither the commonwealth nor the plaintiffs considered civil unions an acceptable resolution. Francis Spina was an unlikely vote for either marriage or civil unions. A former legal aid attorney and dedicated pro bono advocate, "Saint Francis" (so dubbed by colleagues because of his selfless service and generosity to others) appreciated the Catholic natural law vision of marriage and family and supported the commonwealth's position. (As late as *Adoption of Tammy*, there were three justices who voted consistently with Catholic doctrine. By 2003, there was just one.)

GLAD's fourth vote would have to come from either Martha Browning Sosman or Judith Cowin. On paper, Sosman seemed like a good bet, as she was unmarried and had devoted her career to women's rights, especially reproductive rights. She had founded the first all-women law firm in Massachusetts.

Although personally unconventional, even quirky, as a judge she favored strict adherence to precedent and neutral principles derived from precedent. She did not entertain a heroic view of judging. Neither did Judy Cowin. Unlike Cordy, a fellow Harvard Law graduate, she had absorbed little of its legal process philosophy, partly because she had taken her first year elsewhere and was married with a child while in law school. Like Marshall's, Cowin's SJC appointment had initially been opposed by the Catholic Church, because as a trial judge she had increased the counsel fees in a case where a gay man had demonstrated employment discrimination by a Catholic hospital. Her first opinion for the SJC, refusing to enforce a contract to allow a wife to use frozen embryos over her divorced husband's objection, had relied on the constitutional principle that judges should respect "freedom of personal choice in matters of marriage and family life." A nonobservant Jew, she viewed family through a liberal, individual-rights perspective and not through the communitarian perspective of the Catholic Church.[36]

At oral argument on March 4, 2003, six justices tipped their hands. Sosman, the jurist most likely to go for the jugular, pressed Bonauto on her fundamental-right-to-marry argument. Didn't all of the right to marry precedents "deal[] with government attempts to further restrict marriage, even beyond the definitions that have long been sort of inherent in the underlying definition? You're trying to change the definition." Bonauto answered that *Loving* had invalidated long-standing southern bars to interracial marriages, but Sosman was not persuaded: such bars had never been universal, even within the United States. Moreover, what neutral principle would support changing the definition? GLAD said that marriage was about recognizing relationships based on the romantic choices made by consenting adults. Why then, Sosman wondered, would that principle not require the commonwealth to recognize polygamous marriages? GLAD was not getting Sosman's vote—nor those of Cordy or Spina. Marshall, Greaney, and Ireland revealed friendly interest in the *Loving* parallel, so there was reason for optimism with those three. Cowin's questions, however, suggested skepticism: Has any state ever recognized same-sex marriages? Is there evidence that legislators intentionally excluded lesbian and gay couples from civil marriage? The answer to both questions was, essentially, no.[37]

The commonwealth was represented by Assistant Attorney General Judith Yogman. (As in other cases, the attorney general left the appellate file on a shelf, so that a lawyer especially interested in the issue could take the case. But no one did, until Yogman picked it up weeks later—only because she felt that *someone* needed to defend the statute.) At oral argument, Marshall, Greaney, and Ireland questioned her aggressively: What is the *public-regarding* justification for excluding lesbian and gay couples from civil marriage? The primary public justification, she answered, was that "limiting marriage to opposite-sex couples furthers the state's interest in fostering the link between marriage and procreation." Most of the justices thought this was the commonwealth's worst argument because it was not logical. There was no evidence that the commonwealth's family law linked procreation to marriage. It was a matter of record that many straight married couples had no desire to procreate or to raise children, yet no one begrudged them the freedom to marry. And none of the justices understood how denying marriage rights to lesbian and gay couples would encourage straight couples to find a connection between procreation and marriage.

Yogman also argued that by giving one-man, one-woman unions special treatment, "the legislature could conceivably believe that an optimal setting for childrearing and procreation is a family where there are one parent of each sex." Some justices did not quite see the logic behind this claim, either. Marshall wondered why the commonwealth's stance was not inconsistent with *Adoption of Tammy*, "which the legislature has not sought to amend in any way." Had experience with second-parent adoptions "not [been] a powerful recognition that childrearing, in fact, of single-sex couples is optimal for certain children?" Yogman did not have a good answer, and the commonwealth's brief had provided no peer-reviewed study refuting the dozens of studies cited in the social science amicus brief, which maintained that children flourished with lesbian and gay co-parents just as much as with straight co-parents. By this point, the commonwealth had lost four justices, who could not even begin to accept the optimal-parenting justification without some evidence that lesbian and gay parenting was problematic. Even if all the social scientists were wrong, and these parents did fail as role models, how would denying them marriage rights do anything but harm the children, like Annie Goodridge, being raised in lesbian and gay households? Did the commonwealth want the court to overrule *Adoption of Tammy*? That was unthinkable to all the justices, except maybe Spina. Some of the justices felt the government was grasping at straws.

After oral argument, the justices retired to their small, book-lined conference room in the John Adams Court House to discuss the case around a rectangular table. Four of the chairs had leather cushions; the others were bare to accommodate three bad backs. Each associate justice spoke in order of seniority, starting with Greaney. He, Ireland, and Cowin were convinced that the commonwealth was discriminating against lesbian and gay couples without a reasonable justification. They found the commonwealth's brief unpersuasive: it was long on rhetoric about tradition and the virtue of husband-wife families, but short on evidence that expanding marriage to include committed lesbian and gay couples would in any way harm the public interest. Additionally, the discrimination was inconsistent with the commonwealth's general policy respecting lesbian and gay citizens, especially the 1989 comprehensive anti-discrimination statute. If the commonwealth already allowed lesbian and gay couples to form families with children (*Adoption of Tammy*), how could it reasonably deny recognition of the romantic relationships between the same-sex parents? Cordy, Spina, and Sosman saw greater rationality in the commonwealth's reasons and were more willing to defer to legislators' reluctance to make a big change in civil marriage without stronger evidence that the expansion would not harm either children or the institution itself. As was the SJC's custom, the chief justice was the last to speak (she voted to invalidate the discrimination) and controlled the assignment of the opinion, which she took for herself. There would be dissenting opinions. For the next seven-and-a-half months, the justices worked on their opinions in an atmosphere of strict secrecy. No one outside their seven chambers even knew about the decision until just before it was issued.

At 10:00 a.m. on November 18, 2003, the SJC released its opinions in *Goodridge v. Department of Public Health*. Delivering the SJC's judgment and an opinion joined by Justices Ireland and Cowin, Chief Justice Marshall found the exclusion of same-sex couples from marriage a violation of the constitutional principle of equality under the law. "The Massachusetts Constitution affirms the dignity and equality of all individuals. It forbids the creation of second-class citizens." The commonwealth "failed to identify any constitutionally adequate reason" for denying civil marriage to same-sex couples. "We are mindful that our decision marks a change in the history of our marriage law. Many people hold deep-seated religious, moral, and ethical convictions that marriage should be limited to the union of one man and one woman, and that homosexual conduct is immoral. . . . Our concern is with the Massachusetts Constitution as a charter of governance for every person properly within its reach. 'Our obligation is to define the liberty of all, not to mandate our own moral code.'"[38]

Like Jeffrey Amestoy in *Baker*, Margaret Marshall did not decide whether strict scrutiny applied, because she found that none of the public goals identified by the commonwealth rationally supported the exclusion of lesbian and gay couples from marriage. She started with the responsible procreation argument. Marshall found nothing in the Massachusetts statutory scheme declaring procreation to be the central purpose of civil marriage, a point made in amicus briefs filed by the historians of marriage and by the authors of the leading Massachusetts family law treatise, Charles Kindregan and Monroe Inker. Moreover, that argument "singles out the one unbridgeable difference between same-sex and opposite-sex couples, and transforms that difference into the essence of legal marriage." Indeed, Marshall found the marriage exclusion similar to Colorado's disparaging exclusion of "homosexual persons," which had been invalidated by the US Supreme Court in *Romer v. Evans* (1996). The marriage restriction "impermissibly" identified "persons by a single trait and then denies them protection across the board. In so doing, the State's action confers an official stamp of approval on the destructive stereotype that same-sex relationships are inherently unstable and inferior to opposite-sex relationships and are not worthy of respect."[39]

The second goal advanced by the commonwealth was encouragement of optimal family arrangements: a married mom and dad raising their biological children. But the commonwealth "offered no evidence that forbidding marriage to people of the same sex will increase the number of couples choosing to enter into opposite-sex marriages in order to have and raise children," and common sense suggested that the children of lesbian and gay couples would be better off if their parents were married. Marshall also rejected the commonwealth's third justification, that refusing marriage to same-sex couples would advance efficient government (i.e., save money), and the argument of religious amici that changing the definition of marriage would further its decline. Because the "marriage ban works a deep and scarring hardship on a very real segment of the community for no rational reason," it was "rooted in persistent prejudices against persons who are (or who are believed to be) homosexual."[40]

As to the remedy, Marshall followed the approach taken by the Ontario Supreme Court, which in June 2003 had ruled that the exclusion of lesbian and gay couples from marriage violated Canada's Declaration of Rights. Rather than strike down the discriminatory marriage law, the court had extended its terms to include same-sex couples and gave the parliament two years to revise its laws accordingly. In *Goodridge*, the SJC stayed its judgment for 180 days so that the Massachusetts General Court could take any necessary action. Marriage licenses for same-sex couples would have to be issued by May 17, 2004—the fiftieth anniversary of *Brown v. Board of Education* (1954).[41]

Justice Greaney, the fourth vote for the majority's invalidation and remedy, wrote a concurring opinion that found both a fundamental right to marry and discrimination based on a suspect classification, namely, sex. He suggested that the majority was distorting the rational basis approach by requiring a tighter fit between an exclusion and its rationale than the court usually required and by giving the legislature no deference. The dissenting opinions of Justices Spina, Sosman, and Cordy agreed with that criticism but disagreed, in detailed analyses, with Greaney as to whether the exclusion implicated a fundamental right or a suspect (sex-based) classification. For example, when Massachusetts added an ERA to its state constitution in 1978, the voter pamphlet assured the electorate that it would not be interpreted to require same-sex marriages. Each of the three dissenters forcefully argued that the commonwealth had a rational basis for hewing to the traditional definition of marriage. Cordy's influential dissent maintained that it was not irrational for the commonwealth to create an institution (marriage) seeking to channel potentially procreating (different-sex) couples into such an institution that would assure children born of their conjugal behaviors a relatively secure home with their married biological parents.[42]

The jurists in the majority expected criticism for their big move, but the reaction was worse than they imagined. Ireland was shocked to find himself and his colleagues called "dumb," "nuts," "deplorable," "shameful," "sick," "an abomination," "traitors," "communists," and "atheist liberals" who had "lost [their] minds" and were bringing ruin on the United States, just as "God destroyed Sodom and Gomorrah." One person wrote, "We pray every day that you all get cancer and rought [sic] in HELL." The Pawlicks hired airplanes to fly over the Eastern States Exposition (New England's largest state fair) in West Springfield and in communities where each of the majority justices lived, carrying banners condemning the justices by name and Marshall as a "witch." On successive Sundays, a Pawlick-sponsored gang disrupted services in Ireland's church with loud demands that his congregation expel him and his family. "Although no physical violence actually erupted, the group's presence was disconcerting. I have often wondered," Ireland wrote, "about the group's sense of entitlement and privilege in coming to a black church, in the heart of a black community, and whether it would have done the same in a white church, in an upper-income community."[43]

However deflated MCC was in the wake of the sexual abuse scandal in 2002, it mobilized once homosexual marriage was imminent. On January 16, 2004, Massachusetts's four Catholic bishops held a joint press conference and mailed a statement to more than a million households: "[T]he Supreme Judicial Court declared in the *Goodridge* case that marriage will no longer be linked to children and their wellbeing. According to the court, it is the 'act of self-definition' of adults in choosing relationships, and 'not the begetting [and rearing] of children,' that is the new essence of legal marriage in Massachusetts." Recognizing same-sex marriages in this way would delink the institution from children and their welfare, open up recognition to any kind of "self-defining" hedonic relationship, and threaten private groups with discrimination claims. Gender neutrality was unnatural, socially unproductive, and ungodly, the statement informed readers. "The value of sexual difference and complementarity, especially in relation to children, gives marriage its special status. To affirm these uniquely important goods is not prejudice." In 2003, the Vatican had issued "Considerations Regarding Proposals to Give Legal Recognition to Unions Between Homosexual Persons," which called upon all Catholics who were public officials to resist homosexual marriage as "harmful to the public good" and "gravely immoral." The Massachusetts bishops implored Catholic lay leaders to resist what their faith considered an unholy redefinition of marriage.[44]

An opinion poll before *Goodridge* reported that Massachusetts residents supported marriage equality, 50 percent to 44 percent. Polls immediately after the decision was announced revealed that between 50 and 59 percent of the population supported it. After months of criticism and outrage, however, increasing majorities began to support a referendum. Governor Romney joined Evangelicals and Catholics in demanding a popular vote on the issue. A February 2004 poll reported that residents opposed marriage equality, 53 percent to 35 percent, and 71 percent favored a referendum. Surprisingly, 60 percent endorsed Vermont-style civil unions for lesbian and gay couples.

Would *Goodridge* survive religious censure, Republican entrepreneurship for a new wedge issue, and sinking poll numbers? Would the Cinderella moment for marriage equality collapse into one big orange pumpkin?

9 • Cinderella Under Siege

Winning a landmark constitutional victory is usually not as hard as making something of it or, sometimes, even preserving that triumph against political pushback.

The evening *Goodridge* was handed down, lesbian and gay activists and their many allies gathered to celebrate their Cinderella moment at the Colonnade Hotel, near Fenway Park. People were cheering, laughing, drinking, and hugging and kissing one another. Some were crying: for the first time in their lives, they felt like first-class citizens and not moral lepers. Arline Isaacson, the movement's chief lobbyist, was crying out of sadness as well as celebration. By postponing the remedy until May 17, 2004, the Massachusetts Supreme Judicial Court (SJC) ensured that the next six months would be a struggle for everyone and a special hell for her, just after she and her partner had their second child.[1]

Goodridge was delivered into a political environment full of minefields. After the 2002 elections, no more than fifty of the two hundred members of the Massachusetts General Court (the legislature) supported marriage equality for lesbian and gay couples. Moreover, the top three state officials were opponents: Governor Mitt Romney, a devout Latter-day Saint, and Senate President Robert Travaglini and House Speaker Thomas Finneran, both Catholic Conserva-Dems. Cinderella's reunion with Princess Charming was delayed, and all three of these officials were determined that it should be denied altogether.

Raised in an Irish working-class household in Dorchester and South Boston, Finneran was a much-feared politician. "Watching Finneran, you get the sense that a major source of his power as a politician is his cold hard stare– 'the ice face,' as one legislator calls it. Then, as he moves among his fellow members of the House of Representatives, you see that he's got something else, as well: a rollicking, head-thrown-back laugh. His eyes light up and the laugh seems to come from down deep. It moves in instants right up his spine and then into the noisy chamber." Although he had voted for the 1989 anti-discrimination law, "King Tom" gave *Goodridge* the ice face and was determined to mobilize both threats and charm to head off the homosexual marriages the Vatican had condemned just a few months earlier.[2]

The new senate president was Bob Travaglini, an Italian Catholic who had lived all his life in East Boston. (He served on the Boston City Council for ten years, until his election to the senate in 1993.) Not as colorful as the house speaker, Travaglini was just as much a traditional family man. Although he, too, supported the 1989 anti-discrimination law, opposed by the Massachusetts Catholic Conference (MCC), his faith and his constituents prevented him from supporting marriage equality. After *Goodridge,* however, he was open to Vermont-style civil unions, as was Minority Leader Brian Lees.

Governor Romney, the lantern-jaw executive from central casting, had supported equal treatment of gay people in his 1994 campaign against Senator Ted Kennedy. He promised to work for a federal anti-discrimination law as well as integration of gays into the military and even the Boy Scouts. The 2002 Winter Olympics, which Romney brilliantly managed, was LGBT-welcoming; Romney's team included both local and national gay groups in planning. Like Travaglini and Finneran, and consistent with his Mormon faith, however, Romney saw traditional marriage as a matter of definition, not discrimination. Indeed, the governor was eager to lead the charge against *Goodridge,* a stance that would help him with cultural conservatives if he ran for president in 2008.[3]

In this political context, the SJC's six-month delay, intended to give the legislature time to implement the *Goodridge* mandate, became an occasion for intense political maneuvering. In December 2003, MCC joined forces with the Massachusetts Family Institute (MFI) and the Black Ministerial Alliance to create a grand Coalition for Marriage that would coordinate grassroots support for traditional marriage and family values. Before *Goodridge* was decided, grassroots constitutionalism supported GLAD's constitutional lawsuit. Afterward, the constitutional debate shifted to the general court, where grassroots sentiment favored stopping marriage licenses from being issued on May 17, 2004, or else cutting them off soon after that.

Norma Shapiro of the Massachusetts ACLU, Josh Friedes and the Freedom to Marry Coalition of Massachusetts (FMCM), Arline Isaacson and Gary Daffin of the Gay and Lesbian Political Caucus, the GLAD lawyers, and other allies formed the MassEquality Coalition to coordinate a political campaign to protect *Goodridge*. Marty Rouse was its first campaign coordinator; Marc Solomon was its political director. Marty and Marc were determined to mobilize the lesbian and gay community to make legislators aware that they had constituents who were politically invested in this issue. A political contest between gay people and the powerful Catholic-Evangelical-Mormon alliance seemed like David versus Goliath, but they were buoyed by the fact that David prevailed in the biblical matchup.

The Possibility of Civil Unions

On November 20, Attorney General Reilly suggested that the SJC decision and its six-month window gave the general court leeway to satisfy the equality mandate with a Vermont-style civil unions law. Senator Travaglini introduced Senate Bill 2175, a constitutional amendment barring same-sex marriages but establishing civil unions. In December 2003 the senate asked the SJC for an advisory opinion on whether S. 2175 would satisfy the *Goodridge* mandate. The majority justices were astounded that anyone would seriously believe that their decision was ambiguous on this point. On February 4, 2004, the SJC ruled, in another 4-3 decision, that "marriage" meant *marriage*. Chief Justice Marshall's opinion held that civil unions would be a "separate but equal regime" that "would have the effect of maintaining and fostering a stigma of exclusion that the Constitution prohibits." Dissenting justices Sosman, Cordy, and Spina objected that civil unions would remedy the massive discrimination in state benefits and rights identified in *Goodridge* and that it was entirely rational for the legislature to provide a different name to relationships that would have a distinctive legal status under DOMA and in the states with junior-DOMAs.[4]

In a *Wall Street Journal* op-ed the next day, Governor Romney raised the stakes of the debate, and his own profile among social conservatives, by comparing *Goodridge* to *Dred Scott* (the 1857 US Supreme Court decision striking down Congress's effort to limit slavery). Both, he wrote, were offensive, divisive decisions by activist judges. Just as the Reconstruction Amendments overrode *Dred Scott*, so the Massachusetts Constitution should be amended to override *Goodridge*. The comparison of *Goodridge* with the infamous judicial endorsement of human slavery inflamed the lesbian and gay community. It was Romney, they believed, who was making the *Dred Scott* move of dehumanizing a class of people. On February 6, Bonauto requested a meeting with the governor. When his staff declined the request, she and seven of the plaintiffs went to Romney's office, on the third floor of the Massachusetts State House, to hold an impromptu press conference. Surrounded by reporters and a television crew, the delegation started their press briefing—but before they got very far, the governor's calendar magically cleared.[5]

The plaintiffs and their lawyer were shown into a conference room and seated at the end of a long table. Romney entered the room, smiled sheepishly, and sat at the other end, several feet away from the nearest homosexual. Bonauto explained that the governor's op-ed treated his gay constituents unfairly. Would he reconsider that unforgiving stance? Each plaintiff gave a short account of his or her path toward family and the reasons why their families were worthy of being cherished and celebrated. David Wilson and Rob Compton described their interracial family, with five adult children and a growing number of grandchildren. David said that being unable to marry felt like the same kind of discrimination that he and other African Americans had felt from laws barring different-race marriages. Julie Goodridge recounted her daughter's incredulity that her mothers were not already married; Romney seemed not to care. For most of the meeting, he looked down at the table as if he found the whole subject distasteful.

As they were leaving, Goodridge asked the governor, "What would you suggest I say to our daughter about why her mommy and her mom can't get married because you, the governor of her state, are going to block her marriage?" As Julie recalled the conversation later that day, Romney responded, "Well, how old is she?" Goodridge: "Oh, she's eight." Romney: "Well, what have you been telling her for the last seven years? Just keep telling her that." The mother dissolved into tears at the insensitivity of that answer. "In other words, ignore the last year of this historic decision, ignore the fact that she's been so excited that finally her mommy and her mom could be able to get married." Afterward, Romney was all smiles as he told the press that he had enjoyed a "good discussion" with the couples and their lawyer.[6]

The Coalition for Marriage enlisted hundreds of ministers and priests as well as on-the-ground volunteers to mobilize significant grassroots opposition to gay marriage. Legislators were flooded with phone calls, letters, and visits from constituents outraged by *Goodridge*. MassEquality was just getting organized and could not match the resources and political energy of the clergy group. But reinforcements were on hand. In early 2004, grassroots organizer Marc Solomon started work as the legislative director of FMCM, and needed funding came from Tim Gill and other national sources. Would MassEquality be able to hold off the waves of legal and political challenges between February and May 2004?

2004 CONSTITUTIONAL CONVENTION

On February 8, the Coalition for Marriage held a huge rally on Boston Common, just down the hill from the State House. Thousands cheered Archbishop Sean O'Malley as he demanded a marriage protection amendment to the constitution. Three days later, on February 11, members of the general court assembled as a constitutional convention ("Con Con") in the house chamber to consider that and other proposals. Swarmed by lobbyists and deluged with constituent letters, most legislators seemed opposed to *Goodridge*. The worst-case scenario would be a constitutional Super-DOMA like the Pawlick amendment that had failed in 2002. (Even worse would be a Super-DOMA that retroactively nullified existing same-sex marriages.) The least-worst amendment would bar same-sex marriages but write civil unions, with all the legal benefits associated with marriage, into the constitution.

This least-worst alternative was what Senate President Travaglini and Minority Leader Lees had unveiled on February 10 as a "Leadership Amendment." In a collegial gesture at the beginning of the convention the next day, Bob Travaglini, as the presiding officer, recognized Tom Finneran, who surprised his colleague by jumping his more conservative proposal ahead of the Leadership Amendment. Working with MCC's Gerry D'Avolio and MFI's Ron Crews, Speaker Finneran introduced an amendment that would bar same-sex marriages in the commonwealth and would allow (not require) the general court to enact a civil unions law.[7]

From his office in the State House, Governor Romney walked down the hall to urge House Minority Leader Bradley Jones Jr. to mobilize Republicans to support Finneran's proposal. Romney suggested that the party might later support something like the Hawai'i nonsexual reciprocal beneficiaries law. The GOP house caucus was on board. When he heard about the gambit, however, Brian Lees (the GOP's leader in the senate) was furious with Romney for going behind his back. Despite Romney's, MCC's, and MFI's support, Finneran's amendment was defeated that afternoon, 98–100. The main reason it lost was that the senators voted against it 9-30, with five of the six Republicans following Lees. The house voted for the amendment 89-70, with the GOP representatives in favor, 18-7.[8]

Next up was the Travaglini-Lees Leadership Amendment, adding to the constitution a bar to same-sex marriages and a requirement that civil unions "shall provide entirely the same benefits, protections and responsibilities that are afforded to couples married under Massachusetts law." MCC and MFI believed that these provisions diluted rather than reaffirmed the unique and powerful meaning of marriage and urged their supporters to vote no. GLAD and MassEquality believed the provisions were malleable enough to allow a reluctant executive branch to create a separate and deeply unequal regime, and they also urged their allies to vote no. In the end, the compromise lost by a larger margin, 94–104, than the Finneran amendment. (Senators voted for the Leadership Amendment, 32–7, and house members voted against it, 64–97.)[9]

The Con Con continued the next day, February 12. Representative Shaun Kelly, an Irish Catholic Republican from the Berkshires, opened the session with an emotional appeal to treat his friend Representative Liz Malia, a partnered lesbian, the same as everyone else. "If you believe that the love Liz has for her partner is less than the love you have for your spouse, I would suggest that you're wrong." Even though his motion to adjourn the convention was rejected, his speech transformed the debate. Continuing to personalize the issue, Senator Jarrett Barrios reflected on an episode when his child was sick with a fever. He and his partner called the hospital. "My seven-year-old was screaming. I reached a nurse and started going into the symptoms. She said are you the parent. The parent they had listed was Doug. She said you are not listed. Are you married? What ensued seemed like an eternity when my child with a 104.5 fever, I thought he could die on my watch while I was fighting with a nurse over whether I was his parent or not." This, he said, was the human cost of nonrecognition. "There are real harms which are incurred by this. . . . Children do get sick. We need to have health coverage and services for them. Their parents need to be treated as equals. Marriage makes this possible."[10]

Moments like these leached away support from the pro-DOMA forces, as some fence-sitting legislators could not bring themselves to disrespect lesbian and gay families. Representative Phil Travis, representing the Coalition for Marriage, offered a proposal that would entrench one-man, one-woman marriage in the state constitution without requiring any parallel institution for lesbian and gay families. The Travis amendment lost, 96–103. Were the pro-amendment forces losing ground? The convention recessed shortly before midnight and agreed to resume on March 11. On March 11, the Con Con voted for the Leadership Amendment, and a final vote could take place when the Con Con reconvened on March 29. Altogether, two-thirds of the legislators had voted for one of the proposed amendments. This Con Con was already one of the longest and most acrimonious in the commonwealth's history.[11]

When Senate President Travaglini gaveled the convention to order on March 29, legislators were under tremendous pressure to take action, as *Goodridge*'s six-month grace period was running out. It got personal for Representative Barbara L'Italien, whose family belonged to the St. Augustine Catholic Church in Andover. The Sunday after the initial Con Con session, she had been the cantor, sharing the altar with her priest as he delivered a blistering attack on Catholic legislators for departing from the 2003 Vatican admonition that Catholic officeholders must do all they could to prevent any redefinition of marriage. Afterward, Barbara's family started receiving abusive phone calls at home, and the children were taunted at school. This abuse repelled Barbara's seventy-nine-year-old mother, who had been opposed to homosexual marriage. "This is the right thing to do," to stand up to bigots and bullies. The next Sunday, Barbara again performed as the cantor, and her priest lambasted her and other legislators by name. As before, she responded with a crystal-clear rendition of "Table of Plenty." Soon after that, the priest suggested that she and her family find another church.[12]

The stakes kept getting higher. That winter, *Boston Globe* polls showed that large pluralities opposed marriage for lesbian and gay couples—an apparent erosion in support since *Goodridge*. In a confidential analysis delivered in early March, Harvard law professor Mary Ann Glendon warned MCC that the Travaglini-endorsed compromises would destroy marriage and would undermine religious liberty as well. "Even while maintaining a nominal distinction between marriage and civil unions," she wrote, "an amendment transforming civil unions into a constitutional principle is likely to have far-reaching and negative consequences on the right of citizens and institutions to disagree on questions of sexual ethics," generating "perhaps more serious and more permanent harm than *Goodridge* itself."[13]

Over MCC's opposition, an updated Travaglini-Lees amendment was called up for a third reading at the Con Con's March 29 session. As before, Mass-Equality whipped its supporters to vote (1) yes, (2) yes, (3) no—(1) in favor of this amendment over more objectionable alternatives, (2) then to substitute the new amendment in place of the earlier version, and (3) to turn against the amendment in the final vote. The first two votes proceeded as planned, with large majorities for the revised Leadership Amendment. The debate preceding the final vote was dominated by marriage equality supporters, with the most dramatic speech of the day given by Senator Marian Walsh. Representing Irish-Catholic Roxbury, Walsh had once been MCC's most reliable vote, but the predatory-priest scandal had shaken her willingness to follow the Church's moral guidance. On March 29 she came out as a deeply religious person whose faith tradition supported one-man, one-woman marriage but whose civic responsibility was more inclusive. Standing on a box to reach the microphone at the lectern and speaking firmly in her thick Boston accent, she appealed to the universal rights guaranteed to all her constituents by the state constitution and endorsed *Goodridge*. The same social compact that protected freedom of religion also protected the freedom of gay people. "The gay individual is owed the promise and the hope of America equally and fully because that is our compact and that is our Constitution," she said, her voice cracking. "This compact with one another has always required us to reach beyond our moral and emotional grasp, then we actually do become the nation we want to be." Her speech received a standing ovation. In the elevator afterward, the MFI lobbyists could not even look her in the eye.[14]

Watching the speeches, which were broadcast live on public television, one might have thought that the Travaglini-Lees amendment would once more go down—but it was approved by the convention, 105-92 (supported 88-70 in the house, rejected 17-22 in the senate). Some Democrats supported the amendment because they wanted the people to decide the issue and felt that civil unions would be an acceptable alternative. Critically important was another surprise from Governor Romney, whose office urged the GOP house caucus to vote for the Leadership Amendment. Although Minority Leader Jones could not bring himself to support the compromise, fifteen house Republicans who had opposed both civil unions and marriage on earlier votes provided the key votes to change the outcome. As Representative Jeffrey Perry put it, "At the end of the day, this was the best we could do. I felt obligated to give something to the people." Because the Travaglini-Lees amendment would require another affirmative vote in the next session of the general court, the earliest it could have gone to a vote was November 2006. Based upon its lobbying and outreach by lesbian and gay constituents, Marty Rouse estimated that MassEquality had doubled its legislative support during the six weeks between the first and last week of the 2004 Con Con.[15]

THE GOVERNOR'S GAMBITS

Immediately after the Con Con vote, Governor Romney held a press conference calling for a stay in the *Goodridge* mandate until the voters had a chance to weigh in during the 2006 election. "At the core of American democracy is the principle that the most fundamental decisions in society should ultimately be decided by the people themselves." Attorney General Reilly responded that his office, the only legally authorized representative of the commonwealth, would not support such a request. Hence, the governor could not bring suit in the name of the commonwealth. On April 15, Romney asked the general court to authorize him to petition the SJC. To demonstrate how complicated the matter would be, he invoked a 1913 law barring out-of-state couples from securing a Massachusetts marriage license if their marriage would be "void" if contracted in their home state. The 1913 law had been adopted to prevent Massachusetts from giving marriage licenses to different-race couples from the South.[16]

The general court declined to give Romney such authority. Last-minute petitions by legislators and by former Boston mayor (then ambassador to the Vatican) Raymond Flynn to intervene in *Goodridge* and to seek a stay also failed. Liberty Counsel, representing various religious organizations and eleven legislators, brought an eleventh-hour action in federal court. Judge Joseph Tauro dismissed the lawsuit on May 13, and the federal court of appeals summarily affirmed. Liberty sought a stay from Justice David Souter, who referred it to the full US Supreme Court. Without dissent, the justices denied the petition on Friday, May 14. Dozens of "countdown parties" were held that weekend, including a celebration in the Jamaica Plains home of the Reverend Anne Fowler, an Episcopal priest and leader in the religious leaders' committee for marriage equality.[17]

MFI's Ronald Crews implored the governor to defy the general court and the SJC and act on his own to stop the issuance of marriage licenses on May 17. Romney was unwilling to breach the rule of law. Instead, he directed the Department of Public Health to revise the marriage application forms, making them gender-neutral but requiring out-of-state applicants to sign, under penalty of perjury, a declaration that there was no impediment in their home state to their Massachusetts marriages. Also, clerks were authorized (but not required) to ask for proof, such as a driver's license, for applicants claiming to be residents. Provincetown disobeyed the governor and announced that its clerks would issue licenses to out-of-state couples without inquiring whether their home states would recognize their marriages. Traditionalists condemned the governor for not defying the SJC.[18]

MARRIAGE LICENSES FOR GAY AND LESBIAN COUPLES

On May 17, 2004, all seven plaintiff couples went to the marriage license offices in their communities. With a police escort and marksmen atop the surrounding buildings, Mary Bonauto led Julie and Hillary Goodridge, Dave

Wilson and Rob Compton, and Ed Balmelli and Mike Horgan to city hall in Boston to apply for their marriage licenses—then to probate and family court to request a waiver of the waiting period. Judge Nancy Gould asked the plaintiffs for a reason. Bonauto responded: "They've waited seventeen years. They'd like not to have to wait an additional three days." The judge granted the waiver, and the three couples returned to city hall to receive their licenses immediately. On May 17 and 18, Boston issued marriage licenses to 213 lesbian and gay couples.[19]

The first wedding was David Wilson and Rob Compton's, at the Arlington Street (Unitarian) Church in Back Bay, near the Boston Public Garden. Their extended family now included Mary Bonauto. "I was sitting next to Rob's mother, and she kept handing me tissues. It was *her* son, and *I* was the one who was a total mess." A founding member of the coalition of ministers supporting marriage equality, the Reverend Kim Crawford Harvie concluded the ceremony with the declaration that she sealed this marriage "by the power vested in me by the Commonwealth of Massachusetts." The congregation cheered. "Hearing those words and knowing it was true just changed everything," Mary recalls. "It felt like the cage had been lifted off, and it was just a different world from that point forward."[20]

Sitting in church that day, Mary was joined by her longtime partner and the co-parent of their two daughters, Jenny Wriggins. As a law professor, Jenny marked the irony that she and Mary could not take advantage of *Goodridge* because they lived in Portland, Maine. Maine considered same-sex marriages void, so it was covered by Governor Romney's interpretation of the 1913 law. The two women could have secured a marriage license despite the statute. Four communities—Provincetown, Somerville, Worcester, and Springfield—openly embraced out-of-state couples, and dozens of couples in other towns secured licenses from clerks who looked the other way. But like Mitt Romney, the two women were sticklers for the rule of law. So May 17 was not a wedding day for Mary and Jenny.[21]

More Constitutional Conventions

The availability of licenses coincided with a changing of the guard in the politics of marriage. The big news was the resignation of Speaker Finneran in September 2004 after he pled guilty to perjury and obstruction of justice during a federal investigation into a corrupt redistricting process. The new speaker was Arline Isaacson's buddy, Salvatore DiMasi, a liberal Democrat. This was a lucky break for MassEquality. On May 17, the same day marriage licenses were first issued, the Reverend Kris Mineau assumed command of MFI as its "interim president" (a post he held for ten years), after being personally vetted by Focus on the Family's James Dobson. Reflecting the views of his Evangelical network, Mineau's strategy was to lead a grassroots coalition of voters to override *Goodridge*. The Catholic bishops were on board, as they authorized the creation of Catholic Citizenship, a grassroots mobilization group that was formally launched in June 2004.[22]

The new MFI president had an unbeatable journey story of his own. A graduate of the Air Force Academy, young Captain Kris Mineau had been a tall, lanky, handsome top gun who flew more than one hundred combat missions in Vietnam in 1966. He later flew F-4Cs in Europe. On March 25, 1969, his F-4 Phantom II fighter jet malfunctioned and started a nosedive at fifteen thousand feet. Plummeting at the speed of sound, the pilot was unable to eject from his seat. "My life passed before me. Although never a religious person, I cried out, 'Please, God, help!' Instantly, the ejection seat fired." But at one thousand feet, Kris ejected too late to avoid serious injury. He broke dozens of bones when he landed and ended up flat on his back for a year, suffering through a series of operations and therapies. During a conversation with chaplain James Holmes, his mind was "flooded with a vision of Jesus on the cross," and "a deep warmth and wondrous love enveloped me" and transformed his life with the power of the Lord. Miraculously, he resumed flying in 1975. Kris's near-death experience changed his inner life. Before 1969, he says he lived a Hugh Hefner playboy lifestyle of sexual freedom, even during the early years of his marriage. After the accident, he became a born-again Evangelical Christian, joyfully faithful to his wife and to his Lord, Jesus Christ.[23]

THE 2004 ELECTION AND THE 2005 CONSTITUTIONAL CONVENTION

In 2004, traditional marriage supporters viewed defeating some of the marriage equality legislators as imperative. A special election in March 2004 had seen a traditionalist Republican take a Democrat-held seat. Seeing an opportunity to increase the pitifully small GOP representation in the general court, Governor Romney raised $3 million to elect Republican candidates, almost all of whom supported a constitutional amendment. The MFI's political action committee and Catholic Citizenship pledged funding, volunteers, voter guides (distributed in churches and mailed to parishioners), and pulpit support for Romney's effort.[24]

MassEquality raised $700,000 to finance a grassroots effort to shore up its legislative supporters and, importantly, to knock off a few opponents, the daring strategy insisted upon by Marty Rouse, who had applied it eight years earlier in Vermont. Their best opportunity was in the Democratic primary challenge to veteran Somerville-Medford representative Vinny Ciampa by Carl Sciortino, a young gay man. Located right outside Boston, Somerville was a traditional blue-collar, Catholic community that was attracting lesbian and gay professionals who wanted to raise their families in an affordable neighborhood. Marc Solomon, who had joined Josh Friedes at FMCM, and Rouse urged Sciortino to base his campaign on nonmarriage issues; Ciampa was out of touch with his constituents. In addition to mailings and ads, MassEquality volunteers made phone calls and person-to-person pitches for a fresh face in the legislature. On primary day, September 14, Ciampa was routed—as was traditionalist representative Mark Howland in New Bedford. All of the marriage-equality representatives were renominated.[25]

These candidates were more vulnerable in the general election, and the Coalition for Marriage worked especially hard to defeat Barbara L'Italien. Her opponent, Andover businesswoman Maria Marasco, was an excellent candidate. As director of the Digital Mammography Center, Marasco had supported the "Just a Squeeze Please" campaign for early and regular breast examinations by women over forty. Although personally opposed to gay marriage, she explained her position as pro-democracy, not anti-gay. A Romney fundraising speech for Marasco focused on her proposal to give free scholarships to talented students. "Whether it is education reform, reforming the state budget, or reforming the Turnpike Authority, without the help of legislators like Maria, Massachusetts will be stuck with business as usual, taxing and spending on Beacon Hill."[26]

This was a powerful challenge to L'Italien's tenure in the legislature—yet the Andover Democrat had advantages of her own. She embraced constituents of all backgrounds and orientations, was a caregiver for her mother who lived with her family as she was dying from Alzheimer's, and inspired great loyalty by fighting for measures that helped children and families. MassEquality invested dozens of volunteers and modest sums of money in a door-to-door campaign to educate voters about her work in the legislature. Her reelection chances were enhanced by the presidential race, which in 2004 pitted Bay State senator John Kerry against President George W. Bush. In November, L'Italien was reelected by a large margin, 58-42 percent. Surprisingly, the Republicans could not unseat any Democrats and lost two house members of their own. Several traditionalist house members who did not run for reelection were replaced by marriage equality supporters. As the Gay and Lesbian Political Caucus's Gary Daffin explained, once marriage licenses were being issued and the sky did not fall, traditional marriage lost a lot of political steam. "In the end, people didn't see any harm to themselves" and their families. Many traditional marriage defenders "just didn't really care" anymore.[27]

Kris Mineau believed that time was running out for one-man, one-woman marriage. Like the Catholic bishops, he had little enthusiasm for the Travaglini-Lees amendment endorsed by the 2004 Con Con—but after the disastrous 2004 election, the legislature would be less receptive than ever to a stronger defense of marriage amendment. The best strategy, he decided, was to start all over with a citizens' petition to amend the state constitution to entrench one-man, one-woman marriage, with no room for civil unions. On the morning on June 16, 2005, Mineau hosted a press conference at the Nurses Hall of the Massachusetts State House. Speaking for a coalition that included MFI and MCC as well as the Black Ministerial Alliance, Concerned Women for America, and Focus on the Family, he renounced the Leadership Amendment, announced the formation of a ballot committee to launch a citizens' constitutional initiative, and proposed a gender-neutral reciprocal beneficiaries measure similar to the compromise adopted by Hawai'i in 1997. Standing with Mineau on the platform were Bishop Gilbert Thompson of the Black Ministerial Alliance and pastor Roberto Miranda of the Fellowship of Latino Pastors.[28]

Missing from the platform was Mineau's strong ally, Mitt Romney. "MFI had an open door to the governor and his chief of staff" essentially any time Mineau wanted it. When he pitched the idea of starting over with an amendment without civil unions, the governor did not need much convincing. Most Catholics, Evangelicals, and Mormons believed that civil unions were too much like gay marriage. Supporters of marriage equality, of course, wanted to kill the Leadership Amendment to prevent a popular vote in November 2006. On September 14, the 2005 Con Con formally rejected the Travaglini-Lees amendment, 39-157. MassEquality allies joined Catholics and Evangelicals allied with Marriage Coalition to sink it. Brian Lees voted against his own amendment. Observers wondered whether Senator Travaglini's opposition was waning, as he had warmly toasted Senator Barrios and his husband at their wedding celebration, held right after the 2004 election.[29]

2006 CONSTITUTIONAL CONVENTION

For the rest of 2005, MFI and its allies in voteonmarriage.org worked around the clock to gather and verify the 65,825 signatures they needed for a new initiative-generated constitutional amendment. The amendment they proposed was simple and sweeping: "When recognizing marriages entered into after the adoption of this amendment by the people, the Commonwealth and its political subdivisions shall define marriage only as the union of one man and one woman."

In addition to a professional ballot firm and three thousand public policy advocates working at the parish level for Catholic Citizenship, more than 1,200 Evangelical and Catholic churches helped collect signatures. Mineau asked the governor if he would sign the petition. Why not? Mineau brought a signature sheet to Romney's office in October. When Romney's legal adviser suggested that he should not sign it in his office, Romney said, "Let's do this on the street!" So he and Mineau went down to the street behind the State House, and the governor signed the petition—one of 170,000 signatures collected by MFI, more than any previous Massachusetts petition effort.[30]

Succeeding Rouse as head of MassEquality, Solomon launched a "Read Before You Sign" anti-fraud education campaign, which detected some fraudulent signatures that recalled the Pawlicks' 2001–2002 signature-fraud scandal. In addition, GLAD challenged the petition in court and urged the attorney general not to certify the initiative, on the ground that Article 48 of the Massachusetts Constitution explicitly disallowed initiative amendments that attacked the authority of the judiciary or amounted to a "reversal of a judicial decision." Because the MFI initiative sought to reverse *Goodridge*, it fell within the plain meaning of the exclusion. (In GLAD's view, a legislative amendment could "reverse" *Goodridge*, but not a citizens' petition amendment.) MFI persuaded the attorney general that the original meaning of Article 48, adopted in the 1918 Constitution, was to bar initiatives that sought to "recall" specific decisions, not those that added constitutional language prospectively overriding such decisions. In *Schulman v. Attorney General* (2006), the SJC would unanimously agree with MFI and the attorney general. Justice Greaney, in a provocative concurring opinion joined by Justice Ireland, noted that the court was not deciding the further claims (not raised by GLAD) that *Goodridge* "may be irreversible because of its holding that no rational basis exists, or can be advanced, to support the definition of marriage proposed by the initiative and . . . that the *Goodridge* holding has become part of the fabric of the equality and liberty guarantees of our Constitution." Chief Justice Marshall asked questions at the oral argument suggesting that she might be open to such claims as well as a federal constitutional challenge under *Romer v. Evans*.[31]

In December 2005, the secretary of state certified 123,356 signatures, almost twice the number needed for the constitutional junior-DOMA to be placed on the calendar for the 2006 Con Con. As Gary Daffin had predicted, the proliferation of *married* lesbian and gay couples had transformed the political landscape, and MassEquality enjoyed support from a growing majority of legislators. But under the terms of the state constitution, MFI needed support from only one-quarter of the legislators (fifty votes) in successive 2006 and 2007 Con Cons to send the *petition-based* (rather than legislative-based) constitutional junior-DOMA to the voters in November 2008. Mineau was confident that traditional marriage would still prevail among voters five years after *Goodridge.*

Once again, the marriage equality coalition seemed to be fighting an uphill battle. Arline Isaacson urged the same strategy that had worked in 2002, the last time pro-gay strategists had faced a constitutional amendment proposed by a citizens' petition. To begin with, their legislative allies should pack the Con Con schedule with other amendments. Representative Emile Goguen had proposed a legislative constitutional amendment but never put it on the Con Con calendar because his Catholic allies were supporting the MFI-sponsored amendment. Isaacson went to Senator Barrios and asked him to file the Goguen amendment on the calendar before the MFI amendment could be added. If the Con Con calendar could be filled up with other proposals, the MFI amendment would not come up until late in the session, when a recess or adjournment motion could kill it, as in 2002. If legislators had already defeated the Goguen amendment by a majority vote, they could consider their constitutional duty discharged. In May 2006, Barrios asked that the Goguen amendment be listed on the Con Con calendar, with no objection from its sponsor.[32]

Next, Isaacson asked Senator Travaglini to help on a procedural issue. This surprised your authors: Wasn't he on the other side? As his toast at the Barrios wedding suggested, the senate president may have been ambivalent by 2006—critical of *Goodridge* but more comfortable with marriage equality and less enthusiastic about a constitutional response. Indeed, Travaglini was surrounded by MassEquality allies in the senate, including his whip and close buddy, Senator Robert Havern of Arlington. So Havern and DiMasi pitched this idea to Travaglini: work through the Con Con calendar as slowly as possible, leaving the MFI's amendment for the end of the session, when it might be cut off without a vote on the merits. The Con Con presiding officer was willing to go along with the first part of the scheme but did not commit to the rest. In July 2006, the Con Con recessed to November 9—way too early for MassEquality's comfort, but the senate president was no one's puppet.[33]

If all went according to plan, Speaker DiMasi would move for a recess to the last day of the legislative session, January 2, 2007, when MassEquality's allied legislators could run out the clock. This tactic drew pushback from those allies. They were sick of voting for postponements and avoidances, complained legislators who were eager to go on record in favor of marriage equality. On November 9, Travaglini called up the Goguen amendment, which was swiftly voted down. DiMasi moved to recess the session to 2:00 p.m. on January 2, 2007. The motion was approved by a surprisingly close margin, 109-87. Two weeks later, Governor Romney and several legislators brought a lawsuit asking for an injunction directing the president of the senate to comply with Article 48's command that the Con Con continue "until final action has been taken upon all amendments pending." On December 27, just days before the January 2 finale, the SJC unanimously ruled in *Doyle v. Secretary of the Commonwealth* that the general court, sitting as a constitutional convention, had an obligation to take an up-or-down vote on the amendment. The SJC did not enter the mandamus requested by the petitioners but left it to the good faith of the legislators to consider all amendments on its Con Con calendar.[34]

MassEquality felt the ruling was "devastating." Joined by Governor-elect Deval Patrick, MassEquality's lobbyists (Isaacson, Daffin, Shapiro, Solomon) spent the weekend before New Year's Day in a frustrating series of phone calls to their legislative allies, many of whom "were skittish about voting against what the court said was their duty." To hell with the SJC, Sal DiMasi said; full steam ahead with the strategy of a quick adjournment. But Travaglini had stopped talking with him and Isaacson, who feared that the senate president was completely rogue. Even before *Doyle,* Travaglini had called the Gay and Lesbian Political Caucus clueless and, in a tipsy rant, had told Isaacson that everyone was fed up with her recesses and adjournments.[35]

At the January 2 Con Con, Travaglini, the presiding officer, was not inclined to ignore the SJC's constitutional advice. Although MassEquality still hoped to run out the clock, Travaglini rushed through the process and, after midnight, called a quick vote on the MFI initiative amendment. It survived by a vote of 62-134, almost exactly the numbers counted by DiMasi and Isaacson. As predicted, senators voted against the amendment, 7-32, and representatives voted against it, 55-102. Former fans of civil unions like Brian Lees voted no, as did former stalwarts for the Catholic bishops such as Marian Walsh and John Rogers. Still, the amendment needed only fifty yesses in this session and then the next session to go to a popular vote. Cinderella was fighting her way through the crowd to reunite with Princess Charming, but sixty-two legislators stood in her path. Could she push aside thirteen of them and live happily ever after?

The 2006 elections had given pro–marriage equality Deval Patrick the governorship by a landslide. MassEquality gained four seats in the general court. The sixty-two votes cast for the MFI amendment in 2006 thus fell to no more than fifty-eight in the new legislature. On March 19, when Bob Travaglini abruptly resigned from the senate, Kris Mineau found his core group reduced to fifty-seven. He considered those votes rock-solid, but MassEquality did not agree. Armed with a $200,000 gift from the Gill Action Fund, followed by other large donations, Marc Solomon led an all-hands-on-deck campaign, described in his 2015 book *Winning Marriage*. With chapters in virtually every part of the state and dozens of field operatives and engaged families, MassEquality's goal was to convert nine to twelve legislators from yes to no on the MFI-sponsored amendment by June 14, when Senate President Therese Murray (a marriage equality ally) would convene the showdown Con Con. Winner takes the glass slipper.[36]

MassEquality lobbyists and activists held one-on-one meetings with representatives who had voted for the MFI initiative-amendment in January. A typical constituent meeting was organized by a pastor for Worcester County representative Paul Kujawski, a pro-life, pro-gun Catholic Conserva-Dem who went by the nickname Kujo. In the midst of a pleasant meet-and-greet session with the affable legislator, Deb Grzyb and Sharon Murphy identified themselves as a married couple. Kujo wanted to know more about them. In tears, the women talked about their twenty-seven years together and their wedding in Rockport. "Wow," Kujo responded. "Why didn't you say that sooner?" He had never confronted the realities of a lesbian family in person. Solomon had a follow-up meeting with him in which they talked about baseball, marriage equality, and Governor Patrick, whom Kujo liked tremendously. Solomon arranged for the governor to meet with Kujo, and on June 4 Deb and Sharon entertained him at their house. His faith pulled him in the other direction, however. Father Michael Roy, his spiritual mentor, prayerfully urged him to reaffirm traditional marriage. Kujo was undecided.[37]

By April, MassEquality had arranged no fewer than thirteen meetings between legislators like Kujo and families like Deb and Sharon's, as well as dozens of other meetings between legislators and community leaders. Forty field operatives were working the ground game. Dozens of pastors, rabbis, priests, businessmen, and labor leaders were writing op-eds and speaking out publicly in favor of marriage equality. Norma Shapiro and Ann Lambert (ACLU) teamed up with Mary Bonauto and Gary Buseck (GLAD) and Marc Solomon and Matt McTighe (MassEquality) to persuade legislators. Senator Stan Rosenberg told Bonauto that two of MFI's rock-solid house votes had already switched and that a couple of his fellow senators could be turned as well. Rosenberg said he wanted no more procedural dodges and was receptive to GLAD's constitutional pitch. As Justices Greaney and Ireland suggested in *Schulman,* the MFI initiative-amendment was fundamentally inconsistent with the core equality values of the state constitution, a view supported by the new attorney general, Martha Coakley. When Bonauto and Buseck carried that message to other legislators in April, they also claimed that the MFI amendment would probably be interpreted to foreclose civil unions and perhaps even domestic partnerships.[38]

Nonetheless, by the weekend before the June 14 Con Con, MassEquality had only three firm commitments to switch their votes, with Kujo and several others still in play. One long shot was Republican representative Richard Ross, a mortician from Wrentham whose Baptist wife had persuaded him to vote for the MFI amendment in January. A meeting on June 12 with his former colleague Patrick Guerriero, now with the Gill Action Fund, unsettled his thinking. Guerriero casually asked about the family funeral home—and Ross flashed back to advice from his late father: "Folks from all walks of life are going to ring that doorbell. When you open that door, don't look them up and down and judge them by what you think you see. You look them in the eye and you find one thing about their character or their makeup that you like about them, and you build a relationship around that. And I promise you this: nobody will ever leave your life as an adversary." The memory brought him to tears. Ross made up his mind at that moment, sitting in the parlor right below his father's portrait. It was two days before the vote.[39]

On June 13, Representative Anthony Verga, an elderly Conserva-Dem from Gloucester, fell on the stairway outside the house chamber and was hospitalized—meaning that there were now, at most, fifty-three votes for the MFI's amendment. That night, Kujo told his wife and sons that he was switching. Their response: About time, Dad! On the morning of the vote, Thursday, June 14, Springfield representative Angelo Puppolo told Marc Solomon that he was changing his vote to no. Later, Kris Mineau saluted his MFI ally, Representative Paul Loscocco, as he was walking into the house chamber for the Con Con. As Mineau gave him a thumbs up, Loscocco looked away. Mineau got a sinking feeling in his stomach. MFI had focused on securing a vote on the merits, and he realized that he had not been tracking his fifty-seven or fifty-eight "rock-solid" votes carefully enough. If Loscocco had turned, it was possible his side would sink below the fifty needed to get on the 2008 ballot.[40]

With thousands of supporters for each side chanting and waving signs outside the State House and hundreds lining the halls inside, Senate President Murray gaveled the convention to order at 1:08 p.m. The senate vote had to be taken by an alphabetical roll call because the electronic voting system was only wired for the representatives. Springfield senator Gale Candaras had always voted against MassEquality as a house member, but Therese Murray persuaded her to switch. Her "no" early in the roll call was a surprise to both sides. When Senator Mike Morrissey also switched, Mineau's jaw tightened and his shoulders slumped. "Mineau knew, right then, that he was going to lose the whole thing." The senators voted 34 no, 5 yes.[41]

Next the house members voted electronically. Everyone pushed a button, green for yes or red for no, and the boards on either side of the presiding officer's podium slowly lit up. With only five senators, the Marriage Coalition needed at least forty-five house members to vote for the MFI initiative-amendment. At the back of the chamber, Richard Ross was assuring Paul Loscocco that he was voting no when the clerk ordered them back to their desks to vote. "Richard Ross pushed the red button," reports Solomon. "He felt as if his was the deciding vote and . . . also was sure this would mark the end of his career. He burst into tears." Barbara L'Italien and Alice Wolf comforted him. The board revealed 116 red lights, 40 green lights.[42]

The MFI initiative-amendment failed on a 45-150 vote. Seven Conserva-Dems and two Republicans changed their votes between January and June 2007, and two freshmen representatives who had promised to support the amendment voted no. MassEquality had outhustled MFI, which had mobilized no significant grassroots effort beyond weaponizing pastors and priests. "We were naïve to think that we had the upper ground," Mineau told us. "My hat's off to them" for their remarkable effort to turn supporters of the amendment into no votes. This was the worst moment of his post–air force life, yet he could not have been more generous. Grace under fire is the hallmark of the military hero. Grace in the wake of crushing disappointment is the hallmark of a true mensch. Kris Mineau is both.[43]

Why *Goodridge* Was the Critical Moment

The period between when *Goodridge* was handed down and the last Con Con concluded—November 18, 2003, to June 14, 2007—was the most critical period in this book's story. If Hawaiʻi was the marriage equality movement's Dunkirk, Massachusetts was its Normandy, the beachhead from which the marriage equality forces would radiate—but only if its supporters could protect *Goodridge* against a constitutional amendment overriding it. Because supporters were successful, millions of gay Americans who felt alone, disparaged, and outcast enjoyed the validation that came with marriage recognition. It was their Cinderella moment, too.

The *Goodridge* debate also created the conditions for falsifying the stereotypes about lesbian and gay people and their families of choice. The lawsuit and the resulting political battles publicized the stories of hundreds of couples and their children. No longer were they "virtually normal." They became simply normal. Were many gays selfish, hedonistic, predatory, and unfaithful to family values? Of course—as were many straights, from Bill Clinton to Newt Gingrich to Donald Trump. After *Goodridge,* stereotypes of diseased gay men preying on boys were being displaced by images of lesbian and gay couples raising children (sometimes children unwanted by their heterosexual parents) in healthy environments.

Goodridge also offered a real-world test of the defense of marriage argument. Would expanding (or redefining) marriage undermine the institution? In the four years before 2004, the Massachusetts marriage rate averaged 5.85 per one thousand residents (a sharp decline from the 1990s). In 2004, when the commonwealth started to issue marriage licenses to gay couples, the rate jumped to 6.5, and it held at 6.2 the next year. The divorce rate dropped. Both rates declined over the next five years. Taking the country's overall erosion in marriage and divorce rates in this period as the baseline, Massachusetts in 2009 looked better, from a marriage-is-good perspective, than it looked in 2003. It is not clear that *Goodridge* caused this modest development—but neither did gay marriage finish off a declining institution.[44]

When the sky did not fall upon the commonwealth, when polygamy did not gain traction, when children reared in lesbian and gay families turned out fine, and when marriage rates went up and divorce rates fell in the years after the decision, the standard Pandora's box arguments against marriage equality took a hit. To be sure, the deeper defense of marriage argument—the one actually developed from Christian premises—was impervious to short-term tests. But in light of the tangible needs of lesbian and gay families, the traditional definition of marriage could not easily rest upon abstract theology.

Most important for the marriage equality movement, *Goodridge* inspired activists all around the country to think that they, too, could enjoy this Cinderella moment: they could persuade judges, legislators, governors, and administrators to support the idea of opening marriage to lesbian, gay, bisexual, and transgender couples. The Massachusetts and Vermont activists had shown how to do grassroots constitutionalism. Their success was not possible without a massive organizational effort at the community level and without significant infusions of money, but success started with and rested upon personal journey stories like Mary Bonauto's, which opened the previous chapter: I am a good person, and I love persons of the same sex. My partner and I are raising children, and we are doing a good job. Can you find it in your heart and conscience to support our full inclusion in the state's family law? Do unto others as you would have them do to you. As Representative Byron Rushing of Suffolk put it at the end, "The best argument for gay marriage is gay marriage."[45]

Recall that Bonauto—who led the team of lawyers, activists, and allies to win the *Goodridge* case—could not advance her journey story all the way to marriage because she and her family lived in Maine, a junior-DOMA state. She insisted, as Mitt Romney did, that she and Jenny secure their marriage through the proper legal process. So in 2005, GLAD brought a constitutional lawsuit to invalidate the 1913 law excluding most out-of-state couples from *Goodridge* marriages. With only Justice Ireland in dissent, the SJC upheld the law as a reasonable regulation of marriage licensing. Governor Deval Patrick, Mass-Equality, and their allies persuaded the general court to repeal the 1913 law in 2008. At that point, Jenny and Mary became a lawfully wedded couple—long after they and their daughters had become a family.[46]

10 • The New Maginot Line

Maggie Gallagher has the eyes of an unheeded prophet. They are dark brown, and they glow with intelligence, moral sense, and sadness. They are frustrated because knowledge comes too late, and the prophet who speaks inconvenient truths goes unheard.

Cassandra was the raven-haired daughter of King Priam and Queen Hecuba of Troy. Because she refused sexual favors to Apollo, the vengeful deity granted her the gift of foreseeing the future but without credibility. Cassandra warned her brother Paris not to kidnap the beautiful Helen. She warned her parents that Troy would be destroyed if they allowed Helen to remain. She warned her fellow citizens that the Trojan horse was a gift bearing Greeks. Cassandra lived to see every unheeded prophecy come to pass: the Trojan War, the sack of Troy, the death of her parents. So many losses that could have been avoided, if only people had listened.

Maggie Gallagher's prophecy is that America's consumerist culture is the cause of our national malaise, reflected in the decline of marriage. The hedonistic siege on the culture of self-giving marriage has been laid by liberals, feminists, lawyers; they are modern Greeks whose Trojan horse is gay marriage. Maggie warns her countrymen not to bring the horse into the walls of the city. What could go wrong? For the last seventeen years, she has answered: Plenty.

Maggie Gallagher's journey began in Lake Oswego, Oregon, an affluent suburb of Portland. Married in July 1956, William Walter Gallagher and the former Darrilyn Doris Stentz raised Maggie and her siblings as a closely knit family. On their first date, Bill Gallagher and his future wife chose names for their future kids (Kathleen, William, Maggie, Colleen). He taught his children to think for themselves and to see problems in light of the broader world.

Maggie Gallagher

Faithful husband, devoted—indeed doting—father, and public-spirited citizen, Bill Gallagher was the model of manhood and fatherhood that would inspire and haunt Maggie for the rest of her life.[1]

Maggie was an inward kid and a voracious reader. In the 1970s, she discovered Ayn Rand's libertarian philosophy. Maggie especially admired Dagny Taggart, the bold, complicated individualist at the center of *Atlas Shrugged* (1957). A member of the Yale College Class of 1982, Maggie was active in the Yale Political Union, where she starred in the Party of the Right and met future conservative luminaries like Steven Calabresi, Lee Liberman Otis, and David McIntosh—who later founded the Federalist Society at Yale Law School. Her classmates remember her as intense and socially awkward, but Maggie was well respected for her brains and debating skill.[2]

Maggie views her younger self as a naïve woman who uncritically accepted liberal views about sexual freedom. In her junior and senior years, she had a serious boyfriend, a younger Party of the Right student who wrote editorials for a Yale magazine. In spring 1982, she discovered she was pregnant. That was a shock and a turning point in her personal and intellectual life. Sexual expression and pregnancy were supposed to be separate, but here she was carrying a child she was not prepared to abort (love of family trumped Ayn Rand). So she had a heart-to-heart with her boyfriend. Right before spring break, "I was in his room and he had to go do something, and I was going to fly out in a couple of hours, had to get to the airport. And the last thing he said to me was, 'I'll be back in 30 minutes.' And then he wasn't." The soon-to-be-father left her sitting in his room. That summer, Maggie returned to Lake Oswego and bore her son, Patrick, as the autumn leaves were dropping. The father, now a doctor with a second family, recalls that he and Maggie agreed that he should be involved with their son, but "she had an idea of how she wanted things to go," and he backed away.[3]

With cause to be angry with the cad from college, Maggie instead blamed the liberal feminist culture. She and her boyfriend were enjoying their version of sexual liberation, and their future was a matter of each partner's individual choice. Pregnancy messes up that liberal script—especially for the woman carrying the new human life. The man still enjoys a lot of freedom, and Maggie's Yale boyfriend took advantage of it, but what choice did the soon-to-be-mother have? After bearing and raising a child, "the limitations of Randianism became obvious: life is a gift. Unearned love is the basis of all Being."[4]

Providing a home for Patrick Gallagher meant getting a job. Maggie became a successful writer for the *National Review*. In 1989, she published *Enemies of Eros,* an indictment of liberal feminism—especially the notions that women and men are basically the same and that traditional gender roles and sexual taboos are just made-up conventions. "A society which tries to reduce sex to its pleasures, to cut off gender from sex, sex from Eros [the deep sexuality of human nature], Eros from children, cuts itself and its people off from the resources we need to survive and to triumph. For these are . . . the only bonds strong enough to build a future which our children may enjoy." In the chapter titled "Sex and Justice," she assailed the liberal feminist view that marriage was just a contract between consenting adults. Bill and Darrilyn Gallagher had it right. Women's liberation and the sexual revolution—coincidentally, the twin forces that propelled the gay rights movement—were a big cultural mistake.[5]

Written in an aggressive style, with confident and provocative barbs sharply lobbed against liberal platitudes, *Enemies of Eros* was a jeremiad that made Maggie Gallagher a mini-celebrity in conservative intellectual circles. Following that success, she married Raman Srivastav, whom she had known from her

Party of the Right days at Yale, and had a second son, Bair Srivastav, in 1995. Although by the 1980s she had returned to the Catholic faith of her childhood, her husband is Hindu. Her personal and professional success continued when she found a home at the Institute for American Values (IAV).

Founded in 1987 by David Blankenhorn, the IAV sought common ground for proposals that protected core American values and institutions such as marriage. A southern liberal, Blankenhorn believed that the root of much unhappiness and social decay in our country is that increasing numbers of children are being raised without fathers. Gallagher, nostalgic for her own father, who passed away in 1991, and focused on providing father figures to her son Patrick, admired and agreed with Blankenhorn. "What David did was extraordinary," she says. "He forged a genuinely cross-ideological coalition of people who disagree about non-marital sex and abortion and other things around a key question: Is it good or is it not good so many children are growing up outside intact marriages and with diminishing contact with fathers and with women shouldering the burden of parenting alone? [If] you said yes we would like more mothers and fathers raising children together in marriage, you were in regardless about what else we disagreed about." Blankenhorn brought social conservatives, academic progressives, and nonaligned policy wonks together in a common mission: to help children by supporting means to assure all of them fathers as well as mothers, but without demonizing single parents. His "marriage movement" offered more sophisticated policy arguments for traditional marriage than those advanced by government officials and lawyers in marriage equality lawsuits.[6]

Moreover, Blankenhorn and Gallagher were anti-anti-gay. Religion-based defenders of traditional marriage often demonized homosexuals in abusive, stereotype-driven terms. An example from 1997: "Homosexual living arrangements under the guise of marriage are not only sterile, incapable, and insufficient, they are destructive to the very fabric of our society. The strategy to inculcate active homosexual practice into our society as a favored institution is synonymous with injecting a cancer into a healthy body." In contrast, Blankenhorn began most debates about gay marriage by saying that discrimination against lesbian and gay persons was flat wrong. Likewise, Gallagher treated gay people with respect and, in person, great affection. Though she has irritated gay people with her blunt rhetoric and take-no-prisoners debating style, we urge the reader to evaluate her based upon her actual theories and arguments.[7]

As a marriage theorist, Gallagher rejected the liberal-feminist theory of the family, especially insofar as it assumed the following:

(1) *The Liberal State.* The state ought to be neutral regarding individual romantic and parenting choices.

(2) *Individual Happiness.* Sexual happiness is necessary for human flourishing, and there is a natural variation in sexual preferences.

(3) *Sex Sameness.* Men and women are essentially the same. Traditional gender roles stem from irrational stereotyping.

The consequences of this theory were that the state should recognize a wide array of family forms, including cohabitation and domestic partnership, and should let people freely exit relationships (including marriages) that no longer suit them.

Against the foregoing individualistic theory of the family, Gallagher set forth a marriage-centered theory of the state and of the family:

(1) *The Normative State.* The state ought to provide a prescriptive, values-based structure for family formation. Because private relationship choices have third-party effects, the state ought to support the optimal structure, namely, one-man, one-woman marriage.

(2) *Relational Joy.* Interpersonal commitment is necessary for human flourishing. Marital sexuality seals and deepens the connection between the spouses and, at the same time, deepens their connection with their children.

(3) *Sex/Gender Complementarity.* Men and women are essentially different, and their difference is rooted in the gendered nature of marital (procreative) sexuality. It is essential to offer children both male and female parenting styles and role models.

Under that theory, no-fault divorce laws, decriminalization of cohabitation and sex outside of marriage, and reproductive choice regimes had drained marriage of much of its cultural strength. Marriage as a social institution, centered on the well-being of children, was being lost—through no fault of gay people. But the one-man, one-woman definition of marriage was its Maginot Line, the last line of defense against total collapse. Gay marriage, as the ultimate cultural symbol of the separation of marriage from children and their needs, would obliterate that line.[8]

Gallagher's marriage-based theory of the family and her Maginot Line understanding of its fragile status were part of an intellectually and spiritually diverse response by traditionalists to the marriage equality movement in the first decade of the twenty-first century. Their goal was to accomplish what liberal feminists had failed to do in the 1970s: amend the US Constitution. They never came close to that, but they did transform the marriage debate into a serious discussion of family law in America.

The New Party of the Right

In *The Case for Marriage* (2000), Gallagher and social scientist Linda Waite mounted an empirical attack on the liberal norm of marriage as a contract between consenting adults, each seeking to maximize her or his happiness. Waite and Gallagher assembled an impressive social science case supporting lifelong traditional marriage: married women as well as men were happier, more productive, and healthier than single or even cohabiting persons—and the benefit was largest for spouses who viewed their union as a lifetime commitment and not in contractual, till-the-sex-gets-boring terms. Moreover, there were social costs to contract-based marriage, and third-party costs to children whose lives were rendered less secure. The authors proposed that divorces should be harder to obtain, tax policy should support married families, and the state should discourage cohabitation and domestic partnerships. While Gallagher and Waite convincingly showed a correlation between marriage and good health and so forth, they did not prove that marriage *caused* those effects. Selection effects could be at work: healthy, prosperous adults might be more likely to get married in the first place.[9]

In January 2000, Blankenhorn hosted a meeting of more than one hundred scholars and policy intellectuals concerned with declining marriage rates and rising cohabitation rates, rising rates of nonmarital births, and high rates of divorce. These trends constituted what Harvard sociologist Andrew Cherlin called the *deinstitutionalization of marriage*. As Figure 1 illustrates, the percentage of Americans who were married was steadily eroding, and the percentage of births outside of marriage was skyrocketing. The convening institutions summarized their views in *The Marriage Movement: A Statement of Principles* (2000): "Marriage is a productive institution, not a consumer good. Marriage does not simply certify existing loving relationships, but rather transforms the ways in which couples act toward one another, toward their children, and toward the future." The more marriage became privatized, the less effective it would be as a productive institution that helped couples "achieve their goal of a lasting bond."[10]

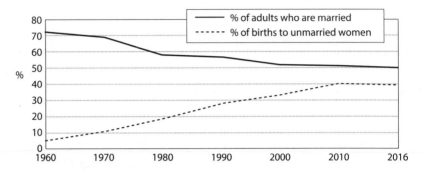

Figure 1 Percentage of married adults and nonmarital births, 1960–2016.
(Chart by Bill Nelson.)

Because privatized marriage generated social and third-party harms, the state should encourage marriage and not remain neutral, should not recognize or provide marital benefits to competing institutions, and should discourage hasty divorces. On April 6, 2000, shortly after the conference, the Southern Baptist Convention, the US Conference of Catholic Bishops, and the National Association of Evangelicals entered into an ecumenical accord along much the same lines as the marriage movement's statement of principles.[11]

Gallagher was the most prolific secular author pressing a normative theory of the family. In *What Is Marriage For?*, she articulated the movement's shared vision: "Marriage is the way in which every society attempts to channel the erotic energies of men and women into a relatively narrow but highly fruitful channel—to give every child the father his or her heart desires. Above all—normal marriage is normative. Marriage is not primarily a way of expressing approval for an infinite variety of human affectional or sexual ties" such as friendship or a sexual relationship. "It consists, by definition, of isolating and preferring certain types of unions over others." Gallagher and Waite's *Case for Marriage* had discussed marriage for lesbian and gay couples. Waite favored it, while Gallagher did not. They agreed that "same-sex couples would reap some, but not all, the benefits of marriage" and that the effect on children would depend on whether "gender is irrelevant to the public project of marriage." Social science had nothing to tell us about that, they said, so policy makers must fall back on religious and moral views. Gallagher's views were shaped by her family background, her faith, and her regret that Patrick was not reared by his biological father.[12]

Another intellectual movement provided a secular theory of sexuality and gender that complemented Gallagher's conception of marriage. The parent of that movement was Robert George. Born in Morgantown, West Virginia, Robby was the oldest of five boys raised by Joseph and Catherine George, both children of coal miners. Joseph earned a good living as a liquor dealer, treasured his wife, and invested all his free time in his flock of kids; Catherine presided over the household and instilled in the boys a sense of Roman Catholic moral responsibility. Channeling his mother's disapproval of sexual license, Robby watched with judgmental eyes as men wooed women with arguments that they should join the sexual revolution, "covering over lust with a patina of significance," he recalls. "It was my first but by no means my last experience with liberal hypocrisy." Some of his female schoolmates remember him as a moralistic and intellectual bully.[13]

From parochial school, Robby graduated in swift succession to Swarthmore College, Harvard University, and Oxford University. At Swarthmore, he met Cindy Schrom, whom he would date and marry. At Oxford, he studied under Professor John Finnis, the founding philosopher of "new natural law," an effort to derive universal moral rules from the necessary first principles of human existence, namely, foundational basic goods. Finnis argued that the great thinkers of Western civilization—from Plato and Aristotle through St. Augustine and St. Thomas Aquinas and beyond—had converged on certain universal moral truths that could be logically derived from human nature. George devoured this body of learning at Oxford and brought it with him to Princeton University, where he was appointed to the political science department in 1986. After stormy meetings in which the department's liberals wrung their hands over promoting an out-of-the-closet religious and moral conservative, Princeton awarded George tenure in 1993. He rapidly consolidated his position as the country's premier conservative philosopher by writing a series of influential articles and books and by raising money to fund his James Madison Program in American Ideals and Institutions. A brilliant classroom teacher and academic mentor, he has been training the next generation of conservative theorists and policy makers.[14]

In 1998, George published "Marriage and the Illusion of Moral Neutrality." Like Gallagher, he maintained that marriage ought to be a normative institution, channeling people's choices into good relationships. In *Making Men Moral* (1993), he had claimed that law inevitably took sides in moral debates and that an important purpose of law was to preserve what he would later call the polity's "moral ecology." The earlier book endorsed "pluralistic perfectionism," in which the government endorsed and instructed but the citizens ultimately made their own choices. In the 1998 essay, George contrasted marriage and friendship. The state did nothing to encourage friendships—but strongly encouraged marriages. Why? Liberals didn't have a good answer, because they understood marriage as an *instrumental good*, existing for the happiness or fulfillment of the partners or, as Gallagher and Blankenhorn argued, for the best interests of children. George claimed that the best justification was that marriage was an *intrinsic good*, an end in itself that yielded public happiness beyond its benefits in providing fleeting pleasure, higher income, or longer lives. The state itself would be unworthy if it did not protect, nurture, and reward intrinsic goods such as marriage.[15]

Why was marriage an intrinsic good? As a matter of natural logic, George argued, marriage was a uniquely *comprehensive* union, meaning that it was shared at several levels at once—emotional, spiritual, and bodily. "And the really interesting evidence that it is comprehensive is that it is anchored in bodily sharing," he suggested in a subsequent interview. "Ordinary friendships wouldn't be friendships anymore if they involved bodily sharing." Sex was the key to this "comprehensive unity." Only "procreative-type" sex acts could consummate this "multilevel" mind-body union. Each opposite-sex partner was incomplete for the task; yet together they created, in the language of Scripture, a "one-flesh union." Procreative intercourse between a sterile couple could still deliver this comprehensive union, but oral or anal sex, even between husband and wife, was morally objectionable because it treated our bodies as instruments of pleasure rather than as participants in the essential marital act of self-giving.[16]

Gay people found George's analysis baffling and off-putting, as it seemed to deny them access to the deepest expression of their humanity. Recall April DeBoer, the Michigan nurse introduced in our prologue. At the same time that George was spelling out the details of his natural law theory of sexuality and gender, April responded to the law's encouragement by marrying a young man, in 1992. She wanted to have children, but the experience of procreative intercourse with a man was, for her, unnatural, unpleasant, and alienating. She and her husband separated after seven years of marriage and then divorced. For April DeBoer, marriage did not represent an intrinsic good, and she did not partake of the noninstrumental joy Robby George described until she made a lifetime commitment to Jayne Rowse. Why should the virtuous state *not* encourage marriage for couples like April and Jayne? Would marriage not provide a more stable environment for their children?[17]

The Federal Marriage Amendment

In October 1998, Catholic University's Marriage Law Project called a meeting of traditional marriage supporters to discuss strategy in Scottsdale, Arizona. Representatives of the US Conference of Catholic Bishops, the Church of Jesus Christ of Latter-day Saints, the Alliance Defense Fund (ADF), and the National Coalition to Protect Marriage joined law professors and marriage activists from several key states. David Orgon Coolidge, the Marriage Law Project's director, proposed that the coalition consider a constitutional amendment to permanently bar same-sex marriage. "Advocates of [Coolidge's] proposal noted that there would likely be a moment of strong reaction against the legalization of same-sex marriage when it happened and they thought that would be the golden moment to introduce and get passed a constitutional amendment to outlaw same-sex marriage." With strong Republican support and acquiescence from Clintonian Democrats, the advocates optimistically hoped for congressional approval within months and swift ratification by the needed thirty-eight states. Family law scholar Lynn Wardle opposed the idea, because such an amendment would further federalize family law and because it was inconsistent with their message that state voters and legislators, not judges, should resolve marriage issues.[18]

Coolidge's proposal was taken up by a tall, darkly handsome paladin with his own compelling journey story. Born in 1964, Matt Daniels was raised in a rough neighborhood in New York's Spanish Harlem by a single mother, who emphasized education as Matt's only way out of poverty. He had, he says, "a survival-driven work ethic" that helped him graduate from Dartmouth College in 1985. In 1991, after the death of his beloved mother, he underwent a conversion experience: inspired by his mixed-race half brother, he "found his epiphany of faith in the black church." Following his mentors, he came to believe the biggest problem afflicting minority youth was that they grew up in homes without fathers. The idea of marriage as the most effective force for imposing some obligations on deadbeat dads was personal to him. Because his own father ("an aspiring intellectual and irresponsible man") walked out on the family when Matt was two years old, his working mother and the family were left unprotected in an unsafe neighborhood.[19]

In 1999, Daniels founded the Alliance for Marriage. At a press conference in August 2000, the Reverend Lois Poag-Ray of the Pilgrim African Methodist Episcopal Church introduced the Alliance and its six-foot-five-inch executive director. Daniels emotionally declared that "marriage is what makes fatherhood something more than a biological event, by connecting men to children that they bring into the world." But society was not doing well at this, because one-third of all children were being raised in fatherless households, triple the number from thirty years ago. He wanted to make sure that every child would have a father, to encourage unwed parents to get married, and to caution married couples not to divorce. This agenda was attractive to minority communities of faith, who were well represented within the Alliance. Important advisory board members included former representative Walter Fauntroy of the National Black Leadership Roundtable and President David DeLeon of the Hispanic Association for Bilingual and Bicultural Ministries.[20]

From his service with the Massachusetts Family Institute, Daniels believed that gay marriage could soon come to the Bay State and asked former judge Robert Bork to draft a constitutional amendment. Bork recruited a dream team: Robby George (Princeton), Gerry Bradley (Notre Dame), and Mary Ann Glendon (Harvard)—among the most distinguished Catholic intellectuals in America. In what Bradley recalls as "round-table electronic discussions," they considered three different strategies:

(1) *DOMA-Lite.* Bar same-sex marriage, but allow Hawai'i reciprocal beneficiaries, Vermont civil unions, and municipal or state domestic partnerships.

(2) *Super-DOMA.* Consider conjugal marriage the only legitimate situs for sexual relationships. Bar civil unions but not reciprocal beneficiaries or modest domestic partnership ordinances.

(3) *Super-Duper-DOMA.* Deny homosexual couples all couples-based state benefits, rights, or duties.

In 1995, George and Bradley had coauthored an important statement of the new natural law on marriage, in which they argued that any union sealed by nonprocreative sodomy is degrading and ought not to be endorsed or in any way encouraged by the normative state. So they wrote off option (1), DOMA-Lite.[21]

Daniels and the other drafters felt that option (3), the Super-Duper-DOMA, went too far. Legislatures, in their view, ought to be free "to extend benefits/protection/duties to unmarried couples (including but not only same-sex couples)," such as hospital visitation rights. The Alliance's political advisers believed it would be impossible to sell such an ambitious constitutional amendment to legislators, who would feel no urgency until some state actually began issuing marriage licenses. So the drafters went with option (2), a Super-DOMA that would reaffirm marriage as the special normative baseline for state recognition of adult relationships but allow friends and caregivers some benefits that no one would mistake for marriage.[22]

A Super-DOMA would bar judges from imposing civil unions. Should it also bar legislators from enacting comprehensive domestic partnership or civil union laws? Bork thought not: "To try to prevent legislatures from enacting permission for civil unions by constitutional amendment would be to reach too far. It would give opponents the opening to say we do not trust the people when, in fact, we are trying to prevent courts from thwarting the will of the people." Bradley, on the other hand, *argued* for the view that by limiting 'marriage' to [one] man and [one] woman the [proposed amendment] implicitly excluded state recognition of any other *sexual* relationship (as such) as properly the predicate of benefits and privileges and rights." Although this view was consistent with George's natural law philosophy, in the final analysis it appears that George went along with Bork's view that their language would permit legislatures to adopt civil union laws.[23]

While the drafting team was deliberating, Matt Daniels was coordinating with his allies in Congress, such as Texas representative Joe Pitts, the chair of the House Values Action Team. Congressional staffers advised the drafting team to keep it simple and to avoid any suggestion that the amendment was anti-gay. In July 2001, Daniels unveiled his proposed Federal Marriage Amendment (FMA):

> Marriage in the United States shall consist only of the union of a man and a woman. Neither this Constitution or the constitution of any State, nor state or federal law, shall be construed to require that marital status or the legal incidents thereof be conferred upon unmarried couples or groups.

The goal of the FMA was to entrench one-man, one-woman marriage at all levels of government and to prevent judicial decisions requiring recognition of same-sex unions or marriages. There were several ambiguities. Would the 2000 Vermont civil unions law violate the FMA, as written? Bradley thought it violated the first sentence, because civil unions were "marriage in all but name," but Bork thought otherwise. The ACLU feared that the first sentence went even further than Bradley thought it did. Would the FMA bar a state court from interpreting state laws or the state constitution to extend some benefits to lesbian and gay couples? The Alliance's website made explicit its expectation that the FMA would allow legislatures (but not courts) to create civil unions, domestic partnerships, and ad hoc distribution of marriage rights to unmarried couples.[24]

On May 15, 2002, the FMA (H.J. Res. 93) was introduced into the US House of Representatives by Mississippi Democrat Ronnie Shows, supported by twenty-two cosponsors, including Texas Republican Joe Pitts and Indiana

Republican Mike Pence. It languished in the House Judiciary Committee, and Shows lost his reelection bid in November. But later that month, the FMA caught a break when Focus on the Family's James Dobson hosted Daniels on his radio show and endorsed the FMA as necessary to save the American family. In his 2003 *Newsletter*, Dobson asserted that gay marriage was "D-Day, or the Gettysburg or Stalingrad" for the family values movement. With an audience of millions and credibility within traditionalist circles, Dobson's endorsement was momentous, especially in light of grumbling by other family values organizations that the FMA did not go far enough.[25]

On May 21, 2003, the FMA was introduced once again in the House of Representatives (as H.J. Res. 56), this time by Representative Marilyn Musgrave, representing Colorado Springs, home to Focus on the Family. As in the previous Congress, there seemed to be very little interest in moving the FMA to a vote in the House or even introducing it in the Senate. But 2003 proved to be a watershed year for both marriage equality and the FMA.

The Conference at Osprey Point

In April 2003, David Blankenhorn hosted a retreat for fifty marriage-policy experts at the Osprey Point Conference Center, a scenic Maryland resort facing the Chesapeake Bay. The agenda was to discuss social and political strategies for reviving marriage. On the last day, Diane Sollee, the founder of Smart Marriages (a marriage education network), brought up the topic of gay marriage. Blankenhorn had structured the conference to avoid that very topic, for he knew it would create a fissure between the social liberals like himself and social conservatives like Gallagher. But his colleague Elizabeth Marquardt had flagged the issue in a note to the participants: "By avoiding the topic of same-sex marriage, we may appear to be sidestepping what many view as the central civil rights issue of our time. In addition, by avoiding discussion of same-sex marriage, we are also avoiding the question of how children in those unions fare."[26]

Blankenhorn tried to postpone the discussion, but Gallagher objected: "This is about to happen. Look, we are the 'Marriage People'! What do we think about it?" Most of the participants were nodding their heads: Why shouldn't they talk about the elephant in the room? So the conference officially adjourned—but a few dozen participants who wanted to discuss the issue were invited to retire to an adjoining room. Bill Doherty led the discussion fishbowl style: start with five people, and then five more, until everyone has had a chance to participate.

Doherty opened: "What do we think about homosexuality? What should be the government's stance?"[27]

Gallagher was on the first panel; naturally, she resisted the question: "I don't care about policy toward homosexuality. What really matters is marriage. Once 'Adam and Steve' can get married, it will be obvious that procreation and rearing biological children by mom and dad is not what marriage is about." Many in the room had not thought about this possibility. Gallagher's comments kickstarted an intense discussion of the broader issues raised by same-sex marriage. As Blankenhorn remembers it, some participants, such as Sollee, embraced the possibility of marriage for lesbian and gay couples. They had the same concerns as straight couples, including child-raising responsibilities. The academic conveners of the conference—Blankenhorn, Doherty, and Don Browning of the University of Chicago's Divinity School—were undecided about the consequences of gay marriage for their pro-marriage movement.

But most of the participants agreed with Gallagher. Same-sex marriage, they thought, was not only an issue they *might* be interested in—it was an issue they *must* be interested in. The ability of two women to get married would be a "civilizational rupture" that would confirm the cultural message that marriage is all about two people's romantic relationship—not about children, society, or the future of the human race. How about lesbian couples raising children? Just as concerning, Gallagher said, because that would entrench the social message that fathers were not necessary for families. She looked at Blankenhorn, whose life project was promoting fatherhood. The participants found the issue more urgent than they had anticipated: the policy wonks had a lot to contribute to this debate.

Osprey was a turning point. Previously, private opposition to same-sex marriage was overwhelmingly dominated by faith-based groups, and its most respectable arguments were those developed by prominent Catholic and Mormon intellectuals who emphasized some combination of tradition and history, religious doctrine, and morality. After Osprey Point, opposition to same-sex marriage was reinforced and sometimes led by social policy institutions represented at the conference—the Bush-Cheney administration, the marriage projects at Rutgers and Catholic Universities, and the Institute for American Values—and its arguments increasingly came from family policy analysts such as Gallagher, Marquardt, Horn, and ultimately Blankenhorn. These intellectuals tended to emphasize the deinstitutionalization of marriage and the importance of reinforcing or reestablishing a public culture in which marriage was understood as a social institution and as a durable and optimal structure for families, especially those with children. Because they were focused on social science evidence and culture, the policy advocates were more easily able to avoid sectarian arguments and anti-gay stereotyping.

Afterward, Maggie Gallagher met with David Blankenhorn back at the IAV offices. He was inclined to avoid the gay marriage issue and keep the IAV focused on the positive agenda of supporting a marriage culture. In full Cassandra mode, Gallagher was frustrated that Blankenhorn could not see how stopping same-sex marriage *was* the positive agenda for reinvigorating a marriage culture. If we succeeded in stopping the redefinition of marriage, she argued, we could pivot to turning back no-fault divorce and stigmatizing deadbeat dads.

"You cannot do that work here," David lamented. So Maggie resigned as the head of the IAV's marriage project. They both cried. "I really don't function well with bosses," Maggie told us. David smiled when he heard that. In July 2003, Gallagher founded the Institute for Marriage and Public Policy, which immediately became a one-woman think tank for the FMA.[28]

The Vatican and the Arlington Group

That the FMA had been drafted by leading Catholic intellectuals meant that the Catholic Church would support the measure—even though it could be read as allowing legislation recognizing civil unions. Gerry Bradley and Bowie Kuhn, the former commissioner of Major League Baseball, contacted dozens of Catholic bishops to drum up support for the FMA and, ultimately, to secure an official endorsement from the US Conference of Catholic Bishops. Meanwhile, the Vatican was following these developments, presumably guided by Mary Ann Glendon, an FMA drafter who later served as the US ambassador to the Holy See.[29]

On June 3, 2003, Cardinal Joseph Ratzinger issued the Vatican's "Considerations Regarding Proposals to Give Legal Recognition to Unions Between Homosexual Persons." "Considerations" reaffirmed that "sexual complementarity and fruitfulness belong to the very nature of marriage" and that association of this sacramental institution with sinful homosexual acts would be an unthinkable heresy. Its final paragraphs were addressed to "Catholic politicians," who had "a moral duty" to oppose homosexual marriages. If a law permitting such marriages were already in force, as in the Netherlands, "the Catholic politician must oppose it in the ways that are possible for him and make his opposition known; it is his duty to witness to the truth. If it is not possible to repeal such a law completely, the Catholic politician . . . could licitly support proposals aimed at limiting the harm done by such a law." The US Conference of Catholic Bishops called for support of "marriage as a unique, essential relationship and institution."[30]

Evangelicals were also focusing on the marriage amendment, through a more ad hoc organizational structure. In spring 2003, the Reverend Donald Wildmon sounded the alarm in an email to Paul Weyrich: "If we all went our separate ways we would not amount to much. However, if we could all sing off the same sheet of music, we could be a significant force." Weyrich, the cofounder of the Moral Majority and "the Lenin of social conservatism," proposed that the top guns of the leading traditional values groups try to pool their resources. Sandy Rios, the president of Concerned Women for America (CWA), volunteered her condominium in Arlington, Virginia, and they met there in June 2003. By Weyrich's account, about fourteen organizations were represented.[31]

The attendees "viewed the prospect of gay marriage not only as a genuine threat, but also as a likely catalyst for rousing the Evangelical grass-roots from their slumber." The idea was to fund a marriage project and coordinate their efforts around a collective strategy. The "Arlington Group" met about every six weeks after that, usually in Washington, DC. By 2006, its membership had grown to seventy-five organizations. Dobson was the national chairman and the key figure. "If it had not been for Dr. Dobson, the FMA would have been discarded in the fall of 2003."[32]

Unlike the pragmatic Catholics, Evangelicals tended to take the perfectionist position that God allowed no tactical compromises. As Rios put it, a constitutional amendment barring same-sex marriage but allowing legislatures to create civil unions would be "like a [Thirteenth] Amendment that said you can own people but just don't call it slavery." At its October meeting, the Arlington Group voted 22-2 to seek broader language than that reflected in the current version of the FMA. Dobson, Rios, and Richard Land of the Southern Baptist Convention pressed the FMA's sponsors to revise the proposed amendment to make clear that state legislatures could not pass laws recognizing same-sex marriages, civil unions, or domestic partnerships. In November, Rios led a delegation of twenty Christian conservative groups to Capitol Hill. "I deal in political reality," retorted Marilyn Musgrave. "That's why I've been firm." A constitutional amendment was going nowhere without a two-thirds vote in both chambers of Congress. Joe Pitts told the Arlington Group that protection-of-life and flag-burning amendments had stalled for exactly this reason. After intense discussions, Musgrave and Daniels "persuaded most—but not all—of the activists to their way of thinking. Dobson says he remains 'bothered' by the prospect of an amendment that would tolerate civil unions. But, he adds, 'I fear it's not possible to get more than that.'" Although the CWA left the Arlington Group over this issue, most of the other organizations followed Dobson's lead. Between 2003 and 2004, donations to Focus on the Family increased by $30 million, to about $147 million.[33]

Lawrence v. Texas (2003)

Meanwhile, the US Supreme Court was considering a case that would raise the stakes of the marriage debate. The Texas Homosexual Conduct Law made it a crime for consenting adults of the same sex (but not different sex) to engage in private anal or oral sex. Representing two Houston men arrested under the law, Lambda Legal asked the Supreme Court to overrule *Bowers v. Hardwick* (1986), which had upheld consensual sodomy laws as consistent with the due process clause of the Fourteenth Amendment. Lambda also argued that the law was inconsistent with *Romer v. Evans* (1996), where the Supreme Court had ruled that state measures singling out lesbian and gay citizens for special exclusion were vulnerable to attack under the equal protection clause. Lambda's case for overruling *Bowers* was buttressed by amicus briefs from the American Bar Association (ABA) and several unexpected allies, including the Republican Unity Coalition and the Cato Institute.[34]

Although twenty-nine churches and faith groups filed briefs supporting the challengers, no denomination filed in support of Harris County, Texas—not the US Conference of Catholic Bishops, not the Southern Baptist Convention, not the Church of Jesus Christ. Already opposing gay people in the marriage cases, these denominations were not eager to condemn them as criminals, too. Focus on the Family believed it was a big mistake to pass on the issue, and its amicus brief, authored by Gerry Bradley and Robby George, linked the state's authority to criminalize sodomy with its traditional definition of marriage. Bradley and George argued that the Supreme Court had always treated conjugal marriage as the only normative framework justifying the regulation of adult relationships. Consensual sodomy laws were constitutionally permissible because a legislature could reasonably believe that barring nonprocreative sodomy would advance the state's legitimate interest in procreative intercourse and strengthen the many state policies that recognized the special status of conjugal marriage.[35]

After an oral argument on March 26, 2003, where the Harris County district attorney fumbled away his legal and policy arguments in defense of the Texas law, the conference among the justices reflected an intellectual tug-of-war between the Lambda brief and its libertarian amici versus the natural law amicus submission from Bradley and George. On a personal level, the conference also reflected greater judicial acquaintance with lesbian and gay families. Having joined *Bowers* and dissented from the court's abortion decisions, Bill Rehnquist surprised no one by rejecting Lambda's due process claim and reaffirming *Bowers*—but he reserved judgment on the equal protection issue, which would not have involved overruling *Bowers*. A Lutheran who worshipped alongside gay couples, he was open to the equality claim. Sally Rider, the assistant to the chief justice from 2000 to 2006, often brought her partner, Betsy, and their two children to Supreme Court social events, where the chief sometimes played peekaboo with the kids. Could the state make his lesbian friends criminals?[36]

A stickler for stare decisis, John Paul Stevens also expressed reservations about overruling *Bowers*. Yet he voted to overturn the homosexual conduct law. Not only did the Texas law penalize only homosexuals, the equal protection concern, but Texas almost never enforced the law against consensual sodomy within the home. He wondered whether the court might narrow *Bowers* without completely overruling it. Like her old law school classmate Bill Rehnquist, Sandra Day O'Connor had also joined the *Bowers* majority, but like Stevens she was open to an equal protection holding without addressing *Bowers* at all. Her former law clerk Stuart Delery had come out to her in 1999 when he invited the justice to his wedding to Richard Gervase and, again, when they adopted a child two years later. "Good for you both to make a loving home for a child who might not otherwise have one," she wrote. Cheered by her staff, O'Connor gave Stuart and Richard's baby a T-shirt identifying him as a "Grandclerk."[37]

Still relatively oblivious of his small number of gay acquaintances, Antonin Scalia defended *Bowers* as correctly decided because legal tradition regulated sexual activities around the conjugal marriage norm, as George and Bradley had shown, and because he felt the state had a broad power to regulate morals. He considered the equality arguments preposterous because the equal protection clause targeted only racial discrimination. To update the Reconstruction Amendments to protect homosexuals would be absurd: "What's next?" he asked at conference, "Same-sex 'marriage?'"[38]

Well acquainted with lesbian and gay persons, the recent appointees were more critical of *Bowers* than the four most senior justices. Recall our understanding of Anthony Kennedy as a rule-of-law Hayekian (chapter 5). At the center of his constitution of liberty was preserving opportunities for citizens to make their own life choices and preventing the government from planning their lives for them. Kennedy had embraced this vision in his portion of the joint opinion in *Planned Parenthood v. Casey,* the 1992 decision reaffirming *Roe v. Wade:* "At the heart of liberty is the right to define one's own concept of existence, of meaning, of the universe, and of the mystery of human life." State compulsion on such matters struck at the heart of such freedom—and compulsory heterosexuality was precisely what Texas was legislating in its homosexual sodomy ban. There was no reason gay people should not receive the benefit of these neutral principles.[39]

Scalia maintained that consensual sodomy laws were supported by custom and tradition—but Kennedy found the Cato Institute's history a persuasive rebuttal: state sodomy laws had not traditionally targeted private activities between consenting adults. Like Hayek, Kennedy believed that custom itself evolved, and he had witnessed society's evolving view of homosexuals like his mentor, Gordon Schaber. Every summer, Kennedy taught a constitutional law course, sponsored by Dean Schaber's McGeorge School of Law, in Salzburg, Austria. Soon after *Bowers,* he taught a segment comparing the Supreme Court's opinion to the European Court of Human Rights ruling in *Dudgeon v. United Kingdom* (1981) that consensual sodomy laws violated Article 8 of the European Convention. (Article 8 protected one's "right to respect for his private and family life, his home and his correspondence.") Whatever justification sodomy bars once had as a matter of public morality had been overtaken by new knowledge of homosexuals as productive human beings. As he told us, that experience confirmed his intuition that *Bowers* was an embarrassment to American constitutionalism. Kennedy found the *Dudgeon* reasoning quite compelling. The equal-protection implications of sodomy laws, unmentioned in *Bowers,* also bothered Kennedy in this case, as they had in *Romer.* Such laws had extensive collateral effects. During conference, he observed that in four states, conviction for consensual sodomy would require a defendant to register as a sex offender, a penalty more liberty depriving than the fine imposed by the Texas law or than brief imprisonment imposed by other states.[40]

David Souter, the laconic New Hampshire bachelor whose jurisprudence leaned libertarian, flatly declared that *Bowers* was wrong the day it was decided. *Bowers* held that the criminal sanction could be justified by moral disapproval of conduct that harmed no one—a proposition that would have required a different result in *Romer.* He would have extended *Romer* to hold that the state cannot deny people liberty—much less render them criminals—based on moral disapproval. Moreover, *Bowers* was pernicious, for reasons the ABA amicus had developed. Everyone knew sodomy laws were not consistently enforced and were mainly used to blackmail or bully sexual minorities. Like the other younger justices, Clarence Thomas felt that these laws were stupid policy, but he apparently agreed with the Bradley and George analysis of the constitutional precedents: legislators could reasonably believe that making consensual homosexual sodomy a misdemeanor would reinforce the conjugality norm undergirding marriage. Ruth Bader Ginsburg picked up where Souter left off: *Bowers* was wrong the day it was decided and ought to be overruled. Moral disapproval was not a rational basis for the state to penalize people for activities that cause no harm. Speaking last, Stephen Breyer believed that *Bowers* should be overruled or eviscerated, as it was a dangerous precedent to say that the state can criminalize conduct that harms no one. Former law professors at Harvard and Columbia, respectively, Breyer and Ginsburg had many LGBT friends and colleagues.

If Kennedy was channeling Hayek's *Constitution of Liberty* (1960), Souter, Ginsburg, and Breyer championed the libertarian presumption associated with John Stuart Mill's *On Liberty* (1859). They believed that the constitutional purpose of the regulatory state was to provide all citizens the freedom to arrange their lives as they saw fit and not as the government mandated. In its due process clauses, the Constitution carved out spaces of personal liberty that government could not regulate without a showing of harm to third parties. Neither philosophical inconsistencies nor departure from tradition counted as constitutional harms to these justices, so the George-Bradley amicus brief did not move them.[41]

As in *Romer*, Stevens was the assigning justice, and he gave the case to Kennedy, who wrote an opinion that was an ode to freedom. He read it in open court on the last day of the term, June 26, 2003. He drew gasps and whispers when he stated that *Bowers*'s framing of the issue as a "right [of] homosexuals to engage in sodomy" reflected "the Court's own failure to appreciate the extent of the liberty at stake. To say that the issue in *Bowers* was simply the right to engage in certain sexual conduct demeans the claim the individual put forward, just as it would demean a married couple were it to be said marriage is simply about the right to have sexual intercourse"—a dig at the Bradley and George amicus. Closely following the Cato amicus brief, the opinion recounted the evolution of sodomy laws, from nineteenth-century proscriptions enforced exclusively against nonconsensual or public activities to twentieth-century laws frequently targeting homosexuals. Once sodomy laws lost their exclusive focus on nonconsensual or public conduct, they came under increasing criticism. Such statutes "seek to control a personal relationship that, whether or not entitled to formal recognition in the law, is within the liberty of persons to choose without being punished as criminals." As a matter of constitutional liberty, consenting adults of all sexual orientations "may choose to enter upon this relationship in the confines of their homes and their own private lives and still retain their dignity as free persons." Echoing similar libertarian text in the *Casey* joint opinion, this language also recalled Hayek's Cairo Lectures.[42]

Romer, too, was relevant to *Bowers*'s validity. The equality and liberty claims "are linked in important respects," foundational to both the rule of law and fairness to minorities. Thus, "when homosexual conduct is made criminal by the law of the State, that declaration in and of itself is an invitation to subject homosexual persons to discrimination both in the public and the private spheres." *Romer*'s invalidation of anti-gay discrimination, adopted for its own sake, was relevant to the court's reevaluation of *Bowers*. Kennedy concluded with the Souter-Ginsburg point: "*Bowers* was not correct when it was decided, and it is not correct today. It ought not to remain binding precedent. *Bowers v. Hardwick* should be and now is overruled." No one could remember a case where the Supreme Court had announced that one of its precedents had been wrong *the day it was decided*. To hear a Catholic Republican jurist denounce *Bowers* as demeaning was emotionally overpowering for the gays in the courtroom. For some, it was the first time in their lives they felt like acceptable American citizens.[43]

Declining to overrule *Bowers* because of stare decisis, Justice O'Connor wrote a separate opinion applying *Romer* to sustain Lambda's equal protection claim. "Moral disapproval of this group [homosexuals], like a bare desire to harm the group, is an interest that is insufficient to satisfy rational basis review under the Equal Protection Clause." Indeed, "a legislative classification that threatens the creation of an underclass" cannot be sustained. *Lawrence* was a double victory for gay rights: it not only extended the privacy right to bar consensual sodomy laws, it also (implicitly) extended *Romer* to overturn liberty-denying statutes grounded on nothing more than moral disapproval.[44]

Justice Scalia's lacerating dissent (joined by Chief Justice Rehnquist, notwithstanding his pass at conference, and Justice Thomas) lambasted his colleagues for striking down a law adopted by the elected legislature, and in the face of contrary precedent (*Bowers*). He thought the decision spelled doom for morals legislation generally. The court's logic, he wrote, swallowed the "so-called homosexual agenda, by which I mean the agenda promoted by some homosexual activists directed at eliminating the moral opprobrium that has traditionally attached to homosexual conduct." The culmination of the "homosexual agenda" was same-sex marriage, which courts in Canada were in the process of forcing upon that nation's population and which was a logical consequence of the majority's opinion. "If moral disapprobation of homosexual conduct is 'no legitimate state interest' for purposes of proscribing that conduct," then "what justification could there possibly be for denying the benefits of marriage to homosexual couples?" He added: "Surely not the encouragement of procreation, since the sterile and the elderly are allowed to marry."[45]

We once asked Nino Scalia whether he saw himself as a modern Cassandra, anticipating the overruling of *Bowers* in his 1996 *Romer* dissent and accurately forecasting constitutional marriage equality in his 2003 *Lawrence* dissent—but finding his prophecies dismissed at the time he wrote them. The allusion amused him, but he knew we were wrong. Whatever liberal academics or the media thought about his prophecy, his target audience—Fox News, the Federalist Society, and congressional Republicans—embraced and ran with it as hard as they could.

Three days after *Lawrence*, Dr. William Frist, the Senate majority leader, announced his support for the FMA, even though no one had filed a Senate bill. In July, the GOP's Senate Policy Committee issued a detailed report, "The Threat to Marriage from the Courts," predicting that Massachusetts judges would follow *Lawrence* to impose gay marriage on that state. This would stimulate dozens of copycat lawsuits in other states, as well as lawsuits challenging DOMA. Unless the FMA was adopted, DOMA was doomed, precisely as Scalia had warned. Although senior Republican senators worried that the FMA was premature or excessive, Catholic and Evangelical senators Rick Santorum, Jeff Sessions, and Sam Brownback were eager to amend the Constitution.[46]

The Senate Judiciary Committee's Subcommittee on the Constitution, chaired by former Texas Supreme Court justice John Cornyn, held a series of hearings on the need for a new Maginot Line—a constitutional amendment to protect DOMA. Former Texas solicitor general Gregory Coleman assured the senators that the logic of *Romer* and *Lawrence* was fatal to DOMA. "It would be very simple for a court to say that, once we have recognized a freedom and liberty under *Lawrence* of certain same-sex relationships, Congress acted with the same animus that the voters of Colorado acted with [in *Romer*], and that it would thereby be struck down under the United States Constitution." All the other witnesses (except for Dale Carpenter, an openly gay law professor) agreed that DOMA was in grave constitutional peril.[47]

Maggie Gallagher made a broader point: DOMA and the FMA were essential responses to the marriage crisis. Assuming the accuracy of Scalia's nightmare, she testified: "In endorsing same-sex marriage, law and government would thus be making a powerful statement our government no longer believes children need mothers and fathers. Two fathers or two mothers are not only just as good as a mother and a father, they are just the same." The logic concluded: "If two mothers are just as good as a mother and a father, for example, why can't a single mother and her mother do just as well as a married mom and dad?" Behind the scenes, Gallagher was quarterbacking strategy for faith-based groups and lecturing congressional staff and representatives on the best social-science arguments to make—and the gay-bashing points to avoid. She was known to arrive late to strategy meetings, somewhat disheveled and her hair still wet, and would then transform the meeting with brilliant insights and strategic vison.[48]

Gallagher insisted that the FMA be strictly nonpartisan and that supporters had to focus on protecting marriage, not on disparaging gay families. In July 2003, pollster Richard Wirthlin confirmed her analysis. He reported that a third of voters were concerned about the decline of marriage and the plight of children but did not want to be seen as anti-gay. In his view, the campaign's motto should be, "Gays and lesbians have a right to live as they choose, but don't have a right to redefine marriage for our entire society." Matt Daniels had deployed this precise language in the May 2002 unveiling of the FMA and would make it the centerpiece of his September 2003 press conference. On the other hand, many faith-based allies, like Robert Knight (the primary drafter of DOMA), opposed the FMA because it was not sufficiently disapproving of homosexual relationships. Contrary to *Lawrence,* many Evangelicals did not think gay people had a "right to live as they choose."[49]

The Marriage Bomb

Matt Daniels believed his constitutional amendment would not catch fire with the public until a court actually insisted on gay marriage. "I don't think the bomb has gone off yet. It will go off and go off soon. It's the marriage bomb." The bomb did indeed explode on November 18, 2003, when the Massachusetts Supreme Judicial Court handed down its *Goodridge* decision.[50]

On November 23, just days after *Goodridge,* Senator Wayne Allard, a Colorado Republican allied with Focus on the Family, introduced the FMA in the Senate. In early 2004 he submitted a new version, with language Representative Musgrave also vowed to add to her House bill:

> Marriage in the United States shall consist solely of the union of a man and a woman. Neither this Constitution, nor the constitution of any State, nor state or federal law shall be construed to require that *marriage* or the legal incidents thereof be conferred upon *any union other than the union of a man and a woman.*

Judge Bork explained that the deletion of the phrase "nor state or federal law" was meant to make clear that legislatures could adopt civil union laws. The new (italicized) wording narrowed the FMA in another way. If given its ordinary meaning, the new text placed the burden of protecting marriage entirely on excluding lesbian and gay couples, while allowing judges to extend "legal incidents" of marriage to unmarried straight couples, a huge population whose cohabitating practices were actually driving the deinstitutionalization of marriage.[51]

Led by Richard Land and James Dobson, the Arlington Group demanded a full-throated presidential endorsement of the FMA. Within the White House, Karl Rove and Press Secretary Tony Snow resented Evangelical nagging but went along for a pragmatic reason: in the wake of *Goodridge,* failure to speak out would be read as a retreat from the family values that born-again Christian George W. Bush accepted as a matter of faith. Also, President Bush's endorsement would motivate Evangelicals to support his reelection. After he was briefed by Maggie Gallagher and Mary Ann Glendon, President Bush on February 24 announced his support for the FMA. It was a brief endorsement, delivered with a somewhat pained expression. His wife, Laura Bush, felt that the FMA was unwise and mean-spirited, and the president's twin daughters, Barbara and Jenna Bush, were reportedly "livid" that their dad was disrespecting lesbian and gay unions. Like most other college students, they saw gay marriage as a civil rights issue.[52]

The House Judiciary Committee's Subcommittee on the Constitution held five substantive hearings on the constitutional threat to marriage. The dramatic story line was that *Lawrence* and *Goodridge* were paving a constitutional path for the homosexual invaders to circumvent DOMA's Maginot Line, just as the Germans circumvented the historic Maginot Line by marching through Belgium in 1939. Congress needed to build a new firewall: voilà, the FMA.

Judge Bork told the subcommittee that DOMA could be gone within three years, after which homosexual marriage would be imposed on the entire country. Liberals exaggerated in the other direction. In parallel Senate committee hearings, law professor Cass Sunstein testified that same-sex marriage was a "reckless conception of what was on the horizon" given the Supreme Court "as currently constituted," with five conservative justices (Rehnquist, O'Connor, Scalia, Kennedy, Thomas). Even the Republicans chuckled when he told them that the odds were better for the Chicago Cubs to meet the White Sox in Game 7 of a World Series than for the Supreme Court ever to announce a right for gay people to get married. (In 2016, the Cubs won Game 7 of the World Series, albeit not against the White Sox.)[53]

Reflecting Gallagher's pervasive influence, these hearings focused on family law data and not on homosexual relationships, which the GOP witnesses insisted they did not want to disturb. Researcher Stanley Kurtz, for example, reported that registered partnership (civil union–type) laws in Denmark, Norway, and Sweden blew up the Maginot Line for marriage in those countries. Scandinavians pretty much stopped getting married, he claimed, and nonmarital births soared. Kurtz's testimony was wildly inconsistent with the actual data, which suggested that marriage in Scandinavia had rebounded rather than collapsed after the new laws. He gave a more accurate account of rising nonmarital birth rates after the Netherlands recognized same-sex marriage in 2000–2001 but did not offer any empirical evidence that marriage recognition caused the rising rates. The nonmarital birth rate had been soaring since the 1970s, and European demographers thought that women's life choices were driving those numbers.[54]

Between July 9 and 14, 2004, the Senate debated whether to cut off the Democrats' filibuster of Senate Joint Resolution 40, the FMA. The Alliance for Marriage hoped to get close to the sixty votes needed to break a filibuster, which could be a prelude to the sixty-seven votes needed to approve a constitutional amendment. Polls showed that large majorities of Americans disagreed with *Goodridge*, though smaller majorities or pluralities favored addressing the decision with a constitutional amendment. If all the Republicans and the Baptist-state Democrats (such as West Virginia's Robert Byrd) voted for the FMA, it would surpass sixty votes.

During the FMA debate, the Republicans' substance was all Gallagher almost all the time, surely owing to her ongoing educational campaign with the staffers who wrote the speeches that were delivered on the Senate floor. The senators emphasized her utilitarian arguments, grounded in natural gender roles and the best interests of children. FMA sponsor Wayne Allard invoked one-man, one-woman marriage as "the ideal union from which people live and children best blossom and thrive. Is it discrimination to hold as ideal that a child should have both a mother and a father?" As Gordon Smith put it, "Boys and girls need moms and dads." Making the cultural argument that gay marriage would disrupt the link between marriage and procreation, Rick Santorum and Sam Brownback displayed posters documenting the decline of marriage in the Netherlands between 1989 and 2003.[55]

The Democrats focused entirely on process: the FMA was premature; let the states make their own choices; consider other measures to strengthen marriage. Few FMA opponents said anything positive about lesbian and gay families. Minority Leader Tom Daschle maintained that marriage ought to be limited to one man, one woman—but it was premature to amend the Constitution and cut off state debate on the issue. Hillary Rodham Clinton boasted that she had repeatedly stood up for "the sanctity of marriage" but could not support the FMA when there were so many more obvious threats to the institution, such as no-fault divorce. Only Ted Kennedy could bring himself to say he supported, without equivocation, the Massachusetts decision in *Goodridge*.

On July 14, the Senate voted 48-50 against cloture, failing by twelve votes to cut off debate. As the Human Rights Campaign's vote count had predicted, forty-three Democrats were joined by one Independent and six Republicans. Forty-five Republicans and three Democrats voted to move the amendment forward. On September 30, the House passed the FMA by a vote of 227-186, nowhere near the two-thirds supermajority needed to send the amendment to the states for ratification. Congressional insiders in both parties believed that the 2004 vote was the high tide of the traditional marriage response to *Goodridge* and that its defeat meant that marriage equality was now unstoppable.[56]

The State Constitutional Super-DOMAs

Between 1994 and 2004, thirty-eight states adopted statutes barring recognition of same-sex marriages validly entered in another state or reaffirming the definition of marriage as one man, one woman (appendix 1 to this volume). These junior-DOMAs faced the same issue the federal DOMA did in the wake of *Lawrence* and *Goodridge*. Marriage equality supporters could evade the statutory Maginot Line by taking the constitutional road around it, as the Massachusetts gay rights activists had done in *Goodridge*. The impulse to create a judge-proof Maginot Line generated proposals to amend many state constitutions.

Some pundits assumed that the Republican Party or the Bush White House were orchestrating the state junior-FMA campaigns. In fact, the opposite was the case. State constitutional initiatives came first, with successful campaigns funded by the Church of Jesus Christ to bar marriage equality efforts in Hawai'i and Alaska. When the Nebraska legislature failed to enact a junior-DOMA statute, Mormon activists gathered enough signatures to put this constitutional initiative on the 2000 ballot:

> Only marriage between a man and a woman shall be valid or recognized in Nebraska. The uniting of two persons of the same sex in a civil union, domestic partnership, or other similar same-sex relationship shall not be valid or recognized in Nebraska.

Adopted with 70 percent of the vote, the nation's first successful Super-DOMA was also the first to be successfully challenged, but an appeals court reinstated it the next year. In two successive popular votes, the Latter-day Saints replicated their Nebraska success by adding a junior-DOMA to the Nevada Constitution in 2002.[57]

To the extent that state constitutional initiatives were coordinated after 2002, it was by the Arlington Group, not the Bush White House. In most states, the ballot measures were sponsored by state policy councils associated with the Family Research Council (FRC) or Focus on the Family, and they were drafted and defended by ADF-affiliated lawyers. In Ohio, for instance, a founding member of the Arlington Group, Phil Burress, and his Cincinnati-based Citizens for Community Values (CCV) secured legislative enactment of a junior-DOMA in February 2004, but Burress worried that the Ohio Supreme Court could breach his Maginot Line if it interpreted the Ohio Constitution to follow *Goodridge*.

CCV's ADF-affiliated attorney, David Langdon, drafted Issue 1, a ballot initiative to add a new paragraph to Article XV of the Ohio Constitution:

> Only a union between one man and one woman may be a marriage valid in or recognized by this state and its political subdivisions. This state and its political subdivisions shall not create or recognize a legal status for relationships of unmarried individuals that intends to approximate the design, qualities, significance or effect of marriage.

Broader than the FMA, Issue 1 resembled the Nebraska Super-DOMA. It would have prevented legislative as well as judicial recognition of straight cohabiting relationships as well as gay marriages, civil unions, and domestic partnerships.

In a herculean effort, CCV and its extensive family values network gathered 575,000 signatures, more than enough to secure Issue 1 a spot on the 2004 ballot.[58]

Burress's strategy was to build on the enthusiastic network created by Lori Viars and her pro-life allies. With a budget of $2 million, mostly from the Arlington Group, Burress and Viars ran an impressive grassroots and media campaign to protect marriage as an institution "critical to the well-being of our children and to the maintenance of the fundamental social institution of the family." Their opponents, by contrast, were timid, disorganized, and poorly funded. Their messaging emphasized the possibility that Issue 1 would deny needed rights to retired straight couples and "would have a negative impact on our struggling economy." All of the top Republican officeholders opposed Issue 1 except for Secretary of State Ken Blackwell, the state's highest-ranking black official, who recorded a hard-hitting, end-of-days message that was robo-called to 850,000 Ohio households right before Election Day.[59]

These efforts in Ohio were part of a broader grassroots movement. Four states voted on state constitutional junior-DOMAs in 2004, and nine others voted on constitutional Super-DOMAs like Ohio's Issue 1. Most were initiated by faith-based groups associated with the Arlington Group, whose leaders had periodic conference calls with the president's reelection team, including Karl Rove, the master strategist. The Arlington Group callers—Dobson, Land, and others, like Chuck Colson—aggressively offered to press voter turnout and pro-GOP messages from the pulpit. Ironically, the Bush campaign organizers were originally reticent, but they became more engaged as they grew impressed with the Arlington Group's resources and grassroots reach. Focus on the Family and the Southern Baptist Convention, for instance, mailed eight million voter guides and "I Vote Values" kits to more than twelve thousand churches across the country. Focus's outreach director contacted perhaps one hundred thousand pastors, many of whom talked up family values from the pulpit on the eve of the election.[60]

Unlike the other ballot initiatives, Michigan's Super-DOMA campaign was funded in large part by the Michigan Catholic Conference. Like Ohio's Issue 1, Michigan's Proposal 2 was broadly and vaguely worded, prohibiting recognition not only of same-sex marriages but of all "similar unions." We asked the DeBoer-Rowse family whether they remembered the Proposal 2 campaign. Wendy DeBoer remembers Proposal 2 because she talked about it with Kevin, her gay neighbor. Like other voters, she was confused by the initiative's wording. She meant to vote yes for gay and lesbian relationships, but her yes vote meant that Proposal 2 would pass—so she voted completely contrary to her true opinion. Her miscast vote still bothers her. Although the Michigan gay community had successfully opposed five of seven local ballot measures between 1997 and 2003, it had neither the funding, nor the organizational structure, nor the messaging to compete with the Proposal 2 forces, which enjoyed local grassroots support from Catholic and Evangelical churches. Adding injury to insult, Michigan's Evangelical attorney general, Bill Schuette, and its Republican-dominated supreme court interpreted Proposal 2 to bar public domestic partnership contracts, a reading contrary to the text of the amendment and to assurances made during the campaign.[61]

At the same time the traditional marriage forces were implementing their grand plan, the National Gay and Lesbian Task Force, HRC, and Freedom to Marry had developed their own plan for a national marriage equality campaign. "The battle for equal marriage rights will be won on the ground," the plan document read. Through public education, recruitment of religious and other non-gay allies, and stepped-up state organizing, the groups aimed to "increase awareness of issues facing LGBT families who are not allowed to marry" and to "change hearts and minds." As the Task Force had learned, such a campaign required early organization, effective communication on matters of concern to voters, fundraising, grassroots strategies (including "door-to-door and other voter contact activities"), and serious efforts to identify allies and to get out the vote on election day. But the marriage equality campaign plan did not anticipate the numerous, widely dispersed state ballot initiatives that hit in 2004.[62]

Most of these proposals were put forward in states with weak LGBT organizations: Arkansas, Georgia, Louisiana, Mississippi, Missouri, Montana, North Dakota, Ohio, Oklahoma, and Utah. HRC, the Task Force, and the Gill Foundation provided significant funding for Ohio and Utah, but the proponents got organized much earlier, were usually better funded, and started out with large public-opinion advantages. Marriage equality's best hope for victory was Oregon. With HRC and Task Force investments of $640,000 and loans of field organizers, Roey Thorpe and Basic Rights Oregon ran a textbook campaign—big media buys, identification of core supporters as well as conflicted voters, an extensive grassroots effort by well-trained and -directed volunteers, and an excellent get-out-the-vote operation on Election Day. Given this effort and the state's relatively liberal electorate, there was hope for a victory here.[63]

An unlikely battleground was Kentucky. Because the Super-DOMA proposal caught them by surprise, the gay community only had twenty-four weeks to put together and implement a statewide campaign, and do so in a state with a large Evangelical churchgoing population. The Task Force's Sarah Reece, proud to have been born and raised in Kentucky, assembled an impressive campaign. They emphasized that the Super-DOMA would sweep well beyond marriage and would needlessly harm lesbian and gay families (including children) and also pressed the positive message that marriage was an institution rooted in love and commitment, values that lesbian and gay couples shared with straight married couples. On the other hand, the proponents had both financial and grassroots advantages, thanks to church support. Southeast Christian Church, a mega-church in Jefferson County, rallied thousands of parishioners for the amendment and spent a million dollars on a media campaign called "One Man, One Woman: God's Plan for Marriage." Kentucky was trending Republican, but even its leading Democrats supported the amendment.[64]

All thirteen constitutional amendments won thumping majorities, ranging from 57 percent in Oregon to 78 percent in Louisiana. Reece and the Task Force were crushed that the Super-DOMA won 75 percent of the vote in Kentucky. The most discussed victory was in Ohio, where the Super-DOMA won by 62-38 percent. Phil Burress believes that Issue 1 was critical to President Bush's reelection. Bush would have been defeated if he had not carried Ohio, which he won by only 118,601 votes—a margin Burress attributes to the thousands of new Amish and other voters the CCV campaign brought onto the rolls; a higher Evangelical turnout on Election Day; and the appeal of tradition to African American voters (Bush's share of the black vote in Ohio went from 9 percent in 2000 to 16 percent in 2004). Massachusetts senator John Kerry reportedly expressed the same thought—but as a bitter complaint, for he would have become president if he had carried Ohio. (By the way, Massachusetts politicians have frequently been nominated for the presidency, but only one ever carried Ohio. For a clue, read the endnote.)[65]

Respected political scientists reject the Burress claims. Kenneth Sherrill points out that the president increased his share of the national vote by 2.8 percent between 2000 and 2004, but he increased his vote share in the states voting on state constitutional DOMAs by 2.5 percent and his vote share in Ohio by only 1.0 percent. D. A. Smith's analysis of Ohio county data suggests that the Bush-Cheney ticket did not significantly increase its vote in counties with high concentrations of Evangelical voters. For us, the most intriguing evidence was the president's larger share of the black vote. The inner circle of the GOP campaign team told us, however, that they had been micro-targeting black voters in swing states—Florida, Ohio, North Carolina, Pennsylvania, and Wisconsin—for most of the Bush presidency and that the issues moving those voters to the president were jobs, national security, and the volunteer army, not marriage. (Micro-targeting is data-based identification of issues that appeal to specific voters.) The 2000 and 2004 election data support the campaign team's account. The president's estimated share of the black vote rose from 9 percent to 16 percent in Ohio, but it went up just as much in the other targeted states, none of which had a marriage initiative on the ballot: Florida, from 7 percent to 13 percent; North Carolina, 9 percent to 14 percent; Pennsylvania, 7 percent to 16 percent; and Wisconsin, from an unknown figure to 14 percent. In short, Phil Burress and Lori Viars enjoyed a great electoral and moral victory in November 2004—but their triumph did not include securing a second term for George W. Bush, the foot-dragging FMA supporter.[66]

A New Round of Super-DOMAs

With massive assistance from Arlington Group members in 2004, the Republicans defeated Senate Minority Leader Tom Daschle (South Dakota), picked up five Senate seats where Democrats in southern states were retiring, and reelected Kentucky's troubled GOP senator Jim Bunning. Republicans dominated the new Senate, 55-44-1. On January 24, 2005, Senator Allard introduced the Marriage Protection Amendment (MPA), with the same language as the revised FMA. In November 2005, grassroots organizers associated with Focus on the Family and FRC secured voter approval, by margins greater than 70 percent, for new state constitutional Super-DOMAs in Kansas and Texas. But as Maggie Gallagher lamented, the MPA had become fatally associated with partisan politics. Supporters of traditional marriage needed to reclaim bipartisan support if they hoped to achieve anything significant.[67]

By 2005, Gallagher was emphasizing the tangible harms marriage equality posed to religious freedom, a point also made by the Witherspoon Institute's "Princeton Principles" (2006), signed by Robby George and almost six dozen other scholars. The threat marriage equality posed to religious liberty had already been raised in the *Baehr* litigation and during legislative deliberations in California, Vermont, and Massachusetts. Marriage equality supporters responded that it was anti-discrimination laws, and not marriage recognition, that sometimes burdened religious institutions. Gallagher replied that the "Marriage Line" played a special role. "Precisely because support for marriage is public policy, once marriage includes gay couples, groups who oppose gay marriage are likely to be judged in violation of public policy, triggering a host of negative consequences, including the loss of tax-exempt status.

Because marriage is not a private act, but a protected public status, the legaliza-tion of gay marriage sends a strong signal that orientation is now on a par with race in the nondiscrimination game. And when we get gay marriage because courts have declared it a constitutional right, the signal is stronger still." An example of these consequences was Catholic Charities of Boston, licensed by the state to make adoption placements. Before *Goodridge,* it satisfied the Mas-sachusetts anti-discrimination law by restricting its adoptions to married couples, but *Goodridge* would have required it to include married lesbian and gay couples. So in March 2006, Catholic Charities terminated its adoption ser-vices. Who were the biggest losers? Maggie's answer: the children—worse off in many ways when the marriage culture was weakened.[68]

A poised and confident public intellectual, Gallagher still faced some un-comfortable moments. In a 2006 CNN interview, she fielded telephone calls with aplomb—until the last caller, from Longford, Kansas. She beamed as he reported that his town of 150 people had passed an ordinance banning same-sex marriages. But when the caller then complained, "This all started when we allowed marriage between blacks and whites," Gallagher's expression shifted: her lips pursed, her eyebrows went up. She closed her eyes and shook her head as he continued, "That really opened up this thing to perverts." "I'd like to disassociate myself from those remarks in [their] entirety," she inter-rupted. The caller from Longford reminded the audience that many of the MPA's most enthusiastic supporters were unashamed bigots—including rac-ists who also hated homosexuals.[69]

More importantly, the fate of the MPA declined with the Bush administra-tion's sinking poll numbers. On June 7, 2006, the Senate voted 49-48 in favor of cloture. Seven Republicans joined forty Democrats and one Independent to sustain the filibuster. Not only did cloture fail by eleven votes, but the MPA would need eighteen senators to switch to yes in order to pass the Senate by the two-thirds required for a proposed constitutional amendment. That aspi-ration soared far out of reach after the November election, in which the Demo-crats defeated six incumbent Republican senators, including MPA sponsors Rick Santorum, Gordon Smith, and George Allen. The Democrats also recap-tured the House, which had voted 236-187 in favor of the MPA in July. Ironi-cally, in the same election, voters added Super-DOMAs to constitutions in eight more states: Alabama, Colorado, Idaho, South Carolina, South Dakota, Tennessee, Virginia, and Wisconsin; Kansas and Texas had voted for Super-DOMAs in 2005. In 2006, a Super-DOMA narrowly lost in Arizona, the first time a marriage initiative failed anywhere in the country. Arizona and three other states would add modest marriage protection amendments to their state constitutions in 2008. As documented in appendix 1, voters in thirty-one states endorsed constitutional junior- and Super-DOMAs between 1998 and 2009, usually by huge margins.

Because the marriage debate was now truly national, Gallagher asked Focus on the Family and other organizations to fund a national political structure for public education, grassroots work, and campaign contributions. She pointed out that Tim Gill and his allies were funding stealth campaigns to unseat conservative legislators in key states like Massachusetts, Iowa, and New York. In 2007, she told Robby George that the traditional marriage supporters needed a political organization to counter the juggernaut they were seeing in Massachusetts. "Our side needed the marriage equivalent of the NRA." George agreed, and they identified a donor who would provide seed money for the National Organization for Marriage (NOM). The donor asked Gallagher whether she could manage NOM's day-to-day business. Probably not, she replied, but Brian Brown, who had been running the Family Institute of Connecticut, could do it. He had an Oxford degree, was a charismatic speaker, and got things done. The donor knew Brown and had complete confidence in his leadership abilities. NOM was up and running by the summer. Gallagher was its president, George headed the board of advisers, which also included Evangelicals and Latter-day Saints, and Brown was the executive director. Although she realized that marriage equality was picking up support, especially among young people, Gallagher hoped that the one-man, one-woman Maginot Line would hold and that NOM could then launch efforts to roll back some of the family law liberalization that had already occurred.[70]

How did Michigan's 2004 Super-DOMA affect April DeBoer and Jayne Rowse, the nurses in Hazel Park, Michigan? By 2005, they had formed a serious relationship, and the next year April moved into Jayne's home. They remained discreet, in large part because of the hubbub surrounding Proposal 2. They even considered moving to another state, but both had excellent jobs in Detroit hospitals. The Super-DOMA could frighten them, but it could not make either woman want to be married to a man, nor could it kill their love for one another. In classic Romeo-and-Juliet (or Juliet-and-Juliet) fashion, their outlaw love brought the women closer together.

One of the things that bonded April and Jayne to one another, and endeared Jayne to April's mother, was that they shared an empathy toward vulnerable persons. In 2008, the couple decided to adopt a child. To their frustration, two potential adoptions fell through, but in January 2009, Hutzel Hospital, where April worked, told her about a woman who wanted to give up her unborn son. Nolan was born at Hutzel on January 25, 2009, and the mother agreed to adoption by Jayne, which was formalized on November 9, 2009. The family bonded with little Nolan. For a while, he suffered from terrible acid reflux and would quietly throw up—but then he would just look up and smile. No big deal. He was a very easygoing little guy. And very happy to have two loving parents who were also experienced nurses.

Nothing in Michigan's Super-DOMA prohibited Jayne from adopting Nolan or having children through donor insemination, which April had tried without success. As we saw in the prelude to this volume, Michigan would not allow both women to be Nolan's legal parents. Before 2002, some Michigan judges had authorized second-parent adoptions, but a state judge exposed and ended that process—and the 2004 Super-DOMA slammed the door on judicial compassion for families like April, Jayne, and Nolan. For some of the same reasons Maggie Gallagher wanted two parents for her son, April and Jayne wanted two parents for Nolan. In the meantime, they thought they could raise their children without state interference. It was not until their near-miss in the automobile accident of February 2011 that they learned how vulnerable the Super-DOMA culture left their family.

11 • The Winter of Love

Following marriage equality's Cinderella moment in 2003, California enjoyed a Winter of Love in 2004 that led, in 2008, to a Spring of Recognition and Summer of Weddings.

On January 10, 2003, California's legal gayocracy met for an all-day roundtable hosted by the Williams Institute at UCLA. The organizers were lawyers who had worked on the campaign for domestic partnership legislation, including Jon Davidson and Jenny Pizer from Lambda Legal, Matt Coles for the ACLU, Toni Broaddus of Californians for Civil Marriage, and Geoff Kors from the lobbying organization soon to be renamed Equality California (EQCA). Two of the key players, Kate Kendell and Shannon Minter, had worked together at the National Center for Lesbian Rights (NCLR) since 1996. They were a contrasting pair. The athletic Kate was outgoing, larger-than-life, and dynamic—a gregarious power lesbian. She had been raised as a Mormon and presided over a largish family, including two young children she had with her domestic partner, Sandy Holmes, and an older daughter. Shannon was shiny-headed, shy, thoughtful, and visionary. A transgender man who had begun transitioning during his early years at NCLR, he found his feminist colleagues warmly supportive, and Kate was proud that the center was at the forefront of the movement to integrate transgender rights into the lesbian, gay, and bisexual rights movement—the ongoing effort that put the *T* into *LGBT*.[1]

One purpose of the roundtable was to dissuade Broaddus from sponsoring a constitutional lawsuit to challenge Proposition 22, the 2000 initiative that had hardwired the definition of marriage as one man, one woman into California law. Because a popular initiative amending the California Constitution could be passed by a simple majority vote, any *Goodridge*-style lawsuit had to

face the question: If marriage equality were to win in court, could its supporters protect that victory in an election? Broaddus felt that the time was coming
more quickly than her colleagues expected. In June 2002, Decision Research
reported that 45 percent of respondents supported same-sex marriage, with
49 percent opposed, a big increase in support from previous polls. The pollsters found that some marriage skeptics could be persuaded by public education and testimonials that LGBT persons formed committed relationships that
would benefit from the rights and duties of marriage.[2]

Nonetheless, the roundtable reached a consensus that the time was not ripe
for a marriage lawsuit and that the priority should be Assembly Member Jackie
Goldberg's comprehensive domestic partnership bill, which would be enacted
in September 2003. A few months later, the Massachusetts Supreme Court's
decision in *Goodridge* stoked interest in a constitutional lawsuit, and Assembly Member Mark Leno told Geoff Kors that the time was ripe for introducing
a marriage equality bill in the legislature. The Lambda, ACLU, and NCLR
lawyers opposed both a marriage lawsuit and a marriage bill: let's stick with
the incremental strategy that has been working well for us, they said, and defend the domestic partnership law. Nonetheless, Kors and Leno prepared a
marriage equality bill, which Leno expected to introduce around Valentine's
Day 2004. They did not know that another San Francisco politician was planning an even bolder move.[3]

When handsome thirty-six-year-old restauranteur Gavin Newsom was narrowly elected mayor of San Francisco in 2003, he was billed as the pro-business
candidate, but upon taking office he wooed minority communities with progressive appointments. In January 2004, Mayor Newsom was Nancy Pelosi's
guest at George W. Bush's State of the Union address in the US Capitol. Much
of the speech was a triumphalist account of the invasion of Iraq, but President
Bush concluded by calling on Congress to protect the nation's children against
three major threats: sexually transmitted diseases, gay marriage, and the loss
of adult mentors for kids with incarcerated fathers. It was important, Bush said,
to "send the right messages to our children," which meant defending "the
sanctity of marriage" against lesbian and gay couples, by a "constitutional process" if need be. Pelosi and Newsom were dumbfounded by the entire address, but especially what they considered its insulting conclusion.[4]

As the chamber emptied, the mayor could hear GOP legislators exchang-
ing anti-gay slurs, and the whole experience made him angry. In taking office, he had sworn to uphold the US Constitution, including the equal protection
clause. How were lesbian and gay couples receiving equal protection when

284 THE WINTER OF LOVE

officials demonized them because they asked for access to the central institution of family life? Why shouldn't he stand up for his constituents? Gavin
Newsom and Joyce Newstat, his policy director, came up with a dramatic
answer.[5]

On Friday, February 6, Newsom called Steve Kawa, his chief of staff, and said,
"I want to start issuing marriage licenses on Monday." Kawa asked whether
that would not be political suicide. The mayor said he did not care, but his plan
was not politically crazy. Corporations were okay with gay marriage, and Bush's
position was unpopular with young people, including his own daughters.
This was an issue waiting for an ambitious statesman to seize it. To be sure,
public support for marriage equality by the mayor of a liberal city would be
ho-hum news—but if the mayor started issuing marriage licenses, that would
cause a sensation. It was a high-stakes gamble—but even if he failed, progressives would appreciate that a straight dude stood up for his queer constituents, and the mayor thought history would judge him generously.[6]

Kawa got permission to give a heads-up to their ally Kate Kendell. She was
parking her car in front of her daughter's preschool that afternoon when she
received the call: "Kate, I am just calling to tell you that Monday morning Gavin
Newsom is going to be issuing marriage licenses to same-sex couples." Kendell
was surprised, then frightened, then elated, then panicked by this news:
"Whoa, wait, I need to talk to my colleagues here and back east." What might
be the consequences? Would a fait accompli out of way-left San Francisco stir
up more opposition to *Goodridge*, which was then under assault in Massachusetts? Would it add fuel to the Federal Marriage Amendment or spark an
initiative-amendment to the California Constitution? Although the mayor was
not seeking permission from the lawyers, Kendell asked whether he would
hold off until he could meet with LGBT leaders on Monday. Sure.[7]

Kate Kendell immediately called Shannon Minter and then Mary Bonauto
of GLAD, Geoff Kors of EQCA, and a few others. The mayor's proposed actions disrupted the carefully wrought master plan developed at UCLA the year
before, and Shannon was both skeptical and more than a little irritated. But
Geoff believed this would supercharge the public education campaign to which
EQCA was dedicated. Mary was attracted to the notion of opening a second
front on the West Coast and starting a serious national conversation about marriage. By Sunday, Kate says she "had come to a place of *Game On*. Every movement needs a provocateur," and who better than this charismatic young
heterosexual mayor, who was married to a glamorous television newscaster?
"Why should we try to talk him out of it?" she concluded. "Who are we to do

that? We agree with him on the substance. This could be a game-changing moment." Although Shannon remained "nervous about where it would end up," he thought it could be "the right thing to do." There would be serious dissent within the marriage equality movement. When he later learned of the plan, Jon Davidson believed a strategy grounded in maverick marriage licenses was likely to boomerang; others in Lambda and the ACLU agreed.[8]

Although Kendell was willing for NCLR to jump aboard the Newsom Express, she wanted to help steer it. Monday, she suggested, was definitely not the right day. Why not Thursday, February 12, which was National Freedom to Marry Day? The leaders of Marriage Equality California (MECA), Molly McKay and Davina Kotulski, staged protests at city hall every February 12, so there might be some ready-to-marry couples on hand. The mayor's office loved this idea—and it would give the office more time to prepare for when they opened the floodgates. Not least important, the courts would not be open that day.

City Attorney Dennis Herrera and Chief Deputy City Attorney Terry Stewart learned of the mayor's plans on Monday. As a lesbian who had defended domestic partnership and had registered with her partner, Carole Scagnetti, Stewart was personally moved by the idea, but as a lawyer she was concerned that it would be hard to defend in court. At her and Herrera's urging, the mayor directed County Clerk Nancy Alfaro to develop new application forms appropriate for same-sex couples. For *Groom* and *Bride,* the revised forms substituted *1st Applicant* and *2d Applicant.* Stewart cracked that if the couples had to decide who was the bride and who was the groom, some would never get any further. She also added this notice to the application forms for same-sex couples:

> By entering into marriage you may lose some or all of the rights, protections, and benefits you enjoy as a domestic partner * * *.

> Marriage of lesbian and gay couples may not be recognized as valid by any jurisdiction other than San Francisco, and may not be recognized as valid by any employer. If you are a same-gender couple, you are encouraged to seek legal advice regarding the effect of entering into marriage.

Hundreds of new marriage license application forms were printed up for the big day.[9]

In a meeting in the mayor's office, Joyce Newstat posed the question of who should be the first couple to receive a marriage license. Kate smiled and replied, "Well, you know who the first couple has to be!" In unison, Joyce and

Gavin Newsom marries Del Martin and Phyllis Lyon on
June 16, 2008. (Photo by Nick Gorton, Creative Commons
License, https://commons.wikimedia.org/wiki/File:Lyonmarti
nweddingholdinghands.jpg.)

Kate shouted out: "Del Martin and Phyllis Lyon!" The founders of the Daughters
of Bilitis, the first lesbian rights group, and the editors of *The Ladder,* the first
lesbian magazine, seventy-nine-year-old Phyllis Lyon and eighty-three-year-old
Del Martin had been living as partners in the Noe Valley section of the city
for half a century. Kate knew that Phyllis and Del were old-fashioned feminists,
who considered marriage a patriarchal institution. But they had spent their
lives arguing that lesbian and gay Americans should be treated the same as
straights. When Kate called them from city hall, she emphasized what a "trans-
gressive" act the mayor was proposing. Phyllis took the call and briefly discussed the matter with Del, her ailing partner. They were up for it, and they
retrieved the pastel lavender and sky-blue pantsuits they had worn for their
commitment ceremony decades earlier. With Mayor Newsom presiding, city
assessor Mabel Teng married Martin and Lyon in a private ceremony inside
city hall at 11:00 a.m. on February 12, 2004.[10]

Once the elderly newlyweds appeared outside the door to city hall, the marriage license office was open for business. As predicted, there were many gay
people assembled to join MECA's Freedom to Marry Day protests. One of the
protesters was John Lewis, from Oakland. He spotted Molly McKay, who was
wearing the wedding dress she always wore at marriage protests, and she

shouted: "You can walk right into San Francisco City Hall and get married." The wildfire was lit. With a borrowed cell phone, John called and proposed to his partner of seventeen years, Stuart Gaffney (who was at work). Get over here, before someone gets an order stopping the mayor! The guys stood in line with dozens of other couples. The clerk gave John and Stuart family planning and pregnancy information, which they considered quite a hoot. After filling out the form, as Applicant 1 and 2, they were sent into the hall, where they chose an officiant authorized to conduct the ceremony. Before they knew it, Stuart and John were one of the first ten same-sex couples to be married. "For the first time, we experienced our government treating us as fully equal human beings . . . and recognizing us as a loving couple worthy of the full respect of the law."[11]

By the end of the day, eighty-seven lesbian and gay couples, some with children, had married. When the clerk's office opened its doors the next day, Friday, February 13, hundreds of couples were lining the streets. In the spirit of Walt Whitman's "Song of Myself," the crowd represented a broad cross-section of San Francisco—some women wearing Prada, others in slacks and flannel shirts; men in business suits or jeans or leather; interracial as well as white, black, and other minority couples; drag queens and nonbinary persons, butch-femme couples, men and women who could pass as straight; teachers and plumbers and custodians and mechanics and out-of-work writers; parents with their children, many children; people in wheelchairs. The mood was festive. Saturday would be Valentine's Day, and city hall would remain open all weekend for marriage license applications.

The mayor was racing against time. Representing the Campaign for California Families (CCF), Mathew Staver and Liberty Counsel filed a request with superior court for an immediate injunction barring the city from issuing further licenses to same-sex couples. Within hours, Glen Lavy, counsel for Alliance Defense Fund (ADF), filed a similar lawsuit on behalf of Andy Pugno's Proposition 22 Fund. Representing San Francisco, Terry Stewart filed a counter-complaint, seeking a declaratory judgment that the state exclusion of same-sex couples from marriage violated the California Constitution. Would the Winter of Love (as the media dubbed it) be a short season? Not at all. Under the leadership of Gavin Newsom, Joyce Newstat, Steve Kawa, Dennis Herrera, and Terry Stewart, San Francisco drove the state government toward several dramatic showdowns in the handsome Beaux Arts building that was catty-corner to San Francisco City Hall, at the intersection of McAllister and Polk Streets: the Earl Warren Building, which housed the California Supreme Court.

The Stormy Winter of Love

Over the long weekend after the CCF and ADF lawsuits had been filed, the county clerk had issued 2,340 marriage licenses. Mayor Newsom deputized a host of public officials to officiate these weddings so that marriages could be performed on the spot. On Tuesday, February 17, Judge James Warren (Earl Warren's grandson) heard and denied ADF's motion for a temporary restraining order, because the Proposition 22 Fund had not suffered an injury that could not be redressed after a proper hearing or trial. Judge Ronald Quidachay followed Warren's reasoning to deny Mat Staver's motion in CCF's case. Both cases were scheduled for a hearing on the merits.[12]

The city attorney's office had secured valuable breathing room so that the mayor's initiative could gather momentum. Newsom had the pleasure of marrying Carole Migden and her longtime partner, Cristina Arguedas. Earlier, he had joined Steve Kawa and his partner, Dan Henkle, in civil matrimony. Migden herself performed dozens of marriages. Sheila Kuehl officiated the marriage of Jackie Goldberg and Sharon Stricker as well as the marriage of Kuehl's own former partner, Torie Osborn, and Lydia Vargas. Couples were flying in from all over the United States. By February 20, the number of same-sex marriages performed at city hall was more than three thousand.

The same day, February 20, Green Party mayor Jason West of New Paltz, New York, created new marriage licenses that were issued to twenty-one lesbian and gay couples. New York prosecutors quickly put a stop to that, but marriage resistance popped up elsewhere, whack-a-mole style. After reading New Mexico's gender-neutral marriage law, Victoria Dunlap, the clerk for Sandoval County, announced she would issue marriage licenses to same-sex couples, also on February 20. "This has nothing to do with politics or morals," the clerk said, echoing Boulder county clerk Clela Rorex a generation earlier. "If there are no legal grounds that say this should be prohibited, I can't withhold it." Twenty-one couples received licenses that day and were immediately married by ministers stationed outside the courthouse. The state attorney general shut down the process by informing Dunlap that the state would not recognize those marriages.[13]

On March 3, San Francisco was joined by Multnomah County, Oregon. Roey Thorpe, the executive director of Basic Rights Oregon, had asked county officials why they should not issue marriage licenses to same-sex couples. County Commission chair Diane Linn and Commissioners Lisa Naito, Serena Cruz, and Maria Rojo de Steffey were open to the idea, and County Counsel Agnes

Sowle opined that the state family law bar to same-sex marriages violated the Oregon Constitution. On March 3, the commissioners opened the doors of the marriage office to lesbian and gay couples—and four hundred of them received marriage licenses that day.[14]

At the same time it was generating national headlines, San Francisco's Winter of Love generated a lot of pushback. During a Thomas Road Baptist Church's Sunday service, the Reverend Jerry Falwell solemnly announced that San Francisco had received some applications that went beyond the homosexual couples folks had read about. When a brother and sister and then a quadruple (two lesbians and two gay men) asked for licenses, the mayor was surprised but agreeable. But just as he thought he had seen everything, Falwell continued, a single man showed up. "My psychiatrist says I have a split personality, and I want to marry myself." The pastor paused. "Well, you've got me there. I'd better close up shop and go home." The sanctuary erupted with cheers, thunderous laughter, and ferocious foot stomping. Falwell's point was that once anyone redefined marriage to recognize gay couples just because they love each other, there was no place to stop.[15]

Bay Area Evangelical pastors and Catholic archbishop William Levada shared Falwell's alarm, though not his sly sense of humor. Every day a handful of religious protesters objected to the weddings with chants and signs. On April 3, Levada led a one-thousand-person prayer march at St. Peter and Paul Church in North Beach to protest the heretical marriage licenses, but he did not direct that Newsom, a practicing Catholic, be denied communion. The mayor claimed that most lay Catholics and many priests supported his action. The archbishop was presiding over a church increasingly divided on this issue—and diverted by a child sexual abuse scandal.[16]

Nonetheless, the mayor did have an acting-out-of-order problem. Expressing objections felt by most conservatives, Mat Staver fumed that the mayor had no greater authority to issue marriage licenses to same-sex couples than he had to declare war on a foreign nation. Republican governor Arnold Schwarzenegger vowed to "abide by the oath" he took to "uphold California's laws." He challenged the mayor: What if a renegade mayor decided to distribute assault rifles or drugs because he disagreed with state law? "I believe this makes the national situation much more complicated and gives ammunition to those who are pushing for a constitutional amendment," worried Democratic senator Dianne Feinstein, who as mayor had vetoed San Francisco's first domestic partnership ordinance.[17]

Openly gay representative Barney Frank of Massachusetts went even further. A week after the Winter of Love commenced, the acid-tongued congressman was in San Francisco for a fundraiser. A local reporter caught him on a street corner, where Frank lambasted the marriage licensing as an "illegitimate act" that was unnecessary in light of *Goodridge*. "The argument that you need to do this in order to get the discussion going isn't right. The discussion's going," without the mayor's intervention. *Goodridge*'s mandate for same-sex marriage licensing did not take effect until May 17, and Frank noted that some opponents were threatening civil disobedience to stop them. "In Massachusetts it's very important for us to say, 'No, no, we're going to follow the law.'" He added, in a parting shot, "Nobody thinks what they're seeing here is marriage. We're going to have actual marriage in Massachusetts." Snap![18]

Shortly after the first Winter of Love licenses were issued, President Bush formally endorsed the Federal Marriage Amendment. One reason for supporting the amendment, he said, was to quell the outside-the-law activities of gay marriage supporters—specifically mentioning San Francisco and Sandoval County. Amendment supporters saw the renegade marriages as evidence that society would unravel once the central institution of marriage lost its age-old definition and meaning.

While the CCF and ADF lawsuits were tied up in the trial court, pressure mounted for Attorney General Bill Lockyer to petition the California Supreme Court to stop the mutiny. Only the attorney general could represent the state before the court. Lockyer personally supported marriage equality, but lawyers all over the state were imploring him to petition the court. There was even a movement to recall Lockyer, a possibility Californians took more seriously after Governor Davis was recalled in 2003. On February 27, Lockyer filed a petition with the California Supreme Court for an injunction to halt the marriages, then in their third week. Terry Stewart bought more time by persuading the court to give the city a chance to file extensive opposition papers.[19]

While Lockyer's petition was pending before the high court, couples kept showing up across the street, in city hall. On March 9, David Knight and Joe Lazzaro, a Baltimore couple, were Winter of Love–married. David was the son of Senator Knight, the legislative paladin for traditional marriage and sponsor of Proposition 22. Just months before he died, Knight rejected the Winter of Love: "We've had homosexuals since time immemorial, and nobody cared as long as they did their work and they didn't flaunt their sexuality and didn't try to push it on you and say, 'You have to accept me.' But now they are going to say they want to be classified as normal, and I can't accept the fact that two men, married, is normal."[20]

On March 11, Baltimore Gonzalez and his partner, Robert, stood in line for their marriage licenses; they had driven up the night before from Fresno. Raised in Madera and in the Catholic Church, Baltimore remained a spiritual person, and he was sure God had created him to be gay and to be married. Although still not out to his family, he had been a marriage activist in Fresno—and was excited to be getting married. Once inside city hall, the couple heard a frenzied cry, "Go get your papers signed; they just put a halt on the marriages." "They" were the California Supreme Court, which had issued a stay that required the city to stop issuing the marriage licenses pending the court's determination whether the mayor's actions were legal and the licenses legitimate. Baltimore and Robert got married that day. It was one of the last Winter of Love marriages.[21]

March 11, however, was not the end of the Winter of Love. Multnomah County, Oregon, continued to issues licenses until a state judge ordered the county to cease and desist in April—six weeks and more than three thousand licenses after the commissioners opened their county's doors to lesbian and gay couples.[22]

Why the Winter of Love Couples Got Married

Between February 12 and March 11, 2004, a total of 4,037 same-sex couples were married under authority of the San Francisco licenses. Who were they? Nine-tenths of them were from California, about a third from the Bay Area. A significant majority of the couples were female (57 percent) and were between thirty-six and fifty-four years old (55.4 percent). Two-thirds had college degrees. Around a quarter of the couples included at least one partner who had an ethnic or racial minority background. Some of the newly minted spouses, like Martin and Lyon, were leaders of the marriage equality movement. Most of the couples were in serious cohabiting relationships, and one-fifth of the female couples were raising children within their households, as were some of the male couples.[23]

Why did they get married? The application form alerted them that their marriages might not have legal validity, yet thousands of couples were eager to get Winter of Love–married. Katrina Kimport interviewed one or both partners in forty-two of the couples. Two-thirds of them, she reported, cited political reasons for participating. They "characterized their marriages as acts of civil disobedience that challenged the assumption that marriage is reserved for different-sex couples. The marriages were an opportunity to show solidarity with one another, make same-sex couples . . . visible, and build on the gains made by lesbian and gay activists who came before."[24]

The political motivation linked the Winter of Love spouses to the gay marriage pioneers profiled in chapter 1. The couples in both eras were rebels who intentionally challenged the core understandings about marriage—especially its insistence on rigid gender roles and heterosexual intercourse—but the Winter of Love couples were also pushing back against comprehensive domestic partnership, which many had entered as a second-best option. Unlike the marriage pioneers, these couples enjoyed the warm support of their surrounding community. Employees volunteered their time to keep the county clerk's office open; officiants made extraordinary efforts to accommodate all the services and to make them feel special. The experience of standing in a line that snaked around the block became the sweetest example of municipal solidarity. Some couples dropped by city hall just to stand in the line for a while. Everyone in the line waited happily, making friends with everyone else. Kids and dogs played in the field. People handed out Valentine's Day candy. One midwestern florist ordered flowers to be delivered to couples at city hall, and by March 11 other florists joined in sending hundreds of huge bountiful bouquets to the newlyweds.[25]

Like most of the marriage pioneers, these Winter of Love couples also got married to express their love and commitment in a public setting. The couples Kimport interviewed had been together an average of ten years. Marvin Burrows and William Duane Swenor had been together since 1953 and had registered as domestic partners in 2000. But when they got married on February 15, the occasion was surprisingly emotional. "That ceremony changed and revitalized our relationship." Half of the couples cited social and cultural legitimacy as a reason to Winter of Love–marry. Being married made your life legible to others, including your own blood family, in a way being domestic-partnered did not. "The San Francisco weddings marked [the first] time many respondents felt entirely a part of society." For many couples, Winter of Love marriages expressed a commitment to secure for their children the social, cultural, and legal benefits of marriage.[26]

The Winter of Love Meets the California Supreme Court

Every day for a month, the California Supreme Court justices could see Winter of Love couples, their friends, and protesters carrying on right outside their offices across the street. What effect, if any, would this have on their deliberations in *Lockyer v. City & County of San Francisco*? At the January 2003 Williams Institute roundtable, Lambda had provided an in-depth profile of the seven justices, six of whom had been appointed by Republican governors. The overall assessment was not optimistic, nor was it completely accurate.

Before joining the court, Marvin Baxter had been Republican governor George Deukmejian's appointments secretary. He was deferential to the political process, with a strong rule-of-law edge. Comfortable dealing with openly gay professionals, Baxter joined court opinions recognizing the co-parenting rights of lesbian domestic partners and cohabiting partners, as did Ming Chin, the youngest of eight children in a Chinese immigrant household. Chin was considered a wizard of the law because of his ability to master complicated bodies of doctrine. His jurisprudence was similar to Baxter's: "I don't think we're here to make laws. We're here to give the public and attorneys guidance on how to proceed on a given piece of legislation. We can put up signposts along the path to keep them on the path, but I don't think we're here to create a whole new freeway. I think that's up to the legislature."[27]

Janice Rogers Brown, the daughter of an Alabama sharecropper, was appointed by Governor Pete Wilson in 1996, two years after she advised him to issue his first veto of a domestic partnership bill. A fan of Ayn Rand and a favorite of the Federalist Society, Brown was conservative on social issues. In 2000, she told law students that big government leads to the atrophy of civil society and that in America it had fostered a "debased, debauched culture which finds moral depravity entertaining and virtue contemptible."[28]

Kathryn Werdegar and Ronald George, also appointed by Governor Wilson, were harder to pigeonhole. A brilliant legal mind whom the future governor had admired from the back of the class at Boalt Hall (the University of California, Berkeley's School of Law), Werdegar believed in following precedent without making major changes in the law. Lambda described her as a "true conservative and a believer in judicial restraint." In 2003, however, she wrote the 6-1 majority opinion in *Sharon S. v. Superior Court*, which held that a lesbian may adopt the child of her female partner without the mother's loss of legal rights. The legal effect of the decision was to allow lesbian and gay couples to secure joint parental rights without registering as domestic partners. As Massachusetts and Vermont judges had learned earlier, the experience of reading the record and briefs on appeal, researching the social science and policy materials, conferring with colleagues, and writing or joining a second-parent adoption opinion had a transformative effect on judges as well as on the law.[29]

An affable jurist with finely honed political instincts, appointed by Wilson to the supreme court in 1991 and promoted by Wilson to chief justice in 1996, Ron George often looked like the cat that caught the canary, a feat he accomplished by thinking two steps ahead of the canary. Lambda, somewhat superficially, called him "extremely ambitious" and a "believer in judicial restraint even when it results in injustice," but also a "centrist." A deeper look at George's jurisprudence would have revealed an appreciation of limited government—but also of the government's need to adapt to changing social circumstances. Consistent with his adaptive view of the law, he joined Werdegar's opinion in *Sharon S.* and later opinions recognizing two lesbians as de facto co-parents.[30]

Although appointed by conservative Governor Deukmejian, Joyce Kennard was, as Lambda reported, "a maverick voice of liberalism in a court that tilts right." A mixed-race immigrant of Dutch-Indonesian ancestry, an amputee, and a woman in a male-dominated profession, she and her mother spent a short time in a World War II internment camp. She understood the perspective of society's outsiders. But she was also smart and tough, having earned college and law school degrees with high honors from the University of Southern California and respect as a rigorous judge. She was infamous for asking long, complicated questions in a thick Dutch accent.[31]

Carlos Moreno, the only Democrat on the court, had grown up in an East Los Angeles working-class Latino family and worked his way through Yale College and Stanford Law School. Humble, unassuming, gregarious, warm, and shrewd, Moreno was an out-of-the-closet liberal. In 2005, he wrote the opinion for a unanimous court in *Elisa B. v. Superior Court,* which extended the reasoning of *Sharon S.* to enforce parental responsibilities against the lesbian partner of a child's biological mother. He also wrote for the court in *Koebke v. Bernardo Heights Country Club,* which unanimously held that the country club violated the Unruh Act when it denied lesbian domestic partners the privileges offered married members. Agreeing with Lambda's Jon Davidson, the court read the Unruh Act in light of the 2003 domestic partnership statute, which gave partners all the rights and duties of married spouses. Dissenting in part, Werdegar maintained that the lesbian golfers were entitled to relief even before the 2003 partnership law took effect.[32]

In 2003, Lambda had opined that this collection of judges was not likely to follow *Goodridge*—and such a group would be even less likely to sustain the action of a mayor acting in defiance of a statutory initiative that had been adopted by an overwhelming vote. The chief justice's memoirs recall this political cartoon: "Two fairly identifiable figures are depicted, Mayor Newsom and myself. Mayor Newsom is standing on top of city hall—as he swings a large wrecking ball toward the building across the street, namely, the Supreme Court's quarters, with me on top of that building—and the caption is, 'The ball is in your court.'" That sums up the way Ron George saw the Winter of Love: the mayor's actions were "a wholesale defiance of the law" that, if tolerated, would unleash legal chaos. This was also the understanding held by Marvin Baxter, Ming Chin, and Janice Rogers Brown; and so there was a clear majority for the view that the mayor had acted unlawfully and the marriage licenses were all void. On August 12, 2004, Chief Justice George delivered this as the judgment of the court in *Lockyer v. City & County of San Francisco*. The court did not, however, rule on the constitutional issue. It restricted itself to the immediate question of whether Newsom had the authority to issue the licenses.[33]

For the suddenly unmarried couples, the ruling was a kick in the gut, but a more complete report of the case offers some interesting twists. In partially dissenting opinions, Justices Werdegar and Kennard would have set the constitutional issues for full review by the court. Based on our conversations with court personnel, we believe that Justices Werdegar, Kennard, and Moreno were already inclined to think that Proposition 22 violated the equality guarantees of the California Constitution. Justices Baxter, Chin, and Brown were baffled that anyone could think homosexuals had a constitutional right to marry. Chief Justice George had no settled thoughts about the constitutional merits. In short, Lambda's 2003 memorandum was too pessimistic about the chances that the court would recognize marriage equality under the California Constitution.[34]

Because the marriage equality movement could not win a constitutional initiative in 2004, Kate Kendell was relieved that the court avoided the constitutional marriage issue. On the other hand, those magical months had changed her views. She had seen excitement and joy in the faces of Winter of Love–married couples, and as executive director of NCLR she naturally was interested in working on issues that met the needs of her community and that excited its members and their families. Being married really was a different emotional experience—not just a different social status—from being domestic-partnered. Because of her public role as a gay rights lawyer, Kate had not taken advantage of Gavin Newsom's offer to marry her and Sandy in city hall—but she now wanted to be *legally* married.

Shannon Minter's views evolved in response to what he called a "chemical chain reaction" within the LGBT community. "Domestic partnership and civil unions as an alternative to marriage died on February 12, 2004," he told us. Unlike Kate, Shannon was already legally married. He and his wife, Robin, were married in 2001 and were raising a daughter in their household. Recall that in *Littleton v. Prange* (chapter 5), Texas in 1999 refused to recognize the marriage of Christie Littleton, a trans woman, to a cisgender man. California in 2001, however, had no problem recognizing the marriage of Shannon, a trans man, to Robin, a cisgender woman. "Being able to marry transformed my life in ways I never could have imagined," Shannon says. "Not only did being married bring me great personal joy, it also enabled me to heal my relationship with my parents and extended family [in Texas], who were able to understand my life for the first time."[35]

The *Marriage Cases*

The California Supreme Court's March 11 order had specifically invited a separate constitutional challenge. "Within hours," the chief justice wrote in his memoir, "the mayor and his subordinates did what they should have done at the outset, namely, proceed with a lawsuit to have the superior court determine the constitutionality of the marriage statutes." The city attorney's office was determined to vindicate Gavin Newsom's bold move when it filed its marriage equality constitutional challenge in *City & County of San Francisco v. State of California*. The LGBT-advocacy organizations were divided on the issue, with EQCA and NCLR in favor of an immediate constitutional challenge and the ACLU opposed because its leaders thought any judicial victory would be overridden by a constitutional initiative.[36]

Lambda's Jon Davidson and Jenny Pizer had been primary architects of the 2003 strategy of incremental progress, but they concluded that their strategy had been overtaken by events. The constitutional train had already left the station, because women's rights attorney Gloria Allred had filed a marriage lawsuit on behalf of the Reverend Troy Perry, Robin Tyler, and their partners on February 22. On March 12, NCLR (through Minter), Lambda Legal (Davidson and Pizer), the ACLU (Matt Coles and James Esseks), and Equality California (Dave Codell) jointly filed a complaint for twelve same-sex couples in *Woo v. Lockyer*.

The Judicial Council of California consolidated the San Francisco, Perry/Tyler, and Lambda/ACLU/NCLR lawsuits with the two earlier CCF and ADF lawsuits as *In re Marriage Cases* and assigned them to San Francisco Superior Court judge Richard Kramer. The consolidation meant that Allred, Codell,

Coles, Davidson, Minter, Pizer, and Stewart became a marriage equality Dream Team. They worked together brilliantly despite strong disagreements over strategy and argumentation. For example, Minter and Codell set forth the argument that Proposition 22 only barred officials from recognizing out-of-state same-sex marriages, similar to DOMA, and did not bar California clerks from issuing such licenses. Stewart and Pizer considered this argument a long shot (as would we), because the initiative sweepingly said that same-sex marriages were neither "valid" nor "recognized" in the state.[37]

Everyone agreed that the constitutional arguments were front and center, and the lawyers put together a synergistic, unified set of claims: (1) marriage was more than a word: it was a fundamental social as well as legal institution that was far from the same as domestic partnership, which was not rich in tradition; (2) yet a judicial ruling for marriage would be a "small step" and a natural development after the 2003 comprehensive domestic partnership law and its legislative findings; and (3) discrimination against LGBT people ought to receive heightened scrutiny under the state constitution, *either* because sexual orientation ought to be a suspect classification *or* because excluding same-sex couples discriminated on the basis of sex, which was already a suspect classification. Points (1) and (2) would receive a boost on April 4, 2005, when the California Court of Appeal in Sacramento, a collection of relatively conservative jurists, unanimously agreed with Codell's argument that comprehensive domestic partnership did not violate Proposition 22 because domestic partnership fell far short of "marriage," which was Senator Knight's object of protection.[38]

A primary disagreement among counsel centered on the sex discrimination argument for marriage equality. Minter and Kendell saw this argument as the unifying constitutional vision supporting equality for women, for trans persons, and for lesbian and gay folks. Stereotypes about the capabilities of gender and sexual minorities, as well as women, rested upon beliefs that there are two sexes, each directed by natural law into traditional patterns of marrying one's sex complement and bearing children through natural procreative intercourse. Stewart agreed with that view but felt that few judges would be able to apprehend the connection among sex, gender role, and sexuality. At about the same time, one of us participated in a program where even a liberal US Supreme Court justice was unable to understand how discriminating against a gay man treated him differently because of his sex (and not just because of his sexual orientation).[39]

The counsel also disagreed over whether they should seek a trial or ask for summary judgment, based upon briefs and affidavits. Stewart really wanted a trial, with witnesses who could be cross-examined in person. She was confident that no witness could successfully explain how expanding marriage to committed LGBT couples would hurt anyone or represent bad public policy. Minter was skeptical, because he believed the challengers' case was strong on the law, and judges could take judicial notice of historical and social science evidence refuting the state's justifications for the exclusion. In any event, Judge Kramer had no interest in a trial with witnesses. Instead, the challengers submitted detailed affidavits from academic experts on the history of marriage (Nancy Cott) and anti-gay discrimination (William Eskridge), the *Loving* parallel (Randall Kennedy), and the similarity of gay and straight couples (Gregory Herek).

While the challengers' team engaged in intense internal debates, the defense team was in open civil warfare. ADF's Glen Lavy and CCF's Mat Staver litigated like bitter rivals, even though they emphasized the same argument: marriage was a unique institution designed to channel straight people into responsible family patterns that were optimal for children. The main substantive distinction between them was that Staver and CCF openly embraced the natural law view that marriage was eternally and universally tied to procreation, while Lavy and ADF emphasized instrumentalist, policy-based arguments of the sort that the justices might actually find persuasive.

Associate Attorney General Christopher Krueger represented the state—but Governor Schwarzenegger was represented by his own counsel. Both government lawyers rejected the CCF/ADF arguments, which they considered offensive. They saw committed lesbian and gay couples as no threat to marriage and conceded that lesbian and gay households were just as good for children as straight married households. The ADF and CCF lawyers found these concessions maddening, as did traditional values amici like the California Catholic Conference, the Church of Jesus Christ of Latter-day Saints, and Focus on the Family. But the government attorneys were professionally required to consider the entire corpus of state public law—including the 2003 domestic partnership law and the recognition of second-parent adoptions in *Sharon S.* If California approved and supported lesbian households where each domestic partner had legal spousal duties and rights and where each was a legal parent of each child, how could its attorneys maintain that California was committed to the policy that the defects of such households were so significant that they supported the exclusion of such couples from civil marriage?

Although the attorney general conceded that the marriage exclusion should be subjected to intermediate scrutiny because sexual orientation was a quasi-suspect classification, he and the governor argued that the overwhelming vote for Proposition 22 meant that society was not ready for gay marriage and that the public interest in gradual legitimate change justified the separate status reflected in domestic partnership. Just as the CCF and ADF counsel were frustrated by the government's concession that gay and lesbian couples were good parents, so the government's counsel were frustrated by the CCF/ADF argument that marriage was special and unique. That moral stance undercut the government's argument that domestic partnerships were sufficient.

Adopting NCLR's sex discrimination argument, Judge Kramer ruled in favor of the challengers as a matter of law, but a divided court of appeals reversed him. The appellate court ruled that Proposition 22 did not deny the plaintiffs a fundamental right, did not rely on a suspect classification, and was justified by the state policy of preserving marriage as a special institution for couples capable of procreation. Despite a strong dissenting opinion, the NCLR, Lambda, and ACLU lawyers seriously considered not appealing, given the losses the movement was suffering in courts all across the country (see our next chapter). But San Francisco filed an appeal on November 13, and the litigating groups followed the next day. The attorney general urged the supreme court to take the case. It usually takes the justices fifteen or twenty minutes of discussion to decide to hear a case. For *In re Marriage Cases*, Ron George reports that the process lasted only as long as it took for seven of his colleagues to utter the word "Grant."[40]

The 2005 and 2007 Marriage Bills

Mark Leno (San Francisco) and John Laird (Los Angeles) were the first openly gay men to serve in the California legislature. Both were elected to the assembly in 2002, joining the lesbians already in the legislature. Leno had served on the San Francisco Board of Supervisors, where he was impressed by the broad domestic partnership law. "For the first time we're talking about our lives not in terms of sex or disease, but in how we love and how we live our lives." He performed more than one hundred commitment ceremonies— and he grew ever more certain that these couples should have the option of getting married. Then came *Goodridge*. Now was the time, he thought. Geoff Kors met with him in Sacramento and promised EQCA's full support.[41]

Leno introduced his marriage bill, A.B. 1967, on National Freedom to Marry Day—the same day Newsom started handing out marriage licenses. Speaker Fabian Núñez proceeded cautiously because of the brouhaha surrounding the

Winter of Love. A third of the Democrats in the legislature were Latino American, and most of their constituents were culturally conservative Catholics. The Democrats did not want to squander their huge advantage with Latino voters by handing the Republicans same-sex marriage as a wedge issue. Assembly Bill 1967 received a favorable committee report on April 20, but it got no further per the Speaker's agreement with Leno.[42]

Marriage equality received a boost in the 2004 elections. The Democrats retained the same majorities in the legislature, and Carole Migden returned as a state senator (after being term-limited out of the assembly in 2002). The state voted overwhelmingly against President Bush, whose description of marriage equality as a threat to children had triggered the Winter of Love. In December 2004, Leno introduced a proposed Religious Freedom and Civil Marriage Protection Act, A.B. 19, making the same arguments to the assembly's judiciary committee that the ACLU, Lambda, and NCLR lawyers were making in the *Marriage Cases:* Proposition 22 did not bar the legislature from extending marriage to same-sex couples; the state's exclusion of such couples, confirmed in *Lockyer,* denied dignitary as well as legal benefits to deserving couples and their children; and domestic partnerships were a "separate but equal" (thus unconstitutional) regime. To make these arguments, EQCA assembled a rainbow coalition of civil rights groups—including the NAACP and dozens of organizations representing women, Mexican Americans, African Americans, Asian Americans, Jewish Americans, people with disabilities, and immigrants—as well as scores of churches, labor unions, and bar associations.[43]

Opposing A.B. 19 were the California Catholic Conference, the California Family Alliance, the Christian Coalition, Concerned Women for America, and several dozen churches. The opposition was almost exclusively religious, and most of their witnesses' testimony before the assembly's judiciary committee reflected the sectarian views that "homosexuals want to destroy marriage as an institution—not benefit from it" and "marriage is a sacred institution with unique attributes to be realized and shared only by the union of one man and one woman." The opponents also made important democratic process arguments: the people had spoken clearly in Proposition 22, which entrenched traditional marriage in state law, and the legislature could not amend a law adopted by the initiative process. At the same time, Andy Pugno's Protect Marriage committee and Randy Thomasson's CCF were also working on voter initiatives to override the domestic partnership law and entrench one-man, one-woman marriage in the California Constitution, but there was insufficient political support for such a strong measure.[44]

On June 2, 2005, Leno's marriage bill secured a 37-36 vote on the floor of the assembly, with seven abstentions. Under the chamber's rules, a measure needed an absolute majority—forty-one out of eighty possible votes—to pass. Kors and Leno were not ready to give up, and they believed the key to success was the Latino caucus; most of those abstaining were Latino legislators. Christine Chavez joined the EQCA team and would ultimately bring with her the support of the United Farm Workers (UFW). Founded in 1962 by Dolores Huerta and Cesar Chavez (Christine's grandfather), the UFW was both a union and a civil rights movement for ethnic minorities traditionally exploited by corporate farmers and food companies. Huerta had been an early supporter of Leno's marriage bill. She and Chavez carried this message: civil rights that protected immigrants, farm workers, and ethnic minorities ought to protect LGBT people, too.[45]

Leno and Kors resolved to start over, in the senate. Sheila Kuehl persuaded the Senate Judiciary Committee to add the Leno bill into A.B. 849, a farm bill, and the committee favorably reported it on July 12. On the floor, Senators Kuehl and Migden were joined by Richard Alarcón, who represented the San Fernando Valley. A devout Catholic whose teaching career had started in parochial schools, Alarcón was touched by the death of his cousin Jimmy from AIDS. "All [Jimmy's] boyfriends came forward" at the funeral. "It opened the doors to who Jimmy was. That was sort of a declaration that constitutional rights are not limited to people of color." When his stepdaughter came out as a lesbian in 2005, Richard embraced her. "If my daughter chose to marry her girlfriend, I would like to perform the wedding."[46]

The Catholic Church did not press Alarcón very hard on this issue, as its leaders were dealing with the predatory priests scandal. In February 2004, the Los Angeles archdiocese issued a report detailing the sexual abuse accusations made by 656 persons against 244 priests, deacons, and other officials. Evangelical lobbyists like Ben Lopez for TVC and Karen England for the Capitol Resource Institute applied strong pressure to legislators from conservative districts. But with Hispanic legislators, these lobbyists had much less clout than Catholic lobbyists would have had, and the LGBT lobbyists easily undermined their credibility with references to homophobic statements by Lou Sheldon, the controversial leader of TVC.[47]

With the Catholic Church's voice muted and new support from Senator Alarcón, the UFW, Huerta and Chavez, Los Angeles mayor Antonio Villaraigosa, and even the Spanish Parliament (which enacted a marriage equality law), A.B. 849 came to the senate floor with a great deal of momentum to persuade Latino legislators that it was safe to vote for marriage equality. On September 1,

A.B. 849 passed in the senate with exactly the number of votes needed, 21-15. The big challenge was to secure a majority in the assembly.

Equality California had been working since June to win over at least four of the assembly members who had passed or abstained on June 2. Assembly Member (and former lieutenant governor) Mervyn Dymally had missed the June 2 vote but was a certain yes in September. Three others represented predominantly Latino districts. Huerta and Chavez personally reassured them that their electoral prospects would not be harmed by supporting marriage equality. EQCA applied sticks as well as carrots. Assembly Member Gloria Negrete McLeod, representing conservative San Bernardino County, was term-limited and planning to run for the senate, where Senator Nell Soto was also term-limited. At a Labor Day event, she watched with great interest as scores of EQCA and MECA supporters lavishly praised Soto for supporting marriage equality. McLeod became a yes.[48]

On September 6, electronic voting in the assembly proceeded quickly, with forty yes lights appearing—but for forty-five long seconds the yes lights were stuck on forty, which would have defeated the measure. Finally, the light for Assembly Member Simón Salinas lit up. He represented rural Monterey County, in the Central Valley, and had not voted in June. A solid civil rights supporter, he had supported comprehensive domestic partnership in 2003 when his vote was needed, and he promised Kors that he would hew to that commitment. His vote meant that the California legislature became the first state legislature to pass marriage equality legislation.[49]

Assembly Bill 849 went to Arnold Schwarzenegger's desk. EQCA invested $100,000 in ads and commercials urging the "Governator" to sign the bill, but Schwarzenegger's interests were not aligned with EQCA's. He wanted a full term in 2006, and signing gay marriage into law would kill him in the GOP primary—so he vetoed A.B. 849 on September 29, saying in his veto statement that "I do not believe the Legislature can reverse an initiative [Proposition 22] approved by the people of California." After reaffirming his support for equal treatment of lesbian and gay couples, the governor noted that Proposition 22's validity would soon be decided by the supreme court. "This bill simply adds confusion to a constitutional issue. If the ban of same-sex marriage is unconstitutional, this bill is not necessary. If the ban is constitutional, this bill is ineffective."[50]

In June 2006, the Democratic primary returned all the marriage equality supporters, and the Democrats maintained their overwhelming 25-15 and 48-32 legislative majorities in November. With support from EQCA, Gloria

McLeod handily won the open senate seat in conservative Riverdale, and Simón Salinas won his race for county commissioner. Governor Schwarzenegger coasted to another term against a weak Democratic nominee. One reason he prevailed is that he installed a savvy liberal Democrat, open lesbian Susan Kennedy, as his chief of staff and took moderate positions on most issues in the year before the election.

In 2007, Mark Leno filed A.B. 43, the same religious freedom and marriage bill that had passed in 2005. Because no legislator who supported marriage equality had lost her or his reelection bid, the path through the legislature was smoother this time. On June 5, A.B. 43 passed in the assembly, 42-34. It passed the senate on September 7 by a vote of 22-15. Both assembly and senate judiciary committee reports listed hundreds of groups that submitted letters or testimony in support of the bill but only a handful of groups stating their opposition. Unlike 2005, the California Conference of Bishops did not register formal opposition in 2007; the senate report listed only four in opposition, all Evangelical groups. The Catholic Church had not altered its doctrine, but it may have quietly reordered its priorities.[51]

On October 12, more than a month after final legislative action, Governor Schwarzenegger vetoed A.B. 43. "In 2000, the voters approved Proposition 22, a challenge which is currently pending before the California Supreme Court. I maintain my position that the appropriate resolution to this issue is to allow the Court to rule on Proposition 22."[52]

The Supreme Court's Decision in the *Marriage Cases*

The California Supreme Court that considered *In re Marriage Cases* included six of the seven justices who had decided *Lockyer*. In 2005, Justice Brown resigned to become a federal judge, and Governor Schwarzenegger named Carol Corrigan as her replacement. Raised in a traditional Catholic household in Stockton, California, she had attended parochial secondary school and graduated from Holy Names College, a Catholic all-women's college in Oakland. She was the third Catholic on the court and the only justice who had never been married.

Terry Stewart and Shannon Minter were the lead counsel for the challengers, and they anchored their case on *Perez v. Sharp* (*Perez v. Lippold*), the California Supreme Court's famous 1948 decision invalidating the state law barring different-race marriages, two decades before the US Supreme Court did so in *Loving v. Virginia* (1967). Justice Roger Traynor's plurality opinion reasoned that the fundamental "right to marry is the right to join in marriage with the person of one's choice" and that the state law restricting choice based upon race was arbitrary. As a constitutional matter, Stewart and Minton argued, lesbian and gay partners were entitled to the same choices. Justices Kathryn Werdegar, Joyce Kennard, and Carlos Moreno would have found *Perez* persuasive if the court had taken up the constitutional merits of the issue in *Lockyer,* and their inclination was only confirmed by events since 2004: not only the media coverage of the happy Winter of Love couples, the lesbian co-parents raising children after *Sharon S.,* and the success of the marriage bills but also the virtual disappearance of nonsectarian opposition to marriage equality. With the implosion of Catholic moral authority on these issues, the leading family values lobbyist was Karen England, a policy lightweight prone to gaffes.[53]

Kate Kendell had heard through the grapevine that Ron George was inclined to think that the comprehensive domestic partnership law satisfied the California Constitution's nondiscrimination mandate. This was the centerpiece of the government's position and its reason for distinguishing *In re Marriage Cases* from *Perez.* Minter, Stewart, and their allies focused their briefs on this issue, demonstrating that the domestic partnership law did not vest the same legal rights and duties as marriage:

- Domestic partners, but not married spouses, were required to have an intimate relationship *and* a common residence before they could apply for state recognition.
- Marriage, but not domestic partnership, was required to have a ceremonial element.
- Domestic partners did not have the right to certain long-term care benefits that married spouses had.
- Short-lived domestic partnerships without children could be dissolved merely by filing a form, in contrast to marriage, which could be dissolved only by divorce.
- For those domestic partnerships that could be dissolved by filling out a form, there were few protections for dependent partners.
- Some other states would recognize California same-sex marriages, but there was no evidence any would recognize California domestic partnerships.

These fundamental differences constituted a regime that was separate and deliberately unequal, arguably even disrespectful.[54]

More important, domestic partnership, Minter and Stewart argued, did not carry the cultural signals and social significance of civil marriage. Domestic partnerships would mark lesbian and gay couples as distinct and second-class, signifying that their relationships were not as serious as those of straight married couples. "By placing all lesbian and gay couples in a separate class with a separate name and status, the domestic partnership law highlights their sexual orientation and places the sexuality of these people in a constant, unwelcome spotlight that perpetuates the invidious stereotype that same-sex relations are presumably about sexual gratification rather than love and commitment." Stewart's brief offered examples of kids who considered themselves "bastards" because their parents were partnered but not married. For a child, "his parents' marriage not only legitimized them, it legitimized *him*."[55]

Because the California Supreme Court was required to decide cases, with a written opinion, within ninety days of oral argument, it had a distinctive process for deliberation. After studying the briefs, the justices met and usually reached a tentative decision for the case before argument. One justice circulated a tentative opinion, called a calendar memorandum. Each chambers responded with comments and an indication whether the justice agreed. Following that drafting and deliberative process, the court heard oral argument, after which the calendar memorandum would be revised into an opinion for the court. The three-and-a-half-hour argument in the *Marriage Cases*, held on March 4, 2008, is available on C-SPAN and is worth watching. The justices and the eight counsel—Terry Stewart, Shannon Minter, Michael Maroko, and Waukeen McCoy for the challengers, versus Christopher Krueger, Ken Mennemeier, Glen Lavy, and Mat Staver for the defenders— were exceptionally well prepared. They engaged in a wide-ranging exploration of the democratic theory, family law, and equality issues discussed in the briefs. But by the time the lawyers spoke, a tentative decision in the case had already been reached.[56]

Marvin Baxter and Ming Chin did not see why the gays were not satisfied with having almost all the legal rights and duties of marriage. Because she had lesbian friends in committed relationships, Carol Corrigan fully understood Stewart and Minter's argument that domestic partnership denied these couples important rights as well as equal respect. She agreed that the children of lesbian couples would benefit from state recognition of their parents' marriages. And she found the arguments for excluding those couples speculative and far-fetched. The sticking point for Corrigan was that California's citizens— the authors and beneficiaries of the state constitution—had recently deliberated and voted on the issue before the court. "The law doesn't belong to lawyers and judges, it belongs to all of us," she said in an interview about her formative college years. "In a democracy, the system doesn't work unless the citizenry can think critically and can debate. If that doesn't happen, the whole society flounders." She and her unelected colleagues were not the right people to decide a meta-constitutional issue that intensely but evenly divided the citizenry. The decision to take marriage off the table for lesbian and gay couples was a judgment about who has a place at the table. As she repeatedly asked at oral argument, "Who decides who we are as Californians?"[57]

Ron George says in his memoirs that had he been a legislator, he would probably have deferred to the voters. But as a judge he was bound by *Perez*, a super-precedent whose result as well as reasoning had borne up brilliantly over time. Assistant Attorney General Chris Krueger argued that *Perez* was distinguishable because California offered all the rights and benefits of marriage to same-sex couples, but George and his assistant Hal Cohen engaged in a series of thought experiments. "Imagine if marital relationships between a Black man and a Black woman were to be given the name domestic partnership and the same relationship between a Caucasian man and a Caucasian woman were to be called a marriage, would we find that passed constitutional muster? . . . I don't think a court would uphold that." Justice Traynor had written that the "right to marry is the right to join in marriage with the person of one's choice," and the right to marry precedents reflected a pro-choice reading of constitutional equality. Ultimately, George considered the separate but unequal domestic partnership regime fatal to, rather than supportive of, the state's defense of the status quo.[58]

The only plausible distinction between *Perez* and *In re Marriage Cases* was that the former struck down a law that openly discriminated because of race. One answer to that challenge was Minter's argument that the exclusion of woman-woman couples from civil marriage was *sex* discrimination in the same way that the exclusion of black-white couples from civil marriage was *race* discrimination. In each case, the regulatory variable—the item that changed the state's action—was the sex or race of one partner. Under the California Constitution, sex was a suspect classification, just as race was. Joyce Kennard, Kathryn Werdegar, and Carlos Moreno agreed with the sex discrimination argument—but Ron George did not. He believed that a law discriminated because of sex only if it treated women differently from men, and all of his court's sex discrimination decisions could be understood that way. But he

agreed with his liberal colleagues that sexual orientation was a suspect classification that ought to be subject to strict scrutiny, and he recalled that the
Proposition 22 campaign was all about homosexuality and gay people and not
about gender role and women.

The initial calendar memorandum circulated by the chief justice took no
firm position on how to resolve the constitutional issues. "I informed all of
them I was giving serious consideration to recommending that the court invalidate the marriage statutes [including Proposition 22] that limited marriage
to the officially recognized relationship between a man and a woman, and that
I would, in the next day or two, be circulating a draft with both options." He
would welcome reactions from all colleagues before casting his vote. Marvin
Baxter was gracious, but he glumly expected that George was being so carefully deliberative because he was making a big move. Ming Chin's eyes grew
wide with incredulity as he listened to George's explanation. Carlos Moreno,
Joyce Kennard, and Kathryn Werdegar submitted their comments and encouragement very quickly. George hoped he could persuade Carol Corrigan to join
a moderate opinion striking down Proposition 22, but she ultimately weighed
in with Chin and Baxter.[59]

With the court divided 3-3, George revised and circulated the final calendar
memorandum as an opinion striking down the exclusion. Three justices
joined, and oral argument was set for March 4. Terry Stewart was up first, and
she could tell immediately, from the justices' expressions and body language,
that the court had decided in her favor: Carlos Moreno looked quite happy, Marvin Baxter was uncharacteristically dour, Ming Chin seemed angry, Joyce
Kennard and Kathryn Werdegar struck her as satisfied, and Ron George, sitting in the center of the bench and gently dominating the questioning, had
the aura of a judicial maestro. By the end of the argument, everyone in the
majestic courtroom had come to the same conclusion.

On May 15, 2008, the California Supreme Court announced its much-
anticipated decision for *In re Marriage Cases*. Chief Justice George delivered
the opinion for the court. He ruled that Proposition 22 and other statutory exclusions of lesbian and gay couples from civil marriage violated the California
Constitution. For the first time since *Baehr*, a state appellate court announced
strict scrutiny for the marriage exclusion. Specifically, the court held that the
exclusion was subject to fatal strict scrutiny both because it denied LGBT
couples their fundamental right to marry and because it deployed a suspect
classification. To Minter's chagrin, the chief justice explicitly rejected the sex

discrimination argument but ruled that sexual orientation was also a suspect classification, the first time a state supreme court had so ruled in a published opinion. Justices Baxter, Chin, and Corrigan wrote thoughtful, serious dissents. Consider some distinctive features of the justices' debate.[60]

Accepting the traditionalists' point that marriage is a cornerstone of society, the chief justice's opinion analyzed marriage as a positive, affirmative right of citizenship, not as just a negative liberty. The state, he suggested, had a duty to provide families with some legal scaffold that would enable them to build the lives of their choosing. The dissenters argued that the domestic partnership law provided that scaffolding, but the majority found no compelling public justification for treating lesbian and gay couples as second-class citizens. The state never met its burden of showing who was harmed by including lesbian and gay couples in civil marriage. The chief justice's memoir quips: "If you don't like gay marriage, don't get gay married."[61]

The court could have ended the opinion with this right-to-marry analysis, but the majority felt it useful to announce that sexual orientation was a suspect classification under the state constitution. Invoking the criteria articulated by the US Supreme Court, the California Supreme Court found that (1) sexual orientation had been the basis for pervasive discrimination, (2) even though it had no relationship to one's ability to contribute to and participate in society, and (3) was a trait that was a core part of one's identity, and that (4) LGBT people were politically disadvantaged by social prejudice and stereotypes. Though it was unnecessary to the resolution of the case, the court also ruled that the marriage exclusion was not a sex discrimination. The chief justice felt it appropriate to emphasize that the decision was protecting gay and lesbian couples and was not a collateral consequence of precedents focused on other groups.

In response to the concern that marriage equality would send a message that marriage was not important or was not needed to raise children, the majority answered that "we do not alter or diminish either the legal responsibilities that biological parents owe to their children." Instead, the court held that "a stable two-parent family relationship, supported by the state's official recognition and protection, is equally as important for the numerous children in California who are being raised by same-sex couples as for those children being raised by opposite-sex couples (whether they are biological parents or adoptive parents)." The court pointedly rejected the ADF-CCF argument that children should be reared by their biological parents. Knowing that Carlos Moreno and his wife were proud parents of an adopted daughter, most of the justices were personally offended by that claim. This was an example of how Glen Lavy and (especially) Mat Staver were tone-deaf toward their judicial audience.[62]

The California Supreme Court's opinion in the *Marriage Cases* was the result of three convergent phenomena: an ascendant LGBT social movement aligned with the dominant Democratic Party that prevailed over a traditional family values countermovement tied to the waning GOP; a brilliant campaign that combined public opinion with mastery of the legislative process; and a rainbow coalition of women, LGBT people, and racial and ethnic minorities. The Winter of Love played a key role. A month of lesbian and gay couples and their children waiting joyfully in line for marriage licenses and on-the-spot weddings transformed people's attitudes about marriage equality and revealed the chasm between real marriage and domestic partnerships. As Minter told us, the Winter of Love was the death of civil unions and domestic partnerships as acceptable alternatives to marriage.

The Winter of Love also helped energize the civil rights super-coalition that would propel marriage equality to success in both the legislature and the judiciary. Gavin Newsom's challenge called for straight people to see gay and lesbian couples as committed to serious, long-term relationships, often with children, that deserved respect and support for the same reason that straight marriages deserved respect and support. The deepening alliance with Hispanic leaders was especially important. Without the support of Assembly Speaker Fabian Núñez, lobbyists Dolores Huerta and Christine Chavez, Latino and Latina legislators, and Justice Carlos Moreno, marriage equality would not have arrived in 2008.

Even the renegade nature of the outside-the-law marriage licenses created a productive dynamic. The Winter of Love forced the gayocracy to abandon its carefully laid plans in the face of thousands of queer as well as gay people claiming their space in the public debate. There were echoes all over the country. In the same year the *Marriage Cases* were decided, April DeBoer and Jayne Rowse held a commitment ceremony to celebrate their spiritual and romantic union. Jayne especially wanted a public expression of their love. It was held in a boutique shop owned by their buddy Scott Bailow.

Dozens of LGBT friends came to make this a festive and gay-supportive occasion—but at heart it was just an old-fashioned midwestern family event, just like a marriage. An ordained minister, Dana Shaw, officiated, in defiance of the 2004 Michigan Super-DOMA. Jayne's family came up from Indiana;

they had not been supportive, but now were warming to the idea. April's family was there in full force, with not a little drama. Wendy and Ken DeBoer had divorced in 2006, and when Ken showed up with his second wife, Kimberly, there were strains between the former spouses. Wendy also thought that her son, Ken, was not on his best behavior.[63]

Resplendent in a traditional white wedding dress, April was nervous about the public event and the tension between her parents. Jayne was nervous because April was nervous. She was dressed in a traditional groom's suit, except that she left the pants at home and had to borrow a pair from Dana. The pants matched well enough, even if some attendants noticed that they were really too tight on Jayne. Their great-niece Kayleigh was the flower girl. The couple exchanged vows of lifetime commitment, with food and drinks afterward. Everyone at the ceremony thought of the nurses as a married couple. To top things off, April was pregnant with triplets, by way of donor insemination. She was 37, an age when pregnancy was riskier, and suffered a miscarriage later in the year. As we noted in the last chapter, Jayne adopted Nolan in 2009, and he made their family complete.

Like April DeBoer, Kate Kendell was raising children with her partner, Sandy Holmes, in San Francisco. The Winter of Love had moved Kate, and NCLR had been lead counsel in the marriage litigation. But she was worried. Having grown up in the Church of Jesus Christ of Latter-day Saints, she knew that if the Mormons mobilized in favor of the constitutional initiative already posed to override *In re Marriage Cases,* her side was in trouble.

12 • Latter-day Constitutionalists

Social movements are guided by their own constitutional interpretations and become most effective when they can change prevailing narratives in support of those principles. In the first decade of the new millennium, the marriage equality movement made some headway on that project. Traditionalists needed to express their own constitutional theory in defense of the status quo, and the most successful arguments came out of Provo, Utah, home to Brigham Young University (BYU).

Lynn Wardle and his five siblings were born and raised in Provo in a devout Mormon household. He graduated from BYU, where he met his wife, Marian Eastwood, and in 1974 he earned a law degree from Duke. Joining the BYU law faculty in 1978 as a scholar of family law, Lynn brought a faith-based perspective to the subject, arguing that pro-choice reforms such as no-fault divorce and sexual cohabitation were undermining marriage and imposing huge costs upon children raised without fathers. Wardle and his mentor, Bruce Hafen, established BYU as a center for criticizing the liberalization of family law at the same time that Gordon Hinckley was bringing the Church of Jesus Christ of Latter-day Saints (which controls BYU) into the ERA and same-sex marriage debates. Like other Mormons, Wardle had dedicated two years of his youth to mission service—and as a law professor he became a missionary for traditional family law. On April 16, 1994, that role brought him to a conference held at the Drake Law School in Des Moines, Iowa.[1]

In one presentation, Frances Olsen argued that liberalizing state regulation had made the family less hierarchical and more individualistic; in "the war between the sexes," she urged feminists to push harder against traditional hierarchy. In the ensuing discussion, Wardle objected to her "conflict" focus: in his view, the law ought to encourage altruistic, cooperative relationships and parenting. The time-tested strategy for such relationships was the special institution of marriage, which Olsen and Martha Fineman (the conference keynote speaker) were challenging. Panelist Evan Wolfson agreed with Olsen and Fineman that marriage ought to be less central—but so long as it remained an important state-supported institution, there should be no "arbitrary exclusions" from it, as the lesbian and gay couples were then claiming in the Hawai'i marriage litigation.[2]

Wardle responded to Wolfson: "Isn't there a good reason to distinguish and not extend family marital status to homosexual relations? From a perspective of the state and society, they simply don't contribute the same way that husband-wife relationships do to the well-being of society." Professor Maura Strassberg objected: she and her partner were raising a child in a "two-mother household." Agreeing with Strassberg, the other panelists evaluated family law based on the norms of individual choice and the happiness of adult couples and their families. Wardle grounded his theory on communitarian premises and emphasized the well-being of children. What regime of family law best assured the good of society and the best environment for rearing children? It was not unusual for Wardle to be the only voice for a faith-based or a communitarian understanding of marriage at law school conferences, but at Drake he had an ally on the faculty.[3]

Professor Gregory Sisk identified a "missing theme" in the conversation: *responsibility*. "Becoming a part of a family means that you adopt certain responsibilities, that your freedom is bounded and that it is a healthy thing to be part of a situation where your freedom is bounded because of your concern for others." Sisk expanded upon Wardle's framing of the challenges facing family law: How does the state provide incentives for men, in particular, to "remain part of these families and not to become the roaming nomads of society, bringing with them all of the pathological problems we face today"? Professor Dorothy Roberts responded that all of the speakers, not just Sisk and Wardle, were focused on "protecting and supporting responsible relationships." Why shouldn't the traditional focus on men's responsibilities and privileges as heads of households give way to a more egalitarian understanding of the family? The issue Sisk raised was whether a liberal, egalitarian approach to the family did not sacrifice the essence of what made the family great—namely, its capacity to inspire fathers as well as mothers to look beyond their own preferences and happily make sacrifices for the greater good, especially the well-being of children. A feminist response is that wives have carried most of the burden of the altruistic family.

Returning to Utah, Wardle reported his alarm over the Hawai'i marriage litigation to the leadership of the Church of Jesus Christ. The Church's leadership, guided by Gordon Hinckley, had warned the country that the ERA would impose homosexual and lesbian marriage (HLM) on all states. Wardle alerted the Church that if the homosexuals won the Hawai'i lawsuit, the full faith and credit clause of the Constitution might do what the "Latter-day constitutionalists" had prevented by intervening in the ERA debate. Early in 1995, the Church mobilized against HLM in the Aloha State. As explored in chapter 4, Professor Wardle was the primary legal adviser for Hawai'i's Future Today, the marriage commission's dissenters, the legislators favoring traditional marriage, and the campaign to amend the Hawai'i Constitution.

Wardle and other Latter-day constitutionalists articulated a view of marriage as a social institution defined by a child-centered system of gendered responsibility. The responsible adult is someone who considers the consequences of her or his actions on other people and who altruistically assumes the duty of caring for others. As a matter of faith, Latter-day Saints believed that family responsibilities worked for the benefit of children and society and operated differently for husbands and wives, fathers and mothers. Marriage as a system of gendered responsibility suggested constitutional reasons why it should not be redefined to include lesbian and gay couples.[4]

Responsible Parenting. According to Wardle, the best households for raising children were ones where the biological parents were married, a status that encouraged family altruism and the most self-sacrificing approach to parenting. Hence, lesbian and gay households deprived children of gendered role models and stable emotional environments. During the Hawai'i marriage debate, Wardle published an article suggesting that the state should not permit lesbian and gay persons and couples to adopt or raise children. In a separate article, his Mormon colleague Monte Stewart (the first graduate of BYU's law school to clerk on the Supreme Court) wrote that, as a matter of international human rights, children had a right to be raised by their biological mothers and fathers. That right would be lost if marriage were redefined.[5]

Responsible Procreation. Earlier defenders of one-man, one-woman marriage had claimed that procreative intercourse consummating marriage was central to the institution's special, privileged role in human lives and societies. Wardle argued that marriage was a mechanism by which the state "channeled" men's sexual desires in responsible directions. Stewart maintained that marriage could have only one meaning—a society could not have "regular marriage" and also "same-sex marriage"—and that any legal change in the meaning of marriage would destabilize its cultural significance for men who would become husbands, women who dreamed of bearing children, and parents who were devoted to their biological children.[6]

Responsible Partnering. In the Hawai'i campaign, Wardle learned that lesbian and gay persons were capable of responsible partnering, namely, mutual support and caregiving. Wardle thus considered it acceptable for the state to create a legal structure for mutual responsibility—but not one grounded in a sexual relationship that could be mistaken for marriage. With his acquiescence, the Church of Jesus Christ went along with the 1997 Hawai'i law creating reciprocal beneficiary relationships for relatives and same-sex buddies who were ineligible to marry but whose mutual caregiving might be supported by the state.[7]

Professor Wardle claims he does not remember his exact role, but church documents establish that he was a constant adviser to his church on these issues, starting no later than the Drake conference. In litigation documents, he and other Latter-day Saints developed their arguments in much greater depth than other defenders of traditional marriage, including counsel for state and local governments, the Evangelical lawyers in the Alliance Defense Fund (ADF), and representatives of Catholic bishops and institutions.[8]

One venue for these arguments was the state constitutional junior-DOMAs. In 2004, Utah voters endorsed Amendment 3, which Wardle drafted. Two central players in that campaign were William Duncan and Monte Neil Stewart. They knew that the marriage debate was far from finished, and they respected the acuity and sophistication of their adversaries in GLAD, the ACLU, and Lambda Legal. Duncan had written amicus briefs in the Vermont and Massachusetts marriage cases; Stewart had just completed a thesis at Oxford on the international marriage debate. Realizing how complex the arguments had become and how ill-equipped most state attorney general offices were to deal with such litigation, at the end of 2004 they established the Marriage Law Foundation (MLF) in Provo.[9]

Like ADF, MLF offered legal advice and services to state and local attorneys defending traditional marriage laws. Duncan and Stewart were the perfect partners for this enterprise. When we met them in Provo, they reminded us of the film critics Gene Siskel and Roger Ebert, who hosted *At the Movies*. Bill's high forehead and quiet thoughtfulness lent him an owlish dignity, while the chunkier Monte was more expressive, even dramatic as he eagerly explained issues and made self-deprecating asides. More important than their easy camaraderie, they were experienced litigators with deep knowledge of the constitutional issues from traditionalist, communitarian, comparative law, and religious perspectives.[10]

One illustration of their acumen was a jointly authored article offering an imaginative rethinking of *Loving v. Virginia* (1967), which most academics interpreted to support a wide-ranging right to marry. Stewart and Duncan framed the decision as a judicial rebuff to earlier efforts to change the definition of marriage! The Virginia law against different-race marriages, they wrote, was an effort by segregationists to highjack traditional marriage and deploy it as a tool of white supremacy. Marriage equality advocates "redefining" marriage were thus more like the Virginia segregationists than the integrationists who had persuaded the Court that interracial couples were entitled to marriage rights accorded other conjugal couples.[11]

As it played out in key states like Colorado, New Jersey, New York, and Washington between 2003 and 2009, the jurisprudence of gendered responsibility evolved a great deal. The Supreme Court's decisions in *Romer v. Evans* (1996) and *Lawrence v. Texas* (2003) convinced government lawyers that they needed strong secular arguments to defend the exclusion of same-sex couples from civil marriage, and this jurisprudence provided many of these arguments, grounded in a popular philosophy of personal responsibility as applied to family law. Moreover, their jurisprudence responded to the perception by supporters of traditional marriage that they needed to avoid any whiff of anti-gay rhetoric. The pollster Richard Wirthlin, another Latter-day Saint, reported that a third of the country was "torn between their strong desire to be tolerant and non-judgmental of others ('live and let live') yet stand up for their belief in traditional marriage. *They will avoid at all costs taking a position or supporting a cause that is perceived to be intolerant or anti-gay/lesbian/homosexual.*"[12]

This was a key reason why Wardle, Duncan, and Stewart emerged as important figures: personally, they oozed congeniality; professionally, they were impeccably respectful; philosophically, they emphasized responsibility-linked themes that reflected an inspiring and attractive understanding of what marriage might mean for a well-ordered society centrally concerned about its children. They also represented an ironic convergence: many lesbian and gay couples harbored the same romantic aspiration for marriage, and the LGBT rights groups also deployed a de-gendered understanding of family responsibility to make their case for marriage equality or, failing that, another institution enabling lesbian and gay couples to take responsibility for one another. The goals of marriage equality and traditional marriage advocates intersected around the idea of caregiving responsibility.

Consider an interesting historical wrinkle. Marriage equality's Cinderella moment had come in Massachusetts, from the pen of Margaret Marshall, the commonwealth's first female chief justice. The marriage debates in the first decade of the twenty-first century occurred during the tenures of the first women to lead the highest courts in the four states we are examining: Deborah Poritz (chief justice, New Jersey Supreme Court, 1996–2006), Judith Kaye (chief judge, New York Court of Appeals, 1993–2008), Barbara Madsen (justice, Washington Supreme Court, 1993–2010; chief justice, 2010–2017), and Mary Mullarkey (chief justice, Colorado Supreme Court, 1998–2010). The debate in Iowa, which we'll discuss in the next chapter, also coincided with the tenure of its first female chief justice, Martha Ternus (2006–2010). Each of these women had raised children within a traditional marriage, just like the Latter-day constitutionalists (Monte Stewart had ten kids). Nonetheless, these women had different ideas about parental, sexual, and personal responsibility from those of Wardle, Stewart, and Duncan—though their understandings played out differently in each state.

Responsible Parenting and the Optimal Child-Rearing Argument

The only argument seriously pressed by Hawai'i at the 1996 *Baehr* trial was the claim that the best household for children was one where their biological parents were married to one another. Judge Kevin Chang ruled that the state had not carried its heavy burden of showing that excluding lesbian and gay marriages would advance the state's interest in providing optimal households for raising children. Criticizing Judge Chang's opinion in *The Potential Impact of Homosexual Parenting on Children* (1997), Professor Wardle argued that the social science upon which the judge relied may have shown that some children were well served by lesbian and gay parents, but it did not establish that parenting by lesbian and gay couples was, *on average,* as effective as parenting by straight married couples. Those studies had big methodological limitations: the sample size was usually very small (five to fifty participants); no study took a random sample of the population, and many included participants who were self-selected or came from friendship networks; few of the studies had a control group carefully matched to the test group (many of them compared households headed by well-to-do lesbian parents with those headed by single mothers); almost none of the studies followed the children's development over a long period of time; and most evaluated the children along soft criteria based upon potentially biased self-reporting.[13]

These methodological points were astute ones. Because government and other databases did not include sexual orientation breakdowns, American social scientists relied on nonrandom methods. In the United Kingdom, however, Susan Golombok was able to replicate the American results in studies that had access to random samples. More important, the limitations of the American studies were a weak basis for criticizing Judge Chang's decision, because the Hawai'i Supreme Court placed the burden on the state to show that there was a compelling public interest that could only be served by excluding lesbian and gay couples from marriage. After its own experts testified that such couples were generally good parents, the state was left with no empirical evidence supporting its (and Wardle's) view that the marriage exclusion was needed to ensure the optimal household structure for child-rearing. The state failed to meet its burden of proof. Stewart told us that this kind of burden shifting is the worst possible way to make important changes in marriage, and he has a point.[14]

In a response to Wardle's article, militantly titled *Warring with Wardle*, Carlos Ball and Janice Farrell Pea suggested that "the social science literature, despite its shortcomings, supports the rather limited proposition that gay and lesbian parents (or prospective parents) are entitled to be evaluated individually on the basis of their ability to be good parents instead of being assessed based on assumptions about their sexual orientation." Indeed, the studies were virtually unanimous in showing that lesbian and gay parents were capable of the same responsible caregiving as straight parents. The burden *ought* to be on the state to demonstrate otherwise. A meta-analysis of 619 parents and 572 children confirmed the similar findings of the smaller studies, though it did not involve a random sample or resolve other problems. As Professor Ball documented in a 2014 update, subsequent empirical studies, many involving random samples, have confirmed and reinforced this hypothesis.[15]

By 1997, professional associations were moving toward a consensus that parental sexual orientation made no difference for successful child-rearing. In June 1999, the American Academy of Child and Adolescent Psychiatry adopted this resolution: "There is no evidence to suggest or support that parents with a gay, lesbian, or bisexual orientation are per se different from or deficient in parenting skills, child-centered concerns and parent-child attachments, when compared to parents with a heterosexual orientation." Similar "no differences" resolutions were adopted by the American Psychological Association (1998), American Academy of Pediatrics (2002), National Association of Social Workers (2002), American Psychiatric Association (2002), and American Medical

Association (2003). That level of academic and professional agreement was probably hastened by individual members' sympathy for lesbian parenting especially, but the consensus itself was driven by the fact that neutral or even skeptical experts, using a variety of professional techniques, found lesbian and gay families to be supportive environments where loving parents happily made sacrifices for their children's benefit.[16]

Wardle rejected the "no differences" hypothesis, in part for moral reasons. His article compared lesbian and gay relationships to "extramarital sexual relationships" where "selfish choices" by parents made their children "innocent victims." He was "concerned that a parent who makes a calculated decision to deprive a child of a parent of the opposite gender may be making a decision that shows insufficient regard for the needs of children." These were moral assumptions, not statements of fact. Wardle and allied scholars believed that lesbian and gay families lacked the deep capacity for altruism characteristic of straight couples who consummated their marriages with procreative intercourse. Statements like these disrespected lesbian and gay parents like April DeBoer and Jayne Rowse. We concluded chapter 10 with their 2009 adoption of Nolan. The mothers were deliriously happy to have a family, and colicky little Nolan needed loving care. Jayne and April eagerly comforted him through nightmares, late-night hunger, and health problems. Their second adopted child, Ryanne, was born at home in February 2010 to a nineteen-year-old mother who brought Ryanne to the intensive care unit and said she wanted to give her up for adoption. With the mother's consent, April brought Ryanne home; she formally adopted the child on April 6, 2011.[17]

Between November 2009 and February 2010, April was also a primary caregiver for Jacob, who was in the neonatal ICU because of complications of his mother's drug use during her pregnancy. Jacob was born three months premature, weighing only one pound nine ounces. The baby was fighting against great odds. His liver was failing, and his spleen was three times the normal size. April held his tiny hand and told the infant, "You try to live, and I'll try to find you a good foster home." Two weeks later, he rallied. The foster care agency tried to place the child with a Detroit family, but his medical issues were too overwhelming. Crossing jurisdictional lines, the agency called the Rowse-DeBoer house in February 2010, and they tearfully accepted. Jacob was placed with them on March 2 and formally adopted on October 28, 2011. He flourished that first year only through constant care.

We recall Jacob's, Nolan's, and Ryanne's stories to suggest why many observers were bothered by Wardle's moral objections to lesbian and gay families.

DeBoer and Rowse epitomized the highest virtue sought by marriage advocates: complete self-sacrificing, other-regarding love and devotion to their children. Years ago, we asked Wardle if he had ever gotten to know a lesbian couple who had adopted children like Nolan, Ryanne, and Jacob. He could not identify anyone by name, but hundreds of lawyers and social scientists did get to know such couples and their families, and they came away with a deep appreciation of the love undergirding the partnered relationships and their joint devotion to their children.

The dearth of social-science support for Wardle's optimal parenting argument, and the cascading opposition to it among professional and academic associations, rendered that argument constitutionally suspect in light of the Supreme Court's decision in *Romer v. Evans* (1996), which called into question any law that targeted lesbian and gay persons for exclusion: Was there a harm-based need for such exclusion, or was it simply an expression of *animus* (the term used in *Romer*)? In the Vermont marriage case, Beth Robinson and Susan Murray relied on the social-science evidence to persuade the state to concede that lesbian and gay parenting was good for children, and then invoked responsible parenting as an argument for striking down the marriage exclusion of altruistic couples who were raising children within their households. Wouldn't those children be better off if their parents could get married? In the Hawai'i marriage trial, the state's own experts had testified to that effect.[18]

In the Massachusetts marriage case, the commonwealth conceded that same-sex couples may be excellent parents but argued that the legislature could have reasonably believed that the state should nonetheless favor husband-wife households. The commonwealth cited a meta-analysis of all previously published studies, reported in 2001 by sociologists Judith Stacey and Timothy Biblarz. The meta-analysis showed no evidence of lower levels of educational attainment and no tendency toward criminal behavior—but it did show that the gay-household children had less gendered attitudes than straight-household children. They were much less likely, for example, to think that girls should be nurses and boys should be doctors or that married men should work outside the home and leave childcare duties to a wife. And adolescent girls raised by lesbian parents tended to be more sexually active and "adventurous" than girls raised by opposite-sex parents.[19]

The majority justices in *Goodridge* were not bothered by the Stacey-Biblarz meta-analysis because they understood the Massachusetts Constitution as set against the traditional idea that women and men are biologically fated to assume gendered roles. In other states entertaining marriage equality lawsuits, judges were committed to the norm that the state was constitutionally barred from socially engineering gender roles in order to head off the possibility of a new generation of adventurous females. In Provo, however, the Latter-day constitutionalists were not at all discouraged. At a 2006 BYU conference on parenting and marriage, Monte Stewart argued for recognition of an international human right of each child to be supported and, preferably, raised by her or his biological mother and father. Same-sex marriage would undermine the child's bonding right by normalizing marriage around sexual consummation that, in his view, placed the spouses' pleasure above the creation of new life bonded to each parent.[20]

Responsible Procreation and Heterosexual Conduct

Between 1999 and 2009, most state attorney general offices either abandoned or offered a watered-down version of the responsible parenting argument. The door was open for a new argument that fit the conservative case for traditional marriage but was immune to charges that it was trading on phony evidence or anti-gay stereotypes. The argument that emerged was called the *responsible procreation* argument, but as Edward Stein suggested, it morphed into an argument based on *accidental procreation*. Under either name, the argument scored impressive successes with state appellate judges. Its key architects were our Latter-day constitutionalists Lynn Wardle, Bill Duncan, and Monte Neil Stewart.[21]

FROM PROCREATION TO RESPONSIBLE PROCREATION

In the early marriage cases, judges accepted as sufficient the state's argument that "our society as a whole views marriage as the appropriate and desirable forum for procreation and the rearing of children." Well into the new millennium, the primary argument made by academic supporters of traditional marriage was that procreation was essential to the integrity of marriage, unlike marginal features such as racial purity that had been tacked onto the institution but then discarded. The ideas advanced by David Blankenhorn and Maggie Gallagher's marriage movement, discussed in chapter 10, provided an intellectual boost for this argument. They offered secular reasons why marriage might be limited to one man and one woman.[22]

The problem with the marriage-as-procreation argument is that it did not fit with the sociology and law of marriage, and the uneven fit between marriage and procreative intercourse was getting worse every year. States had never required straight couples to demonstrate procreative purposes or ability, nor did any state question the right of elderly couples to civil marriage. Increasing numbers of married couples had biological children through artificial reproductive technologies (ART), and many couples adopted children. ART and adoption by lesbian and gay couples made their families look a lot more like traditional marital families, while cohabitation and late-in-life marriages made more straight relationships look more like gay and lesbian ones. However persuasive marriage-as-procreation had been in the 1970s, it needed an update to remain relevant in light of the rapidly changing American family. Latter-day constitutionalists provided some important ideas for modernizing the argument, and faith-inspired lawyers popularized these ideas through amicus briefs filed all over the country.[23]

In 2001, Wardle updated the argument. "Society has compelling interests in protecting the social institution that has best furthered social interests in procreation, in maintaining the clear social identity of that institution, and in preserving the linkage that institution forges among sex, procreation, and child rearing." Lesbian and gay relationships did not fit within this scheme. Wardle provided a broad policy context that drew from Carl Schneider's idea that a central role for family law is to channel people's conduct into productive relationships. "Traditional marriage strengthens the social interest in channeling and limiting procreative sexual behavior to responsible relationships of parental commitment and complementarity." The *responsible procreation* terminology echoed the views articulated by the Vatican's "Instruction on the Dignity of Procreation" (1986), the House Judiciary Committee's report for the Defense of Marriage Act (1996), and the Personal Responsibility and Work Opportunity Reconciliation Act of 1996.[24]

This argument found a partial parallel in philosopher John Rawls's last major book, *Justice as Fairness: A Restatement* (2001). In a well-ordered society, Rawls maintained, marriage "addresses the social problem that men and women are sexually attracted to each other and that, without any outside guidance or social norms, these intense attractions can cause immense personal and social damage. If law and culture choose to 'do nothing' about sexual attraction between men and women, the passive, unregulated heterosexual reality is multiple failed relationships and millions of fatherless children." Conjugal marriage, for Rawls, served a channeling purpose similar to that proposed by Wardle. Rawls did not reject the desirability of marriage equality for LGBT relationships, however, and Ronald Dworkin maintained that Rawlsian principles actually supported these claims.[25]

Justice Robert Cordy's dissent in *Goodridge* made a procreative marriage argument that included a Rawlsian discussion: "An orderly society requires some mechanism for coping with the fact that sexual intercourse commonly results in pregnancy and childbirth. The institution of marriage is that mechanism." Marriage prevented demographic chaos by channeling procreative intercourse into relationships in which the father would be motivated to stick around and contribute to the children's well-being. Because LGBT relationships, however loving and committed, did not advance this plausible theory of marriage, Cordy concluded that the commonwealth had a rational basis for limiting marriage to one-man, one-woman unions and that it was neither irrational nor ill-motivated not to include same-sex couples.[26]

FROM RESPONSIBLE TO ACCIDENTAL PROCREATION

In an influential 2004 article adapted from his Oxford thesis, Monte Stewart elaborated on the responsible procreation argument. Marriage has traditionally channeled procreative activities into responsible commitments, either before the fact (encouraging couples to hold off intercourse until marriage) or after the fact (marriage once there was a pregnancy, as Wendy and Ken DeBoer did in 1967). Straight couples needed this encouragement more than ever before because of their increasing tendency toward *accidental* procreation and because of the gender disparity (such as Maggie Gallagher experienced) in the event of accidental pregnancies. Lesbian and gay couples, by contrast, did not need state encouragement because they inevitably procreated more responsibly. For them, children could arrive only through purposeful acts of adoption, artificial insemination, and surrogacy. If channeling potentially irresponsible sexual behaviors into the productive state regime of duties and responsibilities was an important purpose for marriage law, then it made little sense for progressives to insist that lesbian and gay couples had to be included. Such an accidental procreation argument had first been made by Canadian Supreme Court Justice Charles Gonthier, dissenting in a 1999 marriage discrimination case.[27]

Stewart's argument was a creative advance in the argument from procreation. It provided a policy reason that a court might attribute to legislators who supported the one-man, one-woman understanding of marriage—and it did so without demonizing lesbian and gay couples as unworthy of marriage or as incompetent parents. The argument even presented lesbian couples as more responsible than mistake-prone straight couples and irresponsible straight boys, like the Yale College cad who deserted Maggie Gallagher and their son in 1982. MLF and ADF attorneys pressed this analysis all over the country.

In *Sadler v. Morrison* (2005), the Indiana Court of Appeals upheld the state's limitation of marriage to one man, one woman, based largely upon Stewart's article. The court emphasized the expense and planning required by ART or adoption as opposed to natural procreation, which was often unplanned. Gay and lesbian couples did not need the protections of marriage "because of the high level of financial and emotional commitment exerted in conceiving or adopting a child or children in the first place." By contrast, "even where an opposite-sex couple enters into a marriage with no intention of having children, 'accidents' do happen, or persons often change their minds about wanting to have children. The institution of marriage not only encourages opposite-sex couples to form a relatively stable environment for the 'natural' procreation of children in the first place, but it also encourages them to stay together and raise a child or children together if there is a 'change in plans.'" The New Jersey Court of Appeals followed Stewart's argument to reject marriage equality claims in *Lewis v. Harris* (2005). The next year, the first federal court of appeals decision addressing the constitutionality of a state Super-DOMA upheld Nebraska's constitutional exclusion based upon the accidental procreation theory advanced in an amicus brief Stewart wrote for MLF.[28]

But there was a difficulty with the accidental procreation argument: How would including lesbian and gay couples, many of them raising children, thwart the beneficent policy by which marriage channeled the chaotic sexuality of straight couples? In 2006, Stewart gave his argument a social institutional feature that responded to the riddle. "Marriage, like all social institutions, is constituted by a web of shared public meanings," which "teach, form, and transform individuals" and thereby "provide vital social goods." Marriage channeled procreative sexual activities and modeled optimal households where children were cared for by their biological mothers and fathers. The law had the power to create as well as suppress social meanings and thus could "radically change and even deinstitutionalize man/woman marriage, with concomitant loss of the institution's social goods." Because Stewart believed there was no room in law or society for multiple understandings of marriage, opening marriage to same-sex couples would transform the institution for everyone— in a way that would have pervasive effects on individual expectations and conduct. "Genderless marriage," as Stewart called it, would be "a radically different institution than man/woman marriage" and would not yield the social goods

that traditional marriage had produced—including the regulation of accidental procreation by heterosexuals. Although Stewart had no empirical evidence
suggesting that his speculation actually occurred, he had created a non-
animus theory for not recognizing same-sex marriages.[29]

THE RESPONSIBLE OR ACCIDENTAL PROCREATION
ARGUMENT IN STATE MARRIAGE CASES

The first state supreme court to entertain a marriage equality case after *Goodridge* was the Washington Supreme Court, which heard oral argument in *Andersen v. King County* on March 8, 2005. Eight lesbian and gay couples sought
to overturn Washington's 1998 junior-DOMA law. The legislators and pastors
who intervened to defend the law were represented by ADF-affiliated attorney
Steve O'Ban, who followed the argument developed in the MLF amicus brief
filed by Stewart and Duncan. "Society," O'Ban told the court, "needs to deal
with the challenge that heterosexual intercourse presents," namely, that from
"a single, unplanned encounter a child may result, and society needs to have
a coping mechanism to deal with that particular policy concern. Marriage provides a powerful incentive, through endorsement and through these benefits,
to channel that heterosexual conduct into marriage." Justice Bobbe Bridge
noted that the state had paternity rules and support obligations to motivate
putative fathers to be responsible. O'Ban responded that the legislature had
discretion to include traditional marriage as a further motivation. Assistant
Attorney General William Collins endorsed the accidental procreation argument, noting that "only sexual relations between a man and a woman can
create children—planned or unplanned."[30]

The court that would decide the case consisted of five men and four women,
spanning the ideological spectrum. Because liberal Tom Chambers favored a
constitutional right for the plaintiff couples, they would prevail if all four female justices agreed. Between 1993 and 2010, an appellate judge's sex (not race,
age, or political party) was the best predictor of whether that judge would vote
to invalidate state discrimination against lesbian and gay couples. Female
judges almost always voted to invalidate, male judges split fifty-fifty. On the
other hand, unlike their counterparts in Massachusetts and Vermont, Washington Supreme Court justices had to run for reelection every six years; three
of the four female justices had been forced into runoff elections, which they
had narrowly won.[31]

A former public defender and then a prosecutor in domestic abuse cases,
Barbara Madsen was a feminist lawyer who supported the state's laws protect-

ing gay people from hate crimes and job discrimination. She celebrated Bobbe Bridge's 2005 opinion for the court recognizing de facto parenting rights among lesbian couples. Nonetheless, she could not bring herself to make a big constitutional move and was the fifth vote to sustain the junior-DOMA. On July 26, 2006, Justice Madsen delivered the court's judgment in *Andersen* and wrote a plurality opinion for herself and two others. No state appellate court had found that lesbian and gay couples enjoyed a fundamental right to marry, and Madsen felt hers should not be the first. Nor was she willing to rule that the exclusion rested on a suspect classification. The state, therefore, needed only a rational basis for the exclusion, and she deferred to legislative judgments that conjugal marriage was justified by plausible concerns with accidental procreation and responsible parenting. Justices Jim Johnson and Richard Sanders concurred only in the judgment, based on an assortment of public interests, including ADF's claim that husband-wife households were best for children and that lesbian or gay households were demonstrably inferior.[32]

Writing for four dissenters, Justice Mary Fairhurst questioned the state's responsible procreation and parenting justifications. How "would giving same-sex couples the same right that opposite-sex couples enjoy injure the State's interest in procreation and healthy child rearing?" Several of the plaintiff couples were raising children in a nurturing environment. Because the legislative history, including Wardle's testimony, demonstrated that the legislature acted in the belief that lesbian and gay households were morally as well as practically inferior to straight households, Fairhurst found the junior-DOMA motivated by animus and therefore invalid under *Romer*.[33]

Other states were wrestling with the same issues. In New York, the Wardle-Stewart-Duncan jurisprudence of gendered responsibility had as much traction as it did in Indiana and Washington. Robert Smith's plurality opinion for the New York Court of Appeals in *Hernandez v. Robles* (2006) accepted the state's accidental procreation and optimal parenting justifications, and Victoria Graffeo's concurring opinion went along with the accidental procreation argument. Judith Kaye wrote a heartfelt dissent, which we shall discuss in chapter 16. Just a few months before her death in January 2017, she told us that her failure to persuade a majority in *Hernandez* was among the most painful experiences of her professional life. She lamented the contentious nature of the court's deliberations and the oral argument. Judge Smith, a former corporate lawyer, snickered at the plaintiffs' counsel during argument and delivered what many considered a perfunctory plurality opinion.[34]

In *Conaway v. Deane* (2007), a closely divided (4-3) Maryland Court of Appeals followed the Maryland attorney general and the MLF amicus brief to rule that because only different-sex couples could accidentally procreate, the legislature had the discretion to limit marriage to this mistake-prone social group. In *Lewis v. Harris* (2006), the New Jersey Supreme Court unanimously invalidated the exclusion of lesbian and gay couples from marriage-based rights, but a 4-3 majority was persuaded by Stewart's amicus brief that requiring full marriage recognition was too big a move for the unelected judiciary. Changes in "the shared societal meaning of marriage," the court ruled, paraphrasing the brief, "must come about through civil dialogue and reasoned discourse, and the considered judgment of the people in whom we place ultimate trust in our republican form of government."[35]

Responsible Partners and Designated Beneficiaries

Between *Goodridge* (November 2003) and California's *Marriage Cases* (June 2008), Lambda Legal and the ACLU lost all of their high-profile marriage equality lawsuits to the MLF's jurisprudence of gendered responsibility. Nonetheless, some religious supporters of conjugal marriage were open to arguments that the state might recognize lesbian and gay caregiving relationships. Their primary model was Hawai'i's 1997 reciprocal beneficiaries law, which the Latter-day Saints had agreed to as part of the compromise that put marriage on the 1998 ballot. For LGBT persons, the model was the AIDS-inspired domestic partnership concept pioneered by Matt Coles in the 1980s. He viewed domestic partnership as a new form for responsible family or relationship recognition—and religious groups were open to the idea so long as it was not "marriage-lite," a backdoor recognition of what they considered immoral sexual relationships. Overall, the debate about responsible partnering involved a tug-of-war between lesbian and gay rights advocates, who saw responsible partnerships as sexual relationships, and traditional-values advocates, who saw them as caregiving relationships and sought to suppress any suggestion of sexual activity.

The blurred line between caregiving and sexual partnership also made religious traditionalists ambivalent about whether to oppose particular innovations. In 2003–2004, supporters of a Family Equality Act in the New Jersey legislature revised the bill to address Catholic concerns. Passed as the Domestic Partnership Act of 2004, the law extended a few benefits to older couples and to same-sex couples, the precise approach Catholics and Latter-day Saints supported in the Hawai'i beneficiaries law—but New Jersey's Catholic bishops ultimately opposed the law as too close to marriage. In Rhode Island, on the other hand, we could not find any public pushback from Catholic bishop

Thomas Tobin when Providence's maverick GOP mayor Buddy Cianci negotiated domestic partnership insurance coverage with four municipal employee
unions in 2000 or when the legislature passed a statute affording such benefits to state employees in 2001. But when the legislature tried to expand state
employees' domestic partnership to include retirement benefits and to allow
domestic partners to plan their loved ones' funerals, Bishop Tobin opposed
the measures as "gateways" to marriage, and Catholic GOP governor Dan Car-
cieri successfully vetoed both bills.[36]

Like the debate over responsible parenting, the debate over responsible relationships was a dispute about who should count as *family*. Traditionalists
believed family should be viewed in terms of biology—blood and conjugal
marriage—while increasing numbers of Americans, and especially LGBT persons, saw family in social terms—interpersonal commitment and support. It
was hard for the two sides to reach common ground. Ironically, the pas de deux
between marriage equality and traditional marriage forces generated the most
interesting new family law experiment of this period.

Booming Denver, collegiate Boulder, and resort Aspen, Colorado, attracted
a rising tide of LGBT persons, couples, and activists. In 2004, Pat Steadman,
the executive director of Equal Rights Colorado, was pleased that many LGBT
families enjoyed domestic partnership benefits from their private or public
employers, were able to have children through adoption or ART, and could expect their wills and powers of attorney to be respected by hospitals, judges,
and agencies. Many considered themselves married, but the state did not: Republican governor Bill Owen had secured a junior-DOMA from the legislature
in 2000. Although the Colorado Supreme Court would have been receptive to
a state constitutional challenge to Colorado's junior-DOMA, Steadman and his
colleagues did not bring such a claim. Why not? The long answer is that the
Colorado Constitution was easy to amend through a voter initiative, and public
opinion did not favor marriage equality. The short answer is Tim Gill.

The multimillionaire founder of the software maker Quark, Gill was described in *Rolling Stone* as a tall, trim, openly gay introvert "with a thatch of
silver-black hair and a wide, toothy smile" who was, "genetically, a Republican." After Colorado voted for the gay-scapegoating Amendment 2 in 1992
(invalidated in *Romer*), Gill funded institutions to implement data-driven political strategies. The organizations reflected his two passions: coding and
snowboarding. "As an engineer, Gill believes in experimentation, in method-
ically testing lots of different things to see what works, and then dispassion-
ately choosing the best approach. But as a snowboarder who, by some accounts,

328 LATTER-DAY CONSTITUTIONALISTS

can be harrowing to ski with, he believes in aggressively going for it, even if the risks of a wipeout are high."[37]

In 1994, the Gill Foundation started to fund academic research, polling, field organizing, and list creation. Later, Gill created OutGiving, a club of super-wealthy gay and lesbian donors (including Coloradans Jared Polis, Rutt Bridges, and Pat Stryker) who sought to apply their money in targeted ways to advance specific objectives. Gill Political Action was a direct political group that helped elect hundreds of pro-equality lawmakers at the local, state, and federal levels. Gill's organizations helped finance MassEquality, and his group's expertise contributed to its favorable 2004 and 2006 election results that helped head off legislative proposals for a constitutional amendment overriding *Goodridge* (see chapter 9). His money also opened doors for a generation of brilliant grassroots activists—Marc Solomon, Josh Friedes, and Marty Rouse.

Ted Trimpa, dubbed the Karl Rove of LGBT rights, was Gill's strategic mastermind in a data-driven 2004 campaign that fueled a Democratic takeover of the Colorado legislature. The Trimpa-Gill strategy was to combine political activism with public education—not through a go-for-broke marriage lawsuit but through the kind of equality practice that was successful in California. Enact a small-scale domestic partnership law, build on it until the state had the equivalent of civil unions, and then go for marriage—maybe at that point by constitutional litigation. The Gill network's goals for the 2006 election were to help the Democrats retain their majorities in the legislature and win back the governorship and head off a constitutional Super-DOMA initiative.[38]

But a constitutional Super-DOMA was exactly what Focus on the Family was planning. Focus's James Dobson had created Colorado Family Action, headed by his associate James Pfaff, with the intent of assembling a grand coalition with the Reverend Ted Haggard's National Association of Evangelicals (NAE) and the Colorado Bishops Conference, headed by Denver archbishop Charles Chaput, a rising star among conservative clerics. The Gill plan was to persuade Focus's coalition partners that a Super-DOMA was not in their interests. Perhaps surprisingly, Trimpa and Gill had warm relationships with Haggard and officials in the Catholic archdiocese such as Tim Dore. Gay Ted and Tim reminded devout Ted and Tim that Focus had been the driving force behind Amendment 2 (1992), which had been a constitutional and moral disaster for the state. A broadly written Super-DOMA would appear mean and spiteful (and possibly unconstitutional), and it could preempt laws protecting elderly Coloradans and their caregivers. Observers who remembered Focus's sweeping success with Super-DOMAs in 2004 were surprised when the *Denver Post* reported in December 2005 that Ted Haggard and the three Catholic bishops were insisting upon a simple junior-DOMA, not a Super-DOMA. Their proposed constitutional Amendment 43 codified the traditional definition of marriage as one man, one woman, but left civil unions and domestic partnerships to the legislature.[39]

Ironically, once Focus had agreed to the Amendment 43 compromise, it also signed onto Colorado senator Shawn Mitchell's Senate Bill 166, proposing reciprocal beneficiary contracts for two adults ineligible to marry because they were closely related or because they were of the same sex. Such contracts would allow them to access legal rights needed for caregiving and other responsibilities. Mitchell was a Latter-day constitutionalist, and the inspiration for his bill was the 1997 Hawai'i reciprocal beneficiaries law that Lynn Wardle and the Church of Jesus Christ had helped negotiate. *National Review* author Ramesh Ponnuru had suggested a similar "friends with benefits" idea in 2005, and Dobson publicly endorsed it in February 2006. Ironically, Paul Cameron of the Family Research Institute (FRI, also in Colorado Springs) assailed Dobson for this modest move: "This is madness," he wrote on the FRI website. "Is the 'marriage-lite' bill an attempt by Dobson and Focus on the Family to compromise with homosexuals over the issue of gay marriage?" Not accustomed to attacks for being pro-gay, the placid Dobson admitted he was "close to being ticked" and insisted he had never endorsed the idea that same-sex partners should have "the same benefits that are reserved for the traditional family." Still, "homosexuals should not be deprived of a job or the right to buy a house, they are governed by the same laws that everyone else is." This was a significant evolution in Focus's position since 1992, when it had sponsored the constitutional initiative invalidated in *Romer*.[40]

Under its new president, Jim Daly, Focus supported Mitchell's bill as an occasion to reinvent itself as a vigorously pro-marriage institution that was not anti-gay. Was it Christian to sit in judgment of gay people and scapegoat them for society's problems with marriage and family? Paul Cameron and FRI were perfect foils for this new Focus: We are responsible voices of Christian family values, and not crazy homophobes like Cameron! At a committee hearing on February 27, 2006, Cameron attacked S.B. 166 as state promotion of homosexuality, which he described as rife with disease and predation. Representing Focus, Jim Pfaff rebuked Cameron for being anti-Christian and supported the bill as a measured response to the needs of mutually responsible couples of all sexual orientations. The Catholic Conference also endorsed the bill. Equal Rights Colorado expressed appreciation for the proposal but instead supported

House Bill 1344, which proposed a registry and some legal benefits for same-sex domestic partners, a measure Focus and the Catholics opposed. An evenly split committee killed the bill.[41]

In January 2006, Trimpa and Gill announced a bold counter to Amendment 43. They proposed a legislature-initiated referendum to adopt a Domestic Partnership Benefits and Responsibilities Act, which would vest all the legal rights and duties of marriage with lesbian and gay couples who registered as domestic partners. The Colorado legislature, which can send ballot measures to the voters without having to get signatures, passed the referendum proposal with narrow bipartisan majorities (19-16 in the senate, 38-27 in the assembly), and it went directly to the voters as Referendum I. Gill Political Action was betting that moderate voters inclined to support the marriage amendment (Amendment 43) might hedge their moral bets by also supporting the domestic partnership referendum (Referendum I). If they valued traditional marriage as an institution that encouraged responsibilities associated with procreation, they might also back the personal responsibility norm for lesbian and gay couples. "Establishing legal standards of responsibility and a framework for resolving disputes for same-sex couples is in the state's interest," the legislature declared. "By holding same-sex couples accountable for legal commitments made in raising children, incurring debt, and owning property, domestic partnerships benefit individuals, their families, and the broader community." The Gill network raised more than $5 million for a massive media and grassroots effort to pass Referendum I and defeat Amendment 43.[42]

For the first time, Focus was vastly outspent on a high-stakes marriage referendum—but Jim Pfaff ran an effective campaign on behalf of the Colorado Family Action issue committee. His foot soldiers were hundreds of Evangelical and Catholic volunteers, and local parishes and churches were centers for public education and get-out-the-vote efforts. Dobson hosted him on his radio program three times, giving Pfaff ample time to make his case. Vote no on Referendum I, he argued, and yes on Amendment 43 for precisely the same reason: comprehensive domestic partnerships and same-sex marriages were both counterfeit marriages whose recognition would devalue real marriages. He made what we call the Jenga argument: Marriage as a great institution was like a Jenga block tower; every time you removed a block, you weakened the tower. If you removed a few keystone blocks from the foundation, the whole tower would fall down. Pfaff thought Colorado had already removed one foundation block when it adopted no-fault divorce, and removing the second block would send the wobbly institution into moral and social collapse.

Focus also raised its own equal treatment argument: Why shouldn't other unmarried (heterosexual) couples enjoy the benefits that Referendum I reserved for lesbian and gay couples? The *Denver Catholic Register* pointed out that siblings who assumed responsibility for each other, mothers who cared for their disabled children, and even best friends who wanted to grow old together would not receive the benefits of Referendum I, which was a special measure benefiting no one but lesbian and gay couples. Implicitly, the Catholic and Evangelical opponents were contrasting Referendum I with the "friends with benefits" proposal they had endorsed in February. This coordinated argument suggests to us that Senator Mitchell's bill might have been a countermove by Colorado Family Action to Tim Gill's January announcement of a referendum proposal. Jim Pfaff could play political chess, too.[43]

Polling in late October suggested that Amendment 43 would prevail by a comfortable margin and that Referendum I was a close call. In a radio interview the Wednesday before the election, sex worker Mike Jones identified Reverend Haggard as a regular client who had obtained crystal meth for their trysts. Jones said he wanted to expose the hypocrisy of a renowned critic of the homosexual lifestyle. That evening, the pastor issued a blanket denial. After Jones produced an incriminating voicemail from Haggard, the backtracking started. He resigned as NAE president one day before the election and was later relieved of his duties as chief pastor of his New Life mega-church in Colorado Springs. Mike Jones said he wanted to discredit Amendment 43 and bolster Referendum 1. If so, the move did not succeed.[44]

On November 7, 2006, Amendment 43 swept to a 55-45 percent victory, and Referendum I suffered a narrower but decisive defeat, 47.65-52.35 percent. Ted Trimpa and Pat Steadman believe that the Haggard scandal was pivotal in the defeat of Referendum I, because it mobilized the "ick factor": people's disgust with the details of the "homosexual lifestyle." Jim Pfaff thinks it unlikely that the scandal turned the tables on Referendum I. Most people had made up their minds weeks before the election, and by the time the scandal broke there were not enough undecided voters to yield a decisive majority against Referendum I. He thinks the scandal deprived his own side of votes, because Haggard was, with his good friend Dobson, the most prominent supporter of Amendment 43 and opponent of Referendum I.

In any event, the Gill-funded Democrats retained big majorities in the Colorado legislature and elected Bill Ritter governor. Ironically, the night of his election, Ritter was asked whether he would push for a comprehensive domestic partnership law (like the 2003 California law), and he said he would not support such a measure once it had been decisively rejected by the voters. In retrospect, Colorado might well have had comprehensive domestic partnership or civil unions in 2007, had Referendum I not been put to the voters. In politics as in snowboarding, sometimes you just wipe out.

Openly lesbian senator Jennifer Veiga worked with Pat Steadman and Equal Rights Colorado to enact other LGBT rights laws, including a second-parent adoption law (2007) and a law adding sexual orientation and gender identity to the state's comprehensive anti-discrimination code (2008). Emboldened by the Democrats' strong electoral performance in 2008, Veiga sponsored a bill to give state employees domestic partnership benefits, but that measure also mobilized objections that it defied the voters' judgment on Referendum I. Strategizing over coffee, Pat Steadman and Ted Trimpa came up with a proposal that minimized the Referendum I problem, provided lesbian and gay partners with legal responsibilities and benefits, and borrowed from the Mormon-Evangelical-Catholic "friends with benefits" bill. They called their new idea "designated beneficiaries."

Steadman took the idea to Veiga, openly gay representative Mark Ferrandino, and the legislature's drafting experts. They crafted a Designated Beneficiaries Agreements Act, which Ferrandino introduced at the beginning of the 2009 session as House Bill 1260. With the apparent acquiescence of the Catholic Conference and only token opposition from Colorado Family Action, the bill swept through the assembly on a bipartisan vote of 41-23 and the senate 23-10. Governor Ritter signed it into law on April 9, 2009. It was a novel experiment in American family law.[45]

The legislative purpose was to empower "individuals to care for one another and take action to be personally responsible for themselves and their loved ones," thereby "enabling self-determination and reducing reliance on public programs and services." To that end, the statute authorized competent unmarried adults to enter into designated beneficiary agreements that were legally enforceable unless trumped by a superseding legal document like a will. (Different-sex as well as same-sex couples could enter such agreements, a feature that earned support from groups representing unmarried couples and elderly persons.) The parties to such an agreement could choose from a menu of rights and responsibilities listed in the statute. Those opt-in rights included joint property ownership, rights to be a dependent for health insurance purposes, hospital visitation and access, authority to make medical decisions and anatomical gifts, inheritance and trusteeship rights, workers' compensation benefits, and the right to sue for the wrongful death of one's partner-beneficiary.[46]

The month after the law passed, Jennifer Veiga resigned her senate seat for family reasons, and Pat Steadman was named to replace her. He entered into a designated beneficiary agreement with his longtime partner, David Misner. The rights secured by the law gave Pat's family much-needed security as they planned their lives as a couple. In 2011, with Dave cheering him on, Senator Steadman introduced legislation to recognize civil unions for lesbian and gay couples, but the bill died in the house, which had a narrow GOP majority after the 2010 election. In June the next year, Dave was diagnosed with pancreatic cancer, and he died in September.

Latter-day constitutionalists raised serious objections to same-sex marriage that resonated with many judges, legislators, and voters. Post-*Goodridge* losses in court forced marriage equality groups to settle for civil unions or comprehensive domestic partnerships. On December 14, 2006, just weeks after *Lewis v. Harris* was decided, the New Jersey legislature passed the Civil Unions Act, vesting all the legal rights and benefits of marriage with couples who joined in civil unions. Thousands signed up, in addition to the more than four thousand who had registered as domestic partners. As we shall explore in chapter 14, Latter-day constitutionalism also drove California voters' override of court-imposed marriage equality on Election Day in 2008; same-sex couples still had access to comprehensive domestic partnership rights, however. Although full marriage equality would be thwarted everywhere outside Massachusetts and Connecticut by November 2008, equality practice made significant headway. Ten states and the District of Columbia vested same-sex relationships with some or all marriage rights and benefits by the end of 2008. In addition to those relationship-recognition states, Arizona vested domestic partners with medical decision-making rights, and the domestic partners of state employees in Alaska, Illinois, Iowa, Montana, New York, and Rhode Island enjoyed some or all the benefits of married state employees.[47]

Consider a successful example of equality practice. In the wake of *Andersen,* and fueled by gains in the legislature (abetted by Gill Political Action funds), Equal Rights Washington and openly gay senator Edward Murray in 2007 sponsored a domestic partnership law that could provide a structure for building equal benefits and, ultimately, marriage. Like the Colorado legislators in 2006, the Washington legislators in 2007 rejected a Focus-inspired alternative that would have recognized blood relatives, same-sex partners, and different-sex partners as mutual beneficiaries entitled to a short list of caregiving rights. Like the California law, Washington's Legal Benefits for Domestic

Same-sex marriage recognized
Civil unions, domestic partnerships, etc.
No recognition for same-sex marriages, unions, etc.

Figure 2 Marriage map, November 5, 2008. (Cartography by Patricia Page and Bill Nelson.)

Partners Act included different-sex couples if one partner was sixty-two or older.[48]

In 2008, the Washington legislature added several dozen marriage-based rights to the domestic partnership law. Although the amendments were controversial, the 2008 elections returned every legislator who had supported them, thanks to an enthusiastic grassroots effort led by Josh Friedes (who had relocated from Boston to Seattle) and funded by Gill Political Action. Senator Murray opened the 2009 session with a proposed Domestic Partners Rights and Responsibilities Act, which he dubbed "everything but marriage." It passed with surprising ease and without significant amendment. Governor Christine Gregoire signed it on May 15. Equality practice had proven very effective—but would it survive a referendum? At the last minute, traditional marriage supporters submitted just enough signatures to force a November vote on the measure.[49]

The hastily assembled coalition supporting the new statute was Washington Families Standing Together, with Friedes as its campaign manager. He was able to mobilize the broad network of LGBT volunteers and organizational allies, including feminist stakeholders like the Northwest Women's Law Center, the Religious Coalition for Equality, and various churches and synagogues, Asian American civil rights groups, and several prominent labor unions. The coalition's message was that LGBT people formed serious relationships that deserved respect and support from the state. The primary mechanism for conveying that message was door-to-door conversations by volunteers whom Friedes trained. His advice was to respectfully tell your life story in your own words and try to engage your neighbor with the reality that lesbian and gay persons formed committed relationships, sometimes with children, that were the same or similar to those of married couples. Many of his volunteers were parents of LGBT children, and their stories about how their kids helped them appreciate the value of gay relationships were especially persuasive. The campaign did not back away from talking about marriage.[50]

With a surprising $2 million in donations, the coalition could afford television and radio ads. Its best ad featured Charlene Strong, who had lost her partner Kate in a freak flood. Sipping a cup of coffee and staring out the window, as if waiting for her beloved to come home, Charlene turned to the camera and reminded voters that "now we have important legal protections for gay and lesbian couples in committed relationships." Referendum 71 might take many of them away, she lamented, as a photo of her and Kate filled the screen. "We need to vote approve on Referendum 71." The campaign against comprehensive domestic partnership was run by a thrice-married traditionalist barred from proximity to his second wife because of spousal abuse. Voters approved the new law, 53-47 percent.[51]

Were themes of personal responsibility and good parenting finally tipping in favor of marriage equality by 2009? The answer is complicated.

13 • Love Makes a Family

What makes a family? Is it conjugal marriage, with children generated by the consummation of Mom and Dad's union? Or do love and commitment, regardless of gender or sexuality, suffice to make a family?

The marriage equality movement believed the latter. Notwithstanding the many challenges that followed the *Goodridge* decision, its leading strategists in 2003 were hopeful that love would win, and soon. Mary Bonauto and GLAD had initiated marriage lawsuits or political campaigns throughout New England. Evan Wolfson had left Lambda Legal in 2001; two years later, with a $2.5 million grant from the Evelyn and Walter Haas Jr. Fund, he launched Freedom to Marry as an organization to coordinate local efforts and press activists toward marriage. In January 2004, Matt Coles, the director of the ACLU's Lesbian & Gay Rights and AIDS Project, outlined his plan for winning marriage equality. Phase one would secure marriage in six to eight "economically important, friendly states" through constitutional litigation; phase two would expand that momentum into "the more moderate states," winning marriage or civil unions through litigation or legislation in 60 percent of the country; phase three would involve federal constitutional litigation to overturn DOMA and bring "holdout states" into national conformity. "Part of making victories sustainable would be choosing states wisely (choosing states where constitutional amendments are unlikely). But the most important thing would be convincing the American public that excluding same-sex couples from marriage is unfair." The plan hoped for nationwide marriage equality by 2020. It was obsolete before the year was out.[1]

As we saw in chapter 10, the November 2004 elections were a big win for supporters of one-man, one-woman marriage. Those elections were a strong wake-up call for Tim Gill's team: his political guru, Ted Trimpa; Rodger Mc-Farlane, who headed the Gill Foundation; and Linda Bush, a consultant who wrote an analysis of the 2004 disaster. Unlike the Arlington Group, Bush reported, the marriage equality side had no national strategy, was undermined by infighting and rivalry among national groups, lacked funds and an organizational superstructure, and did not have a data-based approach to persuasive messaging. Related to the last criticism, most marriage equality campaigns were still relying on messaging and grassroots strategies that had been developed by HRC and state groups in the 1990s but were not working in the new millennium.[2]

Alarmed by Bush's report, Gill put out a call to the leaders of the movement: come to Denver, and let's figure out a way forward. In February 2005, twenty-six leaders of LGBT organizations assembled in a conference room at the Gill Foundation's Denver offices. Joining them were representatives from institutional funders who in 2004 had created the Civil Marriage Collaborative, including the Arcus Foundation, the Haas Fund, the Bohnett Foundation, and the Gill Foundation. The six-foot-six McFarlane was the physically intimidating host of the meeting. Bush was intellectually intimidating, with her confident, well-documented analysis and her demand that the movement decide what it wanted and figure out how to persuade a skeptical population that LGBT couples deserve it. Notwithstanding some pushback, most participants found her analysis persuasive.[3]

The next step was to form a marriage working group, consisting of ten thoughtful participants hand-picked by Matt Coles, who was also the scribe. The working group met in Jersey City on May 10–11, 2005, to figure out what the LGBT rights movement should be seeking and how it should achieve that goal. Attending the Jersey City meeting were Michael Adams (Lambda Legal), Mary Bonauto (GLAD), Toni Broaddus (Equality Federation), Rea Carey (NGLTF), Matt Coles (ACLU), Seth Kilbourn (HRC), Shannon Minter (NCLR), Alexander Robinson (Black Justice Coalition), Roey Thorpe (Basic Rights Oregon), and Evan Wolfson (Freedom to Marry). Everyone agreed that the marriage issue was not going away, but there was a wide range of ideas about goals and strategy: Should marriage be the goal? Or statewide domestic partnership? Was marriage an achievable goal? Or should the marriage debate be leveraged toward securing more anti-discrimination laws? In what Coles describes as a "lightbulb moment," it was suggested that the group start with a more concrete and less charged thought experiment: What relationship recognition could be achieved in the next decade? Recasting the question in practical terms let everyone offer ideas, and soon they had come up with the 10-10-10-20 strategy:

in the next fifteen to twenty years, gain marriage equality in ten states, civil unions or comprehensive domestic partnerships in another ten, some other recognition in ten more, together with some progress in public opinion in the remaining twenty. This consensus was reported in a May 25 concept paper, "Winning Marriage," that Coles circulated after the summit.[4]

None of the LGBT rights organizations was bound by the concept paper, but most immediately agreed with the ingenious 10-10-10-20 strategy. Consensus also emerged that success depended on "winning the public" through a national political campaign of education and persuasion. That marriage equality had to involve an ongoing educational and political campaign was a lesson that California, Vermont, and Massachusetts activists had applied successfully. The concept paper did not explain how to persuade skeptical Americans to think differently, other than that they needed to create a media "echo chamber" repeating "our messages over and over again until they are rolling off the tongues of those in the movable middle as reflections of their own values."[5]

To carry out their strategic vision, the campaign for marriage would have to engage the media, state and federal judges, legislators, allied groups, and the LGBT community on both the national and local levels. An institutional idea floated in "Winning Marriage" was the need for a new national organization formally coordinating the political and educational campaign. There was much disagreement as to how the national campaign should be structured. After further deliberation, the working group on June 21, 2005, produced a final plan, titled "Winning Marriage: What We Need to Do." The plan outlined two different ways for creating a national campaign. One mechanism was the "Collaborative," a vehicle for state and national organizations to "share research, intelligence, and plans for the work they hope to do." The other mechanism was an independent organization that would focus on message development and dissemination. Wolfson felt that Freedom to Marry could be adapted to fit the latter role, a notion that did not have universal support.[6]

A follow-up meeting was held at the Gill Foundation. With funders as their audience, the different organizations announced their willingness to cooperate and help fund the plan for "Winning Marriage." Participants recall that HRC was reluctant to agree to a plan that essentially rejected its inside-the-Beltway approach and demoted it within the movement's pecking order. The ACLU, GLAD, NCLR, and Lambda offered enthusiastic support. Other organizations, such as the National Black Justice Coalition, were supportive but not inclined to elevate marriage to a priority. On the whole, however, most of the LGBT groups focusing on marriage equality accepted the June 2005 plan.

There was uncertainty, rather than disagreement, about what the best messaging should be, but Coles had some ideas. In a pre-summit email to the working group, he had suggested that public education must be "showing (not saying) that same-sex couples are, in many ways that appeal to people, similar to opposite-sex couples, and most critically, that they commit to each other" and "showing (not saying) that couples suffer horrible consequences when treated as strangers." Specifically, the marriage equality campaign needed to show how LGBT couples were committed to one another in ways similar to the commitment of straight married couples and that such commitment enabled them to raise children and get through the hard times faced by families everywhere. These ideas had been suggested by a 2003 report to the ACLU by a professional opinion research firm, which strongly urged marriage equality advocates to shift their focus away from gay people and their rights and toward a focus on the value of marriage and commitment. Armed with this evidence, the ACLU and its allies made "marriage as commitment" the centerpiece of state constitutional litigation in the years after *Goodridge*. As chapter 12 reported, one lawsuit after another failed in state supreme courts—until the California Supreme Court's marriage decision in May 2008, examined in chapter 11.[7]

Right after the Jersey City meeting, HRC's Seth Kilbourn asked Anna Greenberg's firm to conduct polling in California and Wisconsin. The firm's conclusions: "Most voters in both states seem ready to accept this debate in terms of love and commitment. . . . [D]espite a broadly hostile reaction to gays and lesbians throughout the survey, a majority of Wisconsin voters agree with the statement: 'Love is what makes a family, and it doesn't matter if parents are gay or straight, married or single.'" *Love is what makes a family* was not an entirely new strategy, as it was the operating assumption of GLAD's marriage cases and the explicit motto of the marriage campaign in Connecticut. Its chief strategist was Anne Stanback, a cheerful, energetic pro-choice organizer based in New Haven. Anne was a feminist before she was an LGBT activist, but it was through meeting her life partner, Charlotte Kinlock, in 1983 that her lesbian identity came into focus. Since 1993, Charlotte and Anne have shared a home in woodsy Avon, Connecticut. In 1999, Anne, with Charlotte's support, worked with others to create Love Makes a Family. As the national movement was taking shape, the Connecticut and other New England campaigns had already developed the themes of love and commitment and were deploying them successfully—as did Lambda in Iowa, where marriage equality scored an unexpected breakthrough in 2009.[8]

Charlotte Kinlock and Anne Stanback

Love Makes a Family in Connecticut

In 1985, activists formed the Connecticut Coalition for Lesbian and Gay Rights to combine grassroots support with focused lobbying for legislation barring sexual orientation discrimination. Charlotte Kinlock was a codirector of the coalition's statewide steering committee, and Anne Stanback was the founding chair of the New Haven chapter. In 1987, their part-time lobbyist Betty Gallo secured the coalition's first legislative hearing. There, a legislator from Gales Ferry remarked that his district did not have any homosexuals—which inspired Charlotte, Anne, and the other activists to identify lesbian and gay individuals all over the state willing to host small house meetings for their representatives. The goal was to create a safe, nonconfrontational space where legislators could get to know lesbian and gay persons and couples. In turn, the meetings would enable the coalition to understand why particular legislators were not with them and what might be done to change their minds.[9]

The coalition also developed a list of supporting clergy to show that there were people of faith on both sides of the debate. Although the list included no Catholic priests, a significant omission in a heavily Catholic state, Father John Barry of the Hartford archdiocese took a pastoral approach to the issue and may have helped persuade Archbishop John Francis Whealon to say this in April 1991: "The Church clearly teaches that homosexual men and women should not suffer from prejudice on the basis of their sexual orientation. Such discrimination is contrary to the Gospel of Jesus Christ and is always morally wrong." This statement—combined with Bridgeport representative Joe Grabarz's decision in 1990 to come out as the legislature's first openly gay member as well as the burgeoning support from individuals, house meetings, and organizations across the state—helped win healthy majorities for the anti-discrimination bill in both chambers of the legislature (21-14 in the senate, 81-65 in the house). Governor Lowell Weicker happily signed the bill into law in 1991. Sponsors claimed that the lack of strong ecclesiastic opposition was decisive in their efforts to focus discussion on the concrete harms of discrimination and away from an abstract threat gay people posed to family values. But church acquiescence came at a price: the new law provided that it should not be read to suggest that the state "condones" homosexuality, authorizes the "promotion of homosexuality or bisexuality" in schools as "an acceptable lifestyle," or recognizes "the right of marriage between persons of the same sex."[10]

Many of the coalition members were in committed relationships, and some couples were raising children. New Haven attorney Maureen Murphy represented lesbian and gay couples who wanted to be co-parents through second-parent adoptions. Bucking the trend in other northeastern states, the Connecticut Supreme Court ruled that the state adoption law barred such adoptions in *In re Adoption of Baby Z* (1999). Responding to *Baby Z,* the coalition, the Connecticut Civil Liberties Union, the Connecticut Women's Education and Legal Fund, and other progressive organizations and individuals formed the umbrella group they called Love Makes a Family (LMF) in February 1999. Executive Director Anne Stanback and lobbyist Betty Gallo immediately sought legislative action.[11]

PARENTING AND PARTNERSHIP BILLS

Rarely does significant legislation result from an initial push, but Love Makes a Family came close to winning a legislative override of *Baby Z* on its first try. In committee, however, traditionalist legislators added a provision reaffirming that marriage was limited to one man, one woman and imposing a fine on clergy who performed same-sex unions. Stanback and her allies withdrew their support for the bill—but the threat of fining clergy motivated more than one hundred Buddhist, Episcopalian, Jewish, Lutheran, Methodist, Presbyterian, and United Church of Christ (UCC) clergy to support the second-parent adoption bill in the 2000 session. Also, the house meetings were paying off, and the bill had bipartisan support, including that of New Haven representative Chris Pino, the Republican Party chairman. As a compromise with Catholic legislators, the preamble to the new law included a one-man, one-woman definition of marriage but did not bar recognition of out-of-state marriages and imposed no penalties on celebrants of same-sex unions.[12]

After the 2000 statute, Love Makes a Family turned its energies to relationship recognition and marriage. On January 30, 2001, it filled the Wesleyan College auditorium with 350 people to hear Mary Bonauto and Evan Wolfson. Bonauto advanced three reasons why marriage should be a goal of the LGBT rights movement: it was a gateway to hundreds of legal rights and benefits, its special status would be a social boon to committed couples, and inclusion was a badge of equal citizenship. The event fired up the core group and attracted new volunteers. With an expanded army of couples, their parents, clerics, civil libertarians, pro-choice feminists, and other allies, Stanback employed the same strategy her group had followed for the second-parent adoption effort: through office visits, letters, and house meetings, lesbian and gay couples, as well as allied messengers, told legislators their stories of commitment to one another and to their children.

As before, LMF got the attention of progressive legislators. In March 2001, the joint judiciary committee, chaired by two openly gay legislators—Senator Andrew McDonald of Stamford and Representative Mike Lawlor of East Haven—held a series of hearings and issued a report on the hundreds of legal benefits and duties associated with marriage and denied to lesbian and gay families. LMF won a few rights from the legislature during the 2002 session, dealing with issues related to serious illness and death. There was no mention of same-sex couples, even though the new rights benefited them. In 2003, McDonald and Lawlor sponsored a comprehensive domestic partnership bill, which stirred up opposition from Archbishop Daniel Cronin of Hartford and Brian Brown, the head of the Connecticut Family Institute. On April 9, 2003, the joint committee rejected GOP proposals to add junior-DOMA language to the bill, only to vote 26-16 against the bill. The silver lining was that Mary Bonauto gave the green light to a state constitutional lawsuit in Connecticut, whose nickname is the Constitution State after its early charter of rights.[13]

KERRIGAN V. STATE

On August 23, 2004, Ben Klein filed GLAD's marriage lawsuit, *Kerrigan v. State*. The original plaintiffs were "seven same-sex couples, each of whom has made a personal commitment and assumed responsibilities for the other, and in [five] cases, their children." The lead couple were Hartford residents Beth Kerrigan and Jody Mock, partnered since 1994 and raising twin boys adopted from Guatemala in 2002. Both parents had good jobs in the insurance industry and provided a loving home and rich extended family for their sons—but both worried about being able to manage their finances and even to travel, because their unmarried status imposed unnecessary expenses on them and would render them vulnerable in health emergencies away from home. Another committed couple, Janet Peck and Carol Conklin, had been together and had assumed mutual responsibilities for twenty-eight years. As an older couple, they confronted escalating health challenges (including a liver operation)—challenges that were much harder to meet because the state treated them as unmarried. Reflecting the same philosophy of love and commitment that the ACLU was coming to appreciate on the eve of "Winning Marriage," Klein's complaint alleged that denying marriage to these seven committed couples and their children violated the freedom to marry and equal protection guarantees of the Connecticut Constitution.[14]

The *Goodridge* decision and the *Kerrigan* complaint had immediate ripple effects. Attorney General Richard Blumenthal, a liberal Democrat, refused to make the optimal-parenting, responsible-procreation, and deference-to-the-political-process arguments in defense of the marriage exclusion. Because court-imposed marriage for lesbian and gay couples suddenly seemed quite possible, pragmatic Republicans discovered that they really liked the idea of Vermont-style civil unions. This prospect thrilled Betty Gallo, Andrew McDonald, and Mike Lawlor because such legislation would give their side 75 percent of the benefits their couples wanted. (But because of DOMA, not 100 percent.)

On December 7, 2004 (Pearl Harbor Day), Stanback and Gallo drove to Boston to meet with Mary Bonauto, Beth Robinson, and Evan Wolfson. Gallo suspected a sneak attack, and she was right. The meeting's unstated agenda was to pressure Love Makes a Family to oppose civil unions legislation. Robinson explained how rotten she felt to have settled for anything less than marriage; civil unions were like riding in the back of the bus. GLAD and its allies worried that Connecticut would be a tipping point in the wrong direction. With two statutes, "civil union becomes the wave," worried Bonauto and Wolfson, and "it might take a generation [before] we eventually get back to marriage, and to really draw that line and say, this is about equality. It's not just about rights and protections." Separate but equal was not equal.[15]

During the drive back to Hartford, Stanback and Gallo had an intense discussion about what LMF should do. Gallo, avid to pass a statute, argued that a civil unions law would immediately give needed rights and benefits to thousands of couples and their children. Stanback could not shake the view that civil unions were a "dignitary insult" to committed lesbian and gay families and that if LMF endorsed civil unions legislation it might be viewed as supporting conservative legislators who were anti-equality. On December 11, Love Makes a Family held a retreat to decide whether to accept a civil unions compromise. Stanback's style was to be both deliberative and nonconfrontational, but on this issue she could not have both. Her colleagues were torn between the two courses—and so was Stanback, who spent many sleepless nights agonizing over the right course of action. After intense deliberation, the members rejected Gallo's pragmatic advice and agreed with GLAD's insistence on complete equality. "We don't need two lines at the town clerk's office, one for marriage and one for civil unions"—a quip Stanback attributes to Wolfson, who encouraged her in numerous phone conversations.[16]

THE CIVIL UNIONS SHOWDOWN

Anne Stanback privately informed Andrew McDonald and Mike Lawlor that Love Makes a Family would not support civil unions. On February 7, 2005, the joint judiciary committee held a hearing on marriage and civil unions before a packed room. Brian Brown submitted a petition signed by ninety thousand voters imploring legislators to submit the issue to a popular referendum. Stanback then dropped LMF's bombshell. Catholic Republican lawmakers who felt that civil unions were the perfect compromise responded like jilted fiancés. On the other hand, LMF's position received strong support from progressive married couples like Jennifer Gerarda Brown and Ian Ayres, law professors who provided a straightforward defense of full marriage rights: for their lesbian and gay friends, marriage entailed the same mutual love, commitment, and responsibilities that their traditional marriage did.[17]

On February 23, after defeating a proposal to add a junior-DOMA, the joint committee voted 25-13 in favor of the civil unions bill. On March 3, Stanback published an op-ed in the *Hartford Courant*, announcing that LMF would neither oppose nor support the civil unions bill. The coalition continued to educate legislators about gay and lesbian couples' families. While LMF and McDonald disagreed on the strategy of supporting civil unions, McDonald's remarks opening the senate debate on April 6 focused on the importance of marriage. That his bill was not a "marriage bill" was an "unfortunate limitation," because marriage was an institution with special cultural resonance that would benefit these couples and, especially, their children. With several Republicans embracing equal rights for lesbian and gay families, the senate approved the civil unions bill, 27-9.[18]

The house debated it on April 13. Republican Larry Cafero praised LMF for its house meetings and other ways of helping him get to know lesbian and gay families—but then proposed an amendment reaffirming the state's limitation of marriage to one man, one woman. The Cafero amendment passed with bipartisan support. The Act Concerning Civil Unions, as amended, passed the house 85-63, and on April 20 the senate signed onto the house changes. Brian Brown had organized a massive email and letter campaign urging Governor Jodi Rell to veto the bill, but she firmly supported a measure that ended legal discrimination against lesbian and gay couples, and she signed it into law within an hour.[19]

THE PAS DE DEUX OF LITIGATION AND LEGISLATION

Assistant Attorney General Jane Rosenberg invoked the new civil unions law as the state's defense against GLAD's marriage equality challenge in *Kerrigan v. State*. Ben Klein's response: separate was not equal. Judge Patty Jenkins Pittman ultimately agreed with the state. GLAD filed an appeal, which the Connecticut Supreme Court permitted to skip the intermediate court. Meanwhile, Love Makes a Family worked to improve its political position.[20]

With grants from the Gill Foundation and the Civil Marriage Collaborative (including $650,000 in 2007), LMF hired more staff, deepened its penetration into all parts of the state, grew its mailing and volunteer list, and created a social media presence on Facebook. MassEquality lent Amy Mello to help train volunteers and field organizers. The grants also financed focus groups and polling to determine what messages worked with middle-of-the-road voters and legislators. These sources, together with results from a joint GLAD/LMF poll, confirmed the 2005 decision to turn marriage messaging away from rights and benefits and toward love and commitment. The "conflicted" straight voter (religious but with gay friends or relatives) felt that her own marriage was founded on love and commitment, while gay marriage demands were based on securing benefits. LMF had to persuade such voters that, like them, lesbian and gay couples were motivated by love, commitment, and altruism.[21]

Fueled with contributions from Gill Action and its network of donors, LMF's political arm helped assure the reelection of its allies in November 2006. GOP Governor Rell, pro–civil union but not yet for marriage equality, was reelected;

Democratic legislators (most of them gay friendly) returned to Hartford with veto-proof majorities (24-12 in the senate, 107-44 in the house). Stanback and her colleagues stuck with the lobbying and education strategies that had gotten them this far. On February 14, 2007, McDonald and Lawlor introduced House Bill 7395, authorizing the state to issue marriage licenses to same-sex couples. The parade of witnesses supporting marriage equality in the joint judiciary committee hearings was unmatched in legislative memory: officials, organizations, and citizens assured legislators that lesbian and gay couples were just as committed to one another and assumed the same mutual responsibilities as traditional married couples. On April 12, the committee favorably reported the marriage bill by a bipartisan vote of 27-15. The marriage coalition did not press the bill any further, as leadership was not willing to call the bill for a vote before the entire chamber.[22]

THE CONNECTICUT SUPREME COURT'S DECISION IN *KERRIGAN*

On May 14, 2007, the Connecticut Supreme Court heard oral argument in the marriage case, now captioned *Kerrigan v. Commissioner of Public Health*. As in the original complaint, GLAD's brief for the plaintiff couples emphasized their mutual love, commitment, and responsibilities—features of their families that were disrespected and even undermined by their unequal status. GLAD's constitutional case led with the sex discrimination argument and then maintained that under the Connecticut Constitution, sexual orientation, like sex, was a suspect classification requiring strict or intermediate scrutiny. In characteristic GLAD fashion, Ben Klein and Mary Bonauto coordinated an array of amicus briefs. Representing the state and the commissioner of public health (the lead defendant on appeal), the attorney general argued that the civil unions law gave the plaintiff couples all the rights and benefits of civil marriage. The responsible procreation and optimal parenting arguments for traditional marriage were pressed in amicus briefs filed by the Connecticut Catholic Conference, the Family Institute of Connecticut, and the Family Research Council, all of which had opposed civil unions.[23]

Before hearing the case, the Connecticut Supreme Court engaged in a dramatic game of musical chairs. Chief Justice Chase Rogers recused herself and was initially replaced by Senior (Retired) Justice William "Tocco" Sullivan, a tradition-minded Catholic who had privately declared himself unwilling to "redefine marriage" to accommodate "the homosexual lifestyle." Upon reflection, Sullivan recused himself as well, perhaps out of collective concerns that he would not be considered a neutral voice. His substitute was Judge Lubbie Harper Jr. from the intermediate appeals court. At oral argument on May 7, 2007, Justice David Borden presided. He had directed the law reform commission that drafted a comprehensive new criminal code for the Connecticut legislature in 1969. Its most controversial move was to decriminalize consensual sodomy, which Borden defended against strong pushback from Catholic senators—men like Tocco Sullivan.[24]

The seven participating justices brought a variety of philosophies to the case. A close ally of Sullivan, Peter Zarella, approached the issue from a traditionalist perspective: Why should the court "redefine" this sacramental institution? Other justices thought the case hinged on individual civil rights: was it valid for the state to exclude lesbian and gay couples from the unique institution of marriage? Justices Richard Palmer, Joette Katz, Flemming Norcott, and Lubbie Harper felt the case resembled *Loving v. Virginia* (1967). If Virginia had offered civil unions, but not marriage, to interracial couples, would the supreme court not have ruled the same way? These four justices viewed marriage as an evolving institution and its traditional definition as requiring justification in light of social and legal changes, including the anti-discrimination law (1991), second-parent adoption (2000), and civil unions (2005). Unlike the trial judge, these justices thought the civil unions law did not save the day for the state; even the law's supporters conceded that it created a separate but unequal regime of rights.[25]

David Borden, the only justice appointed by a Democratic governor, also understood this as a civil rights case but was not persuaded that his court had to provide a remedy. Why not defer to the political process, which seemed to be working just fine? Civil unions might prove sufficient, and if not, legislators would adopt a marriage statute—probably sooner rather than later, given the success of the 2007 marriage bill. Christine Vertefeuille, a Catholic appointed by GOP governor John Rowland, agreed.

The Connecticut Supreme Court was thus divided 4-3, with a majority voting to strike down the discrimination. Dick Palmer, a liberal in the Lowell Weicker mold, took on the job of drafting the court's opinion. Because no state supreme court had followed *Goodridge* in striking down a marriage exclusion when he started working on his opinion in late 2007, Palmer wanted to focus on the argument that he, Katz, Norcott, and Harper all found most convincing: that state exclusions because of sexual orientation ought to be subjected to heightened scrutiny that the state did not pretend to satisfy.

In October 2008, seventeen months after oral argument in *Kerrigan*, the Connecticut Supreme Court released its decision sustaining the plaintiffs' claim. In his majority opinion, Justice Palmer's big analytical move was to hold that sexual orientation was a "quasi-suspect" classification for state equal protection purposes. His opinion applied the criteria usually invoked by state as well as federal judges for determining what classifications were suspect or quasi-suspect. First, the majority found, with no disagreement from the state or from the dissenters, that lesbian and gay people "have been subjected to and stigmatized by a long history of purposeful and invidious discrimination." Second, again without controversy, the court concluded that the discrimination had been based upon a trait that "bears no logical relationship to their ability to perform in society, either in familial relations or otherwise as productive citizens." Third, sexual orientation is "an essential component of personhood, [and] even if there is some possibility that a person's sexual preference can be altered, it would be wholly unacceptable for the state to require anyone to do so." Most in dispute was the further ruling that gay people continued to "face an uphill battle" to correct injustices through the political process. These "immutability" and "political powerlessness" elements, the court maintained, were not core features of the inquiry but were relevant to the court's judgment.[26]

In separate dissents, Justices Zarella and Borden argued that changing the long-standing definition of marriage was "a decision for the legislature or the people of the state and not this court." As Borden showed, LGBT people had enjoyed many legislative successes between 1991 and 2008. Changing the definition of marriage was such a big deal that it should be done through the democratically accountable legislature—as LMF was already doing with great success. The majority's response was that sex had been a suspect classification since the 1970s, even though women were far from powerless at the time. Like sex, sexual orientation ought to be suspect because it would be unfair to impose upon a minority subject to entrenched discriminations the burden of cleaning up so many legislated disadvantages.[27]

Justice Palmer ruled that the state's various administrative convenience rationales did not even constitute a rational basis for discrimination. The legislative history of the civil unions and second-parent adoption laws confirmed the wisdom of the state's concession that lesbian and gay households were good for children and ought to be encouraged. Conversely, they also confirmed the depth of the discrimination: marriage was special and endowed with unique cultural and social meaning. If the attorney general's office harbored any doubt about that, it should have lost it after reading the Zarella dissenting opinion, which adopted the marriage-is-unique viewpoint of the Catholic and Evangelical amicus briefs.[28]

Although polls indicated that most citizens supported the court's October 2008 ruling in *Kerrigan*, there was one more hurdle. Every twenty years, Connecticut voters have an opportunity to authorize the legislature to call a constitutional convention with the power to propose constitutional amendments or an entire new constitution, subject to voter ratification. The next vote would be November 4, 2008, just weeks after *Kerrigan* was handed down. For almost a year, Stanback had quietly built up a network of alliances to turn out citizens to vote no on the constitutional convention. The Family Institute did not mobilize on the issue until the summer, and the Catholic Church not until *Kerrigan*. Because voters generally reject constitutional ballot initiatives, especially broad ones like this, the proposal was defeated, 59.4 to 40.6 percent.[29]

On November 12, 2008, the Constitution State started issuing marriage licenses to same-sex couples—and the sky did not fall. Instead, the heavens embraced the supreme court's bold move.

Love Makes a Family petitioned the legislature to codify *Kerrigan* in the statute books and to terminate civil unions. Governor Rell and moderate legislators supported allowances for Catholic and other religious organizations; reluctantly, LMF went along, and they were added to the bill. On April 22, 2009, legislators voted overwhelmingly for marriage equality: 100-44 in the house and 28-7 in the senate. Governor Rell, who had evolved from civil unions at the same pace as her legislature, happily signed the bill on April 23. Ironically, it was a Republican who was the first governor to sign a marriage equality law. But Connecticut was not the first state to recognize same-sex marriages by statute.[30]

Love, Commitment, and Religious Accommodation in New England

The same year the Connecticut legislature enacted its marriage statute, the Vermont, New Hampshire, and Maine legislatures (as well as the District of Columbia council) also passed laws recognizing same-sex marriages and creating religious allowances and exemptions. In the spirit of equality practice, each of the marriage laws built upon earlier civil union or domestic partnership statutes that, as one legislator put it to us, "brought gay families out of the shadows" and revealed the love and commitment they embodied. The Vermont and New Hampshire legislatures had passed civil union laws in 2000 and 2007, respectively; in 2004, Maine had adopted a domestic partnership law with limited benefits. The District of Columbia's council enacted a domestic partner ordinance in 1992 and had steadily expanded its array of benefits and rights. In all three states and the District, the earlier statutes empowered and encouraged lesbian and gay couples, attracted straight allies to their cause, influenced the persuadable middle that these relationships represented serious families, and ameliorated opposition. It was harder to be angry about gay marriage when your barber, your neighbor, your city council member, your aunt, your kid's teacher, or your daughter was gay-partnered.[31]

Vermont, the first state to enact a marriage equality statute, was also the first to include explicit religious allowances and exemptions. All of the other New England statutes except that in Maine followed Vermont's law to allow churches to celebrate only those marriages permitted by their faith traditions, religious societies to limit their membership, religious charitable or educational societies to restrict insurance benefits to different-sex spouses, and nonprofit organizations controlled or operated by a religious organization to limit their marriage-related services to traditional couples. Professor Robin Fretwell Wilson says that the early marriage statutes would not have been adopted without these religious allowances and exemptions. Is she right?[32]

Start with Vermont, the Green Mountain State. Between July 2000 and January 2009, almost twelve thousand couples were joined in civil unions, including Beth Robinson and Kym Boyman. The easy integration of these families into the life of the state fueled increasing interest in marriage equality. In July 2008, Robinson; Shapleigh Smith, the next speaker of the Vermont House; and Peter Shumlin, the president of the Vermont Senate, were delegates to the Democratic convention. Both legislators were receptive to Robinson's plea for full marriage equality. Respect for lesbian and gay couples had motivated Smith to enter politics in the first place, and Shumlin, a veteran legislator, felt guilty that they did not already have marriage rights. Smith and Shumlin worked with five lesbian and gay colleagues, including Bill Lippert, chair of the house judiciary committee. "It's simply not possible for people to pretend they don't know gay and lesbian people in Vermont anymore," Lippert observed. For that reason, many citizens, businesses, newspapers, and churches that had been skeptical of civil unions now supported gay marriage. The Catholic Church, mired in lawsuits charging cover-ups of predatory priests, was a less formidable opponent than in the past.[33]

Senators Shumlin and Claire Ayer sponsored Senate Bill 115, an Act to Protect Religious Freedom and Recognize Equality in Civil Marriage, while Representatives Mark Larson and David Zuckerman were the primary house sponsors. Although there were many Vermonters opposed to marriage equality, the joint hearings held by the judiciary committees on March 18, 2009, revealed little of the Take Back Vermont fervor that had roiled the state nine years earlier. On March 23, the senate voted 26-4 for the marriage bill. Two days later, after GOP governor James Douglas announced his intention to veto it, the sponsors scrambled to attract moderate Republican support for the measure in Lippert's house judiciary committee. A key committee member was Republican Heidi Scheuermann, a devout, married real estate manager representing a French-Catholic district in northern Vermont. She was moved by the committee testimony, orchestrated by the indefatigable Beth Robinson, showing the dignitary harms of separate-but-not-quite-equal civil unions. The couples Scheuermann met at these hearings had families very much like hers, and they shared her sense of marital commitment and self-sacrifice. They faced the same problems as more traditional families. "I wanted to ensure that equality was there, but at the same time, I wanted to make sure that the language in the public accommodations act allowed [religious organizations] to keep doing the things they've always done." She and Lippert added three clusters of conscience protections to the bill.[34]

First, the amended marriage bill reaffirmed the freedom of churches and clergy to perform only those weddings sanctioned by their faith traditions and explicitly prohibited civil suits against members of the clergy for declining to perform same-sex marriages. Second, the bill exempted religious institutions and organizations from having to provide health insurance benefits to same-sex couples. Third, it amended the public accommodations law to provide that religious institutions, or nonprofits controlled by religious institutions, would not be required to provide services related to the solemnization of a marriage or celebration of a marriage. A church refusing to lease a public space for a gay wedding would not violate the public accommodations law, though a florist who refused to supply flowers might be in violation.

On April 3, the house passed its amended version of S.B. 115 by a vote of 94-52, several votes shy of a veto-proof two-thirds majority. Three days later, the senate overwhelmingly approved the house's amendments. Governor Douglas promptly vetoed the legislation. An affable, old-fashioned guy whose role model was Calvin Coolidge, Douglas says he believed "the institution of marriage is worth preserving in its traditional form. The civil union law gave gay couples the same privileges as married folks in the eyes of the state; this new proposal was really a debate over nomenclature." Given his own faith tradition (the gay-friendly UCC in Middlebury), the governor was not deeply invested in this veto, which was probably a bow to his increasingly dogmatic party and to the traditionalist voters who first elected him.[35]

On April 7, the senate overrode the veto by a 23–5 vote, but the sponsors faced a much tougher challenge in the house, where they had to hold all five Republican yes votes and add six more yeses. Three were easy: Speaker Shap Smith and two other supporters had not voted on April 3 and would support the override. Smith and his team—including Majority Leader Floyd Nease, Representatives Tim Jerman and Bill Lippert, and Senators Claire Ayer, Peter Shumlin, and Dick Sears—had to persuade three more Democrats to vote yes on the marriage bill just four days after they had voted no. Through ordinary persuasion, the boyish thirty-three-year-old speaker reeled in liberal Catholic Debbie Evans as well as Bob South, a conservative but a union man and a party man. The hardest vote was Jeff Young, representing conservative St. Albans County. Nease put a strong arm on him: Do you want to have a future as a leader in the Democratic Party? In the legislature? Young agreed to provide the hundredth vote, but with a reluctance that made Nease and Smith nervous. They also had to keep the five Republican votes, including Minority Leader Patti Komline, who told Smith she was a firm override vote because she had been moved by handwritten letters from gay constituents.[36]

Another question mark was Republican Richard Westman, a conservative farmer from tiny Cambridge who had voted against civil unions in 2000 and 2002. His friend Tom Little had helped persuade him to support the marriage bill on April 3. Westman had his eyes on a state senate race, and a yes vote might help him appeal to a larger constituency. On the other hand, his big legislative initiative that year was to repair bridges and other infrastructure, accompanied by an increase in the gas tax. Would pinch-penny Governor Douglas insist that Westman support his veto of the marriage bill in return for signing the gas tax bill?[37]

Shap Smith walked into the state house on April 7 not knowing whether he had pulled off one of the great legislative coups of the new century—or whether marriage equality in Vermont would suffer another near miss. To prolong the drama, the roll was called alphabetically, with Westman and Young at the end. They both went along, and the veto was overridden, 100-49. Governor Douglas graciously moved on to the business of the state—including signing the gas tax bill.

The Vermont House of Representatives would not have overridden the veto without the conscience allowances. Shap Smith considered them "very important. People needed to really see that we were not requiring religions who didn't think gay marriage was right, that we weren't going to force it on them." House sponsor David Zuckerman felt the allowances "persuaded some people [and] gave others cover." We cannot believe that all five Republicans (especially Heidi Scheuermann) and numerous Catholic Democrats representing conservative districts (like Jeff Young and Bob Smith) would have voted for the override without those provisions. They may have been one reason Jim Douglas did not insist that Dick Westman vote no on April 7.[38]

The success of conscience protections in Vermont stimulated two separate letter-writing efforts by law professors urging that these and other protective provisions be included in subsequent marriage equality statutes. One set of letters came from Robin Wilson and her allies; they took no position on the merits of marriage equality but urged that legislation include protections not only for clergy performing marriages, for churches and other religious institutions, and for religiously affiliated institutions but also for individuals and small businesses that provided goods or services for weddings. Wilson's letters contained draft text, tailored for each state, that could easily be added to marriage bills. Another set of letters came from Douglas Laycock and his allies; those letters supported marriage equality and argued that Wilson's proposed conscience protections would be good for gay rights as well as the rights of religious persons and institutions. Laycock argued that lesbian and gay couples would not be impeded in their wedding plans, while religious persons and institutions would enjoy welcome relief from having to participate. Did marriage equality supporters want to make martyrs of churches, bakers, and florists who did not want to lend their grounds or services to weddings their faith traditions considered sinful?

In response to specific inquiries from Catholic legislators, the first such letters were written on April 16 (Wilson group) and April 17, 2009 (Laycock group), to the speaker of the Connecticut assembly. The leaders did not want to slow down their bill with a long debate over religious liberty, and they feared that Governor Rell might veto the bill if there were no accommodations. Codifying constitutional guarantees, the house judiciary committee added a provision assuring clergy and churches that they remained free to solemnize only those marriages consistent with their faith traditions. Taking language from the Wilson letter, legislators also went beyond the religion clauses and added an allowance that religious or religiously affiliated institutions could not be required to provide goods or services if they were "related to the solemnization of a marriage or celebration of a marriage and such solemnization or celebration is in violation of their religious beliefs and faith." Finally, the bill protected religious organizations such as Catholic Charities in the provision of adoption, foster care, and social services, so long as the specific service was not government funded.[39]

We are not sure that the Connecticut marriage equality law would have been thwarted without conscience protections. The state was already handing out marriage licenses, putting the religious-accommodation advocates in a weaker bargaining position. Governor Rell and many legislators felt religious allowances were symbolically important and helped them express generosity toward LGBT families—but these allowances had little practical effect. The governor probably would have signed the marriage bill without them. Like her own Congregationalist (UCC) faith tradition, she had moved from civil unions and equality practice all the way to marriage equality by 2009. While the Connecticut marriage bill may have been enacted without religious accommodations, including them made its passage much more robust.

For the New Hampshire marriage law, there is no doubt that the religious accommodations were necessary. Here as elsewhere, the Democratic Party swept the 2006 and 2008 elections, twice reelecting Governor John Lynch and winning huge majorities in the legislature. In 2009 the Democratic leadership introduced a marriage bill to a legislature evenly divided on the issue. On March 26, the house narrowly defeated the measure, immediately voted to reconsider, and then passed it, 186-179. In the senate, Majority Leader Maggie Hassan rescued the bill with an amendment explicitly recognizing the rights of clergy and churches to celebrate only those marriages recognized by their faith traditions. After the senate narrowly passed the bill with the Hassan amendments, 13-11, the house repassed it on May 6.[40]

A businessman, environmentalist, and dedicated Catholic husband and father, Governor Lynch was a pragmatist and a pluralist. Relying on the Vermont and Connecticut laws that had just been signed, he announced that he would veto the marriage bill without further accommodations for religious liberty. The Granite State's motto was "Live Free or Die," and its citizens took the idea seriously. The law professors agreed: "Exemptions for religious conscience protect a fundamental human liberty. And they ameliorate social conflict in cases such as this, when Americans with radically different views on fundamental moral questions seek to live together in peace and equality in the same society." After intense negotiations, the legislature passed a bill with the requested accommodations, and the governor signed it on June 3, 2009.[41]

Following the Connecticut law, the New Hampshire marriage law provided that religious or religiously affiliated institutions could not be required to provide goods or services related to the celebration of a marriage that was inconsistent with their faith tradition. New Hampshire expanded this allowance to include solemnization, celebration, and "promotion of marriage through religious counseling, programs, courses, retreats, or housing designated for married individuals." Also going beyond the earlier laws, the statute explicitly protected those persons and institutions against both private lawsuits and any kind of "government penalty," exempted insurance programs for religious fraternal benefit societies like the Knights of Columbus, and assured religious institutions the freedom to allocate housing to married persons according to their faith traditions.[42]

The Maine legislature also had the option of adopting civil union legislation first—but longtime marriage activist Betsy Smith and Equality Maine decided to oppose civil unions and lobby only for marriage equality. Like the other New England groups, Equality Maine benefited each year from grants made by the Civil Marriage Collaborative and Gill Action, which enabled the organization to professionalize its lobbying and grassroots efforts. And the 2006 and 2008 elections gave gay-friendly Democrats control of the legislature and the governorship. Governor John Baldacci, a Catholic, strongly preferred a civil union law over a marriage law, but his party was united on the issue, and the marriage bill sailed through the legislature on party-line votes. Baldacci signed the bill into law on May 6, 2009, and the Pine Tree State became the fourth to adopt marriage equality by legislation. The law's minimal conscience protections simply duplicated federal constitutional guarantees.[43]

Even though the Wilson and Laycock groups overlooked the marriage debate in the District of Columbia, its Religious Freedom and Civil Marriage Equality Amendment Act of 2009 was laden with religious accommodations. The most important opposition came from African American Evangelical pastors, and council members in this racially diverse city wanted to accommodate their needs. Without significant controversy, the marriage equality bill included explicit protections for clergy and churches to solemnize only those marriages consistent with their faith traditions and for religious or religiously affiliated institutions to limit their services, facilities, goods, programs, counseling, courses, and retreats in ways consistent with their religious beliefs. The new law immunized such institutions from both lawsuits and government penalties, but despite a proposal from the Catholic Church, it did not give adoption agencies the freedom to limit their services. On December 18, 2009,

Mayor Adrian Fenty signed the marriage bill at All Souls Church, a Unitarian Universalist Church that welcomed and married lesbian and gay couples.[44]

The Golden Rule in Iowa

Lambda Legal had opened a Midwest regional office in 1993, and Camilla Taylor joined it nine years later. Like many of her generation, Taylor was a straight person who strongly supported equal rights for LGBT persons. "I do feel a compulsion," she later confessed, "to try to make the world a better place for my sister," who was a lesbian.[45]

But Taylor was not focused on the marriage issue until she received a cold call from Janelle Rettig, a partnered lesbian in Iowa City, asking when Lambda planned to bring a marriage case in the Hawkeye State. Normally, the Lambda lawyer would have explained the cautious and lengthy process required for bringing such a lawsuit, and that would be that. But Rettig did not take we-have-a-process for an answer, and before she knew it, Taylor was researching Iowa law. With the exception of David Buckel, the head of Lambda's Marriage Project, her colleagues were skeptical about a lawsuit in the Midwest. Wasn't Iowa the state where crazy fundamentalists grilled GOP presidential candidates every four years to weed out moderate conservatives?[46]

Taylor learned that Iowa enjoyed a progressive history on civil rights that sometimes put it ahead of northeastern states—consistent with the state motto: "Our liberties we prize and our rights we will maintain." In 1869, for example, Iowa was the first state to admit a woman (Arabella Mansfield) to practice law. The University of Iowa was the first public university to admit women (1849) and to recognize a gay student group (1970). In March 2004, Taylor reported to Lambda that Iowa was the most hospitable forum for a marriage lawsuit in the Midwest, with Illinois a distant second. An important consideration was that the state constitution could only be amended if two successive sessions of the legislature voted to place a constitutional amendment on the ballot and a majority of the voters then approved it. The Iowa Supreme Court was a favorable forum because of its tradition of close scrutiny of discriminatory laws and a willingness to protect a greater range of individual rights under the Iowa Constitution than the US Supreme Court protected under the US Constitution. Indeed, the Iowa Constitution had broad equality protections. Article I, section 1 required equal treatment of all people, and section 6 required the legislature to adopt only "general laws," without special exemptions favoring or disfavoring minority groups.[47]

After a great deal of marriage movement deliberation, Camilla Taylor would bring Lambda's marriage crusade to Iowa—where the constitutional litigators applied the love-and-commitment messaging that Lambda and the ACLU had been internalizing in the wake of "Winning Marriage" (2005). That is, straight married people needed to be convinced that lesbian and gay couples felt the same love and commitment they felt and that their families faced the same challenges, which in the American religious heartland mobilized the Golden Rule.

IOWA'S PROPOSED CONSTITUTIONAL
DOMA AND *VARNUM V. BRIEN*

Taylor told Rettig that Lambda would not file a constitutional lawsuit if the Iowa legislature initiated the process for a constitutional amendment in its 2004 session. That process was already underway, spearheaded by Chuck Hurley, president of the Iowa Family Policy Center, an organization associated with Focus on the Family. Father to ten children as well as several foster children, Hurley was a born-again Christian with the earnest demeanor of a small-town lawyer. In December 2003, he and GOP house speaker Christopher Rants agreed on a plan to pass a constitutional DOMA that would head off an Iowa version of *Goodridge*. That February, the GOP leadership introduced Senate Joint Resolution (SJR) 2002 to amend the Iowa Constitution to provide that "only a marriage between a man and a woman will be valid or recognized in the State of Iowa."[48]

Rettig was determined to stop this juggernaut. She alerted her network to contact their legislators, come out to them and others as couples, attract media attention, and stage polite requests for marriage licenses. One couple who participated in such a "marriage-in" was Jennifer and Dawn BarbouRoske of Iowa City. The former Jen Barbour was a nurse who had been raising two children with her committed partner since 1990, the former Dawn Roske. In 2003, their five-year-old daughter McKinley broke into tears when she heard her Mommy (Jen) and Mema (Dawn) discussing their nonmarital status. "Does that mean you're splitting up?" Aghast, Dawn and Jen tried to reassure her, "We're married in our hearts." But they were not married in the eyes of the law, and that made the child anxious. Months later, *Goodridge* raised their hopes that they could satisfy McKinley's yearning for family recognition, and in March 2004 they responded to Rettig's call by applying for a marriage license. With an apologetic look, the clerk politely declined.[49]

Although the Republicans controlled the Iowa Senate, 29-21, Rettig saw openings. Senator Mary Lundby of Cedar Rapids, whose son Daniel was gay, told her friend Janelle she would not vote for the DOMA resolution. Senator Maggie Tinsman voted against the resolution in committee based upon her reading of the Iowa Constitution, which had no provision taking away rights from a minority. In the Democrats' caucus, Senator Matt McCoy came out as gay and explained to his colleagues how the amendment would harm LGBT people and their families. When Minority Leader Michael Gronstal urged his caucus to stand with Matt against SJR 2002, not one Democrat objected. Every senator was asking whether she or he could "sit with a colleague [and] then say to him he wasn't worthy of protection," as Rettig put it. With GOP defections and Democrat solidarity, there were twenty-three votes against the resolution, two votes shy of the twenty-five needed to defeat it.[50]

On the day SJR 2002 was debated, several Republican senators shared Lundby's and Tinsman's discomfort with singling out a minority and hanging the decline of marriage around their necks. Because many senators knew Matt McCoy and Daniel Lundby to be first-rate people, it made the vote more personal. At the end of the day, the forty-nine senators cast their votes electronically. Twenty-four immediately voted no, including Don Redfern, another socially moderate Republican. But only twenty-four yes votes were on the board. Taking his time was GOP senator Doug Shull.

Born and raised in Iowa, Shull was the tenth of eleven children. His mother was Catholic and his father Mormon, so each child chose his or her own faith. Doug went with Methodist. He and a brother established a successful accounting firm in the small college town of Indianola. A practical man, he did not find the religious objections to gay marriage sufficient to support a constitutional amendment, nor did he see his friend Matt McCoy as a threat to marriage. He knew that voting against his party on this issue would foreclose any possibility of winning statewide office as a Republican, but like Maggie Tinsman he was unwilling to carve a minority group out of the Iowa Constitution. When the clerk called out "ten seconds" before the vote tally would close, Doug pressed the no button, and SJR 2002 failed, 24-25.[51]

After the vote, no fewer than three Republican senators came up to Shull to thank him for saving the state from the constitutional amendment. Surprised and disappointed, Rants and Hurley were confident the November elections would pad their majority in the Senate, giving them another shot in 2005. In November 2004, Iowa voted for President Bush's reelection but gave the Democrats a 25-25 tie in the state senate and a close, 49-51 minority in the house.

There would be no constitutional amendment now that Mike Gronstal was the co–majority leader. (Shull was offered a prominent position if he would switch parties in 2005, but he prized loyalty and Iowa-nicely declined the offer.)

After the dramatic senate vote, the coast seemed clear for Taylor to file a constitutional lawsuit—until the disastrous 2004 election results and donor nervousness motivated Lambda executive director Kevin Cathcart to impose a moratorium on new marriage lawsuits. At the Jersey City meeting in May 2005, the informal list created by one of the participants assumed that Maryland, New Jersey, New York, Oregon, Rhode Island, and Washington would precede Iowa to the altar. Overall, Jersey City revved up Lambda's enthusiasm for marriage, and Cathcart lifted the moratorium. Taylor filed the lawsuit on December 13, 2005.[52]

The plaintiffs included a nurse, a business manager, an insurance analyst, a bank agent, a stay-at-home parent, a church organist and piano teacher, a museum director, a federal employee, a social worker, a teacher, and two retired teachers. Some had children and others hoped to have them. The lead couple, Katherine Varnum and Patricia Hyde, were a committed couple raising two children as a family in Cedar Rapids. Janelle Rettig and Robin Butler could not be plaintiffs because they had already gotten legally married in Canada. But their colleagues in the grassroots campaign against the constitutional amendment, Jen and Dawn BarbouRoske, were eager to step in. In June 2004, former Iowa solicitor general Dennis Johnson had agreed to represent the six plaintiff couples. Timothy Brien, the Polk County recorder who had denied the couples marriage licenses in Des Moines, was the defendant in *Varnum v. Brien*.[53]

THE TRIAL COURT HEARING AND DECISION

Polk County's assistant county attorney Roger Kuhle represented the defendant. On March 6, 2006, the Alliance Defense Fund (ADF) filed a motion to allow nineteen Republican legislators to intervene as defendants. Because his office was not sufficiently staffed to handle major constitutional litigation, Kuhle welcomed ADF counsel as needed reinforcements and signed onto the standard ADF arguments: marriage had always been one man, one woman, and only the legislature could significantly redefine it; marriage ought to remain one man, one woman, because it channeled procreation into the best households for rearing children.

Camilla Taylor could understand the power of the defer-to-the-legislature claim, but she was dismayed by the optimal-parenting claim. She did not see any difference between her plaintiff families and the best husband-wife families. The BarbouRoskes gave her an idea. They believed that their inability to marry was more costly for their daughters than for themselves. As an example, they cited an interview with the principal of a private school they were considering for McKinley. When they casually asked if it was alright that she had two mothers, the principal replied: "Well, she wouldn't be able to give a presentation during the unit on families because we wouldn't want to upset the other parents." They found another school. For Jen and Dawn, "the state's law declaring their family unworthy of marriage sent a message even to the youngest children that there was something wrong and inferior about their family." Even in the more gay-friendly school, McKinley encountered teasing and ridicule about her two moms. A fearless child, she pushed back and defended her family. Taylor was so impressed by the girl's pluck that she amended the *Varnum* complaint to add McKinley, her sister Breeanna, and another child as plaintiffs—the first time a marriage equality lawsuit had done so.[54]

When a few movement lawyers objected that gay people raising children made straight people too nervous, Taylor stuck to her guns. Why run away from the fact that over a third of Iowa's lesbian and gay couples were raising children? ADF and Polk County made fatherless households the centerpiece of their defense, and Taylor was relying on the social science evidence demonstrating "no differences" because of parental sexual orientation. McKinley BarbouRoske was the "heart and soul" of the case, for she showed how important marriage law was in everyday life—and not just because of the material benefits and conveniences denied these genuine families. By pointedly excluding lesbian and gay couples from marriage, the state was telling schools, teachers, parents, and classmates that McKinley came from a disapproved family and could be treated differently from other children. This was cruel unless it was justified by something more than "marriage has always been this way."[55]

Plaintiffs demanded a trial on the county's justifications. Require the defendants to prove that lesbian and gay households were inferior—and refute their claims with the testimony of the plaintiffs and Lambda's respected expert witnesses. The attorneys spent a year deposing one another's witnesses. One of the defendants' experts, University of Virginia professor Steve Rhoads, filed a declaration describing the disadvantages of fatherless households. Late in pregnancy with her first child, Taylor conducted his deposition. Rhoads lectured her that when she gave birth, she would enjoy increased levels of oxytocin, an interpersonal-bonding hormone that would make her want to stay home and care for her child full-time, rather than continue working on this case. Like some other ADF-recruited witnesses, Rhoads saw the world and even science through faith-based beliefs that women's "natural" role was to marry a man, engage in procreative intercourse, and raise children. Like the plaintiff couples, Taylor wanted both children and a career, and hormones accompanying the births of her two children did not dampen her enthusiasm for those twin goals. (In 2018, oxytocin and all, she was named Lambda's legal director.)

Each side moved for summary judgment—a decision based only on undisputed facts derived from depositions and affidavits. Taylor and Johnson's statement of material facts opened with the theme consistent with the "Winning Marriage" research: "Plaintiffs each have chosen and consented to marry the one unique person who is irreplaceable to them and with whom they have formed a deeply intimate bond and share daily family life, but have been denied this right by the government." In detail, the lawyers documented the dozens of disadvantages the denial of marriage imposed upon these families—ranging from situations where plaintiffs and their children were treated disrespectfully because they were unable "to communicate the depth and permanence of their commitment to others, or to obtain respect for that commitment, as others do simply by invoking their married status," to the many tangible rights and benefits the state provided married couples to support their committed relationships and responsibilities.[56]

Polk County district judge Robert Hanson was deeply moved by the evidence presented in declarations and depositions demonstrating the seriousness of the plaintiffs' committed relationships and the harms the marriage exclusion was imposing upon their families. Conversely, the judge was underwhelmed by the county's factual submissions and found that five of the defendants' proffered witnesses did not qualify as social science "experts," including Professor Rhoads and Magill University professors Katherine Young and Paul Nathanson. On August 30, 2007, Judge Hanson granted the plaintiffs' motion for summary judgment. He accepted all three of the constitutional claims made by Lambda and its amici: Iowa's 1998 junior-DOMA, excluding same-sex couples from civil marriage, (1) deprived the couples of their fundamental right to marry without a strong justification, (2) was a sex discrimination that could not meet the heightened scrutiny the Iowa Constitution required, and (3) did not even rest upon a rational basis required of all laws creating distinctions. The judge rejected the county's responsible-procreation and optimal-parenting arguments as unsupported by any evidence. Polk County filed an immediate appeal.[57]

While *Varnum* was on appeal, One Iowa (founded in 2005) engaged in a concerted political campaign. Funded by Tim Gill and other donors in the

Marriage Collaborative, One Iowa retained field organizers, a communications/messaging director, and a lobbyist. In 2008, it hosted forty-nine marriage equality house meetings, created steering committees in ten communities, confirmed sixteen important institutional allies, and networked with stakeholders, legislators, and allies to generate popular and media attention to lesbian and gay couples' need for the freedom to marry. Gill Action and other groups provided funding and political advice for the 2006 and 2008 elections, which returned Democratic majorities to both chambers of the Iowa legislature. We do not think any of this directly affected the justices, but these efforts may have helped create a political climate helping all Iowans to see "LGBT people and families as relatable, as part of their communities," who "want the same things that all families want—dignity and security."[58]

THE IOWA SUPREME COURT'S DECISION
IN *VARNUM V. BRIEN*

The Iowa Supreme Court took *Varnum v. Brien* immediately, and the justices spent much of the autumn of 2008 reading the parties' briefs, twenty-six amicus submissions, and the case's five-thousand-page record. The court that heard the case on December 9, 2008, was relatively young, hardworking, collegial, and nonpartisan. Three older justices serving in 2005 had retired by 2008, a development that improved plaintiffs' opportunities. Marsha Ternus and Mark Cady, appointed by GOP governor Terry Branstad, seemed just as open to the plaintiffs' claims as the five colleagues appointed by Democratic governors: Brent Appel, Michael Streit, David Wiggins, Daryl Hecht, and David Baker.

Taylor and Johnson's target audience was Marsha Ternus, the chief justice. She had grown up on a farm in a large traditional Catholic household, had been the first in her family to graduate from college, and as a judge enjoyed a sterling reputation for care, analytical clarity, and neutrality. She demanded reasons. Her opinion in *Racing Association of Central Iowa v. Fitzgerald* (2004) had invalidated Iowa's discriminatory tax treatment of racetrack and riverboat gambling; the state's strained reasoning satisfied the US Supreme Court but not Marsha Ternus. In *Varnum*, counsel's goal was to help her understand that the plaintiff couples and their children represented genuine families grounded in the same love and commitment as the Ternus family. An engaged plaintiff, McKinley BarbouRoske sat in the front row at oral argument, carefully recording the proceedings in a notebook. Taylor told her not to react to any of the

statements made about her family, and McKinley kept a poker face for the entire hour—as did the justices.[59]

The Iowa Supreme Court treated the plaintiffs like neighbors and not like
strangers to the law. During oral argument, Roger Kuhle repeatedly conceded
that marriage had changed in many ways in the last fifty years, and the justices wondered why it could not accommodate couples who seemed so much
like their own families. Kuhle also stumbled on the central issue: Was sexual
orientation discrimination constitutionally suspect, as the California and Connecticut Supreme Courts had just ruled? If so, Polk County would lose,
because the record did not demonstrate that excluding lesbian and gay couples
was necessary to protect a compelling public interest. After reading the record and engaging in oral argument, some justices wondered whether Polk
County had even offered a rational basis for excluding lesbian and gay couples
from civil marriage.[60]

Kuhle's main justification for the discrimination was that redefining marriage would undermine the institution itself and deny children the mom-dad
parenting that was best for them. Consider the incentives for couples in a world
where procreative intercourse was not the state's primary aspiration for marriage. In such a brave new world, "[I]t doesn't matter whether you're with your
biological parents or not. Anybody can raise a child; a child doesn't need a
father; a child doesn't need a mother." The Iowa legislature had the discretion to
say its members and their constituents didn't want to live in such an alienated
world. Were the justices really certain that a child did not need a daddy? As Chuck
Hurley would later put it: Did they think they were smarter than nature?[61]

Near the end of the argument, Mark Cady asked Denny Johnson: Why
wouldn't civil unions, with all the legal rights and benefits of marriage, satisfy constitutional equality requirements? Johnson nailed the answer—twice.
"Sometimes the easiest way to analyze these arguments is to turn them on
yourself, you know. I'm happily married to a woman I dearly love. If the state
told me that we couldn't be married anymore but I could have a civil union, I
feel some loss there." Every Iowan knew the Golden Rule: "Do unto others as
you would have them do unto you" (Matthew 7:12). Was that not a guide to the
requirements of equal protection?[62]

But Johnson had not finished his answer. Civil unions would not just affect
the romantic couple. "We have McKinley BarbouRoske here, ten years old in
the courtroom with her parents. You know, she found out that her parents
weren't married and that upset her. She started to cry because she wondered
why her family was different than others. And then, they tried to find a day

care situation for her pre-school, and they were told by the teacher that McKinley could participate but she wouldn't be allowed to talk about her family during family week because they weren't married. That hurts people in a serious way." Several justices had noticed McKinley sitting quietly in the front row, listening intensely, and this touched them deeply.[63]

At conference right after the argument, Mark Cady had responsibility for leading the discussion, based upon a random drawing of names and cases out of a black bag. A strict constructionist who had dissented in *Racing Association*, Cady was persuaded that lesbian and gay couples were similarly situated to straight couples for purposes of the state's marriage law and that Polk County had not demonstrated any persuasive reason to exclude them. For him, the strongest justification was that the traditional definition of marriage promoted the best possible environment for rearing children—but amicus briefs by professional groups and family law professors demonstrated that gay and lesbian parents were no less fit or capable than heterosexual parents and that their children were no less psychologically healthy and well-adjusted. Icing on the equality cake was Cady's further conclusion that, given the criteria established in both federal and state equal protection precedents, sexual orientation was a quasi-suspect classification requiring especially skeptical examination. This made the decision easy: unconstitutional. No civil unions, just marriage.

Taking turns around the table, each justice expressed similar views. There was consensus in favor of heightened equal protection scrutiny and skepticism about the state's responsible procreation argument. "Why would you let old people get married over 50 or 60? Why would you let people get married if they don't intend to have children?" They also dismissed the optimal-child-rearing rationale as inconsistent with the voluminous record and with state policy. Iowa already allowed lesbian and gay couples to adopt and raise children, and they were doing so capably. "Why not make the households even more secure with marriage?" They were not going to ignore McKinley. Recalls Justice Baker: "This was not *Brown v. Board of Education*, where Earl Warren had to basically browbeat some of the Southern Justices in order to have a unanimous decision. This truly was a unanimous decision."[64]

A product of dozens of drafts, Justice Cady's opinion for the unanimous court in *Varnum* found that the plaintiff couples were "in committed and loving relationships, many raising families, just like heterosexual couples." Moreover, these couples fit within the core purposes of marriage, which did not depend on conjugality. "Society benefits, for example, from providing same-sex couples a stable framework within which to raise their children and the power to make health care and end-of-life decisions for loved ones, just as it does when that framework is provided for opposite-sex couples." Like Palmer in *Kerrigan,* Cady ruled that the discrimination against those couples was because of their sexual orientation, which he found to be a quasi-suspect classification under the Iowa Constitution. None of the county's stated justifications was valid, but the opinion concluded with a discussion of the "unspoken" justification, religious objections. Reaffirming the freedom of religious groups to recognize only different-sex marriages, he ruled that this right did not justify a civil exclusion.[65]

Camilla Taylor was with McKinley BarbouRoske when they all learned that they had won. McKinley's elated face and upraised arms are her most lasting memory from that day. That summer, her parents were legally married in Iowa City. Breeanna was the ring bearer and flower girl; McKinley played Johann Pachelbel's soulful Canon in D on the violin.

Driving back to Chicago after the Iowa celebrations subsided, the Lambda lawyers stopped to get gasoline. Noticing the banner headline in the local newspaper, Camilla Taylor asked the woman who filled their tank what she thought of the marriage ruling. She smiled broadly, "I think I'm gonna get me some of that." In Iowa, hers was a minority viewpoint, however. One post-*Varnum* poll found only 28 percent of Iowans supported marriage equality. Iowa's Catholic bishops issued a statement expressing sadness that the court was redefining civil marriage in a way that would undermine the institution. (Marsha Ternus, a lifelong Catholic, was no longer comfortable attending church.) Lobbied by One Iowa and by Tim Trimpa, who guaranteed that Gill Action would raise money to support pro-marriage Democrats, Governor Chet Culver rejected Chuck Hurley's call for an executive order preventing clerks from complying with the court's mandate and even backed away from his earlier statement that he would support a constitutional amendment. But given the pollsters' report that 67 percent of Iowa voters wanted a constitutional referendum so they could decide the question, the GOP seized upon this issue in 2010.[66]

When the LGBT leaders met in Jersey City in May 2005, things looked bleak for the marriage equality movement. With powerful forces narrowing in on a strategy to put marriage equality to a popular vote, it was not clear whether Massachusetts would be the movement's Normandy or another Dunkirk. Four years later, the marriage map had expanded well beyond the parameters faced in Jersey City. Indeed, the marriage map had added quite a few states in the year after the November 2008 election, the modest state of affairs depicted in Figure 2, which closed the last chapter. Court-ordered marriage licenses were being issued in Connecticut and Iowa, and marriage legislation had passed in Connecticut, the District of Columbia, Maine, New Hampshire, and Vermont. (In November 2009, Maine's voters would override that state's marriage law.) The Jersey City "Winning Marriage" blueprint, the money from the Civil Marriage Collaborative and the Gill network, and the coordination afforded by the ACLU, Lambda Legal, Freedom to Marry, HRC, and GLAD were helpful in securing marriage equality in these post-*Goodridge* states.

Yet marriage equality would not have come to Connecticut, Vermont, or Iowa in 2008–2009 had it not been for the efforts of Anne Stanback, Beth Robinson, and Camilla Taylor, as well as their powerful networks. The chief players in those networks were not the billionaire donors or the national groups, valuable as they were, but lesbian and gay couples themselves, their parents and children, friends and neighbors, media advisers and inquisitive reporters, dedicated social workers, inclusive preachers and priests and rabbis, academics and unpaid or underpaid experts, grassroots field organizers, openly lesbian and gay legislators, progressive law professors, and feminist judges.

Most essential to the success of these local marriage movements was the average straight person—not just people like Ivy-educated Camilla Taylor and her architect-husband Rusty Walker, but also the local union steward, the neighborhood druggist, the popular barber and hairdresser, the schoolteacher, and the farmers, accountants, parents, and lawyers serving in state legislatures. Marriage would not have come to Iowa in 2009, for instance, if Doug Shull, Mary Lundby, Maggie Tinsman, and Don Redfern had not voted against the constitutional junior-DOMA in 2004. Taylor, Robinson, and Stanback figured out what persuaded these straight people: love and commitment make a family. Lesbian and gay people form committed relationships for the same reasons my spouse and I got married. A lot of them have children: Who knew? How would I feel if the government told me that my relationship was not good enough to be called marriage? And told our children that our committed union was not morally different from adultery? The lesbian and gay couples also reminded straight married couples of all the tangible ways the state supported them in times of trouble.

The Michigan nurses who opened this volume illustrated the messaging insights reflected among marriage equality supporters both before and after the Denver and Jersey City meetings. Recall, from chapter 12, Nolan and Ryanne, the son and daughter adopted by Jayne Rowse and April DeBoer.

Ryanne was a very needy baby, and April and Jayne stayed up many nights caring for her. Who could match the love, commitment, and responsibility offered by these partners and parents? And don't forget Jacob, the child brought back from near death and into the DeBoer-Rowse household in March 2010. Jacob and his mothers struggled with one physical issue after another through his infancy. After about a year, April brought him with her back to Hutzel Hospital, where baby Jacob had hovered between life and death. A doctor asked April whatever became of the boy who weighed just a pound and a half when he was born. April pointed toward Jacob, who was playing on the other side of the room. The doctor's jaw dropped; it was a medical miracle. Could this baby have survived without constant care and expertise from his nurse-parents? How could Michigan explain to Jacob Rowse (Jayne adopted him in October 2011) that his parents could not get married because the state wanted to channel straight people into responsible procreation? How well did that channeling work for Jacob, whose crack-addicted mother did not pick up all those signals the state was sending?

In 2010, however, marriage equality was the last thing on April and Jayne's minds. Their main concern was saving Jacob's life and making sure their children's health problems were addressed. That year, they purchased a two-story, three-bedroom house on East Granet Avenue in Hazel Park, Michigan. Situated on a corner lot of a tree-lined street with lots of families, the new house had a central living room, a large kitchen, and a big backyard for the menagerie of pets that April and the children collected.

This was the house we visited in 2015. After spending the afternoon and early evening with the whole family, including Grandma Wendy, we were saying our goodbyes when five-year-old Ryanne, wearing a deep-pink "IT Girl" shirt, escorted us to the door. She gave us a parting gift, a piece of paper with this message, which she read to us: "Family IS LOVE." Who wrote this lovely message? She studied the paper intently and pronounced: "Nolan did 'Family,' and I did 'IS LOVE.'" She gave us a sideways look. We appreciated the expression and that the gift was a collaborative project.[67]

14 • "Restore Marriage"

Like Matt Coles, an architect of the "Winning Marriage" blueprint for marriage equality in the last chapter, Maggie Gallagher, the intellectual paladin for one-man, one-woman marriage introduced in chapter 10, believed that the marriage debate's center of gravity shifted in 2004 away from judges and courts and toward voters and legislatures. The next stage in building a new post-DOMA Maginot Line would be harder to achieve than past victories. The remaining state constitutions were harder to amend, the Federal Marriage Amendment was a lost cause, and the LGBT community was becoming better organized and better funded.

In July 2007, Gallagher had cofounded (with Brian Brown and Robby George) the National Organization for Marriage (NOM), with a focus on Congress and state legislatures. She was skeptical of ballot initiatives as the firewall for traditional marriage, but that was a minority view among her allies. In 2005, Andy Pugno had launched a new organization to support a California constitutional ballot initiative: ProtectMarriage.com. Its executive committee included Ron Prentice of the California Family Council, Ned Dolejsi of the California Catholic Conference, and Mormon and Evangelical businessmen Mark Jansson and Doug Swardstrom, respectively.[1]

Soon after establishing NOM, Gallagher met with San Diego bishop Salvatore Joseph Cordileone. The son of Italian immigrants, the bishop had the heart of a lion (*cor di leone*) and the soul of a doctrinal purist. Despite a thinning layer of white hair, Cordileone had a youthful appearance thanks to his radiant pink skin, sparkling eyes, and effervescent smile. "Bishop Sal" viewed marriage equality as an existential threat generated by "the Evil One" himself. It would, he feared, erode civil, religious rights in America as in other

countries. In a society where homosexual relationships were completely accepted, Bishop Sal feared that faith-based supporters of traditional marriage
would be considered bigots.[2]

In October 2007, while the California Supreme Court was deliberating in
the *Marriage Cases,* ProtectMarriage.com submitted a constitutional junior-
DOMA proposal to the attorney general for his approval, after which the
sponsors would have to submit petitions signed by 694,354 California voters
(8 percent of the 2006 gubernatorial vote). The estimated $1.5 million cost of
hiring professional signature-collection firms was one reason constitutional
initiative proposals had died in 2005–2006. On December 23, Bishop Sal
called Maggie. A Catholic donor was offering $100,000 to kick things off.
Could Maggie and NOM help the Church match that donation? Absolutely!
Gallagher called NOM's executive director, Brian Brown, who was spending
the Christmas holidays with his family in San Diego. Why don't you, your wife,
Sue, and your children just stay put, so that you can work on raising money
for the cause? Through small meetings with wealthy donors, Gallagher, Brown,
and Cordileone raised more than $1.5 million to launch the signature campaign
in early 2008. Attending the March 4 oral argument in the *Marriage Cases,*
Pugno reported that ProtectMarriage.com was acting just in time, as it was
clear to everyone at the argument that the California Supreme Court was ready
to impose gay marriage on the state.[3]

ProtectMarriage.com sponsored the campaign for the constitutional initiative, denominated "Proposition 8" by the secretary of state. Because preliminary polling showed that California voters were not enthusiastic about taking
away gay people's rights, winning would be a struggle, but ProtectMarriage
.com made three critical decisions that improved its odds. The first was to keep
the proposed amendment simple, short, and limited. Earlier proposed amendments had sought to revoke state domestic partnership laws as well as bar
same-sex marriages. This idea was a nonstarter. Faced with the threat of marriage equality, the Catholic Church had given up its earlier strong opposition
to domestic partnerships. At the suggestion of consultant Gary Lawrence, the
proponents just copied Proposition 22 (which had been a statutory initiative).
"Only marriage between a man and a woman is valid or recognized in
California."[4]

In May 2008, ProtectMarriage.com retained Schubert Flint Public Affairs
to manage the campaign. A Sacramento firm created in 2003, Schubert Flint
had successfully represented corporations seeking to defeat voter initiatives to
impose new regulatory burdens, such as higher tobacco taxes. Although they

Frank Schubert

had never been involved in a "values" campaign, Frank Schubert agreed with the message: "Restore marriage." His Catholic faith had taught him that marriage, the procreative union of a husband and a wife, had a timeless core. In its May 5 decision in the *Marriage Cases,* the California Supreme Court had "overthrown" marriage as it had always been understood and as We the People had reaffirmed in 2000.[5]

Schubert Flint would oversee the entire campaign. It would develop a strategy and message, create radio and television ads, and coordinate grassroots field organizers and volunteers. Based on its earlier experience in tobacco campaigns, Schubert Flint understood that the issue was now framed around the rights of committed lesbian and gay couples. To succeed, Yes on 8 would need to reframe the issue by publicizing negative consequences of these rights. Some Evangelicals were urging ProtectMarriage.com to rely on old tropes of homosexuals as diseased and predatory, but Schubert believed that such a message was both politically counterproductive (polling supported that view) and morally squalid. His sister, Anne Marie Schubert, was raising her two children in domestic partnership with another woman, and Frank respected their family. Ned Dolejsi, Bishop Sal, and other Catholics concurred. They took seriously the Church's pastoral concern for all God's children. In any event, Andy Pugno (also a devout Catholic) had a better messaging idea, based on his experience in the Proposition 22 campaign. Parents had not thought about the effect of marriage equality on what the public schools would teach their kids. Pugno's reading of the state education code suggested that, if schools opted for the state sex education curriculum, they were required to teach about marriage, which after the supreme court decision had to include respect for gay marriage on a par with traditional marriage, a message that many parents would find disturbing.[6]

To prevail, Proposition 8 would need a super-coalition of diverse family values constituencies. Accordingly, its official signatories for the state-issued ballot materials included Bishop George McKinney, the director of the Coalition of African American Pastors, and Rosie Avila, the governing board member of the Santa Ana Unified School District. Most African American and Latino American voters were Evangelicals and Catholics (respectively) who would tend to agree with the Yes on 8 message. Many pastors agreed with Bishop McKinney that the needs of minority communities were better met by reaffirming the traditional understanding of marriage than by expanding that understanding in ways that would be "confusing" to the next generation.[7]

But Ned Dolejsi warned his colleagues: "Except the Latter-day Saints are involved in this, it will fail." Andy Pugno confirmed that the Church of Jesus Christ of Latter-day Saints had been the most effective participant in the 2000 campaign. Unfortunately, President Gordon Hinckley, the mastermind of the 2000 campaign, had died in January 2008. Would his successor, Thomas Monson, support the new campaign? Monson's advisers cautioned that their church had carried most of the load in 2000, while the Catholics and Evangelicals were reputed to have been free riders. In May, the ProtectMarriage.com executive committee turned to William Weigand, the bishop of Sacramento, and George Niederauer, the archbishop of San Francisco. Both men had previously served as bishop for Salt Lake City and were friends with Monson. In early June, a letter was sent to Monson setting out the high stakes of the California initiative, which could be a needed firewall against the expansion of "homosexual and lesbian marriage," and the importance of the Church of Jesus Christ in a united religious effort to preserve traditional marriage.[8]

Although some advisers complained that the Church of Jesus Christ had carried more than its share of the load in the Proposition 22 campaign, President Monson immediately dispatched church officials M. Russell Ballard,

L. Whitney Clayton, and Bill Evans to California for two days to gather facts and report on what should be done. The delegation met with Archbishop Niederauer, Bishop Weigand, and other leading Catholics as well as Andy Pugno and members of ProtectMarriage.com's executive committee. They came away favorably impressed with the campaign, which was already well organized. Based on their report, the Council of the First Presidency and the Quorum of the Twelve Apostles on June 20 formally committed the Church of Jesus Christ to support Proposition 8. It was unusual for the Church to act so quickly on such a major investment in resources on a matter of sensitive political debate. Elder Clayton was named as the liaison with the Yes on 8 campaign.[9]

The marriage equality side was better organized than it had been in 2000. After the 2004 Winter of Love put the issue front and center, Geoff Kors of Equality California organized Equality for All Californians; its executive committee consisted of Kors, Kate Kendell, Lorri Jean, Andy Wong, Delores Jacobs, and Maya Harris. Although ProtectMarriage.com did not secure approval and signatures for a constitutional initiative until spring 2008, there was already a No on 8 structure in place to respond to them. The executive committee retained the Dewey Square Group to manage the campaign against the expected constitutional initiative. Steve Smith, the lead consultant, had managed initiative campaigns in California for a quarter century and told the coalition that he had never lost a "no" campaign. He had recently managed campaigns that defeated parental-notification ballot measures, but he had never managed a campaign involving LGBT rights.

Equality for All/No on 8 brimmed with optimism that they would conduct the best-funded, most grassroots-savvy, most intelligently messaged ballot campaign, with the most diverse leadership and minority outreach, in the history of LGBT rights. We believe it was pretty successful—not as successful, to be sure, as Kyrsten Sinema's Arizona Together campaign against a constitutional Super-DOMA in 2006 or Hans Johnson's campaign against an Idaho initiative to preempt gay rights ordinances in 1994. But pretty successful. Nevertheless, Yes on 8 prevailed: "marriage" was "restored."

Ultimately, the Proposition 8 campaign was a referendum on the normalization of LGBT persons and families and on the prescriptive role of marriage in society. Frank Schubert and Yes on 8 articulated a clear, consistent message about those issues: gay people and their families deserved love and respect, but conjugal marriage remained the normative ideal, identifying families that the state, society, and religion should endorse, subsidize, and celebrate with the most vigor. This was a message that excited millions of voters and motivated hundreds of thousands of people to donate their money, their time, and their enthusiasm. Geoff Kors, Kate Kendell, and No on 8 believed that society should embrace the families formed by gay and lesbian couples for the same reasons it celebrated traditional marriage—but they were afraid to rest their campaign on that viewpoint. Most Californians were not there yet, and the No on 8 campaign never figured out how to change their minds by Election Day 2008.

Restoring Marriage Versus Eliminating Rights

On October 7, 2007, ProtectMarriage.com, Dennis Hollingsworth, Gail Knight (Pete Knight's widow), Martin Gutierrez, Dr. Hak-Shing William Tam, and Mark Jansson submitted the California Marriage Protection Act to the attorney general's office to supply a title and summary of its proposal so that they could start collecting signatures. On November 27, Attorney General Jerry Brown gave the proposal its title and summary:

LIMIT ON MARRIAGE. CONSTITUTIONAL AMENDMENT.

Amends the California Constitution to provide that only marriage between a man and a woman is valid or recognized in California. * * *

Months later, ProtectMarriage.com turned in almost twice the required number of signatures, and on June 2 the California secretary of state certified Proposition 8 for the November 2008 ballot. After the California Supreme Court decided the *Marriage Cases* and declared marriage a fundamental right not to be denied to same-sex couples, Attorney General Brown changed the title and summary of Proposition 8:

ELIMINATES RIGHT OF SAME-SEX COUPLES TO MARRY.
INITIATIVE CONSTITUTIONAL AMENDMENT.

Changes the California Constitution to eliminate the right of same-sex couples to marry in California. * * *

The new title would benefit the No on 8 campaign because voters were much more reluctant to take something away from a minority group than to grant it new rights. The proponents, represented by Pugno, sued the attorney general, but Judge Timothy Frawley ruled that the California Supreme Court's *Marriage Cases* ruling justified the new title.[10]

Yes on 8 had submitted to the secretary of state the following arguments to be included in the state's official voter information guide:

> It [the amendment] restores the definition of marriage to what the vast majority of California voters already approved and human history has understood marriage to be.

> It overturns the outrageous decision of four activist Supreme Court judges who ignored the will of the people.

> It protects our children from being taught in public schools that "same-sex marriage" is the same as traditional marriage.

The original submission went on to say that the supreme court's decision would *require* teachers to tell their students, as young as kindergarten age, that same-sex marriage was the same as opposite-sex marriage. Judge Frawley ruled that this statement was misleading because the California Education Code did not require instruction on marriage and permitted parents to withdraw their children from such instruction if it were offered. Proposition 8's proponents ultimately gave their ballot materials a more conditional wording:

> The narrow decision of the California Supreme Court isn't just about "live and let live." State law may require teachers to instruct children as young as kindergarteners about marriage. (Education Code § 51890.) If the gay marriage ruling is not overturned, TEACHERS COULD BE REQUIRED to teach young children there is *no difference* between gay marriage and traditional marriage.

Having researched and developed this line of argument, Pugno was disappointed by the judicial editing.[11]

Judge Frawley left intact Yes on 8's explanation of the moral balance struck by Proposition 8:

> Proposition 8 is about preserving marriage; *it's not an attack on the gay lifestyle.* Proposition 8 doesn't take away any rights or benefits of gay or lesbian domestic partnerships. Under California law, "domestic partners shall have the same rights, protections, and benefits" as married spouses. (Family Code § 297.5.) There are NO exceptions. Proposition 8 WILL NOT change this.

This statement was controversial among Evangelicals. Randy Thomasson's Campaign for California Families (CCF) and its lawyer Mat Staver would have taken a harder line against homosexuality, which they considered an aggressive Trojan horse that would destroy America if not contained. Although ProtectMarriage.com systematically excluded CCF from participation in the official Yes on 8 campaign, similar points of view were expressed within the Yes on 8 coalition. On June 11, ProtectMarriage.com hosted a meeting for supporters in Newport Beach, attended by major contributors as well as representatives from the American Family Association (AFA) and the Family Research Council. Several participants told the coalition's leaders, "You haven't been stern enough." Reverend Donald Wildmon, the AFA's founder, led the hard-liners. As late as 2010, AFA programs advocated the imprisonment of sexually active homosexuals, whom they labeled threats to public health and morality.[12]

Reverend Wildmon's insistence that Proposition 8 should have targeted domestic partnerships as well as marriage and that the gay-tolerant rhetoric was too soft on homosexuality gained him few fans in Newport Beach. The Yes on 8 board members rolled their eyes at the AFA's attitude, not appropriate for California. "We knew exactly what they wanted," a meeting participant recalled: "they wanted to take everything back to 1959. That wasn't going to happen. The reason why it wasn't going to happen was because of what had happened demographically, in the shift of the attitude of the voters." Frank Schubert and ProtectMarriage.com would have been ashamed to be associated with a campaign that made bigoted statements about their lesbian and gay coworkers, relatives, and neighbors.[13]

That ProtectMarriage.com rejected Wildmon's anti-gay rhetoric did not mean that conservative values were not central to their campaign. For faith-based reasons, the leaders believed that homosexual behavior was morally wrong. Where they differed from Wildmon was that they accepted the social consensus (and the Roman Catholic reading of Scripture) that LGBT people ought to be treated with friendship and compassion rather than demonized and shunned. But compassion did not mean social approval, religious endorsement, or government encouragement of homosexual relationships as equivalent to marriages. Marriage as traditionally defined contributed to human flourishing in a distinctive way, and the executive committee and campaign officials associated with ProtectMarriage.com believed that redefining marriage would dilute its value. However, many gay Californians felt disrespected and disparaged by this line of argument.

Proposition 8 in Plain English, a video cartoon posted on the ProtectMarriage .com website in mid-October, captured the prevailing Yes on 8 philosophy. Jan and Tom had two children, a dog, and a minivan. They were a traditional white, middle-class, gender-conforming cartoon couple ("Tom mows his lawn on Saturday. Jan likes to cook"), and they lived next door to Dan and Michael, a hand-holding, offbeat-looking but inoffensive gay cartoon couple. "When Jan and Tom were on vacation, Dan and Michael watched their dog. When Dan was sick, Jan brought him soup." After they learned about Proposition 8, Jan and Tom became what consultants call *conflicted voters.* "On the one hand, they believed in and wanted to teach their children traditional values. On the other hand, they felt that Dan and Michael should be treated fairly and equally, regardless of their lifestyle choice." The tolerant traditionalists then engaged in some carefully guided research. Tom discovered that the California domestic partnership law already gave Dan and Michael *all* of the rights and benefits of marriage. So if the gay neighbors already had all the rights they need, what was this all about?[14]

Jan talked to her sister Nancy, who lived in Massachusetts, where same-sex marriage had been legal since 2004. In 2006, two sets of parents objected to their children's being read *King & King,* a kids' book that romanticized same-sex marriage. Judges and school administrators allegedly rebuffed the parents' efforts to withdraw their children from this particular instruction. "Tom was now starting to understand. Changing the definition of marriage was a big deal and could have some very serious consequences. If Proposition 8 were to fail, would their church be required to perform same-sex marriages? What would their children be taught at school?" Yikes! Tom and Jan decided to vote for Proposition 8—but they "are still good friends with Dan and Michael." Emotional conflict resolved: "Tom and Jan have come to an important conclusion: they can respect Dan and Michael's lifestyle choice without affirming and embracing their lifestyle." Yes on 8 knew from pollster Richard Wirthlin that this toleration-but-not-endorsement message was exactly what would appeal to conflicted voters.[15]

The No on 8 ballot materials opened with the same claims that had prevailed with the California Supreme Court:

OUR CALIFORNIA CONSTITUTION—the law of our land—SHOULD GUARANTEE THE SAME FREEDOMS AND RIGHTS TO EVERY-ONE—NO ONE group SHOULD be singled out to BE TREATED DIFFERENTLY.

In fact, our nation was founded on the principle that all people should be treated equally. EQUAL PROTECTION UNDER THE LAW IS THE FOUNDATION OF AMERICAN SOCIETY.

The signatories to the statement were Sam and Julia Thoron, a straight couple married for thirty-five years, with three children. Daughter Liz was a lesbian, and her parents "never treated our children differently, we never loved them any differently, and now the law doesn't treat them differently, either." Please don't take away Liz Thoron's life choices.[16]

In June 2008, Steve Smith and Dewey Square distributed *Equality for All . . . A Roadmap to Victory* to the No on 8 leadership. The authors expressed confidence that Proposition 8 was doomed. It had started with support from only half the electorate (successful initiatives usually started with at least 60 percent support); more than four months of happy lesbian and gay weddings would generate tons of free media; and the presidential race was sure to attract Democratic voters to the polls. The *Roadmap* identified three general themes it would use in mobilizing opposition:

(1) People should not be treated "differently."
(2) It's wrong to deny people fundamental rights and freedoms. The Constitution should guarantee equal protection for everyone.
(3) Government should not determine who can and who cannot get married—or the more libertarian way of saying it: government should stay out of our lives.

The managers promised a campaign focusing on "cherished American values like equal treatment under the law, fundamental freedoms like speech, religion and yes, marriage, and our rights to be treated fairly and equally by all, rather than emotional messages about love and commitment." The consultants assumed that Yes on 8 would focus on democratic process rather than values. "Their strongest argument is that the court has overridden the will of the people and the people need to exercise their will—again." They minimized the role of other messages—including the consequences of same-sex marriage for the rights of churches, religious persons and organizations, and parents with school-age children.[17]

There were many dissenters from the Dewey Square assumptions. In 2007, Ineke Mushovic of the Movement Advancement Project (MAP) and Sean Lund of the Gay & Lesbian Alliance Against Defamation (GLAAD) had made a thorough review of the existing empirical and focus group studies of which arguments actually persuaded conflicted voters to support rights for LGBT persons. Summarizing the synthesis that had been documented in a detailed "Toolkit" they had distributed to LGBT rights organizations, MAP and GLAAD in January 2008 jointly circulated a pamphlet *Talking About Marriage and Relationship Recognition for Gay Couples.* "[W]e must make an emotional connection and establish that gay couples want to marry for the same reasons as straight couples—namely, to make a lifelong promise to take care of and be responsible for each other"— and that "good people care about the well-being of others and oppose putting committed couples in harm's way." This strategy was at odds with the *Roadmap for Victory* strategy. MAP and GLAAD concluded: "Marriage isn't about 'rights.' It's about love, commitment, and responsibility. It's about the things we give, not the things we get. Straight and gay couples want to marry for the same reasons."[18]

Geoff Kors expressed interest in the MAP-GLAAD strategy. In 2007, his Equality California Institute teamed up with the Task Force, HRC, and Freedom to Marry to conduct an experiment, "Let California Ring," to figure out what motivated conflicted voters on the marriage issue. Mushovic, Lund, and other researchers surveyed in the Toolkit had concluded that conflicted voters, like Tom and Jan in the Proposition 8 video, could not be won over by abstract rights-based arguments but might respond to an approach that emotionally invited them to think about Proposition 8 from the perspective of gay couples who were in many respects quite like straight married couples. The California Ring campaign developed a *Garden Wedding* video vividly depicting silly obstacles placed in the path of a bride as she tried to make her way to the altar. The ad invited the audience to empathize with the bride and her father, and only at the end did it reveal its message: committed lesbian and gay couples faced equally frustrating obstacles. The ad engaged conflicted voters emotionally and invited them to translate their empathy for the bride in the ad to the bride who wanted to marry another woman. In the ensuing ballot campaign, however, No on 8 did not pursue a Garden Wedding strategy, while Yes on 8 perfected the intuitions underlying the Tom and Jan story.[19]

On Monday, June 16, at 5 p.m., county clerks all over the state opened their offices to take applications for marriage licenses from lesbian and gay couples. At 5:01 p.m., San Francisco mayor Gavin Newsom officiated at the legal wedding of Del Martin (then eighty-seven years old) and Phyllis Lyon (eighty-three), the pioneer couple whose wedding had kicked off the Winter of Love four years earlier. Robin Tyler and Diane Olson, one of the plaintiff couples in the *Mar-*

riage Cases, were lawfully married by a rabbi in Los Angeles. Hundreds of couples got married that day, and 18,600 lesbian and gay couples followed them between June 16 and Election Day, November 4. Frank Schubert sagely decided that Yes on 8 should not disrupt the happy occasions in any way.[20]

Latter-day Saints and Evangelicals Mobilize

On June 29, the letter from the First Presidency announcing the Church of Jesus Christ's formal involvement in Proposition 8 was read in the sacrament meetings for the 1,181 wards (congregations) throughout California. "The Church's teachings and position on this moral issue are unequivocal. Marriage between a man and a woman is ordained of God, and the formation of families is central to the Creator's plan for His children. Children are entitled to be born within this bond of marriage." The letter then issued a call to action to the state's 750,000 Latter-day Saints. "We ask that you do all you can to support the proposed constitutional amendment by donating of your means and time . . . to preserve the sacred institution of marriage."[21]

Evangelicals mobilized in a more diffuse manner, through appeals to pastors and their congregations. On June 25, the Reverend James Garlow promulgated *Ten Declarations for Protecting Biblical Marriage.* Blaming selfish straight couples for the decline of marriage, *Ten Declarations* pulled no punches on the matter of God's Will: "Biblical texts assert, and contemporary sociological research confirms, that maximal sexual fulfillment occurs within one man-one woman monogamous, covenantal relationships" and that "boys and girls need and deserve to have a daddy and a mommy" who are married. "God established marriage between Adam, a male, and Eve, a female, as the pattern for all time." Garlow also established the Pastors Rapid Response Team. On June 28, he led a conference call that included more than one thousand pastors, who committed themselves and their congregations to spread the word as set forth in *Ten Declarations.* This and other calls informed ministers about the resources available from the ProtectMarriage.com website—including statements of principle, evidence that traditionalists would be harmed by gay marriage, and forms for contributing to the campaign.[22]

In a simulcast to California's Latter-day Saints interested in working on the campaign, Lance Wickman described Proposition 8 as "the Gettysburg of the culture war." Once mobilized, that church's members dominated the Yes on 8 campaign. Yes on 8 had a big head start in fundraising, but its advantage became a chasm after a summer of Mormon mobilization. In July, the Salt

Lake City leadership issued directives to each of the 175 stakes and 1,181 wards (congregations) in California, with invitations for supporters to make donations directly to ProtectMarriage.com. A key idea was for stake and ward leaders to ask their wealthiest members to consider giving $25,000 each; in July and August a stream of $25,000 contributions (many from Utah) showed up in the Yes on 8 reports. Middle-income families, including some that were not wild about Proposition 8, felt social pressure to contribute. "Some Mormons who declined to donate," the *Wall Street Journal* reported, "said their local church leaders had made highly charged appeals, such as saying their souls would be in jeopardy if they didn't give. Church spokesmen said any such incident didn't reflect Mormon Church policy."[23]

In late August and early September, the Church organized conference calls in which members of the Quorum of the Seventy invited well-to-do Latter-day Saints to consider donations to ProtectMarriage.com. In addition, Maggie Gallagher's NOM ultimately contributed around $3 million, the Knights of Columbus kicked in $1 million, and Focus on the Family gave $400,000. On September 30, the official tally had $25.4 million in contributions to Yes on 8, compared with $15.8 million to No on 8. This financial advantage allowed Yes on 8 to buy more airtime in more markets—and hence to define the issues in the minds of voters.

Gary Lawrence was the grassroots director for the Yes on 8 campaign, which he conducted brilliantly. In an August 7 memorandum, Lawrence advised Mormon stake and ward members that their grassroots efforts would unfold in three overlapping stages:

(1) *Identification.* On "Walk Saturdays," volunteers and their friends should walk through their neighborhoods to identify potential supporters. Thousands did the Saturday walks, starting on August 16.
(2) *Advocacy and Persuasion.* Volunteers would provide information, such as Lawrence's *Six Consequences if Prop 8 Fails,* to voters "who are in the Mushy Middle."
(3) *Get Out the Vote.* Volunteers would engage in one-on-one efforts to persuade those who said they were voting by early mail (starting on October 6) and then would assemble into one big get-out-the-vote drive on November 4.

Lawrence's grassroots command provided training and talking points to local coordinators and detailed directives on how to do the walks, phone calls, and get-out-the-vote efforts. Church leaders directed stake presidents and bishops to announce, and implicitly to endorse, the Walk Saturdays. Schubert estimates that these and other volunteers distributed 1.25 million Yes on 8 yard signs and as many bumper stickers. He thinks that as many as 250,000 volunteers worked for Yes on 8 at some point during the campaign.[24]

By August, Yes on 8 was having weekly meetings of grassroots organizers, with organized outreach to various minority groups, including groups where the No on 8 grassroots effort was less effective. Latino neighborhoods were added to the Walk Saturday for August 16. Heading the Latino outreach, Jesse Romero planned to contact all relevant Catholic parishes and to make more materials available in Spanish. Latter-day Saints played a critical role in minority outreach through the efforts of Glen Greener, the former Salt Lake City commissioner who worked with Evangelical pastor Derek McCoy to drum up support among black voters.[25]

The Traditional Values Coalition's Bill Tam arranged Chinese-language radio ads and flyers and worked with allies to dispel the notion that marriage was a civil rights issue. Because many of his materials were discovered during litigation, we know a lot about the Chinese-outreach messaging. In a widely distributed flyer, "What If We Lose?," Tam characterized the "gay agenda" this way: "After legalizing same-sex marriage they want to legalize prostitution," followed by "legalizing having sex with children." His literature was obsessed with the idea that gay people were predatory and promiscuous. "If Proposition 8 loses, one by one other states would fall into Satan's hand." The under-the-radar campaign within individual Evangelical churches encouraged parishioners to see Proposition 8 as a holy war, a skirmish between the forces of Jesus and the army of the Evil One.[26]

Schubert reports that materials such as these did not reflect ProtectMarriage .com's messaging strategy and were not approved by the campaign team. Although Tam was an official proponent of Proposition 8, he attended none of the executive committee meetings. But Ron Prentice (the chair of the executive committee) organized a number of public rallies with similar, albeit milder, apocalyptic messages. At a rally in Cupertino that summer, Yes on 8 supporters distributed a flyer that read: "It is time the Church rise up against the forces of evil that are destroying the families and young souls."[27]

Glen Greener and Gary Lawrence were responsible for the most talked-about document of the campaign. *Six Consequences If Proposition 8 Fails* first appeared as a blog post on August 24, 2008, and was distributed to voters as part of the Mormon outreach. Drawing from the Church's August 13 press release explaining *The Divine Institution of Marriage,* Greener and Lawrence predicted that, if traditional marriage was not restored, (1) children in public schools would have to be taught that same-sex marriage was just as good as traditional marriage; (2) churches would lose their tax-exempt status if they refused to perform same-sex marriages; (3) religious adoption agencies would have to give up their policy of placing children in homes with one mother and one father; (4) religious schools would have to open their married-student housing to same-sex couples; (5) ministers preaching against same-sex marriage could be charged with hate speech; and (6) everyone would have to pay for the many lawsuits engendered by same-sex marriage advocates. This document was an intellectual blueprint for Schubert's planned ad campaign showing that lesbian and gay weddings had negative consequences for Californians. Morris Thurston, also a Latter-day Saint, promulgated a detailed response to *Six Consequences,* arguing that claims (1), (2), and (4) were not accurate statements of the law, claim (5) was so at odds with established First Amendment doctrine as to be irresponsible, and claims (3) and (6) were speculative or overstated.[28]

A closer examination of the first claim is in order. As Andy Pugno had discovered, the California Education Code required that if the school district included sex education instruction, teachers had to include discussion of the "legal and financial aspects and responsibilities of marriage and parenthood" and could not include instruction reflecting a "discriminatory bias," including anti-gay bias. Because almost all school districts opted to teach sex education, Pugno and Lawrence concluded that teachers would have to say something about marriage and would have to treat all forms of marriage as morally equivalent. Thus, they claimed, schoolchildren would be "indoctrinated" into the "ideology" of "homosexual rights." To clinch their case for the bad consequences of marriage equality for parents, the supporters of Proposition 8 had an emotionally resonant real-world parent-school drama.[29]

In 2006, a federal judge had dismissed the claims of two sets of Massachusetts parents—Robert (Robb) and Robin Wirthlin and David and Tonia Parker—that they had a right to receive notification and to withdraw their young children when there was instruction that included mention of same-sex marriage. The judgment was affirmed in January 2008, and *Parker v. Hurley* became a central talking point in the marriage debate. The great-nephew of Mormon elder Richard Wirthlin and a graduate student at MIT, Robb Wirthlin moved his family into the school district where the Parkers were already objecting to the diversity curriculum, which included *King & King,* the story of the marriage of two princes. Tapes of Dave Parker's encounter with police officers show that he refused to leave the building until he was arrested; he was apparently itching to generate publicity photos of a parent handcuffed while trying to protect his kindergarten-age son. In October 2008, Ron Prentice hosted a Bus Tour for Marriage. Starting in Sacramento and winding its way south, the Marriage Bus carried the Wirthlins, who lamented that their parental rights had been violated and their family had been driven out of Massachusetts by politically correct persecution. (Their main reason for leaving was that Robb completed his MIT degree.) In California, parents had a statutory right to remove their children from public school health instruction that "conflict[ed] with their religious beliefs." "So what they're angry about," educator Christine Allen claimed, "is that Massachusetts doesn't have the same opt-out educational code option that California has had for a very long time."[30]

The Yes on 8 campaign stepped up its intensity after October 6, when early voting began in California. Two days later, Elder Clayton hosted a satellite broadcast called *The Divine Institution of Marriage.* Clayton urged Latter-day Saints to donate time, money, and text messages to the cause and announced a new website (www.preservemarriage.com) with materials that the faithful could download and distribute. He and other church leaders warned that homosexual marriage would produce a "tyranny of tolerance," whereby diversity today would evolve into tomorrow's condemnation of churches and parents whose disapproval of state-sanctioned marriages would be "discriminatory." Like the Wirthlins, parents would have to endure teachers' equating "gay marriage" with "traditional marriage." Families felt increasing pressure from their lay leaders to give money, donate time, and spread the word among their friends that Proposition 8 was an important constitutional moment for people of faith.[31]

Some Latter-day Saints pushed back. Morris Thurston was one; Barbara Young was another. The wife of the former San Francisco 49ers quarterback Steve Young, Barbara felt that the Church was demonizing decent human beings like her gay brother. She was part of a network of women who criticized the Yes on 8 campaign within the Church and, by the end of the campaign, in public. The week before the election, Barbara, eight months pregnant with her second child, spent a day putting No on 8 signs all over her yard. Internal debate within the Church intensified. Reports of disrespectful rhetoric within some of the stakes included claims that marriage equality supporters were "trying to force their perverted lifestyles on the rest of us." As we shall document in chapter 23, there was also a lot of invective and vandalism directed against the Church of Jesus Christ and its members.[32]

Meanwhile the Evangelicals responded with holy drama. Reverend Garlow invited the Reverend Lou Engle to move his family to San Diego so that he could organize "The Call": forty days of fasting and one hundred days of prayer to ensure the defeat of "Antichrist Legislation." Thousands participated. (Fasting meant no food during daytime hours.) At the Skyline Church in La Mesa, Reverend Engle created a Room of Travail, where fifty young adults fasted and prayed 24/7 (with occasional naps on the hard floor) for those forty days. The fasting and prayer ended right before the election.[33]

Broadcast Messaging For and Against

In a sprawling, heavily populated state like California, the conventional wisdom is that television, radio, and internet ads were critical. Both sides spent most of their budgets on television advertisements. Given the brevity of an ad, message and presentation were key. Here, Yes on 8 earned a decisive advantage.[34]

On September 22, No on 8 aired its first major ad, *Thorons,* showing a conversation between Julia and Sam Thoron about how much they loved their lesbian daughter and her partner. Conflicted voters could relate to the Thorons, a typical married couple who had made the journey to acceptance of marriage equality because they loved their daughter and wanted her to have the same family choices they enjoyed. Because fundraising was lethargic, No on 8 could afford airtime only in a few big-city markets. It could not reach the small-town and rural voters for whom the ad could have been most effective.

Ironically, marriage equality supporters also provided much of the content of the Yes on 8 ads—starting with the first one, suggested by Pugno after he saw a tape of San Francisco's Mayor Newsom reacting to the marriage ruling. On September 29, Yes on 8 began running its *Newsom* ad, with an expensive three-week purchase in media markets all over California. The ad began with Newsom gloating over the triumph of marriage for LGBT people: "This door's wide open now!" he hollered gleefully. "It's gonna happen, *whether you like it or not.*" The ad warned that the decision imposed upon California by "four unelected judges" was not about tolerance. A law professor explained: "People sued over their personal beliefs!" "Churches lose their tax exemptions!" "Gay marriage taught in public schools" (with a *Parker v. Hurley* folder in the background). The ad ended with a repeat shot of a smug-looking Newsom: *"Whether you like it or not."* No on 8 did not air immediate responses.[35]

Yes on 8 began running its *Two Princes* ad on October 6 (a small buy on Spanish-language networks) and October 8 (a large buy on English-speaking networks). In that ad, a Latina girl with double ponytails proudly announced to her alarmed mother, "I want to marry a Princess!" The aspiring bride explained that she and her classmates had just learned (from reading *King & King*, the book the Wirthlins had sued over) that a prince can marry another prince. Mom looked concerned, confused, defeated. Between October 8 and 20, Yes on 8 dominated the airwaves, alternating among *Newsom, Two Princes,* and a third ad, *Massachusetts,* featuring the earnest, clean-cut Wirthlins and warning gravely about *Parker v. Hurley.*[36]

Lake Research Associates conducted daily tracking polls for No on 8. Between October 11 and 14, when *Two Princes* saturated the media, opposition to Proposition 8 among women with children at home fell from 52 percent to 38 percent. Overall, Lake Associates found, Yes on 8 pulled ahead with all voters, 50-38 percent. Its tracking polls showed Yes on 8 with 50 percent or more of voters every day that month until October 28, when the race narrowed. Experts believed that the surge in support for Proposition 8 was based upon parental (especially maternal) concerns about what their children would learn in school about gay marriage. This realignment worried the No on 8 campaign— which, not coincidentally, was in a dramatic transition.[37]

Equality for All was in a panic. Steve Smith and his team seemed thoroughly outmatched by Frank Schubert and his thousands of grassroots volunteers. On September 29, Patrick Guerriero took a leave from the Gill Action Fund to run the No on 8 campaign. In early October, he brought in a new team: Mark Armour (who created new TV ads), Rick Claussen, Guy Cecil, Marc Solomon, Mary Breslauer, Marty Rouse, and Thalia Zepatos. Guerriero worked with Geoff Kors and the executive committee to put out the word among LGBT Californians and their Hollywood allies that their side was about to be clobbered at the polls.

Blunt candor paid off. Alarmed at the prospect of losing everything they had gained in the *Marriage Cases,* tens of thousands of small donors made online donations to the campaign. These donations ultimately amounted to around $17 million of the approximately $44 million raised to oppose Proposition 8. Nonetheless, most of the publicity went to more famous donors. Hollywood and Beverly Hills became just as important for No on 8 as the Church of Jesus Christ and Salt Lake City were for Yes on 8. The celebrities were also more alert than the campaign managers about effective messaging. Lesbian comedian Ellen DeGeneres was an especially effective advocate. "I don't know what people are scared of," she joked on her top-rated daytime television show. "Maybe they think their children will be influenced, but I've got to tell you, I was raised by two heterosexuals. Everywhere I looked—heterosexuals. And they did not influence me." That's pretty funny, not particularly threatening, and true. It deftly set Ellen up for her punch line, delivered with her trademark innocent smile: "It's time we love people for who they are and let them love who they want." This soft sell was, in our view, more persuasive to straight, married parents with children than *Lies* and *Unfair*, the dark, hard-edged ads run by No on 8 at the same time as *Two Princes* and *Massachusetts*. Lake Associates found that opposition to Proposition 8 continued to erode during the period *Unfair* was competing with *Two Princes* and *Massachusetts*.

By October 18, No on 8 had caught up in the money race, having raised $27 million and retained $4 million cash on hand, compared with $28.2 million and $7.2 million, respectively, for Yes on 8. Three days later, supermarket billionaire Ron Burkle hosted a lavish reception and dinner for No on 8 at Green Acres, his Beverly Hills estate. Pat Guerriero shared hosting duties with Mayors Newsom and Villaraigosa. Melissa Etheridge and Mary J. Blige were the headliners; Etheridge donated a song at one couple's wedding in return for an extra $50,000 to No on 8. Because Burkle paid for all the food and service, the gala event took in at least $3.9 million.[38]

Suddenly flush with money, No on 8 was able to make extensive media buys. On October 22, it flooded the state's television sets with its belated response to *Two Princes*. California's superintendent of public instruction Jack O'Connell explained that the state did not require any particular curriculum regarding the definition of marriage and that the *Marriage Cases* had nothing to do with schools. From an academic perspective, this was a thoughtful ad—but it lacked emotional punch. Conflicted voters who had children—like cartoon couple Tom and Jan, still agonizing on the ProtectMarriage.com website—were concerned about their children's moral education. *Two Princes* got them thinking about the effects of gay equality on their own children, and *O'Connell* did not allay their visceral fears. Mark Armour and his team were not producing messaging that persuaded wavering voters—but they also ran into a bit of bad luck and more Frank Schubert wizardry.[39]

On October 10, a Creative Arts Charter School first-grade class surprised their teacher, Erin Carder, by showing up at San Francisco City Hall to see her marry her female partner, Kerri McCoy. (Mayor Newsom presided over the wedding.) As the brides walked down the steps outside city hall, the children tossed rose petals and blew bubbles. The outing was organized by the parents, and eighteen kids participated after receiving their parents' permission (two parents opted out of the trip). The event was filmed and publicized in the local news media. The next morning, October 11, Paul Cobb, the owner of various newspapers and radio networks serving Latino and African American audiences, told Glen Greener that McCoy's wedding was political gold, because the episode demonstrated how "innocent" grade schoolers could be "recruited" to celebrate "homosexuality." Greener took the idea back to Yes on 8, which issued a press statement: "This is overt indoctrination of children who are too young to have an understanding of its purpose." Schubert Flint worked the episode up into an ad.[40]

Aired in ten major media markets (including four in Spanish) within forty-eight hours of Jack O'Connell's ad, *Field Trip* was Yes on 8's lightning response. "A public school took first-graders to a lesbian wedding, calling it a 'teachable moment.'" Responding to O'Connell's insistence that schools would not have to teach anything about gay marriage, the ad revealed that it had already happened: first-graders were being taught to *cheer* a lesbian couple after they got married. "Children *will* be taught gay marriage unless we vote 'yes' on Proposition 8." Kors despaired that *Field Trip* was very effective messaging, though it was also controversial. On October 26, the parents of two of the field trippers called a press conference to denounce the exploitation of their children in the No on 8 campaign. "This field trip was about sharing a special moment with a teacher these kids love," said Jen Press, whose daughter, Lucy, was prominently featured in the ad. "To turn around and distort images of our children is outrageous." Nonetheless, the ad continued for the rest of the campaign on both Spanish- and English-language stations.[41]

Between October 15 and 28, No on 8 spent $7.4 million on media purchases, compared with $5.5 million for Yes on 8. Yet experienced observers thought the Yes on 8 ads were more effective. Conflicted voters were especially unmoved by "vouching" ads, in which famous people—Senator Dianne Feinstein, Governor Arnold Schwarzenegger, and Senator Barack Obama—urged voters to say no to Proposition 8.[42]

The Grand Finale

The Green Acres fundraiser assured No on 8 of a cash-on-hand advantage for the remainder of the campaign—and it was Schubert's turn to feel financial panic. "We're going to lose this campaign if we don't get more money," he warned the ProtectMarriage.com executive committee. With the committee's support, Schubert emailed a "Code Blue for Marriage," begging for more money from 92,000 supporters registered on the ProtectMarriage.com website. Prentice, Jansson, and Dolejsi made personal pitches to wealthy Evangelical, Mormon, and Catholic donors, respectively. By November 2, Schubert estimates, the Code Blue email had generated as much as $7.5 million for last-minute ad buys and get-out-the-vote efforts. Most of the donations came from Latter-day Saints, including seven $100,000 contributions from out-of-state families (mostly in Utah). On October 28, Yes on 8 announced a $1 million donation from Alan Ashton, a founder of WordPerfect and a grandson of David McKay, the former president of the Church of Jesus Christ.[43]

Still raking in thousands of online donations a day as well as hefty sums from Beverly Hills and Silicon Valley, No on 8 saved its most hard-hitting ad, *Internment,* for the last week. Samuel L. Jackson narrated the terrible history of discrimination against racial minorities in California, culminating in the internment of Japanese American citizens during World War II, and suggested that Proposition 8 was a legacy of this exclusionary history. We doubt that *Internment* was effective messaging. To the extent that it engaged voters' emotions, it invited them to feel guilty about past atrocities—but guilt rarely motivates people to change their minds. The ad may even have been counterproductive. LGBT messaging experts believed that heavy-handed civil rights comparisons turned off minority voters, who considered analogies to their brutal past treatment strained or insulting.[44]

Frank Schubert understood this last point better than his No on 8 counterparts. Like his NOM colleagues, he saw religious black voters as natural supporters of Proposition 8. In August, he had received another break: presidential candidates Barack Obama and John McCain joined the Reverend Rick Warren for a televised conversation at his Evangelical church in Lake Forest, California. In a play for middle-of-the-road voters, Obama explained that his reading of Scripture convinced him that marriage is inherently the union of one man and one woman—and Schubert used a recording of that remark in robocalls to more than 850,000 households in the last days of the campaign.

Reverend Engle's Forty Days of Fasting ended the weekend before the election, and on Saturday, November 1, "The Call" held a large public rally in San Diego's Qualcomm Stadium. Some 33,000 people prayed and demonstrated against "Antichrist Legislation." More than eight thousand young adults lay face down on the playing field, praying for God to deliver the state from a sinful path. According to Reverend Garlow, at the end of an intense prayer session, around 4:50 a.m., "We felt something snap. We knew that God had moved!" He had decided to pass Proposition 8. The next day, Sunday, November 2, congregations all over California heard priests, lay leaders, and pastors read letters imploring the faithful to vote yes on November 4 and to make sure their families, friends, and neighbors did the same. Focus on the Family broadcasts and mailings offered the same message.[45]

Schubert estimates that on November 4, one hundred thousand Californians got out the vote and worked the polls for Proposition 8, an unheard-of number of Election Day volunteers for an initiative. Geoff Kors could not make such a claim for No on 8, but tens of thousands of LGBT people and their friends and families walked their neighborhoods the same day. At the end of a dramatic campaign, both Schubert and Kors expected that Proposition 8 would win, and it did, 52.3 percent to 47.7 percent. Reverend Garlow—or God—had called it right.[46]

Because Latinos and African Americans provided supermajorities for the initiative, pundits opined that race was the critical variable driving the votes. But the race effect largely went away when one controlled for how regularly voters went to church. The main variables suggesting that a voter would support Proposition 8 were conservative ideology, Republican Party affiliation, regular church attendance, lack of a college degree, residence in a small town or rural area, and an age of sixty-five or older. Conversely, No on 8 voters tended to be liberal Democrats, have college degrees, attend church rarely, live in the San Francisco Bay Area, and be forty-five years or younger. Evangelicals were more likely to vote for Proposition 8 than any other major demographic group, and Jews were most likely to vote no.[47]

So why did Proposition 8 prevail in a relatively gay-friendly state like California? The most popular theories have been that No on 8 ran a poor campaign and that Yes on 8 ran a ruthless one. While overstated, there is something to be said for both arguments. As gay activist David Fleischer found in his detailed postmortem, the No on 8 campaign team was caught flat-footed when Schubert unleashed the kids-in-schools message, and it was slow and ineffective in responding to those ads. It did not exploit the messaging ideas that MAP and GLAAD had synthesized in their Toolkit. Conflicted voters did not hear much from No on 8, and its ads did not move them nearly as profoundly as the Yes on 8 ads did. Although there was outreach to Latino and black voters, it was often ineffective, partly because of a decision-making structure that did not effectively integrate minority representation. Activist Doreena Wong explained to us the many ways the marriage equality movement effectively reached Chinese American communities between 2000 and 2008—and we did not detect that kind of deep and creative outreach into African and Latino American communities.[48]

Most LGBT Californians saw the Yes on 8 campaign as a series of personal attacks on gay people: How could a lesbian couple raising children not take it personally when the official campaign materials constantly urged voters to "protect children from homosexuality"? Yes on 8 supporters like Dr. Tam and Reverend Engle openly appealed to anti-gay stereotypes, spread claims that the "homosexual agenda" was to legalize sex with children, and called marriage equality "Antichrist Legislation." Progressive Catholics and Mormons (such as Barbara Young) were offended by the milder rhetoric coming from their faith communities, which were more central to the Yes on 8 campaign.

Frank Schubert has a persuasive theory for why his side won: there were more devout conservatives who were eager, enthusiastic, and morally hungry to "take back" marriage than there were supporters of marriage equality who were enthusiastic about protecting their new rights and status. The 2004 Winter of Love and the 2008 *Marriage Cases* left both hot and cold anger in their wake. To a lot of regular Californians, Gavin Newsom seemed arrogant and condescending as he defied state law to hand out marriage licenses (2004) and then gloated when gay marriage actually became legal (2008). They thought the definition of marriage and the status of LGBT people were important questions that should not be decided by the San Francisco mayor or by unaccountable judges. That was the hot anger. The cold anger was fueled by anxieties that parents were losing control of their children's moral education, that churches promoting traditional morality would be demonized as examples of discrimination and bigotry, and that marriage, family structure, and communities were falling apart. People's anger chilled because they believed that public officials were dismissing their point of view as ignorant prejudice. Proposition 8 gave them an opportunity to express both anger and values, and millions of Californians did so.[49]

Our take on Schubert's theory for the triumph of Proposition 8 is that most Californians agreed with its normative message from the outset, and No on 8 did not have an effective strategy for overcoming that advantage. Neutrally stated, Proposition 8's message was tolerance, but not endorsement, of LGBT families. Most Californians were okay with LGBT families, a position Yes on 8 respected: its sponsors did not propose to roll back second-parent adoption or comprehensive domestic partnerships. But did Californians also believe that

LGBT families were entitled to the special honor that society gave to marriage? Polls throughout 2008 suggested that most did not. Marriage was unique, the best way to channel people's sexual activities and family formation. LGBT couples had domestic partnerships, with all the legal rights, benefits, and duties of marriage, and most Californians thought that was sufficient.

As researchers were learning, most straight Californians felt that their marriages were grounded upon a special love and mutual commitment, both to one another and to children they wanted to raise—but they believed LGBT couples wanted to get married just to secure legal benefits and rights. No on 8 was not responsive to these feelings, and the campaign put forth many ads starkly inconsistent with lessons learned by the LGBT movement's messaging experts like Mushovic and Lund: Don't talk about a right to marriage. Don't get trapped in the opponents' framework; make your affirmative case. Engage the audience's emotions, using regular folks (like the Thorons) who can take the audience through their journey toward the embrace of marriage for their LGBT daughters, friends, neighbors, and coworkers.[50]

And Ned Dolejsi was right: Proposition 8 would not have won without the Latter-day Saints. Yes on 8 would have been shorted half or more of its $39–$40 million budget; tens of thousands of volunteers every weekend, and as many as one hundred thousand on election day, would not have campaigned for the initiative; the Wirthlins might not have come to the state to dramatize the threat to parents; and the campaign would have lacked the brilliant advice offered by Gary Lawrence, Glen Greener, and other Mormon consultants. The Church of Latter-day Saints was also important to the victory of Arizona's Proposition 102, which reversed the 2006 result and prevailed, 56.2-43.8 percent. On the same day, Florida voters added a junior-DOMA to their state constitution, 62-38 percent.[51]

Ultimately, the most important reason for Proposition 8's triumph was Frank Schubert. He ran an effective campaign and proved to be a master strategist. After Maine enacted a marriage equality law in 2009, Brian Brown and Maggie Gallagher brought NOM's resources to support a popular referendum to override that law as well. "We will win," Gallagher promised, "by using techniques and arguments developed in the big victory last year in California." That meant working with the Catholic Diocese of Portland and leading Evangelical pastors in Schubert's encore campaign. His first two ads were *Real Consequences*, which focused on how gay marriage might affect the rights of churches, religious parents, and small businesses, and *Everything to Do with Schools*, which trotted out Robb and Robin Wirthlin to warn about homosexual indoctrination of the state's children. His most controversial ad was *Gay Sex,* in which a Brookline, Massachusetts, teacher explained how kids asked a lot of questions about "what is gay sex," which the teacher answered "thoroughly and explicitly." Although the marriage equality advocates raised a lot more money than NOM and rapidly responded to Schubert's protect-the-children ads, the result was the same: marriage equality was revoked by the popular vote, 52.9 percent to 47.1 percent.[52]

Confirming 2008 electoral victories in California, Arizona, and Florida, Maggie Gallagher claimed that the 2009 vote in Maine "interrupts the story line that is being manufactured that suggests the culture has shifted on gay marriage and the fight is over. Maine is one of the most secular states in the nation. It's socially liberal. They had a three-year head start to build their organization, and they outspent us two-to-one. If they can't win there, it really does tell you the majority of Americans are not on board with this gay marriage thing." In 2010, she could add that Frank Schubert and Brian Brown, together with NOM funding, were instrumental in a lopsided Iowa vote against retaining Chief Justice Ternus and two of her *Varnum* (marriage equality) colleagues. Also losing was Democratic governor Culver, and so new justices appointed by a GOP governor might be willing to overrule *Varnum* if NOM could oust a fourth justice whose retention vote would come in 2012. In NOM's biggest disappointment that year, a narrowly divided (5-4) District of Columbia Court of Appeals held that a referendum on the 2009 marriage equality law was barred by the DC charter.[53]

For Gallagher and Brown, the stakes had never been higher. They not only continued to believe that marriage for same-sex couples would entrench an "anti-family culture" in the United States, they also thought that it would be "the weapon that will be and is being used to marginalize and repress Christianity and the Church. What does the gay marriage idea mean once government adopts it? It means faith communities that promote traditional families should be treated in law and culture like racists. It means that the authority of parents to transmit moral values to children will be eroded." Ironically, NOM's smashing electoral victories between 2008 and 2010 unleashed a great deal of anger against its religious allies and galvanized political energy for marriage equality.[54]

The great gay pushback began no later than Thursday, November 6, 2008, when Lorri Jean led a few thousand demonstrators to protest at the Mormon Temple in Westwood, Los Angeles. The following day, a few thousand more appeared in Salt Lake City's Temple Square, and tens of thousands rallied in San Francisco. The next ten days saw protests in more than one hundred cities, as well as vandalism of at least seventeen Latter-day Saints' houses of worship in Utah and California. Pushback also came from within their faith community. Angry that their church was demonizing their families, some Mormon parents and their gay sons and daughters unloaded on church officials, including an emotional encounter with Elder Marlin Jensen at a meeting in Oakland on September 19, 2009.[55]

Marc Mutty, the Catholic official who chaired the executive committee for the NOM campaign in Maine, was the unexpected star of a documentary film about the campaign. In public debates, he hewed to the Schubert playbook, arguing that gay marriage would be forced upon schoolchildren—but several minutes later he told the filmmakers that this was "a lousy approach, but it's the only thing we got." How, he asked, can I forgive myself for my role in this travesty? By the end of the campaign, when Schubert Flint cut an ad saying that schools would teach the kids how to use sex toys, Mutty was appalled: "I cringed." He soldiered on, but confessed, "I feel like I have been thrown under the bus. I hate it."[56]

Mutty was one of the winners. The losers felt even worse—and their anger motivated activism. Typical of this new energy was Dustin Lance Black, the screenwriter for the Hollywood movie about martyred San Francisco supervisor Harvey Milk. Black was frustrated by the No on 8 campaign's reluctance to talk about LGBT families and to attempt a grassroots engagement with a broad range of communities. *Milk* premiered in San Francisco on October 28, 2008. Black felt that Milk's lesson for politics was that gay people would make progress only by coming out to friends and family and standing up to prejudice and stereotyping. "If you don't show respect for yourself, no one will respect you." The movie depicted Milk's successful opposition to a 1978 ballot initiative that would have barred teachers who were gay affirming. Many young people agreed with Black that the No on 8 campaign should have been more Harvey Milk and less Caspar Milquetoast. Fred Karger, a conservative gay activist, said that Proposition 8 was "the greatest thing that could have happened" because it "awakened Godzilla." The devastating defeat "lit a fire under the gay community" and its allies. Just as important, thousands of straight people understood, for the first time, the sting LGBT people felt at once again being singled out for exclusion based upon stereotypes. "Discrimination is not a family value" became a rallying cry for straight allies such as conservative

Republican mayor Jerry Sanders, who joined his wife and his lesbian daughter as a constitutional critic of Proposition 8.[57]

In retrospect, Maggie Gallagher believes that Proposition 8 undermined NOM's mission. Neither she nor her opponents expected that Yes on 8 would politicize so many LGBT people and so many families with gay kids or relatives or make so many straight people feel embarrassed and guilty for their yes votes. In her view, Proposition 8 revealed the gay David as a political Goliath. The marriage equality movement had raised a lot of money, called on thousands of celebrities, and enjoyed favored treatment by the media. To her surprise, Gallagher found that she no longer had an automatic outlet on Fox News, which backed away from the marriage issue after Proposition 8. When she appeared on CNN or MSNBC, she felt the hosts treated her like a crackpot. Donors told her that they could not be associated with NOM for fear of product boycotts or retaliation. Defending old-fashioned marriage became socially and politically radioactive almost overnight.[58]

The consequences for Frank Schubert were also mixed. In March 2009, Proposition 8 dominated the Pollie Awards ceremony of the American Association of Political Consultants. In an Oscars-like evening, Schubert Flint won eighteen awards, including the top award as Team of the Year. As he walked onstage to accept the Pollie, Frank was struck that the woman introducing him went out of her way to signal support for marriage equality, and the room gave him a chilly reception. "I represent those who read the Bible and believe in God," he stubbornly responded. His work on the campaign did not sit well with Schubert Flint's corporate clients, especially those like Reynolds American (owner of R.J. Reynolds Tobacco) that had strong pro-gay corporate policies. "The LGBT community should take a good hard look at any company that's using any suppliers actively working against LGBT equality," wrote the National Gay & Lesbian Chamber of Commerce. "We'd hope that when this is brought to [a company's] attention, that they'll rectify the situation." Slowly, firms shifted their business away from Schubert Flint.[59]

In April 2012, Frank separated from Schubert Flint and created Mission: Public Affairs, focusing on "social issues such as protecting life, strengthening families, preserving traditional marriage and protecting religious liberties, along with pursuing conservative public policies that promote prosperity and liberty." He also became the political director of NOM and best friends with the gregarious Brian Brown.

Before Proposition 8, Frank says, he "didn't spend five minutes thinking about marriage—not in a deep way." Afterward, he reflected on his involvement in the marriage issue. "Was this an accident? That here I am, a political consultant who happens to believe in the cause, on the scene at the very moment that this debate is occurring." He says his NOM projects have deepened his faith, his second marriage, and his ability to be a good father to his two (adult) children from his first marriage. How about his relationship with his sister, Anne Marie Schubert, who is today (2020) the district attorney for Sacramento County? "I love my sister deeply and I love her children," he said. "That doesn't require me to accept that marriages should be redefined because my sister is in a gay relationship with two kids. I worry about anybody who doesn't have the benefit of a loving, active father in their lives. And those kids won't have that; I pray for them."[60]

15 • 8, the Trial

Proposition 8 did not end the marriage debate in California. Instead, it marked the beginning of a new chapter, one that would dramatically unfold in the federal courts.

County clerks stopped issuing marriage licenses to same-sex couples on November 5, the day after the election. On the same day, the City of San Francisco, NCLR, Lambda Legal, the ACLU, and Equality California filed a new state constitutional lawsuit, *Strauss v. Horton*. The California Constitution distinguished between a constitutional *amendment* and a constitutional *revision;* the latter was an amendment so fundamental that it altered the Constitution's basic structure. A revision could be adopted only upon the recommendation of the legislature followed by popular ratification; because Proposition 8 had been initiated by citizen petitions, it did not qualify as a revision. The plaintiffs' counsel knew that this was a Hail Mary lawsuit. The California Supreme Court had rarely invalidated a popular constitutional initiative for this reason, and the one-sentence addition made by Proposition 8 struck few observers as a fundamental revision in the constitutional structure. Yet the lawsuit served an important strategic purpose. So long as *Strauss v. Horton* was pending, marriage equality lawyers could wave off federal constitutional challenges to Proposition 8 until the state constitutional litigation was completed. With just two states recognizing marriage equality in November 2008, the freedom-to-marry movement wanted to avoid federal lawsuits that might reach the US Supreme Court, which they felt was not ready to deliver nationwide marriage equality.[1]

The movement lawyers did not reckon with the combustible outpouring of anger and mission that followed the electoral verdict on Proposition 8. Thousands of activists wanted an immediate federal response and felt that it was time for their movement to claim its *Brown v. Board of Education* moment. Two of those impatient progressives were Rob Reiner and Michele Reiner. Once the bearish Michael Stivic (Meathead) in the television series *All in the Family*, Rob Reiner had become an award-winning movie director and producer. He was so depressed by the Proposition 8 vote that he could not get out of bed for days after the election. Michele roused him to have lunch at the Polo Lounge of the Beverly Hills Hotel with two younger friends, Kristina Schake and Chad Griffin, partners at a Los Angeles communications firm who had worked on the No on 8 campaign's messaging strategy. Their discussion focused on the very measure the litigation groups had rejected: a federal constitutional challenge. So started a process that would upend the movement lawyers' plans.[2]

The Reiners' friend Kate Moulene stopped by their table to chat. At that lunch or afterward (accounts differ), Kate told Michele: "My ex-brother-in-law is a constitutional lawyer," Ted Olson. "And knowing him as I do, I bet he'd be on your side on this." Michele was flabbergasted. A top Department of Justice official in the Reagan administration, Olson was then the most famous conservative Republican lawyer in America not on the US Supreme Court. In 2000, when he persuaded the court to halt ballot counting in *Bush v. Gore,* he handed the presidency to Governor George W. Bush, who named him solicitor general. Michele answered, "Why on earth would I want to talk to *him*?"[3]

Afterward, Kate called Ted, who was receptive to her idea. He had grown up and attended law school in California, and he had known lesbian and gay people throughout his career. Kate also knew him as a kind man, with the easy friendliness of a golden retriever. Marriage equality was not an issue he had thought about at great length, but Ted does remember that he and his late wife, Barbara, debated the issue over dinner in February 2001 with David Frum and his family. The Frums echoed the conventional wisdom that gay couples were not suited for marriage, which was inherently one man, one woman. Ted did not agree: marriage was about love and commitment. Why shouldn't gay couples enjoy the same encouragement for their committed relationships that straight people took for granted? Ted did not see any material difference between gay and straight relationships.[4]

After Kate gave Michele a heads-up, Chad flew to Washington and met with Ted at the Gibson Dunn law offices. The grizzled Republican super-lawyer from California and the eager, young gay political operative from Arkansas hit it off. Ted cleared the likely representation with his law partners—but more importantly, he consulted his eighty-eight-year-old mother; his fourth wife,

Lady Booth; and his adult children. All were enthusiastic. In December, Ted traveled to the Reiners' Brentwood estate to meet with Rob, Michele, Kristina, Chad, and Bruce Cohen, the producer of the hit movie about Harvey Milk that had debuted the previous autumn. Ted told the group that he considered sexual orientation, like race and sex, a trait that should not be the basis for any kind of government penalty or exclusion, including relationship recognition. "Gays and lesbians crave the right to be married, in the same way and for the same reasons as other citizens." It was "un-American" to deny them this fundamental right.[5]

Olson promised to throw the entire weight of Gibson Dunn into a federal constitutional lawsuit. The plan was to negate Proposition 8 with a preliminary injunction, which could be immediately appealed by the other side to the court of appeals and then to the Supreme Court, where he was confident of victory. He knew that many of his old conservative allies would be shocked by his representation, but he declared it would not bother him. "I've been in the eye of the storm before, and if I believe in something, I do it. I will not be just some hired gun. I would be honored to be the voice for this cause." Everyone agreed. Afterward, he put together a team of top Gibson Dunn lawyers, anchored by Ted Boutrous, a constitutional litigator and partner in the Los Angeles office, and Chris Dusseault, a younger partner in the Washington, DC, office.[6]

On March 5, 2009, the California Supreme Court heard argument in *Strauss v. Horton*. Chief Justice George and his colleagues were clearly not persuaded that Proposition 8 was an unconstitutional constitutional amendment. As George later wrote in his memoirs, his three marriage equality cases reflected the deep principle that each branch of government operated under constitutional limits: the executive branch had to faithfully execute state statutes (*Lockyer*, invalidating the Winter of Love licenses), legislators were bound by constitutional limits (*Marriage Cases*), and the judiciary must likewise faithfully enforce the California Constitution, as amended (*Strauss*). Because the court was expected to dismiss the marriage equality movement's claims within three months, the federal constitutional challenge needed to be prepared, funded, and ready to file no later than May 2009.[7]

Kristina Schake and Chad Griffin created the American Foundation for Equal Rights (AFER) to sponsor the lawsuit. As chairman of the board and treasurer, respectively, Bruce Cohen and Michele Reiner raised millions of dollars at celebrity-packed events. On February 22, 2009, their federal constitutional challenge received a shout-out at the Academy Awards. Dustin Lance

Black won the Best Original Screenplay Oscar for *Milk*. In a moving acceptance speech, he urged gay youth to take heart from the bravery of forebears
like Harvey Milk and assured them that they would soon enjoy, "federally,"
equal rights across the land. In-the-know viewers took this as a reference to a
federal constitutional lawsuit—an idea that inflamed many in the gayocracy,
some of whom privately waved him away from the issue.[8]

On March 21, Griffin and Black attended Tim Gill's annual OutGiving conference of mega-donors at the Ritz-Carlton Lake Las Vegas, where Black delivered a keynote speech. He directly addressed the go-slow, state-by-state
approach reflected in "Winning Marriage," the 2005 roadmap for securing
marriage equality state by state (discussed in chapter 13). "This is no time to
engage in the luxury of cooling off," he quoted from Dr. Martin Luther King Jr.'s
"I Have a Dream" address to the 1963 March on Washington, "or to take the
tranquilizing drug of gradualism." This was also the lesson of Harvey Milk,
the San Francisco politician who had been discouraged from running for office as an openly gay man by some of "the very same people" now calling for
gradualism. "It has been 30 years since Harvey Milk gave his life in our struggle for equality, and we will not wait 30 years more. It is time for us to stop
asking for crumbs and demand the real thing." The speech drew a chilly reception from many veteran funders and gay rights leaders (including Evan
Wolfson) in the audience. The next night, Gill delivered a rebuttal. Using "gradualism as a pejorative denigrates the hard work of tens of thousands of
people" who had achieved great advances in the rights of all LGBT persons
over the years, he admonished.[9]

Meanwhile, Olson was looking for a litigating partner who would give him
credibility with the gayocracy. An obvious candidate was Paul Smith, who argued for the gay defendants in *Lawrence v. Texas* (2003). A genial redhead who
had been a Yale classmate of Sonia Sotomayor (nominated to the US Supreme
Court on May 26), Smith told Olson that he had discussed a possible federal
lawsuit with some colleagues and recent Supreme Court clerks. They reached
the same conclusion as the LGBT rights movement lawyers: with just a handful of marriage equality states, the court was highly unlikely to impose nationwide gay marriage anytime soon. In the wake of *Brown*, even the liberal
Warren court had declined to invalidate state laws barring different-race marriages and did not act until all such laws were confined to the Deep South.
Specifically, Justice Kennedy (essential to any majority opinion) was famously
attentive to the number of states whose laws would fall if the court were to
recognize novel constitutional claims.[10]

Olson also called Kathleen Sullivan, a lesbian who had been Stanford Law School's dean. Like Smith, she was aware of the hostility that AFER's efforts were receiving from movement lawyers—but Sullivan was even more keenly aware of the risks of premature constitutional claims. She had been part of the team that had litigated the legality of consensual sodomy laws in *Bowers v. Hardwick* (1986), constitutional litigation that, in retrospect, had been brought too early. In any event, however, Sullivan was being considered for appointment to the Ninth Circuit, and so everyone concerned felt that the search had to continue.[11]

A federal lawsuit would probably receive no help from prominent gay rights lawyers. During a conference call, the perfect partner occurred to Olson: Why not David Boies? They had been adversaries in *Bush v. Gore,* but had since become good friends, sharing a taste for fine wine and taking family vacations together. Boies Schiller in New York was one of the toniest trial firms in the country. Tall, balding, and brilliant, Boies was the "Mozart of cross-examination," while Olson had argued more Supreme Court cases than anyone else, and with great success. The idea of these Republican and Democratic super-lawyers teaming up to bring the case that would be the *Loving v. Virginia* for LGBT rights was immediately compelling. On May 10, Ted called David, who signed on without hesitation. Later, Boies learned that movement lawyers were horrified by the risky litigation. He observed that attorneys were going to file federal lawsuits if he and Olson did not act, and "we were confident we could prepare, try, and appeal the case as well as, and probably better than, any alternative team."[12]

As Olson was finalizing research for the case and completing the legal team, AFER and Enrique Monagas, a Gibson Dunn lawyer with a male partner and a daughter, searched for plaintiff couples. One couple, Jeff Zarrillo and Paul Katami of Burbank, came to AFER's attention after they released a home-made video (*Weathering the Storm*) parodying a doomsday video against gay marriage. The Reiners recommended Kris Perry and Sandy Stier from the San Francisco Bay Area. Partnered since 1999, they were raising four boys— Sandy's two sons from her marriage to a man, and Kris's two sons from a previous relationship with a woman. Olson and Boies were delighted. "Just like Paul and Jeff, Kris and Sandy seemed very much like the people you would meet at a neighborhood block party or in the aisle of a suburban supermarket."[13]

Griffin had discussed a federal challenge with "dozens of individuals," including San Francisco's city attorney Dennis Herrera, who had encouraged the idea. Leading movement litigators were left out of the loop, however. This could be a big problem. The Reiners again came to the rescue with a May 14 luncheon to explore the possibilities of cooperation with Lambda, represented by Legal Director Jon Davidson (another Sotomayor classmate) and Jenny Pizer, and the ACLU of Southern California, represented by Ramona Ripston and Mark Rosenbaum. Ted Boutrous presented the case for AFER's federal lawsuit. Griffin boasted that the lawsuit would be gay people's *"Brown v. Board of Education* moment,"* a comment that rankled the movement attorneys. Were these folks not aware of the work the established groups had been doing for two decades? The incremental approach had worked in *Loving*, where the US Supreme Court acted only after all but sixteen states had repealed their bars to different-race marriages, and it was working for marriage equality. In the five weeks before the luncheon, marriage equality statutes had been passed in Vermont, Connecticut, New Hampshire, and Maine, and the Iowa Supreme Court had delivered Lambda's go-slow attorneys a huge victory in *Varnum v. Brien*. But there were still only six marriage equality states, and the newest addition (Maine) faced a referendum that would ultimately override the law in November 2009. There were more states with civil unions and marriage-lite institutions for LGBT couples, a pattern suggesting that the Supreme Court might, at best, follow *Baker* rather than *Goodridge*.[14]

Davidson peppered Boutrous with challenging questions: Have you considered the risks of reaching the Supreme Court too early? The Lambda and ACLU lawyers understood that a Supreme Court decision rejecting marriage equality would have constitutional ripple effects undermining arguments against state discrimination in employment, child custody, and public benefits. Angered by Davidson's defensiveness, Griffin pointed to the money AFER had raised, thereby "saving" the LGBT groups the cost of a hugely expensive litigation. Davidson responded that excitement around federal constitutional litigation would pay for itself and that fancy firms like Irell & Manella, where he had been a partner, would line up to work on the case pro bono. "Well, you get what you pay for," Griffin cracked. "We have the Cadillac of law firms." This was an unfortunate comment. If Gibson Dunn was a classic Cadillac, Irell & Manella was a snazzy Maserati. Davidson then played the Olson-is-too-conservative card, which angered Boutrous and the AFER representatives. Who could move public opinion better than a conservative vouching for gay couples? On that note, the luncheon concluded, and the bristling lawyers departed. "Well, that was a disaster," concluded Michele Reiner.[15]

On May 22, the Friday before Memorial Day, the California Supreme Court announced that it would release its decision in *Strauss* the following Tuesday.

Gibson Dunn was ready. Its two plaintiff couples had already applied for marriage licenses in San Francisco (Kris and Sandy) and Los Angeles (Jeff and Paul), and the clerks had refused the requests. The complaint was drafted and signed, and Enrique Monagas went to the federal courthouse in San Francisco to file the papers that afternoon—right before the court closed for the long weekend, so that the media would not pick up on the filing. At 3:25 p.m., Monagas submitted the short complaint and supporting papers in *Perry v. Schwarzenegger.*[16]

On Tuesday, May 26, the California Supreme Court upheld Proposition 8 in *Strauss v. Horton.* The next day, AFER held a press conference at the Biltmore Hotel in Los Angeles. Olson and Boies announced their federal constitutional lawsuit, to great media fanfare and a bevy of American flags. Basking in the moment, Olson said he expected *Perry* to make a swift trip to the US Supreme Court, where he was right at home and pretty sure his side would prevail, perhaps by a lopsided vote. Based on the same intimate knowledge of the justices, one of us wrote a sharp rebuttal: not a single justice was very likely to vote for nationwide marriage equality as early as 2009–2010. On the same day that Olson and Boies filed their lawsuit, the ACLU, Lambda, and seven other national LGBT-rights groups issued a joint statement warning that premature federal litigation, before there was a critical mass of marriage equality jurisdictions, "is likely to lead to bad rulings."[17]

As we shall see, the gayocracy that AFER and Gibson Dunn were defying ensured that the case would be delayed for years beyond its original timetable— but they also helped ensure that *Perry* would become an excellent trial. While Davidson was right to accuse Olson and Boies of both hubris and innocence about the complexities of gays in court, he also admitted to his colleagues (and to us) that they were damned good attorneys whose prestige would discourage other federal constitutional lawsuits. Damned good attorneys would adjust their initial strategy, if needed, to respond to an audience and a real-world environment that they would come to know ever more deeply as they litigated their case. Starting out with a sound structure and some good intuitions, the plaintiffs' legal team improved their position at every stage—unlike the political team that had unsuccessfully opposed Proposition 8.

Dustin Lance Black had been frustrated that the stories of LGBT families were invisible during the Proposition 8 campaign and that unfounded claims and stereotypes went unanswered. The "8 trial" offered an opportunity to put those families front and center, require the other side to document its objections, and subject their claims to rigorous cross-examination. We find Black's point compelling but add that trials are not perfect venues for deep debates between competing republican visions of American constitutionalism and family law. And the 8 trial would not emerge as a redefining trial in American history, in part because the other side of the debate did not offer its leading thinkers, such as Maggie Gallagher and Robby George. David Blankenhorn was the only defense witness at their intellectual level—and he received rough treatment from a trial process that demanded narrow, fact-based expertise and punished broad philosophizing based upon experience in the world.[18]

Judge Walker's Thirst for Facts and Empirical Evidence

As he was submitting the *Perry* complaint, Enrique Monagas peeked over the clerk's shoulder and saw the initials VRW. He knew that the case was assigned to Chief Judge Vaughn R. Walker. The plaintiffs could scarcely have been luckier. Tall and elegant, with thinning gray hair and a salt-and-pepper Vandyke beard, Judge Walker looked like a southern colonel, but with a soft midwestern accent, a dry sense of humor, and a sharp memory for detail and precedent. His appointment to the bench by President Reagan had been blocked by gay-friendly legislators because of his successful lawsuit to deny the Gay Olympics use of the trademarked word *Olympics*. (President George H. W. Bush successfully appointed him in 1989.) It was known in some circles that Walker was gay and had been partnered with a male doctor for almost a decade. Although closeted judges had generally voted against marriage equality claims in earlier cases, Walker was socially out and was comfortable with his sexuality.

Vaughn Walker had studied economics at the Universities of Michigan and California (Berkeley) and had been an avid student of law and economics professors Dick Posner and Bill Baxter at Stanford Law School. Like Posner, he would view the constitutional issues in *Perry* through the cost-benefit lens suggested by most forms of economic analysis: What harms were suffered by the plaintiffs because they were excluded from civil marriage? Inflicted upon their children? What would be the harms to third parties or to society if California were required to give marriage licenses to the plaintiff couples? What evidence was there for such harms, and how credible was it by social science standards? These were precisely the inquiries that the plaintiffs and their lawyers wanted to be the focus of the case.[19]

If Walker was a great judge for the plaintiffs, Governor Arnold Schwarzenegger and Attorney General Jerry Brown were the perfect defendants. The governor had a casual attitude toward marriage generally, and his counsel took no position on the constitutional merits of the marriage exclusion. In his June 12 answer to the complaint, Brown (a liberal Democrat) conceded that Proposition 8 violated the Fourteenth Amendment. Although counsel for the governor and the attorney general were present every day of the trial, they seldom participated. Under California law, the proponents of a successful statutory or constitutional initiative were welcome participants in proceedings challenging the law, and so ProtectMarriage.com sought to intervene as a party in the case to defend Proposition 8.[20]

Andy Pugno, ProtectMarriage's general counsel, and his ADF lawyers, Brian Raum and James Campbell, had successfully defended Proposition 8 in *Strauss* and asked their appellate counsel in that case, former solicitor general Ken Starr, to continue the representation. Claiming personal reasons but perhaps sensing a difficult case on the merits, Starr begged off. Robby George recommended Chuck Cooper, who had succeeded Ted Olson as the head of the Office of Legal Counsel under President Reagan and had represented the state on appeal in the Hawai'i marriage litigation. Olson describes Cooper as "an Alabama-born son of the South who wore French-cuff shirts, elegant suits, and spoke with a formality that one political writer called 'Victorian copy book prose.'" Cooper had clerked for Chief Justice Rehnquist and shared his strong aversion to the view of constitutional rights generally held by elite law professors and the clerks they sent to the court. Like Pugno and the ADF lawyers, Cooper believed that constitutional law must be applied consistent with tradition and original meaning. Cooper liked things orderly and was irritated when the Yes on 8 banner fell off his podium during the press conference that kicked off his defense. Was this an omen?[21]

On June 30, Judge Walker ruled that ProtectMarriage.com and the individual proponents of Proposition 8 (Dennis Hollingsworth, Martin Gutierrez, Hak-Shing William Tam, Gail Knight, and Mark Jansson) could intervene as defendants. The same day, the judge surprised both Olson and Cooper by denying Olson's motion for a preliminary injunction and, instead, announcing that he would conduct a trial to determine whether sexual orientation met the criteria to be considered a suspect classification, what public interests the marriage exclusion might serve, and other issues of fact. These rulings dashed Olson's hope for a quick trip to the US Supreme Court, and Cooper suddenly faced the prospect of extensive exchanges of documents and other information (what is called *discovery*), a process that would strain the resources of Cooper & Kirk, a firm with only twelve lawyers. David Boies felt that a trial on the merits would be good for the plaintiffs, as any judgment resting upon tested factual findings would be more robust on appeal. Also, Gibson Dunn could overwhelm the opposition with its abundance of legal talent; as many as fifty Gibson Dunn lawyers and paralegals ultimately worked on the lawsuit.[22]

Meanwhile, more parties wanted to get into this blockbuster case. Lambda, the ACLU, and NCLR filed a motion to intervene as parties in support of the plaintiffs. "With perhaps a little too much zeal" (say Olson and Boies), Griffin issued a public rebuke: "You have unrelentingly and unequivocally acted to undermine this case, even before it was filed. In light of this, it is inconceivable that you would zealously and effectively litigate this case if you were successful in intervening." Because Dennis Herrera had been a friendly adviser, Griffin was not opposed to San Francisco's entering the case as a party on the side of the plaintiff couples. Indeed, San Francisco's leadership in the *Marriage Cases* would give the plaintiffs instant access to the leading expert witnesses supporting marriage equality. Hence, Olson and Boies strongly opposed Lambda's motion to intervene but suggested that, if the judge were to let any new party into the case, it should be San Francisco, which had a distinctive public interest in the issue. Wink, wink. On August 19, Judge Walker granted San Francisco's motion and dismissed that of the movement lawyers. He also went along with Cooper's opposition to the intervention motion filed by Mat Staver and Liberty Counsel for the Campaign for California Families. (Cooper worried that Staver's history of gay-bashing comments would undermine the case for 8.)[23]

On September 19, Cooper filed a motion for summary judgment, arguing that undisputed facts supported the one-man, one-woman definition of marriage. A skeptical Judge Walker heard argument on October 14. The judge peppered him with questions, including the ultimate question: What was the neutral, rational basis for excluding LGBT couples from civil marriage? Cooper and his team had decided not to emphasize Yes on 8's harm-to-schoolchildren argument, which they felt would not be well received by his ultimate audience, Justice Kennedy, the decisive vote on the Supreme Court. Instead, Cooper & Kirk argued "responsible procreation," an idea that could be expanded, if need be, to embrace an optimal parenting argument as well. Walker was skeptical. "What is the harm to the procreative purpose or function of marriage that you outline of permitting same-sex marriage?" Cooper answered too quickly: "Your Honor, my answer is: I don't know. I don't know," words that surprised the judge, delighted the plaintiffs' counsel, and would repeatedly come back to haunt Cooper. His point was that no one had a data-based foundation for saying exactly what would happen if marriage were entirely delinked from procreation. The consequences could be really bad—and the people of California had exercised their right in both 2000 and 2008 to avoid that risk.[24]

Cooper's underlying assumption was a standard one in constitutional law: the challengers had a high burden of proof to demonstrate a constitutional violation. If the law could be applied to any set of plausible facts, the judge was supposed to reject the constitutional challenge. Cooper assumed that the onus was on the plaintiffs to demonstrate to the judge that redefining marriage would not have *any* bad consequences. To prevail, the defendants needed only to point out uncertainty—I don't know and neither do they. But neither Vaughn Walker nor Anthony Kennedy analyzed gay rights cases this way. Kennedy's *Romer* and *Lawrence* opinions implicitly but unmistakably imposed a tougher burden of proof. Because Colorado and Texas were depriving an unpopular minority group of basic equal protection (*Romer*) and personal liberty (*Lawrence*), the Supreme Court had placed the burden of uncertainty on the state, not on the challengers. Even worse, from Cooper's point of view, the plaintiffs were arguing that Proposition 8 denied LGBT people a fundamental right (marriage) because of a suspect classification (sex or sexual orientation). If they were right on either point, Supreme Court precedent made the defendants' burden of proof even higher: Was the exclusion of same-sex couples from civil marriage necessary for the state to advance a compelling public interest? On October 14, Cooper all but admitted that if the judge applied heightened scrutiny, Proposition 8 was invalid.

The Cooper-Walker colloquy should not be understood as a moment when counsel misspoke and sank his case. But at that moment, the ProtectMarriage team should have realized that they needed tangible evidence of genuine harm that would occur if the court burst the traditional marriage bubble. They should have spent the discovery period coming up with that evidence. But the trial was scheduled to start in three months. Walker believed in efficiency: hold the lawyers to a strict timetable and get to the point. Cooper called the discovery schedule a "Bataan death march," an unfortunate metaphor suggesting that his team would not survive it.[25]

Pretrial Discovery and Motions

Between October and January, the parties exchanged thousands of pages of documents. In a case of this magnitude, one would expect intense disputes about what documents and information each side could demand from the other. In *Perry v. Schwarzenegger,* the judge and the magistrate assisting him ruled on more than fifty such disputes. The parties also conducted thirty-four depositions—examinations of the other side's witnesses under oath. Depositions were an opportunity to learn, through questioning and personal observation, what each witness knows, what holes may be in her account, and how well she holds up under cross-examination. Finally, the period before trial allows the judge to hear from the parties and decide important procedural issues. In *Perry,* the big issue was whether the trial would be live-broadcast on YouTube. That, in turn, would affect Cooper's ability to put on a defense.

The most intense disputes involved the communications within the Yes on 8 campaign regarding messaging, commercials, and outreach. Terry Stewart and Matt McGill (of Gibson Dunn) thought these communications were highly relevant because they would reveal that responsible procreation had nothing to do with Proposition 8. Instead, Yes on 8 was a barely concealed appeal to stereotypes of gay people as predatory and out to recruit children into their lifestyle. Ted Olson felt the matter was more complicated, and he doubted that a Supreme Court victory would rest upon a finding of animus. Such evidence would raise the emotional stakes of the case. Traditionalist organizations and individuals, already nervous about being stigmatized for their opposition to marriage equality, saw the prospect of turning over indiscreet or emotionally raw internal communications as embarrassing at least, and threatening as well.

Judge Walker ordered the disclosure of most of ProtectMarriage's internal communications. Outraged at what he considered a judge-sanctioned lynch mob for his clients, Chuck Cooper pushed back hard. The order not only violated his clients' free speech rights but would have a chilling effect on any politically incorrect political group, he argued. As Mark Jansson stated in an affidavit, if he knew that private communications during a political campaign could be disclosed in a court proceeding, he would curtail his political activities. Cooper took the unusual step of seeking a mandamus (an order mandating legal action) from the Ninth Circuit Court of Appeals. Normally, district court orders in the course of discovery or trial could not be appealed until final judgment has been entered, but if a judge made a clear and serious error the appeals court had jurisdiction to direct the lower court to follow the commands of the law. On December 11, just a month before trial would commence, the Ninth Circuit ruled that Walker's order violated the proponents' free speech rights and directed that the discovery orders be withdrawn. On January 4, the

Ninth Circuit amended its order to allow discovery of documents Yes on 8 had made available to third parties.[26]

Each side was required to identify its proposed expert witnesses early, so that the experts could be deposed by lawyers for the other side. The plaintiffs ultimately named nine experts, most of whom Dennis Herrera and Terry Stewart brought into the case based on their work with them during the earlier *Marriage Cases*. The defendants identified six experts. David Boies conducted the depositions of Paul Nathanson and Katherine Young, both academics at McGill University, in Montreal. They were scholars of the history of religion who had submitted reports in the Iowa marriage litigation and had participated as experts on the history of marriage in Canada's constitutional litigation. Professor Young's report asserted that there were very few examples of same-sex marriage in human history, and most of the commonly cited examples were ambiguous as to what the cultures were recognizing: Were they really marriages or something else? But that was not the main focus of the deposition.[27]

As he had earlier done with Nathanson, Boies's strategy was to unnerve Young through picking apart her qualifications, disciplining her when she tried to provide a complex answer to yes-or-no questions, pouncing on any mistake and blowing it up into a major humiliation. For example, when Young testified that she had a "secondary expertise" in cultural anthropology, she "opened herself to the full Boies treatment." Boies repeatedly pressed her to identify her peer-reviewed publications in anthropology. She finally identified "Future of an Experiment" as an article in which she based her cultural argument on anthropological work. It was published in *Divorcing Marriage* (2004), an edited collection of essays on marriage equality in Canada. After a series of questions whether *that* was peer-reviewed, she answered no and admitted a contradiction. Boies and Olson provide a triumphalist account of this examination: it exposed an unreliable "expert." We note that the editors of *Divorcing Marriage* were prominent family law scholars who did provide an initial peer review of Young's chapter; the book was published by McGill-Queen's University Press, which would have secured peer reviews before committing to publication. Moreover, Professor Young told us that she had intended to reference an article on "Redefining Marriage" that had been published in the peer-reviewed *Journal of Family Studies*. Had a smart lawyer rattled a serious scholar into understating her own credentials? Young ruefully recalls that "Boies exhibited no desire to cross-examine me on my actual research," including the data and analysis across historical cultures. "I had been subject to a legal 'game' as the handbooks on cross-examination put it."[28]

On September 25, 2009, Judge Walker had announced that he was interested in allowing the trial proceedings to be broadcast. The plaintiffs' counsel endorsed the idea, and the defendants' counsel opposed it. The local rules governing civil cases in the Northern District of California did not allow cameras in the courtroom under these circumstances—but the matter was under consideration within the Ninth Circuit. On December 17, the Ninth Circuit Judicial Council announced that it had approved a pilot program for "the limited use of cameras in federal district courts within the circuit." The next week, the Northern District of California amended Civil Local Rule 77-3 to allow broadcast of proceedings in pilot projects authorized by the judicial council. On January 6, 2010, Judge Walker informed the parties that an audio and video feed of trial proceedings would be streamed live to courthouses in other cities.[29]

On January 7, Cooper filed a petition with the Ninth Circuit, seeking to prohibit or stay enforcement of the order to televise. A three-judge panel denied the petition the next day, and Cooper appealed to the Supreme Court. On January 9, the Supreme Court issued a stay, barring the lower courts from broadcasting the proceedings until the court could rule on the merits. On January 13, two days after the *Perry* trial commenced, a closely divided (5-4) Supreme Court invalidated revised Local Rule 77-3 and rebuked the district court for trying "to change its rules at the eleventh hour to treat this case differently from other trials in the district." Writing for three other dissenters, Justice Breyer argued that the lower courts had given everyone plenty of notice and that the public interest in televising the proceedings outweighed objections by the Proposition 8 proponents.[30]

This was a high-stakes procedural tempest. AFER and its attorneys understood the 8 trial as a media event and an ongoing process of public education and entertainment. Continuous YouTube broadcast would create opportunities for extensive internet engagement, commentary, satire, and discussion. They were confident that their witnesses would shine and those making the case for 8 would not. Cooper saw this gambit as an effort to create a backlash against Proposition 8 and to publicly shame his witnesses. Five of his six experts were professors. The academy overwhelmingly supported marriage equality. When the trial commenced on January 11, Cooper told the court that four of his expert witnesses had dropped out: Loren Marks, an expert on religion and the sociology of the family; Nathanson and Young; and Oxford professor Daniel Robinson, a neuroscientist.

Olson and Boies boast that these witnesses were scared off by Boies's fierce cross-examination skills on display in the Young and Nathanson depositions.

After contacting all four witnesses, Kenji Yoshino believes the matter is more complicated; we corresponded with three of them and share his ambivalence. Marks told us that the trial in San Francisco gave a "home court advantage" to marriage equality supporters, "but Judge Walker's decision to allow video cameras in the courtroom seemed to me a little beyond the bounds of 'blind justice' and fair play—a perceived effort to amplify the already significant home court advantage. This was a tipping point for me." Robinson told us, with typical British asperity: "A journey to appear before this judge was to be fit into a very busy Oxford term and to expose myself to the nonsense so carefully crafted by those hostile to the proposition." Rather than travel thousands of miles, he thought an amicus brief from him would suffice.[31]

Young inferred from her experience at the deposition that her cross-cultural research would not be taken seriously, but the key point for her was "the fact that the trial might be televised. I knew that in Canada emotions over this case had run so high that one public intellectual . . . received threats to her safety on several occasions, which were assessed" by the Royal Canadian Mounted Police. "Because of the threats, the speaker on one occasion travelled in a kidnap-proof car and was booked under another name into a hotel, which was far away from the venue and was asked to quickly leave the grounds after the event." In short, the professor feared that "I too might be in danger if I were publicly recognized after extensive American television coverage. I concluded it was not worth the risk."[32]

The saga of the four withdrawn witnesses illustrated the anxieties of intellectuals who supported what academics considered the wrong side of history. Supporters of one-man, one-woman marriage increasingly viewed themselves as victims of persecution by an elite consensus. The traditional marriage movement wove this meta-narrative through its own publicity outlets, to compete with the triumphalist meta-narrative of AFER and its allies. On January 10, the day before trial started, former attorney general Edwin Meese wrote an editorial excoriating Judge Walker for his rulings on discovery and videotaping—immediately reversed on appeal—that seemed slanted to help the case against 8. (Ironically, Meese had been Walker's biggest booster when he was nominated to the bench.) With controversy and media attention swirling, the 8 trial started on January 11.[33]

The 8 Trial

The 8 trial lasted twelve days, between January 11 and 27, 2010. The first day saw opening arguments by Ted Olson for the couples, Terry Stewart for

San Francisco, and Chuck Cooper for the proponents. Lawyers representing Governor Schwarzenegger and Attorney General Brown declined to speak. The first ten days of the trial saw the plaintiffs present their case. Proposition 8's defenders made their case on days 10–12. Closing arguments came months later, on June 16, after post-trial discovery and after the judge had digested the transcript, exhibits, and post-trial submissions.[34]

There were three big arenas of constitutional contention. First, the plaintiffs claimed they were discriminated against because of their sex or sexual orientation in violation of the equal protection clause. Sex was a classification requiring heightened equal protection scrutiny, and the plaintiffs argued that sexual orientation should require it as well. Any heightened scrutiny would be fatal to Proposition 8. The proponents responded that there was no real discrimination and that, if there were, it was not grounded in sexual orientation, which in any case should not be a suspect classification. Two key criteria for heightened scrutiny—the immutability of the trait and the political powerlessness of the minority group—were missing. Second, the plaintiffs maintained that they were denied their constitutional right to marry, which would also require strict scrutiny. The proponents responded that because marriage was fundamentally about procreation, same-sex couples did not fit within the marital tradition. Finally, the plaintiffs maintained that Proposition 8's discrimination had no neutral justification grounded in the public interest but was based entirely on private feelings of anxiety or animosity toward sexual and gender minorities. Thus, even if the court did not apply heightened scrutiny, Proposition 8 could not satisfy equal protection's minimal requirement that every legal distinction have a neutral and rational basis. Proponents responded that rejecting the traditional definition of marriage would go against its core (procreative) purpose, undermine its cultural support, and disrupt the state's interest in assuring as many children as possible the optimal household headed by their biological mothers and fathers.[35]

By 2010 these issues had been seriously debated by excellent judges all over the country—most notably, Jeff Amestoy and Denise Johnson in Vermont; Margaret Marshall, John Greaney, Martha Sosman, and Robert Cordy in Massachusetts; Barbara Madsen and Mary Fairhurst in Washington; Judith Kaye and Victoria Graffeo in New York; Ron George and Carol Corrigan in California; Dick Palmer and David Borden in Connecticut; and Mark Cady in Iowa. Chapters 7–8 and 11–13 in this volume have discussed these debates.

Intellectually, what the 8 trial added was a sustained response to Maggie Gallagher and Robby George. They had maintained that civil marriage was a normative institution and that the state could not be neutral about that institution's structure. In the 8 trial, the plaintiffs themselves testified that the state should have a moral stake in their thriving, virtuous families. If marriage was not for us, what was its point? The proponents had difficulty articulating their vision that only conjugal marriage could yield the public benefits traditionally expected of marriage—perpetuating the human race, providing an optimal household in which to rear children, and teaching citizen virtues such as generosity, selflessness, and cooperation. Judge Walker would not uphold a measure that hurt thousands of families while serving no demonstrable public interest.

The 8 trial also linked the marriage debate to constitutional citizenship. Nancy Cott (one of the experts San Francisco brought into the case) described the importance of marriage as a microcosm of democratic citizenship throughout American history. "The individual's ability to consent to marriage," she testified, "is the mark of a free person in possession of basic civil rights." Given the state's persecution of sexual and gender minorities in the twentieth century, full civil rights were important for this group. The proponents did not clearly articulate their perspective: citizenship was a zero-sum game. State approval of homosexuality entailed state disapproval of traditional values and would turn the ubiquitous Wirthlins, most churches, and many religious employers into bigots overnight. In the *Marriage Cases*, Justice Corrigan had asked who got to define family and marriage for the state of California. If marriage equality were a watershed moment in the history of civil marriage, was it legitimate for such a big change to be made by federal judges, rather than by the legislature or by the people acting through the constitutional initiative process?[36]

The *Perry* trial suggested the outlines of a great debate—but did not produce that debate because the Yes on 8 side did not field its "A team." Maggie Gallagher and Frank Schubert were in the courtroom, available as witnesses to explain the Yes on 8 messaging; Robby George was an adviser to Cooper's team. The Wirthlins could have testified that marriage equality harmed them as parents. Were there no Massachusetts or Connecticut ministers and priests who could have testified about the harms visited upon their churches in the wake of marriage equality? We asked Vaughn Walker what surprised him most about the trial, and he said it was the proponents' failure to present witnesses talking about the tangible, concrete harms that marriage equality would bring to traditionalist parents, churches, employers, teachers, and neighbors.[37]

Domestic Partnership and Discrimination

Recall that one prominent argument in both the California *Marriage Cases* and the Yes on 8 campaign was that same-sex couples could secure all the legal rights and benefits of marriage through domestic partnerships. This argument spoke to two features of what it meant to discriminate. On the one hand, American constitutional culture has understood discrimination as treating similar things differently; the proponents maintained that potentially procreative different-sex couples were not similar to nonprocreating same-sex couples. Marriage was reserved for the former. On the other hand, the proponents also argued that, despite this difference, domestic-partnered couples were getting the same legal rights and benefits as different-sex couples. Just not marriage.

The plaintiffs' counsel opened the trial with their two couples. This would humanize their case and offer the kind of personal stories that messaging experts found most persuasive. "We would win or lose this case by the testimony of the four plaintiffs," Olson reflects. On day one of the trial, January 11, Boies examined Jeff Zarrillo and Paul Katami, followed by Olson's examination of Kris Perry and Sandy Stier. We shall focus on Kris and Sandy.[38]

Fair, blond-haired Sandy Belzee was born and raised in Iowa, where she was on the cheerleading squad and spent the summers detasseling corn. She came to California for college, where she met and wed Matt Stier. Although they reared two wonderful sons, Sandy was not happy. They didn't click romantically, and her husband's drinking problem made matters worse. Through work, Sandy met Kris, who had grown up in California and had two sons of her own from a previous relationship with a woman. They became fast friends. As Sandy recalls it, "I began to realize that the feelings I had for [Kris] were really unique and different from . . . feelings I normally had towards friends. And they were absolutely taking over my thoughts and my—sort of my entire self. And I grew to realize I had a very strong attraction to her and, indeed, I was falling in love with her." She had cared for her husband when she married him, but she realized that she had never *loved* him. But she had love tingles for Kris.[39]

In 1999, Sandy walked out of her marriage and into the arms of her soul mate. They established a household in North Berkeley and raised their four sons as a family. They lived near Indian Rock, from which one could see the entire Bay Area; it was there that Kris proposed to Sandy in December 2003. A few months later, they got Winter of Love–married in San Francisco, followed by a great wedding celebration. The honeymoon was terminated by an official letter informing them that the California Supreme Court had nullified their marriage licenses. "I'm not good enough to be married," Sandy recalled thinking. Realizing their family was vulnerable without some legal recognition, they signed up for domestic partnership. It was "just a legal agreement," not anything special. "We don't remember the day it happened [nor did we] invite people over" to celebrate the occasion. Her jaw clenching, Kris put it this way: "I have been in love with a woman for ten years, and I don't have a word to tell anybody about that." When Olson asked what difference marriage would make in the family's life, Sandy answered that it would provide them with social respect. "I want our children to feel proud of us. I don't want them to feel worried about us in any way, like our family isn't good enough."[40]

The messaging they remembered from the Yes on 8 campaign was the protect-the-children ads. As parents, Sandy and Kris understood the impulse to protect children against germs and illness, drugs, and predatory priests. But the ads were saying that California's children had to be protected against the likes of Sandy and Kris. Sandy recalls that "the very notion that I [would] be a part of what others need to protect their children from was just—it was more than upsetting. It was sickening, truly. I felt sickened by that campaign."[41]

Sandy and Kris's testimony was heartfelt and powerful. In the courtroom, Sandy's mother and Kris's two sons wept openly. The plaintiffs' counsel underscored the couples' testimony with that of UCLA professor Letitia Anne Peplau, who testified on day three that lesbian and gay couples like the plaintiffs would benefit from marriage for the same emotional, cultural, and religious reasons that straight couples found value in it. This testimony raised a point that the No on 8 campaign had neglected: to persuade conflicted voters, marriage equality advocates needed to show that lesbian and gay couples wanted to get married for the same reasons as straight couples. On day six of the trial, Dennis Herrera examined San Diego mayor Jerry Sanders. A conservative Republican, Sanders testified that he originally supported domestic partnerships because they assured equal rights for LGBT persons, such as his daughter Lisa. He changed his mind after meeting with those constituents who told him about the pain they felt from their treatment as second-rate families and from their demonization in the Yes on 8 campaign.[42]

On cross-examination, Peplau admitted that her "just like straights" testimony was backed up by no empirical evidence and that when marriage equality was enacted in Belgium and the Netherlands, few lesbian and gay couples had taken advantage (suggesting that such couples were not entirely like straights). The professor also conceded that "some scholars also suggest that a growing emphasis on individualism and personal fulfillment has eroded an earlier emphasis on the importance of obligation and commitment in marriage." If the reasons marriage was eroding were a matter for differences among informed opinion, why should an unelected judge substitute his judgment for that repeatedly announced by California voters?[43]

The Normative History of Marriage

The plaintiff couples maintained that the discrimination deprived them of their constitutionally fundamental right to marry and that this denial required strict scrutiny. Even though the Supreme Court had ruled that convicted felons and deadbeat dads owing child support enjoyed a constitutional right to marry, the proponents argued that such a right was limited to conjugal couples. A witness who had provided expert reports supporting marriage equality in Vermont, Massachusetts, and Iowa, Nancy Cott was the plaintiffs' first expert witness and easily their best.[44]

Unflappable, polite, but diffident, Cott commanded the courtroom by sheer force of deep learning and precise exposition. Testifying as a leading feminist historian, she explained how marriage evolved as society and the state evolved, so there was no such thing as "traditional marriage" that the state could salvage from a stable, nirvanic past. Procreative intent or capacity has never been a requirement for marriage, it was not "the prime mover in states' structuring of the marriage institution in the United States, and it cannot be isolated as the 'main' reason for the state's interest today." Instead, the history of marriage was all about the formation of households and the evolving meaning of constitutional citizenship.[45]

Cott's key evidence for the last proposition was *Dred Scott v. Sandford* (1857), where the Supreme Court ruled that free persons of African descent could not constitutionally be citizens of any state. Chief Justice Roger Taney relied primarily on America's then-traditional definition of marriage to conclude that Africans were a "subordinate and inferior class of beings" incapable of citizenship. He cited colonial marriage laws to show that "intermarriages between white persons and negroes or mulattoes were regarded as unnatural and immoral, and punished as crimes, not only in the parties, but in the person who joined them in marriage. And no distinction in this respect was made between the free negro or mulatto and the slave, but this stigma, of the deepest degradation, was fixed upon the whole race." Such a "stigma, of the deepest degradation" was how the plaintiff couples understood the message of Proposition

8. *Dred Scott* was an exemplar of the constitutional "anti-canon": Don't make this kind of mistake again! The Reconstruction Amendments explicitly repudiated its holdings, and *Loving* extended the equal citizenship norm to assure people of color full marriage rights.[46]

The Fourteenth Amendment's citizenship protections were not limited to racial minorities, and feminists invoked the citizenship idea as central to their critique of coverture. Common-law coverture rules restricted the rights of wives to enter into contracts, hold property, or even protect themselves against domestic violence. All of these restrictions were once considered fundamental to marriage based upon "the sexual division of labor," where "men were suited to be providers" while "women were suited to be dependent" and to deal with the household and raising children. By 1920, when the Nineteenth Amendment assured women the franchise, coverture had been at least partially revoked virtually everywhere. After Title VII barred employment discrimination against women, the workplace offered for women (including wives) many occupations traditionally closed to them. In most marital households, both wife and husband now work outside the home (though wives still do most of the work inside the home).[47]

Cott concluded her historical survey with an important observation on how the evolution of American society paved the way for the current constitutional moment. "The more symmetrical and gender-neutral spousal roles have become . . . the more that the marriage between couples of the same sex seem[s] perfectly capable of fulfilling the purposes of marriage." This encapsulated a central theme of this book: the key variable driving the marriage debate has been the changing social status and roles of women. As women have secured more educational, employment, political, financial, and other opportunities, they have made different decisions about family, marriage, and children—and those decisions have eroded the sexual division of labor on which traditional marriage was founded. At the same time, the evolution of women's status opened doors for lesbians as well as straight and bisexual women—and for gay men, whose deviation from traditional gender roles grew more acceptable as those roles were considered more flexible.[48]

Marriage equality for LGBT couples would be a "turning point" in the history of marriage, Cott testified. On cross-examination by David Thompson, she added that law and ideas have "an impact on the social meaning of marriage" and that "it is far easier to say that the social meaning of marriage has consequences than to measure the consequences." Thompson was providing context to Cooper's "I don't know" blooper earlier in the case. If society considered marriage to be one man, one woman, as the yes vote for Proposition 8 suggested, and the law then expanded that definition, one might expect new and unpredictable consequences. Although Cott believed marriage equality was creating a "new reverence" for marriage, she had no hard evidence for that opinion.[49]

The Politics of Homosexuality

In addition to denying gay couples a fundamental right to marry, the plaintiffs argued, that denial was based upon a suspect classification under the Supreme Court's race and sex discrimination jurisprudence. To satisfy the court's criteria for suspect classifications, counsel offered evidence that (1) gays had been subject to pervasive discrimination (2) based on a trait (sexual orientation) having no bearing on their capacities; (3) sexual orientation was as immutable as race; and (4) gays were underrepresented in the political process.[50]

HISTORY OF UNFAIR DISCRIMINATION

The first two requirements were a gimme. In the earlier marriage cases, state attorneys general had conceded that LGBT persons had been subject to a long history of unfair discrimination, and Chuck Cooper was not inclined to contest the point. Nevertheless, Terry Stewart conducted a thorough examination of Yale historian George Chauncey on this issue.[51]

Chauncey read Yes on 8's protect-the-children message the same way the plaintiff couples did, as disparagement of gay people. The campaign "evokes, for me, the language of saving our children, the need to protect children from exposure to homosexuality; not just from exposure to homosexuals as presumed child molesters, but protecting them from the idea of openly gay people." On cross-examination, Thompson recalled President Obama's long-standing opposition to redefining marriage: Was Obama prejudiced? He then walked the witness through repeated admissions on how the last ten years had seen a "sea change" in public attitudes toward gay people. Chauncey conceded that medical organizations, the press, and leading universities had abandoned anti-homosexual views and now supported LGBT rights. Federal and state governments had adopted laws and executive orders repealing anti-gay discriminations and providing affirmative protections for sexual minorities. Although Chauncey had opined that most religious denominations rejected the anti-gay positions of the religious right, he disavowed that on the witness stand. "I do occasionally make mistakes." Had he been conducting the cross-examination, Boies would then have humiliated the witness: Could you identify one mistake you have made where confessing error would lend support to Proposition 8? Weren't all your mistakes efforts to walk back earlier statements that might be read to support 8? Didn't you testify that you strongly support gay marriage? So your testimony is just advocacy?[52]

GAY POLITICAL CLOUT

One of Thompson's last questions for Chauncey was this: "As a result of both individual and collective efforts, gay political clout has grown in many parts of the country, correct?" Chauncey agreed. Gay political clout was constitutionally important for two reasons. On the one hand, it was relevant to the argument that Thompson had launched from Cott's testimony, that gay marriage would be a "watershed" change in American family law that ought to be made through the democratic process. On the other hand, it was relevant to whether sexual orientation should be a suspect classification. If gay people had political clout, why did they need constitutional protection from unelected judges?[53]

On day seven, the plaintiffs' counsel responded with Stanford political scientist Gary Segura. Based on the results of ballot initiatives and an undersupply of anti-discrimination laws and public officials, Segura testified, "gays and lesbians do not possess a meaningful degree of political power" and were less powerful than blacks and women were when race and sex were established as suspect and quasi-suspect classifications. Even though gay groups had assembled a powerful array of allies in California, most Americans still did not like LGBT people, a large minority despised or feared them, and some Americans were obsessed with them and actively sought to harm or assault them.[54]

David Thompson, who had emerged as a stellar cross-examiner, led Segura through the political process by which LGBT people and their allies secured comprehensive domestic partnership in California in 2003 as well as marriage statutes in Vermont, Connecticut, New Hampshire, Maine, and the District of Columbia in 2009. Did they utterly lack political power in those states? Segura felt the case had not been made even for those states, a conclusion we find incredible. A few days later, Thompson offered the defendants' expert on California politics, political scientist Kenneth Miller of Claremont McKenna College. In terms of a group's ability to raise money, organize itself into effective lobbying and litigating organizations, gain access to legislators, secure allies and form coalitions, and persuade policy makers, Miller testified that lesbian and gay Californians constituted a group with great political power. In more than forty pages of testimony, Miller guided the judge through the LGBT community's many successes in California and the enormous support generated from the Democratic Party and most of the leading social and economic groups in the state. He showed better knowledge than Segura did about the politics of homosexuality in California. David Boies belittled him for not knowing a few pieces of gay arcana (Who was Alan Spear?) but also pointed Miller to an article he had coauthored saying that anti-gay prejudice and stereotyping played a role in Proposition 8's triumph.[55]

Key to applying Segura's and Miller's testimony to constitutional doctrine would be one's understanding of "political powerlessness." Segura and the plaintiffs' counsel equated *powerlessness* to "didn't win all the time" or "generated a lot of intense opposition," neither of which strikes us as quite correct. Miller and the proponents' counsel equated *powerlessness* with "never won in the legislature," which slighted the fact that most LGBT wins were to eliminate discriminatory baselines that did not affect other social groups. The dueling experts revealed the paradox of minority power: much of what held sexual minorities back politically—that they were few in number, clustered in big cities, and disliked by many of their fellow citizens—also contributed to their political potency, as they were motivated to organize around a small number of issues, like marriage equality, and had effectively nested within the Democratic Party. Armed with numerous allies, money, and political mobilization, the LGBT community also faced huge political obstacles.[56]

THE IMMUTABILITY OF SEXUAL ORIENTATION

Immutability was another tricky criterion relevant to suspect classification analysis. Excluding a group of people because of a trait they cannot change is often unfair, but some immutable traits (like intelligence) are a legitimate basis for public policy, while many mutable traits (like religion) are off-limits. As Dr. Gregory Herek testified on day nine, sexual orientation was not a trait that people could consciously change. They could not choose it the way they shopped for jeans or chose an occupation. On the other hand, sexual orientation was not quite like race or sex, both of which were, by most accounts, genetically hardwired. On cross-examination, Herek conceded that there was no scientifically accepted genetic basis for homosexuality and that sexual orientation had a large cultural component.[57]

The ADF position, reflected in the daily trial commentary by senior counsel Austin Nimocks, was that gay people could change their sexual orientation through "reparative therapy." Herek testified that reparative therapy had been professionally discredited, but Terry Stewart felt that her side should demonstrate how positively harmful such treatments could be. On day seven, the plaintiffs' counsel offered the testimony of Ryan Kendall, a young police officer whose disapproving parents sent him to "reversal therapy" when he was fourteen. The experience was a nightmare—he compared it to torture—and it assuredly did not cure him of homosexuality. This testimony touched Judge Walker more deeply than any other, because it explored the psychic costs of the closet and the cruelty that some families visited upon their own gay children.[58]

Following Segura to the stand on day eight was Dr. Bill Tam, one of the official proponents. A hostile witness called by Boies, Tam testified that "science proves that homosexuality is a changeable sexual preference" and said he agreed with the Yes on 8 campaign documents warning that "gay marriage will encourage more children to experiment with the gay lifestyle, and that the lifestyle comes with all kinds of disease." There was even a link between gay marriage and Satan's agenda. Dr. Tam's testimony suggested that the philosophy of reparative therapy, belief in the susceptibility of children to the lure of homosexuality by mere exposure to the concept, and the intensity of opposition by otherwise laid-back Californians were strongly linked. The Yes on 8 campaign had emphasized how the amendment would protect parental and religious liberties, but Tam represented a shadow campaign that appealed more openly to anti-gay prejudice and helped the official campaign gain emotional traction with voters. Tam's experience on the stand was unpleasant; as he told his lawyers, "I felt like a naughty boy being put in front of a classroom and being mocked at."[59]

Did Proposition 8 Serve Public Interests?

In his opening statement, Chuck Cooper had identified three central reasons being used to justify the restoration of one-man, one-woman marriage, to the exclusion of lesbian and gay couples: (1) Because marriage was most useful as an institution channeling straight men toward "responsible procreation," its core meaning did not have to include same-sex couples who could never procreate between themselves. (2) Redefining marriage would accelerate the institution's downward spiral, what social scientists called the "deinstitutionalization" of marriage. Such a change in the institution should be decided by the larger body politic, not by an unelected judge. (3) Limiting marriage to one man, one woman signaled the state's endorsement of mom-dad marital households as the optimal structure for child-rearing. Cooper did not, however, make the Yes on 8 argument that children must be protected against normalizing homosexuality in schools and public culture, because he worried that Justice Kennedy would find this point too close to animus.[60]

After other witnesses dropped out, the proponents rested their defense largely on the testimony of David Blankenhorn, the president of the Institute for American Values. With degrees from Harvard and Warwick, Blankenhorn was a public intellectual, but not a full-time scholar. That he carried the weight of the proponents' case was the most remarkable feature of a trial populated with drama and odd twists. Cooper and his allies had contacted academics all over the world, but most did not even return their calls. Gallagher found the process frustrating: "It doesn't matter what the social science says, if there are no social scientists willing to say it." In the summer of 2009, she called her old friend David, who was happy to testify, even after he heard the trial might be televised. "Serious discussions are being made about national policy, and people ought to hear my information on an issue I care about."[61]

Blankenhorn had seen Boies cross-examine earlier witnesses, such as Dr. Tam, and thought that "it was kind of like watching a train wreck coming." Needless to say, he considered his culminating performance something of a challenge. On voir dire, Boies ridiculed his lack of traditional academic qualifications, and Judge Walker treated him condescendingly. Still, Blankenhorn was excited to explain what marriage is for and why intellectuals and policy scientists should agree with him. His mission was to rescue marriage, not save the ballot initiative. Boies's mission was to destroy his credibility and demolish the case for 8. Train wreck ahead.[62]

On direct examination, Blankenhorn emphasized what a unique institution marriage has enjoyed in human history. "There is only one institution in the world that performs the task of bringing together the three dimensions of parenthood: the biological, the social, and the legal. That institution is marriage." He reported a consensus among anthropologists that marriage was unique in that it rested upon the husband-wife dyad and served as the social and legal mechanism for creating, recognizing, and raising children. As the 1951 edition of *Notes and Queries on Anthropology* put it, family "is based on marriage, which is defined as a union between a man and a woman such that children born by the woman are recognized as the legitimate offspring of both partners." (Apparently unknown to Blankenhorn and the lawyers, the community

422 8, THE TRIAL

of anthropologists rejected the *Notes and Queries* definition after 1961, based upon woman-woman and berdache marriages documented for many African and Native American cultures.)[63]

Drawing from the anthropological theory of kin altruism, Blankenhorn explained why conjugal marriage afforded the optimal environment for raising children. "You typically sacrifice more for people to whom you are related. You typically extend yourself, whether it's risking your life or loaning money or inconveniencing yourself, on their behalf." Sociologists have concluded, he said, that "the optimal environment for children is if they are raised from birth by their own natural mother who is married to their own natural father."[64]

Finally, Blankenhorn testified that Proposition 8 was necessary to prevent the further decline of marriage. Easier divorce, extramarital cohabitation, and other liberalizations had all made marriage better suited to the individual flourishing of the spouses but had made the rules that govern marriage "less comprehensible and clear and less authoritative. And when its structure becomes less stable, less able to give robust shape to the institution, it's like a— kind of a shrinking process." Liberalized family law undermined marriage's ability to fulfill its traditional public or social goals. If the courts catered to the demands of gay and lesbian couples to get married, the public purpose of marriage would be further diluted.[65]

In a brutal cross-examination, David Boies dismantled this testimony. Repeatedly mispronouncing the witness's name as "Blankenthorn" and sarcastically ridiculing him, Boies was not above petty tactics, but the power of his questioning lay in his exposure of the shaky empirical foundation for Blankenhorn's theoretical assertions—starting with the claim that redefining marriage would speed its decline. Dr. M. V. Lee Badgett had earlier testified that nothing of the sort had occurred in Massachusetts. After *Goodridge,* the marriage rate had actually risen. As we shall see in chapter 21, the story was more complicated for the Bay State, but neither side in the 8 trial had figured this out.[66]

On direct examination, Blankenhorn had identified Andrew Cherlin and Norval Glenn as leading scholars who documented the decline of marriage because of liberalizations that shifted its social meaning away from children and toward the adult relationship. Boies queried: Among the scholars identified with the deinstitutionalization thesis, could you identify the ones "who have asserted that permitting same-sex marriage would cause a reduction in heterosexual marriage"? Boies knew that Cherlin and Glenn had never said any such thing, and his team suggested that none of Blankenhorn's other sources did, either. That would undermine the case for 8.[67]

But the witness made it worse. He might have cited Maggie Gallagher and David Popenoe, whom his cross-examiner would have criticized for lacking rigorous empirical evidence. Or he could have responded that the deinstitutionalization hypothesis did not claim immediate effects; marriage's decline would be slow. Massachusetts might experiment with gay marriage, but that did not justify forcing it upon California. Blankenhorn did none of this. Instead, for too many transcript pages, he sparred with counsel. What are you asking for, exactly? I cannot really answer "yes" or "no" or "I don't know." It depends on a variety of factors. And so on. The exchange between the lawyer repeatedly asking the same question and the witness hemming, hawing, dodging, and being admonished by the judge was like the teacher from hell repeatedly trapping the too-smart-for-his-own-good student who would not admit he had lost his homework.[68]

Boies attacked the procreation argument with the same relentless gusto. Blankenhorn had gleaned three rules about marriage that he said were universal in human societies: opposite sex, just two people, and sexual relationship. So no society has *ever* recognized same-sex marriages? wondered Boies. Well, not exactly. The opposite-sex rule had recently been relaxed in Massachusetts, Spain, and Canada. Before that? Well, maybe three or four civilizations in human history. Professor Young's deposition, read into evidence by the plaintiffs' counsel, had stated there have been some such cultures. (Boies failed to read Young's explanation for why she thought most of them were not relevant to modern marriage equality.) So much for the universal opposite-sex rule. Counsel led the witness through counterexamples for the other two "universal" rules. As Young had testified, polygamy has been practiced in dozens of cultures throughout human history—inconsistent with Blankenhorn's "universal" rule of two.[69]

More was going on here than a repeat game of gotcha, and it illustrates why his associates compared Boies to Mozart. The super-lawyer tested, taunted, ridiculed, and entrapped Blankenhorn to order to expose the intellectual ambivalence that had haunted him ever since Gallagher had pressed the marriage movement to oppose gay marriage at Osprey Point in April 2003. Blankenhorn was both politically liberal and culturally pro-marriage. His engagement in the marriage equality debate had created a moral schizophrenia. On the one hand, his celebrity in family values circles impelled him to explore the cultural and anthropological arguments for traditional marriage. On the other hand, his engagement with Jonathan Rauch and other gay intellectuals had taught him that there were many committed lesbian and gay couples whose unions were worthy of respect, which his liberal side embraced. For example, Blankenhorn agreed with Professor Michael Lamb, who had testified on day five, that (in David's words) "adopting same-sex marriage would be likely to improve the well-being of gay and lesbian households and their children." Lamb's testimony, endorsed by the proponents' best witness, undermined the optimal parenting argument for traditional marriage.[70]

In *The Future of Marriage,* Blankenhorn had written that "we would be *more* American on the day we permitted same-sex marriage than we were on the day before." When asked about this statement on cross-examination, of course he confirmed it. Boies bragged that he had turned Blankenhorn from a witness for the defense into one for the plaintiffs. We'd be more nuanced. The plaintiffs' legal team had uncovered more than enough vehicles for Blankenhorn to reaffirm his liberal, pro–gay rights side, but it had discredited the academic support Blankenhorn, as a traditional marriage booster, was adducing to limit the definition of marriage.[71]

The Opinion and the Appeal

After Blankenhorn left the witness stand, the trial just . . . ended. There was no jury, and the closing arguments would not come until June.

The plaintiffs' team could not have been more pleased. Working with excellent expert witnesses, thanks to Terry Stewart and the movement lawyers whom AFER had disrespected, the San Francisco city attorney's office, Gibson Dunn, and Boies Schiller had done a splendid job of presenting the already established constitutional case for marriage equality as a trial record and, simultaneously, as a publicity campaign. On the proponents' side, Cooper and Kirk were certain that Judge Walker would invalidate Proposition 8 as inconsistent with the Fourteenth Amendment. Cooper felt that the judge (whom he discovered was gay) was biased against Proposition 8 from the beginning— but he agreed with Olson that a broadly written opinion would be perfect for purposes of appellate review. Cooper was sure that the Supreme Court would not swallow a nationwide right to marry in 2010. While Olson seemed just as certain the other way, we think Cooper had it right.

In August 2010, Judge Walker ruled that Proposition 8 violated the Fourteenth Amendment. Starting with eighty detailed findings of fact, each annotated to the trial's three-thousand-page transcript and dozens of exhibits, the published opinion read the evidence largely the way the plaintiffs' counsel had pitched it. Walker found their witnesses credible while completely dismissing

Blankenhorn's two days on the stand as "inadmissible opinion testimony that should be given essentially no weight." The findings of fact drew extensively from the testimony of Professor Cott and the plaintiffs' other expert witnesses. For example, Finding 35 set forth the many public purposes served by civil marriage, including encouragement of cohesive and stable households, assuring caregiving for persons, offering a safe space for romantic couples, legitimation of children, and facilitating property ownership. Findings 36–40 detailed the benefits of marriage to society and, especially, to the spouses. Finding 41 mentioned that children benefited from their parents' marriage.[72]

Judge Walker found that California's lesbian and gay couples generally considered domestic partnership unsatisfactory and wanted to get married for the same reasons straight couples did. Accordingly, Proposition 8 denied those couples an important right—and "place[d] the force of law behind stigmas against gays and lesbians, including: gays and lesbians do not have intimate relationships similar to heterosexual couples; gays and lesbians are not as good as heterosexuals; and gay and lesbian relationships do not deserve the full recognition of society." In return, Proposition 8 did not advance any discernible public interest. Left undisturbed, marriage equality would "not affect the number of opposite-sex couples who marry, divorce, cohabit, have children outside of marriage or otherwise affect the stability of opposite-sex marriages." Referencing Yes on 8's ads, voter information guides, pamphlets, and speeches, Walker more or less found that the Proposition 8 campaign relied on unfounded fears, anti-gay stereotypes, and prejudice "to show that same-sex relationships are inferior to opposite-sex relationships."[73]

Judge Walker invalidated Proposition 8 from every constitutional angle: it was a denial of the fundamental right to marry, plus an unsupported deployment of quasi-suspect classifications (both sex and sexual orientation), plus an exclusion of a minority without even a rational basis. As to the last point, Walker examined six different justifications and found that they all lacked evidence demonstrating harm from including lesbian and gay couples in the marriage law. "Proposition 8 was premised on the belief that same-sex couples simply are not as good as opposite-sex couples. Whether that belief is based on moral disapproval of homosexuality, animus towards gays and lesbians or simply a belief that a relationship between a man and a woman is inherently better than a relationship between two men or two women, this belief is not a proper basis on which to legislate."[74]

Susan Kennedy, Governor Schwarzenegger's lesbian chief of staff, told AFER that the governor would not appeal the decision. David Boies spoke to his old

Yale Law School buddy, Attorney General Brown, who assured him that he would not appeal, either. Representing the proponents, Chuck Cooper filed an appeal in October 2010. On April 25, 2011, he also filed a motion to vacate the judgment on the ground that Judge Walker had not been impartial. Earlier that month, Vaughn Walker, recently retired from the federal bench, had told Reuters that he was gay and had enjoyed a ten-year relationship with a male physician. Cooper argued that the judge had violated the first rule of judicial neutrality: he had been "a judge in his own case," as his judgment would allow him and his partner to get married. Judge James Ware rejected the argument, on the well-established ground that personal traits did not constitute per se evidence of bias. Indeed, if Cooper were right that gay marriage might harm marriage for straight people, then straight-partnered as well as gay-partnered judges ought to be recused.[75]

On appeal, the Ninth Circuit panel followed the lead of Olson and Boies's frenemies, the gayocracy. To begin with, the panel took seriously the argument that Proposition 8's proponents had no constitutional standing to take an appeal. Judge Walker's judgment was against state and local officials, who could take an appeal—but chose not to do so. Could the Proposition 8 proponents stand in for the state? The judges followed the suggestion in David Codell's amicus brief for Equality California to ask the California Supreme Court to tell the federal judges what legal status initiative proponents had under state law. The California court took a year and finally answered the question in November 2011. The justices said that the proponents had an interest sufficient to participate in a state court challenge to their constitutional initiative but stopped short of saying that they were delegated representatives with fiduciary responsibilities to the people of California. At least some justices believed that their ruling would not be sufficient to justify Article III standing for the intervening defendants to take an appeal.[76]

The gayocracy had succeeded in slowing the appeal, but even in 2011 they were not sure their side had five Supreme Court votes for nationwide marriage equality. In a third coup, the Ninth Circuit panel agreed with Dennis Herrera and Terry Stewart's brief for San Francisco, as well as with amicus briefs filed by Lambda, NCLR, the ACLU, and Professor Eskridge (for leading constitutional law professors). By a vote of 2-1, the court ruled that because the initiative took back constitutional rights from a minority, *Romer v. Evans* required a close look at the justifications. As in *Romer*, the case for Proposition 8 rested on rationales that did not hold up, suggesting that the exclusion enforced antigay stereotypes or animus. The symbolic disrespect inherent in denying the name *marriage* to unions that were marriages in all but name sealed the fate of Proposition 8. AFER's members and counsel were irritated (some were furious) that the Ninth Circuit had diluted their great victory by sidestepping Judge Walker's arguments for strict scrutiny. His embrace of the sex discrimination argument for marriage equality was especially notable, as it validated the feminist inspiration for many of the ideas and the enthusiasm in the marriage equality campaign. Diplomatically, Vaughn Walker told us that trial judges should never complain when their judgments are affirmed.[77]

After the *Perry* trial was over, Dustin Lance Black proposed that he create a play out of the transcripts and interviews. *8 the Play* was a montage of actors reading excerpts from the trial transcripts, videos of Yes on 8's protect-the-children ads, and interviews with the plaintiffs, their children, and their counsel. It premiered as an AFER fundraising event on September 19, 2011, at the Eugene O'Neill Theatre in New York City. Binding the story together were Kris Perry (read by Ellen Barkin) and Sandy Stier (Christine Lahti), together with their teenage sons, Spencer and Elliott. They sounded the great theme of the trial, namely, that marriage was important to these couples because it was the only word that could express their relationship, reflect the state's and society's acceptance of their family, and assure their sons that they were committed to them just as much as to each other. Rob Reiner read the part of David Blankenhorn, whom he presented as stubborn, foolish, evasive, and broadly comical, the butt of sarcastic cross-examination by David Boies (Morgan Freeman). Like 8 the trial, *8 the Play* ended with Blankenhorn's testimony that, of course, gay people were capable parents and America would be better off if they could marry. Black had been in tears at that point in the trial.[78]

When the play was performed a second time, on March 3, 2012, at the Ebell in Los Angeles and streamed live to a larger and permanent audience, Black's advocacy theatre became a celebrity event. Brad Pitt read the judge, George Clooney the cross-examiner, Martin Sheen was Ted Olson, and Kevin Bacon was Chuck Cooper. Jane Lynch re-created Maggie Gallagher, and Chris Colfer was the victim of conversion therapy. At the end of the Los Angeles reading, the plaintiffs, Kris's sons, the plaintiffs' lawyers, and Rob Reiner joined the actors on the stage. Speaking directly to the audience, David Boies underscored a point that George Clooney had made in the play: "The witness stand is a lonely place to lie." It was easy for public intellectuals like Blankenhorn to sound dire warnings about how marriage would suffer if gay people were allowed to join that fundamental social and legal institution—but it was another thing for them to defend those easy predictions under close questioning and demands for evidence. While Boies's earlier statement that "we put fear and prejudice on trial" was an overstatement, his main point stuck.[79]

Black's play also illustrated the new politics of the marriage debate. Gone were the days when lawyers like Mary Bonauto and lobbyists like Arline Isaacson called the shots through appeals to a handful of judges or legislators. The debate was now fully public, and the marriage equality side was making great strides. At the Broadway performance, David Blankenhorn sat in the audience, fascinated by the refracted version of the 8 trial and by Rob Reiner's brutal rendition of him as a witness. Afterward, he talked with a lesbian couple about their family, and several cast members engaged him as well. He told us that 8 the Play helped push him to write an op-ed in the New York Times titled "How My View on Gay Marriage Changed." In it, he wrote: "I don't believe that opposite-sex and same-sex relationships are the same, but I do believe, with growing numbers of Americans, that the time for denigrating or stigmatizing same-sex relationships is over. Whatever one's definition of marriage, legally recognizing gay and lesbian couples and their children is a victory for basic fairness." This volte-face was a gutsy move—in our view, a profile in courage. As David expected, his institute immediately lost its board of directors, led by Robby George, as well as its funding.[80]

Consider another wrinkle in the public relations story. After Cooper filed a petition asking the Supreme Court to review the Ninth Circuit's ruling in Perry, the law professors who had urged the Ninth Circuit to write a narrow opinion drafted an amicus brief urging the Supreme Court to deny review and let the issue percolate. In a conference call bringing together Terry Stewart, Jeremy Goldman from Boies Schiller, and various Gibson Dunn folks, Chris Dusseault implored the law professors to recognize that the court and the country were now ready for marriage equality: "We [the lawyers and AFER] have created the favorable climate that is making marriage recognition possible, and you don't want to ruin all the work that we have done." Speaking for the law professors, William Eskridge responded icily, "Ellen DeGeneres has done more to create a favorable climate for marriage equality than you and all the other lawyers."[81]

As we saw it, the public's increasingly favorable attitudes toward marriage equality were not primarily the result of lawyers. Thousands of marriage equality activists, supportive academics, funders and volunteers, journalists, legislators, and judges brought America toward the freedom to marry. If any lawyers were primarily responsible for changing public opinion, they were the GLAD lawyers Mary Bonauto, Gary Buseck, and Jennifer Levi, who prevailed in

Goodridge. The day Massachusetts started issuing marriage licenses, May 17, 2004, was the empirical turning point—the Cinderella moment. Because one state opened the door to gay marriage and the sky did not fall, lesbian and gay couples came out all over the country, and public opinion began to change. Other lawyers also dramatically advanced the cause of marriage equality— Beth Robinson and Susan Murray in Vermont, Josh Friedes in Massachusetts and Washington, the ACLU's Matt Coles, Evan Wolfson of Freedom to Marry, Kate Kendell and Shannon Minter at NCLR, and Jon Davidson, Jenny Pizer, David Buckel, and Camilla Taylor of Lambda Legal. The *Perry* team were not the only important attorneys.[82]

The law professors filed their amicus brief opposing Supreme Court review, as did Gibson Dunn. Viewing the issue as far from ripe, Justices Kennedy, Ginsburg, Breyer, Sotomayor, and Kagan voted against taking up *Hollingsworth v. Perry,* but Chief Justice Roberts and Justices Scalia, Thomas, and Alito voted to take the case for the 2012 term. Only four votes were required. On December 12, 2012, the court announced that it would review *Hollingsworth.* The same day, it unanimously accepted for review a Second Circuit decision striking down the core of DOMA, which the gayocracy did consider ripe for review and a likely Supreme Court win, *United States v. Windsor.*[83]

16 • Three Men in a Room

On Wednesday, March 24, 2003, Daniel Hernandez and Nevin Cohen, along with eight other plaintiffs, sued the city clerk in the New York State Supreme Court. They asked the court to declare New York's Domestic Relations Law unconstitutional "insofar as it denied marriage licenses and access to civil marriage to same-sex couples." On February 4, 2005, Justice Doris Ling-Cohen found in their favor, which set off a long journey through New York's labyrinthine government.[1]

Hernandez v. Robles eventually joined other marriage equality challenges in the New York Court of Appeals; briefs and oral arguments were scheduled for the last day of May 2006. (The court of appeals is New York's highest court—higher than the state's supreme court.) The oral arguments in *Hernandez* were nothing short of a spectacle. The normally seven-judge court was reduced to six for this case, as Albert Rosenblatt, the affable former district attorney of Dutchess County, recused himself from consideration of the case (probably for a family-based conflict of interest). Representing forty-four same-sex couples, seventeen lawyers participated in an argument that ran over two hours. Detailed briefs were filed by the ACLU, Lambda Legal, GLAD, the Catholic Conference, the Family Research Council, and Attorney General Eliot Spitzer. Judge Robert Smith, a former corporate lawyer, dominated the oral argument, aggressively pressing counsel to demonstrate why New York did not have a rational basis to treat same-sex and opposite-sex couples differently with regard to the special institution of marriage. His style of interjection, interrupting counsel with lengthy questions which he then doggedly pursued, created tension and some ill feelings in the court of appeals's majestic courtroom.[2]

The court issued its 4-2 decision in *Hernandez v. Robles* on July 6, with Judge Smith announcing the judgment of the court and authoring a plurality opinion. He concluded that reasonable legislators could rationally believe that the traditional definition of marriage was useful to channel straight couples into "responsible procreation" and to valorize marital mom-dad families as the optimal arrangement for child-rearing. "We therefore express our hope that the participants in the controversy over same-sex marriage will address their arguments to the Legislature . . . and that those unhappy with the result—as many undoubtedly will be—will respect it as people in a democratic state should respect choices democratically made." Judge Victoria Graffeo's concurring opinion accepted only the responsible procreation justification. The court's judgment left any final decision on marriage equality firmly within the purview of the New York legislature. Yet Smith's dismissive opinion was controversial within that body. Assemblywoman Deborah Glick wrote an op-ed and sent a private letter to Smith deriding his opinion as laced with anti-gay stereotyping and hostile terminology that the legislature had pointedly rejected.[3]

In a detailed dissent, Judith Kaye, joined by Carmen Ciparick, lamented that the plurality judges had failed to understand that "fundamental rights . . . are not defined in terms of who is entitled to exercise them" and that marriage has never had the "single and unalterable meaning" the plurality attributed to it. "I am confident that future generations will look back on today's decision as an unfortunate misstep." Kaye also argued that the exclusion of gay couples from civil marriage was an invidious discrimination with no rational basis.[4]

Chief Judge Kaye took pride in her statement in *Hernandez*, particularly because of the importance of marriage, family, and children in her own life and the lives of those she loved. She saw the question of marriage equality through the lens of her own past struggles as a woman trying to find a job at a law firm. After law school, she had worked as an associate at the venerable Sullivan & Cromwell before leaving to start a family. Upon returning to legal practice, she started at Olwine, Connelly, Chase, O'Donnell & Weyher in 1969, becoming the firm's first female partner in 1975. The early rejections she faced in her professional life gave her a deep sympathy for the experiences of gay and lesbian couples whose life commitments and families were rejected by the state. When we spoke with her, she reminisced about having officiated at the marriage of her law clerk, Megan Wolfe Benett, to David Ratzen just days after hearing oral arguments in *Hernandez*. Opening a scrapbook that she kept detailing all the weddings she had performed, she asked us, "How can you not feel touched seeing this?" It was her reflection on the opposite-sex marriage of a person in her judicial family, her own law clerk, that inspired her most memorable paragraph about same-sex marriages in *Hernandez*: "For most of us, leading a full life includes establishing a family. Indeed, most New Yorkers can look back on, or forward to, their wedding as among the most significant events of their lives. They, like plaintiffs, grew up hoping to find that one person with whom they would share their future, eager to express their mutual lifetime pledge through civil marriage." She lamented that the forty-four plaintiffs were denied those rights solely because of their sexual orientation. "This State has a proud tradition of affording equal rights to all New Yorkers. Sadly, the Court today retreats from that proud tradition."[5]

If anything were to be done about marriage equality, however, it was up to the famously gridlocked New York legislature. *Hernandez* set the stage for an ensemble of key players from the executive and legislative branches who would strive to deliver what the judiciary had not. Could the rights of a minority be vindicated by the legislative process?[6]

New York's Legislature and Gay Rights

Albany, the state capital, is easily reached from New York City by the Empire Service train. Almost any person in New York politics—from legislators like Tom Duane and Danny O'Donnell to judges like Judith Kaye to executive officials like Alphonso David—has enjoyed many memories of traveling back and forth between New York City and Albany via the 7:15 a.m. Amtrak from Pennsylvania Station. "Some of the most vivid writing in America is on the walls of restrooms," Truman Capote once mused. "The men's room in the Albany, N.Y. railroad station, for instance, should be preserved as a national shrine: there is more wit there than in any Broadway hit!"[7]

Less than two years after the Stonewall riots of 1969, various people within the organs of government began their often tortuous dance toward marriage equality. In February 1971, Assemblyman Al Blumenthal and state senator Manfred Ohrenstein proposed the Sexual Orientation Non-Discrimination Act (SONDA). Two decades later, the proposal still had not passed, and in 1990 Deborah Glick, the first openly gay member of the state assembly, made the passage of SONDA the chief goal of her election platform. In February 1993, Glick won assembly approval of SONDA by a lopsided vote of 90-50, but the senate refused even to bring it to the floor for a vote. Nine years later, SONDA was enacted and signed into law. In her 2006 letter to Judge Smith, Assemblywoman Glick invoked the lengthy and painstaking legislative process of passing SONDA and ridiculed Smith's claim in *Hernandez* that the court needed to "defer" to the legislature. Indeed, Smith's own opinion failed to follow the guidance from the legislature, referring to homosexuality as a chosen "sexual preference" and ignoring SONDA's finding that this minority "sexual orientation" was not chosen.[8]

Historically, the New York legislative chambers had been at a perpetual impasse on gay rights issues, while the court of appeals was the primary government body taking proactive steps to protect LGBTQ+ persons. In *People v. Onofre* (1980), the court of appeals invalidated a state law making consensual sodomy a misdemeanor. The 5-2 court held that it was not the function of the state's criminal penal laws to dictate moral or religious values. In *Braschi v. Stahl Associates* (1989), the court ruled that New York City's rent control laws applied to LGBTQ+ couples living together in long-term relationships. As Chief Judge Kaye told us when asked about the case, "That was their home . . . he was his family." For similar reasons, she dissented when the court two years later held that a woman with no biological ties to a child had no legal standing to seek visitation rights, even though she had been a caregiver since the child's birth.[9]

The same year, Thomas Duane was elected to New York City's council as an openly gay and HIV-positive man. He was born at French Hospital in Manhattan in 1955; came from a large Irish Catholic family from Flushing, Queens; attended Holy Cross High School; and secured a college degree from Lehigh University. During his time on the city council, Duane watched the legal evolution of the court of appeals but also the continued blockage of SONDA in the state senate. He became increasingly convinced of the importance of local action and activism—something he had learned from serving on the local community board. In 1998, Duane was elected to the New York Senate, becoming its first openly gay member and first openly HIV-positive member.[10]

Senator Duane immediately struck up a friendship with Republican senate majority leader Joseph Bruno, a powerful friend to have. In New York, the governor, senate majority leader, and speaker of the assembly were dubbed the "three men in a room" who made all the important political decisions for the Empire State. Most legislation was never even brought to the floor of each chamber for a serious vote unless all three agreed to it. Until 2019, they were always men.[11]

As the 2001 legislative session was to begin, Duane pulled Bruno aside and made an appeal to his friend's kindness. Would Bruno allow domestic partner benefits to be extended to senate employees? Despite what felt like a quick brush-off, Duane later learned that the majority leader silently granted his request, without debate or discussion. He attributed this nonpartisan demonstration of support to the fact that Joe Bruno, like many other New York Republicans, did not personally object to equal benefits for gay and lesbian couples.[12]

Weeks after the life-changing attacks of September 11, 2001, GOP governor George Pataki issued an executive order to ensure that surviving partners of LGBTQ+ victims would receive equal benefits as spouses from the New York State Crime Victims Board. The legislature passed bills to include same-sex partner survivors in other state benefits, including state worker's compensation. In December, the American Red Cross changed its official policy and opened up its disaster relief programs to same-sex partner survivors. On January 28, 2002, SONDA passed the assembly by a 113-27 vote. At the end of the year, December 27, Bruno scheduled a senate vote, with the same bipartisan result, 34-26. Pataki signed the bill the same day.[13]

One additional topic was on Duane's mind: Would New York consider marriage equality? This was particularly important to him because so many states were copying the federal law to bar lesbian and gay relationship recognition through junior-DOMAs and even Super-DOMAs. Just as he had before, Duane approached Majority Leader Bruno. Would it be possible to move toward marriage after September 11? Bruno was swift and unapologetic: he saw no reason to roil state politics and create trouble for his party's senators by placing this issue on the legislative agenda. Moving to the second of the three men in a room, Duane approached Assembly Speaker Sheldon Silver and got the same response: no way. So he changed the question. If you are not going to allow marriage equality, he asked both men, are you planning to enshrine inequality in our state laws by considering a defense of marriage law? Bruno and Silver were again in agreement: No, absolutely not, not here in New York. Duane knew that a New York junior-DOMA had no chance, two years before the national junior- and Super-DOMA electoral sweep in 2004.

Unlike the soft-spoken Senator Duane, Assemblyman Danny O'Donnell was the epitome of the brash New York politician. Less of a consensus maker and far less apologetic, O'Donnell was also born in Queens. Like Duane he hailed from a large family, and he attended Catholic University before transferring and completing his bachelor's degree at George Washington University and his law degree at City University of New York. After winning election to the assembly in late 2002, he quickly grasped how to navigate its choppy waters and joined Deborah Glick in the fight for marriage equality legislation.[14]

First Marriage Equality Bill, 2007

In November 2006, after twelve years of Republican control, Attorney General Eliot Spitzer was elected governor, and Danny O'Donnell felt that the time was ripe for the legislature to answer the challenge laid down in *Hernandez*. He and Deborah Glick represented part of Manhattan, as did Speaker Silver, and they knew that a fellow elected official from New York City would, at a minimum, let them start collecting and counting the votes he would need for a marriage equality bill. They also felt that having the Speaker on their side would be a powerful asset in dealing with Governor Spitzer. If O'Donnell could gain at least the tacit support of the new governor, gay rights would have enlisted two of the three men who make Albany function. Only weeks after his election, Spitzer received O'Donnell, whose question was simple: Was the governor okay with his proposing legislation to allow for marriage equality in New York? O'Donnell assured the governor that he and Glick could get the assembly speaker to agree, and by the spring of 2007 Spitzer had given them the green light: "Now go out there and get the votes." Spitzer may have thought he would never hear of the bill again. O'Donnell and Glick needed seventy-six assembly votes to pass it, and at the time they were assured of only twenty-seven.

O'Donnell and Glick planned a three-step strategy to enlist the support of Speaker Silver. First, O'Donnell had his staff implement a polling and vote-count procedure. Every week, they would take the temperature of the assembly and send an updated count to the Speaker. Second, Glick and O'Donnell had to show that a marriage equality bill was politically viable. Every week, the Democrats in the assembly were sent a letter about representatives who had moved on the issue without being penalized by the voters. Most important, they realized they needed to make the issue personal rather than abstract. The letters O'Donnell sent were signed "John and I would like to thank you for your vote," and Danny's partner, John Banta (now his husband), was assigned to speak personally each week to targeted members.[15]

Assembly members also received letters and other communications from gay constituents and their families. Since the 1990s, Marriage Equality New York had taken the lead in grassroots organizing on this issue, joined by the Empire State Pride Agenda, the largest LGBTQ+ rights organization in the state. Under President Joe Solmonese and National Field Director Marty Rouse, the Human Rights Campaign (HRC) became an enthusiastic supporter of marriage equality and devoted millions of dollars to grassroots organizing. Staunchly opposed to Glick and O'Donnell's bill were Archbishop Edward Egan and the Catholic Conference of New York, still the most potent lobbying force in Albany.

By early June 2007, the sponsors believed they had reached the seventy-six yes votes their bill needed to pass, and the time had come to court people across the aisle. Glick and O'Donnell started with Assemblywoman Teresa Sayward, a Republican from upstate New York with an openly gay son. Despite knowing she was putting herself in electoral jeopardy, Sayward felt that it was important that a parent of a gay or lesbian child speak up in support of the legislation. On June 17, O'Donnell and Glick told the Speaker that they had some Republican support and were confident that a bill would pass in the assembly by a respectable margin. They had in hand a June 12 letter by Mildred Loving, half of the interracial married couple in *Loving v. Virginia* (1967). Specially pegged to the fortieth anniversary of that decision, Loving affirmed that "all Americans, no matter their race, no matter their sex, no matter their sexual orientation, should have that same freedom to marry." On June 18, O'Donnell attached Mildred's "Loving for All" letter to a note he addressed to all assembly members, in which he wrote: "Today we are at a similar crossroads for marriage equality."[16]

The next day, Speaker Silver sent the marriage equality bill to the floor, and the assembly voted 85-61 to pass it. Given the meager start and perceived electoral perils, securing eighty-five votes for marriage was an extraordinary accomplishment by Glick and O'Donnell. While Majority Leader Bruno declined to schedule the marriage bill for debate in the senate, getting it passed in even one chamber was a momentous legislative feat and show of strength for marriage equality. A New York marriage statute was now a distinct possibility.

Second Marriage Equality Bill, 2009

On March 10, 2008, press accounts named Governor Spitzer as a client of a high-priced escort service, the Emperors Club VIP. The young Icarus of New York politics fell even faster than he had ascended, and he resigned on March 17. Lieutenant governor David Paterson was sworn in by Chief Judge Kaye the same day. Almost immediately, the new governor presented himself to gay legislators as both a willing ally and, ultimately, an unwitting obstacle to marriage equality.[17]

Buoyed by Senator Obama's presidential candidacy, the Democrats saw the November 2008 election as an opportunity to flip the New York Senate, which had been controlled by the Republicans for four decades. The Gill Action Fund,

HRC, and wealthy gay donors funded challenges to vulnerable GOP senators. The senate did indeed flip, returning a 32-30 majority for the Democrats. O'Donnell spent the early months of 2009 whipping votes in the assembly to improve on the 2007 vote, but he took notice on April 15, when Timothy Dolan was installed as the tenth Catholic archbishop for New York City. Surrounded by the state's top elected officials, the affable and politically astute archbishop (untouched by the predatory priest scandal) was the perfect prelate to reassert the Church's political authority in Albany.[18]

Within twenty-four hours of leaving Archbishop Dolan's installation, Governor Paterson introduced a marriage equality bill. He did so, however, without obtaining the blessing of the longtime legislative supporters of marriage equality. While O'Donnell felt the governor had not done the needed preparatory work, he won approval in the assembly in May, with a whopping 89-52 majority. In the senate, however, Duane was pessimistic about the bill's chances. Paterson had neither conferred with the new leadership nor confirmed majority support; the Catholic Church and the minority GOP leadership were adamantly opposed.

With a Democratic Party majority in control of the senate calendar, marriage equality appeared likely to come to a vote in June. But you can never take anything for granted in the New York Senate. On June 8, the Democrats' 32-30 majority collapsed. By flipping two conservative Democrats, Republican Dean Skelos was able to install himself as the new senate majority leader. Lawsuits between the parties flew like paper airplanes, senators played musical chairs with party alignments, Paterson appointed a new lieutenant governor to preside over the senate, and judges left the legislative mess to the political process. In the turmoil, the well of goodwill between the parties ran dry.[19]

When the political and legal dust settled in July 2009, Democrats once again enjoyed a tenuous 32-30 majority in the senate; and their new majority leader, Pedro Espada Jr., was willing to bring marriage to a floor vote later in the session. The Pride Agenda had retained legendary lobbyist Emily Giske to head a team to whip the senators. Governor Paterson called a special session of the legislature to consider the bill. It would surely pass the assembly, but Duane still worried about the senate: Would there be enough Democratic votes? Would Minority Leader Skelos allow GOP senators to vote their consciences? If so, would enough Republicans vote for marriage equality to overcome the expected no votes from conservative Democrats? Or would they bow to pressure from the Catholic Church and fear of primary challenges funded by the National Organization for Marriage (NOM)? Privately, Duane felt that the marriage bill was heading for a dramatic failure.

On December 2, 2009, the assembly passed bill A40003 by a margin of 88-51, a thumping majority that made O'Donnell proud. That afternoon, Senator John Sampson (head of the Democratic Conference) met with Giske and Duane in his office; they concluded that there was no path to thirty-two votes in the senate. Sampson wanted to pull the bill: Why put some members of his caucus in electoral jeopardy for a bill that was sure to fail? Alan van Capelle, Pride Agenda's executive director, joined the meeting and insisted that the senators go on record, yea or nay. "I don't know how we go into the next election cycle in 2010 without a work plan, and the only work plan I can think of is targeting the people who voted no."[20]

In the senate, the vote was by roll call, in alphabetical order. The second to vote was Joseph Addabbo, a Queens County Democrat who had been elected in 2008 with LGBTQ+ support and money. To Duane's surprise, he voted no. A devout, traditionalist Catholic like most of his constituents, Senator Addabbo did not believe he had *promised* that he would vote yes, and the governor had not pressured him to do so. Watching on the sidelines, O'Donnell, like Duane, now knew defeat was certain; he was furious that the bill had even been allowed to get to the floor.

Jim Alesi, a moderate Republican of Rochester, was the next to vote. He and his whole family were gay friendly, but his caucus had decided earlier to oppose the bill as a block. His tear-filled eyes closed, his hands holding his head, Senator Alesi blurted out his no, and it was clear that the vote would not only fail, but fail spectacularly. Duane muttered under his breath that he could not believe the history of LGBTQ+ rights in New York would be written with the help of Joe Bruno but not Dean Skelos. As Governor Paterson trudged back to his office and Duane pondered how his chamber had delivered a severe rebuke to gay rights, O'Donnell and his partner drove down the New York State Thruway seething that their hard work culminated in such a dramatic loss. The ultimate vote was 24-38. Eight Democrats had deserted their governor, and all thirty Republicans voted no.

This was a demoralizing defeat, but early the next year Bill Smith from the Gill Action Fund and Emily Giske formed a political action committee (PAC) called Fight Back New York. As van Capelle had predicted, marriage equality supporters now knew who their enemies were—and some of them were Democrats. As Rouse and Solomon had learned in Massachusetts, an effective strategy for motivating legislators to "do the right thing" was to punish those who betrayed their commitments. The first casualty was Hiram Monserrate, a Queens County Democrat who had been expelled from the senate for improprieties but was a candidate in a special election on March 16, 2010. Fueled by Gill money, Fight Back invested in grassroots support for Jose Peralta, a marriage equality assembly member running for the seat. Assisted by negative ads against Monserrate, Peralta won the primary by a 39 percent margin. Targeting longtime senator Bill Stachowski of Buffalo in the Democratic primary, the PAC supported young Tim Kennedy, who prevailed by thirty-seven points. In the general election, the targets were Republicans.

Third Marriage Equality Bill, 2011

Alphonso David's background did not mark him as destined for an instrumental role in New York state government. Born in Silver Spring, Maryland, in 1970, he returned to his family's home country of Liberia when he was just one year old. His father became the mayor of Monrovia (Liberia's capital) in 1977. Together with his great-uncle William Tolbert as president of Liberia and his mother working in a national agency, David was keenly attuned to political life from the start. On April 12, 1980, a military coup overthrew the elected government—assassinating his uncle and jailing his father. Upon his release from prison, his father sought political asylum and relocated Alphonso and two other children in the United States. Amid this tumultuous time for his family, Alphonso David was haunted by a vivid worry: his feelings of same-sex attraction could be a great risk both socially and legally.[21]

As a student at Temple Law School, David began to see a painful disconnect between his family's own courage to forge a life in a foreign country and his own difficulty finding the courage to admit his identity as a gay man. In his published law student note, he found a connection between civil rights law and the AIDS epidemic then ravaging the community of which he was secretly a member. "The Supreme Court has spoken and yet remains silent," he wrote, even as he thought the same idea applied to himself.[22]

After graduating from law school and clerking for a federal trial judge, David worked in various civil positions before accepting an offer at Lambda Legal and moving to New York. One of his first Lambda cases was *Hernandez*. Similar to the *Hernandez* plaintiffs, David overcame his childhood fear that a public life in government would entail a personal life relegated to secrecy. In 2007, he joined the New York State Division of Human Rights. Under Attorney General Andrew Cuomo, Alphonso David became the bureau chief for civil rights. He and his boss watched the 2009 legislative marriage meltdown with horror—and determination to reverse that result.

PATERSON'S FALL, CUOMO'S RISE

With the colossal failure of the marriage bill, Governor Paterson lost most of the political mojo needed for a viable campaign to win election to a four-year term in 2010. Meanwhile, Attorney General Cuomo's star was ascending. Born in Queens in 1957, Andrew Cuomo was the eldest son of legendary former Governor Mario Cuomo (1983–1995). He worked as the campaign manager for his father's 1982 run for the governorship and then became an assistant district attorney in Manhattan. By 1990 he was the chair of the New York City Homeless Commission. During his father's tenure as governor, Andrew went to Washington, DC, where he was an assistant secretary, and then secretary, of the Department of Housing and Urban Development under President Clinton. He made his first run for governor in 2002, but after some political missteps he withdrew.[23]

Andrew Cuomo had his own journey story on issues of gay rights. For many years, he had been in a romantic partnership with Sandra Lee, the star of *Semi-Homemade Cooking with Sandra Lee,* a ratings bonanza on the Food Network. From an early age, Sandra Lee was responsible for helping to raise her siblings. Despite a sick mother and absent father, she was able to finish high school and briefly attend college. By 1988, she had moved to Los Angeles to live closer to her family, and her youngest and closest sibling, John Paul Christiansen, moved to Los Angeles as well. Johnny eventually came out to Sandra, who gave him the comfort and support one would hope for from a protective older sister. In late 2005, after her marriage ended in divorce, Sandra Lee moved to New York, where she fell in love with up-and-coming Attorney General Cuomo. The father of three children from a previous marriage, Cuomo and Sandra Lee became inseparable. Cuomo welcomed Sandra's brother Johnny into his family.[24]

Faced with Cuomo's ascendance and abandoned by donors and political supporters, Paterson withdrew from the governorship race in February 2010. In May, Cuomo announced his second campaign for governor, with marriage equality as a central plank in his platform. He told the Empire State Pride Agenda the month before the election: "I want to be the governor who signs the law that makes equality a reality in the State of New York." His Republican opponent, businessman Carl Paladino, landed in hot water when he disparaged lesbian and gay couples who were raising children. Responding to a media firestorm, he appeared on the *Today* show and made matters worse when he lambasted Cuomo for taking his daughters to a gay pride parade. "I think it's disgusting." On November 2, Cuomo won by a 2-1 landslide.[25]

Ironically, 2010 was a wave election for the Republicans across the country, and New York was only partly exceptional. Although Fight Back New York took out one Republican senator, the GOP gained assembly seats and, after recounts in three races, ended up controlling the senate by a 32-30 margin. (Gay-friendly legislators were tossed out all over the country. In Massachusetts, marriage equality supporters Barbara L'Italien and Paul Kujawski lost their races.) After the election, the three men in a room included an ambitious, determined Democratic governor facing a canny, cautious Republican senate majority leader from Long Island, Dean Skelos.[26]

GOVERNOR CUOMO TAKES COMMAND

Momentum in Albany politics is rarely as strong as it was going into 2011. Governor Cuomo had run on a platform of changing the culture of Albany, and at the very top of his priorities was the need to show that he could navigate the legislature well enough to pass game-changing legislation—like marriage equality. Assemblyman O'Donnell remained confident that his ongoing vote tally in the assembly was accurate, but Senator Duane, confronting the new 32-30 Republican majority in the senate, felt it would be an uphill battle there. To make matters worse, he did not trust Majority Leader Skelos.[27]

Alphonso David, planning to return to private practice, was floored when the governor-elect offered to appoint him to the newly created position of deputy secretary for civil rights—and to make marriage equality his first legislative priority. For the first time, the executive was going to firmly take command—and David was going to be the point man. Because it would be the governor's first major legislative push, David realized how important it was to control the bill, control the vote, and control the message. This was going to require a new approach, relying on trusted allies while also targeting specific individuals, particularly senators. Cuomo would have to be at the heart of all discussions, negotiations, drafting, and tactics. The governor's team included David and four others: Secretary to the Governor Steven Cohen, Counsel Mylan Denerstein, Assistant Counsel Katherine Grainger, and Director of Legislative Affairs Betsey Ball.

Almost immediately, David and Ball let O'Donnell and Glick know that they trusted them to continue to count votes in the assembly, lobby new and old members, and maintain that legislative chamber's solid majority in support of marriage equality. But the governor's team demanded that nothing should be introduced in either chamber until they were sure the bill was going to pass. What O'Donnell did not want to tell David was that his vote count in the assembly was down to seventy-seven because of losses in the 2010 election, and now the governor's team was asking him to maintain a solid majority for a bill that did not exist. Counting votes without a bill is not how one maintained support. Still, he and Deborah Glick were determined to press forward.

As for the senate, Duane told David that several Republicans had said privately that they were open to marriage equality. Duane insisted that it was important not only to put pressure on the renegade Democrats and on targeted Republicans but also to ensure that Skelos would actually allow a floor vote. The Republican senators whose votes were seemingly within reach included James Alesi of Rochester and Stephen Saland of Poughkeepsie, both of whom reluctantly opposed marriage equality in 2009. But, as in 2009, both were worried about GOP primary challenges and opposition from the Conservative Party if they voted for the bill. David told Duane that the executive, through Betsey Ball, would round up GOP senators and that Duane should focus on Democrats.

The governor's team was mindful that the civil rights groups in 2009 had sometimes worked at cross-purposes because of rivalries and lack of a centralized leadership. Following Duane's advice, David suggested a plan for the executive and the groups to work together on gettable senators. On Fridays from early 2011 until June 2011, David assembled representatives from all the key groups in one place to discuss what all parties were doing. Included were Ross Levi of the Empire State Pride Agenda, Marc Solomon of Freedom to Marry, Brian Ellner of HRC, and Bill Smith of the Gill Action Fund. As with any good Albany legislative push, a number of lobbyists were often in attendance as well—not just Emily Giske, but also Mike Avella and Jeff Cook, lobbyists for the gay rights–supporting Log Cabin Republicans.[28]

From the start, Team Cuomo set a different tone. Taking his cue from his focused, data-driven boss, David let the gay rights groups know that the governor's office would control the agenda and direct a lot of the group activities. David demanded to know: How many postcards were going out in each district? How many calls were being made? Who was reaching out to organized labor, religious groups, and key officials outside the senate? He did not want to hear that some group was veering off message or stepping on another's efforts. Team Cuomo made clear that they were aiming for a cushion of five Republican votes and that no bill would be brought to the senate floor with fewer than three Republicans on board. The governor's office wanted GOP senators to be aware that there was value in voting yes and that the governor would reward those who joined him. Furthermore, the gay rights groups would need to be unified in targeting those Democrats who had voted no in 2009—especially Senator Addabbo. Duane and O'Donnell recalled how they knew that the 2009 vote was over as soon as his vote (the second on the roll call) was a no.[29]

While his advisers and officials helped manage the vote tally and the interest groups, the governor himself set out to neutralize what was expected to be intense opposition from the Catholic Church. Raised in a devout Catholic household, Cuomo realized that given the Church's importance in New York, and particularly the incredible political sway Archbishop Dolan held, it was critical to engage the church leadership from the beginning. On February 15, 2011, in the middle of state budget negotiations, the governor met in Albany with the archbishop.[30]

In that meeting, Cuomo described his overarching vision for his tenure. He told Dolan that he wanted a more general audience with the bishops in the coming weeks, something Dolan agreed to broach with his flock. The cleric left with this message from the chief executive: the Catholic Church was going to have to make a choice about its priorities. The legislature was considering two measures the bishops would not like: the forthcoming Marriage Equality Act and the Child Victims Act, which would open up new windows of liability for sexual abuse of minors. Cuomo suggested that he did not intend to push for the Child Victims Act and that the Church's legislative focus should be on defeating that legislation, not on defeating marriage. If the Church went hard after the marriage bill, the governor could always change his mind about which bill he would prioritize. He was determined to pass major legislation, and it was expanding either marriage or the statute of limitations. He was not asking for the Church's support for the marriage bill, just relative neutrality. At the same time, other members of Team Cuomo engaged leaders of New York's powerful Orthodox Jewish community not to fight any marriage equality proposal. While Cuomo did not expect explicit support from traditionalist faith communities, he did ask for what could be deemed as discreet religious acquiescence.[31]

Brian Silva of Marriage Equality New York noticed how the governor was bringing together the self-interested mentalities that frayed the 2009 campaign. Silva also realized that this time, there was no need to cast a wide net. On the contrary, the goal was to target specific individuals, to get legislators, not their staffers, on the record, and to ensure that everyone used the same data-driven metrics. HRC field director Marty Rouse was ready to deploy postcards, phone calls, and boots on the ground where the senators lived. There was a unified plan among the many parties to the cause, but some LGBTQ+ leaders were not wild about giving up their autonomy and felt the governor's office operated with a heavy hand. Pride Agenda and HRC were nervous about the governor's demand that they commit to support whatever bill his office drafted, sight unseen. Nonetheless, the new approach provided needed focus, and everyone was working together to target legislators who actually might flip in favor of marriage equality. Senate Democrats were mindful that Fight Back New York had taken out two marriage equality opponents in the 2010 Democratic primary and that significant majorities of voters supported marriage equality.

WHIPPING THE SENATORS

In 2009, the 24-38 senate vote against the marriage equality bill had included eight Democrats who voted no and zero Republicans who voted yes. Marriage equality supporters had to secure support from all the Democrats, except unmovable Senator Rubén Díaz, an Evangelical minister, and to flip several Republicans. There was no other path to a majority in that chamber. Cuomo's team set about reviewing detailed maps and polls of various senate districts, looking for "weak spots" among the GOP incumbents. Recall that no bill would be brought to the senate floor with fewer than three Republican votes. LGBTQ+ rights and marriage equality organizations worked hard to target friendly Republicans and each of the remaining Democrats who had voted no in 2009.

At least ten Republican senators, including Alesi and Saland, were pegged as possible yes votes, perhaps for a compromise bill. David and Ball wanted John Flanagan of Long Island added, as polls showed that close to 70 percent of the electorate in his district supported marriage equality. Senator Mark Grisanti of Buffalo was included because grassroots activists noted that they had constantly engaged with him off-line. Grisanti privately admitted to Cuomo that his views on marriage equality were evolving. Alesi said his wife and children had been adamant that marriage equality was a foregone conclusion. Alesi would be the first Republican to vote in a roll call, and a yes from him would influence his colleagues down the alphabet. In the short term, the governor's office made clear that it would handle these Republicans and urged the gay rights groups to focus on reluctant Democrats.

On March 8, 2011, the governor hosted a large luncheon at the executive mansion in Albany. In attendance were Archbishop Dolan, thirteen bishops from all over the state, and staffers from the New York State Catholic Service. During the lunch, Cuomo stressed the importance of supporting the Catholic Church and protecting religious liberty. At the same time, he emphasized how important it was to him personally that his administration protect the civil rights of same-sex couples. The next day, the governor convened a meeting of his marriage coalition, including Duane, O'Donnell, Giske, and representatives of Freedom to Marry, HRC, Empire State Pride Agenda, SEIU Local 1199, and Equality Matters. Cuomo assured the civil rights groups that a marriage bill was his top priority and gently suggested that all the groups should follow a unified game plan coming out of his office. Each representative pledged support. Cuomo then turned the meeting over to Steve Cohen, who suggested regular meetings with the allied groups and officials. There was a general sense of the executive leading the pack.[32]

As March moved into April and the annual state budget process came to a rare on-time close, the governor held a large thank-you reception at the executive mansion. It was clear to attendees that with the budget now behind them, the governor's office intended to turn its full attention to the bills that would come up at the end of the legislative session—especially a marriage equality bill. Led by Bill Smith of Gill Action, Marc Solomon of Freedom to Marry, and Ross Levi of Pride Agenda, the leading stakeholder groups were coming together to pool their efforts in the kind of unified campaign encouraged by the governor. After a meeting with Steve Cohen, the umbrella group, New Yorkers United for Marriage, went public on April 20. Cohen envisioned a $1.5 million media and public education campaign. Pride Agenda, HRC, and Freedom to Marry were each pledging $250,000, with no idea where the next half of the budget was coming from.[33]

The previous autumn, Ken Mehlman, the former chair of the Republican National Committee who had come out of the closet, had organized a fundraiser for the California federal marriage case. Among the generous supporters of that effort were billionaire Republicans Paul Singer and Dan Loeb; they and their friends had become patrons of the equality movement. On April 28, 2011, Singer hosted a meeting of investors with Mehlman, Smith, Cohen, and Linda Cunningham (who was running the media campaign). The marriage campaigners made their pitch—and a week later the investors pledged $1 million for New Yorkers United, which gave the campaign more than the amount Cohen had optimistically demanded.[34]

On May 6, Singer hosted Majority Leader Skelos and Deputy Majority Leader Tom Libous. Joined by Mehlman and GOP donors, the group argued that the marriage issue was important to them and that allowing it to come to a vote was consistent with Republican values. Skelos responded: "This could wreak havoc on our conference politically, so we need to understand the playing field." Marriage equality votes could cost legislators the support of New York's Conservative Party in the general election, and Brian Brown of NOM had pledged to defeat Republican yes votes in their primaries. Bill Smith reassured Skelos that no GOP legislator who had voted for marriage equality had ever been defeated for reelection. Representing the fundraising muscle of Gill Action, and with Singer and his colleagues nodding in agreement, Smith promised Skelos that "we will continue to have peoples' backs." Later in May, GOP mayor Mike Bloomberg went public with his strong financial and personal support for marriage equality. Mehlman made several trips to Albany to meet with Republican senators who were making up their minds on the issue.[35]

Meanwhile, there was drama in the assembly. Because there was still no marriage bill that legislators could focus on, O'Donnell felt that support was softening—and on May 10, 2011, the impulsive legislator introduced his own rogue marriage bill. The reaction was swift and brutal, through a phone call from Steve Cohen. Unleashing every profanity in the dictionary, and some that were not, Cohen impressed upon O'Donnell that the governor felt betrayed. O'Donnell desperately tried to explain that he could no longer whip votes without a bill to count votes for—but that got him nowhere with the infuriated secretary to the governor. The next call was from Alphonso David, who was gentler. Acknowledging the difficulty of tracking votes for a bill that did not exist, David implored O'Donnell to respect the agreed-upon strategy, whereby Team Cuomo controlled the message, the bill, and the votes. Although insulted by Cohen's angry profanity and dismayed by the transparent good cop–bad cop routine, O'Donnell had worked too hard for marriage equality to indulge his own ego. Cohen and David represented the leader of his party and the best hope for marriage equality in Albany. He swallowed his pride and soldiered on.

Armed with polls showing majority support for marriage equality, Governor Cuomo on Friday, May 20, taped a video urging New Yorkers to let their legislators know how they felt. Only ninety seconds long and released to the public the following Monday, the video emphasized that this was a matter of civil rights, fairness, and equality—not a question of religion or culture. Behind the scenes, some Republicans were warming up to the governor, but not one had publicly stated that he or she was planning to support marriage equality. Cuomo was taking a large risk, as there was no bill drafted and no Republican publicly signed on, but he had no choice. Skelos had indicated that he would not call a marriage bill to the senate floor unless the governor lined up almost all the Democrats and at least a few Republicans.[36]

When it came to the recalcitrant Democrats, Senator Addabbo was critical. Marty Rouse, who had sharp expertise from years on the ground in Joe Addabbo's Bronx district, knew from the start that he and the other field organizers needed to make the senator aware that his constituents were adamant on the issue; hence, letters, emails, phone calls, and thousands of postcards flooded Addabbo's office. HRC and Empire Pride Agenda also whipped up constituent pressure on Senator Shirley Huntley of Queens. In late May, they called in celebrity power: world-renowned poet Maya Angelou called a shocked Huntley, asking her to reconsider her public position against any marriage bill. By creating a cocoon of protection around the vote, New Yorkers United was helping move the needle among the remaining Democrats to yes.[37]

On June 13, the governor's office announced that Democratic Senators Huntley, Kruger, and Addabbo were *yes* for marriage equality. That meant that twenty-nine of the thirty Democrats were on record for a marriage bill. Later that Monday afternoon, Senator Alesi told the governor that he was going to vote yes as well—the first pledge from a Republican. Cuomo called his team together, including David, Duane, O'Donnell, and members of the gay rights groups and unions, to present his Republican "get." Alesi emphasized that he needed a marriage bill that contained generous exemptions for religious organizations. As Alphonso David and Katherine Grainger continued to quietly circulate draft bills (containing religious allowances) to undecided senators, Cuomo that evening dined with Republican senators and told them he was ready to introduce a bill. It was time for them to fish or cut bait: decide what side of history they wanted to be on.[38]

On the morning of June 14, Senator Roy McDonald from Saratoga became the second Republican to announce, privately, to Team Cuomo that he would support a marriage bill. His switch was motivated in part by his faith: What would Jesus want me to do? As Cuomo told Smith that morning, "You never start the train unless you know how you're going to get to the station." McDonald was the thirty-first vote. With the lieutenant governor available to break a 31-31 tie, the train was ready to start.[39]

The Marriage Equality Act of 2011

On the afternoon of June 14, the governor's office released the text of the proposed Marriage Equality Act. David and Grainger, conducting shuttle diplomacy among numerous senators, had helped craft exemptions to protect members of the clergy, churches, religious nonprofits, and religious benevolent organizations from having to solemnize or celebrate same-sex marriages. These protections, lacking in the 2009 bill, were an attempt to persuade undecided Catholic Republicans such as Skelos, Lanza, and Saland that there was "a middle path that allows the Legislature to balance compelling, competing interests in a plural democratic society." The civil and gay rights groups pushing for marriage equality were dismayed at being left out of the discussions over the religious exemption language, but Cuomo and Cohen had no patience for backseat driving. New Yorkers United was hostage to the governor's judgment about what was needed to seal the deal.[40]

By Wednesday, June 15, Governor Cuomo was ready for the marriage equality bill to go to the floor of the assembly, giving O'Donnell the chance to finally whip up the votes with an actual bill. While he remained disappointed that his own bill was sidelined and was shocked that there were so many religious allowances in the governor's bill, he also knew that this was the time for the legislature to deliver marriage equality to the Empire State. In the assembly, the marriage equality bill passed 80-63, a smaller margin than in prior sessions because of increased GOP strength in the chamber. Immediately, Cuomo issued a message of necessity allowing the senate to waive the three-day aging period between passage in one chamber and consideration in the next.

Then came a moment when the marriage bill's strength popped out of the governor's closet. In response to persistent press inquiries about his vote and the pressure he was receiving from other Republicans, Senator McDonald blurted out: "Well, fuck it, I don't care what you think. . . . I come from a blue-collar background. I'm trying to do the right thing, and that's where I'm going with this." Opponents now realized the full power of the governor's behind-the-scenes maneuvering. Although Brian Brown and NOM had unleashed an extensive ad campaign and hundreds of thousands of constituent calls to potentially wavering legislators, there was little pressure inside the capitol (not even from the Catholic lobbyists) to resist the governor. Archbishop Dolan was out of town as the bill advanced through the legislature. Coordinating with NOM, however, the Conservative Party threatened retaliation against Republicans who supported the bill.[41]

The same day, June 15, the Republican senators' conference met for four hours behind closed doors and agreed to demand further religious exemptions. That evening, GOP senators Steve Saland, Andrew Lanza, and Kemp

Hannon met with the governor to press for those exemptions. Cuomo, in turn, lectured them that it was time for them to be on the right side of history. These three senators were on his final target list as they moved into the last week of the legislative session, and they were promised the full weight and power of the executive branch if they were to publicly support the pending bill. Saland told the governor that if they reached agreement on further religious exemptions, he would supply the thirty-third vote for the bill. (Senator Grisante had privately assured Cuomo he would be vote number thirty-two.)

Majority Leader Skelos got cold feet about letting the issue go to a vote, so it was not immediately put on the senate calendar. Protests from both sides engulfed the capitol building. While the bill was held up in the senate, David and others continued to fine-tune amendments to the religious freedom language in the hope of deflecting any criticism of wavering senators by religious organizations. He and Grainger knew it was important that Cuomo be seen at the start of his term as someone who would work with members of the legislature to craft language that could accommodate the concerns of various interests.[42]

Archbishop Dolan finally uttered some strong criticism of the marriage equality bill, but only as a caller to an Albany radio show. In an interview in the *National Catholic Register,* he claimed the Church was facing "a real David and Goliath battle." As for the governor, the archbishop acknowledged: "He's a shrewd politician, and I have to say that with a certain amount of envy and admiration—but you talk about twisting arms, you talk about using every political tool in the book; he's doing it, and he's doing it effectively."[43]

When more versions of the religious exemption language started coming from David and Grainger, Speaker Silver called O'Donnell and asked if the language would be acceptable to him and the majority coalition. The amendments had gone well beyond the initial assurances that clergy and churches would not have to celebrate marriages inconsistent with their religious principles. Section 3 of the revised bill exempted religiously controlled nonprofit institutions and benevolent associations, including the controversial Knights of Columbus, from SONDA's anti-discrimination rules with regard to facilities or services in connection with marriages. It also exempted religious institutions and religiously controlled charitable or educational institutions from SONDA's employment and service nondiscrimination rules if these conflicted with the institution's religious principles. O'Donnell found the exemptions highly objectionable, and he knew that HRC and the other gay rights groups would hate them as well. But he took a deep breath and resigned himself to this final compromise. He kept his name on the assembly bill. In the tradition of Albany, the three men in a room would decide whether the bill would reach its destination—but the man in the governor's mansion was driving the car.[44]

With pressure mounting from the Catholic Church, NOM, and the Conservative Party, but with a broad set of religious exemptions in the marriage bill, Dean Skelos convened the Republican conference to decide whether the proposed legislation should be brought to the floor. Most of the thirty-two almost-all-white, older male senators were uncomfortable with the topic to start with. They had been raised in good Catholic mom-and-dad marital households: Why was that not the best for everyone? Jim Alesi responded: "There's another side of life that's just as real. Do you understand that there are people who are raising children in same-sex households now?" In the wake of Judith Kaye's 1995 opinion upholding second-parent adoptions, many children had two mothers. How would denying marriage to their mothers help those children? As many as ten senators felt this point had weight. Dean Skelos and his colleagues were also aware of Ken Mehlman's arguments that voters would punish their party if they were responsible for disrespecting gay families. And they felt the financial heat from Paul Singer and other donors. The bill would proceed to a vote.[45]

On Thursday, June 23, Governor Cuomo called a final formal meeting of the team, including Steve Cohen, Mylan Denerstein, Betsey Ball, Alphonso David, and representatives from New Yorkers United. The bill was going to the senate floor for a vote, and he wanted all hands on deck. Skelos the next day announced that marriage equality would be the final bill of the legislative session. As part of the deal to schedule the bill, Cohen had pledged that there would be no long "haranguing" speeches on the floor. Skelos's counsel and Cohen agreed to this limited choreography: Saland would explain the religious exemptions, Duane would introduce the bill, Díaz would speak in opposition, and Grisanti would justify his decision to support the bill.[46]

On the day of the vote, however, twenty-three Democrats demanded the right to speak, and their leaders were disinclined to enforce the Cohen-Skelos deal. The gallery watched in bewilderment as Lieutenant Governor Duffy stalled, while Cohen tracked down Senator Sampson. If the minority floor leader allowed his senators to speak, Skelos was going to pull the bill, and Cohen would go public with the blame: "I'm going to tell every reporter that it failed because of you. . . . And I'm going to do it forever until your political career is over." Sampson stalked away—and told his caucus that there would be no speeches.[47]

The senate chamber and gallery were dead silent as the roll call commenced. First to vote was Eric Adams, who voted yes, as he had done in 2009. Next up was Joe Addabbo, who also voted yes, after a show-stopping no only two years before. Then came Republican Jim Alesi, who was visibly relieved to cast his affirmative vote. David could feel the flush of emotion that a baseball player must feel as his struck ball soars over the center field fence. With four Republicans voting yes and one Democrat voting no, the final tally was 33-29: the marriage equality bill passed the senate with votes to spare. Watching the roll call from the sidelines, Andrew Cuomo took a bow and received a standing ovation from the chamber.

That night, at 11:55, the governor signed the bill into law. New York became the sixth marriage equality state, joining three New England states and the District of Columbia as jurisdictions where the freedom to marry was established by the legislature. Overnight, the number of Americans living in a marriage equality jurisdiction doubled. In July 2011, some town clerks objected that they should not be forced to issue marriage licenses, but the courts rejected their pleas.[48]

After Marriage . . . Excelsior?

With his most important achievement behind him, Tom Duane would leave the senate in 2012. Danny O'Donnell still serves in the assembly and is married to his husband, John. Alphonso David would become the longest-serving member of Cuomo's senior staff and for several years was counsel to the governor, the most powerful and prominent LGBTQ+ person in the state's government. In 2019, he was chosen to lead the Human Rights Campaign.

As NOM's Brian Brown had predicted, and contrary to the assurances from Gill Action, none of the Republican senators supporting marriage equality survived their votes. In 2012, Roy McDonald was narrowly defeated in the Republican primary, Jim Alesi retired rather than face a similarly bruising primary, and Steve Saland lost his bid for reelection in November. In 2014, Mark Grisante was routed in the GOP primary and lost as an independent candidate in November. Loyal to his allies, Governor Cuomo rewarded each one with appointments to other high offices.

After the dust settled on the marriage battle, Joe Bruno, Dean Skelos, and Sheldon Silver were indicted for federal or state crimes, as were John Sampson, Pedro Espada Jr., and Carl Kruger (indicted during the marriage debate). They all pled guilty or were convicted. Among the three men in a room who

Judith Kaye, middle, officiates at the wedding of Danny O'Donnell and John Banta. (© Julie Skarratt 2019.)

delivered marriage equality to New York, only Andrew Cuomo—the man who dominated the room—remains in office. In 2018, he was elected to a third term as governor, fending off a primary challenge from actress Cynthia Nixon and coasting to a landslide win in November.[49]

Securing marriage equality through the legislative process in New York was a shot in the arm for the freedom to marry movement, which was by 2011 organized on a national level and aspired to victories outside of court. In the following four years, executive and legislative branch officials would play an increasingly important role in the campaign for marriage equality. Indeed, the next chapter will focus on national officials in the White House and the Department of Justice.

But judges would remain important figures in the debate, and few were as important in the long run than Judith Kaye, who had retired from the court of appeals when she reached the mandatory retirement age of seventy in 2008. Her 1995 opinion for the court in New York's second-parent adoption case opened the door to legal recognition of lesbian and gay families with children, and the landmark decision is still taught in law schools all over the country— as is her dissenting opinion in *Hernandez*. That heartfelt opinion set forth the case for lesbian and gay couples to enjoy the same freedom to marry that everyone else did. As she noted, there were enough marriage licenses for everyone. She was gratified that she got to see her *Hernandez* dissent become state law. And she personally officiated at the wedding of Danny O'Donnell and his spouse, depicted in the accompanying photograph.

Chief Judge Kaye's vision of family law was the embodiment of New York's motto, *Excelsior* ("ever upward"). If sexual and gender minorities wanted to assume responsibility for raising children and to lift up their lives through these commitments, she emphatically believed that the law should support them. In January 2017, just weeks after we interviewed her for this volume, Judith Kaye passed away from cancer.

17 • Obama's Team Gay

A social movement that cannot move popular opinion or that ignores the legislature cannot significantly change the law. In the last chapter, we saw how important a governor can be. But no executive can compare to the nation's president.

One of the greatest presidential nomination battles in our lives was the 2008 contest between Barack Obama and Hillary Clinton. Because LGBT leaders overwhelmingly supported Senator Clinton, Senator Obama's campaign felt it had to one-up her on marriage. Clinton vowed to repeal section 3 of the Defense of Marriage Act (DOMA), which excluded same-sex married couples from federal benefits—but Obama, in February 2008, also promised to repeal section 2, which protected traditionalist states against lawsuits to enforce valid same-sex marriages entered in sister states.[1]

That Obama was opposed to DOMA, however, did not mean he supported marriage equality. When he ran for the Illinois Senate in 1996, the thirty-five-year-old candidate wrote that "I favor legalizing same-sex marriages, and would fight efforts to prohibit such marriages." Two years later, running for reelection, he answered, "Undecided." In his 2004 campaign for the US Senate, Obama endorsed "domestic partnership and civil union laws" and was "not a supporter of gay marriage. To the extent that we can get the rights, I'm less concerned about the name." In 2006 he opposed the Federal Marriage Amendment but reiterated that "marriage is between a man and a woman." Starting with a candidates' forum in August 2007, as a presidential candidate he took a consistent approach to the issue: he favored full equality of rights and benefits (i.e., civil unions), but "we should try to disentangle what has historically been the issue of the word *marriage*, which has religious connotations to some people, from the civil rights that are given to couples."[2]

In June 2008, the presumptive Democratic nominee opposed California's Proposition 8 and wrote the Alice B. Toklas Club in San Francisco, "I want to congratulate all of you who have shown your love for each other by getting married." His stance was somewhat different in the general election. At a candidates' forum hosted by the Reverend Rick Warren at the Saddleback Church in Lake Forest, California, Senators McCain and Obama were both asked: "Define marriage." The Obama campaign knew this question would come up, and Tobias Wolff, the campaign's LGBT policy adviser, implored the handlers to ask the candidate not to throw over gay couples entirely. Yet Obama answered: "I believe that marriage is the union between a man and a woman. Now, for me as a Christian, it's also a sacred union. You know, God's in the mix." This drew cheers and applause. When speaking to an Evangelical audience, the candidate was for traditional marriage, but when speaking to an LGBT audience, he was for equal treatment. Could this difference be reconciled?[3]

Obama's longtime friend and adviser Valerie Jarrett told us that he was genuinely committed to equal treatment of gay persons in all civil matters—but that his religious faith instructed him that the sacred understanding of conjugal marriage required the exclusion of nonprocreating same-sex couples as a matter of definition. That is why he was attracted to civil unions, which gave LGBT couples the same legal rights and benefits straight couples could secure through marriage—nondiscrimination as a matter of legal rights—while respecting the sacred space of marriage in our society. If you frame marriage equality as a civil rights issue akin to employment bars, you are likely to consider the marriage exclusion "discriminatory." But if you frame it as a family or religion issue, you are likely to consider the marriage exclusion "definitional" and not discriminatory. Jarrett supported marriage equality, but she respected her friend's faith-based reasons for preferring civil unions.[4]

Obama says he did not see the restrictive definition of marriage as discrimination in the same way that the military exclusion was. In 2008 he felt that civil unions were "a sufficient way of squaring the circle." Within the LGBT community, however, 2008 was the moment when a relative consensus solidified: civil unions and domestic partnerships were not enough; nothing less than full marriage equality was acceptable. Between 2008 and 2012, most straight Americans came around to that viewpoint—and Barack Obama says he was one of them, because he saw "the pain and the sense of stigma that was being placed on same-sex couples who were friends."[5]

David Axelrod, the master strategist for Obama's 2004 Senate and 2008 presidential campaigns, says the candidate was not being completely candid. "Opposition to gay marriage was particularly strong in the black church, and as he ran for higher office, he grudgingly accepted the counsel of the more pragmatic folks like me, and modified his position to support civil unions rather than marriage, which he would term a 'sacred union.'" So Obama kept his true views about marriage equality in the closet. "Having prided himself for forthrightness, though, Obama never felt comfortable with his compromise and, no doubt, compromised position." He said to Axelrod about his masquerade on the marriage issue, "I'm just not very good at bullshitting."[6]

Axelrod's account resonates with the recollections of LGBT activists and bloggers, who claim credit for Obama's coming out of the closet on the marriage issue. Lawyer-blogger Kerry Eleveld and marriage strategists Marc Solomon and Evan Wolfson provide a roadmap of the president's evolution that closely tracks pressure applied by freedom-to-marry activists—including bloggers who monitored the Obama administration on LGBT issues, lawyers who lobbied for it to abandon DOMA, and political operatives who persuaded leading Democrats to demand a marriage equality pledge in the 2008 party platform. Referring to civil unions, Wolfson claimed that "nobody believes it's his real position. It can't be his real position," because it was so blatantly unconstitutional. These activists assumed that Obama was their ally all along but needed constant nudging and occasional outrage to do the right thing. The subtitle of Solomon's book *Winning Marriage* sums it up: "The inside story of how same-sex couples took on the politicians and pundits—and won."[7]

While we cannot deliver the final verdict on Barack Obama's personal evolution on this issue, an early episode suggests a more nuanced understanding. On March 28, 2008, Kevin Jennings and his partner, Jeff Davis, hosted the first major LGBT fundraising event for Senator Obama at their loft apartment in a renovated factory building in the Chelsea neighborhood of Manhattan. The son of a Southern Baptist preacher in Lewisville, North Carolina, Jennings had pioneered the idea of high school gay-straight alliances and had founded the Gay Lesbian Straight Education Network (GLSEN). The senator arrived resplendent in a charcoal suit, crisp white shirt, bright crimson tie, and lean confident presence. More than 150 well-heeled attendees packed the loft and cheered the candidate.[8]

Obama revealed sympathetic fluency with LGBT issues. His priorities as president would be to enact a hate crimes bill and to repeal the law barring gay people from military service. (Most of the audience knew that President Bill Clinton had promised but had not delivered hate crimes legislation and had supported the 1993 statutory ban of gays in the military.) He favored the inclusion of transgender persons in the pending employment discrimination bill, but observed that there were not enough votes for that in the Senate. This was a priority for the future. The audience listened with rapt attention.

Inevitably, someone asked: What about marriage? "Well, the country is not ready for same-sex marriage," Obama explained. "And it is not ready for a president who supports same-sex marriage." He could only support civil unions at this point. The hosts bit their tongues; it was a hard moment for them. But the senator did not stop there. "When my parents got married in the 1960s," he said, "marriages between men and women of different races were illegal in many states. Civil rights leaders were marching against segregation; racism was under fire from religious, political, and street activists. Legislators and judges were listening." Most of the audience understood the implicit references to the Civil Rights Act of 1964 and *Loving v. Virginia* (1967). "I'd urge you to pay attention to that example," the candidate suggested. Jeff and Kevin looked at one another: Did he just tell us he was for marriage equality?[9]

Some attendees took away the message that marriage equality was a process they needed to advance socially and culturally, abetted when politically possible by their ally in the White House. If this inspiring man were elected, they felt, LGBT people would for the first time have a place at the table in the national government, such as they had secured in California. Kevin Jennings viewed Obama's address as a challenge for gay people to build up enough political support to make it possible for the president to close the deal on marriage equality when the country was ready for it. After the event, Jennings and his friend Joan Garry, former executive director of GLAAD, agreed to be cochairs of the LGBT finance committee for the Obama campaign.

Consider another angle. Any candidate for a major contested public office is forced to separate private opinions from public ones. As citizens and parents, Barack and Michelle Obama were happy to talk sympathetically with their daughters, Sasha and Malia, about lesbian and gay families and marriage. But what they as president and first lady officially expressed about the marriage issue as a matter of public policy was necessarily refracted through conversations with religious as well as secular friends, political advisers, and the anticipated responses of political allies, adversaries, and undecided voters.

Throughout his life, Barack Obama has been idealistic—but he has also been an astute and strategic thinker. You aren't elected president of the United States at age forty-seven—or president of the savagely competitive *Harvard Law Review* at age twenty-eight—without a superlative ability to detect political danger and steer around it, while also pursuing your affirmative agenda through persuasion and coalition building.[10]

In 2008, Senator Obama and his advisers detected considerable political danger in the marriage issue. It was safer to support civil unions, which were less threatening to most faith traditions, acceptable to a majority of voters, and consistent with the widely shared norm of nondiscrimination. As Proposition 8 illustrated, even gay-friendly California was not quite ready for full marriage equality in 2008, and most other states strongly opposed the idea—including such presidential battlegrounds as Florida and Ohio. Between 2009 and 2012, both the president and the country moved from civil unions to marriage. The Obama administration played an important role in that shift by pervasively normalizing lesbian and gay relationships and by interring two problematic legacies from the Clinton administration: DOMA and the no-gays-in-the-military statute.

President Obama surrounded himself with legal and policy advisers who were committed egalitarians on issues of sexuality and gender. They included, among others, Vice President Joe Biden, presidential adviser Valerie Jarrett, Attorney General Eric Holder, and Solicitor General Elena Kagan. Openly gay and lesbian persons served in the White House and the Department of Justice. Openly straight, White House counsel Greg Craig had advised the 1993 grassroots campaign advocating for gays in the military. When Elena Kagan was dean of Harvard Law School, she had led her faculty to oppose the Bush-Cheney administration's efforts to bully universities into welcoming gay-excluding military recruiters onto campus.[11]

In the Obama administration, LGBT people and their allies not only had a place at the table, they occupied almost all the chairs. They moved first cautiously, then dramatically, toward an open embrace of marriage equality. Their progress is a good example of *presidential constitutionalism,* where leadership on a national meta-constitutive debate comes from the White House. The rhetoric and actions of the Obama administration mobilized the power of the presidency to elevate equal rights for sexual and gender minorities to a prominent position on the national agenda, to persuade Congress to adopt gay-friendly legislation, to normalize gay people and same-sex couples through the regulatory process, and to stand up for equal rights in the federal courts, ultimately defending those rights in two major Supreme Court cases (chapters 19 and 21).

The Obama White House and Marriage Equality

When President Obama took the oath of office in January 2009, LGBT issues were not his top priority. The financial crisis and the campaign for health care reform occupied most of the administration's attention. With regard to LGBT issues, Valerie Jarrett, associate White House counsel Alison Nathan, and deputy director of the Office of Public Engagement Brian Bond developed the administration's strategy for passing hate crimes legislation and repealing the armed forces exclusion (the top priorities). The president met with Secretary of Defense Robert Gates and Admiral Mike Mullen, chairman of the Joint Chiefs of Staff, and indicated his firm intention to repeal the 1993 statutory ban. Gates approached the issue more cautiously than the president did, but he understood the inevitability of integrating openly gay soldiers into the modern armed forces. As a central part of the internal deliberative process, the secretary agreed to study the views of rank-and-file soldiers to determine whether the opposition that fueled the 1993 law was still strong.[12]

The marriage issue could not be completely ignored, however. A week before Obama's inauguration, Ninth Circuit chief judge Alex Kozinski interpreted a federal employee health care law to cover same-sex spouses—DOMA notwithstanding. And soon after the inauguration, Mary Bonauto met with Ali Nathan to give her a heads-up that GLAD would soon file a massive federal lawsuit challenging the application of DOMA's section 3 to deny federal benefits and rights to legitimately married lesbian and gay couples in Massachusetts. On March 3, GLAD filed its equal protection challenge to DOMA, *Gill v. Office of Personnel Management*. Four months later, the commonwealth of Massachusetts filed a federalism-based challenge to DOMA. Also in the first half of 2009, the Vermont, Connecticut, New Hampshire, and Maine legislatures passed marriage equality statutes, and the Iowa Supreme Court required marriage equality under the state constitution, as we discussed in chapter 13.[13]

The administration caught sharp criticism from the gay blogosphere because it did not properly celebrate those marriage equality victories and seemed to have no plan for advancing relationship recognition. There was movement behind the scenes, however. On May 18, 2009, for example, the *New York Times* ran a story about Janice Langbehn and Lisa Pond, longtime partners who had been enjoying a Rosie O'Donnell cruise with their three children when Pond collapsed from a brain aneurysm. The Miami hospital that received Pond refused Langbehn access to her dying partner, even after she produced medical-power-of-attorney documents. Chief of Staff Rahm Emanuel and President Obama were outraged by the incident. Danielle Gray, associate counsel to the president, worked with deputy White House counsel Daniel Meltzer to develop a proposal that family visitation, broadly defined, be required of all hospitals receiving federal Medicare or Medicaid funds. Kathleen Sebelius, the secretary of Health & Human Services, strongly endorsed that proposal—though the White House held off from implementing it until the Affordable Care Act was passed, with critical support from the Catholic Church, in March 2010. A White House memorandum was issued the next month.[14]

Smeltdown and the Birth of Team Gay

The Obama Department of Justice (DOJ) recalibrated its approach to litigation in cases challenging armed forces and civil service discriminations against gay persons and couples. Tony West, the head of the department's civil division that litigates cases against the government, personally reviewed briefs to make sure that they presented only arguments that did not disparage LGBT persons and their relationships. Responding to a DOMA challenge brought by Arthur Smelt and Christopher Hammer, DOJ attorneys drafted a comprehensive memorandum supporting a motion to dismiss. Part of the draft memorandum argued that states did not have to recognize marriages contrary to their public policy and cited cases where states declined to recognize incestuous or child marriages. Another part argued that DOMA was consistent with equal protection's rational basis test (applicable to sexual orientation classifications in the Ninth Circuit), because encouraging responsible procreation was rational policy and Congress had discretion to adopt a wait-and-see attitude toward innovations in state marriage law. By maintaining neutrality—neither banning nor endorsing same-sex marriages—DOMA respected state autonomy and self-governance and preserved scarce enforcement resources. West, reviewing the draft, eliminated the responsible procreation argument. In the White House, Nathan flagged several problems with the document's language, but her last-minute changes were not made.[15]

DOJ filed its memorandum and motion on June 11, 2009—and the blogosphere lit up with indignation. On the AMERICAblog, John Aravosis and Richard Socarides complained that the Obama administration was repeating the objectionable arguments the Bush administration had made. DOJ could have chosen to raise purely procedural objections, but "what Obama did was throw the legal kitchen sink at us in a brief that could have been written by Antonin Scalia," a comparison that both Obama and Scalia found offensive. "Where in the law does it say that Obama was required to compare gay marriage to incest?" West groaned when he read that; he had missed the indirect reference to incest. On June 12, six gay rights organizations publicly condemned the neutrality justification for DOMA. "There is nothing 'neutral' about the federal government's discriminatory denial of fair treatment to married same-sex couples."[16]

The bloggers blamed the president, who of course had not read the brief. Valerie Jarrett met with freedom to marry activists and assured them that the White House was listening. Increasingly, she turned to Brian Bond to help her spot flashpoints like this. After June 11, DOJ filed nothing in any gay rights case unless it was carefully reviewed by the White House counsel, where Ali Nathan, Katherine Shaw, and Ian Bassin could spot sensitive statements and arguments. This tripled the office's workload—and generated what the lawyers and Bond would call *Team Gay:* White House officials who specialized in delivering on the administration's promise to promote equal rights for LGBT Americans. Soon after Smeltdown, the Team Gay lawyers started researching and discussing the constitutionality of DOMA and Don't Ask, Don't Tell and the administration's duties to defend those measures (or not) in court.[17]

Later in June, Tony West, Elena Kagan, and other DOJ attorneys met in the civil division's conference room with representatives of LGBT organizations and private counsel. West made sure that the relevant civil division attorneys were present, including those working in civil appellate (briefing the federal position on appeals) and federal programs (relations between DOJ and other agencies). He wanted these attorneys to understand why the LGBT community read some DOMA arguments as endorsing the view that lesbian and gay unions were inferior to those of straight couples. That view was inconsistent with the administration's vision that LGBT persons were entitled to exactly the same legal rights and responsibilities as everyone else. Within the civil division there was some dissent from this sort of accommodation. Joseph (Jody) Hunt, one of the directors of federal programs, argued that catering to the gay rights movement was inconsistent with DOJ's carefully cultivated neutrality. West's view was that neutrality demanded dignified treatment of gay persons and couples.[18]

Team Gay was also tasked with identifying deliverables—tangible recognition and benefits for lesbian and gay families within existing statutory directives.

462 OBAMA'S TEAM GAY

Nathan, Shaw, Bassin, and Bond started having weekly meetings around the White House to come up with ideas. With the assistance of Team Gay, the Office of Personnel Management (OPM), and the State Department, the White House on June 17 issued a memorandum, "Federal Benefits and Non-Discrimination." Although the administration was "not authorized by Federal law to extend a number of available Federal benefits to the same-sex partners of Federal employees," the White House had "identified areas in which statutory authority exists to achieve greater equality for the Federal workforce through extension to same-sex domestic partners of benefits currently available to married people of the opposite sex." Secretary of State Clinton extended relocation and other benefits to same-sex partners the next day. After considering overwhelmingly supportive public comments, OPM expanded bereavement and other leave policies to include same-sex domestic partners as family members, though it ultimately concluded that it had no statutory discretion to extend spousal insurance benefits to such partners. The June 17 memorandum directed all other executive departments and agencies to work with OPM to determine whether they could extend same-sex domestic partnership benefits to their employees. This memorandum was a major advance, but other equally important ones percolated below the radar. For example, Team Gay's "forms project" edited hundreds of federal forms to make them more accommodating to different identities and partnership arrangements.[19]

On June 29, 2009, Barack and Michelle Obama hosted a reception at the White House to celebrate Gay Pride Month. At the suggestion of Mara Keisling, Obama acknowledged the importance of equal rights for gender as well as sexual minorities. On the military and marriage issues, the president conceded that "many in this room don't believe that progress has come fast enough. It's not for me to tell you to be patient, any more than it was for others to counsel patience to African Americans who were petitioning for equal rights a half century ago. But I say this: We have made progress and we will make more." The next week, he called a meeting in the Roosevelt Room, the large West Wing conference room catty-corner to the Oval Office. The room is dominated by two large portraits, one each of Teddy and Franklin Roosevelt, aggressive chief executives who wielded the presidential bully pulpit for progressive causes. Attendees included President Obama and his senior advisers Valerie Jarrett, Rahm Emanuel, David Axelrod, and Jim Messina; Vice President Biden and his chief of staff, Ron Klain; Tina Tchen and Brian Bond; Greg Craig and Ali Nathan; and several DOJ lawyers, but not Tony West.[20]

There was consensus that the administration was committed to equal rights for LGBT Americans, but no unanimity as to how hard and where to press for those rights. Emanuel and Axelrod were reluctant to sacrifice other priorities. Floating above the strategic differences, the commander-in-chief issued some marching orders: "I am not going to act like the previous administration; we are going to follow the law. What I want you to do is find me a legal path to advance the rights of gay and lesbian families. I am willing to take hits in the political arena"—a comment that made Emanuel and Axelrod cringe—"but I am not willing to violate the law."[21]

In the wake of the Roosevelt Room meeting, not a single official we spoke to felt that the administration would defend DOMA before the US Supreme Court. How to get from DOMA to no DOMA was uncertain, however. In the short term, DOJ agreed not to invoke public morality, responsible procreation, or optimal parenting as rational justifications for DOMA. Instead, it would defend DOMA along procedural lines: the administrative convenience of having a stable definition of marriage as states experimented in various ways, and an avoidance of putting a federal thumb on the scales in state debates. Left open, but on the minds of the lawyers, was whether DOMA's sexual orientation discrimination should be subject to heightened constitutional scrutiny. If so, was the administration required to defend its constitutionality? These were questions on which Team Gay focused after the Roosevelt Room meeting.

On August 17, DOJ filed its reply brief in *Smelt*. It opened by stating that "this Administration does not support DOMA as a matter of policy, believes that it is discriminatory, and supports its repeal. Consistent with the rule of law, however, the Department of Justice has long followed the practice of defending federal statutes as long as reasonable arguments can be made in support of their constitutionality, even if the Department disagrees with a particular statute as a policy matter, as it does here." The White House released a personal statement from the president: "I have long held that DOMA prevents LGBT couples from being granted equal rights and benefits. While we work with Congress to repeal DOMA, my Administration will continue to examine and implement measures that will help extend rights and benefits to LGBT couples under existing law." On August 25, the judge dismissed the *Smelt* case on one of the procedural grounds advanced by the government.[22]

On September 18, when DOJ moved to dismiss the equal protection claims in *Gill* (the GLAD challenge), it explicitly abjured the responsible procreation and optimal parenting arguments. Under First Circuit precedent, the government was only required to justify DOMA's sexual orientation discrimination by demonstrating a rational connection to the public interest, the same test applicable in *Smelt*. The rational basis was administrative convenience. "Given the evolving nature of this issue," DOJ argued, Congress foresaw that the meaning of federal rights based upon marriage "would vary dramatically from State to State. Congress could reasonably have concluded that there is a legitimate government interest in maintaining the status quo and preserving nationwide consistency in the distribution of marriage-based federal benefits."[23]

Equal Citizenship for LGBT Americans

Like racial minorities and women, sexual and gender minorities had been subjected to a long history of unfair state discrimination, and the Obama administration was determined to translate its support for the equal dignity of LGBT Americans into tangible progress against that discrimination.

GENDER IDENTITY AND SEXUAL ORIENTATION AS SUSPECT CLASSIFICATIONS

Supreme Court precedent suggested that a classification might require heightened equal protection scrutiny if (1) the burdened group had suffered an unfair history of arbitrary discrimination, (2) based on an immutable trait that (3) was generally irrelevant to proper public policy, and (4) those suffering the discrimination were unable to remedy it through the normal political process. Early on, the Obama administration signaled that discrimination against transgender persons was flat-out sex discrimination and therefore presumptively unconstitutional. As soon as Elena Kagan took office as solicitor general, she vetoed an appeal from an injunction barring the Library of Congress from firing a transgender employee, on the ground that gender-identity bias was "discrimination because of sex" under Title VII and probably under the Constitution as well.[24]

On September 10, 2009, lawyers from GLAD, Lambda Legal, the ACLU, NCLR, and HRC came to the White House to discuss the marriage issue with DOJ and White House lawyers. In a detailed memorandum setting forth their constitutional analysis, the movement lawyers urged the administration to concede that sexual orientation was a suspect or quasi-suspect classification, because it met the requirements developed by the Supreme Court to justify race and sex as fishy classifications. No federal appeals court had accepted this analysis, in large part because it was inconsistent with *Bowers v. Hardwick*

(1986)—but that precedent had been overruled in *Lawrence v. Texas* (2003). If DOJ adopted the movement's analysis, some of the appeals courts would reconsider their precedents, which might help persuade the Supreme Court as well. The visitors also asked: Why was the administration still defending DOMA, a statute saturated with anti-gay animus of the sort that *Romer v. Evans* (1996) and *Lawrence* condemned? The lawyers strongly urged DOJ to "disavow morality as a justification for DOMA Section 3" and to disavow "conservation of resources" as well.[25]

Tony West had already abandoned morality and best-family arguments, as reflected in DOJ's memorandum in *Gill*. But he was not prepared to give up the department's standard conservation-of-resources or progress-one-step-at-a-time arguments. As for suspect classification, there was scant support in the civil division to press that argument in the eight federal courts of appeals that had rejected it (including the First Circuit), but West was already considering such an argument for the Second Circuit, which had not addressed the issue. His guru on these matters was Bob Kopp, the longtime director of appellate staff in the civil division. Kopp thought sexual orientation met the Supreme Court's criteria for essentially the same reasons Judge Vaughn Walker would advance in *Perry v. Schwarzenegger* (chapter 15). Greg Craig and Ali Nathan strongly agreed, even before the September 10 meeting, and younger lawyers considered this a no-brainer: it made no more sense to exclude gay people from anything than it would to exclude people of color or women. No one in the White House represented a more traditional perspective, including the president, who was delighted whenever Ali Nathan brought her twin boys to the office.[26]

If the executive branch thought DOMA was unconstitutional, what should its officials actually do? Some commentators maintain that the president has a duty *not* to apply statutes he or she considers unconstitutional. Article II requires the president to "take Care that the laws be faithfully executed" and to "preserve, protect and defend" the Constitution. How is the president satisfying either obligation by defending a statute she or he strongly believes is unconstitutional? Other scholars and almost all government lawyers, however, believe that the president should usually continue to apply unconstitutional laws until there is an authoritative judicial declaration of their invalidity. The proper functioning of the rule of law depends upon each branch's deferring to the Supreme Court as the decider of constitutional issues. The Office of the Solicitor General has long considered this its gospel, and there is a tradition of solicitors general defending statutes their presidents believed unconstitutional. One famous example was Title III of the Voting Rights Act of 1970, which guaranteed eighteen-year-old citizens the right to vote in state and federal elections. During congressional hearings, top DOJ officials had testified that Title III was unconstitutional, and President Nixon, when he signed the bill, expressed the same view. Although informing the Supreme Court that the president believed that only a constitutional amendment could solve the problem, Solicitor General Erwin Griswold defended the law in *Oregon v. Mitchell* (1970). Although the Court struck down the requirement as applied to state elections, it upheld its application to federal ones. This declaration of professional independence made The Grizzer (as Harvard law students called him when he was their dean) a legend in the Solicitor General's Office.[27]

Team Gay's lawyers were impressed by the practical wisdom found within DOJ's Office of Legal Counsel (OLC), which had sent them a collection of historical letters notifying Congress that DOJ was not going to defend the constitutionality of a federal statute. For example, the executive branch had declined, on separation-of-powers grounds, to defend the independent counsel statute and the legislative veto. In both instances, Congress itself defended the laws. Even the solicitor general recognized, as an exception to the duty to defend, statutes that reflected congressional aggrandizement at the expense of the executive branch, but this principle could not be applied to DOMA. However, another precedent could be. As OLC's Marty Lederman reminded everyone, Acting Solicitor General John Roberts had in 1989 refused to defend the FCC's policy favoring race diversity in programming, because the first Bush administration considered race-based preferences a fundamental violation of equal protection.[28]

OLC pointed to another possible exception. In 1995, Congress passed a Department of Defense budget that included a provision that would have required the armed forces to dismiss any soldier who was HIV-positive. President Clinton vetoed that bill, but Congress retained the provision in the successor bill. To keep the armed forces funded, Clinton signed the bill into law, accompanied by a statement that the provision was "blatantly discriminatory and highly punitive," a constitutional atrocity. OLC developed the administration's stance toward the HIV ban: the executive branch would implement the discriminatory provision but would not defend its constitutionality. Under that approach, the courts would have the final say, but with input and a political nudge from the president. The courts never reached that issue, because Congress repealed the HIV ban before it took effect.[29]

As an academic, Dawn Johnsen (Obama's initial choice to head the OLC) had written in favor of what we'd call a "Don't Defend, Do Enforce" approach, and Lederman elaborated on it within the Obama OLC. There was pushback from the White House counsel's office, where Dan Meltzer made an institutional counterargument. The duty to defend ought to be a strong baseline, and exceptions rare, because of the president's constitutional obligation to "take Care" to enforce and defend enacted laws. Presidential objections were best expressed through the veto power or efforts to repeal offensive legislation, like the HIV ban. Any departure from this baseline threatened to politicize the enforcement of statutes and raised separation-of-powers issues. If the current administration felt DOMA was indefensible, what would prevent the next administration from refusing to defend the Affordable Care Act? Team Gay called this the Sarah Palin argument: Would a refusal to defend DOMA embolden President Palin's DOJ to abandon any defense of Obamacare?[30]

ADMINISTRATIVE RECOGNITION
OF LESBIAN AND GAY UNIONS

Team Gay's primary agenda was still to figure out deliverables for lesbian and gay couples. Between July 2009 and July 2011, the administration took three kinds of actions that assured new benefits and rights for many families: (1) liberally interpreting broad statutory terms to include same-sex couples and their families; (2) promulgating rules, such as the hospital visitation rule, that created new regulatory categories to include LGBT families; and (3) exercising discretion not to apply existing law against such families. On April 27, 2010, for example, DOJ interpreted the Violence Against Women Act (VAWA) to include gender-motivated violence against persons of the same sex. Because of DOMA, VAWA's protection of spouses could not apply to lesbian and gay couples, but the law also protected "intimate partners" and "persons," which OLC interpreted to include same-sex partners. On June 22, the Department of Labor interpreted the Family and Medical Leave Act to assure mandatory leave for same-sex couples caring for children and one another.[31]

On June 2, 2010, the president ordered all agencies to work with OPM to interpret *families* expansively. His memorandum directed OPM and the General Services Administration to make sure that a child raised in a lesbian or gay household qualify as a "child" for federal childcare subsidies, that federal employee assistance programs include domestic partners, that federal retirement programs award annuities on the death of retirees to their same-sex partners, that LGBT families receive appropriate relocation expenses, and that lesbian and gay federal employees be eligible for unpaid leave to care for their families. "In the future, all agencies that provide new benefits to the spouses of Federal employees and their children should, to the extent permitted by law, also provide them to the same-sex domestic partners of their employees and those same-sex domestic partners' children."[32]

Many of the LGBT persons harmed by DOMA were binational couples, where one partner was a US citizen but the other was not. Immigration law throws up all sorts of barriers to such relationships, but the Obama Department of Homeland Security exercised enforcement discretion in a number of cases involving undocumented LGBT persons or families. That discretion included instances in which border agents failed to exclude such persons or families from entering the country, police or prosecutors delayed or failed to initiate removal proceedings against undocumented spouses and partners, and officials declined to enforce removal orders or decisions regarding detention or parole. Recall, from chapter 2, that federal authorities had kicked Australian immigrant Tony Sullivan out of the country, but he and his spouse, Richard Adams, sneaked back in. In 2009, they came out of the "undocumented closet." The Obama administration left them alone and ultimately apologized to Sullivan for the disrespectful treatment he had received.[33]

LEGISLATION AGAINST LGBT DISCRIMINATION

As promised at the Jennings-Davis fundraiser in March 2008, the Obama administration made hate crime legislation a priority in the 111th Congress (2009–2011), which was packed with large Democratic Party majorities. To get around dogged opposition from Senator Jeff Sessions and Representative Ike Skelton, the Matthew Shepard and James Byrd Jr. Hate Crimes Prevention Act of 2010 was attached as a rider to the National Defense Authorization Act. (Shepard was a gay man tortured and murdered in 1998 because of his sexual orientation.) With the support of five Republicans, the bill survived a Senate filibuster and breezed through both chambers with bipartisan majorities. The president signed it on October 28, 2009. The statute expanded the 1969 federal hate crime law to enhance the penalties for crimes motivated by a victim's actual or perceived gender, sexual orientation, gender identity, or disability.[34]

In his second State of the Union address, delivered on January 27, 2010, President Obama emphasized his proposal to repeal the exclusion of gay and bisexual persons from the armed forces. On February 2, Secretary of Defense Gates testified before the Senate Armed Services Committee that he had ordered the military to work out a plan for transitioning to open LGBT personnel.

Admiral Mullen told the senators that he thought gay people ought to serve openly. On October 12, in *Log Cabin Republicans v. United States,* federal district judge Virginia Phillips ruled that the statutory exclusion of openly gay soldiers violated the First Amendment rights of gay people who wanted to serve in the armed forces.[35]

Although Judge Phillips's injunction was stayed pending appeal, this was a wake-up call for Secretary Gates and the Joint Chiefs of Staff, who understood that the transition to an armed forces where gay soldiers could serve openly was inevitable. Did the Defense Department want to manage the transition itself, or have it judicially supervised? On November 30, the department released an exhaustive study concluding that soldiers were ready for openly gay and lesbian colleagues. Even after the Democrats had taken a shellacking in the midterm elections, the president insisted on pressing for repeal legislation in the lame duck session of the 111th Congress. Three days before Christmas, he signed the Don't Ask, Don't Tell Repeal Act of 2010, which set in motion a process for repeal of the 1993 law (a process completed by September 21, 2011).[36]

The repeal of the military exclusion left DOMA stranded as the only major federal discrimination against lesbian and gay Americans. Team Gay now concentrated its efforts on same-sex marriage and LGBT families, and they had a surprising new ally. During the Defense Department's working group deliberations, Colonel James Clapsaddle argued that once gays were "our men and women," DOMA would have to go. The top brass wanted all soldiers to enjoy the same rights and responsibilities of citizenship. Additionally, the military exclusion had brought a surprising show of Republican support for constitutional LGBT rights. Ken Mehlman, a former chairman of the Republican National Committee, had come out as gay earlier in 2010. He personally lobbied ten Republican senators, eight of whom joined the Democrats in voting for the Don't Ask, Don't Tell Repeal Act.[37]

The repeal of the military exclusion further undermined the credibility of the Pandora's box argument against LGBT rights. Ever since Jack Baker and Mike McConnell raised the possibility of gay marriage, Pandora's box was repeatedly deployed against it: if you redefine marriage, you will unleash untold evil consequences. This had been the last-ditch argument against repealing Don't Ask, Don't Tell. In March 2009, a statement ultimately signed by 1,167 retired generals and admirals predicted that allowing gays in the military would break the all-volunteer armed forces by crippling recruitment, retention, and cohesion. Yet when the exclusion ended on September 21, 2011, few even noticed. The new policy resulted in two verified resignations, both by chaplains, and the most thorough study of the effects found zero impact on military recruitment and retention and no net change in perceived unit cohesion. In 1993, it was feared that the mere presence of open homosexuals might scare away recruits, render young soldiers hysterical, and destabilize the barracks. In 2011, Pandora actually opened the box, and nothing came out. This was a big moment in the normalization of gay people, much as President Truman's desegregation of the armed forces (over hysterical claims of institutional collapse that were immediately falsified) helped integrate people of color into the body politic.[38]

The repeal of the military exclusion also sent an important symbolic message. Chief Justice Taney's infamous opinion in *Dred Scott*, denying citizenship to free black people, invoked state laws criminalizing interracial marriage as well as barring free black persons from serving in the militia. "Nothing could more strongly mark the entire repudiation of the African race. [H]e is not, by the institutions and laws of the State, numbered among its people. He forms no part of the sovereignty of the State, and is not therefore called on to uphold and defend it." Taney also cited the first federal militia law, passed in 1792, which limited service to "free able-bodied white male citizen[s]." The "African race" did owe "allegiance to the Government, whether they were slave or free; but it is repudiated, and rejected from the duties and obligations of citizenship in marked language." *Dred Scott* shows how our nation's cultural tradition links marriage, military service, and citizenship. Just as blacks could not claim completely equal citizenship until armed forces segregation, southern apartheid, and anti-miscegenation laws had been repudiated, so LGBT persons could not be equal citizens until consensual sodomy laws, the armed forces exclusion, and marriage bars were repudiated.[39]

Eric Holder's Letter of February 23, 2011

Although few officials expected DOMA to outlast the Obama administration, few had a clear idea how it might end. Lawsuits by LGBT movement groups forced the administration to take public actions informed by the recommendations of White House counsel. Several days each week, Rahm Emanuel assembled top White House advisers in the Oval Office to brief the president; White House counsel Bob Bauer (January 2010 to June 2011) kept Obama up-to-date on the status of the DOMA lawsuits, his and DOJ's thoughts on the level of scrutiny that ought to be applied, and the possibility that the executive branch might enforce DOMA but not defend it in court. A former professor of constitutional law, Obama understood all the arguments and said nothing to discourage the plan of action being developed by White House counsel and DOJ. It is striking to us that the president still did not support marriage equality as a political matter, but if his lawyers were right that sexual orientation was a constitutionally suspect classification, state marriage exclusions, and not just DOMA, were unconstitutional.

GLAD'S MASSACHUSETTS DOMA CASES

On July 8, 2010, federal district judge Joseph Tauro issued twin rulings that section 3 of DOMA (the pervasive denial of federal marriage or spousal rights or duties) violated both the Fifth Amendment's equality guarantees (*Gill v. Office of Personnel Management*) and the constitutional limitations on Congress's authority to burden the states (*Massachusetts v. U.S. Department of Health & Human Services*). Because the latter holding threatened other congressional programs and laws, the government's lawyers would certainly appeal *Massachusetts*. Whether to appeal Judge Tauro's decision in *Gill* was a more contentious matter altogether. Normally, the solicitor general makes that decision, but this was a matter on which other divisions of the department weighed in as well.[40]

The civil rights division, headed by Tom Perez, viewed *Gill* through the prism of human rights. Perez argued against appealing *Gill* and, if DOJ did appeal, in favor of strict scrutiny for exclusions based on sexual orientation. Like Nancy Cott at the *Perry* trial, which had just concluded, the civil rights division framed the marriage issue as a question of equal citizenship for LGBT Americans. Its lawyers also believed there was a third big exception to the duty to defend (in addition to cases where federal law was clearly invalid and where Congress was usurping presidential authority): cases where federal law treated an honorable minority as outcasts. As the only federal official with a national mandate and an accountability to all the people, the president not only was free to abandon class-based laws, but ought to do so.[41]

The solicitor general's office, representing the federal government in appellate litigation, took the opposite point of view. Acting Solicitor General Neal Katyal and Deputy Solicitor General Edwin Kneedler argued for a strong duty to defend—the argument earlier advanced within the White House by Dan Meltzer, who had returned to his Harvard professorship. Katyal and Kneedler also worried about how the president would justify abandoning the statute. Because the government pervasively relied on the rational basis test to defend federal statutes and policies, they did not want to invite heightened scrutiny, even in a good cause. Only once in recent history had DOJ argued for courts to upgrade scrutiny from rational basis to heightened scrutiny, and the Roberts brief in the FCC affirmative action case was not a precedent they wanted to build on.

Tony West's civil division remained internally divided, with Jody Hunt arguing for the duty to defend the law and Bob Kopp arguing that sexual orientation classifications ought to be subjected to heightened scrutiny. West and Kopp also pondered whether DOMA satisfied an intermediate standard they dubbed "rational basis on steroids," drawn from *Romer*. (The rational basis test required only a *plausible* connection to a legitimate state interest; *Romer* seemed to require that anti-gay policies needed a *demonstrable* connection, to avoid the impression that they were motivated by animus.) Probably not, but they worried whether the civil division should concede that the rational basis test sometimes had teeth—a concession that might come back to bite the government in another case. Reflecting his academic background, President Obama, in an interview, gave a shout-out to rational basis on steroids: "certain groups may be vulnerable to stereotypes, certain groups may be subject to discrimination, and . . . the court's job historically is to pay attention to that." Was discrimination against this minority really needed to advance public policy for everyone? Or was it just the scapegoating of a disliked minority?[42]

Sidestepping the departmental debate, Attorney General Eric Holder decided that in the Massachusetts appeals DOJ should follow the First Circuit's precedents, which required only a rational basis for reviewing sexual orientation–based discrimination. On January 13, 2011, DOJ filed its appellate brief in *Gill*, arguing that Congress could plausibly have concluded that DOMA (1) preserved a national status quo at the federal level, while states engaged in a period of experimentation, (2) created a uniform and easy-to-administer statutory rule, or (3) respected the authority of each state to choose its own course. These justifications all boiled down to administrative convenience—an interest that no one thought would meet any kind of heightened scrutiny.[43]

THE NEW YORK DOMA CASES

On November 9, 2010, two challenges to DOMA were filed in the Second Circuit, where the level-of-scrutiny question was still open. Robbie Kaplan, working with the ACLU, filed *Windsor v. United States* in New York federal court; Mary Bonauto and GLAD filed *Pedersen v. United States* in Connecticut federal court (see chapter 19 for a detailed account of these lawsuits). Reflecting Team Gay's research and a consensus among his closest advisers (Kathryn Reummler, Donald Verrilli, Kate Andrias, and Kathleen Hartnett), White House counsel Bauer strongly recommended to the president that sexual orientation ought to be considered a suspect classification, that DOMA was unconstitutional, but that the administration should enforce DOMA until the Supreme Court invalidated it. Bauer was also meeting weekly with Holder, who no doubt knew that the White House counsel and probably the president were prepared to abandon DOMA in the Second Circuit. In the fall of 2010, Obama met with gay bloggers who took him to task for opposing marriage equality; he responded, "attitudes evolve, including mine." Bob Bauer and his office were prime movers in that evolution.[44]

After the Second Circuit lawsuits were filed, the attorney general asked the relevant divisions whether DOJ should continue to defend DOMA. Tom Perez and the civil rights division weighed in with a detailed memorandum arguing that sexual orientation easily met the criteria for heightened scrutiny. Perez and Christopher Schroeder, who headed the Office of Legal Policy, strongly endorsed Don't Defend, Do Enforce. Marty Lederman (back at Georgetown but still working with OLC on some issues) lent support to the Perez-Schroeder position by demonstrating that the duty to defend was more of a strong presumption that could be overridden by the president. In a conference call with Tony West, civil division attorneys reached a rough consensus that the Constitution required heightened scrutiny of sexual orientation discrimination. This was a new stance for the civil division.[45]

In a series of tense departmental meetings, Acting Solicitor General Neal Katyal carried the flag for the Meltzer position. At one such meeting, where Perez, Schroeder, and West formed a united front in favor of Don't Defend, Do Enforce, Katyal pressed the Sarah Palin argument for a strict duty to defend. Now at the civil division after her service with White House counsel, Danielle Gray marveled to Marty Lederman at how much process DOJ was devoting to this debate. That was all well and good, "but if you think that, at the end of this process, the president is going to concur in the department's filing a brief saying DOMA should be subjected to rational basis review, then you obviously don't know anything about Barack Obama."

Katyal persisted. He did not know Obama well but felt that Holder, who was his mentor, would back him up on this matter. What he did not know was what a heavy thumb White House counsel Bauer had put on the scale. A memorandum from Kathleen Hartnett (who had succeeded Ali Nathan), Ian

Bassin, and Kate Shaw to Bauer and President Obama summarized the arguments and conclusions within DOJ and provided a detailed analysis in support of Don't Defend, Do Enforce. Holder hosted a conference call with the various divisions and offices in January 2011, and the strong weight of departmental opinion was consistent with Team Gay's analysis and Bauer's personal recommendation.

ERIC HOLDER'S LETTER SUPPORTING STRICT SCRUTINY

Journalist Jo Becker reported that the decision to abandon DOMA was made at the White House's Super Bowl party on February 6, 2011. Barack Obama raised the issue with his old friend Eric Holder and suggested that DOJ not defend DOMA but that the government continue to apply it. Eric laughed and said that this is exactly what DOJ had decided—and that he thought it the right thing to do. "And, as is typical of [Obama], he just kind of said, 'Yeah, it is right. I think it's the right thing to do, Eric, so let's get back to the game.'" The reality, of course, was that both men knew, weeks and even months earlier, what White House counsel and the various divisions were recommending—Don't Defend, Do Enforce—and both were comfortable with the recommendation. And each knew that the other was okay with it. So whatever conversation they had at the 2011 Super Bowl party only confirmed a White House–driven consensus that had been consolidated in 2010.[46]

On February 23, 2011, Attorney General Holder delivered a letter to House Speaker Boehner. "After careful consideration, including a review of my recommendation, the President has concluded that given a number of factors, including a documented history of discrimination, classifications based on sexual orientation should be subject to a heightened standard of scrutiny. The President has also concluded that Section 3 of DOMA, as applied to legally married same-sex couples, fails to meet that standard and is therefore unconstitutional." DOJ was not going to defend DOMA, but federal agencies would "continue to comply with Section 3 of DOMA, consistent with the Executive's obligation to take care that the laws be faithfully executed, unless and until Congress repeals Section 3 or the judicial branch renders a definitive verdict against the law's constitutionality." Despite some partisan objection, there was much more support or acquiescence than opposition. For the first time since it began polling on the issue, the Gallup Poll found in early 2011 that most Americans favored marriage equality, 53-45 percent.[47]

On April 9, the House of Representatives' Bipartisan Legislative Advisory Group (BLAG) voted 3-2 to defend DOMA. Former solicitor general Paul Clement and his law firm, King and Spalding, were retained to represent BLAG. There was an immediate kerfuffle. After accepting the representation, King and Spalding got heat from some gay-friendly corporate clients, egged on by HRC, and the firm's chairman told Clement that they could not represent BLAG. Clement resigned as a partner that day, with this statement: "Representing unpopular defendants is what lawyers do. When it comes to lawyers, the surest way to be on the wrong side of history is to abandon a client in the face of hostile criticism." He joined Bancroft PLLC, which ably represented BLAG. Intervening in the First, Second, and Ninth Circuit cases, BLAG opposed heightened scrutiny and argued that DOMA was a rational response to problems of statutory administration in the face of changing state law and could also be justified as encouragement of responsible procreation. On February 22, 2012, in *Golinski v. OPM*, federal district judge Jeffrey White rejected those arguments.[48]

Pressure on the President to Come Out of the Marriage Closet

In the wake of Holder's letter to Congress, observers both inside and outside the administration wondered why President Obama did not take that opportunity to complete his evolution on the issue of marriage equality. If DOMA were unconstitutional under heightened scrutiny, then how could state junior-DOMAs and (worse) Super-DOMAs be constitutional? The president, apparently, wanted to proceed slowly and not to get ahead of public opinion. DOMA enjoyed virtually no public enthusiasm, but state-defined marriage remained a polarizing issue.

On July 27, 2011, however, Joel Benenson, the Obama campaign's pollster, and Jan van Lohuizen, a pollster for George W. Bush, discussed public opinion in a Freedom to Marry event at the National Press Club. Both reported that a majority of respondents now supported marriage equality. The pollsters had never seen such a rapid volte-face on such a divisive social issue. They were seeing increases in support from every age, religion, party, and income category. Also, "supporters of marriage for gay couples feel as strongly about the issue as opponents do, something that was not the case in the recent past." The rise in the poll numbers would very likely continue "as Americans currently under the age of forty make up a greater percentage of the electorate." Freedom to

Marry made sure that the White House had all of this information and argued that the American public was comfortable with equal marriage rights, so long as it was presented to them in a persuasive manner.[49]

The poll numbers were complemented by tangible results in the state-by-state campaigns for marriage equality. When Obama was elected president, there were two states handing out marriage licenses—one of which stopped the next day because of Proposition 8 (to be replaced by Connecticut, which started issuing marriage licenses soon after the election). Five states had civil unions or comprehensive domestic partnerships, and five had some other institution granting some marriage rights to registered couples. In 2009, during Obama's first year in office, a net of three states (Vermont, New Hampshire, and Iowa) and the District of Columbia granted full marriage rights, two more established comprehensive domestic partnerships, and one created limited partnership rights. In 2010–2011, while the Obama administration was moving toward its constitutional renunciation of DOMA, four more states adopted civil unions. In California, Judge Walker's August 2010 decision in the Proposition 8 case promised to flip that state back to marriage equality. On June 15, 2011, the New York legislature passed and Governor Cuomo signed the Empire State's Marriage Equality Act. In February and March 2012, governors signed marriage equality laws in Washington and Maryland. It was expected that those laws would be subject to referenda in November 2012, when an initiative to establish marriage equality would also be on the ballot in Maine.

Pending the results of the referenda, there were by May 2012 as many as eight marriage states and the District of Columbia, eight civil union or comprehensive domestic partnership states, and three states with lesser forms of relationship recognition. These nineteen states, as illustrated in Figure 3, were the core jurisdictions for President Obama's reelection campaign, but they were not enough to win the Electoral College. How would the marriage issue play in Florida, Pennsylvania, and Ohio? The president had won all of them in 2008 and would need to win at least one in 2012.

In September 2011, Barack Obama had lunch at the White House with Ken Mehlman, his Harvard Law School classmate and Republican ally on the Don't Ask, Don't Tell repeal. Contrary to the president's super-cautious reelection team, Mehlman made a political case for a presidential endorsement of marriage equality. "People vote based on attributes, not issues," the GOP strategist argued. And what voters liked most about Obama was his authenticity and his ability to unite Americans around his positive vision. Young voters were wondering why he was not already supporting the freedom to marry. On No-

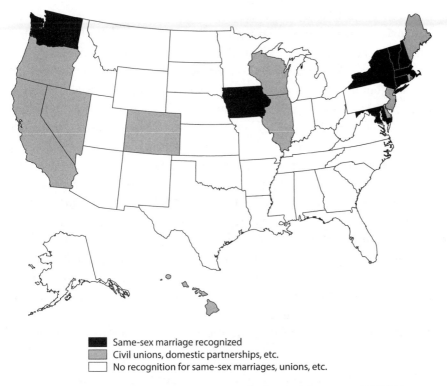

Same-sex marriage recognized
Civil unions, domestic partnerships, etc.
No recognition for same-sex marriages, unions, etc.

Figure 3 Marriage map, May 5, 2012. (Cartography by Patricia Page and Bill Nelson.)

vember 10, Mehlman sent campaign strategist David Plouffe an email outlining a scenario for the president to come out in favor of marriage equality. His
scenario reflected the sophisticated messaging research that his colleagues in
the Proposition 8 team and Freedom to Marry had provided him and that
struck him as politically savvy.[50]

To frame the issue, Mehlman suggested language like this for the president:
"I've said before that my position has been evolving, and Michelle and I have
been having a similar conversation in our family that lots of American families have been having on marriage equality." After admitting his earlier preference for civil unions, Obama should suggest that he and his wife "teach
Sasha and Malia about America's greatness and how we've constantly enlarged
the circle and expanded freedom, [and] we no longer feel we can make an exception that treats our gay friends differently just because of who they love."
Why not? "Many of them have made life-long commitments to people they love,
just like Michelle and I have. And they should be treated the same by their
government."[51]

Jim Messina, Obama's 2012 campaign manager, and other political advisers preferred that the move come after the election, especially if the Republicans nominated former Massachusetts governor Mitt Romney. Because of his chilly reaction to the *Goodridge* decision, Romney would attract little LGBT backing, but his likely support for civil unions would not energize religious conservatives unless the president came out for full marriage equality. In contrast, Democratic National Committee (DNC) chair Debbie Wasserman Schultz and executive director Patrick Gaspard were committed to endorsing marriage equality in the party platform. In February, Freedom to Marry launched a "Democrats: Say I Do!" campaign. House Minority Leader Nancy Pelosi was among the first to take the pledge: "We support the full inclusion of all families in the life of our nation, with equal respect, responsibilities, and protections under the law, including the freedom to marry." Los Angeles mayor Anthony Villaraigosa, slated to chair the party's nominating convention, openly supported marriage equality, as did many of the other honorary cochairs of the Obama reelection campaign. The "Say I Do" campaign ramped up the pressure on a president who had probably already decided to come out of the constitutional closet and endorse marriage equality sometime in 2012.[52]

The Vice President and President Come Out

On Friday May 4, 2012, Vice President Biden taped a segment of *Meet the Press* that would air the following Sunday. Although his staff preparation had focused almost exclusively on the economy, gay families were on his mind. In April, he had appeared at a Los Angeles fundraiser held at the home of HBO executive Michael Lombardo and his husband, Sonny Ward. Biden came into their house through the kitchen—and was immediately set upon by their two children, ages four and seven. His face lit up as he interacted with the kids. "I wish everybody could see this," he later said to the donors. "All you got to do is look into the eyes of those kids. And no one can wonder, no one can wonder whether or not they are cared for or nurtured and loved and reinforced. . . . Things are changing so rapidly, it's going to become a political liability in the great near term for an individual to say, 'I oppose gay marriage.' Mark my words."[53]

Yet Biden's staff were caught entirely off guard when he launched into a discussion of marriage during his *Meet the Press* taping. Marriage, he said, is very simple: "Who do you love, and will you be loyal to the person you love?" That's "what all marriages at their root are about, whether their marriage is of lesbians or gay men or heterosexuals." Host David Gregory followed up: "Are you comfortable with same-sex marriage now?" Joe Biden answered: "I am absolutely comfortable with the fact that men marrying men, women marrying women, and heterosexual men marrying women are entitled to the same exact rights, all the civil rights, all the civil liberties. And quite frankly I don't see much of a distinction beyond that." Rambling a bit, he gave a shout-out to *Will & Grace* (a popular TV show featuring zany gay men and the straight women who loved them) and closed with the joy he felt when visiting a male couple and their children in Los Angeles. "I wish every American could see the look of love those kids had in their eyes for [their two dads]. And they wouldn't have any doubt about what this is about."[54]

This was seen at the time as another example of Biden's lovable-but-aggravating spontaneity—but we don't buy it. Sources close to the vice president believe his remarks were far from a goofy gaffe and were, instead, a sincere expression of a long-considered policy position and a gambit to turn up the heat on the president. As the most politically experienced person in the Obama administration, the vice president was frustrated that the campaign was ignoring his advice that the time was ripe for the president to support full marriage equality and to release an executive order barring sexual orientation and gender identity discrimination by government contractors. Like Mehlman, Biden was certain the marriage issue would energize the president's base of support. The people who reacted most negatively would not have voted for Obama in the first place.

The campaign team still did not see it that way. Axelrod tried to walk back Biden's remarks, and Messina told the DNC to take the position that there was nothing new here. A DNC official responded that the press considered the walk-back laughable, and so the reelection team was stuck. Obama reacted more mildly than his protective campaign officials. He joked that Biden had "gotten ahead of his skis" on the issue, but also seemed relieved. The day after *Meet the Press,* education secretary Arne Duncan came out in favor of marriage equality on *Morning Joe.* Because Duncan was personally close to the Obamas, his endorsement was a signal that the president was prepared to make the same move. The White House put together a media event for the afternoon of Wednesday, May 9.[55]

Before facing the camera, however, the president arranged a conference call with eight or nine leading African American ministers. Obama felt he owed them a heads-up before he dropped the marriage bomb, but it may have also been an opportunity for him to face his personal demons. Was it inconsistent for a person of faith to support marriage for lesbian and gay couples? Not only did he finally answer no to that question, he was willing to take the heat for it from faith mentors. Only a few of the pastors on the call welcomed the president's conversion on this issue, and more than one gave him fire and brimstone. After facing their anger, Obama turned to a more embracing encounter with Robin Roberts, the charismatic lesbian of color who hosted *Good Morning America*.

Drawing from Ken Mehlman's suggestions, Barack Obama offered his journey story: "I had hesitated on gay marriage, in part because I thought civil unions would be sufficient. I was sensitive to the fact that, for a lot of people, the word marriage was something that evokes very powerful traditions, religious beliefs, and so forth." But this was not a stable belief. Over several years, he had discussed the issue with friends, family, and White House coworkers, some raising children within their relationships or marriages. He contemplated the gay soldiers, laying down their lives for their country yet "constrained" by their inability to get married like everyone else. "At a certain point, I've just concluded that, for me personally, it is important for me to go ahead and affirm that I think same-sex couples should be able to get married." The president emphasized the influence of his wife, Michelle, and his daughters, Malia and Sasha. "You know, Malia and Sasha, they have friends whose parents are same-sex couples. There have been times where Michelle and I have been sitting around the dinner table and we're talking about their friends and their parents. And Malia and Sasha, it wouldn't dawn on them that somehow their friends' parents would be treated differently."

Because he supported *both* complete equality for LGBT people *and* respect for the special role of religion-based conjugal marriage, Barack Obama was a classic example of a conflicted voter on this issue. Like Tom and Jan (Yes on 8's cartoon couple who talked over the issue when it was put before California voters in 2008), Obama that year had tilted toward civil unions as a way to resolve the conflict. But like many Californians who voted Yes on 8, he was not entirely happy with his stance and did not believe it was his final resting place. That Michelle and their children supported marriage equality put pressure on Barack, as did the hundreds of lesbian and gay couples, and their children, that he encountered. Interacting with them, the president grew ever more certain that their families were no different from married families—and that civil unions were no longer an honorable way to respect those couples, their children, and their equal citizenship.

Obama's journey from civil unions to marriage for LGBT couples was America's journey. And the 2012 election was an immediate test: Would the marriage-embracing president turn back the challenge of Governor Romney, who rejected marriage equality? One of the battleground states that year was Michigan, where April DeBoer and Jayne Rowse were suing Governor Snyder to recognize their family of two moms, three young children, and a doting grandmother. The nurses' attorneys, Dana Nessel and Carole Stanyar, had amended the complaint to add a marriage equality claim in September—and they were sure that their claim was righteous. Key reasons for their optimism were the Holder letter in 2011, the briefs filed by the Obama administration in the DOMA cases, and the president's warm embrace of marriage equality that May. Obama gave them hope that they were not wasting their time. Would socially conservative Michigan deliver its electoral votes for the president after he took a position that neither he nor the country was ready for in 2008? Would the voters in Maryland and Washington overturn the marriage laws enacted by their legislatures? Would the voters in Maine opt for marriage equality, after rejecting it in 2009? Would Minnesota's voters amend the state constitution with a proposed DOMA?

Between 2008 and 2012, the marriage equality movement took its own conceptual and political journey. How can marriage be won at the ballot box? How can marriage equality supporters persuade enough conflicted voters to come down on the side of marriage rather than the status quo? Social scientists, political messaging specialists, grassroots organizers, and campaign managers on the marriage equality—or freedom to marry—side suggested a strategy for taking the nation on the same journey as that taken by Barack Obama.

18 • Behind the Glass

What makes people change their minds about deep-seated values? We don't do it often. When people do change their minds, emotions and values play a bigger role than facts and reasoning.

The National LGBTQ Task Force holds an annual conference called Creating Change. The 2009 conference in Denver (January 29–February 1) focused on finding a way forward on marriage equality in the wake of Proposition 8. Attending the conference to share the results of their synthesis on how to do pro-LGBT messaging on a wide array of policies (the "Toolkit"; chapter 14), Sean Lund from GLAAD and Ineke Mushovic from MAP met their friend Thalia Zepatos for coffee. All three had suggested a different approach from that taken by the California No on 8 campaign. Conflicted voters—those who knew and liked LGBT people but were reluctant to tinker with traditional marriage—were not moved by No on 8's legal rights-and-fairness arguments nearly as much as judges were. Mushovic and Lund's synthesis of existing research suggested that marriage equality advocates needed to appeal to voters' values and emotions. Among the lessons the Task Force had learned from the marriage initiatives in 2004–2008 was that the most persuasive approach was lengthy conversations with conflicted voters about the reality of lesbian and gay families and the harms inflicted when they were denied basic freedoms.[1]

From her own experience with the Task Force and with earlier ballot campaigns, Thalia Zepatos had a clear view of the next step. The daughter of second-generation immigrants, she grew up in a closely knit Greek Orthodox community in Yonkers, New York, and had been involved in a wide range of progressive causes. As a young organizer, she did grassroots support for the ERA in Florida in 1978, where she encountered echoes of the 1977 "Save Our

Children" campaign against gay rights. When she moved to Oregon to work on reproductive freedom issues, Zepatos became directly involved with opposition to the 1988 and 1992 anti-gay ballot measures. She was a central strategist for the 1992 campaign against Ballot Measure 9, which would have added to the state constitution a directive that the government must educate "Oregon's youth" that "homosexuality, pedophilia, sadism or masochism" are "abnormal, wrong, unnatural and perverse and they are to be discouraged and avoided." Morally offended by its anti-gay message, Zepatos threw her heart and soul into opposing Measure 9. One day in southeast Portland, she was at a stoplight, her car adorned with No on 9 stickers, when guys in a pickup truck started lesbian-bashing her. She got out of her car and dared the rednecks to confront her face-to-face. The truckers drove off shouting homophobic epithets. Apart from revealing her insane bravery, this incident illustrated both the hysterical bigotry of some Yes on 9 Oregonians and many feminists' emotional commitment to lesbian and gay rights. Measure 9 failed, 55.5 to 44.5 percent.[2]

As a feminist, Zepatos was skeptical of the value of fighting for a right to marry but warmed to it once she realized that it was a frontal assault on homophobia: the foundational anti-gay prejudice was, she realized, the feeling that homosexuals were dirty and promiscuous, and the central stereotype was that they were incapable of family and commitment. In 2004, she was a consultant to Basic Rights Oregon's textbook campaign to defeat a ballot measure to add a junior-DOMA to the state constitution. Zepatos felt the messaging was not quite right. The campaign's biggest ad purchase showed a judge talking about the many marital rights denied to lesbian and gay couples. These ads did not resonate with undecided voters. Voters told canvassers that they were more persuaded by an episode from the television series *ER*, where a lesbian surgeon, devastated by the death of her partner, faced an effort by the partner's blood family to seize custody of the child the couple had been raising together. In November 2004, the junior-DOMA initiative won comfortably, 56.6-43.4 percent.

After the disastrous 2004 election results, new polls suggested reasons why the rights-and-fairness messaging was not working. A 2005 Gill Foundation study reported that 57 percent of respondents believed that lesbian and gay Americans did not share their basic values. "We were shocked when we discovered this values gap," said the foundation's Tim Sweeney. "As it turned out, our opponents had successfully painted us as unconnected, free-floating atoms who weren't connected to family, society or society's institutions." How could those attitudes be changed? HRC's Seth Kilbourn and Geoff Kors (Equality

California's executive director) thought that focus groups and field experiments, in which different neighbors received different mailings or messages, might be a good way to secure more precise information and figure out better tactics.[3]

At the same time, progressive message experts were turning to psychological research into the way people formed ideas and reached conclusions. A pioneer in this field was Dr. Phyllis Watts, a Sacramento applied psychologist who understood human decision-making and opinion formation as complicated processes of emotional reaction, identification and values affirmation, and fact processing. Her research was based on her in-depth, systematic review of videotaped interviews of individuals, dyads (such as spouses), and small focus groups. Typically, these interviews were conducted by a professional mediator, while experts studied people's facial and body reactions, as well as their language, from behind the glass—namely, a half-silvered mirror in the interview room. Because moral judgments followed emotional connections and reactions for most humans, Watts looked for cues to deep emotional and self-identification concerns that people had about public issues. The insights Watts gained from this method helped the Dewey Square Group prevail against 2005–2006 ballot campaigns seeking to impose parental vetoes on their daughters' right to secure abortions.[4]

To figure out better messaging on the marriage issue, EQCA suggested an experimental campaign of public education funded by the Civil Marriage Collaborative (CMC). Freedom to Marry and the Task Force, partners in the project, nominated Zepatos to be the lead consultant for "Let California Ring." Zepatos worked with Margaret Conway's firm to develop new messaging for a limited market, Santa Barbara in Southern California. The idea that tested the best among focus groups was a commercial called *The Garden Wedding*. Produced in 2007, the ad started with a tender scene between a father and his daughter, decked out in her wedding dress. In short order, the bride and her father encountered obstacles as they walked to the wedding site—a door that wouldn't open, tightly parked cars blocking the bridal path, a tree limb that knocked off the bridal veil, a misbehaving flower girl, and a nasty old lady whose cane tripped the bride at the last minute. As the disheveled bride looked sadly at the groom, the caption appeared: "What if you couldn't marry the person you love? Every day gay and lesbian couples are prevented from marrying. Support the freedom to marry." The ad avoided preachy talk about rights and instead invited conflicted voters to empathize with people prevented from marrying. In early 2008, California Ring ran *The Garden Wedding* as a public

education ad in Santa Barbara County and coordinated its message with intense on-the-ground organizing and grassroots events, such as house parties
to view and discuss the ad. Santa Barbara was the only county in Southern
California to vote No on 8.[5]

While the *Garden Wedding* experiment was playing out in Santa Barbara,
Phyllis Watts was telling the statewide No on 8 campaign that it needed to develop messaging that appealed to conflicted voters' self-identifications, values, and emotional commitments. Lund and Mushovic reported to the
campaign that the focus group studies summarized in their 2007–2008
Toolkit showed the futility of the campaign's fairness-and-rights-based strategies and suggested that a better focus would be how the love and commitment in lesbian and gay families resembled that of traditional families. These
arguments were not entirely new. The marriage campaigns in Hawai'i, Vermont, Massachusetts, and (especially) Connecticut had made similar
claims. What was most novel was the experts' suggestion that rights-based
arguments were actually counterproductive and that the best messengers for
gay marriage were almost never gay couples themselves but married straight
couples, with whom conflicted (straight) voters could identify.[6]

Complementing these ideas about messaging content were ideas about how
to deliver the messages face-to-face. The Task Force's David Fleischer and Sayre
Reece had concluded that the best way to reach conflicted voters was through
long one-on-one conversations with neighbors, friends, and well-trained volunteers or paid canvassers. Follow-up was important. They had learned this
lesson the hard way: under the auspices of the Los Angeles LGBT Center,
Fleischer spent night and day working to defeat California's Proposition 8;
Reece had managed the campaign against the 2004 Kentucky Super-DOMA
and was the statewide field director for No on 8. Conflicted voters were not
persuaded by short ads, robocalls, or scripted conversations. They were moved
by conversations that allowed them to explain their reservations about opening up marriage to LGBT persons, with gentle suggestions about other viewpoints they might consider. At the Creating Change conference, Zepatos, Lund,
and Mushovic agreed that these conversations, as well as public advertisements,
had to avoid any talk of rights and should reboot with a focus on values. Also
on the same page was Lanae Erickson, who headed the Commitment Campaign of Third Way, a center-left think tank. She and Zepatos met at the conference and became collaborators.[7]

In 2008–2009, Phyllis Watts and San Francisco pollster Amy Simon felt
that the voters' verdict on Proposition 8 required marriage equality supporters

Thalia Zepatos. (Photo by Barbara Gundle. Used by
permission of Thalia Zepatos.)

to engage in new research on how to persuade conflicted voters to reconsider
their emotional reluctance to expand marriage. Zepatos agreed. At the 2009
Denver conference, she proposed a Marriage Research Consortium, which
would collect studies and tests for effective messaging; would immediately
share that research with all member groups, thereby preventing duplication
of effort; and would conduct its own research to address key unanswered
questions. What was their proactive message, and what language delivered it
best? How should they respond to parental fears that gay marriage would undermine their families? What delivery mechanism worked best to persuade
conflicted voters? Third Way, MAP, GLAAD, and other groups agreed to participate in the consortium, which was a major advance in the creation of a national message to support the freedom of LGBT persons to marry. Regular
conference calls made sure that all participating groups were working together
in what Erickson and Zepatos dubbed "radical cooperation."[8]

Complementing Simon and Watts's research, Lisa Grove's firm assembled
dozens of focus groups in Portland, Oregon. Watching from behind the glass,
Grove and Zepatos confirmed the distressing news that gay-friendly straight
people viewed lesbian and gay relationships as based on rights and benefits—

unlike their own, which they described in terms of love and commitment. How could they convince these nice people that lesbian and gay couples wanted to marry for the same reasons they did? Showing them videos of lesbian and gay couples was not persuasive. Grove learned that the most effective advocates for lesbian and gay couples were straight people with whom the ambivalent audience could identify—older relatives or parents, pastors or priests or rabbis, and ordinary neighbors or colleagues. In earlier campaigns, the Task Force had relied on straight allies, including faith leaders, though it had caught criticism for not having LGBT people speak for themselves.[9]

This research suggested the value of a particular kind of *journey story*, in which mature, gay-friendly heterosexuals explained how they changed their minds about marriage equality once they engaged with lesbian and gay couples and discovered that they partnered out of love, commitment, and family—the same reasons married couples did. Once conflicted straights began to ask themselves how they would feel if they, too, could not have gotten married, and once they connected that insight with their faith tradition's teaching of the Golden Rule (do unto others as you would have them do unto you), they were better able to understand and sometimes to support claims for marriage equality.[10]

These insights had ample precedents, as discussed in previous chapters of this volume. The New England campaigns for marriage and the California campaign for domestic partnership relied on life stories like that of Julie and Hillary Goodridge. In Massachusetts, Josh Friedes had touted the value of "unexpected messengers," clerics who vouched for the idea that lesbian and gay families were just like straight families. Building on these insights and prior research, the new messaging researchers empirically honed the basic insights of earlier psychological studies for the marriage issue, developed specific ad campaigns based on those insights, tested those ads with new focus groups and polling, and then shared the research with the movement groups that joined the consortium. In May 2010, the consortium launched *Why Marriage Matters,* a national public education effort that offered Internet-accessible materials for persuading conflicted voters to support LGBT couples' freedom to marry. The materials included sample journey stories and ads that were run in various jurisdictions based on those stories.[11]

The institutional host for the consortium and for *Why Marriage Matters* was Evan Wolfson's Freedom to Marry. After Proposition 8, Wolfson persuaded the Gill Foundation, the Haas Fund, and other donors to invest in what he called Freedom to Marry 2.0. This allowed the organization to expand from five employees to forty and its annual budget to grow from $3 million to $12 million. Its goal was to guide funders to the states where it felt marriage equality could be achieved and then to provide strategic and messaging assistance to those campaigns. In 2011, Freedom to Marry published *Moving Marriage Forward*, which summarized the new research and its implications for values-based messaging—love and commitment, the Golden Rule—and personal conversations and outreach in minority communities. Armed with these materials, Amy Simon, Phyllis Watts, Thalia Zepatos, and Marc Solomon (Freedom to Marry's national campaign director) worked directly with state marriage campaigns to develop their own commercials, videos, training manuals, and messaging tools.[12]

Freedom to Marry 2.0 brought together state and national groups into a more unified educational and political campaign at the very moment when marriage equality was picking up steam from the Obama election, the New England triumphs, the events in California, and the *Varnum* decision in Iowa. In 2011 and early 2012, major legislative victories in New York, Maryland, and Washington were driven by local organizing but were strongly assisted by the national organizations (especially regarding fundraising and, in the case of New York, strategic assistance). And 2012 was shaping up to be a watershed year: the North Carolina and Minnesota legislatures had placed constitutional DOMAs on the ballot, Maine's freedom to marry group put a marriage equality initiative on that state's ballot, and traditional marriage groups forced referenda that might veto Maryland's and Washington's marriage equality laws from going into effect.

All but the North Carolina campaign ultimately followed the messaging ideas synthesized in the MAP-GLAAD Toolkit and honed into ad strategies developed by the new researchers and shared through the consortium. The campaigns also followed the Task Force's innovations regarding grassroots canvassing. Organizationally, the campaigns revealed some variety. The consortium, CMC, and Freedom to Marry incentivized a more uniform, disciplined approach to messaging and canvassing in the Maine, Minnesota, and Washington campaigns. The Maryland campaign was less directed by the national coordinators. Although HRC played a major role, Governor O'Malley and local leaders drove the campaign in the Old Line State. Importantly, Maryland was the most racially diverse state of the four voting in November 2012. LGBT marriage movement organizations had traditionally not been attuned to minority communities, and black Evangelical voters were the most skeptical audience. A challenge for both the old politics of marriage and the new messaging research was how to persuade these voters.[13]

The Five 2012 Marriage Initiatives and Referenda

The 2012 elections were the first time the national electorate pondered the marriage equality issue with both sides vigorously represented in the debate. With some local variation, the National Organization for Marriage (NOM) directed one side while Freedom to Marry and HRC coordinated the other, with input from the Task Force and Gill Action. Overall, the electoral terrain was much more favorable for the marriage equality side than it had been in 2008. Having scored just one victory in a direct marriage vote (Arizona, 2006), however, the LGBT coalitions were taking nothing for granted. They faced Frank Schubert—the maestro of marriage campaigns—in all five states.

THE UNIFIED CAMPAIGN FOR ONE-MAN, ONE-WOMAN MARRIAGE

Led by charismatic Brian Brown, today the father of nine children, NOM was the force unifying the one-man, one-woman marriage campaigns that year. Its new national political director, Frank Schubert, was the effective campaign manager for all five ballot measures. Schubert was well versed in the psychology-of-voting literature, and his experience in initiative campaigns gave him an edge on messaging. As in 2008–2009, his plan was to mobilize a big turnout from the religious base by grassroots efforts at the congregational level and to persuade conflicted voters that changing the definition of marriage would affect them as parents, business persons, and church members. At the end of the campaign, he planned to run advertisements dramatically featuring children whose lives could be ruined if marriage were unsettled. Schubert also counted on grassroots support from African American and Hispanic voters, groups that had supported Proposition 8.

The NOM campaigns confronted three big changes between 2008 and 2012. The most important was the overall shift of public opinion. By September 2011, there was majority support for the freedom to marry—partly because of President Obama's initiatives, partly because of the 8 trial in California, but mainly because of the post-2004 flood of married lesbian and gay couples and the fact that the sky had not fallen upon the increasing number of marriage equality states. The more normal LGBT marriages and families became for middle America, the harder Schubert's job would be. Normalization also affected his campaigns financially. Contributions to NOM fell from $9.1 million in 2010 to $6.2 million in 2011 (most of that reduced sum came from just two megadonors). This reflected a growing concern that contributors to one-man, one-woman marriage campaigns would encounter pushback, shaming, intimidation, and even retaliation from angry gay people. NOM and its allies reported several dozen examples of illegal retaliation after Proposition 8. Schubert considered bullying by gay people and their allies to be the number one challenge to success for his side in 2012.[14]

Second, the freedom to marry campaigns had the advantage of organizational and grassroots head starts in three of the five states. Minnesota and North Carolina followed the California scenario, where one-man, one-woman marriage supporters got organized early, put the issue on the ballot, and formed umbrella organizations to conduct the campaigns: Minnesota for Marriage and the North Carolina Values Coalition. The organizational landscape in the other states was less favorable. Freedom to Marry Maine initiated the ballot proposal in that state, Question 1, and NOM's allied organization, Protect Marriage Maine, spent much of 2012 on the defensive. In Washington and Maryland, marriage equality supporters mobilized grassroots support to persuade their state legislatures to pass marriage laws early in the year. By the time Preserve Marriage Washington and the Maryland Marriage Alliance (NOM's affiliated organizations) secured enough signatures to put the new laws to a vote in Referendum 74 (Washington) and Question 6 (Maryland), the marriage equality supporters had political momentum.

A third big change was the nature and strength of the support for NOM from organized religion. After the Proposition 8 backlash outside and within the Church of Jesus Christ of Latter-day Saints, its leadership terminated formal involvement in marriage ballot campaigns. The Church's retreat created a huge gap that Schubert could not entirely fill, despite strong support from Catholic dioceses, state organizations affiliated with Focus on the Family, and Evangelical churches. Although NOM helped fund each of the 2012 state campaigns, its treasury was spread too thin to make up for the missing Mormon donations. The freedom to marry campaigns outspent the traditional marriage campaigns in all five states, by margins ranging from 2-to-1 in North Carolina to almost 5-to-1 in Washington. Schubert also missed the tens of thousands of well-educated, on-message Latter-day volunteers.

In their place, Catholic and Evangelical volunteers eagerly gathered signatures, pounded the pavement, made phone calls, and delivered the crusade's ecumenical message. In November 2009, fifty Catholic bishops and theologians had joined one hundred Evangelical, Protestant, and Orthodox Christians to sign the "Manhattan Declaration: A Call of Christian Conscience." Drafted by Robby George and his associates, the Manhattan Declaration emphasized three interconnected values: the sanctity of life, traditional marriage, and religious freedom. Invoking Martin Luther King Jr.'s letter from a Birmingham jail, the document advocated "resistance to the point of civil disobedience against any legislation that might implicate their churches or charities in abortion, embryo-destructive research or same-sex marriage." At the same time that the marriage equality movement was asserting a values-based claim for marriage recognition, an expanded Christian conscience movement was joining abortion, marriage, and religious liberty into a meta-normative commitment uniting Catholics and Evangelical Protestants. The NOM-sponsored executive committees in all five ballot states included Catholic and Evangelical representatives, with the campaign leadership vested in prominent Evangelicals.[15]

Evangelical leadership created complications for Schubert, whose campaigns emphasized the bad social consequences that allegedly would flow from recognizing a broad freedom to marry. His local Evangelical leaders sometimes veered off script, depicting their campaigns as holy wars pitting God and His Christian soldiers against Satan and his handmaidens of evil. Pastor Derek McCoy, executive director of the Maryland Marriage Alliance, preached that the push for homosexual marriage was "an assault on the very essence of who God is in our culture." At one event, he listened appreciatively as another minister decried homosexual relationships as more deserving of death (the Levitical punishment for "men lying with men") than of state recognition. The Reverend Bob Emrich, who headed the Protect Marriage Maine campaign, described freedom to marry supporters as "mocking God," and other officers in that campaign referred to homosexual relations as "insidious and evil" and a "culture of death." Director of the Minnesota Family Council John Helmberger led Minnesota for Marriage as a holy crusade to "restrain evil" and to restore marriage as an institution reflecting the dignity of the Lord. His lieutenants claimed that "the homosexual agenda and the homosexual movement" preyed on innocent children. "Satan knows that if he gets the kids he gets the future. Even Adolf Hitler knew that." Comparing Hitler and Satan with lesbian couples raising children was cruel on top of crazy.[16]

Other Evangelical leaders stuck to the Schubert game plan. Director of the Washington Family Council, youthful Joseph Backholm was the spokesman for Preserve Marriage Washington. Calling it hubris for people to think they can change the "natural, physical, moral laws of the universe," he compared same-sex marriage to "walking on our hands and eating with our feet." You might say people ought to have that choice, he argued, but it's a nutty choice, because human beings were not designed that way. The universe was designed a certain way—you are meant to walk on your feet and marry someone of the opposite sex—and it was unnatural and inefficient to pretend otherwise. Although North Carolina was a more religiously conservative state than the other four, Tami Fitzgerald and the North Carolina Values Coalition did not claim that homosexual marriage was the work of Satan. Instead, Fitzgerald emphasized rhetoric from the previous decade's Federal Marriage Amendment campaign: "Everyone, gay or straight, is free to live as they choose, but nobody has the right to redefine marriage."[17]

THE UNIFIED CAMPAIGN FOR MARRIAGE EQUALITY AND THE FREEDOM TO MARRY

The 2012 campaigns supporting marriage for LGBT couples were better organized, more professional, better funded, and strategically smarter than before. Although most funds were raised locally, CMC, Freedom to Marry, and HRC provided a huge boost to the campaign treasuries. Flush with money, the state campaigns devoted more resources to neighborhood canvassing with well-trained volunteers as well as paid canvassers, developed focus group–tested television and radio ads, and bought lots of airtime for those ads. In three of the five states, Freedom to Marry launched public education media programs, including ads featuring the journey stories of unexpected messengers. In those states, Freedom to Marry participated in the structuring and operation of the local campaigns and assigned experienced staff members and allies to work directly with them. For four states (all but North Carolina), the local campaigns were integrated into a national network of daily research sharing, fundraising, and strategizing.[18]

Schubert was impressed that his opponents' messaging was much better than in 2008–2009. Integrating messaging experts like Watts and Zepatos and pollsters such as Simon into their operations, the 2012 campaigns emphasized values-based arguments and evocative journey stories by straight allies, who discussed why they had moved from skepticism to acceptance of marriage for LGBT couples. By offering regular folks with whom conflicted voters could identify, the ads provided emotional cues allowing those voters to open their minds to gay marriage. One controversial feature of the ads is that the only people who spoke were usually heterosexuals. Gays were largely unseen and almost entirely unheard, a phenomenon that bothered many in the local LGBTQ+ communities. However, virtually without exception, focus groups did not like ads featuring lesbian and gay couples because they cued visions of "icky" sexual activities in the minds of straight people.[19]

One lesson the Task Force's Sayre Reece and Dave Fleischer had drawn from earlier campaigns was that conflicted voters were not moved by short conversations in which a nice neighbor vouches for marriage equality or by strangers leaving voice mails endorsing the freedom to marry. Between 2009 and 2012, Kathleen Campisano and Regina Clemente of the Task Force honed what they called the "deep canvass," and Amy Mello perfected it in 2012. The 2012 campaigns trained volunteers to engage in longer conversations that encouraged conflicted voters to explain where they were coming from, related their personal experiences to the voters' values, and suggested a path forward in their thinking. Even when voters were opposed to marriage equality for faith-based reasons, canvassers were encouraged to listen to them and to connect with their deeply held commitments: "Jesus is all about inclusion, not [about] leaving anyone out."[20]

Finally, the local campaigns were more diverse and heterogeneous than earlier campaigns had been. Most important were aggressive and well-organized outreach efforts to communities of color and to faith communities. As early as 2005, HRC had documented that the LGBT rights movement lacked deep engagement with minority communities. Typically, gay rights organizations dominated by white voices funded LGBT leaders of color to support a rainbow understanding of equality. Outreach would have been more successful if Latinx, African American, and Asian American persons had been in positions of leadership and actively helped shape the agenda of marriage advocacy while they worked as ambassadors to their larger minority communities. All of the 2012 campaigns (especially Maryland's) made progress on that front, although the gays who called the shots nationally were not a notably diverse crowd. Diversity also included religion. For more than a decade, the Task Force and the New England activists like Friedes had emphasized the importance of having faith leaders who supported marriage equality, and all of the 2012 campaigns had prominent religious supporters. Three of the five ballot campaigns had faith directors whose sole responsibility was to coordinate religion-based endorsements and messaging ideas.[21]

Offering itself as the linchpin of a national campaign, Freedom to Marry supported and advised local campaigns and made sure they were all learning from one another. For example, Wolfson and Zepatos pressed campaigns to abandon *marriage equality* and speak only about the *freedom to marry*. Based on research, they argued that *marriage equality* was confusing to voters and that freedom-based messaging appealed to the libertarian instincts of most conflicted voters. If an equal treatment argument were needed, canvassers could invoke the Golden Rule. Nonetheless, HRC and the Maryland campaign continued to emphasize marriage equality. Equality Washington and the Task Force used both terms.

Determined to stop the string of losses in ballot campaigns and to prove to donors that their money was being wisely deployed, Freedom to Marry and CMC were selective about the state campaigns they were willing to fund. As benchmarks to determine which states were good bets, Zepatos and Solomon considered (1) whether freedom to marry consistently polled above 50 percent in a state, (2) how strong and well organized the state LGBT rights groups were, and (3) whether there was a sound fundraising plan that included local money. In 2011, Maine nailed all three benchmarks, and Freedom to Marry committed money, expertise, and the services of Marc Solomon to assist his old Mass-Equality associate Matt McTighe, the campaign manager of Mainers United for Marriage. Amy Simon and Phyllis Watts persuaded McTighe and, with greater effort, the board of Mainers United that the campaign should rely on values-based messaging, delivered by straight couples in ads to be produced by Simon. Also important, the Pine Tree State had an abundance of volunteers who were eager to have the longer, voter-friendly conversations that the new strategy demanded. Amy Mello, who had also worked with Solomon in Massachusetts and had been the field director for Equality Maine, segued into a similar role for Mainers United and conducted the most extensive deep-canvassing operation of the year: volunteer and paid canvassers reached as many as one in seven Mainers. Donald Sussman, the local businessman who had funded the 2009 ballot contest, contributed generously to the 2012 contest as well. Together with money from the national groups, McTighe enjoyed ample resources to cover extensive polling, voter research (which he shared with the Marriage Research Consortium), field organizers, trainers of volunteers, and advertising.[22]

While polling for marriage equality hovered at or below 50 percent, Minnesota was Freedom to Marry's other target of opportunity in 2011. Although local activists Monica Meyer and Ann Kaner-Roth founded Minnesota United for All Families, the national coordinators supplied many key players, led by Zepatos and Solomon, who served on the Minnesota United board and supported the choice of Richard Carlbom as the campaign manager, in part because he intuitively understood the new messaging strategy. Lisa Grove was the campaign's pollster, and Phyllis Watts was a messaging consultant. Grass-roots Solutions helped orchestrate a massive field campaign.[23]

Freedom to Marry wrote off North Carolina because polling was very weak and the local activists would not follow its guidelines for a successful campaign. HRC invested about $1 million in what everyone felt was a losing battle. In 2011, neither Maryland nor Washington met the benchmarks for probable success, either. In both states, marriage equality organizations were focused on legislative campaigns but had not prepared for the more expensive ballot campaigns that would follow. As Solomon had learned, legislative campaigns aimed at finding supporters and getting them to weigh in with their legislators was a different and less expensive enterprise than ballot campaigns aimed at trying to persuade conflicted voters to resolve their conflict in favor of the freedom to marry. Moreover, the stakes were high: with DOMA cases and the Olson-Boies Proposition 8 case heading to the US Supreme Court, marriage movement attorneys, activists, and funders were determined to break the lock that NOM seemed to have on ballot initiatives.[24]

Wounded by this lack of confidence, Josh Friedes of Equal Rights Washington called his old MassEquality colleague Marty Rouse, now at HRC. Friedes implored him to see that Washington was on the verge of marriage equality. HRC funded a comprehensive poll, which confirmed that optimism. Rouse flew to Seattle and met with state senator Edward Murray, who explained why the time was ripe for a marriage statute. His coalition had a broad base of support, including feminist groups, labor unions, and civil liberty organizations. They had won the ballot referendum in 2009 and were confident they could win again. HRC immediately sent $250,000 to help fund the lobbying campaign, with more money promised for the electoral campaign likely to follow.[25]

As predicted, the marriage bill succeeded in the Evergreen State—but not without an intense political struggle (where HRC's advance came in handy). The main hurdle was the state senate, where the Democrats' 27-22 majority included several senators from the socially conservative southern and western counties. On January 23, Senator Mary Margaret Haugen, a Catholic Democrat from a conservative district, announced that after years of praying about the issue and discussing it with Ed Murray, she had completed her political journey. "For me personally, I have always believed in traditional marriage between a man and a woman," she explained in a written statement. "That is what I believe, to this day. But this issue isn't about just what I believe. It's about respecting others, including people who may believe differently than I. It's about whether everyone has the same opportunities for love and companionship and family and security that I have enjoyed." A week later, the senate passed the marriage bill with a large bipartisan majority, 28-11, and the house followed, 55-43. Herself a Catholic convert to marriage equality, Governor Christine Gregoire signed Senate Bill 6239 into law on February 23, 2012.[26]

By the time Referendum 74 was certified for the November ballot, Freedom to Marry was persuaded that Zach Silk, who became Washington United's campaign manager near the end of the legislative process, had a sound institutional base and a promising plan for raising money and conducting a ballot campaign that could be sold to picky funders. With advice from Solomon, Silk managed the campaign. He was assisted by Amy Simon, Phyllis Watts, and Thalia Zepatos on messaging and media and Thomas Wheatley and Josh Friedes on the field efforts.[27]

As in Washington, Maryland's Catholic governor Martin O'Malley, whose gay brother had died of AIDS, was a key supporter of marriage legislation. The 2011 marriage bill fell short, in part because black Democrats in the house of delegates splintered, a fracture that was addressed by two unexpected messengers: the Reverend Delman Coates and Bishop Donté Hickman. A strikingly handsome man with caramel skin and a shaved head, Coates led the Mt. Ennon Baptist Church in Prince George's County. With degrees from Morehouse (B.A.), Columbia (Ph.D.), and Harvard (M.Div.), Coates read the Bible in its original Hebrew and never found anything to suggest that God condemned lesbian and gay marriages. Surmounting early life challenges, Hickman had risen to lead the Southern Baptist Church in Baltimore. Unlike Coates, he did not find scriptural support for marriage equality, but he believed Christ wanted His faithful to support committed lesbian and gay unions.

In January 2012, Reverend Coates had lunch with Governor O'Malley and recommended some changes to the marriage bill that would make it more acceptable to persons of faith: add *civil* marriage to the title and explicit religious exemptions to the body of the bill, similar to those that had succeeded in Connecticut in 2009. O'Malley eagerly adopted these suggestions. Before they knew it, Coates and Hickman were testifying alongside the governor before a senate committee. With the critical support of black legislators, some of whom the pastors lobbied personally, the bill passed the house of delegates, 72-67, and then the senate, 25-22. Governor O'Malley signed the Civil Marriage Act on March 1.[28]

While the Maryland Marriage Alliance was gathering signatures to support a referendum on the new law (which would ultimately get on the ballot as Question 6), Marylanders for Marriage Equality organized itself for a grueling campaign. On April 11, the organization released an HRC-funded poll showing support for marriage equality running 52-43 percent, much better than expected. HRC invested as much as $2 million to support the ballot campaign, but fundraising and campaign strategy remained predominantly local. The Marylanders emphasized equality arguments and worked closely with the NAACP to find apt civil rights parallels. Like the other campaigns, the Maryland campaign made its case through the journey stories of unexpected messengers. The stars of the campaign were Coates and Hickman, who were Evangelical, learned, and earnest in their support for marriage equality.

AMENDMENT 1 IN NORTH CAROLINA:
THE PROPOSITION 8 DEBATE REVISITED

Vote for Marriage North Carolina relied on Catholic and Evangelical support for North Carolina's Amendment 1, which was on a special May 2012 ballot. Although the campaign's message was that "everyone, gay or straight, is free to live as they choose, but nobody has the right to redefine marriage," Amendment 1 was phrased more broadly: "Marriage between one man and one woman is the only domestic legal union that shall be valid or recognized in this State." The Coalition to Protect North Carolina Families objected that this broad language would make it harder to protect women from domestic violence, which Schubert considered a dubious claim and which did not speak to the family issues that concerned the voters.[29]

HRC helped the coalition raise $2.5 million—more than twice the amount raised by the supporters of Amendment 1—and that funding advantage gave the coalition more airtime for its ads. But the coalition did not benefit from the new messaging philosophy, nor did it have the services of Zepatos, Simon, and Watts. As in previous ballot losses, it was doubtful that argumentative messaging would offset the amendment's solid support from churches in the Southern Baptist Tar Heel State. The week before the election, the Reverend Billy Graham, an Evangelical hero retired in Montreat, North Carolina, emphatically endorsed Amendment 1. On May 8, the voters ratified the Super-DOMA by an overwhelming margin, 61-39 percent. Every state in the South was now constitutionally committed to limiting marriage to one man, one woman, and most would not recognize lesbian or gay unions (or domestic units) of any sort. The next day, May 9, President Obama came out in favor of marriage equality.

Question 1 in Maine: Truth or Consequences Versus the New Messaging

Working closely with Marc Solomon, Thalia Zepatos, Amy Simon, and Amy Mello, Matt McTighe and Mainers United ran a campaign straight out of the new playbook: deploy values-based messaging, with an emphasis on straight citizens, faith leaders, and married couples explaining their journeys toward acceptance of gay people's freedom to marry; train thousands of volunteers to engage in long, personal conversations with their neighbors, with follow-up conversations from paid canvassers; exceed the generous national donations with aggressive local fundraising—more than $5 million by the end of the campaign. Protect Marriage Maine was not able to match Mainers United in either fundraising or in the number of volunteers.[30]

Maine was one of the least religious states in America, with only 27.6 percent of its population affiliated with a church. Half of those were members of the Catholic Church—but support from that denomination was initially weak. Portland bishop Richard Malone issued a statement opposing the ballot initiative, but his stance generated little Catholic money or support from the pulpits. Some Catholics were embarrassed by the 2011 release of *Question 1: The Documentary*, which displayed what they considered un-Christian tactics that had buoyed the traditional marriage side in the 2009 referendum. The Evangelicals and FRC provided strong support, but less than 5 percent of Maine's population identified as Evangelical.[31]

Mainers United used its financial advantage effectively, funding Mello's army of 150 paid canvassers and more than 3,500 trained volunteers and saturating the airwaves with a professionally honed ad campaign. Its masterpiece was a thirty-second ad, dubbed *Harlan*, which first aired in July 2012. The camera panned across four generations of the Gardners, an old northeastern Maine family assembled at a round farmhouse dining room table with a patterned violet tablecloth. White-bearded and looking cool in a fire-engine-red shirt and suspenders, ninety-year-old Harlan Gardner recalled his World War II military service. His gray-haired wife, Dorothy, said she would like her granddaughter Katie to have the opportunity to marry Alex, her female partner. "We want for her what we have, not a domestic partnership, but a marriage."

Holding his wife's hand, Harlan concluded: "What has been so good for Dorothy and I is too good not to share with the people that we love."[32]

We were also impressed with two September ads. In *Brotherhood*, three volunteer firemen discussed the surprising news that their fourth colleague was gay. The crew-cut buddies were not fazed—they were a brotherhood of firefighters, not a straights-only club. They were urging their wives and girlfriends to vote yes in November. In *Redikers*, an elderly married couple reminisced about their lives together. "We weren't always so gay-friendly," remarked Paul, his eyes closing as though recalling a bad dream. They had never talked about homosexuality until they learned their daughter was gay. "There was a lot of emotions. We went to see a priest, and I will never forget the answer that he told me: she is the same person that you loved yesterday." Their love for their daughter trumped their fears and impressions about homosexuality. "I would be very happy if my oldest daughter could get married at home," Jeanette stated matter-of-factly. Like the Gardners and the firefighters, the Redikers were authentic, plainspoken Mainers whose heartfelt messages spiked support for marriage equality to 55-57 percent in mid-October.[33]

In October, NOM and the Knights of Columbus invested an additional $1.5 million to salvage ProtectMarriage's flagging effort. This infusion enabled Schubert to run a wave of powerful ads that would appeal to Maine's older and religious voters. Don Mendell, a decorated school guidance counselor in Maine, had cut an ad for traditional marriage in its successful 2009 campaign. In Schubert's October 7 ad for the 2012 campaign, the avuncular, gray-bearded Mendell spoke calmly about efforts made to have him fired and to revoke his license because he had spoken out. The ad claimed that everywhere gay marriage had been recognized, skeptics had been harassed, fired, and fined. "This is not a live-and-let-live proposition," explained a representative of ProtectMarriage. "There's no tolerance for anyone who dares to speak out against their definition of marriage. Don Mendell is the perfect example." Schubert was still the maestro of *truth-or-consequences* ballot campaigns: either accept the natural truth of one-man, one-woman marriage or face the disastrous consequences of expanding marriage's long-standing definition.[34]

In *The O'Reillys*, which ran in mid-October, a salt-of-the-earth couple who operated the Wildflower Inn in Vermont reported that they had been sued after they declined to make their facilities available for a lesbian wedding. They were assessed a $30,000 fine and could no longer host weddings for anyone. At the end of October, ProtectMarriage started airing its *Local Schools* ad, featuring David and Tonia Parker once again recounting their painful experience with

King & King being forced upon their son in politically correct Massachusetts. "If gay marriage happens here," in Maine, "schools could teach that boys can marry boys." Similar ads, featuring the Parkers, were run by Schubert in Maryland, Minnesota, and Washington in late October.[35]

Would *Local Schools* be the Waterloo for freedom to marry in 2012 that *Two Princes* had been in Schubert's campaign for Proposition 8? As Thalia Zepatos tells the story, Lanae Erickson and Third Way in 2011 figured out the best answer to Schubert's appeals to parental fears that their kids might pick up bad values from schools where gay marriage had been normalized. As Matt McTighe tells it, Mainers United learned from the Marriage Research Consortium that teachers were effective in responding to the *Two Princes* ad, so the Mainers worked up some scripts that were tested with focus groups. From behind the glass, Amy Simon and Phyllis Watts figured out that what was effective was to have a teacher who was also a parent talk about how we can all protect our children against harmful things and ideas in the world. So Simon developed ads featuring Maine teachers talking parent to parent. Don't rely on schools to teach values, one way or the other. It was the responsibility of parents to instill in their children the values that they wanted them to learn. Because it spoke directly to the heart of parental concerns and suggested a productive path that made sense to many parents, this was a relatively effective response to the *Local Schools* ad. Similar ads were run by freedom to marry campaigns in Minnesota and Washington in late October.[36]

Less than two weeks before the vote, a middle school in Gorham, Maine, held a diversity day. Proud Rainbow Youth of Southern Maine made three presentations to eighth-grade students about sexual and gender diversity and the effects of anti-gay discrimination, including its impact on teens. In the question-and-answer period, the topic of safer sex came up, and the presenter ventured into a detailed description of safer practices—from foreplay to Saran wrap. Teachers and parents vigorously objected, and the school profusely apologized. Fox News gave the story nationwide publicity. Building on the concerns raised by *Local Schools*, Protect Marriage Maine issued a press release: "If there was any doubt that gay marriage would be taught to young children in Maine schools just as it is in Massachusetts and Canada, that doubt should be removed now. If they are willing to teach our kids how homosexuals engage in foreplay, do you really think they won't force gay marriage instruction of young children when it is the law of the land?" The controversy erupted too late in the campaign for Schubert to turn it into a last-minute "we told you so" ad, as he had done in Proposition 8.[37]

This sort of incident aroused fearful emotions—the famous "ick" factor triggered when older straight people contemplated what gay people did in the bedroom. McTighe recalls that, although Mainers United enjoyed polling majorities throughout the campaign, "support was slipping" in the last couple of weeks. "Undecideds were kind of still uncomfortably too high, and all past campaign experience led us to believe that undecideds were still going to go the other way." Would three years of hard work go down the sink because of a middle school diversity day snafu? Buoyed by an outpouring of faith-based support and knowledge that Maine's electorate was one of the oldest in the country, Schubert thought so.[38]

Amendment 1 in Minnesota: Catholics Divided

Minnesota was much like Maine in several respects: its aging, overwhelmingly white electorate tended to vote for moderate or liberal candidates of both parties, and it had a broad anti-discrimination law that included sexual orientation and gender identity. Both states also had one large, pro-gay metropolitan area—Portland in Maine and Minneapolis–St. Paul in Minnesota—but most of the votes would be cast in smaller towns and rural counties. Even if opponents of Minnesota's Amendment 1 prevailed in the Twin Cities, the constitutional junior-DOMA would prevail if its supporters won the rest of the state. After winning a contentious 2011 vote in the legislature to place Amendment 1 on the 2012 ballot, marriage conservatives found that the long Minnesota winter gave their opponents ample time to raise money and create a campaign to defeat the constitutional initiative.[39]

Thirty-year-old campaign manager Richard Carlbom stunned Minnesota United's board by proposing a budget of $12 million—but then he raised that sum from more than sixty-seven thousand donors as well as from Freedom to Marry, which reports raising and investing $1.75 million. Minnesota United would need every penny for Carlbom's ambitious campaign: a massive field effort of long door-to-door conversations, extensive outreach to religious communities, and smart social media, radio, and television messaging. As a result, the ad campaign was dominated by Amendment 1's opponents. Indeed, before the formal campaign commenced, Freedom to Marry in mid-August bought weeks of airtime for *Grandparents*. Yvonne and Fred Peterson, a Duluth couple who had been married for fifty-nine years, observed that "the world is changing" and gays and lesbians wanted to get married for the same reason they did in 1953. (Unmentioned in the ad, they had a gay grandson.) "Love is love, and it does belong to everybody," concluded Yvonne, as she walked hand in hand with Fred into the closing credits of the commercial.[40]

Minnesota for Marriage had a fraction of the freedom to marry budget, and almost all of its money came from NOM, the Minnesota Catholic Conference, and the Minnesota Policy Council. Unlike Maine, the North Star State was pretty religious—with 32 percent of the churchgoing population mainstream Protestant, 28 percent Catholic, and 22 percent Evangelical—and Schubert focused his grassroots strategy in the churches willing to mobilize their pastors and parishioners to contribute time and money to campaigning for traditional marriage. His anchor was John Nienstedt, the ruggedly handsome, steel-gray-haired archbishop of Minneapolis. No Catholic prelate in America devoted more energy to the issue than Nienstedt did. In April, he reached out to Evangelicals and other Protestants in order to assure that the Amendment 1 campaign had their united and vigorous support. Overall, he funneled as much as $1 million in church funds to the campaign. The archdiocese distributed forty thousand copies of a DVD sounding the alarm against redefining marriage. "We wouldn't have gotten very far without him," Schubert confessed. "It's hard to overstate his importance."[41]

But Archbishop Nienstedt did not speak for all Catholics. In May, eighty priests publicly spoke out against Amendment 1. Clergy United for All Families, the faith-based outreach of the freedom to marry campaign, included Catholic clerics and lay leaders and was even more successful with other denominations. By the end of the campaign, more than one hundred of Minnesota United's seven hundred official coalition members were churches, synagogues, and faith-based organizations. In early 2012, the Minnesota Rabbinical Association, the Minneapolis and the St. Paul Synods of the Evangelical Lutheran Church (the second-largest denomination, after the Catholics), and the Minnesota Conference of the United Methodist Church all adopted resolutions, by lopsided votes, opposing Amendment 1. The Reverend Leith Anderson, the Minnesota pastor who was the head of the National Association of Evangelicals, remained neutral in the campaign.[42]

Starting on January 3, Minnesota for Marriage posted weekly YouTube videos called the *Minnesota Marriage Minute,* hosted by Kalley King Yanta, a former newscaster with a calming voice and a rainbow wardrobe of pastel suits. Appealing to the "Minnesota nice" voters, the Marriage Minutes explained the virtues of marriage and responded to questions people had about the amendment. Yanta also warned of the bad consequences of redefining marriage: some children would lose the benefit of having an intact family with married parents; parents would be helpless to stop schools from teaching same-sex marriage to their children; and churches, religious institutions, and devout individuals would have to support marriages they did not endorse or else face legal consequences.[43]

As he did in the other states, Schubert saved his campaign funds for truth-or-consequences ads to run continuously at the end of the campaign. His third ad, aired in mid-October, was *Not Live and Let Live*. It explained what happened in other jurisdictions that recognized same-sex marriages: supporters of traditional marriage were fined (the O'Reillys, who could no longer host weddings at their Vermont inn), had to close down adoption services (Catholic Charities), and saw their children taught the virtues of gay marriage in schools, with no recourse for concerned parents (the Parkers). On November 1, fueled by an eleventh-hour infusion of NOM donations, Minnesota for Marriage started airing radio ads in Spanish and English that emphasized the consequences for children, "who could be taught about gay marriage in school, against the desires of parents." Schubert's *Broken Promises* ad launched on November 2. "There have been a lot of broken promises elsewhere about gay marriage," the ad warned, "like it won't affect anyone else, even as small businesses are fined, charities closed, and people fired. Or 'it won't be taught to young children in public schools' even though it was in Massachusetts and Canada. Don't trust broken promises," and vote to protect all marriages by a yes on Amendment 1.[44]

Minnesota United responded to the late-October ads but closed its media campaign with a strong, positive, values-based ad. It opened with a video of the floor speech opposing the amendment by GOP representative John Kriesel, a decorated veteran. In an emotional statement, he testified that his feelings changed after fighting alongside gay soldiers in Iraq. He passed around the chamber a photo of Corporal Andrew Wilfahrt, a Minnesotan who was the first gay solider to die in combat after the repeal of Don't Ask, Don't Tell. "I cannot look at this family and look at this picture and say, 'You know what, Corporal, you were good enough to fight for your country and give your life, but you were not good enough to marry the person you love.' I can't do that." Minnesotans identified with Kriesel, who looked like an ordinary middle-aged guy with a comb-over. In thirty seconds, he had effectively conveyed his journey: once Kriesel got to know an openly gay colleague selflessly serving his country, fairness required him to treat Wilfahrt as he and his wife would want to be treated. We found this ad particularly moving.[45]

With powerful closing ads like *Kriesel* and more than twenty-seven thousand volunteers working on Election Day, Carlbom and his team were optimistic heading into election Tuesday. The final poll showed a small majority opposed to the amendment, but Schubert was cautiously optimistic as well. In past campaigns, concerned parents had broken his way at the end, and he was using the same triggers for parental concern that had worked before. On November 2, Minnesota for Marriage announced a mega-coalition of more than five hundred faith leaders endorsing Amendment 2. Billy Graham's endorsement ran in major newspapers all over the country.

Referendum 74 in Washington: Big Funders and Unexpected Messengers

The marriage equality movement in Washington treated the 2012 ballot measure as the extension of a long campaign that its members had conducted since 2006 and that had triumphed in a 2009 referendum upholding the comprehensive domestic partnership law (described in chapter 12). The ongoing effort for public education involved a rainbow coalition of stakeholders and leaders. Equal Rights Washington, led by George Cheung and Josh Friedes, did the most but saw itself as collaborating with other partners. Lisa Stone and the Northwest Women's Law Center as well as Lambda Legal and Jamie Pedersen did much of the legal work, as did the local ACLU. Marsha Botzer, an openly transgender woman, was the chair of the local Task Force, which was critical to generating grassroots and public education activities. Labor unions and various ethnic groups, such as the Japanese American Citizens League, had a place at the table. Senator Murray was the most influential leader. By 2012, he had three lesbian and gay colleagues in the Washington legislature.

Zach Silk, Washington United's campaign manager, created an ambitious and expensive game plan. The campaign raised most of its funds from corporations and executives of Microsoft, Amazon, Nike, Starbucks, and Google. On July 22, Jennifer Cast, the finance cochair, wrote a three-thousand-word email to Jeff and MacKenzie Bezos, the founders of Amazon, for whom Cast had worked early on. She poured out her life story and asked the multibillionaire couple to consider a "big/generous/hmm-I-surprised-myself donation," say, $100,000–$200,000. The next day, she found a response: "Jen, this is right for so many reasons. We're in for $2.5 million." With additional funds streaming in from Freedom to Marry, CMC, and HRC, Washington United ultimately raised $12.6 million, and its website listed more than five hundred allied or contributing organizations, including more than one hundred churches and religious organizations.[46]

Flush with money, Washington United and its allies dominated the airwaves, starting in July, when Freedom to Marry sponsored its ad *Pflug* during the opening ceremony for the 2012 Olympics. Senator Cheryl Pflug explained why she voted for marriage equality. She knew a number of lesbian and gay families who were sharing their lives and values just like her family. "As a Republican, I believe in freedom, and that includes the freedom to marry the person you love." Another married-with-children GOP legislator, Steve Litzow, recorded a moving video that was released earlier in July. These Republican lawmakers, emphasizing freedom from government coercion and recognition of marital choice, were unexpected messengers that made moderate voters think twice before voting against marriage equality. On August 27, Silk made an advance purchase of $5 million in television-ad time for September and October, when GOP representative Maureen Walsh would endorse the freedom to marry.[47]

The messaging that moved us to tears, however, was an independently produced three-minute video, *Cougs for Marriage Equality*. Dozens of Washington State University students (Cougars) held handwritten signs expressing their support in their own words. One young woman stood in front of the Cougar monument with this message: "Because my friend deserves HAPPINESS!" A Mona Lisa smile hovered above another sign: "Because the government shouldn't decide who you get to spend the rest of your life with." Another, "Love is like air. It is for everyone." All of those messages were held by women of color, and many others were offered by male and white students. A gentle rapping voice singing "Same Love" gave the video a neat tempo: "When I was at church they taught me something else/When you preach hate at the service those words are not anointed/No freedom until we are equal."[48]

The Bezoses' donation alone exceeded the total amount raised by Preserve Marriage Washington. To conserve resources, Preserve Marriage did not start airing television ads until mid-October, but from the beginning it was active in local churches—including many Catholic parishes, some Mormon stakes, and Evangelical churches. Schubert's leading television ad, *Examples*, first aired on October 23. "Experience shows how Referendum 74 can harm people who oppose gay marriage," it said. The ad offered examples of persecution: Vermont innkeepers Jim and Mary O'Reilly and Damian Goddard, a Canadian sportscaster fired for tweeting his agreement with a traditional marriage post. A five-minute video, *Don't Redefine Marriage,* posted on October 19, featured FRC's Tony Perkins explaining how Referendum 74 would normalize "homosexual marriage" and require schools to "indoctrinate" children to believe that "homosexual marriage is the very same as your marriage." The Parkers and the Wirthlins told their stories of childhood "indoctrination" one final time.[49]

On its website, Washington United listed around six hundred local institutions supporting marriage equality—including more than 120 churches and religious organizations. Among the religious supporters were Catholics for Marriage Equality, Seattle's First Baptist Church, and Mormons for Marriage Equality. Given its impressive coalition of unexpected messengers, vast fundraising advantage, and consistent albeit narrow majorities in Amy Simon's tracking polls, Washington United had the same winning feeling it had in 2009. According to NOM's blog, however, Referendum 74 lost its modest lead once Schubert's truth-or-consequences and danger-to-children ads started airing, and the question was a toss-up heading into November. On the weekend before the election, the website of the Catholic Archdiocese of Seattle was headlined by videos of Archbishop Sartain arguing against same-sex marriage as well as by a "Prayer in Defense of Marriage": "May your Holy Spirit enlighten our society to treasure the heroic love of husband and wife, and guide our leaders to sustain and protect the singular place of mothers and fathers in the lives of their children."[50]

Question 6 in Maryland: Race and Religion

In 2012, dependably Democratic Maryland was represented by one of the most liberal congressional delegations in the country. While Montgomery County and the Baltimore suburbs were gay friendly, rural Maryland could be expected to vote against marriage equality. Founded as a religiously tolerant colony and a haven for Catholics, the Old Line State boasted a proud faith tradition, with 15 percent of the population Catholic, 10 percent mainstream Protestant, and 13 percent Evangelical. Socially conservative African American Evangelicals dominated Prince George's County and Baltimore.

As in Minnesota, the Catholic Church's internal divisions were on sharp display. Governor Martin O'Malley led the campaign for the marriage equality referendum, while William Lori, archbishop of Baltimore, was the most erudite of the traditional marriage supporters. On September 26, hosting a meeting of several dozen Catholic, Evangelical, and Muslim faith leaders at St. Mary's Seminary, Archbishop Lori observed that the Bible both opened and closed with one-man, one-woman marriage: Adam and Eve in Genesis, and the wedding feast of the lamb at the end of Revelation. He warned that mar-

riage equality would directly threaten religious liberty and urged all faith traditions to contribute money and mobilize grassroots support against the
referendum. On the other hand, Sister Jeannine Gramick of the New Sisters
of Mercy created Catholics for Marriage Equality. She maintained that "Catholic social teaching requires that all people be treated with dignity, regardless
of their state in life or their beliefs." The Church promotes "stable family units,"
which ought to include "same-sex couples and their children." Sister Jeannine
argued that lesbian and gay couples enjoyed the same kind of supportive love
and family formation as straight married couples.[51]

Black pastors mostly opposed the marriage law. Reverend McCoy and Bishop
Jackson were the leading spokesmen for the Marriage Alliance—but Reverend Coates and Bishop Hickman provided a counterpoint to their views within
that faith community. President Obama joined Coates and Hickman on May 9,
when his interview with Robin Roberts brought him and his family out of the
marriage closet. The polling bounce from the president's announcement was
reinforced ten days later when the NAACP's board of directors, led by its chair,
Roslyn Brock, and president, Benjamin Jealous, adopted a resolution opposing any discrimination against LGBT people and supporting marriage equality. The resolution also denounced a secret NOM memorandum, widely
reported in the media, suggesting that traditional marriage supporters used
the opposition of African American and Latinx parishioners to create a wedge
among civil rights groups. On June 9, the National Council of La Raza (the
largest Latinx civil rights organization) unanimously endorsed marriage
equality—followed within a month by the League of United Latin American
Citizens.

The Obama bounce partially melted over the summer, and fundraising
lagged. Governor O'Malley asked Delegate Maggie McIntosh to take over the
campaign. A quietly effective lesbian representing Baltimore, McIntosh created a bipartisan kitchen cabinet and recruited her buddy, Chip DiPaula, a gay
Republican. DiPaula helped Marylanders for Marriage to recruit big donors,
including Mayor Mike Bloomberg ($250,000), hedge-fund manager Paul
Singer ($250,000), and former NFL commissioner Paul Tagliabue ($100,000).
HRC says it contributed as much as $2 million in funds and services to the
campaign. As a result, Marylanders for Marriage was able to spend $800,000
a week on media ads for the last month of the campaign.[52]

While Archbishop Lori was whipping the Catholic vote and Reverend Mc-
Coy and Bishop Jackson calling forth the Evangelicals against Question 6,
Marylanders for Marriage deployed Sister Jeannine, Reverend Coates, and

Bishop Hickman in their autumn counteroffensive. In September 2012, Coates, Hickman, and ten other black ministers held a press conference to express their support for civil marriage equality, even though most congregants in their churches accepted the conjugal understanding of marriage. Later that month, both pastors taped companion television spots that would kick off marriage equality's "It's All About Fairness" media campaign in early October. Coates: "I would not want someone denying my rights based upon their religious views; therefore, I should not deny others' based upon mine." Hickman: "I support this law because it does not force any church to perform a same-sex marriage if it's against their beliefs." These television ads were hits with the public. Focus groups were electrified by the eloquent pastors. Speaking from their hearts and from a spiritual perspective, they turned things around for Marylanders for Marriage.[53]

The last weeks of the campaign saw a barrage of television and radio ads, and the race tightened, as pastors and priests rallied their flocks to oppose Question 6. With a last-minute gift of $400,000 from NOM, the Marriage Alliance purchased additional advertising time in the expensive Baltimore-Washington media market. Schubert's biggest coup was a radio ad featuring Dr. Alveda King, the niece of the late Reverend Martin Luther King Jr. Alveda King not only reaffirmed the one-man, one-woman definition of marriage but criticized the "unholy alliance" between the NAACP and "gay activists" on the issue. "It's possible to be tolerant of gay and lesbian rights," she explained, "without redefining marriage, [which is] God's holy union. I believe we are on the right side of history—and the right side of eternity."[54]

No Frank Schubert campaign would have been complete without David and Tonia Parker, still traumatized because gay-affirming Massachusetts had forced *King & King* upon their now-teenage son. We were particularly moved, however, by the video dubbed *Crank*. Fourteen-year-old Sarah Crank had testified against changing the definition of marriage before the Maryland General Assembly. Homeschooled by Evangelical parents, she was the definition of adorably well-spoken, with her light-blue eyes sparkling behind neat glasses and a winsome smile that showed she was unashamed of the braces over her teeth. In the video, her mother, Kathleen, reported death threats, sexual speculations, and vicious name-calling against her daughter. One lowlife wrote Sarah: "I hope you get raped by your married parents." The video closed with this: "Question 6 threatens freedom of speech and freedom of religion. Stop the Intimidation. Vote Against Question 6." A television ad, *We Will Not Be Intimidated*, showed three women talking about being bullied and called bigots for supporting traditional marriage. During the campaign, Gallaudet University suspended its diversity officer, Dr. Angela McCaskill, for signing a petition supporting the Question 6 referendum. Schubert turned the episode into a powerful truth-or-consequences ad.[55]

Marylanders for Marriage Equality's closing ad was *Maryland, It's Time.* The thirty-second spot started: "Question 6 strengthens protections for our churches and guarantees the civil right to commit to the one you love." Marylanders of all political and religious persuasions should join together in support of this balanced legislation. The commentary was accompanied by a slideshow of handsome, smiling marriage equality supporters, including President Obama, the NAACP's former president Julian Bond, Reverend Coates, Bishop Hickman, and former lieutenant governor Kathleen Kennedy Townsend.[56]

In 1973, Maryland had been the first state to pass a statute that banned civil marriage between people of the same sex. In 2006, Baltimore trial judge M. Brooke Murdock declared the statute unconstitutional, but Judge Glenn Harrell Jr. wrote for the court of appeals in *Conaway v. Deane* (2007) to overturn Murdock's decision and uphold the traditional definition of marriage based on Maryland's constitution. Judge Harrell ended the court's opinion by noting that nothing in the decision precluded the legislature from voting to change the statute. In 2012, when the legislature had voted to change the statute and when presented with the opportunity to vote on the subsequent referendum, Judge Harrell voted for Question 6. He explained to us that he personally felt that all people should have the responsibilities and opportunities that family life, and marriage, provide.[57]

Was marriage equality an idea whose time had come?

Lessons from the 2012 Referenda

The DeBoer and Rowse family in Michigan had not been very politically engaged, but 2012 was different. President Obama had come out of the constitutional closet for them, and nothing could have prevented April DeBoer, Jayne Rowse, and April's parents from voting for the president on Tuesday, November 6. By midnight, his reelection was assured. Would 2012 be a reprise of 2008, when Obama romped and marriage equality tanked? It was not until the morning of November 7 that there was a clear answer.

Because Portland reported early, Question 1 raced off to a big lead in Maine, but supporters watched the lead erode as results from rural counties trickled in. Shortly before midnight, however, Mainers United declared victory, ultimately winning 52.7 to 47.3 percent. Minutes after that, the pundits concluded that, when all the votes were counted, Maryland would have decided 52.4 to 47.6 percent to ratify its marriage equality law. Support was strongest in Montgomery County and Baltimore, with Prince George's County about even and the Eastern Shore and southern Maryland against. Two-thirds of women with children supported the law. Although black voters narrowly rejected it, the margin would have been much greater and would have sunk the law if it were not for the journey stories from Reverend Coates, Bishop Hickman, and President Obama.

Around 2:00 a.m. Central Time, it was official that Minnesota's constitutional junior-DOMA, Amendment 1, was headed for defeat, 47.4 to 52.6 percent. The Twin Cities, their suburbs, and Duluth anchored the no vote; the state's northern ridge and other rural areas supplied most of the yes vote. The presidential and initiative-opposing coattails brought Democrats back into majorities in the Minnesota legislature. Washington, the last state to report final results because so many were mailed, saw marriage equality triumph by the largest margin: 53.7 to 46.3 percent. King County (Seattle) and its suburbs voted yes by large margins, while western and southern Washington opposed Referendum 74. Marriage equality supporter Jay Inslee won the governorship, handily defeating a GOP critic.

As the Task Force's Rea Carey told us, no one expected that marriage for LGBT persons would sweep all four states on election night. Among the most optimistic had been Marc Solomon, who predicted three out of four. Interestingly, their side's wins were by pretty much the same margins everywhere, regardless of the state and its local politics, the organizational structure and dynamics, or the precise terminology and messaging used. So why did marriage for LGBT couples finally win at the ballot box?[58]

President Obama's endorsement was helpful with black voters, especially in Maryland. More important, his campaign raised electoral turnout among young people, progressives, Democrats, and well-educated persons—all more likely to support marriage equality. Additionally, the Obama administration had fueled a constant stream of messages supporting the image of LGBT Americans as responsible citizens. Without the repeal of the military exclusion, Representative Kriesel would not have known that Corporal Wilfahrt was gay, and the experience of serving with him would not have changed Kriesel's mind on marriage equality. The association of citizenship, military service, and family is powerful in American culture, and Obama did more than anyone else to clinch that association for LGBT persons. Conversely, Ken Mehlman's group estimated that Obama's support for marriage equality netted him 233,000 extra votes in the battleground states that he carried by 504,422. Only one in twenty of Obama's supporters had second thoughts because of his stance, while more than one in ten of Romney's supporters disliked his stand on the marriage issue.[59]

Persuasive advertisements and deep grassroots canvassing contributed to the ballot victories. Frank Schubert lamented that the freedom to marry campaigns overwhelmingly dominated the media, crowding out his truth-or-consequences warnings with messaging that was much more effective than it had been in 2008–2009. Maine, Minnesota, and Washington saw higher than expected turnout in base geographic areas, which the Center for American Progress attributed in part to the public education and canvassing campaigns in those states. The educational campaign in Maryland split the black vote fairly evenly, which saved Question 6. Conversely, the absence of the Church of Jesus Christ of Latter-day Saints deprived the protect marriage campaigns of funds, excellent strategists, and many neighborhood volunteers. The Catholics were divided, and while Evangelicals supported one-man, one-woman marriage, their messaging sometimes undermined the Schubert campaigns with sectarian and strident rhetoric.[60]

Also important was affirmative religious support for marriage equality. Faith leaders from the Methodist, Reformed Jewish, Lutheran, Presbyterian, Universalist Unitarian, and Quaker denominations not only endorsed marriage as a religious institution for LGBT people but also argued that religious liberty cut both ways. The state's failure to recognize marriages that those faiths celebrated was discrimination against *their* religious freedom. Prominent Catholics (including Governors Gregoire and O'Malley) persuasively supported marriage equality with heartfelt endorsements and their own journey stories, as did many priests and nuns (like Sister Jeannine). Although Evangelicals saw many fewer breaks in their ranks, the support of Reverend Coates and Bishop Hickman was critical in Maryland.

Another important reason marriage equality swept those four states in November 2012 was the fact that more Americans than ever—a majority in all those states—were open to or okay with same-sex marriage to start with. Young voters who grew up watching *Will and Grace* on television, admiring their gay relatives and teachers, and laughing with their diverse array of buddies at the wry humor of Ellen DeGeneres favored marriage equality by large margins. Because the political demography was slanted toward an expanded freedom to marry, all age groups expected marriage equality to prevail sooner rather than later. Although Evan Wolfson correctly maintains that a sense of inevitability created complacency in the 2008 California campaign, our impression is that in 2012 inevitability sapped opponents of some energy and, for the first time, helped motivate undecided voters to break for marriage equality rather than stick with the status quo.[61]

Recall that focus groups are typically conducted in a room with a one-way mirror so that researchers can observe from behind the glass.

On March 13, 2013, Jorge Mario Bergoglio was selected as pope. From behind the glass in the Vatican, Pope Francis viewed with dismay the behavior of the Catholic Church's officials in the United States—especially Archbishop Nienstedt, who was embroiled in investigations and lawsuits for covering up the sexual misbehavior of priests; there were also reports that the archbishop had long been sexually active with young men, with the Vatican looking the other way. In 2015, Francis would request Nienstedt's resignation. As doctrinally hardline bishops in the Pope Benedict XVI mold retired after 2013, Pope Francis replaced them with pastoral bishops in the Pope John XXIII mold. He passed over Seattle's doctrinaire Peter Sartain and appointed the progressive Blase Cupich to the Archdiocese of Chicago, and in 2017 he hemmed in Sartain with the appointment of a progressive auxiliary bishop, Daniel Mueggenborg. Also watching from behind the glass were Leith Anderson, the Minnesota pastor who headed the National Association of Evangelicals, and Dallin Oaks, an influential member of the Church of Jesus Christ's First Presidency. Like the Catholics, the Evangelicals and the Latter-day Saints planned to adapt to a new regime.[62]

The critical figures relishing the ballot victories from behind the glass were Thalia Zepatos, Kathleen Campisano, Lanae Erickson, Dave Fleischer, Josh Friedes, Sean Lund, Amy Mello, Ineke Mushovic, Sayre Reece, Marty Rouse, Amy Simon, Marc Solomon, Phyllis Watts, and others. Although Freedom to Marry's Evan Wolfson, HRC's Chad Griffin, and the Task Force's Rea Carey were the public faces of the marriage campaign, it was these messaging and canvassing innovators who were key to the unexpected electoral sweep in November 2012. The nation's path toward marriage equality reflected not just a generational shift and increasing political power for sexual and gender minorities but also one-by-one transformations in people's attitudes when confronted with lesbian, gay, and transgender families and (importantly) their straight parents, relatives, coworkers, and friends.

Many feminists were soul-searching behind the glass. One was law professor Nancy Polikoff. She had taken up the feminist critique of marriage equality pioneered by Paula Ettelbrick, explored in chapter 3 of this volume. As Polikoff observed the 2012 ballot campaigns, she was happy that LGBT persons and groups succeeded in defeating discriminations against them, but she was deeply disturbed by the process by which victory was secured and by the people marriage equality left behind. All of Ettelbrick's prophecies had come to pass. The marriage politics of "just like straights" not only de-radicalized queer politics and culture but seemed to embrace assimilation on straight terms. Worse, such politics succeeded by denigrating alternative institutions such as domestic partnerships as "not the real thing," inferior to marriage, which was sold as the gold standard for love, commitment, and happiness. The embrace of marriage was occurring just as marriage was receding out of reach for working class and poor Americans. Worst of all, from Polikoff's point of view, the LGBT rights movement was consumed by this strategy, perhaps at the expense of goals that would help most LGBT people much more than marriage: greater protection against hate crimes, the adoption of anti-discrimination laws, and support for nonmarital families. In 2006, Polikoff had been one of the first to sign the "Beyond Same-Sex Marriage" statement of principles supporting government recognition of a variety of relationships, not just marriages. By 2012 she was dismayed at how irrelevant they seemed, as lesbian and gay couples themselves seemed to disrespect any relationship outside of marriage.[63]

Also watching behind the glass were dozens of attorneys who had marriage cases pending for review with the US Supreme Court. That summer, Chuck Cooper had applied for review of the Ninth Circuit's decision in *Perry v. Hollingsworth,* and Ted Olson was praying that the Supreme Court would grant it. That the marriage equality candidate won the presidency was significant, but the mandate from ballot victories in four different states was stunning. Olson had dialed back his earlier suggestion that six or more justices were in the bag for marriage equality—but his critics in the gayocracy were now saying a 5-4 majority was in sight. While the *Perry* petition for review was pending, so were petitions in three cases where lower courts had ruled that DOMA was unconstitutional. Mary Bonauto and her GLAD colleagues represented plaintiff couples in two cases, and James Esseks of the ACLU and Robbie Kaplan were the lawyers in a third case. The plaintiff in that third case was an iconic grande dame, Edie Windsor.

19 • The Perfect Wife

The perfect wife is not always married to a man. And the perfect plaintiff is not always the one savvy lawyers imagine. Edith Schlain Windsor was both.

Born in 1929 Philadelphia, the youngest of three children of Russian Jewish immigrants, Edith Schlain was an American original. With vivacious dark-brown eyes and matching hair that she wore in a bob whose curls turned outward, Edie was a flirty, feminine, and fantastic young lady. After receiving her bachelor's degree from Temple University in 1950, she married her persistent suitor, Saul Wiener. "He was exactly what most girls wanted," she reminisced decades later. "He was big, handsome and strong yet sweet. I think that if I had been straight," he would have been "the love of my life." Because she did not want to be known as Edie Wiener, she insisted that Saul change his name to Saul Windsor, and she took that last name. But marriage to a man was not her destiny. "Anytime I would see two women walking on the street on a Saturday night, I would be so jealous." Less than a year after the wedding, she and Saul amicably divorced. (Saul took back his last name, but she kept Windsor.) As she confessed to her broken-hearted husband, it was not Prince Charming she wanted to sweep her off her feet, but a charming princess.[1]

After her divorce, Edie secured a series of jobs that culminated in a computer programming position at IBM, where she labored in the corporate closet. Although she wore the mask at work, Edie tore it off in her free time, when she perused the city for women. She found them in the merry-go-round of the West Village's lesbian hangouts. Edie was the Belle of the Bagatelle, an Eleventh Street bar. Although she flirted with and dated many women, none moved her deeply—until 1963, when some friends introduced her to Thea Spyer at the Portofino restaurant on Thompson Street, where Fridays were a special kind of ladies night. A handsome raven-haired heiress, Thea was two years younger and several inches taller than Edie, who stood an even five feet. Her family had made a fortune in the pickle business in Amsterdam, where Thea was born; their wealth and connections allowed them to flee a few steps ahead of Hitler's invading army and make their way to the United States in the early 1940s. Thea crushed on girls almost immediately. Her first love affair was with a woman nine years her elder, while she was a student at Sarah Lawrence College. A night watchman spotted them making out in the parking lot one night and reported them to the dean, who promptly expelled the Dutch coed. She rebounded with a bachelor's degree from the New School for Social Research, and then a master's degree from City University of New York and a Ph.D. in clinical psychology from Adelphi University.[2]

Instantly attracted to one another that night at the Portofino, the two women ended up in Thea's apartment, where "Edie kicked off her shoes and danced until she had worn a hole in one of her stockings." Thea recalled, "We immediately just fit. Our bodies fit." Edie swooned as Thea spun her around the improvised dance floor. "First lesbian I ever met who could lead," Edie reported. For the next two years, the two ran into one another occasionally, but in the summer of 1965, Edie surprised Thea at the Long Island farmhouse of some mutual friends, and they became lovers. Like many other lesbian couples of that era, they had a butch-femme relationship: Thea took the lead on the dance floor and in the bedroom, while Edie, a classic lipstick lesbian, often made their plans. Later in her life, when people would refer to Thea as her wife, Edie would adamantly correct them. No! "I was the wife." The perfect wife, writes journalist Ariel Levy.[3]

One Friday in 1967, while driving to the Hamptons, Thea stopped the car, pulled over, and got out. "I did kneel down in classical fashion, and I proposed to her," or tried to. Thea started, "Will you," and Edie answered "Yes. Yes! Yes!! YES!!!" before Thea even finished the sentence. Remember, from chapter 1, that 1967 was also the year that Jack Baker proposed to Mike McConnell and the US Supreme Court decided *Loving v. Virginia*. Although Jack and Mike spent half a century trying to validate their 1971 marriage, licensed by Blue Earth County, Minnesota, Edie and Thea assumed that New York would never legally recognize their union. Indeed, Edie feared she would lose her job if people knew she was partnered with another woman. Thea thoughtfully sealed and concealed what would be a very long engagement with a circular diamond brooch, which Edie could wear pinned to her blouse.[4]

For the next forty-two years, Edie and Thea lived in a three-bedroom apartment at 2 Fifth Avenue, a stately building just north of Washington Square Park. In 1968, Edie purchased a cottage in Southampton as a birthday gift to her beloved. Although Thea considered it insufficiently swanky at first, the cottage soon became their refuge and playground. When not in the Hamptons or at work in Manhattan, they were traveling all over the world. The evening after the Stonewall riots, just a few blocks from their apartment, they returned from Venice. When Edie went to Seventh Avenue to purchase cigarettes, she learned that the fearful world of the homosexual closet had been unhinged by two nights of protests. They threw fundraisers for some of the new lesbian and gay organizations that blossomed after Stonewall. After the LGBT Community Center opened in 1983, Edie donated time and expertise to do programming and bug removal for its computers.[5]

"Happily ever after" hit a snag in 1977, when Thea was diagnosed with chronic progressive multiple sclerosis, a deterioration of her muscles that started in her legs and gradually moved to her arms and hands. Only forty-five years old and still possessed of a regal glamour, she had to use a cane to steady herself, then two forearm crutches, then a manual wheelchair, and eventually, for the rest of her life, a motorized wheelchair. The illness brought the women closer together and hardly diminished their effervescent partnership. Thea continued to see patients four days a week, and the couple continued to travel, entertain friends, and swim and summer in the Hamptons. The dancing never stopped. Even after Thea had become a quadriplegic, Edie would sit on the arm of the motorized wheelchair, and they would zip and turn in a pantomime of dance.

On May 22, 2007, at Thea's suggestion, they were legally married in Toronto, Canada, which had recognized same-sex marriages by statute in 2005. Justice Harvey Brownstone (Canada's first openly gay judge) presided over their ceremony at an airport hotel. Edie wore a cream-colored silk pantsuit and a boutonnière of small white roses. Thea wore a black tuxedo, white turtleneck, and a boutonnière of small red roses. (The wedding cake echoed their attire, with little replicas of Edie in a dress and Thea in a tuxedo.) The couple exchanged vows and rings. When the judge pronounced them "legally married spouses and partners for life," their very long engagement was over.[6]

State court precedents indicated that their Canadian marriage was valid in New York as well. Thea believed that the summer of 2008 would be her last, because the doctors had told her she was suffering from a gradual closing of her aorta. They spent the summer in their Hamptons cottage and the winter

Thea Spyer and Edith Windsor. (Photo by Joan Abrahams
from the Estate of Edith S. Windsor, donated by The Judith M.
Kasen-Windsor Trust.)

in their Fifth Avenue apartment, where Thea died, held and loved by her life
partner, on February 5, 2009. A few weeks after that, Edie suffered the first
of two heart attacks, what the doctors call stress cardiomyopathy. Yet she became a celebrity after the release of a documentary about her life with Thea.
"If you have to outlive a great love, I can't think of a better way to do it than
being everybody's hero. Suddenly I'm exalted, instead of being this goofy old
lady, which is what I feel like."[7]

In the glow of her new celebrity, Edie, the brilliant financial planner, was
hit with a huge tax bill. Because the Defense of Marriage Act (DOMA) prevented Edie from taking advantage of the spousal allowance that would have
eliminated estate tax liability for Thea's sizeable estate, she owed $363,000 in
federal estate taxes that the survivor of a traditional marriage would not have
owed. She decided to sue, and mutual friends connected her with Roberta Kaplan, one of the lawyers who had represented the gay marriage plaintiffs in
Hernandez v. Robles (2006), the unsuccessful New York marriage case. When
they met at Windsor's apartment, Kaplan was impressed by this "knock out—a
slender, impeccably dressed woman with a blond bob, a string of pearls, and
perfectly manicured nails." Hearing Windsor's remarkable story, she wanted
to represent this firecracker septuagenarian in what she realized would be an
offbeat DOMA challenge. In the New England marriage cases, movement
lawyers had carefully curated a representative array of couples seeking access
to large federal programs, such as social security and health care insurance,
that the average straight family relied on themselves. The strategy was to

demonstrate how DOMA affected everyday lives and undermined families. Windsor was a childless multimillionaire whose inheritance justified a tax bill higher than many Americans' lifetime earnings. Still, Edie Windsor had this Betty White thing going. By 2010, the marriage equality message focused on love, commitment, and family—and Edie's half-century love affair with her spouse, her caregiving for the last thirty years of their life together, and her resemblance to everyone's favorite grandmother convinced Kaplan that she was, in her unique way, the perfect plaintiff.[8]

To coordinate with GLAD, which was planning its own DOMA challenge in Connecticut, Kaplan did not file a complaint in *Windsor v. United States* until November 9, 2010. Together, the two lawsuits pulled together all of the arguments for and against DOMA and its relationship to marriage equality, as well as important institutional players that had been battling over the issue for decades. Several weeks after her complaint was filed, Windsor had another heart incident—but she was determined to outlive DOMA. The story of her success starts with Mary Bonauto, the earnest architect of marriage equality in Massachusetts and a lawyer Edie adored from the day she met her.

The DOMA Challenges

DOMA was constitutionally assailed even before its enactment. A few weeks after the US Supreme Court held in *Romer v. Evans* (1996) that a state constitutional amendment was invalid because it reflected "animosity" toward gay people, one of us argued in *The New Republic* that the Fourteenth Amendment barred states from invoking anti-gay sentiment to deny acceptance of same-sex marriages recognized in another state. As the Supreme Court had just declared, "a classification of persons undertaken for its own sake" violated constitutional equality rules. Because Congress did not have the authority to authorize state violations of the equal protection clause, Eskridge maintained that both section 2 (which authorized states to discriminate against valid same-sex marriages) and section 3 (barring federal recognition of valid same-sex marriages) of the defense of marriage bill "raise[d] grave constitutional concerns." Amherst professor Hadley Arkes, a supporter of the bill, worried that *Romer* could, indeed, be applied by the Supreme Court to mean that a government "may not incorporate anywhere in its laws or public policy any adverse judgment on the status of homosexuality" and that a state could not single out homosexual relationships and declare them inferior to straight relationships. Other scholars suggested that the proposed legislation was an affront to federalism—the constitutional principle assuring state governments independent regulatory authority over local governance matters such as family law. None of these concerns deterred Congress from passing and President Clinton from signing DOMA into law in September 1996.[9]

Constitutional questions were largely academic until the *Goodridge* decision required Massachusetts to start handing out marriage licenses to gay and lesbian couples in May 2004. Based on research from GLAD's working group, Mary Bonauto began to talk with policy makers, movement litigators, and academics about a constitutional challenge to DOMA, and the idea was featured in several sessions of the twice-a-year Litigators' Roundtable. DOMA was also discussed at the 2005 Denver and Jersey City meetings of LGBT leaders, described in chapter 13. The May 2005 "Winning Marriage" strategy accepted GLAD's view that a constitutional challenge to DOMA would be easier to win than a challenge to the exclusionary laws of forty-nine states, because the federal government could be presented as undermining valid state marriages and families. The collective wisdom, however, was that such a challenge was premature. Movement leaders grew even more pessimistic as the US Supreme Court turned sharply to the right with the 2005 appointments of John Roberts and Samuel Alito, constitutional lawsuits were rebuffed in gay-friendly jurisdictions, and most states voted to add junior-DOMAs and Super-DOMAs to their constitutions.[10]

GLAD BUILDS THE CASE AGAINST DOMA

In January 2001, GLAD's attorneys circulated a memorandum, "Is DOMA Doomed?," outlining three constitutional arguments against DOMA: it violated the equal protection guarantee the US Supreme Court had read into the Fifth Amendment; it rewrote the full faith and credit clause; and it improperly nationalized domestic relations law, in violation of the Constitution's federalist structure. In a series of memoranda distributed in 2003, Michele Granda (a young GLAD lawyer) explored federalism-based challenges to DOMA. While GLAD did not ultimately pursue such a challenge, its lawyers shared this research with the Office of the Massachusetts Attorney General and deployed it to support the equal protection challenge by demonstrating how anomalous as well as sweeping DOMA was.[11]

First, the Tenth Amendment provided that Congress could only act pursuant to a power granted it in the Constitution. Otherwise, the power to legislate on that matter was constitutionally reserved to the states or to the people.

Because DOMA's section 3 operated only on the definition of spouse or marriage in laws that Congress had already enacted under one or more enumerated powers, its legitimacy could rest upon the constitutional authorization for the preexisting statutes. Most of those statutes were authorized by the spending clause of Article I. In *South Dakota v. Dole* (1987), the Supreme Court had interpreted the spending clause as not authorizing conditions (1) that were coercive against the states, (2) that were not germane to the federal purpose of the spending program, or (3) that required the states to violate the Constitution. The third condition could be integrated with GLAD's basic argument that DOMA violated the equal protection rights of Massachusetts-married couples and their families.[12]

The Tenth Amendment might be the textual marker for a more general limitation derived from the constitutional structure: the federal government could not deprive the states of their sovereign status or interfere with their abilities to carry out core governance functions. Because regulation of marriage has traditionally been a core state function, one might argue that Congress cannot adopt a global, rather than targeted, regulation of marriage. But no constitutional precedent cleanly articulated state family law as a monopoly that posed a hard limit on federal power. The best analogy was *Erie Railroad v. Tompkins* (1938), in which the Supreme Court announced that neither Congress nor the court had authority to create "federal general common law" displacing state law on a global basis. The totalizing effect of DOMA could be the basis for a claim that Congress was unduly interfering with state law and the families created thereunder. Bonauto and her colleagues were dubious that such a claim could succeed, but it might be useful in support of the equal protection claim.[13]

Finally, the Supreme Court had recently interpreted the constitutional structure to bar Congress from commandeering state governments by telling them how to legislate or by usurping the services of their executive officials. This line of cases was also hard to mobilize against DOMA, which did not command the states to do anything. Overall, Granda thought GLAD's best federalism pitch was that "Congress cannot define marriage because the subject matter addressed by DOMA's Section 3 . . . impinges on an essential state function—one of 'the most fundamental sort for a sovereign state'—namely, the regulation of domestic relations." GLAD's leaders considered this argument respectable enough to share with movement lawyers at the autumn 2003 session of the Litigators' Roundtable. By 2005, Bonauto was openly discussing the possibility of a constitutional challenge to DOMA, primarily grounded on equal protection but with a federalism angle as well.[14]

The national organizations were not enthusiastic. HRC worried that a DOMA challenge would revive interest in the sagging Federal Marriage Amendment. ACLU and Lambda liked the *Romer*-based equal protection argument but believed the Supreme Court was not ready for it—especially after Justice O'Connor (a federalism-loving justice who wrote an equal protection concurring opinion in *Lawrence*) and Chief Justice Rehnquist (a federalism fan who was warming up to gay rights before his death in 2005) were replaced by federal court of appeals judges Samuel Alito and John Roberts, Catholic Republicans who kept their distance from gay rights. Any equal protection claim against DOMA would probably apply to state constitutional DOMAs. With just one state recognizing same-sex marriage, even a more liberal Supreme Court would not impose nationwide marriage equality. In 2006, after consultation with former law clerks to Justice Kennedy (whose vote was essential to any majority), Lambda's David Buckel and the ACLU's Matt Coles and James Esseks decided not to seek Supreme Court review for the lightly reasoned Eighth Circuit decision upholding Nebraska's constitutional Super-DOMA in *Citizens for Equal Protection v. Bruning* (2006).[15]

But the ACLU and Lambda feared a rogue lawsuit that might vault onto the Supreme Court's docket before the issue was ripe for consideration. A GLAD challenge to DOMA would discourage such suits. Buckel considered the federalism argument "a respectable but losing claim, but which has the significant advantage of presenting absolutely no threat to state DOMAs." Ironically, GLAD had discovered that, in the First Circuit, the only claimant with standing to make a Tenth Amendment or general federalism argument would be the commonwealth of Massachusetts, not the individual plaintiffs whom GLAD was assembling.[16]

Notwithstanding the reluctance of the other movement litigation groups— the same groups that strongly resisted the federal Proposition 8 challenge discussed in chapter 15—Bonauto proceeded with preparation for a cautious attack on DOMA. To improve the odds of prevailing, she proposed that GLAD bring an "as-applied" challenge, maintaining that DOMA was unconstitutional as applied to large federal programs and leaving open the possibility that DOMA was also unconstitutional on its face. A series of plaintiff couples would offer their stories of being denied access to family health benefits, social security protections for surviving spouses, and family medical leaves—situations where it made no sense, in terms of federal policy, to exclude married same-sex couples. This would allow judges to see, concretely, how DOMA harmed the lives of good American couples—and Justice Kennedy could write as broad or narrow an opinion as he desired. If he did not want to invalidate section 3 entirely, he could write an opinion holding that DOMA could not constitutionally be applied, for example, to social security benefits. GLAD could build on that precedent, adding more federal programs, until the Supreme Court felt comfortable striking down section 3 in all applications. From a practical lawyering perspective, this was an excellent idea, as was Bonauto's recruitment of Massachusetts attorney general–elect Martha Coakley to bring a separate lawsuit. Massachusetts could present the federalism claims as a broad attack on DOMA, while GLAD would present its equal protection claims as a surgical strike against DOMA's most harmful applications.[17]

Expanding upon its approach in the Massachusetts and Connecticut marriage lawsuits, GLAD envisioned the DOMA litigation as a major public relations campaign, made possible by contributions from local donors, HRC, and the Civil Marriage Collaborative. To frame the issue properly, publicists Stephanie Cutter and Erik Smith advised a sharp distinction between the rights-based and federalism arguments GLAD would make in its constitutional briefs and the emotion-and-values-based messaging that should saturate the media. The media campaign, which began a year before the case was filed, focused on how DOMA's sweeping exclusion harmed lesbian and gay families, grounded in the same mutual commitment and encountering the same problems as everyone else's families. GLAD's message was also informed by its own experiences in the states and by private polling, which revealed strong popular support for both traditional marriage and for equal benefits to married lesbian and gay couples, with social security and insurance benefits being paramount. The polling also boosted the federalism argument against DOMA (Republicans liked it) and arguments based on harms DOMA inflicted on children raised in LGBT households.[18]

GLAD was ready to file its lawsuit by mid-2008, but it wanted Massachusetts to file its own DOMA challenge at roughly the same time. In December 2006, Bonauto had met with Attorney General–elect Coakley, and GLAD's attorneys had several meetings with Maura Healey, chief of the civil rights division. In 2007, Bonauto forwarded a massive memorandum to the attorney general's office, laying out the contours of its potential federalism claims. DOMA section 3 undermined Massachusetts's constitutional right to define its own citizens' marital status and forced the state government to spend money and act in ways discordant with the state's fundamental public policy. Most important, by tying federal benefit programs to DOMA's discriminatory policy, Massachusetts was being "coerced" to violate the US Constitution as well as its own.

Buckel had suggested in 2005 that the equal protection and federalism arguments could cross-fertilize, and GLAD's attorneys had, independently, come to the same conclusion. DOMA's "unprecedented nature in the federalist system of government" could also support a finding of animus, as in *Romer*. Its "extraordinary expansion of congressional authority" could motivate a Hayekian libertarian like Justice Kennedy to look closely at the equal protection issue and more skeptically at the demonstrable harms DOMA visited upon legitimate families. After a great deal of lobbying by GLAD, the Massachusetts attorney general agreed to file a federalism challenge to DOMA.[19]

BONAUTO AND HEALEY AGAINST DOMA

Mary Bonauto and GLAD filed their complaint in federal district court on March 3, 2009. The plaintiffs in *Gill v. Office of Personnel Management* included five married lesbian couples, three married gay couples, and three gay men who were surviving spouses. The lead plaintiffs were Nancy Gill and Marcelle LeTourneau, who were raising two kids in Bridgewater. Struggling to make ends meet, the family could ill afford the extra expense incurred because Marcelle could not be added to Nancy's federal health insurance. In characteristic GLAD fashion, the nineteen plaintiffs were a cross section of the ten thousand same-sex married couples in Massachusetts—representing all parts of the state and different social and economic backgrounds, ethnicities, ages, and religious traditions. The lengthy *Gill* complaint focused on how DOMA created "second-class marriages" for lawfully wed same-sex couples who paid into federal safety-net programs but were unable to share in their benefits on an equal basis.[20]

This complaint was accompanied by a press conference in which Bonauto introduced the case in terms that had been informed by poll testing as well as by GLAD's experience in the trenches. "Love and commitment brought them to marry. Federal discrimination and the harms it has caused them brought them to GLAD." Looking back at the assembled couples, she lamented that the "federal government bars these people from programs that would enable them to take better care of each other and their children. The federal safety net has been pulled from them alone." Hurting these families was bad enough, but Congress had "stepped beyond its proper role" when it passed DOMA: Do we really want Washington making decisions about families here in Massachusetts?[21]

In July 2009, Maura Healey filed the commonwealth's complaint in *Massachusetts v. Department of Health & Human Services*. She argued that the statute interfered with the commonwealth's ability to maintain a unified, coherent family law regime. Under DOMA, Massachusetts had to create a two-track system: marriages with federal benefits and pseudo-marriages with none. Massachusetts also made an enumerated powers argument. Most of the federal statutes affected by DOMA were enacted under Congress's spending clause authority, which could not be used to induce states to commit constitutional violations. Under DOMA, for example, Massachusetts could not receive federal funds if it authorized the burial of a same-sex spouse in a federally funded veterans cemetery or if it recognized the marriages of same-sex spouses in assessing eligibility for Medicaid health benefits. But if the commonwealth were to disregard the lawful marriages of same-sex couples when administering these programs, it would violate the equal protection clause, because DOMA's section 3 failed rational basis scrutiny, as applied by the Supreme Court in *Romer* and by Justice O'Connor's concurring opinion in *Lawrence*.[22]

Both cases were assigned to federal district judge Joseph Tauro. Counsel to GOP governor John Volpe in the 1960s, Tauro was no rebel but was a no-nonsense fact finder. His first big case involved a civil rights complaint to clean up conditions at a state school for the mentally disabled. The commonwealth's attorneys told him it was not so bad there. Okay, he replied, let's pay a visit—and so without warning the federal judge, trailed by the attorneys, dropped in on the Belchertown State School, where he found the conditions and the treatment of its youthful residents inhumane and appalling. He ended the commonwealth's defense on the spot. Many trial judges start their decision-making by reading the complaint and then working through the record. Tauro's judgment in the DOMA cases was set in motion when he read the statute. "I said to myself, 'This is intolerable.'" Just like his visit to Belchertown, his review of the GLAD affidavits only deepened his sense of injustice. On July 8, 2010, he ruled for the plaintiffs in both cases. His opinions were filled with discussion of precedent and evidence, but he recalls that the result, "the way it was going to come out—that was right from my soul."[23]

In *Gill*, Judge Tauro found DOMA section 3 to be a violation of the equal protection component of the Fifth Amendment, because its exclusion of lesbian and gay married couples lacked any rational basis. He rejected the responsible procreation justification, for example, not just because government lawyers disavowed it but also because harming lesbian and gay families did not, in any plausible way, encourage straight people to behave more responsibly. Following *Romer*, he did not accept the government's administrative convenience argument: DOMA created administrative complexity, and its legislative history suggested that it accomplished nothing beyond scapegoating gay people. Judge Tauro's opinion in *Massachusetts v. U.S. Department of Health & Human Services* paralleled his opinion in *Gill*. By conditioning "the receipt of federal funding on the denial of marriage-based benefits to same-sex married couples" in programs like Medicaid and veterans cemeteries, DOMA "induce[d] the Commonwealth to violate the equal protection rights of its citizens." Tauro also held that DOMA violated the Tenth Amendment because "compliance with DOMA would impair the Commonwealth's ability to structure integral operations in areas of traditional governmental functions" such as Medicaid. DOMA interfered with Massachusetts' ability to develop and apply a coherent law of marriage and family.[24]

WINDSOR AND KAPLAN AGAINST DOMA

While GLAD and Massachusetts were litigating the validity of DOMA in the First Circuit, which was committed to rational basis review for sexual orientation exclusions, Robbie Kaplan was lobbying the ACLU's James Esseks to be cocounsel in Edie Windsor's case. Esseks, Matt Coles's successor as head of the ACLU's LGBT and AIDS Project, thought a DOMA lawsuit should not be brought until a fair number of states were handing out same-sex marriage licenses *and* national polling revealed close to a 50-50 split on marriage equality. In September 2010 there were still only five marriage equality states, and national polling remained less than 50-50. But GLAD and Massachusetts had won smashing judgments from a conservative judge in July, and Vaughn Walker had issued his judgment invalidating California's Proposition 8 in August. So the ACLU was suddenly open to a DOMA lawsuit, and Kaplan persuaded Esseks that Edie Windsor would be the perfect DOMA challenger. In September, Esseks signed on as cocounsel. He notified GLAD at the end of October, just as Bonauto was preparing to file a second DOMA challenge in Connecticut.[25]

On November 9, 2010, GLAD filed *Pedersen v. United States*, a DOMA challenge involving legally married Connecticut couples, while the ACLU filed *Windsor v. United States* in the Southern District of New York. The Connecticut and New York district courts were in the Second Circuit, which had not decided the level of constitutional scrutiny for sexual orientation discrimination. Unlike the *Gill* and *Pedersen* complaints, which had a Walt Whitman "We are America" comprehensiveness, the *Windsor* complaint echoed Patricia Highsmith's *The Price of Salt*, in which the lesbian romance breaks with convention to deliver a happy ending. Notwithstanding "pervasive discrimination and homophobia that Edie and Thea encountered on a routine basis," the two women had fallen in love, formed a committed relationship, and lived "lives of great joy, full of dancing, love, and celebration." As GLAD was claiming in *Gill* and *Pedersen*, Windsor's legal claim was that DOMA discriminated against her marriage without even a rational basis, much less a compelling governmental interest that would pass strict scrutiny, and so violated the equal protection guarantee of the Fifth Amendment.[26]

When the White House's Team Gay read the *Windsor* complaint, they cried like plutocrats at tax time. They were cheered by the expectation that the Obama administration would not defend DOMA and would probably support heightened scrutiny for all sexual orientation–based discriminations. Kaplan and Esseks did not know any of this—only that Windsor had suffered another heart incident during Thanksgiving week, soon after her federal complaint was filed. Kaplan deluged federal district judge Barbara Jones and Magistrate Jay Francis with requests for an expedited process, which Francis accommodated with a brisk schedule that required the government to file its expected motion to dismiss by February 9, 2011. Kaplan reluctantly agreed to a personal plea from Assistant Attorney General Tony West to postpone the government's motion until March 11.

On February 11, 2011, West scheduled a conference call with Bonauto, Buseck, Kaplan, and Esseks. He calmly dropped his bombshell: the Department of Justice (DOJ) had concluded that discrimination because of sexual orientation was constitutionally suspect, that DOMA's discrimination could not survive heightened scrutiny, and that the United States would urge federal judges to invalidate DOMA's section 3. The shocked advocates treated this as cause for great celebration. But this volte-face, which Attorney General Holder made public with his famous letter to Speaker Boehner on February 23, would considerably delay and complicate GLAD's and the ACLU's constitutional challenges to DOMA.[27]

There would be no motion to dismiss by the United States, but the Bipartisan Legal Advisory Group (BLAG) of the House of Representatives immediately voted to defend DOMA and to retain former solicitor general Paul Clement to represent them. On June 2, Magistrate Francis granted BLAG's motion to intervene, and Clement would need much of the summer to prepare BLAG's defense. On June 24, Kaplan and Esseks filed their motion for summary judgment, featuring a lengthy affidavit from Windsor telling her story and explaining how DOMA harmed her. The plaintiff's counsel also filed affidavits from the same experts GLAD had assembled for *Gill* and who had testified in the

Proposition 8 trial: Nancy Cott, George Chauncey, Michael Lamb, Letitia Peplau, and Gary Segura. On August 1, BLAG filed its own motion to dismiss. As the exchange of motions and affidavits consumed the remainder of the year, Kaplan fretted over Windsor's health more than she did over BLAG's justifications.[28]

Eric Holder's February 23 letter announcing DOJ's new stance on DOMA had broad ramifications. The California Supreme Court in *Strauss v. Horton* (2009) had recognized the validity of eighteen thousand same-sex marriages performed in the state between June and November 2008. Most of those couples were affected by DOMA. For example, Gene Douglas Balas and Carlos Morales were validly married in California in August 2008. During the economic collapse of 2008–2009, the family filed a joint petition for Chapter 13 bankruptcy. The US Trustee moved to dismiss the Balas-Morales joint petition because DOMA barred a finding that they were entitled to take advantage of special bankruptcy rules for marital families. On June 13, just as the *Windsor* case was back on track in New York, bankruptcy judge Thomas Donovan of the Central District of California ruled that DOMA was unconstitutional as applied to the Bankruptcy Code. In a show of judicial solidarity, twenty of the Central District's twenty-four bankruptcy judges signed onto Judge Donovan's opinion, adopting the rationale of the Holder letter. They also ruled that the exclusion was an instance of sex discrimination. Holder's letter also played a key role in the long-running travails of Karen Golinski, the Ninth Circuit employee who had administratively petitioned for the federal government to include her female spouse in her government health plan. Represented by Susan Sommer and Jon Davidson of Lambda, Golinski had brought a federal lawsuit. In February 2012, district judge Jeffrey White ruled DOMA unconstitutional and ordered the Office of Personnel Management (OPM) to provide the spousal benefits.[29]

By 2012, several of the aforementioned cases were candidates to be the occasion for the US Supreme Court to review and, the lawyers hoped, bury DOMA. To the lawyers outside the government, the Massachusetts cases seemed to be on the fastest track to the Supreme Court. Enjoying her role as the Grand Old Lady, Edie Windsor hoped that hers would somehow reach the highest court, and Robbie Kaplan was working hard to make that happen.

BOUDIN'S MARRIAGE DECISION
FOR THE FIRST CIRCUIT

The DOJ's volte-face of February 23, 2011, meant that BLAG would bear the burden of defending DOMA in all the aforementioned lawsuits. Paul Clement and his colleagues crafted a much harder-hitting brief in *Gill* than DOJ had filed earlier. BLAG asserted no fewer than six public-regarding justifications that might meet the rational basis test applied in the First Circuit: DOMA served (1) to freeze the status quo as states experiment; (2) to protect the public fisc and to respect the original assumptions of earlier statutes; (3) to provide uniformity and ease of administration; (4) to encourage responsible procreation; (5) to preserve the link between marriage and children; and (6) to encourage optimal households for childrearing. The brief's Achilles' heel was that it did not deeply engage with the US Supreme Court's gay rights precedents that had applied the rational basis test with bite. The First Circuit could follow its own precedent in applying rational basis scrutiny, yet it could reject any or all of those justifications if it gave *Romer*-like bite to the rational basis test.[30]

Although he pointedly refused to mention the responsible procreation justification at oral argument, Paul Clement strongly pressed the rationality of BLAG's proffered justifications. Arguing for GLAD, Mary Bonauto claimed *Romer*'s more demanding version of rational basis review—and added the anomalies entailed in the federal disrespect for only these marriages and disruption of families recognized under state law as a constitutional booster shot. The Clement-Bonauto debate about what the rational basis test required to justify DOMA's wide discrimination put Assistant Attorney General Stuart Delery in a bind. Arguing for the federal government, he was urging the First Circuit to overturn or distinguish its own precedent on level of scrutiny. Should he admit that *Romer* required the government to provide evidence of tangible harm in order to justify anti-gay discrimination? Such a concession could be used against the DOJ in future cases. His colleagues agreed that Delery could follow Justice O'Connor's view that government exclusions of gay people were subject to "a more searching form of rational basis review."[31]

The appeals court, it turned out, needed no prompting on the issue. Writing for the unanimous panel in *Massachusetts v. Department of Health & Human Services* was circuit judge Michael Boudin, a former antitrust attorney who had no interest in constitutional law but had a sophisticated theory of judging: "Appellate judges have the peculiar burden of seeking to do three different things at the same time: first, to determine and respect 'the law,' this vast collection of constitutional provisions, statutes, precedents, canons, and other paraphernalia; second, to reform doctrine, if permissible and when appropriate, in light of new insights, experience, and social imperatives; and finally, to get the specific quarrel settled in a just and practical way." Boudin's opinion, handed down on May 31, 2012, started with the proposition that this was not an ordinary rational basis case, because it had a federalism dimension and a more-serious-than-usual equal protection dimension. Together, these two dimensions "require a closer than usual review based in part on discrepant impact among married couples and in part on the importance of state interests in regulating marriage." Boudin was suggesting that *Romer* required more searching review because of the pervasive discrimination against gay people, while the federalism precedents required a more careful look at the congressional rationales because DOMA interfered with state family law.[32]

Boudin's searching version of rational basis required a "*demonstrated* connection between DOMA's treatment of same-sex couples and its asserted goal of strengthening the bonds and benefits to society of heterosexual marriage." The responsible procreation and optimal families arguments were too speculative to meet this standard, and BLAG's other justifications were either more attenuated or rested on impermissible considerations. "If we are right in thinking that disparate impact on minority interests and federalism concerns both require somewhat more in this case than almost automatic deference to Congress' will, this statute fails that test." Particularly impressive was Judge Boudin's invalidating a major federal statute without casting aspersions on the intelligence, motivations, or wisdom of the enacting Congress. Within a week of Boudin's disposition, Judge Jones took a similar approach in Windsor's case: DOMA's interference with state family law gave the rational basis approach greater bite, which the law did not survive. BLAG and DOJ immediately filed notices of appeal to the Second Circuit.[33]

THE RACE TO THE US SUPREME COURT

By mid-2012, there were five DOMA cases in the pipeline to the US Supreme Court—the GLAD and Massachusetts cases in the First Circuit, the ACLU and GLAD cases in the Second Circuit, and the Lambda case in the Ninth Circuit. Also racing toward the court was the federal Proposition 8 case. Ironically, David Boies and Ted Olson—the winners in Judge Walker's court—wanted the Supreme Court to take their case as much as Paul Clement and BLAG did. On July 3, Solicitor General Donald Verrilli filed a petition for review of Judge Boudin's decision and asked the court to take review in *Golinski* even before the Ninth Circuit's review. In the wake of Windsor's heart attack on March 12, her attorneys filed their own petition before judgment, as did GLAD in *Pedersen*.[34]

Meanwhile, Robbie Kaplan and James Esseks clamored for the Second Circuit to set an accelerated briefing and argument schedule for Windsor's case. Chief Judge Dennis Jacobs (DJ) gave them almost everything they asked for. A native of Queens, New York, DJ was a classic live-and-let-live libertarian. He and his colleagues wanted the case to be Supreme Court–worthy. In record time for a major case, Jacobs delivered an opinion for a divided court that adopted the DOJ's arguments and ruled that sexual orientation classifications required heightened scrutiny under the Supreme Court's precedents: gay people had suffered an unspeakable history of discrimination based on a trait having nothing to do with their capacity to contribute to society; the trait was not easily altered and was important to their personhood; and the political process remained slanted against their claims for decent treatment and fair laws. Paul Clement had conceded that DOMA could not survive heightened scrutiny, so that was that. With the Second Circuit's judgment, BLAG and DOJ immediately sought review through a regular petition for certiorari (which superseded the earlier petition before judgment).[35]

THE US SUPREME COURT GRANTS REVIEW
IN TWO MARRIAGE CASES

The nine justices met on December 7, 2012, for a regular conference to determine which among hundreds of petitions for review they should choose. The marriage issue was the hottest constitutional topic of the term. Following the referendum victories a month earlier, marriage equality was now the law in nine states and the District of Columbia. The president had been reelected on a marriage equality platform. Polls showed that most Americans favored the freedom to marry.

Since President Bush's appointments, two new members had joined the court. One was Sonia Sotomayor, a Second Circuit judge nominated by President Obama in April 2009. Like Justice Alito, a graduate of Princeton University and Yale Law School, Justice Sotomayor had been a prosecutor under the legendary Robert Morgenthau, a corporate attorney and law firm partner, a civil libertarian (serving especially the Latinx community), and the beloved district court judge who in 1995 had saved baseball from a crippling players' strike. She was more liberal and had more extensive legal experience than any of her new colleagues. Raised in the Bronx by her widowed Puerto Rican mother, Celina, Sotomayor was known to keep an inclusive circle of friends and law clerks.

Solicitor General Elena Kagan replaced retiring Justice Stevens in August 2010. Before that, she had been one of the most successful deans in the storied history of the Harvard Law School. Her elevation to the Supreme Court created an unexpected wrinkle for the marriage petitions. Recall that DOJ was involved in ongoing conversations about the *Gill, Massachusetts,* and *Golinski* cases at the trial courts in 2009 and 2010. Solicitor General Kagan had participated in some of those conversations. A judge is not supposed to adjudicate a case or controversy in which she has been personally involved, so Kagan would recuse herself from any deliberations regarding the First Circuit or California DOMA cases, a fact well understood by the DOJ when it endorsed *Windsor* as the best vehicle for judicial review of DOMA's section 3.

Before December 7, Chief Justice Roberts had circulated a helpful memorandum to his colleagues. Noting that Kagan was recused from *Massachusetts* and *Golinski,* Roberts urged his colleagues to take *Windsor* so that there would be a full court to decide the case. Also, the Second Circuit had nicely teed up the DOMA issue, rendering an authoritative opinion that New York would recognize the Windsor-Spyer Canadian marriage. Following Roberts's logic, the justices unanimously voted to grant review in *Windsor* and (also at his suggestion) added two new questions for the parties to address: Did the executive branch's refusal to defend DOMA deprive the Supreme Court of jurisdiction? Did BLAG have standing to take its appeal? Hedging their bets as always, the justices left the First Circuit petition in limbo: it was neither dismissed nor granted, as it could be disposed of after the court decided *Windsor.*[36]

Hollingsworth v. Perry, the Proposition 8 case, was not so urgent, as a coalition of law professors had written an amicus brief opposing review. The Ninth Circuit had written a narrow opinion, and it was not clear that the private proponents of Proposition 8 were proper parties to defend the constitutional amendment. Five justices (Kennedy, Ginsburg, Breyer, Sotomayor, and Kagan) voted against review for these reasons—but you only need four, and the chief justice and three others (Scalia, Thomas, and Alito) felt there were issues of interest to them. Roberts was especially intrigued by the procedural issue, and so the court added a new question for the parties to brief: Did the private Proposition 8 proponents have standing to appeal the judgment against the state?[37]

Windsor and *Perry* at the Supreme Court

Edie Windsor and her legal team were elated that her case was going to the Supreme Court. Mary Bonauto not only graciously accepted the personal disappointment of seeing her deeply researched case sidelined, but she redoubled her efforts in support of the only goal that mattered, the end of DOMA. At Kaplan's request, Bonauto managed the amicus briefs, a task she performed brilliantly, securing many briefs from *not* the usual suspects: 278 large employers from Amazon to Zynga, who maintained that DOMA imposed burdens on them and poisoned American workplaces; former cabinet officials such as Donna Shalala and Louis Sullivan, who demonstrated that DOMA did nothing to make administration of federal programs more uniform and only operated to exclude some marriages; General Wesley Clark and other defense experts, detailing DOMA's burdens on military personnel; James Clapper, Michael Flynn, and fourteen former top intelligence officials, arguing that DOMA's burdens on national intelligence agencies undermined national security; and the libertarian Cato Institute, arguing that DOMA was blatantly inconsistent with equality under the law. In *Perry*, the big news was an amicus brief by former GOP National Committee chair Ken Mehlman and more than one hundred other leading Republicans who argued that Proposition 8 undermined the conservative values of commitment and family.

Although the Second Circuit had adopted the Obama administration's view favoring heightened scrutiny of laws discriminating because of sexual orientation, Team Edie (Robbie Kaplan, James Esseks, Pam Karlan and Jeff Fisher from the Stanford Law School, as well as Mary Bonauto on amici) did not assume that the Supreme Court would follow that approach. As GLAD's briefs had done in its cases, Windsor's brief emphasized how DOMA failed the rational basis test. DOMA raised three red flags that had accompanied earlier Supreme Court rulings that laws lacked a rational basis: (1) the legislative process was not deliberative and was saturated with statements of animus toward LGBTQ+ persons; (2) the exclusion was sweeping and not carefully linked to particular harms; and (3) the law was unprecedented, especially in its disregard for the federal structure. Karlan and Kaplan then argued that the goals BLAG asserted as rational were neither distinctively federal interests nor advanced by DOMA's sweeping exclusion.[38]

Paul Clement believed that Team Edie started with five justices inclined to strike down DOMA. The law had been renounced by its sponsors and had been mocked in Andrew Koppelman's famous article, "Dumb and DOMA." Once hailed as a super-statute, DOMA now stank like a rotting fish, and in such cases Anthony Kennedy was notorious for following his olfactory reactions. (In the *Romer* argument, he literally scrunched up his nose at the beginning of Tim Tymkovich's presentation for Amendment 2.) Given the justices' leanings, we asked Clement why he took the case in the first place. Speaking like a lawyer born to be solicitor general (as he was, 2004–2008), he reflected that every serious federal statute deserves a defense, and he was professionally disappointed that President Obama's DOJ was abandoning the law. In his view, DOMA was defensible under established constitutional criteria—and in our view, his merits brief for BLAG made an excellent case for its validity.[39]

Clement devised a smart strategy in response to his adversaries in the Obama administration, the media, the legal academy, and Team Edie. He believed the justices would not be eager to use the *Windsor* case to recognize a new suspect or quasi-suspect classification, and he thought DOMA passed traditional rational basis review because it created an administratively easy to follow, predictable, and uniform rule for federal agencies, a point that the Shalala-Sullivan amicus undermined. Perhaps a better justification for DOMA was Clement's argument that it pushed pause on federal policy while the marriage debate raged in the states. Now that LGBTQ+ Americans were persuading their neighbors to vote for marriage equality, it was only a matter of time before DOMA was repealed, just as the military exclusion had been repealed in 2010–2011. Let the people continue to deliberate, he urged, and let gay marriage come through the legitimating democratic process.[40]

Clement's partial blind spot was that he believed the rational basis test would be applied here roughly as it was applied in economic regulation cases. If Windsor were challenging a routine estate tax distinction, administrative convenience arguments would have sufficed—but she was alleging serious discrimination through an unprecedented deployment of congressional authority, which made the case look a lot like *Romer*. Clement understood that *Romer* applied rational basis with greater bite, but he believed that the two cases were vastly different. *Romer* had struck down a badly drafted state initiative adopted after a gay-bashing campaign, while *Windsor* involved a precisely drafted congressional super-statute enacted by enormous bipartisan majorities after intensive public debate. It was endorsed by a president who counted gay people as his friends and supporters.

Although many lawyers did not quite see what *Romer*'s added bite meant for judicial review, Judge Boudin explained it lucidly: rational basis with bite meant that defenders of a broad anti-gay statute had to demonstrate something more than administrative convenience. They had to point to some tangible harm that the statute actually addressed and produce some evidence that the discriminatory statute would probably reduce the harm. If Boudin's reading was correct, BLAG would likely lose. The 2012 Boudin opinion also handed Team Edie an additional reason to apply rational basis with bite: the states' interest, under federalism, in the federal government's not disrespecting their legal marriages across the board.[41]

Because the president had signed on to heightened scrutiny in 2011, Solicitor General Verrilli was committed to that stance in *Windsor,* but he and his colleagues realized that Boudin's opinion could render the Obama administration's three-year odyssey toward heightened scrutiny immediately passé. The United States' brief on the merits made a strong case for heightened scrutiny but also maintained that BLAG's reasons for the exclusion did not even satisfy the "searching inquiry" with which the Supreme Court had applied the rational basis test in *Romer* and *Lawrence.* This was the first time the solicitor general's office had admitted that the rational basis test was sometimes applied with greater bite than the deferential version that served the federal government so well.[42]

By pairing *Windsor* with *Perry,* the Supreme Court created a dilemma for the government. Heightened scrutiny for marriage exclusions under the Fifth Amendment (*Windsor*) would automatically carry over to the Fourteenth Amendment (*Perry*), which would be fatal for all the remaining state marriage exclusions. But the DOJ lawyers did not think that five justices were prepared to render a fifty-state solution in *Perry,* and they worried that such reluctance could undermine the government's chances for sweeping away DOMA in *Windsor.* The Ninth Circuit had written a decision that was basically a one-state solution: Proposition 8 was unconstitutional for reasons that could be confined to that one constitutional initiative. That was too stingy for the administration.

After consulting with President Obama and White House counsel, Solicitor General Verrilli decided to adopt a middle-ground solution that would apply heightened scrutiny but not require the entire nation to immediately recognize same-sex marriages. The government's amicus brief in *Perry* argued for an eight-state solution: under heightened scrutiny, the eight states (like California) that gave all or most marital benefits to same-sex couples through comprehensive civil union or domestic partnership laws were in an especially weak position because they were endorsing gay relationships but giving them second-class status. This was an ingenious threading of the constitutional needle—but Assistant Attorney General Delery, whose memorandum had laid out the 1-8-50-state framework, thought the eight-state solution would be a hard sell to the Supreme Court.[43]

ARGUMENT AND DECISION IN *PERRY*

On March 26, 2013, the Supreme Court devoted a full morning for oral argument in *Perry*. Chuck Cooper (for Proposition 8's proponents), Ted Olson (for the plaintiff couples), and Don Verrilli (for the United States) all started their arguments with the equal protection issue—and Chief Justice Roberts immediately walked each of them back to the question whether the proponents had the "personal stake" in the issue that the court required for a party to have standing to press a claim in federal court. The California Supreme Court had opined that California law authorized the initial proponents of a state ballot initiative "to appear and assert the state's interest in the initiative's validity and to appeal a judgment invalidating the measure" if the state's attorneys declined to do it. Was the state law authorization for the private parties "to assert the state's interest" sufficient to meet the more stringent "case or controversy" requirements imposed by Article III of the Constitution?[44]

Several justices were skeptical, and their skepticism was fueled by an excellent amicus brief filed by former acting solicitor general Walter Dellinger, written principally by Irving Gornstein, with input from Martin Lederman, both of the Georgetown University Law Center. The bedrock precept was that an interest shared by everyone was "generalized" and did not represent the concrete "personal stake" required for a claiming party to launch a constitutional case or controversy, either by initiating a lawsuit or taking an appeal. Because everyone in California had an interest in the fate of Proposition 8, the interest of the proponents was not unique as a matter of legal right. Government officials, by the nature of their offices, had a legally cognizable personal stake in defending state law, and private parties legally deputized and vested with fiduciary responsibilities to the public interest could defend state law for similar reasons. But the proponents had not been deputized by state law to represent all the people of California, nor had they taken an oath or assumed fiduciary responsibilities to the public. Thus, amicus explained, states could authorize private parties to defend state laws, but only through a process of public delegation. This argument skillfully played the music of Article III. It sang a beautiful tune to John Roberts—but also appealed to justices wanting to push off the merits of marriage equality for a few more years.[45]

Although entirely happy to postpone a decision on the constitutional merits, Anthony Kennedy was a Californian who appreciated the special status of initiatives and their proponents under the state constitution. For him, the proponents did have a personal stake in the initiative they had sponsored that was not shared by the general population. They had a distinctive state constitutional interest as well. The point of the initiative process was to impose popular measures that elected representatives were not willing to adopt; thus to allow the representatives to thwart the will of the people by refusing to defend the initiatives, as the California officials had done, would be an anti-democratic deployment of Article III, and Justice Kennedy wanted no part of it. He was joined in his skepticism by Justices Thomas, Alito, and Sotomayor, none of whom shared Chief Justice Roberts's enthusiasm for creating new and more intricate doctrine limiting federal court jurisdiction. For them, Article III was satisfied because the proponents provided a strongly adversarial controversy and better represented the state on this distinctive issue than the state's own attorney general would have done.

All counsel that morning were frustrated by the justices' interest in procedural issues, to the detriment of the great marriage debate all sides hoped to have. Ted Olson had the most to gain from an Article III disposition, because it would leave Judge Walker's 2010 judgment in place and his clients would secure their marriage licenses. But because he wanted to win a landmark marriage decision, not a dull decision about standing, Olson's brief had made the Article III argument in the most perfunctory manner possible. In two paragraphs of a fifty-three-page brief, Olson and Boies asserted that the proponents did not have a "direct stake" in the controversy and cited a few relevant Article III precedents. At oral argument, Olson tried to interest the court in the merits but only succeeded in rousing Justice Scalia into a series of questions about original meaning.[46]

Consistent with what they had shown at the oral argument, the justices' conference focused on process. Opening the discussion, Roberts made a strong pitch for dismissing the appeal because the proponents did not have the concrete injury required by Article III for precisely the reasons set forth in the Dellinger-Gornstein-Lederman amicus brief. Scalia enthusiastically agreed, and Roberts's opinion for the 5-4 court in *Hollingsworth v. Perry* closely followed Gornstein's reasoning. Once the California Constitution was amended, the proponents had no more of a personal stake in defending its enforcement than any other citizen of California. That was fatal. "Article III standing is not to be placed in the hands of concerned bystanders, who will use it simply as a vehicle for the vindication of value interests." The majority opinion contrasted the proponents, who at most were authorized to argue the state's interests, from public officials and private persons officially deputized to act as official agents of the state with fiduciary responsibilities to the public. Ginsburg, Breyer, and

Kagan filled out the majority. Impressed by the Dellinger-Gornstein-Lederman brief, they were happy enough to join Roberts's fine opinion, but with varying degrees of enthusiasm. It was persuasive enough for each of them to avoid what they strongly considered a premature decision on the merits. Kennedy wrote an equally fine dissent, joined by the three justices who graduated from the Yale Law School (Thomas, Alito, and Sotomayor)—the only time those three justices have ever voted together in a dissenting opinion.[47]

ORAL ARGUMENT AND CONFERENCE IN *WINDSOR*

The next day, March 27, the Supreme Court heard counsel in *United States v. Windsor*, the case that everyone had been waiting for. No one had waited longer than Edie Windsor, who sat right behind the counsel's table and was treated to one of the most intellectually exciting oral arguments of the twenty-first century. The jousting pitted Solicitor General Verrilli and his powerhouse deputy, Sri Srinivasan (now a judge) and Edie's paladin Robbie Kaplan on one side. Arguing against them on the merits was Paul Clement. Arguing against both Verrilli and Clement on the Article III issue was Harvard law professor Vicki Jackson, who had been appointed to argue that the United States and BLAG had no standing to take their appeals.

Jackson opened the Article III conversation by responding to the argument that the $363,000 debt Uncle Sam owed to Windsor gave the government a tangible stake in the case sufficient to support its standing to appeal. She had no problem with a lawsuit against the United States for $363,000, where the government conceded the liability. Where Article III presented difficulty was the next step, when the government appealed a judgment it helped persuade the judge to enter. The United States had no standing to take such an appeal, Jackson argued, and by adjudicating it, the lower court was only accepting the president's invitation to give cover to the executive branch's constitutional vision. That's not what courts were for. Article III's case or controversy requirement gave federal courts the authority to resolve adversarial disputes by reference to settled law, not to participate directly in the political process.[48]

Srinivasan defended the United States's standing to appeal, but he could not cite any previous decision exactly on point. "So this is totally unprecedented," Roberts replied. "You're asking us to do something we've never done before to reach the issue in this case?" Scalia was mighty peeved. A former DOJ official, he objected that DOJ had traditionally defended any federal statute, except those which invaded the president's authority or where no rational argument could be made under the precedents. Many in the courtroom turned to look at Roberts, who as acting solicitor general had declined to defend the FCC's affirmative action policy. His perpetually placid poker face revealed no sign of self-consciousness.[49]

Equally unflappable, Srinivasan tacked back to standing. In *Immigration and Naturalization Service (INS) v. Chadha* (1983), the Supreme Court had invalidated the one-house legislative veto. Representing the agency, DOJ had agreed with the Ninth Circuit that the veto was unconstitutional, but appealed its "loss" to the SCOTUS nevertheless. The majority opinion had treated the INS as a proper petitioner and held that it was "aggrieved" for purposes of a jurisdictional statute: even though it agreed with the judgment below, the INS was under a court order to do something, and that was enough. *Chadha* did not quite hold that the INS had constitutional standing to appeal, because the House and Senate had intervened as defendants to defend the law, and they had standing.[50]

In the last sixty seconds of her rebuttal, Jackson eviscerated the proposition that BLAG had standing. In *Chadha,* the House and Senate suffered a concrete and institutional harm by the lower court's invalidation of their institutional prerogative (the legislative veto), but in *Windsor,* BLAG was acting just like the Proposition 8 proponents, defending a law the executive branch would not defend. The Supreme Court had repeatedly rejected the possibility of legislator standing to protect laws he or she had voted for. Indeed, BLAG was barred by the constitutional separation of powers from asserting an interest in the "execution" of the law, because Article II left that solely in the hands of the president.

Jackson had given an intellectually breathtaking performance. In any case but a major constitutional showdown, like *Chadha* or *Windsor,* one would have said that a majority would follow her reasoning the way they followed the Dellinger-Gornstein-Lederman reasoning in the case argued the day before. At conference in *Windsor,* Roberts and Scalia stuck to the same strict understanding of Article III they announced in *Perry.* And as before, Kennedy and Sotomayor endorsed the justiciability of this oddball appeal. Kennedy had written the Ninth Circuit opinion that was affirmed in *Chadha.* He had invited the House and Senate to participate in the case, and his opinion ruled that they provided the adversariness that he found central to Article III; his vote was driven by *Chadha,* as was that of Alito, who accepted that BLAG had constitutional standing.[51]

Ginsburg, Breyer, and Kagan flipped on Roberts, however, and agreed with Kennedy in this case. The late Yale law professor Alexander Bickel had famously argued that the Supreme Court's Article III jurisprudence had never been principled and instead was one of the "passive virtues" deployed by the court when it needed to duck a combustible issue. In *Perry*, Article III served that passive virtue admirably, as it avoided controversy that would have accompanied any decision on the merits. In *Windsor*, however, the gay-friendly justices felt no need to be passive and every desire to be virtuous.[52]

On the merits, Clement defended DOMA as a permissible administrative decision to follow a uniform understanding of federal marriage-based benefits and obligations. Kennedy was bothered by DOMA's broad reach, affecting more than 1,100 federal rights and duties that are "intertwined with citizens' day-to-day lives." Clement responded that DOMA was a garden-variety definitional provision, an amendment to the Dictionary Act, and this provided another rational justification. All of the marriage-based federal rights and duties were adopted by Congress or by agencies under the assumption that marriage was one man, one woman. When this long-standing definition was called into question in the 1990s by Hawai'i, it was rational for Congress to protect the original expectations of its predecessors. But, Ginsburg asked, did that justify such a broad exclusion? The federal stance toward marriage touched every aspect of people's lives. A federal rule refusing to respect valid state marriages thus created, as Kennedy put it, a "real risk of running in conflict with what has always thought to be the essence of the state police power, which is to regulate marriage, divorce, and custody." DOMA's pervasive regime of excluded benefits and duties created a new institution, what Ginsburg called "skim milk marriages," which differed from the full-blown marriages available to most couples.[53]

Breyer and Kagan—former law professors—raised the question whether rationality-with-bite review (*Romer* and *Lawrence*) presented problems for DOMA, especially in light of the House Judiciary Committee's language announcing the statutory goal of disapproving homosexuality. Reflecting his experience as solicitor general, Clement vigorously rejected the suggestion that there was a new tier of judicial scrutiny. Ginsburg reminded him that the Supreme Court had struck down the sex discrimination in *Reed v. Reed* (1971) under the rational basis test, even though there were perfectly good administrative convenience arguments supporting the preference for male relatives as executors of estates.

The bench was just as aggressive with the solicitor general. Alito posed this devilish hypothetical to Verrilli. Soldier 1 was legally married to someone of the same sex; Soldier 2 was legally joined in a civil union; Soldier 3 was in a committed relationship but lived in a state that had neither same-sex marriage nor civil unions. The administration's position was that Soldier 1 should receive marriage benefits, contrary to DOMA. Under the government's theory, Soldier 2 had also been treated unfairly, right? And so had Soldier 3. Alito was raising the stakes of the DOMA argument: invalidation of the federal statute on equal protection grounds would carry over to the state defense-of-marriage rules such as Proposition 8. Verrilli did not strongly resist this analysis, as it was consistent with the president's interpretation of the Constitution, as reported in the 2011 Holder letter.

On the equal protection issue, Verrilli argued that DOMA was generated by "moral disapproval" of homosexuality, to quote the House Judiciary Committee's report. The law had nothing to do with cost saving, ease of administration, or uniformity in federal policy. There was a reason it was not called the Uniform Federal Marriage Benefits Act: not a single supporter cared about uniformity, and opponents were worried that they would be tarred with the "promotes homosexuality" smear. "This is discrimination in its most basic aspect," Verrilli concluded, and it was deeply inconsistent with the constitutional guarantee of equal treatment under the law.[54]

Kaplan's best moment was her response to BLAG's argument that DOMA was simply Congress's effort to remain neutral in the culture wars. From Windsor's point of view, Kaplan argued, Congress was mocking neutrality. Passing such a sweeping and punitive law, years before a single state had accepted marriage equality, was an effort to stop the debate. It was a giant national rally for the view that homosexuals were different from the rest of Americans and unfit for marriage and the other badges of citizenship. The antithesis of federal neutrality, DOMA was aimed at stigmatizing gay people generally and isolating and stigmatizing lesbian and gay families once they could get married. Kaplan could not tell whether her oration touched any of the justices, all of whom stared impassively at her from behind their elevated bench. But she knew that Windsor had tears in her eyes.

In his rebuttal, Clement revealed that he had been listening to the conversation carefully. When a bipartisan majority in Congress legislated through an open process to define terms in valid federal statutes, and their bill was endorsed and signed by a president who claimed gay people among his friends, what was there for the Supreme Court to fix? And with what doctrinal tools can the court deploy to fix a statute that did not deny people fundamental rights or deploy a suspect classification? The remedy was through the political process, where LGBTQ+ groups were, by 2013, fully empowered. Colorado, the state that adopted Amendment 2, had just created civil unions at the behest of those groups. Congress, which had earlier passed the military exclusion and DOMA, had just repealed the former. Legislatures or popular referenda in seven states and the District of Columbia had voted for marriage equality (two more states had done so exclusively by judicial decree), and another ten recognized their civil unions and domestic partnerships. "Allow the democratic process to continue," he implored the court.[55]

Clement's argument earned a warm embrace when Chief Justice Roberts opened the justices' private conference. Kaplan had told the justices that there had been a "sea change" in public attitudes about homosexuals since 1996. Roberts did not see why courts needed to bend the Constitution to do work that the political process was doing more than adequately. Although he was not as naïve about homophobia as he wanted to sound, he argued that DOMA met the basic requirements of the Constitution. He was saddened by the ironic twist that he believed would produce upside-down constitutional law. He expected that Kennedy and Ginsburg would lead his colleagues to strike down DOMA as a bad statutory innovation—while swallowing the Article III innovation represented by the Don't Defend, Do Enforce policy. The pride of ordinary LGBTQ+ persons (including Roberts's own cousin) was not the business of the Supreme Court, but policing the limits of Article III was central to its legitimacy. At conference, Scalia, Thomas, and Alito agreed with Roberts on the merits and on the United States' lack of standing. Following *Chadha*, Alito believed that BLAG had standing.[56]

On the merits, the big winner at conference was someone who had been absent from the courtroom—Mike Boudin. His opinion in *Massachusetts v. HHS* subjected DOMA to rationality-plus review because of the interplay between the federalism concerns and the law's minority-scapegoating features, and that proved to be stable legal ground on which most of the justices could rest. Kennedy's and Sotomayor's questions at oral argument had been directly inspired by Boudin's opinion, and at conference both suggested that they would affirm the Second Circuit based on Boudin's analysis. Ginsburg, Breyer, and Kagan said that the rational-basis-with-bite approach the court had followed in *Romer* and *Lawrence* was completely applicable here. Interestingly, none of the justices revealed any interest in recognizing sexual orientation as a new suspect (or quasi-suspect) classification—the issue that had consumed thousands of hours of discussion and memo writing in the Obama administration. Not only was such a move not required to decide the case, but Kennedy was loathe to invigorate equal protection doctrine with more suspect classifications.

Nor did anyone press the *Baehr* argument that DOMA was flat-out sex discrimination. That argument remained in a constitutional closet because it would decide too much: it would open up federal sex discrimination statutes (especially Title VII and Title IX) to LGBTQ+ claims. No one wanted to risk unraveling the tentative majority in *Windsor*.

THE COURT'S DECISION IN *WINDSOR*

As the senior justice in the majority, Tony Kennedy assigned himself the task of writing the majority opinion in *United States v. Windsor*. He started with the Article III issue and wrote a nice, clear analysis based upon *Chadha*. The opinion then explored the social and constitutional background of the DOMA challenges. "When at first Windsor and Spyer longed to marry, neither New York nor any other State granted them that right," Kennedy started. "Many citizens had not even considered the possibility that two persons of the same sex might aspire to occupy the same status and dignity as that of a man and woman in lawful marriage." But a new world was upon us, and Edie Windsor was asking the court to validate her marriage under federal law.[57]

The majority opinion was launched with clarity and eloquence, but when it reached the merits Kennedy recast Boudin's approach in a way that left most readers and some of his colleagues confused. Rather than openly announcing that the majority was applying rational-basis-with-bite because of DOMA's unusual combination of sweeping national interference with state family law and with the lives of LGBTQ+ people, as Boudin did, Kennedy started with a lengthy, heartfelt paean to state primacy in the recognition and regulation of families. The other justices in the majority went along with this odd ode to federalism because of an informal but ironclad agreement that, in gay rights cases, their Catholic Republican colleague from Sacramento spoke for them all.[58]

Echoing David Buckel's suggestion eight years earlier, Kennedy's ode to federalism ended with this quotation from *Romer*: "Discriminations of an unusual character especially suggest careful consideration to determine whether they are obnoxious to the constitutional provision." The survey of state domestic relations law suggested how central the definition of marriage and family was to "the daily lives and customs of its people," like Windsor and Spyer. DOMA's sweeping disavowal of state law harmed actual families in ways the Supreme Court had never seen before. And its targeting a minority group was "strong evidence" that the law's purpose was "to impose a disadvantage, a separate status, and so a stigma upon all who enter into same-sex marriages made lawful by the unquestioned authority of the States." The impression that DOMA was overwhelmingly aimed at denigrating and harming lesbian and gay families was confirmed by the language of the committee report, by the title of the law, and by its structure, which wrote "inequality into the entire United States Code." Following the arguments made by Verrilli and Kaplan, this part of the court's opinion featured analysis that Boudin had avoided: the prejudiced motives of DOMA's supporters.[59]

Once he found that DOMA's intended effect was to entrench lesbian and gay unions as "second-class marriages," Kennedy dismissed Clement's administrative convenience arguments. The effect of the law on liberty was fundamental and broad. "The differentiation demeans the couple, whose moral and sexual choices the Constitution protects, and whose relationship the State has sought to dignify. And it humiliates tens of thousands of children now being raised by same-sex couples. The law in question makes it even more difficult for the children to understand the integrity and closeness of their own family and its concord with other families in their community and in their daily lives." DOMA's section 3 violated the Fifth Amendment.[60]

Sam Alito wrote a thoughtful dissent, joined by Clarence Thomas. In contrast to Kennedy's framing of family law through the lens of federalism, Alito framed it through the prism of society. Family and marriage were a fundamental part of society; they influenced and were affected by everything else going on in that society. Fundamental changes in the institution would have "far-reaching consequences." Courts could not effectively tackle polycentric problems (those with many dimensions and connections to the rest of society), because they could not foresee or regulate the ripple effects of their policy decisions. More deeply, Alito observed that the majority was purporting to "resolve a debate between two competing views of marriage," the traditional or "conjugal" view—the "solemnizing of a comprehensive, exclusive, permanent union that is intrinsically ordered to producing new life, even if it does not always do so"—and a newer, "consent-based" view that "primarily defines marriage as the solemnization of mutual commitment—marked by strong emotional attachment and sexual attraction—between two persons." Unelected judges had neither the democratic mandate nor the philosophical wisdom to commit the country to one view and to ban the other.[61]

Windsor was Nino Scalia's last star turn in a gay rights case, though he would participate in several more. His dissenting opinion (joined by Roberts in part and Thomas entirely) was saturated with colorful language as well as keen, take-no-prisoners reasoning. This case, he wrote, "is about the power of our people to govern themselves, and the power of this Court to pronounce the law. Today's opinion aggrandizes the latter, with the predictable consequence of diminishing the former." The majority was reaching out to take an appeal forbidden by the limitations of Article III. The losing party in the lower court ought to have had an opportunity to petition the Supreme Court—but not the winning party. End of case. But if you wanted to reach the merits—and what judicial oligarch would not?—Scalia lambasted the majority for an opinion that swerved like a drunk driver from one justification (federalism!) to another (liberty!!) to yet another (why not equality?) and then indicted DOMA as a law persecuting lesbian couples and their children, when in Scalia's opinion the statute was a garden-variety administrative measure signed by a pro-homosexual president.[62]

In concluding, Scalia assailed the majority for trying to pull the wool over America's eyes with "legalistic argle-bargle." The good justice jumped the shark with his invocation of that archaic Scottish term, popularized in James Joyce's *Ulysses*. In Joyce's "Cyclops" chapter, a gang of angry Irish drinking buddies denigrated Bloom, the novel's protagonist, as a "perverted jew," an effeminate "mixed middling," a greedy cheat who covered his tracks with "argol bargol," or obfuscating nonsense. Joyce was using the old language ironically: the drunks are the ones talking "argol bargol," as their prejudiced epithets have no connection to the Bloom the reader knows. They see Bloom, and the world, through one, jaundiced eye. As critics have observed, "Cyclops" explores the interaction among anti-Semitism, misogyny, and homophobia. Borrowing this marked language to demean a "homosexual rights" opinion joined by the three Jews and three women on the Supreme Court, Scalia, an angry Catholic male, unwittingly suggested a linkage among classic prejudices that formed an unmentionable theme of the deliberations in the LGBTQ+ rights cases.[63]

Scalia's lacerating dissent ended with a Cassandric bang. Forget about the ode to federalism, he demanded. Five justices were prepared to strike down all remaining state laws and constitutional provisions patterned on DOMA. As evidence, he edited several passages from Kennedy's flowery opinion, as they might be repurposed for the next case, where the same majority would impose marriage equality on all fifty states. One example, with cross-outs being Scalia's deletions and italics representing his additions, is the following:

"~~DOMA's~~ *This state law's* principal effect is to identify a subset of ~~state-sanctioned marriages~~ *constitutionally protected sexual relationships*, see *Lawrence*, and make them unequal. The principal purpose is to impose inequality, not for other reasons like governmental efficiency. Responsibilities, as well as rights, enhance the dignity and integrity of the person. And ~~DOMA~~ *this state law* contrives to deprive some couples ~~married under the laws of their State~~ *enjoying constitutionally protected sexual relationships,* but not other couples, of both rights and responsibilities."

Scalia closed his dissent on an operatic note: "By formally declaring anyone opposed to same-sex marriage an enemy of human decency, the majority arms well every challenger to a state law restricting marriage to its traditional definition." Distancing himself from this part of Scalia's dissent, the chief justice lamented that his acid-tongued colleague would spill so much bile onto the Supreme Court.[64]

As Scalia saw it, the majority's decision was an assault on democracy, the family, and the Constitution itself. Windsor did not see it that way at all. Soon after her victory, she held a press conference at New York City's Lesbian and Gay Center, of which she was a founding member. "I thought our arguments were sound and everyone else's were insane," she said. "I think ultimately it's the end of suicide. It's the end of teenagers falling in love and not knowing it's okay." When someone asked how it felt to be compared to Rosa Parks and Harvey Milk, she was silent, honored that she would be compared to such brave constitutional pioneers.[65]

The Implementation of *Windsor*

No one was more gratified by the Supreme Court's decision than Assistant Attorney General Stuart Delery, who attended the June 26 session with his spouse, Richard Gervase. Their eyes misted during the reading of Kennedy's opinion. When Delery returned to the Justice Department, the attorney general's chief of staff called him to duty. The president wanted DOJ to coordinate the implementation of *Windsor.* How did Delery feel about taking charge of that? "I was enjoying all this so much more a few hours ago!"[66]

Delery assembled a *Windsor* Implementation Team (WIT), with attorneys from all over the department to coordinate the effort. Each attorney was assigned to work with one or more agencies and their counsel. Delery met with each agency, most of them more than once, and reported regularly to Attorney General Holder and to the White House counsel. He also met with any group submitting informed advice; often working through Valerie Jarrett's office, GLAD's Mary Bonauto and Lambda's Susan Sommer lobbied hard, with deeply researched memoranda, for a broad approach to spousal rights for LGBTQ+ couples. Delery also relied on an informal advisory group of top-level officials (including Deputy Solicitor General Kneedler and Virginia Seitz, who headed the Office of Legal Counsel) to provide additional advice on the legal issues the agencies would confront.[67]

More than 11,000 regulatory provisions involved marriage—including statutes, agency rules and adjudications, guidance and policy documents, and websites. As WIT worked with each agency, there were a few major recurring legal issues. With the fall of DOMA, the government reverted to state law to determine valid marriages: Which state law should be determinative? With the immediate addition of California based on the Supreme Court's disposition in *Perry*, thirteen states recognized marriage equality. Even before June, however, Delery and other officials had decided to apply the "celebration rule" wherever possible: same-sex couples living in nonrecognition states could still enjoy federal recognition if their marriages were valid in the place of celebration, such as Massachusetts, New York, Iowa, or Canada (Windsor's place of celebration). The celebration rule was already followed by most agencies, and it would be consistent with the White House mandate that the law be interpreted generously to support LGBTQ+ families.

On June 26, 2013, eight states that did not hand out marriage licenses did offer domestic partnership or civil unions; on June 27, California dropped off the list. Four of the remaining state laws only applied to same-sex couples. Because the Holder letter suggested that *all* laws discriminating on the basis of sexual orientation should be subjected to heightened scrutiny, Delery felt the federal government ought not provide a boon to those couples without a compelling justification. The Hawai'i, Illinois, and Nevada laws included different-sex couples as well as same-sex couples. Adding those relationships to federal spousal benefits would include straight couples who had opted against marriage, a move that Delery also considered beyond his mandate.

Except for social security (governed by a unique statutory scheme), Bonauto, Sommer, and other LGBTQ+ representatives did not insist that WIT apply *Windsor* to civil unions or comprehensive domestic partnerships, because the post-DOMA benefits gap between those institutions and marriage would be so enormous that state courts would have to strike down civil union laws—which is exactly how New Jersey Superior Court judge Mary Jacobson ruled on September 27, 2013. After she refused to stay the effect of her judgment, and the state supreme court declined to intervene, the conservative Republican governor, Chris Christie, threw in the constitutional towel and permitted marriage licenses starting on October 21. In Illinois and Hawai'i, the disparity between civil unions and marriages fueled legislative efforts to enact marriage legislation, and Democratic governors Pat Quinn (Illinois) and Neil Abercrombie (Hawai'i) signed marriage bills on the same day, November 21, 2013. Within eighteen months of *Windsor,* all eight states that had comprehensive domestic partnership or civil union laws were issuing marriage licenses to lesbian and gay couples. Ironically, the combination of *Windsor's* reasoning, ongoing marriage litigation, and Delery's decision to continue to exclude civil union and domestic partners from more than one thousand federal marriage-based rights delivered the eight-state solution that Solicitor General Verrilli's amicus brief had proposed to an uninterested Supreme Court in *Perry.*[68]

Every federal agency cooperated with WIT; most had been working on the issue before June 26. On July 1, less than a week after *Windsor,* Secretary of Homeland Security Napolitano "directed U.S. Citizenship and Immigration Services to review immigration visa petitions filed on behalf of a same-sex spouse in the same manner as those filed on behalf of an opposite-sex spouse." On August 2, Secretary of State Kerry announced that consulates would process visa applications for same-sex marriages abroad the same as for different-sex marriages. On July 17, OPM issued an omnibus memorandum on marriage rights for federal employees. Those who were validly married to a spouse of the same sex could henceforth include the spouse and their family in the federal health benefits program, group life insurance, the dental and vision program, long-term care insurance, and flexible spending accounts that were previously available only to different-sex spouses. OPM made clear that the state of residency did not matter; any marriage validly entered would qualify. Civil unions would not.[69]

On August 29, the IRS issued Revenue Ruling 2013–17, providing that the terms *spouses* or *marriage* when used in the tax code would thereafter include same-sex marriages valid in the state of celebration. Additionally, the IRS said, even when the statute used gendered terms (*husband* and *wife*), it would interpret those terms to include valid same-sex married spouses in order to avoid the constitutional problems *Windsor* would pose for a narrower view. *Windsor* was a tax case, and the Supreme Court's opinion indicated that its ruling applied throughout the tax code. Following DOJ's lead, the IRS did not extend this treatment to couples joined in civil unions or domestic partnerships. Based upon this ruling, the Department of Health and Human Services advised health insurance exchanges under the Affordable Care Act that same-sex spouses were eligible for advance payments of the premium tax credit and cost-sharing reductions.[70]

The Social Security Act presented some distinctive issues of statutory interpretation. Section 416(h)(1)(A)(i) provided a definition of "family status" to include the insured individual's husband or wife if the courts of the domicile state "would find that such applicant and such insured individual were validly married." This provision seemed to foreclose the administration's policy of recognizing valid marriages even if the state of domicile did not. Bonauto and her allies devised ingenious statutory and constitutional arguments to ameliorate the force of this provision and a similarly restrictive statutory rule governing spousal veterans benefits, but Delery was firm: the administration was not going to rewrite statutes. Attorney General Holder and White House counsel backed him up 100 percent.[71]

The Social Security Act also provided that even if the state did not recognize the marriage, the applicant should be "deemed" a spouse of the insured individual "if such applicant would, under the laws applied by such courts in determining the devolution of intestate personal property, have the same status with respect to the taking of such property as a wife, husband, widow, or widower of such insured individual." Acting Social Security Administration Commissioner Carolyn Colvin agreed with Bonauto and Sommer that a couple joined in civil union could satisfy this clause, and Delery was glad to extend benefits under those circumstances.[72]

On June 20, 2014, less than a year after *Windsor*, Attorney General Holder reported to President Obama that the executive branch had implemented *Windsor*'s equal treatment mandate "to the greatest extent possible under the law." An appendix to the memorandum contained a summary of specific measures taken by dozens of agencies to assure that lesbian and gay married couples would be afforded all the rights and responsibilities associated with marital status. In October 2014, Holder bestowed his Award for Exceptional Service on twenty-eight attorneys involved in WIT.[73]

June 26, 2013, was the culmination of decades of constitutional activism on the part of LGBTQ+ people and their allies in support of their right to marry. Consider some of the historical ironies that day's Supreme Court's decisions represented.

The first is that the constitutional dream team of Ted Olson and David Boies won their Supreme Court case on technical grounds, not the merits, and were immediately eclipsed by the gayocracy's triumph in *Windsor*. Olson's vision of becoming an iconic constitutional lawyer in the tradition of Thurgood Marshall was overtaken when Edie Windsor became the iconic movement plaintiff. *Windsor* would bring a whirlwind of constitutional challenges, almost all under the watchful eyes of the movement litigation groups that had been excluded from formal participation in *Perry*, as we saw in chapter 15.

A deeper irony is the way DOMA boomeranged to wound the social movement that had generated it. Chapter 5 explained how the statute was the product of traditional values constitutionalism just as idealistic as marriage equality constitutionalism. But when DOMA was handed off to Congress, whatever was inspirational about it got worn down by a rushed legislative process, intemperate rhetoric, and the nitty-gritty of shin-kicking politics. There was a scapegoat quality to a law whose biggest boosters inside the Beltway—President Clinton, Speaker Gingrich, and Majority Leader Dole—were adulterers purporting to protect marriage against committed partners and unselfish parents like the Hawai'i couples DOMA disparaged. In 2013, the US Supreme Court was not quite ready for a Fourteenth Amendment lawsuit seeking nationwide marriage equality. Given DOMA's unprecedented breadth, the ignorant and sometimes prejudice-laced comments by legislators, and its tension with federalism principles, DOMA was constitutionally vulnerable, and the marriage equality movement made the most of its opportunity. If Edie Windsor was the perfect wife and the perfect plaintiff, DOMA was the perfect constitutional target. Yet it came within one vote of surviving.

That brings us to another irony. The Republican Party propelled DOMA into law in 1996—but it was Republican-appointed judges who buried it. The first big strike against DOMA was an administrative ruling for Karen Golinski by Chief Judge Alex Kozinski of the Ninth Circuit, appointed by President Reagan, who also put Anthony Kennedy on the US Supreme Court. President George W. Bush appointed Judge Jeffrey White, who wrote the district court decision for Karen Golinski. The author of the first judgments declaring DOMA unconstitutional, Judge Tauro, was appointed by President Nixon. His judgments were affirmed by Judge Boudin, nominated by the first President Bush. Bush also nominated Chief Judge Jacobs, who hurried his Second Circuit opinion so as to let Edie Windsor have her shot at the Supreme Court. It was remarkable that the nation's leading conservative Republican jurists wrote the opinions that were fatal to DOMA. They did so for the same reason that Republican Mark Cady wrote *Varnum* for a unanimous Iowa Supreme Court: the statute denigrated decent people and denied legitimate families rights and benefits across the board, without congressional findings or plausible arguments that the discrimination served a neutral public interest.

Many Republican judges, of course, did not agree with Justice Kennedy, Judge Boudin, or the others. This is yet another irony. At their moment of greatest triumph, the marriage equality movement faced a formidable new critic. Although Fox News and conservative bloggers reveled in Antonin Scalia's headline-grabbing *Windsor* dissenting opinion, the more thoughtful critical analysis was penned by Samuel Alito. A deep normative debate was occurring between the communitarian philosophy associated with conjugal marriage and the liberal philosophy associated with marriage as contract. DOMA was constitutional, Alito argued, because Congress was entitled to support the traditional understanding. Given this great normative debate, We the People, not Us the Judges, were the proper forum for deliberations. Alito's dissent also suggested that principled critics of marriage equality should enjoy all the free speech and associational rights that the ACLU had championed for other righteous minorities. The Alliance Defending Freedom (a religious counterpoint to the ACLU) had hundreds of attorneys who were taking Alito's philosophy into the trenches. Their theory was that Americans whose identity was bound up in the philosophy of conjugality had First Amendment rights to refuse to accommodate lesbian and gay couples whose matrimony was an existential affront to their lives and their families.

This irony leads to an oddity of cosmic proportions. Old-fashioned Catholics, Alito and Scalia saw marriage equality as a national defiance of God's Will. As any student of the Old Testament knows, defiance of God has consequences, such as His judgment raining fire and sulfur on Sodom and Gomorrah (Genesis 19:23–25). Another classic punishment was God's sending locusts to punish the Egyptians for their shameful treatment of the Jews in exile (Exodus 10:5). Most locusts emerge and wreak destruction every seventeen years. Like locusts, as David Codell instructed us, gay rights advocates in this period operated on a seventeen-year clock. DOMA was enacted in 1996, and its time ran out seventeen years later with *Windsor*. *Bowers v. Hardwick*, the Supreme Court decision that had confirmed gay people's status as outlaws, was handed down in 1986 and overruled seventeen years later in *Lawrence v. Texas* (2003), which seriously launched the constitutional process by which lesbian and gay couples could be considered in-laws. President Clinton signed the infamous Don't Ask, Don't Tell statute in 1993, and that policy was revoked through a statute President Obama signed in 2010. Count the years.

At the moment of her Supreme Court triumph, Edie Windsor reduced a room full of reporters to laughter as she told them her and Thea's mantras for a good relationship: "Mine was 'Don't postpone joy,' and Thea's was, 'Keep it hot!'" She then quoted from a poem by W. H. Auden: "For now I have the answer from the face / That never will go back into a book / But asks for all my life, and is the place / Where all I touch is moved to an embrace / And there is no such thing as a vain look." Edie was in love with being in love. Three years after her judicial triumph, she married a second love of her life, Judith Kasen-Windsor. Hours after an enthralling conversation with her spouse, Edie died of heart failure on September 12, 2017.[74]

20 • Hijacking Science

After their near-death experience in early 2011, April DeBoer and Jayne Rowse just wanted to protect the integrity of their family: two-year-old Nolan, as well as Jacob and Ryanne, both just a little over a year old at the time. April was Ryanne's legal mother, and Jayne had parental rights to the boys, but Michigan would not give them joint parental rights unless they were a male-female married couple. Recall, from the prelude to this volume, that the nurses had engaged Detroit civil rights lawyers Dana Nessel and Carole Stanyar to represent them in a federal constitutional challenge to Michigan's refusal to recognize second-parent adoptions.[1]

To help them on the federal constitutional claim, Stanyar enlisted Ken Mogill, and Nessel brought in her former constitutional law professor, Bob Sedler. He believed that the nurses' basic grievance was that Michigan did not allow them to get married; under state law, stepparent adoption by legal spouses was routine. Why not bring a marriage case in the Great Lakes State? Jayne and April emphatically vetoed the idea because they wanted the lawsuit to be about the children. A marriage lawsuit would be about the adults. In Nessel's experience, second-parent adoption was a more important issue for lesbian families than marriage equality.

The lawyers filed the complaint in *DeBoer v. Snyder* on January 23, 2012. By denying second-parent adoptions to families headed by lesbian and gay parents, they argued, Michigan discriminated against the children of those unmarried parents and against the parents themselves. "The undisputed sociological and psychological evidence demonstrates that there are some significant sociological and psychological benefits for children having two parents rather than one," and children also derived legal benefits from having two parents. The social science evidence demonstrated that "unmarried persons, straight, gay or lesbian, are no less loving, caring and effective parents than those parents who are married to each other." The state thus had no rational justification for this discrimination, much less the significant state interests the US Supreme Court required for discriminations affecting parental rights.[2]

A conservative, fundamentalist Republican aligned with the Alliance Defending Freedom (ADF), Michigan's attorney general, William Schuette, turned the case over to assistant state's attorney Kristen Heyse, his longtime protégée. Although Heyse was a true believer who would give the state policy a more vigorous and heartfelt defense than state counsel had done elsewhere, she had never tried a case. Presiding over the case was federal district court judge Bernard Friedman, a Reagan appointee and a fact-oriented rule-of-law jurist, not a constitutional boat-rocker. A stickler for fair process, he wanted everyone to feel welcome and comfortable in his courtroom, as we learned when we spent a day there. He insisted that people call him Bernie, was avuncular and schmoozy on the bench, and greeted court participants personally, including (the day we visited) a criminal defendant being sent away for a major parole infraction. Local lawyers described him as *hamishah,* Yiddish for a friendly fellow who treated everybody like family.

Bernie knew a family like April and Jayne's. One of his all-time favorite law clerks was Judy Levy, a lesbian who was raising a child with her partner when she started her clerkship in 1996 and who had twins during the first of the three years she clerked for Judge Friedman. (Levy is now a federal district judge sitting in Ann Arbor.) But the judge thought the nurses were pushing the Constitution further than the appellate courts had taken it. The Supreme Court had rejected the argument that people had a constitutional right to adopt, and precedent supported the rationality of a state policy that limited adoption to married couples. Friedman felt that the plaintiffs' real grievance was that Michigan would not allow them to marry, as that would have given them stepparent adoption rights. At the August 29 hearing on the state's motion to dismiss, Judge Friedman expressed skepticism about the nurses' second-parent adoption claim and asked if they wanted to amend their complaint to add a marriage claim.[3]

Everyone on the plaintiffs' side retired to a conference room. Bob Sedler found the prospect of a marriage challenge an exciting, once-in-a-lifetime opportunity. Dana Nessel was disappointed, elated, and frightened. She thought Michigan's refusal to recognize parental rights for nonbiological, nonmarital caregivers was pigheaded, bad for children, and unconstitutional, but she was also attracted to the idea of an in-your-face marriage suit. Carole Stanyar was mainly terrified. A marriage suit would be expensive. They would have to en-list expert witnesses and file tons of paperwork, perhaps without help from the national gayocracy. The local ACLU and Equality Michigan had bad-mouthed their case. April DeBoer was inconsolable: "We didn't sign up for this!" Jayne Rowse asked: "Does this mean we'd lose the adoption challenge not just for us, but for everyone else?" We're afraid so, the lawyers replied. In the end, the nurses deferred to the reluctant judgment of their counsel—but they were resigned to leaving the state if they lost. "If the state will not allow you to take care of your own family, how can you stay here?"[4]

With the permission of the court, the amended complaint was filed on Octo-ber 3, 2012. The first count was the same as before: Nolan, Jacob, and Ryanne had a constitutional right to two parents, whether married or not. The second count was the claim that April and Jayne's exclusion from the state marriage law (and the accompanying stepparent adoption right) violated the Fourteenth Amendment. Three months later, on December 7, the Supreme Court accepted both *Perry* (the Proposition 8 case) and *Windsor* (the DOMA case) for review, and Friedman pushed the pause button for the nurses' case until after the Supreme Court decided those cases, June 26, 2013.

On October 16, 2013, Judge Friedman heard oral argument on the state's mo-tion to dismiss the amended complaint. Heyse argued that the court should defer to the voters' adoption of the 2004 constitutional Super-DOMA, which implicitly reaffirmed that, as Heyse put it, the "ideal home environment is to have children raised by both a mother and a father together in marriage. Hav-ing both role models from both sexes is viewed by many as the optimal situa-tion." The judge asked: Isn't there an issue of fact, whether lesbian and gay households are just as good as straight households for raising kids? Heyse called the social science evidence "debatable," but Stanyar disagreed, citing the consensus among professional associations that the sex of the parents made "no difference" for childhood flourishing. Well, thought Friedman, why not have a trial, where the experts can be subjected to cross-examination?[5]

He set the trial date for February 25, 2014, giving the parties just four months to prepare their cases. At the plaintiffs' request (because counsel did not have enough funds to secure experts needed to make out a case for heightened scru-tiny), the judge limited the trial to whether the state had a rational basis for excluding lesbian and gay couples from marriage. Networked with ADF, the attorney general's office planned to defend the traditional definition of marriage as rationally reaffirming the optimal environment for raising children: because biology was destiny, and every child had a right to a father as well as a mother, lesbian and gay partners were bound to be inadequate parents. With professional associations solidly arrayed against the ADF position, however, even conservative judges were backing away from that argument. Traditionalists grumbled that progressive scholars had "hijacked science," in other words, that the scientific consensus reflected an academic echo chamber, not the real world. In *Marriage and the Public Good* (2006/2008), the Witherspoon Institute claimed that there was no statistically rigorous study based upon a random sample of the population confirming that children raised in lesbian or gay households were, on average, as well off as those raised in mom-and-dad marital households.[6]

Witherspoon cohosted gatherings of scholars in Washington, DC, in order to explore the possibilities for sponsoring a large-scale empirical study that its officials expected would show how the life outcomes of children in lesbian and gay households were inferior to those of children raised in intact marital households. In 2009, they found a promising candidate to conduct such a study—a dorky, thoughtful, politically naïve young man with expertise in empirical sociology who saw the world the way they did. Raised in a traditionalist Presbyterian household, Mark Regnerus was an associate professor of sociology at the University of Texas. Having just completed an insightful book on religion and the sex lives of teenagers, he was searching for a new empirical project. A colleague alerted him to the debate on lesbian and gay parenting. Upon a bit of reading, he concluded that this was an important topic and that the leading studies could not be generalized because they did not rely on random samples of the population. So why not generate a random sample of young adults that would allow comparisons of different household structures? He would need a large grant to accomplish such a survey. At a Washington meeting for supporters of traditional marriage, Regnerus discussed his idea with Maggie Gallagher and Luis Tellez, Witherspoon's president.[7]

In 2010, the Heritage Foundation hosted an event attended by Tellez, Gallagher, and Regnerus. Generalizing from his experience in the Proposition 8 trial, David Blankenhorn reported that judges were not satisfied with abstract, philosophical, or theological accounts of family and child-rearing; they wanted data-driven science. Unless supporters of traditional marriage came up with data, the marriage issue would be lost. The Witherspoon grant of $695,000 for what Regnerus called the New Family Structures Study (NFSS) was finalized before Blankenhorn's Code Blue, which confirmed Witherspoon's belief that its side of the marriage debate needed an empirical study its lawyers could take to the Supreme Court. Regnerus's plan was their best shot.[8]

The NFSS would be developed in cooperation with a team of consultants, including Brad Wilcox, an assistant professor at the University of Virginia who was identified as the director of the Witherspoon Family and Marriage Project in 2010–2012. In an email of September 21, 2010, Regnerus sought Wilcox's approval for the scope of the proposed study. "I would like," he wrote, "to get more feedback from Luis and Maggie about the 'boundaries' around this project, not just costs but also their optimal timelines . . . and their hopes for what emerges from this project, including the early report we discussed in DC." Wilcox forwarded the email to Tellez, who emailed Regnerus the next day: "We would like you to move along as expeditiously as possible but experience suggests that we ought not get hung up with deadlines, do what is right and best, move on it, don't dilly, dolly, etc. It would be great to have this before major decisions of the Supreme Court, but that is secondary to the need to do this and do it well."[9]

Originally, Wilcox and Regnerus had described a plan to sample one thousand young adults from same-sex households, one thousand young adults from adoptive households, and one thousand young adults from heterosexual households and compare the lifestyle characteristics, problems, and achievements of the people in each group. This strikes us as a promising methodology—but there was no available data set that would identity one thousand young adults from same-sex households. Because such a data set would have to be created, the original plan would have cost a lot of money and would have taken years to accomplish. In January 2011, the researchers came up with a new study design that could be completed quickly enough to provide evidence in the cases headed toward the Supreme Court in 2012.[10]

Under the new plan, Knowledge Networks gathered a random sample of fifteen thousand Americans born between 1972 and 1993. The researchers ultimately surveyed more than three thousand of those persons, 248 of whom had lived with what Regnerus deemed a "lesbian mother" (175 respondents) or "gay father" (73 respondents). The NFSS defined "lesbian mother" and "gay father" as any mother and father who had *ever* enjoyed a romantic relationship with someone of the same sex. While the researchers were still gathering the data, Luis Tellez was securing an additional grant from the Bradley Institute. "We are confident," he wrote, "that the traditional understanding of marriage will be vindicated in this study as long as it is done honestly and well." Bradley kicked in $90,000.[11]

The 175 respondents with "lesbian mothers," the NFSS found, suffered from more sexually transmitted diseases and had lower levels of education and employment, greater use of drugs and tobacco, greater likelihood of arrest and sexual abuse, and more sexual partners than respondents raised in intact marital households. Respondents with lesbian mothers compared favorably, however, to respondents raised by single parents and to those with gay fathers, and they were similar to respondents with stepparents. All of these results were statistically significant, and some reflected staggering differences between the "gay" and "lesbian" households and the intact marital households. With Wilcox's encouragement, the study was submitted for publication in February 2012, and it was accepted by *Social Science Research* six weeks later; rushed into print in near-record time, Regnerus's article was published in the July 2012 issue. Wilcox was a member of the journal's editorial board and wrote one of the three supportive peer reviews. A second favorable review was written by Paul Amato, who revealed in his review that he had consulted at an early stage of the project.[12]

Defenders of one-man, one-woman marriage incorporated the NFSS findings in their briefs for the marriage cases in the Supreme Court's 2012 term. Although Regnerus says that the NFSS was not aimed at influencing the marriage debate, he signed an ADF amicus brief in the pending Supreme Court cases to support the claim of "significant differences in the outcomes of children raised by parents in a same-sex relationship and those raised by a married biological mother and father." Regnerus's brief then recommended: "The State of California [*Perry*] and the federal government [*Windsor*] thus have a rational interest in supporting that proven parenting structure by reserving the title and status of marriage to unions comprised of a man and a woman." At the *Perry* oral argument, Justice Scalia echoed Regnerus's claim that (in Scalia's words) "there's considerable disagreement among . . . sociologists as to what the consequences of raising a child" in a same-sex household might be, "whether that is harmful to the child or not."[13]

Supporters of marriage equality saw the NFSS as an effort by Witherspoon to hijack science. On June 29, 2012, Dr. Gary Gates and two hundred other social scientists sent a letter to the editors of *Social Science Research*. The NFSS included any mother with "same-sex relationship experience," with about half of the lesbian mothers being women who left their husbands to date women. This design created a population in which family instability could not be separated from sexual orientation; the poor results were very probably generated by household instability. In contrast, the NFSS carefully avoided family instability for the children of different-sex parents: it counted only those persons who were raised in a stable marital family. Just as it was unfair to compare apples and oranges, so it was unfair to compare this array of unstable family structures with intact married couples.[14]

Gates's letter was published in the November 2012 issue of *Social Science Research*, as was a response by Regnerus. He disputed Gates's insistence that "instability" was an independent variable driving the results and claimed, instead, that it was a dependent variable driven by sexual orientation: lesbian relationships, he wrote, were inherently less stable and long-lasting than male-female marital ones. In a subsequent conversation, Regnerus agreed that a better apples-to-apples comparison would have been young adults who had been raised in intact lesbian households and those raised in intact straight households, but he said there were simply not enough of the former, a fact he interpreted as evidence that lesbian households were unstable. After an internal audit, *Social Science Research* concluded that the methodological flaws should have precluded publication of the original article. Inverting Gates's view, Maggie Gallagher considered his letter and the internal audit a hijacking of science by the politically correct academy of sociologists. The NFSS, she said, "has limitations: It cannot tell you how children do when they are raised by two moms in a stable lesbian partnership their whole childhood—because it can tell you: This is an incredibly rare experience for children," given Regnerus's evidence of the instability of lesbian relationships. Other social scientists disputed that conclusion.[15]

Bill Schuette and Kristin Heyse thought the NFSS established that it was not unreasonable for legislators and voters to conclude that the special status and legal benefits of marriage should not be conferred on couples who were not the best parents. Team Michigan's attorneys believed that the ability of husbands and wives to procreate matched the synergy of special virtues that each sex contributed to good child-rearing. For Team Nurses, the issue was even more personal. Devoted to their children, DeBoer and Rowse were appalled by this argument. Had Professor Regnerus actually engaged with real lesbian parents who were raising their children in intact, stable households that were marital in all but name? Could his evidence be used by Michigan to take away their children? The issue was also personal for Stanyar and Nessel. Stanyar had biological children from her marriage to a man, which had ended in divorce. Nessel's children were conceived during her relationship with another woman.

The optimal parenting argument had been the subject of the Hawai'i marriage trial in September 1996. In light of equivocal testimony by the state's witnesses and the strong testimony by the plaintiffs' witnesses, Judge Chang had accepted the "no differences" hypothesis and had ruled the marriage discrimination unconstitutional. Sixteen years later, Justice Kennedy's chambers dismissed the similar claim made in Regnerus's amicus brief. Instead, Kennedy's majority opinion in *Windsor* found that DOMA "humiliates tens of thousands of children now being raised by same-sex couples" and "makes it even more difficult for the children to understand the integrity and closeness of their own family and its concord with other families in their community and in their daily lives." *Windsor* applied the liberty and equality protections of the Fifth Amendment with considerable bite, putting to rest the notion that the Supreme Court would apply the highly deferential version of the rational basis test in the next marriage case, an implication amplified in Scalia's dissenting opinion. Armed with the NFSS, Kristin Heyse was determined to be a more effective advocate for the "significant differences" hypothesis, but problems with her witnesses and her inexperience as a trial lawyer undermined her ability to do that.[16]

Each side in the debate thought the other had hijacked science. But when the experts themselves disagreed, not merely about interpretation but also about which studies were even sound enough to interpret, how could lawyers and judges separate good science from bad? The answer to that question would have important ramifications for the national marriage debate.

After *Windsor*

When *Windsor* was decided on June 26, 2013, there were pending federal constitutional challenges to state marriage exclusions in Hawai'i, Illinois, Nevada, New Jersey, New Mexico, Ohio, Utah, and Michigan. After *Windsor*, lawyers brought dozens of new federal and state challenges to invalidate state DOMAs. In April 2014, Lambda Legal counted seventy-two pending constitutional lawsuits: forty-six in federal court (ten on appeal) and twenty-six in state court (six on appeal). By the end of the year, every non–marriage equality state had at least one lawsuit. Typically, one or more of the national litigating organizations—Lambda, ACLU, NCLR, or GLAD—teamed up with local attorneys to represent the plaintiff couples. Even when local attorneys had filed their own lawsuits, as in Utah and Ohio, national organizations typically volunteered their services after *Windsor* fueled marriage-equality optimism.[17]

In almost all the cases, counsel argued that the marriage laws excluding same-sex couples were unconstitutional because they (1) denied those couples a fundamental right to marry, (2) invidiously discriminated against them based upon either their sex or sexual orientation (both claimed to be fishy classifications triggering heightened scrutiny), and/or (3) lacked even a rational basis for the exclusion of lesbian and gay couples, à la *Windsor*. Any one of these arguments could be fatal to the challenged exclusions. Whatever doctrine judges applied, the disrespect and typically the tangible harm to gay couples and their children would require the state to demonstrate, with evidence and not just speculation, that the exclusion of those couples actually solved some problem or prevented specific persons or groups from being harmed. *Windsor* put the exclusions under a constitutional cloud—and immediately killed New Jersey's marriage exclusion. Recall from the previous chapter that the Obama administration extended federal spousal benefits only to married same-sex couples, not those joined in civil unions. New Jersey's lesbian and gay couples complained that the 2006 civil unions law had, overnight, become an example of separate but grossly unequal rights for their families. In October 2013, Governor Christie declined to appeal a lower court judgment, and New Jersey became the fourteenth marriage equality state.[18]

Supporters of one-man, one-woman marriage expected a public backlash when the Supreme Court struck down DOMA—but pollsters suggested a frontlash instead. The Pew Research Center reported that, between 2013 and 2015, support for marriage equality steadily increased from 50 percent to 55 percent, and opposition steadily declined from 43 percent to 39 percent. With the momentum of swiftly evolving public opinion, it was now safer for elected officials to support marriage equality. Governor Neil Abercrombie, for instance, called a special session of the Hawai'i legislature to respond to *Windsor,* which had rendered that state's civil unions law immediately unequal. When Abercrombie signed the Marriage Equality Act on November 13, 2013, the Aloha State became the fifteenth marriage equality state. One of the first couples to apply for a license was Genora Dancel and Kathryn Dennis. Their marriage license was issued by Irene Takeda, the same clerk who had apologetically turned down the request by Genora and Ninia Baehr twenty years earlier. Governor Pat Quinn signed Illinois's Religious Freedom and Fairness Act on November 20, making the Prairie State the sixteenth to accept marriage equality. One month after that, the New Mexico Supreme Court unanimously invalidated that state's junior-DOMA, and there were suddenly seventeen states and the District of Columbia distributing marriage licenses to lesbian and gay couples.[19]

Reflecting the new political climate, Oregon's attorney general, Ellen Rosenblum, and Pennsylvania's attorney general, Kathleen Kane, agreed with marriage equality plaintiffs and refused to defend marriage exclusions, as Attorney General Eric Holder had done in *Windsor*. Virginia's attorney general, Mark Herring, and Nevada's attorney general, Catherine Cortez Masto, switched sides in the middle of litigation in their states, as did Nevada's GOP governor Brian Sandoval. When they did defend, government lawyers put forward the let's-be-cautious arguments the Obama administration had originally made for DOMA and refused to make the optimal parenting argument, or made it in the most perfunctory manner, as Texas's Republican attorney general, Greg Abbott, did. That argument was still made by some traditional values attorneys representing court clerks or legislators as well as by some amicus briefs submitted by churches, religious organizations, and Professor Regnerus.[20]

Lawyers on the defense of marriage side were increasingly those affiliated with ADF, which had become an ACLU-style powerhouse network dedicated to litigating Christian values into American public law. By 2013, ADF employed several dozen staff attorneys and was fast approaching three thousand allied attorneys around the country. To become an allied attorney, one had to subscribe to ADF's statement of faith, which in 2013 included a commitment to believing that God designed marriage for one man and one woman and that homosexual behavior was "sinful and offensive to God." Many ADF-affiliated attorneys viewed the defense of marriage as something like a holy crusade to save the country from damnation.[21]

But the crusaders were routed everywhere. Justice Scalia's sarcastic prediction that *Windsor* was a harbinger for nationwide marriage equality began to look prescient. Between June 26, 2013, and June 26, 2015, a total of forty-three reported federal district court decisions in twenty-eight states (listed in the endnote) supported relief for marriage equality plaintiffs. Only one court, in Louisiana, sustained the exclusion of same-sex couples. Republican judges appointed by President Bush joined Democratic judges appointed by President Obama in striking down state junior- and Super-DOMAs.[22]

The first of the post-*Windsor* opinions was that of Utah district judge Robert Shelby, a registered Republican and decorated veteran appointed by President Obama, with the warm support of GOP senators Orrin Hatch and Michael Lee. Delivered on the eve of Christmas 2013, his decision in *Kitchen v. Herbert* ruled that Utah's constitutional DOMA unconstitutionally infringed on the plaintiffs' due process right to marry *and* denied them equal protection. There was a synergy between these two strains of constitutional analysis, which paralleled the debate among LGBT groups between the "freedom to marry" rhetoric appealing to libertarians and "marriage equality" resonant with civil

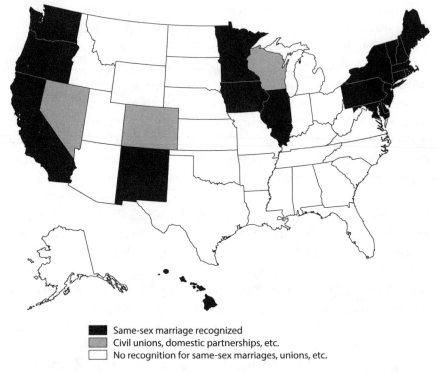

Same-sex marriage recognized
Civil unions, domestic partnerships, etc.
No recognition for same-sex marriages, unions, etc.

Figure 4 Marriage map, June 1, 2014. (Cartography by Patricia Page and Bill Nelson.)

rights advocates. Shelby's opinion suggested that both terms could appeal to moderate judges. Shelby also ruled that the Beehive State had not even offered a rational basis for excluding these couples. In particular, he found the NFSS irrelevant and reasoned that the state's interest in the welfare of children was best served by recognizing same-sex marriages (thereby helping the three thousand children being raised in lesbian and gay households) and regulating adoption and surrogacy for everyone.[23]

To Utah's surprise, Judge Shelby refused to stay (delay the effect of) his judgment, and so marriage licenses were immediately available to lesbian and gay couples. Tenth Circuit judges Jerome Holmes and Robert Bacharach—appointed by Presidents Bush and Obama, respectively—summarily rejected an emergency stay. On January 6, 2014, however, the Supreme Court granted Monte Stewart's motion to stay the district court order, but only after 1,360 marriage licenses had already been issued. Following the Supreme Court's lead, most district judges after January 6 put their marriage judgments on hold so the states could pursue their arguments on appeal.[24]

A few district court judgments were not appealed, and those states immediately converted to marriage equality. On May 19, 2014, federal district judge Michael McShane invalidated Oregon's constitutional junior-DOMA in *Geiger v. Kitzhaber.* Applying the rational basis standard, with considerable bite, the judge rejected the optimal child-rearing justification because Oregon's official policy was to protect all children, including those being reared in the households before the court. As the state immediately disclaimed any intention to file an appeal, Multnomah County issued marriage licenses that afternoon. The Beaver State was the eighteenth to recognize marriage equality, and the nineteenth came the next day, when Pennsylvania governor Tom Corbett (a Republican) declined to appeal a district court order invalidating the Keystone State's junior-DOMA in *Whitewood v. Wolf.* By June 1, 2014, the District of Columbia and nineteen states were handing out marriage licenses to same-sex couples, as illustrated in the accompanying marriage map.[25]

The Michigan Marriage Trial

By February 2014, when the *DeBoer* trial commenced, the focus on the optimal parenting rationale by the attorney general's office was being overtaken by events. The NFSS had been methodologically trashed by dozens of experts, and academic psychologists and sociologists had closed ranks behind the no differences hypothesis. Even if Mark Regnerus's findings were plausible as social science, their constitutional relevance remained elusive: How did denying children raised in lesbian and gay households the benefits of married parents encourage straight couples to provide more stable homes for their children?

Nonetheless, Attorney General Schuette was not backing away, and Team Nurses was determined to lay to rest the notion that lesbian and gay parents did a poor job raising children. Between October 16 and February 23, the plaintiffs' counsel worked eighteen-hour days preparing for trial, which included finding and paying expert witnesses, who cost thousands of dollars. Where would the money come from? An immediate offer came from the American Foundation for Equal Rights (AFER), the Proposition 8 conquerors still eager to litigate the case that would bring marriage equality to all fifty states. If Team Nurses would allow AFER to bankroll the case, Ted Olson would lead the team to victory. Carole Stanyar seriously considered the offer until she spoke with a lawyer who had worked with AFER on the Proposition 8 case. It was a devil's bargain, that lawyer warned: Gibson Dunn would completely take over the case and push Stanyar and her colleagues to one side, not always respectfully. She declined the offer, as well as a more tempting one from the ACLU. Stanyar petitioned for financial help from the Civil Marriage Collaborative and Freedom to Marry, but without success.

Team Nurses largely financed their own case, with old-fashioned midwestern hustle, thrift, and sacrifice. Stanyar sold her house in Plymouth, Michigan. Nessel's first fundraising event was "shot night" at a local gay bar. She networked furiously, and many local groups and allies came through for her. Behind the scenes, Mary Bonauto pitched the Michigan case to Jon Stryker, a gay philanthropist whose Arcus Foundation gave the largest donation, which rescued the team near the end of the pretrial process. Later in the process, Bonauto again intervened to raise money to pay the lawyers and their expenses. Seeking to repair sour relations between Team Nurses and the national LGBTQ+ rights organizations, Bonauto reached out to Camilla Taylor in Lambda Legal and Leslie Cooper at the ACLU. GLAD's expert witnesses in its New England cases also made themselves available, namely Gary Gates, George Chauncey, Gregory Herek, and Nancy Cott.

The Nessel-Stanyar-Mogill partnership struggled against these financial limits and a whisper campaign denigrating their "rogue" litigation. Because the local ACLU was hostile, Stanyar reached out to the national ACLU. Lisa Brummel, one of her college basketball teammates, and her business colleague Anne Levinson told the national ACLU "to put their big boy pants on" and get behind the Michigan trial. The upshot of the backdoor cajoling was a conversation between Stanyar and Cooper, the nation's premier lawyer on the social science issues. (Additionally, Mary Bonauto personally vouched for the Michigan lawyers.) Leslie Cooper agreed to work with Team Nurses and also contributed David Brodzinsky, the go-to expert witness for the no differences hypothesis. Through a cold call, Mogill won the support of Stanford professor Michael Rosenfeld, who had done his own study on the no differences issue. The expert witnesses agreed to take partial payments or late payments, and Rosenfeld declined to bill for his invaluable services.[26]

Not least important, the plaintiffs' lawyers relied on enthusiastic law student volunteers: Abbye Klamann, Wayne Fore, Derek Turnbull, Alanna Maguire, and others from Michigan Law and Irina Vaynerman, Steven Kochevar, Bryn Williams, and Jonas Wang from Yale Law. As Abbye described the collaboration, Team Nurses molded itself into an ad hoc version of a traditional high-powered law firm. Carole Stanyar and Dana Nessel were the senior partners—the lead advocates before Judge Friedman and the mama bears who cheered everyone up and kept them going. Mogill was their trusted law partner, Sedler was of counsel, Bonauto and GLAD were cooperating lawyers, and Cooper was a valued outside consultant. The law students acted as junior associates, paralegals, and secretaries, doing most of the basic research, legwork, and typing. In our view, this jerry-rigged operation, with a shoestring budget, put on as excellent a case as the powerhouse big-city firms in AFER's lavishly funded case against California's Proposition 8.[27]

At the same time the plaintiffs' counsel were drawing upon the national marriage equality network, Michigan's attorneys called upon four social scientists whom Witherspoon had brought together for its 2010 meetings in Washington: Regnerus and three empirical economists—Joseph Price of BYU, Loren Marks of Louisiana State University, and Douglas Allen of Simon Fraser University in Vancouver, Canada. All clean-cut youngish white men with straight teeth, sharp haircuts, and traditional family values, these sophisticated social scientists were determined to upend the conventional wisdom reflected in the no differences hypothesis. Kristin Heyse's case focused on optimal family structure, which the state presented through the lens of gender rather than sexuality: a marital mom-dad household was superior to a mom-mom household because mothers and fathers brought different gender-based aptitudes and skills to parenting and because children's development benefited differently but deeply from both paternal and maternal styles. Although heartfelt and zealous, Michigan's defense of one-man, one-woman marriage was weak to begin with and lost steam in the course of the trial.

THE PLAINTIFFS' CASE

The Michigan marriage case played out during a record-setting polar vortex that covered the Detroit area, with almost eight feet of snow and temperatures as low as 30 degrees below zero. The trial commenced on a super-frigid Tuesday, February 25, 2014, in Detroit's magnificent and well-heated federal courthouse.[28]

The plaintiffs' first witness was Professor Brodzinsky, the Rutgers professor (now emeritus) who had been the lead witness in the 1996 Hawai'i trial. Summarizing the vast literature on parenting in a soft, avuncular voice, he agreed that mothers tended to have different parenting approaches from fathers, but testified that whenever there were two parents, of any sex, each tended to fill in the emotional gaps left by the other. Having surveyed as many as 150 peer-reviewed articles, he testified that there were no discernible differences in life outcomes or developmental characteristics between children raised by lesbian or gay parents and those raised by straight parents. This result held even though lesbian and gay persons were more likely to adopt special needs kids. As the plaintiffs and the state had stipulated before trial, Judge Friedman was aware that DeBoer and Rowse were A+ parents. Upon sharp cross-examination, state attorney Joseph Potchen walked Brodzinsky through the methodological limitations of those 150 studies. None of them had secured random samples of the population, most had no heterosexual control group, and the samples were generally all white.[29]

Complementing Professor Brodzinsky's psychological testimony, Professor Rosenfeld testified as a sociologist about the professional consensus supporting the no differences hypothesis. While Brodzinsky came across as your therapeutic grandfather, the younger, bearded Rosenfeld looked like your hip, tech-savvy cousin. Drawing from 2010 Census data, which provided a random sample of families, he testified that the grade-school progress of children raised in same-sex households was indistinguishable from that of children raised in traditional marital households. Family instability and poverty created hardships for children, he said, but same-sex parenting did not. The NFSS findings were easily attributable to family instability, not to the sex of the parents. He was aware that Professor Regnerus claimed that household instability was directly correlated with sexual orientation and that lesbian couples broke up at alarming rates. On this issue, too, Rosenfeld had conducted an empirical study. Based upon a random sample from national data, his 2011 report for the National Science Foundation found that couples in lesbian and gay civil unions broke up at about the same rate as couples in traditional one-man, one-woman marriages.[30]

These were the plaintiffs' most important witnesses, and Team Nurses could not have been happier. They had explained the professional consensus in both child psychology and sociology, had corrected for the lack of random samples in earlier studies, and had identified the major defect in the NFSS. The second day closed with a final witness, Vivek Sankaran, who directed the child advocacy clinic at Michigan Law. He praised DeBoer and Rowse as parents "who have done just a tremendous job with kids who, ordinarily, the system would have problems finding someone to take care of them." Sankaran's testimony framed the case for the judge: while the nurses were dutifully pressing their constitutional marriage claim, the case was really about the kids.[31]

On the third day of the trial, Thursday, February 27, Dr. Gary Gates, the leading demographer of LGBT families, documented the explosion in lesbian and gay households raising children. From the 2010 Census data, it appeared that 19 percent of same-sex households included children, and that number was bound to increase. Not only did more LGBT people than ever before want to get married, they wanted to raise children—and a lesbian or gay couple like DeBoer-Rowse was more likely to adopt or foster a child, especially a child with special needs, than a straight cohabiting couple or a straight married couple.

The next day was the testimony of Nancy Cott. As she had done in *Perry*, Professor Cott described the historical purpose of civil marriage as the state's structuring of family governance and political citizenship. In no state at any period of American history, she asserted, had marriage been denied because the couple disclaimed procreation as their goal. She spent the bulk of her testimony describing the three great changes in American civil marriage: the end of coverture and the instantiation of companionate marriage between legal equals; the end of laws barring different-race marriages, which freed the institution from obsession with racial purity; and no-fault divorce. The marriage equality movement would not change marriage any more, and probably would produce somewhat smaller changes, than those earlier developments. All of these movements have rendered marriage both more egalitarian and more libertarian. People marry whom they choose and dissolve those marriages when they choose.[32]

THE DEFENDANTS' CASE

Michigan opened its case on day five of the trial, March 3, and it got off to a rocky start. The state's lead-off witness was Yale law student and Princeton Ph.D. candidate Sherif Girgis, who was a protégé of Princeton philosopher Robby George (and a stellar student of an author of this volume). Girgis was planning to testify in support of the historical and philosophical basis for the view that conjugality was at the core of marriage, unlike other past restrictions such as race. On voir dire, probing the witness's qualifications to be an expert, Ken Mogill established that Girgis had few professional accomplishments other than coauthored papers that echoed George's natural law philosophy. Based on Girgis's youth and modest accomplishments, Judge Friedman refused to qualify him as an expert. Because its next witness was not in court, the state had to ask for a recess. Friedman, as always, was accommodating.[33]

For the afternoon of day five and most of day six, the state presented its key witness, Professor Regnerus. He got off to a strong start, confidently summarizing the problems with existing studies Brodzinsky had cited for the no differences hypothesis; the biggest flaw was the lack of random samples. The NFSS, based on a large random sample, was meant to generate results that could be statistically generalized to the entire population. Kids with lesbian mothers or gay fathers compared unfavorably across many dimensions to kids of intact mom-and-dad marital families. Children did need both a mother and a father! Team Michigan was pleased.[34]

Day six consisted mostly of Leslie Cooper's cross-examination. Like David Boies in the Proposition 8 case, Cooper was thoroughly prepared, in part because she had conducted a seven-hour deposition of Regnerus during the discovery period before trial, but mainly because she had mastered the social science and had developed an effective manner of cross-examination. While Boies was relentless and sarcastic in *Perry*, Cooper was matter-of-fact, even pleasant in *DeBoer*. Boies left witnesses feeling they had been publicly mocked and humiliated, often for minor gaffes, but Cooper left them feeling pretty good. (If Boies was the Mozart of cross-examination, as we suggested in chapter 15, Cooper was its Verdi, just as brilliant but more down-to-earth.) Regnerus told us his testimony was weak on direct and pretty good on cross-examination. But the judge, his law clerks, and the court reporter all believed his cross-examination was a disaster for the state's case.

Cooper started with the NFSS's biggest problem: it included as a lesbian or gay parent anyone who had intercourse with persons of the same sex. Few of the parents so defined lived in stable same-sex relationships, and most had left different-sex marriages, a transition likely to be traumatic to the children. Regnerus conceded that only two of the households screened by the NFSS had a child who was raised from birth by co-parents of the same sex. So his study was not an apples-to-apples comparison of children raised from birth by intact lesbian families with those raised by intact marital families. And it offered no evidence to support the proposition that excluding same-sex couples from marriage actually promoted "the ideal environment for children."[35]

"You compared two groups in which the majority of the respondents had been through a family breakup," namely the "lesbian mother" and "gay father" groups, Cooper said. "You compared them to a group that was defined by the stability of the group, the intact biological family group." Yes, Regnerus answered. As Friedman and other listeners interpreted this exchange, the professor was admitting that his survey was designed to produce bad results for lesbian mothers and gay fathers, because everyone agreed that household instability and parental strife created the worst conditions for child-rearing. As Cooper cajoled admission after admission, it became ever clearer that the study was evidence that family breakups and other transitions (and not stable same-sex parent households) were bad for children—a point made explicitly by Paul Amato, a key NFSS consultant. So what relevance did the NFSS have for the marriage exclusion? The professor looked down at his hands and ceased making eye contact with the judge or the lawyer. Court reporter Joan Morgan could see the witness's legs shuffling around as he grew increasingly fidgety. Based upon Stanyar's opening argument, the Brodzinsky and Rosenfeld testimony, and this cross-examination, plaintiffs had won their case even before Cooper dropped her bombshell.[36]

She presented Regnerus with a copy of a public statement issued the day before (March 3) by Professor Christine Williams, the chair of his department of the University of Texas. The statement announced that the NFSS findings "do not reflect the views of the Sociology Department" because they "are fundamentally flawed on conceptual and methodological grounds and . . . findings from Dr. Regnerus' work have been cited inappropriately in efforts to diminish the civil rights and legitimacy of LBGTQ partners and their families." The American Sociological Association and two hundred eminent social scientists had already criticized the study as worthless, but now his own colleagues had renounced his work. Lamenting that the statement was "regrettable," Regnerus seemed to sink in the witness chair.[37]

In light of these problems, why did Regnerus devote so much effort to presenting lesbian and gay households in such a negative light? Did he think the state should not allow gay people to adopt children? Not particularly, he answered. Nor did he think the state should prohibit straight divorced persons from remarrying, which prompted Cooper to remind him that the NFSS claimed to show that stepparent households were just as bad for children as same-sex households. Why then, she asked, was Regnerus so strongly opposed to same-sex marriage? Was his opposition entirely faith driven? "Yes," he answered. God created Adam and Eve as sexual opposites, and their yin-and-yang conjugality was essential for the destiny of the human race. Regnerus had converted to the Catholic faith because it offered a deeper theory for the regulation of sexuality and gender.[38]

Although Regnerus was not willing to admit that he tailored his research design to fit his religious beliefs, Cooper reminded him that he had earlier portrayed himself as a Christian professor, with these words: "I believe that if your faith matters it should inform what you teach and what you research." Yes, he replied, he had written that ten years ago, but he was more discreet about his faith nowadays. As Cooper led him deeper into his own motivations, he conceded that the idea for the NFSS had come from conversations with Luis Tellez and Maggie Gallagher, two of the nation's most ardent foes of same-sex marriage.[39]

Regnerus insisted that Witherspoon's sponsorship had not affected his research, but conceded that he collaborated with Brad Wilcox, then the director of Witherspoon's family, marriage, and the law project. Cooper introduced a 2010 email to Wilcox in which Regnerus suggested they seek explicit "feedback" from Tellez and Gallagher regarding "their optimal timelines (for the coalition meeting, the data collection, etc.), and their hopes for what emerges from this project, including the early report we discussed in D.C." (Because Regnerus taught at a state university, which had hosted the research, emails relating to the NFSS were available through freedom of information requests.) Responding to this, Tellez wrote to Regnerus: "It would be great to have this before a major decision of the Supreme Court but that is secondary to the need to do this and do it well."[40]

For the remainder of day six and the next two days (March 4–6), the state called three empirical economists: Joe Price, Loren Marks, and Doug Allen. Professor Marks was the best witness, in our view, and he flipped the hijacking-science charge that Cooper was making against the NFSS. He sharply criticized the "groupthink" of liberal social scientists and asked how many social scientists authoring no differences studies were supportive of marriage equality. All or almost all. In Marks's view, the studies everyone celebrated were not as good as the NFSS, which relied on a random sample and focused on hard variables.

With Professors Allen and Pakaluk, Professor Price had published a paper criticizing Professor Rosenfeld's finding that kids who resided with two same-sex parents for at least five years had similar educational outcomes as those residing with different-sex parents. Rosenfeld's restriction produced too small a sample, Price argued, and relaxing the restrictions produced a much larger sample of children to compare. Their study found statistically significant differences in outcomes; for example, children from same-sex households had less educational achievement than those from marital households. As Dana Nessel established on cross-examination, however, relaxing Rosenfeld's assumptions created an apples-and-oranges problem: Price was comparing stable marital households with same-sex households that had seen some form of instability for the children. Nessel also established on cross-examination that Price first met his coauthor Allen at the 2010 Witherspoon seminar featuring Blankenhorn. (Marks and Regnerus were also there, as were representatives of ADF and NOM.) Professors Allen and Price started work on their paper three months later.

Even before counsel offered their summations, on March 7, Judge Friedman had heard enough to make up his mind. Plaintiffs had demonstrated that lesbian and gay parents did an excellent job raising children, that many foster kids and children available for adoption would benefit from that parenting, and that recognizing their families through marriage would harm no one. *Windsor* seemed to dictate a judgment invalidating the constitutional exclusion, unless the state could show a good reason for it. But as the judge explained in his *DeBoer v. Snyder* decision of March 21, 2014, the state's case for the Michigan Marriage Amendment had died in the cross-examination of Professor Regnerus. "The Court finds Regnerus's testimony entirely unbelievable and not worthy of serious consideration." The study was designed to assure findings that satisfied the agenda of the professor's funder and his own religious beliefs. "The funder clearly wanted a certain result, and Regnerus obliged." Regnerus feels that this judgment was unnecessarily harsh, because he was testifying honestly, even if unpersuasively; Joan Morgan, the court reporter who was watching him like a hawk, agrees with Friedman that Regnerus was not being entirely forthright with the court.[41]

"Taken together," Friedman wrote, "both the *Windsor* and *Loving* decisions stand for the proposition that, without some overriding legitimate interest, the state cannot use its domestic relations authority to legislate families out of existence." Because their exclusion from marriage and even second-parent adoption undermined the stability of lesbian and gay households, the state was unnecessarily harming the children being reared in those households. In light of the harm to children like Nolan, Jacob, and Ryanne, Friedman dismissed the state's other defenses, such as the advantages of incremental change or deference to the democratic process. Aware that Attorney General Schuette was planning to delay enforcement of any injunction, the judge announced his decision on a Friday afternoon and did not issue a stay. Some clerks immediately started granting marriage licenses to lesbian and gay couples—until the attorney general secured a stay from the Sixth Circuit the next week. (The panel divided along party lines: Two judges appointed by President Bush supported a stay. Judge Helene White, originally nominated by President Clinton but ultimately appointed by President Bush, dissented.)[42]

The Race to the United States Supreme Court

Judge Friedman's decision in *DeBoer* was the last hurrah for the NFSS and the argument that the state should not recognize same-sex marriages because it should not give its approval to households that were toxic for children. District court opinions after *DeBoer* gave this argument less attention or ignored it altogether, and the NFSS played virtually no role in the federal appeals that played out in the Tenth, Fourth, and Seventh Circuits. Federal judges were following Justice Scalia's lament that *Windsor* raised the bar for state exclusions of lesbian and gay couples from marriage. Did the *Windsor* majority really go as far as Scalia charged? Only the justices themselves could answer that question—and counsel for the many plaintiff couples scurried to position their cases to be the vessel for a nationwide marriage equality decision.

The Utah marriage case had a head start. On April 10, 2014, the Tenth Circuit heard oral argument on Utah's appeal of Judge Shelby's order. The panel hearing the appeal consisted of Judges Paul Kelly from New Mexico (appointed by the first President Bush in 1992); Carlos Lucero from Colorado (appointed by President Clinton in 1995); and Jerome Holmes from Oklahoma (appointed by the second President Bush in 2006). Press reports suggested that this panel, with two Republican appointees, leaned to the right, but counsel for Utah knew it leaned the other way. Judge Kelly was sure to uphold Utah's definition of marriage, and liberal judge Lucero clearly favored invalidating its exclusion. Judge Holmes had been on the motions panel that had denied a stay in December. This had been a surprise to everyone, as Holmes was a judicial conservative who had been sponsored by Oklahoma senators Tom Coburn and James Inhofe, two of the most outspoken opponents of rights for LGTBQ+ citizens in American history.

Washington lawyer Gene Schaerr represented Utah; he was joined on the brief by Monte Stewart (like Schaerr, a Latter-day constitutionalist) and John Bursch (former Michigan solicitor general). The state's excellent brief argued that including same-sex couples in marriage would create a new institution that would be less child-centric, less supportive of the gold standard for parenting (an intact mom-dad marriage), and less able to channel young heterosexuals into responsible decisions about procreation. More than any other state, Utah adhered to traditional marriage—and was rewarded by a low rate of nonmarital births, high levels of education, and low crime rates. Federal judges, Schaerr and his colleagues maintained, should not disrupt this successful regulatory regime![43]

Schaerr had cited the NFSS in his brief, but on April 9, 2014, the day before oral argument, he submitted a letter to the court disavowing it because of its methodological flaws. "The state's principal concern is the potential long-term impact of a redefinition of marriage on the children of heterosexual parents," he wrote, and so the social science debate over "same-sex parenting" was largely beside the point. At oral argument, Judge Holmes brought up the letter. The state really had no firm evidence that bad things would happen if same-sex marriage were allowed, right? Shouldn't the state lose if the court applied heightened scrutiny? Schaerr resisted the idea, but the case seemed to turn on whether there would be heightened scrutiny.[44]

The Tenth Circuit had previously ruled that sexual orientation discriminations required only a rational basis, but Jerome Holmes was persuaded that Utah was denying the couples a fundamental right to marry, which was an alternate trigger for strict scrutiny. The first African American judge on the Tenth Circuit, he may have been sensitive to the fact that *Loving v. Virginia* (1967) had relied on the substantive due process right to marry in order to overrule the state's longstanding interracial marriage prohibition—a law that Holmes himself would have violated by marrying his girlfriend Jeri Towler, as he would do within several years of *Kitchen*. His relationship with Towler may have been relevant in another way. Towler and her daughter Alexandra were strongly committed to an inclusive community. Indeed, after Alex Towler graduated from law school, she joined her mother, by then Jeri Holmes, in Nonprofit Solutions, which provided legal advice to public interest organizations. One of their clients would be the Pride Alliance that sponsored Oklahoma City's annual gay pride celebration.[45]

Whatever the reason, Judge Holmes was open to an expansive understanding of the fundamental right to marry, tethered to mutual commitment and not just procreation. Indeed, such an understanding was not out of line with his strict rule-of-law jurisprudence, for the Supreme Court had recognized a broad right to marry in opening wedding doors to deadbeat dads and convicted prisoners. In the prisoners case, *Turner v. Safley* (1987), the court extended the right to some inmates who would never sexually consummate their marriages. In the deadbeat dads case, *Zablocki v. Redhail* (1978), the court's articulation of the right to marry brought forth a complaint from Justice Powell that its reasoning might be broad enough to call into question state exclusions for "incest, bigamy, and homosexuality." On June 25, 2014, Judge Lucero delivered the opinion of the 2-1 panel in *Herbert v. Kitchen*, striking down Utah's statutory and constitutional junior-DOMAs as a violation of the constitutional right to marry.[46]

A month later, the same panel affirmed Judge Kern in the Oklahoma case, *Bishop v. Smith*. Judge Holmes wrote a concurring opinion commending the district court for declining to find that the Oklahoma Super-DOMA was motivated by animus. In his view, courts should rarely find that legislatures or electorates acted with animus toward a minority. Measures lacking the novelty and sweeping exclusions of Colorado's Amendment 2 and DOMA should be examined under the regular precepts of strict scrutiny (where applicable) and rational basis review. As in the Utah case, Holmes's vote was the decisive one against Oklahoma's marriage bar. There was a personal sequel. In 2018, Holmes's stepdaughter Alex married Kristen Bliss and changed her name to Alex Towler Bliss.[47]

On the same day the Tenth Circuit announced *Bishop*, the Fourth Circuit released its decision invalidating Virginia's marriage exclusions in *Bostic v. Rainey*. As in the Tenth Circuit, the majority subjected the exclusions to strict scrutiny because they denied the couples a fundamental right to marry. Echoing the ADF's brief, Judge Niemeyer dissented, arguing that the right to marry was a social right embedded in tradition and associated with procreation and child-rearing. At oral argument, Judge Gregory had opined that marriage with children had never been limited to procreative intercourse between the spouses and that the children reared in lesbian and gay households would benefit from their parents' right to marry. Like Jerome Holmes, Roger Gregory was the first African American to serve on his court of appeals and was appointed by President Bush (after a recess appointment by President Clinton in his case). Gregory agreed with Henry Floyd (appointed by President Obama) that *Loving*'s fundamental right to marry was an individual right, an entitlement to choose the spouse who best suited one's needs and desires. Notably absent from the dueling majority and dissenting opinions was any mention of the NFSS or the comparative competence of lesbian and straight parents.[48]

As the summer wore on, matters only got worse for the optimal parenting argument. On August 26, 2014, the Seventh Circuit heard oral argument for Indiana's and Wisconsin's appeals of district court orders invalidating their junior-DOMAs. The panel was a most learned trio: Judges Richard Posner, Ann Williams, and David Hamilton. Both states and the ADF ignored the NFSS, abandoned the optimal parenting argument, and revived the responsible procreation argument, which was revealing a Terminator quality (it got smashed repeatedly yet always bounced back), because it did not demonize gay people, couples, or parents. Wisconsin threw in justifications grounded in tradition, Burkean prudence, and the virtues of incrementalism. Cranky and impatient under the best of circumstances, the owlish, sharp-tongued Dick Posner demolished those justifications, mocked counsel's inability to answer his factual questions, and suggested that both junior-DOMAs boiled down to hate legislation. Appointed to the bench by President Reagan, Judge Posner had long been skeptical that gay marriage was a good idea and incredulous that the Constitution would require it. But he changed his mind when confronted with the reality of lesbian and gay families.[49]

An estimated three thousand children had been adopted by lesbian or gay persons in Indiana. Wouldn't these kids be better off, Posner asked, if their parents could get married? How about the ten thousand Indiana youth in foster care? What does the state have against these children? Indiana insisted that preventing homosexual couples from marrying was key to its policy of encouraging responsible procreation by accident-prone heterosexuals. All three judges were incredulous. Indiana allowed sterile male-female couples to get married, right? It barred first cousins from marrying—unless they were over sixty-five years old, when the state presumed they could not produce children like the Hapsburgs. If Indiana could accommodate nonprocreating first cousins, why not nonprocreating lesbians? David Hamilton sealed the state's doom when he observed, at the end of a long morning for the defenders of one-man, one-woman marriage, that between 1990 and 2009 the percentage of births outside marriage in Wisconsin soared 53 percent, in Indiana a whopping 68 percent. Was this anti-gay state policy really preventing irresponsible procreation? Or was it state policy just because it was anti-gay?

Posner's opinion in *Baskin v. Bogan*, handed down with lightning speed a week after the argument, contained one swipe after another at the state's justifications. The most-quoted swipe was this one: "Indiana's government thinks that straight couples tend to be sexually irresponsible, producing unwanted children by the carload, and so must be pressured (in the form of governmental encouragement of marriage through a combination of sticks and carrots) to marry, but that gay couples, unable as they are to produce children wanted or unwanted, are model parents—model citizens really—so have no need for marriage. Heterosexuals get drunk and pregnant, producing unwanted children; their reward is to be allowed to marry. Homosexual couples do not produce unwanted children; their reward is to be denied the right to marry. Go figure."[50]

In October 2014, when the Supreme Court returned from its summer recess, the justices faced petitions from Utah, Virginia, Oklahoma, Indiana, and Wisconsin seeking review of these appeals court decisions striking down state constitutional amendments limiting marriage to one man, one woman. If at least four justices voted to accept a petition for review, the court would take the case. On October 6, 2014, the court issued its list of cases accepted for review and those denied—and the "certiorari denied" list included all five marriage appeals. No one had predicted this.

Justices Scalia, Thomas, and Alito had been strongly in favor of taking one or more of these appeals, because they found the lower court decisions legally erroneous and constitutionally toxic. Marriage for lesbian and gay couples was a big deal and should be decided by the citizens of each state; the Constitution, in their view, had nothing to say about it. Justices Ginsburg, Breyer, Sotomayor, and Kagan were just as strongly opposed to taking any of these cases. The marriage equality issue was, in their view, not ripe for Supreme Court review and should continue to percolate among the appeals courts. They may also have believed that the more marriage licenses were given to same-sex couples, the smaller would be the political backlash against the nationwide marriage equality decision they now favored. Let the nation get accustomed to lesbian and gay marriage, as it had done with interracial marriage in the 1950s and 1960s, before the Supreme Court put its constitutional stamp on a conclusion the popular majority had already reached. Justice Kennedy also opposed review for Hayekian reasons: let the lower court judgments stand, and see if the popular reaction supports or refutes the hypothesis that cultural norms had decisively changed in favor of marriage equality.[51]

The biggest surprise was that Chief Justice Roberts declined to vote for review. Personally, he was more persuaded by the dissenting opinions in *Kitchen* and *Bostic,* and he found Dick Posner's sarcastic opinion in *Baskin* a shade injudicious. So why did he not vote for review, as he had done in *Perry?* We have a couple of theories. The court usually denies review when there is no split in the circuits. From Roberts's institutionalist perspective, the Supreme Court's job was to resolve divisive constitutional and statutory issues when the lower courts could not reach consensus, not to correct every erroneous decision. Because all of the post-*Windsor* appeals court decisions had struck down marriage exclusions, it was premature for the court to terminate the discussion— especially because the conservative Fifth, Sixth, and Eighth Circuits had not yet weighed in on the marriage appeals before them. Another possibility, widely believed among the Supreme Court bar, is that the chief's vote was a "defensive denial." Roberts believed that there then were five votes for nationwide marriage equality, a controversial result that he wanted to avoid. If you were 95 percent certain that you would lose in October 2014, but there was even just a 20 percent chance things would change decisively by April 2015, then your best strategy would be to avoid taking the cases in October. Although no justice would openly admit to voting in this manner, political scientists have shown that strategic voting is common on the Supreme Court, especially for discretionary decisions on whether to take review.[52]

The legal community was "flabbergasted" that the Supreme Court denied review in all five cases. Neither Monte Stewart nor Gene Schaerr could think of a case where the justices had imposed a stay on a lower court judgment striking down a state or federal law, yet ultimately denied review—which is what the justices did in *Kitchen*. Olson and Boies were sorely disappointed, as *Bostic* was their last shot at glory. LGBTQ+ rights organizations were delighted with the court's action, because it signaled possible majority sympathy with the results in the five cases and because it immediately expanded the orbit of marriage equality.

On October 5, there had been nineteen marriage equality states, the same states mapped out earlier in Figure 4. On October 6, after the three courts of appeals dissolved their stays, five more states were under judicial injunctions to issue marriage licenses to same-sex couples, and all five did so promptly. Because *Kitchen* and *Bishop* were now binding precedent in the Tenth Circuit, three other Tenth Circuit states would soon be required to issue licenses: Colorado, Kansas, and Wyoming. *Bostic* would require district courts in North Carolina, South Carolina, and West Virginia to do the same. The Colorado attorney general immediately directed its county clerks to follow *Kitchen*, and most of the other states soon followed.

South Carolina (Fourth Circuit) and Kansas (Tenth) dragged their feet. District courts required both states to issue marriage licenses to lesbian and gay couples, and the courts of appeals refused to stay those orders. On November 12, an internally divided Supreme Court (over objection from Justices Scalia, Thomas, and Alito) denied Kansas a stay pending appeal, giving the state no choice but to comply with a district court judgment requiring the issuance of marriage licenses. On November 20, an internally divided court (with Scalia and Thomas publicly dissenting) denied South Carolina a stay pending appeal, and that state also fell into line. Five justices would have been required to grant a stay in these cases, meaning that Justice Kennedy voted with Justice Ginsburg and her liberal bloc to deny those stays.[53]

On October 7, the day after the Supreme Court's denied review in the five appeals, the Ninth Circuit released its decision striking down the marriage exclusions in Idaho and Nevada. Monte Stewart, who was handling the appeals in those states, had expected this result and immediately sought a Supreme Court stay pending a petition for review in *Otter v. Latta,* as he had done in *Kitchen.* On October 10, a majority of the court rejected the request. Marriage licenses were issued forthwith in Idaho and Nevada—as well as Alaska, Arizona, and (after some stalling) Montana, the three Ninth Circuit states whose marriage exclusions were being litigated in federal district courts.[54]

In the wake of judicial actions on October 6 and 7, 2014, the number of states issuing marriage licenses to lesbian and gay couples increased, in just weeks, from nineteen to thirty-five. The number of states in Figure 4's marriage map almost doubled—by Thanksgiving marriage equality had arrived in all the states of the Northeast, five states in the Midwest, and all the states of the Rockies and West Coast. Suddenly the map looked a lot like the one the Supreme Court had faced in *Loving v. Virginia* (with mostly the same holdout states). October 6, 2014, was the day that national marriage equality came out of the closet as inevitable. By voting no, the Supreme Court was in effect saying yes.

November 2014 was also a special month for the DeBoer-Rowse family. In July 2012, a baby named Rylee was born to a mother who was in physical and emotional distress. Social services almost immediately contacted April and Jayne, who agreed to provide a nurturing foster home. Thus, during the trial before Judge Friedman, the nurses were raising four small kids, several dogs, and a stray cat. Money was tight. Jacob and Ryanne had developmental issues that were being addressed by ongoing therapy, and Rylee was coping with the effects of maternal health problems. With Wendy DeBoer's help, April and Jayne created a secure place for all of them to flourish.

In 2015, we visited the household and interviewed each of the children. Six-year-old Jacob, a towheaded charmer, told us all about his family, including Grandma. We asked him what was special about him, and he gave us a shy smile: "It's because I'm, well, handsome." Ryanne was wearing a red sweatshirt that said "IT Girl," but she denied being an "It Girl" herself. Giggling, she was more reticent but admitted that she loved going to the park with Mom and Mama and Grandma. Six-year-old Nolan explained how he was working on a project that Mommy could help him load onto his iPad. Was he able to use the iPad? Oh sure, "I can do any kinda thing, and I can do a whole bunch," he replied proudly. Only three years old and still very shy, Rylee had to be coaxed by Mommy but introduced us to her stuffed animal, a dog named Da Da. When we asked about her brothers and sisters, she became more animated, identifying her siblings and announcing that Nolan had a seventh birthday coming up. So what's special about you, Rylee? She looked us in the eyes, with some skepticism about the question, and answered: "Mommy."

When you actually meet the families of lesbian and gay couples who have fostered or adopted children, you learn that the NFSS was even more deeply flawed than its scientific critics suggested. As he had frequently done when he was a full-time faculty member at the University of Chicago's law school, Dick Posner posed the killer question during oral argument in the Indiana and Wisconsin marriage cases: Does a society recognizing lesbian and gay marriages provide adopted or fostered children the possibility for better life opportunities than a society that does not recognize those marriages or that affirmatively disrespects and even penalizes such families?

21 • Self-Determination

The Leviathan enjoys a fearsome power to command our lives. But it cannot tell us whom to love.

Shortly after 10:00 a.m. on June 26, 2013, Americans learned that the United States Supreme Court had required the federal government to recognize valid same-sex marriages. John Arthur and Jim Obergefell of Cincinnati watched as NBC's Pete Williams (an openly gay newscaster) described the court's opinion in *United States v. Windsor*. "Jim kissed John lightly, loving the feel of his face, and then, because it seemed as if the country was changing, Jim looked at his dying partner and said for the first time in twenty years, 'Let's get married.' John said yes."[1]

Jim and John were both born in the *Loving v. Virginia* year of 1967. When they were twenty-five, they met at a 1992 New Year's Eve party in John's Cincinnati mansion. It was "love at third sight," as they had crossed paths before, but that night they shared a New Year's kiss and the beginning of a lifetime together. Tall and gangly, John could be the life of the party and had a great social sense, but was in his soul very lonely. After a childhood filled with taunts and paternal rejection, the most important people in his life remained Marilyn Arthur, his mother; his younger brother Curtis; and his aunt Paulette Roberts. Jim, the youngest of six kids with two adoring parents in Sandusky, Ohio, grew into a nice-looking man with brown hair, hazel eyes, and Clark Kent glasses. When he saw John again on New Year's Eve, he felt warm all over—and when John made an overture to get to know him better, he ended up staying at the house most of the week. "Jim had never met anyone with such a sharp wit, with one-liners about his broken family that made Jim laugh or cringe or both."[2]

After they had dated long distance for seven weeks, John gave Jim a gold ring with five diamonds; it was not quite a proposal, but it sealed a relationship that would last for two decades. They made their life together in the Mount Washington neighborhood of Cincinnati, at precisely the same time that Phil Burress was leading the campaign to override the city's anti-discrimination ordinance, as noted in chapter 5 of this volume. Jim and John became politically active and did their part to transform Cincinnati into a pro-gay city. In November 2004, the voters decisively reinstated the anti-discrimination ordinance. Burress attributed the result to an exodus of conservatives to the suburbs and to the global decline of traditional values. "The city is going belly up as to values," he said. "The left has taken over." Jim and John disagreed with the first statement and hoped the second was true. The city was growing more inclusive each year.[3]

In the winter of 2011, John felt a tingling in his left foot, which was an early sign of amyotrophic lateral sclerosis (ALS), known as Lou Gehrig's disease. ALS causes a loss of motor ability; by the time he accepted Jim's proposal, John was completely bedridden. With the aid of Aunt Paulette, Jim was determined to get legally married. Because of the 2004 ballot initiative and earlier statutes, Ohio would not issue a marriage license to two men—but by July 2013, thirteen states and the District of Columbia were willing to do so. Most of them were a short airplane ride away from Cincinnati (John was too fragile to travel by automobile). Maryland was the perfect destination: the state recognized same-sex marriages and would give licenses to out-of-state couples; only one partner was required to appear at the clerk's office to make the application.

On July 11, 2013, an ambulance brought John, Jim, and Paulette to the Cincinnati Municipal Lunken Airport. Buckled onto a narrow gurney, John was transferred into a Learjet specially equipped for medical transport. Jim had the marriage license in hand. After a ninety-minute flight, the airplane landed at Baltimore/Washington International Airport (BWI). With Paulette conducting the ceremony, Jim and John exchanged vows while parked on the tarmac at BWI. Jim had written his own marriage vows: "As you recently said, it was love at third sight. And for the last twenty years, six months, and eleven days, it has been love at every sight. You've loved me when it was easy and when it was difficult. You've made me a better person. Thank you—for seeing in me someone you could spend your life with. Thank you—for allowing me to love you when you thought you were lost and beyond love."[4]

Alphonse Gerhardstein, the Cincinnati lawyer with the big eyeglasses who had challenged the 1993 charter amendment overriding Cincinnati's gay-rights ordinance, was inspired by *Windsor*. With the support of his wife, Mimi, and their three grown-up children, Al felt the time was ripe for a marriage lawsuit in conservative Ohio. An effective strategy might be a challenge to the state's refusal to recognize valid out-of-state marriages. The parallel to *Windsor* was striking: just as the Supreme Court invalidated the federal government's refusal to recognize a valid same-sex marriage, so a lower court might invalidate Ohio's refusal to recognize same-sex marriages validly entered in other states. Gerhardstein put out the word to his friends in the LGBTQ+ community. Within days of their marriage, John and Jim contacted him. Never one to dawdle, Al filed *Obergefell v. Wymsylo* three days later—the first federal lawsuit focusing on a state's refusal to recognize a valid out-of-state marriage between two women or two men.[5]

Gerhardstein asked for a court order directing that, in due course, Obergefell be listed as Arthur's spouse on the county-issued death certificate. On July 22, 2013, federal district judge Timothy Black issued a temporary restraining order to that effect. John Arthur died at home on October 22, 2013, and as ordered, his death certificate identified him as married and Jim Obergefell as his surviving spouse. David Michener, a widower, and Robert Grunn, a funeral home director, were added as plaintiffs in *Obergefell*. James Esseks of the ACLU worked with Gerhardstein and ultimately joined him as cocounsel. On December 23, 2013, Judge Black found that Ohio's Super-DOMA violated the widowers' due process "right not to be deprived of one's already-existing legal marriage and its attendant benefits and protections" and granted the permanent injunction. The state appealed that ruling to the Court of Appeals for the Sixth Circuit.[6]

Sitting in the back of the courtroom during the December hearing were Shannon Fauver and Dawn Elliott, two young lawyers from Louisville. On July 26, 2013, they had filed a federal constitutional case for four plaintiffs: Greg Bourke and Michael DeLeon, a Louisville couple, and their two adopted teenage children, Isaiah and Bella. Like April DeBoer and Jayne Rowse, Greg and Michael wanted joint parental rights like those enjoyed by spouses. Although they were legally married in Canada, Kentucky did not recognize that marriage. The lawyers ultimately added as cocounsel Dan Canon and Laura Landenwich, who in turn brought in two other legally married couples, Paul Campion and Randy Johnson, and Kim Franklin and Tammy Boyd. This marriage-recognition lawsuit was controversial within the national gayocracy, whose disapproval surprised the plaintiff couples. Like Michigan, Kentucky was not on the agreed-upon "marriage map," the jurisdictions where litigators and Freedom to Marry wanted to concentrate resources to challenge junior- and Super-DOMAs.[7]

Nonetheless, on February 12, 2014, federal district judge John Heyburn III granted relief in *Bourke v. Beshear,* ruling that in light of *Windsor,* the state had no serious justification for refusing to recognize these valid marriages and bestowing the benefits of joint parenting to the six children being raised in these households. The 2004 Kentucky Super-DOMA was therefore unconstitutional. Agreeing with the judge, Kentucky attorney general Jack Conway declined to appeal the judgment. Governor Beshear retained Leigh Landerow as outside counsel to take the appeal on the state's behalf. There were then two marriage cases on appeal to the Sixth Circuit—and more to come.[8]

Dr. Valeria Tanco and Dr. Sophie Jesty had been together since they met at Cornell's veterinary school, but their jobs took them to Tennessee. The day after *Windsor,* Val became pregnant through artificial insemination, and the couple immediately focused on the possibility that their child would be born in a state that would not recognize either their marriage or their joint parental rights. (Tennessee law stipulated that the names of both *spouses* would be listed on the child's birth certificate, so marriage was important to assure Sophie's parental rights.) They joined a lawsuit brought on October 21 by Regina Lambert and legendary Nashville attorney Abby Rubenfeld (formerly Lambda's legal director). Two other plaintiff couples were Ijpe DeKoe and Thomas Kostura, and Matthew Mansell and Johno Espejo, the parents of an adopted daughter and son. Working with Bill Harbison of the Sherrad and Roe firm and with Shannon Minter of NCLR, Rubenfeld won a preliminary injunction from district judge Aleta Trauger on March 14, two weeks before Val gave birth to Emilia. Because of the order, both mothers were listed on the birth certificate. Tennessee appealed immediately, the third marriage appeal to be lodged with the Sixth Circuit. Michigan appealed Judge Friedman's *DeBoer* judgment to the Sixth Circuit on March 21.[9]

A fifth appeal was another brainchild of Al Gerhardstein. In 2011, Joe Vitale and Rob Talmas were married in their home jurisdiction of New York. They arranged to adopt a child born in Ohio on April 19, 2013. They named him Cooper Talmas-Vitale and brought him home to New York City. In January 2014, the adoption agency told them that Ohio would only put one of their names on Cooper's birth certificate. This snafu would assure confusion for years to come, so they called Gerhardstein, who felt that the perfect complement to his death certificate case would be a birth certificate case. One of the plaintiffs would be Cooper Talmas-Vitale, the person most injured by Ohio's exclusion. Three married female couples, in each case with one of the part-ners pregnant and the baby due to be delivered in June 2014, contacted Ger-hardstein about being plaintiffs in the new nonrecognition lawsuit: Pam and Nicole Yorksmith, Brittani Henry and Brittni Rogers, and Kelly Noe and Kelly McCracken. On February 10, 2014, Gerhardstein filed a complaint for these four couples, little Cooper, and an adoption agency. In this case, he partnered with Susan Sommer from Lambda Legal. Expanding upon his earlier *Oberge-fell* decision, Judge Black on April 14 issued a statewide injunction in *Henry v. Himes*. Two days later, he followed other judges in staying the effect of his broad injunction pending the appeal, but he insisted that the individual relief not be affected. The three babies born to plaintiffs later that spring all had both mothers' names on their birth certificates.[10]

The sixth and final appeal was another Kentucky case brought by Fauver and Elliott. *Love v. Beshear* was a lawsuit by three long-term committed couples who unsuccessfully applied for marriage licenses in Kentucky: Tim Love and Larry Ysunza, an older "bear couple" (gay slang for beefy males); Maurice Blanchard and Dominique James, a younger, very stylish Baptist couple; and Jim Meade and Luke Barlowe, a well-to-do couple who had been together since 1968. Like the Michigan case, this was a regular marriage equality case, not a lawsuit seeking recognition of valid out-of-state marriages. It was filed on Valentine's Day 2014. Judge Heyburn ruled in their favor on July 1, and the state took an appeal.[11]

The Sixth Circuit consolidated all six cases for oral argument. The plain-tiffs in these six lawsuits included fourteen couples, three children, two wid-owers, a funeral home director, and an adoption agency. Eight of the couples were male, six female. Altogether, the adult plaintiffs started with twenty children, most of whom were children of color, and more would be born or adopted in the course of the appellate litigation. The families came from all social classes, races, ethnicities, and ages, with a wide range of health histo-ries and occupations. All were asking for state recognition of families that seemed little different from traditional married families, except for the sex of the couples.

Their doctrinal claim was that the states had a constitutional obligation to accord their marriages and family commitments the same respect that different-sex marital families enjoyed. In a democracy, they suggested, citizen-ship entailed self-governance as well as participation in governance of the political community. Self-governance entailed the freedom that each adult ought to enjoy, in order to determine her/his/their own careers, goals, and relationships—and a correlative responsibility to pursue those personal objectives without harming other citizens. *Self-determination* was the moral center for all six marriage cases, which were pushing back against the many ways state governments were discouraging the families they chose, the families that were best for them.

As you read the following account of the complicated process culminating in the Supreme Court's famous decision in Jim Obergefell's case, consider the broader lessons his journey portends for American constitutionalism. The last three chapters demonstrated a dialectic among the three moral faces of the marriage debate: our nation's commitment to individual *liberty*, which we understand as self-determination, and which embraces religious free exercise as well as the freedom to marry; reconstruction's dedication to *equal protection* of all citizens, which extends to new minority and fading majority groups; and the needs of the political, social, and economic *community*, which justify bold government actions that compromise preexisting liberties and protect some citizens more than others. Anyone who says that one of these is the only legitimate ground for decision is not being true to American constitutional history.

Sixth Circuit Argument and Decision in *DeBoer v. Snyder*

The Tennessee, Kentucky, Ohio, and Michigan marriage cases were heard together at the federal courthouse in Cincinnati on August 6, 2014. April DeBoer, Wendy DeBoer, and Jayne Rowse drove down from Detroit; Valeria Tanco drove up from Knoxville. "The courtroom was filled with babies," Jim Obergefell wrote. April and Jayne, having left their kids at home, "walked over to see Orion Yorksmith, sleeping in a sling crisscrossed across Pam Yorksmith's chest." Obergefell himself sat alone, reminiscing about his life with John Arthur and staring at the bald eagle, wings spread wide, perched above the leather chairs reserved for the three judges. Joe Vitale sat next to him. "We all have someone except for Jim," he sadly recalled.[12]

Defending the Super-DOMAs were Michigan solicitor general Aaron Lindstrom, Ohio solicitor Eric Murphy, Kentucky's appointed counsel Leigh Latherow, and Tennessee's Associate Solicitor General Joseph Whalen. Representing the plaintiff couples were Carole Stanyar, Al Gerhardstein, Laura Landenwich, and William Harbison. The panel consisted of Judge Martha (Cissy) Daughtrey from Nashville, appointed by President Clinton in 1993, and Judges Deborah Cook of Akron, Ohio, and Jeffrey Sutton of Columbus, Ohio, both appointed by President Bush in 2001 but confirmed after a delayed process. At oral argument, Daughtrey was skeptical of the state positions, and it was clear she would vote to affirm the various injunctions; Cook asked a few elementary questions that reflected tentativeness or confusion, but everyone expected her to vote to reverse; Sutton asked probing questions to each side, but his philosophical reluctance to second-guess the democratic process made him a likely vote to reverse as well. He would write the majority opinion overturning all the injunctions; Daughtrey would dissent. The briefs, oral arguments, and the written opinions revealed the highest level of legal analysis and constitutional deliberation.[13]

DEMOCRACY AND RATIONALITY

The meta-theme of Jeff Sutton's opinion was that fundamental normative debates should be worked out through the normal democratic process, and courts should be reluctant to intervene. At oral argument, he said that "the best way to get respect and dignity is through the democratic process, forcing everyone's neighbors, co-employees, friends [to understand] that these unions deserve the same respect as traditional heterosexual couples." That process was working well for the marriage equality side, which ran the table in the November 2012 election. If you really want to change "hearts and minds," Sutton cautioned, a judicial opinion was not the way to go.[14]

Deference to the popular will was the reason the Supreme Court has required the judiciary to accept most legislation or popular initiatives so long as there was a rational basis for its policy determinations. Suppose that Michigan adopted a law giving special tax credits to steelworkers for the purpose of subsidizing workers in a struggling industry. A judge might believe the legislature was mistaken to use tax policy in this way, or that it ought to apply the same policy to auto workers, but the judge's job was not to tell the legislature (or the voters) what the best policy might be. She should defer to the legislature's judgment about the wisdom of the policy. The judge should *not* ask: Would excluding auto workers be unfair, because including them would not (in her opinion) impede the steel industry protective policy? This is how Sutton saw the marriage equality cases: the voters had made a reasonable choice to avoid experimenting with the established definition of marriage, and even if (contrary to popular belief) same-sex couples would not undermine the institution, it was not the judicial role to write them into the law.[15]

Cissy Daughtrey saw the matter through a civil rights lens, expecting judges to be less deferential when fundamental liberties were apportioned unequally to a social group long subject to government discrimination and exclusions. After 1971, the Supreme Court had not told women that they should work through the political process to purge the law of blatant sex discriminations, even though women were a majority of the voters. For example, assume Michigan granted a tax credit limited to all self-avowed heterosexuals and required admitted homosexuals and bisexuals to pay higher taxes. The rationale that saved the steelworkers' tax credit could apply here: the legislature or the voters wanted to encourage a struggling sexual orientation—heterosexuality!—which was useful and maybe necessary for the perpetuation of the human race. As Daughtrey saw it, this application of the rational basis approach would be inconsistent with *Romer* and *Lawrence,* which held that government endorsement of heterosexuality and implicit denigration of gay people did not satisfy the rationality requirement of the Fourteenth Amendment. Consider another variation: Could Michigan pass a statute imposing a poll tax just on admitted homosexuals? Surely not, because that would infringe on the fundamental right to vote, and we cannot imagine such a tax serving a compelling public interest.[16]

ORIGINAL MEANING AND TRADITION

Sutton's majority opinion described the four states' legal backgrounds in the following way: (1) each state's common law and long-standing statutory law defined marriage as one man, one woman; (2) after that definition was called into question in the 1990s, these states reaffirmed the traditional definition in statutory junior-DOMAs; and (3) once civil unions and domestic partnerships became prominent, the states all adopted constitutional Super-DOMAs. Given this legal context, Sutton thought he could easily distinguish the marriage cases from something like our gay-excluding tax and voting hypotheticals above. Our hypotheticals involve novel statutes targeting gay people, while the Super-DOMAs in Michigan, Ohio, Kentucky, and Tennessee did nothing more than reaffirm a tradition that was never designed to harm gay people. Likewise, the fundamental right to marry invoked by the plaintiff couples based upon *Loving v. Virginia* (1967) was historically premised upon the conjugal understanding that undergirded the idea of marriage as a foundation of civil society. States had invested legal benefits and rights to recognize and reward marriages—but not friendships, caregiving arrangements, or sexual cohabitation—in order to channel procreation into committed, lasting relation-ships that would be the best situses for raising children.[17]

The bridge between democracy and tradition was Sutton's view of the Con-stitution "as a covenant between the governed and the governors, between the people and their political leaders," which meant that "the originally understood meaning of the charter generally will be the lasting meaning of the charter. . . . The written charter cements the limitations on government into an unbend-ing bulwark, not a vane alterable whenever alterations occur—unless and until the people, like contracting parties, choose to change the contract through the agreed-upon mechanisms for doing so." Who among the framers of the Fourteenth Amendment would have "originally understood" same-sex unions to be marriages? No one. Under this approach, *Loving* was also wrongly de-cided, for none of the framers originally understood different-race unions to be marriages, either. A fundamental problem with Sutton's "original under-standing" approach is that it would bind the country to the prejudices of the past. Is that really required by an originalist methodology?[18]

As the late Justice Scalia insisted, an originalist ought to focus on "original public meaning" (an objective standard) rather than the more subjective "orig-inal understanding." What was the original public meaning of the equal pro-tection clause? The Fourteenth Amendment's term *equal protection,* taken from the Ohio Constitution of 1851, had a widely accepted legal meaning in 1868. Ohio's equal protection clause asserted that "all men are, by nature, free and independent, and have certain inalienable rights, among which are those of enjoying and defending life and liberty . . . and seeking and obtaining happi-ness and safety" and that "[g]overnment is instituted for their equal protection and benefit." The equal protection clause protected against what nineteenth-century lawyers called "class legislation." Iowa's 1857 Constitution, for exam-ple, put it this way: "All laws of a general nature shall have a uniform operation; the general assembly shall not grant to any citizen, or class of citizens, privi-leges or immunities, which, upon the same terms shall not equally belong to all citizens." As applied by judges, equal protection clauses protected against laws creating special privileges for political insiders or targeting "odious indi-viduals or corporate bodies" with special legal burdens.[19]

The great abolitionist Charles Sumner provided a classic elaboration of this norm against class legislation in his argument against public school racial seg-regation in *Roberts v. City of Boston* (1849). Applying the provision recognizing the equality of all citizens in the Massachusetts Constitution, he wrote (em-phasis added):

This is the Great Charter of every person who draws his vital breath upon this soil, whatever may be his condition and whoever may be his parents. He may be poor, weak, humble, black; he may be of Caucasian, of Jewish, of Indian, or of Ethiopian race; he may be of French, of German, of English, or of Irish extraction—but before the Constitution of Massachusetts all these distinctions disappear. He is not poor, nor weak, nor humble, nor black—nor Caucasian, nor Jew, nor Indian, nor Ethiopian—nor French, nor German, nor English, nor Irish; he is a Man,—the equal of all his fellow men. *He is one of the children of the State, which, like an impartial parent, regards all its offspring with an equal care.* To some it may justly allot higher duties, according to higher capacities, but it welcomes all to its equal, hospitable board.

Introducing the proposed Fourteenth Amendment in Congress, Senator Jacob Howard said that the equal protection clause "establishes equality before the law, and . . . gives to the humblest, the poorest, and most despised . . . the same rights and the same protection before the law as it gives to the most powerful, the most wealthy, or the most haughty." It plainly "abolishes all class legislation in the States and does away with the injustice of subjecting one caste of persons to a code not applicable to another." The public debate for state ratification confirmed this reading of the amendment's language—but also confirmed that the principle against class legislation did not apply to laws classifying people based upon traits relevant to regulation that served the public good or prevented harm.[20]

If original public meaning were to be credited, the Fourteenth Amendment's mission was to transform the nation, to equalize citizenship, and to create a process to get the country beyond the limitations of racism and other caste-based thinking. Under an original public meaning approach, the Super-DOMAs might be considered class legislation excluding a well-defined social group from the benefits and duties of state family law—and not just reaffirmations of traditional marriage. Take Michigan, whose regulatory regime looked very different from Judge Sutton's description. The Michigan Court of Appeals had ruled that the state could deny a lesbian mother custody of her biological child because of her sexual orientation. Although some states offered unmarried lesbian and gay couples the possibility of second-parent adoption, Michigan judges had pulled back from that practice around 2002. Its courts also ruled that a child's caregiver from birth could be cut out of the child's life at any time. In 2004, the voters amended the state constitution to assure that "the union of one man and one woman in marriage shall be the only agreement recognized as a marriage *or similar union* for any purpose." The Michigan Supreme Court applied this sweeping bar to deprive lesbian and gay municipal employees of health insurance and other contract-based benefits. Municipalities were barred from offering domestic partnership registries.[21]

"Under a system of caste," read another Fourteenth Amendment background source, "personal liberty and the right of property are controlled by laws restraining the activity of a class of persons, more or less strictly defined, to a particular course of life, and allowing only a limited enjoyment of property and relative rights." This sounds like an anti-commandeering principle, whereby the state cannot deny opportunities for self-determination and flourishing to a class of citizens. By reading lesbian and gay families out of most of the protections of family law through increasingly novel mechanisms, Michigan's government and its voters had restrained the relationships of a "class of persons" to a "particular course of life, and allowing only a limited enjoyment" of property and contract rights. Does this not raise concerns under the original public meaning of the Fourteenth Amendment, especially as interpreted in *Romer?* Even a democracy-loving judge should, at the very least, have considered invalidating the Super-DOMAs or remanding the matter to the legislature to create a legal regime for these families, like the Vermont Supreme Court did in *Baker v. State* (1999). As in *Baker,* however, this was not a remedy plaintiffs were seeking.[22]

RATIONALITY AND RESPONSIBLE PROCREATION

Jeff Sutton dismissed the optimal parenting justification for the Super-DOMAs as factually unsupported, but he accepted a Rawlsian version of the responsible procreation justification, as explained in chapter 12. Sutton's written opinion hinged on a thought experiment. Assume that "governments got into the business of defining marriage, and remained in the business of defining marriage, not to regulate love but to regulate sex, most especially the intended and unintended effects of male-female intercourse." Think about the society-wide "problems that might result from an absence of rules about how to handle the natural effects of male-female intercourse: children. May men and women follow their procreative urges wherever they take them? Who is responsible for the children that result? How many mates may an individual have? How does one decide which set of mates is responsible for which set of children?" Given these core issues, "one can well appreciate why the citizenry would think that a reasonable first concern of any society is the need to regulate male-female relationships and the unique procreative possibilities of them. One way to pursue this objective is to encourage couples to enter lasting relationships through subsidies and other benefits and to discourage them from ending such relationships through these and other means." Under the rational basis precedents, government is allowed to give priority to core concerns; legislatures have a lot of discretion with regard to step-by-step regulation, what Sutton called "pacing."[23]

Carole Stanyar responded that Michigan was not the state to sustain marriage discrimination in order to reinforce a child-centric, responsible procreation policy. The trial court had found, as a matter of fact, that Michigan's marriage law did not require procreative capacity or intent and had never done so. In past days, Michigan had criminalized procreative sex outside of marriage and had required a showing of fault for married couples to divorce—but that child-protective regime was long gone. By 2014, the Great Lakes State allowed procreative sex outside of marriage, legalized sexual cohabitation, permitted no-fault divorce, encouraged adoption by single persons as well as married couples, and permitted the use of artificial reproductive technologies. None of this assured responsible procreation. Michigan had been liberalizing family law like there was no tomorrow—until confronted with lesbian and gay couples like DeBoer and Rowse, who were the poster parents for child-centric families.

Cissy Daughtrey's dissenting opinion argued that "an exclusionary law violates the Equal Protection Clause when it is based not upon relevant facts, but instead upon only a general, ephemeral distrust of, or discomfort with, a particular group." Recall Charles Sumner's explanation of the constitutional admonition that the government must treat all social groups as "the children of the State, which, like an impartial parent, regards all its offspring with an equal care." Michigan and the other states were showing the opposite of equal care to lesbian couples and their children. As Justice Scalia once put it, the equal protection clause "requires the democratic majority to accept for themselves and their loved ones what they impose on you and me."[24]

NONRECOGNITION

All of the Ohio and Tennessee plaintiffs and half of the Kentucky plaintiffs just wanted their states to recognize their valid out-of-state marriages. Even if the state could constitutionally deny marriage licenses to same-sex couples, they argued that it was constitutionally required to recognize valid out-of-state marriages, such as the Obergefell-Arthur wedding on the tarmac. Although none of the lawyers argued that the full faith and credit clause required recognition of any and all marriages validly celebrated in other states, Al Gerhardstein maintained that full faith and credit did require Ohio to recognize out-of-state adoption decrees, because they were judgments, which the Supreme Court insisted that states respect (and Ohio had not). The Tennessee lawyers claimed that the Super-DOMA burdened their clients' fundamental right to interstate travel.[25]

Jeff Sutton found the separate arguments against nonrecognition "odd." If Ohio and Kentucky could constitutionally limit their own marriages to one man, one woman, and they considered that an important public policy, why should they be required to recognize out-of-state same-sex marriages? This requirement would negate the states' policies, as those states' residents could simply fly to Maryland and get married, as Obergefell and Arthur had done. This was a persuasive point—but Sutton topped it when he stumped Bill Harbison, counsel for the Tennessee couples, at oral argument: You are challenging Tennessee's Super-DOMA, but shouldn't you also be challenging section 2 of the Defense of Marriage Act, which authorized state nonrecognition policies? Article IV of the Constitution permitted Congress to "prescribe . . . the effect" of state licenses and such in the courts of sibling states. Didn't the plaintiffs have to demonstrate that section 2 was unconstitutional as well? *Windsor* had invalidated only section 3. Touché![26]

Supreme Court Briefing and Oral Argument in *Obergefell*

Notwithstanding initial reluctance from the national LGBTQ+ rights organizations to encourage marriage litigation in the conservative Sixth Circuit, they were by 2014 working with local counsel for the plaintiff couples in all four states: GLAD and Bonauto were cocounsel in the Michigan case, ACLU lawyers were cocounsel in Ohio and Kentucky, Lambda was cooperating in one of the Ohio cases, and NCLR was assisting in Tennessee. Also involved were Douglas Hallward-Driemeier of Ropes and Gray (Tennessee); Jeffrey Fisher and Stanford's Supreme Court clinic (Kentucky); and Robert Sedler (Michigan). After the Sixth Circuit's opinion was issued on November 6, 2014, the lawyers had sixty days to file petitions for Supreme Court review. Hallward-Driemeier urged the four teams of lawyers to hold off for all or most of the sixty-day period so that the Supreme Court would have to schedule the marriage cases for the term commencing in October 2015, not the current term. Marriage equality was already the law in thirty-five states, with more to come in 2015. Counsel did not follow this advice and agreed to file their petitions on November 14, 2014, seven weeks earlier than necessary. Eager-beaver Al Gerhardstein filed his petition in *Obergefell v. Hodges* at the beginning of the day, immediately followed by Hallward-Driemeier's petition in *Tanco v. Haslam* and then Carole Stanyar's in *DeBoer v. Snyder*. Dan Canon's petition in *Love v. Beshear* came four days later. Also supporting review, Michigan's response urged the court to clear up the conflict in the circuits by affirming Judge Sutton. Counsel for Kentucky and Ohio filed similar responses. Only Tennessee opposed review.[27]

While the plaintiffs waited for the Supreme Court to act on their petitions, the court delivered an important procedural decision. In August 2014, federal district judge Robert Hinkle had invalidated Florida's constitutional Super-DOMA. He agreed to a stay of the injunction in *Brenner v. Scott* until the Supreme Court ruled on then-pending appeals, but after the court denied all the petitions on October 6, Judge Hinkle announced his intent to terminate the stay after January 5, 2015. On December 19, the Supreme Court denied Florida's request for an extension of the stay beyond January 5. Justices Kennedy, Ginsburg, Breyer, Sotomayor, and Kagan voted against the stay; Chief Justice Roberts and Justices Scalia, Thomas, and Alito voted for a stay. Scalia and Thomas published a dissenting opinion. On January 6, 2015, Florida became the thirty-sixth marriage equality state. That Kennedy was no longer willing to grant stays suggested to court-watchers that he was ready to support nationwide freedom to marry.[28]

Ten days later, on January 16, 2015, the Supreme Court unanimously voted to grant review for all four of the Sixth Circuit cases—but the justices were sharply divided as to when they should hear the appeals. Kennedy, Ginsburg, Breyer, Sotomayor, and Kagan wanted the cases scheduled for the October 2015 term, which would have meant that the marriage issue would percolate for another year or so before being decided in June 2016. Roberts, backed by Scalia, Thomas, and Alito, was ready to schedule the cases for later in the 2014 term; there was plenty of room in the court's schedule. Because it only takes four votes to grant review, the chief justice prevailed. The conservative justices may have been turning up the heat on Kennedy: Would their Catholic colleague dare to require fifty-state marriage equality right now?

Chief Justice Roberts also suggested that the grant include two questions for the parties to address. First, did the Fourteenth Amendment require a state to license marriage between two people of the same sex? Second, did the Fourteenth Amendment require a state to recognize a marriage between two people of the same sex when their marriage was lawfully licensed and performed out of state? Roberts was intrigued by a possible compromise, in which Ohio would not have to give Obergefell and Arthur a marriage license but would have to recognize their valid Maryland marriage. Would there be any takers for this split-the-baby solution?

THE KENTUCKY BARBEQUE AND THE ANN ARBOR AMBUSH

Given the high-profile constitutional issues raised by the cases, the Supreme Court granted counsel ninety minutes to argue question one, and sixty minutes to argue question two, to be divided evenly among the parties. The defending states explored the possibility of representation by one of Washington's established Supreme Court advocates, but they encountered reluctance from the large firms because of concerns about backlash from gay-friendly corporate clients. After a series of amicable conference calls, the consensus among counsel was that Michigan's former solicitor general John Bursch should represent the states on question one. Bursch had argued eight Supreme Court cases for Michigan and won six of them, secured the relief requested in one more, and despite losing the last one was able to narrow the lower court's reasoning. A man of faith, married with five kids, this boyish attorney combined Christian congeniality with a level of preparation few could match. (He had trained himself to recognize the voices of all nine justices, so that when one of them spoke through microphones that distorted location, he could turn immediately to address the speaker.) Tennessee's deputy solicitor general, Joe Whalen, who had demonstrated acumen in his briefs and argument before the Sixth Circuit, would handle question two.[29]

For the plaintiffs, the choices were not so easy.

In a joint letter of March 17, addressed to Scott Harris, the clerk of the Supreme Court, the four counsel of record for the petitioners requested that argument be split four ways: Michigan (Carole Stanyar) and Kentucky (Dan Canon) would each have fifteen minutes for question one, with the remaining fifteen minutes ceded to Solicitor General Verrilli, an invaluable ally who had requested argument time. Ohio (Al Gerhardstein) and Tennessee (Doug Hallward-Driemeier) would each have fifteen minutes for question two. Reflecting the court's policy, the clerk discouraged this request and asked the plaintiffs' lawyers to nominate one counsel for each question. So they decided to hold two moots, or practice arguments before a panel of knowledgeable faux judges, to determine their choices.[30]

The first moot, to determine who would argue question two, the nonrecognition issue, was held in a conference room of the Louisville Bar Association and was dubbed the Kentucky Barbeque. Doug Hallward-Driemeier (Tennessee) and Al Gerhardstein (Ohio) each presented his argument, punctuated frequently by questions and skepticism from a panel of judges anchored by Mary Bonauto. As he had done before the Sixth Circuit, Gerhardstein emphasized the compelling stories of the families in the case, but the questions came too fast for him to keep track of his affirmative constitutional case. Although the Ohio clients felt that Al deserved the argument, the panel of judges and the attorneys believed that Doug was the superior advocate—and upon watching a video of the arguments, Al agreed. That Doug was experienced (fifteen Supreme Court arguments) and intellectually nimble was decisive, but he also brought a certain charisma to the task. Tall, tanned, dimpled, and blessed with a full head of rusty walnut hair, he looked like a Supreme Court advocate out of central casting.[31]

The session to choose the counsel for question one was held on Sunday, March 29, 2015, in the moot court practice room of the majestic gothic building housing the University of Michigan's School of Law in Ann Arbor. Room 232 had an elevated bench in front for the judges, with a jury box to the judges' right and seats in the back and to the left. Carole Stanyar (Michigan) and Jeff Fisher (Kentucky) were the contestants, facing these judges, sitting from left to right:

- Leah Litman, a 2010 Michigan law graduate who had clerked for Judge Sutton and then Justice Kennedy.
- Irving Gornstein, former deputy solicitor general who had argued thirty-six Supreme Court cases and who had authored the decisive brief on standing in Hollingsworth v. Perry (2013).
- David Codell, who had worked with NCLR on the California state and federal marriage cases and who had persuaded the federal appeals court in Perry to certify the standing issue to the state supreme court.
- Michigan professor Margo Schlanger, the host and a prominent constitutional law scholar.
- Diane Soubly, an Ann Arbor employment relations attorney who had filed amicus briefs for constitutional law professors in more than fifteen appellate marriage cases.

In addition, the room held more than twenty stakeholders involved in the four marriage equality cases—including the Michigan couple and at least one Kentucky couple; Jim Esseks and Dan Canon for the Kentucky team; Shannon Minter, Abby Rubenfeld, and Scott Hickman for the Tennessee team; Al Gerhardstein for the Ohio team; and Dana Nessel, Ken Mogill, and Mary Bonauto for the Michigan team. The participants came into Room 232 with a wide array of assumptions about the ground rules: some believed the judges would decide the matter by vote; others thought they would only provide feedback while the clients or stakeholders would make the decision.[32]

The panel's questions focused on issues the justices might raise. Weren't petitioners asking the Supreme Court to redefine marriage? Wasn't this too big an issue for judges to decide? If the court required marriage for gay couples, why not sibling marriage and polygamy? Was discrimination because of sexual orientation suspect under the court's precedents? Was this sex discrimination, subject to heightened scrutiny? Did the plaintiffs lose under rational basis review? Four of the five panelists thought that Jeff Fisher was the superior advocate, because he was more conversant with Supreme Court precedents, was quicker on his feet, and gave more responsive answers—but two of the five felt that Stanyar would be a better representative of the LGBTQ+ rights movement because she was a lesbian attorney clearly capable of making a good argument. Having read a rough transcript of the argument, we think they both did an outstanding job, but Stanyar sometimes gave superior responses. Did first cousins have a right to marry? Fisher answered that the state had a genetic interest in barring first cousin marriages. Geneticists say that is not quite right as a matter of biology, and family law experts would add that this justification did not explain why incest statutes applied to relatives by marriage and to older relatives. Stanyar had a better answer: the state had an interest in keeping the family a sex-free zone because there were issues of abuse and consent even among first cousins.[33]

The panel praised both counsel but gave a nonunanimous nod to Fisher. The Kentucky and Tennessee representatives agreed with this recommendation, but the Michigan representatives did not. There was no consensus, and some participants on both sides feared what we term an "Ann Arbor Ambush" if the discussion veered away from their expectations. In the general conversation following the panel's evaluation, April DeBoer asked Fisher: What was your personal interest in this case? He replied that he supported marriage equality as a matter of civil rights. Emotionally exhausted by the day's proceedings, DeBoer and Rowse found his answer cold and analytical. It showed he had not bled for marriage equality the way Stanyar had. "This is my family we are talking about," DeBoer told him. "I am raising two black daughters, and I am teaching them that nothing is going to hold them back from doing great things. I don't want to look back five or ten years from now and tell my daughters that I was part of the decision-making process that let five white heterosexual men argue this case!" The solicitor general and counsel for the states were straight white men, as were Hallward-Driemeier and Fisher.[34]

Several women in the room thought the discussion was exposing some traditional gender stereotypes. A nice-looking straight man carried a presumption of competence, while a lesbian had to be better than the man to get the job. Women had sacrificed for the Michigan case, Carole had sold her house, and now the boys were trying to hog the glory. Others in the room were amazed at how well Fisher had mastered the details of the record and were irritated by Michigan's kvetching. With tensions mounting, the Michigan plaintiffs and their lawyers moved to a table in the hallway. Mary Bonauto and Ken Mogill conducted shuttle diplomacy to try to bring the sides together. Identity politics threatened to blow up the case.

If we could not come to agreement, shouldn't we report that to the clerk and allow the justices to appoint someone to represent us? No one liked that idea. Another lawyer suggested a coin flip, which the Michiganders considered insulting. With desperation filling the room, Dave Codell tossed out an idea: Why not Mary Bonauto? She was a member of the Michigan team and had helped them when almost no one else would. An out lesbian now lawfully married, Bonauto had won *Goodridge* and had created the winning strategy for *Windsor*. Plus, everyone really liked her, and many would have walked off a cliff for her, including some of the lawyers on the Tennessee team.

Bonauto disclaimed interest in displacing Stanyar from the case. Indeed, when the Michigan lawyers had sought her assistance in drafting their petition for Supreme Court review, they had elicited a promise that Bonauto would not seek to represent the nurses in oral argument. The GLAD lawyer had no problem sticking by that agreement, but she and Mogill dutifully brought Codell's suggestion back to the Michigan delegation. Stanyar still did not want to give up her chance to represent the nurses in their landmark Supreme Court case, and her clients would have stood by her to the end. But what alternatives were there? Nessel, an utter loyalist, looked at Stanyar and implored, "Can you go with Mary?" With resignation, Stanyar said okay.

Now some of the lawyers on the Kentucky team took their turn to complain. Why should we compromise, when our guy won the moot? As Kentucky fumed and some participants left to catch flights back home, Scott Hickman, one of the private-firm Tennessee counsel, stood up and made a speech: "Stop leaving! We need to make a decision, and Mary is the right choice. We are on the verge of winning marriage equality—don't blow this opportunity." Dan Canon, a founding partner of the Clay Daniel firm that worked on the Kentucky cases, agreed with Hickman and urged his colleagues to go along. They did.

On March 31, counsel of record informed the clerk that Douglas Hallward-Driemeier would argue question two and Mary Bonauto would argue question one. Unlike Stanyar and Fisher, Bonauto had never argued before the United States Supreme Court.[35]

MARRIAGE EQUALITY AND THE FREEDOM TO MARRY

The Fourteenth Amendment protects people's life, liberty, and property (under the concept of substantive due process) and assures them the equal protection of the laws. Reflecting the lives of the couples, the plaintiffs' counsel in *Obergefell v. Hodges* (the caption given to the four consolidated cases, because the Ohio petition was first-filed) saw the liberty and equality arguments as synergistic—like the Supreme Court had framed them in *Lawrence* and *Windsor*. The plaintiffs articulated their liberty interest as a "freedom of personal choice in matters of marriage and family life." *Lawrence* recognized that "our laws and tradition afford constitutional protection to personal decisions relating to marriage, procreation, contraception, family relationships, child rearing, and education" and that gay and lesbian persons "may seek autonomy for these purposes, just as heterosexual persons do." The constitutional liberty interest was grounded in a philosophy of personal self-determination: the romantic, marital, and family decisions of LGBTQ+ Americans should be respected by the state.[36]

Of course, the couples already enjoyed some freedom of personal choice. All four states allowed them to get married in a private religious service and raise children (though not as joint parents), so at bottom, the liberty the *Obergefell* plaintiffs wanted was the freedom to join the same state institution (marriage) that everyone else could join. That was essentially an equal protection claim— as was the *dignitary* harm (Kennedy's beloved term) suffered by the couples and their children when they alone were excluded from this broadly welcoming government institution. Central to their claim was equal citizenship, the theme of Cott's testimony in the *DeBoer* trial. Three of the four couples' briefs gave primacy to equality arguments: the Super-DOMAs discriminated against them and their families based on a (quasi-)suspect classification (either sex or, they argued from the precedents, sexual orientation), denied them a fundamental right to marry (*Zablocki v. Redhail* [1978]), and/or excluded them without even a rational basis (as that approach was applied in *Romer* and *Windsor*). Even the briefs challenging nonrecognition of out-of-state marriages were dominated by equality arguments. The Kentucky brief, for example, claimed that nonrecognition triggered heightened equal protection scrutiny because it singled out and demeaned lesbian and gay families (*Windsor*) and was an unprecedented departure from the celebration rule Kentucky applied to all other out-of-state marriages (*Romer*). The Tennessee brief, reflecting NCLR's input, made the sex discrimination argument the center of its equal protection claim. Also focusing on equal citizenship claims were the solicitor general's brief for the United States, Ken Mehlman's amicus for three hundred prominent conservative Republicans, and William Eskridge and Steve Calabresi's original meaning amicus brief for the Cato Institute.[37]

DEMOCRATIC FREEDOM AND RELIGIOUS LIBERTY

John Bursch opened his brief for Michigan: "This case is not about the best marriage definition. It is about the fundamental question regarding *how* our democracy resolves such debates about social policy: Who decides, the people of each state, or the federal judiciary?" When he was Michigan's solicitor general, Bursch had prevailed in *Schuette v. Coalition to Defend Affirmative Action* (2014), which upheld a voters' initiative barring race-based affirmative action by state actors in Michigan. In his plurality opinion, Justice Kennedy found it "demeaning to the democratic process to presume that the voters are not capable of deciding an issue of this sensitivity on decent and rational grounds." For Kennedy, the First Amendment included the freedom "to engage in a rational, civic discourse in order to determine how best to form a consensus to shape the destiny of the Nation." Bursch applied the same idea to the marriage cases. "The liberty to engage in self-government is the fundamental right at stake in this case, a right held by all members of society in common."[38]

The states did not rely on religious liberty as a public justification for their Super-DOMAs, but amici made precisely that argument. Although the primary legal bases for burdens on faith groups were anti-discrimination laws, marriage equality created more occasions for religious persons to have a reason to identify and treat LGBTQ+ persons differently. For example, Catholic Charities had closed its adoption services in several states because it was not prepared to place children with married same-sex couples. In a judicious amicus brief, Douglas Laycock, Thomas Berg, David Blankenhorn, Marie Failinger, and Ed Gaffney urged the Supreme Court to recognize both gay people's marriage rights and religious people's conscience-based liberties, as almost all the state marriage equality statutes had done. More broadly, they implored the court to avoid any decision resting upon state "animus," the language Kennedy had used in *Windsor* to denigrate DOMA. As Alexander Dushku put it for the Evangelicals and Latter-day Saints, "a decision that traditional marriage laws are grounded in animus would demean us and our beliefs. It would stigmatize us as fools or bigots, akin to racists. In time it would impede full participation in democratic life, as our beliefs concerning marriage, family, and sexuality are placed beyond the constitutional pale."[39]

Traditionalists like Dushku had good reason to fear that their voices would be marginalized while gay marriage was celebrated. In early 2014, they were astounded when what they considered a routine religious-protection bill passed by the Arizona legislature was nationally denounced as a gay-bashing measure; similar crises occurred in staunchly Baptist Arkansas, Georgia, and Indiana, as we shall discuss in chapter 23. The Church of Jesus Christ of Latter-day Saints was determined to refute the idea that it was anti-gay or intolerant. Even the Evangelicals were nervous that a society embracing gay marriage would consider them bigots. In April 2015, ABC News reported that 61 percent of Americans supported marriage equality for lesbian and gay couples.

IMPACT ON MARRIAGE AND CHILDREN

Dr. Gary Gates told the Supreme Court that there were as many as 690,000 same-sex couples in America, that their committed relationships rested upon the same need for mutual love as those of married straight couples, and that their relationships were approximately as stable as those of different-sex couples. At least 122,000 of those households were raising as many as 210,000 minor children. Married same-sex couples were five times likelier than different-sex married couples to be raising adopted or foster care children. Amicus briefs from social science associations reaffirmed the scholarly consensus that the life outcomes and achievements of children reared in lesbian and gay households compared well with those of children reared in male-female households. Although Mark Regnerus and Loren Marks filed an amicus brief claiming the opposite, Judge Friedman's findings of fact closed the door on that argument, even among many true believers.[40]

Although there was little debate about the prevalence and child-rearing ability of LGBTQ+ families, there was sharp dispute among the amici about their effect on marriage generally—a matter most observers considered premature. Massachusetts attorney general Maura Healey and the attorneys general of fifteen other marriage equality states and the District of Columbia maintained that their "experience with marriage equality suggests that the institution is better off for it." The seven jurisdictions with available data (Connecticut, the District, Iowa, Massachusetts, New Hampshire, New York, Vermont) saw an immediate surge in the marriage rate after marriage equality began, and in six of those states the marriage rate in 2011 was the same or higher than it had been before marriage equality. In the same period, the national marriage rate declined. Six of those seven jurisdictions had divorce rates at or below the national average. In 2012, twelve of the seventeen marriage equality jurisdictions had lower percentages of nonmarital births than the national average.[41]

Not so fast, responded Gene Schaerr, who filed a brief for one hundred marriage scholars. Examining the marriage rates for only different-sex couples in states with such data, they reported a 5 percent decline, during a period when national marriage rates were stable. Over a thirty-year period of national marriage equality, they predicted, six hundred thousand more children would grow up in nonmarital different-sex households. Schaerr's brief also reported that different-sex marriage rates in the Netherlands declined 5 percent after marriage equality. According to one expert, the decline was sharpest among urban populations, where women typically worked outside the home and traditional religion was weak, while marriage held rates up in rural, more religious communities.[42]

NO ROOM FOR COMPROMISE

After an internal debate, the petitioners' counsel followed Bonauto's advice to deemphasize the arguments for question two (nonrecognition of valid out-of-state marriages). She felt that the couples would prevail on question one (complete marriage equality), a judgment confirmed on February 9, 2015, when the Supreme Court refused to grant a stay of federal district judge Callie "Ginny" Grande's injunction in the Alabama marriage case *Searcy v. Strange*. In dissent, Justices Scalia and Thomas expressed alarm and puzzlement that the court would not push pause for all the outstanding marriage cases. Chief Justice Roberts and Justice Alito also disagreed with the majority but did not join the public dissenting statement.[43]

Accordingly, the Ohio, Kentucky, and Tennessee petitioners attacked the nonrecognition rules with substantially the same right to marry and equal protection arguments they used against the non-issuance rules. The main point that was distinctive to question two was that none of the states had created constitutional nonrecognition rules until the gay marriage controversy appeared, and all recognized marriages they considered incestuous (first cousins) or underage but that were lawful in the states where they were celebrated. However, no one answered Judge Sutton's objection that the challengers had to show *both* that the nonrecognition rules violated the Fourteenth Amendment *and* that Congress exceeded its authority under the take effect clause of Article IV when it authorized the states not to give full faith and credit to sibling-state marriages for lesbian and gay couples (DOMA section 2).[44]

Neither the parties nor amici suggested another obvious compromise: strike down the Super-DOMAs as inconsistent with *Romer* and *Windsor* but leave it to state political processes to create civil unions or marriage for the excluded couples. Shannon Minter told us that, for the marriage equality side, the idea of civil unions as an acceptable compromise died in 2004, with California's Winter of Love, and had virtually no support within LGBTQ+ rights circles after Proposition 8. The states, meanwhile, were not willing to concede that civil unions could be their backup position. Recall that the Catholic Church, the Church of Jesus Christ, the Southern Baptist Convention, Focus on the Family, and the Republican Party considered civil unions or comprehensive domestic partnership the functional equivalent of marriage. Any state attorney general or traditionalist amicus suggesting domestic partnership as a "compromise" would have suffered brutal pushback from the interconnected network of traditional family values activists, funders, and political operatives.[45]

ORAL ARGUMENT IN THE MARRIAGE CASES

The Supreme Court scheduled the entire morning of April 28, 2015, for oral argument in *Obergefell v. Hodges*. Jim Obergefell and other plaintiffs assembled outside the Supreme Court and entered the building, walked up a flight of white marble stairs, passed through the Great Hall, and entered the chamber where the justices would hear their case. Mary Bonauto arrived breathless because her taxi got lost. John Bursch arrived early and followed his ritual from previous Supreme Court arguments. He solemnly approached the huge bronze statue of a seated John Marshall on the building's ground floor, bent down, and rubbed the tip of Chief Justice Marshall's boot. He believed this ritual would give him luck—and he needed it. Because only Justices Scalia and Thomas had published a dissent from the denial of the stay in *Searcy v. Strange*, he feared that as many as seven justices were inclined to reverse the Sixth Circuit.[46]

Also expecting this to be the clinching moment for marriage equality, a big chunk of the gayocracy begged or cajoled insiders for tickets. Outside, we chatted with Sandy Stier and Kris Perry, plaintiffs in the Proposition 8 trial. Dozens of people were holding equality signs or rainbow flags—but the gendarmerie enforcing the court's strict security rules pushed most of them to the small sidewalk off First Street. Inside, Carole Stanyar joined Mary Bonauto at the counsel table, with their other lawyers right behind them. Also on hand were Jon Davidson of Lambda Legal, Shannon Minter of NCLR, James Esseks of the ACLU, former assistant attorney general Stuart Delery, Paul Smith, Robbie Kaplan, Evan Wolfson, and other interested parties. We also spotted Ryan Anderson and other traditional marriage supporters.

Mary Bonauto's opening sentence summed up the plaintiffs' case: "The intimate and committed relationships of same-sex couples, just like those of heterosexual couples, provide mutual support and are the foundation of family life in our society." These couples wanted to join the institution of marriage. Chief Justice Roberts immediately raised his central concern: "The argument on the other side is that you're seeking to redefine the institution," not join it. "You're seeking to change what the institution is." As Bonauto started to explain how marriage was an institution in constant flux, Justice Kennedy jumped in: "This definition has been with us for millennia. And it—it's very difficult for the Court to say, oh, well, we—we know better." No, she responded, it's a matter of society as a whole learning that gay people are decent, normal citizens entitled to the same rights as everyone else. More interruptions. Justice Breyer complained that counsel had not answered Roberts's initial question.[47]

This was the great challenge for a Supreme Court advocate: unless you could provide the nub of your answer in the first sentence, you might never be able to score your point amid the crossfire from across the bench. And yet you had to be careful not to overstate your point or give hostile justices an opening to divert the discussion. Responding to the chief justice's redefinition-of-marriage question, one might have started with "the requirement of equal protection we advocate represents no greater revolution or change in the meaning of marriage than this Court's decisions in *Loving* and *Zablocki*." That would invite justices to ask about those decisions, which were favorable terrain for the plaintiff couples. Or "we do rely on a consent-based rather than conjugality-based understanding of marriage—but we are echoing family law policies long followed in all four states and reflected in this Court's precedents, such as *Griswold* [spousal contraception] and *Turner* [prisoners' right to marry]." If any of the conservative justices doubted that proposition, Bonauto could have reminded them of Professor Cott's testimony and Judge Friedman's helpful findings of fact in the Michigan case, other favorable terrain for exchanges.

Justice Alito introduced a new topic: If the states were doing nothing more than following tradition, how did that demean the people who had never before qualified? Finding her footing, Bonauto responded that this was a lot like sex discrimination. For hundreds of years, our country considered women and men inherently different in their natural capabilities and legal rights, but in less than a decade, most of these long-established exclusions and discriminations were invalidated or repealed because they demeaned the status of women in an egalitarian society. As *Lawrence* said, "Times can blind us to certain truths and later generations can see that laws one thought necessary and proper in fact serve only to oppress." Justice Ginsburg helpfully added that the institution of marriage had already redefined itself when it moved from a regime of gendered domination, and that egalitarian move made the plaintiffs' aspiration possible. Bonauto then deftly sidestepped the justices' mistaken belief that marriage had universally been one man, one woman throughout human history.[48]

Why, Chief Justice Roberts asked, should "nine people outside the ballot box" tell states they have to redefine marriage? Wouldn't it be in the deeper interest of gay people to let the democratic process work longer, given the remarkable success that this minority group had in the 2012 election? Bonauto's rejoinder appealed to the human dimension of constitutional rights: Because Michigan did not allow April DeBoer and Jayne Rowse joint parental rights over the children the state allowed them to adopt, were their children not constantly at risk of losing their entire family if one of the parents died? Did those children not need legal protections now, while they were still children? Justice Scalia asked whether faith traditions opposed to gay marriage would not be compelled to perform such ceremonies. Bonauto repeatedly affirmed that the religion clauses protected those faiths against any penalty, an unimpeachable answer that did not satisfy Scalia, whose persistence on the topic ate up the rest of her time.

As Mary Bonauto sat down after the longest twenty-five minutes of her life, a gray-haired man with crazy eyes, sitting a row or two behind us, stood up and started shouting: "If you support gay marriage, you will burn in hell!" Gay marriage was an "abomination to God." As he bellowed the Lord's judgment, dark-suited marshals swooped down like pigeons on bread crumbs. The man was swiftly removed from the stately courtroom, but for several minutes you could hear his screams echoing from the marbled hallway. Justice Scalia cracked, "It was rather refreshing, actually." He was trying to lighten the mood, but many of the gay persons in the room had suffered such verbal assaults as a prelude to being physically attacked or fired from a job. Could the justices not recognize animus when it was screamed in their faces?

Solicitor General Verrilli put it to the court: if you dismiss the constitutional claims, you are saying that this second-class citizenship is consistent with the equal protection of the law. "That is not a wait-and-see. That is a validation." Leaving the matter to the political process would not yield a legitimate consensus but a long-standing division of the country between have and have-not states, much like apartheid on the eve of *Brown*. The Supreme Court had rejected wait-and-see in *Lawrence*, which was "an important catalyst that has brought us to where we are today. . . . [W]hat *Lawrence* did was provide an assurance that gay and lesbian couples could live openly in society as free people and start families and raise families and participate fully in their communities without fear." The earlier homophobic outburst had been eclipsed by the solicitor general's simple eloquence.

Chief Justice Roberts reminded the government that *Lawrence* prevented the state from intruding into people's private lives, while marriage was about public recognition. Verrilli turned the point around. At its core, *Lawrence* set gay people free to "lay claim to the abiding promise of the Fourteenth Amendment in a way that was just impossible when they were marginalized and ostracized." Once gay people were no longer outlaws, they could aspire to become in-laws and enjoy the same right of self-determination that everyone else enjoyed. This was the perfect synthesis of freedom and equality, and the audience was ready to stand up and cheer the solicitor general. Respecting courtroom decorum and stern looks from the marshals, however, they just sat there. Some wept.

Justice Alito asked whether the federal policy of denying federal tax exemptions and benefits to charitable and educational institutions that discriminate because of race could be applied to these institutions if they discriminated because of sexual orientation. The solicitor general explained that the government was not prepared to take a position on that issue. In fact, no one had thought of it in the mooting process, and no one in the Justice Department knew the answer.

John Bursch opened the states' argument much as he had opened his brief: "This case isn't about how to define marriage. It's about who gets to decide that question. Is it the people acting through the democratic process, or is it the federal courts?" Judicial usurpation of the issue would deny every "individual's fundamental liberty interest in deciding the meaning of marriage." Sonia Sotomayor failed to see how anyone's interest in the democratic process was a liberty similar to the freedom of choice sought by the plaintiffs. Apart from tradition and moral objections, which he and his colleagues had disavowed in *Lawrence,* Stephen Breyer asked what was the state's interest in excluding these couples from civil marriage. Following Sutton's opinion, Bursch replied that marriage was an institution to channel procreative sexual activities into a set of civilizing rules and practices; thus, the social purpose of marriage did not necessarily entail nonprocreative unions.

Justices Ginsburg, Sotomayor, and Kagan pressed him: Didn't Michigan have to show that *including* same-sex couples in marriage would *harm* married couples or the institution? "How does withholding marriage from one group, same-sex couples," Sotomayor asked, "increase the value to the other group?" As Bursch was whipsawed by these three justices, all demanding an answer but giving him little time to speak, Scalia tossed him a lifeline: "Is it your burden to show that it will harm marriage between a man and woman if you allow two men or two women to marry? I thought your burden was simply to show that the State's reason for this institution is a reason that has nothing to do, that is inapplicable to same-sex couples." Yes, Bursch responded.

Bursch's larger point was that the states were trying to preserve something of the self-sacrificial, altruistic understanding of marriage that had been lost when the institution was updated in terms of mutual choice by the spouses, choices that have often been detrimental to their children. "But," Kennedy intervened, that answer "assumes that the same-sex couples would not have the noble purpose, and that's the whole point" of these cases, where so many children were being raised in households dedicated to their needs. Bursch responded that it was not unreasonable for the voters who overwhelmingly endorsed the four Super-DOMAs to believe that marriage equality would undermine the child-centric aspirations of traditional marriage. Breyer and Sotomayor wanted to know, what *evidence* was there that including lesbian and gay couples would *actually* encourage straight couples to forsake their commitment to children and consider their marriages in purely selfish terms? We found it curious that Bursch failed to mention the empirical evidence in Gene Schaerr's amicus brief, but he was committed to the democracy-based claim that the justices must defer to the electorate's acceptance of what we have dubbed the Jenga argument: marriage was like a Jenga tower of blocks, and many key blocks had already been removed through state tolerance of cohabitation, the decriminalization of fornication and adultery, and no-fault divorce. Abandoning the conjugality requirement for marriage would knock away that last critical block and send the wobbly Jenga tower tumbling down.

Bursch's pitch for deference to the majority's will rested upon the Kennedy opinion in *Schuette*. Kennedy, however, saw affirmative action in workplaces (the *Schuette* issue) as a zero-sum game (one race advances at the expense of another) not involving a fundamental right—in contrast to marriage exclusions, which took away a fundamental right from one group and gratuitously harmed their children without advancing the well-being of other groups or society. Schaerr's amicus brief provided some evidence that the states' defense of marriage argument might actually be true, and some basis for the states to argue that there was harm on both sides of the equation, but no one mentioned that during the oral argument.[49]

Eighty-two-year-old Ruth Bader Ginsburg asked whether it would be constitutional for Michigan to prohibit marriages between men and women over the age of seventy. [Laughter in the room.] That would advance the state's interest in using marriage as a vehicle to encourage procreation, right? She had raised a similar hypothetical in the *Windsor* argument, and Justice Scalia had retorted that longtime senator Strom Thurmond had fathered a bunch of children in his seventies (albeit with a much younger wife). Aware of that retort, Bursch had a subtler response: only same-sex marriages, by definition, excluded the possibility of procreation. The point of marriage was to encourage straight couples toward a committed union before they had kids, and that point held as a general matter even if there were exceptions. Unless the Supreme Court applied heightened scrutiny, judicial review allowed a fair amount of overinclusion (i.e., a statute protects some people incidentally).

The plaintiffs claimed a fundamental right to marry, which the court had recognized in *Loving* (interracial couples), *Zablocki* (deadbeat dads), and *Turner v. Safley* (prisoners). Kagan asked why she should not follow those precedents, which would require a strict scrutiny that did not tolerate much overinclusion. Bursch responded that all the precedents involved couples who could procreate. But what about the life prisoners, asked Sotomayor: they could not procreate. Bursch sought to reframe the *Turner* decision by referring to the court's earlier summary disposition in *Butler v. Wilson* (1974), upholding New York's law imposing marriage restrictions on convicted rapists as part of their sentences.

No one contradicted Bursch on this point, but his characterization was debatable. Because it was a summary disposition, *Butler* was not accompanied by a statement of reasons, and in any case it was superseded by *Turner*, which cited *Butler* for the idea that the state could restrict the right to marry if there were a tangible reason to protect future spouses against a dangerous partner. A subsequent district court decision treated *Butler* as limited in precisely this way.[50]

Bursch ended on a strong note: *Lawrence* protected gay people's liberty the same way *Roe v. Wade* protected women's liberty: the state could not put people in jail for consensual activities. But tolerance and protection for liberty did not mean the government had to celebrate and subsidize the activity. Since the late 1970s, the court had said that the government did not have to fund or otherwise participate in a woman's choice to have an abortion, and Bursch maintained that the court should make the same distinction in this case: toleration did not entail state approval and participation. Michigan ought to tolerate April and Jayne's sexual cohabitation and their adoptions, but it was not required to subsidize their family with the special rights and privileges of marriage.

The last forty-five minutes of argument were devoted to question two: If Ohio, Kentucky, and Tennessee could constitutionally decline to offer marriage licenses to same-sex couples, might there still be a constitutional violation if they refused to recognize valid out-of-state marriages, such as that of Jim Obergefell and John Arthur? Reflecting the team consensus, Doug Hallward-Driemeier reiterated some of the arguments relevant to question one, something an irritated Sam Alito immediately noticed. He made the further argument, drawn from *Windsor,* that a couple validly married in a state might have a strong liberty interest in that marriage, which might justify a greater evidentiary burden on receiving states such as Ohio. Representing the states, Joseph Whalen provided a lucid account of the Supreme Court's full faith and credit jurisprudence. The court had imposed strong recognition requirements only for out-of-state "judgments" and had allowed nonrecognition of out-of-state laws, licenses, and public acts. Whalen then made a most interesting argument: Tennessee presumed that children born within a marriage were the biological progeny of the married couple. If it were forced to recognize a California gay marriage, not only would its marriage policy be thwarted, but its parentage policy would be confused as well. Could a state refuse to recognize the birth certificate of another state? Whalen did not know.

As planned, Hallward-Driemeier dedicated his rebuttal to describing the consequences of nonrecognition for the families in these appeals. Tanco and

Jesty fell in love with one another in veterinary school and were legally married. Their best academic employment opportunity came in Tennessee, so they moved there and had a child. Last week, Hallward-Driemeier told the court, that child was hospitalized. Because she was not the birth mother and because Tennessee did not recognize their marriage, Jesty was, in the hospital's view, a stranger to the child. She had to get Tanco, the biological mother, on the phone to vouch for her. Until then, the crying child received no treatment. "These laws have real import for real people." Bravo, thought Al Gerhardstein, his eyes moist and his adrenaline racing. Surely, his and Bonauto's arguments had won the case for the couples, the widowers, the funeral director, and kids named Isaiah, Bella, and Cooper.

The Supreme Court's Decision

On Friday May 1, the justices met in conference to decide the marriage cases. The Supreme Court's disposition and opinions would be announced on June 26, 2015, exactly twelve years after the court handed down *Lawrence* and two years to the day after *Windsor*.

THE JUSTICES' CONFERENCE

The conference was civil and tame, unlike the fireworks blasting in the media. Eight of the nine jurists had approached these appeals with a pretty firm idea how they were going to vote and why. This was not entirely true of the chief justice. Consistent with his interest in enforcing Article III limits on federal jurisdiction, John Roberts saw himself as the custodian of the Supreme Court's political capital. Like Jeff Sutton and John Bursch, he felt it deeply unwise for the court to make big moves that went against the political process, a view that inspired his compromise judgment in the Obamacare case, his dissent in *Windsor,* and his majority opinion in *Hollingsworth*. But he also understood that marriage equality was inevitable. Did he want to be the judge who stood against history? Nino Scalia and Clarence Thomas relished that role if they thought it was required by constitutional principle; John Roberts did not.[51]

Thus, he flirted with the idea that the Constitution allowed states to decline to issue marriage licenses to same-sex couples, but not to refuse to recognize valid out-of-state same-sex marriages absent a stronger justification than public morality or administrative convenience. Unfortunately, the parties had not given him much legal argumentation to support such a resolution, and he could discern in his colleagues no interest in a split-the-baby resolution. By the way, there was yet another way of approaching the cases that we were told that Roberts may have considered. *Romer* suggested that all four constitutional Super-DOMAs and the denial of second-parent adoptions violated the equal protection clause because they denied a class of worthy citizens access to the ordinary protections of state family law. A conservative jurist believing that complete marriage equality was not required by the Constitution could have struck down the Super-DOMAs but left in place the previous laws limiting marriage to one man, one woman in all four states. Or he could have remanded the matter to the state legislatures to create a family law regime for these families (like civil unions). Admittedly, this position was not taken by any party or any amicus, but a Solomonic judge is allowed to consider creative answers.

In any event, John Roberts opened the conference with a careful and detailed statement to uphold all four Super-DOMAs. There was no basis, he calmly argued, for applying heightened scrutiny here: the right to marry cases were premised on the possibility of procreation, and sexual orientation was not a suspect classification because LGBT people were far from "politically powerless," so their remedy was with the democratic process. Even the *Romer* rational-basis-with-bite approach was not on point, as the long-standing definition of marriage was not inspired by animus against anyone. With no reason to give heightened scrutiny, states were entitled to follow long-standing marriage rules. Conceding that marriage equality was not a divisive issue for younger generations—including many of his former law clerks—Roberts urged his colleagues to leave it to the political process: not just legislation, but popular initiatives like the ones marriage equality groups won in 2012.

Nino Scalia put the matter more confrontationally. Speaking for Tony Kennedy's benefit, he predicted that the author of an opinion imposing homosexual marriage on America would be dogged to his grave just as Harry Blackmun had been haunted by *Roe v. Wade*, in Scalia's view a lawless decision that had embroiled judges in bitter but needless controversy for decades. History, he declared, would give a homosexual marriage opinion the same respect that President Lincoln accorded *Dred Scott*, another poorly reasoned and anti-democratic blunder that was swiftly overridden. He urged his colleagues to consider the consequences of reversing Jeff Sutton (who had been one of his favorite law clerks). It would be a disaster for religious traditionalists. Clergy would be forced to perform homosexual marriages. Schools like Notre Dame and BYU would lose their charitable tax exemptions because they would not tolerate homosexual cohabitation in their housing. Knowing that none of this parade of horribles was likely, colleagues bit their tongues.

Having already taken conservative heat for *Lawrence* and *Windsor,* Tony Kennedy was impervious to Scalia's fulminations and to Roberts's appeal to democracy. As in *Windsor,* he worried that the lesbian and gay couples and their children were doing nothing more than asking the state to treat them with the same dignity it afforded other couples and their families. Reflecting his strongly libertarian approach to the Constitution and his close attention to the amicus briefs from various faith traditions, he rested his vote on the fundamental right to marry and disagreed with Roberts's view that that right was invariably tied to procreation. Like the liberties protected in *Casey* and *Lawrence,* this was a "right to define one's own concept of existence" and one's own concept of family. Because the right to marry was fundamental, the court did not need to discuss animus; the best-intended legislation, such as the deadbeat-dads law in *Zablocki,* could not easily meet strict scrutiny.[52]

Where Tony Kennedy saw a freedom and liberty case, Ruth Bader Ginsburg saw an equality and anti-discrimination case much like the sex discrimination cases she had litigated in the 1970s. She was not as worried as Roberts about "redefining" marriage, since marriage was constantly evolving. At conference, Ginsburg answered the concerns Roberts, Scalia, and Clarence Thomas (who agreed with the chief) had raised against heightened equal protection scrutiny. Heightened scrutiny did not require that the oppressed group be entirely powerless, as the case of sex discrimination made clear: women were not politically powerless, yet the Supreme Court (at Counsel Ginsburg's urging) had applied heightened scrutiny to sex-based classifications since 1976. The First Amendment strongly protected clergy and churches against conformity, as in *Hosanna-Tabor.* With respect to the court's political capital, Ginsburg observed that courts had applied heightened scrutiny to same-sex marriage exclusions in Canada and South Africa without dire results. The political process in those countries had swiftly come around to support marriage equality after judicial nudging, just as it was doing in the United States.

Stephen Breyer was unimpressed with the state's justifications for excluding same-sex couples. Neither tradition nor religious belief could be a license to exclude fellow citizens from an important state institution and its benefits—and he found the responsible procreation justification comical. Samuel Alito worried that the Supreme Court's imprimatur on gay marriage would drive traditional marriage supporters out of the public sphere. They would be silenced not only by social pressure but by legitimate fears of losing their charitable tax exemptions. Canada even punished traditionalists for engaging in "hate speech."

Commenting more briefly, Sonia Sotomayor supported Ginsburg's equal protection approach, and Elena Kagan diplomatically observed that she agreed with everything that had been said in favor of nationwide marriage equality. Both of these junior justices had been considered likely yes votes on the marriage issue: they were appointed by a president who favored marriage equality, and both had a wide and diverse circle of friends and law clerks. Neither understood the constitutional precedents to hold that civil marriage must be conjugal. Like Ruth Ginsburg and Sandra O'Connor, Elena Kagan had previously officiated a wedding of her male former law clerk and his husband.

THE COURT'S OPINION: A CONSTITUTIONAL FREEDOM TO MARRY

Once again the assigning justice, Tony Kennedy took the case for himself and asked for drafting assistance from his openly gay law clerk, Joshua Matz, who had coauthored a law review essay on the "constitutional inevitability" of marriage equality. Kennedy instructed his clerk to work on a libertarian opinion based upon the fundamental right to marry that had been recognized in *Loving, Zablocki,* and *Turner.* Ironically, the four other justices in the majority would have been more sympathetic to Matz's article, emphasizing equal access to marriage, than they were to a fundamental right to marry approach.[53]

The central feature of the opinion was a rebuttal of the view that the fundamental right to marry applied only to potentially procreative—and therefore different-sex—marriages. Why is the right to marry fundamental? The opinion identified several reasons, all of which supported marriage rights for same-sex couples:

- *Freedom to make choices that give meaning to one's life.* "Marriage responds to the universal fear that a lonely person might call out only to find no one there. It offers the hope of companionship and understanding and assurance that while both still live there will be someone to care for the other." Only the individual, and not the state, could make that decision about whom to marry.
- *Protecting families and children.* Lesbian and gay couples were raising children who benefited from their caregiving. "Without the recognition, stability, and predictability marriage offers, their children suffer the

stigma of knowing their families are somehow lesser" as well as lose important benefits and the protection of joint parenting.

- *Social order and good citizenship.* "Marriage remains a building block of our national community." This was the ancient notion that spousehood was a school for responsibility that trained husbands and now wives to be good citizens. Lesbian and gay unions ought to be encouraged as marriages for the same community-building reasons as one-man, one-woman marriages.

Because the plaintiff couples had been denied a fundamental right, the four states were required to show that the deprivation was uniquely necessary to effectuate a compelling public purpose. Their justifications for excluding same-sex couples were speculative (the defense of marriage argument) or tautological (responsible procreation, tailored to exclude only lesbian and gay couples, even though many were raising children).[54]

The other majority justices nudged Kennedy to include more nods to equal protection. "The right of same-sex couples to marry that is part of the liberty promised by the Fourteenth Amendment is derived, too, from that Amendment's guarantee of the equal protection of the laws." This paragraph and those following were added to the opinion at the behest of Ginsburg, and Kennedy knitted that analysis into his liberty analysis as he had done in *Lawrence* and as the court had done in *Loving* and *Zablocki*. "In interpreting the Equal Protection Clause, the Court has recognized that new insights and societal understandings can reveal unjustified inequality within our most fundamental institutions that once passed unnoticed and unchallenged." For example, "invidious sex-based classifications in marriage," like the idea of husband as lord and master of the household, "remained common through the mid–20th century. These classifications denied the equal dignity of men and women," and the Supreme Court had overruled all of them.[55]

In response to the states' argument that such fundamental policy decisions should be left to the normal democratic process, Kennedy's opinion observed that the country had been deliberating about the issue for decades, and it was ripe for decision. "The petitioners' stories make clear the urgency of the issue they present to the Court. James Obergefell now asks whether Ohio can erase his marriage to John Arthur for all time. April DeBoer and Jayne Rowse now ask whether Michigan may continue to deny them the certainty and stability all mothers desire to protect their children, and for them and their children the childhood years will pass all too soon."[56]

The Obama administration was surprised that the court did not rely centrally on the equal protection clause and disappointed that it missed an opportunity to say that sexual orientation was a fishy classification that presumptively ought not to be a basis for state policy making. When we asked John Bursch whether he thought Michigan could constitutionally set a special, higher minimum wage just for steelworkers, he said it surely could. Could it set a higher minimum wage just for heterosexuals? Not so clear. He suggested that an opinion announcing heightened scrutiny for state laws excluding sexual and gender minorities would have been more consistent with precedent and the rule of law than yet another Kennedy opinion protecting the individual's dignity and his/her/their reflection on the "sweet mystery of life." We think Bursch has a valid point, that a constitutional liberty right grounded in each person's self-evaluated dignity is either limitless or is limited to the values held by a majority of the judges considering the claim. "If the Constitution guarantees me the power to define myself and the universe, why can't I define my work as having the value of $15 an hour rather than $5?"[57]

Although we (personally) agree with Bursch and Verrilli on the virtues of an equal protection approach and the dangers of a "sweet mystery of life" jurisprudence, there is much to be said in favor of Kennedy's exploration of the deep connection between liberty and equality that his *Lawrence* opinion had foregounded. Consensual sodomy laws were both a state intrusion into people's intimate lives and a justification for discrimination against gay people. Super-DOMAs limiting marriage and "similar unions" to heterosexuals left LGBTQ+ families vulnerable to attack and were a mechanism for discrimination against those minorities. Indeed, the synergy between liberty and equality linked *Lawrence* and *Obergefell* with the Fourteenth Amendment's core principle: states cannot be allowed to commandeer the lives of an unpopular class of citizens and exclude them from normal legal rights and benefits. Pam Karlan calls this the "stereoscopic Fourteenth Amendment." We call it original meaning.[58]

At the heart of liberty is the authority of each human being, not just the privileged few, to figure out her/his/their own life and career path, without government commandeering or discrimination. Philosophers as different as Amartya Sen, Friedrich von Hayek, and John Rawls might agree with that general statement of constitutional obligation. Recall Charles Sumner's metaphor for the state constitutional provisions that were the basis for the equal protection clause. Every human being "is one of the children of the State, which, like an impartial parent, regards all its offspring with an equal care." As Jonathan Rauch suggested to us, *Obergefell* honored the moral seriousness of the plaintiffs' claims and invited Americans of all orientations to ask themselves: What would your life be like right now if your marriage, or the prospect of marrying, were erased? Many Americans could not imagine their lives that way. Well, that's what committed gay couples and their children faced.[59]

Consider the world imagined by the Constitution, as interpreted in *Lawrence* and *Obergefell*. Everyone should have the same opportunities for flourishing. For a fundamental institution like marriage, the baseline would presume decentralized experimentation and discovery by many individuals over time. Cultural changes would result from mass trends in those individual decisions, and the assurance of liberty would expand to accommodate new cultural norms. Following Hayek, Kennedy was skeptical of social engineering by the government, which would augur against top-down national uniformity. By 2015, cultural norms had reached a new equilibrium in which marriage for everyone was recognized as something best left to individual choice. Many Hayekians (like Sutton) disagreed with this analysis, but Kennedy relished his role of occasionally announcing new constitutional baselines that advanced the liberty everyone should enjoy. Although Kennedy oversold marriage as an institution suitable for everyone, his opinion was inclusive in important ways. Not only did it invite LGBTQ+ Americans to join the nation's family culture, but it did so without disrespecting Americans of faith or declaring that the constitutional Super-DOMAs reflected anti-gay animus, prejudice, or stereotypes. His opinion did not escape sharp criticism, however.[60]

THE THOUGHTFUL CHALLENGES POSED
BY THE *OBERGEFELL* DISSENTS

The Supreme Court issued its decision on Friday, June 26, 2015. Justice Kennedy read most of his opinion to a thrilled courtroom, and Chief Justice Roberts read most of his dissenting opinion, the first time he had done so in ten years on the court. When the published opinions were issued the same morning, observers were impressed by the anger expressed by two of the four dissenters. Justice Scalia's dissenting opinion denounced "today's judicial Putsch." In a footnote, he vented outrage at this most recent Kennedy opinion relying on "sweet mystery of life" individualism: "If, even as the price to be paid for a fifth vote, I ever joined an opinion for the Court that began: 'The Constitution promises liberty to all within its reach, a liberty that includes certain specific rights that allow persons, within a lawful realm, to define and express their identity,' I would hide my head in a bag. The Supreme Court of the United

States has descended from the disciplined legal reasoning of John Marshall and Joseph Story to the mystical aphorisms of the fortune cookie." (Several justices, dissenting from as well as joining Tony Kennedy's opinion, implored Nino Scalia to delete the head-in-a-bag footnote, but he was adamant.) Moreover, he and Justice Alito departed from the etiquette of ending dissenting opinions with the phrase, "I respectfully dissent," as Roberts and Thomas did. Scalia's last words were "our impotence," and Alito ended his dissent by warning that all Americans "should worry about what the majority's claim of power portends."[61]

As explained above, the majority opinion was more profound than a fortune cookie—but in our view three of the four dissenting opinions raised fundamental concerns that the majority should have discussed. Indeed, their criticisms gave the majority missed opportunities to deepen its historical and constitutional analysis.

Chief Justice Roberts wrote the primary dissenting opinion, joined by Justices Scalia and Thomas. Five unelected, life-tenured judges were changing the long-standing, indeed ancient, definition of marriage without proper support in either the Constitution or the democratic process. "Just who do we think we are?" Roberts worried that the Supreme Court was making the same institutional mistake it had made in *Lochner v. New York* (1906), which interpreted the due process clause to protect liberty of contract and, ultimately, market freedom. As Alito had said in *Windsor,* there were two normative theories of family law: a consent-based theory and a conjugal theory. Like the *Lochner* majority, the *Obergefell* majority read one of these theories into the Constitution— thereby blocking democratic majorities from adopting the other. Citing his mentor, the celebrated jurist Henry Friendly, Roberts quipped that "the Fourteenth Amendment does not enact John Stuart Mill's *On Liberty* any more than it enacts Herbert Spencer's *Social Statics.*"[62]

The majority was engaged in illegitimate lawmaking, the chief argued. Just as he thought big issues like universal health care ought to be decided by the democratic process, so ought the definition of marriage, an issue where LGBTQ+ rights groups had already demonstrated an ability to persuade both legislators and voters to redefine marriage under state law. Marriage equality supporter Jonathan Rauch put it this way two years earlier: "Gay Americans are in sight of winning marriage not merely as a gift of five referees [judges] but in public competition against all the arguments and money our opponents can throw at us. A Supreme Court intervention now would deprive us of that victory. Our right to marry would never enjoy the deep legitimacy that only a popular mandate can bring."[63]

Lochner is an example of the "anti-canon," illegitimate precedents whose disastrous reasoning was to be avoided in the future—but the champion of the anti-canon is *Dred Scott v. Sandford* (1857), in which the Taney court read the Fifth Amendment's due process and anti-takings clauses to protect the property interests of slaveholders and held, further, that free persons of African descent could not constitutionally be "citizens" of any state for purposes of Article III. Roberts's dissent claimed that the *Obergefell* majority was making the same mistake the majority made in *Dred Scott*. Although Roberts discussed only *Dred Scott*'s Fifth Amendment holding, he should have considered the entire opinion, which enriched the case for marriage equality (a point Nancy Cott made in the *DeBoer* trial, part of the record on appeal). To support the second holding, that free persons of African descent could not be citizens of any state, Chief Justice Taney relied on colonial statutes where "intermarriages between white persons and negroes or mulattoes were regarded as unnatural and immoral, and punished as crimes, not only in the parties, but in the person who joined them in marriage. And no distinction in this respect was made between the free negro or mulatto and the slave, but this stigma, of the deepest degradation, was fixed upon the whole race." *Dred Scott* expressed the historical connection between citizenship and marriage. Just as the promise of *constitutional* citizenship for African Americans was not delivered until *Loving*, the promise of *constitutional* citizenship for sexual and gender minorities was not delivered until *Obergefell*. Although not fully responsive to Rauch's powerful point about "deep legitimacy," the negative example of *Dred Scott* undermined the dissenters' view that defining marriage was a policy judgment best left to the legislative process, not a matter of constitutional citizenship and civil rights.[64]

Justice Thomas wrote a separate dissent (joined by Justice Scalia) elaborating on the original constitutional meaning of *liberty* as protection against government interference with people's property and their freedom to walk around unrestrained. Liberty was decidedly not an entitlement to government benefits, he maintained. The majority saw the Constitution as protecting the dignity of gay people and their children—but "the Constitution contains no Dignity Clause," and "even if it did, the government would be incapable of bestowing dignity." Thomas argued that the original meaning of liberty—as a negative right, protecting against governmental interference with walking-around freedom—was consistent with the court's right to marry precedents. *Loving* was a liberty precedent because Virginia had made it a crime for a married interracial couple to live in the commonwealth. Criminal

penalties were also involved in *Zablocki*, and *Turner* of course involved convicted criminals.[65]

Thomas's opinion missed half of the majority's constitutional claim, for the
original public meaning of the equal protection clause could have supported
the majority, as we observed above. On the matter of liberty, the majority also
had an answer to doubting Thomas: denying one class of citizens access to a
state-supported institution could well be a denial of liberty. For example, "property" and "freedom of contract" have always been state-supported institutions, as they existed only insofar as the government stood ready to exclude
people from your property and enforce your contracts. If the state legislated
that it would no longer protect property or contract rights of gay people, even
the most conservative jurist would admit that there was a denial of liberty. Likewise, the four Super-DOMAs, excluding most LGBTQ+ relationships from
state family law, denied those persons access to a fundamental state institution (civil marriage) open to almost everyone else. Consider another angle.
Given the huge legal and social incentives to get married, it might be said that
the state was trying to commandeer the lives of these citizens and channel
their energies away from relationships they would freely choose.[66]

Justice Alito's dissenting opinion (joined by Justices Scalia and Thomas) lamented that the majority's decision "will be used to vilify Americans who are
unwilling to assent to the new orthodoxy." By comparing the four Super-
DOMAs to laws requiring racial segregation and coverture, the court was unnecessarily demonizing religious traditionalists. "I assume that those who
cling to old beliefs will be able to whisper their thoughts in the recesses of their
homes, but if they repeat those views in public, they will risk being labeled as
bigots and treated as such by governments, employers, and schools." Social
censure, combined with state disapproval, would chill religious expression. Indeed, Alito was suggesting that a country with constitutional marriage equality plus sexual orientation and gender identity anti-discrimination laws would
commandeer the lives of religious Americans. They would be "forced" to sacrifice their lives of faithful adherence to God's Word when the politically correct state insisted that they become "complicit" in marriages that they believed
to violate that Word. In 2015, Kim Davis, a county clerk in Kentucky, went to
jail because she closed her office rather than issued marriage licenses to same-
sex couples.[67]

In his opinion, Justice Kennedy assured traditionalist Americans that their
churches could not be compelled to perform gay weddings and that the First
Amendment protected their ability to defend religious views in the public

sphere. The dissenters treated these assurances as cheap talk, but three years later Justice Kennedy delivered the opinion for a 7-2 court in *Masterpiece Cakeshop, Ltd. v. Colorado Civil Rights Commission* (2018). The court held that state adjudicators could not denigrate religion-based reasons as inferior to other kinds of reasons to deny service to gay weddings. Kennedy's analysis was attentive to the liberties of traditionalists as well as gay people—but left open broader challenges to marriage-related applications of state anti-discrimination laws (explored in chapter 23).[68]

Was *Obergefell* a legitimate exercise in judicial review in a constitutional democracy? As Judge Sutton opined, the freedom to marry had succeeded in persuading many straight Americans that marriage for LGBTQ+ persons was a good idea. Marriage equality secured through the democratic process would enjoy a "deep legitimacy" not possible from the judicial process. Wouldn't persuading your neighbors and your legislators entrench marriage equality much better than persuading the judges?

Thirty-seven states were handing out marriage licenses by the time the Supreme Court handed down *Obergefell*. Although we think Michigan would have been gettable through the political process within the decade, the last dozen states would have been very hard to secure—and in the interim the country would be confusingly divided between the new normal and the old holdouts. Moreover, the court could easily—and perhaps by a lopsided margin—have invalidated the four Super-DOMAs based upon *Romer* and remanded the cases to the state legislatures to provide a suitable family law regime for LGBTQ+ persons (including but not limited to marriage). Such a judgment would have yielded a great deal more public deliberation—though probably not marriage equality in the near term.

The Sutton-Roberts challenge highlights a central tension in constitutional judicial review between the rule of law and democratic accountability. Both are sources of legitimacy, and in *Obergefell* the majority felt the democratic process had run its course. What we should add is that Michigan, Ohio, Kentucky, and Tennessee were undermining the conditions of democracy. By undermining the capacity of LGBTQ+ citizens to determine the structure of their own lives and build a stable home for their children, these four states were treating them as second-class citizens who were apt targets for social stigma and political scapegoating.

Was there any point to further deliberation? The country had been intensely focused on the marriage debate for at least a dozen years—at the state as well as federal level, in legislatures as well as courts, and in scores of ballot campaigns. What arguments were left to deny these couples full equality? Ably representing the states, John Bursch had declined to make the faith-based and protect-the-children arguments that probably motivated most of the Super-DOMA voters, had abandoned the optimal parenting argument in the wake of Judge Friedman's *DeBoer* opinion, and worked Judge Sutton's responsible procreation argument into a stance that could not withstand even slightly heightened scrutiny. Outside the court, signs declared that every child had a right to a father, and inside the court, the advocate declared that every voter had a right to decide fundamental issues. Both arguments bombed, ignored even by the dissenters.

Ultimately, the best justification for *Obergefell* was that democratic deliberation in our constitutional democracy is subject to substantive baselines. Precisely as the text, background history, and precedents interpreting the Constitution of 1789, the Bill of Rights, and the Fourteenth Amendment suggest, those baselines are both libertarian and egalitarian. As James Madison appreciated at the founding of our constitutional democracy, government must respect the constitutional liberties of all citizens that allow each of them to determine the contours of her/his/their lives and families to the greatest extent consistent with the liberties of others. As Charles Sumner appreciated prior to and during the reconstruction of our constitutional democracy, no group of productive citizens should be excluded from core public institutions—the franchise, marriage, military service, freedom to contract and own property—that allow citizens to determine their own life projects and engagements.

After intense deliberation, liberal Democrats and some conservative Republicans, legislators as well as judges, and hundreds of independent scholars concluded that the Super-DOMAs met none of these constitutional baselines. In our view, Justice Kennedy wrote a righteous, even if incomplete, opinion accounting for national freedom for sexual and gender minorities to marry the persons of their choice. After he retired, we asked him which of his hundreds of judicial opinions was his favorite. Answer: his concurring opinion in the flag-burning case, where the court defied the democratic process in virtually all the states and the Congress but reaffirmed the Constitution's meta-commitment to free expression for everyone. Flag burning remains deeply unpopular: Did the court's reaffirmation of First Amendment principles undermine the court's or the Constitution's legitimacy? He certainly did not think so, nor did Scalia, who voted with him in the flag-burning case. Could the same be said after *Obergefell* (an opinion Kennedy mentioned as another one he was proudest of, right after flag burning)?[69]

On June 12, 2007, the fortieth anniversary of *Loving v. Virginia*, Mildred Loving had expressed her gratitude for her marriage to Richard, and for the children and grandchildren it brought them, "even if others thought he was the wrong kind of person for me to marry. I believe all Americans, no matter their race, no matter their sex, no matter their sexual orientation, should have that same freedom to marry" as a civil right. "I support the freedom to marry for all." Less than five years later, President Obama's second inaugural address linked the freedom and equality promised in the Declaration of Independence with the civil rights and marriage reform movements of people of color, women, and gay people: "We, the people, declare today that the most evident of truths— that all of us are created equal—is the star that guides us still; just as it guided our forebears through Seneca Falls, and Selma, and Stonewall."[70]

At 11:06 a.m. on June 26, 2015, soon after the Supreme Court had released the *Obergefell* opinions, President Obama placed a call from the Oval Office to Jim Obergefell's cell phone. Standing on the steps of the court, wearing a lavender and white bow tie and a gray suit with a small American flag on its lapel, Jim received Barack Obama's congratulations: "Your leadership on this has changed the country." With Isaiah DeLeon (the son of Greg Bourke and Mike DeLeon) listening over his right shoulder, Jim responded that he was living up to the commitment he had made when he married John Arthur. "I appreciate everything you have done for the LGBT community," he said to the president, "and it has been an honor for me to be part of that fight." Scribbling some notes with his left hand, Obama suggested that Jim's efforts would "bring about a lasting change in this country." That night, the White House was lit up in rainbow colors.[71]

Still, Jim Obergefell's soul ached for his late husband. For him, like all of us, self-determination does not mean that life will turn out the way we hope and plan.

22 • From Outlaws to In-Laws

On March 7, 1967, forty million Americans watched *CBS Reports: The Homosexuals,* network television's first documentary on homosexuality. Mike Wallace, the host, opened the show by describing homosexuals as "the most despised minority in the United States." Over the next sixty minutes, therapists explained homosexuality as a mental illness, and cloaked homosexuals expressed anguish at their condition. In a token effort at balance, CBS included a short interview with Jack Nichols, a dashing twenty-eight-year-old man who considered his sexual orientation completely natural and was untroubled by it. After the interview, Wallace allegedly told Nichols: "You seem to be able to answer all my questions very nicely, but I don't believe that in your heart you actually believe what you've been saying."[1]

In 1967, what government documents described as "homosexuals and other sex perverts" were social outcasts and legal outlaws. Every state but Illinois made consensual sodomy and solicitation a serious crime. Homosexuality disqualified one for the federal and state civil service, teaching and most other professions, liquor licenses, and military service. Sexual and gender nonconformity were formally classified as mental illnesses or, to use the primary legal term, evidence of a "psychopathic personality." Homosexuals and cross-dressers "wore the mask" or hid "in the closet" and could offer little political opposition to the outlaw regime. After World War II, a tiny group of quasi-open homosexuals and sympathetic experts argued that homosexuals were relatively harmless misfits. While heterosexuality was natural and much to be preferred, pathetic homosexuality ought to be tolerated rather than persecuted, as the CBS documentary suggested. A third perspective, reflected in the interview with Jack Nichols, had emerged by 1967. Its leading exponent was Nichols's mentor, Dr. Franklin Kameny.[2]

After serving his country during World War II, Kameny had earned an astronomy Ph.D. from Harvard in 1956. Two years earlier, in May 1954, he had come to the realization that he was homosexual, and after years of repressed desire he took to sex with men "like a duck to water," as he typically put it. In 1957, however, Kameny was discharged from his job with the Army Map Service and subsequently rendered unemployable in his field because the government discovered a recent arrest for homosexual solicitation. Assisted by the ACLU, he challenged his discharge as irrational and took his case all the way to the Supreme Court. The petition he wrote, filed on January 27, 1961, announced a radically novel constitutional framework for homosexuals. Anticipating jurisprudence a generation into the future, Kameny argued that the government's action unconstitutionally limited his freedom and violated his right of equal protection. The government had no business imposing an "odious conformity" and penalizing people for their private affairs that harmed no one. It was unconstitutional for the state to "tell the citizen what to think and how to believe." The federal employment exclusion, he wrote, "makes of the homosexual a second-rate citizen, by discriminating against him without reasonable cause."[3]

This brief anticipated *Obergefell*'s view that freedom in our constitutional democracy was founded upon each citizen's right of self-determination and equal treatment. The anti-homosexual terror was as antithetical to our constitutional democracy as apartheid and coverture had been. Asserting that "the average homosexual is as well-adjusted in personality as the average heterosexual," Kameny argued that because such persons were capable of excellent government service, excluding them was presumptively irrational. That irrationality stood in contrast to the American government's purpose "to protect and assist *all* of its citizens, not as in the case of homosexuals, to harm, to victimize, and to destroy them." The government's exclusionary policy, whether based on private conduct or admitted status, was a "discrimination no less illegal and no less odious than discrimination based upon religious or racial grounds."[4]

On March 20, 1961, the Supreme Court unanimously denied Kameny's petition. That ended the lawsuit but marked the beginning of fifty years of his political activism. Later that year, Kameny, Nichols, and fourteen other gay men revived the Mattachine Society of Washington, with the mission of securing for homosexuals the same "rights and liberties established by the word and

Table 1: The Social Movement Continuum (Gays)

Outlaw regime	Tolerance regime	In-law regime
Sexual perverts are predatory and dangerous	Homosexuals are sad but tolerable	Gay people are good
Sexual variation is malignant	Sexual variation is tolerable	Sexual variation is benign
Compulsory heterosexuality	Straight preferred	No material differences
Predators and criminals	Misfits and addicts	Full citizens and relatives
Criminalization; mental institutions	Decriminalization; "no promo homo"	Anti-discrimination; marriage
Due process rights; criminal procedure	Privacy rights; First Amendment	Equality rights; freedom to marry

spirit of the Constitution" as well as "equality under law, equality of opportunity." Mattachine's constitutional vision was "to secure for the homosexual the right, as a human being, to develop and achieve his full potential and dignity, and the right, as a citizen, to make his maximum contribution to the society in which he lives." This language sounds a lot like the language deployed half a century later in the Supreme Court decisions invalidating DOMA and state Super-DOMAs.[5]

Kameny and his allies pressed the message "Gay is Good" in court cases, legislative hearings, and executive branch deliberations. The Mattachine activists advocated a sea change in American beliefs about and attitudes toward gay people. Through public education, protest and agitation, and institutional maneuvering, they pushed to move American law away from the outlaw regime and even the tolerance regime, toward the regime of completely equal citizenship. Table 1 illustrates the precepts associated with each regime.[6]

Although he originally felt that marriage was too constraining for gay people, by 1974 Kameny was defending gays' freedom to marry as a corollary to the constitutional guarantees of "first class citizenship to all of its citizens, the right of the pursuit of happiness to all of its citizens, and the right to be different and to be unpopular without disadvantage to all of its citizens." Gay marriages would "impair or interfere with no societal interest. In fact, they further some societal interest" by supporting stable relationships. In 1975, he led the Gay Activists Alliance to support District of Columbia council member Arrington Dixon's marriage liberalization bill. When Craig Dean and Patrick Gill brought a lawsuit seeking marriage equality from the District in 1991, Kameny was one of the few prominent gay leaders to support them. In a 2011 ceremony in the House of Representatives, he was memorialized as the rebellious homosexual who would not sit in the back of the bus, a relentless grassroots organizer and public educator, and the visionary constitutional advocate who challenged the legitimacy of the old regime.[7]

In Kameny's memory, we now step back and consider the freedom to marry from the perspective of the social movement propelling that revolution in American constitutional and family law. Most social movements do not achieve such dramatic changes so swiftly, and few worked against as much emotional distaste and backlash as the marriage equality campaign. For years, the prevailing wisdom even among academics was that it was crazy to think that despised, "icky" homosexuals could overcome social hostility to secure marriage rights. Why did marriage equality suddenly succeed? How did it overcome the backlash that paralyzed the civil rights and abortion-choice movements?[8]

The rapid success of the marriage equality movement owes much to changes in society. In the last half-century, as women's economic and social options have expanded, marriage has lost its sacred status among straight persons at the same time gay persons have formed committed relationships, often with children. In other words, straight and gay families substantially converged, and with that convergence the definition of marriage as one man, one woman was understood as obsolescent by increasing numbers of Americans. In our view, these social changes (explored in chapter 24) have been the driving force. But we also think the marriage equality movement has been unusually successful because of three other phenomena, each of them linked with one of the faces of the marriage debate suggested in the previous chapter:

(1) *Liberty: Dispersed Minority Emerging from the Closet.* The beneficiary group was widely and randomly dispersed; they could pop up anywhere. Once large numbers of gay persons came out to their straight parents, pastors, and friends, these "unexpected messengers" were persuasive advocates for social, religious, and legal recognition of their freedom to form committed relationships supported by the state.

(2) *Community: No Harm, No Cost.* Over time, most people were persuaded that the sought-after right to marry did not directly

impose negative "externalities," or costs, on society nor did it seem to harm other people. Instead, they were convinced that marriage equality created positive externalities, or advantages to society, such as linkages between this minority and their straight relatives, neighbors, and coworkers.

(3) *Equality: Organization Matters.* As the twenty-first century progressed, freedom to marry was supported by an increasingly well-funded, coordinated effort that operated effectively at the state and federal levels and developed ever-more sophisticated appeals to executives, legislators, and voters, as well as to judges.

We do not maintain that all three features were essential for marriage equality to prevail nationwide, but the coming together of all three features—on top of the social trends, plus a great deal of good fortune (i.e., Tony Kennedy rather than Bob Bork replaced Lewis Powell on the Supreme Court)—were essential for it to prevail so rapidly.

Ironically, and for some lamentably, the process by which marriage equality prevailed—the deployment of straight messengers, downplaying the effects of gay marriage on the institution, and the lavish public education campaign— sacrificed much that was once radical or progressive about the sexual liberty undergirding the freedom to marry and even generated social, religious, and legal pressure toward the "odious conformity" that Kameny objected to in 1961. The success of marriage equality reflects Derrick Bell's important thesis that social movements achieve major political or legal changes only when the mainstream is persuaded that minority interests "converge" with their own. On the other hand, the marriage equality movement has also helped integrate gender minorities into the gay rights social movement—not only adding more letters to the LGBT acronym but also pressing the movement into a more radical challenge to gender roles and stereotyping.[9]

One meta-lesson of marriage equality for other social movements is that campaigns to change public opinion and to secure constitutional protections are very difficult and, even if successful, risk blunting messages dear to the movements. Another meta-lesson is that prejudice in this country is hydraulic: when one group seems to triumph, anger and negative attitudes will reemerge, as by undermining the group's gains or by targeting another group. Thus, the most immediate consequence of *Obergefell* was to motivate leaders of the Republican Party, lawyers with the Alliance Defending Freedom (ADF), and officials of the country's leading religious denominations to pirouette away

from rhetoric denying LGBTQ+ persons the freedom to marry to rhetoric protecting the freedom of religious persons to the free exercise and expression of
their traditionalist faith. Relatedly, substantial social and political acceptance
of gay marriage may have driven the Republican Party toward greater demonization of immigrants, "abortion doctors," and Muslims. (Indeed, charges of
homophobia have fueled animus against Muslims, whose conservative beliefs
about sexuality and gender are wielded to persecute and humiliate them.) Although the marriage campaign suggests strategies for the abortion-choice
and immigration debates, it also suggests that these social movements face
even higher hurdles. Undocumented immigrants and women who have had
abortions are widely dispersed, but severe penalties have discouraged their
coming out of the immigration and abortion closets, respectively. Also, neither the pro-choice nor the immigration social movement has come up with
effective strategies for dealing with deep prejudices and stereotypes about
women's sexuality and geographic and racial boundaries that fuel resistance
and counter-mobilization.[10]

As a general matter, efforts to help marginalized social groups protect their
members' liberties and ensure their equal protection will not be successful
unless unexpected mainstream messengers can persuade the community (i.e.,
middle-of-the-road voters) that it is in their interests to recognize the dignity
and needs of the marginalized group. A successful social movement also needs
to do what Frank Kameny pioneered for gay people: come up with a new
vocabulary and normative framework that galvanizes your group to think
that they are normal and their lives are valuable and that can persuade mainstream Americans as well. Relatedly, such success may depend on the social movement's ability to generate a massively funded media campaign to
create a counter-narrative of community benefits that would flow from equal
treatment.

Equality Practice: Why Marriage Equality Prevailed

When Frank Kameny turned eighty-five years old in May 2010, there were
a series of birthday celebrations befitting his status as a founder of the modern gay rights movement. The painting below was featured at a celebration
hosted by David Bradberry and Don Patron in Washington's Dupont Circle
neighborhood. We asked Kameny how the gay rights movement was able to accomplish so much. Slicing the air with emphatic hand gestures, he said that
the secret to constitutional success was bludgeoning power with truth. The

Franklin Kameny. (Portrait art by Don Patron.)

truth had always been that gay people are human beings worthy of the same rights and respect everyone else enjoys. Gay is good, he insisted: not evil, not pathetic, not just okay, but good. Once you have your hands on the truth, he insisted, you make a lot of noise and never let officials and the media forget it.[11]

The early marriage activists—Donna Burkett and Manonia Evans; Jack Baker and Mike McConnell; Del Martin and Phyllis Lyon; Troy Perry and Robin Tyler—had the same idea Kameny did, but for many years the nation was not ready to listen. Philosopher Miranda Fricker has a term for what Kameny and other activists were fighting: *hermeneutical marginalization.* Simply stated, they were responding to the minority's helplessness when there was no intelligible framework of words, ideas, and morality to express the pain and harms society and individuals were inflicting upon the minority group. Before 1961, there was no widely available conceptual framework for homosexuals even to view themselves as functional human beings who deserved to be treated better than society's dregs. That lack of a framework generated feelings of self-loathing and worthlessness and fed the regime of the closet. In a process theorists call *hermeneutical dissent,* rebellious homosexuals like Kameny provided a new vocabulary (*gay* rather than *homosexual*) and a new conceptual and normative framework ("Gay is Good") that not only redefined their community but created a moral space where people could be okay with gay or proud to be queer. Kameny saw as his life's work the enterprise of insisting that a hostile society acknowledge, then tolerate, then accept the new vocabulary and the new moral framework. In law, that project was the movement of LGBTQ+ persons from *outlaws* (bad, sick, disgusting criminals outside the law) to *in-laws* (good, productive people who could be your relatives). This is why we found the marriage debate very important for LGBTQ+ rights thirty years ago.[12]

The low point for marriage activism was also its moment of regeneration: the AIDS epidemic, which thrust thousands of gay and bisexual men out of the closet, revealed caregiving capacities that gays often did not realize they had, and impelled a new generation of LGBT persons to think about serious relationships the way Tom Stoddard did at the end of his life. During the epidemic's early stages, a new generation of leaders like Mary Bonauto, Anne Stanback, Evan Wolfson, Beth Robinson, James Esseks, Jenny Pizer, and Shannon Minter were in college and/or law school. Partly because of efforts by pioneers like Kameny to provide a vocabulary and moral framework, their generation found it easier to accept their sexual or gender orientation as natural and to conclude it was the world that was crazy, not them. They saw the marriage issue as important—and they became leaders in organizations like GLAD, Freedom to Marry, Love Makes a Family, ACLU, Lambda Legal, and NCLR and created a genuine campaign for full marriage rights. The 1990s were a more hospitable decade for such a campaign, because the connection between AIDS and homosexuality receded, because most Americans knew at least one openly lesbian or gay person, because marriage itself had evolved away from rigid gender roles and a focus on conjugality, and because many religious leaders and some denominations were okay with marriage equality.[13]

Nonetheless, between 1985 and 2015, the larger campaign for LGBTQ+ rights saw more defeats than victories. As a volunteer and then a staff member at Lambda Legal, Evan Wolfson was involved in three of the biggest defeats: *Bowers v. Hardwick* (1986), in which the Supreme Court ruled that homosexual sodomy between consenting adults in the home could be a felony; *Baehr v. Lewin* (1993), the early marriage case that inspired DOMA and ended with a 1998 state constitutional amendment allowing the Hawai'i legislature to limit marriage to one man, one woman; and *Boy Scouts of America v. Dale* (2000), in which the Supreme Court held that the Boy Scouts had a First Amendment right to exclude gay people from their organization. Like Kameny, who suffered his share of defeats, Wolfson rationalized these efforts as "losing forward," a term first suggested by another gay rights pioneer, San Francisco supervisor Harvey Milk, martyred in 1979. These losses put gay rights on the national agenda, set forth a defensible normative position, encouraged more sexual minorities to come out of their closets, and attracted straight allies. Losing forward, however, works only when you are certain your idea is deeply true and that the next generation will find merit in it.[14]

In our view, the moment when widespread, even nationwide, marriage equality became likely was when Massachusetts started issuing marriage licenses, on May 17, 2004 (the fiftieth anniversary of *Brown v. Board of Education*). That moment was a collective effort combining activism and deliberation, involving not just Mary Bonauto (GLAD), Arline Isaacson (Caucus), Norma Shapiro (ACLU), and Josh Friedes, Marty Rouse, and Marc Solomon (MassEquality) but also ACLU's Matt Coles, Evan Wolfson of Lambda, Dan Foley in Hawai'i, Vermont's Beth Robinson and Susan Murray, Anne Stanback of Connecticut, historian Nancy Cott, litigators such as Shannon Minter and Kate Kendell from NCLR, gay rights scholars and authors, and the Williams Institute in Los Angeles.[15]

Consider evidence for *Goodridge* as the turning point. Marriage equality would not have arrived so long as two-thirds of the American people were dead set against it, as they were in the 1990s. Master statistician (and gay genius) Nate Silver collected all of the polls on the marriage issue from 1996 to 2013, averaged them, and then arrayed the results in a graph. The turning point was 2004: before that, national public support for marriage equality was low and steady; after that, support ticked up about 2 percent a year. Support increased even in the years the marriage equality movement was losing almost all the court cases and ballot initiatives (2004–2008). By 2011, the polls revealed a plurality and then a majority supporting marriage equality. In 2015, the Williams Institute confirmed Silver's analysis and documented how support accelerated after 2012, especially in states that were handing out marriage licenses.[16]

Why did marriage equality win in Massachusetts? And why did support for it spread steadily afterward? As to the first question, marriage equality won through a combination of excellent leadership, enthusiastic followership, and lucky breaks. The efforts of GLAD, ACLU, MassEquality, and the Gay and Lesbian Caucus helped inspire gay people from all over the commonwealth to come out as couples, many responsibly raising children, and channeled their straight relatives, their neighbors and employers, and a wide array of religious leaders to champion their relationships. Lucky breaks included the disorganized, amateurish push for a state constitutional amendment in 2002 and the tendency of Republican governor William Weld to appoint social progressives to the state supreme court. The Catholic Church's struggle with revelations about its cover-ups of predatory priests undermined the movement's most powerful adversary.[17]

As to the second question, reflecting lessons learned from Hawai'i, the marriage campaigns in Massachusetts, Vermont, and Connecticut represented a path forward. First, they were bottom-up, not top-down political campaigns; they were responsive to the needs and demands of the LGBT community. The plaintiff couples, as well as the lawyers and leaders, deeply represented the community. Second, the campaigns were institutionally sophisticated. Filing a social impact lawsuit requires a legal, political, and institutional foundation. Legislatures in all three states had amended their anti-discrimination laws to include sexual orientation and had codified a right to second-parent adoption for lesbian and gay couples. The marriage campaigns built on those advances and the political alliances they reflected—and they revealed political muscle by protecting supportive legislators and knocking off a few vulnerable opponents. Importantly, the three state constitutions were hard to amend, and the marriage campaigns had smart strategies for heading off such a process. Third, it was essential to have allied groups—such as feminist and reproductive rights associations, businesses with domestic partnership policies, sympathetic religious leaders and faith communities, and academics, historians, social workers, child psychologists, and medical professionals.[18]

Not least important was the New England campaigns' ability to work around the politics of disgust, the "ick" factor associated with homosexuality. At every opportunity, the campaigns offered representatives who would be relatively unthreatening to mainstream audiences. It was no coincidence that the public leaders in all three states—Mary Bonauto, Susan Murray and Beth Robinson, Anne Stanback and Maureen Murphy—were charming, well-spoken, earnest lesbians whom homophobes could easily imagine as their sisters. In Massachusetts, Arline Isaacson, Amy Hunt, and their gal pals had an edge as lobbyists, because the aging altar boys in the legislature were the opposite of disgusted by sexy lesbians. The plaintiff couples in all three marriage cases were carefully curated and coached to be as mainstream as apple pie. In their interviews and public appearances, the couples offered a completely domesticated ("just like straight") view of their relationships: they all worked hard at their jobs and struggled to make ends meet, they made sacrifices for their partners and their children, they volunteered for an endless list of community services, they went to church, and so forth. Who had time for disgusting sex?[19]

The more lesbian and gay people who were out of the closet and willing to talk about their lives and extended families, the better. This is one reason the successful marriage lawsuits were in states that had repealed their consensual sodomy laws, added sexual orientation to their anti-discrimination laws, and enjoyed domestic partnership recognition from many private and public employers. These policies encouraged more people to be out of the closet—which provided opportunities for other citizens to temper their feelings of disgust. Massachusetts pioneer Elaine Noble, the first openly lesbian legislator, had said in 1974 that "if homosexual marriages were legalized," she and her partner "would be able to participate in the community in a very full and complete way" and would have a positive impact "in terms of shaping people's attitudes, making them change their minds and view homosexual relationships as a valid life style." When wedding bells rang for lesbian and gay couples thirty years later and the sky did not fall, it was harder for skeptical straights to begrudge the freedom to marry.[20]

Consistent with Noble's prophesy, civil unions (Vermont in 2000, Connecticut in 2005) and comprehensive domestic partnerships (California in 2003) contributed powerfully to the cause through *equality practice*. In Europe, Kees Waaldijk had deployed this "small steps" strategy to secure marriage equality in the Netherlands. In 2006, William Eskridge and Darren Spedale predicted which states were most likely to recognize the freedom to marry for LGBT people. Eskridge and Spedale developed a table setting forth, for each state, whether it (1) had decriminalized consensual sodomy, (2) had included sexual orientation in its hate crime and (3) employment anti-discrimination laws, (4) had local governments with domestic partnership policies, (5) had recognized joint caregivers through second-parent adoptions or in other ways, and (6) had given limited statewide recognition to same-sex partnerships. Appendix 2 in this volume updates the data through December 2007, when Massachusetts was still the only marriage equality state. The jurisdictions at the top (Massachusetts, Vermont, California, District of Columbia, Connecticut) were those the model considered, in 2006, most likely to recognize marriage equality; those at the bottom (such as Alabama, Idaho, Mississippi) were least likely.[21]

Of the nineteen states that recognized the freedom to marry by October 2014, eighteen had checked off five or all of our six categories in 2007. All of the states with fewer than four categories had to await a federal court order in 2014–2015. States where gay rights groups and their allies had already enjoyed some success in both the legislatures and the courts were the most likely to recognize same-sex marriages. In those states, there were legislative allies who had not suffered at the polls, proven grassroots enthusiasm, and repeated instances where pro-gay measures had not only defied predictions of Armageddon but had produced positive effects.

The gay-friendly legal and political culture in those score-five or score-six jurisdictions contributed to an environment where lesbian and gay citizens were more willing to come out of the closet to their families, coworkers and bosses, neighbors, and their children's schoolteachers. States checking off the family-recognition columns directly contributed to the ability of lesbian and gay couples to raise children. If one of the partners worked for an employer with domestic partnership coverage, then her partner and their children usually had affordable health insurance, a key need for a well-planned family. If both partners enjoyed parental rights with the children and relationship rights to one another, each would have greater assurance that the enormous endeavor of raising children would be a joint effort—one that would engage straight relatives. Few parents can resist the lure of grandchildren, and Parents, Families, and Friends of Lesbians and Gays (PFLAG), founded in 1973 and now boasting more than two hundred thousand members, has been a highly effective lobbying group for marriage equality. Other straight couples can relate to PFLAG parents, who have been a consistent force for humanizing lesbian and gay families.[22]

The gay-friendly states also brought America's attention to the fact that LGBT persons were widely dispersed throughout the population. Because gay people usually come from straight parents, they can pop up almost anywhere—from the Cheney household (daughter Mary) to the Republican National Committee (Ken Mehlman) to the US Senate (allegedly, Larry Craig and several others). One of these "pop-up homosexuals" invites us to recall Mrs. Phyllis Schlafly's campaign against the ERA. After the ratification period for the amendment formally closed, on June 30, 1982, STOP ERA celebrated with a gala dinner held for 1,400 guests in the Regency Ballroom of the stately Shoreham Hotel in Washington, DC, down the road from the National Zoo. The theme for the evening was "Over the Rainbow," from The Wizard of Oz. Unaware that the rainbow and the song were being appropriated by her adversaries, the homosexuals, Mrs. Schlafly basked in the attention of leading Reagan-era conservatives as her son John played a rousing piano medley of show tunes on a centrally located grand piano. As he later acknowledged, John Schlafly was gay, but that did not seem to matter to his mother. John was her trustee until her death in September 2016. John opposes gay marriage, yet his being out of the closet as a gay conservative illustrates that homosexuality is not a choice for most people. One reason public homophobia is disappearing is the presence of openly gay persons in churches, gun clubs, and conservative political organizations like the Schlafly Eagles, where Phyllis's tall, soft-spoken, piano-playing son is a top official (as of 2020).[23]

How Constitutional Litigation Advanced Marriage Equality

In 2008, political scientist Gerald Rosenberg claimed that resorting to the courts had not been productive for proponents of marriage equality. Instead, he argued, it had produced the kind of backlash that haunted *Roe v. Wade*. His thesis was immediately falsified. As illustrated in Figure 5, marriage equality came to twenty-four states by court orders issued before December 2014, including nineteen by federal courts. The last fifteen nonrecognition states converted to marriage equality by federal court orders in 2015. The eleven states where marriage equality was delivered by either legislation or ballot referendum were important to the Supreme Court's willingness to sweep the boards in *Obergefell*, but without constitutional litigation, marriage equality would not have arrived in the 2010s and might not have come to Mississippi and Alabama for many decades. Political scientists have documented that proper timing and preparation of constitutional lawsuits resulted in a decline in anti-gay attitudes and other frontlash effects in states that acted early. Consider some concrete ways constitutional litigation contributed to the advance of marriage equality.[24]

GETTING ON THE PUBLIC LAW AGENDA

The courts' biggest contribution was to create overnight publicity (and some intelligibility) for marriage equality—essentially, to elevate the issue to a more prominent spot in public discussion. Before 1993, the gayocracy ruminated about the possibility of gay marriage—but not until the Hawai'i Supreme Court decided *Baehr v. Lewin* did the issue make the front page of the *New York Times,* engage the highest echelons of the nation's major religions, and become a topic of conversation among lesbian and gay couples across the nation. Gwendolyn

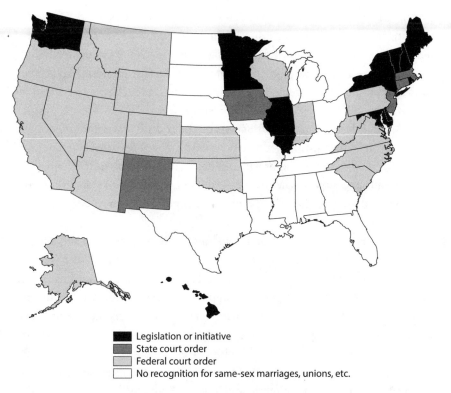

Legislation or initiative
State court order
Federal court order
No recognition for same-sex marriages, unions, etc.

Figure 5 Progress of marriage equality by legislation, state court order, and federal court order, December 1, 2014. (Cartography by Patricia Page and Bill Nelson.)

Leachman has shown that the mainstream media has been much more likely to publicize and explain a judicial opinion on marriage equality than any other government action, and the publicity impelled people to rethink their assumptions. Phyllis Watts told us this story. One of her close lesbian friends all of a sudden decided to get married. Why the new interest? The friend said: "Well, I never had the slightest desire to visit Paris—until I learned that it would be possible for me to visit Paris—and now I cannot think of anything else. Same thing with marriage to my partner: we cannot stop thinking about it!" This story illustrates the movement from cognitive marginalization to normalization: once lesbians and gay men had a moral framework that gave them a place in American culture, more of them wanted to participate.[25]

Without the commotion surrounding *Baehr*, serious discussion and grass-roots organizing around marriage would not have begun in New England when it did. Without the partial but breakthrough success of *Baker v. State*

(1999), GLAD would not have pressed *Goodridge* as early as it did. *Goodridge,* in turn, raised the marriage issue in the public consciousness and inspired tens of thousands of lesbian and gay couples—as well as the mayor of San Francisco, whose Winter of Love inspired yet more marriage proposals and constitutional lawsuits. The intense discourse that judicial decisions generated for marriage equality also generated a lot of controversy: DOMA and state junior-DOMAs were direct responses to *Baehr,* and the Federal Marriage Amendment rose to prominence only after *Lawrence* and *Goodridge.* Marriage and civil unions were an issue in the presidential elections of 2004, 2008, and 2012. DOMA and state Super-DOMAs were litigation targets for the Obama administration, and erasing them is one of President Obama's most consequential legacies.[26]

But even the negative attention intensified the public's interest and affected the English language. Before *Baehr,* there was no widely utilized term for committed homosexual relationships, and most Americans found the idea incomprehensible. After *Baehr,* even devout opponents had to develop a terminology to refer to what was once without a name. The term *partner* already had wide currency among straight as well as gay Americans. Opponents used the terms *homosexual* or *same-sex* "*marriage,*" with scare quotes—while supporters just called it *marriage.* By 2015, almost everyone in the country had heard LGBTQ+ unions referred to as *marriages,* and Justice Kennedy's *Obergefell* opinion treated their freedom to marry as a fundamental right embedded in the normative history of the institution. Justice Scalia gagged on that analysis, but his dissenting opinion referred to *same-sex marriages* without quotation marks. Chief Justice Roberts's dissent used the term *marriage equality* and conceded that "the people of a State are free to expand marriage to include same-sex couples." The lack of self-consciousness, even among conservative Catholic jurists, about coupling *marriage* with same-sex spouses signaled the depth of the moral revolution and the end of the linguistic isolation of same-sex couples.[27]

REVERSING THE BURDEN OF INERTIA

Inertia in our political system disadvantages minorities who have been subject to discriminatory laws and policies. Few groups have the clout to move their agendas past the many gatekeepers of the legislative process, especially if there is intense opposition. Courts are more attentive to minority claims, but judges have neither the clout nor the legitimacy to impose an important social change upon a polity that considers that change completely "off the wall."

There is, however, a large policy space where changes in society make it reasonable for a minority to feel it is unlawfully being discriminated against but does not have the clout and the needed allies to secure legislation ratifying its emerging social status. In that policy space, courts might announce that social conditions and the political system as a whole justify a revised interpretation, and the popular majority might go along or be unable to override the court.

Consider the following question: Who bears the political burden of inertia on an issue? The burden rests on the group that loses if it cannot bestir the political process to do something. If the minority bears the burden, it will not be able to protect its members' freedom or secure equal treatment. If those disparaging the minority bear the burden, the minority at least has a fighting chance to keep those rights. Its odds are better if the burden of inertia is high, as in jurisdictions where amending the constitution is difficult. Even where the burden of inertia is low, the minority can prevail if it has made enough headway in public education to persuade people that its rights are fairly debatable. Under those conditions, the body politic might accept a judicial decision as the product of the regular operation of the system.[28]

This helps us understand the state marriage litigation in Hawai'i, New England, and California. In each instance, judges recognized marriage rights for the excluded minority—and the majority could override those court decisions only by amending the state constitution. In Hawai'i, the justices were too far ahead of public opinion. A religious coalition was able to secure a constitutional amendment, but to do so they had to agree to a new reciprocal beneficiaries institution, as we saw in chapter 4. In Vermont, Massachusetts, and Connecticut, court recognition of marriage equality was the final word because the burden of inertia was pretty high (their state constitutions were very hard to amend), and marriage equality advocates were able to persuade a lot of straight people that the court decisions were defensible (chapters 7–9 and 13). In 2008, the California Supreme Court understood that the burden of inertia in that state was low but believed public opinion was ready for their verdict in the *Marriage Cases* (chapter 11). Proposition 8 proved them wrong, but only because of Frank Schubert's brilliant campaign and critical support from the Church of Jesus Christ of Latter-day Saints. The subsequent federal lawsuit was an effort to reset the burden of inertia at a higher level (chapter 15). That is, a US Supreme Court decision declaring marriage equality could be overridden only by the Supreme Court's overruling its own decision, or else by the arduous process of amending the US Constitution, a virtually impossible burden.[29]

CREATING CONDITIONS FOR FALSIFICATION

Reversing the burden of inertia would not have advanced the cause of marriage equality if only a few lesbian and gay couples had gotten married, nor would public opinion have warmed up to a marriage equality regime in which couples treated the matter as a lesbian version of *The Bachelorette*. There would have been problems if states recognizing the freedom to marry had seen straight couples desert the institution in droves. But the brides showed up, and the sky did not fall.

When Massachusetts started issuing marriage licenses on May 17, 2004, the immediate consequence was that thousands of lesbian and gay couples got married, many in churches and synagogues. All seven of the *Goodridge* couples got married. They integrated their new status into their family, friends, and professional networks, and four couples bore or adopted children within those relationships. A fifth couple, David Wilson and Rob Compton, had five children from previous marriages to women. For many years, the seven couples held a "family reunion" around May 17—just their families together with Mary Bonauto and her family. They have prospered as individuals and as families, with but one divorce, that of the Goodridges, who remain close friends. Their delightful daughter, Annie Goodridge, graduated from Oberlin College in 2018 with a degree in mathematics and a brilliant career in track and field.

One of the couples, Heidi Norton and Gina Smith, created a blended name—Nortonsmith—for their children and then adopted that name for themselves. Now in their fifties, they live in Northampton and have raised two young men, Avery (born 1996) and Quinn (born 2000). The Nortonsmiths reflect two revolutions that would not have been possible so early if courts had not created the conditions for falsifying stereotypes. In 1993, the Massachusetts Supreme Judicial Court ruled in favor of second-parent adoption. After Heidi Norton bore Avery, Gina Smith was able to secure equal parenting status because of that ruling. Avery was a star student-athlete in high school and graduated from MIT in 2019. His brother, Quinn, is a member of Yale College's Class of 2022. The Nortonsmith sons find the idea that every child needs a father bewildering. As Avery put it to us, "The idea of having two moms just seems normal to me." When asked what he appreciated most about his two parents, Avery immediately cited the unconditional love they showed both sons. "I've never worried that my parents would not be there for me." He and Quinn appreciate that their parents brought different strengths to the family. While the Nortonsmiths are unusually successful parents, in other ways Avery and Quinn are typical. The most effective voices favoring a flexible view of gender roles have been children reared in lesbian and gay households.[30]

Marriage, the second revolution illustrated by the Nortonsmith family, presents another opportunity to falsify stereotypes and even ameliorate prejudice. The classic American stereotype about homosexuals—the notion that inspired the state terror and private denigration against them—follows a peculiar emotional logic: because they are sterile, they are selfish and hedonistic; because they are sterile, selfish, and hedonistic, they are predatory; because they are sterile, selfish, hedonistic, and predatory, they are anti-family. The ongoing prejudice against gay people owes much to disgust at their presumed sexual behavior, but Dr. Angela Simon concludes that the disgust is also deeply rooted in the idea that they are "promiscuous recruiters and corrupters of children, who cannot have committed relationships."[31]

The politics of anti-gay disgust and contagion flourishes in a society where the dominant image of LGBTQ+ people is of pleasure seekers and stylish narcissists who don't care about family, faith, or the community. In such a society, DOMA sponsor Bob Barr could invoke the "flames of narcissism, the flames of self-centered morality" in dismissing gay marriage in 1996. After Massachusetts and other marriages were entrenched and he became aware that lesbian and gay families were a serious matter, Barr supported the Respect for Marriage Act, which would have repealed DOMA. In 2013, Bill Clinton joined Barr in denouncing DOMA—the first time a former president had publicly urged the Supreme Court to declare a statute he had signed unconstitutional.[32]

This classic stereotype affected gay people's lives for most of the twentieth century. The majority opinion in *Bowers v. Hardwick* (1986) held that the right-to-privacy precedents did not extend to *homosexual sodomy*. The majority read the precedents as protecting families and marriages but found "no connection between family, marriage, or procreation on the one hand and homosexual activity on the other." A concurring opinion emphasized that Sir William Blackstone, the great synthesizer of the common law, described "the infamous *crime against nature*" as an offense of "deeper malignity" than rape; sodomy, but not rape, was a heinous act "the very mention of which is a disgrace to human nature." In the family regime of coverture and conjugality, one might understand this ranking of harm, but in today's culture of consent and companionate marriage, Blackstone's hierarchy appalls us. Justice Powell, the critical fifth vote in *Bowers*, wrote in a draft of his concurring opinion that homosexual "sodomy is the antithesis of family."[33]

By the time the Supreme Court revisited the issue in *Lawrence v. Texas* (2003), the nation had enjoyed ten years of intense debate about same-sex marriage, and more of the justices were personally acquainted with committed same-sex couples. Justice O'Connor had joined the brutal majority opinion in *Bowers* but was happy to strike down the Texas homosexual sodomy law on equal protection grounds in 2003. Her bold concurring opinion in *Lawrence* owed something to the fact that her beloved law clerk, Stuart Delery, came out as gay in 1999, when he told her he was having a church wedding with his partner, Richard Gervase, and came out as a gay parent when he told her he and Richard were adopting a child in 2001. On both occasions, O'Connor responded warmly. Archconservative chief justice Rehnquist initially passed on the equal protection issue in *Lawrence,* surely because of his affection and respect for Sally Rider, his married-with-children lesbian chief of staff. It is also noteworthy that none of the nation's leading traditionalist religions filed an amicus brief supporting the Texas law. They strongly opposed same-sex marriage but worried that their support for continued criminalization of this minority's characteristic behavior would be seen as too much anti-gay activism by denominations that considered themselves Christian. In this context, it was not deeply controversial when the Supreme Court refused to treat "homosexual conduct" as merely pleasure-seeking activity but understood it as integral to the constitutionally protected liberty gay people (like straight people) enjoyed as they structured their lives and formed relationships.[34]

Nondiscrimination and the Survival of Traditional Attitudes

In *Obergefell,* the plaintiff couples and most of their supporting amici agreed with the Obama administration's argument that government discrimination because of sexual orientation should be subjected to heightened equal protection scrutiny. In other words, sexual orientation should join race and ethnicity as a suspect classification, or it should be a quasi-suspect classification like sex. Because *Obergefell* relied on the fundamental right to marry, it did not offer an opinion on the level of scrutiny for anti-gay measures. Nonetheless, our constitutional culture is moving toward a consensus that Frank Kameny's 1961 Supreme Court petition got it right: sexual orientation ought not be the basis for governmental discrimination or exclusion. Whatever their announced approach, the Supreme Court's precedents—*Romer, Lawrence,* and *Windsor*—gave anti-gay statutes and state constitutional amendments a level of scrutiny clearly higher than standard rational basis review. At most, it would be a short step from rational basis *with bite* (the mildest statement of review in those cases) to *heightened* scrutiny like that applied to sex-based classifications.

At oral argument in *Hollingsworth,* Chuck Cooper (representing the Proposition 8 proponents) confessed he could think of no state discrimination against gay people that would pass constitutional muster. In the Indiana marriage case, the state's lawyer told presiding judge Richard Posner he knew of no example of justifiable state discrimination. Based upon our conversation with John Bursch, counsel for the states in *Obergefell,* we think he would have, at most, a short list of acceptable discriminations. Many constitutional conservatives would agree with the overwhelming majority of constitutional liberals that the state cannot discriminate against gay people in employment and civil service hiring and promotion, public funding for welfare and other services, immigration and naturalization policy, and service in the armed forces. Many conservatives find it much easier to take these positions as a matter of public policy rather than as a matter of constitutional law.[35]

History supports this emerging consensus. Like society as a whole, and national politics to a significant extent, American constitutional law has moved from treating lesbians, gay men, and bisexuals as *outlaws,* with no expectation of equal or dignified treatment, to treating them as *in-laws,* accepted members of the political community. This constitutional regime change resembles earlier revolutions in the treatment of racial minorities and women. Just as the Supreme Court swept away all remnants of explicit apartheid and coverture, so it should carry forth the project initiated in *Romer* and sweep away explicit anti-gay rules and policies: they irrationally denigrate a worthy class of citizens and exclude them from fundamental freedoms everyone else takes for granted. As Kameny put it in 1974, "our society belongs to all of its members and segments. It is our society as homosexuals quite as much as yours as heterosexuals." This honors the tradition of Charles Sumner's famous argument against apartheid, and it epitomizes the Supreme Court's decisions in *Romer, Lawrence, Windsor,* and *Obergefell.*[36]

Some conservatives might hesitate, however, if they knew the full reach of American laws and policies that discriminate against gay people. Between 1990 and 2015, as the nation worked its way toward marriage equality, anti-gay discriminations in public education law actually increased. Most states responded to the AIDS epidemic by revamping their sex education programs, and many included anti-gay curricular rules in that reform. These changes had a discernable effect: according to the Gay, Lesbian, and Straight Educational

Network (GLSEN), gay and queer teens are subject to more bullying and harassment (and risk of suicide) in jurisdictions having such laws.[37]

These laws and policies illustrate what Kameny warned about traditional attitudes: they are hydraulic. Rights for LGBTQ+ persons have not made traditional fears about sexual and gender minorities disappear; often, they have gone underground or have reemerged in new initiatives. In 2017, for example, seventeen states required teachers to emphasize the benefits of abstinence from sexual activity outside of marriage; Title V of the Social Security Act (added in 1996) provides block grants to states for abstinence-until-marriage education. So long as these programs provide accurate information, they are constitutional exercises of state authority to engage in values-based education. The difficulty is that those states and the federal government still have statutes or constitutional provisions providing that marriage is one man, one woman. A chief lesson of the marriage debate is that these laws cannot be constitutionally applied if they insist on one-man, one-woman marriage as the only moral situs for sexual activity. Their invalidity ought to affect state educational agendas, but in practice this is not always the case.[38]

Obergefell held that the Constitution entitles same-sex couples to civil marriage "on the same terms and conditions as opposite-sex couples." Two years (to the day) after *Obergefell*, the Supreme Court applied that point of law in *Pavan v. Smith* (2017). When a married woman gave birth in Arkansas, state law required that the name of her husband appear on the birth certificate, whatever his biological relationship to the child. Arkansas declined to apply this rule to a same-sex spouse. Summarily reversing the state courts, the Supreme Court held that the Arkansas practice violated *Obergefell*'s commitment to provide same-sex couples "the constellation of benefits that the States have linked to marriage." As interpreted in *Pavan*, the freedom to marry presumptively renders all the state junior-DOMAs and Super-DOMAs unconstitutional. Because they are facially invalid, and because every state now has recognized same-sex marriages (even if through court orders), those laws cannot be applied to impose discrimination in abstinence education.[39]

There may be some judicial resistance to the normal application of precedent in this arena. For example, Justice Gorsuch (joined by Justices Thomas and Alito) dissented from the court's summary reversal in *Pavan*. They argued that "nothing in *Obergefell* indicates that a birth registration regime based on biology, one no doubt with many analogues across the country and throughout history, offends the Constitution." This was a puzzling point. For married couples, Arkansas's birth certificate regime was based entirely on marriage, not on biology. Arkansas carved out an exception to its own rules in order to exclude same-sex married couples. That not only violated the reasoning in *Obergefell* but violated the holding, even narrowly defined. Recall that the issue in *Henry v. Himes* (one of the six cases consolidated for appeal in *Obergefell*) was whether Ohio could prefer biology over marriage on its birth certificates where the married parents were of the same sex at the same time that it was preferring marriage over biology for different-sex married parents. The Supreme Court's mandate left no doubt that Ohio could not discriminate in this way.[40]

Based on nothing more than the requirements of ordinary stare decisis, *Pavan* was correctly decided, and we remain puzzled that the disposition was not unanimous. More important, there are good reasons why *Obergefell, Lawrence,* and *Romer* should be considered super-precedents, foundational decisions that deeply reflect the needs of society and affect the evolution of the law. This cluster of decisions effected the constitutional transition from outlaws to in-laws for lesbian, gay, and bisexual persons. *Lawrence* held that gay people could not be considered presumptive criminals because of their intimate relationships; *Romer* held that they could not, as a class, be excluded from the ordinary protections of the law; *Obergefell* held that states could not deny them fundamental freedoms like marriage. Every one of these decisions was justified by the original public meaning of the Fourteenth Amendment, by analogous Supreme Court precedent, and by the democratic pluralism that undergirds the Constitution.[41]

Consider another species of anti-gay regulations: statutes and policies barring sex educators from encouraging or promoting homosexuality. A classic "no promo homo" law is a 1992 Alabama statute imposing this duty on public schools: "Classes must emphasize, in a factual manner and from a public health perspective, that homosexuality is not a lifestyle acceptable to the general public and that homosexual conduct is a criminal offense under the laws of the state." This law is at war with the Fourteenth Amendment—but it is not clear whether the Alabama or US Supreme Court would invalidate the law.[42]

To begin with, the second clause of the law is flatly unconstitutional. Although Alabama does in fact criminalize homosexual conduct, its consensual sodomy law cannot be constitutionally enforced after *Lawrence*. As a corollary to *Lawrence*, the consensual sodomy law cannot be the predicate for normative instruction in public schools. There are equal protection as well as due process problems with the first clause. From a "public health perspective," lesbian relationships are virtually AIDS-free and have lower rates of STDs than straight or gay male relationships. To the extent that the law demonizes safe homosexual activities, it is so much at odds with responsible sex education that the policy is arbitrary in that respect. Such a law, if actually enforced, would mislead and harm students. Consider the validity of the remainder, the core, of the statute: Is it constitutional for Alabama to teach schoolchildren that "homosexuality is not a lifestyle acceptable to the general public"?[43]

As a description of public opinion, the Alabama statute would be defensible, but as a mandatory subject of moral instruction to students, this command seems like precisely the kind of "class legislation" that was the object of the equal protection clause. Recall Charles Sumner's explanation of the equal protection concept: every citizen ought to be treated by the polity as "one of the children of the State, which, like an impartial parent, regards all its offspring with an equal care." Alabama's gratuitous demonization of gay people violates this standard and imposes real harm. Federal health experts have concluded that depression, estrangement, and suicide among gay teens remain serious social problems that are made worse by anti-gay curricula and policies.[44]

To be sure, the Supreme Court defers to state and local public school policies, and its deference decisions provide some arguments even for objectionable sexuality-based guidelines. In *Hazelwood School District v. Kuhlmeier* (1988), for example, the court allowed educators to censor a high school newspaper's story about experiences with teen pregnancies—an action that under almost any other circumstance would violate the press clause of the First Amendment. On the other hand, the stark denigration of and discrimination against an entire class of citizens in the Alabama statute poses a deeper equal protection problem than was presented in cases like *Hazelwood*. Suppose, for instance, that Alabama allowed public schools to teach the history of religion but included a directive that "Islam is not a lifestyle acceptable to the general public." Such a statute ought to be considered unconstitutional under the religion clauses of the First Amendment or (if there were no such clauses) the equal protection clause of the Fourteenth.[45]

In *Romer*, the Supreme Court found relevant "the absence of precedent" for the Colorado anti-gay initiative and ruled that "discriminations of an unusual character especially suggest careful consideration to determine whether they are obnoxious" to the equal protection clause. Although the court has not explained exactly what it meant by "careful consideration," this can only be a more demanding standard of review than the classic rational basis approach, and it might counteract the justices' customary deference to local education policy. We now pose a related question: Should courts take review of anti-LGBTQ+ policies to the next level?[46]

The Second and Ninth Circuits have held that sexual orientation meets the requirements the Supreme Court has announced for considering a classification suspect or quasi-suspect and therefore subject to heightened scrutiny. In the marriage cases decided in 2008–2009, the Connecticut, Iowa, and California Supreme Courts made such findings under their state constitutions. The four *Frontiero* factors (named after the leading Supreme Court decision) for determining whether a discriminatory classification triggers heightened scrutiny under the equal protection clause are (1) whether the excluded class has been historically subject to pervasive discrimination; (2) whether the classification "frequently bears [a] relation to ability to perform or contribute to society"; (3) whether the classification reflects "obvious, immutable, or distinguishing characteristics"; and (4) whether the class is "a minority or politically powerless." In the years since these factors were articulated, the US Supreme Court has created new suspect classifications only twice, for sex and nonmarital birth.[47]

Although not resting upon heightened equal protection scrutiny, *Obergefell* gave gay rights lawyers ammunition for satisfying those four factors. Justice Kennedy's opinion described the country's long history of discrimination against lesbian and gay people in criminal law, government employment, military service, and immigration law (relevant to item (1)). The opinion found "powerful confirmation" that "gays and lesbians can create loving, supportive families," showing an important way in which sexual orientation is not relevant to an individual's abilities and capacities for good citizenship (item (2)). And the *Obergefell* majority declared that "sexual orientation is both a normal expression of human sexuality and immutable" (relevant to item (3)). Just as religious faith is "bred in the marrow" because it is so natural to people that it seems to be in their bones, so, too, is heterosexuality or homosexuality.[48]

Obergefell justices were keenly divided as to whether sexual minorities are "politically powerless" (item (4)). Supreme Court decisions recognizing race as a suspect classification and sex as a quasi-suspect classification came in the mid-1960s and mid-1970s, respectively—just when both racial minorities and women were scoring much greater successes in Congress and in state legislatures than sexual minorities are scoring today. The Civil Rights Act of 1964 and Congress's endorsement of the ERA in 1972 were but two examples. The court in that era considered political powerlessness to include situations where, because of pervasive discrimination against a stigmatized group, it was fair to reverse the burden of inertia with regard to discriminatory laws. This resembles the way state judges Ron George and Richard Palmer treated that factor in the California and Connecticut marriage cases, respectively.[49]

Ironically, the state and federal political gains achieved by the LGBTQ+ minority were impressive during the campaign for marriage equality. By 2008, twenty states had enacted employment anti-discrimination laws, and thirty states had hate crime laws. Marriage equality brought many more people (including many straight persons) into the gay rights movement, excited funders more than other issues did, and directly addressed anti-gay stereotypes. At the grassroots level, the marriage campaign persuaded increasing numbers of Americans that Kameny had been right all along: gay is not just tolerable but good. The nationwide triumph of marriage equality coincided with political victories at the national level, including a hate crime law and the repeal of the military exclusion. In 2015, Utah became the first conservative Republican state to enact a sexual orientation, gender identity (SOGI) anti-discrimination law.[50]

In some respects, political progress has stalled since *Obergefell*. Most LGBTQ+ persons are not married but are employed, and job discrimination protections have lagged. The proposed Employment Non-Discrimination Act passed the House of Representatives in 2007 and 2009. A broader Equality Act passed the House on May 17, 2019, but has not been taken up by the Senate. Federal judicial decisions interpreting Title VII's sex discrimination protections to protect sexual and gender minorities have been very controversial. (The Supreme Court will resolve the conflict among lower federal courts this year.) With bitter party polarization paralyzing state legislatures, SOGI laws have hit a brick wall since 2015. Republican voters are turned off by anti-discrimination discourse and issue framing; marriage *equality* and the liberty-plus-equality holding of *Obergefell* have contributed to gridlock by raising the stakes of SOGI laws. Because most clashes between religious liberty and marriage equality are litigated under SOGI laws, conservative faith traditions and their allies fervently oppose new laws.[51]

Interest Convergence and Minorities Left Behind

The marriage equality movement conforms to Derrick Bell's thesis that social movements tend to succeed only when their demands coincide with mainstream economic or ideological interests. Professor Bell described *Brown v. Board of Education* (1954) not as a great triumph of judicial compassion for a badly treated minority but as the convergence of the interests of people of color with the interests of the white military-industrial establishment, which feared that apartheid was holding the country back in the Cold War and in economic development. "The interest of blacks in achieving racial equality," he prophesied, "will be accommodated only when it converges with the interests of whites."[52]

So long as most Americans felt that lesbian and gay couples did not want the same thing married couples did or believed that gay marriage was a threat to their children or even to marriage itself, freedom to marry triggered significant resistance and backlash. Only after most Americans concluded that expanding marriage would not harm treasured institutions or unduly influence children and that it would benefit relatives and neighbors who shared their values did the idea take off among judges, legislators, government lawyers, and voters. As described in chapter 18, the 2012 ballot campaigns epitomized this interest convergence. Crusty Maine patriarch Harlan Gardner, war hero John Kriesel in Minnesota, the Reverend Delman Coates and Bishop Donté Hickman in Maryland, and dozens of Washington State Cougars all spoke up for their gay relatives, military colleagues, parishioners, and fellow students. Their message: They're just like straight, and we love 'em.[53]

Constitutional marriage litigation was an important mechanism by which interest convergence operated. Doctrinally, sexual and gender minorities' best hope for securing marriage rights was through the prism of constitutional protections for either liberty or equal protection. Both constitutional doctrines funneled the movement's arguments into the rhetoric of sameness. The due process liberty argument rested on *vertical sameness:* lesbian and gay couples were a fit for the traditional purposes of marriage (with procreation morphing into raising children). The equal protection argument rested upon *horizontal sameness:* lesbian and gay unions were similar to straight couples' marriages. The *Obergefell* oral argument was a ritualized dance where one justice after another demanded that Mary Bonauto explain why marriage for gays and lesbians was not disturbingly different from traditional marriage, and she struggled to find new ways to say that nothing will change; you are safe with us.

The flip side of interest-convergence theory is that any social movement asking for a *redistribution* of rights, status, benefits, or resources faces a steep uphill battle. The welfare rights social movement of the early 1970s rested on a robust moral theory of decent treatment, generated media attention, and enjoyed support among academics, but it fizzled and may have set the cause of welfare recipients back politically. Generally, when racial integration has threatened to impose significant costs on white people, opposition has increased and advances have stalled. Once the opponents of any social movement persuasively translate its goals into a zero-sum game, the social movement's advances are slowed, thwarted, or reversed. In the marriage equality debate, supporters of one-man, one-woman marriage were originally able to frame the issue as zero-sum—but by 2012, marriage equality advocates had turned the tables.[54]

An important consequence of Professor Bell's theory is to minimize Justice Alito's concern that marriage equality for LGBT couples would slide inevitably into constitutionally required incestuous and plural marriages. There is no social movement on the horizon to orchestrate a social, political, and legal campaign to expand marriage along those lines. In light of concerns by both religious conservatives and feminist liberals, any such campaign would face long odds to persuade Americans that polygamy would be costless and would not create risks for women, children, and the institution of marriage. For these practical reasons, Alito's slippery slope was more of a statement of political philosophy than a serious constitutional prediction.[55]

The interest-convergence thesis also reinforces the warnings Paula Ettelbrick made in the 1980s: marriage equality would mostly benefit a subset of the gay community—specifically, the subset already most like the mainstream (chapter 3). In the last generation, marriage rates have held up pretty well for higher-income Americans but have plummeted for lower-income and jobless Americans. The latter often cannot afford to get married and set up a stable household, and they secure fewer economic benefits from marriage. The economic effect also contributes to a race effect: people of color are much less likely to marry than white people. Unmarried lower-income gays could be worse off than they were before *Obergefell* because the triumphalist account of winning marriage obliterated concerns that marriage itself has become a privatized welfare system and an excuse for not devoting resources to the economically disadvantaged. As far back as 1982, Dr. Amos Cleophilus Brown opposed San Francisco's domestic partnership ordinance because it did nothing to address the problems confronting the city's black community, including gays and lesbians of color. Marriage equality, posed as the great civil rights issue of our time, has attracted black support with little (if any) tangible commitment by the marriage movement to economic equalization or safety-net justice.[56]

On the other hand, marriage equality may have contributed to more positive attitudes toward sexual minorities and may contribute to greater racial diversity in the long-segregated institution of marriage. Analyzing the 2010 census data, UCLA's Williams Institute found that 20.6 percent of lesbian and gay couples were different-race, compared with 18.3 percent of straight unmarried couples and 9.5 percent of straight married couples. The study also showed that mixed-race lesbian and gay couples were more likely to be raising children, and we know from the *Obergefell* case that many white lesbian and gay couples are raising children of different races. Those new images will contribute to an unpredictable array of changes and will complicate any simple view of marriage equality as nothing more than interest convergence. Marriage equality has also interacted with—and perhaps facilitated—a broader social movement that is upending gender norms in our society and expanding the acronym under which gay rights has been parading of late.[57]

Beyond Gender: Beyond Marriage?

Transgender persons feel an incongruity between their sex assigned at birth and their gender identity. They have been important participants in the marriage equality movement—starting with Neva Heckman, the first freedom-to-marry plaintiff, and continuing with Christie Littleton, the plaintiff in the first DOMA case, and Shannon Minter, who argued the California *Marriage Cases*. In the 1990s, Littleton's lawyer, Phyllis Frye, strenuously objected to the gay rights movement's neglect of gender identity issues. If Kameny was the parent of the gay rights movement, Frye was the parent of the transgender rights movement. More than any other lawyer, she added the *T* to *LGBT*, while younger queers and gender dissenters have added the *Q* and other letters to the expanding acronym. Frye and her allies have spent decades creating a vocabulary, social framework, and normative valence to help transgender persons express their identities and create productive lives for themselves in a more tolerant or accepting society.[58]

The marriage equality movement generated messaging insights that have been deployed in similar campaigns seeking to preserve anti-discrimination rights for transgender persons. As part of a national LGBT movement public education campaign, the Movement Advancement Project (MAP) developed *Restaurant*, a sixty-second ad that aired on the Fox News channel during the last night of the 2016 Republican National Convention. Exploiting insights from MAP's post-*Obergefell* messaging research on LGBT nondiscrimination, the ad told an evocative story of a transgender woman enjoying coffee with her friends. When she excused herself to use the restroom, the restaurant's manager interceded and demanded that she use the men's room; two young men sneered at her menacingly. A female customer joined them outside the restrooms and implored the manager to respect the woman's needs; a third woman emerged from the restroom and ushered the trans woman inside, followed by the supportive customer. In her voice-over, the transgender woman conceded that the law cannot change attitudes, but it could help her meet such basic needs as using the restroom safely. This ad confronted the main concern voiced by people objecting to trans-protective laws and emotionally engaged the viewer to join the cisgender women in resolving the situation productively.[59]

In 2018, Massachusetts voters overwhelmingly rejected an initiative to override a 2016 trans-inclusive anti-discrimination law. Freedom for All Massachusetts, an umbrella coalition of LGBTQ+ groups, mounted a campaign right out of the 2012 freedom to marry playbook: encourage transgender youth to come out to their parents, friends, and teachers; deploy parents and other cisgender speakers as unexpected messengers supporting equal treatment; and saturate the airwaves and churches with appealing advocates and messages. We were moved by an ad featuring Ian, a transgender boy, and his mom, Trish. She was concerned that Ian would not be allowed the same fair opportunities as his sibling. Speaking parent to parent, Trish concluded simply, "I want both my kids to be protected against discrimination." In contrast to the 2012 marriage equality messaging, the 2019 trans equality messaging also included ads where trans persons (like Ian) spoke for themselves and not just through the filters of their cisgender parents and other unexpected messengers.[60]

The evolving gender debate has already broadened beyond the use of restrooms by transgender persons. The same process of hermeneutical dissent that generated positive vocabularies and frameworks for gay and trans persons is now being developed by individuals with nonbinary gender identities, who do not exclusively identify with either sex. Such persons may identify as gender-fluid, genderqueer, or other self-definitions. Sayre Reece, who masterminded the grassroots activism key to the 2012 ballot victories, is a nonbinary person who was important for the marriage equality movement. After *Obergefell*, not only can nonbinary and transgender persons marry the partner of their choice without having to worry about sex-matching, but because marriage is linked with so many laws and regulations, marriage equality removes many marital rules from the matters that might be hassles for gender minorities.[61]

Theorists of gender and sexuality have offered a variety of suggestions for legal reform. Perhaps the simplest approach would be *recognition of gender pluralism,* allowing the individual choice as to which category they/he/she falls into. Sonia Katyal advocates more than two categories on official and other documents. Dean Spade and Heath Fogg Davis, among others, argue for government *neutrality or anti-classification.* They would eliminate sex as a government classification altogether, a proposal that is more feasible in the post-*Obergefell* world but might impose burdens on medical research and diagnostics, for example. Practical lawyers and academics like Jessica Clarke take an *ad hoc, context-dependent approach.* They make the more limited claim that government impositions of sex-binary rules upon unwilling individuals are arbitrary or even due process violations unless they can be justified by a reasonable public policy.[62]

More generally, the emergence of a variety of gender minorities has queered the larger social movement, pressing it toward more radical proposals that enable marginal members of the political community the same freedom of self-determination that marriage equality has brought to some lesbian and gay couples. Because the social movement for sexual and gender minorities now covers so much variety, with potentially more letters for the LGBTQ+ acronym, Jonathan Rauch has proposed a simplification: drop the *LGBT* and call the cluster of minorities *Q.* The fate of such proposals rests with the next generation of Americans.[63]

As Table 2 speculates, younger nonbinary and transgender persons are also pressing this expanded social movement to embrace more radical conceptualizations of sexuality and gender. Long flanked on the right by natural law thinking, the liberal philosophy that undergirds the marriage equality movement is now flanked on the left by a radical philosophy maintaining that sex as well as gender are social more than biological creations and that self-determination at the personal and relationship levels ought to trump conventional categories.[64]

The progressive principle of self-determination presses a great body of progressive thinking "Beyond Marriage," a statement of principles signed by more than 250 scholars and intellectuals since it was promulgated in 2006. "Beyond Marriage" argues that society ought not privilege marriage based on tradition or religious endorsement but, instead, ought to support a variety of caregiving relationships. The marriage movement teaches us that the law can construct new mechanisms, and we shall explore them in chapter 24.[65]

Table 2: The Social Movement Continuum (LGBTQ+)

Natural law	Liberal	Radical
God/Nature made man and woman sexual and gender complements	Natural variation in sex, gender, and sexuality	No natural baseline for gender and (perhaps) sex
Sexual perverts and gender inverts are predatory and dangerous	Sexual and gender minorities are basically the same as mainstream persons	Queers or nonbinary persons happy to be not mainstream; value in diversity
Compulsory cisgender heterosexuality	Compulsory regimes wrong when overriding personhood	Sexuality, sex, gender are all about individual choice and expression
Predators and criminals	Full citizens; in-laws and relatives	Full citizens; evolving human beings
Criminalization; mental institutions	Anti-discrimination rules; marriage or partnership	Self-determination; caregiving and community
Due process rights; criminal procedure	Equal protection; privacy rights	Diminution or erasure of sex and gender as classifications; First Amendment (expression)

Marriage Equality and Other Social Movements

Despite its unique features, marriage equality offers important lessons for other social movements in the new millennium. To recap, the marriage campaign suggests that a social movement is most likely to change public opinion if (1) its beneficiaries are widely dispersed and out of the closet so that they can generate unexpected messengers to vouch for basic liberties for those persons; (2) its proposals are not perceived to impose significant social costs on the community or harms on third parties, in part because society is already moving in the direction of its moral vision; and (3) it can back up its petition for equal protection with a coordinated campaign of public education and government support at the state and federal levels and among executives and legislators as well as judges. This last point exploits the notion of *polycentric constitutionalism*—the possibility of floating constitutional proposals at differ-

ent levels (local, state, federal) and different institutions of government (judicial, legislative, executive). Consider the implications for several different social
movements.[66]

THE NEW RELIGIOUS MINORITY

A traditional family values social movement emerged in the 1970s to oppose
the broad social changes brought by the previous decade's sexual revolution,
including most prominently gay rights and abortion. Many religious Americans saw gay marriage as an existential threat. Mrs. Phyllis Schlafly wrote in
1974 that any state recognition of same-sex marriages would "be a grave interference with the rights of the rest of our citizens" to religious freedom and to
control of their children's education. Because conjugal marriage and gender
complementarity were central tenets of their faiths, the Church of Jesus Christ
of Latter-day Saints, the Southern Baptist Convention, and the Catholic Church
supported STOP ERA and opposed same-sex marriage. With the advance of
marriage equality as a constitutional right, would traditionalist religion be demoted from the dominant cultural position its members had long enjoyed to
a tolerance or even outlaw status? In other words, religious conservatives fear
that their normative fate will move in reverse—away from the traditional view
that faith is the backbone of America and toward the view that religious institutions are the incubators of prejudice. This is why Justice Alito asked Solicitor General Verrilli during the *Obergefell* oral argument whether churches
declining to celebrate same-sex marriages would lose their tax exemptions as
charitable institutions.[67]

The religious family values movement parallels the marriage equality movement, with a powerful central message (religion is good, and your eternal
salvation depends on following God's directives); an ongoing campaign that
has been influential in every branch and at every level of government; and
some unexpected messengers, including hedonistic capitalists and social progressives. The religious values movement enjoys a wealth of funding and institutions that advance its agenda—ranging from established churches and
religious persons to litigation organizations such as ADF, which now has more
money and affiliated lawyers than the ACLU, to the Republican Party, whose
electoral interests are intimately tied to the movement. By the way, the foregoing analysis provides an explanation for the Evangelicals' embrace of Donald Trump, notwithstanding his disinterest in theology and defiance of
biblical norms of discourse and behavior. Trump is the ultimate unexpected

messenger and as president offers the added bonus of opening the doors of executive and judicial power to religious values supporters. (Politics makes strange bedfellows. The Democratic Party of the New Deal brought south-ern segregationists, Catholic workers, and urban minorities and liberals into a mega-coalition.)

Widely reviled at tony law schools, ADF lawyers have learned valuable stra-tegic lessons from Frank Schubert (the architect of the Proposition 8 victory) and from Evan Wolfson (the longtime champion of marriage as a goal for the gay rights movement). Americans don't like denying basic freedoms to decent citizens, and they do like the Golden Rule. Marriage equality foundered when Americans believed that it would impose unwanted rules on traditionalist par-ents and churches; marriage equality prevailed once most Americans were convinced that gay couples and their extended families really would benefit from a freedom to marry. The endless stream of ADF-sponsored post–marriage equality cases returns to the earlier Schubert narrative, but with more cogency because of perceived intolerance on the marriage equality side. Should a reli-gious pastry artist be forced to create a wedding cake with two women on top? Faced with a $100,000 fine for refusing? ADF lawyers feast on these scenar-ios like famished dieters.

Like the marriage equality campaign, ADF's campaign for ever-expanding conscience exemptions would entail normative trade-offs. Recall from earlier chapters that, since 2003, traditional religious values organizations had been on notice that anti-gay rhetoric turned away potential supporters. In order to press for the Federal Marriage Amendment and the state Super-DOMAs, the traditional values movement jettisoned outmoded leaders (like Reverend Sullivan and, ultimately, Dr. Dobson) and retired the "abominable vice" tropes that were the bread and butter of ADF's founder, Alan Sears. The new genera-tion of ADF leaders, such as John Bursch (who argued for the states in *Oberge-fell* and in 2018 became the ADF's chief appellate litigator), not only treat gay people more like in-laws than outlaws but internally deliberate the prospect that they ought to acquiesce in the legitimacy of *Obergefell* itself.[68]

REPRODUCTIVE FREEDOM

Broadly understood, the reproductive freedom movement may have been America's most successful social movement of the last century. Margaret Sanger, the founder of Planned Parenthood (the movement's mother ship), was one of the greatest norm entrepreneurs in American history. Through relentless organizing, publicity, and support among families from all walks of life, her notion of constitutional privacy triumphed over state and federal restrictions on contraceptives, and the positive norm of family planning swept aside religion-based objections. Marriage equality was one by-product of this social movement: Sanger advocated to a receptive population that marriage is about love, commitment, and sexual pleasure that is delinked from procreation. Conservative Republicans vied with liberal Democrats to endorse her project.[69]

A corollary of Sanger's movement has been women's freedom to choose abortion—a more controversial idea than contraception-based family planning. The pro-choice social movement shares many features that fueled the success of marriage equality, including a beneficiary group (women) that is widely dispersed and way more numerous; a sharply focused norm appealing to freedom from government control of women's lives and of families; well-funded organizations conducting a coordinated campaign to support pro-choice policies and constitutional principles; and some unexpected allies among religious leaders and conservative politicians.

An important difference is that while queer people have been streaming out of their sexual and gender closets, women have retreated into abortion closets. One consequence of women's reticence about discussing their abortion decisions is that people have incorrect understandings about the basic facts: the typical American thinks that 10 percent of women will have an abortion (the real number is around 25 percent) and that abortion is a risky medical procedure (many women die in childbirth; virtually none during medical abortions). Few Americans think they know a woman who has had an abortion, and those who do know someone often have no idea of the complicated moral journey she took before having the procedure. Younger Americans are more likely to know these journey stories and are correspondingly more supportive of pro-choice policies.[70]

Although large majorities of Americans support *Roe v. Wade* (1973), the pro-choice movement has been losing most of its twenty-first-century battles. One reason is that the pro-life movement has adopted a brilliant strategy: focus attacks on the supply of abortion, such as the availability of doctors, clinics, and funds, rather than on the demand for abortion by pregnant women. (Demand-side attacks have homed in on parental concerns about their daughters' sexual behaviors, another smart strategy.) Another reason is that pro-life voters in the last thirty years seem to care about the issue much more than pro-choice voters—so politicians know they are more likely to face retribution at the polls if they go against the pro-life stance. A final reason may be that a lot of Americans, including some who are pro-choice, are uncertain about the moral status of the fetus. The charge of murder makes them anxious.[71]

The pro-choice movement needs creative strategies if its leaders want to reverse the political tide. A Supreme Court decision openly overruling *Roe v. Wade* would be a judicial gift to the pro-choice movement because it would be a mega-public event that would galvanize tens of millions into more aggressive political mobilization. Short of that, the movement needs to build on experience with persuasive argumentation. Consider a lesson Victoria Nourse taught us from the congressional deliberations over the Violence Against Women Act of 1994 (VAWA), Joe Biden's signature accomplishment as a senator. The ranking Republican on Biden's Judiciary Committee, Utah senator Orrin Hatch led the opposition—until his counsel and Nourse organized a public hearing in Salt Lake City. One Mormon woman after another spoke from the heart about violence she had suffered. These were people Hatch identified with, and he was in tears by the end of the hearing. VAWA passed by acclamation in the Senate. Moments like this are a start.[72]

Katha Pollitt suggests a deeper reason why pro-life positions are doing so well, especially compared with the opponents of marriage equality. Marriage equality benefited men as well as women, while abortion choice is understood to benefit only women, and at a cost to husbands, fathers, and boyfriends, who perceive that they lose some degree of control over the fetuses they helped create and over the bodies and sexuality of women. As our account of the marriage equality campaign suggests, Pollitt's challenge is central to the pro-choice movement: not only do women need to come out of the abortion closet, but they need to persuade some of their fathers, husbands, and boyfriends that abortion choice is in their interests as well. "[Men] suffer when a pregnancy pushes them into marriage, or into marriage with the wrong person," Pollitt suggests. "For men as for women, ill-timed or unwanted children can mean giving up ambitions and dreams." So men need to talk about that—and they need to speak out about how their lives and their families' lives have been improved by responsible choices made by their daughters, wives, and girlfriends.[73]

Such a double-edged campaign—women coming out of the abortion closet and men telling their journey stories toward abortion choice—would have to be massively funded. Research-based messages would need to saturate the media, become available to educators and schools, influence medical schools, agencies, and state legislatures—and it would need to do all that without triggering a significant backlash. Opinion might soften as a result of testimony by religious mothers about how their lives were shattered when their sisters or daughters died of pregnancy complications, by husbands who could not support a growing family and bonded with their wives over family planning, and by fathers who respected their daughters' decisions not to bear children conceived as a result of sexual assault or supervisor pressure. The value of these unexpected messengers is that conflicted voters could identify with them and thereby be more susceptible to their arguments that abortion is a social good and not a moral embarrassment. Ironically, abortion-rights campaigns seeking to erode the power of patriarchy might need to deploy the patriarchs themselves as spokesmen. As we suggested earlier, however, women's voices are central and critical to any successful campaign.[74]

THE IMMIGRATION CLOSET

Australian citizen Tony Sullivan spent most of his marriage to Richard Adams hiding in the immigration closet because he was an inadmissible and deportable "alien" after he sneaked back into the country in 1986, as we reported in chapter 2. An estimated eight to ten million undocumented visitors inhabit the *immigration closet,* with pervasive effects on their and their families' lives. Although several organizations represent their interests and the human costs of American immigration policy are felt by these immigrants' American relatives, employers, priests, neighbors, and friends, the social movement to help these families has enjoyed mixed success, at best. Most Americans harbor inaccurate views about the relative costs of this population; in fact, because most undocumented immigrants pay income taxes but do not collect many federal or state benefits, their net contribution is greater than that of most citizen families.[75]

Several reasons underlie the lack of success: because they could be deported, few undocumented immigrants are able to come out of the closet, and fewer still get to tell their journey stories to help attract unexpected messengers. When they do tell their stories, opponents are able to marginalize them as lawbreakers. Businessman Donald Trump has relied on undocumented workers to staff his resort properties, but that has not prevented him, as president, from stereotyping such immigrants and making open appeals to ethnicity-based prejudice. When they dare to come out of the closet and accuse him of hypocrisy, he dismisses them as deceitful criminals. Even the images and stories about immigrant children separated from their parents and housed in cages has caused little shift in overall public opinion. As with gay people before Stonewall, the nascent social movement for undocumented immigrants will have to rely on legal groups enforcing procedural protections. This movement will not be able to make big gains until large numbers of allied American citizens become energized in coalition with unexpected messengers. Not until immigrants can command a campaign that combines lawyers and lobbyists, grassroots mobilization and campaign contributions, and dramatic public education will they be able to transform American public norms.[76]

Frank Kameny lived to see the tide turn in favor of a gay-friendly Constitution. In August 2009, he was invited to the White House to participate in President Obama's signing of a memorandum to provide a number of nonmarital federal benefits to same-sex couples. Kameny died on October 11, 2011, just months after the Obama administration announced its view that sexual orientation was constitutionally suspect as a discriminatory classification—half a century after his Supreme Court brief introduced that very precept. Less than four years later, with *Obergefell,* Kameny's vision of an America where gay people would be treated like in-laws rather than outlaws was vindicated. Gay was officially Good.

But there were double edges to Kameny's vindication. To begin with, none of those benefits could help Frank himself. Since the 1950s, when he lost track of the love of his life, this lone wolf had no special partner; there was an ambiguous relationship with a young man living in the basement of his house, but his friends report that the relationship provided neither care nor concern for Frank's well-being. If Frank was married to anything, it was to the gay rights movement, which was a fickle lover. Because he sacrificed a career, together with a 401(k) account and a regular source of income, he spent his twilight years in penury. Even as he was feted and honored downtown by the White House and HRC, he sometimes could not pay for a taxi to get back to his home in Northwest Washington. A small group of donors and volunteers provided him with essentials and company in his last years.

Moreover, the constitutional campaign that brought marriage equality to all fifty states, the District of Columbia, and Puerto Rico (but still not American Samoa) relied on a messaging strategy inconsistent with the self-determination strain of Frank Kameny's activism. Recall that in 1961 he deplored the conformity that society and the state imposed on sexual and gender outlaws. The campaign to turn LGBTQ+ people from outlaws to in-laws did not benefit all such Americans and, more important, rested on television ads, videos, and interviews in which unexpected messengers vouched for their "just like straight" gay children, parishioners, and military colleagues. Long retired from a guiding role in the movement, Kameny understood how such a campaign, saturated with interest convergence, would not only leave behind many sexual and gender rebels but would for many of them impose a social conformity that in his younger days he would have denounced as odious.[77]

23 • The Golden Rule

The gay population and many faith traditions have sharply contrasting moral visions. For that reason, zealous advocates in both communities often understand religious liberty and marriage equality as a zero-sum exchange in a "culture war." The Golden Rule (Matthew 7:12) offers the terms for a less adversarial exchange: "Do unto others as you would have them do unto you."[1]

During research for this volume, we spoke with dozens of faith leaders and visited churches all over America. On November 15, 2015, just months after *Obergefell*, one of us attended services at St. Paul's Lutheran Church in St. Claire Shores, Michigan—the church where Ken and Wendy DeBoer were married and in which they raised their children, Ken Jr. and April. A member of the traditionalist Lutheran Church—Missouri Synod, St. Paul's displays a framed statement of faith in its fellowship hall. Belief #11 is that "God creates each person as male or female" and that to "reject one's gender is to reject the Creator's work." Belief #12 is that marriage is an "institution of God, and is defined by uniting one man with one woman unto one flesh." In 2015, the pastor and officers of St. Paul's were all men. (Recently, the Missouri Synod gave local churches the option to include women as officers.) Ken DeBoer was the vice president of the congregation. His former wife, Wendy, and his daughter, April, no longer worshipped at this church, in large part because of the clash between April's lesbian marriage and Belief #12.[2]

We were warmly greeted by the president of the congregation. When we inquired about April DeBoer, he told us that the congregation was proud of her commitment to the children she and her partner were raising so wonderfully. He hoped that April would ask St. Paul's to baptize her children within the church. We also met the Reverend David Rutter, his wife, Susan, and their two teenage kids. Drawing from Matthew 25:31–46, the pastor's sermon that morning drew a sharp distinction between the sheep saved by Christ and the goats damned for eternity.

At the adult Sunday school class, we sat next to Dave, a former Catholic who married into the Lutheran Church. We talked about same-sex marriage, which he opposed because the Bible taught him that marriage was all about procreation. If marriage were just about love and desire, there would be no reason not to allow relatives or threesomes to marry. But lesbian and gay couples do raise children, we suggested. He was okay with civil unions and spoke warmly about his gay brother-in-law, who absolutely, he believed, would make a great father someday. He said St. Paul's was concerned that its traditionalist stance would earn it the label of a hate group. We pooh-poohed the idea, but less than a year later the US Commission on Civil Rights issued a report called *Peaceful Coexistence* in which the chair of the commission worried that *religious liberty* and *religious freedom* are sometimes deployed as "code words for discrimination, intolerance, racism, sexism, homophobia, Islamophobia, Christian supremacy or any form of intolerance."[3]

At the end of Sunday school, we asked Reverend Rutter about April DeBoer's children, and he thoroughly endorsed the idea of baptizing them. When Ken DeBoer remarried within the church, he and his second wife met with the pastor. The new wife reportedly inquired: "From the church's point of view, how should I interact with my lesbian stepdaughter?" Rutter responded: "Love her! She's family and a child of God." This theologically conservative congregation seemed fine with gay people and surprisingly acquiescent in civil marriage for lesbian and gay couples.

Our visit to St. Paul's helped us understand how culture war rhetoric mischaracterizes the dynamic marriage debate and the relationship between faith communities and gay families. The expanded freedom to marry has created more possibilities for conflict between the equal treatment of more open LGBTQ+ persons and the religious liberty of a diminishing number of persons and institutions. The Alliance Defending Freedom (ADF) and other organizations have seized upon conflicts between traditionalist wedding vendors and same-sex couples to publicize battles in a conflict they are hyping—but the wedding vendor cases ought not overshadow the common ground between LGBTQ+ equality and religious liberty. By the way, the focus on wedding vendors also obscures the more important interaction of anti-discrimination rules with employment and screening policies in institutions substantially controlled or managed by churches and organized religions—parochial schools and universities, religious nonprofits, and so forth.

We did not feel embattled at St. Paul's, and its congregants and pastor did not seem under siege. The main effect of marriage equality for their congregation and for most other traditionalist churches has been more encounters with real LGBTQ+ families, including families linked with their own congregants, such as Ken DeBoer. These families have destabilized exclusionary practices and are softening doctrinal lines. The presence of gay families, especially marriages with children, tends to move the conversation away from sinful sexual practices toward family-based commitment, support for children, and love for your neighbor. When the gay families come from within the church (pop-up families), church leaders create internal tensions and hard feelings if they condemn and exclude. Once congregants come out of the closet as parents of gay children and grandparents of their kids, the conversation moves further away from centuries-old dogma toward pastoral concerns: How can we be helpful? The Golden Rule kicks in.[4]

For these internal reasons, there will continue to be variety and evolution in how faith communities respond to marriage equality and *Obergefell*. These responses will vary both among denominations and within them. In contrast to the Lutheran Church—Missouri Synod, the Evangelical Lutheran Church in America (ELCA) has adopted a policy of allowing local congregations to celebrate lesbian and gay marriages. Martin Luther himself was, conceptually, on both sides of the issue: he believed that marriage was between one man and one woman and that sodomy was sinful, but he rejected the Roman Catholic tradition of marriage as a sacrament focused primarily on procreation and also viewed it in terms of companionship, love, and mutual support, modern ideas reflected in *Obergefell*. Even within the Missouri Synod, attitudes have moved. The Pew Research Center found the synod's members split 44-47 percent against affirming attitudes toward homosexuality in 2007—but 56-37 percent the other way by 2014.[5]

There was anxiety within St. Paul's that the new constitutional and social norms would limit their free exercise of religion. Would their church have to celebrate same-sex weddings? Nope, nor would it lose its tax-exempt status. Their church would not be required to hire a qualified gay man (or a woman of any sexual orientation) as its minister, or perhaps as its organist. What mainly concerned Reverend Rutter, however, was that his faith community would be shamed and shunned because it hewed to traditionalist marriage. These are realistic concerns.

One of the earliest religious thinkers to address the legal issues systematically was a remarkable member of the Quorum of the Twelve Apostles, part of the governing structure of the Church of Jesus Christ of Latter-day Saints. In 1984, Dallin Oaks wrote a statement of "Principles to Govern Possible Public Statement on Legislation Affecting Rights of Homosexuals." He synthesized church doctrine and its deeply gendered understanding of marriage and family, and he commented on these issues' legal and practical dimensions. For example, he urged the Church not to single out "homosexual sodomy" for criminalization but instead to focus its opposition on "homosexual marriage," which was most deeply inconsistent with Latter-day theology. Although no state in 1984 included sexual orientation in its comprehensive anti-discrimination statute, Elder Oaks saw growing support for such laws. Rather than oppose such legislation "across the board," he proposed that the Church support "well-reasoned exceptions" to protect faith concerns. Exactly thirty years later, the Church created an ad hoc committee on religious liberty and decided to support a Utah law protecting LGBT persons against discrimination, along with securing generous religious accommodations. Embodying the lessons of the Golden Rule, this statute of principles has been the foundation of a "Fairness for All" movement seeking intergroup dialogue to reconcile equality for LGBT persons with religious liberty for conservative persons of faith.[6]

In May 2018, the Michigan Civil Rights Commission ruled that its comprehensive civil rights law would consider LGBT exclusions to be sex discriminations. The commission opined that henceforth, employers, landlords, and public accommodations could not exclude sexual and gender minorities. By affording equal protection to these minorities, however, the commission raised religious liberty concerns among faith groups such as the Lutherans we met at church. How should the community achieve a balance between equality for LGBT persons and liberty for religious persons and institutions? Can the law constitutionally require a baker, florist, or photographer to provide goods or services for a same-sex wedding, notwithstanding faith-based or expressive objections? Does such a law require the government to terminate subsidies for or contracts with faith-based adoption or foster care agencies that will not place with LGBT families? Would it require religious schools to hire lesbian janitors or gay teachers or transgender administrators?[7]

The most publicized cases are those where a state anti-discrimination commission requires a private person or small business to provide a wedding-related service that runs against her/his/its faith tradition. Overshadowed by these cases, the larger issue is whether the state should legally require religiously affiliated schools, charitable institutions, and other nonprofits to provide their services or make employment decisions on a nondiscriminatory basis. Recall, from chapters 13 and 16, that New York and other states have largely refrained from pressing their anti-discrimination laws so far. Some states, like Michigan, have narrower statutory allowances. What constitutional limits might there be? In the wake of *Obergefell,* these issues are front and center.

We shall discuss the deep issues raised by these cases and the meta-principle that should help resolve them, namely, the Golden Rule's principle of reciprocality. Come up with a code of conduct for others that you would happily apply to yourself. To help figure that out, you need to discern the other person's point of view and accompany her or him on the moral journey taken to get to that point of view. The Golden Rule, therefore, entails a process as well as a precept. That process and precept are transforming American religion and seek to transform the public law of both conservative red states like Utah and blue states like New York. As law professors, we implore lawyers and judges not to get in the way. This chapter lays out the case for legislatures, more than courts, to take the lead to resolve or ameliorate conflicts involving religion, sexuality, and gender.

Social Norms, Constitutional Equality, and Religion

In 1975, when Clela Rorex issued marriage licenses to six lesbian and gay couples in Boulder, Colorado, all of them celebrated their marriages in religious ceremonies. Most American churches and synagogues at the time excluded lesbian and gay persons and families, but the Metropolitan Community Church, founded by the Reverend Troy Perry in 1968, focused on the faith needs of gay people and specialized in gay marriages and unions. The Congregationalists (United Church of Christ), Unitarians, Quakers, and Reformed Jews were dialoguing with and embracing openly lesbian and gay persons and their families. Some pastors, such as Roger Lynn (the Methodist minister who married Jack Baker and Mike McConnell), were willing on their own to officiate at lesbian and gay weddings. In the half century since 1968, there has been significant movement toward toleration and even acceptance among American religious denominations.

The most dramatic development has been an increased understanding of sexual and gender variation as natural and not matters of "perverse choice" and with that understanding a rejection of discrimination against LGBTQ+ persons because of who they are. As early as the 1970s, Reform and Conservative Jews, Congregationalists, Unitarians, Episcopalians, Presbyterians, and Lutherans condemned anti-gay discrimination as a matter of religious principle. In the last generation, they have been joined by the Catholics, Methodists, Latter-day Saints, the Islamic Society of North America, and many Evangelical Protestant denominations and independent megachurches. These developments are consistent with the Golden Rule, a precept embraced by the Old and New Testaments, the Prophet Muhammed, and most other religious and ethical traditions.[8]

That so many faith traditions condemn discrimination because of a person's self-identification as lesbian or gay does not mean that they accept the moral legitimacy of consensual sodomy or same-sex marriage. For example, the four largest denominations in this country—the Roman Catholic Church, the Southern Baptist Convention (SBC), the Church of Jesus Christ, and the United Methodist Church—remain committed, as a matter of religious doctrine, to the propositions that homosexual relations are sinful and same-sex marriage unacceptable. Likewise, Greek and Russian Orthodox Christianity, Islam's Sunni and Shiʻa sects, and Orthodox Judaism (major religions in the world) take the same positions as a matter of scriptural interpretation. On the other hand, the Methodists and other denominations are moving toward greater pastoral concern for and even acceptance of LGBTQ+ persons, especially those whose families are devoted worshippers.[9]

Among Jewish and mainstream Protestant traditions, the emerging norm is acceptance of LGBTQ+ congregants and clergy *and* recognition of same-sex unions as marriages those denominations will celebrate and recognize. The debate within the Presbyterian Church USA is illustrative. In the twentieth century, that denomination maintained that God made men and women as physical and gender complements, that the Bible sanctioned only conjugal marriage between one man and one woman, and that homosexual relations were morally wrong. The Reverend Mark Achtemeier led the Presbyterians to issue, in 1997, a ban on ordination of gay persons as ministers. Afterward, he had a series of encounters with anguished seminarians who felt torn apart by the conflict between their natural feelings and their devotion to God's Word. These individuals were dedicated Christians, yet Achtemeier discovered that "the result of this faithfulness was a depth of despair and brokenness that was very different from anything the Bible would lead us to expect." These experiences led him to reexamine the Bible—and to change his mind. Achtemeier not only led the campaign within the Presbyterian Church to ordain openly gay ministers but also supported a 2015 church rule allowing ministers and congregations to celebrate same-sex marriages.[10]

Reverend Achtemeier's journey story offers insight into the process that pressed American religion toward inclusion. Religious doctrine and practice have influenced social attitudes and constitutional law—but the converse is also true: evolving social norms and constitutional rulings have influenced pastoral practices, vocabularies for addressing LGBT persons, and even religious doctrine. The pastor's conversations could not have happened without these changes, as the gay seminarians would have been afraid to open up to a straight moralist. His willingness to revisit the Bible was encouraged by his wife, Katherine Morton Achtemeier, and their children, who understood that many lesbian and gay persons were committed partners and excellent parents. That Reverend Achtemeier went public with his views was fueled by ever greater and friendlier interest in the subject than we had found in the 1990s, when we documented the support for marriage equality among religious leaders in the Washington, DC, area.[11]

Our overall thesis is that, just as religion played a large role in the social and legal marriage equality debate, so, too, social norms and constitutional principles are playing a large role in deliberations regarding doctrine and pastoral practice within the country's religious denominations. The dialectic relationship among religious doctrine, social norms, and constitutional law was originally suggested to us by the Presbyterian Church's history on issues of race (one of us is Presbyterian). Nineteenth-century Southern Presbyterians justified slavery based on Noah's curse against the family of his son Ham (Genesis 9:22–27), supposedly the father of the African race—a gloss southerners tendentiously read into Genesis. After slavery's end, Presbyterian pastors invoked the Bible to justify racial segregation and bans on interracial marriage. Motivated by the increasingly sharp conflict between apartheid and human rights, during the twentieth century the Southern Presbyterians and other denominations revisited the Bible on these issues. By the 1960s, most Presbyterian and mainstream Protestant ministers supported civil rights. The Southern Baptists dragged their feet but ultimately got there as well.[12]

When social norms and constitutional status change, faith traditions come under pressure to update their doctrines and practices. Churches that disparage lesbian and gay couples risk social ostracism, as Justice Alito feared in *Windsor* and *Obergefell*. But most of the pressure to conform to social norms comes from within the faith community, not from the government or from

Table 3: Continuum of Religious Acceptance for Lesbian and Gay Faithful (2020)

Exclusion/Denial	Tolerance/Pastoral	Acceptance/Marriage
Benedict XVI Catholics	Francis I Catholics and Jesuits	New Ways Ministry
Russian/Greek Orthodox	Old Anglicans	Episcopalians
Old Southern Baptists	New Southern Baptists	Alliance of Baptists
Dr. Land and Dr. Mohler	Dr. Moore and Rev. Greear	Cooperative Baptist Fellowship
Thomas Road Baptist Megachurch	North Point Megachurch	EastLake Megachurch
Assemblies of God	United Methodists	Metropolitan Community Churches
Evangelical Presbyterians	Presbyterian Church in America	Presbyterians (USA)
Jehovah's Witnesses	Lutherans—Missouri Synod	Evangelical Lutherans
Conservative Pentecostals	National Ass'n of Evangelicals	Congregationalists (UCC)
Many Orthodox Jews	Conservative Jews	Reform Jews
Old Mormons	Modern Latter-day Saints	Affirmation (Latter-gay Saints)
Nation of Islam	Islamic Society N.A.	Muslims for Progressive Values
Shi'ite Muslims	Sunni Muslims	Unity Mosques
Lakewood Megachurch		Quakers
Westboro Baptists		Unitarian Universalists

gay organizations. Nor do these internal as well as external pressures mean that all faith traditions will follow; like niche markets, there will be space in the great American religious smorgasbord for denominations that hew to a traditionalist approach to issues of sexuality and gender. Table 3 suggests the current map of that smorgasbord in this country, and the ensuing discussion will focus on three great conservative faith traditions.

Variation Among Evangelical Protestants

Table 3 reveals wide variation both among and within denominations and exposes the error made by scholars who treat Evangelicals as a homogenous anti-gay group. Because Evangelical Protestantism tends to be institutionally decentralized and emphasizes the individual's encounter with God's Word and personal salvation, this broad cluster of denominations—ranging from the huge SBC (more than sixteen million strong) to the more modest Assemblies of God and Jehovah's Witnesses to single-church or internet denominations—offers endless variety: from open loathing of gay people to "love the sinner, hate the sin" to open embrace and doctrinal rethinking.[13]

Some independent (unaffiliated with an established denomination) Evangelical churches preach anti-gay prejudice. The most famous is the Westboro Baptist Church, in Topeka, Kansas. Founded by the late Reverend Fred Phelps, Westboro Baptists believe that "God hates fags" and "God hates America" because it tolerates homosexuals. They are best known for protesting at military funerals. Even scarier is the Faithful Word Baptist Church in Tempe, Arizona. Its pastor, Steve Anderson—a lifelong Baptist with a remarkable memory for Bible verses—zealously derides "horrible wicked" homosexuals, who "keep molesting and destroying people." So, he urges, they should put a bullet in their heads; if they don't take advantage of self-help, God will deal with them, per the death penalty directed by Leviticus 20:13. On YouTube, he can be seen joking to his congregation that *LGBT* stands for Let God Burn Them. And *LGBTQ* means Let God Burn Them Quickly. The video shows the congregation laughing.[14]

More representative of the Evangelical perspective is the SBC, which since 1976 has regularly adopted resolutions condemning "the evils inherent in homosexuality." In June 1996, the SBC passed its first Resolution on Homosexual Marriages, condemning such relationships as "completely and thoroughly wicked" (Leviticus 20:13; Romans 1:26–28). No fewer than seven times since then, the SBC has adopted new resolutions condemning homosexual relationships, including domestic partnerships and civil unions. Other resolutions supported the Federal Marriage Amendment (2004, 2006) and DOMA (2011) and condemned *Obergefell* (2016).[15]

The intellectual leaders of the SBC's doctrinal stance were Dr. Richard Land, the founding president of its Ethics & Religious Liberty Commission (ERLC), and Dr. Albert Mohler, the president of the Southern Baptist Theological Seminary. After being ensnared in race-baiting and plagiarism scandals, Land was replaced in 2013 as ERLC's president by the mediagenic moderate conservative Dr. Russell Moore. In June 2012, the SBC's marriage resolution avoided "wickedness" rhetoric and instead announced that "all people, regardless of race or sexual orientation, are created in the image of God and thus are due respect and love (Genesis 1:26–27)." The resolution respectfully asserted that same-sex marriage went beyond biblical and other traditions.[16]

The change in the SBC's approach became apparent in its conference "The Gospel, Homosexuality, and the Future of Marriage," held in Nashville, October 27–29, 2014. More than 1,300 ministers and theologians attended the event, which was packed with Evangelical all-stars: Moore and Mohler, Jim Daly and Glenn Stanton of Focus on the Family, Kristen Waggoner and other ADF counsel for Barronelle Stutzman (the florist who was penalized for declining to service a gay wedding in Washington state), and J.D. Greear, the charismatic pastor of the Summit Church in Raleigh-Durham, North Carolina. The conference offered neither anti-gay condemnations nor any doctrinal softening. LGBT persons were concentrated into a panel of Christians struggling with same-sex attraction but following God's rules as to sexual conduct. The panel, hosted by Moore, accepted the premise that sexual orientation is not a choice, a novel idea for most Baptists.[17]

Especially dramatic was Reverend Greear's address that closed the conference, "Preaching Like Jesus to the LGBT Community and Its Supporters." The pastor announced that the Church owed that community an apology for not opposing anti-gay discrimination and abuse. He implored parents not to abandon their LGBT kids, Christians not to shun gay neighbors and relatives, and the Church to admit that all its members are sexual sinners—no different from gay people. Invoking Christ's admonition that His followers not judge lest they be judged for their own failings (Matthew 7:1), Greear urged a middle path between alienation of gay people from the Church and affirmation of homosexual relationships. Both, he said, were contrary to Scripture. The middle way would be pastoral concern and friendship: share the Good News with your gay friends, but let their hearts be guided by God and not by human shaming or discrimination. Focus on the Family's cheerful president, Jim Daly, had delivered a similar message earlier in the conference.[18]

It remains to be seen how the SBC will respond to this call for friendship and pastoral concern. As a general matter, most Southern Baptists still consider pastoral care to include the practice of "pray the gay away" conversion therapy, a set of controversial practices that have proven emotionally bruising to many minors involuntarily subjected to them. SBC president Ronnie Floyd, who once preached that homosexuality was a tool of Satan, announced "spiritual warfare" against the Supreme Court's decision in *Obergefell*. On June 12, 2018, however, the SBC elected Reverend Greear as its president, over strong opposition from the old guard.[19]

The First Baptist Church of Decatur, Georgia, was kicked out of the SBC in 2009 for calling a woman, the Reverend Julie Pennington-Russell, to be its senior pastor. During her tenure, this church has had as many as forty LGBT members, some of them couples raising children. First Baptist Decatur is a member of the Cooperative Baptist Fellowship, an assembly of 1,800 churches that allows a great deal of pastoral and doctrinal diversity on issues of sexuality and gender. Like the progressives who formed the Alliance of Baptists in 1987, the moderates who formed the cooperative in 1990–1991 were reacting to conservative domination of the SBC since 1979 and especially to Dr. Land's dogmatic activism.

Worshipping at the Decatur church is Dr. David Gushee of Mercer University, a leading Evangelical ethicist. He dropped a bombshell with his 2014 book, *Changing Our Mind,* an account of how the marriage equality debate and encounters with gay Christians inspired him to revisit the Bible, which he found surprisingly open to committed lesbian and gay unions. His book provides a thoughtful examination of the "clobber verses" used to demonize gay people. Referring to Levitical condemnation of men lying with men, Dr. Gushee observes that there are 117 things identified as "abominations" in the Old Testament—including the charging of interest on loans, which Ezekiel 18:10–13 says is punishable by death. He challenges traditionalists to defend their principle of selection: Why emphasize one Levitical crime and ignore the rest? Christ's teachings sidestepped the Levitical commands for the most part. Does His life or teachings provide a principle for selection?[20]

Ezekiel condemned adultery as an abomination, and Jesus referred to adultery with disdain in Matthew 19:9, where He defined it to include a man who divorces his wife without cause and then remarries. When we visited St. Paul's Church in Michigan, we asked Reverend Rutter: Wasn't Ken DeBoer's second marriage, performed in their church? Of course it was. Wasn't that celebration of a remarriage inconsistent with Matthew 19:9? Reverend Rutter gave us a Mona Lisa smile and a lame answer, "Well, that's a *very* good question." Gushee's point is that reading the Bible should not be an exercise in looking over the crowd and picking out your friends. Evangelicals need a Christ- and Scripture-based principle for emphasizing one abomination over all the others. Gushee finds that principle in Scripture's understanding of marriage as a "lifetime covenant." He agrees that the union of April DeBoer and Jayne Rowse epitomizes Christ's vision of selflessness, generosity, fidelity, devotion to vulnerable children, and charity.[21]

The Adam and Eve creation narrative is the favored basis for the traditional Judeo-Christian view of marriage. Genesis 1–2 instructs that men and women carry out God's design when they marry and have children, but Gushee suggests that these chapters do not tell us how to treat a minority population that had no specification in biblical times. Additionally, Genesis 3 tells us that the world described in Genesis 1–2 came crashing down after Adam and Eve's original sin, their decision to eat the forbidden fruit. Inspired by Dietrich Bonhoeffer's "Creation and Fall" lectures, Gushee maintains that in a post–Genesis 1–2 world, everyone's sexuality is depraved, and no adult is a sexual innocent. "Our task, if we are Christians, is to attempt to order the sexuality we have in as responsible a manner as we can. We can't get back to Genesis 1–2, a primal sinless world."[22]

The biggest development in American religion in the last generation has been the explosion of nondenominational megachurches that combine crowd-pleasing Bible stories, entertaining services, and ethical leadership that avoids fire and brimstone. Because churches do not become mega without attracting scores of younger parishioners, these megachurches avoid gay bashing and are often gay friendly. Noteworthy is the Reverend Andy Stanley, pastor of the North Point Community Church outside of Atlanta. A boyishly handsome sixty years old, with well-trimmed sandy hair, a ready smile, and a Tom Sawyer aw-shucks demeanor, he is the son of the Reverend Charles Stanley, the pastor of Atlanta's First Baptist Church for more than four decades who proclaimed AIDS to be God's judgment on homosexuals. In 1995, Andy Stanley established his own church in an effort to appeal to the unchurched—what is called the seeker approach pioneered by the Willow Creek Community Church in Illinois. Though it celebrates only one-man, one-woman marriages, North Point generally welcomes lesbian and gay worshippers, and Stanley regularly confers with individual parishioners or groups. Other megachurches and their pastors have been gay affirming. EastLake Community Church, a megachurch in Bothell, Washington, for example, performs same-sex marriages.[23]

Pew Research reports that as many as two-fifths of Evangelicals now support marriage equality for LGBT persons, and young Evangelicals are particularly supportive. The founder of the Reformation Project, Matthew Vines sponsors conferences and training sessions for affirming Evangelicals. Openly gay musicians Trey Pearson and Vicky Beeching have amassed large followings by introducing gay-friendly lyrics to contemporary Christian music. Justin Lee founded the Gay Christian Network and helped persuade Alan Chambers, the former head of Exodus International, to stop asserting that homosexuality can easily be flipped and to apologize for the psychological harm that Exodus visited upon gay people and their families. In 2016, Texas Evangelical author and HGTV star Jen Hatmaker came out in favor of LGBT relationships as holy.[24]

In October 2018, the executive committee of the National Association of Evangelicals endorsed a fairness-for-all motion to support federal anti-discrimination legislation combined with strong religious protections. In a sermon delivered on January 27, 2019, Reverend Greear opined that gay colleagues such as those he had welcomed into his home could enrich the Church and that homosexual intimacy was no greater sin than greed—comments that brought protests from conservative Baptists, including intemperate charges that the "depraved" SBC president was a "false prophet" for befriending "wicked, vile, disgusting reprobates." Reverend Greear was channeling the Golden Rule, while his more thoughtful critics insisted that Christ's directive did not permit sanctioning sinful behaviors.[25]

The Roman Catholic Church: Doctrinal Stability and Pastoral Evolution

Before 1965, Catholic theology followed St. Thomas Aquinas's emphasis on the procreative purpose of marriage. But in *Gaudium et spes* (1965) the Second Vatican Council elevated its unitive purpose, valuing marriage as a "community of love." The Catholic chaplain who, in chapter 1, told Jack Baker and Mike McConnell that Christ would approve their proposed marriage reflected this shift in moral emphasis. In 1975, however, the Vatican's Congregation for the Doctrine of the Faith closed the book on this possibility in its declaration *Persona humana*. The declaration reaffirmed traditional doctrine that sexual intercourse, as responsive to God's requirements and "those of human dignity," can only be legitimate in the context of "conjugal" marriage. Although individual homosexuals deserved the Church's "pastoral care," homosexual relations lacked the productive connection to human life that would give them value. "In Sacred Scripture [homosexual acts] are condemned as a serious depravity and even presented as the sad consequence of rejecting God." They are "intrinsically disordered and can in no case be approved of."[26]

John McNeill, SJ, said in *The Church and the Homosexual* (1976) that homosexual relations were consistent with Scripture and Catholic tradition, liberally understood (as in *Gaudium et spes*). Arguing that *Persona humana* was 180 degrees backward, Father McNeill's book, which was approved by his Jesuit superiors, was a sensation. In 1977, Sister Jeannine Gramick and Father Robert Nugent established New Ways Ministry, a "gay-positive ministry of advocacy and justice for lesbian and gay Catholics and reconciliation within the larger Christian and civil communities." Because even *Persona humana* recognized that some people were innately homosexual, Sister Jeannine and Father Robert reasoned that no moral blame could be attributed to them and that it was unjust to discriminate based upon an innate feature. From that premise, they argued that it was morally indefensible to deny these human beings the basic right to connect with one another and form families. "How can we have a *be* but *don't do* theology," Sister Jeannine asked. "How can you say, it's okay to be a bird, but you can't fly?" (For statements like these, the Vatican officially barred New Ways from speaking as representatives of the Church in 1999.)[27]

Imbued with what many called "the spirit of Vatican II," some Catholic officials interpreted *Persona humana* as a doctrinal affirmation that left room for the view that homosexuals ought to be the beneficiaries of a more open-minded pastoral concern. Archbishops Jack Quinn of San Francisco, Raymond Hunthausen of Seattle, and John Roach of Minneapolis, among others, expanded the Church's outreach to lesbian and gay persons and supported the principle that they should not be subject to discrimination because of their sexual orientation. In strong language, however, Cardinal Ratzinger discouraged this kind of pastoral outreach in the Vatican's "Letter to the Bishops of the Catholic Church on the Pastoral Care of Homosexual Persons" (1986). "Pastoral Care" raised questions about how accepting the Church should be for Christians whose orientation was homosexual. "Although the particular inclination of the homosexual person is not a sin, it is a more or less strong tendency ordered toward an intrinsic moral evil; and thus the inclination itself must be seen as an objective disorder."[28]

Popes John Paul II and Benedict XVI (former Cardinal Ratzinger) appointed doctrinally conservative American bishops who mobilized church resources against homosexual marriage all over the United States. Those most relevant to the state debates examined earlier in this volume were Kenneth Angell in Vermont, Bernard Law in Massachusetts, Adam Maida in Michigan, Charles Chaput in Colorado and Pennsylvania, Salvatore Cordileone in California,

Richard Malone in Maine, Peter Sartain in Washington, Timothy Dolan in New York, John Nienstedt in Minnesota, and William Lori in Maryland. The US Conference of Catholic Bishops, dominated by these bishops and archbishops, strongly supported the Federal Marriage Amendment, opposed efforts to repeal or invalidate DOMA, and filed a hard-hitting amicus brief in *Obergefell*.

Notwithstanding the conservative clerical leadership, Catholic lay opinion between 2007 and 2017 moved from 40 percent supporting marriage equality to 67 percent. Attentive to Jesus's example of befriending social outcasts, Pope Francis (selected in 2013) has introduced a new era in the Catholic Church's stance toward gay people. He wrote his gay friend and former student Yayo Grassi, "In my pastoral work, there is no room for homophobia." He is the first pope to use the term *gay*, as he has many times. "Who am I to judge?" he humbly confessed: We are all sinners, so why single out one set of sinners for denigration? How does that advance God's plan? The dignity God has conferred upon each human life? The work of the Lord requires discernment into the souls of His children, as the shepherd accompanies them on their journeys. In 2018, the Vatican invited James Martin, SJ, to address the World Meeting of Families on the topic of "Showing Welcome and Respect in Our Parishes for LGBT People and Their Families," one of the first official uses of the term *LGBT* in any Vatican setting. Sister Jeannine told us that a gay couple in Rome was anguished because of admonitions from their parish priest. Should we split up? they asked Pope Francis. He reportedly called them late at night on his pope-phone, "No, find a new parish."[29]

Pope Francis has asserted values of inclusion through his public pronouncements and through appointments of bishops dedicated to gay-welcoming pastoral themes. Among the most notable have been Cardinals Blase Cupich in Chicago and Joseph Tobin in Newark, as well as Archbishop Wilton Gregory in Washington, DC. The pope has also set a deliberative agenda aimed at advancing the Church's understanding, starting with the Extraordinary Synod of Bishops on Family, held at the Vatican in October 2014. Pope Francis opened this assembly of 170 clerics with a plea for the Church to include a broader rainbow of persons and families, and strong voices for the dignity of LGBTQ+ people came from Germany, England, and Australia. On the eve of the synod, German cardinal Walter Kasper urged church recognition for "homosexual unions," too controversial a move for most bishops and anathema to those representing African, East European, and many Asian churches. Cardinal Lorenzo Baldisseri, Francis's handpicked secretary general of the synod, supported efforts to "open doors and windows" of the Church to gay families.

These efforts received strong support from European, Canadian, and Australian bishops but very little from the American delegation, led by Archbishop Joseph Kurtz of Louisville, head of the US Conference of Catholic Bishops.[30]

Orchestrated, some have said, by Baldisseri and his allies, the synod's midterm report proposed significant changes in pastoral thinking. "Homosexuals have gifts and qualities to offer to the Christian community: are we capable of welcoming these people, guaranteeing to them a fraternal space in our communities?" While reformers were not suggesting changes in the Church's doctrine on conjugal marriage, they emphasized gay families in which "mutual aid to the point of sacrifice constitutes a precious support in the life of the partners. Furthermore, the Church pays special attention to the children who live with couples of the same sex, emphasizing that the needs and rights of the little ones must always be given priority." Gone were characterizations of homosexuality as "depraved" or "disordered," replaced by language about "gifts and qualities." This language was not included in the final report, however, because it failed to secure approval by two-thirds of the participants. Strongest opposition came from Eastern European and African bishops. The Catholic Church is truly worldwide, and the growing Catholic populations in Africa and Asia place limits on its ability to liberalize doctrine.[31]

Pope Francis called a second Synod on the Family for October 2015, and he made sure that it included more clerics sympathetic to the Kasper-Baldisseri philosophy. The 263 attending bishops included progressives such as Blase Cupich of Chicago (added to the American delegation as a personal selection by Pope Francis), Mark Coleridge of Brisbane, and Heiner Koch of Berlin. Although the progressives were frustrated by their colleagues' unwillingness to soften long-standing doctrine, they made some progress toward a pastoral embrace of sexual minorities. The final report avoided describing homosexuality as disordered, welcomed homosexual persons, denounced unjust discrimination against them, expressed pastoral concern for families "experiencing" homosexual persons, and called for the Church to "accompany" such families—in the words of Father Martin, "not simply to repeat church teaching to them, or to scold them; but to get to know them, to be with them, to listen to them." This is a thoughtful expression of the Golden Rule: don't just treat others as you would like to be treated, but internalize *their* point of view.[32]

Pope Francis was actively engaged in the synods and inferred from their discussions how far he could go in his "small steps" approach toward a welcoming Church. On March 19, 2016, he issued his apostolic exhortation—a document traditionally used to sum up a synod and to build on its deliberations to speak to the entire Church—*Amoris laetitia* ("The Joy of Love"). Its main innovations concerned the Church's relationship with divorced and remarried Catholics, but a handful of paragraphs concerned gay Christians. "Every person, regardless of sexual orientation, ought to be respected in his or her dignity and treated with consideration, while 'every sign of unjust discrimination' is to be carefully avoided, particularly any form of aggression and violence." But "as for proposals to place unions between homosexual persons on the same level as marriage, there are absolutely no grounds for considering homosexual unions to be in any way similar or even remotely analogous to God's plan for marriage and family." *Amoris laetitia* rejected an absolute rule against all "irregular" relationships, however, as some of them bring a "stability" that ought to be respected. For such relationships, which implicitly included "same-sex unions," Pope Francis counseled pastoral discretion and support.[33]

Amoris laetitia reaffirmed traditional Catholic doctrine, recognized valuable lesbian and gay relationships that the Church was not prepared to consider marriages, and endorsed at the pastoral level what we have been calling equality practice. Parish priests and other counselors were urged to understand lesbian and gay unions in a broader context that might consider their mutual support and the needs of their children. The process has proceeded unevenly. Father Martin reports that a mother was overjoyed that her gay son was willing to give the Church another chance, and they attended Easter services together. After the priest "proclaimed the story of Christ's Resurrection," his homily focused on the "evils of homosexuality. The son stood up and walked out of the church. And the mother sat in the pew and cried." Father Martin's *Building a Bridge* (2017) laments this kind of dogmatism as undermining Christ's mission and argues for greater outreach to and support for gay families, a stance that has brought him controversy but also explicit endorsement from a number of bishops as well as Cardinals Cupich, Tobin, and Kevin Farrell, the current prefect for the Dicastery for Laity, Family, and Life in the Vatican. Father Martin's bridge-building project has the implicit support of Pope Francis.[34]

Feeling the whiplash of the intramural debate were Greg Bourke and Michael DeLeon, plaintiffs in *Obergefell*. Legally married since 2004, they raised their children, Bella and Isaiah, in the Church of Our Lady of Lourdes in Louisville, Kentucky. As an openly gay family, they found widespread support from "people in the pews," including parishioners in their nineties who encouraged their participation in the Kentucky marriage litigation. Their priest could not have been more welcoming. After *Obergefell,* the *National Catholic Reporter* named Michael and Greg its Persons of the Year, as an exemplary Catholic family.[35]

As they confess, the church hierarchy was "a different story." They applied for a joint burial plot in St. Michael Cemetery in Louisville, where Greg's parents were buried. After consulting with their priest, they submitted this design for their joint headstone: their names at the top, separated by intertwined wedding rings, with a sketch of the Supreme Court underneath their names. Archbishop Kurtz vetoed this on the ground that the design was inconsistent with the Church's teaching about marriage. As Newt Gingrich (the husband of our ambassador to the Holy See, Callista Gingrich) lectured us after a recital at the Basilica of the National Shrine of the Immaculate Conception, the Catholic Church will continue to reach out to sexual and gender minorities in a pastoral manner, but one should not expect doctrinal change or even softening from the Church's leadership in the near future.[36]

In that spirit, Archbishop Kurtz was looking for opportunities to reassert the Church's understanding of marriage as the union of one man and one woman. In September 2015, he offered encouragement to Rowan County (Kentucky) clerk Kim Davis, who went to jail rather than follow a court order directing her to issue marriage licenses to same-sex couples. The archbishop praised her eagerness "to bear witness to the truth." When Pope Francis visited the United States that month, he met privately with Kim Davis. The Vatican stated that the Davis meeting was arranged under false pretenses, and the removal of Carlo Vigano as papal nuncio to the United States was a sign of papal displeasure. Indeed, immediately after the Davis meeting, the Vatican promoted a video of Pope Francis's meeting with his gay friend Grassi and his partner. The pastoral message was implicit but unmistakable.[37]

While the Kim Davis event and other symbolic actions have been frustrating to followers of Pope Francis's approach, what equality practice entails is ongoing Golden Rule conversations among gay Catholics such as DeLeon and Bourke, supportive priests and parishioners such as those in the Church of Our Lady of the Lourdes, and traditionalists like Archbishop Kurtz. Perfectionists on either side—gay Catholics who leave the Church and clerics who would exclude them—thwart the capacity of the Church to survive the troubled times that have followed decades of revelations about predatory priests long tolerated or protected by diocesan officials.

The Church of Jesus Christ of Latter-day Saints

Like the Roman Catholic Church, the Church of Jesus Christ has a central-ized structure: doctrine, procedure, and pastoral practices are all subject to di-rectives from the main offices in Temple Square, Salt Lake City. The Council of the First Presidency and the Quorum of the Twelve Apostles, acting in con-cert, constitute the governing authority. Theologically, the Church is strictly traditionalist on sexuality and gender. The best statement of doctrine was gen-erated during the Hawai'i marriage litigation, when the Church was, unsuc-cessfully, trying to intervene as a party formally defending one-man, one-woman marriage. In September 1995, Gordon Hinckley, acting on behalf of the First Presidency and the Quorum, promulgated "The Family: A Procla-mation to the World." Its premise was that "gender is an essential character-istic of individual premortal, mortal, and eternal identity and purpose." Thus, you are a son or daughter of God from the beginning of time; after you are born, you are supposed to live your mortal life in conformity with your pre-mortal gender role. God's central commandment is "for His children to multiply and replenish the earth," and "the sacred powers of procreation are to be employed only between man and woman, lawfully wedded as husband and wife." The Church maintains that marriage on earth parallels the heav-enly union between God the Father and God the Mother; the Mother in Heaven is a belief distinctive to this faith. The eternal plan entails a gendered division of labor within the family. "By divine design, fathers are to preside over their families in love and righteousness and are responsible to provide the necessities of life and protection for their families. Mothers are primarily responsible for the nurture of their children."[38]

The proclamation and its underlying cosmology generate connections among gender, sexuality, and marriage. If God has bestowed a sex and gen-der upon each of us, as Latter-day Saints believe, both transgender feelings and "same-gender attraction" are mistaken or perverse conditions that can be reversed back to one's eternal, "natural" state. Hence some organs of the Church (such as BYU) sanctioned conversion therapy through the 1970s, and many Latter-day Saints cannot accept that there is more than one sexual ori-entation or that gender identity might not match sex assigned at birth. For these reasons, the Church in the mid-1970s mobilized against the ERA and embraced Mrs. Phyllis Schlafly's argument that a constitutional bar to sex dis-crimination would require states to recognize homosexual marriages. Church money, organization, and volunteers were critical to the defeat of the ERA in several of the last key contests—Utah, Nevada, and Virginia—and were significant in Florida, North Carolina, and Missouri. The conceptual and organizational apparatus undergirding the anti-ERA campaigns is the same one the Salt Lake City leadership deployed to oppose same-sex marriage in Hawai'i in 1994–1998 as well as in California, Nebraska, and Nevada in 2000. Their campaign in support of California's Proposition 8 was their greatest triumph, but a surprisingly Pyrrhic victory.[39]

In the wake of Proposition 8, the Latter-day Saints found themselves the object of intense animosity from LGBT people and their allies. A harbinger of protests to come was *Home Invasion,* a video produced by the Courage Campaign. The thirty-second ad started with two white-shirted missionaries who cheerfully announced to a married lesbian couple, "We're here to take away your rights." After seizing the women's wedding rings, the missionaries ransacked the couple's home until they found their marriage license, which they ripped in half. "Hey, we have rights," one woman insisted—to which a smirking missionary replied, "Not if we can help it." Yes on 8 supporters called the Courage Campaign an appeal to prejudice against Latter-day Saints, but *Home Invasion* foreshadowed an even harsher backlash.[40]

On November 7, 2008, about a thousand protesters marched around the Los Angeles Temple and plastered its fences with signs demanding that the Church stop persecuting gay people. Similar protests occurred elsewhere in California and in Salt Lake City, the latter drawing more than two thousand people. In the ten days after the election, at least seven Mormon houses of worship in Utah and ten in California were vandalized. A peaceful candlelight vigil by six hundred parents of LGBTQ+ persons at the Salt Lake City Temple on November 8 was a more effective sign of the anguish church opposition had engendered. "I don't think anyone thought through the consequences," recalled a top church official. "They really didn't anticipate the backlash, and they were not prepared for it. It hurt us, and it really hurt us with the young people."[41]

Much of the criticism came from within the Church. During the Yes on 8 campaign, Barbara Young, Carol Lynn Pearson, and other Mormon women reported dozens of disturbing episodes where stake (congregation) leaders pressured or bullied reluctant faithful to give money to Proposition 8. Barbara and her husband, football quarterback Steve Young, became active in Affirmation, a support group for "Latter-gay Saints." Large numbers of gay and lesbian youth came out to their parents, many of whom were anguished by the perceived pressure to choose between their religion and their children. Wendy Montgomery voted for Proposition 8 and did not understand why "the gays" were so upset: "Marriage is for us. Marriage is for straight people," she thought. Later, when her son came out as gay, Wendy felt "shame and regret over that, and the pain that I caused my son," who interpreted her Yes on 8 yard sign as a signal she didn't love him. "Some of the most atrocious things I have ever heard about gay people," she recalled, "were in that time period. I sat there silently." Through social media, she knows of three hundred to four hundred Latter-day Saints who left the Church over this issue.[42]

The church leadership was listening. Although senior apostle Boyd Packer emphasized traditional attitudes, Apostles Dallin Oaks, Dieter Uchtdorf, Todd Christofferson (whose brother Tom is openly gay), and Jeff Holland led the Church of Jesus Christ toward a more moderate stance. Concerned that post-2008 public opinion was judging them harshly, they pondered the standing offer from the gay rights organization Equality Utah to meet with church representatives. Public affairs officers Bill Evans and Michael Purdy were eager to have such a meeting, but the Church does not act without consensus within the First Presidency and the Quorum.[43]

A kiss accelerated that process. On July 9, 2009, Matthew Aune kissed his boyfriend Derek Jones right in front of the gleaming Mormon Temple, on a part of Main Street that had been deeded to the Church. According to Aune and Jones, private security guards yelled at them, body-slammed them to the ground, handcuffed them, and called the police, who charged the young men with criminal trespass. The Church vigorously denied that the men had been assaulted and claimed that their conduct, on church property, was lewd and drunken. Former council member Deeda Seed (who had opposed the sale of that part of Main Street to the Church) organized a crowd of sixty to a hundred straight and gay people to stage a Kiss-In in front of the temple the next Sunday. Kiss-Ins ridiculing the Church continued all summer in cities all over America. *The Colbert Report* ran a five-minute *Nailed 'Em* clip featuring Matt and Derek as a comically unthreatening couple and a video of four big security officers berating the couple and then pushing them to the ground. The *Report* gave equal time to a cute law professor who explained that the Mormons were *not* "stickin' it to the gays." Why, those rascals were criminal *trespassers*, desecrating a sacred space with lewd behavior. The suggestion was that the Church would not tolerate public lewdness by any couples, straight or gay. But the Colbert staff filmed a bunch of romantic straight couples caressing and wildly making out in front of the temple in broad daylight, with nary a peep out of the Latter-day gendarmes. Colbert's hip audience found all this mighty amusing.[44]

The kiss controversy was the public relations disaster that broke the inertia. Deeda Seed urged the Church to establish a dialogue with Equality Utah, and Bill Evans of Public Affairs said yes. At a private home, Brandie Balken, Jim Dabakis, Stephanie Pappas, Valerie Larabee, and Jon Jepson met with Evans and Michael Purdy. After someone suggested that each person say something about her- or himself, the participants chatted away for two-and-a-half hours, discovering that they had much in common. Other meetings followed, but trailed off later in the summer.[45]

Discussions reopened after Dabakis paid a visit to the Human Rights Campaign (HRC) in Washington. HRC was considering a number of themes for its next round of public education and fundraising. The front-runner was "Slam the Door." Riffing on the classic Latter-day Saint missionary visits, like the one in *Home Invasion*, the campaign planned to urge families to slam the door on these young missionaries because the religion they represented was dedicated to taking away rights from gay people. Dabakis tipped off the Public Affairs Office: Shouldn't the Church try to head this off? Evans reported this to the leadership, which gave an okay for a deal. Dabakis asked HRC to back off the campaign, which it did, and Evans asked the Church to respond with a good faith gesture, which it did.[46]

In November 2009, Michael Otterson of the Church's Public Affairs Office testified in favor of a sexual orientation anti-discrimination bill before the Salt Lake City Council. This was the first time the Church had *endorsed* a gay rights measure, and it signaled to the Utah legislature that it should not use its authority to nullify the ordinance. Cued by apparent church approval, at least eleven other Utah municipalities copied the Salt Lake City ordinance. In the ensuing years, as the Church deliberated on what, if anything, to do next, its leaders decided to take a vacation from marriage initiatives. Professor Robby George reportedly made an emphatic personal pitch to some of the church elders not to abandon the marriage issue, which would be in play during the 2012 election. As always, George was articulate, insistent, and polite—but the leadership was unmoved.[47]

In 2012, the Church launched an official website, now called mormonandgay.churchofjesuschrist.org. That the site used the term *gay* rather than *same-gender affection* was significant. More important, however, the Church stepped away from its previous dogma that homosexuality was a perverse choice, and not a fact of life for most gay persons. Dozens of videos of church members and leaders populate the website today, including one featuring Dallin Oaks, now a counselor in the First Presidency. A doctrinal traditionalist, he urged that the primary response of parents with gay children should be to reaffirm parental love and support. Like some Evangelicals and progressive Catholics, President Oaks has advocated doctrinal stability but pastoral outreach and flexibility.[48]

Although the Church had earlier in 2015 supported a statewide anti-discrimination law (discussed below), four months after *Obergefell*, Salt Lake City made a change in the *Handbook of Instructions* that is supposed to guide stake and mission presidents in their pastoral responsibilities. Even though there was not complete consensus, the leadership approved the addition of "homosexual relations (especially sexual cohabitation)" to the list of apostasies calling for a disciplinary council; other items on the list were murder, rape, serious assault, adultery, and fornication. The implication was that legally married same-sex couples were subject to expulsion from the Church. Moreover, the *Handbook* was amended to instruct presidents that they could not offer baptism in the Church for "a child of a parent who has lived or is living in a same-gender relationship," unless the president were satisfied that the child is a legal adult *and* "the child accepts and is committed to live the teachings and doctrine of the Church, and specifically disavows the practice of same-gender cohabitation and marriage."[49]

Church leaders told us that the model for the change was its stance on polygamy: having multiple wives is an apostasy, and the Church will not baptize children raised in polygamous relationships without a disavowal of plural marriage. Moreover, the First Presidency claims it routinely waived the baptism requirement for any stake or mission president who requested a waiver. From the outset, however, many devout families and some church leaders were anguished and embarrassed by the changes. Some would have followed the Church's advice to single parents instead: they are not apostates, nor do their children have to disavow their parents. "Regardless of their family situation, all Church members are entitled to receive all the blessings of the gospel of Jesus Christ." The *Handbook* allows unwed mothers to join the Relief Society and to participate in religious activities.[50]

The Church of Jesus Christ is rethinking its stance toward lesbian and gay married couples. Reportedly, 40 percent of Latter-day Saints supported gay marriage in 2017, up from 27 percent in 2014. Support was 52 percent for respondents aged eighteen to twenty-nine. Latter-gay Saints report that attitudes of stake presidents vary widely; in urban and university communities, presidents and stake members tend to be welcoming and supportive of lesbian and gay couples and their children. Almost no one expects the official doctrine to change anytime soon, but the Church has altered doctrine in the past, as in 1978, when President Kimball and his colleagues enjoyed a Revelation from the Lord to abandon their long-standing rule barring persons of African descent from full church membership. Kimball's son says that one reason for the doctrinal shift was that the "American conscience was awakened to the centuries of injustice toward blacks; the balance had tipped socially against racism and toward egalitarianism." To be sure, the Church's race-based understanding of marriage was not as central to its doctrine and cosmology as its gender-based understanding of marriage. But that doctrine does not foreclose a tolerant interpretation of President Hinckley's proclamation to include the same Golden Rule support for lesbian and gay families that it shows for single-parent families and divorced families. In April 2019, as we were revising our manuscript for publication, the First Presidency and the Quorum of the Twelve reversed the 2015 changes to the *Handbook:* no longer is same-sex marriage an apostasy, and children raised by such parents can be baptized within the Church. Notice the parallel to the stance taken by St. Paul's Church in Saint-Claire Shores, Michigan.[51]

Constitutional Dialogue Involving Faith, Gender, and Sexuality

Many religious traditionalists fear that marriage equality will create social pressure for their faith communities to provide equal treatment to devout gay persons and their families. They are likely correct, but the main pressure will be internal: from colleagues who plead for a welcoming attitude because they have decent gay friends, relatives, or coworkers; from parents whose children come out as gay or transgender; and from scholars and theologians who question traditional doctrine from within the premises of the faith community. Religion is changing from the inside more than from the outside.

Nonetheless, we have heard concerns from St. Paul's and other churches that they will lose their tax exemptions and will be hit with anti-discrimination lawsuits—maybe even hate crime prosecutions. They fear that religious schools might have to hire lesbian and gay employees and pay spousal benefits to support relationships their faith tradition considers sinful; that religious institutions might have to withdraw from activities funded or licensed by the government; and that religious entrepreneurs could be forced to participate in gay weddings that violate their consciences. In our view, the most serious effects have involved Catholic adoption and foster care services in Massachusetts, the District of Columbia, New York, Pennsylvania, and Michigan because of governmental pressure to place children with married lesbian and gay couples. Where religiously affiliated institutions are performing traditional governmental functions outright or in partnership with the government, they should expect to treat LGBTQ+ persons and families the same as everyone else. On the other hand, private religiously affiliated schools and other institutions have stronger moral objections to having their employment (including benefits) policies second-guessed by state civil rights commissions.[52]

Nevertheless, we caution against exaggerating the scope of these conflicts: most gay people do not want to force their marriages onto unwilling churches and wedding-service providers, and most conservative Christians, Muslims, and Jews do not begrudge the happiness of their LGBT neighbors and coworkers. Indeed, traditionalist faith communities should be more worried about alienating young people—the future of any denomination—than about avoiding social pressure to be nice to gay people. And LGBTQ+ groups ought to be more worried about charges that they are bullying or shunning persons of faith, precisely the kind of social pressure that kept gay people in painful closets during the last century.

In any event, the Constitution affords persons and institutions of faith substantial protection. The due process, equal protection, and religion clauses require government neutrality (and nondiscrimination) with regard to religious minorities. The neutrality principle underwrites both *Obergefell* and the Supreme Court's decision in *Masterpiece Cakeshop, Ltd. v. Colorado Civil Rights Commission* (2018), which overturned an administrative penalty against a baker who invoked religious conscience reasons not to serve a gay wedding. Because the justices found that the Colorado Civil Rights Commission's deliberations treated religion-based reasons as illegitimate compared with secular reasons, the court ruled that the penalty violated the neutrality required by the religion clauses. Justice Kennedy's opinion for the court ducked the broader issue, whether the First Amendment's free speech or free exercise clause protected crafting a special order wedding cake, which the baker considered to be conduct expressing and central to his faith.[53]

The court was wise to duck these issues, which require a great deal more public deliberation. On personal matters that are bred in the marrow the way religion, gender, and sexuality are for most people, the government should give its citizens liberty to create a personal structure in which they can flourish, and it should not tell them what to do, what to believe, whom to associate with, whom to marry, or (consistent with child welfare) how to raise their children.

The companion principle, however, is civic collegiality. In the public sphere, it is fair for the government to demand that we be tolerant and cooperative. The widely accepted anti-discrimination norm establishes a legal duty to treat one another with respect in the workplace, in public accommodations, in government, and in commercial services. The controversial cases are the quasi–public, quasi–private sphere cases like commercial vendors serving private weddings or religious institutions reserving leadership positions for persons of their faith. Inspired by the Golden Rule, we shall suggest some neutral principles that might accommodate both religious freedom for traditionalists and equal treatment for sexual and gender minorities.

THE RELIGION CLAUSES AND FREEDOM OF ASSOCIATION

At oral argument in *Obergefell*, Justice Scalia asked Mary Bonauto whether constitutional marriage rights for gay and lesbian couples would impose a duty upon traditionalist faiths to celebrate their marriages. Bonauto answered that the religion clauses would protect those faith traditions. In *Hosanna-Tabor Evangelical Lutheran Church and School v. EEOC* (2012), a unanimous Supreme Court held that the religion clauses bar the federal government from applying anti-discrimination laws to church personnel decisions regarding ministers and similar faith officials. Chief Justice Roberts's opinion relied on the First Amendment principle that the state cannot regulate any "internal church decision that affects the faith and mission of the church itself." Justice Alito's concurring opinion emphasized the need to protect "certain key religious activities, including the conducting of worship services and other religious ceremonies and rituals, as well as the critical process of communicating the faith." In *Obergefell*, Justice Kennedy observed: "The First Amendment ensures that religious organizations and persons are given proper protection as they seek to teach the principles that are so fulfilling and so central to their lives and faiths."[54]

The *Obergefell* oral argument raised a more worrisome issue. Churches are exempt from federal income tax because they are charitable institutions. The tax code defines *charitable institution* to include those "organized and operated exclusively for religious, charitable, scientific, testing for public safety, literary, or educational purposes." Justice Alito asked Solicitor General Verrilli whether marriage equality would affect the tax status of churches that refused to perform same-sex marriages. Verrilli had no answer; the issue had never come up in his preparation for the argument.[55]

686 THE GOLDEN RULE

Behind the Alito-Verrilli exchange was *Bob Jones University v. United States* (1983). In 1971, the IRS decided that a private school whose admissions policy discriminated because of race was not charitable within the Internal Revenue Code's exemption. By the time its case reached the Supreme Court, the university admitted students of color but still prohibited interracial dating or marriages, based upon its reading of Scripture. All nine justices saw this policy as discriminating because of race, and all nine rejected the university's constitutional claim. Would *Bob Jones* be extended to deny tax-exempt status to churches refusing to celebrate same-sex marriages? In his *Obergefell* dissenting opinion, Chief Justice Roberts warned that it might. We think he is wrong about that.[56]

Bob Jones held that the national policy against race discrimination was so powerful that it overwhelmed the public policy encouraging private charity, religion, and education. No court has expanded *Bob Jones* to penalize private educational institutions that discriminate on any ground other than race, nor has any court ever applied *Bob Jones* to churches for any reason (even race-based discrimination). Within a month of *Obergefell*, the IRS announced that it "does not view *Obergefell* as having changed the law applicable to section 501(c) (3) determinations or examinations."[57]

If the IRS were to apply the *Bob Jones* exception more broadly, churches are the last place it would start. Sex discrimination is a quasi-suspect constitutional classification, yet the IRS has consistently applied section 501(c)(3) to churches that openly discriminate on the basis of sex, such as denominations like St. Paul's in Michigan that will not ordain women as priests or ministers. Additionally, the tax code requires the IRS to give churches special treatment. Most charitable organizations must apply to the IRS for tax-exempt status— but churches are entitled to their tax exemption automatically, by virtue of being churches. Churches even enjoy special procedural protections that discourage IRS audits. "Even in the area of racial discrimination, where it has the strongest explicit mandate and has, in fact, revoked exemptions, [the IRS] has not revoked the exemption of a single discriminatory church."[58]

Finally, the Religious Freedom Restoration Act of 1993 (RFRA) prohibits the federal government from taking any action that "substantially burden[s] a person's exercise of religion," unless the government proves that the burden "is in furtherance of a compelling governmental interest" and "is the least restrictive means of furthering that compelling governmental interest." Although the Supreme Court has struck down the application of RFRA to state discrimination (as beyond Congress's authority to enforce the Fourteenth Amendment), it has treated RFRA as binding on the federal government. Even if, as we think, *Bob Jones* could be decided the same way under RFRA, existing Supreme Court precedent suggests that the public policy against sexual orientation discrimination may not rise to the same compelling level. *Boy Scouts of America v. Dale* (2000) held that a state policy against sexual orientation discrimination was not sufficiently compelling to justify a milder infringement on the Boy Scouts' First Amendment right of expressive association. A broad reading of *Obergefell* could call that feature of *Dale* into question. Because many clashes between gay rights and religious liberty will involve employment with or services from normative institutions like the Boy Scouts or associations or nonprofits controlled by religious denominations or societies, *Dale* will be relevant in future cases.[59]

Under the statute, the IRS will not and should not penalize churches, synagogues, mosques, and other religious institutions that authorize only conjugal marriages. If it did so, there might be constitutional concerns under *Hosanna-Tabor*, where the Supreme Court ruled that a statute of general application could not constitutionally be applied to a church's decision about officials and practices central to worship and faith. Does the *Hosanna-Tabor* reasoning also assure churches that the state cannot constitutionally take away a tax benefit? Current constitutional doctrine says not. In *Employment Division v. Smith* (1990), the Supreme Court upheld the application of laws of general application, like anti-discrimination laws, in ways that might substantially burden religious freedom, unless such application were inspired by anti-religious animus (as in *Masterpiece*). Admittedly, *Hosanna-Tabor* narrowed *Smith*'s rule that laws of general application do not raise religion clause concerns absent a showing of animus. Might the Roberts Court overrule *Smith* altogether? Most scholars would argue against such a course because RFRA and other statutes have built upon and responded to *Smith* and because the statutory protections for religious liberty are more robust in any event.[60]

Masterpiece suggests another angle. Jack Phillips believed that he would be committing a sin by "participating" in a gay marriage ceremony. The Colorado Civil Rights Commission threw the book at him—but showed leniency in other cases. A Christian ally, William Jack, had asked three other bakeshops for wedding cakes in the shape of a Bible, with two grooms accompanied by a big red *X* and text opining that homosexuality is a "detestable sin." When all three bakeshops refused to do those decorations, the commission provided no remedy because it believed the refusal was based on the offensive message, not the customer's religion or sexual orientation. Raising constitutional red flags, however, two commissioners in Phillips's case suggested that religious beliefs could not legitimately be carried into the commercial domain, disparaged Phillips's faith, and compared his invocation of his religious beliefs to defenses of slavery. A 7-2 Supreme Court majority ruled that this lack of neutrality violated the religion clauses. Dissenting, Justices Ginsburg and Sotomayor objected that the commission properly distinguished the Jack cases, which were denials of service because of message and not because of a protected trait. Later the same month, the Supreme Court dismissed religion clause objections to President Trump's immigration travel ban, which he had repeatedly touted as anti-Muslim. Justices Sotomayor and Ginsburg's dissent in the travel-ban case claimed that the court was not treating the different religious liberty claims in a neutral manner.[61]

SERVICES TO THE PUBLIC AND FREEDOM OF SPEECH

In *Masterpiece*, Phillips also claimed that Colorado violated the First Amendment's free speech clause because the directive requiring him to make cakes for gay weddings was an example of government-coerced speech that was not justified by a compelling public interest (as required by strict scrutiny). In *Hurley v. Irish-American Gay, Lesbian and Bisexual Group of Boston* (1995), for example, a unanimous Supreme Court invalidated the application of a state anti-discrimination law to require that Boston's St. Patrick's Day Parade include an LGBT marching group. The court treated the parade as classic expressive conduct, and Phillips's ADF lawyers claimed that, as a "cake artist," he was engaging in similarly expressive activity. Solicitor General Noel Francisco (formerly an ADF-affiliated lawyer) offered a narrower ground: there is a First Amendment violation when the government compels a person *both* to "create" speech he doesn't believe *and* to "participate" in an "expressive event." A concurring opinion by Justice Thomas (joined by Justice Gorsuch) agreed with ADF.[62]

The ADF-Thomas argument stretches First Amendment doctrine and threatens to eviscerate anti-discrimination laws. In *Masterpiece*, all nine justices recognized that religious and philosophical "objections do not allow business owners and other actors in the economy and in society to deny protected persons equal access to goods and services under a neutral and generally applicable public accommodations law." Nor can wedding vendors "who object to gay marriages for moral and religious reasons put up signs saying 'no goods or services will be sold if they will be used for gay marriages.'" An early example of this liberty-equality clash was *Newman v. Piggie Park Enterprises* (1966). Anne Newman, a woman of color, sued Piggie Park for refusing to serve her, in violation of the public accommodations title of the Civil Rights Act of 1964. Piggie Park's owner, Maurice Bessinger, claimed that applying the statute would violate his First Amendment rights because he believed that racial mixing was contrary to Scripture. Bessinger saw his refusal to desegregate as protected expression, but a unanimous Supreme Court viewed it as conduct that the government can regulate.[63]

Bob Jones had the same conceptual structure as *Piggie Park*: the university's defense invoked the expressive-religious features of its refusal to admit; the government focused on the action based upon a race-based classification. Many public accommodation cases can be understood in precisely this way— including *Masterpiece* and *Hurley*. So why did *Piggie Park* and *Bob Jones* come out differently from *Hurley*? It may be that judges in the earlier cases found the elimination of race discrimination a more compelling interest than judges found elimination of sexual orientation discrimination in the later cases (the *Dale* point), but such reasoning would be at odds with *Romer's* and *Obergefell's* holding that gay people are entitled to at least many of the same civil rights as racial minorities and with the analysis in *Masterpiece*. Writing for seven justices and referencing *Piggie Park*, Justice Kennedy's majority opinion rejected the claim made by ADF and the Conference of Catholic Bishops that sexual orientation and race are on separate constitutional tracks. Following the long-standing national consensus, Kennedy applied the Fourteenth Amendment's version of the Golden Rule: whatever exemption judges create for religious defendants in anti-gay discrimination cases will presumptively be applicable in race- and sex-discrimination cases as well.[64]

A more authoritative doctrinal distinction between *Piggie Park* and *Hurley* is provided by the Supreme Court's decision in *Rumsfeld v. Forum for Academic & Institutional Rights (FAIR)* (2006). A unanimous court rejected law school objections to a statute cutting off government funding for their universities unless they hosted military recruiters who excluded LGBT applicants from consideration. The law schools (1) refused to provide host services (2) because hosting a recruiter having a particular institutional identity based on its excluding gay people (3) would convey an offensive message (that anti-gay employment discrimination is okay). The *FAIR* court rejected the First Amendment claim because "the compelled speech to which the law schools point is plainly incidental to the [statute's] regulation of conduct." As an example of a conduct regulation with a permitted ancillary restriction of expression, the court cited laws barring "employers from discriminating in hiring on the basis of race." *Hurley* was also distinguishable because "the complaining speaker's own message was affected by the speech it was forced to accommodate." *FAIR* characterized *Hurley* as direct regulation of a core form of political expression protected by the First Amendment. Under *Hurley,* a state public accommodations law cannot tell parade organizers what marchers and banners to include— but under *FAIR* it can tell a business that sells banners and flags that it must sell to all comers, gay or straight. Under *FAIR,* however, it is not clear whether the state can require a vendor to make customized banners that say things inconsistent with her core beliefs.[65]

Unless *Piggie Park, Bob Jones,* and *FAIR* must be rewritten or overruled, the ADF-Thomas free speech argument does not work in *Masterpiece.* The court may be willing to sacrifice doctrinal coherence to reassure religious traditionalists that the state will not bully them in repeated exercises of political correctness. Given our analysis in this chapter, we think that these disputes will go the way of the dispute in *Piggie Park:* after social norms shift toward equality, most people will go along with the new requirements. Another lesson of *Masterpiece* is that anti-discrimination laws protect religious minorities against discrimination, so reciprocity ought to be considered. Under the ADF's broad understanding of protected expression, traditionalist Christians, Jews, and Muslims could face discrimination from service providers whose faith tradition insists upon the equal dignity of LGBTQ+ persons. In our view, anti-discrimination laws ought to vigorously protect religious minorities just as they ought to protect sexual and gender minorities.

Indeed, a useful First Amendment heuristic suggested by *Masterpiece* is the Golden Rule: impose upon others only those restrictions you would gladly accept for yourself. Consider this thought experiment. Can a religious customer go to a progressive baker and ask her to do a cake for a male-female wedding that has icing spelling out "Thank God We're Straight" and then complain of religion-based discrimination when the baker refuses? We think the baker enjoys First Amendment protection from application of the anti-discrimination law to require affirmative expression of an idea antithetical to one's core beliefs. Conversely, if a gay couple asks a traditionalist baker to do a cake for a same-sex wedding with icing spelling out "Gay is Good," the baker has the same First Amendment justification for refusing to serve. But neither the progressive baker nor the religious baker ought to be able to refuse to sell a wedding cake simply because of the identity of the spouses or because of what they plan to do with the cake. In *Masterpiece,* Phillips said he would have been happy to sell the couple a generic wedding cake. In a subsequent controversy, however, he was unwilling to make a cake with a pink inside and blue outside once he learned that it celebrated a gender transition. Although the state agency ultimately declined to prosecute, Phillips's claim may be inconsistent with *FAIR.* The law schools claimed an expressive interest in denying interview rooms to a gay-excluding federal employer, but Chief Justice Roberts held that the law schools were over-reading the meaning of such access.

Robin Wilson would separate the service from the provider. LGBTQ+ customers might have a statutory right to service for their weddings—but traditionalist providers ought to be able to subcontract the service to another provider but remain responsible for the service. In the spirit of the Golden Rule, this remedy has the virtue of asking each side to accommodate the needs of the other: the indignity of being denied service is ameliorated by the behind-the-scenes arrangement, and the complicity with an unholy event is ameliorated by allowing another enterprise to have the business. We worry that the Wilson proposal would often be cumbersome to implement, but some jurisdiction should try it and see how it works. *Masterpiece* suggests a different procedural amelioration, consistent with this chapter's analysis of denominational deliberations. An agency enforcing an anti-discrimination law against a service provider who seriously claims an expressive interest (whether religious or not) has an implicit constitutional obligation to work with the complainant and the provider to devise a remedy that accommodates both (perhaps Wilson's farming-out idea) and *not* to impose ruinous financial or business penalties on the enterprise unless it engages in bad faith behavior. From a gay-friendly point of view, what value is served by imposing financial martyrdom on small businesspeople?[66]

First Amendment scholars have floated a variety of other ideas about where the line should be drawn. Douglas Laycock would exempt all small businesses providing any same-sex marriage or wedding services to which the owner has a faith-based objection, so long as another provider can be found without substantial hardship. He would provide a constitutional defense for Jack Phillips as well as Barronelle Stutzman, the florist who was sanctioned in *Arlene's Flowers and Gifts* (2017), and Elaine Huguenin, the wedding photographer sanctioned in *Elane Photography* (2013). Kent Greenawalt, reflecting a different balance, would exempt only those businesses where the religious owner is directly involved with the wedding ceremony—the photographer and caterer, but not the baker and the florist. Michael McConnell would exempt any commercial provider who has a sincere religious objection to performing a particular service. Douglas NeJaime and Reva Siegel would not exempt any religious provider if it would significantly harm a third party in a dignitary or financial manner.[67]

The foregoing suggestions are grounded in theories of fairness rather than in accepted sources of law. We have sought to provide a rule based on nothing more than the precedents already decided by the Supreme Court—but we cheerfully admit that a rule grounded in past decisions might not be the best rule moving forward. The best approach may not even be a bright-line rule. Consider the theory recently proffered by Lance Wickman, the general counsel of the Church of Jesus Christ. He organizes various First Amendment religious freedoms and free speech rights into concentric circles, in which claims to constitutional protection weaken as one goes outward. The strongest protection should be reserved for core religious activities: personal and family worship, internal church affairs and doctrine, the free exercise of religion in public spaces, and nonprofit status. *Hosanna-Tabor* protects religious activities within this inner circle, he argues. Wickman's second circle would include decisions about nonministerial personnel, the operation of religious schools, and the activities of religious charities, all of which can be regulated so long as they do not unduly burden the religious mission. The outer circle would encompass "commercial settings," where "our expectations of unfettered religious freedom must be tempered." Secular businesses are properly limited by long-standing civil rights laws and regulations. This circle includes religious dress and observances, which Wickman believes should be reasonably accommodated, but "a county clerk may need to perform marriages contrary to her religious beliefs if no one else can easily take her place."[68]

Wickman's approach combines (1) bright-line rules for the inner circle with (2) standards balancing freedom and community needs in the middle circle, and (3) regulatory allowances in the outer circle. It calibrates the freedom to exclude with the expectation of privacy that accompanies traditional religious practice. The more an institution or individual participates in the market or in public or governmental activities, the smaller the freedom to exclude. This is a promising approach—but one better calibrated by legislatures than by judges, for legislators can engage in an open give-and-take with the relevant stakeholders. Deciding where to draw the line between *Hurley* and *FAIR* is a matter of policy where judges have fewer comparative advantages and lack accountability to the democratic process.

Fairness-for-All Statutes

Legislatures are a much better forum than courts for working out clashes between a sexual orientation and gender identity (SOGI) anti-discrimination law and conscience claims because they bring all the stakeholders together and because they have more policy tools to ameliorate conflict. Thus, anti-discrimination laws often deflect conflict through "carve outs" from statutory mandates of small businesses or landlords with only a handful of apartments, through special defenses tied to the purposes of the enterprise, and through allowances for specified institutions to engage in classifications that might otherwise be considered discriminatory. For example, New York's 2011 marriage equality law reaffirmed the autonomy of churches and synagogues and also exempted religiously affiliated institutions (like parochial schools) and benevolent associations (like the Knights of Columbus) from public accommodations regulation, allowing them to limit their facilities and halls to marriage celebrations that their faith tradition accepts. For another example, the 1993 RFRA was a consensus statute barring the state from imposing substantial burdens on a person's free exercise unless needed to accomplish a compelling state interest. In *Burwell v. Hobby Lobby Stores, Inc.* (2014), the Supreme Court significantly expanded RFRA to protect religious expression for closely held commercial enterprises opposing governmental equality mandates. Alarmed at the court's expansive move, LGBTQ+ groups retracted their willingness to provide additional religious allowances in their proposed federal anti-discrimination law. State supreme courts interpreting junior-RFRAs have been reluctant to follow the Supreme Court, and when legislatures have tried to codify or follow *Hobby Lobby,* they have been rebuked in all but the reddest of states.[69]

For the last two decades, the most powerful lobbyist in Arizona has been Cathi Herrod, the executive director of the Center for Arizona Policy (CAP). In 2014, responding to concerns that new municipal anti-discrimination ordinances might apply to wedding vendors, CAP and ADF proposed an Act Relating to the Free Exercise of Religion. Senate Bill 1062 would have expanded free exercise protections to include companies as well as persons and would have protected this expanded class against private discrimination lawsuits as well as government actions. The Arizona Chamber of Commerce had concerns about the bill because any whiff of homophobia would scare away the high-tech companies the state was trying to attract.[70]

Backed by the Arizona Conference of Catholic Bishops and Republican leadership, S.B. 1062 passed on party-line votes in the Arizona Senate (17-13) on

February 19 and in the House (33-27) the next day. After house passage, however, thousands of queer folk angrily protested on the green lawn in front of the state capitol. National LGBTQ+ groups and the media lampooned S.B. 1062, and businesses like Apple and Google publicly deplored it. There was talk of yanking the 2015 Super Bowl from Arizona. The Chamber of Commerce staff in charge of tourism and technology warned that the law's repercussions would be immediate, severe, and lasting, as it would revive business's fears generated by earlier anti-immigrant measures sought by the governor and adopted by the legislature. Backed up by moderate GOP senators who regretted their votes, Chamber of Commerce president Glenn Hammer met with Governor Jan Brewer, who listened attentively as Hammer warned that S.B. 1062 would significantly set back the Arizona economy. Most Arizonans saw it as a provocative anti-gay discrimination measure.

A staunch conservative, Governor Brewer vetoed S.B. 1062 on February 26, 2014. The rout was so complete that legislators refused to consider a more moderate religious freedom bill that session. Arkansas and Indiana went through similarly painful experiences in 2015. Arkansas governor Asa Hutchinson, an even stauncher conservative, vetoed a broad religious freedom bill on March 31, and the legislature responded with a more moderate bill resembling a traditional junior-RFRA. Indiana governor Mike Pence, the staunchest conservative of all, signed a broad junior-RFRA on March 27, 2015, but faced such a tremendous business backlash that he and the legislature moderated the law in April.[71]

While these states were swamped in public relations nightmares, Utah and the Church of Jesus Christ were approaching the issue more productively. In 2014, the Church created an ad hoc committee on religious liberty, which sought common ground between equality for LGBT persons and liberty for religious persons and organizations. After October 6, 2014, when the Supreme Court denied its petition for review, Utah was required by court order to distribute marriage licenses to same-sex couples—a development that motivated the First Presidency and the Quorum to support a state law barring SOGI discrimination while also affirming important religious liberty protections. The leadership acted after years of discussions between its public affairs officers and Equality Utah.[72]

On January 22, 2015, Senate Majority Whip Stuart Adams got a phone call from the Public Affairs Committee: the Church wanted him to pass a SOGI law, to be paired with a statute assuring marriage licenses for gay couples *and* conscience allowances for county clerks. A small businessman representing

Ogden, Adams had no experience with civil rights legislation but did not hesitate to take it up. On January 27, 2015, Elders Dallin Oaks, Jeffrey Holland, and Todd Christofferson and Mrs. Neill Marriott of the Relief Society held a press conference at the state capitol to announce the Church's support for SOGI legislation. Legislators saw this as a game changer—a reality missed by the national press accounts, which emphasized Oaks's lament about attacks on religious freedom.[73]

In the three months remaining in the legislative session, Senator Adams, the Church, and Equality Utah would have to draft the bill from scratch, figure out what religious accommodations to include and how to phrase them, consult the Chamber of Commerce and social conservative organizations like the Eagle Forum, and persuade the nation's reddest state legislature to pass a law protecting sexual and gender minorities, who seemed to violate every sentence of the 1995 Proclamation on the Family that hung in most of their houses. The process was a legislative opera. Until the end, no one knew whether it would be a tragedy or a comedy.

Act one involved a basic question: How should SOGI anti-discrimination protections be added to the Utah Code? Reflecting their conviction that sexual orientation and gender identity were completely different classifications from race or sex, the Republican leadership and the Church felt that there should be a special law just for gays. Cliff Rosky, counsel to Equality Utah, insisted that discrimination based on sexual orientation or gender identity was as harmful and irrational as other forms. In late February, Equality Utah was prepared to walk away from negotiations if the legislators did not agree to integrate SOGI protections into the existing anti-discrimination law, which had generous religious exemptions. Bill Evans and Mike Purdy helped persuade the Church's leadership that an integrated law made sense, and Robin Wilson showed Senator Adams how most other states had followed the integrated approach. Act one closed on February 26, when Alexander Dushku (outside counsel for the Church) came back with a draft bill that integrated the new protections into existing law. Dueling divas, singing in entirely different registers, could still harmonize.[74]

Act two, full of dramatic conflict, involved working out the exact coverage of the bill. The Church, the GOP leadership, and Wilson all wanted relatively broad exemptions for religious institutions, religiously affiliated institutions, expressive institutions like the Boy Scouts, and religious persons. To their left, Equality Utah, the ACLU, and the handful of Democrats in the legislature wanted only to add SOGI protections to the existing anti-discrimination law.

To their right, Representative LaVar Christensen, the sponsor of Utah's 2004 constitutional DOMA, strongly opposed SOGI protections and instead favored a Religious Freedom Restoration Act of the sort Arizona was considering. There were many anguished conversations about covering the Boy Scouts and BYU (the Church's flagship university) and about defining gender identity and employers' discretion over their bathrooms.

On Sunday, March 1, a meeting of the main negotiators worked out substantial agreement on the religious allowances and the gender identity provisions. Section 1 of the bill would exempt from the definition of *employer* not only religious organizations, associations, and societies but also their affiliates, leaders, and educational institutions (left undefined). In a last-minute concession to seal the deal, the Church agreed to limit the expressive association exemption to just the Boy Scouts, and Equality Utah agreed to exempt them. Section 5 allowed religious schools to make employment decisions based on religion. Sections 7 and 8 gave employers latitude on dress codes and bathrooms if they provided reasonable accommodations based on gender identity (defined by reference to medical standards). Section 14 gave nonprofit and educational institutions wide latitude in making distinctions with regard to housing, which meant that BYU could keep its sex-segregated dorms and continue to offer married-student residences only to different-sex couples. Exemptions for the Boy Scouts and BYU were hard pills for Equality Utah to swallow. In a series of conference calls to gay rights leaders around the country, Rosky suggested that these exemptions were needed for the legislation to pass, and the national leaders reluctantly went along.[75]

In an important innovation, section 10 assured employees they could express their "religious or moral beliefs and commitments in the workplace in a reasonable, non-disruptive, and non-harassing way on equal terms with similar types of expression of beliefs or commitments allowed by the employer in the workplace." GOP legislators recalled the plight of Eric Moustos, a Salt Lake City police officer who was discharged because he criticized his bosses for bullying officers to work overtime for the 2014 Gay Pride Parade. Because section 10 protected LGBTQ+ as well as traditionalist straight employees, Equality Utah was okay with it.[76]

Act two concluded with the big reveal of S.B. 296, and the chief actors joined hands at the front of the stage. The senate approved S.B. 296 on March 6 by a vote of 23-5-1. Although the cast was exhausted and ready for the opera to end, there would be an explosive act three. While the various stakeholders were working out their disagreements regarding S.B. 296, Dushku and Wilson were drafting S.B. 297 for Senator Adams. The point of this bill was to give religious allowances that states like Connecticut and New York had given and to ensure that same-sex couples could get marriage licenses while allowing individual clerks to opt out of the process for conscience reasons. House Republicans, however, were worried that there were not enough votes to pass S.B. 296. And the chair of the relevant committee, LaVar Christensen, was unfriendly to say the least. In a side plot worthy of Mozart, Brad Dee (who managed S.B. 296 in the house) and Stuart Adams asked Christensen to be the house sponsor of S.B. 297 in return for his tacit acquiescence in S.B. 296. Wilson and Adams finalized S.B. 297. Their bill contained several faith-based exemptions, including a bar to government penalties against religious individuals or organizations who invoked "religious or other deeply held beliefs . . . regarding marriage, family, or sexuality" as a defense to a claim under the SOGI antidiscrimination law. Also added were protections for religious counseling.[77]

Equality Utah and Rosky did not get the text of S.B. 297 until the evening of March 5. They went ballistic nine seconds later. They interpreted the new exemptions as creating a religious belief defense to S.B. 296 claims and as possibly opening the door to reparative therapy, which they considered a combination of voodoo medicine and waterboarding. Dushku and Wilson insisted that this was not their intent and that Equality Utah was over-reading the new provisions. Without quite comprehending why S.B. 297 was so inflammatory, church leaders still wanted a deal, so Dushku and Wilson reworked and tightened the anti-penalty and other offending provisions. Behind the scenes, the Church was the deus ex machina that magically made everything come together, with no more last-minute hitches. Casting aside all doubts, the house voted 65-11 for S.B. 296 on March 11. With a chorus of hundreds singing hosanna, Governor Herbert signed it into law in a huge public ceremony in the capitol the next day.[78]

Utah's Anti-Discrimination and Religious Freedom Amendments Act of 2015 might be a template for future legislation. Its approach of adding specific exemptions, after legislative deliberation, strikes us as a productive strategy for protecting religious freedom. The Church and its allies have created a movement dubbed "Fairness for All." The plan is to persuade other red states to follow Utah's example of bringing stakeholders together—leading religious denominations, the business community, and LGBTQ+ organizations and civil rights groups—to work out statutory schemes, state by state, that ensure equal treatment for sexual and gender minorities while also entrenching protections for religious minorities.[79]

Consistent with Fairness for All, we believe the 2015 Utah law is a statute of principles and not just a set of political compromises:

- *Nondiscrimination.* LGBT citizens need assurance that the state disapproves of discrimination because of sexual orientation and gender identity in employment, housing, and public accommodations. As the Supreme Court said in *Romer* and repeated in *Masterpiece,* a baseline of nondiscrimination is taken for granted by most Americans today—and that group should include sexual and gender minorities as well as racial minorities.

- *Religious Free Exercise.* Free exercise of religion should extend beyond churches, stakes, synagogues, and mosques to include religiously affiliated or controlled institutions, such as seminaries, charity associations, madrassas, and schools. One reason we support leeway for BYU in the 2015 Utah law is that BYU is effectively a seminary for the Latter-day Saints, who have no formal clergy.

- *Freedom of Speech and Association.* Utah's exclusion of the Boy Scouts from the employment protections can be justified by the freedom that expressive associations ought to have to pick their own officials. Without state compulsion, the Boy Scouts have responded to internal pressure to integrate sexual and gender minorities.

Professor Wilson lays down this challenge. In three-fifths of America, there are no statewide sexual orientation or gender identity protections in public accommodations laws. Hence, LGBT people can be told "We don't serve people like you." In two-fifths of the country, there are no statutory conscience protections, so people of faith can be told "Get over your faith or get out of business." "Across all of America," she says, "the public square belongs only to one side. Unless America finds new ways to share the public square, it will remain a checkerboard of injustice to someone."[80]

On December 6, 2019, a proposed Fairness for All Act was introduced in the House of Representatives. Going beyond the Utah statute, H.R. 5331 would add SOGI protections to federal laws barring discrimination in public accommodations, public funding, and education, as well as laws barring workplace and housing discrimination. The proposed legislation would also expand the coverage of the federal public accommodations law. In return, each arena of anti-discrimination protections would be limited by allowances for churches, religious associations, and religiously affiliated or controlled nonprofits and educational institutions to operate according to the dictates of their faith traditions. Some of the new religious allowances in H.R. 5331 are procedurally very complicated, such as the creation of a process to allow child-placement agencies to receive public funds even though they exclude LGBT families from their services. Some allowances just apply to claims of discrimination because of religion, sex, sexual orientation, and/or gender identity. Added at the last minute, one new provision specifically says that a broad range of institutional carve-outs will not apply to claims involving discrimination because of race, color, or national origin.[81]

As of 2020, Congress has not acted on the proposed Fairness for All Act, nor has any red state replicated Utah's statute. Indeed, the public reception of H.R. 5331 was frosty, if not subzero. The ACLU, Lambda Legal, the NAACP, HRC, the Leadership Conference on Civil and Human Rights, and other civil rights organizations roundly condemned the proposal because of its many religious allowances and its different treatment of SOGI discriminations. Their joint statement labeled the bill "an affront to existing civil rights protections" and a denial of just treatment for sexual and gender minorities. At the same time, Focus on the Family's President Daly, Dr. Moore of the Southern Baptists' ERLC, and dozens of other faith leaders have rejected the need for any protections for sexual and gender minorities. Fearing that the religious allowances would melt away over time, Princeton professor Robby George labeled the bill a "legislative wolf in sheep's clothing." Representative Christopher Stewart, a Utah Republican who is the chief sponsor, admitted that his bill was dead on arrival—but he held out hope that it could be the basis for a future statute. In light of the strongly negative reaction, is his hope realistic? We are not sure, but there is a path forward.[82]

To make any progress, leaders and staff of conservative religious and gay rights groups would at some point need to sit down together and start the process of creating common ground based upon a Golden Rule attitude where each group appreciates the core needs of the others. Gay rights leaders would need to understand that conscience claimants are not just ADF puppets seeking to revoke *Obergefell*. They are speaking from their hearts and expressing their faith as animating all of their dealings in the world. Religious leaders would need to understand that LGBTQ+ people are not just engaged in political correctness; many of them are still not at home in an America that persecuted them until very recently. Both sets of leaders would need to understand the limits of a substantially subjective understanding of rights. For the same reason the ADF's John Bursch objects to constitutional liberty based upon subjective views about dignity and the "mystery of life," so GLAD's Mary Bonauto objects to constitutional expression based upon subjective views about complicity with the "homosexual agenda." In other words, both groups of Americans need to understand that an expansive, subjective understanding of *harm* is neither constitutionally acceptable nor socially productive in our pluralist polity.[83]

Why should leaders of these contending social forces consent to such a process? Each group must be strongly motivated to *want* a fairness-for-all statute. Today, neither group seems motivated, but the future may bring new incentives. The religious groups' motivation might be that their future depends on the interest and allegiance of young people—who are turned off by even mildly anti-gay stances and who want a faith that stands for something positive. Evangelicals and Catholics need to do more than just say nice things about LGBTQ+ people: like the Latter-day Saints, they need to work with sexual and gender minorities before the ship sails without them. Gay rights leaders need to remember that most Americans live in states without public accommodation laws applicable to sexual and gender minorities. If they want such laws and if they want to entrench marriage equality against an increasingly conservative Supreme Court, they need to meet red state religions halfway. The court is unlikely to interpret existing civil rights statutes to include sexual and gender minorities, and if LGBTQ+ rights organizations want national protections, federal legislation is essential. To secure federal legislation, a bill needs sixty votes to cut off a senate filibuster. The LGBTQ-preferred Equality Act cannot win that many votes in the US Senate, while the Fairness for All Act might do so. The Equality Act has already passed the US House of Representatives, but legislation agreed to by both chambers would require some senate accommodations along the lines of the Fairness for All Act.

As this volume has demonstrated, popular support for SOGI anti-discrimination protections is strong and will not abate, but this should not lead the gayocracy to believe that a gridlocked Congress will bow to public opinion—or to believe that the Supreme Court will not announce new constitutional exemptions. ADF has recruited hundreds of bakers, florists, wedding planners, photographers, and marriage counselors who have brought or want to bring lawsuits—and *Masterpiece* is just the first of a string of victories ADF may win, notwithstanding existing First Amendment doctrine. Moreover, First Amendment doctrine (namely, the Boy Scouts case) protects Americans' freedom of association in normative groups. Following *Hobby Lobby*, the next wave of religious freedom cases will be those brought by or for religiously affiliated institutions. Armed with actual doctrine, the court will probably narrow civil rights protections even more vigorously. On the other hand, if the Supreme Court perceives that state and federal legislators are working out religious conscience accommodations on their own, the conservative majority will be more reluctant to announce sweeping new doctrines.

A theme that pervades this chapter is a contrast between unyielding doctrine—whether it be dogmatic understandings of marriage or dogmatic insistence upon equal treatment—and on-the-ground governance of a church or a society whose members have seemingly inconsistent normative commitments. Following the lead of SBC president J.D. Greear, Pope Francis, and the Latter-day Saints' President Dallin Oaks, we suggest the value of Golden Rule deliberations, where people of good will try to understand the lives and commitments of those with whom they disagree. Deep deliberation requires a commitment to reciprocity, takes time and patience, and considers novel accommodations and principles. Although we think deliberation works best in administrative or legislative settings, it can also work in judicial settings if judges use evidentiary hearings, trial testimony, and oral arguments to listen empathically to perspectives not their own and to seek common ground rather than lobby for their personally preferred policy. Whether one's model is the Golden Rule, the original meaning of the equal protection clause, or the soaring rhetoric of *Romer* and *Masterpiece*, the goal ought to be building bridges rather than blowing them up.

24 • Families We Choose

Joan Ruth Bader was born on March 15, 1933, into a world where women were expected to marry, bear and raise children, and cook meals and keep house for their husbands. She and thousands of other female icons remade that world into one where women are encouraged to become professors, athletes, mechanics, and notorious justices.

Ruth's mother, Celia, gave her excellent advice. "I should be a lady," namely, "be in control of your emotions and don't give way to anger, to remorse, to envy; those emotions just sap strength. And [this will] enable you to move forward. And her other message was, be independent. I suppose she hoped that someday I would meet and marry Prince Charming. Nevertheless, she emphasized the importance of being able to fend for myself." The daughter needed little prodding to become a top student. When Ruth started public high school, in 1946, her mother was diagnosed with cervical cancer. She graduated with top honors one day after her mother died.[1]

At Cornell University, Ruth Bader was a quiet, light-brunette-haired beauty. She found the boys insufficiently serious—until she met Marty Ginsburg on a blind date. Although he charmed her with his goofy smile and self-deprecating humor, what won her over was that "Marty was the first boy I ever knew who cared that I had a brain." In 1954, Ruth and Marty got married, right after Ruth completed her degree at Cornell and Marty finished his first year at Harvard Law School. Soon thereafter they had a child, Jane. To satisfy Marty's military obligations, their family relocated in Oklahoma for two years. They seemed like the typical postwar family: breadwinning husband, housekeeping wife, and a tow-haired child born of the couple's conjugal union.

But Ruth's nature was not domestic, and Marty always said she was the brains of the family. After his wife's unfortunate encounter with a tuna casserole, Marty often took over the kitchen (especially when there were guests), as she planned her entry into Harvard Law School in 1956. Although law school dean Erwin Griswold wondered whether the nine women in the class of 1959 should take the places of qualified men, and most professors refused to call on female students, Ruth earned top grades. She attributes much of her success to Jane. Because they had a sitter only until 4:00 p.m., Ruth would focus hard on her classwork until then, when she would return home to play with Jane. After the infant went to sleep, the mother would stay up much of the night preparing for the next day's classes. During her second year of law school, Marty was diagnosed with testicular cancer, which required toxic doses of radiation. Ruth's ability to multitask expanded as she took care of both Marty and Jane, kept up with her classwork, and typed up the class notes taken by Marty's friends.

Marty survived, his humor intact, and secured an excellent job at a New York law firm starting in 1958. Ruth asked Harvard if she could spend her last year at Columbia Law School and use those credits to complete her Harvard degree. Harvard refused, and she transferred to Columbia Law School, where she tied for first in her class in 1959. Even though she had top grades and made law review at two Ivy League schools, Ruth found no law firm willing to hire her. She had a summer job at Paul, Weiss, Rifkind, Wharton and Garrison, a progressive firm looking for a female attorney. But she did not get a permanent offer because the firm latched on to a black woman who satisfied two diversity needs at once. Little did they know.[2]

Anna Pauline (Pauli) Murray came from a very different background. Born in 1910 and of Cherokee, African, and European ancestry, she fell between the cracks of the American dream. Pauli lost her mother at age three, and a guard at a segregated mental institution in Alabama murdered her father. Aunt Pauline Fitzgerald Dame adopted her and raised her in the Durham, North Carolina, home of Pauli's maternal grandparents. She was "a thin, wiry, ravenous child" who devoured books and food in equal measure. By the time she graduated from high school at fifteen, "she was the editor-in-chief of the school newspaper, the president of the literary society, class secretary, a member of the debate club, the top student, and a forward on the basketball team." Refusing to attend a "colored" college in North Carolina, she learned about sexism when Columbia College told her it did

Joan Ruth Bader. (Portrait art by Don Patron.)

not admit women. She ended up at Hunter College and lived in Harlem, where she befriended Langston Hughes, listened to Nat King Cole, and soaked up the Harlem Renaissance.[3]

While Ruth Bader Ginsburg was a research fellow at the Columbia Law School, hoping for a tenure-track academic appointment, Pauli Murray was struggling with poverty and hunger, the oppression of racism and a short stint in jail, and denigration for being a woman—though a very striking woman who could outthink the racists and the sexists. At a Richmond fundraiser for a death-row inmate, she impressed Thurgood Marshall and Howard Ransom, who got her admitted to Howard University Law School. (She also applied to the University of North Carolina's law school, which rejected her because of her race.) Older than most students and smarter than most faculty, she figured out at Howard that "Jane Crow" (her term) was just as oppressive a system as Jim Crow. She graduated first in her class.

Pauli maintained that America would never be a legitimate democracy so long as African Americans were disenfranchised and excluded from public institutions and private opportunities. To pursue her idea, she applied to do graduate work at the Harvard Law School, which rejected her because

Anna Pauline Murray. (In the Portrait Collection
#P0002, North Carolina Collection Photographic
Archives, The Wilson Library, University of North
Carolina at Chapel Hill.)

of her sex. Pauli responded with a witty (though unsuccessful) petition for
reconsideration:

> Gentlemen, I would gladly change my sex to meet your requirements,
> but since the way to such change has not been revealed to me, I have no
> recourse but to appeal to you to change your minds on this subject. Are
> you to tell me that one is as difficult as the other?

She was only half joking. Pauli did not identify as a woman, and she might
indeed have corrected her sex if it had been feasible for her. She described
herself as a "male head and brain (?), female-ish body, mixed emotional

characteristics." In her words, she was "one of nature's experiments; a girl who should have been a boy." Just as Ruth was naturally left-handed, feminine, and attracted to funny boys, Pauli was naturally aggressive, outspoken, and attracted to nice white girls. She did not see herself as a lesbian, for she regarded her "very natural falling in love with the female sex" as consistent with her identity as a man. Today she would probably self-identify as transgender, nonbinary, or queer.[4]

In 1950, she joined the Paul, Weiss firm. Pauli found the legal work and professionalism inspiring and the mostly white, male atmosphere too confining. She lingered long enough to become intimately involved with the firm's office manager, Irene Barlow, a social justice Episcopalian who was Pauli's best friend and the closest she would come to a life partner. During the 1960s, Pauli was a rambunctious, brilliant, often outraged participant and theorist in both the civil rights and women's rights movements. In 1961, she was named to the Committee on Political and Civil Rights of the President's Commission on the Status of Women. In 1962, she wrote a prophetic memorandum arguing that the equal protection clause could be interpreted to question sex-based discrimination for the same reasons the Supreme Court had applied strict equal protection scrutiny to race-based discrimination. Like race discrimination, sex discrimination rested upon a natural-law argument about "inherent differences" between men and women that had been deployed to support the disadvantages and social inferiority of women, a class of capable citizens. In 1965, while a graduate student at Yale Law School, she coauthored an article called "Jane Crow and the Law" in which she wrote: "Discriminatory attitudes toward women are strikingly parallel to those regarding Negroes." The Fourteenth Amendment had to stand against this kind of irrationality. It ought to guarantee women both "equality of opportunity," unimpeded by traditional gender stereotypes, and "freedom of choice" to form and participate in families where they could flourish. Anticipating the dialectical relationship between liberty and equality that the Supreme Court would valorize in its recent gay rights precedents, Pauli also explored the ways in which sexism and racism were synergistic: dismissed by black men as well as whites, black women suffered more than twice over.[5]

After two years as a research fellow at Columbia, that law school declined to offer Ruth Ginsburg the academic appointment it had frequently tendered to male fellows. Reportedly, professors at Columbia recommended that Ruth apply to the Rutgers School of Law because "they wouldn't mind having a woman." In 1963, she started her academic career at Rutgers and eventually taught a course about women and the law. Plunging into the new area of inquiry, she was dazzled by Pauli Murray's charge that gender stereotypes held women back in the same irrational ways that racial stereotypes harmed people of color. Because of the massive radiation from Marty's treatment for testicular cancer, the Ginsburgs were surprised when Ruth became pregnant with their second child. Concerned that employers pervasively discriminated against pregnant female employees, Ruth wore her mother-in-law's one-size-larger dresses so that she would not show until the summer break. James was born at the end of the summer, right before the once-again trim professor went back to work.[6]

Thurgood Marshall, the NAACP's constitutional litigator, considered Murray's *States' Laws on Race and Color* (1950) to be "the Bible" for the civil rights movement, as it documented (in 750 pages) the massive array of race-based laws buttressing apartheid. Similarly, Ginsburg discovered that there were thousands of federal, state, and local laws buttressing the apartheid of the household. These laws created a massive regime of sex discrimination—starting with family law, which situated husbands as the lords and masters of the family, required wives to change their names, and insulated husbands from culpability for rape and sexual assault of their wives. The Ginsburg family considered these legal atavisms appalling and outmoded. Jane and James grew up believing a natural family arrangement could be, as Marty put it (with characteristic hyperbole), one where "Daddy did the cooking, and Mother did the thinking."[7]

At the same time she was cofounding the National Organization for Women (NOW), Murray was serving on the ACLU's Equality Committee and pushing it to challenge government sex discriminations as violations of the Fourteenth Amendment. Ginsburg volunteered with the ACLU, which asked her to write its brief for the appealing party in *Reed v. Reed* (1971). Idaho law mandated that a qualified man should be the administrator of the decedent's estate, ahead of an equally qualified woman. Believing herself best qualified to administer her deceased son's estate, Sally Reed challenged that discrimination, which favored her estranged husband, Cecil. The ACLU took Sally's appeal to the Supreme Court. Ginsburg listed Murray on the brief, as Murray had put forward the central idea: sex was a suspect classification for the same reasons race was. Both were natural traits that the dominant culture had treated as a badge of inferiority and stigmatized legally, based upon inaccurate stereotypes. The ACLU did not press Murray's claim that racism and sexism were not just parallel phenomena but interactive and mutually reinforcing, as Murray had learned in her encounters with prestigious universities, tony firms, and the police in Richmond, Virginia.[8]

Although the Supreme Court unanimously agreed that Sally Reed's sex discrimination was constitutionally arbitrary, the court did not address the Murray-Ginsburg argument that government discrimination because of sex ought to be constitutionally suspect. The next year, the Tenth Circuit followed *Reed* in a tax case that Ruth and Marty briefed and argued as a team, *Moritz v. Commissioner* (1972). Charles Moritz was the caregiver for his invalid mother and tried to deduct the expenses of a nurse. The IRS denied the deduction because it was only allowed for women and formerly married men. At Ruth and Marty's behest, the court of appeals overruled the agency on the ground that the statutory distinction was an invidious discrimination.[9]

The same year as the *Moritz* decision, the ACLU installed Ginsburg as the codirector of its new Women's Rights Project (WRP), which won a series of landmark Supreme Court rulings, including *Frontiero v. Richardson* (1973), where a plurality accepted her argument for strict scrutiny, and *Craig v. Boren* (1976), where a majority held that sex was a "quasi-suspect" classification. Among Ginsburg's favorite rulings were those involving the family. After she left the ACLU to become a judge, the Supreme Court followed the WRP's analysis to invalidate a Louisiana law requiring that the husband be "lord and master" of the household and barring wives from entering into mortgage agreements.[10]

One of Ginsburg's own family law victories involved Stephen Wiesenfeld, whose wife died during childbirth. Stephen resolved that he would personally care for his infant and would not work full-time until the child started school. He was aware that the Social Security Act provided childcare supplements for bereaved spouses who wanted to work part-time so they could care for their children—but these benefits were not available to fathers. As she had done in *Moritz*, Ginsburg could show the all-male judiciary that men also suffered unfairly from sex discriminations, and she could show society that there were fathers (like Marty) who *wanted* to do childcare and domestic work out of love for their children and concern for their well-being. She won the case on a 9-0 vote. The majority opinion focused on the harm to both female employees (whose social security contributions did not benefit their survivors) and male survivors and caregivers. Ginsburg managed a smile when she read the concurring opinion of conservative Justice William Rehnquist, who focused on the arbitrary harm to children.[11]

At the same time the WRP was attacking government sex discriminations, the ACLU was attacking state restrictions on people's private sexual activities and their nonmarital relationships. Table 4 compares traditional religion-inspired family law with the agenda pursued by the ACLU and its allies, prominently including Dr. Franklin Kameny, who cofounded the National Capital chapter of the ACLU in Washington. We also include progressive thinking that emerged after *Loving v. Virginia* (1967) and Stonewall (1969). Murray was a harbinger of radical or progressive critiques. Her life illustrated how American family law operated to destroy relationships of unconventional citizens, at the same time it claimed to be supporting marriage and family.[12]

The liberal vision of family law espoused by Ruth Bader Ginsburg (a Supreme Court justice since 1993) has triumphed socially, politically, and constitutionally in the last half century. Marriage equality for LGBTQ+ couples is a part of this larger story. Thus, when Justice Ginsburg cast her vote for the plaintiff couples in *Obergefell v. Hodges,* she was carrying forth the ACLU's constitutional vision for the family. Although the parent of the ACLU's feminist constitutionalism, Murray would not have been satisfied with just marriage equality, because it neglected people like her—many of them women, many racial minorities—who did not want to get married and did not appreciate the government's lavish array of marriage-based benefits and rights. She and her partner sustained one another, but the law did nothing to support their relationship. Irene Barlow died in 1973, and in 1985 pancreatic cancer took Pauli Murray, still striving, always thinking ahead, and penniless to the end.[13]

The liberal vision has been a powerful articulation of both libertarian and egalitarian norms as applied to families: the state should be neutral with regard to people's romantic choices and should not discriminate or exclude social groups from the fundamental protections of family law. The liberal vision rests upon a theory of the community's well-being that valorizes individual choice—but traditionalists have responded that any effort to deviate from the baseline of gender complementarity and marital conjugality would be disastrous for the institution of marriage, for children, and ultimately for society. Some critics predicted that few gay people would take advantage of same-sex marriage if it were offered. With marriage licenses having been offered in Massachusetts since 2004 and in other states after that, all of these propositions can be tentatively evaluated based on experience. Marriage is doing better than expected, and there are some promising developments for those who believe that children are usually better off with two parents rather than just one.

Table 4: Competing Assumptions About Marriage and the Family, 1972

Topic	Natural law baseline (Catholic Church, Southern Baptists)	Liberal baseline (ACLU, NOW)	Radical baseline (Nat'l Ass'n of Gay Orgs.)
Normative yardstick	Human nature. God's commands.	Human happiness. Liberal: no harm.	Reconstructed equality. Radical critique.
Gender assumptions	Biology is destiny. Men and women different.	Presumptive equality. Men and women pretty much the same.	Sexuality and gender categories as arbitrary forms of social power.
Permitted sexual expression	Conjugal marriage is only situs of valid sex: sex outside marriage wrong; sodomy very wrong.	Consent by two adults. Fornication, consensual sodomy okay.	Critical understanding of *consent* and power relations. Focus on genuine mutuality.
Marriage	Conjugal marriage as exclusive institution for family. Lifetime commitment.	Marriage as one option for romantic partners. Expand definition of marriage.	Expand both eligibility for marriage and for state benefits (to nonmarital families).
Children	Biological children central to marriage. Gendered role modeling.	Children by choice can enrich marriage. Best interests of the child.	Caregiving > biology and marriage. State support for caregiving.
State regulation	Marriage monopoly. Mandatory rules to support marriage for life.	Guided choice; family law pluralism. Default rules > mandatory rules.	Family law pluralism, with marriage less central. Few mandatory rules, softer default rules.

Progressives have responded to the liberal vision with a more capacious understanding of equal protection: under conditions of oppressive social power, state neutrality is itself unfair, and its pro-choice regime will not serve the overall good of the community. Notice how both traditionalists and progressives focus on community needs and allocation of resources, but with different theories of what is good for the community. Like traditionalists, progressives found much to criticize in Justice Kennedy's *Obergefell* opinion. The day it was handed down, a noontime discussion was hastily convened at a family law conference sponsored by the American Association of Law Schools. Most of the speakers were disappointed, and some were shocked, by Kennedy's praise for "the transcendent importance of marriage," which responded to our "most basic human needs" and was "essential to our most profound hopes and aspirations." Only marriage allowed children "to understand the integrity and closeness of their own family and its concord with other families in their community and in their daily lives." The professors felt that this romanticized account glossed over the ways marriage has been an institution where women did more of the work and reaped less security for their efforts. Kennedy extolled the marital aspirations of April DeBoer and Jayne Rowse but seemed unaware that they did not want to marry until the judge nudged them into it.[14]

Most of the academic criticism of *Obergefell* has focused on the message these passages send to the many Americans, like Pauli Murray, who do not want to get married or cannot afford to do so. As Serena Mayeri puts it, "Kennedy's opinion elevates and ennobles marriage in terms that implicitly disparage non-marriage." Melissa Murray (no relation to Pauli) infers from *Obergefell* the message that alternatives to marriage "are less profound, less dignified, and less valuable. On this account, the rationale for marriage equality rests— perhaps ironically—on the fundamental inequality of other relationships and kinship forms." Like Pauli Murray decades earlier, feminist, critical race, and queer critics see the Supreme Court's celebration of marriage as casting a disparaging shadow on families of poverty, many of which are headed by single black and Latina women. Drawing from parallel marriage normalization for freed slaves after the Civil War, Katherine Franke warns that normalization of marriage for sexual and gender minorities invites increased government regulation and discipline into the intimate relationships of LGBTQ+ people.[15]

The democratic vision shared by Pauli Murray and Ruth Ginsburg provides a counterpoint to both the Mayeri-Murray pessimistic understanding of *Obergefell* as disrespecting unmarried Americans (a group that included all three of the court's female justices in 2015, including the widowed Ruth Bader Ginsburg) and the Thomas-Scalia insistence that constitutional liberty only offers protections against negative prohibitions, such as the criminal sanction in *Loving*. Like Ginsburg, Murray would have favored the equality-based challenge to the state Super-DOMAs—but the experience of women, people of color, and LGBTQ+ people also led them to appreciate a deeper reading of *Obergefell*. The liberty protected in *Obergefell* is not freedom from state penalty but freedom from state efforts to commandeer the lives of minority groups by inflexibly channeling their most personal decisions into a government-approved mold. Freedom from state commandeering (*Obergefell*, following *Lawrence*) dovetails with an originalist anti-caste reading of equal protection (*Windsor*, following *Romer*) to yield a robust constitutional regime that assures us all opportunities to form relationships that foster the many faces of human flourishing. This understanding of *Obergefell* best captures the constitutional vision and Hayekian leanings of its author, Anthony Kennedy. But it also synthesizes the lessons we draw from the lives of Ruth Bader Ginsburg and Pauli Murray. Under the old coverture regime of family law, neither would have been allowed to go to law school, and even the milder regime of domesticity would have discouraged their careers and their writings. America would have been deprived of two of the greatest legal minds of the last century.[16]

Our account in this volume supports an anti-commandeering reading of *Obergefell* as consistent with both developments in society and the larger constitutional space of "equal liberty" within which the decision rests. It remains to be seen how the Supreme Court will interpret *Obergefell* and apply it to new issues, including some we discuss below, but much of our audience for equal liberty is state judges and legislators, who are the primary architects of American family law. "Families we choose" (Kath Weston's term) are now embedded in American culture, and the legitimacy of the modern state depends upon the capacity of family law to meet as well as shape the needs of our diverse population.[17]

From "Traditional" Marriage to Families We Choose

In 1967, the year Wendy Brown married Ken DeBoer, American family law looked a lot like what people now deem "traditional." If two consenting adults wanted to enjoy sexual relations, marriage had a legally protected monopoly: fornication (sex outside of marriage), adultery (sex between two people, at least one of whom is married to someone else), and sexual cohabitation outside of marriage were crimes in almost all states. Agreements between cohabiting partners were legally unenforceable. Children born within marriage were presumed to be the progeny of the husband and wife; children born outside of marriage were "illegitimate" and were denied family-based benefits. The law assumed that husbands and wives were married for life; divorce in most states required a showing of spousal fault such as adultery. The marital union was a zone of privacy that the state could not regulate, whether through anti-contraceptive rules or protections against some spousal assaults.[18]

For social as well as legal reasons, marriage in 1967 was well-nigh compulsory for romantic couples. More than two-thirds of American adults were married in 1967, and most of them were raising or had raised their biological children. Most wives and mothers did not work outside the home. Divorce rates were on the rise, but most marriages were still lifetime affairs. The lives of Ginsburg and, especially, Murray were harbingers, for the next half century witnessed a radical change in the economic opportunities, social status, and political clout of American women—and the American family changed correspondingly. Family pluralism begat family law pluralism, as the legitimacy of the marriage monopoly collapsed. Endowed with social, religious, and legal significance, marriage in its decline became a magnet for the equality claims of LGBTQ+ people. Their clamor to join marriage has possibly renewed that flagging institution.

SOCIOLOGY OF THE FAMILY: WOMEN'S OPTIONS AND CHOICES

Historian Carole Shammas teaches us that, from the eighteenth century onward, America has seen a steady decline in fertility and household size and an overall decline in marriage rates. The economic foundation for those trends has been the displacement of our largely rural, agrarian economy with an urban, industrial one and then by a postindustrial service economy. These developments, augmented by technological advances in contraception and assisted reproduction, have freed increasing numbers of women to assert their personal needs and interests outside the home and to demand changes in male-empowering legal baselines.[19]

Consider historian Nancy Cott's analysis in *Public Vows* (2000). The common law understanding of marriage the colonies inherited from England—the coverture regime—yoked wives to an indentured servitude. The American republic slowly weaned itself from that regime as the urbanizing polity moved toward a more egalitarian understanding of marriage, but with strong role differentiation based on sex. The long transition took place under the banner of complementarity, positing that men and women were sexually, physically, mentally, and dispositionally complements to one another. Affection and love replaced obedience to the master of the house, and coverture gave way to the idea that the husband represented the household in the public sphere while the wife ruled the private sphere. The Proclamation on the Family from the Church of Jesus Christ, declarations from the Vatican, and the resolutions by the Southern Baptist Convention all reflected the complementarity that was central to what is now called "traditional marriage" but which Cott describes as "marriage as constituted by society between 1927 and 1967."[20]

In the late twentieth century, complementarity came under fire as women steadily increased their public presence. Pauli Murray worked traditional male jobs during World War II, and Ruth Ginsburg demonstrated she could outlawyer the boys after the war. With keen media awareness, a boom in public education, and new job opportunities, postindustrial America produced a steady stream of women wanting careers and participation in the public sphere. (With more divorces and insufficient alimony, some women had to seek work outside the home to support themselves and their children.) After 1960, women increasingly postponed marriage or did not marry, had fewer children and bore them later in life, and split with their husbands when relationships soured. More Americans had sex outside of marriage. Under the banner of the sexual revolution, a lot of women got pregnant, and a lot of men got lost. Recall Figure 1 from chapter 10, which maps the declining percentage of Americans who were married in any given year and the increasing percentage of births outside of marriage.

These social and economic changes were particularly liberating for lesbian, bisexual, gender-noncomforming, and queer women. Before jobs opened up for women in large numbers, such women were under tremendous pressure to marry men. Although Pauli Murray never made much money in her various careers, she was the first woman or first black woman to work as an attorney at Paul, Weiss, to teach at Brandeis University, or to become an ordained Episcopal priest. By the time she died, women had unparalleled employment opportunities, and lesbians seized them, sometimes divorcing their husbands. In the 1990s, April DeBoer was unhappily married to a man; in 1999, after separating from her husband, she met Jayne Rowse, who would be her life partner. Once both secured jobs as nurses, they enjoyed the economic foundation for a life together and the resources to raise lots of children.

Women's improving economic and social status contributed to the marriage equality movement even more tangibly. Starting with Clela Rorex, the clerk who knowingly issued marriage licenses to same-sex couples in 1975, female public officials have overwhelmingly supported equal treatment. For the most dramatic example, twenty-one out of twenty-six female state supreme court judges voted for constitutional equality claims between 1993 and 2013. Male high court judges divided more evenly, 24-19. In federal constitutional litigation, all but one female judge voted for marriage equality, and all three female Supreme Court justices who had the opportunity to do so voted repeatedly for marriage equality. Given the post-*Windsor* timing of the federal cases, a large majority of male judges also voted for marriage equality, though only two of six male Supreme Court justices did so. Of course, the most prominent judicial voice for marriage equality was that of Justice Ginsburg.[21]

CHANGING SOCIAL NORMS OF THE FAMILY

In our substantially liberal society, American couples nowadays tend to separate three things that the traditionalist, natural law approach joins together as a normative package: sexual intercourse, marriage, and procreation. Most Americans have openly engaged in sexual activities outside of marriage and without the possibility of procreation; they have increasingly procreated without either sexual intercourse or marriage; and some have married without any intent or capacity to procreate. (There remains an assumed connection between sexual activities and marriage, but that may loosen as well.) Sociologist Andrew Cherlin views the shift as a decline of "institutional" marriage, replaced by "companionate" marriage, which is being supplanted in turn by "individualized" marriage.[22]

The shift in attitudes has been part of a generational movement away from communitarian and morals-based assumptions and toward individualistic assumptions: What lets me chart a life path that will allow me to flourish? Be happy? America is now a consumerist society, and even religion has become more consumerist. As early as Margaret Sanger, popular thinkers were advocating sex for pleasure. Americans have gradually minimized sex for marital procreation and increasingly but discreetly have admitted that they enjoy it for pleasure or sociability. In the 1960s, the liberal understanding came out from the shadows and saturated American culture. It even reached the Supreme Court, which in *Griswold v. Connecticut* (1965) announced a constitutional right to sexual privacy and consensual pleasure for married couples—a right it soon

broadened to mean the "right of the *individual,* married or single, to be free
from unwarranted governmental intrusion into matters so fundamentally affecting a person as the decision whether to bear or beget a child." Today, political conservatives join liberals in asserting that pleasure and sociability are
legitimate justifications for sexual activities.[23]

The power of the liberal baseline for constitutional law was revealed when
the 1987 nomination of Robert Bork for the Supreme Court was defeated in
large part because he acidly criticized the constitutional right to sexual privacy. "If the Bork hearings accomplished anything," wrote Gary McDowell, "it
was the enshrinement of *Griswold v. Connecticut* as 'a fixed star in our constitutional firmament.'" Six years after the Bork hearings, five justices appointed
by Republican presidents reaffirmed a constitutional right of privacy and abortion choice in *Casey v. Planned Parenthood of Southeastern Pennsylvania* (1992).
In his portion of the per curiam opinion, Justice Kennedy (who got the Bork
seat) wrote: "At the heart of liberty is the right to define one's own concept of
existence, of meaning, of the universe, and of the mystery of human life. Beliefs about these matters could not define the attributes of personhood were
they formed under compulsion of the State." He relied on the same broad understanding of liberty in his gay rights opinions for the Supreme Court in
Lawrence, Windsor, and *Obergefell.* Justice Scalia ungenerously found this reasoning godless, lawless, and hopeless—culminating in his dyspeptic "hide my
head in a bag" dissent from the majority opinion in *Obergefell.* We view the
language to reflect an anti-commandeering and egalitarian understanding of
the Fourteenth Amendment: the neutral state sets up a legal structure that
allows everyone to structure his/her/their life and relationships without undue pressure from the state.[24]

The change in Americans' attitudes toward sexual freedom, procreation, and
marriage had a direct effect on gay people and their rights. Straight Americans escaped the natural law regulatory regime through laws creating no-fault
divorce, police and prosecutors' policies not to enforce laws against fornication and cohabitation, legislators' votes to deregulate consensual sex crimes,
and constitutional decisions like *Griswold* and *Casey.* Between 1965 (*Griswold*)
and 2015 (*Obergefell*), the legal latitude for straight people to define and live
out their personal understandings of the sweet mystery of life grew ever more
inconsistent with the statutory restrictions discouraging gay people from defining and living out their personal understandings. Often estranged from
their blood families and strangers to the law, lesbians and gay men created
what social anthropologist Kath Weston dubbed "families we choose" from

friends, lovers, life partners, neighbors, community organizations, and accepting relatives. Assisted reproductive technology (ART) allowed them to create families with blood ties between one parent and the child. In the new millennium, a lot of straight people have followed the families-we-choose approach rather than that dictated by either natural law or liberal marriage. This is one reason for the revival of interest in Pauli Murray, for whom marriage was irrelevant and friendship networks deeply sustaining.[25]

FAMILY LAW PLURALISM

The liberal understanding of sexuality, gender, and relationships has placed pressure on American family law to rely more on individual choice and less on convention. The biggest change has been the no-fault divorce revolution, which made marriages much easier to dissolve if one or both spouses wanted to move on. There can be no return to "traditional" marriage so long as the country remains wedded to no-fault divorce, which has thus far remained politically impregnable. Our focus here will be the erosion of marriage's monopoly on legitimate sexual intercourse, relationship recognition, and parent-child bonds. In its place has emerged a burgeoning family law pluralism, where the state offers romantic couples more choices outside of marriage and recognizes parental rights for unmarried biological parents and for caregivers who are not related to their children by either marriage or blood. All of these changes are responses to the families-we-choose social norm. None has absolved the state from regulatory duties to protect partners and children from harm and from facilitating choices that reflect a productive way forward for the community.[26]

(1) *Ending Marriage's Monopoly on Sexual Intercourse.* Apart from no-fault divorce, the biggest development has been the decriminalization of sex with a consenting adult outside of conjugal marriage—consensual sodomy, fornication, cohabitation, or adultery. Most of the decriminalization was through state adoption of the Model Penal Code, which reflected a quintessentially liberal approach to sex crimes. After that initial sweep, gay rights organizations contributed to a second wave of decriminalization, which culminated in *Lawrence v. Texas,* where the Supreme Court invalidated consensual sodomy laws. Justice Kennedy began his opinion with an echo of his anti-commandeering passage from *Casey:* "Liberty presumes an autonomy of self that includes freedom of thought, belief, expression, and certain intimate conduct."[27]

Natural law scholars Robert George (Princeton) and Gerard Bradley (Notre Dame) recognized that if the state could not channel the sex lives of its citizens into conjugality (*Lawrence*), the next step would be to bar the state from channeling its citizens' relationships into conjugal marriage. Their brief for Focus on the Family implored the Supreme Court to respect the normative anchor of conjugal marriage. No one on the court completely agreed with their brilliantly articulated position: even Justice Thomas, in dissent, ridiculed the law as uncommonly silly, and Justice Scalia deferred to the Texas legislature to make moral judgments and invested all his energies into lambasting the majority opinion. After the court majority broadly endorsed a baseline rooted in individual choice rather than moral convention or marriage, religious leaders and philosophers failed to mount an effective campaign against it. George and Bradley had drafted the Federal Marriage Amendment and hoped that the constitutional discussion would rally America to their perspective on natural law—but the proposed amendment fizzled badly, and its defeat opened the door for marriage equality.[28]

(2) *A Menu of Relationship Options.* Because contracts and wills involving cohabiting partners had been subject to legal objection on the ground that the underlying relationship was meretricious, decriminalization potentially legitimated those contract and property rights. In *Marvin v. Marvin* (1976), the California Supreme Court ruled that courts should enforce contractual obligations, including implied contracts, between sexually cohabiting partners. Almost all state courts have followed this anti-commandeering precedent. A few states recognize *Marvin* claims only if they are founded on explicit contracts. A larger minority not only recognize implied contract claims but also infer the partners' agreement to share income or property from the fact that one partner took care of the household, allegedly in return for the other partner's willingness to support the household financially. In those states, the finding that a couple is cohabiting more or less creates a new default rule in which the partners are presumed to be mutually supportive or to share property.[29]

Once sexual cohabitation became legal, and thus subject to normal rules of contract and property, most states created rules to regulate these relationships. Thus, domestic violence admonitions and procedures often apply to cohabiting as well as married couples. A few states have imposed duties upon third parties through recognizing tort claims by cohabiting partners for death or harm to their loved ones. Following developments in Europe and Canada, Grace Ganz Blumberg has proposed that legislatures create a "cohabiting partners" status and set forth rights and responsibilities that the partners should know before moving in together.[30]

Consistent with the anti-commandeering norm, sexually active American adults can now choose among three regulatory regimes: dating, with few regulations outside of tort and criminal law; cohabitation, regulated by contract doctrine and some statutory rules; and marriage, an institution vesting the spouses with many rights, benefits, and duties. The marriage equality movement added new institutions to the menu in particular states: domestic partnerships for employees; reciprocal beneficiaries; designated beneficiaries; and comprehensive statewide domestic partnerships or civil unions. Most municipal and corporate domestic partnership policies included different-sex as well as same-sex partners, as did the civil union/comprehensive domestic partnership laws in Colorado, Illinois, and Nevada. In California and Washington, comprehensive domestic partnership laws reached all couples where one partner was age sixty-two or older.

On the eve of *Obergefell,* many states offered all couples a menu of options. Partners could choose the regime that best fit their level of commitment and the range of benefits and duties they wanted. Table 5 offers the potential range of such a menu. All options rest upon mutual consent: if romantic couples do not choose to live together or to register as partners or beneficiaries, they are regulated only by the ordinary rules of criminal and tort law; if they choose to marry, they enjoy more benefits but also more duties. Thus, the menu is also a regulatory regime, for the choice of relationship form often involves a trade-off between benefits and obligations. The state can nudge but not commandeer couples' choices. Getting married, for instance, provides many benefits but imposes fidelity and support obligations and is difficult and expensive to terminate. The menu includes covenant marriages, which require waiting periods and counseling before spouses can secure divorces.

(3) *The Independence of Parenthood from Biology and Marriage.* The anti-commandeering and equal treatment principles have profound implications for parent-child relationships. The coverture regime gave marriage a monopoly over this relationship: any children born within the marriage were conclusively presumed to be the progeny of the married couple; the father was master of the children as well as of the wife-mother; and any children born outside of marriage were illegitimate. In most states, illegitimate children had no legal parents, and their fathers had no legal obligations to them. In *Levy v. Louisiana* (1968), the Supreme Court invalidated a law denying wrongful death benefits to nonmarital children. The court ruled that "these children are not 'nonpersons.' They are humans." The state's policy to channel sexual and

Table 5: Menu of Relationship Options

Duty or benefit	Dating	Cohabitation	Domestic partnership	Designated beneficiary	Civil union/ marriage	Covenant marriage
Tort	Yes	Yes	Yes	Yes	Yes	Yes
Contract		Yes	Yes	Yes	Yes	Yes
Domestic violence		Yes	Yes	Yes	Yes	Yes
Employee benefits			Yes	Yes	Yes	Yes
Decision rules				Yes	Yes	Yes
Inheritance rules				Yes	Yes	Yes
Support and fidelity					Yes	Yes
Portability					Maybe/Yes	Yes
Divorce process					Yes	Yes
Divorce waiting period						Yes

parental energies into civil marriage was an insufficient justification to impose such harm on children—an anticipation of the anti-commandeering reasoning in *Windsor* and *Obergefell*. In subsequent cases, the Supreme Court held that nonmarital children could not be denied support from their biological parents or welfare assistance from the state. *Stanley v. Illinois* (1972) ruled that unmarried biological fathers could not be automatically barred from establishing a parental relationship with their children. In all these cases, liberalization deployed biology to trump state marriage law.[31]

Consistent with *Levy* and *Stanley*, the 1973 Uniform Parentage Act (UPA) sought to assure legal recognition "equally to every child and to every parent, regardless of the marital status of the parents." The UPA suggested that the presumption of fatherhood for a married couple be rebuttable with appropriate biological evidence. The 2002 version of the UPA was an effort to make it easier for unmarried biological fathers to establish paternity through voluntary acknowledgment or through an agreement with the mother. These were important liberalizing proposals to allow biology to trump the legal regime of

marriage, whose monopoly was fast eroding. The Supreme Court accommodated some of this conceptual shift but often acquiesced in state paternity policies that harmed indigent unmarried mothers.[32]

Adoption was another engine of liberalization. By the 1960s, most states permitted single as well as married persons to create families through adoption,
and stepparents could adopt their spouse's children. But joint adoptions were
not available to unmarried couples until progressive lawyers started pushing
social workers and state judges to allow second-parent adoptions, whereby a
lesbian could become the second parent to her partner's children. Nancy Polikoff wrote a blockbuster law review article defending the idea in 1990, and
in 1995 the New York Court of Appeals interpreted the state statutes to allow
second-parent adoptions by unmarried different-sex as well as same-sex
couples. Chief Judge Judith Kaye's opinion for the court in *In re Jacob* and *In
re Dana* was a classic elaboration of the anti-commandeering principle in
American family law.[33]

By 2013, a majority of states allowed either second-parent adoptions or what
were variously called equitable or de facto parenting rights. Most reported cases
have involved lesbian relationships where the partners agreed to raise children
as a couple. A leading case was *In re Custody of H.S.H.-K.* (1995), where the
Wisconsin Supreme Court rejected second-parent adoption but recognized as
de facto parents caregivers who were part of the household and assumed obligations of parenthood, with the consent of the legal parent, "for a length of
time sufficient to have established with the child a bonded, dependent relationship parental in nature." As the New Jersey Supreme Court later held,
children "have a strong interest in maintaining the ties that connect them to
adults who love and provide for them. That interest, for constitutional as well
as social purposes, lies in the emotional bonds that develop between family
members as a result of shared daily life." These state judges homed in on the
key variables for the current era: the best interests of the child and the caregiving conduct of the adult—not the traditional ties of marriage and blood.
Grounded upon social science research, the emerging norm is that children
bond with adults who provide early caregiving, and removing those adults from
the children's lives can be deeply harmful.[34]

The lesbian and gay parenting cases have also highlighted the importance
of ART, which is increasingly used by straight couples as well. *Donor insemination* can be done with a turkey baster, or it can involve medically sophisticated hormone therapy, sperm washing, and other techniques that improve
the chances of pregnancy. *Traditional surrogacy* is a way for a gay male couple

(for example) to have children with a genetic link to one of the partners. The intended male parent donates sperm to a female donor who contributes both genetic material and gestation but does not intend to be the child's parent. *Gestational surrogacy* involves a gestational mother who is different from the genetic mother (the latter is typically the intended mother); the process involves in vitro fertilization of the genetic mother's egg and then insertion into the biological mother. All of these methods—what Naomi Cahn calls "the new kinship"—take sexual intercourse out of procreation and complicate any biology-based rule of parental recognition. Many states have no laws or relevant judicial decisions for the various practices, and the rules are sometimes inconsistent even within a state. In practice, would-be parents who conform to traditional gender and sexuality roles—married men and women—find that the law usually meets their expectations. Parents who conform less well to traditional gender and sexuality roles—women and men who form families with a same-sex partner, and women who use surrogacy to separate motherhood from biology—sometimes find that state law thwarts their expectations. From a "best interests of the child" perspective, these discriminations are questionable, especially given the thesis, entrenched since the *DeBoer* trial, that children do about as well with either same-sex or different-sex parents.[35]

Reflecting these developments in family formation and the constitutional considerations suggested in *Obergefell,* the Uniform Law Commission revisited the UPA through a committee chaired by Washington representative Jamie Pedersen (an openly gay sponsor of the state's marriage equality law) and assisted by reporter Courtney Joslin, a leading family law scholar. The revised UPA, promulgated in 2017, sought to achieve completely equal treatment for children of LGBTQ+ parents. To do so, the drafters moved the model law *away* from marriage and biology as the only linchpins of legal parenthood *toward* a regime that emphasizes the needs of children and the consent and conduct of adult caregivers. While the 2017 UPA retains a gender-neutral marital presumption of parenthood and recognizes the interests of biological parents, it explicitly endorses other paths toward parental recognition: an adult's public "holding out" as a parent, a "voluntary acknowledgment of parentage," de facto parenthood, and "intended" parenthood secured through ART agreements. The 2017 UPA is a roadmap for an LGBTQ-friendly legislative response to *Obergefell*'s equal protection reasoning.[36]

On the whole, the 2017 UPA is a liberal regime along Ruth Bader Ginsburg lines. Its provisions and commentary do not address the larger normative debate between progressives who would abolish civil marriage and channel more state resources toward caregivers, and traditionalists who believe that the state's best strategy for community welfare is to channel romantic couples into marriage. Among traditionalists, there is now an *Obergefell*-inspired debate whether their marriage-is-best policy should include same-sex couples. Social scientists like Linda Waite and David Blankenhorn are in favor, while natural law and religious thinkers like Robert George and Gerard Bradley would still not consider unions of nonconjugal couples to be legitimate marriages.

Obergefell and Partners We Choose

The public discourse regarding American family law has moved from status to contract: adults choose their own sexual or life partners, select a regime that fits their level of commitment, and decide whether and how to bear or raise children. As a matter of sociology, there is no persuasive reason for American family law not to offer LGBTQ+ couples the same choices and the same rules that it offers straight couples. *Obergefell* explicitly requires equal treatment for all married couples, as the majority opinion required the states to offer same-sex couples civil marriage "on the same terms and conditions as opposite-sex couples."[37]

As a matter of *Obergefell*'s narrow holding (its precise disposition of the six appeals adjudicated by the court), states must issue marriage licenses to same-sex couples, must include same-sex married couples on the birth certificates of children born within their marriages, and must include the surviving spouse on death certificates. Does *Obergefell* also require states to provide the same benefits to same-sex married couples as they do to different-sex married couples? Most state and local governments have equalized benefits—but not yet (as of 2020) in Texas, where state law forbids local government from spending taxpayer money on any benefit "asserted as a result of a marriage between persons of the same sex." In *Pidgeon v. Turner*, a state district judge ruled that Houston had to provide regular spousal benefits to its employees in valid same-sex marriages. In the wake of local GOP outrage, the all-Republican state supreme court remanded the issue to the district court to determine how broadly to read *Obergefell*. The court felt that *Obergefell* "did not hold that states must provide the same publicly funded benefits to all married persons."[38]

At the heart of liberty is the authority of each human being, not just the privileged few, to figure out her/his/their own life and career path, without discriminatory government commandeering. Recall Charles Sumner's metaphor for the state constitutional provisions that were the basis for the equal protection clause. Every human being "is one of the children of the State, which, like an impartial parent, regards all its offspring with an equal care." *Obergefell's* analysis of the *fundamental* right to marry emphasized the "constellation of benefits that the state has linked to marriage" and held that the exclusion of same-sex couples from these benefits was integral to the constitutional holding. The court also ruled that singling out gay families for exclusion imposes "stigma and injury of the kind prohibited by our basic charter." *Obergefell* requires the state to recognize and validate mature lesbian and gay choices of marital partners—and also bars the state from discriminating against those marriages. For the same reason that Kim Davis was not allowed to close the courthouse in Rowan County, Kentucky, because she didn't like same-sex marriage and Chief Justice Roy Moore was not allowed to obstruct its implementation in Alabama, the Supreme Court ought to be prepared—without dissent, please—to clear away the constitutional fog created by the Texas Supreme Court in *Pidgeon v. Turner*.[39]

In the remainder of this part, we shall consider the consequences of *Obergefell* and its underlying sociology for the future of the law governing adult relationships. Has the time come to divorce the state from marriage? Should the state create a minimalist institution to replace or supplement marriage? Should government vest cohabiting couples with marriage-lite rights and/or obligations? The experience of LGBTQ+ couples is relevant to all these issues.

MARRIAGE AFTER OBERGEFELL?

Between 2003 and 2015, the traditional marriage movement made stopping marriage equality a headline issue that was key to its campaign to reverse the cultural and demographic slide away from marital families. Maggie Gallagher and her allies maintained that every child has a right to a mother and a father and that "changing the definition of marriage" would wound the institution—and for no reason, as they did not think many gay people would even get married. Ironically, the marriage equality debate did revive proposals to abolish civil marriage entirely. David Boaz, the president of the Cato Institute, asked in 1997, "Why should the government be in the business of decreeing who can and cannot be married?" Why not make this issue like freedom of religion: each person makes her/his/their own choice, consistent with that person's faith tradition (or lack of it), and the government just enforces promises as contracts. Likewise, from feminist and lesbian perspectives, respectively, Tamara Metz and Nancy Polikoff have proposed to "disestablish" marriage, divorcing its connection to the state. In 2019, the Alabama legislature passed a statutory proposal to discontinue state licensing of marriages and to recognize only contracts filed with the state. Baptist Republicans, meet the Radicalesbians.[40]

The social sequel to *Obergefell* makes us doubtful that marriage is or ought to be sunsetting as a civil institution, however. To begin with, a lot of lesbian and gay couples have gotten married. Because there is no national database of marriages and few states break down marriage statistics by sex, we don't know exactly how many have done so. The best data come from the tax collectors. The Treasury Department counted at least 183,280 joint tax returns filed by same-sex married couples for tax year 2014, the first tax year after *Windsor*. That undercounted the number of same-sex marriages, because many Americans were outside the income tax network, some taxpayers did not know they could file jointly, and others found it advantageous to file separately. A tax records study by the Urban Institute and Brookings estimated that 250,450 joint federal income tax filings for tax year 2015 were by same-sex married couples. That also understated the total, but it gives us a benchmark.[41]

A more recent basis for estimating married couples was a June 2017 poll. Drawing from a large random sample, Gallup reported that 10.2 percent of LGBT respondents were married to a same-sex spouse (up from 7.9 percent in June 2015), in contrast to only 6.6 percent cohabiting with a same-sex partner (down from 12.8 percent in June 2015). In June 2017, 7.5 percent were divorced or separated and 2.2 percent widowed. Interestingly, 55.7 percent of the LGBT respondents were single, an increase from 47.4 percent in June 2015. These data suggest that most LGBT Americans were in no hurry to get married—but that most of the cohabiting couples were destined for the altar. Surprisingly, more than one in six LGBT persons were married or cohabiting with someone of a different sex; the "B" (for bisexual) in LGBT includes a lot of people.[42]

The Williams Institute estimated that there were 197,000 same-sex marriages on the eve of *Windsor*, 347,000 on the eve of *Obergefell*, and 547,000 by the middle of 2017. Given the benchmarks established by the 2014 and 2015 income tax joint filings, that estimate strikes us as high but not out of the ballpark. Overall, the statistics refute claims that LGBTQ+ persons and couples would not get married in significant numbers. Family data assembled by the Census Bureau in its American Community Surveys show that, in most states, more than half of the cohabiting lesbian and gay couples have gotten married, a number that will probably continue to rise slowly. Because half or more LGBT

Americans remain single, we surmise that they will not marry at the same rate as straight Americans.

Will marriage equality speed the institution of marriage into irrelevance? Because so many variables are involved, it would be hard to establish a causal link between marriage equality and any decline of marriage. In any event, the short-term data point the other way, with a similar lack of causal certitude. According to the Centers for Disease Control and Prevention (CDC), there were 2.3 million marriages in the United States (8.1 per thousand people) in 2001, a number and rate that sank almost every year of the decade, to 2.08 million (6.8 per thousand people) in 2009, when a cascading number of states embraced the freedom to marry. After 2009, the marriage rate held steady at 6.8 per thousand until there was a small uptick in 2014, the year after *Windsor,* when 2.14 million Americans got married (6.9 per thousand), followed by 2.22 million in 2015, 2.45 million in 2016, and 2.24 million in 2017 (steady at 6.9-7.0 per thousand people). During the same period, the divorce rate declined, from 4.0 per thousand people in 2001 to 2.9 per thousand people in 2017.[43]

The CDC numbers for early marriage equality states tell a more precise story. In Massachusetts, the marriage rate plummeted from 7.9 per thousand people in 1990 to 5.6 in 2003, a decline of almost one-third. In 2004, when *Goodridge* licenses commenced, the rate jumped to 6.2 per thousand and settled between 5.4 and 5.8 for the next twelve years, before bumping up again in 2016–2017. The other New England states showed similar trends. In the District of Columbia, the marriage rate nosedived from 8.2 to 4.7 per thousand between 1990 and 2009, but in the next year marriage licenses issued to same-sex couples sent the rate to 7.6. It stayed between 8.1 and 11.8 for the next seven years. (The District has the highest percentage of LGBTQ+ residents of any state-level jurisdiction.) Iowa's marriage rate fell from 9.0 to 6.5 per thousand between 1990 and 2008, then jumped to 7.0 in 2009, when *Varnum v. Brien* opened the door to marriage equality. Iowa's marriage rate remained relatively high until 2015, when it fell to 6.1 and has remained there since then. Illinois, which started issuing marriage licenses in 2014, has followed the New England pattern: a huge and steady fall in the marriage rate until 2014, when it received a jolt upward, followed by a new plateau well above the pre-2014 rate.[44]

California saw its marriage rate tumble from 7.9 per thousand people in 1990 to 6.2 in 2007. In 2008, the *Marriage Cases* opened a summer window when more than eighteen thousand same-sex couples got married before Proposition 8 cut them off. Almost exactly reflecting the new same-sex marriages (in a state with thirty-seven million people), the state's marriage rate for 2008 jumped up to 6.7—but in the wake of Proposition 8 plummeted to 5.8 for the next four years, the lowest rates for the 1990–2017 period covered by the CDC table. If anything, Proposition 8 was very bad news for the institution of marriage in the Golden State of California. As Dierdre Bowen has documented for the country as a whole, state constitutional junior-DOMAs (like Proposition 8) and Super-DOMAs (like the constitutional initiatives invalidated in *Obergefell*) as a statistical matter had no discernible effect of stimulating marriage but, instead, were correlated with depressed marriage rates in the jurisdictions that adopted them between 1995 and 2010. As Bowen would predict, *Hollingsworth v. Perry* (2013), the decision finally burying Proposition 8, set off a mini-renaissance in marriage, sending the rate back up to 6.5 in 2013. California's marriage rates for the next four years were 6.4, 6.2, 6.5, and 6.3 per thousand persons. The average yearly post-*Perry* marriage rate has been almost 10 percent higher than the average yearly rate between Proposition 8 and *Perry*.[45]

In short, the raw numbers do not support a narrative that court-mandated marriage equality spelled the end of marriage, either in the early marriage equality states or in the country as a whole. DOMA and state junior- or Super-DOMAs corresponded to depressed marriage rates, while marriage equality has corresponded to upward bounces or, at worst, stability in those rates. So far, marriages have not fallen back to their previous levels—and marriage has certainly not followed the dramatic decline that the statistics suggest before 2009. There is another way of evaluating the data, however. Gene Schaerr's *Obergefell* amicus brief examined the rate at which *straight* couples were marrying—and that rate, he argued, was in alarming free fall. We don't embrace the premise that only different-sex marriages count toward a marriage rate. While a diminishing minority of the country view same-sex marriages as not real, many Christians (following Matthew 19:9) do not believe that most remarriages are valid, either. We do not know of any demographer who has recalculated the marriage rate to exclude remarriages—an exercise that would surely depress the marriage rate much more.[46]

As appendix 3 to this volume documents, Schaerr was right that the number of different-sex marriages in Connecticut, Iowa, Massachusetts, Vermont, and Hawai'i fell in the years after marriage equality. But he did not control for the sharply declining numbers before marriage equality; the earlier trends would have suggested a sharper decline than what he found. In Massachusetts, for example, the CDC-calculated marriage rate declined from 7.9 to 5.6 between 1990 and 2003 (when *Goodridge* was decided); after 2003, the CDC-calculated marriage rate has stabilized around 5.6 or 5.7. Not only does

Schaerr make little if any progress on the claim that marriage equality caused the *further* decline of marriage, but the evidence is consistent with the hypothesis that marriage equality coincided with a halt in the marriage free fall that was going on before *Goodridge*. Also, Oregon and perhaps New York and California saw their different-sex marriage rate go up or stabilize after marriage equality. In Massachusetts, the marriage rate (including the rate for different-sex couples) rose sharply in 2016–2017.

So marriage, whether straight or gay, has not been collapsing. If anything, marriage remains relevant for the population as a whole. Couples are voting with their feet, and pairs of feet are still headed toward the altar. In practice, and we think as a prescriptive matter, marriage equality throws cold water on proposals to abolish civil marriage.

DOES MARRIAGE MATTER TOO MUCH?

While Maggie Gallagher and Gene Schaerr worry that the *redefinition* of marriage after *Obergefell* will undermine the institution, Serena Mayeri and Melissa Murray worry that the Supreme Court's *reaffirmation* of marriage will undermine the rights of the unmarried and their children. Romantic couples of all orientations choose not to get married because they are not sure they are committed for life, because marriage has historical associations they don't like, and even because the federal tax code penalizes married couples whose spouses have roughly equal income. Because the IRS does not recognize civil unions or domestic partnerships as marriages, in some states such couples can have their cake (wedding/marital benefits of state law) and eat it too (lower federal tax rates).[47]

According to demographers, the commonest reason romantic couples do not get married is that they cannot afford it. June Carbone and Naomi Cahn have shown that marriage is now a two-track system: well-to-do Americans get married (and divorced) almost as much as they did a generation ago, but poor and working-class Americans have children out of wedlock. "In today's system," they write, "married two-parent families have become a marker of privilege, characterizing a disproportionately better-educated and wealthier upper third of the country." If reformers want to restore a marriage culture, their efforts will be futile unless they also tackle poverty and working-class economic insecurity, as David Blankenhorn urges. One of us (Eskridge) has proposed that legislatures genuinely wanting to support marriage as a situs for child-rearing might consider income-linked tax credits for married couples raising children if they agree to mandatory counseling and a waiting period before divorcing.

Few straight couples entered covenant marriages in the states that adopted that option, but more would do so with a tax incentive. And the state would provide tangible support for working- and middle-class Americans raising children in a marital household.[48]

Because a lot of Americans have legitimate reasons not to get married and are more concerned with the public safety net than with the privatized safety net (which is one way to think about marriage), some progressives have claimed that marriage equality does not meet the needs of many LGBTQ+ couples and, if anything, marginalizes them further. Echoing the progressive-pluralist agenda in the last column of Table 4, the 2006 statement "Beyond Same-Sex Marriage," signed by hundreds of prominent intellectuals and scholars, urged much greater social and government support for nonmarital families. Some law professors worry that *Obergefell* not only reinforces a cultural narrative that marriage is the only responsible family structure but also makes it more difficult for unmarried persons to seek legal rights. We find their reading of *Obergefell* incomplete.[49]

Melissa Murray, for example, says that *Obergefell* will make it harder to challenge the constitutional bars to civil unions that exist in some twenty states. The Supreme Court struck down the challenged Super-DOMAs "to the extent they exclude same-sex couples from civil marriage on the same terms and conditions as opposite-sex couples" and said nothing about civil unions. Although *Obergefell* works against efforts to create civil unions limited to same-sex couples, we don't see a demand for that anymore. But if a state tried to create civil unions as an alternative for all couples, the Supreme Court would surely strike down a Super-DOMA carving out same-sex unions because they were "similar" to marriage. Even a conservative court would require that state to make the institution available to same-sex couples on the same terms as different-sex couples. *Obergefell*'s emphasis on equal treatment of sexual minorities would be strong constitutional ammunition against discriminatory civil union bars.[50]

Murray also argues that *Obergefell* will discourage state courts from recognizing contract and property rights for cohabiting couples. In *Blumenthal v. Brewer* (2016), for an excellent example, the Illinois Supreme Court declined to revisit a 1979 precedent holding that a person could not sue her cohabiting partner for an allocation of property. Citing *Obergefell*'s recognition of "the centrality of marriage," the court found it "more imperative than before that [courts] leave it to the legislative branch to determine whether and under what circumstances a change in the public policy governing the rights of parties in nonmarital relationships is necessary." Resting mainly on stare decisis, *Blumenthal* did not question the *Marvin* line of cases. But Murray may be correct in suggesting that state judges will be more cautious about applying *Marvin* precedents in the wake of *Obergefell*. Stay tuned.[51]

Nonetheless, there is much more in *Obergefell* than a valentine to marriage, especially when it is read in light of the Supreme Court's earlier gay rights precedents. Read together, those precedents support the following propositions. First, states presumptively cannot treat gay couples differently from straight couples, either in their marriage law (*Obergefell*) or in their nonmarriage law (*Lawrence* and *Romer*). Some of the early *Marvin* cases treated cohabiting lesbian or gay couples more skeptically than straight couples, but recent Supreme Court cases, as well as global changes in social norms, have discredited that practice. For example, the Illinois Supreme Court treated *Blumenthal* (involving two women) as the same kind of case as the earlier precedent (involving a man and a woman).

Second, states cannot punish unmarried couples or exclude them or their children from social programs because of animus (*Romer, Windsor,* and *Levy*). The case law suggests that certain signals trigger heightened judicial suspicion of animus: a novel legal mechanism; a measure that was rushed through the legislature without the usual deliberative process; and one that disproportionately penalizes a small group in a manner that seems like scapegoating. Following *Levy* and *Obergefell*, courts ought to be especially skeptical when a policy harms children in order to penalize or incentivize their parents. *Blumenthal* does not seem to reflect animus, because the rule was developed in a logical judicial manner, respected the legislature's role, has been sustained by stare decisis, and has been applied to lesbian, gay, and straight couples alike.

Third, the state has a responsibility to provide a regulatory baseline of common law property, contract, tort, and fundamental rights protections to all social and economic groups in our society. This responsibility was the foundation for both *Romer* and *Lawrence,* and we think it was a background norm undergirding *Windsor* and *Obergefell* as well. This is a potential Achilles' heel of *Blumenthal*. More than 10 percent of American couples are cohabiting, and 40 percent of American children are being reared by cohabiting parents. The state has a Fourteenth Amendment obligation to provide these households with a basic legal framework, and that includes enforcement of promises and anti-assault rules. To the extent that *Blumenthal* denies cohabiting couples in Illinois these basic legal rights, it may violate the Fourteenth Amendment. *Obergefell* provides support for that conclusion. Like *Levy* and other early nonmarital children cases, *Obergefell* emphasized the precept that the Constitution is concerned with providing a legal structure that considers the interests of children as well as their parents. It remains to be seen whether the US Supreme Court will enforce this constitutional baseline, but that does not relieve state judges from doing so, especially when they interpret the equality guarantees of state constitutions.[52]

WHAT WILL BECOME OF ALTERNATIVE INSTITUTIONS?

The campaign for marriage equality generated new institutions for family recognition and benefits: (1) employer and municipal domestic partnerships, (2) reciprocal or designated beneficiaries, and (3) civil unions or comprehensive domestic partnerships. Family law theorists tend to understand these new institutions as promising developments, for they meet the needs of unmarried couples. Elizabeth Brake, for example, maintains that the state should "minimize marriage," essentially replacing lavishly subsidized marriages with institutions that facilitate caretaking and other limited objectives. Others find these new institutions attractive as alternatives to rather than replacements for marriage. A richer array of choices furthers individual liberty and equality interests by allowing couples to craft and define their relationships as they see fit. Traditionalists objected that these new institutions would compete with marriage and thereby deny children optimal households and undermine the community's flourishing. Conversely, progressive critics predicted that marriage equality would render these new institutions obsolete.[53]

Consistent with the progressive critique, equal marriage rights have already retired some of these alternative institutions. In Arizona, for example, state employees enjoyed domestic partnership benefits by an executive order that was withdrawn in 2009. In a constitutional lawsuit, Lambda Legal won reinstatement of the benefits in 2011. After the Ninth Circuit invalidated marriage exclusions in Idaho and Nevada in October 2014, a federal district court required Arizona to issue marriage licenses to same-sex couples, and the state attorney general chose not to appeal. But the state immediately notified its employees that "because same-sex couples may now marry in Arizona, same-sex domestic partners will no longer be eligible for [health insurance] coverage effective January 1, 2015." Marriage equality statutes adopted in Vermont (2009), Connecticut (2009), New Hampshire (2009), Washington (2012), and Delaware (2013) repealed earlier statutes that had established statewide domestic partnerships or civil unions and provided a process for converting the earlier relationships into marriages or for opting out.[54]

On the other hand, most alternative institutions have survived—especially those that were open to different-sex as well as same-sex couples. When the Maryland, Hawai'i, and Illinois legislatures adopted marriage equality statutes in 2012–2013, they left in place the laws creating noncomprehensive domestic partnership (Maryland) and comprehensive civil unions (Hawai'i and Illinois). When Maine adopted marriage equality by voter initiative in 2012, its voters left the domestic partnership law in place. New Jersey's noncomprehensive domestic partnership law survived adoption of its civil unions law in 2007, and both remained intact when the state declined to appeal a state court decree for marriage equality. In 2013, Colorado enacted a civil unions law that left designated beneficiaries in place, and when the federal district court struck down its constitutional junior-DOMA, the ruling did not affect the earlier statutes. Oregon's comprehensive and Wisconsin's noncomprehensive domestic partnership laws survived federal judicial invalidation of their marriage exclusions in 2014. In July 2019, the California legislature expanded its domestic partnership regime to include all different-sex couples. Its sponsor explained that it was intolerable to discriminate against straight couples now that LGBTQ+ couples had the option of getting married. Many couples of all orientations still prefer not to be married, because they object to the normative baggage associated with marriage or simply because they want federal tax advantages. Hence, the legislature expanded rather than repealed the state's comprehensive domestic partnership law.[55]

In short, most of the new institutions of family recognition remain in effect, and some have expanded, contrary to the expectations of many family law scholars. But few couples are signing up for these new institutions; they are choosing either marriage or cohabitation. Based on data for the ten largest counties in Colorado, reported in appendix 3 to this volume, we found that the 2009 designated beneficiaries law never really caught on, securing only 403 registrations in its first year. Registration dropped to double digits in 2011, when the legislature created civil unions. These generated a lot more interest—until the federal district court required marriage equality in 2014. Once every couple could get married, very few signed up for either designated beneficiaries or civil unions. In every state we surveyed for appendix 3, the year in which same-sex couples could receive marriage licenses was also the year the numbers for alternate institutions plummeted. (In Maine, registrations for domestic partnerships dropped but then rose again.)

We were surprised by the poor numbers for Colorado's designated beneficiaries law, because that legal regime would have been ideal for couples like
Pauli Murray and Irene Barlow. The fiercely independent Murray would likely
never have agreed to anything like marriage, but being Irene's designated beneficiary would have sealed one of the few relationships that gave Pauli emotional peace. "This conflict [between my sex and my gender identity] rises up
to knock me down at every apex I reach in my career," she wrote in 1943. "And
because the laws of society do not protect me, I'm exposed to any enemy or
person who may or may not want to hurt me." Irene was her bulwark in that
struggle. They nursed one another in sickness and worked together in health.
The decision-making rules of a designated beneficiary agreement would have
been useful to them. Apparently, most couples like Murray-Barlow today do
not feel the need for a more formal recognition of their cohabiting relationships, while other such couples are opting for marriage. The Colorado experience was a natural test whether marriage should be replaced by something
minimal. Voting with their feet, same-sex couples have said yes to marriage
and no-thank-you to minimal institutions, so far.[56]

For many unmarried couples, the most important marriage alternative is the
health insurance and other benefits offered to domestic partners (usually both
same-sex and different-sex) by employers in both the private and public sector.
Pauli Murray might have found this option attractive, because her friend/part-
ner Irene Barlow worked at Paul, Weiss. One of New York City's toniest and
most progressive law firms, Paul, Weiss was one of the earliest to offer domestic
partnership benefits, starting in 1995. Recall, from chapter 3, that Walter Rieman's Paul, Weiss benefits afforded excellent medical care for his dying partner,
Tom Stoddard. Paul, Weiss partner Roberta Kaplan successfully represented
Edie Windsor in the case where the Supreme Court overturned the Defense of
Marriage Act. Responding to the court's 2015 marriage equality ruling, however, Paul, Weiss no longer offers health insurance to domestic partners; only
spouses and dependents now qualify. How common is this firm's response?

After *Obergefell*, employee domestic partnerships have been steadily declining, perhaps approaching a stable floor. In 2014, 51 percent of employers
reporting to the International Foundation of Employee Benefit Plans said
they provided benefits to LGBT employees joined in civil unions, 59 percent
gave spousal benefits to domestic partners, and 59 percent gave spousal
benefits to same-sex married employees. After *Obergefell* was decided, more
than a third of the employers reported that they were considering dropping the
program, and some had already done so when their states adopted marriage

equality. For 2016, the foundation reported that 31 percent of employers provided benefits to LGBT employees joined in civil unions, 48 percent gave spousal benefits to domestic partners, and a whopping 86 percent gave spousal benefits to same-sex married employees. By 2018, the foundation reported that 37.9 percent of employers provided health care benefits to LGBT employees joined in civil unions, 35.6 percent gave spousal benefits to same-sex domestic partners, and 86.9 percent did so for same-sex married employees. In its 2019 *Corporate Equality Index,* HRC reports that 49 percent of the companies in the Fortune 500 offer domestic partner benefits. Based on the available information, we think that firms offering the domestic partnership option to all employees, not just those in same-sex relationships, will continue these policies, as will larger employers and universities. In 2018, 33.2 percent of the foundation's surveyed employers offered domestic partnership benefits for different-sex as well as same-sex domestic partners. One-third might be the stable floor for such policies. As before, stay tuned.[57]

In the wake of *Obergefell,* marriage is holding its own and continues to inspire Americans of all sexual and gender orientations. But nonmarriage is also holding its own, and many children are being reared in nonmarital families. Does *Obergefell* have implications for those children?

Obergefell and Children We Choose

Obergefell also prompts our polity to recognize the value of families from the perspective of children, not just the adult partners. Judge Friedman's opinion in *DeBoer v. Snyder* (affirmed in *Obergefell*) effectively settled the issue of whether lesbian and gay parenting is bad for children and suggests that the state cannot constitutionally discourage lesbian and gay families. In 2017, Justice Ginsburg wrote for the Supreme Court that statutory rules relating to parenthood and the rights of children "granting or denying benefits 'on the basis of the sex of the qualifying parent'" differentiate "on the basis of gender, and therefore attract heightened review under the Constitution's equal protection guarantee." Precedents like this one support the 2017 revisions of the UPA that removed sex-based classifications from the model act and expanded legal parenting recognition for lesbian and gay caregivers.[58]

Does *Obergefell* allow the state to discriminate in favor of marital parents? Justice Kennedy's ode to marriage suggests that it might be read that way— but his equally heartfelt invocation of the best interests of children could be read to support caregiving outside of marriage, as Courtney Joslin and Douglas NeJaime have argued. *Obergefell's* recognition that lesbian and gay couples provide "loving and nurturing care to their children" can be the starting point for an argument that the state should not discriminate against parenting couples where at least one partner is not biologically related to the child and the further argument that this nondiscrimination principle ought to apply to unmarried same-sex couples as well as married ones. It was for this reason that the 2017 UPA, for which Professor Joslin was the reporter, expanded the rights of caregivers who are neither biologically related to the child nor married to the child's legal parent. Especially when read in light of *Romer* and *Windsor, Obergefell* casts a possible constitutional shadow on state laws penalizing lesbian and gay families because one partner is related to the child by neither biology nor marriage. This is motivation for states to revise their laws to adopt the 2017 UPA, as several have already done.[59]

DONOR INSEMINATION AND MARITAL PRESUMPTIONS OF PARENTHOOD

From the beginning of their relationship, April DeBoer and Jayne Rowse wanted to bear children and raise them as a couple. As nurses, they knew the medical options and chose donor insemination: April became pregnant with triplets through sperm donation, but miscarried. Their Supreme Court case has been the occasion for clarifying and (in states like Michigan) expanding the rights of lesbian couples who want to create families through ART. If the partners marry, the spouse can easily become a stepparent to the children of the other spouse, and the latter does not lose parental rights.

When a married woman gives birth, the law in most states requires that the name of the mother's spouse appear on the birth certificate, whatever the biological relationship to the child. Arkansas officials declined to include the names of lesbian spouses. On the second anniversary of *Obergefell,* the Supreme Court summarily reversed the state supreme court on this issue. Reflecting the connection between liberty and equality rights, the court's per curiam opinion in *Pavan v. Smith* (2017) said that Arkansas's practice violated *Obergefell's* commitment to give same-sex couples the same "constellation of benefits that the States have linked to marriage." Although three dissenting justices read *Obergefell* more narrowly, *Pavan* confirms our suggestion that the Texas judges should dismiss the *Pidgeon* complaint and allow Houston to provide spousal benefits to same-sex spouses.[60]

When a woman married to a man bears a child, most states have a statutory presumption of the husband's paternity. Does the same presumption apply to the nonpregnant spouse in a married lesbian couple? In Arizona, one set of judges viewed the presumption of paternity as a simple rule for assuring that parenthood followed biology, while another set of judges viewed it as a marriage-based rule for assuring that two parents will be available to support the child and for assuring the integrity of the marital family. In *McLaughlin v. Jones* (2017), the Arizona Supreme Court applied *Obergefell* and *Pavan* to hold that "the state cannot deny same-sex spouses the same benefits afforded opposite-sex spouses." Family law experts agree. The 2017 UPA presumes that an individual is the parent of a child if "the individual and the woman who gave birth to this child are married to each other and the child is born during the marriage." At last count, seventeen states and the District of Columbia have statutes with gender-neutral marital presumptions, and based on *Obergefell* and *Pavan,* other states will follow.[61]

Obergefell supports a family law regime in which lesbian partners will both be legal and certified parents of a child from birth, if they are married to one another. What if they are not married? The New York Court of Appeals has read *Obergefell* to support parental rights under those circumstances as well. Relying on *Obergefell*'s emphasis on the needs of children raised in lesbian and gay households, the court of appeals in *Brooke S.B. v. Elizabeth A.C.C.* (2016) overruled a 1991 precedent barring an unmarried lesbian caregiver from seeking parental rights. Following *Brooke S.B.,* the 2017 UPA internalizes the principle of "equal treatment of children born to same-sex couples," whether married or not. The 2017 UPA authorizes nonbiological mothers and fathers to sign voluntary acknowledgments of parentage (VAPs) to signify that they are a child's intended parents. Thus, by agreement, unmarried partners can replicate the marital presumption of parenthood. Even before 2017, the District of Columbia and some states permitted unmarried partners to identify the parent-by-choice (in the place of a biological parent) on a child's birth certificate.[62]

SURROGACY AND INTENDED PARENTS

Lesbian couples can form biological families through donor insemination, which, if they are married, is legally straightforward. Gay male couples have formed biological families through surrogacy, where a man provides sperm to a woman who bears the child and gives it to the intended parents (the man and his partner or spouse). Because most state laws are silent on this issue, the intended parents must rely on the willingness of the surrogate to waive her parental rights to the adoptive parents. There is greater legal recognition for, and regulation of, gestational surrogacy, where a man donates his sperm to inseminate an egg donated by one woman, and a second woman carries the fertilized embryo until delivery. Gay couples, such as celebrities David Burtka and Neil Patrick Harris, are the intended parents for as many as half the children born through gestational surrogacy arrangements.[63]

When their kids were born, Burtka and Harris lived in California, which allows gestational surrogacy so long as the sperm donor father, the intended father or mother, the egg donor, and the gestational surrogate have all signed a surrogacy agreement, which the statute makes enforceable under state law. An earlier statute provides forms that can be used to create an intended parent who is not biologically related to the child. California is exceptional in this regard. As of 2017, only ten other states and the District of Columbia had explicit statutes allowing this arrangement, but the 2017 UPA has helped motivate New Jersey, Oklahoma, Rhode Island, Vermont, and Washington to allow and regulate gestational surrogacy. (Doug NeJaime provided these updates.) The details of these statutes remain to be worked out. In Arkansas, for example, a surrogate mother is the legal parent of the child unless the father is married, in which case his wife becomes the other legal parent. If two men married to one another engage a surrogate in Arkansas, does this provision apply to them, providing the child two legal fathers and no legal mother at birth? *Pavan* suggests that as the logical answer.[64]

There are a few states where surrogacy contracts are a criminal offense, and moral objections are still made by both feminist and religious thinkers. We are not aware of recent prosecutions, but there may be a constitutional liberty objection grounded upon *Lawrence:* criminalizing such an intimate family-creating act—literally, expressing people's understanding of and participation in the "mystery of life" protected in *Casey*—requires something more than a moral objection. *Obergefell* and *Griswold* would add constitutional oomph for a married (gay or straight) couple turning to surrogacy as a means of forming a family.[65]

SECOND-PARENT ADOPTION

Adoption is the classic example of children we choose: a single adult or a married couple select a child for whom they will take parental responsibility. Traditionally, many adoptions were made by close relatives, such as Aunt Pauli's adoption of Pauli Murray after her mother died. States also allow stepparent adoptions as a routine matter within marriage. Second-parent adoption extends the stepparent exception to committed cohabiting couples. Before *Goodridge*, the highest courts of California, the District of Columbia, Massachusetts, New Jersey, New York, Pennsylvania, and Vermont had interpreted their family codes to permit such adoptions. After 2003, other state supreme courts followed.[66]

On the other hand, state supreme courts in Connecticut, Kentucky, Nebraska, North Carolina, Ohio, and Wisconsin interpreted their adoption statutes not to allow second-parent adoption: under the plain meaning of the statutes, if the child's other mother wanted to adopt, the biological mother would have to give up her parental rights. That, of course, would defeat the purpose of the adoption. In most of these states, some lower court judges were known to allow second-parent adoptions if the local department of child welfare persuaded them that such a move was in the child's best interest. That had been the practice in Michigan until 2002, when the chief judge in one county called out the practice and directed other judges to refuse such adoptions in the future. The publicity did discourage the practice—which is why DeBoer and Rowse brought their lawsuit.[67]

By requiring all states to recognize same-sex marriages, *Obergefell* also required them to apply their stepparent adoption laws for the benefit of married lesbian and gay couples. Mississippi, for instance, has a law limiting adoptions to married couples. If the state tried to exclude married lesbian and gay couples from joint adoption, *Obergefell* and *Pavan* would require a state or federal court to rule that to be inconsistent with the Fourteenth Amendment. While those precedents would not necessarily invalidate Mississippi's exclusion of unmarried couples from adoption, they would call into question a law excluding only lesbian or gay unmarried couples.

The state-to-state variation in second-parent adoption law has given rise to an important constitutional ruling. A lesbian couple secured a second-parent adoption in Georgia and moved their family to Alabama. When the couple split up, the Alabama Supreme Court refused to recognize the joint parental rights. In *V.L. v. E.L.* (2016), the US Supreme Court unanimously reversed the Alabama court and enforced the full faith and credit clause. Georgia's adoption order was a judgment rendered by a court of competent jurisdiction—and eighteen years earlier, Justice Ginsburg had written for a unanimous court that "the full faith and credit obligation is exacting" with respect to *court judgments*. After *V.L.*, unmarried lesbian and gay couples wishing to establish joint parental rights can do so in an increasing number of states—and then carry those rights with them if they move into a state (like Alabama) that would not have granted them.[68]

DE FACTO OR PSYCHOLOGICAL PARENTING

Melissa Murray's account of *Obergefell*'s consequences for liberalized family law concluded with a concern that "nonmarital routes to parenthood, like *de facto* parenthood, may also be imperiled." Some of the de facto parenthood cases relied on the fact that the co-parents were not eligible to marry and, hence, had a better case for the exercise of courts' equitable authority. *Obergefell*, she worried, would undermine existing precedents and render state courts less likely to follow the Wisconsin Supreme Court's *H.S.H.-K.* decision. Logically, she has a point, but the point is blunted if you read *Obergefell* in light of the broad anti-commandeering principle of the Fourteenth Amendment, as the revisers of the 2017 UPA have done.[69]

Michelle and Brittany Conover conceived a child through donor insemination prior to their marriage in 2009. In their subsequent divorce, Brittany demanded sole parental rights because Michelle was not biologically related to the child and had never second-parent-adopted the child. Michelle relied on the de facto parent doctrine, and the Maryland Court of Appeals unanimously overruled a precedent to sustain her claim—based in large part on marriage equality. Writing for the court in *Conover v. Conover* (2016), Court of Appeals judge Sally Adkins was persuaded that the earlier case had rested on shaky premises and was decisively undermined by Maryland's 2012 marriage equality law, which "illustrates the greater acceptance of gays and lesbians in the family unit in society." The court adopted the Wisconsin de facto parenting doctrine for both married and unmarried couples. Five of the seven judges who decided the case, including the chief judge, were women.[70]

The Maryland Court of Appeals was, essentially, following the post-*Obergefell* reasoning pioneered by the New York Court of Appeals's decision in *Brooke S.B.* The New York court was also overruling a pre-*Obergefell* precedent that limited nonmarital parental recognition to biological fathers and mothers. As the late Judge Sheila Abdus-Salaam's opinion for the court explained, a family law regime that recognizes a liberty interest for unmarried biological fathers who did not marry children's biological mothers, but does not recognize an interest for unmarried gay caregivers, treats lesbian and gay families unequally. "Under the current legal framework, which emphasizes biology, it is impossible—without marriage or adoption—for both former partners of a same-sex couple to have standing [as legal 'parents'], as only one can be biologically related to the child." To treat lesbian and gay nonmarital families the same as straight nonmartial families, the court ruled that unmarried lesbian or gay caregivers must sometimes be recognized as parents. Other judges in "blue" (liberal Democratic) states agree with Judge Abdus-Salaam that *Obergefell* and earlier precedents support recognition of de facto parenthood.[71]

In *Eldredge v. Taylor* (2014), the Oklahoma Supreme Court evaluated a co-parenting agreement entered between two lesbians. When they split up, the nonbiological mother petitioned to enforce her rights as a second parent under the agreement; the biological mother argued that the agreement was contrary to Oklahoma's constitutional Super-DOMA. The Oklahoma judges unanimously rejected the latter argument and enforced the contract. Because the Tenth Circuit had invalidated that state's Super-DOMA, it could not be used as a basis for a public policy objection. In a subsequent case, the Oklahoma Supreme Court recognized a de facto lesbian parent but limited its holding to "unmarried same-sex couples" who could not (at the time) get married. The court's implication was that once lesbian and gay couples could get married, the de facto parenting doctrine would not be available to them. As Melissa Murray demonstrates, many judges in other "red" (conservative Republican) states agree with the Oklahoma judges. Another eminent family law scholar, however, now argues that such judgments may violate the due process clause of the Fourteenth Amendment.[72]

DO UNMARRIED CAREGIVERS HAVE DUE PROCESS LIBERTY RIGHTS?

Building on the foregoing developments in family law, Douglas NeJaime argues for recognition of a strong substantive due process liberty interest for caregivers in a continued connection with their children, including caregivers who have neither biological ties to the child nor marital ties to the child's recognized parent. In *Stanley v. Illinois* (1972), the Supreme Court recognized a liberty interest for biological fathers seeking a relationship with their non-marital children. Subsequent decisions declined to enforce such an interest where biological fathers had not established close bonds with their progeny and/or where their interest was outweighed by that of nonbiological fathers married to children's mothers and providing homes for those children. In *Windsor* and *Obergefell,* the court recognized a fundamental liberty interest for lesbian and gay couples raising children to have the option of getting married.

In light of the equal treatment baseline for sexual and gender minorities, supported by *Romer, Lawrence,* and *Windsor,* NeJaime argues that equal treatment for LGBTQ+ parents justifies the short step from these precedents to a constitutional ruling that caregivers with neither a marital nor a biological relationship have a liberty interest deserving explicit constitutional protection.[73]

For many judges, such a constitutionally protected interest for nonbiological, nonmarital caregivers would be a rather complicated step, and NeJaime himself recognizes that the Roberts Court is most unlikely to take it. Although easily distinguishable, earlier precedents declined to recognize constitutional liberty interests of caregiving foster parents or of blood-related grandparents when at the expense of biological parents. A tribunal that divided 6-3 (in *Pavan*) on whether to apply the narrowest understanding of *Obergefell's* holding will not be eager to extend its logic in the wake of Justice Kennedy's retirement, and very probably not to a family law issue that has divided state court judges. We admire the reasoning in *Brooke S.B.* but recognize that the court did not exactly create a hard-and-fast "constitutional" rule when it interpreted the common law of the family. Judges in red states like Oklahoma hesitate to follow the New York judges because they feel that a constitutional right for unmarried parents would be inconsistent with their pro-marriage public policy. Even judges in blue states might be uncertain about the effects of constitutionalizing a parenting issue. Subjecting parenting issues to case-by-case evolution would be a judge-empowering step not to be taken lightly, and surely not at the national level without more deliberation and experience.[74]

Recall from our prelude and chapter 20 that April DeBoer and Jayne Rowse did not want to assert their own constitutional interests in parenting: from their perspective, as dedicated parents, the only relevant matter was the best interests of their children—which is the common law's litmus test for parenting issues. Where the overall welfare of children is concerned, individual liberty and social equality ought to take a back seat to communitarian concerns, precisely as traditionalists have urged. The difficult question is this: What legal rule or standard best serves the interests of children in the long run? Until this question is answered, most judges will be chary of creating new constitutional rights.

Consider legal strategies suggested by the DeBoer-Rowse point of view. In chapter 3, we introduced Paula Ettelbrick and Nancy Polikoff, who (among others) pioneered second-parent adoption and other consent-based mechanisms for co-parents to devise their own family structure, including caregiving responsibilities and rights. The rights of parents are best developed by contract-making rather than by constitutional decision-making—but the rights of vulnerable children ought to be subject to moral and constitutional judgments that fly under the banner of "the best interests of the child." Two big developments require judicial sensitivity to the claims of nonbiological caregivers: family pluralism, where many children are raised outside of marriage notwithstanding the state inducements to the contrary, and overwhelming social science evidence that separating a young child from his/her caregiver is harmful. This area of research is called "attachment theory."[75]

Inspired by Ettelbrick and Polikoff, whose academic work reflected their social and political engagement, we should urge state legislatures to address these issues. The 2017 UPA represents one promising approach. Assuming that it is usually good for a child to have more than one parent and that straight, gay, lesbian, and other parents ought to be treated equally, the UPA creates rebuttable presumptions of parenthood (e.g., spouses), a process for voluntary acknowledgment, and exacting standards for determining whether a claimant is a de facto parent. One virtue of the UPA approach is its flexibility and attentiveness to the best interests of the child; another virtue is its creation of a parental registry and bright-line rules or strong presumptions that provide clarity for family planning. Several UPA standards, however, must be applied by judges, an expensive and less predictable process. In our view, legislators should also consider nonjudicial processes. Hawai'i, for example, has had success with family mediation procedures, which are less expensive and on the whole more cooperative than litigation.[76]

POLYPARENTING AND POLYGAMY

In her concurring opinion in *Conover*, Judge Shirley Watts cautioned that she would not extend the de facto parenting doctrine to families where there were already two legal parents, for that "could result in a second existing parent having no knowledge that a *de facto* parent, *i.e.*, a third parent, is created. Such situations may result in a child having three parents vying for custody and visitation, and being overburdened by the demands of multiple parents." Judge Watts was concerned about an institution we dubbed *polyparenting* in 1999. Two decades later, "the three-parent family is here. Once states accept that parenthood does not depend on either biology or marriage, then three parents are inevitable unless the states go out of their way to rule that adults who otherwise meet their definition of parenthood will not be recognized."[77]

Legislative solutions to the issues raised by polyparenting might be useful, especially if the solutions were grounded on (or delegated authority to) expert evaluation of experience in jurisdictions where legislatures or courts have recognized the possibility of more than two parents. Responding to a state appellate court refusal to recognize a caregiver's relationship to a child with two parents, the National Center for Lesbian Rights worked with California legislators in 2013 to amend the state family code to authorize the recognition of more than two parents. Legislators concluded that "most children have two parents, but in rare cases, children have more than two people who are that child's parent in every way. Separating a child from a parent has a devastating psychological and emotional impact on the child, and courts must have the power to protect children from this harm." The statute allows recognition of more than two parents "if the court finds that recognizing only two parents would be detrimental to the child." Courts should consider "the harm of removing the child from a stable placement with a parent who has fulfilled the child's physical needs and the child's psychological needs for care and affection, and who has assumed that role for a substantial period of time." The 2017 UPA offers legislatures statutory language similar to that in California. Delaware, Maine, Vermont, and Washington also authorize courts to find de facto parents even if the child already has two legal parents. New authorizations for de facto parents enacted by the District of Columbia Council apparently allow more than two parents as well.[78]

Consider a variation on Pauli Murray's life. If her mother had lived but had been unable to take care of six children while her husband was institutionalized, Pauli's aunt could have qualified as a de facto parent if she had raised and cared for Pauli in her household. The young girl might have suffered psychological harm if Aunt Pauline were not considered a de facto parent under those circumstances. One or both of the grandparents might also have qualified. None of those relatives would have wanted to terminate the parental rights of Pauli's mother and father, however. When lesbian couples use known sperm donors, the biological father sometimes brings litigation to enforce parental rights, and a 1994 New York case saw judges recognize parentage rights for a sperm-donating gay father, in addition to the parentage rights of the lesbian partners raising the children. Going forward, many of the cases will be battles between a lesbian couple raising children and a former partner who was a caregiver for one or more children.[79]

It remains to be seen how often a genuine need for polyparenting arises— and how often it leads only to family conflict and turmoil. Polyparenting will often empower a third party in ways the primary caregivers do not agree with. Also, if polyparenting statutes or court decisions generate litigation among the caregivers, the costs may outweigh the benefits. Not only are lawsuits expensive, but they provide public forums for escalating emotional conflict that can harm the very children the law is supposed to protect. These are potentially prohibitive costs of recognizing polyparents.[80]

If three adults can jointly parent, can they also get married? Both conservative and liberal pundits are fascinated by legalized polygamy both before and after *Obergefell*, though the body politic remains largely uninterested. Most traditionalists as well as feminists strongly oppose expanding marriage in this way, and there is no strong polygamy social movement pressing the issue. Nevertheless, Ronald Den Otter argues that the same liberty and equal treatment arguments that would win same-sex marriage in *Obergefell* provide an obvious constitutional basis for a right to plural marriage. The individual autonomy, interpersonal commitment, and child-rearing values undergirding marriage might just as easily apply to two women and a man as to two women joined in matrimony. We should caution that polygamy would be a nonstarter under these criteria unless it were heavily regulated. For example, the state should bar the addition of new spouses without the genuine consent of existing spouses. How to accomplish such regulation would be a difficult task, and the nation's experience with easy divorce suggests that "consent" within the family setting is fraught with opportunities for bullying and deceit.[81]

Even with effective regulation and a social demand, we remain skeptical because of social costs that would likely ensue from a polygamy-recognizing regime. In our society, most polygamous marriages would be polygynous (one man and two or more women). Polygyny has a track record that is strongly inconsistent with women's equal citizenship. In an exhaustive cross-cultural survey, Rose McDermott reports that, in polygynous societies, women are less likely to receive an education and more likely to die in childbirth, sustain much more physical and sexual abuse, and are more vulnerable to sexual trafficking. She also finds that such societies offer their citizens fewer liberties and less safety-net infrastructure. Neither Den Otter nor the other leading apologists for polygamy have provided data refuting McDermott's analysis.[82]

For now, scholarship such as McDermott's forecloses any kind of constitutional right to plural marriage. Recall that four of the five justices in the *Obergefell* majority preferred the equal protection challenge to the exclusion of LGBTQ+ couples from marriage—and they persuaded Justice Kennedy to add several pages of equality-based reasoning. Ruth Ginsburg's life work has been constitutional recognition of women's equal citizenship. So long as plural marriage is considered antithetical to women's equal citizenship, it is a nonstarter. Justice Alito's concern that *Obergefell* opens the door to plural marriage is, for now, constitutionally unfounded.

On the other hand, if the door were to be cracked open, the best strategy would be one founded on the arguments in this chapter. Two lesbians and a gay man can now commit to become joint parents; there are some families where each lesbian bears the child of the gay man. Should marriage be open to this "thrupple"? Or to two gay men and a woman who bears their children? These relationships may find more social approval than traditional plural marriages. Although this alone cannot be sufficient to open marriage to plural partners, it might become the basis for an alternate institution of some sort, perhaps along the lines of designated beneficiaries. As Martha Ertman points out, such relationships can also be established by contracts that should ordinarily be enforced by courts.[83]

Obergefell untethers civil marriage from religious doctrine and natural law but demands that the polity seriously ask the question posed twenty-one years ago by E.J. Graff: What is marriage for? Marriage is a constantly evolving institution, responsive to social demands and changing preferences. The challenge laid down by David Blankenhorn, Monte Stewart, and Maggie Gallagher in the marriage debate is that the polity should think about marriage from an ex ante perspective: Because its definition, regulation, and encouragement create incentives for romantic couples, what mix of legal rules and subsidies have the best overall effect on American families and our society? As *Obergefell* reminds us, the interests of children must be front and center, and they ought to be studied rigorously and without an ideological agenda. For example, under what circumstances does polyparenting work to the advantage of children? Do the risks outweigh the benefits even in best-case scenarios? The future of polyparenting allowances or regulation ought to be driven or influenced by objective case studies and neutral data analysis.

From a policy perspective, the legal regulation of marriage and the benefits associated with the institution contribute to no fewer than three social goals: mutual commitment, responsible decision-making, and a social safety net. To begin with, legal requirements of mutual support and fidelity, as well as the difficulty of divorce, create an institution where each spouse offers commitment and receives the security of the other spouse's commitment. This is why marital households might, all else being equal, be the best situs for raising children. As the DeBoer-Rowse marriage illustrates, the mutual commitment can and ought to extend to the children as well. Many other marriage-linked legal rules are decision-making defaults—for example, if I am incapacitated and have no medical power of attorney, my spouse makes decisions for me. This efficiently selects appropriate decision-making rules but also respects the dignity of those needing decisions. Finally, marriage-linked benefits, starting with health insurance, constitute important features of people's social safety nets. Indeed, marriage itself is a privatized safety net, as spouses are expected to be the first line of care for people as they become infirm or enfeebled.[84]

In the long marriage to her late husband, Marty, Ruth Ginsburg most treasured the first benefit of marriage and enjoyed the other two as well. Americans like her reveal the continuing appeal that *marriage* enjoys for a new generation. In a world of anomie and isolation, shouldn't the state support mutual commitment, especially when a couple is raising children within their relationship? After *Obergefell*, it should not matter whether the couple is straight, lesbian, or gay. The state should support their enterprise, especially if the spouses are raising children. But, as Pauli Murray would argue, the state should also support the efforts of biological parents to cooperate in child-rearing even if they are not married. For example, the Supporting Father Involvement (SFI) program is an intervention where teams of counselors work with fathers and mothers who are raising or responsible for infant children. Researchers have, tentatively, found the approach successful: fathers who engage with mothers or other parents as collaborators in an altruistic team effort will be more engaged with the lives of their children. Why shouldn't scholars and legislators advocating child-centric family law support programs like this one?[85]

The marriage rules that might have most benefited Murray would have been decision-making defaults. She and Barlow should have been treated as default decision makers for one another. Notice that Colorado's designated beneficiaries law, the reciprocal beneficiaries law in Hawai'i, and the state domestic partnership laws in New Jersey and Maine make the marital decision-making rules the centerpiece of a limited family regime—but one that might best meet the needs of couples like Barlow-Murray, who did not want to be spouses but who did want to support one another. The menu reflected in Table 5 illustrates how the different relationship regimes divvy up the purposes of marriage: covenant marriage seeks to improve upon the commitment goal, designated beneficiaries satisfy the decision-making goal, and municipal-employer domestic partnership benefits cater to the social safety-net goal. Murray would also be sympathetic to the progressive agenda of delinking more safety-net benefits from marriage and extending them to nonmarital families and single people.

Just as we don't know exactly how marriage will fare with the next generation, so, too, we don't know how well these alternative institutions will operate to meet individual and social needs. A central virtue of the federalist system of government is that states and municipalities can experiment, and the rest of us can learn from their successes—just as the nation has learned from the virtuous family created by Jayne Rowse and April DeBoer.

Postscript • And It Ends with Family

As was the case with untold numbers of loving couples for centuries, April DeBoer and Jayne Rowse got married on August 22, 2015.[1]

The Hazel Park nurses and their four children had been together through an intense family journey. In an express effort to protect the legal rights of their children, April and Jayne had gone from providing care and comfort to those in need, as two nurses in Detroit and its environs, to helping ensure the constitutional freedom for all other families looking to protect their own loved ones, as plaintiffs in a landmark lawsuit. By the time of their wedding, April and Jayne had already been living together for over a decade, sharing in household expenses and splitting the responsibilities of maintenance. They jointly owned a home, various cars, and pieces of furniture. Between the two of them, they had adopted four children. And they were about ready to adopt a fifth child, whom they named Kennedy. (They told us she was named after April's father, Kenneth, and not Anthony Kennedy.) Their relationship already looked identical to many marriages by the time their case was decided by the Supreme Court.

Before they had children, April and Jayne had already celebrated their union through a commitment ceremony. They were both uninspired by marriage at the time, and they simply wanted to celebrate their long-standing commitment to each other. Jayne had worn a black suit, April a simple white dress. At the time, they were expecting children but had not thought about the way their family would fit, or not fit, into Michigan family law. This reality did not hit them until the winter of 2011, when they were almost obliterated by an oncoming truck, the episode that started this volume. In those four years between 2011 and 2015, they grew as a family and engaged the public as a family ask-

748

ing to be treated right by the state. By August 22, 2015, April and Jayne remained in love with each other, but they were now inspired by their shared journey to have a proper wedding—nuptials blessed by the US Supreme Court, in their case.

This time, Jayne wore a dashing black tuxedo with a beautiful deep-purple vest. With her graying hair in a handsome crew cut, she was a dashing bride. April, her red hair coifed in a fetching beehive, was dressed in a dazzling cream-colored wedding gown. The venue was updated to a large hall in Southfield, Michigan. As the crowd stood in awe, April and Jayne walked down the aisle to the sound of George Harrison's "Here Comes the Sun." April was joined by her father, Kenneth DeBoer, and her two young daughters dressed in matching cream-colored dresses of their own. Jayne was joined by her two young sons in matching tuxedos. This was one of the proudest moments in the life of Wendy Brown DeBoer, who had done more than anyone else to support this family and this marriage. Wendy looked resplendent in her crimson dress, showing off her trim figure and covering her shoulders in lace. More than two hundred guests, including their lawyers, friends, and family, stood as supporting witnesses to the joining of April DeBoer and Jayne Rowse as legal spouses.

Presiding over the wedding ceremony, just as he had presided over their marriage case and trial, was Judge Bernard Friedman. Bernie remarked to everyone gathered that he would never forget the look of surprise on April's and Jayne's faces, or the look of shock on their lawyers' faces, when he told them all that he had decided that their case was going to have to be a case about marriage. Bernie waxed poetic as he noted that all citizens of the United States appreciated what April and Jayne had done in order to ensure equal protection under the law and that everyone in the room owed them "a big debt of gratitude." Those gathered, including family, friends, and well-wishers, stood in an ovation. Robin Tyler and Diane Olson, who married as one of the first couples in California in June 2008, had tears in their eyes. April, in her always affable style, noted during the course of her vows that after meeting Jayne she could never have imagined that Jayne would bring her the four beautiful children surrounding them at their feet, and she also could never have imagined that Jayne would also drag her into the United States Supreme Court. The crowed laughed and appreciated April's joke, and the impact of this marriage was lost on no one.

No one had forgotten that April and Jayne's case was originally brought *only* to assure joint parental rights for the sake of their children and *not* to establish

April DeBoer and Jayne Rowse, and their daughter Ryanne

rights between the two partners. Even after they had, reluctantly, consented to add a marriage claim, they had always represented the case as one whose focus should be the welfare of their kids. Judge Friedman had his way back in 2012, when he pressured the nurses into making their case a marriage case—but in 2015 they called the shots. The judge opened the ceremony with the confession that he was under strict orders to put the children first; everyone applauded; the kids were standing with their parents.

At the beginning of the exchange of vows, April expressed her appreciation and devotion to Jayne. Tearing up, she interrupted herself: "Dad? Potty!" Everyone cheered the father of the bride as he took Jacob for a needed restroom break. "I can't imagine my life without you and my life without our kids," she summed up. Jayne, too, said that she could not imagine life without her wife and kids. "I promise to take care of us, forever and always." After Ken returned from Jacob's potty break with the rings, April and Jayne exchanged rings.

Before Bernie declared them legal spouses, April took the microphone and kneeled down to address Ryanne and Rylee. Do you take me to be your legal Mommy, and Jayne to be your legal Momma? I will love you forever! Each girl repeated the vow, little Rylee in her own words, "Wuve *ever!*" Jayne repeated the same vows with the boys. Not only were April and Jayne joined matrimonially to each other; they were also joined maternally to their children.

After Bernie pronounced April and Jayne "lawfully married," by authority vested in him by the Michigan Constitution and under order of the US Supreme Court, the wedding ended to the tune of The Beatles' "All You Need Is Love." As the judge had earlier announced, there would be five additional witnesses who would sign the marriage license. They were called to the front of the room: Carole Stanyar, Dana Nessel, Ken Mogill, Bob Sedler, and Mary Bonauto. Under the scrutinizing eye of federal district judge Judy Levy, each of the five signed the certificate, "All you need is love; love is all you need" playing in the background.

As April and Jayne knew only too well, their marriage did not establish joint parental rights: they would still need to legally cross-adopt all four children, allowed under the state stepparent adoption law. On Thursday, November 5, 2015, Oakland County Circuit Court judge Karen McDonald presided over a room brimming with energy and excitement. After the required legal questions were asked of both April and Jayne, Judge McDonald noted how honored she was to announce that each of them would now be the adopted parents of six-year-old Nolan, five-year-old Jacob, five-year-old Ryanne, three-year-old Rylee, and their newest addition, one-year-old Kennedy. After formally announcing the adoption, Judge McDonald came down from the bench to give huge hugs to April and Jayne as she congratulated them. Judge McDonald, like Wendy, April, and Jayne, is a hugger. After the formal adoption ceremony, people enjoyed celebratory cake in the courthouse. For April and Jayne, with all five little members of their family being adopted on the same day, November 5 is an anniversary that they will continue to celebrate. April DeBoer, who always brought every critter, bird, and worm in need into the house, had finally reached her goal of a legally recognized family along with Jayne Rowse, the woman she loves.

As we followed the winding and unpredictable path trod by the Michigan nurses toward legal marriage, we have been struck by what a difference legal formalities make in people's lives. The *legal* recognition of their joint parental relationship with all their children was important to Jayne and April for practical reasons but also for symbolic and social reasons. It was a public declaration of their commitment, a declaration that found an echo in their wedding ceremony. They didn't know how meaningful the lawful marriage would be to them and their families and friends until they undertook the legal journey with Dana and Carole, Ken and Bob, Bernie and Mary.

But theirs is not the last chapter in our story. More chapters are being written each month.

On September 17, 2018, the Minnesota District Court for Blue Earth County ruled that Mike McConnell and Jack Baker's September 1971 marriage "was in all respects valid" and should be recorded by the clerk as a legal marriage. Stubbornly, Mike and Jack had refused to be (re)married after Minnesota passed its marriage equality law in 2013 because they thought they had been married all along. On October 3, 2018, Blue Earth complied with the order and recorded the marriage—making it "the earliest same-gender marriage ever to be recorded in the public files of any civil government"—and confirmed it as lawful in open court. Bravi![2]

In storybooks, including *King & King,* the fable that set off the Wirthlins and the Parkers in Massachusetts, the spouses live happily ever after. In real life, that is not always so. Marriage does not prevent life's tragedies, even though it enables people to cope with those difficulties more constructively and makes hardships more bearable. Dashing Jack Baker remains handsome in old age, but he has lost the sharpness of mind that spurred the couple to be the first gay marriage celebrities. As we learned, most of the earliest same-sex marriage applicants and plaintiffs have died, some from AIDS, several from suicides; a few live alone; one languishes in prison. Most of the post-1990 plaintiffs, however, remain married to women and men they love, but love does not solve all of life's problems.

Life has not been easy for April DeBoer and Jayne Rowse, even after the wonderful memories of their marriage struggle and celebration. With more and growing children, their home in Hazel Park was no longer adequate, so they found a fixer-upper that was large enough for the entire family. According to April, Jayne, and Wendy, the home is a constant work in progress, more financially and emotionally draining than they expected. As the kids have grown up, the family has adopted the favorite midwestern pastimes of learning to play cards together like euchre, Uno, and rummy. For a time in 2017 and 2018, April and Jayne took on a sixth foster child, but ultimately they did not adopt him. For the first time the family realized that a family of seven was just right for them. While their hearts and home are open, April and Jayne have realized that while they always will be welcoming to those in need, their nuclear family unit has crystallized.

After a few health scares, Jayne decided it was necessary to take a step back and find an easier employment situation. Leaving her intense work as an emergency room nurse in Detroit, she now works for the Oakland County Health Department. This has given her more regular hours, allowing for a more stable family unit and giving April the freedom to continue her work providing care and comfort for needy children in intensive care. Grandma Wendy has continued to assist and frequently has the children over for sleepovers when possible. Money is tight, but time with your kids and grandkids is priceless.

On August 22, 2018, the family gathered at a Benihana outside Detroit in order to celebrate Jayne's fifty-fourth birthday. As is customary for all great family celebrations, they invited friends, family, and even the legal eagles who took them all the way to the Supreme Court only a few years earlier. The DeBoer-Rowse family had helped to pave the road from outlaws to in-laws.

Appendix 1 • Evolving State Rules Pertaining to Same-Sex Couples

State	Statutory DOMAs	Constitutional DOMAs	State benefits for unmarried LGBTQ couples	Legal authority for marriage equality and first legal licenses
Alabama	H.B. 152, 1998 Ala. Laws 1077, Ala. Code § 30-1-19 (1998)	Amendment 774, Ala. Const., art. I, § 36.03 (passed by voters in 2006)	N/A	*Searcy v. Strange*, 81 F. Supp. 3d 1285 (S.D. Ala. 2015) First licenses: Feb. 9, 2015
Alaska	S.B. 308, 1996 Alaska Sess. Laws ch. 21, Alaska Stat. §§ 25.05.011, 25.05.013 (1996)	Ballot Measure 2, Alaska Const., art. I, § 25 (passed by voters in 1998)	*Alaska Civil Liberties Union v. State*, 122 P.3d 781 (Alaska 2005) (mandating extension of benefits to state employees' domestic partners)	*Hamby v. Parnell*, 56 F. Supp. 3d 1056 (D. Alaska 2014) First licenses: Oct. 13, 2014
Arizona	S.B. 1038, 1996 Ariz. Laws 1839, Ariz. Rev. Stat. §§ 25-101, 25-112 (1996)	Proposition 102, Ariz. Const., art. XXX, § 1 (passed by voters in 2008)	Act Relating to Living Wills and Healthcare Directives, H.B. 2247, 1992 Ariz. Sess. Laws ch. 193 (signed June 8, 1992) (codified as amended at Ariz. Rev. Stat. § 36-323l) (medical decision-making rights for domestic partners); 14 Ariz. Admin. Reg. 1420-34 (April 25, 2008) (health insurance benefits for domestic partners of state employees), overridden by Proposition 102 but reinstated by *Diaz v. Brewer*, 656 F.3d 1008, 1014 (9th Cir. 2011) (suspended after Oct. 2014)	*Majors v. Horne*, 14 F. Supp. 3d 1313 (D. Ariz. 2014) First licenses: Oct. 17, 2014

State	Statute	Constitutional Amendment	Domestic Partnership	Case / First Licenses
Arkansas	H.B. 1004, 1997 Ark. Acts 825, Ark. Code Ann. §§ 9-11-107, 9-11-109, 9-11-208 (1997)	Amendment 3, Ark. Const., amend. 83 (passed by voters in 2004)	N/A	*Obergefell v. Hodges*, 135 S. Ct. 2584 (2015) First licenses: June 26, 2015
California	Proposition 22, formerly codified at Cal. Fam. Code § 308.5 (passed by voters in 2000)	Proposition 8, Cal. Const., art. I, § 75 (passed by voters in 2008) (overriding *In Re Marriage Cases*, 183 P.3d 384 (Cal. 2008), which had invalidated Proposition 22 under the California Constitution)	Act Relating to Domestic Partners, A.B. 26, 1999 Cal. Stat. 4157 (signed Oct. 10, 1999) (codified as amended at Cal. Fam. Code §§ 297 et seq. and other portions of the code) (domestic partnership for same-sex and older couples), frequently amended, e.g., A.B. 25, 2001 Cal. Stat. 7283 (2001); A.B. 205, 2003 Cal. Stat. 308 (2003); S.B. 651, 2011 Cal. Stat. 5604 (2011) (ultimately providing all the state benefits and duties of marriage); S.B. 30, 2019 Cal. Stat. (signed July 30, 2019) (codified at Cal. Fam. Code § 297) (expanding domestic partnership to include all different-sex couples)	*In re Marriage Cases*, 183 P.3d 284 (Cal. 2008), superseded by Proposition 8 (2008), invalidated by *Perry v. Schwarzenegger*, 704 F. Supp. 2d 921 (N.D. Cal. 2010), aff'd, *Perry v. Brown*, 671 F.3d 1052 (9th Cir. 2012), vacated and remanded, *Hollingsworth v. Perry*, 133 S. Ct. 2652 (2013) (reinstating district court decision), codified by Act Relating to Marriage, S.B. 1306, 2014 Cal. Stat. 1965 (signed July 7, 2014) First licenses: June 16, 2008 (following *Marriage Cases*, suspended after enactment of Prop. 8); June 27, 2013 (following *Perry*)

(continued)

State	Statutory DOMAs	Constitutional DOMAs	State benefits for unmarried LGBTQ couples	Legal authority for marriage equality and first legal licenses
Colorado	H.B. 00-1249, 2000 Colo. Laws 1054, Colo. Rev. Stat. § 14-2-104 (2000)	Initiative 43, Colo. Const., art. II, § 31 (passed by voters in 2006)	Colorado Designated Beneficiary Agreement Act, H.B. 09-1260, 2009 Colo. Laws 428 (signed April 9, 2009) (codified at Colo. Rev. Stat. §§ 15-22-101 et seq.) (private agreements to designate a same-sex or different-sex partner to enjoy certain rights and benefits); Colorado Civil Union Act, S.B. 13-011, 2013 Colo. Laws 147 (signed March 21, 2013) (codified at Colo. Rev. Stat. §§ 14-15-101 et seq.) (same-sex and different-sex civil unions)	*Burns v. Hickenlooper*, 2014 WL 3634834 (D. Colo. July 23, 2014) (applying 10th Circuit's *Kitchen* decision to invalidate Colorado's same-sex-marriage ban, but staying effect until certiorari denied in *Kitchen*); *Brinkman v. Long*, No. 2013-CV-032572, 2014 WL 7722910 (Colo. Dist. Ct. July 9, 2014) (same) First licenses: July 10, 2014 (civil disobedience by county clerk, despite stay order); Oct. 7, 2014 (after stay was lifted)
Connecticut	S.S.B. 963, 2005 Conn. Acts 19 (Reg. Sess.), formerly codified at Conn. Gen. Stat. §§ 46b-38aa et seq. (2005) (marriage defined as one man, one woman)	N/A	Office of Conn. Comptroller, Memorandum No. 2000-13 (2000) (extending health care and pension benefits to same-sex domestic partners of state employees and retirees); An Act Concerning Civil Unions, S.S.B. 963, 2005 Conn. Acts 19 (Reg. Sess.) (signed April 20, 2005) (codified at Conn. Gen. Stat. §§ 46b-38aa et seq.) (civil unions for same-sex couples) (repealed 2009)	*Kerrigan v. Comm'r Pub. Health*, 957 A.2d 407 (Conn. 2008), codified by Act Implementing Equal Protection for Same Sex Couples, S.B. 889, 2009 Conn. Acts 78 (Reg. Sess.) (signed April 23, 2009) First licenses: Nov. 12, 2008

State	Statutory prohibition	Constitutional amendment	Civil union / domestic partnership	Marriage equality
Delaware	H.B. 503, 70 Del. Laws 835, formerly codified at Del. Code. Ann. tit. 13, § 101 (1996)	N/A	Civil Union and Equality Act, S.B. 30, 78 Del. Laws ch. 22 (signed May 11, 2011) (codified at Del. Code. Ann. tit. 13, § 201 et seq.) (providing for civil unions as equivalent in rights and benefits to marriage)	Civil Marriage Equality and Religious Freedom Act, H.B. 75, 79 Del. Laws ch. 19 (signed May 7, 2013) (amending Del. Code. Ann. tit. 13, § 101) First licenses: July 1, 2013
District of Columbia	No explicit provision, but D.C. Code §§ 30-101 to 30-121 interpreted to exclude gay couples from marriage in *Dean v. District of Columbia*, 653 A.2d 307 (1995).	N/A	Health Care Benefits Act, C.B. 9-162, 39 D.C. Reg. 2861, D.C. Code § 32-701 et seq. (1992) (domestic partners health care rights, unfunded in 1990s); Domestic Partnership Equality Amendment Act, C.B. 16-52, 53 D.C. Reg. 1035, amended by Omnibus Domestic Partnership Equality Amendment Act, C.B. 17-135, 55 D.C. Reg. 6758 (2008) (providing virtually same rights as marriage)	Religious Freedom and Civil Marriage Equality Amendment Act, C.B. 18-482, 57 D.C. Reg. Act 18-29 (signed Dec. 18, 2009) (codified at D.C. Code §§ 46-401 et seq.) First licenses: March 9, 2010
Florida	H.B. 147, 1997 Fla. Laws 4957, Fla. Stat. § 741.212 (1997); S.B. 352, 1977 Fla. Laws 465, Fla. Stat. § 741.04 (1977)	Amendment 2, Fla. Const., art. I, § 27 (passed by voters in 2008)	N/A	*Brenner v. Scott*, 999 F. Supp. 2d 1278 (N.D. Fla. 2014), stay denied, *Armstrong v. Brenner*, 135 S. Ct. 890 (Dec. 19, 2014) First licenses: Jan. 5, 2015
Georgia	H.B. 1580, 1996 Ga. Laws 1025, Ga. Code. Ann. § 19-3-3.1 (1996)	Amendment 1, Ga. Const., art. I, § 4, ¶ 1 (passed by voters in 2004)	N/A	*Obergefell v. Hodges*, 135 S. Ct. 2584 (2015); *Inniss v. Aderhold*, 80 F. Supp. 3d 1335 (N.D. Ga. 2015). First licenses: June 26, 2015

(continued)

State	Statutory DOMAs	Constitutional DOMAs	State benefits for unmarried LGBTQ couples	Legal authority for marriage equality and first legal licenses
Hawaiʻi	H.B. 2312, 1994 Haw. Sess. Laws 217, formerly codified at Haw. Rev. Stat. § 572-1 (1994)	Amendment 2, Haw. Const., art. I, § 23 (allowing legislature to restrict marriage) (passed by voters in 1998)	An Act Relating to Unmarried Couples, H.B. 118, 1997 Haw. Sess. Laws 1211 (became law without governor's signature, July 8, 1997) (codified at Haw. Rev. Stat. §§ 572C-1 et seq.) (reciprocal beneficiaries benefits for same-sex and older couples); An Act Relating to Civil Unions, S.B. 232, 2011 Haw. Sess. Laws 1 (signed Feb. 23, 2011) (codified at Haw. Rev. Stat. §§ 572B-1 et seq.) (civil unions for all couples)	Hawaiʻi Marriage Equality Act, 2013 Haw. Sess. Laws 1 (signed Nov. 13, 2013) (amending Haw. Rev. Stat. §§ 572-1 et seq.) First licenses: Dec. 2, 2013
Idaho	H.B. 176, 1995 Idaho Sess. Laws 334, Idaho Code §32-201 (1995); H.B. 658, 1996 Idaho Sess. Laws 864, Idaho Code §32-209 (1996) (nonrecognition)	Amendment 2, Idaho Const., art. III, § 28 (passed by voters in 2006)	N/A	Latta v. Otter, 771 F.3d 456 (9th Cir. 2014) First licenses: Oct. 10, 2014
Illinois	S.B. 1140, 1996 Ill. Laws 504, formerly codified at 750 Ill. Comp. Stat. 5/212 et seq. (1996)	N/A	Ill. Admin. Order No. 1 (May 8, 2006) (extending medical benefits to domestic partners of state employees); Illinois Religious Freedom Protection and Civil Union Act, S.B. 1716, 2010 Ill. Laws 7567 (signed Feb. 1, 2011) (codified at 750 Ill. Comp. Stat. 75/1 et seq.) (civil unions for both same-sex and opposite-	Religious Freedom and Marriage Fairness Act, S.B. 10, 2013 Ill. Laws 7141 (signed Nov. 20, 2013) (codified as amended in scattered sections of 750 Ill. Comp. Stat.) First licenses: June 1, 2014

Indiana	H. 1265, 1997 Ind. Acts 2897, Ind. Code § 31-11-1-1 (1997)	N/A	N/A	*Baskin v. Bogan*, 766 F.3d 648 (7th Cir. 2014) First licenses: June 25, 2014 (stay ordered next day), resumed Oct. 7, 2014
Iowa	H.F. 382, 1998 Iowa Laws 182, Iowa Code § 595.2 (1998)	N/A	2003–2005 Collective Bargaining Agreement Between the State of Iowa and AFSCME Council 61, art. IX § 4 (July 1, 2003) (extending health care benefits to state employees' domestic partners and their children)	*Varnum v. Brien*, 763 N.W.2d 862 (Iowa 2009) First licenses: April 27, 2009
Kansas	S.B. 24, 2011 Kan. Sess. Laws 95, Kan. Stat. Ann. § 23-2501; S.B. 515 1996 Kan. Sess. Laws 438, Kan. Stat. Ann. § 23-2508 (nonrecognition)	Amendment 1, Kan. Const., art. 15, § 16 (passed by voters in 2005)	N/A	*Kitchen v. Herbert*, 755 F.3d 1193 (10th Cir. 2014); *Marie v. Moser*, 65 F. Supp. 3d 1175 (D. Kan. 2014) First licenses: Nov. 13, 2014
Kentucky	H.B. 13, 1998 Ky. Acts 984, Ky. Rev. Stat. Ann. §§ 402.005 et seq. (West 1998)	Amendment 1, Ky. Const. § 233A (passed by voters in 2004)	N/A	*Obergefell v. Hodges*, 135 S. Ct. 2584 (2015) First licenses: June 26, 2015
Louisiana	H.B. 1480, 1999 La. Acts 2503, La. Civ. Code. Ann. art. 3520 (1999)	Question 1, La. Const., art. XII, § 15 (passed by voters in 2004)	N/A	*Obergefell v. Hodges*, 135 S. Ct. 2584 (2015); *Constanza v. Caldwell*, 167 So.3d 619 (La. 2015) (moot after *Obergefell*) First licenses: June 29, 2015

(continued)

State	Statutory DOMAs	Constitutional DOMAs	State benefits for unmarried LGBTQ couples	Legal authority for marriage equality and first legal licenses
Maine	I.P. 1, 1997 Me. Laws 326, formerly codified at Me. Stat. tit. 19-A, §§ 650, 701 (1997)	N/A	Act to Promote the Financial Security of Maine's Families and Children, H.P. 1152, 2004 Me. Laws 2126 (signed April 28, 2004) (codified at Me. Stat. tit. 22, § 2710) (creating domestic partnerships for same-sex couples, with some marriage rights)	Act to End Discrimination in Civil Marriage and Affirm Religious Freedom, S.P. 384, 2009 Me. Laws 150 (signed May 6, 2009), repealed by Question 1 (passed by voters on Nov. 3, 2009); Act to Allow Marriages for Same-Sex Couples and Protect Religious Freedom, Ratified by Maine Question 1 (passed by voters, Nov. 6, 2012) (amending Me. Stat. tit. 19-A, § 650-A) First licenses: Dec. 29, 2012
Maryland	H.B. 1, 1984 Md. Laws 1847, formerly codified at Md. Code Ann., Fam. Law § 2-201 (West 1984)	N/A	Act Concerning Visitation and Medical Decisions—Domestic Partners, S.B. 566, 2008 Md. Laws 4597 (signed May 22, 2008) (codified at Md. Code Ann. Health-Gen. § 6-101 (West 2008)) (creating domestic partnerships for same-sex couples, with some marriage rights)	Civil Marriage Protection Act, H.B. 438, 2012 Md. Laws 9 (signed March 1, 2012), ratified by Maryland Question 6 (passed by voters, Nov. 6, 2012) (codified at Md. Code Ann., Fam. Law § 2-201 (West 2012)) First licenses issued: Dec. 6, 2012, but did not take effect until Jan. 1, 2013

State				
Massachusetts	No explicit provision, but Mass. Gen. Laws ch. 207, §§ 19, 20 assumed to bar same-sex marriages in Goodridge v. Dept. Pub. Health, 798 N.E.2d 941 (Mass. 2003)	N/A	Executive Order No. 340, Comm. of Mass. (1992) (extending some domestic partnership benefits to senior civil service employees; broadened by executive order in 2000)	Goodridge v. Dept. Pub. Health, 798 N.E.2d 941 (Mass. 2003), reaffirmed by Opinions of the Justices to the Senate, 802 N.E.2d 565 (Mass. 2004) (civil unions would not satisfy the Massachusetts Constitution) First licenses: May 17, 2004
Michigan	S.B. 937, 1996 Mich. Pub. Acts 1026, Mich. Comp. Laws § 551.1 (1996)	Proposal 2, Mich. Const., art. 1, § 25 (passed by voters in 2004)	N/A	Obergefell v. Hodges, 135 S. Ct. 2584 (2015) First licenses: June 26, 2015
Minnesota	S.F. 1908, 1997 Minn. Laws 1587, codified at Minn. Stat. § 517.01 (1997); S.F. 966, 1977 Minn. Laws 1206, codified at Minn. Stat. § 517.01 (1977)	N/A	N/A	H.F. 1054, 2013 Minn. Laws 74 (signed May 14, 2013) (amending Minn. Stat. § 517.01) First licenses: July 31, 2013
Mississippi	S.B. 2053, 1997 Miss. Laws ch. 301, Miss. Code Ann. § 93-1-1 (1997)	Amendment 1, Miss. Const., art. 14, § 263A (passed by voters in 2004)	N/A	Obergefell v. Hodges, 135 S. Ct. 2584 (2015) First licenses issued: June 29, 2015

(continued)

State	Statutory DOMAs	Constitutional DOMAs	State benefits for unmarried LGBTQ couples	Legal authority for marriage equality and first legal licenses
Missouri	S.B. 768, 1996 Mo. Laws 741, Mo. Rev. Stat. § 451.022 (1996)	Amendment 2, Mo. Const., art. 1, § 33 (passed by voters in 2004)	N/A	*Obergefell v. Hodges*, 135 S. Ct. 2584 (2015) First licenses: June 25 and Nov. 7, 2014 (rogue licenses issued by two different counties); June 26, 2015 (lawful licenses issued statewide)
Montana	H.B. 323, 1997 Mont. Laws 2088, Mont. Code Ann. § 40-1-401 (1997); S.B. 5, 1975 Mont. Laws 1514, Mont. Code Ann. § 40-1-103 (1975)	Initiative 96, Mont. Const., art. XIII, § 7 (passed by voters in 2004)	*Snetsinger v. Mont. Univ. Sys.*, 104 P.3d 445 (Mont. 2004) (mandating extension of benefits to state employees' domestic partners)	*Latta v. Otter*, 771 F.3d 456 (9th Cir. 2014); *Rolando v. Fox*, 23 F. Supp. 3d 1277 (D. Mont. 2014) First licenses: Nov. 20, 2014
Nebraska	L.B. 165, 1978 Neb. Laws 87, Neb. Rev. Stat. § 42-102 (1978)	Initiative 416, Neb. Const., art. I, § 29 (passed by voters in 2000)	N/A	*Obergefell v. Hodges*, 135 S. Ct. 2584 (2015); *Waters v. Ricketts*, 48 F. Supp. 3d 1271 (D. Neb. 2015) First licenses: June 26, 2015
Nevada	A.B. 262, 2009 Nev. Laws 1503; Nev. Rev. Stat. § 122.020 (2009)	Question 2, Nev. Const., art. I, § 21 (passed by voters in 2000 and 2002)	Domestic Partnership Responsibilities Act, S.B. 283, 2009 Nev. Laws 2183 (veto overridden June 1, 2009) (codified at Nev. Rev. Stat. §§ 122A.010 et seq.) (domestic partnerships for same-sex and different-sex couples)	*Latta v. Otter*, 771 F.3d 456 (9th Cir. 2014), codified by Act Authorizing the Marriage of Two Persons of Any Gender Under Certain Circumstances, A.B. 229, 2017 Nev. Laws 755 (signed May 26, 2017)

State				
New Hampshire	N/A	S.B. 115, 1987 N.H. Laws 192, formerly codified at N.H. Rev. Stat. Ann. §§ 457:1, 457:2 (1987)	Act Permitting Same Gender Couples to Enter Civil Unions, H.B. 437, 2007 N.H. Laws 57 (signed May 31, 2007) (codified at N.H. Rev. Stat. Ann. § 457-a) (civil unions, identical to marriage in legal effect) (repealed 2009)	Act Relative to Civil Marriage and Civil Unions, H.B. 436, 2009 N.H. Laws 60 (signed May 3, 2009) (codified at N.H. Rev. Stat. Ann. § 457:1-a) First licenses: Jan. 1, 2010
New Jersey	N/A	N/A	Domestic Partnership Act, A. 3742, 2003 N.J. Laws 1675 (signed Jan. 12, 2004) (codified at N.J. Stat Ann. §§ 26:8A-1 et seq.) (domestic partnerships for same-sex and older couples); Lewis v. Harris, 908 A.2d 196 (N.J. 2006), implemented by Act Concerning Civil Unions, A. 3787, 2006 N.J. Laws 975 (signed Dec. 21, 2006) (codified at N.J. Stat. Ann. §§ 37:1-28 et seq.)	Garden State Equality v. Dow, 82 A.3d 336 (N.J. Super.), stay denied, 79 A.3d 1036 (N.J. 2013), and state acquiesces First licenses issued: Oct. 21, 2013
New Mexico	N/A	N/A	Uniform Health-Care Decisions Act, H.B. 483, 1995 N.M. Laws 1496 (signed April 6, 1995) (codified at N.M. Stat. Ann. § 24-7A-5) (medical decision-making rights for persons in "long-term relationships" similar to marriage); N.M. Executive Order No. 2003-010 (April 9, 2003) (providing domestic partners of state employees with the same benefits as those provided to married spouses)	Griego v. Oliver, 316 P.3d 865 (N.M. 2013) First licenses: Dec. 19, 2013

(continued)

State	Statutory DOMAs	Constitutional DOMAs	State benefits for unmarried LGBTQ couples	Legal authority for marriage equality and first legal licenses
New York	No explicit provision, but N.Y. Dom. Rel. Law §§ 10 et seq. interpreted to exclude same-sex couples from marriage, *Hernandez v. Robles*, 855 N.E.2d 1 (N.Y. 2006)	N/A	Family Health Care Decisions Act, A. 7729-D, 2010 N.Y. Laws 17 (signed March 16, 2010) (codified at N.Y. Pub. Health Law § 2994-a) (medical decision-making rights for domestic partners); Ian Fisher, *Cuomo Decides to Extend Domestic-Partner Benefits*, NYT, June 29, 1994, B4 (medical benefits for domestic partners of state employees, secured in collective bargaining agreement)	Marriage Equality Act, A. 8354, 2011 N.Y. Laws 749 (signed June 24, 2011) (codified at N.Y. Dom. Rel. Law §§ 10-a, 10-b) First licenses: July 24, 2011
North Carolina	S.B. 1487, 1996 N.C. Sess. Laws 67, N.C. Gen. Stat. § 51-1.2 (1996)	Amendment 1, N.C. Const., art. XIV, § 6 (passed by voters in 2012)	N/A	*Bostic v. Shaefer*, 760 F.3d 352 (4th Cir. 2014); *General Synod of the United Church of Christ v. Resinger*, 12 F. Supp. 3d 790 (W.D. N.C. 2014) First licenses: Oct. 10, 2014
North Dakota	S.B. 2230, 1997 N.D. Laws 755, N.D. Cent. Code § 14-03-01 (1997)	Measure 1, N.D. Const., art. XI, § 28 (passed by voters in 2004)	N/A	*Obergefell v. Hodges*, 135 S. Ct. 2584 (2015); *Ramsay v. Dalrymple*, No. 3:14-cv-57 (D.N.D. June 29, 2015) First licenses: June 26, 2015

State	Statute	Constitutional provision	Domestic partner benefits	Judicial decision
Ohio	H.B. 272, 2004 Ohio Laws 3403, Ohio Rev. Code Ann. §3101.01 (West 2004)	Issue 1, Ohio Const., art. XV, § 11 (passed by voters in 2004)	2010 Ohio Reg. 1018007 (promulgated Oct. 28, 2010) (codified at Ohio Admin. Code 3349-7-30) (specified benefits to domestic partners of employees in state university system)	*Obergefell v. Hodges*, 135 S. Ct. 2584 (2015) First licenses: June 26, 2015
Oklahoma	S.B. 73, 1996 Okla. Sess. Laws 473, Okla. Stat. tit. 43, § 3.1 (1996); S.B. 399, 1975 Okla. Sess. Laws 186, Okla. Stat. tit. 43, § 3 (1975)	Question 711, Okla. Const., art. II, § 35 (passed by voters in 2004)	N/A	*Bishop v. Smith*, 760 F.3d 1070 (10th Cir.), cert. denied, 135 S. Ct. 271 (2014) First licenses: Oct. 6, 2014
Oregon	S.B. 118, 1975 Or. Laws 1377, Or. Rev. Stat. § 106.010 (1975)	Measure 36, Or. Const., art. XV, § 5a (passed by voters in 2004)	39-1 Or. Bull. 29 (Jan. 1, 2000) (codified at Or. Admin. R. 101-015-0005 et seq.) (medical benefits for domestic partners of state employees); Oregon Family Fairness Act, H.B. 2007, 2007 Or. Laws 425 (signed May 9, 2007) (codified at Or. Rev. Stat. §§ 106.300 et seq.) (domestic partnerships with same rights/benefits as marriage)	*Geiger v. Kitzhaber*, 994 F. Supp. 2d 1128 (D. Or. 2014), codified by Act Relating to Gender Neutrality in Laws, H.B. 4127, 2016 Or. Laws 2641 (signed March 14, 2016) First licenses: May 19, 2014
Pennsylvania	S.B. 434, 1996 Pa. Laws 706, 23 Pa. Cons. Stat. §§ 1102, 1704 (1996)	N/A	N/A	*Whitewood v. Wolf*, 992 F. Supp. 2d 410 (M.D. Pa. 2014) First licenses: May 21, 2014

(continued)

State	Statutory DOMAs	Constitutional DOMAs	State benefits for unmarried LGBTQ couples	Legal authority for marriage equality and first legal licenses
Rhode Island	N/A	N/A	Act Relating to Public Officers and Employees' Insurance Benefits, H. 5339A, 2001 R.I. Pub. Laws 694 (signed July 9, 2001) (codified at 36 R.I. Gen. Laws §§ 36-12-1 et seq.) (benefits for domestic partners of state employees); Act Relating to Civil Unions, H. 6103A, 2011 R.I. Pub. Laws 1134 (signed July 2, 2011) (codified at 15 R.I. Gen. Laws §§ 15-3.1-1 et seq.)	Act Relating to Persons Eligible to Marry, S. 38A, 2013 R.I. Pub. Laws 15 (signed May 2, 2013) (amending 15 R.I. Gen. Laws § 15-1-1) First licenses: Aug. 1, 2013
South Carolina	H.B. 4502, 1996 S.C. Acts 2048, S.C. Code Ann. § 20-1-15 (1996)	Amendment 1, S.C. Const., art. XVII, § 15 (passed by voters in 2006)	N/A	Bostic v. Shaefer, 760 F.3d 352 (4th Cir. 2014); Bradacs v. Haley, 58 F. Supp. 3d 514 (D.S.C. 2014) First licenses: Nov. 19, 2014
South Dakota	H.B. 1143, 1996 S.D. Sess. Laws 221, S.D. Cod. Laws § 25-1-1 (1996); H.B. 1163, 2000 S.D. Sess. Laws 169, S.D. Cod. Laws § 25-1-38 (2000) (nonrecognition)	Amendment C, S.D. Const., art. XXI, § 9 (passed by voters in 2006)	N/A	Obergefell v. Hodges, 135 S. Ct. 2584 (2015); Rosenbrahn v. Daugaard, 61 F. Supp. 3d 862 (D.S.D. 2015) First licenses: June 26, 2015
Tennessee	S.B. 2305, 1996 Tenn. Pub. Acts 822, Tenn. Code Ann. § 36-3-113 (1996)	Amendment 1, Tenn. Const., art. XI, § 18 (passed by voters in 2006)	N/A	Obergefell v. Hodges, 135 S. Ct. 2584 (2015) First licenses: June 26, 2015

Texas	S.B. 334, 1997 Tex. Gen. Laws 8, Tex. Fam. Code § 2.001 (1997)	Proposition 2, Tex. Const. art. I, § 32 (passed by voters in 2005)	N/A	*Obergefell v. Hodges*, 135 S. Ct. 2584 (2015); *De Leon v. Perry*, 975 F. Supp. 2d 632 (W.D. Tex. 2014), aff'd, *De Leon v. Abbott*, 791 F.3d 619 (5th Cir. 2015) First licenses: June 26, 2015
Utah	S.B. 24, 2004 Utah Laws 1158, Utah Code § 30-1-4.1 (2004); H.B. 3, 1977 Utah Laws (1st Sp. Sess.), 1, Utah Code § 30-1-2 (1977); H.B. 366, 1995 Utah Laws 461, Utah Code § 30-1-4 (1995) (nonrecognition)	Amendment 3, Utah Const. art. I, § 29 (passed by voters in 2004)	N/A	*Kitchen v. Herbert*, 961 F. Supp. 2d 1181 (D. Utah 203), aff'd, 755 F.3d 1193 (10th Cir. 2014), cert. denied, 135 S. Ct. (Oct. 6, 2014) First licenses: Dec. 20, 2013, stayed 134 S. Ct. 893 (Jan. 6, 2014), stay lifted Oct. 6, 2014
Vermont	No explicit provision, but Vt. Stat. Ann. tit. 15, ch. 1 and tit. 18, ch. 105, interpreted to exclude same-sex couples from marriage in *Baker v. State*, 744 A.2d 864, 868–869 (Vt. 1999)	N/A	Act Relating to Civil Unions, H. 847, 2000 Vt. Acts & Resolves 72 (signed April 26, 2000) (codified at Vt. Stat. Ann. tit. 15, §§ 1201 et seq.) (civil unions for same-sex couples; reciprocal beneficiaries for same-sex couples and older couples); *Vermont Workers Win Health Benefits*, NYT, June 13, 1994, A13 (medical benefits for same-sex and opposite-sex domestic partners of state employees, secured in collective bargaining agreement)	Act to Protect Religious Freedom and Recognize Equality in Civil Marriage, S. 115, 2009 Vt. Acts & Resolves 3 (passed over veto, April 7, 2009) (amending Vt. Stat. Ann. tit. 15, §§ 8 et seq.) First licenses: Sept. 1, 2009

(continued)

State	Statutory DOMAs	Constitutional DOMAs	State benefits for unmarried LGBTQ couples	Legal authority for marriage equality and first legal licenses
Virginia	H.B. 751, 2004 Va. Acts 1920, Va. Code Ann. § 20-45.3 (2004) (same-sex unions, partnerships); H. 1470, 1975 Va. Acts. 1336, Va. Code Ann. § 20-45.2 (1975), amended by S.B. 884, 1997 Va. Acts 513 (nonrecognition)	Question 1, Va. Const., art. I, § 15-A (passed by voters in 2006)	N/A	*Bostic v. Shaefer*, 760 F.3d 352 (4th Cir.), stay granted, *McQuigg v. Bostic*, 135 S. Ct. 32 (2014), stay lifted, 2014 WL 4960335 (4th Cir. Oct. 6, 2014) First licenses: Oct. 6, 2014
Washington	H.B. 1130, 1998 Wash. Sess. Laws 1, formerly codified at Wash. Rev. Code §§ 26.04.010 et seq. (1998)	N/A	01-01 Wash. Reg. 126 (Jan. 3, 2001) (codified at Wash. Admin. Code § 182-12-119) (medical benefits for domestic partners of state employees); Act Relating to Protecting Domestic Partnerships, S.B. 5336, 2007 Wash. Sess. Laws 616 (signed April 21, 2007) (codified at Wash. Rev. Code §§ 26.60.010 et seq.) (domestic partnerships for same-sex and older couples), amended by Domestic Partners Rights and Responsibilities Act, S.B. 5688, 2009 Wash. Sess. Laws 3065 (signed May 18, 2009), ratified by Referendum 71 (passed by voters in Nov. 2009) (expanded domestic partnership, all	Marriage Equality Act, S.B. 6239, 2012 Wash. Sess. Laws 199 (signed Feb. 13, 2012), ratified by Referendum 74 (passed by voters Nov. 6, 2012) (amending Wash. Rev. Code §§ 26.04.010 et seq.) First licenses: Dec. 9, 2012

West Virginia	H.B. 2199, 2001 W. Va. Acts 374, W. Va. Code §§ 48-2-101, 48-2-104, 48-2-603 (2001)	N/A	N/A	*Bostic v. Schaefer*, 760 F.3d 352 (4th Cir. 2014); *McGee v. Cole*, 66 F. Supp. 3d 747 (S.D. W. Va. 2014) First licenses: Oct. 9, 2014
Wisconsin	N/A	Referendum 1, Wis. Const., art. XIII, § 13 (passed by voters in 2006)	A.B. 75, 2009 Wis. Sess. Laws 179 (signed June 29, 2009) (codified at Wis. Stat. § 770.01) (domestic partnership for same-sex couples)	*Wolf v. Walker*, 986 F. Supp. 2d 982 (W.D. Wis.), aff'd, *Baskin v. Bogan*, 766 F.3d 648 (7th Cir.), cert. denied, 135 S. Ct. 316 (Oct. 6, 2014) First licenses: June 6, 2014, stayed June 13, 2014, stay lifted Oct. 6, 2014
Wyoming	S.F. 76, 1977 Wyo. Sess. Laws 479, Wyo. Stat. Ann. § 20-1-101 (1977)	N/A	N/A	*Guzzo v. Mead*, 2014 WL 5317797 (D. Wyo. Oct. 17, 2014) First licenses: Oct. 21, 2014

APPENDIX 2 • GAY-FRIENDLY LAWS IN THE UNITED STATES, DECEMBER 2007

State	Consensual sodomy no crime	Sexual orientation hate crime law	Laws against public/private employment discrimination	Municipalities with domestic partnership registration	Second-parent adoptions, de facto parenting	Limited state recognition of same-sex partnerships
Massachusetts	1974/2002	1996	1989/1989	Boston	1993	2000
Vermont	1977	1989	1991/1991	Burlington	1993	2000
California	1975	1991	1979/1979	Los Angeles	2003	1999
District of Columbia	1994	1994	1977/1977	Washington	1995	1992
Connecticut	1969	1990	1991/1991	Hartford	2000	2005
New Jersey	1978	1995	1991/1991	Newark	1995	2004
Oregon	1971	1989	1987/2007	Portland	2007	2007
Maine	1975	1995	2005/2005	Portland	2004/2007	2004
Iowa	1972	1992	2007/2007	Iowa City		2003
New York	1980		1983/2002	New York City	1995	1994
Illinois	1961	1991	1996/2005	Chicago	1995	2006
Minnesota	2001	1989	1986/1993	Minneapolis	2000	
Rhode Island	1998	1991	1985/1995	Providence		2001
Hawai'i	1972	2001	1991/1991	Honolulu		1997
Washington	1975	1993	1985/2007	Seattle		2007
Wisconsin	1983	1988	1982/1982	Milwaukee	1995	
New Hampshire	1973	1991	1997/1997		2007	2007
New Mexico	1973	2003	1985/2003	Albuquerque		1995
Pennsylvania	1980	2002	1975/None	Philadelphia	2002	
Maryland	(1999)	2005	1993/2001	Baltimore		
Colorado	1971	2005	2001/2007	Denver		
Arizona	2001	1997	2003/None	Tucson		
Indiana	1976		2004/None	Bloomington	2003/2005	
Nevada	1993	2001	1999/1999			
Ohio	1972		1983/None	Toledo		

(continued)

State	Consensual sodomy no crime	Sexual orientation hate crime law	Laws against public/private employment discrimination	Municipalities with domestic partnership registration	Second-parent adoptions, de facto parenting	Limited state recognition of same-sex partnerships
Michigan	(1990)		2003/None	Kalamazoo		
Kentucky	1992	1998	2003/None			
Missouri	(1999)	2001		Saint Louis		
Florida	(1971)	1991		Miami		
Louisiana	1997	1997	2004/None	New Orleans		
Delaware	1972	2001				
Montana	1997		2000/None			
Alaska	1978		2002/None			
Nebraska	1977	1997				
Georgia	1998			Atlanta		
Texas		2002		Houston		
Tennessee	1996	2001				
North Dakota	1973					
South Dakota	1976					
West Virginia	1976					
Wyoming	1977					
Kansas		2002				
Virginia				Arlington		
North Carolina				Carrboro		
Alabama						
Arkansas						
Idaho						
Mississippi						
Oklahoma						
South Carolina						
Utah						

Appendix 3 • Number of State Marriages, Civil Unions, and Domestic Partnerships, 2000–2018

	2000–2003	2004	2005	2006	2007	2008	2009
Colorado							
Marriages	ND	ND	ND	ND	ND	28,796	28,579
Beneficiaries	NA	NA	NA	NA	NA	NA	403
Civil Unions	NA	NA	NA	NA	NA	NA	NA
Connecticut							
Marriages	20,088	20,371	20,514	19,320	19,499	19,028	20,857
Same-Sex	NA	NA	NA	NA	NA	543	2,706
Hawai'i							
Marriages	ND	ND	ND	ND	ND	25,464	23,170
Same-Sex	NA	NA	NA	NA	NA	NA	NA
Civil Unions	NA	NA	NA	NA	NA	NA	NA
Iowa							
Marriages	20,924	20,455	20,419	20,060	19,895	19,566	21,139
Same-Sex	NA	NA	NA	NA	NA	NA	1,783
Not Stated	NA	NA	NA	NA	NA	NA	902
Maine							
Marriages	ND	11,288	10,938	10,325	9,870	9,858	9,497
Same-Sex	NA	NA	NA	NA	NA	NA	NA
Dom P'ships	NA	373	205	163	184	211	170
Massachusetts							
Marriages	38,152	41,571	39,507	37,993	37,897	36,923	36,407
Same-Sex	NA	6,121	2,060	1,442	1,524	2,168	2,814
Upstate New York							
Marriages	72,252	66,663	64,322	62,369	61,319	60,386	57,101
Same-Sex	NA	NA	NA	NA	NA	NA	NA
Unknown	NA	NA	NA	NA	NA	NA	NA
Oregon							
Marriages	25,615	25,789	26,471	26,715	26,664	26,139	25,239
Same-Sex	NA	NA	NA	NA	NA	NA	NA
Dom P'ships	NA	NA	NA	NA	NA	2,636	716
Vermont							
Marriages	6,063	5,834	5,532	5,355	5,320	4,937	5,434
Civil Unions	1,670	712	452	429	352	268	NA
Washington							
Marriages	41,306	40,169	40,802	41,536	41,375	41,643	40,318
Dom P'ships	NA	NA	NA	NA	3,159	1,719	1,898

2000–2003: Yearly average for 2000, 2001, 2002, 2003

NA: Not applicable (e.g., domestic partnerships had not been recognized)

ND: No data available from the state.

2010	2011	2012	2013	2014	2015	2016	2017	2018
28,751	29,921	29,268	30,159	33,026	34,257	34,819	35,637	ND
214	131	136	66	48	32	17	21	ND
NA	NA	NA	1,970	580	74	82	93	ND
19,946	19,504	19,216	19,428	19,350	20,924	ND	ND	ND
1,791	1,262	668	1,356	1,057	ND	ND	ND	ND
23,896	24,135	23,723	22,813	25,130	22,820	22,219	21,908	9,942 (½ year)
NA	NA	NA	533	2,710	1,661	1,375	1,147	ND
NA	NA	730	388	32	23	29	39	ND
20,880	20,567	20,986	22,841	21,327	19,540	19,277	ND	ND
1,594	1,302	1,247	3,397	1,813	534	415	ND	ND
814	774	773	1,140	794	536	677	ND	ND
9,451	9,530	9,703	11,039	10,302	10,117	10,149	10,139	ND
NA	NA	NA	1,774	1,021	526	598	522	ND
156	162	176	97	121	117	128	156	ND
36,429	36,327	37,055	36,820	36,284	37,450	39,652	ND	ND
2,335	2,212	1,913	3,196	2,657	1,997	2,030	ND	ND
57,145	60,114	60,394	60,053	61,278	60,319	61,176	ND	ND
NA	ND	2,796	4,031	3,193	2,044	2,056	ND	ND
NA	ND	7,771	5,334	4,767	4,578	4,416	ND	ND
25,067	25,530	25,641	24,951	27,735	27,794	28,023	27,604	ND
NA	NA	NA	NA	2,027	1,704	1,901	1,547	ND
593	550	634	538	189	103	71	83	ND
5,811	5,198	5,217	5,778	5,455	5,119	5,190	ND	ND
NA	NA	NA	NA	NA	NA	NA	NA	NA
ND	41,509	43,238	49,590	45,841	44,622	45,456	ND	NA
1,567	1,316	NA	NA	NA	NA	NA	NA	NA

Notes

Archives

AFER ARCHIVES: American Federation for Equal Rights, transcripts of the trial, *Perry v. Schwarzenegger,* http://afer.org/our-work/hearing-transcripts/.

CLINTON PAPERS: Presidential papers of William J. Clinton, https://clinton.presidentiallibraries.us.

DEBOER TRIAL: Exhibits and testimony from *DeBoer v. Snyder,* Federal Court, Detroit, 2014, MI #12-Civ-10285, https://web.stanford.edu/~mrosenfe/DeBoer_docs.htm.

ETTELBRICK ARCHIVES: Papers of Paula Ettelbrick, New York City and Cornell University Library.

F2M ORAL HISTORY: Freedom to Marry Oral History Project, archived at the University of California, Berkeley, https://update.lib.berkeley.edu/2017/04/10/freedom-to-marry/.

GLAD ARCHIVES: Papers of LGBTQ Advocates & Defenders (formerly Gay & Lesbian Advocates & Defenders), Boston and Portland, ME, to be deposited at Yale University Library.

HRC ARCHIVES: Papers of the Human Rights Campaign, Cornell University Library.

LA GLBT ARCHIVES: Gay Lesbian Bisexual and Transgender Historical Society Archives, http://oac.cdlib.org/findaid/ark:/13030/kt158023t6/.

LA LAMBDA ARCHIVES: Files maintained in the Los Angeles office of Lambda Legal.

MCC ARCHIVES: Records of the Massachusetts Catholic Conference, https://www.macatholic.org/children.

MCCONNELL ARCHIVES: University of Minnesota Library, Tretter Collection, papers of Michael McConnell.

PRINCE ARCHIVES: Library of Mormon history in the home of Gregory and JaLynn Prince, River Road, Potomac, MD, to be deposited at the University of Virginia Library.

SCHLESINGER LIBRARY: Arthur and Elizabeth Schlesinger Library on the History of Women in America, Harvard University, Cambridge, MA.

TASK FORCE ARCHIVES: Papers of the LGBTQ Task Force, Washington, DC, and Cornell University Library.

Prelude

1. Our account of the Michigan nurses and their family is mainly based upon a series of interviews we conducted at their home in November 2015, together with telephone interviews conducted at various points in 2015 and 2017 with April DeBoer, Jayne Rowse, Wendy DeBoer (April's mother), and their attorneys Dana Nessel, Carole Stanyar, and Ken Mogill. We also met with Stanyar and Nessel in their offices in August 2017. Another useful source is "Interview with Jayne Rowse and April DeBoer," Eclectablog, Dec. 2, 2013.

2. In 1999, Renee Harmon and her partner, Tammy Davis, had their first child, a girl, followed in 2003 by twin boys. After nineteen years as partners and a decade as co-parents, they split up in 2008, and Davis and her new partner cut off Harmon from all contact with the kids in 2009. Harmon lost her case by a 4-3 vote of the Michigan Supreme Court. Lesbians who co-parent with a child's biological or adoptive parent, said the judges, have no rights.

1. Coming Out of the Constitutional Closet

1. The introductory story is assembled from Michael McConnell, with Jack Baker, as told to Gail Langer Karwoski, *The Wedding Heard 'Round the World: America's First Gay Marriage*, 1–22 (2016); Michael McConnell, "Marriage—My Childhood Dream Comes True" (Nov. 2013), in McConnell Archives, Box 20; William Eskridge interviews of Jack Baker and Michael McConnell, Minneapolis (week of June 7, 2015), as supplemented by emails and telephone conversations.

2. On the closet, see George Chauncey, *Gay New York: Gender, Urban Culture, and the Making of the Gay Male World, 1840–1940* (1994) and *Why Marriage? The History Shaping Today's Debate Over Gay Equality*, 15–22 (2004); William Eskridge Jr., *Gaylaw: Challenging the Apartheid of the Closet* (1999).

3. McConnell, *Wedding*, 1 (quotation in text).

4. McConnell, *Wedding*, 21–22 (quotations in text).

5. Minn. Stat. §§ 517.01–517.02 (West 1970) (first quotation in text; emphasis added); McConnell, *Wedding*, 66 (second quotation).

6. David Carter, *Stonewall: The Riots That Sparked the Gay Revolution* (2004); Martin Duberman, *Stonewall* (1993). See William Eskridge Jr., *Dishonorable Passions: Sod-*

omy Law in America, 1861–2003 (2008); Lillian Faderman, *The Gay Revolution: The Story of the Struggle* (2015); Joanne Meyerowitz, *How Sex Changed: A History of Transsexualism in the United States* (2002).

7. After the November 1966 police raid, officers called the parents, schools, and employers of the men arrested that night. McConnell, *Wedding,* 7, 11 (quotations in text).

8. Betty Friedan, *The Feminine Mystique,* 27 (1963) (quotation in text). See Stephanie Coontz, *A Strange Stirring: "The Feminine Mystique" and American Women at the Dawn of the 1960s* (2011); Chauncey, *Why Marriage?,* 30–35 (feminism, civil rights, and the sexual revolution encouraged gays to come out).

9. McConnell, *Wedding,* 40–45. On Kameny, see Eric Cervini, *The Deviant's War: The Homosexual vs. the United States of America* (2020); David Johnson, *The Lavender Scare: The Cold War Persecution of Gays and Lesbians in the Federal Government* (2009).

10. Lillian Faderman, *Surpassing the Love of Men: Romantic Friendship and Love Between Women from the Renaissance to the Present* (1981) (discreet female relationships); Jonathan Ned Katz, *Gay American History* (1976) (women passing as men and marrying other women).

11. E. B. Saunders, *Reformers' Choice: Marriage License or Just License?,* One, Aug. 1953, 10–11 (first two quotations in text); Randy Lloyd, *Let's Push Homophile Marriage,* One, June 1963, 5–10 (latter quotations in text). See Nathaniel Frank, *Awakening: How Gays and Lesbians Brought Marriage Equality to America,* 11–15 (2017).

12. Kate Millett, *Sexual Politics,* 85–86 (1969) (quotation in text); Adrienne Rich, *Compulsory Heterosexuality and Lesbian Existence,* 5 Signs 631, 645 (1980). On women's and gay liberation as oppositional to patriarchy, see Sidney Abbott and Barbara Love, *Sappho Was a Right-On Woman: A Liberated View of Lesbianism,* 139 (1972); Dennis Altman, *The End of the Homosexual,* 53 (2013); Jack Onge, *The Gay Liberation Movement,* 33–35 (1971); Donn Teal, *The Gay Militants* (1971).

13. William Eskridge interview of Martha Shelley, New York City (May 1, 2019); Lillian Jimenez interview of Daisy De Jesus, Hunter College (Jan. 16, 2008), http://voces .prattsi.org/items/show/96.

14. Scott Bloom, director, *Call Me Troy* (Tragoidia Moving Pictures, 2007) (quotation in text). See also Troy Perry, *The Lord Is My Shepherd, and He Knows I'm Gay* (1972).

15. Rob Cole, *A Marriage for Liberation?,* The Advocate, April 2, 1972.

16. Email from Rev. Troy Perry to William Eskridge, Oct. 4, 2017 (quotations in text); John Zeh, *Perry Plans Marriage Test,* The Advocate, June 24, 1970, 2; Rev. Dr. Nancy Wilson, "SCOTUS and Gay Marriage—The Sky Is Not Falling," *The Blog,* HuffPost, April 28, 2015.

17. *Marriage Stalls: He-She Loves She-He,* San Jose News, Aug. 10, 1973 (quotations in text). Patricia Page discovered Neva's subsequent history, and Alex Lichtenstein tracked down Jason.

18. R. S. Redmount, *A Case of a Female Transvestite with Mental and Criminal Complications*, 14 J. Clin. & Exper. Psychopathy 95, 96–97, 110–111 (1953) (satisfying marriage of female-passing-as-male transgender person and cisgender female); *Anonymous v. Anonymous*, 325 N.Y.S.2d 499 (Supreme Ct. Queens Cnty. 1971) (annulling marriage between cisgender man and man-passing-as-woman transgender person); *M.T. v. J.T.*, 355 A.2d 204 (N.J. App. 1976) (upholding validity of marriage between post-op male-to-female transgender person and cisgender male).

19. Dan Mjolsness, *"Gay Is Good" Outdates Myth*, The Concordian, April 24, 1970, in McConnell Archives; [Revised] Constitution of FREE (Feb. 5, 1970), in McConnell Archives; McConnell, *Wedding*, 55–63.

20. McConnell, *Wedding*, 65–70 (account of marriage plans and quotation in text).

21. McConnell, *Wedding*, 70–72 (first-person account of the application as well as the quotation in text).

22. Minn. Stat. § 517.07 (first provision, quoted in text) and § 517.09 (solemnization provision) (West 1971); Memorandum from George Scott to Gerald Nelson, "Requested Opinion Concerning Marriage License Application: Richard John Baker and James Michael McConnell" (May 22, 1970), McConnell Archives, Box 26 (second quotation in text).

23. McConnell, *Wedding*, 72–73 (first quotation in text), 74–81 (remaining quotations).

24. McConnell, *Wedding*, 96. Assistant county attorney David Mikkelson informed the couple that he was personally okay with same-sex marriage and gave Baker some helpful advice (e.g., counseling against filing a federal lawsuit). See Jack Baker's handwritten notes on the planned marriage lawsuit (1970–1971), McConnell Archives, Box 21.

25. Plaintiffs' memorandum, pp. 15–17, Fourth Jud. Dist., No. 671379 (District Court, Hennepin County, filed Nov. 12, 1970), McConnell Archives, Box 15; *Reed v. Reed*, 404 U.S. 71 (1971); brief for the appellant, *Reed*, 1971 WL 133596 (No. 70-4, filed June 25, 1971) (ACLU/Ginsburg brief).

26. See McConnell Archives, Box 21, vol. 2b (marriage license lawsuit materials, including Judge Kane's opinion, quoted in text).

27. Jack Star, *The Homosexual Couple*, LOOK, Jan. 26, 1971, 69 (quotation in text).

28. *Baker v. Nelson*, 191 N.W.2d 185 (Minn. 1971). On the oral argument, see Ken Bronson, *A Quest for Full Equality* (2004); Email from Jack Baker and Mike McConnell to Bill Eskridge, Feb. 23, 2005. Justice Kelly was a Catholic Republican who would later write the opinion outlawing workplace sexual harassment. *Continental Can Co. v. State*, 297 N.W.2d 241 (Minn. 1980).

29. Jurisdictional statement, pp. 14–15, *Baker v. Nelson* (US Supreme Court, No. 71-1027) (first quotation in text), p. 12 (second quotation, invoking *Loving*).

30. Appellee's motion to dismiss appeal and brief, p. 6, *Baker v. Nelson* (US Supreme Court, No. 71-1027) (quotation in text); *Baker v. Nelson*, 409 U.S. 810 (Oct. 10, 1972) (dismissing the appeal for lack of a substantial federal question).

31. Catherine Fosl, *It Could Be Dangerous! Gay Liberation and Gay Marriage in Louisville, Kentucky, 1970*, 12 Ohio Valley History 46 (2012). See Michael Boucai, *Glorious Precedents: When Gay Marriage Was Radical*, 27 Yale J.L. & Humanities 1, 29–34 (2015).

32. Catherine Fosl interview of Marjorie Jones (2012). See Fosl, *Dangerous!*, 55, 63–64; Geoffrey Brown, *County Attorney Rules Out Woman-Woman Wedding*, Louisville Times, July 8, 1970, 10.

33. Email from Catherine Fosl to William Eskridge, April 21, 2019; Fosl, *Dangerous!*, 46 (first quotation in text), 55 (second quotation); Boucai, *Glorious Precedents*, 34 (third quotation, "we couldn't let the boys"); Frank Clifford, *2 Local Women Apply for Marriage License*, Louisville Times, July 7, 1970 (last quotation).

34. Letter from Bruce Miller, county attorney, to James Hallahan, county clerk, July 8, 1970, appendix 1 to brief for appellees, p. 23, *Jones v. Hallahan*, No. W-152-70 (Ky. Ct. App. 1973) (quotations in text); Boucai, *Glorious Precedents*, 30–32.

35. Bill Peterson, *Without Fee or Fear: The KCLU Picks Cause, Then a Lawyer Who's Not Afraid of Controversy*, Louisville Courier-Journal, July 17, 1970, B1 (quotation in text); Complaint, *Jones v. Hallahan*, No. CR 140,279 (Jefferson County Circuit Court, filed July 10, 1970); Fosl interview of Jones (account of the wedding).

36. Transcript of trial, *Jones v. Hallahan*, No. C 140,279 (Jefferson Cnty. Cir. Ct. Nov. 11, 1970) (first quotation in text); Catherine Fosl interview of Bruce Miller (Dec. 22, 2011) (second quotation); Peter Wallenstein, *Tell the Court I Love My Wife: Race, Marriage, and Law*, 286 n.1 (2010) (Judge Schmid's race-based ruling).

37. Transcript of trial, *Jones v. Hallahan* (first quotation in text); Fosl interview of Jones (remaining quotations).

38. Fosl interview of Miller (quotation in text).

39. *Jones v. Hallahan*, 501 S.W.2d 588, 589–90 (Ky. 1973) (both quotations in text).

40. James Stephens Jr., *Two Women Plan to Get Married; File Suit; Make It Federal Case*, Jet, Nov. 4, 1971, 20–26 (first quotation in text); Julia Kleppin interview of Donna Burkett (July 14, 2007), Milwaukee LGBT Oral History Project, http://collections.lib.uwm.edu/cdm/ref/collection/lgbt/id/20 (second quotation).

41. William Eskridge telephone interview of Manonia Evans Glass (Nov. 29, 2018); Stephens, *Two Women*.

42. Kleppin interview of Burkett (first two quotations in text); Eskridge interview of Evans Glass (third quotation).

43. Kleppin interview of Burkett (quotations in text).

44. *Two Milwaukee Women Fight for Marriage License*, The Advocate, Dec. 8, 1971, 7 (quotation in text); Stephens, *Two Women*.

45. *Burkett v. Zablocki*, 54 F.R.D. 626 (E.D. Wis. 1972).

46. Jim Stingl, *Milwaukee Woman Broke Ground on Gay Marriage—In 1971*, Milwaukee Journal Sentinel, Oct. 4, 2014 (first quotation in text); Kleppin interview of Burkett (second quotation); Eskridge interview of Evans Glass.

47. Eli Sanders, *Gay Marriage's Jewish Pioneer: Faygele ben Miriam*, Jewish News, June 6, 2012 (first quotation in text); Kristin Hayman, "John Singer's and Paul Barwick's Selfless Pursuit of Marriage Equality" (2017) (second quotation). See Gary Atkins, *Gay Seattle: Stories of Exile and Belonging*, 293 (2003); Jill Bateman interview of Faygele ben Miriam (aka John Singer), Seattle Univ. Communication & Community Project (1995); Boucai, *Glorious Precedents*, 38–41.

48. Hayman, "Selfless Pursuit" (first quotation in text); Lornet Turnbull, *Gay Man Sees Big Changes Since '72 Lawsuit*, Seattle Times, April 4, 2006 (second quotation); William Eskridge telephone interview of Michael Withey (May 23, 2019).

49. Cf. *Sailor Inn, Inc. v. Kirby*, 485 P.2d 529 (Cal. 1971) (following Herma Kay's argument for treating sex as a suspect classification under the state constitution).

50. Brief of appellants, p. 14, *Singer v. Hara*, No. 1879-I (Wash. Ct. App. 1973) (quotation in text). See pp. 2–42, 44–52 (sex discrimination argument).

51. *Singer v. Hara*, 522 P.2d 1187, 1192, and n.8 (Wash. App. 1974), review denied (Wash. Oct. 1974) (quotation in text).

52. Fosl interview of Jones (quotations in text).

53. Kay Tobin and Randy Wicker, *The Gay Crusaders*, 144 (1972) (first quotation in text, from an interview of Baker and McConnell); Brief of appellants, p. 17, *Singer v. Hara*, No. 1879-I (Wash. Ct. App. 1973) (second quotation).

54. Tobin and Wicker, *Gay Crusaders*, 144 (quotation in text); Nancy Farber, *Lesbians Sandy Schuster and Madeleine Isaacson Find "Marriage" Happy but Hardly Untroubled*, People, July 9, 1979.

55. Boucai, *Glorious Precedents*, 57 (Singer/ben Miriam's quotation in text); Transcript of trial, *Jones v. Hallahan*, 36–37 (Knight's quotation); Stephens, *Two Women* (Evans's quotation); Boucai, *Glorious Precedents*, 57 (Baker's quotation).

56. Boucai, *Glorious Precedents*, 58 (Barwick's quotation in text); Sanders, *Gay Marriage's Jewish Pioneer* (ben Miriam's quotations).

57. Lars Bjornson, *Appeal Planned: Judge Nixes Marriage Bid*, The Advocate, Dec. 9, 1970 (quotations in text); Eskridge interviews of Baker and McConnell.

58. Garance Franke-Ruta, *The Prehistory of Gay Marriage: Watch a 1971 Protest at NYC's Marriage License Bureau*, The Atlantic, March 26, 2013 (GAA zap and quotations in text); Memorandum from Rob Teir to Bill Eskridge and Craig Dean, "District of Columbia Marriage Legislation [1975]," 11–16 (Aug. 4, 1991) (Washington, DC, GAA's support for a marriage bill).

59. Margot Canady, *The Straight State: Sexuality and Citizenship in Twentieth-Century America* (2009); Eskridge, *Gaylaw*.

60. *Dred Scott v. Sandford*, 60 U.S. 393, 409 (1957) (quotations in text), 413–416 (collecting early American marriage laws and policies marking "negroes" as inferior).

61. Jack Baker, memorandum, "Leaders Rejected Same-Sex Marriage" (draft Jan. 21, 2019) (quotation in text).

62. McConnell, *Wedding*, 115–118 (account and quotations in text). See also McConnell Archives, Box 31 (legal documents relating to the adoption and name change).

63. McConnell, *Wedding*, 123–138; Eskridge interviews of Baker and McConnell.

64. Doug Belden, *Gay Marriage Landmark? Minnesota Pastor Who Conducted 1971 Ceremony Thinks So,* Twin Cities Pioneer Press, Nov. 11, 2015 (quotations in text).

65. Belden, *Gay Marriage Landmark?* (quotations in text); *Jury Halts Action on Gay Couple,* Minneapolis Star, Mar. 28, 1972, in McConnell Archives, Box 31.

66. *McConnell v. Anderson,* 451 F.2d 193 (8th Cir. 1971) (McConnell's First Amendment lawsuit); McConnell, *Wedding,* 83–93, 156–159; *Married Males Apply for a Child,* The Advocate, July 3, 1974, A-12; McConnell Archives, Box 15 (Gay House and IRS matters); McConnell Archives, Box 26 (both adoption and veterans benefits applications and subsequent lawsuits). Correspondence and notes related to Baker's frustrations with the bar exam, including evidence that the chief justice tried to block him, are contained in the McConnell Archives, Box 26.

2. Opening Pandora's Box

1. Ken Bronson, *Quest for Full Equality,* 18 (2004) (quotations in text).

2. Our account in the text and in the next two paragraphs is based on telephone conversations and emails with Clela Rorex in 2015–2017.

3. Letter from David McCord to William Eskridge, Nov. 27, 2017 (quotation in text).

4. Kyle Harris, *Clela Rorex Planted the Flag for Same-Sex Marriage in Boulder 40 Years Ago,* Denver Westword, Aug. 13, 2014 (quotation in text).

5. Eskridge telephone interview of Clela Rorex (2015) (first quotation in text); WNYC, *Meet the Clerk Who Started the Same-Sex Marriage Revolution,* NPR, April 2015, http://www.wnyc.org/story/county-clerk-who-made-history/ (subsequent quotations in text).

6. 1975 Ariz. House Bill 2024 (emergency response that did not become law); 1980 Ariz. Senate Bill 1033 (law limiting marriage to one man, one woman); Richard Ruelas, *This One Marriage Is the History of Ariz. Gay Rights Movement,* The Republic, April 10, 2015.

7. Anita Morse, *Pandora's Box: An Essay Review of American Law and Literature on Prostitution,* 4 Wis. Women's L.J. 21 (1988). Cf. Stephen Macedo, *Homosexuality and the Conservative Mind,* 84 Geo. L.J. 261, 265 (1995) (lamenting the widespread belief that "homosexuals, more than any other group in society, reject the basic guideposts that nature offers to human conduct").

8. Carol Taylor, *Boulder Was a Trendsetter for Same-Sex Marriage,* Boulder Daily Camera, May 24, 2013 (quoting *Daily Camera* editorial from 1975).

9. *Colorado Clerk Recalls Issuing Same-Sex Marriage Licenses—In 1975,* NPR, July 18, 2014 (quotations in text).

10. Carol Taylor and Glenda Russell, *Boulder's LGBT History: From "The Hate State" to the Supreme Court*, Boulder Magazine, Fall 2016 (quotations in text).

11. *Marriage License Issued to Gay Couple*, Colo. Daily, March 26, 1975, 2 (quotation in text).

12. Clela Rorex, as told to Jack Holmes, *How One Woman Married Gay Couples Forty Years Ago*, Esquire, June 24, 2016.

13. *Colorado Clerk Recalls*, NPR, July 14, 1974 (quotations in text); Sylvia Pettem, "Your Boulder History Byte: 'Lonesome Cowboy' Tried to Marry His Horse," Facebook post, June 15, 2009 (publicity, including *Tonight Show*).

14. Thomas Miller, director, *Limited Partnership* (PBS, 2014) (documentary of Sullivan and Adams's life together, including quotation in text).

15. William Eskridge telephone interview of Annice Joan Ritchie (Oct. 12, 2017) (quotation in text).

16. *Rorex to Stop Issuing Gay Marriage Licenses*, Colo. Daily, April 28, 1975, 9 (quotation in text). Clela Rorex was in and out of the hospital because of disabling migraines. She left her job and Boulder before the end of her term in order to marry a man from California, where she relocated briefly. The marriage lasted but a year, and she later returned to Colorado for a successful career doing public interest work.

17. Memorandum from Rob Teir to Bill Eskridge, "District of Columbia Marriage Legislation [1975]," 13–16 (Aug. 4, 1991). See *Dixon Set to Amend Bill on No-Fault Divorce*, Washington Afro-American, Dec. 30, 1975 (Dixon quotation in text); *A Public Scandal*, Editorial, The Catholic Standard, July 17, 1975 (archdiocese quotation); *Ministers Oppose Bills*, Washington Post, Sept. 24, 1975 (ministers' quotation); *Dixon Drops Bill for Homosexuals*, Washington Post, Dec. 24, 1975.

18. William Eskridge and Christopher Riano telephone interview of Wendy Brown DeBoer (March 12, 2015) as well as subsequent emails and telephone conversations by Riano with DeBoer.

19. Annotation, *Presumption of Legitimacy, or of Paternity, of Child Conceived or Born Before Marriage*, 57 A.L.R.2d 729, 732 (1958) (presumption of paternity everywhere); Sally Goldfarb, *Divorcing Marriage from Sex: Radically Rethinking the Role of Sex in Marriage Law in the United States*, 6 Onati Socio-Legal Series 1276, 1279 n.2 (2016) (quotation in text).

20. John Stuart Mill, *On Liberty* (1857) (Mill quotation in text); Jean-Jacques Rousseau, *Emile, or On Education*, 327 (Allan Bloom, trans., 1979) (Rousseau quotation). See John Rawls, *A Theory of Justice*, 409–410 (rev. ed. 1999); Walter Berns, *Marriage Anyone?*, First Things, April 1996; Andrew Koppelman, *Sex Equality and/or the Family: From Bloom vs. Okin to Rousseau vs. Hegel*, 4 Yale J.L. & Hum. 399 (1992). For a version of the argument from the perspective of an "egalitarian family," see Susan Miller Okin, *Justice, Gender, and the Family*, 18–19 (1989).

21. Letter from a female heterosexual to Jack Baker, Oct. 12, 1972, McConnell Archives, Box 26 (first quotation in text); *Christian*, Colo. Daily, April 24, 1975, 7 (second quotation).

22. William Eskridge Jr., *The Case for Same-Sex Marriage: From Sexual Liberty to Civilized Commitment*, chap. 2 (1996) (same-sex marriage recognition in many non-Western cultures, including marriages involving gender-bending Native American *berdaches*).

23. Letter from US senator Walter Mondale to Jack Baker, June 1974, McConnell Archives (quotation in text).

24. Rorex, *How One Woman Married Gay Couples* (quotations in text).

25. Marie Conn, *Pandora and Eve: The Manipulation and Transformation of Female Archetypes*, in Marie Conn and Therese McGuire, eds., *Balancing the Scales* (2003). Our Old Testament quotations are from the King James Version.

26. *Ethic*, Colorado Daily, April 30, 1975, 7 (quotation in text). For examples of readings of the Bible that were tolerant of homosexual relationships, see Derrick Sherwin Bailey, *Homosexuality and the Western Christian Tradition* (1955); Robert Wood, *Christianity and Homosexuality* (1960). According to the marriage licenses as recorded in Boulder County, one marriage was celebrated in the Boulder Unitarian Church (Prince-Hagan); two were in MCC ceremonies (Adams-Sullivan and Hough-Guillen); and two were performed by a "Minister of the Gospel" (Ritchie-Garcia and Mele-Sernovitz).

27. *Christian*, Colo. Daily, April 24, 1975, 7 (first quotation in text); *Standard*, Colo. Daily, April 23, 1975, 7 (second quotation).

28. *Christian*, Colo. Daily, April 24, 1975, 7 (first quotation in text); *Commitment*, Colo. Daily, May 8, 1975, 7 (second quotation).

29. Ira Mark Ellman, *Dissolving the Relationship Between Divorce Laws and Divorce Rates*, 18 Int'l Rev. L. & Econ. 341, 347–348 (1998) (no-fault divorce laws); William Eskridge Jr., *Dishonorable Passions: Sodomy Laws in America 1861–2003*, 387–407 (2008) (repeals of consensual sodomy laws). Yena Lee, Yale law class of 2019, compiled the data for fornication and cohabitation laws—e.g., Gerhard Mueller, *Sexual Conduct and the Law*, 116–120 (2d ed. 1980); Richard Posner and Katharine Silbaugh, *A Guide to America's Sex Laws*, 98–110 (1996).

30. *Eisenstadt v. Baird*, 405 U.S. 438 (1972) (right of sexual privacy is an "individual" right not tied to marriage); *Roe v. Wade*, 410 U.S. 113 (1973) (right of abortion choice for unmarried pregnant plaintiff); *Doe v. Commonwealth's Attorney of Virginia*, 425 U.S. 901 (1976) (summary affirmance of Virginia's law stigmatizing consensual sodomy as a felony).

31. Cardinal Franjo Seper, prefect, Congregation for the Doctrine of the Faith, *Persona humana*, chap. 11 (Dec. 29, 1975) (first quotation in text), chap. 8 (second quotation). Pope Paul VI approved, confirmed, and ordered the publication of this declaration, "On certain questions concerning sexual ethics."

32. Germain Grisez, *The Way of the Lord Jesus: Living a Christian Life*, 580 (1993) (first quotation in text); Rev. Warren Heidgen, *Letter to the Editor*, Denver Catholic Register, May 8, 1975, 6 (second quotation). See John Finnis, *Law, Morality, and "Sexual Orientation,"* 69 Notre Dame L. Rev. 1049 (1994); Mary Catherine Geach, *Lying with the Body*, 91 Monist 523 (2008) (recent synthesis).

33. John McNeill, SJ, "Address to First National Dignity Conference" (Los Angeles, 1973), National Catholic Reporter, Oct. 5, 1973 (quotation in text). See McNeill's three 1970 articles published in *Homiletic and Pastoral Review;* Timothy Potts, *Homosexuality,* in Adrian Hastings, ed., *Modern Catholicism: Vatican II and After* (1991) (arguing that acceptance of homosexuality was a necessary implication of Vatican II's logic). For mediationist statements, see Charles Curran, *Transition and Tradition in Moral Theology* (1979); Denver Catholic Register, July 18, 1979, 9 (Cardinal Humberto Sousa Medeiros of Boston); Denver Catholic Register, Nov. 25, 1975, 3 (Archbishop Joseph Bernardin of Cincinnati); *Homosexuality and Civil Rights: Neither Side Helped Things Any*, Denver Catholic Register, July 13, 1977, 11 (advocating a tolerant, pastoral approach toward homosexuals).

34. Hal Longmont, *Letter to the Editor*, Denver Catholic Register, July 29, 1977, 19 (quotations in text).

35. Didi Herman, *The Antigay Agenda: Orthodox Vision and the Christian Right* (1997); Oran Smith, *The Rise of Baptist Republicanism*, 52–67 (1997); see 215–231 (SBC's anti-homosexual resolutions, quoted in text).

36. Dan Gilgoff, *The Jesus Machine: How James Dobson, Focus on the Family, and Evangelical America Are Winning the Culture War*, 21 (2007); Dale Buss, *Family Man: The Biography of Dr. James Dobson*, 67–68 (2005). See James Dobson and Gary Bauer, *Children at Risk* (1994); James Dobson, *Bringing Up Boys* (2002); Tim LeHaye, *The Unhappy Gays* (1978).

37. Eskridge telephone interview of Rorex (quotation in text). See David Mathews and Jane Sherron DeHart, *Sex, Gender, and the Politics of the ERA*, 35–53 (1990); Jane Mansbridge, *Why We Lost the ERA* (1986).

38. Equal Rights 1970: Hearing before the Senate Comm. on the Judiciary, 91st Cong., pp. 74–75 (1970) (statement of Professor Paul Freund, quoted in text); Accord, Equal Rights for Men and Women 1971: Hearing before Subcomm. No. 4 of the House Comm. on the Judiciary, 92d Cong. (1971) (Freund); Note, *The Legality of Homosexual Marriage*, 82 Yale L.J. 573, 574 (1973); Paul Freund, *The Equal Rights Amendment Is Not the Way*, 6 Harv. C.R.-C.L. L. Rev. 234 (1971).

39. On the Freund argument in state debates, see *ERA and Homosexual "Marriages,"* Phyllis Schlafly Report, Sept. 1974, 3; Douglas Kneeland, *Amendment Now Needs Only Four More States: Missouri Proponents Elicit White House*, Biloxi Sun Herald, Feb. 15, 1975; Martha Weinman Lear, *Fear Holds More Clout Than Fact in ERA Fight*, Chicago Tribune, April 19, 1976. On the Rousseauian philosophy of Schlafly, see Andrew Koppelman, *Why Phyllis Schlafly Is Right (but Wrong) About Pornography*, 31 Harv. J.L. & Pub. Pol'y 105, 108 (2008).

40. P.H., *Letter to the Editor,* Denver Catholic Register, April 10, 1975, 37 (first two quotations in text); *Marriage License Issued to Gay Couple,* Colorado Daily, March 26, 1975, 2 (remaining quotations).

41. *The Church and the Proposed Equal Rights Amendment: A Moral Issue,* Ensign (Feb. 1980) (quotation in text); Spencer Kimball, *The Miracle of Forgiveness,* 78–86 (1969) (best-selling book on Mormon doctrine, labeling homosexuality as "Satanic"); Gregory Prince, *Gay Rights in the Mormon Church: Intended Actions, Unintended Consequences,* 31–37 (2019) (Kimball's critical attitude toward homosexuality and support for reparative therapy).

42. William Eskridge Jr., *Latter-Day Constitutionalism: Sexuality, Gender, and Mormons,* 2016 U. Ill. L. Rev. 1227, 1234–1235; D. Michael Quinn, *The LDS Church's Campaign Against the Equal Rights Amendment,* 20 J. Mormon Hist. 85 (1994); Neil Young, *"The ERA Is a Moral Issue": The Mormon Church, LDS Women, and the Defeat of the Equal Rights Amendment,* 59 Am. Q. 623 (2007).

43. *Standard,* Colo. Daily, Apr. 23, 1975, 7 (first quotation in text); Letter from Grulinar Sonson to Jack Baker (no date), McConnell Archives, Box 26 (second quotation); Letter from the executive council to James M. McConnell, Feb. 1, 1972, in McConnell Archives (third quotation).

44. See brief of appellants, pp. 2–42, *Singer v. Hara,* No. 1879-I (Wash. Ct. App. 1973) (Withey's refutation of leading anti-homosexual stereotypes).

45. Our account of the lives of Sullivan and Adams, as well as the first quotation in text, draw from Miller, *Limited Partnership.* See letter from INS district director to Richard Adams, Nov. 24, 1975 (reprinted in Rorex's *Esquire* article; second quotation in text).

46. *Adams v. Howerton,* 673 F.2d 1036, 1040, and n.2 (9th Cir. Feb 21, 1982), cert. denied, 458 U.S. 1111 (June 28, 1982), citing *Boutilier v. INS,* 387 U.S. 118, 121 (1967).

47. *Sullivan v. INS,* 772 F.2d 609, 611 (9th Cir. Sept. 30, 1985), citing *Adams,* 673 F.2d at 1040; *Sullivan,* 613 (Pregerson, J., dissenting) (first quotation in text).

48. Letter from Dave McCord to William Eskridge, Nov. 27, 2017 (quotation in text).

49. Erika Stutzman, *Same-Sex Marriage and Boulder,* Boulder Daily Camera, March 28, 2010 (quotation in text). On McCord's activities with minors and governmental inattention, see Paul Rubin, *Sex Education,* Phoenix New Times, Oct. 28, 1992, http://www.phoenixnewtimes.com/news/sex-education-6426184 (quotations in text). Rubin's conclusion: "What emerges is a portrait of a bright, manipulative man unable to control his sexual appetite for boys."

50. McCord letter to Eskridge.

3. Trojan Horses

1. See Monique Wittig, *The Trojan Horse,* in The Straight Mind *and Other Essays,* 68–75 (1992). AIDS as a Trojan horse was suggested to us in a 1995 seminar paper by

Yale law student (now NYU professor) Kenji Yoshino. See Paula Treichler, *AIDS, Homophobia, and Biomedical Discourse: An Epidemic of Signification*, 43 AIDS: Cultural Analysis/Cultural Activism 59 (Oct. 1987).

2. James Simpson, *Gay Marriage: A Trojan Horse Movement*, American Thinker, April 25, 2015 (quotation in text). On homosexuality as a Fifth Column, see David Johnson, *The Lavender Scare: Cold War Persecution of Gays and Lesbians in the Federal Government*, 31–38 (2004) (in the 1950s) and Paul Kengor, *Takedown: From Communists to Progressives, How the Left Has Sabotaged Family and Marriage* (2015) (today). Cf. Jarrod Hayes, *Proust in the Tearoom*, 110 Pub. Mod. Lang. Ass'n Am. 992, 993, 1004 (1995) (the "secret of homosexuality" opens up "like a Trojan Horse" within *Remembrance of Things Past*, exposing a world entirely populated by homosexuals).

3. Centers for Disease Control and Prevention, *A Cluster of Kaposi's Sarcoma and Pneumocystis Carinii Pneumonia Among Homosexual Male Residents of Los Angeles and Orange Counties*, 31 MMWR 305 (June 18, 1982). On the AIDS epidemic, see Randy Shilts, *And the Band Played On: Politics, People, and the AIDS Epidemic* (1987); Stephen Joseph, *Dragon Within the Gates: The Once and Future AIDS Epidemic* (1992); David France, *How to Survive a Plague: The Inside Story of How Citizens and Science Tamed AIDS* (2016). On Trojan horse leukocytes, see Deborah Anderson et al., *Targeting Trojan Horse Leukocytes for HIV Prevention*, 24 AIDS 163–87 (Jan. 2010).

4. *Bowers v. Hardwick*, 478 U.S. 186 (1986) (harsh majority opinion and brutal concurring opinion); William Eskridge Jr., *Dishonorable Passions: Sodomy Law in America, 1861–2003*, 229–251, 261–262 (2008). See Patrick Egan, Nathaniel Persily, and Kevin Wallsten, *Gay Rights, Public Opinion, and the Courts*, in *Public Opinion and Constitutional Controversy*, chap. 10 (2008) (negative attitudes toward homosexual relations and rights for gay people in the 1980s correlated to press coverage of AIDS and its association with homosexuality). Our numbers for the cumulative death toll from AIDS at the end of each year are taken from AmfAR, *Thirty Years of HIV/AIDS: Snapshots of an Epidemic* (2011), http://www.amfar.org/thirty-years-of-hiv/aids-snapshots-of -an-epidemic/.

5. Abby Rubenfeld, *Lessons Learned: A Reflection Upon* Bowers v. Hardwick, 11 Nova L. Rev. 59, 62 (1986) (quotation in text). On how litigation losses can have movement-galvanizing effects, see Steven Boutcher, *Making Lemonade: Turning Adverse Decisions into Opportunities for Mobilization*, 13 Amici 8–13 (Fall 2005); Douglas NeJaime, *Winning by Losing*, 96 Iowa L. Rev. 941 (2011).

6. Martin Meeker interview of Tim Sweeney, p. 26 (Feb. 12, 2016), F2M Oral History (quotations in text).

7. Rhonda Rivera, *Lawyers, Clients, and AIDS: Some Notes from the Trenches*, 49 Ohio St. L.J. 883–928 (1989).

8. William Eskridge telephone interview of John Duran (July 21, 2017); Michael Klarman, *From the Closet to the Altar: Courts, Backlash, and the Struggle for Same-Sex Marriage*, 38–39 (2012).

9. Susan Anderson and David Dunlap, *New York Day-by-Day: From Legal-Rights Past to Homosexual Rights,* New York Times, Dec. 16, 1985 (first quotation in text); Thomas Stoddard, *Gay Marriages: Make Them Legal,* New York Times, Mar. 4, 1988 (second quotation); Robert Murphy, *The Personal Is the Pedagogical: A Very Brief Life of Professor Stoddard,* 72 NYU L. Rev. 1027, 1032 (1997) (duty to love).

10. Larry Kramer, *Reports from the Holocaust: The Making of an AIDS Activist,* 178–179 (1989) (first quotation in text); Andrew Sullivan, *Here Comes the Groom: A (Conservative) Case for Gay Marriage,* The New Republic, Aug. 28, 1989 (remaining quotations). Accord, Bruce Bawer, *A Place at the Table: The Gay Individual in American Society* (1993); William Eskridge Jr., *The Case for Same-Sex Marriage: From Sexual Liberty to Civilized Commitment* (1996); Gabriel Rotello, *Sexual Ecology: AIDS and the Destiny of Gay Men* (1997). On gay marriage as a health measure, see Tomas Philipson and Richard Posner, *Private Choices and Public Health: The AIDS Epidemic in an Economic Perspective* (1993).

11. Walter Rieman, *Tom Stoddard, Marriage Equality, and the Stoddard Fellowships: A Husband's Remembrance,* 19 NYU J. Legis. & Pub. Pol'y 555 (2016) (personal reminiscence, including the quotation in text).

12. Evan Wolfson, "Samesex [*sic*] Marriage and Morality: The Human Rights Vision of the Constitution" (Harvard Law School senior paper, April 1983); Martin Meeker interview of Evan Wolfson, pp. 32–33, 48 (Sept. 21, 2015), F2M Oral History (quotations in text); William Eskridge and Christopher Riano interview of Evan Wolfson, New York City (Aug. 26, 2015).

13. Paula Ettelbrick, *Wedlock Alert: A Comment on Lesbian and Gay Family Recognition,* 5 J.L. & Pol'y 107, 122 (1996) (quotation in text). For other progressive and queer critiques of gay marriage, see Urvashi Vaid, *Virtual Equality: The Mainstreaming of Gay and Lesbian Liberation* (1995); Michael Warner, *The Trouble with Normal: Sex, Politics, and Ethics of the Queer Life* (1999); Kendall Thomas, *Beyond the Privacy Principle,* 92 Colum. L. Rev. 1431 (1992).

14. Shelly Lundburg and Robert Pollak, *The Evolving Role of Marriage: 1950–2010,* The Future of Children 29–50 (Fall 2015); William Eskridge Jr. and Brian Weimer, *The Economics Epidemic in an AIDS Perspective,* 61 U. Chi. L. Rev. 733, 764–768 (1994).

15. Judith Scherr, *Berkeley, Activists Set Milestone for Domestic Partnership in 1984,* East Bay Times, June 28, 2013 (quotations in text); OUT History interview of Tom Brougham (1987), http://outhistory.org/exhibits/show/out-and-elected/late-1980s/tom -brougham. See David Chambers, *Tales of Two Cities: AIDS and the Legal Recognition of Domestic Partnerships in San Francisco and New York,* 2 Law & Sexuality 181–208 (1992); Nathaniel Frank, *Awakening: How Gays and Lesbians Brought Marriage Equality to America,* 37–58 (2017).

16. Douglas NeJaime, *Before Marriage: The Unexplored History of Nonmarital Recognition and Its Relationship to Marriage,* 102 Calif. L. Rev. 87, 114–115 (2014) (quoting Coles); Proposed Ch. 45, S.F. Admin Code, Oct. 1982 (remaining quotations in text).

17. William Eskridge telephone interview of former archbishop John Quinn (Oct. 17, 2016); US Catholic Conference, *The Many Faces of AIDS: A Gospel Response* (Nov. 1987).

18. Eskridge telephone interview of Quinn (quotations in text).

19. US Catholic Conference, *Called to Compassion and Responsibility: A Response to the HIV/AIDS Crisis* (Nov. 1989); Wallace Turner, *Partnership Law Vetoed on Coast,* New York Times, Dec. 10, 1982, A17 (Quinn quotation in text); Diane Whitacre, *Will You Be Mine? Domestic Partnership, San Francisco City Hall, February 14, 1991,* 17 (Coles quotations). See Clarence Johnson, *The New S.F. Supervisors; To Amos Brown, This Job Is Fulfillment of Destiny,* San Francisco Chronicle, May 28, 1996, A-1 (progressive opposition because the Britt-Coles bill did not meet the needs of minority communities).

20. Shilts, *Band Played On,* 204–205; Turner, *Partnership Bill Vetoed,* A17. The Feinstein quotation in text came from an off-the-record interview.

21. Leland Traiman, *A Brief History of Domestic Partnerships,* Gay & Lesbian Review Worldwide, July–Aug. 2008, 23; Columbia Law Sexuality & Gender Clinic, *Compilation of Governmentalities Offering Health Care Benefits* (May 14, 2007).

22. NeJaime, *Before Marriage,* 87–88 (quotations and analysis in text).

23. Archbishop Quinn, *A Letter to Mayor Art Agnos,* Origins, June 8, 2009, 50 (quotation in text).

24. Chuck and Donna McIlhenny, *When the Wicked Seize a City* (1993); William Eskridge and Alex Lichtenstein telephone interview of Chuck McIlhenny (Feb. 24, 2018).

25. Whitacre, *Will You Be Mine?,* 93–94 (quotation in text); Randy Shilts, *Gay Nuptials and Public Health,* San Francisco Chronicle, Oct. 30, 1989; Don Lattin, *Political Minefield: Clergy Pressured on Partners Law,* San Francisco Chronicle, Sept. 18, 1989.

26. Marc Sandalow and Elaine Herscher, *Domestic Partners Defeat Upsets S.F.'s Image as Gay Mecca,* San Francisco Chronicle, Nov. 11, 1989; Marc Sandalow and Elaine Herscher, *Prop. S Defeat a Serious Blow to Gay Power,* San Francisco Chronicle, Nov. 9, 1989 (quotation in text).

27. Whitacre, *Will You Be Mine?,* 93–94; William Eskridge telephone interview of Geoffrey Kors (July 16, 2016). See Roberta Achtenberg, National Center for Lesbian Rights (NCLR), *Preserving and Protecting the Families of Lesbians and Gay Men* (March 1990) (report documenting the need for domestic partnership recognition).

28. Whitacre, *Will You Be Mine?,* 94 (first quotation in text), 90–92 (second quotation); Eskridge and Lichtenstein interview of McIlhenny.

29. Whitacre, *Will You Be Mine?,* 26 (quotation in text).

30. Email from Matt Coles to William Eskridge, July 9, 2019 (quotation in text).

31. Whitacre, *Will You Be Mine?,* 26 (quotation in text).

32. Whitacre, *Will You Be Mine?,* 146–148 (quotations from couples registering for domestic partnership on Feb. 14, 1991).

33. Daniel Winunwe Rivers, *Radical Relations: Lesbian Mothers, Gay Fathers, and Their Children in the United States Since World War II,* 174 (2013) (quotation in text). On the lesbian baby boom, see 174–181; Nancy Polikoff, *Beyond (Straight and Gay) Mar-*

riage: Valuing All Families Under the Law, 49–56 (2008); Gina Kolata, *Lesbian Couples Find the Means to Be Parents*, New York Times, Jan. 30, 1989, A13.

34. Columbia Law Sexuality & Gender Clinic, *Governmentalities Offering Health Care Benefits;* Robert Elbin, Note, *Domestic Partnership Recognition in the Workplace: Equitable Employee Benefits for Gay Couples*, 51 Ohio St. L.J. 1067 (1990); Martin Meeker interview of Professor Barbara Cox (Aug. 23, 2016), F2M Oral History.

35. Alan Finder, *Rights of "Domestic Partners" Broadened by Dinkins Order*, New York Times, Jan. 8, 1993, A1; Paula Ettelbrick, Letter to the Editor, *Domestic Partner Benefits Are a Matter of Law*, New York Times, Jan. 9, 1995, A14; Mike Allen, *Gay Groups Celebrate New Rights Bill*, New York Times, May 13, 1998, B3.

36. Nicole Raeburn, *Changing Corporate America from Inside Out*, 2–3, 47–48 (2004); William Eskridge interview of Elizabeth Birch, Washington, DC (July 6, 2017) (Apple's domestic partnership benefits, 1992–1993); Kim Mills and Daryl Herrschaft, HRC Foundation, *The State of the Workforce for Lesbian, Gay, Bisexual, and Transgendered Americans*, 19 (1999).

37. Kath Weston, *Families We Choose: Lesbians, Gays, and Kinship* (1991); Roberta Achtenberg et al., Mayor's Task Force on Family Policy, *Approaching 2000: Meeting the Challenges to San Francisco's Families* (June 13, 1990) (quotation in text); Barbara Cox, *Alternative Families: Obtaining Traditional Family Benefits Through Litigation, Legislation and Collective Bargaining*, 15 Wis. Women's L.J. 93 (2000) (Madison); NeJaime, *Before Marriage*, 28–39 (Los Angeles, San Francisco).

38. *Braschi v. Stahl Assocs.*, 543 N.E.2d 49 (N.Y. 1989). See Carlos Ball, *From the Closet to the Courtroom: Five LGBT Rights Lawsuits That Have Changed Our Nation*, 21–65 (2010) (excellent account of the litigation).

39. Lambda amicus brief, pp. 4–5, *Braschi* (filed March 9, 1989) (quotation in text); see pp. 7–12, 13–17 (Lambda's facts and arguments). See Catherine Fitch et al., University of Minnesota Population Center, *The Rise of Cohabitation in the United States: New Historical Estimates* (March 2005) (Fig. 5); New York City's amicus brief, pp. 4–5, *Braschi* (filed March 30, 1989).

40. Our account of the *Braschi* deliberations and the quotations in the text draw from Christopher Riano interviews of Henry Greenberg (Kaye's clerk during *Braschi* deliberations) and Steven Mintz (Titone's clerk), New York City (Nov. and Dec. 2017).

41. The quotations in the text are from *Braschi v. Stahl Assocs.*, 543 N.E.2d 53–54 (N.Y. 1989) (Titone's plurality opinion), 56 (Bellacosa's opinion concurring in the judgment), 57–60 (dissenting opinion).

42. Riano interview of Mintz (quotations in text).

43. *In re Guardianship of Kowalski*, 478 N.W.2d 790 (Minn. Ct. App. 1991); Brief amici curiae of Lambda Legal et al., *In re Guardianship of Kowalski*, pp. 3–5, No. C2-91-1407 (Minn. App., filed 1990), quoting *Developments in the Law—The Constitution and the Family*, 93 Harv. L. Rev. 1156, 1285 (1980); Wendy Manning, *Trends in Cohabitation: Twenty Years of Change, 1987–2010*, NCFMR: Family Profiles, FP 13-12 (2012).

44. *Adoptions of B.L.V.B. and E.L.V.B,* 628 A.2d 1271 (Vt. 1993) (Ettelbrick's case); *In re Jacob,* 660 N.E.2d 397 (N.Y. 1995) (Dohrn's case); Daniel Winunwe Rivers, *Radical Relations: Lesbian Mothers, Gay Fathers, and Their Children in the United States Since World War II,* 193–195 (2013). Early articulations of second-parent adoption are Elizabeth Zuckerman, *Second-Parent Adoption for Lesbian-Parented Families: Legal Recognition of the Other Mother,* 19 U.C. Davis L. Rev. 729 (1986); Nancy Polikoff, *This Child Does Have Two Mothers: Redefining Parenthood to Meet the Needs of Children in Lesbian-Mother and Other Nontraditional Families,* 78 Geo. L.J. 459 (1990); Paula Ettelbrick, *Who Is a Parent? The Need to Develop a Lesbian Conscious Family Law,* 10 N.Y.L. Sch. J. Hum. Rts. 513 (1993).

45. Nancy Polikoff, *For the Sake of All Children: Opponents and Supporters of Same-Sex Marriage Both Miss the Mark,* 8 N.Y. City L. Rev. 573, 594–95 (2005) (excerpting Family Bill of Rights, quoted in text).

46. William Eskridge and Christopher Riano interview of Walter Rieman, New York City (March 25, 2016).

47. Eskridge and Riano interview of Rieman (quotations in text).

48. The account in the text quotes liberally from the Ettelbrick and Stoddard articles, which are reprinted in William Eskridge Jr., Nan Hunter, and Courtney Joslin, *Sexuality, Gender, and the Law,* 337–340 (4th ed. 2017).

49. Our discussion of the Litigators' Roundtables is based upon the written agendas and minutes as well as Martin Meeker's interview of James Esseks (ACLU), pp. 7–8 (Nov. 11, 2015), F2M Oral History (quotation in text); Meeker's interview of Kate Kendell, pp. 12–13 (Feb. 23, 2016), F2M Oral History; Meeker's interview of Cox, pp. 17–18; and Meeker's interview of Sweeney, pp. 32–33.

50. Our account of the Dean and Gill case is based on Eskridge's notes, as he was cocounsel in *Dean v. District of Columbia,* 653 A.2d 307 (D.C. 1995). On the Hawai'i plaintiffs, see Ball, *Closet to Courtroom,* 165–166; Michael Sant'Ambrogio and Sylvia Law, *Baehr v. Lewin and the Long Road to Marriage Equality,* 33 U. Haw. L. Rev. 705, 709–711 (2011).

51. Martin Meeker interview of Evan Wolfson, p. 100 (Nov. 11, 2015) (quotation in text); William Eskridge conversations with Paula Ettelbrick (2005–2008) and some of her surviving friends (2016–2018).

52. Our account of Evan Wolfson's firing is drawn from conversations with Wolfson, Paula Ettelbrick, and several Lambda board members. See also Meeker interview of Wolfson, pp. 100–105 (Nov. 11, 2015). No two persons had exactly the same recollection.

53. Richard Cohen, Talk of the Town, *Tom and Walter Got Married,* The New Yorker, Dec. 20, 1993 (first quotation in text); Rieman, *A Husband's Perspective* (second quotation); Eskridge and Riano interview of Rieman.

54. Cohen, *Tom and Walter Got Married,* 56 (quotation in text).

4. Aloha, Same-Sex Marriage

1. Haw. Rev. Stat. § 5-75(a) (quotation in text).

2. Our account is taken from conversations, interviews, and emails between William Eskridge and Genora Dancel and Ninia Baehr, starting on May 8, 1995, and continuing through 2019. See also Carlos Ball, *From the Closet to the Courtroom: Five LGBT Rights Lawsuits That Have Changed Our Nation*, 165–166 (2010); Michael Sant'Ambrogio and Sylvia Law, Baehr v. Lewin *and the Long Road to Marriage Equality*, 33 U. Haw. L. Rev. 705, 709–711 (2011).

3. See Ninia Baehr, *Abortion Without Apology: A Radical History for the 1990s* (1990).

4. William Eskridge interview of Ninia Baehr and Genora Dancel, Baltimore (May 8, 1995) (quotation in text).

5. Linda Hosek, *Lesbian Couple Stand Tall at Trial*, Honolulu Star-Bulletin, Sept. 11, 1996.

6. Cary Goldberg, *Couple Who Started Issue of Same-Sex Marriage Still Hopeful*, New York Times, July 28, 1996 (quotation in text).

7. The parade of applicants and their recollections are captured on film in the April 1994 episode of *In the Life*, https://www.youtube.com/watch?v=uXnimfG805M&feature=youtu.be.

8. William Eskridge interview of Nan Hunter, Washington, DC (July 2016); William Eskridge telephone interview of former judge Daniel Foley (Oct. 26, 2017).

9. *Bowers v. Hardwick*, 478 U.S. 186 (1986); Haw. Const. art. I, § 5, cls. 2–3 (equal protection and nondiscrimination provisions).

10. *Baehr v. Lewin*, 852 P.2d 44, 53–55 (Haw. 1993) (summarizing and quoting from trial court's opinion dismissing the marriage complaint); William Eskridge telephone interview of former justice Robert Klein (July 6, 2017).

11. Our description of the various justices serving on the Hawaiʻi Supreme Court between 1991 and 1993 draws from off-the-record conversations with court insiders.

12. Our account of and quotations from the oral argument in *Baehr* are taken from an audiotape of that argument, available at the Hawaiʻi Supreme Court.

13. Ken Kobayashi, *1993 Ruling Paved Way for Shifting Views on Marriage Equality, Former Justice Says*, Honolulu Star-Advertiser, April 30, 2013 (quotation in text). Our account of the supreme court's deliberations in *Baehr* draws from published interviews supplemented by our off-the-record conversations with court insiders.

14. Haw Const. art. I, § 5, cls. 2–3 (quotations in text).

15. Cf. Evan Wolfson, "Samesex [sic] Marriage and Morality: The Human Rights Vision of the Constitution" p. 8 and n.57 (Harvard Law School senior paper, April 1983) (endorsing the sex discrimination argument for gay people's freedom to marry, suggested to him by a conversation with "Kitty MacKinnon").

16. Leslie Wilcox, Long Story Short (PBS interview series), *Interview with James S. Burns*, Dec. 9, 2016. See *Baehr*, p. 69 (Burns's opinion concurring in the judgment) ("biologically fated" language).

17. *Baehr*, pp. 55–57, 63–67 (quotations in text from Levinson's plurality opinion rejecting the right to marry argument but finding sex discrimination). See *Zablocki v. Redhail*, 434 U.S. 374, 384–386 (1978) (right to marry decision relied on by Levinson to distinguish the unsuccessful marriage challenges in the 1970s).

18. *Baehr*, pp. 68–70 (Burns's concurring opinion). The court's clarification of the mandate on May 27 is reported as *Baehr v. Lewin*, 852 P.2d 74 (Haw. 1993).

19. Eskridge telephone interview of Foley.

20. Martin Meeker interview of Barbara Cox (Aug. 23, 2016), F2M Oral History; Evan Wolfson, Lambda Legal, memorandum, "Winning and Keeping Equal Marriage Rights: What Will Follow Victory in *Baehr v. Lewin*?" (Nov. 1994).

21. GLAD report to New England groups re Sept. 11, 1995, meeting of the National Freedom to Marry Coalition, GLAD Archives (quotations in text). See Freedom to Marry Coalition, "Communications Strategy" (1995); Nathaniel Frank, *Awakening: How Gays and Lesbians Brought Marriage Equality to America*, 98–100 (2017). On pro-gay shifts in public opinion and national politics in the early 1990s, see Patrick Egan, Nathaniel Persily, and Kevin Wallsten, *Gay Marriage, Public Opinion, and the Courts*, in *Public Opinion and Constitutional Controversy*, chap. 10 (2008).

22. First Presidency, the Church of Jesus Christ of Latter-day Saints, "Same Gender Marriages" (Feb. 1, 1994), reprinted in Ensign, April 1994 (quotation in text).

23. *The Gospel According to Gabbard*, Honolulu Weekly, Jan. 27, 1999, 4 (quotation in text); Mike Gabbard, *Gay Marriages Will Hurt State*, Honolulu Advertiser, Aug. 21, 1995, A-6.

24. William Eskridge telephone interview of Dan Foley (Oct. 26, 2017) (quotations in text).

25. Act Relating to Marriage, 1994 Hawai'i Session Laws, Act 217 (H.B. 2312) (quotations in text); *McGivern v. Waihee*, Civ. No. 94-00843 HMF (D. Haw. Jan. 13, 1995) (invalidating the provision authorizing commissioners to be named by the Catholic and Mormon churches); 1995 Hawai'i Session Laws, Act 5 (reconstituting the commission without the church nominations).

26. Martin Meeker interview of Evan Wolfson (Nov. 11, 2015), F2M Oral History.

27. Affidavit of Charles W. H. Goo, president, BYU-Hawaii 1st Stake, *Baehr v. Lewin*, Docket Item 39, Feb. 16, 1995; Answer of defendant-intervenors [Charles Goo and the LDS] to complaint, *Baehr v. Lewin*, Docket Item 39, Feb. 23, 1995 (list of compelling interests, quoted in the bulleted text); *Church Joins Hawaii Fight Over Same-Sex Marriages*, Deseret News, February 24, 1995 (last quotation in text).

28. Haw. Rev. Stat. § 572-12 (statutory protection for religious institutions and officials to conduct marriage ceremonies according to their faith traditions); *Baehr v. Miike*, 910 P.2d 112 (Haw. 1996) (affirming the trial judge's refusal to allow intervention by

the Church of Jesus Christ); Gregory Prince, *Gay Rights and the Mormon Church: Intended Actions, Unintended Consequences*, 49–52 (2019) (account of the Church's effort to intervene in *Baehr*).

29. Gordon Hinckley, "Stand Strong Against the Wiles of the World," address to Relief Society General Conference, Sept. 23, 1995, printed in Ensign, November 1995, 98–101 ("the proclamation," discussed in text); Russell Ballard, "The Sacred Responsibilities of Parenthood," BYU devotional address, Aug. 19, 2003 (quotation in text). See Prince, *Gay Rights*, 52–54.

30. On the sex discrimination argument for gay rights, see Andrew Koppelman, *Why Discrimination Against Lesbians and Gay Men Is Sex Discrimination*, 69 N.Y.U. L. Rev. 197, 208 (1994); Sylvia Law, *Homosexuality and the Social Meaning of Gender*, 1988 Wis. L. Rev. 187; Samuel Marcosson, *Harassment on the Basis of Sexual Orientation: A Claim of Sex Discrimination Under Title VII*, 81 Geo. L.J. 1, 6 (1992).

31. Letter from Elder Loren Dunn to Elder Russell Ballard, "H.L.M. Strategy for California and Hawaii" (March 4, 1997), Prince Archives. Our account of the elevation of Elder Dunn to the Seventy is taken from the diaries of President McKay, March 27–28, 1968, Prince Archives.

32. Loren Dunn, "Report to the Public Affairs Committee on Same-Gender Marriage Issue in Hawaii" (Oct. 24, 1995), Prince Archives.

33. Loren Dunn, "Report to the [Public Affairs Committee] on Same-Gender Marriage Issue in Hawaii" (Nov. 21, 1995), Prince Archives (quotation in text); Memorandum from Loren Dunn to Marlin Jensen (Oct. 24, 1995), Prince Archives (laying out the plan for HFT, including the possible compromise to allow domestic partnerships).

34. Loren Dunn, "Report to the Public Affairs Committee on Same-Gender Marriage Issue in Hawaii" (Dec. 5, 1995), Prince Archives (quotation in text); Prince, *Gay Rights*, 55–56.

35. *Report of the Commission on Sexual Orientation and the Law*, 43–44 (Dec. 8, 1995) (recommendations of the majority), 95, 72 (quotations from the dissenting views).

36. Eskridge interview of Baehr and Dancel (1995).

37. Email from David Coolidge to Lynn Wardle, Feb. 19, 1996 (quotation in text, suggesting that Graulty would insist on strong domestic partnership legislation and would only support a constitutional amendment if required by electoral pressure); Memorandum from Elder Oaks to Elder Dunn (Oct. 31, 1995), Prince Archives.

38. On the 1996 legislative deliberations, see David Orgon Coolidge, *The Hawai'i Marriage Amendment: Its Origins, Meaning and Fate*, 22 U. Haw. L. Rev. 19, 35–41 (2000); Prince, *Gay Rights*, 57–59.

39. Coolidge, *Hawai'i Marriage Amendment*, 37–38 (quotations in text).

40. Letter from Loren Dunn to Neal Maxwell (June 5, 1996), Prince Archives (quotation in text); *The Gospel According to Gabbard*, Honolulu Weekly, Jan. 27–Feb. 2, 1999, 4–7.

41. William Eskridge telephone interview of Rick Eichor (May 26, 2017) as well as daily reports from the *Honolulu Star-Bulletin*, Sept. 10–16, 1996 (available online).

42. In its pretrial memorandum, Hawai'i identified three compelling public interests it claimed were advanced by the traditional definition of marriage: (1) "promot[ing] the optimal development of children," as "it is best for a child that it be raised in a single home by its parents, or at least by a married male and female"; (2) "securing or assuring recognition of Hawaii marriages in other jurisdictions"; and (3) "protecting the public fisc from the reasonably foreseeable effects of approval of same-sex marriage."

43. Eskridge telephone interview of Eichor. Our account of the trial and quotations from witnesses are taken from the trial transcript and supplemented by daily newspaper accounts Eichor shared with us.

44. *Baehr v. Miike*, 1996 WL 694235 (Haw. 1st Cir. Ct. Dec. 3, 1996) (trial court opinion, summarizing and quoting Pruett's trial testimony); Kyle Pruett, *Fatherneed: Why Father Care Is as Essential as Mother Care* (2000); Kyle Pruett and Marsha Pruett, *Partnership Parenting: How Men and Women Parent Differently* (2009).

45. William Eskridge interview of Dr. Kyle Pruett, New Haven, CT (May 24, 2017).

46. The state's witnesses also included BYU psychology professor Richard Williams and Honolulu psychologist Thomas Merrill, who criticized the methodology of studies purporting to show that children of lesbian households are no different from children of straight households. Wolfson accused Williams of coming to court not because he was eager to explore the scientific evidence but "because of their personal axe to grind" against gay people. Eichor retorted that Wolfson's attack was "classic religious bigotry" (because Williams was Mormon).

47. Linda Hosek, *Gay Attorney Has Opposition Taking Notice*, Honolulu Star-Bulletin, Sept. 16, 1996 (first quotation in text); David Orgon Coolidge, *Same-Sex Marriage: As Hawaii Goes . . .* , First Things (Fall 1997) (second quotation).

48. *"My Daughter Is Perfect," Lesbian Parent Argues*, Honolulu Star-Bulletin, Sept. 21, 1996 (Pregil's quotation in text).

49. David Orgon Coolidge, *Marriage on Trial: Leaving It to the Experts?*, Hawaii Catholic Herald, Sept. 20, 1996 (quotations in text).

50. Findings of fact, ¶ 134, *Baehr v. Miike*, 1996 WL 694235 (Haw. 1st Cir. Ct. Dec. 3, 1996) (first quotation in text), ¶¶ 125, 128, 132 (second quotation), ¶ 136 (third quotation). Compare *Dean v. District of Columbia*, 653 A.2d 307, 309–361 (D.C. Jan. 1995) (Ferren, J., dissenting in part).

51. Eskridge telephone conference with Genora Dancel and Ninia Baehr (June 14, 2015).

52. Mike Yuen, *Gay Marriage Foes Target Lawmakers*, Honolulu Star-Bulletin, Sept. 11, 1996; Eskridge telephone interview with Foley (quotation in text).

53. Eskridge telephone interview with Foley (quotation in text). Our discussion of the legislature's 1997 session draws from Elder Dunn's memoranda and from Coolidge, *Hawai'i Marriage Amendment*, 40–49.

54. Coolidge, *Hawai'i Marriage Amendment*, 43 (first quotation in text); Letter from Elder Loren Dunn to Elder Neal Maxwell (Jan. 24, 1997), Prince Archives (second quotation).

55. Coolidge, *Hawai'i Marriage Amendment*, 47–48 (quotation in text).

56. On the 1997 legislative deliberations, see Coolidge, *Hawai'i Marriage Amendment*, 38–66.

57. *Voters Strongly Oppose Gay Unions*, Honolulu Star-Bulletin, Feb. 24, 1997, A5; Coolidge, *Hawai'i Marriage Amendment*, 60–75. On the willingness of the Church of Jesus Christ to compromise in order to get the marriage issue to the voters, see Elder Dunn, "Same-Gender Marriage Status Report" (Feb. 3, 1997), Prince Archives, and letter from Elder Dunn to Elder Ballard (April 10, 1997), Prince Archives (reporting on the house-proposed compromise that HFT representatives had drafted).

58. Reciprocal Beneficiaries Act, 1997 Hawaii Session Laws, Act 383; Letter from Elder Dunn to Elder Ballard (April 17, 1997), Prince Archives (first quotation in text); Letter from Professor Wardle to Elder Dunn (April 22, 1997), Prince Archives (second quotation).

59. See Coolidge, *Hawai'i Marriage Amendment*, 81–83.

60. Memorandum from Marlin Jensen to Public Affairs Committee, "SGM Update" (Oct. 9, 1997), Prince Archives (quotation in text). See Prince, *Gay Rights*, 64–66; Coolidge, *Hawai'i Marriage Amendment*, 97–101.

61. William Eskridge telephone interview of David Smith (April 15, 2019); John Cloud, *Taking the Initiative*, Out, Feb. 1999, 36–38.

62. John Cloud, *For Better or Worse: In Hawaii, a Showdown over Marriage Tests the Limits of Gay Activism*, Time, Oct. 19, 1998 (discussing the role of Jackie Young); Mary Adamski, *Clergy Rebut Charges of Intolerance*, Honolulu Star-Bulletin, Oct. 2, 1998 (quoting Honold).

63. Cloud, *For Better or Worse* (descriptions of the STM'98 ads); Mary Adamski, *Christian Groups at Odds over Ads Against Same-Sex Marriage*, Honolulu Star-Bulletin, Oct. 1, 1998 (Ishibashi quotation in text); Adamski, *Clergy Criticize Campaign Against Same-Sex Marriage*, Honolulu Star-Bulletin, Sept. 30, 1998; Adamski, *Clergy Rebut Charge of Intolerance* (discussing Honold, a supporter of the amendment, criticizing the STM'98 ads as divisive).

64. Op. Haw. Att'y Gen. No. 98-05 (Aug. 10, 1998) (opinion for Duane Black, chair of the Campaign Spending Commission); Mike Yuen, *Same-Sex Marriage: The Entire Nation Is Watching Hawai'i*, Honolulu Star-Bulletin, Oct. 29, 1998, A8.

65. Mike Yuen, *Battle over Same-Sex Unions Takes Last-Minute Twists, Turns*, Honolulu Star-Bulletin, Nov. 3, 1998; Alliance for Traditional Marriage, "The Gabbards" (Oct. 1998), https://twitter.com/urbroyo/status/1084349561324355585?s=21 (quotations in text).

66. John Gallagher, *The Other "M" Word*, The Advocate, June 23, 1998, 55 (HRC's role in the Hawai'i referendum).

67. Linda Hosek, *Will Hawaii Once Again Lead the Way?*, Honolulu Star-Bulletin, Sept. 10, 1996 (quotation in text). The stamp-of-approval argument against gay marriage was widely accepted on the mainland: e.g., Richard Posner, *Sex and Reason*, 311 (1992), criticized in William Eskridge Jr., *A Social Constructionist Critique of Posner's Sex and Reason: Steps Toward a Gaylegal Agenda*, 102 Yale L.J. 333 (1992).

68. David Orgon Coolidge, *Same-Sex Marriage: As Hawaii Goes . . .* , First Things (April 1997); *The Gospel According to Gabbard*, Honolulu Weekly, Jan. 27, 1999, 4. See Alan Hawkins, Lynn Wardle, and David Orgon Coolidge, *Revitalizing the Institution of Marriage for the Twenty-First Century: An Agenda for Strengthening Marriage* (2002).

69. Citizens for Community Values, *The Ultimate Target of the Gay Agenda: Same-Sex Marriage*, 1996 (Woodall's fear of normalization, based on the *Friends* episode).

70. David Orgon Coolidge, *Playing the Loving Card: Same-Sex Marriage and the Politics of Analogy*, 12 BYU J. Pub. L. 201, 201, 205 (1998) (quotations in text). See Lynn Wardle, Loving v. Virginia *and the Constitutional Right to Marry, 1790–1990*, 41 How. L.J. 289 (1998) (presented at the same 1997 conference sponsored by BYU, Catholic, and Howard Universities).

71. Frank, *Awakening*, 98–100; GLAD report on Sept. 11, 1995, meeting (detailed roadmap for a national educational and political campaign).

72. William Eskridge and Christopher Riano telephone interview of Wendy Brown DeBoer (March 12, 2015).

73. Civil Marriage Equality Campaign Plan (draft Aug. 12, 2003), Task Force Archives (quotations in text). See William Eskridge interview of Rea Carey, executive director, LGBTQ Task Force, Washington, DC (Dec. 6, 2018); Email from Evan Wolfson to William Eskridge, Jan. 17, 2019.

5. Defense of Marriage

1. James Dao, *After Victory, Crusader Against Same-Sex Marriage Thinks Big*, New York Times, Nov. 26, 2004 ("double life"). Our account in the text and the next several paragraphs is drawn from William Eskridge's telephone and in-person interviews of Phil Burress (and, on one occasion, his wife, Vickie, and daughter Stephanie) between February and November 2017.

2. William Eskridge and Daniel Strunk interview of Phil Burress, Cincinnati (March 17, 2018) (quotation in text); Cincinnati Human Rights Ordinance, Ord. No. 490-1992 (Nov. 25, 1992), overridden by Issue 3. See *Equality Found. of Greater Cincinnati v. City of Cincinnati*, 128 F.3d 289 (6th Cir. Oct. 23, 1997) (affirming the constitutionality of Issue 3).

3. Letter from former senator William Armstrong for Colorado for Family Values (Fall 1991), reprinted in Stephen Bransford, *Gay Politics vs. Colorado and America: The Inside Story of Amendment 2*, 241–244 (1994) (quotation in text); see 68–69, 73–74 (normalization of homosexuality threatens religion).

4. Bransford, *Gay Politics vs. Colorado;* Sara Diamond, *Not by Politics Alone: The Enduring Influence of the Christian Right,* 34–35, 167 (1998); Suzanne Goldberg and Lisa Keen, *Strangers to the Law: Gay People on Trial* (2000).

5. William Eskridge and Daniel Strunk interview of Reverend K.Z. and Mrs. Connie Smith, Cincinnati (March 18, 2017) (all the quotations in text).

6. Kimberly Dugan, *Just Like You: The Dimension of Identity Presentations in an Antigay Contested Context,* in Jo Reger et al., eds., *Identity Work in Social Movements,* 21, 36–38 (2008); Dagmar Herzog, *Sex in Crisis: The New Sexual Revolution and the Future of American Politics,* 71–72 (2008) (quotations from John Eldridge, representing Focus on the Family).

7. Evan Wolfson, Lambda Legal, memorandum, "Winning and Keeping Equal Marriage Rights: What Will Follow Victory in *Baehr v. Lewin?*" 3–7 (Nov. 7, 1994); Barbara Cox, *Same-Sex Marriage and Choice-of-Law: If We Marry in Hawaii, Are We Still Married When We Return Home?,* 1994 Wis. L. Rev. 1033. Cf. Andrew Koppelman, *Same Sex, Different States: When Same-Sex Unions Cross State Lines* (2006) (southern states sometimes recognized interracial marriages).

8. U.S. Const., art. IV, § 1 (full faith and credit clause); Wolfson, "Winning and Keeping Equal Marriage Rights," 8–9; Evan Wolfson, *Crossing the Threshold: Equal Marriage Rights for Lesbians and Gay Men and the Intra-Community Critique,* 21 NYU Rev. L. & Soc. Change 567, 612 n.196 (1994–1995). But see Linda Silberman, *Decision on Gay Marriages Should Only Affect Hawaii,* New York Times, April 11, 1996; Thomas Keane, Note, *Aloha Marriage? Constitutional and Choice of Law Arguments for Recognition of Same-Sex Marriages,* 47 Stan. L. Rev. 499 (1995). In addition to Silberman, we spoke to other leading choice-of-law scholars from the 1990s.

9. Minutes of the Roundtable for the Freedom to Marry Coalition (July 26, 1995; Sept. 18, 1995), GLAD Archives. The Coalition included representatives from GLAD, Lambda Legal, the ACLU, LLEGO, HRCF, NCLR, NOW, NGLTF, Victory Fund, P-FLAG, Japanese American Citizens League, Log Cabin Republicans, and community centers in Los Angeles and New York City.

10. In the 120 House races where the Christian Coalition participated, thirty Republican victories were by 5 percent or less. John Green et al., *Evangelical Realignment: The Political Power of the Christian Right,* Christian Century, July 5–12, 1995, 676–679. See Diamond, *Not by Politics Alone,* 102–103 (Gingrich's 1995 Contract with the Family).

11. Barney Frank, *Frank: A Life in Politics from the Great Society to Same-Sex Marriage,* 189 (2015) (quotation in text). Our account is based on off-the-record conversations with two gay staffers who attended the meeting with Evan Wolfson.

12. William Eskridge and Daniel Strunk telephone interview of Phil Burress (Feb. 2, 2017) (quotations in text); Daniel Pinello, *America's War on Same-Sex Couples and Their Families—And How the Courts Rescued Them* (2016); Dao, *After Victory.*

13. Eskridge and Strunk telephone interview of Burress (quotation in text).

14. Eskridge and Strunk telephone interview of Burress (quotation in text). The Evangelical activists who met in Memphis reassembled later in Washington, DC, and have met there as the "DC Group" every three months since 1996.

15. Adele Stan, *Showdown in Des Moines,* Mother Jones, Nov.–Dec. 1995 (Des Moines school board campaign); Frank Rich, *Bashing to Victory,* New York Times, Feb. 14, 1996 (role of Horn in Iowa presidential caucuses).

16. Quotations from speeches in this and the next paragraph are taken from the C-SPAN video of the February 10, 1996, Des Moines rally, https://www.c-span.org /video/?69857-1/campaign-protect-marriage-rally.

17. William Horn, producer, *The Ultimate Target of the Gay Agenda: Same-Sex Marriage* (1996) (quotations in text).

18. Robert Knight, FRC, "Answers to Questions About the Defense of Marriage" (March 22, 1996) (quotations in text).

19. The quotation in the text is from an anonymous gay staffer. On Barr, see Thomas Edsall, *Controversial Group Has Ties to Both Parties in South,* Washington Post, Jan. 13, 1999, A2.

20. Our discussion of the DOMA drafting process is based upon off-the-record interviews with DOMA advocates and congressional staff, supplemented by educated guesses to fill in gaps.

21. In 1995, the Flag Desecration Amendment sailed through the House, 312-120 (June 28, 1995), and failed in the Senate, 63-36 (Dec. 12, 1995). The same results recurred in 1997, 1999–2000, 2001, 2003, and 2005–2006. In addition to Barr, the original cosponsors for House Bill 3396 included two Missouri Democrats, Eugene Volkmer and Ike Skelton.

22. Gregory Prince interview of Mike McCurry, Washington, DC (Dec. 19, 2014), Prince Archives (McCurry quotations in text); John Harris, *The Survivor: Bill Clinton in the White House,* 243 (2005) (last quotation).

23. Email from Elizabeth Birch to William Eskridge, April 9, 2019; Memorandum from George Stephanopoulos and Richard Socarides to President Clinton (Sept. 11, 1996), Clinton Papers (support for ENDA deflected attention from the president's support for DOMA).

24. Prince interview of McCurry.

25. Memorandum from Jack Quinn, George Stephanopoulos, Marsha Scott for the president through Leon Panetta: "Gay Marriage Legislation" (May 10, 1996), Clinton Papers. The memorandum suggested that the president should reiterate his opposition to same-sex marriage but not rush to endorse the DOMA bill.

26. Letter from Andrew Fois, assistant attorney general, to Hon. Henry Hyde, chairman, House Committee on the Judiciary (May 14, 1996) (quotation in text), noted and quoted in Defense of Marriage Act: Hearing Before the Subcomm. on the Constitution of the House Comm. on the Judiciary, 104th Cong., 2d Sess. 2 (May 15, 1996); Eskridge interview of Birch.

27. May 15 House DOMA hearing, pp. 10–31, reprinting Evan Wolfson, director, The Lambda Legal Marriage Project, memorandum, "Winning and Keeping the Freedom to Marry for Same-Sex Couples—What Lies Ahead After Hawaii, What Tasks Must We Begin Now?" (April 19, 1996).

28. May 15 House DOMA hearing (testimony of Elizabeth Birch) (quotation in text). See HRC, *A Basic Human Right: Talking About Gay Marriage*, 6 (1996) ("Making a commitment to a life-long relationship is a fundamental human need that should not be denied to anyone").

29. Brief for petitioners, *Romer v. Evans* (Supreme Court Docket No. 94-1039, filed April 21, 1995), 1995 WL 310026 (Colorado's brief, quoted in text).

30. Brief for respondents, *Romer v. Evans* (Supreme Court Docket No. 94-1039, filed June 19, 1995), 1995 WL 17008447 (Lambda Legal and ACLU's brief for challengers to Amendment 2).

31. Amicus brief for Equal Rights, Not Special Rights, *Romer v. Evans* (Supreme Court Docket No. 94-1039, filed April 21, 1995), 1995 WL 17008425 (Bork's brief, quoted in text).

32. Amicus brief for ABA, pp. 4–5, *Romer v. Evans* (Supreme Court Docket No. 94-1039, filed June 16, 1995), 1995 WL 17008433. Mark Agrast was the primary architect of the ABA brief. For the scholars' brief, see amicus brief for Laurence Tribe, John Hart Ely, Gerald Gunther, Philip Kurland, and Kathleen Sullivan, *Romer* (filed June 9, 1995), 1995 WL 862021.

33. Amicus brief for Christian Legal Society, Focus on the Family, et al., p. 5, *Romer v. Evans* (Supreme Court Docket No. 94-1039, filed April 2, 1995), 1995 WL 17008428 (Amendment 2 sought to protect churches which "do discriminate" against practicing homosexuals).

34. *Robert Skolrood Is Dead at 79; Argued Religion Cases*, New York Times, March 3, 2008; William Eskridge Jr., Nan Hunter, and Courtney Joslin, *Sexuality, Gender and the Law*, 1253–1260 (4th ed. 2018) (appendix 7, reprinting the Amendment 2 ballot materials); Bransford, *Gay Politics vs. Colorado*, 37–38 (Tebedo's quotation in text, from an Amendment 2 campaign insider).

35. Transcript of oral argument, *Romer v. Evans* (Supreme Court Docket No. 94-1039, Oct. 5, 1995).

36. William Eskridge Jr., *Dishonorable Passions: Sodomy Law in America, 1861–2003*, 278–289 (2008) (Supreme Court's conference in *Romer*).

37. The descriptions are based upon Eskridge's social interactions with Justices Scalia and Stevens and from his conversations and interviews with Stuart Delery, David Dorsen, Steve Gunderson, and various Supreme Court personnel.

38. The account is based upon Eskridge's conversations with Justice Kennedy and one of his childhood friends (2015–2018).

39. William Eskridge conversation with Mary and Tony Kennedy, Washington, DC (Nov. 20, 2017) (quotations in text). Dean Schaber was a key lobbyist for Kennedy's

Supreme Court nomination appointment after the Senate had rejected Judge Bork in 1987; Schaber helped overcome the doubts of his friend and ally, Attorney General Ed Meese, who decisively supported Kennedy over Edith Jones after Douglas Ginsburg withdrew his nomination.

40. For a video of Kennedy's speech, quoted in the text, see *What a Difference One Man Can Make: A Tribute to Dean Gordon Schaber*, Nov. 10, 1992, https://www.youtube.com/watch?v=ox5eil-dfAw (quotations in text).

41. Justice Kennedy told us he attended the Hayek lectures during the year he spent at the London School of Economics (1957–1958). William Eskridge conversation with Justice Anthony Kennedy, Washington, DC (April 20, 2018). See Friedrich Hayek, *The Political Ideal of the Rule of Law* (Cairo Lectures, 1955); Friedrich Hayek, *The Constitution of Liberty* (1960); Steven Ealy, *The Evolution of Rule of Law in Hayek's Thought, 1935–1955* (Mercatus Center, George Mason University, July 2010).

42. Hayek, *Political Ideal*, 35–36 (quotations in text).

43. *Romer v. Evans*, 517 U.S. 620, 623 (1996), quoting *Plessy v. Ferguson*, 163 U.S. 537, 559 (1896) (Harlan, J., dissenting) (first two quotations in text); p. 631 (third quotation in text); p. 630 (fourth quotation in text).

44. *Romer*, p. 632 (first quotation in text); p. 633, quoting *Sweatt v. Painter*, 339 U.S. 629, 635 (1950) (second quotation); pp. 631, 634–635, quoting *Department of Agriculture v. Moreno*, 413 U.S. 528, 534 (1973) (third quotation).

45. *Romer*, p. 636 (Scalia, J., dissenting) (quotation in text). As Souter's chambers told the Scalia chambers, *Kulturkampf* was not a Pat Buchanan–style "culture war" but was Chancellor Otto von Bismarck's campaign to domesticate the Roman Catholic Church and induce state-imposed conformity upon the devout population. The Scalia clerk dismissed the concern raised by the Souter clerk, but the clumsy *Kulturkampf* reference was an immediate embarrassment.

46. Fax from Walter Dellinger, OLC, to Jack Quinn, White House counsel (May 21, 1996) (analysis of *Romer*); Letter from Melinda Parus, executive director, NGLTF, to William Clinton, President of the United States (May 23, 1996) (quotation in text).

47. Letter from Andrew Fois, assistant attorney general, to Charles Canady, chairman, Subcommittee on the Constitution, House Committee on the Judiciary (May 29, 1996); FRC, "Same-Sex Marriages" (video, July 2, 1996) (Arkes's quotation), https://www.c-span.org/video/?73344-1/gender-marriage.

48. Fax from Dellinger (*Romer* presumably fatal to anti-gay initiatives with similar wording); *Equality Found. of Greater Cincinnati v. City of Cincinnati*, 128 F.3d 289 (6th Cir. Oct. 23, 1997) (upholding Issue 3, a municipal charter amendment, and distinguishing *Romer*, which invalidated a statewide amendment), rehearing en banc denied, 1998 WL 101701 (6th Cir. Feb. 5, 1998), cert. denied, 525 U.S. 943 (Oct. 13, 1998); Carey Goldberg, *Maine Voters Repeal a Law on Gay Rights*, New York Times, Feb. 12, 1998.

49. Jonathan Rauch, *For Better or Worse?*, The New Republic, May 6, 1996 (quotation in text). See Judge Richard Posner, *Book Review*, 95 Mich. L. Rev. 1578 (1997) (skep-

tically reviewing William Eskridge Jr., *The Case for Same-Sex Marriage: From Sexual Liberty to Civilized Commitment* [1996]).

50. Gregory Lewis and Jonathan Edelson, *DOMA and ENDA: Congress Votes on Gay Rights*, in Rimmerman et al., eds., *Politics of Gay Rights*, 206–207 (2000).

51. House Committee on the Judiciary, Report No. 104-664: Defense of Marriage Act, pp. 6–10 (July 9, 1996); see pp. 12–19 (committee's positive justifications for DOMA, including the morality-based justifications, quoted in text); William Eskridge interview of Steve Gunderson, Washington, DC (May 27, 2016). The debate and vote on the modified closed rule, H.R. Res. 474, can be found in 120 Cong. Rec. H7273–7279 (July 11, 1996).

52. The House debate for DOMA, H.R. 3396, is found in 120 Cong. Rec. H7441–7445 (July 11, 1996) and H7481–7505 (July 12). Quotations in text are from H7441 (first quotation, Canady), H7445 (second quotation, Canady), H7481 (third quotation, Barr), H7444 (fourth quotation, Coburn), H7488 (final quotation, Dornan). References to the Wolfson Lambda memorandum can be found at H7275 and H7444 (July 11) and H7486 and H7489 (July 12).

53. 120 Cong. Rec. H7503-7504 (Lewis) (first quotation in text), H7492 (Gunderson) (remaining quotations).

54. 120 Cong. Rec. H7500 (vote on Frank Amendment), H7505 (final House vote on DOMA).

55. Memorandum to Leon Panetta from George Stephanopoulos and Richard Socarides, Aug. 2, 1996 (describing the Iskowitz deal). See Nathaniel Frank, *Awakening: How Gays and Lesbians Brought Marriage Equality to America*, 110–111 (2017) (HRC's enthusiasm for ENDA and its sense of futility with regard to DOMA). Barney Frank had tried to make the same DOMA-ENDA pairing in the House, but he had no political leverage to persuade the GOP leadership to acquiesce.

56. The quotations and descriptions of the Senate debate are taken from the C-SPAN broadcast, Sept. 10–12, 1996, https://www.c-span.org/video/?c4395357/same-sex-marriage-debate. Senator Byrd read into the congressional record William Eskridge Jr., *The Case for Same-Sex Marriage*, 100–104.

57. Senators voting yes on DOMA included at least three suspected closeted lesbian and gay senators as well as such liberals as Senators Biden (D-Delaware), Daschle (D-South Dakota), and Specter (R-Pennsylvania). Voting against DOMA were Democratic senators Akaka (Hawai'i), Boxer (California), Feingold (Wisconsin), Feinstein (California), Inouye (Hawai'i), Kennedy (Massachusetts), Kerrey (Nebraska), Kerry (Massachusetts), Moseley-Brown (Illinois), Moynihan (New York), Pell (Rhode Island), Robb (Virginia), Simon (Illinois), and Wyden (Oregon). Senator Pryor (Arkansas) was absent.

58. Our discussion and quotations from the Senate's ENDA debate on Sept. 10, 1996, are taken from the C-SPAN video, https://www.c-span.org/video/?c4471817/doma-vote-enda-debatevote. See J. Jennings Moss, *Jilted: Gays and Lesbians Lost a Battle for the Right to Marry*, The Advocate, Oct. 15, 1996, 22–29. The quotation in text is from

Senator Coats (Indiana), with similar points being made by Senators Nickles (Oklahoma), Hatch (Utah), and Lott (Mississippi). Republicans voting for ENDA were Senators Chafee (Rhode Island), Cohen (Maine), D'Amato (New York), Hatfield (Oregon), Jeffords (Vermont), Simpson (Wyoming), Snowe (Maine), and Specter (Pennsylvania). Democrats voting against ENDA were Senators Byrd (West Virginia), Exon (Nebraska), Ford (Kentucky), and Nunn (Georgia).

59. Richard Socarides, *Why Bill Clinton Signed the Defense of Marriage Act*, The New Yorker, March 8, 2013 (quotation in text).

60. President William Clinton, signing statement for the Defense of Marriage Act (Sept. 20, 1996) (quotations in text).

61. Compare Bill Clinton, *It's Time to Overturn DOMA*, Washington Post, Mar. 7, 2013 (quotation in text) (claiming that he signed DOMA to "defuse a movement to enact a constitutional amendment"), with Eskridge interview of Birch (strong objection to that posthoc explanation); Michelle Lee He Yee, *Hillary Clinton's Claim That DOMA Had to Be Enacted to Stop an Anti-Gay Marriage Amendment to the U.S. Constitution*, Washington Post, Oct. 28, 2015 (detailed examination of the Clintons' claims, finding them untruthful); and internal campaign email from Jake Sullivan, Oct. 25, 2015 (suggesting that the campaign abandon the constitutional amendment story and focus on Hillary Clinton's more recent support for LGBT families).

62. Prince interview of McCurry (quotation in text); William Eskridge telephone interview of Mike McCurry (June 13, 2016). Dick Morris claims that the possibility of a constitutional amendment never came up during his frequent discussions with Bill and Hillary Clinton. See Dick Morris, "Hillary Lied About DOMA on Maddow Show" (Oct. 29, 2015).

63. Andrew Kaczynski, *Listen to Bill Clinton's 1996 Radio Ad Touting His Passage of DOMA*, CNN (updated version Oct. 10, 2016) (audio version, quoted in text). The different accounts of the decision to pull the ad are taken from Eskridge interview of Socarides and Eskridge interview of Birch. See also Barney Frank, *Frank*, 192 (also claiming credit for killing the ad, based on a phone call to his sister, who worked in the White House).

64. Executive Order 13,087, 63 Fed. Reg. 30,097 (May 28, 1998), amending Executive Order 11,478.

65. See William Eskridge interview of Judge Phyllis Randolph Frye, Washington, DC (Aug. 27, 2016); Phyllis Randolph Frye and Alyson Dodi Meiselman, *Same-Sex Marriages Have Existed in the United States for a Long Time Now*, 64 Alb. L. Rev. 1031, 1047–1048 (2001).

66. *Littleton v. Prange*, 3 S.W.3d 223, 225–226 (Tex. App. Oct. 27, 1999).

67. *Littleton*, pp. 229–231 (majority opinion); pp. 231–232 (Angelini, J., concurring), citing Julie Greenberg, *Defining Male and Female: Intersexuality and the Collision Between Law and Biology*, 41 Ariz. L. Rev. 265 (1999).

68. Petition for a writ of certiorari, p. 17, *Littleton v. Prange*, Docket No. 00-25 (US Supreme Court, filed July 3, 2000), 2000 WL 33999789 (quotation in text); *Turner v. Safley*, 482 U.S. 78 (1987) (constitutional right to marry extends to prisoners).

69. Transgender rights advocates petitioned the ENDA sponsors to expand their bill to include that term. GOP senator Jeffords was open to that suggestion, but HRC and its counsel adamantly opposed changing the bill because it would doom the legislation.

70. In 1973, Phillip Frye met and married his second wife. By 1976, Phillip had become Phyllis, whose public presentation was female.

71. *Estate of Araguz*, 443 S.W.3d 233 (Tex. App. 2014), applying Tex. Family Code § 2.005(b)(8) as an override of the *Littleton* rule that transgender persons can only marry persons who are a different sex from the one on their original birth certificates.

72. States enacting laws reaffirming one-man, one-woman marriage, generally adopted in response to the new claims from lesbian and gay couples, included Montana, Oklahoma, Oregon, Utah, and Virginia in 1975; California, the District of Columbia, Florida, Minnesota, and Wyoming in 1977; and Nebraska in 1978. In the 1980s, Maryland, New Hampshire, and perhaps other states followed with similar laws. Citations to these laws can be found in appendix 1 to this volume.

73. 1995 Utah Laws ch. 146 (H.B. 366), adopted March 14, 1995, effective May 1, 1995, codified at Utah Code § 30-1-4(a)(1) (quotation in text). See Utah Code § 30-1-2(5) (barring marriages between persons of the same sex). For strategies suggested by the Mormons' same-gender advisory committee, see Arthur Anderson to Marlin Jensen, Loren Dunn, Lance Wickman, Richard Wirthlin, Lynn Wardle, "Design and Content of Coalition Organizing Instruction Book," June 1, 1998, discussed in Gregory Prince, *Gay Rights and the Mormon Church: Intended Actions, Unintended Consequences*, 68–69 (2019).

74. In 1996, junior-DOMAs were adopted by legislatures in Alaska, Arizona, Delaware, Georgia, Idaho, Illinois, Kansas, Louisiana, Michigan, Missouri, North Carolina, Oklahoma, Pennsylvania, South Carolina, South Dakota, and Tennessee. In 1997, such measures passed the legislatures of Arkansas, Florida, Indiana, Maine, Minnesota, Mississippi, Montana, North Dakota, and Virginia. They were added in 1998 to family law in Alabama, Iowa, Kentucky, and Washington. See Donald Haider-Markel, *Lesbian and Gay Politics in the States: Interest Groups, Electoral Politics, and Policy*, in Rimmerman et al., eds., *Politics of Gay Rights*, 324–346.

75. Robert Knight, FRC, "Talking Points: Defense of Marriage Act (DOMA)" (May 23, 1996); David Orgon Coolidge, *Playing the Loving Card: Same-Sex Marriage and the Politics of Analogy*, 12 BYU J. Pub. L. 201, 205 (1998); Lynn Wardle, *Loving v. Virginia and the Constitutional Right to Marry, 1790–1990*, 41 How. L.J. 289 (1998). For explicitly anti-gay versions of this argument, see FRC, "Same-Sex Marriages" (Knight's remarks); Horn, *The Ultimate Target*.

6. A Place at the Table

1. Archive of American Television, interview of Sheila Kuehl (Aug. 7, 2015) (quotation in text), available at https://www.youtube.com/watch?v=hPPHUdNGdM4.

2. Jonah Markowitz, director, *Political Animals* (Idiot Savant Pictures, 2016); William Eskridge telephone interview of Sheila Kuehl (June 2017).

3. Bruce Bawer, *A Place at the Table: The Gay Individual in American Society* (1993); Markowitz, *Political Animals* (quotations in text).

4. Markowitz, *Political Animals* (quotation in text).

5. Markowitz, *Political Animals* (quotations in text).

6. Markowitz, *Political Animals* (quotation in text).

7. William Eskridge interview of Jackie Goldberg and Sharon Stricker, Echo Park, Los Angeles (Aug. 10, 2017).

8. 1999 Cal. Stats. (A.B. 537), amending Cal. Educ. Code §§ 220-221.1 (adding sexual orientation as a new category protected by the state hate crime law).

9. Nancy Hill-Holtzman, *Foe of Gay Marriages Says His Son Is Homosexual*, Los Angeles Times, Sept. 11, 1996 (quotation in text); Jennifer Warren, *Initiative Divides a Family*, Los Angeles Times, Nov. 24, 1999. For Colonel Knight's biography, see his career description in the National Aviation Hall of Fame, *William (Pete) Knight* (inducted 1988).

10. Scott Cummings and Douglas NeJaime, *Lawyering for Marriage Equality*, 57 UCLA L. Rev. 1235 (2010).

11. Gregory Lewis, *Domestic Partners Benefits Win in S.F.*, San Francisco Examiner, Oct. 29, 1996; Email from Geoff Kors to William Eskridge, June 9, 2019.

12. *Sunday Interview—Archbishop William Levada*, San Francisco Chronicle, Feb. 23, 1997 (all quotations in text from the transcript of an interview of the archbishop); Martha Minow, *Should Religious Groups Be Exempt from Civil Rights Laws?*, 48 Boston Coll. L. Rev. 781, 829–832 (2007).

13. Ted Gideonse, *Flying the Gay-Friendly Skies*, The Advocate, Sept. 14, 1999, 34.

14. Ryan Patrick Murphy, *United Airlines Is for Lovers? Flight Attendant Activism and the Family Values Economy in the 1990s*, Radical Hist. Rev., Winter 2012, 100–112 (quotation in text).

15. *Air Transport Ass'n v. City and County of San Francisco*, 992 F. Supp. 1149 (N.D. Cal. April 10, 1998).

16. Nicole Raeburn, *Changing Corporate America from the Inside Out: Gay and Lesbian Workplace Rights*, 122–123 (2004); Murphy, *United Airlines Is for Lovers?*, 105–108 (union's pressure and consumer boycott).

17. Kim Mills and Daryl Herrschaft, HRC Foundation, *The State of the Workplace for Lesbian, Gay, Bisexual, and Transgendered Americans*, 19 (1999).

18. Raeburn, *Changing Corporate America*, 68–70 (network effects resulting from widespread corporate adoption of domestic partnership policies), 82–85, 94–98 (HRC's network-effecting efforts, which had synergy with union and employee pressure).

19. William Eskridge interview of Jenny Pizer, Los Angeles (June 29, 2016); William Eskridge interview of Jon Davidson, Los Angeles (June 30, 2016); Cummings and NeJaime, *Lawyering for Marriage Equality*, 1255–1256.

20. William Eskridge telephone interview of former California legislative assistant Alan LoFaso (Sept. 26, 2016).

21. Statement of Assembly Member William (Pete) Knight, A.B. 1982 (Feb. 9, 1996) (quotations in text).

22. See report from Bion Gregory, legislative counsel of California, to William "Pete" Knight, Decision #7063: Marriage (March 28, 1996); Letter from Daniel Lungren, Office of the California Attorney General, to William "Pete" Knight: "Re: Support for Your Measure, A.B. 1982" (June 6, 1996); Statement of Professor Lynn Wardle submitted to the California Senate Judiciary Committee Regarding A.B. 1982, p. 9 (July 3, 1996). On the domestic partnership poison pill added to the bill in the senate, see Carl Ingram, *Bill Opposing Gay Marriages Weakened*, Los Angeles Times, July 11, 1996, A3; Ingram, *Davis Breaks Tie, Backs Domestic Partner Registry*, Los Angeles Times, Aug. 20, 1996, B8.

23. Markowitz, *Political Animals* (Migden's quotations in text).

24. In committee, Catholic and Protestant witnesses testified that the Bible contained "a number of family forms, all centering around the concept of the household," like that in the Migden bill. They also testified that "it is fundamentally just and right that all persons have access to health insurance." California Assembly Committee on Insurance, *Hearing on A.B. 1059 (Migden): Health Coverage; Domestic Partners* (April 17, 1997) (committee summary). See Senate Committee on Insurance, *Hearing on A.B. 1059 (Migden): Health Insurance* (July 2, 1997) (committee summary).

25. Markowitz, *Political Animals* (Migden quotation in text); Cummings and NeJaime, *Lawyering for Marriage Equality*, 1258–1259 (Coles quotation); William Eskridge telephone interview of Matt Coles (July 2016); Eskridge interview of Davidson; William Eskridge telephone interview of Carole Migden (Jan. 18, 2019); California Senate Committee on the Judiciary, *Hearing on A.B. 26 (Migden): Domestic Partnership* (July 7, 1999) (summary by the committee).

26. Eskridge telephone interview of Migden ("too marriagy"); Spectrum Institute, *Domestic Partnership Legislation in California: A Tradition of Gender-Neutral Bills, Proposals, and Laws, to Protect a Wide Range of Unmarried Adults* (July 1999).

27. 1999 Cal. Stats. ch. 588 (A.B. 26 [Migden]).

28. Melissa Murray, *Paradigms Lost: How Domestic Partnership Went from Innovation to Injury*, 37 NYU Rev. L. & Soc. Change 291 (2013); Scott Sayare and Maïa de La Baume, *In France, Civil Unions Gain Favor Over Marriage*, New York Times, Dec. 15, 2010.

29. Markowitz, *Political Animals* (Migden and Goldberg quotations in text).

30. Letter from Loren Dunn to Russell Ballard (Feb. 11, 1997), Prince Archives (quotation in text); Letter from Dunn to Ballard (March 4, 1997), Prince Archives.

31. Memo from Gary Lawrence to California Defense of Marriage Leadership Group (May 12, 1997), Prince Archives (quotation in text).

32. Cal. Const., art. VI, § 16(a)–(d) (to qualify a constitutional initiative, the proponents need to gather signatures amounting to 8 percent of the voters in the previous governorship election); Memorandum from Elders Jensen, Dunn, and Wirthlin to the public affairs committee, Church of Jesus Christ: "Same-Gender Initiatives: Hawaii and California" (July 1, 1997), Prince Archives (quotation in text).

33. Memorandum from Lynn Wardle to SGM [Same-Gender Marriage] Committee members: Marlin Jensen, Loren Dunn, David Sorensen, Lance Wickman, Richard Wirthlin, Arthur and Jan Anderson, and Von Keetch (March 26, 1998), Prince Archives.

34. Memorandum from Marlin Jensen to California SGM referendum file: "California Definition of Marriage Initiative" (Dec. 17, 1998) (first quotation in text), Prince Archives; Memorandum from Marlin Jensen, Cecil Samuelson, and Richard Wirthlin to the public affairs committee, Church of Jesus Christ, "California Definition of Marriage" (Feb. 25, 1999), Prince Archives; Memorandum from North America West Area Presidency et al. to Area Authority Seventies, stake presidents, mission presidents, bishops, branch presidents, and all church members in California (May 11, 1999), Prince Archives (second quotation). See Gregory Prince, *Gay Rights and the Mormon Church: Intended Actions, Unintended Consequences,* 72–79 (2019).

35. Memorandum from Elder Douglas Callister to stake presidents in California (May 20, 1999); *Mormon Money,* Newsweek, Aug. 9, 1999, 6.

36. David Combe email, Oct. 20, 1999, Prince Archives; Prince, *Gay Rights,* 78–79.

37. Lorri Jean and Darrel Cummings, *The Battle Against Proposition 22: Post-Election Analysis of the "No on Knight" Campaign,* 6–7 (2000) (time line for No on Knight); Memorandum from Celinda Lake and Vicki Shabo, Lake Snell Perry Assocs., to California Same-Sex Marriage Team, "Focus Group Findings: Strategic Recommendations on Same-Sex Marriage" (April 9, 1999) (quotations in text). The records for No on Knight are located in the LA GLBT Archives.

38. On December 13, the secretary of state promulgated the informational pamphlet sent to all registered voters, with pro and con arguments supplied by each side. Yes on 22 emphasized the "Don't Redefine Marriage" argument, while No on 22 charged that the initiative would add nothing to California law, was unfair to lesbian and gay partners and their families, and would have malign effects on individuals.

39. Marriage Equality USA, "Our History" (2019), https://www.marriageequality.org/our_history.

40. Toni Broaddus, *Vote No If You Believe in Marriage: Lessons from the No on Knight/No on Proposition 22 Campaign,* 15 Berkeley Women's L.J. 1, 5–10 (2000) (quoting the No on Knight ads); Aurelio Rojas, *Foes of Prop 22 Disagree on TV Ad,* San Francisco Examiner, Feb. 29, 2000 (describing the Jeff Davis ad and quoting a critic).

41. Evelyn Nieves, *Ballot Initiative That Would Thwart Gay Marriage Is Embroiling California*, New York Times, Feb. 24, 2000; Carol Ness, *Tough New Ads Blast Prop 22*, San Francisco Examiner, March 2, 2000 (quotations in text).

42. On suicides of Mormon gay youth, see Carol Lynn Pearson, *No More Goodbyes: Circling Our Wagons Around Our Gay Loved Ones* (2011); Prince, *Gay Rights*, 79–82 (Matis quotation in text).

43. Broaddus, *Vote No*, 6–7, 10–11.

44. Jean and Cummings, *Battle Against Proposition 22*, 9–11 (quotations in text); Broaddus, *Vote No*, 4–5 (campaign faced a choice between trying to win and building the movement; its leaders chose the former but lost anyway).

45. Although all demographic groups (except for Jews) voted for Proposition 22, there was concern that minority communities—African, Asian, and Latino Americans—were more negative or apathetic than one would have expected. Daniel Pinello, *America's Struggle for Same-Sex Marriage and Their Families—And How the Courts Rescued Them*, 96 (2017).

46. Eskridge telephone interview of LoFaso.

47. Proposed A.B. 25 (Migden, 2000); Eskridge telephone interview of Migden (too "marriagy").

48. Markowitz, *Political Animals* (quotations in text).

49. Markowitz, *Political Animals* (quotations in text, from assembly committee hearing).

50. Scott Lively and Kevin Abrams, *The Pink Swastika: Homosexuality in the Nazi Party* (1995); Markowitz, *Political Animals* (quotations in text).

51. Markowitz, *Political Animals* (quotation in text).

52. Letter from the California Catholic Conference to Senator Martha Escutia, chair of the committee on the judiciary, June 28, 2001 (first quotation in text); ACLU of Southern California, "Domestic Partner Rights Expansion Places California at Forefront" (Oct. 15, 2001), https://www.aclusocal.org/en/news/aclu-southern-california-says -domestic-partner-rights-expansion-places-california-forefront (second quotation).

53. Domestic Partnership Amendments Act, 2001 Cal. Stats. ch. 893 (A.B. 25 [Migden]); Saskia Kim and Drew Leibert, chief counsel, assembly judiciary committee, "A Primer on Civil Unions" (Oct.–Nov. 2001).

54. 2002 Cal. Stats. ch. 447 (A.B. 2216 [Keeley]). See California Senate Committee on the Judiciary, *Hearing on A.B. 2216: Intestate Succession; Domestic Partners* (June 25, 2002) (summary prepared by the committee).

55. NCLR, *Evolution of California's Domestic Partnership Law: A Timeline* (circa 2011).

56. Our account is taken from various interviews, especially William Eskridge telephone interview of former EQCA director Geoffrey Kors (July 14, 2016).

57. Draft A.B. 205 (Goldberg, 2003) (quotation in text), LA Lambda Archives. See Grace Ganz Blumberg, *Legal Recognition of Same-Sex Conjugal Relationships: The 2003 California Domestic Partner Rights and Responsibilities Act in Comparative Civil Rights*

and Family Law Perspective, 51 UCLA L. Rev. 1555 (2004). For the movement discussion of a constitutional lawsuit, see Williams Project, "Marriage Litigation on Behalf of Same-Sex Couples in California: A Roundtable Discussion," Jan. 10, 2003; Cummings and NeJaime, *Lawyering for Marriage Equality,* 1270–1271.

58. Assembly Member Jackie Goldberg, memorandum, "AB 205: The Domestic Partner Rights and Responsibilities Act of 2003" (2003) (quotation in text).

59. Senate bill analysis: AB 205, p. 14 (Aug. 27, 2003) (quotations from Catholic Conference); Memorandum from Rev. Louis Sheldon, TVC, to Hon. Ellen Corbett, chair, assembly judiciary committee, "AB 205—OPPOSE" (Mar. 26, 2003) (Sheldon quotations).

60. Eskridge telephone interview of Kors.

61. The quotations and description of the assembly debate and vote are taken from the video of the June 4 debate in Markowitz, *Political Animals.*

62. Letter from Jennifer Pizer, Lambda, and Shannon Minter, NCLR, to Jackie Goldberg: "Deletion from AB 205 of responsibility to provide partner support in appropriate cases would create unwarranted legal, practical and political risks for gay people" (July 2, 2003); Eskridge telephone interview of Kors.

63. Email from Geoff Kors to William Eskridge, June 9, 2019.

64. Domestic Partner Rights and Responsibilities Act of 2003, 2003 Cal. Stats. ch. 421 (A.B. 205 [Goldberg]), codified at Cal. Family Code § 297.5.

65. *Knight v. Davis,* complaint, Case No. 03AS05284 (Super. Ct. Sacramento Cnty., filed Sept. 22, 2003) (Senator Knight's lawsuit to invalidate A.B. 205 as inconsistent with Proposition 22).

66. Eskridge telephone interview of Kuehl (quotations in text).

7. Equality Practice

1. On Bellemarre's case, see Jeff Kaufman, director, *The State of Marriage* (Floating World Pictures 2015); David Moats, *Civil Wars: A Battle for Gay Marriage,* 84–89 (2004).

2. Connie Cain Ramsey, *1989 Custody Case Put Attention on Equal Rights,* Burlington Free Press, Aug. 7, 2014 (quotation in text, from the judge's daughter); William Eskridge telephone interview of Susan Murray (Dec. 9, 2017).

3. *In re B.L.V.B.,* 628 A.2d 1271 (Vt. 1993) (quotation in text); Nancy Polikoff, *This Child Does Have Two Mothers: Redefining Parenthood to Meet the Needs of Children in Lesbian-Mother and Other Nontraditional Families,* 78 Geo. L.J. 459 (1990); *In re R.C.,* Probate Court No. 9088 (Addison Cnty., VT, Dec. 9, 1991) (Murray's second-parent adoption case).

4. Eskridge telephone interview of Murray (quotation in text); William Eskridge interview of Justice Beth Robinson, Ferrisburgh VT (Dec. 1, 2017) (Robinson's classes with feminist visiting professors); Adrienne Rich, *Compulsory Heterosexuality and Lesbian Existence,* 5 Signs 631, 645 (1980).

5. Mary Bonauto, *The Litigation: First Judicial Victories in Vermont, Massachusetts, and Connecticut,* in Kevin Cathcart and Leslie Gabet-Brett, eds., *Love Unites Us,* 73 (2016) (quotation in text).

6. United Church of Christ (UCC), "Social Policy Statements on LGBT Concerns," http://www.ucc.org/lgbt_statements. See Tenth General Synod, UCC, *Resolution on Human Sexuality and the Needs of Gay and Bisexual Persons* (adopted June–July 1975); Fourteenth General Synod, UCC, *Resolution in Response to the Concerns of Same-Gender Oriented Persons and Their Families Within the United Church of Christ* (adopted June 1983); Board of Directors, Homeland, UCC, *Equal Marriage Rights for Same-Gender Couples* (adopted Nov. 1996) (quotation in text); Twenty-Fifth General Synod, UCC, *In Support of Equal Marriage Rights for All* (adopted July 2005).

7. William Eskridge interview of the Reverend Craig and Mrs. Deb Bensen, Cambridge, VT (Dec. 1, 2017). As he had told Phil Burress (see chap. 5), Mike Gabbard warned the Bensens that Vermont would have to recognize Hawai'i same-sex marriages.

8. Congregation for the Doctrine of the Faith, "Letter to the Bishops of the Catholic Church on the Pastoral Care of Homosexual Persons," ¶ 7 (Oct. 1, 1986) (first quotation in text); Eskridge interview of the Bensens (remaining quotations).

9. George Chauncey, *Why Marriage? The History Shaping Today's Debate Over Gay Equality,* 48–49 (2004).

10. The account of Murray and Robinson's grassroots organizing is taken from personal and telephone interviews of them and from the sources in William Eskridge Jr., *Equality Practice: Civil Unions and the Future of Gay Rights* (2002).

11. An Act Relating to Adoptions, 1996 Vt. Session Laws, Public Act 161 (S. 136), § 1-102(b) (May 15, 1996) (allowing second-parent adoptions by unmarried partners); David Cole, *Engines of Liberty: The Power of Citizen Activists to Make Constitutional Law,* 34–35 (2016).

12. Moats, *Civil Wars,* 54–56, 77–78; William Eskridge telephone interview of Stan Baker and Peter Harrigan (Oct. 16, 2000); Joseph Watson, producer, Vermont Freedom to Marry Task Force, *The Freedom to Marry: A Green Mountain View* (1996).

13. William Eskridge and Christopher Riano interview of Marty Rouse, Washington, DC (June 23, 2017).

14. Our description of the meeting and the quotation in text are taken from interviews and conversations with Susan Murray, Beth Robinson, and Mary Bonauto, mostly in 2017.

15. Moats, *Civil Wars,* 89–91, 94–95, 104–105; William Eskridge interview of Stacy Jolles and Nina Beck, Burlington, VT (Oct. 7, 2000).

16. Governor Kunin had appointed feminist-friendly justices John Dooley (her chief of staff), Denise Johnson (head of the civil rights division of the attorney general's office), and Jim Morse (head of the public defender service). See Madeleine May Kunin, *The New Feminist Agenda: Defining the Next Revolution for Women, Work, and Family* (2012).

17. Vt. Const. chap. I, art. 7 (common benefits clause, quoted in text).

18. State of Vermont's motion to dismiss, p. 52, *Baker v. State*, No. S1009-97 CnC (Chittenden Sup. Ct., filed Nov. 10, 1997) (first quotation in text); Judgment dismissing the complaint, *Baker* (Dec. 19, 1997) (second quotation).

19. Eskridge interview of the Bensens.

20. David Goodman, *A More Civil Union*, Mother Jones, July–Aug. 2000 (quotations in text); *Brigham v. State*, 692 A.2d 384 (Vt. 1997) (invalidating the state's formula for school funding).

21. Eskridge interview of Robinson.

22. In this and the next three paragraphs of text, our description of, and quotations from, the *Baker* oral argument are based on the videotape made of that argument. See also Moats, *Civil Wars*, 130–138.

23. See Richard Posner, *Sex and Reason*, 310–312 (1992) (stamp-of-approval arguments against marriage equality accepted by respected scholar and federal judge).

24. Our account of the Vermont Supreme Court's deliberations in *Baker* are based upon off-the-record conversations with knowledgeable observers and participants.

25. *Baker v. State*, 744 A.2d 864, 879 (Vt. 1999) (quotation in text); *San Antonio Independent School District v. Rodriguez*, 411 U.S. 1, 98–99 (1973) (Marshall, J., dissenting) (synthesizing from the Supreme Court's cases a three-factor approach very similar to the one in *Baker*). See William Eskridge Jr., *Some Effects of Identity-Based Social Movements on Constitutional Law in the Twentieth Century*, 100 Mich. L. Rev. 2062, 2269–2279 (2002).

26. *Baker*, p. 887 (quotations in text).

27. The quotations are taken from William Eskridge interviews of the plaintiff couples and of Beth Robinson in Burlington, VT (October 2000). See also Moats, *Civil Wars*, 1–14.

28. John Flowers, *Same-Sex Ruling Celebrated*, Addison Independent, Dec. 23, 1999 (Angell quotation); Abbey Duke, *Opponents Gather Forces for Messy Battle with the Legislature*, Burlington Free Press, Dec. 22, 1999 (TIP quotation). Reverend Bensen felt that the release of the decision just days before Christmas discouraged popular mobilization. Our discussions with court personnel suggest that the disagreements among the justices and the opinion-writing process were responsible for the delays.

29. Adam Lisberg and Nancy Remsen, *Legislators Embrace Idea of "Domestic Partnership,"* Burlington Free Press, Dec. 21, 1999; Jack Hoffman, *Poll: Majority Say No to Same-Sex Benefits*, Rutland Herald, Jan. 2000.

30. The discussion of the deliberations of the house judiciary committee in the text and in the next nine paragraphs is largely taken from William Eskridge Jr., *Equality Practice: Civil Unions and the Future of Gay Rights*, 57–82 (2002). See Moats, *Civil Wars*, 150–152.

31. Memorandum from Thomas Little, chair, to house judiciary committee members, Jan. 4, 2000 (quotations in text).

32. Moats, *Civil Wars*, 157–159 (first quotation in text); Michael Mello, *Legalizing Gay Marriage*, 45–48 (2004) (second quotation).

33. Nancy Cott, *Public Vows: A History of Marriage and the Nation* (2000).

34. Moats, *Civil Wars*, 164–179.

35. Transcript of Vermont House Judiciary Committee hearing, Feb. 9, 2000 (quotations in text); Eskridge interview of Murray (firsthand account).

36. Transcript of Vermont House Judiciary Committee hearing (quotation in text); William Eskridge interview of Tom Little, Burlington, VT (Oct. 2000); Thomas Little, "Summary: Work of the House Judiciary Committee for the Week of February 8–11, 2000."

37. Tom Little's early drafts of a marriage alternative used the term *domestic partnership*, but the last draft or two ended up with *civil union*. See Eskridge, *Equality Practice* (original account of the origins of the term "civil unions" and the deliberations and debate in the Vermont legislature). Although they favored marriage, the minority position within the committee, Robinson and Murray worked with Little and his staff to develop and draft the civil unions bill.

38. Eskridge interview of Robinson; Eskridge telephone interview of Murray.

39. Mello, *Legalizing Gay Marriage*, 48–73 (describing town hall meetings and quoting letters to newspapers).

40. Mello, *Legalizing Gay Marriage*, 82–83; Eskridge telephone interview of Murray.

41. In this and subsequent paragraphs, the description and quotations from the house debates on H. 847 on March 15, 2000, are taken from the audiotapes of those debates, which are available from the Vermont legislature.

42. Ross Sneyd, *Lippert Gives an Impassioned Plea for Justice*, Valley News, March 16, 2000 (quotations in text).

43. The legislative votes in this chapter are taken from Vermont Legislative Bill Tracking System, *Rollcall Vote Detail, 1999–2000 Legislative Session, H.0847: Civil Unions*.

44. Sheltra represented the civil unions bill as encouraging activity (sodomy) that "causes disease and STDs," including AIDS. The house speaker asked Sheltra to stick to the subject of the debate, and she then argued that civil unions would contribute to the "tearing down of traditional marriage." As before, the quotations in the text are taken from the audiotapes of the house debate, available from the Vermont legislature.

45. Mello, *Legalizing Gay Marriage*, 88–93 (all quotations in text; riveting account of TIP's ad and letter campaign after the house vote).

46. Moats, *Civil Wars*, 224–226 (quotation in text).

47. The quotations in the text and in the next paragraph are taken from transcripts of the senate judiciary committee's hearings.

48. Mello, *Legalizing Gay Marriage*, 102–103. See Moats, *Civil Wars*, 230–233; William Eskridge telephone interview of Richard Sears (March 21, 2017).

49. Eskridge telephone interview of Sears.

50. In the text and in the next four paragraphs, the description and quotations from the senate debates on H. 847 and various amendments on April 18–19, 2000, are taken from the audiotapes of those debates, which are available from the Vermont legislature. The Sears anecdote was inspired by Robert Bolt, *A Man for All Seasons*, 65–67 (1962).

51. An Act Relating to Civil Unions (H. 847), 2000 Vt. Laws, Act No. 91.

52. After some complaining, almost all of the county clerks agreeably issued civil union licenses starting July 1, 2000. The first couple joined in civil union was Carolyn Conrad and Kathleen Peterson of Brattleboro; they received their civil union license at 12:01 a.m. See Mello, *Legalizing Gay Marriage*, 126–131.

53. Gerald Rosenberg, *The Hollow Hope: Can Courts Bring About Social Change?* (2d ed. 2008) (applying the famous backlash hypothesis to the same-sex marriage debate). But see William Eskridge Jr., *Backlash Politics: How Constitutional Litigation Has Advanced Marriage Equality in the United States*, 93 B.U.L. Rev. 275 (2013) (arguing that *Baker* and other same-sex marriage decisions had a frontlash effect that was ultimately more important).

54. Our accounts of hot versus cold anger and the Take Back Vermont movement draw from Eskridge interview of the Bensens.

55. Carey Goldberg, *Vermont Residents Split over Civil Unions Law*, New York Times, Sept. 3, 2000 (first quotation in text); Heather Stephenson, *Opponents Target the November Election*, Rutland Herald, July 5, 2000 (second quotation). At the rally, Steve Cable linked homosexuality to a list of social ills, from decreased use of seat belts to increased alcoholism, drug use, AIDS, and child abuse.

56. Elizabeth Mehren, *Voters Oust 5 Who Backed Vermont Civil Union Law*, Los Angeles Times, Sept. 14, 2000.

57. Mello, *Legalizing Gay Marriage*, 142–192 (what's wrong with civil unions). Compare Moats, *Civil Wars* (largely celebratory account of the civil unions law).

58. On equality practice and the virtues of incremental reform, see Eskridge, *Equality Practice*, 127–158; Kathleen Hull, *Same-Sex Marriage: The Cultural Politics of Love and Law*, 204–208 (2006) (defending the civil unions law in a larger context of Eskridge's "equality practice" approach); Kees Waaldijk, *Small Change: How the Road to Same-Sex Marriage Got Paved in the Netherlands*, in Robert Wintemute and Mads Andenaes, eds., *Legal Recognition of Same-Sex Partnerships* (2001).

59. Eskridge interview of Robinson.

8. The Cinderella Moment

1. The Bonauto biography is drawn from conversations with Mary Bonauto in Boston and in Portland, Maine, over a two-year period (from 2016 to 2018) and a telephone conversation between Christopher Riano and Nancy Rabinowitz in 2017.

2. Act of Nov. 15, 1989, ch. 516, 1989 Mass. Acts 796. See § 19, 1989 Mass. Acts at 803 (marriage proviso); Peter Cicchino et al., *Sex, Lies and Civil Rights: A Critical History of the Massachusetts Gay Civil Rights Bill,* 26 Harv. C.R.-C.L. L. Rev. 549 (1991).

3. *Bezio v. Patenaude,* 410 N.E.2d 1207, 1215–1216 (Mass. 1980) (following GLAD amicus supporting custody rights for lesbian and gay parents); Marie-Amélie George, *Agency Nullification: Defying Bans on Gay and Lesbian Foster and Adoptive Parents,* 51 Harv. C.R.-C.L. L. Rev. 363, 384–397 (2016) (account of the Babets-Jean case and the foster-care ban); *Adoption of Tammy,* 619 N.E.2d 315 (Mass. 1993) (approving second-parent adoption); *Adoption of Susan,* 619 N.E.2d 323 (Mass. 1993) (GLAD's companion case); *E.N.O. v. L.M.M.,* 711 N.E.2d 886 (Mass. 1999) (approving child visitation rights for a lesbian de facto parent).

4. Governor William Weld, Executive Order No. 340, Comm. of Mass. (1992); MCC, "Statement on Benefits Package for Homosexual Partners" (Oct. 9, 1992) (criticizing Weld's order); Testimony of Gerald D'Avolio, executive director, MCC, before the joint legislative committee on insurance, April 9, 1997 (opposing domestic partnership bill).

5. William Eskridge Skype interview of Arline Isaacson (Jan. 13, 2018).

6. In addition to our interviews of Mary Bonauto, Anne Stanback, Beth Robinson, and Susan Murray, see Bonauto, *Equality and the Impossible: State Constitutions and Marriage,* 68 Rutgers U.L. Rev. 1481 (2016).

7. MCC, "Family: The Key to a Healthy Society" (1991) (opposing gay marriage or domestic partnerships); Editorial, *A New Cultural Reality,* The Pilot, Nov. 21, 2003. On Catholic influence between 1948 and 1998, see Maurice Cunningham, *Catholics and the ConCon: The Church's Response to the Massachusetts Gay Marriage Decision,* J. Church & State 19, 22–26 (2004).

8. Josh Friedes, "The Beginning of the Movement" (May 17, 2014); William Eskridge interview of Josh Friedes, Palm Springs, CA (Aug. 8, 2017); and documents provided to us by Friedes.

9. H.B. 472, 181st Session Mass. Gen. Ct. (1999) (proposed junior-DOMA) (quotation in text); Adoption Act of March 29, 1999, H.B. 3965, 181st Session Mass. Gen. Ct.

10. William Eskridge Skype interviews of Arline Isaacson (January 13–14, 2018). Because earlier bills were blocked by a tight-knit cluster of Irish Catholic Conserva-Dems, the 1989 landmark statute came only after the caucus was able to play the legislative process game effectively.

11. Eskridge interview of Friedes, and documents provided by Friedes. Founding leaders of the Religious Coalition for the Freedom to Marry included Rev. Reine Abele (UCC), Rabbi Howard Berman (Reform Judaism), Rev. George Welles Jr. (Episcopal), and Rev. Kim Harvie (Unitarian).

12. H.B. 3375, 182d Session Mass. Gen. Ct. (2001) (proposed Super-DOMA) (quotation in text); Eskridge interview of Friedes, and documents provided to us by Friedes.

13. Mary Bonauto, Goodridge *in Context,* 40 Harv. C.R.-C.L. L. Rev. 23–26 (2004); Eskridge Skype interview of Isaacson (Jan. 13, 2018).

14. Bonauto, Goodridge *in Context*, 31–32 (quotation in text).

15. Bonauto, Goodridge *in Context*, 32 (quotation in text). See J. Edward Pawlick, *Libel by New York Times: Gay Marriage Didn't Just Happen in Massachusetts, It Was Engineered by the New York Times* (2003).

16. Verified complaint, *Goodridge v. Department of Public Health*, No. 011647A (Suffolk Super. Ct., filed April 11, 2001); Patricia Gozemba and Karen Kahn, with photographs by Marilyn Humphries, *Courting Equality: A Documentary History of America's First Legal Same-Sex Marriages* (2007); Bonauto, Goodridge *in Context*, 27.

17. Verified complaint, *Goodridge* (first quotation in text); Evan Thomas, *The War Over Gay Marriage*, Newsweek, July 6, 2003 (remaining quotations).

18. Verified complaint, *Goodridge* (descriptions of plaintiff couples); MCC, "Suit Seeks Sanction for Relationship with No Bounds" (April 12, 2001) (quotations in text).

19. MCM, Marriage Protection Amendment (July 2001) (quotation in text); MCM, *MCM Announces Constitutional Amendment: People Will Have a Voice in the Process* (press release, July 31, 2001).

20. Laura Kiritsy, *Both Sides Square Off on Marriage Ban*, Bay Windows, Aug. 10, 2001 (first quotation in text); MCM, *Acting Governor Expands Partner Benefits: Costs Will Unfairly Burden the Taxpayers of the Commonwealth* (press release, Aug. 16, 2001) (second quotation).

21. Brief amici curiae Massachusetts Gay and Lesbian Political Caucus in support of respondents, *Doe v. Reed*, Docket No. 09-0559 (US Supreme Court, filed April 10, 2010), 18–33 and appendices (recounting the signature fraud for the 2001 constitutional initiative); Joshua Israel, *Marriage Equality Almost Didn't Happen: The Strange Tale of How It Started*, ThinkProgress, Dec. 23, 2015.

22. Testimony of Attorney General Tom Reilly, joint committee on public service, Massachusetts General Court, April 10, 2002 (quotation in text).

23. Eskridge Skype interview of Isaacson (Jan. 13, 2018).

24. Letter from Senator Jacques to every member of the Massachusetts General Court, April 9, 2002; FMCM, *Love Makes a Family, Laws Should Protect Them: Stop SuperDOMA, H. 4840, Vote NO!* (April 9, 2002), GLAD Archives (stories and quotations in text).

25. H.B. 4840, 182d Session Mass. Gen. Ct. (2002) (proposed Super-DOMA constitutional amendment); William Eskridge and Christopher Riano telephone interview of Cheryl Jacques (July 2015); William Eskridge telephone interview of Tom Birmingham (Jan. 29, 2016).

26. Eskridge Skype interview of Isaacson (Jan. 14, 2018).

27. Eskridge Skype interview of Isaacson (Jan. 14, 2018); Eskridge and Riano telephone interview of Jacques (quotation in text).

28. Spotlight Team (Matt Carroll, Sasha Pfeiffer, and Michael Rezendes) articles, starting with *Cardinal Allowed Abuse by Priest for Years*, Boston Globe, Jan. 6, 2002.

29. Mass. Const. amend. 48, part 4, § 2 (the process for initiative amendments); *Opinion of the Justices to the Acting Governor*, 780 N.E.2d 1232 (Mass. Dec. 20, 2002) (interpreting Article 48). See also *Answer of the Justices to the Senate*, 780 N.E.2d 444 (Mass. Dec. 20, 2002) (declining to answer the senate's largely hypothetical questions).

30. *Marcoux v. Attorney General*, 375 Mass. 63, 65 n.4 (1978) (quotation in text) (applying rational basis with bite but upholding a regulation of marijuana); Bonauto, Goodridge *in Context*, 34–37.

31. Amicae curiae brief of professors of marriage, family, and the law, *Goodridge* (No. SJC-08860, filed Nov. 8, 2002); Brief of the Massachusetts Psychiatric Society et al., *Goodridge* (No. SJC-08860, filed Nov. 8, 2002) (amicus brief joined by seven professional associations and four doctors). See Nancy Cott, *Public Vows: A History of Marriage and the Nation* (2000); Carlos Ball, *The Right to Be Parents: LGBT Parenthood and the Transformation of the Family* (2012).

32. Eskridge interviews of Bonauto (Dec. 13, 2017) and Isaacson (via Skype, Jan. 14, 2018).

33. Decision Research, *Freedom to Marry Coalition: Massachusetts Survey Report* (2003), GLAD Archives. In the following paragraphs, we draw from and quote off-the-record interviews of SJC insiders.

34. Roderick Ireland, *In* Goodridge's *Wake: The Political, Public, and Personal Repercussions of the Massachusetts Marriage Equality Cases*, 85 NYU L. Rev. 1417, 1435–1436 (2010). Our characterizations of the seven justices who participated in *Goodridge* are taken from personal interactions with four of the justices and off-the-record conversations with SJC insiders.

35. Emily Bazelon, *A Bold Stroke*, Legal Affairs, May–June 2004 (quotation in text).

36. *A.Z. v. B.Z.*, 725 N.E.2d 1051, 1059 (Mass. 1980) (quotation in text).

37. The description and quotations in text and in the next two paragraphs are taken from transcript of the oral argument in *Goodridge*, SJC Docket No. 08860 (March 4, 2003), GLAD Archives.

38. *Goodridge v. Department of Public Health*, 798 N.E.2d 941, 949 (Mass. 2003) (Marshall's plurality opinion), quoting *Lawrence v. Texas*, 539 U.S. 558 (2003).

39. *Goodridge*, p. 962 (Marshall), quoting *Romer v. Evans*, 517 U.S. 620, 633 (1996).

40. *Goodridge*, p. 963 (Marshall) (first quotation in text), p. 968 (second quotation).

41. *Goodridge*, pp. 969–970 (Marshall), following *Halpern v. Toronto*, [2003] O.A.C. 276 (Ontario, Canada).

42. *Goodridge*, pp. 970–974 (Greaney's concurring opinion), pp. 974–978 (Spina's dissent), pp. 978–983 (Sosman's dissent), pp. 983–1005 (Cordy's dissent).

43. Ireland, *In* Goodridge's *Wake*, 1421–1422, 1431 (quotations in text).

44. MCC, "Marriage in Massachusetts: Crisis and Challenge" (Jan. 2004) (first quotations in text); Massachusetts bishops' statement on marriage (mailer, Jan. 16, 2004);

Congregation for the Doctrine of the Faith, "Considerations Regarding Proposals to Give Legal Recognition to Unions between Homosexual Persons" (2003).

9. Cinderella Under Siege

1. William Eskridge Skype interview of Arline Isaacson (Jan. 15, 2018).

2. Dave Denison, *Tom Finneran Is in Control,* Commonwealth: Politics, Ideas, and Civic Life in Massachusetts, Winter 1997 (quotation in text).

3. Staff, *Romney: I'll Be Better Than Ted for Gay Rights,* Bay Windows, Aug. 25, 1994; Stephanie Mencimer, *Mitt Romney's Big, Gay Olympics,* Mother Jones, July 31, 2012.

4. Frank Phillips, *AG Suggests Bill: Same-Sex Benefits Without Marriage,* Boston Globe, Nov. 21, 2003, A1; *Opinion of the Justices to the Senate,* 802 N.E.2d 565 (Mass. Feb. 4, 2004) (quotation in text, from majority opinion), pp. 571–572 (Sosman's dissent), pp. 580–581 (Cordy's dissent); Mary Bonauto, Goodridge *in Context,* 40 Harv. CR-CL L. Rev. 1, 45–48 (2005).

5. Governor Mitt Romney, *A Citizen's Guide to Protecting Marriage,* Wall Street Journal, Feb. 5, 2004. On the meeting between Romney and the plaintiffs, see Marc Solomon, *Winning Marriage: The Inside Story of How Same-Sex Couples Took on the Politicians and Pundits—and Won,* 21–24 (2015); William Eskridge and Christopher Riano interview of Mary Bonauto, Portland, ME (July 2016).

6. Frank Phillips, *SJC Ruling Aftermath; Travaglini Will Call Convention, Promises Vote on Gay Marriage Amendment,* Boston Globe, Feb. 7, 2004 (quotations in text).

7. Letter from Senate President Robert Travaglini and House Speaker Thomas Finneran to colleagues, Feb. 10, 2004; Yvonne Abraham, *National and Local Lobbying Efforts Ratcheted Up,* Boston Globe, Feb. 11, 2004, B6.

8. Rick Klein, *The Constitutional Convention: Impassioned Arguments/Oratory,* Boston Globe, Feb. 12, 2004, B8; Frank Phillips, *The Constitutional Convention: The Governor's Role,* Boston Globe, Feb. 13, 2004.

9. Frank Phillips and Raphael Lewis, *Two Marriage Amendments Fail,* Boston Globe, Feb. 12, 2004, A1.

10. Our quotations from the Feb. 12 session are taken from a transcript of the audiotape, http://www.anderkoo.com/ma_constitutional_convention?wid=138&func =view&pn=5.

11. Solomon, *Winning Marriage,* 35–36; Bonauto, Goodridge *in Context,* 54–55.

12. Solomon, *Winning Marriage,* 36–38 (quotations in text).

13. Letter from Mary Ann Glendon et al. to MCC, "Legal Analysis of the Finneran-Travaglini Amendment" (March 5, 2004) (quotation in text).

14. Video of Walsh's speech, https://www.youtube.com/watch?v=xclwybomHxU (quotations in text); Email from Mary Bonauto to William Eskridge, Jan. 28, 2019.

15. Rick Klein, *Vote Ties Civil Unions to Gay-Marriage Ban; Romney to Seek Stay of SJC Order,* Boston Globe, March 30, 2004 (quotation in text); Raphael Lewis and Yvonne

Abraham, *In Crucial Shift, Governor Sways 15 in GOP to Support Measure*, Boston Globe, March 30, 2004; Raphael Lewis, *Same-Sex Marriage Ban Loses Ground*, Boston Globe, Nov. 5, 2004, B1, B4 (Rouse estimate).

16. Press statement of Governor Mitt Romney, March 29, 2004 (quotations in text). See Raphael Lewis, *Romney Cites Gay-Marriage Tangles*, Boston Globe, April 16, 2004; Pam Belluck, *Romney Won't Let Gay Outsiders Marry in Massachusetts*, New York Times, April 25, 2004.

17. *Largess v. Supreme Judicial Court*, 317 F. Supp. 2d 77 (D. Mass. May 13, 2004), aff'd, 373 F.3d 219 (1st Cir. 2004); Bonauto, *Goodridge in Context*, 56–60; Frank Phillips and Kathleen Burge, *Reilly Gives Governor a Hurdle; Reilly Rebuffs Romney on Possible SJC Appeal*, Boston Globe, March 30, 2004; Elizabeth Mehren, *For Massachusetts Gays, the Wedding Countdown*, Los Angeles Times, May 16, 2004.

18. Scott Greenberger and Yvonne Abraham, *Gay-Marriage Rule Eased: Romney Aide Says Clerks Have Discretion on Residency Proof*, Boston Globe, May 5, 2004; Frank Phillips and Yvonne Abraham, *Defiance, Rebuke on Gay-Marriage: Romney Aide Rips Provincetown*, Boston Globe, May 12, 2004. See Amy Contrada, *Mitt Romney's Deception: His Stealth Promotion of "Gay Rights" and "Gay Marriage" in Massachusetts* (2011) (MassResistance's condemnation of Romney for not bending the legal rules to undermine gay marriage rulings).

19. Pam Belluck, *Hundreds of Same-Sex Couples Wed in Massachusetts*, New York Times, May 18, 2004 (quotation in text).

20. Tovia Smith, *Lawyer Reflects on Nation's First Gay Marriages: "The Cage Had Been Lifted,"* Morning Edition, National Public Radio, May 15, 2014 (quotations in text).

21. Mass. Gen. Laws ch. 207, §§ 11–12 (1913 law barring licenses to couples residing in states where their marriage was illegal; repealed by Act of July 31, 2008).

22. Greg O'Brien, *Finneran Continues to Live Life His Way*, Dorchester Reporter, Aug. 7, 2007; Maurice Cunningham, *A Christian Coalition for Catholics? The Massachusetts Model*, 51 Rev. Religious Research 55 (2009).

23. William Eskridge telephone interview of Kris Mineau (Feb. 5, 2016); Helen Mooradkanian, *Hero in Our Midst: Colonel Kris Mineau, USAF (Ret.): Valley Patriot of the Month*, Valley Patriot, March 2012 (first quotation in text); Dick Rose, *Bailout*, Christian Life, Jan. 1984 (remaining quotations).

24. On the November 2004 "Do or Die Election," see Solomon, *Winning Marriage*, 56–78; Cunningham, *Christian Coalition for Catholics*, 59–64.

25. Solomon, *Winning Marriage*, 56–67.

26. Tommy Duggan, *Romney Endorses Marasco*, Valley Patriot, Nov. 2004 (quotation in text).

27. Cunningham, *Christian Coalition for Catholics*, 62–64; Jaime McCauley, "On the Right Side of History: How Lesbian and Gay Activists Galvanized Culture and Politics to Make Massachusetts the First State with Legal Same-Sex Marriage," 264 (PhD dissertation, University of Windsor, 2012) (quoting Daffin).

28. MFI, "Massachusetts Initiative Petition for a Constitutional Amendment to Protect Marriage" (June 16, 2005).

29. Eskridge telephone interview of Mineau (quotation in text); Yvonne Abraham, *No Court Ruling on Same-Sex Marriage*, Boston Globe, Nov. 30, 2004, B6 (Travaglini's toast at Barrios's wedding).

30. Eskridge telephone interview of Mineau (quoting Romney); Cunningham, *Christian Coalition for Catholics*, 64–65.

31. Mass. Const., art. 48, part II, § 2 (quotation in text); Letter from Assistant Attorney General Peter Sacks to Gary Buseck and Jennifer Levi, Sept. 7, 2005 (rejecting GLAD's constitutional challenge to the MFI initiative); *Schulman v. Attorney General*, 850 N.E.2d 505 (Mass. July 10, 2006) (agreeing with the attorney general), p. 512 (quotation in text from Greaney's concurring opinion).

32. Eskridge Skype interview of Isaacson.

33. Eskridge Skype interview of Isaacson (the caucus's strategy and Travaglini's role).

34. *Doyle v. Secretary of the Commonwealth*, 858 N.E.2d 1090 (Mass. 2006); Eskridge Skype interview of Isaacson.

35. Solomon, *Winning Marriage*, 98–101 (quotation in text); Eskridge Skype interview of Isaacson.

36. Email from Marc Solomon to William Eskridge, May 4, 2019; Solomon, *Winning Marriage*, 102–105. For astute race-by-race analyses by MassResistance, a family values group, see http://www.massresistance.org/docs/govto6/election06/general _races.html.

37. Solomon, *Winning Marriage*, 105–107, 110–111, 114–115, 121–123 (quotation in text).

38. Memorandum from Mary Bonauto and Gary Buseck to Marc Solomon, "Meeting with Senator Rosenberg" (April 6, 2007), GLAD Archives; Letter from Mary Bonauto and Gary Buseck to Senator Michael Morrissey, "The Amendment and Legislative Prerogatives" (June 1, 2007), GLAD Archives. See also memorandum from GLAD to Massachusetts attorney general's office, "The Pending Marriage Amendment: Its Constitutional Vulnerabilities" (April 27, 2007).

39. Solomon, *Winning Marriage*, 124–127 (quotation in text).

40. Solomon, *Winning Marriage*, 128–130; Eskridge telephone interview of Mineau.

41. Solomon, *Winning Marriage*, 137–139 (quotation in text).

42. Solomon, *Winning Marriage*, 139–140 (quotation in text).

43. Eskridge telephone interview of Mineau (quotations in text).

44. The data are taken from the Centers for Disease Control, State Tables.

45. Email from Mary Bonauto to William Eskridge, Feb. 3, 2019 (quoting Rushing).

46. Mass. Gen. Laws ch. 207, §§ 11–12 (1913 law barring licenses to couples residing in states where their marriage was illegal), upheld in *Cote-Whiteacre v. Department of Public Health*, 844 N.E.2d 623 (March 30, 2006) (per curiam), repealed by Act of July 31, 2008.

10. The New Maginot Line

1. See William Eskridge interview of Maggie Gallagher, Mayflower Hotel, Washington, DC (May 13, 2015), as well as emails from Gallagher between May and December 2018.

2. Email from Maggie Gallagher to William Eskridge, May 11, 2018; Ayn Rand, *Atlas Shrugged* (1957).

3. Mark Oppenheimer, *The Making of Gay Marriage's Top Foe*, Salon, Feb. 8, 2012 (quotations in text from Gallagher and her Yale boyfriend).

4. Email from Gallagher to Eskridge (quotation in text).

5. Maggie Gallagher, *Enemies of Eros: How the Sexual Revolution Is Killing Family, Marriage, and Sex and What We Can Do About It*, 270–271 (1989) (quotation in text).

6. William Eskridge and Christopher Riano interview of David Blankenhorn, New York (March 13, 2016); Email from Gallagher to Eskridge (quotation in text). See David Blankenhorn, *Fatherless America: Confronting Our Most Urgent Social Problem* (1996).

7. Keith Fournier, *In Defense of Marriage*, Law and Justice (American Center for Law and Justice), Jan. 1997, 4–5 (quotation in text).

8. For Gallagher's theory of the marriage-based state, we drew from conversations, interviews, and emails we enjoyed with her, as well as her books and articles, especially Maggie Gallagher, *What Is Marriage For? The Public Purposes of Marriage Law*, 62 La. L. Rev. 773 (2001).

9. Linda Waite and Maggie Gallagher, *The Case for Marriage: Why Married People Are Happier, Healthier, and Better Off Financially*, 186, 200 (2000).

10. Coalition for Marriage, Family, and Couples Education; Institute for American Values; and Religion, Culture, and Family Project, University of Chicago Divinity School, *The Marriage Movement: A Statement of Principles*, 9 (2000) (quotations in text). See Andrew Cherlin, *Marriage, Divorce, Remarriage* (1992); James Q. Wilson, *The Marriage Problem: How Our Culture Has Weakened Families* (2002). Among the signatories of *The Marriage Movement* were sociologists Bill Doherty, Steven Nock, David Popenoe, Linda Waite, Judith Wallerstein; students of religion and ethics such as Jean Bethke Elshtain, Richard John Neuhaus, John Witte Jr.; policy theorists James Q. Wilson, Bill Galston, Wade Horn; and family law professors David Orgon Coolidge, Mary Ann Glendon, Katherine Spaht, and Lynn Wardle.

11. Coalition for Marriage, Family, and Couples Education et al., *Marriage Movement*, 10–13 (third-party effects of the decline of marriage), 19–20, 22–23 (proposed reforms). See Judith Wallerstein, Julia Lewis, and Sandra Blakeslee, *The Unexpected Legacy of Divorce* (2000).

12. Gallagher, *What Is Marriage For?*, 781–782 (first quotations in text); Waite and Gallagher, *Case for Marriage*, 200–201 (last quotation).

13. Anne Morse, *Conservative Heavyweight: The Remarkable Mind of Professor Robert P. George*, Crisis, Sept. 2003, 36–42 (quotations in text). We also drew from a telephone

interview of Robby George's high school classmate and from informal conversations with him and his former students over the years. Professor George cordially declined our request for a formal interview.

14. John Finnis, *Natural Law and Natural Rights* (1980); John Finnis, *Law, Morality, and "Sexual Orientation,"* 69 Notre Dame L. Rev. 1049 (1994) (natural law philosophy, drawing heavily from Georgetown theologian Germain Grisez).

15. Robert George, *Marriage and the Illusion of Moral Neutrality*, in T. William Boxx and Gary Quinlivan, eds., *Political Order and Culture: Towards the Renewal of Civilization*, 114–127 (1998); Robert George, *Making Men Moral: Civil Liberties and Public Morality* (1993); Robert George, *In Defense of Natural Law* (1999).

16. David Kirkpatrick, *The Conservative-Christian Big Thinker*, New York Times Magazine, Dec. 16, 2009 (quoting George); Finnis, *Law, Morality, and "Sexual Orientation,"* 1065–1066.

17. Andrew Koppelman, *The Gay Rights Question in Contemporary American Law*, 80–93 (2002); Andrew Koppelman, *Is Marriage Inherently Heterosexual?*, 42 Am. J. Jurisprudence 51 (1997); Stephen Macedo, *Homosexuality and the Conservative Mind*, 84 Geo. L.J. 261 (1995).

18. Memorandum from Lynn Wardle to Elder Marlin Jensen, chair, SGM [same-gender marriage] committee, "A Proposal to Amend the U.S. Constitution to Prohibit Same-Sex Marriage" (Oct. 19, 1998), Prince Archives (quotation in text); Lynn Wardle, *The Proposed Federal Marriage Amendment and the Risks to Federalism in Family Law*, 2 U. St. Thomas L.J. 137 (2004).

19. Karen Peterson, *Man Behind the Marriage Amendment*, USA Today, April 12, 2004 (first quotation in text); Faye Fiore, *Lawyer Was Ready for the Marriage Debate*, Los Angeles Times, Feb. 15, 2004 (second and third quotations).

20. Alliance for Marriage, C-SPAN press conference, Aug. 20, 2000, https://www.c-span.org/video/?159012-1/marriage-family-issues (quotation in text).

21. Jacob Schlesinger, *How Gay Marriage Thrust 2 Outsiders onto Center Stage*, Wall Street Journal, Feb. 23, 2004; Franklin Foer, *Marriage Counselor: Matt Daniels Believes He's Found a Solution to the Political Problem of Gay Marriage. So Why Do His Fellow Conservatives Want to Divorce Him?*, Atlantic Monthly, March 2004; Emails from Gerard Bradley to William Eskridge, June 21 and 30, 2016 (quotation in text); Robert George and Gerard Bradley, *Marriage and the Liberal Imagination*, 84 Geo. L.J. 301 (1995).

22. William Eskridge telephone interview of Gerard Bradley (April 25, 2016) (quotation in text); Dan Gilgoff, *The Jesus Machine*, 145 (2006) (Daniels's opposition to a sweeping amendment).

23. Robert Bork, *Stop Courts from Imposing Gay Marriage: Why We Need a Constitutional Amendment*, Wall Street Journal, Aug. 7, 2001 (first quotation in text); Email from Gerard Bradley to William Eskridge, April 29, 2016 (second quotation, emphasis in the original); Robert George, *The 28th Amendment*, National Review, July 23, 2001.

24. Alliance for Marriage, *Legal Impact of the Federal Marriage Amendment* (May 19, 2003), http://www.allianceformarriage.org/reports/fma/colorchart.cfm.

25. See Gilgoff, *Jesus Machine*, 146–147 (FRC opposition to FMA and quotation in text).

26. Collected talking points for Marriage Leaders' Summit, Osprey Point (ca. March 2003) (memo from Elizabeth Marquardt) (quotation in text).

27. Eskridge and Riano interview of Blankenhorn (quotations in text). In the next four paragraphs of text, our account, including quotations, of the dramatic conversation at Osprey Point is based upon our review of the conference's briefing book and the Eskridge and Riano interview of Blankenhorn.

28. Eskridge and Riano interview of Blankenhorn (first quotation in text); Eskridge interview of Gallagher (second quotation).

29. Email from Gerard Bradley to William Eskridge, April 21, 2016.

30. Congregation for the Doctrine of the Faith, "Considerations Regarding Proposals to Give Legal Recognition to Unions Between Homosexual Persons" ¶¶ 3–4, 10 (June 3, 2003) (initial quotations in text); Administrative committee, US Conference of Catholic Bishops, *Promote, Preserve, Protect Marriage* (Sept. 9, 2003) (last quotation).

31. Paul Weyrich, *The Arlington Group* (Dec. 3, 2004), http://www.renewamerica.com/columns/weyrich/041203 (quotation in text). Among the organizations present at the initial meeting of the Arlington Group were the American Family Association (represented by Wildmon); CWA (Rios); Focus on the Family (Dobson); the Free Congress Foundation (Weyrich); Coral Ridge Ministries (James Kennedy); the Southern Baptist Convention's Ethics & Religious Liberty Commission (Richard Land); the Home School Legal Defense Association (Michael Farris); Citizens for Community Values (Phil Burress); and, we speculate, the Christian Coalition and the Family Research Council.

32. Gilgoff, *Jesus Machine*, 137–141, 156–160 (quotations in text). In addition to the organizations earlier identified with the Arlington Group, subsequent meetings included the Institute for American Values committee (represented by Gary Bauer); the National Association of Evangelicals (Ted Haggard); Alliance Defense Fund (John Sears); Prison Fellowship Ministries (Chuck Colson); the Moral Majority (Jerry Falwell); CommunityHQ.com (Richard Viguerie); and Exodus International (Alan Chambers).

33. Schlesinger, *How Gay Marriage* (quotations in text); David Kirkpatrick, *Conservatives Using Issue of Gay Unions as a Rallying Tool*, New York Times, Feb. 8, 2004. See Gilgoff, *Jesus Machine*, 168; Email from Maggie Gallagher to William Eskridge, April 29, 2016.

34. For a detailed treatment of the Texas sodomy case, see Dale Carpenter, *Flagrant Conduct: The Story of* Lawrence v. Texas (2009).

35. Brief amicus curiae of the Family Research Council, Inc., and Focus on the Family in support of the respondent, *Lawrence v. Texas* (No. 02-102, filed Feb. 18, 2003), 2003 WL 470066.

36. Our discussion and quotations from the justices' conference in *Lawrence v. Texas* are based upon William Eskridge Jr., *Dishonorable Passions: Sodomy Laws in America, 1861–2003*, chap. 10 (2008), supplemented by off-the-record interviews for this volume.

37. William Eskridge interview of Stuart Delery, Washington, DC (March 2019); Letter from Justice Sandra Day O'Connor to Stuart Delery, Jan. 24, 2002 (quotation in text).

38. William Eskridge telephone interview of Hadley Arkes (April 2018).

39. *Planned Parenthood of Southeastern Pennsylvania v. Casey*, 505 U.S. 833, 851 (1992) (joint opinion) (quotation in text, reportedly written by Kennedy).

40. *Dudgeon v. United Kingdom*, No. 7525/76 (Eur. Ct. Hum. Rts. Oct. 22, 1981); William Eskridge conversation with former justice Anthony Kennedy (May 15, 2019); Brief of the Cato Institute as amicus curiae in support of the petitioners, *Lawrence* (No. 02-102, filed Jan. 16, 2003), 2003 WL 152342.

41. Friedrich Hayek, *The Constitution of Liberty*, chaps. 1, 6, 14 (1960); John Stuart Mill, *On Liberty*, chap. 4 (1859).

42. *Lawrence v. Texas*, 539 U.S. 558, 566–567 (2003) (quotations in text), pp. 567–573 (Cato-based history of sodomy laws). See Marc Spindleman, *Surviving* Lawrence v. Texas, 102 Mich. L. Rev. 1615, 1641–1642, n.124 (2004).

43. *Lawrence*, pp. 575–578 (quotations in text from Kennedy's majority opinion).

44. *Lawrence*, pp. 582, 584 (quotations in text from O'Connor's concurring opinion).

45. *Lawrence*, pp. 604–605 (quotations in text from Scalia's dissenting opinion).

46. Mark O'Keefe, *Religious Right, Frustrated Despite Friends in High Office, Rethinks Strategy*, Newhouse News Service, July 14, 2003; US Senate, Republican Policy Committee, Jon Kyl, chairman, "The Threat to Marriage from the Courts" (July 29, 2003).

47. What Is Needed to Defend the Bipartisan Defense of Marriage Act of 1996? Hearing before the Subcomm. on the Constitution, Civil Rights, and Property Rights, S. Comm. on the Judiciary, 108th Congress, p. 17 (Sept. 4, 2003) (quoting Coleman's testimony). Accord, September 2003 Senate hearing, p. 19 (Michael Farris's testimony); Less Faith in Judicial Credit: Are Federal and State Defense of Marriage Initiatives Vulnerable to Judicial Activism? Hearing before the Subcomm. on the Constitution, Civil Rights, and Property Rights, S. Comm. on the Judiciary, 109th Congress (April 13, 2005) (Bradley's and Wardle's testimony). But see September 2003 Senate hearing, pp. 20–21 (Dale Carpenter's testimony that DOMA was in no immediate peril).

48. September 2003 Senate hearing, pp. 13–14 (quotations in text from Gallagher's testimony); William Eskridge telephone interview of Glenn Stanton, Focus on the Family (May 28, 2015). The Reverend Raymond Hammond testified that the African American community has "paid a heavy price for the modern epidemic of family disintegration" and would be especially harmed by any further dilution in the social meaning of marriage. September 2003 Senate hearing, pp. 10–13.

49. Richard Wirthlin and Dee Allsop, Wirthlin Worldwide, "Marriage Strategy for Federal Marriage Amendment" (July 2015) (quotation in text); AFM press statement, *Introduction of the Federal Marriage Amendment in Congress*, May 15, 2002; AFM, C-SPAN press conference at US Capitol, Sept. 17, 2003; Wardle, *Proposed Federal Marriage Amendment*, 137, 146–148 (Knight and other conservatives opposed the FMA).

50. Mark O'Keefe, *Christian Right Frustrated by Lack of Political Progress*, Baptist Standard, July 25, 2003 (quoting Daniels).

51. A Proposed Constitutional Amendment to Preserve Traditional Marriage: Hearing before the S. Comm. on the Judiciary, 108th Cong., pp. 56–60 (March 23, 2004) (ABA testimony that the FMA would bar all forms of legislation, like creating civil unions, supporting lesbian and gay families).

52. David Kirkpatrick, *Conservative-Christian Big Thinker* (conference calls between Land-Dobson and the White House, with the latter committed to FMA endorsement by Feb. 3, 2003). See Gilgoff, *Jesus Machine*, 161–162.

53. Legal Threats to Traditional Marriage: Hearing before the Subcomm. on the Constitution, Civil Rights, and Property Rights, H. Comm. on the Judiciary, 108th Cong., p. 6 (April 22, 2004) (Dwight Duncan's testimony, making the Maginot Line analogy); The Federal Marriage Amendment (Musgrave Amendment): Hearing before the Subcomm. on the Constitution, Civil Rights, and Property Rights, H. Comm. on the Judiciary, 108th Cong., pp. 16–17 (May 13, 2004) (Bork's testimony); A Proposed Constitutional Amendment to Preserve Traditional Marriage: Hearing before the S. Comm. on the Judiciary, 108th Cong., pp. 38–40 (March 23, 2004) (Sunstein's testimony, quoted in text).

54. April 2004 House hearing, pp. 14–22 (Kurtz's testimony and statements). Compare Stanley Kurtz, *The End of Marriage in Scandinavia*, Weekly Standard, Feb. 2, 2004, with William Eskridge Jr. and Darren Spedale, *Gay Marriage—For Better or For Worse? What We've Learned from the Evidence*, chap. 5 (2006) (Scandinavian marriage rates increased and divorce rates fell after registered partnership laws). For the Dutch evidence, compare Stanley Kurtz, *Going Dutch?*, Weekly Standard, May 31, 2004, with Eurostat, *Marriages and Births in the Netherlands*, https://ec.europa.eu/eurostat /statistics-explained/index.php?title=Archive:Marriages_and_births_in_the _Netherlands.

55. Our description and quotations from the Senate's FMA debate are taken from the C-SPAN videos available for July 9 and 12–14, 2004.

56. Republicans voting against cloture on the FMA debate were Senators Campbell (Colorado), Chafee (Rhode Island), Collins (Maine), McCain (Arizona), Snowe (Maine), and Sununu (New Hampshire). Democrats voting for cloture were Senators Byrd (West Virginia), Miller (Georgia), and Nelson (Nebraska), all representing conservative Baptist states.

57. Gregory Prince, *Gay Rights and the Mormon Church: Intended Actions, Unintended Consequences*, 70–72 (2019); *Citizens for Equal Protection v. Bruning*, 368 F. Supp. 2d

980 (D. Neb. 2005) (applying *Romer* to overturn Initiative 416), rev'd, 455 F.3d 859 (8th Cir. 2006) (reinstating Initiative 416).

58. William Eskridge and Daniel Strunk interview of Lori Viars and friends, Cincinnati (March 2017); *168 Days: A Miracle*, https://www.youtube.com/watch?v=LVO-A8bwjHQ (part 1) and https://www.youtube.com/watch?v=aosOnLq9ffg (part 2).

59. Official ballot materials (pro and con) for Ohio Issue 1 (2004) (quotations in text); Daniel Pinello, *America's War on Same-Sex Couples and Their Families: And How the Courts Rescued Them*, 27–28 (2016).

60. Gilgoff, *Jesus Machine*, 184; Alan Cooperman and Thomas Edsall, *Evangelicals Say They Led Charge for the GOP*, Washington Post, Nov. 8, 2004.

61. On the 2004 Michigan Super-DOMA campaign, see Amy Stone, *Gay Rights at the Ballot Box* 93–95, 129–135 (2012); Glen Staszewski, *The Bait-and-Switch in Direct Democracy*, 2006 Wis. L. Rev. 17 (2006). See Christopher Riano telephone interview of Wendy DeBoer (Sept. 2018); *Constitutionality of City Providing Same-Sex Domestic Partnership Benefits*, Op. Mich. Att'y Gen. No. 7171 (Mar. 16, 2005), 2005 WL 639112 (broad interpretation of Proposal 2, preempting employer domestic partnership benefits), followed in *National Pride at Work v. Governor of Michigan*, 748 N.W.2d 524 (Mich. 2008). For a critique of the textual liberties taken in *Pride at Work*, see William Eskridge Jr. et al., *Case and Materials on Legislation and Regulation: Statutes and the Creation of Public Policy* (5th ed. 2014).

62. Draft Civil Marriage Equality Campaign Plan (Aug. 12, 2003) (quotations in text), Task Force Archives, circulated to NGLTF, HRC, FTM, GLAAD, GLSEN, ACLU, Lambda Legal, GLAD, and NCLR. For ballot campaign lessons from the 1990s, see Stone, *Gay Rights at the Ballot Box*, 68–73 (describing the "model campaign" inspired by Basic Rights Oregon); William Eskridge interview of Sayre (formerly Sarah) Reece, NGLTF, Washington, DC (Dec. 7, 2018) (lessons synthesized by David Fleischer of the Victory Fund and the NGLTF: start early, build big teams, be honest with voters, use lots of one-on-one contact).

63. Stone, *Gay Rights at the Ballot Box;* NGLTF, "Assessing How to Confront Marriage-Related Challenges Deploying Scarce Resources in the Most Effective Way Possible" (2003), Task Force Archives.

64. Sarah Reece, executive summary, Campaign 2004 exit report, "NO on the Amendment/Kentucky Families for Fairness" (March 2005), Task Force Archives; Decision Research, "Kentucky Statewide Survey Report" (Aug. 2, 2004); Eskridge interview of Reece.

65. Michael Klarman, *From the Closet to the Altar: Courts, Backlash, and the Struggle for Same-Sex Marriage*, 111–112 (2013) (reasons to think that the marriage initiative "might well" have cost Kerry Ohio). Cf. Jonathan Tilove, *Bush's Small Success with Black Voters Proved Crucial*, Newhouse News Service, Nov. 8, 2004 (if Kerry had polled the same percentage of blacks in Ohio as Gore, that would have meant a 110,000-vote swing). Former Massachusetts governor and US president Calvin Coolidge carried Ohio in 1924.

66. Ken Sherrill, "Same-Sex Marriage, Civil Unions, and the 2004 Election" (NGLTF Policy Institute 2004); D. A. Smith, *Was Rove Right? Ohio's Gay Marriage Ban and the 2004 Presidential Election,* in Samuel Bowler and Aaron Glazer, eds., *Direct Democracy's Impact on American Political Institutions* (2008).

67. Institute for Marriage Public Policy, *Same-Sex Marriage: Trends in Public Opinion* (2005) (surveying the major polls, 2003–2005); Klarman, *Closet to Altar,* 109–111 (marriage issue was helpful to Bunning's reelection and to Republicans who replaced Baptist-state Democratic senators).

68. Maggie Gallagher, *PAC Marriage,* National Review Online, May 3, 2005; Maggie Gallagher, *Banned in Boston,* Weekly Standard, May 15, 2006 (quotations in text); Witherspoon Institute, *Marriage and the Public Good: Ten Principles,* 1 (2008) (published version of 2006 statement). The Witherspoon Institute was established as a conservative think tank on the Princeton University campus, near Robby George's office.

69. C-SPAN, Washington Journal, interview of Maggie Gallagher, May 22, 2006, https://www.c-span.org/video/?192546-5/federal-marriage-amendment (quotations in text).

70. William Eskridge telephone interview of Maggie Gallagher (Dec. 19, 2018) (quotation in text).

11. The Winter of Love

1. See Ann Rostow, *NCLR Earns Its Stripes,* The Advocate, June 7, 2005. Among others also present at the Jan. 20 roundtable were Brad Sears of the Williams Institute; David Codell, a private lawyer; and law professors David Cruz, Isabelle Gunning, and Barbara Cox.

2. Williams Institute, "Marriage Litigation on Behalf of Same-Sex Couples in California: A Roundtable Discussion" (Jan. 10, 2003); Confidential memorandum from Toni Broaddus to roundtable participants, "California Polling Data" (Dec. 20, 2002).

3. See Scott Cummings and Douglas NeJaime, *Lawyering for Marriage Equality,* 57 UCLA L. Rev. 1235, 1274–1276 (2010).

4. William Eskridge telephone interview of Steve Kawa (Feb. 6, 2017); Text of President Bush's 2004 State of the Union Address (Jan. 20, 2004), https://www.washingtonpost.com/wp-srv/politics/transcripts/bushtext_012004.html (quotations in text).

5. The account and quotations in the text and in the next two paragraphs are drawn from William Eskridge's interviews of Kate Kendell, San Francisco (Jan. 5, 2017; Jan. 2, 2019), and of Therese Stewart, San Francisco (Aug. 3, 2017; Jan. 4, 2019). See Joan Walsh, *Winter of Law,* Salon, Feb. 26, 2004; Debra Chasnoff, director, *One Wedding and a Revolution* (New Days Films, 2014); Nathaniel Frank, *Awakening: How Gays and Lesbians Brought Marriage Equality to America,* 150–155 (2017); Daniel Pinello, *America's*

War Against Same-Sex Couples and Their Families: And How the Courts Rescued Them, 76–79 (2016).

6. Eskridge telephone interview of Kawa (quotation in text).

7. Eskridge 2017 interview of Kendell (quotations in text).

8. Eskridge 2017 interview of Kendell (first quotation in text); Cummings and NeJaime, *Lawyering,* 1278 (last quotations).

9. Email from Terry Stewart to William Eskridge, Sept. 6, 2017 (copy of revised marriage license).

10. Eskridge 2019 interview of Kendell (quotations in text); Chasnoff, *One Wedding* (Martin-Lyon wedding inside San Francisco City Hall).

11. Stuart Gaffney and John Lewis, *On the Road to Equality Nationwide,* in Marriage Equality USA, *The People's Victory: Stories from the Front Lines in the Fight for Marriage Equality,* 64–65 (2017) (quotations in text).

12. Therese Stewart, *The Story of* In re Marriage Cases: *Our Supreme Court's Role in Establishing Marriage Equality in California,* Calif. Sup. Ct. Hist. Soc'y Newsletter, Spring/Summer 2018, 4–5; Jeremy Quittner, *Gavin's Gay Gamble,* The Advocate, March 30, 2004.

13. Francie Grace, *New Mexico Jumps on the Gay Marriage Train,* Associated Press, Feb. 20, 2004 (quotations in text).

14. Beth Slovic, *Multnomah County Unleashes Gay Marriage,* Willamette Week, March 2004.

15. Eskridge attended services at Thomas Road Baptist Church during the Winter of Love, and the paraphrased quotations in text are based on his notes from the service.

16. Kelly St. John, *Archdiocese to Pay $16 Million/22 of 23 Cases About San Jose Priest Have Been Settled,* San Francisco Chronicle, July 10, 2005 (hundreds of lawsuits by victims of predatory priests after California relaxed its statute of limitations in 2002).

17. Mark Simon and Carla Marinucci, *Top State Democrats Criticize S.F. Mayor,* San Francisco Chronicle, Feb. 20, 2004 (quotations in text).

18. Joe Dignan, *Way Out Front,* Gay City, Feb. 26–March 3, 2004 (quotations in text from Barney Frank).

19. Stewart, *Story of* In re Marriage Cases, 5–6; Dean Murphy, *California Attorney General Pushed on Gay Marriage,* New York Times, Feb. 25, 2004.

20. *Gay Marriage a Wedge Between Father, Son,* Associated Press, April 5, 2004 (quotation in text); Matthew Baijko, *Gay Groups Press Lawmakers on Marriage,* Bay Area Reporter, April 14, 2004 (Knight's deathbed declaration).

21. Baltimore Gonzalez, *There Are Gay People Everywhere: The Fight for Marriage Equality in California's Central Valley,* in Marriage Equality USA, *People's Victory,* 77–78.

22. Evelyn Nieves, *Now Portland Is Gay-Marriage Capital,* Washington Post, March 19, 2004; *Li v. State,* 110 P.3d 91 (Ore. 2005) (voiding the three thousand marriage licenses issued by Multnomah County).

23. The data are taken from the San Francisco assessor's office.

24. Katrina Kimport, *Queering Marriage: Challenging Family Formation in the United States*, 20–21 (2014) (quotations in text); Marriage Equality USA, *People's Victory* (collection of first-person accounts).

25. Kimport, *Queering Marriage*, 33–34; Email from Terry Stewart to William Eskridge, Jan. 17, 2019.

26. Kimport, *Queering Marriage*, 59 (first quotation in text); Marriage Equality USA, *People's Victory*, 40 (second quotation).

27. Lambda Legal, "Overview of the California Supreme Court" (Jan. 2003), LA Lambda Archives (quotation in text). See *Sharon S. v. Superior Court*, 73 P.3d 554, 575 (Cal. 2003) (Baxter and Chin's opinion, concurring in the judgment allowing second-parent adoptions for lesbian and other unmarried couples); *Balyut v. Superior Court*, 12 Cal. 4th 826 (1996) (Baxter's majority opinion, invalidating police sting targeting gay men); *In re Mathew B.D.*, 232 Cal. App. 3d 1239 (1992) (Chin's majority opinion, denying surrogate mother parental rights in favor of the intended parents, the biological father and his wife).

28. Janice Rogers Brown, "A Lighter Shade of Pale," address to the Federalist Society, University of Chicago, April 20, 2000, http://ejournalofpoliticalscience.org/janicerogersbrown.html (quotation in text).

29. "It is important for the law to evolve in steps and not in great leaps and bounds." Lambda Legal, "Overview" (quoting Werdegar). See *Sharon S. v. Superior Court*, 73 P.3d 554 (Cal. 2003) (Werdegar's majority opinion, upholding second-parent adoption).

30. Lambda Legal, "Overview" (quotation in text). See *Curran v. Mt. Diablo Council of BSA*, 17 Cal.4th 670 (1998) (George's opinion for the court, finding that the Boy Scouts were not a "public accommodation" covered by the state anti-discrimination law).

31. Lambda Legal, "Overview" (quotation in text).

32. *Elisa B. v. Superior Court*, 37 Cal.4th 100, 117 P.3d 660 (2005); *Koebke v. Bernardo Heights Country Club*, 115 P.3d 1212 (Cal. 2005) (Moreno's majority opinion), pp. 1230–1233 (Werdegar's opinion, dissenting in part). See also *K.M. v. E.G.*, 117 P.3d 673 (Cal. 2005) (Moreno's majority opinion, again recognizing parental rights for two women).

33. Ron George, *Chief: The Quest for Justice in California*, 629–630 (2013) (quotations in text); *Lockyer v. City & County of San Francisco*, 95 P.3d 459, 462 (Cal. 2004) (George's opinion for the court).

34. *Lockyer*, pp. 503–508 (Kennard's partial dissenting opinion, arguing that the court should not invalidate the four thousand marriages without hearing the constitutional challenge), pp. 508–512 (Werdegar's partial dissenting opinion, similar), pp. 499–502 (Moreno's concurring opinion).

35. William Eskridge interview of Shannon Minter, Washington, DC (July 5, 2016) (first two quotations in text); Shannon Minter, *California Dreaming: Winning Marriage*

Equality in the California Courts, in Kevin Cathcart and Leslie Gabel-Brett, eds., *Love Unites Us: Winning the Freedom to Marry in America,* 145, 152 (2016) (last quotations).

36. George, *Chief,* 630 (quotation in text).

37. The discussion in the text is based upon our interviews of David Codell, Shannon Minter, Jenny Pizer, and Terry Stewart in Los Angeles and San Francisco and our telephone interviews of Geoff Kors.

38. *Knight v. Superior Court,* 26 Cal. Rptr. 3d 687, 689 (Ct. App. 2005) (review denied June 29, 2005) (upholding comprehensive domestic partnership as consistent with Proposition 22).

39. See our interviews of Shannon Minter, Terry Stewart, and David Codell, as well as Cummings and NeJaime, *Lawyering,* 1285–1289. The encounter of a Supreme Court justice with the sex discrimination argument was prompted by Eskridge a few years before the Winter of Love.

40. *In re Marriage Cases,* 49 Cal. Rptr. 3d 675, 706–714, 718–724 (Ct. App. 2006); William Eskridge interview of James Esseks, New York City (July 2016) (decision to appeal); George, *Chief,* 631 (supreme court's vote to take the *Marriage Cases*).

41. CBS News, *No to Gay Marriage in California,* March 7, 2000 (Leno's quotation in text); Eskridge telephone interview of Kors (EQCA divided on the issue but reaffirmed Kors's leadership).

42. Robert Salladay, *Assembly Goes Slow on Gay Marriage Bill,* Los Angeles Times, April 2, 2004.

43. California Assembly Committee on the Judiciary, report on A.B. 19 (Leno), April 26, 2005 (summarizing testimony in favor of A.B. 19 as well as hundreds of supporting organizations).

44. Report on A.B. 19 (identifying more than one hundred opponents, summarizing testimony against A.B. 19 and providing the quotations in text). See Michael Foust, *California Political Debate Over Same-Sex "Marriage" Intensifies,* SBC Life, Feb. 2005; Staff, *Voters Won't See Domestic-Partnership Rollback Initiatives on the November Ballot,* Capitol Weekly, May 25, 2006.

45. Joe Dignan, *Marriage at Issue in California,* Gay City, June 15–24, 2006 (Huerta's early support for the Leno bill).

46. Joe Dignan, *California Senate Poised on Marriage,* Gay City, Sept. 1–7, 2005 (quotations in text); Jordan Rau and Nancy Vogel, *State Senate Votes to Let Gays Marry,* Los Angeles Times, Sept. 2, 2005.

47. Dignan, *California Senate* (religious lobbying on the marriage bill); Archdiocese of Los Angeles, Office of the Archbishop, *Report to the People of God: Clergy Sexual Abuse Archdiocese of Los Angeles 1930–2003* (Feb. 17, 2004); Joe Mozingo and John Spano, *$660-Million Settlement Set in Priest Abuse,* Los Angeles Times, July 15, 2007 (payouts by the archdiocese for priest-abuse lawsuits).

48. William Eskridge telephone interview of Geoffrey Kors (Aug. 9, 2016).

49. Nancy Vogel, *Legislature OKs Gay Marriage,* Los Angeles Times, Sept. 7, 2005, A1.

50. Governor Arnold Schwarzenegger, veto statement for A.B. 849, Sept. 29, 2005 (quotations in text); Michael Finnegan and Maura Dolan, *Citing Prop 22, Gov. Rejects Gay Marriage Bill*, Los Angeles Times, Sept. 8, 2005.

51. California Senate Judiciary Committee, report on A.B. 43, p. 18 (July 10, 2007) (listing statements of opposition); California Assembly Committee on the Judiciary, report on A.B. 43, pp. 18–19 (April 10, 2007) (longer list in opposition, but not reporting any Catholic opposition).

52. Governor Arnold Schwarzenegger, veto statement for A.B. 43, Oct. 9, 2007 (quotation in text).

53. *Perez v. Sharp*, 32 Cal.2d 711, 720, 198 P.2d 17, 19 (1948) (quotations in text, from Traynor's plurality opinion); GLAAD, *Facts About Karen England*, https://www.glaad .org/cap/karen-england (England dismissed "gender identity" because it was nothing more than "expressing your gender whatever you feel that day").

54. Brief amicus curiae of William Eskridge in support of the parties challenging the marriage exclusion, pp. 1–2, *In re Marriage Cases* (Cal. Sup. Ct. No S147999, filed Oct. 4, 2007), 2007 WL 3307727 (detailed statement of California law).

55. Respondents' consolidated reply brief on the merits, p. 14, *Marriage Cases* (filed Aug. 17, 2007) (first quotation in text); Petitioners City & County of San Francisco opening brief on the merits, p. 50, *Marriage Cases* (filed April 3, 2007) (second quotation). Cf. *Sweatt v. Painter*, 339 U.S. 629, 634 (1950) (invalidating separate law school for blacks because the students did not enjoy the special "traditions and prestige" of the University of Texas).

56. George, *Chief,* 537, 545–546, 554–556, 658–659, 667–669 (process generally followed by the justices before oral argument); Oral argument, *Marriage Cases,* California Supreme Court, March 4, 2008, https://www.c-span.org/video/?199950-1/california -marriage-cases.

57. Association of Independent California Colleges and Universities, *AICCU Portrait of Alumni—Justice Carol Corrigan* (Aug. 19, 2015), https://www.aiccu.edu/2015/08 /19/aiccu-alumni-profile-justice-carol-corrigan/ (first quotations in text); Oral argument, *Marriage Cases* (quoting Corrigan's questions at oral argument).

58. George, *Chief,* 632 (quotations in text).

59. George, *Chief,* 636 (quotation in text).

60. *In re Marriage Cases*, 183 P.3d 384 (Cal. 2008). See William Eskridge Jr., *The California Supreme Court, 2007–2008—Foreword: The Marriage Cases, Reversing the Burden of Inertia in a Pluralist Democracy,* 97 Calif. L. Rev. 1785 (2009).

61. *Marriage Cases,* pp. 426–427 (majority opinion); George, *Chief,* 635 (quotation in text).

62. *Marriage Cases,* p. 433 (quotations in text from George's majority opinion).

63. Our account of the DeBoer-Rowse 2008 commitment ceremony is taken from conversations, emails, and interviews of Jayne Rowse, April DeBoer, and Wendy De-Boer between 2015 and 2018.

12. Latter-day Constitutionalists

1. See Lynn Wardle, *No Fault Divorce and the Divorce Conundrum*, 1991 BYU L. Rev. 79; Bruce Hafen, *The Constitutional States of Marriage, Kinship, and Sexual Privacy*, 81 Mich. L. Rev. 963 (1983).

2. The discussion and the quotations in the text and in the next two paragraphs, reporting on the conference on family law, are taken from Drake University Law School's published transcript of *Changing Perspectives of the Family* (April 16, 1994).

3. Bruce Hafen, *Individualism and Autonomy in Family Law: The Waning of Becoming*, 1991 BYU L. Rev. 1 (advocating a communitarian-based theory of family law).

4. See William Eskridge Jr., *Latter-Day Constitutionalism: Sexuality, Gender, and Mormons*, 2015 U. Ill. L. Rev. 1227.

5. Lynn Wardle, *The Potential Impact of Homosexual Parenting on Children*, 1997 U. Ill. L. Rev. 833, 844–848 (quotations in text); Monte Neil Stewart et al., *Marriage, Fundamental Premises, and the California, Connecticut, and Iowa Supreme Courts*, 2012 BYU L. Rev. 193, 243–256 (published version of a 2006 conference paper).

6. Lynn Wardle, *"Multiply and Replenish": Considering Same-Sex Marriage in Light of State Interests in Marital Procreation*, 24 Harv. J.L. & Pub. Pol'y 771, 779–780 (2001); Monte Neil Stewart, *Judicial Redefinition of Marriage*, 21 Can. J. Family L. 13, 47 (2004).

7. Wardle felt that the Hawai'i Reciprocal Beneficiaries Act of 1997 went too far toward "recognizing" and rewarding homosexual relationships, but he advised the Church that it was an acceptable compromise in return for placing a marriage amendment on the 1998 ballot.

8. Answer of defendant-intervenors [Church of Jesus Christ] to complaint, *Baehr v. Lewin*, Docket Item 39, Feb. 23, 1995 (procreation and parenting arguments); Memorandum from Loren Dunn to Marlin Jensen, Oct. 24, 1995, Prince Archives (domestic partner compromise suggested by Wardle).

9. *Pro-Marriage Foundation Gets First Home*, Deseret News, Feb. 17, 2005.

10. William Eskridge interview of William Duncan and Monte Neil Stewart, Provo, UT (June 20, 2018).

11. Monte Neil Stewart and William Duncan, *Marriage and the Betrayal of Perez and Loving*, 2005 BYU L. Rev. 555.

12. Richard Wirthlin and Dee Allsop, Wirthlin Worldwide, "Marriage Strategy for Federal Marriage Amendment" (July 28, 2003) (quotation in text, emphasis added).

13. Wardle, *Potential Impact*, 844–848. Accord, Dana Baumrind, *Commentary on Sexual Orientation: Research and Policy Implications*, 31 Developmental Psychol. 130, 132–134 (1995); Philip Belcastro et al., *A Review of Data Based Studies Addressing the Effects of Homosexual Parenting on Children's Sexual and Social Functioning*, 20 Divorce & Remarriage 105, 111–116 (1993).

14. Charlotte Patterson, *Children of Lesbian and Gay Parents*, 63 Child Development 1025, 1036–1039 (1992); Eskridge interview of Duncan and Stewart. For early United

Kingdom studies based on random samples, see Susan Golombok et al., *Children Raised in Fatherless Families from Infancy: Family Relationships and Socioemotional Development of Children of Lesbian and Single Heterosexual Mothers*, 33 J. Child Psychol. & Psychiatry 783 (1997) and others discussed in Carlos Ball, *Same-Sex Marriage and Children: A Tale of History, Social Science, and Law*, 88–89 (2014).

15. Carlos Ball and Janice Farrell Pea, *Warring with Wardle: Morality, Social Science, and Gay and Lesbian Parents*, 1998 U. Ill. L. Rev. 253, 277 (quotation in text). See Mike Allen and Nancy Burrell, *Comparing the Impact of Homosexual and Heterosexual Parents on Children: Meta-Analysis of Existing Research*, 32 J. Homosexuality 19 (1996); Ball, *Same-Sex Marriage and Children*, 86–94 (empirical update to *Warring with Wardle*).

16. The resolutions of professional associations described and quoted in the text, are collected on the American Psychological Association's website, http://www.apa.org/pi/lgbt/resources/parenting.

17. Wardle, *Potential Impact*, 897–898 (quotations in text). Compare Ball and Pea, *Warring with Wardle*, 261–272 (identifying anti-gay stereotyping as a recurring theme in Wardle's article); George Dent, *The Defense of Traditional Marriage*, 15 J.L. & Pol. 581 (1999).

18. Brief for respondent (the state), p. 55, *Baker v. State*, Docket No. 98-32 (Vermont Supreme Court, filed 1998); Appellants' reply brief, p. 31 and n.42, *Baker*.

19. *Goodridge v. Department of Social Servs.*, 798 N.E.2d 941, 963–964 (Mass. 2003) (Marshall's plurality opinion, rejecting the optimal parenting argument and noting that four of the seven couples were successfully raising children), pp. 979–980 (Sosman's dissent), pp. 998–1000 (Cordy's dissent) (deferring to the legislature's understandable reluctance to experiment with same-sex marriage); Judith Stacey and Timothy Biblarz, *(How) Does the Sexual Orientation of Parents Matter?*, 66 Am. Soc. Rev. 159, 168–171 (2001) (meta-analysis invoked by the commonwealth to claim that there were real differences in outcomes for children raised in lesbian households). See William Duncan, *The State Interests in Marriage*, 2 Ave Maria L. Rev. 153 (2004); Eric Andersen, *Children, Parents, and Nonparents: Protected Interests and Legal Standards*, 1998 BYU L. Rev. 935 (1998).

20. *Goodridge*, p. 968 (Marshall's plurality opinion), pp. 970–973 (Greaney's concurring opinion); Monte Neil Stewart et al., "Marriage, Fundamental Premises, and the California, Connecticut, and Iowa Supreme Courts" (article presented at a 2006 BYU and Catholic University symposium on the social harms of same-sex marriage; almost half of the panelists were associated with BYU or MLF). See David Blankenhorn, *The Future of Marriage*, 161 (2007).

21. Wardle, *"Multiply and Replenish,"* 779–780 (eight state interests in preserving the traditional definition of marriage, including responsible procreation); Edward Stein, *The "Accidental Procreation" Argument for Withholding Legal Recognition for Same-Sex Relationships*, 89 Chi.-Kent L. Rev. 403 (2009); Ball, *Same-Sex Marriage and*

Children, 48–54 (evolution of the responsible procreation argument into the accidental procreation argument).

22. *Singer v. Hara*, 522 P.2d 1187, 1195 (Wash. App. 1974) (quotation in text). See William Bennett, *The Broken Hearth: Reversing the Moral Collapse of the American Family*, 133–134 (2001); Duncan, *State Interests*, 154–156; Douglas Kmiec, *The Procreative Argument for Proscribing Same-Sex Marriage*, 32 Hastings Const. L.Q. 653 (2004); Lynn Wardle, *A Critical Analysis of Constitutional Claims for Same-Sex Marriage*, 1996 BYU L. Rev. 1, 38–39 (1996); Amy Wax, *The Conservative's Dilemma: Traditional Institutions, Social Change, and Same-Sex Marriage*, 42 San Diego L. Rev. 1059, 1077–1079 (2005).

23. Stein, *"Accidental Procreation,"* 411–414.

24. Wardle, *"Multiply and Replenish,"* 784, 793–797 (quotations in text); Julie Nice, *The Descent of Responsible Procreation: A Genealogy of an Ideology*, 45 Loy. L.A. L. Rev. 781 (2012), citing Congregation for the Doctrine of the Faith, "Instruction for Human Life in Its Origin and on the Dignity of Procreation: Replies to Certain Questions of the Day," part II.A.1 (1987); Personal Responsibility and Work Opportunity Reconciliation Act of 1996, P.L. 104-193 (welfare reform law, centrally concerned with channeling recipients toward responsible procreation, i.e., within marriage); House Report No. 104-664, Defense of Marriage Act, p. 13 (July 9, 1996) (one of DOMA's purposes was to reaffirm the responsible procreation policy of the welfare reform law).

25. John Rawls, *Justice as Fairness: A Restatement*, § 50, pp. 162–168 (Erin Kelly, ed., 2001) (quotation in text). See John Rawls, *The Idea of Public Reason*, 64 U. Chi. L. Rev. 765, 779 (1997) (polity's understanding of marriage must be related to "the orderly reproduction of society over time"); Mathew O'Brien, *Why Liberal Neutrality Prohibits Same-Sex Marriage: Rawls, Political Liberalism, and the Family*, 1 Br. J. Am. Stud. 411 (2012). But see Stephen Macedo, *Homosexuality and the Conservative Mind*, 84 Geo. L.J. 261 (1996) (Rawlsian premises support an expansive understanding of marriage to include lesbian and gay couples); Ronald Dworkin, *Three Questions for America*, New York Review of Books, Sept. 21, 2006 (Rawls-like principles of human dignity require recognition of marriages for lesbian and gay couples).

26. *Goodridge*, pp. 995–996 (quotation in text from Cordy's dissent).

27. Stewart, *Judicial Redefinition of Marriage*, 47; *M. v. H.*, [1999] 2 S.C.R. 3, ¶¶ 156–157, 188–191 (Can. Sup. Ct. May 20, 1999) (Gonthier, J., dissenting) (anticipating the accidental procreation argument).

28. *Sadler v. Morrison*, 821 N.E.2d 15, 24–25 (Ind. App. 2005) (quotations in text); *Lewis v. Harris*, 875 A.2d 259, 276–277 (N.J. App. 2005) (Parrillo's concurring opinion, channeling Stewart), modified, 908 A.2d 196 (N.J. 2006); *Citizens for Equal Protection v. Bruning*, 455 F.3d 859, 867–868 (8th Cir. 2006). Accord, *Stanhardt v. Superior Court*, 77 P.3d 451 (Ariz. App. 2003, review denied 2004).

29. Monte Neil Stewart, *Genderless Marriage, Institutional Realities, and Judicial Elision*, 1 Duke J. Cont'l L. & Pub. Pol'y 1–2 (2006) (quotations in text); see 16–17.

30. *Andersen v. King County*, 138 P.3d 963 (Wash. 2006). Our discussion and quotations from the oral argument are taken from the C-SPAN video, https://www.c-span.org/video/?185874-1/constitutionality-marriage.

31. In state high-court marriage decisions between 1993 and 2010, twenty-one of twenty-six female justices voted to invalidate state exclusions. The judges are identified by name in chapter 24, n.17.

32. *Andersen*, pp. 974–990 (constitutional reasoning in Madsen's plurality opinion), pp. 991–1010 (Johnson's opinion concurring in the judgment). See *In re Parentage of L.B.*, 122 P.3d 161 (Wash. 2005) (recognizing de facto parents).

33. *Andersen*, p. 1012 (Fairhurst's dissenting opinion), p. 1017 (quotation in text), pp. 1032–1040 (Bridge's dissenting opinion). See *Romer v. Evans*, 517 U.S. 620 (1996), discussed in chapter 5.

34. William Eskridge and Christopher Riano interview of Judith Kaye, New York City (Nov. 2016); Roberta Kaplan, *Then Comes Marriage: U.S. v. Windsor and the Defeat of DOMA*, 77 (2015) (describing Smith's snide behavior during oral argument).

35. **Maryland:** *Conaway v. Deane*, 932 A.2d 571, 630–634 (Md. 2007) (majority opinion's rational basis analysis), following brief for appellants [Maryland], pp. 60–63, *Conaway* (Docket No. 44), 2006 WL 2679782 (quotation in text); Reply brief of appellants, pp. 16–20, *Conaway* (filed Sept. 22, 2006), 2006 WL 3905926. Compare *Conaway*, pp. 635–654 (Raker's dissenting opinion, following *Baker v. State*) and pp. 654–693 (Battaglia's dissenting opinion, based on the Maryland ERA) with pp. 585–599 (majority opinion's response to the ERA argument). **New Jersey:** *Lewis v. Harris*, 908 A.2d 196, 222 (N.J. 2006) (quotations in text), following brief amicus curiae of the Family Leader Foundation, *Lewis* (Docket No. 58,389, filed Dec. 21, 2005), 2005 WL 6735471. Accord, New Jersey attorney general's brief, pp. 44–45, *Lewis* (filed Jan. 6, 2006), 2006 WL 6850899.

36. **New Jersey:** Domestic Partnership Act, 2004 N.J. Laws chap. 246, codified in N.J. Stats. 26:8A; Laura Mansnerus, *New Jersey to Recognize Gay Couples*, New York Times, Jan. 9, 2004. Further partnership rights were added by 2005 N.J. Laws chaps. 304 (guardianship rights) and 331 (funeral and inheritance rights). **Rhode Island:** Act Relating to Public Officers and Employees' Insurance Benefits, H. 5339A, 2001 R.I. Pub. Laws 694 (benefits for domestic partners of state employees).

37. Andy Kroll, *Meet the Megadonor Behind the LGBTQ Rights Movement*, Rolling Stone, June 23, 2017 (quoted description of Tim Gill); David Callahan, *No One Left Behind: Tim Gill and the New Quest for Full LGBT Equality*, Inside Philanthropy, 2015 (quotations about Gill's passions).

38. See Adam Schrager and Rob Witwer, *Blueprint: How the Democrats Won Colorado (And Why Republicans Everywhere Ought to Care)* (2010); Kroll, *Meet the Megadonor*.

39. D. H. Dilbeck and William Eskridge telephone interview of James Pfaff (March 9, 2018); William Eskridge telephone interview of Ted Trimpa (June 19, 2015); Eric Gorski, *Push to Nix Gay Nuptials Begins*, Denver Post, Dec. 8, 2005.

40. Ramesh Ponnuru, *Friends with Benefits*, Nat'l Rev., Feb. 16, 2006 (author's 2005 "friends with benefits" proposal and Mitchell's reciprocal beneficiaries bill); Rebecca Waddington, *Compromise Proposed on Civil Unions*, Greely Tribune, Feb. 24, 2006 (Mitchell's bill); FRI, "Focus Marriage Dispute" and "Dobson's On-Air Statement" (Feb. 8, 2006) (quotations in text), www.familyresearchinst.org/category/reciprocal -beneficiaries/.

41. [Colorado] Senate Comm. on Business, Labor & Technology, final bill summary for S06-166 (Feb. 27, 2006).

42. Legislative Council, Colorado General Assembly, analysis of the 2006 ballot proposals, p. 23 (Sept. 17, 2006) (quotations in text).

43. Legislative Council, Colorado General Assembly, analysis of the 2006 ballot proposals, p. 23 (equal protection argument for other unmarried couples); Fr. Thomas Carzon, *And the Two Shall Become One Flesh*, Denver Catholic Register, Oct. 18, 2006.

44. William Eskridge telephone interview of Pat Steadman (July 11, 2017); Eskridge telephone interview of Trimpa; Dilbeck and Eskridge telephone interview of Pfaff.

45. John Gleason, *Busy Legislative Session for Colorado Catholic Conference*, Denver Catholic Register, March 25, 2009 (after its sponsors agreed to a minor change, the Conference dropped its objections to H.B. 1260).

46. Designated Beneficiaries Agreements Act, H.B. 09-1260, codified as new Article 22 of the Colorado Family Code; see § 15-22-102(d) (legislative purpose, quoted in text) and § 15-22-105(3) (listing rights of designated beneficiaries).

47. New Jersey Civil Unions Act, 2006 N.J. Public Laws, chap. 103.

48. Legal Benefits for Domestic Partners, 2007 Wash. Acts, S.B. 5336 (signed April 21, 2007); Josh Feit, *The Education of Ed Murray*, Seattle Met, Dec. 19, 2017; Janet Tu and Andrew Garber, *Domestic Partnerships Likely a Done Deal in State*, Seattle Times, March 2, 2007. See Austin Jenkins, *Outside Gay-Rights Supporters Quietly Targeted Northwest Legislator Races in 2006*, Crosscut, May 7, 2007, https://crosscut.com /2007/05/outside-gayrights-supporters-quietly-targeted-nort.

49. Expanding Rights and Responsibilities for Domestic Partnerships, 2008 Wash. Acts, H.B. 3104 (signed March 8, 2008); Domestic Partners Rights and Responsibilities Act of 2009, 2009 Wash. Acts, S.B. 5688 (signed May 15, 2009).

50. William Eskridge interview of Josh Friedes, New York City (July 1, 2017).

51. "Charlene Strong: Approve Referendum 71" (Oct. 20, 2009), https://www.youtube .com/watch?v=_bSdqAWrGog. See Charlene Strong, *Charlene Strong Calls for Equality and Dignity*, Seattle Gay News, Oct. 23, 2009 (first-person account).

13. Love Makes a Family

1. Memorandum from Matt Coles to the ACLU, "Ending the Exclusion of Same-Sex Couples from Marriage: Long-Term Plans and Short-Term Strategy" (Jan. 2004) (quotations in text).

2. William Eskridge telephone interview of Katherine Peck, former Gill senior vice president for programs, March 18, 2018.

3. Eskridge telephone interview of Peck and conversations with several participants. Attending the meeting were Matt Coles (ACLU), Kevin Cathcart (Lambda), Lee Swislow (GLAD), Joan Geary (GLAAD), Matt Foreman (NGLTF), David Smith (HRC), Toni Broaddus (Equality Federation), Evan Wolfson (Freedom to Marry), Marty Rouse (MassEquality), Kate Kendell (NCLR), Mara Kiesling (National Center for Transgender Equality), Chuck Wolfe (Victory Fund), Lori Jean (Los Angeles LGBT Community Center), and others.

4. Jersey City Working Group (concept paper), "Winning Marriage: What We Need to Do" (May 25, 2005); Matt Coles, *The Plan to Win Marriage,* in Kevin Cathcart and Leslie Gabel-Brett, eds., *Love Unites Us: Winning the Freedom to Marry in America,* 100–106 (2016); Email from Matt Coles to William Eskridge, July 10, 2019; Nan Hunter, *Varieties of Constitutional Experience: Democracy and the Marriage Equality Campaign,* 64 UCLA L. Rev. 1662 (2017).

5. Concept paper, 6–7 (quotation in text, adapting language from a May 5 email from Evan Wolfson to the working group).

6. Jersey City Working Group (final document), "Winning Marriage: What We Need to Do" (June 21, 2005) (quotations in text).

7. Email from Matt Coles to Jersey City Working Group, "Marriage Planning Meeting" (April 28, 2005) (quotations in text); Email from Coles to Eskridge. The earlier report to the ACLU was Belden, Russello & Stewart, "Live and Let Marry: Communicating to Persuadable Voters About Marriage Rights for Gay Couples: Findings from Ten Focus Groups" (2003), discussed in Hunter, *Varieties,* 1685–1686.

8. Memorandum from Anna Greenberg et al. to Seth Kilbourn and HRC's marriage team, "Summary Recommendations" (Dec. 7, 2005) (quotation in text).

9. William Eskridge interview of Anne Stanback and Charlotte Kinlock, Avon, CT (Oct. 2017); Anne Stanback, *Love Makes a Family in Connecticut,* in *Love Unites Us,* 92–94.

10. Archbishop John Whealon, *The Church and the Homosexual Person,* The Catholic Transcript (April 5, 1991) (first quotation in text); Kirk Johnson, *Connecticut Senate Passes Law Protecting Gay Rights,* New York Times, April 18, 1991; An Act Concerning Discrimination on the Basis of Sexual Orientation, 1991 Conn. Public Acts No. 91-68 § 20 ("no promo homo" provisions, quoted in text).

11. *In re Adoption of Baby Z.,* 724 A.2d 1035 (Conn. 1999).

12. An Act Concerning the Best Interest of Children in Adoption Matters, 2000 Conn. Public Acts No. 00-228; Melinda Tuhus, *Easing the Fears of a Parent, Gay or Not,* New York Times, July 30, 2000.

13. Email from Mary Bonauto to Anne Stanback, March 28, 2003, GLAD Archives; Abigail Sullivan Moore, *The View/From Hartford; Parishioners Await a Vocal Protest,* New York Times, March 23, 2003.

14. Verified complaint, ¶ 1, *Kerrigan v. State*, No. CV04-4001813 (Conn. Super. Ct., New Haven, filed Aug. 25, 2004), 2004 WL 5651244 (quotation in text). See ¶¶ 20–21 (risks that Mock and Kerrigan's unmarried status posed to their family), ¶¶ 28–31 (Peck and Conklin's health care worries).

15. Martin Meeker interview of Anne Stanback (April 11, 2016), F2M Oral History (quotation in text); Eskridge interview of Stanback and Kinlock.

16. Eskridge interview of Stanback and Kinlock; Meeker interview of Stanback, pp. 20, 17 (quotations in text); Email from Anne Stanback to William Eskridge, Oct. 22, 2018.

17. Transcript of Connecticut legislature, Joint Judiciary Committee hearing (Feb. 7, 2005) (testimony of Jennifer Brown and Ian Ayres), GLAD Archives; Ian Ayres and Jennifer Gerarda Brown, *Straightforward: How to Mobilize Heterosexual Support for Gay Rights* (2005).

18. Anne Stanback, *Marriage Equality: Unfinished Business*, Hartford Courant (March 3, 2005); Transcript of the Connecticut Senate debate on Raised Bill 963 (civil unions), April 6, 2005, GLAD Archives (McDonald's quotations in text). See Mary Bonauto, *Kerrigan* legal team, memorandum, "Floor Debate on CU Bill No. 963" (April 3, 2005), GLAD Archives.

19. Transcript of the Connecticut House debate on House Bill 963 (civil unions), April 13, 2005, GLAD Archives; Susan Thomas, *The Rise and Fall of Civil Unions: Lessons from the Connecticut Legislature's Abandonment of Gay and Lesbian Citizens*, 58 J. Homosexuality 315 (2011); An Act Concerning Civil Unions, 2005 Conn. Public Acts No. 05-10 (signed April 20, 2005).

20. *Kerrigan v. State*, 909 A.2d 87 (Conn. Super., New Haven, 2006).

21. Eskridge interview of Stanback and Kinlock.

22. Transcript of Connecticut legislature, Joint Judiciary Committee hearing (March 26, 2007), GLAD Archives. Testimony supporting marriage equality came from the Connecticut comptroller, who reported how easy and inexpensive state domestic partnership benefits had been; the Connecticut secretary of state and the treasurer; the Permanent Commission on the Status of Women; the AFL-CIO and other unions; the National Association of Social Workers and the American Academy of Pediatrics, urging marriage for the benefit of the children; Hartford P-FLAG; the mayors of New Haven, Hartford, and Stamford; and others.

23. **Key Briefs Supporting the Plaintiff Couples:** Brief for appellants, *Kerrigan v. Commissioner of Public Health* (Conn. Supreme Court, filed Nov. 22, 2006); Brief amicus curiae professors of history and family law, *Kerrigan* (filed Jan. 11, 2007), 2007 WL 4725460; Brief amicus curiae religious organizations and clergy, *Kerrigan* (filed Jan. 11, 2007), 2007 WL 4725461; Comparative law amicus curiae brief, *Kerrigan* (filed Dec. 12, 2006), 2006 WL 5247960; Brief amicus curiae professors of family law, *Kerrigan* (filed Jan. 11, 2007), 2007 WL 4725447. **Key Briefs Supporting the Statutory or Traditional Definition of Marriage:** Brief for the appellees (state), *Kerrigan* (filed Feb. 11, 2007),

2007 WL 4725470 (civil unions were sufficient); Brief amicus curiae Catholic Conference of Connecticut, *Kerrigan* (filed April 25, 2007), 2007 WL 4725449; Brief amicus curiae Family Institute of Connecticut, *Kerrigan* (filed April 25, 2007), 2007 WL 4729865; Brief amicus curiae Family Research Council, *Kerrigan* (filed April 25, 2007), 2007 WL 4725452.

24. At the end of his tenure as chief justice (2000–2006), Tocco Sullivan had been accused of delaying an important opinion to assure the elevation of Justice Peter Zarella to succeed him. The controversy impelled the governor to withdraw Zarella's nomination and may have played some role in Sullivan's recusal. On Borden and sodomy reform, see William Eskridge Jr., *Dishonorable Passions: Sodomy Law in America, 1861–2003*, 161–163 (2008).

25. Our discussion of the Connecticut Supreme Court's deliberations in *Kerrigan* is based on off-the-record conversations with several court insiders.

26. *Kerrigan v. Commissioner of Public Health*, 957 A.2d 407, 425–454, 472–473 (Conn. 2008) (majority opinion) (quotations in text, arguing that sexual orientation was a quasi-suspect classification), largely following *In re Marriage Cases*, 183 P.3d 384 (Cal. 2008).

27. *Kerrigan*, p. 516 (quotation in text from Zarella's dissenting opinion, maintaining that the marriage law did not even discriminate on the basis of sexual orientation and had "its basis in biology, not bigotry"), pp. 492–505 (Borden's dissenting opinion). Compare with pp. 454–461 (majority's response); William Eskridge Jr. and Philip Frickey, *The Supreme Court, 1993 Term—Foreword: Law as Equilibrium*, 94 Harv. L. Rev. 4, 27–29 (1994) (demonstrating that the US Supreme Court tends to apply equal protection with teeth *only* after a minority group is no longer "politically powerless").

28. *Kerrigan*, pp. 477–478 (quotation from majority opinion). Cf. pp. 516–517 (Zarella's dissenting opinion, agreeing that civil unions and marriage are not comparable institutions).

29. Christopher Keating, *Catholic Bishops Urge "Yes" Vote on Constitutional Convention*, Hartford Courant, Oct. 11, 2008.

30. Act Implementing the Guarantee of Equal Protection Under the Constitution of the State for Same Sex Couples, 2009 Conn. Public Acts No. 09-13.

31. William Eskridge Jr., *Equality Practice: Civil Unions and the Future of Gay Rights* (2002); William Eskridge telephone interview of Shapleigh Smith, June 7, 2017 (quotation in text).

32. Robin Fretwell Wilson and Anthony Michael Kreis, *Embracing Compromise: Marriage Equality and Religious Liberty in the Political Process*, 15 Geo. J. Gender & L. 485 (2014).

33. William Eskridge interview of Beth Robinson, Ferrisburgh, VT (Dec. 1, 2017); Eskridge telephone interview of Smith; Nathaniel Frank, *Awakening: How Gays and Lesbians Brought Marriage Equality to America*, 213 (2017) (Lippert quotation in text); Charlotte Schwartz and William Eskridge telephone interview of Richard Sears

(March 21, 2017); Kevin O'Connor, *Records Show Vermont Church Knew of Child Sex Abuse,* Rutland Herald, July 1, 2007.

34. David Goodman, *Vermont's "Happily Ever After,"* Mother Jones, April 8, 2009; Anthony Michael Kreis, *Marriage Equality in State and Nation,* 22 Wm. & Mary Bill of Rights J. 747, 760–761 (2014) (quotation in text).

35. David Gram, *Vermont House Advances Bill for Gay Marriage,* Associated Press, April 3, 2009; James Douglas, *The Vermont Way: A Republican Governor Leads America's Most Liberal State* (2014) (quotation in text); William Eskridge interview of Rev. Craig and Deb Bensen, Cambridge, VT (Dec. 1, 2017).

36. Kreis, *Marriage Equality,* 759.

37. One legislator told us Dick Westman said he would not vote to override the governor, but another legislator told us that Westman said he would stick with his original vote. Yet another legislator thought that Westman would not show up that day.

38. Kreis, *Marriage Equality,* 762 (quotations from Zuckerman and Smith). Our telephone interviews of Senators Ayer and Sears suggest that the conscience exemptions were irrelevant in the senate, which had more than enough votes to override the governor's veto.

39. Conn. legislature, 2009 session, Raised Bill 899 §§ 10, 17, codified at Conn. Gen. Stat. §§ 46b-35a and 46b-35b (quotations in text).

40. Abby Goodnough, *Vote in Doubt as a Senate Takes Up Gay Marriage,* New York Times, April 15, 2009; Abby Goodnough, *New Hampshire Senate Passes Gay Marriage Bill,* New York Times, April 29, 2009.

41. Kreis, *Marriage Equality,* 774–776; Letter from Thomas Berg (St. Thomas), Robin Fretwell Wilson (Washington & Lee), Carl Esbeck (Missouri), and Richard Garnett (Notre Dame) to New Hampshire legislature and Governor John Lynch (May 1, 2009); Letter from Douglas Layock (Michigan), Andrew Koppelman (Northwestern), Michael Perry (Emory), and Marc Stern (American Jewish Congress) to Governor John Lynch (May 22, 2009) (quotation in text).

42. N.H. Rev. Stat. Ann. § 457.37.II–III (quotations in text).

43. Me. Rev. Stat. tit. 19-A, § 650 (repealed 2009). See Abby Goodnough and Katie Zezima, *Gay Marriage Advances in Maine,* New York Times, May 5, 2009.

44. Religious Freedom and Civil Marriage Equality Amendment Act, § 2(d), 2009 District of Columbia Laws 18-110 (Act 18–248); Tim Craig, *D.C. Council Approves Same-Sex Marriage Bill,* Washington Post, Dec. 16, 2009.

45. Rex Huppke, *"We Really Owe Her." 10 Years after Iowa Same-Sex Marriage Ruling, Chicago Lawyer Carries on the Fight,* Chicago Tribune, June 27, 2019 (quotation in text).

46. Camilla Taylor, *"Our Liberties We Prize": Winning Marriage in Iowa,* in *Love Unites Us,* 131–133; William Eskridge telephone interview of Camilla Taylor (April 5, 2018).

47. Memorandum from Camilla Taylor to Pat Logue et al., Lambda Legal Midwest regional office, "Survey of Midwest Political Context for Marriage Litigation" (March 17, 2004); Iowa Const., art. I, §§ 1, 6 (quotations in text).

48. Senate Joint Resolution 2002 (Iowa, quotation in text).

49. Tom Witosky and Marc Hansen, *Equal Before the Law: How Iowa Led Americans to Marriage Equality*, 1–6, 56–58 (2016) (quotations in text).

50. Witosky and Hansen, *Equal Before the Law*, 59–61 (quotation in text).

51. William Eskridge telephone interview of Doug Shull (April 20, 2018).

52. Email from Camilla Taylor to William Eskridge, April 3, 2018; Camilla Taylor and Pat Logue, Lambda Legal Midwest regional office, "Affirmative Marriage Litigation in Iowa" (Sept. 29, 2005).

53. Witosky and Hansen, *Equal Before the Law*, 65–90, 134–135 (detailed description of all six couples).

54. Witosky and Hansen, *Equal Before the Law*, 135–137 (quotations in text); Eskridge telephone interview of Taylor.

55. Eskridge telephone interview of Taylor ("heart and soul" quotation in text).

56. Statement of material facts in support of all plaintiffs' motion for summary judgment, ¶¶ 1, 26, *Varnum v. Brien*, Case No. CV5965 (Iowa Dist. Ct., Polk Cnty., filed Jan. 30, 2007), 2007 WL 2461127 (quotations in text).

57. District court's opinion, *Varnum* (Aug. 30, 2007).

58. Memorandum from Brad Clark, campaign director, Iowa One, to national stakeholders [funders], "Campaign Update" (Nov. 14, 2008); Memorandum from Campbell Spencer, One Iowa, to Thalia Zepatos, Marriage Collaborative, "Proposed Iowa Marriage Education Paid Media Program" (2009) (quotation in text).

59. Taylor and Logue, "Affirmative Marriage." See *Racing Association of Central Iowa v. Fitzgerald*, 675 N.W.2d 1 (Iowa 2004) (Ternus's majority opinion striking down a state tax on gambling, because it treated riverboat and racetrack gambling differently, without a public-regarding reason), pp. 17–24 (Cady's solo dissenting opinion, which would have applied the same deferential analysis that the US Supreme Court applied to uphold the same tax differential in *Fitzgerald v. Racing Association of Central Iowa*, 539 U.S. 103 (2003)).

60. Transcript of oral argument, *Varnum v. Brien* (Iowa Supreme Court, Dec. 9, 2008), 2008 WL 5454171; Witosky and Hansen, *Equal Before the Law*, 133–145; William Eskridge telephone interview of Marsha Ternus (April 13, 2018).

61. *Varnum* oral argument (quotation in text).

62. *Varnum* oral argument (quotation in text).

63. *Varnum* oral argument (quotation in text).

64. Sharyn Jackson, *Iowa Gay Marriage Ruling a Turning Point for Justices*, USA Today, April 2, 2014 (quotations in text); Eskridge telephone interview of Ternus; Witosky and Hansen, *Equal Before the Law*, 133–135.

65. *Varnum v. Brien*, 763 N.W.2d 862, 883–884 (Iowa April 3, 2009) (quotations from Cady's opinion for the court), pp. 884–896 (sexual orientation is a quasi-suspect classification, and the marriage exclusion did not satisfy its burden on the state).

66. Eskridge telephone interview of Taylor (quoting the gas station attendant); Witosky and Hansen, *Equal Before the Law,* 158; Eskridge telephone interview of Ternus; William Eskridge telephone interview of Ted Trimpa, Gill Action (July 2015).

67. Video of Ryanne DeBoer, Hazel Park, MI, Nov. 16, 2015.

14. "Restore Marriage"

1. The discussion in the introduction to this chapter is based on William Eskridge interview of Maggie Gallagher, Washington, DC (May 13, 2015); Eskridge telephone interview of Gallagher (Dec. 19, 2018); Joshua Green, *They Won't Know What Hit Them,* The Atlantic, March 2007; Political Research Associates, *Profiles on the Right: National Organization for Marriage* (Nov. 11, 2013) (NOM's budget, which escalated from $500,000 in 2007 to $9.1 million in 2010).

2. On Bishop Sal, see Chris Thompson, *The Father of Proposition 8,* East Bay Express, Aug. 12, 2009.

3. Eskridge interview of Gallagher; William Eskridge interview of Andy Pugno, Sacramento, CA (Oct. 22, 2015).

4. One earlier constitutional initiative proposal would have abrogated the state domestic partnership law: "A marriage between a man and a woman is the only legal union that shall be valid or recognized in this state." *Voters Won't See Domestic-Partnership Rollback Initiatives on November Ballot,* Capitol Weekly, May 25, 2006; Joe Dignan, *California Girds for Marriage Fight,* Gay City, Dec. 1–7, 2005.

5. William Eskridge telephone interview of Frank Schubert (July 14, 2017); Erik Eckholm, *One Man Guides the Fight Against Gay Marriage,* New York Times, Oct. 9, 2012.

6. Eskridge interview of Pugno; Richard Wirthlin and Dee Allsop, Wirthlin Worldwide, "Marriage Strategy for Federal Marriage Amendment" (July 2005) (polls suggesting that voters were turned off by anti-gay messaging).

7. George McKinney, *Christian Marriage: An Act of Faith, Hope, and Commitment* (1977) (every marriage is a covenant among God, the husband, and the wife); Politically Speaking, NBC 7 (San Diego), Oct. 10, 2008 (debate featuring Reverend McKinney), https://www.nbcsandiego.com/news/local/30775174.html.

8. Gregory Prince, *Gay Rights and the Mormon Church: Intended Actions, Unintended Consequences,* 128 (2019) (first quotation in text); *Archbishop Niederauer Explains Catholic Involvement in Prop. 8,* Catholic News Agency, Dec. 4, 2008 (second quotation). Our sources inside ProtectMarriage.com suggest that letter was a joint one, from both Weigand and Niederauer, but the public discussion only mentions the latter.

9. Prince, *Gay Rights,* 128–131.

10. Lisa Leff, *Gay Marriage Amendment Headed to California Ballot,* Associated Press, April 24, 2008; Jack Leonard, *Voters Will Decide on Gay Marriage,* Los Angeles Times, June 3, 2008, B1; *Jansson v. Bowen,* Case Number 34-2008-00017351 (Cal. Super. Ct., Sacramento Cnty., Aug. 7, 2008) (Judge Frawley's ruling).

11. California General Election, *Official Voter Information Guide, Tuesday, November 4, 2008*, Prop 8: Argument in Favor of Proposition 8 (emphasis and capitalization in original), reprinted in William Eskridge Jr., Nan Hunter, and Courtney Joslin, *Sexuality, Gender, and the Law*, app. 6 (4th ed. 2017).

12. Our account of the June Newport Beach meeting, and the quotations in text and in the following paragraph, are taken from an off-the-record interview of one of the Yes on 8 leaders. See Bryan Fischer, "Why Homosexual Behavior Should Be Against the Law," AFA blogs, Feb. 3, 2010.

13. See Donald Wildmon, *Speechless: Silencing the Christians: How Secular Liberals and Homosexual Activists Are Outlawing Christianity (and Judaism) to Force Their Sexual Agenda on America* (2009).

14. *Proposition 8 in Plain English* (Oct. 12, 2008, posted on ProtectMarriage.com) (quotations in text), transcript and cartoon frames reprinted in Eskridge, Hunter, and Joslin, *Sexuality, Gender, and the Law*, app. 6. Schubert told us that ProtectMarriage .com did not produce the video but that it was consistent with their "key messaging."

15. *Proposition 8 in Plain English* (quotations in text from Oct. 12 video); Wirthlin and Allsop, "Marriage Strategy" (2005 polling report).

16. California General Election, *Official Voter Information Guide, Tuesday, November 4, 2008*, Prop 8: Argument Against Proposition 8 (quotations in text; emphasis and capitalization in original), reprinted in Eskridge, Hunter, and Joslin, *Sexuality, Gender, and the Law*, app. 6.

17. Dewey Square Group, consultants, *Equality for All . . . A Roadmap to Victory* (June 2008) (quotations in text), reprinted in David Fleischer, LGBT Mentoring Project, *The Prop 8 Report: What Defeat in California Can Teach Us About Winning Future Ballot Measures on Same-Sex Marriage*, app. Q (2010).

18. MAP and GLAAD, *Talking About Marriage and Relationship Recognition for Gay Couples* (Jan. 2008) (quotations in text).

19. William Eskridge telephone interview of Geoff Kors (Aug. 9, 2016); William Eskridge telephone interview of Sean Lund (April 20, 2018); Let California Ring, *The Garden Wedding* (Oct. 2007), https://www.youtube.com/watch?v=GG7ddWLF_Fk (discussed further in chapter 18).

20. Frank Schubert and Jeff Flint, *Passing Prop 8: Smart Timing and Messaging Convinced California Voters to Support Traditional Marriage*, Politics, Feb. 2009, 44.

21. Circular letter to general authorities, area seventies, and the following in California: stake and mission presidents; bishops and branch presidents, June 20, 2008, but read to congregations the week after that (quotations in text), Prince Archives. See Kaimipono David Wenger, *The Divine Institution of Marriage: An Overview of LDS Involvement in the Proposition 8 Campaign*, 26 J. Civil Rights & Econ. Dev. 705, 721–722 (2012). We owe the precise number of wards to comments from Elder Clayton.

22. Dr. James Garlow, *The Ten Declarations for Protecting Biblical Marriage* (June 25, 2008), http://drjamesdobson.org/images/pdf/10declarations.pdf (quotation in text

from Declaration No. 2); Surina Khan, *Tying the Not: How the Right Succeeded in Passing Prop 8*, Pol. Res. Assocs., April 1, 2009.

23. Mark Schoofs, *Mormons Boost Antigay Marriage Effort*, Wall Street Journal, Sept. 20, 2008 (quotations in text). See Monica Youn, *Proposition 8 and the Mormon Church: A Case Study in Donor Disclosure*, 81 Geo. Wash. L. Rev. 2108 (2013).

24. Memorandum from Gary Lawrence, state grassroots director, to all area directors etc. (Aug. 7, 2008) (quotation in text); Eskridge telephone interview of Schubert.

25. Memorandum from Sarah Pollo, Schubert Flint, to ProtectMarriage.com et al., minutes of Aug. 21 grassroots meeting (Aug. 22, 2008).

26. Dr. William Tam, "What If We Lose?" (2008), English translation as plaintiffs' Exhibit 513 in *Perry v. Schwarzenegger* (initial quotations in text); Dr. Tam, "Why Should We Support Proposition 8?" (2008), English translation as plaintiffs' Exhibit 2343 in *Perry* (last quotation).

27. Apocalyptic flyer (summer 2008), plaintiffs' Exhibit 2187 in *Perry* (quotation in text).

28. *Six Consequences If Proposition 8 Fails*, Prop 8 Saving Marriage blog (Aug. 24, 2008), http://prop8savingmarriage.blogspot.com/2008/08/six-consequences-if-proposition-8-fails.html (Lawrence's document adapted from Greener's article in a Mormon online magazine); The Church of Jesus Christ of Latter-day Saints, press release, *The Divine Institution of Marriage*, Aug. 8, 2008; Morris Thurston, *A Commentary on the Document "Six Consequences . . . if Proposition 8 Fails"* (2008), http://www.connellodonovan.com/thurston_response.pdf. See Wenger, *Divine Institution*, 722–724.

29. Cal. Educ. Code §§ 51890(a)(1)(D), 51933(b)(7) (initial quotations in text, duty to teach marriage), § 51500 (barring instruction reflecting a "discriminatory bias"); Eskridge interview with Pugno (last quotations in text). See Ruth Butterfield Isaacson, *"Teachable Moments": The Use of Child-Centered Arguments in the Same-Sex Marriage Debate*, 98 Calif. L. Rev. 121 (2010) (relating the 2008 child-centric ads for Yes on 8 to civil rights debates in the 1950s–1960s); Lynn Wardle, *The Impacts on Education of Legalizing Same-Sex Marriage and Lessons from Abortion Jurisprudence*, 2011 BYU Educ. & L.J. 593 (expanding the gotta-teach-gay-marriage argument beyond California to other school systems).

30. *Parker v. Hurley*, 514 F.3d 87 (1st Cir. 2008); Cal. Educ. Code § 51240 (first quotation in text); Scott Wooledge, *David Parker, the Man Behind Frank Schubert's Deceptive Multi-State Anti-Equality Ad*, HuffPost, Oct. 30, 2012; Dan Aiello, *Mass. Couple Pushes Prop 8*, Bay Area Reporter, Nov. 27, 2008 (second quotation).

31. Elder L. Whitney Clayton et al., *The Divine Institution of Marriage* satellite broadcast (Oct. 8, 2008). See Wenger, *Divine Institution*, 724–727.

32. William Eskridge telephone interview of Barbara Young (July 2017); Wenger, *Divine Institution,* 729–732 (quotation in text); Jessica Garrison and Joanna Kin, *Prop 8*

Protesters Target Mormon Temple in Westwood, Los Angeles Times, Nov. 7, 2008 (anti-Mormon ads).

33. Sarah Posner, *"The Call" Warns of Antichrist Legislation in California and Beyond,* Religion Dispatches, June 15, 2009.

34. Texts for all advertisements quoted in text are from Fleischer, *Prop 8 Report,* app. E.

35. *Newsom* (Sept. 2008) (quotation in text, from Yes on 8 ad). See Fleischer, *Prop 8 Report,* app. E (transcript).

36. *Two Princes* (Oct. 2008) (quotation in text, from Yes on 8 ad). See Fleischer, *Prop 8 Report,* app. E (transcript); Isaacson, *"Teachable Moments,"* 148–151 (child-centric ads central to Yes on 8's media campaign).

37. Fleischer, *Prop 8 Report,* app. D (visuals on the Lake Research daily tracking polls). Accord, Melissa Murray, *Marriage Rights and Parental Rights: Parents, the State, and Proposition 8,* 5 Stan. J. C.R. & C.L. 357 (2009) (analysis of how Yes on 8's appeal to parental fears was the key reason for its electoral success).

38. John Wildermuth, *Prop. 8 Opponents Take Lead in Money Race,* SFGate, Oct. 25, 2008.

39. *O'Connell* (No on 8 ad, Oct. 2008). See Fleischer, *Prop 8 Report,* app. E (transcript).

40. Jill Tucker, *Class Surprises Lesbian Teacher on Wedding Day,* San Francisco Chronicle, Oct. 11, 2008 (quotation in text).

41. *Field Trip* (Yes on 8 ad, Oct. 2008) (quotations in text). See Fleischer, *Prop 8 Report,* app. E (transcript).

42. On October 27, No on 8 started running one of its best ads, *No for Latinos,* featuring Ana Ortiz, Tony Plana, and America Ferrara explaining why they thought Proposition 8 was inconsistent with Latino family values. In the same period, Yes on 8 countered with *Hola,* featuring popular singer Eduardo Verástegui. See Fleischer, *Prop 8 Report,* app. E (transcript of ads).

43. Jesse McKinley and Kirk Johnson, *Mormons Tipped Scale in Ban on Gay Marriage,* New York Times, Nov. 15, 2008 (quotation in text); Schubert and Flint, *Passing Prop 8,* 47. For a similar account, see Fred Karger, *Out of State Mormons Just Gave $3 Million More to End Gay Marriage: New Mormon Total = $22 Million,* Mormon Money Watch, Nov. 2, 2008.

44. Karin Wang, *Parallel Journeys Through Discrimination: Asian Americans and Modern Marriage Equality,* in Kevin Cathcart and Leslie Gabel-Brett, eds., *Love Unites Us: Winning the Freedom to Marry in America,* 157–160 (2015); GLAAD, MAP, et al., *Overall Approaches for Talking About Gay and Transgender Issues* (2008).

45. Talk to Action, "The Call: Spiritual Warfare in the Field of Martyrs" (Nov. 4, 2008) (quotations in text, from the Nov. 1 rally).

46. Eskridge telephone interview of Schubert.

47. Patrick Egan and Kenneth Sherrill, NGLTF Policy Institute, *California's Proposition 8: What Happened, and What Does the Future Hold?* (2009); Public Policy Institute of California, *Post-Election Survey: Proposition 8 Results Expose Deep Rifts Over Same-Sex Marriage* (Dec. 3, 2008).

48. Fleischer, *Prop 8 Report,* 14–15; William Eskridge interview of Doreena Wong and Jenny Pizer, Los Angeles (July 2015); Robert Chang and Karin Wang, *Democratizing the Courts: How an Amicus Brief Helped Organize the Asian American Community to Support Marriage Equality,* 14 Asian Pac. Am. L.J. 22 (2009).

49. William Eskridge interview of Frank Schubert, Washington, DC (June 17, 2017).

50. GLAAD and MAP, with Arizona Together, HRC, Lake Research Partners, Margaret Conway, and P-FLAG, *Talking About Marriage and Relationship Recognition for Gay Couples* (Jan. 2008).

51. Wenger, *Divine Institution,* 734–737.

52. Maggie Gallagher, "National Organization for Marriage: Board Update, 2008–2009," NOM deposition Exhibit 25, *NOM v. McKee,* Civil No. 1:09-cv-00538 (D. Me. 2009) (first quotation in text); Eric Russell, *Question 1 TV Ad Sparks Charges of "Blatant Misinformation,"* Bangor News, Oct. 2, 2009 (describing the ProtectMarriage television ads, including quotations in text from *Gay Sex*); Joe Fox and James Nubile, directors, *Question One: God. Sin. Sex. Love. Equality* (Fly on the Wall Prods. 2012) (Maine marriage referendum, including on-camera interviews with its Evangelical and Catholic leaders).

53. Abby Goodnough, *Gay Rights Rebuke May Change Approach,* New York Times, Nov. 4, 2009 (quotation in text). On the Iowa nonretention campaign, see Barb Heki and Vicki Crawford, *We Overrule: How Iowa Turned Judicial Tyranny into a Triumph for Freedom* (2012); Tom Witosky and Marc Hansen, *Equal Before the Law: How Iowa Led Americans to Marriage Equality,* 166–168 (2016); Todd Pettys, *Letter from Iowa: Same-Sex Marriage and the Ouster of Three Justices,* 59 U. Kan. L. Rev. 715 (2011). On the DC nonreferendum, see *Jackson v. District of Columbia Board of Elections and Ethics,* 999 A.2d 89 (D.C. 2010); NOM, "National Strategy for Winning the Marriage Battle," 12 (n.d.) (NOM's role in DC).

54. NOM, "National Strategy," 6 (quotations in text).

55. Nathaniel Frank, *Awakening: How Gays and Lesbians Brought Marriage Equality to America,* 185–190 (2017) (protests after Proposition 8); Carol Lynn Pearson, *Elder Marlin K. Jensen Listens to Pain Caused by Prop 8,* Rational Faiths, Oct. 27, 2013 (Elder Jensen's Sept. 2009 meltdown when confronted by Latter-day Saints angry about the brutal Proposition 8 campaign).

56. Fox and Nubile, *Question One* (quotations in text).

57. William Eskridge telephone interview of Dustin Lance Black (May 25, 2018) (first quotation in text); Mike Swift, *Gay Rights Regroup After Proposition 8 Passage,* Monterey County Herald, Nov. 9, 2008 (second quotation, from Karger).

58. Eskridge telephone interview of Gallagher (Dec. 19, 2018).

59. *Anti-Gay Marriage Mastermind Keeps Ties to Pro-Gay Companies*, The Advocate, Nov. 11, 2009 (quotations in text).

60. Joe Garofoli, *Strategist Behind Proposition 8 Is Loved, Feared*, SFGate, July 5, 2012 (quotations in text).

15. 8, the Trial

1. On the liberty-democracy issues in *Strauss*, see Anna Marie Smith, *The Paradoxes of Popular Constitutionalism: Proposition 8 and* Strauss v. Horton, 45 U. San Francisco L. Rev. 517 (2010), as well as William Eskridge Jr., *The California Proposition 8 Case: What Is a Constitution For?*, 98 Calif. L. Rev. 1235 (2010).

2. For the prefatory account in text, we draw from Chuleenan Svetvilas, *Anatomy of a Complaint: How Hollywood Activists Seized Control of the Fight for Gay Marriage*, California Lawyer, Jan. 2010, 20–27, supplemented by our interviews and by David Boies and Theodore Olson, *Redeeming the Dream: The Case for Marriage Equality*, 8–14 (2014); Jo Becker, *Forcing the Spring: Inside the Fight for Marriage Equality* (2014).

3. Becker, *Forcing the Spring*, 7 (quotation in text). Svetvilas and Olson and Boies have different accounts of the interaction.

4. William Eskridge interview of Ted Olson, Washington, DC (June 11, 2018).

5. Boies and Olson, *Redeeming the Dream*, 24–25 (quotation in text); Eskridge interview of Olson.

6. Becker, *Forcing the Spring*, 21 (quotation in text).

7. Ron George, *Chief: The Quest for Justice in California* (2013).

8. William Eskridge telephone interview of Dustin Lance Black (May 25, 2018).

9. Becker, *Forcing the Spring*, 28–29 (quotations in text); Nathaniel Frank, *Awakening: How Gays and Lesbians Brought Marriage Equality to America*, 218–221 (2017).

10. *Naim v. Naim*, 350 U.S. 891 (1955) (vacating lower court judgment upholding law barring different-race marriages), on remand 90 S.E.2d 849 (Va. 1956) (reaffirming the law), appeal dismissed, 350 U.S. 985 (1956) (backing away from a confrontation with racist marriage laws in the wake of *Brown*); William Eskridge Jr. and Philip Frickey, eds., *Historical and Critical Introduction* to Henry Hart Jr. and Albert Sacks, *The Legal Process: Basic Problems in the Making and Application of Law*, cix–cx (1994). For Kennedy opinions focusing on the small number of states whose laws were being invalidated, see, e.g., *Lawrence v. Texas*, 539 U.S. 558, 570–573 (2003); *Atkins v. Virginia*, 536 U.S. 304 (2002).

11. William Eskridge Jr., *Dishonorable Passions: Sodomy Laws in America, 1861–2003*, 233–247 (2008) (strategic decision-making in the *Hardwick* litigation); Email from Ted Olson to William Eskridge, Dec. 18, 2018 (multiple reasons Sullivan did not work out).

12. Boies and Olson, *Redeeming the Dream*, 31 (Olson's version), 44–46 (Boies's version, quoted in text); William Eskridge telephone interview of Jeremy Goldman (Aug. 2017) ("Mozart" quotation).

13. Svetvilas, *Anatomy*, 25; Boies and Olson, *Redeeming the Dream*, 50–53 (quotation in text).

14. William Eskridge interview of Jon Davidson, Los Angeles (June 29, 2016) (quotations in text); William Eskridge interview of Jenny Pizer, Los Angeles (July 1, 2016).

15. Eskridge interview of Davidson (quotations in text); Becker, *Forcing the Spring*, 31.

16. Svetvilas, *Anatomy*, 20.

17. Jesse McKinley, Bush v. Gore *Foes Join to Fight Gay Marriage Ban*, New York Times, May 27, 2009; William Eskridge Jr. and Darren Spedale, *Sit Down Ted Olson and David Boies*, Slate, May 29, 2009; ACLU, Equality Federation, Freedom to Marry, GLAAD, GLAD, HRC, Lambda, NCLR, and NGLTF, *Make Change, Not Lawsuits* (May 2009) (quotation in text); Frank, *Awakening*, 228–229.

18. Eskridge telephone interview of Black; Kenji Yoshino, *Speak Now: Marriage Equality on Trial—The Story of* Hollingsworth v. Perry 7 (2015) (virtues of the 8 trial).

19. William Eskridge interview of Vaughn Walker, San Francisco (Dec. 30, 2016).

20. Administration defendants' trial memorandum, *Perry v. Schwarzenegger* (Dec. 7, 2009); Attorney general's answer to the complaint, *Perry* (June 12, 2009).

21. Boies and Olson, *Redeeming the Dream* (quotation in text); Geoffrey Fowler, *The Other Lawyer in Gay-Wed Case*, Wall Street Journal, March 26, 2013; William Eskridge interview of Chuck Cooper, Washington, DC (May 5, 2015); *Baehr v. Miike*, 994 P.2d 566 (Haw. 1999) (Cooper as prevailing counsel).

22. Eskridge interview of Olson.

23. Boies and Olson, *Redeeming the Dream*, 79 (quotation in text); William Eskridge telephone interview of Dennis Herrera (March 29, 2019); Eskridge interview of Cooper; William Eskridge telephone interview of James Campbell, ADF (Feb. 23, 2016).

24. Transcript of the hearing on motion for summary judgment, p. 23, *Perry v. Schwarzenegger* (Oct. 14, 2009), AFER Archives (quotations in text).

25. Eskridge interview of Cooper ("Bataan death march"); Becker, *Forcing the Spring*, 59 (same language).

26. *Perry v. Schwarzenegger*, 591 F.3d 1147 (9th Cir. Dec. 11, 2009), vacating 264 F.R.D. 576 (N.D. Cal. Nov. 11 & Dec. 1, 2009), p. 1165 n.12 (amended decision, Jan. 4, 2010).

27. Professor Young was responding to evidence from Professor Eskridge, the opposing expert, that dozens of cultures in world history had recognized same-sex marriages and unions. William Eskridge Jr., *The Case for Same-Sex Marriage: From Sexual Freedom to Civilized Commitment*, 25–45 (1996).

28. Deposition of Katherine Young, pp. 8–14, *Perry v. Schwarzenegger* (Nov. 13, 2009) (initial quotations in text), referencing Katherine Young and Paul Nathanson, *The Future of an Experiment*, in Daniel Cere and Douglas Farrow, eds., *Divorcing Marriage: Unveiling the Dangers in Canada's New Social Experiment*, 41–62 (2004); Email from Katherine Young to William Eskridge, April 1, 2019, referencing Katherine Young and Paul Nathanson, *Redefining Marriage or Deconstructing Society: A Canadian Case Study*, 13 J. Fam. Studs. (Australia) 133–178 (2007); Email from Katherine Young to William

Eskridge, May 22, 2017 (last quotation in text). See Boies and Olson, *Redeeming the Dream,* 96–102 (triumphal account of the Nathanson and Young depositions).

29. On the Ninth Circuit's and Northern District's process for revising its videotaping rules, as well as the quotation in the text, see the briefs and opinions in *Hollingsworth v. Perry,* 558 U.S. 183 (Jan. 13, 2010) (per curiam).

30. *Hollingsworth,* p. 190 (quotation in text, from the per curiam opinion).

31. Boies and Olson, *Redeeming the Dream,* 102, 163–164; Yoshino, *Speak Now,* 204–209; Email from Loren Marks to William Eskridge, May 19, 2017 (first quotations in text); Email from Daniel Robinson to William Eskridge Jr., May 6, 2017 (last quotation in text).

32. Email from Young to Eskridge (May 2017) (quotations in text). Olson and Boies respond that none of the defense witnesses opted back in to the 8 trial after the Supreme Court slammed the door on its broadcast. But three lived in other countries, and none of them was willing to change her or his plans again, especially in light of the fact that Judge Walker continued to tape the proceedings.

33. Edwin Meese III, *Stacking the Deck Against Proposition 8,* New York Times, Jan. 10, 2010.

34. Becker, *Forcing the Spring* (detailed day-by-day description); Frank, *Awakening,* 233–244. Compare Boies and Olson, *Redeeming the Dream* (trial from the perspective of the winning team) with ADF, Perry v. Schwarzenegger *District Court Trial Blog Posts* (Jan. 12–27 and June 16, 2010), http://www.adfmedia.org/News/PRDetail/4897 (trial from the perspective of the Prop 8 defenders).

35. *Perry* trial transcript (day one, Jan. 11), pp. 18–72 (opening statements by Olson, Stewart, Cooper), AFER Archives.

36. Expert report of Nancy Cott, p. 5, *Perry v. Schwarzenegger,* Case No. 09—CV-2292 VRW (N.D. Cal., filed Oct. 2, 2009) (quotation in text).

37. Eskridge interview of Walker.

38. *Perry* trial transcript (day one), pp. 75–86 (Zarrillo), 86–137 (Katami), 137–160 (Perry), 160–181 (Stier); Eskridge interview of Olson (quotation in text). See Kris Perry and Sandy Stier, *Love on Trial: Our Supreme Court Fight for the Right to Marry* (2017); Boies and Olson, *Redeeming the Dream,* 126–137.

39. *Perry* trial transcript (day one), p. 164 (Stier and Perry quotations in text), pp. 80, 88–90 (similar testimony by Zarrillo and Katami).

40. *Perry* trial transcript (day one), pp. 144–146 (first quotation in text), pp. 153–154 (second quotation in text, from Perry's account), 170–171, 175–176 (last quotation in text, from Stier's account). See pp. 82–83 (Zarrillo's testimony about why he and Katami did not register as domestic partners).

41. *Perry* trial transcript (day one), p. 177 (quotation in text).

42. *Perry* trial transcript (day three, Jan. 13), pp. 568–606 (Peplau testimony), pp. 606–659 (cross-examination); *Perry* trial transcript (day six: Jan. 19), pp. 1264–1285 (Sanders testimony).

43. *Perry* trial transcript (day three), pp. 651–654 (quotation in text, from Peplau cross-examination).

44. *Zablocki v. Redhail*, 478 U.S. 374 (1978) (fundamental right to marry for deadbeat dads); *Turner v. Safley*, 482 U.S. 78 (1987) (right to marry for prisoners); Nancy Cott, *Public Vows: A History of Marriage and the Nation* (2000).

45. Rebuttal expert report of Nancy Cott, pp. 2, 4, *Perry v. Schwarzenegger* (filed Nov. 9, 2009) (quotation in text); *Perry* trial transcript (day one), pp. 220–223 (Cott testimony). See Nancy Cott, *The Grounding of Modern Feminism* (1987).

46. *Perry* trial transcript (day one), pp. 203–204 (Cott testimony), discussing *Dred Scott v. Sandford*, 60 U.S. 393, 404–405, 409 (1857) (quotations in text). See *Dred Scott*, pp. 413–416 (post-independence marriage laws and policies marking "negroes" as inferior). The Fourteenth Amendment overrode *Dred Scott*'s citizenship holding.

47. *Perry* trial transcript (day two: Jan. 12), pp. 242–243 (quotations in text, from Cott).

48. *Perry* trial transcript (day two), p. 244 (quotation in text).

49. *Perry* trial transcript (day two), pp. 268, 312–313, 331 (quotations in text, from the Cott examination and cross-examination).

50. Serena Mayeri, *Reasoning from Race: Feminism, Law, and the Civil Rights Revolution* (2011). See *City of Cleburne v. Cleburne Living Center*, 473 U.S. 432 (1985) (disability ought not be a suspect classification, because it was relevant to public policy and the political process had been responsive to petitions from the disability rights community).

51. *Perry* trial transcript (day two), pp. 357–442 (Chauncey testimony). See George Chauncey, *Gay New York: Gender, Urban Culture, and the Making of the Gay Male World, 1890–1940* (1994). On anti-LGBT discrimination in California, see Nan Alamilla Boyd, *A Wide-Open Town: A History of Queer San Francisco to 1965* (2003); Lillian Faderman and Stuart Timmons, *Gay L.A.: A History of Sexual Outlaws, Power Politics, and Lipstick Lesbians* 14–30 (2006); William Eskridge Jr., *The California Supreme Court, 2007 Term—Foreword: The Marriage Cases*, 97 Calif. L. Rev. 1785, 1789–1802 (2009).

52. *Perry* trial transcript (day two), p. 429 (first quotation in text, from Chauncey examination); (day three), pp. 472, 497 (remaining quotations, from Chauncey cross-examination).

53. *Perry* trial transcript (day three), pp. 486–487 (quotation in text, from Chauncey cross-examination); (day six), pp. 1285–1295 (Sanders cross-examination). Cf. John Hart Ely, *Democracy and Distrust: A Theory of Judicial Review* (1980) (counter-majoritarian judicial review is inconsistent with the Constitution unless needed to correct a dysfunctional political process).

54. *Perry* trial transcript (day seven: Jan. 20), p. 1535 (quotation in text, from Segura testimony), pp. 1585–1646 (the religion-based grand coalition), pp. 1657–1667 (evidence of fierce anti-gay hostility).

55. *Perry* trial transcript (day seven), pp. 1660–1669 (Segura cross-examination); *Perry* trial transcript (day ten: Jan. 23), pp. 2428–2437, 2437–2478 (Miller voir dire and testimony); *Perry* trial transcript (day eleven: Jan. 25), pp. 2608–2631, 2710–2714. See Bruce Cain and Kenneth Miller, *The Populist Legacy: Initiatives and the Undermining of Representative Government,* in Larry Sabato et al., eds., *Dangerous Democracy,* 33–62 (2001) (anti-gay stereotyping in the Yes on 8 campaign); Brief amicus curiae of professors William Eskridge Jr. and Bruce Cain in support of petitioners, *Strauss v. Horton,* Case No. 168047 (Cal. Sup. Ct., filed Jan. 15, 2009) (similar). Forgotten today, Alan Spear was a progressive state senator in Minnesota, one of the first legislators to come out as gay.

56. On the paradox that a truly "discrete and insular minority" will usually not be completely "powerless," see Bruce Ackerman, *Beyond* Carolene Products, 98 Harv. L. Rev. 713 (1985).

57. *Perry* trial transcript (day nine: Jan. 22), pp. 2017–2324 (Herek testimony).

58. *Perry* trial transcript (day seven), pp. 1504–1522 (Kendall testimony); Eskridge interview of Walker.

59. *Perry* trial transcript (day eight: Jan. 21), pp. 1939–1940, 1943, 2003 (quotations in text, from Tam examination).

60. *Perry* trial transcript (day one), pp. 41–43, 62–69 (opening arguments).

61. Email from Maggie Gallagher to William Eskridge, May 12, 2018 (first quotation in text); William Eskridge and Christopher Riano interview of David Blankenhorn, New York (March 13, 2016) (second quotation); Sharon Jayson, *Blankenhorn: A Family Guy with a Cause,* USA Today, March 13, 2007.

62. Eskridge and Riano interview of Blankenhorn (quotation in text); *Perry* trial transcript (day eleven), pp. 2732-40 (Blankenhorn voir dire). See David Blankenhorn, *Fatherless in America* (1997) and *The Future of Marriage* (2007).

63. *Perry* trial transcript (day eleven), p. 2745 (Blankenhorn quotation in text); Royal Anthropological Institute, *Notes and Queries on Anthropology,* 71 (1951 ed.) (second quotation). See Eskridge, *Case for Same-Sex Marriage,* pp. 95–96 (the post-1951 debate in anthropology).

64. *Perry* trial transcript (day eleven), pp. 2766–2772 (Blankenhorn quotations in text). See Sara McLanahan and Gary Sandefur, *Growing Up with a Single Parent* (1994).

65. *Perry* trial transcript (day eleven), pp. 2775–2777 (quotation in text).

66. *Perry* trial transcript (day six) (Badgett examination); M. V. Lee Badgett, *When Gay People Get Married: What Happens When Societies Legalize Same-Sex Marriage* (2009); Brief amicus curiae for professors William Eskridge et al., *Perry v. Brown* (9th Cir. No. 10-16696, filed Oct. 25, 2010) (marriage and divorce data for Massachusetts, 2000–2009).

67. *Perry* trial transcript (day eleven), p. 2806 (quotation in text). See Andrew Cherlin, *The Deinstitutionalization of American Marriage,* 66 J. Marriage & Family 848

(Nov. 2004); Norval Glenn, *The Struggle for Same–Sex Marriage*, 41 Society 25 (Sept./ Oct. 2004).

68. *Perry* trial transcript (day eleven), pp. 2806–2830 (quotation in text, from excruciating Blankenhorn cross-examination).

69. *Perry* trial transcript (day eleven), pp. 2879–2911 (cross-examination on the three "universal rules" of marriage). See Eskridge, *Case for Same-Sex Marriage*, pp. 15–35 (same-sex marriage in pre-modern cultures).

70. *Perry* trial transcript (day five: Jan. 10), pp. 1003–1043 (Lamb examination); (day eleven), pp. 2798–2802, 2803 (quotation in text, from Blankenhorn's cross-examination); *Perry* trial transcript (day twelve: Jan. 27), pp. 2846–2855 (Blankenhorn confirming that gay marriage would have benefits for the children raised by such couples).

71. *Perry* trial transcript (day eleven), p. 2805 (quotation in text, from Blankenhorn, *Future of Marriage*, 2); Boies and Olson, *Redeeming the Dream*, 152–159.

72. *Perry v. Schwarzenegger*, 704 F. Supp. 2d 921, 945–950 (N.D. Cal. 2010) (quotation in text and Walker's analysis of Blankenhorn's testimony).

73. *Perry*, pp. 973, 972, 990 (quotations in text).

74. *Perry*, p. 1002 (quotation in text).

75. *Perry v. Schwarzenegger*, 790 F. Supp. 2d 1119, 1125 (N.D. Cal. June 14, 2011) (quotation in text); 28 U.S.C. § 455(b)(4) (relevant recusal law).

76. *Perry v. Schwarzenegger*, 628 F.3d 1191 (9th Cir. Jan. 4, 2011), certifying question to California Supreme Court, as suggested by brief for amicus curiae Equality California, p. 19 n.2, *Perry v. Schwarzenegger*, No. 77-78 (9th Cir., filed Oct. 25, 2010), 2010 WL 4622580. See William Eskridge interview of David Codell, West Hollywood (June 30, 2016). The California Supreme Court's response to the certified question was *Perry v. Brown*, 265 P.3d 1002, 1006 (Cal. Nov. 17, 2011).

77. *Perry v. Brown*, 671 F.3d 1052 (9th Cir. Feb. 7, 2012), rehearing denied, *Perry v. Brown*, 681 F.3d 1065 (9th Cir. June 5, 2012); Eskridge interview of Walker. See Michael Kavey, *Slighting the Sex-Discrimination Claim in* Hollingsworth v. Perry, 37 NYU Rev. L. & Soc. Change 151 (2013).

78. Eskridge telephone interview of Black. Our references to *8 the Play* are based upon our viewing of the video of the Los Angeles performance on March 3, 2012, https://www.youtube.com/watch?v=qlUG8F9uVgM.

79. *8 the Play* (quotations in text).

80. David Blankenhorn, *How My View on Gay Marriage Changed*, New York Times, June 22, 2012 (quotations in text).

81. Eskridge's notes (quotations in text). See William Eskridge Jr., *The Ninth Circuit's Decision and the Constitutional Politics of Marriage Equality*, 64 Stan. L. Rev. Online 93 (2012).

82. Nate Silver, *Support for Gay Marriage Outweighs Opposition in Polls*, New York Times, May 9, 2012.

83. *Hollingsworth v. Perry*, 133 S. Ct. 786 (Dec. 12, 2012) (granting review); *United States v. Windsor*, 133 S. Ct. 786 (Dec. 12, 2012) (granting review).

16. Three Men in a Room

1. *Hernandez v. Robles,* 7 Misc. 3d 459, 461, 794 N.Y.S.2d 579, 582 (Sup. Ct.), rev'd and vacated, 26 A.D.3d 98, 805 N.Y.S.2d 354 (2005), aff'd, 7 N.Y.3d 338, 855 N.E.2d 1 (2006).

2. Karen Tracy, *How Questioning Constructs Judge Identities: Oral Argument About Same-Sex Marriage,* 11 Discourse Studies 199–221 (2009) (quoting and analyzing Judge Smith). Court of appeals insiders have attributed Judge Rosenblatt's decision to his deep devotion to his openly lesbian daughter, Elizabeth (Betsy).

3. *Hernandez v. Robles,* 7 N.Y.3d 338, 366, 855 N.E.2d 1, 12 (2006) (quotations in text, from Smith's plurality opinion); Letter from Deborah Glick to Robert Smith (2006), Task Force Archives. Accounts of discussions during the deliberations of the case are taken from off-the-record interviews with court insiders.

4. *Hernandez,* 7 N.Y.3d, pp. 382, 396 (quotations in text from Kaye's dissenting opinion). Chief Judge Kaye would foresee, almost ten years before *Obergefell v. Hodges* (2015), that the fundamental right to marry applied to same-sex couples.

5. *Megan Benett, David Ratzan,* Weddings, New York Times, June 11, 2006; William Eskridge and Christopher Riano interview of Judith Kaye, New York City (Nov. 2016) (first and third quotations in text); *Hernandez,* 7 N.Y.3d, p. 380 (second quotation, from Kaye's dissenting opinion).

6. Valuable accounts of the New York marriage campaign from the perspective of LGBTQ+ organizations and activists include Kerry Eleveld, *Don't Tell Me to Wait: How the Fight for Gay Rights Changed America and Transformed Obama's Presidency,* 225–232 (2015); Nathaniel Frank, *Awakening: How Gays and Lesbians Brought Marriage Equality to America,* 259–267 (2017); Marc Solomon, *Winning Marriage: The Inside Story of How Same-Sex Couples Took on the Politicians and Pundits—and Won* (2014). Also essential to understanding the campaign, however, is the important role played by the governor and gay and lesbian legislators.

7. George Chauncey, *Gay New York: Gender, Urban Culture, and the Making of the Gay Male World, 1890–1940,* 291–299 (1994); Lawrence Grobel, *Conversations with Capote* (1985) (Capote quotation in text).

8. New York State Office of the Attorney General, "The Sexual Orientation Non-Discrimination Act ('SONDA')," https://ag.ny.gov/civil-rights/sonda-brochure; Letter from Glick to Smith, referencing Smith's discussion of "sexual preference" in *Hernandez,* 7 N.Y.3d, pp. 364–366.

9. *People v. Onofre,* 51 N.Y.2d 476 (1980); *In the Matter of Alison D. v. Virginia M.,* 77 N.Y.2d 651 (1991), overruled by *Brooke S.B. v. Elizabeth A.C.C.,* 27 N.Y.3d 1026, 61 N.E.3d 488 (2016); Eskridge and Riano interview of Kaye (quotation in text).

10. Discussion of Tom Duane's life and career draws from Christopher Riano's in-person and phone interviews of him from 2015–2017. Duane has mentored the next generation of LGBTQ+ political leaders, including his successor in the senate, Brad Hoylman, and Corey Johnson, an HIV-positive gay man who is the current speaker of the New York City Council.

11. Senator Andrea Stewart-Cousins became New York's first female majority leader in 2019.

12. Christopher Riano interview of Tom Duane, New York City (Nov. 2015).

13. Lou Chibbaro Jr., *Legacy of 9/11*, Washington Blade, Sept. 8, 2011. The New York State Crime Victims Board would further expand benefits to same-sex domestic partners of all homicide victims on a permanent basis in October 2002.

14. Christopher Riano interviews of Danny O'Donnell as well as his staff, friends, and confidants from 2015–2018. Danny's younger sister is celebrity and LGBTQ+ activist Rosie O'Donnell.

15. Letter from Daniel O'Donnell to the New York Assembly's Democratic Conference, May 22, 1007 (quotation in text).

16. Mildred Loving, "Loving for All" (June 12, 2007) (first quotation in text), attached to letter from Daniel O'Donnell to members of the New York Assembly, June 18, 2007 (second quotation).

17. Danny Hakim and William Rashbaum, *Spitzer Is Linked to Prostitution Ring*, New York Times, Mar. 20, 2008.

18. Paul Vitello, *With Pomp and a New Vigor, Dolan Arrives as Archbishop*, New York Times, April 15, 2009.

19. *Skelos v. Paterson*, 13 N.Y.3d 141, 915 N.E.2d 1141 (2009) (4-3 court holding that the governor had authority to appoint a new lieutenant governor, who would preside over the senate).

20. Solomon, *Winning Marriage*, 154–155 (quotation in text).

21. Christopher Riano telephone interview of Alphonso David (Nov. 8, 2015), as well as follow-up with numerous other sources.

22. Alphonso David, Note, Bragdon v. Abbott: *The Supreme Court Redefines "Disability" Under the Americans with Disabilities Act,* 9 Temp. Pol. & Civ. Rts. L. Rev. 109 (Fall 1999) (quotation in text).

23. Richard Pérez-Peña, *Cuomo Quits Primary Race and Endorses McCall for Governor*, New York Times, Sept. 3, 2002.

24. Joshua David Stein, *The Semi Homemade World of Sandra Lee*, Out, April 3, 2011.

25. Solomon, *Winning Marriage*, 169–170 (quotations in text).

26. Frank, *Awakening*, 261–263; Jeremy Peters, *Campaign Goes After Opponents of Gay Marriage*, New York Times, Feb. 24, 2010.

27. Michael Barbaro, *Behind N.Y. Gay Marriage, an Unlikely Mix of Forces*, New York Times, June 25, 2011 (principal players in 2011 marriage campaign).

28. Christopher Riano's off-the-record interviews; Governor Andrew Cuomo's schedules, Feb.–June 2011.

29. Christopher Riano interviews of Alphonso David, Daniel O'Donnell, and Tom Duane, as well as Brian Silva (Marriage Equality New York), Marty Rouse (HRC), and Marc Solomon (Freedom to Marry).

30. Governor Andrew Cuomo's schedule, Feb. 2011.

31. The account of the Cuomo-Dolan meeting is based on off-the-record conversations by executive insiders with your authors.

32. Governor Andrew Cuomo's schedule, March 2011; Solomon, *Winning Marriage*, 174–178.

33. Solomon, *Winning Marriage*, 178–182.

34. William Eskridge telephone interview of Ken Mehlman (July 8, 2019).

35. Solomon, *Winning Marriage*, 187–192 (quotations in text); Eskridge telephone interview of Mehlman.

36. Governor Andrew Cuomo's schedule, May 2011.

37. Jeremy Peters, *Celebrities Champion State's Same-Sex Marriage Bill*, New York Times, May 28, 2009.

38. Nicholas Confessore and Michael Barbaro, *Once Against Gay Marriage, 4 Senators Say They Will Back It*, New York Times, June 13, 2011; Solomon, *Winning Marriage*, 194–201.

39. Solomon, *Winning Marriage*, 201–202 (quotation in text).

40. Letter from Robin Fretwell Wilson to John Saland, June 15, 2011 (quotation in text).

41. *Republican NY State Senator Roy McDonald's Awesome Defense of Gay Marriage*, HuffPost, June 16, 2011 (quotation in text).

42. Danny Hakim, *Exemptions Were Key to Vote on Gay Marriage*, New York Times, June 25, 2011.

43. John Burger, *Archbishop Dolan on Same-Sex "Marriage" Vote*, National Catholic Register, June 24, 2011 (quotations in text).

44. Proposed Marriage Equality Act, Bill 808354, New York Assembly, §§ 3 and 5 (June 14, 2011). For analysis skeptical of the effect of the religious exemptions, see David Wexelblat, *Trojan Horse or Much Ado About Nothing? Analyzing the Religious Exemptions in New York's Marriage Equality Act*, 20 Am. U.J. Gender, Soc. Pol'y & Law 961–993 (2012).

45. Solomon, *Winning Marriage*, 210–212 (quotations in text, Solomon's paraphrases of Alesi's argument).

46. Riano interview of David. We do not know all the reasons why Skelos finally allowed a marriage vote to proceed. Because he was in jail as we finished up the book, he was unavailable for an interview.

47. Solomon, *Winning Marriage*, 212–216 (quotation in text).

48. Marriage Equality Act of 2011, ch. 95, 2011 N.Y. Sess. Laws 95 (McKinney); *Lawsuit Seeks to Set Aside New York Same-Sex Marriage Law Over Open Meetings Violations*, Liberty Counsel, July 25, 2011.

49. Dean Skelos was first convicted in 2015, but his first conviction was overturned in 2017 before he was retried and again convicted. Sheldon Silver was first convicted in 2015, but his first conviction was overturned in 2017 before he was retried and again convicted.

17. Obama's Team Gay

1. "Open Letter from Barack Obama to the LGBT Community" (Feb. 28, 2008), http://bilerico.lgbtqnation.com/2008/02/open_letter_from_barack_obama_to_the _lgb.php.

2. For the pre-2007 quotations, see Tracy Baim, *How Obama's Marriage Views Changed*, Windy City Times, Jan. 14, 2009; David Garrow, *Rising Star: The Making of Barack Obama*, 646, 865, 993, 1030 (2017). For the 2007 quotation, see Lynn Sweet, Chicago-Sun Times, transcript of HRC/LOGO Forum for the Democratic Candidates, Los Angeles (Aug. 7, 2007).

3. Letter from Senator Barack Obama to the Alice B. Toklas Democratic Club, San Francisco, June 28, 2008 (first quotation in text); Transcript of Saddleback Presidential Forum, Aug. 16, 2008, http://www.thirty-thousand.org/pages/Saddleback _16AUG2008.htm#marriage (remainder of the quotations); William Eskridge interview of Tobias Wolff, Philadelphia (Sept. 25, 2018).

4. William Eskridge telephone interview of Valerie Jarrett (April 7, 2017).

5. Barack Obama, *The Audacity of Hope: Thoughts on Reclaiming the American Dream*, 222–223 (2006); Interview with President Barack Obama, Buzzfeed, 2015 (quotations in text).

6. David Axelrod, *Believer: My Forty Years in Politics*, 447 (2015) (quotations in text); Randall Kennedy, *The Persistence of the Color Line: Racial Politics and the Obama Presidency* (2012).

7. Kerry Eleveld, *Don't Tell Me to Wait: How the Fight for Gay Rights Changed America and Transformed Obama's Presidency* (2015); Marc Solomon, *Winning Marriage: The Inside Story of How Same-Sex Couples Took on the Politicians and Pundits—and Won* (2014); Martin Meeker interview of Evan Wolfson, p. 213 (April 14, 2015), F2M Oral History (quotation in text).

8. Our account of Senator Obama's remarks at the Jennings-Davis fundraiser is a synthesis of reports from the hosts and several people who attended.

9. William Eskridge telephone interview of Kevin Jennings (Aug. 31, 2018) (quotations in text are based on the host's recollection).

10. See David Maraniss, *Barack Obama: The Story* (2012) (Obama's ancestors and early life), reviewed by James Fallows, *The Making of the President*, New York Times, June 14, 2012.

11. William Eskridge telephone interview of Brian Bond (April 22, 2017); Brief of Professors William Alford et al. as amici curiae, *Rumsfeld v. Forum Academic Freedom & Institutional Rights*, 447 U.S. 47 (No. 05-1152, filed Sept. 12, 2005), 2005 WL 2367595 (brief by Dean Kagan and her faculty on the statutory issue, unanimously rejected by the justices).

12. David Graham, *Bob Gates, America's Unlikely Gay-Rights Hero*, The Atlantic, July 28, 2015. See Robert Gates, *Duty: Memoirs of a Secretary at War* (2014).

13. *In re Golinski*, 587 F.3d 901 (9th Cir. Jan. 13, 2009); *Gill v. Office of Personnel Management*, Civ. No. 09-10309-JLT (D. Mass., filed March 3, 2009).

14. Eleveld, *Don't Tell Me to Wait*, 65–71; Andrew Sullivan, *Barack Obama's Gay Marriage Evolution*, Newsweek, May 13, 2009. On the Langbehn tragedy and the administration's response, see Tara Parker-Pope, *Kept from a Dying Partner's Bedside*, New York Times, May 18, 2009; William Eskridge telephone interview of Marty Lederman (June 25, 2019); Memorandum from President Obama to HHS Secretary, "Respecting the Rights of Hospital Patients to Receive Visitors and to Designate Surrogate Decision Makers for Medical Emergencies," 75 Fed. Reg. 20,511 (April 15, 2010).

15. William Eskridge telephone interview of Tony West (May 8, 2017); Memorandum in support of motion to dismiss, pp. 18–19 and fn., *Smelt v. United States*, Case No. SACV-09-286 DOC (C.D. Cal., filed June 11, 2009) (part IV), pp. 21–29 (part V).

16. John Aravosis, "Obama Defends DOMA in Federal Court. Says Banning Gay Marriage Is Good for the Federal Budget. Invokes Incest and Marrying Children," AMERICAblog, June 12, 2009 (first quotations in text); Nathaniel Frank, *Awakening: How Gays and Lesbians Brought Marriage Equality to America*, 199–201 (2017) (last quotation).

17. William Eskridge telephone interview of Brian Bond (April 30, 2017) (post-*Smelt* White House monitoring of DOJ marriage filings and the spontaneous generation of Team Gay).

18. Eleveld, *Don't Tell Me to Wait*, 86–88; William Eskridge telephone interview of Brian Bond (April 13, 2017); Eskridge telephone interview of West.

19. President Barack Obama, memorandum for the heads of executive departments and agencies, "Federal Benefits and Non-Discrimination," 74 Fed. Reg. 29,393 (June 17, 2009) (quotations in text); Secretary of State Hillary Rodham Clinton, press release, *Benefits for Same-Sex Domestic Partners of Foreign Service Employees* (June 18, 2009); Office of Personnel Management, "Absence and Leave; Definition of Family Member, Immediate Relative, and Related Terms," 75 Fed. Reg. 33,491 (June 14, 2010).

20. Our account of the July 2009 Roosevelt Room meeting is drawn from conversations with several attendees. See also Eleveld, *Don't Tell Me to Wait*, 87–88 (quotation in text).

21. Eskridge telephone interview with Bond (April 13) (quotation in text, based on Bond's recollection).

22. Reply brief in support of motion to dismiss, p. 2, *Smelt v. United States*, 2009 WL 2610458 (C.D. Cal. Aug. 17, 2009) (quotation in text); Order dismissing complaint, *Smelt*, 2009 WL 10674308 (Aug. 24, 2009).

23. Memorandum of law in support of defendants' motion to dismiss, p. 19, n.10, *Gill v. Office of Personnel Management*, 2009 WL 5803678 (D. Mass., filed Sept. 18, 2009) (disavowing responsible procreation and optimal child-rearing arguments), pp. 16–17 (quotations in text). For a critique of the government's argumentation, see Lynn Wardle, *Section Three of the Defense of Marriage Act: Deciding, Democracy, and the Constitution*, 58 Drake L. Rev. 951, 970 (2010).

24. *City of Cleburne v. Cleburne Living Center, Inc.*, 473 U.S. 432, 442 (1985), classically setting forth the four criteria for heightened scrutiny; *Schroer v. Billington*, 577 F. Supp. 2d 293 (D.D.C. Sept. 19, 2008) (gender identity discrimination against transgender employees is "discrimination because of sex" in violation of Title VII; no appeal taken by the federal government). Subsequently, the Obama EEOC took the position that Title VII's bar to employment discrimination because of sex protected transgender persons.

25. Memorandum from ACLU, GLAD, HRC, Lambda Legal to Tony West, assistant attorney general, civil division, "The Administration's legal position regarding whether government classifications based on sexual orientation trigger heightened judicial scrutiny" (Sept. 9, 2009) (quotation in text); Memorandum from ACLU, GLAD, HRC, Lambda Legal to Tony West, assistant attorney general, civil division, "The Administration's legal position on justifications advanced in the House Report on DOMA and on opposing intervention" (Sept. 11, 2009).

26. Eskridge telephone interview of West; Eskridge telephone interview of Bond (April 13). All but one of the court of appeals' decisions rejecting heightened scrutiny for sexual orientation relied on *Bowers*. The one exception, *Citizens for Equal Protection v. Bruning*, 455 F.3d 859 (8th Cir. 2006), relied on the optimal parenting and responsible procreation arguments.

27. US Const., art. II (quotations in text); *Oregon v. Mitchell*, 400 U.S. 112, 117–118 (1970) (opinion of Black, J., announcing the judgment of the court): Katherine Shaw, *Constitutional Nondefense in the States*, 114 Colum. L. Rev. 213, 232 n.84 (2014). For an audio of Griswold's oral argument, see https://www.oyez.org/cases/1970/43-orig. See Larry Alexander and Frederick Schauer, *On Extrajudicial Constitutional Interpretation*, 110 Harv. L. Rev. 1359 (1997). For academic arguments that the president has a duty not to defend statutes he or she believes are unconstitutional, see Edward Corwin, *Court over Constitution*, 5–6 (1938); Neal Devins and Saikrishna Prakash, *The Indefensible Duty to Defend*, 112 Colum. L. Rev. 507, 509 (2012); Michael Stokes Paulsen, *The Most Dangerous Branch: Executive Power to Say What the Law Is*, 83 Geo. L.J. 217, 228–262 (1994); Saikrishna Prakash, *The Executive's Duty to Disregard Unconstitutional Laws*, 96 Geo. L.J. 1613 (2008).

28. Brief for the United States as amicus curiae supporting petitioner, *Metro Broadcasting, Inc. v. FCC*, 497 U.S. 547 (1990), 1989 WL 1126975; Marty Lederman, *John Roberts and the SG's Refusal to Defend Federal Statutes* in Metro Broadcasting v. FCC, Balkinization, Sept. 8, 2005.

29. Dawn Johnsen, *The Obama Administration's Decision to Defend Constitutional Equality Rather Than the Defense of Marriage Act*, 81 Fordham L. Rev. 599 (2012) (history of the HIV ban); Dawn Johnsen, *Presidential Non-Enforcement of Constitutionally Objectionable Statutes*, 63 Law & Contemp. Probs. 7 (Winter/Spring 2000).

30. Daniel Meltzer, *Executive Defense of Congressional Acts,* 61 Duke L.J. 1183 (2012). On the two noted exceptions to the duty to defend, see "Presidential Authority to Decline to Execute Unconstitutional Statutes," 18 Op. O.L.C. 199, 201 (1994) (Walter Dellinger and Dawn Johnsen); "Attorney General's Duty to Defend the Constitutionality of Statutes," 5 Op. O.L.C. 25, 25 (1981).

31. OLC, memorandum opinion for the acting deputy attorney general, "Whether the Criminal Provisions of the Violence Against Women Act Apply to Otherwise Covered Conduct When the Offender and the Victim Are the Same Sex," 34 Op. O.L.C. 1 (2010); Administrator's interpretation, Department of Labor, No. 2010-3 (June 22, 2010) (FMLA covers lesbian and gay families).

32. White House, presidential memorandum for the heads of executive departments and agencies, "Extension of Benefits to Same-Sex Domestic Partners of Federal Employees," 75 Fed. Reg. 32,247 (June 2, 2010) (quotation in text).

33. Joseph Landau, *DOMA and Presidential Discretion: Interpreting and Enforcing Federal Law,* 81 Fordham L. Rev. 619, 632–642 (2012) (examples of discretionary nonenforcement of immigration bars and commands).

34. Matthew Shepard and James Byrd Jr. Hate Crimes Prevention Act of 2009, enacted as §§ 4701–4713 of the National Defense Authorization Act for Fiscal Year 2010, P.L. 111-84, 123 Stat. 2190 (Oct. 28, 2009).

35. *Log Cabin Republicans v. United States,* 716 F. Supp. 2d 884 (C.D. Cal. Oct. 12, 2010). See Nathaniel Frank, *Unfriendly Fire: How the Gay Ban Undermines the Military and Weakens America* (2009); Tobias Wolff, *Political Representation and Accountability Under Don't Ask, Don't Tell,* 89 Iowa L. Rev. 1633 (2004).

36. Department of Defense counsel Jeh Johnson and General Carter Ham, *Report of the Comprehensive Review of the Issues Associated with a Repeal of "Don't Ask, Don't Tell"* (Nov. 30, 2000); Don't Ask, Don't Tell Repeal Act of 2010, P.L. 111-321, 124 Stat. 3515 (Dec. 22, 2010); Eskridge interview of Wolff.

37. Marc Ambinder, *Bush Campaign Chief and Former RNC Chair Ken Mehlman: I'm Gay,* The Atlantic, Aug. 25, 2010.

38. Aaron Belkin et al., *Readiness and DADT Repeal: Has the New Policy of Open Service Undermined the Military?,* 2, n.3 (2012) (opposition by retired generals and admirals); Aaron Belkin et al., Palm Center, *One Year Out: An Assessment of DADT's Repeal on Military Readiness* (Sept. 30, 2012) (no deleterious effect).

39. *Dred Scott v. Sandford,* 60 U.S. 393, 415, 420 (1857) (quotations in text). On race, sex, and sexual orientation exclusions as a gendered denial of full citizenship, see Kenneth Karst, *The Pursuit of Manhood and the Desegregation of the Armed Forces,* 38 UCLA L. Rev. 499 (1991).

40. *Gill v. Office of Personnel Management,* 699 F. Supp. 2d 374 (D. Mass July 8, 2010); *Massachusetts v. U.S. Dep't of Health & Human Services,* 698 F. Supp. 2d 234 (D. Mass. July 8, 2010). The decisions were consolidated for purposes of appeal and both were

affirmed in *Massachusetts v. U.S. Dep't Health & Human Servs.*, 682 F.3d 1 (1st Cir. May 31, 2012), discussed in chapter 19.

41. Johnsen, *Obama Administration's Decision*, 608–609; former solicitor general Seth Waxman, *Twins at Birth: Civil Rights and the Role of the Solicitor General*, 75 Ind. L.J. 1297 (2000).

42. Eleveld, *Don't Tell Me to Wait*, 212 (quoting the president).

43. William Eskridge interview of former assistant attorney general Stuart Delery, Washington, DC (Sept. 2, 2016); Brief for appellants, *Massachusetts v. U.S. Dep't Health & Human Servs.*, No. 10-2204 (1st Cir., filed Jan. 13, 2011).

44. Complaint, *Windsor v. United States*, No. 1:10CV08435 (S.D.N.Y., filed Nov. 9, 2010), 2010 WL 5647015; Frank, *Awakening*, 257 (quotation in text).

45. Our account of the civil division discussions is based upon off-the-record conversations with civil division attorneys.

46. Jo Becker, *Forcing the Spring: Inside the Fight for Marriage Equality*, 248–249 (2014) (quotations in text).

47. Department of Justice, Office of Public Affairs, letter from the attorney general to Congress on litigation involving the Defense of Marriage Act (Feb. 23, 2011) (quotations in text); 28 U.S.C. § 530D (requiring the DOJ to notify Congress when it is declining to defend the validity of an act of Congress).

48. Dahlia Lithwick, *The Best Offense Is a Good Defense: Why Even Opponents of DOMA Should Want It to Get a Vigorous Defense*, Slate, April 26, 2011 (quotation in text); *Golinski v. United States Office of Personnel Management*, 824 F. Supp. 2d 968 (N.D. Cal. Feb. 22, 2012) (earliest judicial opinion accepting the new DOJ argument for heightened scrutiny).

49. Joel Benenson and Jan van Lohuizen, "The Rapid Increase in Support for Marriage Changes Political Equation; Emerging Majority Supports the Freedom to Marry" (July 27, 2011) (quotations in text); Solomon, *Winning Marriage*, 291–293, referencing Ruth Marcus, *The Good Politics of Marriage Equality*, Washington Post, July 27, 2011.

50. William Eskridge telephone interview of Ken Mehlman (March 8, 2019) (quotation in text).

51. Email from Ken Mehlman to David Plouffe, Nov. 10, 2011, provided in an email from Mehlman to William Eskridge, July 8, 2019 (quotation in text).

52. Solomon, *Winning Marriage*, 296–300.

53. William Eskridge interview of Steve Richetti, Washington, DC (Aug. 25, 2015); Becker, *Forcing the Spring*, 286 (quotations in text).

54. David Gregory interview of Vice President Joe Biden, *Meet the Press*, Sunday, May 6, 2012, https://www.nbcnews.com/meet-the-press/video/flashback-bidens-2012 -endorsement-of-same-sex-marriage-471856195543?v=raila& (quotations in text).

55. Gautam Raghavan, ed., *West Wingers: Stories from the Dream Chasers, Change Makers, and Hope Creators Inside the Obama White House*, 15–18 (2018).

18. Behind the Glass

1. MAP and GLAAD, *Talking About Marriage and Relationship Recognition for Gay Couples* (Jan. 2008) (summarizing the findings of the confidential Toolkit); William Eskridge interview of Rea Carey, National LGBTQ Task Force, Washington, DC (Dec. 6, 2018); William Eskridge interview of Sayre Reece, National LGBTQ Task Force, Washington, DC (Dec. 7, 2018).

2. William Eskridge and Christopher Riano telephone interview of Thalia Zepatos (Oct. 23, 2015); Martin Meeker interview of Thalia Zepatos (Feb. 18–19, 2016), F2M Oral History.

3. Proteus Fund, *Hearts and Minds: The Untold Story of How Philanthropy and the Civil Marriage Collaborative Helped America Embrace Marriage Equality*, 8 (2015) (quotations in text); Memorandum from Seth Kilbourn and Geoff Kors, "Public Education on Marriage Equality in California" (draft, April 25, 2005), HRC Archives.

4. William Eskridge telephone interviews of Dr. Phyllis Watts (June 18, 2018; March 18, 2019); Robert Perez and Amy Simon, *Heartwired: Human Behavior, Strategic Opinion Research and the Audacious Pursuit of Social Change*, 15 (2017), https://www.packard.org/wp-content/uploads/2017/05/Heartwired-digital.pdf.

5. Let California Ring, *The Garden Wedding* (2007–2008), https://www.youtube.com/watch?v=GG7ddWLF_Fk (quotation in text); Meeker interview of Zepatos, pp. 39–46.

6. MAP and GLAAD, *Talking About Marriage* (rights-based arguments don't work to change opinions; values-based and emotion-appealing arguments can work). Accord, David Cole, *Engines of Liberty: How Citizen Movements Succeed,* chap. 5 (2017); William Eskridge Jr., *The Case for Same-Sex Marriage: From Sexual Liberty to Civilized Commitment* (1996).

7. Eskridge interview of Reece; Benoit Denizet-Lewis, *How Do You Change Voters' Minds? Have a Conversation,* New York Times, April 7, 2016.

8. Lanae Erickson Hatalsky and Thalia Zepatos, "The Marriage Movement's Secret Weapon: Radical Cooperation," HuffPost, June 26, 2015 (quotation in text); William Eskridge telephone interview of Thalia Zepatos (Jan. 25, 2019).

9. Steve Law, *Oregon Paved the Way in Support of Gay Marriage,* Portland Tribune, June 25, 2015; Molly Ball, *The Marriage Plot: Inside This Year's Epic Campaign for Gay Equality,* The Atlantic, Dec. 11, 2012.

10. Eskridge telephone interview of Watts (March 2019).

11. Meeker interview of Zepatos, pp. 61–67; Freedom to Marry, *Moving Marriage Forward: Building Majority Support for Marriage* (May 2010). Cf. David Blankenhorn, Institute for American Values, *Why Marriage Matters* (2002) (policy arguments favoring the preservation and revival of traditional marriage).

12. William Eskridge and Christopher Riano interview of Evan Wolfson, New York City (2015); Proteus Fund, *Hearts and Minds,* p. 10; Freedom to Marry, *Moving Marriage*

Forward; Nathaniel Frank, *Awakening: How Gays and Lesbians Brought Marriage Equality to America,* 277–282 (2017).

13. Elizabeth Abbott, *A History of Marriage,* 277–278 (2010) (lack of racial diversity in LGBT advocacy groups "reinforces gayness as a white phenomenon").

14. Email from Frank Schubert to William Eskridge, Feb. 26, 2019, referencing Thomas Messner, Heritage Foundation, *The Price of Prop 8* (Oct. 22, 2009).

15. Robert George, Timothy George, and Charles Colson, drafters, "Manhattan Declaration: A Call of Christian Conscience" (Nov. 20, 2009) (quotations in text).

16. GLAAD, quotations from Rev. Derek McCoy, https://www.glaad.org/cap/maryland-derek-mccoy?response_type=embed (quoting McCoy's anti-gay remarks); Aaron McQuade, GLAAD, *Profiles of Anti-LGBT Activists in Maine, Maryland, Minnesota, and Washington* (Oct. 29, 2012) (remaining quotations in text). See Zack Ford, *Marriage Equality Opponents Distribute Sodomy Based Marriage Truth Pledge,* Think Progress, April 9, 2012; Van Smith, *Inside the Crusade to Kill Maryland's New Marriage-Equality Law,* City Paper, Oct. 3, 2012.

17. Worldwide Ministries, "Washington State Referendum 74" (April 9, 2012) (Backholm's arguments); McQuade, GLAAD, *Profiles* (first quotation in text). The Fitzgerald quotation is taken from "North Carolina Same-Sex Marriage, Amendment 1 (May 2012), TV Ads," Ballotpedia, https://www.ballotpedia.org/wiki/index.php/North_Carolina_Same-Sex_Marriage,_Amendment_1_%28May_2012%29,_TV_ads (third video from the top of the page).

18. Grassroots Solutions, *The 2012 Marriage Campaigns: A Qualitative and Quantitative Analysis* (2013) (for Freedom to Marry) and *Analysis of the 2012 Marriage Campaigns* (July 2014) (for Center for American Progress); Marc Solomon, *Winning Marriage: The Inside Story of How Same-Sex Couples Took on the Politicians and Pundits—and Won,* 229–246 (2014); Freedom to Marry, "Summary of Support for the 2012 Marriage States" (Jan. 2013).

19. Grassroots Solutions, *Analysis of the 2012 Marriage Campaigns;* Irina Vaynerman, "Same-Sex Marriage in Minnesota: An Analysis and Critique of the Campaigns For and Against the Minnesota Marriage Protection Amendment" (Yale Law School, May 23, 2013); Martin Meeker interview of Thomas Wheatley, pp. 14–15, 19–22 (Feb. 20, 2015), F2M Oral History (focus groups did not like ads featuring gay and lesbian couples).

20. Eskridge interviews of Carey and Reece; David Fleischer, *The Prop 8 Report: What Defeat in California Can Teach Us About Winning Future Ballot Measures on Same-Sex Marriage* (Aug. 3, 2010); Grassroots Solutions, *Analysis of the 2012 Marriage Campaigns,* 41–43; Solomon, *Winning Marriage,* 241–244 (quotation in text); Meeker interview of Wheatley, pp. 15–16.

21. Eskridge interview of Carey.

22. William Eskridge telephone interview of Marc Solomon (May 1, 2019); Martin Meeker interview of Matt McTighe (April 10, 2016), F2M Oral History.

23. Martin Meeker interview of Richard Carlbom (May 10–11, 2016), F2M Oral History.

24. Email from Evan Wolfson to William Eskridge, April 30, 2019; William Eskridge telephone interview of Marc Solomon (May 4, 2019).

25. William Eskridge and Christopher Riano interview of Marty Rouse, Washington, DC (June 23, 2017); William Eskridge interview of Josh Friedes, New York City (July 17, 2017).

26. William Yardley, *Washington: Gay Marriage Wins a Crucial Backer,* Washington Post, Jan. 23, 2012 (quotations in text); Email from Thalia Zepatos to William Eskridge, Feb. 11, 2019.

27. Eskridge interview of Solomon (May 4); Meeker interview of Wheatley, pp. 14–15.

28. William Eskridge interview of Rev. Delman Coates, Washington, DC (June 19, 2017); Miranda Spivack, *Speaking Out for Same-Sex Marriage Law, Black Minister Stands Apart,* Washington Post, Feb. 13, 2012.

29. Email from Schubert to Eskridge (quotation in text).

30. Solomon, *Winning Marriage,* 233–238, 241–246; Freedom to Marry, "Summary of Support," 2–3 (support for Maine campaign).

31. Francis DeBernardo, ed., *What Did the Bishop Do in Maine? Depends on Which News Source You Follow,* New Ways Ministry, March 6, 2012.

32. Mainers United, *Harlan,* https://www.youtube.com/watch?v=2dTdP-XLZzk (quotations in text).

33. Eskridge telephone interview of Solomon (May 1); Mainers United, *Brotherhood,* https://www.familyequality.org/2012/09/24/maine-firefighters-for-marriage-equality/ (first quotation in text); Mainers United, *Redikers,* https://www.youtube.com/watch?v=rzGLqWjuu18 (remaining quotations).

34. David Sharp, *Gay Marriage Opponents Launch Two New Ads,* Associated Press, Oct. 7, 2012 (ad description and quotation in text); Email from Schubert to Eskridge.

35. Protect Marriage Maine, *O'Reillys* (Oct. 22, 2012), https://www.huffpost.com/entry/jim-and-mary-oreilly-vermont-wildflower-inn-anti-gay-marriage-maine_n_2002439; Protect Marriage Maine, *Local Schools* (Oct. 30, 2012), https://www.youtube.com/watch?v=MER3qEaQlkY&version=3&hl=en%5FUS&rel=0 (quotation in text).

36. Meeker interview of McTighe, pp. 68–70. For Zepatos's account, see Molly Ball, *The Marriage Plot: Inside This Year's Epic Campaign for Gay Equality,* The Atlantic, Dec. 11, 2012.

37. Ilana Rosen, *Maine: Diversity Day Hijacked by Opponents of Marriage Equality,* SIECUS, Dec. 2012 (quotation in text).

38. Meeker interview of McTighe (quotations in text).

39. Saha Aslanian and Eric Ringham, *Eighteen Months to History: How the Minnesota Marriage Amendment Was Defeated—Money, Passion, Allies,* Minnesota Public Radio, Nov. 9, 2012; Eskridge telephone interview of Frank Schubert (July 14, 2017); Eskridge and Riano telephone interview of Zepatos.

40. Freedom to Marry, "Summary of Support," 3–4 (support for Minnesota campaign); Freedom to Marry, *Grandparents* (Aug. 2012), http://thecolu.mn/8451/freedom-to-marry-debuts-minnesotas-first-vote-no-ad (quotations in text).

41. Rose French and Baird Helgeson, *The Archbishop Draws the Line*, Star Tribune, Oct. 27, 2012 (quotation in text).

42. Rose French, *State's Methodists Vote to Oppose Marriage Ban*, Star Tribune, June 13, 2012.

43. The first Minnesota Marriage Minute was posted on Jan. 3, 2012, https://www.youtube.com/watch?v=7cDUN75OouA, and was followed by weekly postings until Nov. 2012.

44. Minnesota for Marriage, *Not Live and Let Live* (Oct. 2012); Minnesota for Marriage, *Broken Promises* (Nov. 2, 2012), https://www.mprnews.org/story/2012/11/02/politics/pro-marriage-measure-group-releases-new-ads (quotations in text).

45. Eskridge telephone interview of Watts. Minnesota United's *Kriesel* (Oct. 26, 2012, quoted in text) can be accessed at Aslanian and Ringham, *Eighteen Months to History*.

46. Solomon, *Winning Marriage*, 238–239 (quotations in text); Grassroots Solutions, *Analysis of the 2012 Marriage Campaigns*, 19; Washington Public Disclosure Commission, 2012 Public Contributions by Initiative Committees (Statewide).

47. Freedom to Marry, *Pflug* (July 2012), https://www.youtube.com/watch?v=mVqlXACfHVw& (quotation in text).

48. Students at Washington State University, *Cougs for Marriage Equality* (Oct. 20, 2012), https://www.youtube.com/watch?v=N9pfPOkEjPk (quotations in text). The background music is Macklemore & Ryan Lewis, "Same Love," featuring Mary Lambert (Oct. 2, 2012), https://www.youtube.com/watch?v=hlVBg7_o8no.

49. Preserve Marriage Washington, *Examples*, https://www.youtube.com/watch?v=iqcbDVDTTxo (first quotation in text); Preserve Marriage Washington, *Don't Redefine Marriage*, https://www.youtube.com/watch?v=VKGaXe3q93I (remaining quotations). See Preserve Marriage Washington, *Call to Pastors* (Oct. 1, 2012), https://www.youtube.com/watch?v=WDveSPUZ1-0 (Joe Backholm video making the truth-or-consequences arguments against marriage equality).

50. Joel Connelly, *Catholic Bishops Take Campaign to Prayer and Pulpit*, Seattle P-I, Nov. 2, 2012 (quotation in text).

51. *Archbishop Lori, Other Religious Leaders Urge Grass-Roots Efforts to Oppose Redefining Marriage*, Catholic Standard, Archdiocese of Washington, Oct. 10, 2012; Jeannine Gramick and Francis DeBernardo, *A Catholic Case for Same-Sex Marriage*, Washington Post, Feb. 14, 2012 (quotations in text). See also *Mormon Church Sidesteps Question 6*, Washington Post, Oct. 29, 2012.

52. Annie Linskey, *Gay Marriage Supporters Seized Victory After a Tough Start*, Baltimore Sun, Nov. 10, 2012.

53. Eskridge interview of Coates; Marylanders for Marriage Equality, *It's About Fairness* (Rev. Coates, Oct. 9, 2012), https://alchetron.com/Delman-Coates (first quotation

in text); Marylanders for Marriage Equality, *It's About Fairness* (Bishop Hickman, Oct. 9, 2012), https://www.youtube.com/watch?v=-SYSVSQnTnA (second quotation in text).

54. Maryland Marriage Alliance, *Dr. King* (Oct. 24, 2012), https://www.youtube.com /watch?v=h-okT_WSKcA (quotations in text).

55. Maryland Marriage Alliance, *Crank* (Oct. 28, 2012), https://thinkprogress.org /anti-equality-groups-roll-out-more-exaggerated-victim-stories-a40dd7849f92/ (quotations in text).

56. Marylanders for Marriage Equality, *Maryland, It's Time* (Nov. 1, 2012), https:// thinkprogress.org/anti-equality-groups-roll-out-more-exaggerated-victim-stories -a40dd7849f92/ (quotation in text).

57. Christopher Riano interview of Judge Glenn Harrell Jr., Annapolis, MD (Nov. 2012). Judge Harrell was also the author on behalf of the court of a pro-same-sex-divorce opinion, based on comity, in *Port v. Cowan*, 426 Md. 435 (2012).

58. Eskridge interview of Carey; Eskridge interview of Solomon (May 4).

59. Grassroots Solutions, *Analysis of the 2012 Marriage Campaigns,* 22–26 (Obama's positive impact on big pro–marriage equality voter turnout); Memorandum from Alicia Downs and Alex Lundry, Target Point Consulting, to Project Right Side, "10 Key Data Points on Marriage Equality," Nov. 7, 2010 (analysis of marriage issue for Obama's reelection).

60. Grassroots Solutions, *Analysis of the 2012 Marriage Campaigns,* 22; Email from Schubert to Eskridge. In three of the five states, protect marriage campaigns were unlucky to occur just after the installation of new archbishops (Lori in Baltimore, Sartain in Seattle) or during a diocesan vacancy (Portland was in transition after May 10).

61. Joel Benenson (leading Democratic pollster) and Jan van Lohuizen (leading Republican pollster), "The Rapid Increase in Support for Marriage Changes Political Equation; Emerging Majority Supports the Freedom to Marry" (July 27, 2011) (more than 50 percent support for marriage equality in 2011, and growing); Memorandum from Downs and Lundry, "10 Key Data Points."

62. Tim Gihring, *Does It Matter Whether Archbishop John Nienstedt Is Gay?*, Minnesota Post, Aug. 19, 2016.

63. Nancy Polikoff, *Beyond (Straight and Gay) Marriage: Valuing All Families Under the Law* (2008); "Beyond Same-Sex Marriage: A New Strategic Vision for All Our Families and Relationships" (July 26, 2006), https://mronline.org/2006/08/08/beyond -same-sex-marriage-a-new-strategic-vision-for-all-our-families-relationships/.

19. The Perfect Wife

1. Ariel Levy, *The Perfect Wife*, New Yorker, Sept. 23, 2013 (quotations in text); William Eskridge telephone interview of Judith Kasen-Windsor (April 25, 2019). On Windsor's life and great romance with Spyer, see Edie Windsor, with Joshua Lyon, *A*

Wild and Precious Life: A Memoir (2019); Susan Muska and Gréta Olafsdóttir, *Edie and Thea: A Very Long Engagement* (Bless Bless Prods., 2009); Complaint in *Edie Windsor v. United States,* Civil No. 1:10CV08435 (S.D.N.Y., filed Nov. 9, 2010), 2010 WL 5647015.

2. Jill Hamburg Coplan, *When a Woman Loves a Woman: In the Fight for Marriage Equality, It's Edith Windsor vs. the United States of America,* NYU Alumni Magazine, Fall 2011.

3. Muska and Olafsdóttir, *Edie and Thea* (quotations in text); Roberta Kaplan, with Lisa Dickey, *Then Comes Marriage: U.S. v.* Windsor *and the Defeat of DOMA,* 87 (2015); Complaint, *Windsor,* ¶ 21; Levy, *Perfect Wife.*

4. Muska and Olafsdóttir, *Edie and Thea* (quotations in text); Complaint, *Windsor,* ¶ 26.

5. Levy, *Perfect Wife.*

6. Muska and Olafsdóttir, *Edie and Thea* (quotation in text).

7. Levy, *Perfect Wife* (quotation in text). On New York's recognition of valid out-of-state marriages between spouses of the same sex, see *Martinez v. County of Monroe,* 850 N.Y.S.2d 740 (4th Dep't 2008); Memorandum from David Nocenti to agency counsel (May 14, 2008); *Golden v. Paterson,* 877 N.Y.S.2d 822 (N.Y. Sup. Ct. 2008) (rejecting challenge to legality of Nocenti memo).

8. Kaplan and Dickey, *Then Comes Marriage,* 17–21 (quotation in text).

9. *Romer v. Evans,* 517 U.S. 620, 634, 635 (1996) (first two quotations in text); William Eskridge Jr., *Credit Is Due,* New Republic, June 17, 1996 (third quotation in text); Family Research Council, "Media and Congressional Briefing on the Defense of Marriage" (July 2, 1996) (fourth quotation); Scott Ruskay-Kidd, Note, *The Defense of Marriage Act and the Overextension of Congressional Authority,* 97 Colum. L. Rev. 1435, 1481–1482 (1997). Accord, Andrew Koppelman, *Dumb and DOMA: Why the Defense of Marriage Act Is Unconstitutional,* 83 Iowa L. Rev. 1 (1997); Laurence Tribe, *Toward a Less Perfect Union,* New York Times, May 25, 1996; Evan Wolfson and Michael Melcher, *The Supreme Court's Decision in* Romer v. Evans *and Its Implications for the Defense of Marriage Act,* 16 Quinnipiac L. Rev. 217 (1996).

10. Martin Meeker interview of James Esseks, pp. 34–35 (April 12, 2016), F2M Oral History. Before *Goodridge,* the Netherlands had been the first modern country to recognize lesbian and gay marriages, in 2000–2001.

11. *Lawyers Weekly Diversity Heroes: Michele Granda,* Mass. Lawyers Weekly, Jan. 22, 2007.

12. Michele Granda, GLAD, memorandum, "Section 3 of DOMA Violates the Tenth Amendment" (June 2003), GLAD Archives; *South Dakota v. Dole,* 483 U.S. 203, 207–208, 211 (1987). We examined fourteen legal memoranda and two legal overviews of the federalism issues in the GLAD Archives for the period 2003–2009.

13. Michele Granda, GLAD, memorandum, "Further Reflections on a Challenge to Federal DOMA, Section 3" (July 28, 2003), GLAD Archives; Jill Elaine Hasday, *Federalism and the Family Reconstructed,* 45 UCLA L. Rev. 1297 (1998) (extensive federal

regulation of marriage and family today); Julie Murray, GLAD, memorandum, "Historical Precedent of Federal Intervention in Definition of Marriage, Bearing on GLAD's Challenge to Section 3 of Federal DOMA" (May 1, 2009), GLAD Archives; *Erie R.R. Co. v. Tompkins,* 304 U.S. 64, 78 (1938) (quotation in text). Accord, Kristin Collins, *Federalism's Fallacy: The Early Tradition of Federal Family Law and the Invention of States' Rights,* 26 Cardozo L. Rev. 1761 (2005); Courtney Joslin, *Federalism and Family Status,* 90 Ind. L.J. 787 (2015).

14. Granda, "Further Reflections"; Michele Granda, GLAD, memorandum, "Remaining Issues from June 16th Meeting on Federal DOMA, Section 3," p. 4 (July 14, 2003), GLAD Archives (quotation in text); Notes on National LGBT Legal Roundtable, ACLU Headquarters, New York City, Sept. 22–23, 2003. See *Printz v. United States,* 521 U.S. 898, 928 (1997) (no commandeering state and local officials); *New York v. United States,* 505 U.S. 144, 188 (1992) (no commandeering state legislatures).

15. David Buckel, Lambda Legal, memorandum, "Federal DOMA Challenge: Switching Strategy?" (April 25, 2005), LA Lambda Archives; Matt Coles, ACLU, memorandum, "Summary of Our Thinking as of June 20, 2006," HRC Archives; Meeker interview of Esseks, p. 35.

16. Buckel, "Federal DOMA Challenge" (quotation in text); Granda, "Further Reflections."

17. The discussion is drawn from telephone conversations and email exchanges with Mary Bonauto in 2005–2008.

18. Mary Bonauto, GLAD, memorandum, "Public Relations Strategy" (Oct. 22, 2007), GLAD Archives; Notes on Cutter Media Group meeting, Oct. 24, 2007, GLAD Archives; Peter D. Hart Research Associates, Inc., "Messaging the DOMA Section 3 Lawsuit" (Jan. 16, 2008), GLAD Archives.

19. David Buckel, Lambda Legal, memorandum, "Presenting Concerns of Federalism Within the Equal Protection Claim" (Jan. 23, 2005) (quotation in text); GLAD memorandum to Massachusetts Office of the Attorney General, "Proposed State Sovereignty Challenge to Section 3 of 1 U.S.C. § 7" (April 26, 2007); Mary Bonauto, GLAD, memorandum to DOMA team, "Federalism Internal Status Report" (Nov. 1, 2008)—all from GLAD Archives

20. Complaint, *Gill & LeTourneaux v. Office of Personnel Management,* Civil Action No. 1:09-cv-10309-JCT (D. Mass., filed Mar. 3, 2009) (quotation in text); GLAD, "*Gill v. Office of Personnel Management:* Plaintiff Profiles" (March 3, 2009). The other plaintiffs were Dean Hara (Boston), the surviving spouse of former representative Gerry Studds; Bernice Hernandez and Melba Abreu (Brighton), a Latina couple; Marlin Nabors and Jonathan Knight (Boston), a young interracial couple; Bette Jo Green and Jo Ann Whitehead (Jamaica Plain), an older couple; Mary Ritchie and Kathy Bush (Framingham), a longtime couple raising two sons; Herbert Burtis (Sandisfield), the caregiver and survivor of a Parkinson's victim; Doreen and Mary Bowe-Shulman (Acton), raising two children; Randell Lewis-Kendell (Harwich Port), a widower; Keith and Al

Toney (Worcester), an interracial couple raising a daughter; and Martin Koski and Jim Fitzgerald (Bourne), an older couple.

21. "MLB Press Conference Remarks" (March 3, 2009), GLAD Archives (quotations in text).

22. Complaint, *Massachusetts v. U.S. Department of Health & Human Services*, Civil Action No. 1:09-cv-11156-JCT (D. Mass., filed July 8, 2009), 2009 WL 1995808; see memorandum of law in opposition to defendants' motion for summary judgment (filed Feb. 18, 2010), 2010 WL 581804 (fleshing out the commonwealth's claims and integrating the federalism and equal protection arguments).

23. Richard Belin, *Benchmarks XXIV: The Life and Legacy of Joseph L. Tauro* (2011); Beth Schwartzapfel, *The Judge*, Brown Alumni Magazine, Jan.–Feb. 2015 (quotations in text, from Judge Tauro).

24. *Gill v. Office of Personnel Management*, 699 F. Supp. 2d 374, 388–389, 391, 395 (D. Mass., July 8, 2010); *Massachusetts v. U.S. Department of Health & Human Services*, 698 F. Supp. 2d 234, 248, 252 (D. Mass., July 8, 2010) (quotations in text).

25. Meeker interview of Esseks, pp. 35–37.

26. Complaint, ¶ 13, *Windsor* (quotations in text); see ¶¶ 65–69, 85 (constitutional equal protection claims); Kaplan and Dickey, *Then Comes Marriage*, 65–67. Cf. Patricia Highsmith, *The Price of Salt* (1952) (greatest of the lesbian romances, the basis for the movie *Carol*).

27. Kaplan and Dickey, *Then Comes Marriage*, 144–146.

28. Our description of the filings and orders in *Windsor* are taken from the federal district court's docket sheet; the expert affidavits are available from the Westlaw report for *Windsor*.

29. *Strauss v. Horton*, 207 P.3d 48, 119–122 (Cal. 2009) (interpreting Proposition 8 not to affect marriages entered between June and November 2008); *In re Balas*, 449 B.R. 567 (C.D. Cal. June 13, 2011); *Golinski v. Office of Personnel Management*, 824 F. Supp. 2d 968 (N.D. Cal. Feb. 22, 2012).

30. Brief for intervenor-appellant BLAG, pp. 38–58, *Massachusetts v. HHS* (Docket Nos. 10-2204 et al., filed Sept. 22, 2011), 2011 WL 4539095 (rational bases for DOMA); *Romer*, pp. 634–635 (applying the rational basis test "with bite" to Colorado's anti-gay Amendment 2, discussed in chap. 5). BLAG also argued that the First Circuit was bound by the US Supreme Court's summary decision in *Baker v. Nelson*, 409 U.S. 810 (1972). See *Massachusetts v. HHS*; *Hicks v. Miranda*, 422 U.S. 332, 344–345 (1975) (lower courts must follow Supreme Court summary affirmances until instructed otherwise by the Supreme Court).

31. William Eskridge interview of Stuart Delery, Washington, DC (Sept. 2, 2016), referencing *Lawrence v. Texas*, 539 U.S. 558, 580 (2003) (quotation in text, from O'Connor's concurring opinion).

32. Michael Boudin, *Judge Henry Friendly and the Craft of Judging*, 159 U. Pa. L. Rev. 1, 2 (2010) (first quotation in text); *Massachusetts v. U.S. Dep't of Health & Human Servs.*,

682 F.3d 1, 8, 12 (1st Cir. May 31, 2012) (second quotation), referencing *Romer*, pp. 632–633, 635; *U.S. Dept. of Agric. v. Moreno*, 413 U.S. 528, 537–538 (1973) (invalidating statutory exclusion from the food stamp program of households containing unrelated individuals because it reflected a "bare congressional desire to harm a politically unpopular group"); *City of Cleburne v. Cleburne Living Ctr.*, 473 U.S. 432 (1985) (similar, protecting disabled persons).

33. *Massachusetts v. HHS*, p. 15 (quotations in text, with our emphasis added); *Windsor v. United States*, 833 F. Supp. 2d 394 (S.D.N.Y. June 6, 2012).

34. Petition for writ of certiorari, *HHS v. Massachusetts*, Docket No. 12-15 (US Supreme Court, filed July 3, 2012); Petition for writ of certiorari before judgment, *Office of Personnel Management v. Golinski*, Docket No. 12-16 (US Supreme Court, filed July 3, 2012); Petition for writ of certiorari before judgment, *Windsor v. United States*, Docket No. 12-63 (US Supreme Court, filed July 16, 2012); Petition for writ of certiorari before judgment, *Office of Personnel Management v. Pederson*, Docket No. 12-302 (US Supreme Court, filed Sept. 11, 2012). See also brief for the United States, *Windsor* (filed Aug. 31, 2012) (urging the court to take review in the First and Ninth Circuit cases and to hold the Second Circuit cases).

35. *Windsor v. United States*, 699 F.3d 169 (2d Cir. Oct. 18, 2012); Meeker interview of Esseks, pp. 46-47; Chris Geidner, *Meet the Hero of the Marriage Equality Movement*, BuzzFeed News, Jan. 10, 2013. We also draw from off-the-record conversations with Second Circuit judges and staff.

36. *United States v. Windsor*, 568 U.S. 1066 (Dec. 7, 2012).

37. *Hollingsworth v. Perry*, 568 U.S. 1066 (Dec. 7, 2012).

38. Brief on the merits for respondent Edith Schlain Windsor, pp. 32–38, *United States v. Windsor*, Docket No. 12-307 (US Supreme Court, filed Feb. 26, 2013), 2013 WL 701228 (DOMA's three red flags), pp. 39–62 (DOMA's lack of a rational basis).

39. William Eskridge interview of Paul Clement, Washington, DC (July 2017).

40. Brief on the merits for respondent bipartisan legal advisory group of the House of Representatives, *Windsor* (filed Jan. 22, 2013), 2013 WL 267026. Paul Clement deemphasized the responsible procreation argument, which he considered too speculative.

41. BLAG's Second Circuit brief, *Windsor*, p. 36 (quotation in text).

42. Brief for the United States on the merits question, pp. 51–53, *Windsor* (filed Feb. 22, 2013), 2013 WL 683048.

43. Brief of the United States as amicus curiae supporting respondents, *Hollingsworth v. Perry*, Docket No. 12-144 (US Supreme Court, filed Feb. 28, 2013), 2013 WL 769326 (separate-but-equal regime of eight states with civil union laws posed special equal protection problems); William Eskridge interview of former solicitor general Donald Verrilli, Washington, DC (July 2017); William Eskridge interview of former assistant attorney general Stuart Delery, Washington, DC (March 29, 2019).

44. *Perry v. Brown*, 265 P.3d 1002, 1007 (Cal. 2011) (quotations in text).

45. Brief for Walter Dellinger as amicus curiae in support of respondents on the issue of standing, *Perry* (filed Feb. 28, 2013), 2013 WL 768643.

46. Brief for the respondents, pp. 16–17, *Perry* (filed Feb. 21, 2013), 2013 WL 648742 (two paragraphs on the standing issue), pp. 17 n.1, 17–18 (longer defense of the trial court's judgment as consistent with Article III). On the original public meaning argument against Proposition 8, see brief amicus curiae of William Eskridge Jr., Rebecca Brown, Daniel Faber, and Andrew Koppelman in support of respondents, *Perry* (filed Feb. 28, 2013), 2013 WL 840011.

47. *Hollingsworth v. Perry*, 570 U.S. 693, 707 (June 26, 2013) (quotation in text), pp. 712–713 (distinguishing situations where proponents might be legally deputized agents of the state).

48. Our discussion of and quotations from the *Windsor* oral argument draw from the audio version at https://www.oyez.org/cases/2012/12-307?TB_iframe=true&width=914.4&height=921.6. On Jackson's reasoning, see brief for the court-appointed amica curiae addressing jurisdiction, *Windsor* (filed Jan. 24, 2013), 2013 WL 315234.

49. *Windsor* oral argument audio (quotation in text).

50. *Immigration & Naturalization Service v. Chadha*, 462 U.S. 919, 929–930, n.6 (1983).

51. *Chadha v. INS*, 634 F.2d 408, 419–420 (9th Cir. 1980) (Kennedy's discussion of justiciability), aff'd, 462 U.S. 919 (1983).

52. Alexander Bickel, *The Least Dangerous Branch: The Supreme Court at the Bar of Politics* (1962); Fritz Scharpf, *Judicial Review and the Political Question: A Functional Analysis*, 75 Yale L.J. 517 (1966).

53. *Windsor* oral argument audio (quotations in text).

54. *Windsor* oral argument audio (quotations in text).

55. *Windsor* oral argument audio (quotation in text).

56. Our discussion of the justices' conference in *Windsor* is drawn from off-the-record conversations with Supreme Court insiders.

57. *United States v. Windsor*, 570 U.S. 744, 763 (2013) (quotations in text, from Kennedy's majority opinion).

58. *Windsor*, pp. 755–763 (United States had Article III standing to appeal Second Circuit's judgment), pp. 763–769 (leading off the merits holding with an ode to federalism).

59. *Windsor*, p. 768 (quoting *Romer*), pp. 770–771 (remaining quotations in text).

60. *Windsor*, pp. 771–772 (quotations in text).

61. *Windsor*, pp. 809, 813–815 (Alito's dissenting opinion) (quotations in text). See Sherif Girgis, Ryan Anderson, and Robert George, *What Is Marriage? Man and Woman: A Defense*, 23–28 (2012). Girgis would clerk for Justice Alito during the 2018 term.

62. *Windsor*, p. 778 (quotation in text, from Scalia's dissenting opinion).

63. *Windsor*, p. 799 (first quotation in text, from Scalia's dissenting opinion); James Joyce, *Cyclops*, in *Ulysses* (1922) (remaining quotations in text). See Joseph Allen Boone,

A New Approach to Bloom as a "Womanly Man": The Mixed Middling's Progress in Ulysses, 20 James Joyce Q., No. 1, pp. 67, 74 (Fall 1982).

64. *Windsor,* pp. 799, 800 (quotations in text, from Scalia's dissenting opinion), pp. 776–778 (Roberts's dissenting opinion, insisting that the majority was not prejudging state junior-DOMAs).

65. Danielle Tcholakian, "The Unforgettable Edie Windsor," Longreads, Sept. 13, 2017 (quotations in text).

66. William Eskridge interview of former assistant attorney general Stuart Delery, Washington, DC (Sept. 2, 2017) (quotation in text); Eskridge interview of Delery (2019).

67. Our account of *Windsor's* implementation is drawn from the Eskridge interviews of Delery (2017, 2019).

68. *Garden State Equality v. Dow,* 82 A.3d 336 (N.J. Super. Ct. Sept. 27, 2013), stay petition denied, 79 A.3d 1036 (N.J. 2013); Appendix 1 (dates that Delaware, Hawai'i, Illinois, Nevada, Oregon, and Rhode Island converted from civil unions or comprehensive domestic partnership in the wake of *Windsor*).

69. Statement from Secretary of Homeland Security Janet Napolitano (July 1, 2013) (quotation in text); Department of State, announcement on visa changes for same-sex couples (Aug. 2, 2013); Office of Personnel Management's benefits administration letter No. 13-203, "Coverage of Same-Sex Spouses" (July 13, 2013).

70. IRS, Revenue Ruling 2013–17 (Aug. 29, 2013); Commission on Medicare & Medicaid Services, HHS, "Guidance on Internal Revenue Ruling 2013–17 and Eligibility for Advance Payments of the Premium Tax Credit and Cost Sharing Reductions" (Sept. 27, 2013).

71. 42 U.S.C. § 416(h)(1)(A)(i) (quotation in text); Letter from Commission of Medicare & Medicaid Services, HHS, to state health officials and Medicaid directors, *"United States v. Windsor"* (Sept. 27, 2013); Memorandum from Will Gunn, general counsel, Department of Veterans Affairs, "Reliance on State Law to Determine Validity of Same-Sex Marriages" (June 17, 2014).

72. 42 U.S.C. § 416(h)(1)(A)(ii) (quotation in text); HHS letter (Sept. 27).

73. Memorandum from the attorney general to the president, "Implementation of *United States v. Windsor*" (June 20, 2014) (quotation in text).

74. Steven Thrasher, *Good-bye Edie Windsor. Thank You for Never Giving Up,* The Guardian, Sept. 13, 2017 (quotations in text); Eskridge telephone interview of Kasen-Windsor.

20. Hijacking Science

1. Dana Nessel had represented Renee Harmon, a co-parent for her partner's children until the couple split up. The Michigan courts told Renee that she had no legal relationship to her children. *Harmon v. Davis,* 800 N.W.2d 63, 65 (Mich. 2011); Brian Dickerson, *For Her, Marriage Ruling Comes Too Late,* Detroit Free Press, June 28, 2015.

2. Complaint for declaratory and injunctive relief, ¶¶ 20–21, *DeBoer v. Snyder*, No. 12-cv-10285 (E.D. Mich., filed Jan. 23, 2012), 2012 WL 8719652 (quotations in text); William Eskridge and Christopher Riano telephone interview of Carole Stanyar (Nov. 17, 2015).

3. William Eskridge and Christopher Riano interview of Judge Bernard Friedman, Detroit, MI (Nov. 18, 2015).

4. The account and quotations are taken from our interviews of April DeBoer, Jayne Rowse, Carole Stanyar, and Dana Nessel.

5. Transcript of hearing on cross-motions for summary judgment, pp. 18–20, *De-Boer v. Snyder*, Case No. 12-10285 (E.D. Mich. Oct. 16, 2013) (Heyse's quotations in text), pp. 33–36 (Stanyar's pushback), pp. 36–41 (Judge Friedman's conclusion). On the same day, Attorney General Schuette emailed all the Michigan county clerks, instructing them not to issue marriage licenses in the event of a judgment against the state.

6. Mark Regnerus, *Hijacking Science: How the "No Differences" Consensus About Same-Sex Households and Children Works*, Public Discourse, Oct. 14, 2016 (quotation in text); Norval Glenn, *The Struggle for Same-Sex Marriage*, 41 Society, Iss. 6, pp. 25–28 (2004); Witherspoon Institute, *Marriage and the Public Good: Ten Principles* (2008) (principle four, optimal parenting, supported by detailed and skeptical review of the social science).

7. Mark Regnerus, *Forbidden Fruit: Sex and Religion in the Lives of American Teenagers* (2007). For a review of the social science gay parenting literature, see Carlos Ball, *Same-Sex Marriage and Children: A Tale of History, Social Science, and Law*, 86–94 (2014), esp. 88–89 (random samples).

8. Sofia Resnick, *New Family Structures Study Intended to Sway Supreme Court on Gay Marriage, Documents Show*, HuffPost, March 10, 2013.

9. Email from Mark Regnerus to Brad Wilcox, Sept. 21, 2010 (*DeBoer* trial Exhibit R-12) (first quotation in text); Email from Luis Tellez to Mark Regnerus, Sept. 22, 2010 (*DeBoer* trial Exhibit R-11) (second quotation).

10. Philip Cohen, *"More Managerial Than Intellectual": How Right-Wing Christian Money Bought Us the Regnerus Study*, Family Inequality, March 11, 2013. Dr. Gary Gates of the Williams Institute and Professors Michael Rosenfeld (Stanford) and Timothy Biblarz (USC) declined Regnerus's invitation to collaborate on the NFSS because of the Witherspoon sponsorship.

11. William Eskridge telephone interview of Mark Regnerus, July 18, 2018; Cohen, *"More Managerial"* (quotations in text). The study design was the product of discussions among Professors Regnerus and Wilcox and a team of paid consultants: Professors Cynthia Osborne (LBJ School at Texas), Jason Carroll (BYU), and Paul Amato (Penn State) as well as a representative of Knowledge Networks.

12. Mark Regnerus, *How Different Are the Adult Children of Parents Who Have Same-Sex Relationships? Findings from the New Family Structures Study*, 41 Soc. Sci. Res. 752–770 (July 2012). See Mark Regnerus, *Queers as Folk: Does It Really Make No Difference*

If Your Parents Are Straight or Gay?, Slate, June 11, 2012; Philip Cohen, *Amato on Regnerus*, Family Inequality, July 20, 2013 (peer-review process for publishing the NFSS). An interactive cartoon website also publicized the NFSS, http://www.familystructure studies.com/.

13. Amici curiae brief of social science professors in support of Hollingsworth and BLAG, *Perry* and *Windsor*, Docket Nos. 12-144 and 12-307 (US Supreme Court, filed Jan. 29, 2013), 2013 WL 457383 (seven social scientists, including Regnerus), p. 4 (both quotations in text); audio recording of the oral argument in *Perry* (March 26, 2013), https://www.oyez.org/cases/2012/12-144 (last quotation, from Scalia). Accord, brief amicus curiae for the Beverly LaHaye Institute and the National Legal Foundation in support of respondents, BLAG, *Windsor*, Docket No. 12-307 (US Supreme Court, filed Jan 29, 2013). On amicus briefs responding to the NFSS, see Wendy Manning et al., *Child Well-Being in Single-Sex Parent Families: Review of Research Prepared for American Sociological Association Amicus Brief,* 33 Population Res. Pol'y Rev. 485–502 (2014).

14. Gary Gates et al., letter to the editor and advisory editors of *Social Science Research,* June 29, 2012, https://familyinequality.wordpress.com/2012/06/29/200-researchers -respond-to-regnerus-paper/. For a defense of the NFSS, see Mathew Franck, *Mark Regnerus and the Storm Over the New Family Structures Study,* Public Discourse, Oct. 30, 2012.

15. Gates et al., *Letter to the Editor and Advisory Editors of* Social Science Research, 41 Social Science Research 1350 (Nov. 2012) (published version of Gates's June 29 letter); Mark Regnerus, *Parental Same-Sex Relations, Family Instability, and Subsequent Life Outcomes for Adult Children: Answering Critics of the NFSS with Additional Analyses,* 4 Soc. Sci. Rev. 1367–1377 (Nov. 2012); Eskridge telephone interview of Regnerus; Maggie Gallagher, *The Best or the Worst of All Possible Gay-Parenting Studies?*, Nat'l Rev., June 12, 2012 (quotation in text). On the internal review, see Darren Sherkat, *The Editorial Process and Politicized Scholarship: Monday Morning Editorial Quarterbacking and a Call for Scientific Vigilance,* 41 Social Science Research 1346–1349 (2012).

16. *United States v. Windsor,* 570 U.S. 744, 772 (2013) (quotations in text).

17. Lambda Legal, "Pending Marriage Equality Cases" (as of April 24, 2014), Lambda LA Archives.

18. *Garden State Equality v. Dow,* 82 A.3d 336 (N.J. Super. Ct. Sept. 27, 2013), stay petition denied, 79 A.3d 1036 (N.J. Oct. 2013).

19. Pew Research Center, *Attitudes on Same-Sex Marriage* (May 14, 2019), http://www .pewforum.org/fact-sheet/changing-attitudes-on-gay-marriage/; Hawai'i Marriage Equality Act, 2013 Haw. Sess. Laws 1 (signed Nov. 13, 2013); Illinois Religious Freedom and Fairness Act, 2013 Ill. Legis. Serv. P.A. 98-597 (signed Nov. 20, 2013); *Griego v. Oliver,* 316 P.3d 865, 885–886 (N. Mex. Dec. 19, 2013) (striking down New Mexico's junior-DOMA). See also William Eskridge interview of Genora Dancel and Kathryn Dennis, Honolulu (July 2016); William Eskridge interview of former governor Neil Abercrombie, Honolulu (July 2016).

20. For briefs making the optimal parenting argument and relying on the NFSS, see brief of amici curiae professors Lynn Wardle, William Duncan, et al., *Kitchen v. Herbert* (D. Utah, filed Oct. 22, 2013), 2013 WL 8125056; Brief of amici curiae professors of social science [Regnerus et al.], *Sevcik v. Sandoval,* No. 12-17668 (9th Cir., filed Jan. 28, 2014). Cf. brief of amicus curiae Alliance Defending Freedom, *Sevcik* (filed Jan. 28, 2014) (making optimal parenting argument without reference to NFSS).

21. Sarah Posner, *The Christian Legal Army Behind "Masterpiece Cakeshop": A Special Investigation into the Rise of Alliance Defending Freedom,* The Nation, Nov. 28, 2017 (quotation in text).

22. Between June 26, 2013, and June 26, 2015, federal district courts struck down marriage exclusions in Alabama, Alaska, Arizona, Arkansas, Colorado, Florida, Georgia, Idaho, Illinois, Indiana, Kansas, Kentucky, Michigan, Mississippi, Nebraska, North Carolina, Ohio, Oklahoma, Oregon, Pennsylvania, South Carolina, Tennessee, Texas, Utah, Virginia, West Virginia, Wisconsin, and Wyoming. See *Obergefell v. Hodges,* 135 S. Ct. 2584, 2609–2610 (2015) (citing the decisions); appendix 1 for more detailed citations and history. For opinions upholding the Louisiana constitutional Super-DOMA, see *Robicheaux v. Caldwell,* 2 F. Supp. 3d 910 (E.D. La., Sept. 13, 2014); *Merritt v. Attorney General,* 2013 WL 6044329 (E.D. La., Nov. 14, 2013).

23. *Kitchen v. Herbert,* 961 F. Supp. 2d 1181, 1193–1194, 1212–1213 (D. Utah Dec. 20, 2013).

24. *Kitchen v. Herbert,* 2013 WL 6834634 (D. Utah Dec. 23, 2013) (denying stay pending appeal), aff'd, No. 13-4178 (10th Cir. Dec. 24, 2013), rev'd, 134 S. Ct. 893 (Jan. 6, 2014) (granting stay); Portia Pedro, *Stays,* 106 Calif. L. Rev. 869 (2018) (malleability of stay practice).

25. *Geiger v. Kitzhaber,* 994 F. Supp. 2d 1128, 1139 (D. Ore., May 19, 2014) (invalidating Oregon's junior-DOMA); *Whitewood v. Wolf,* 992 F. Supp. 2d 410 (M.D. Pa. May 20, 2014) (invalidating Pennsylvania's junior-DOMA).

26. Email from Carole Stanyar to Christopher Riano, Aug. 23, 2018 (quotation in text).

27. William Eskridge telephone interview of Abbye Klamann (July 2017).

28. Our references to the trial record, including daily transcripts, are taken from "Documents from the *DeBoer v. Snyder* Same-Sex Marriage Trial, Federal Court, Detroit Michigan, 2014, MI #12-civ-10285," https://web.stanford.edu/~mrosenfe/DeBoer_docs.htm.

29. In addition to Dr. Brodzinsky's trial testimony, see the expert witness report of David M. Brodzinsky, Ph.D. (Dec. 13, 2013). The parties' stipulations are in Exhibit 53, *DeBoer* transcript (day two), part 1, pp. 53–58.

30. Michael Rosenfeld, *Couple Longevity in the Era of Same-Sex Marriage in the United States,* J. Marriage & Family (2014); Michael Rosenfeld, Reuben Thomas, and Maja Falcon, "How Couples Meet and Stay Together" (National Science Foundation 2011).

31. *DeBoer* transcript (day two), part 2, pp. 26–28 (quotation in text).

32. Expert report of Nancy Cott, *DeBoer,* No. 12-Civ-10285 (E.D. Mich., filed Dec. 19, 2013).

33. *DeBoer* transcript (day five), part 1, pp. 27–29.

34. Expert report of Mark Regnerus, *DeBoer* (E.D. Mich., filed Dec. 20, 2013), 2013 WL 8719114; Regnerus, *How Different?;* Regnerus, *Parental Same-Sex Relations.*

35. *DeBoer* transcript (day six), part 1, p. 25 (quotation in text).

36. *DeBoer* transcript (day six), part 1, pp. 30–31 (quotations in text); *Paul Amato on Reviewing Regnerus,* Family Inequality, July 20, 2013; William Eskridge and Christopher Riano interview of district judge Bernard Friedman and court reporter Joan Morgan, Detroit (July 2015).

37. *DeBoer* transcript (day six), part 1, pp. 43–44 (quotation in text, from the department's condemnation of the NFSS).

38. *DeBoer* transcript (day six), part 1, p. 75 (quotation in text). See Mark Regnerus, *It Just Makes Sense (Even as a Protestant),* Catholic Sistas, March 22, 2016 (describing the author's conversion to Catholicism).

39. *DeBoer* transcript (day six), part 1, p. 76; Exhibit 16 (quotation in text, from Trinity Christian College profile of Regnerus).

40. *DeBoer* trial, Exhibits 11–12 (email quotations in text).

41. *DeBoer v. Snyder,* 973 F. Supp. 2d 757, 765–768 (E.D. Mich. March 21, 2014) (court's analysis and quotations in text). More surprising, Friedman "was unable to accord the testimony of Marks, Price, and Allen any significant weight," either (pp. 768–769).

42. *DeBoer,* pp. 770–775 (court's analysis and quotation in text); *DeBoer v. Snyder,* Docket No. 14-1341 (6th Cir. March 25, 2014) (granting stay of Judge Friedman's order; Helene White dissented).

43. Brief of appellants Gary Herbert and Sean Reyes, *Herbert v. Kitchen,* Nos. 13-4178 et al. (10th Cir., filed Feb. 2, 2014), 2104 WL 580550.

44. Brief of appellants Herbert and Reyes, pp. 67–68, n.32 (relying on the NFSS); Letter from Gene Schaerr, for the Utah Office of the Attorney General, to Elizabeth Shumaker, clerk of the court, 10th Cir., "*Kitchen v. Herbert:* Rule 28(j) letter regarding press reports of Professor Regnerus's study" (April 9, 2014) (quotation in text); Audio recording of oral argument in *Herbert* (April 10, 2014), https://www.c-span.org/video/?318832-1/utah-marriage-ban-oral-argument; William Eskridge interview of Gene Schaerr, Washington, DC (Aug. 1, 2018).

45. *Loving v. Virginia,* 388 U.S. 1, 4, 12 (1967) (right to marry for different-race couples); Miguel Rios, *Pride Building Pride: Community Members Pooled Resources to Build Oklahoma City Pride Alliance and Its Events from the Ground Up,* Oklahoma Gazette, June 21, 2019 (critical assistance Jeri [Towler] Holmes and Alex Towler Bliss provided for the gay pride organization).

46. *Zablocki v. Redhail,* 434 U.S. 374, 384 (1978) (right to marry for deadbeat dads), p. 399 (Powell's concurring opinion, alarmed that the majority opinion might call into

question state regulation of "incest, bigamy, and homosexuality"); *Turner v. Safley*, 482 U.S. 78, 81–82, 94–95 (1987) (prisoners' right to marry); *Herbert v. Kitchen*, 755 F.3d 1193 (10th Cir. June 25, 2014) (majority's application of strict scrutiny because Utah's junior-DOMA denied the plaintiff couples their fundamental right to marry).

47. *Bishop v. Smith*, 760 F.3d 1070 (10th Cir. July 18, 2014), pp. 1096–1108 (Judge Holmes's concurring opinion); Emails between William Eskridge and Jerome Holmes, Aug. 2018.

48. *Bostic v. Schaefer*, 760 F.3d 353 (4th Cir. July 28, 2014); Transcript of oral argument, *Bostic v. Schaefer*, Nos. 14-1167 et al. (4th Cir. May 13, 2014). Compare brief of amici curiae William Eskridge, Rebecca Brown, Daniel Farber, Michael Gerhardt, Jack Knight, Andrew Koppelman, Melissa Lamb Saunders, Neil Siegel, and Jana Singer, *Bostic v. Rainey*, Nos. 14-1167 et al. (4th Cir., filed April 18, 2014), 2014 WL 1511199 (documenting the commonwealth's pervasive war on lesbian and gay families, many with children) with brief of amici curiae Alan Hawkins and Jason Carroll [BYU professors], *Bostic v. Rainey* (filed by Lynn Wardle and Bill Duncan, April 3, 2014), 2014 WL 1333654 (defending the child-centric regime of traditional marriage).

49. Our description of the oral arguments is taken from the audio recordings for *Baskin v. Bogan*, 7th Cir., Nos. 14-2386 et al. (Aug. 26, 2014), http://media.ca7.uscourts .gov/oralArguments/oar.jsp?caseyear=14&casenumber=2386&listCase =List+case%28s%29 and *Wolf v. Walker*, 7th Cir., No. 14-2526 (Aug. 26, 2014), http:// media.ca7.uscourts.gov/oralArguments/oar.jsp?caseyear=14&casenumber =2526&listCase=List+case%28s%29.

50. *Baskin v. Bogan*, 766 F.3d 648, 662 (7th Cir. Sept. 4, 2014) (quotation in text, from Judge Posner's opinion); Richard Posner, *Eighteen Years On: A Re-Review*, 125 Yale L.J. 533 (2015) (re-review of William Eskridge Jr., *The Case for Same-Sex Marriage: From Sexual Liberty to Civilized Commitment* (1996), and intellectual history of Posner's evolution on the policy and constitutional arguments).

51. Our discussion in the text is based upon off-the-record conversations with Supreme Court insiders.

52. *Citizens for Equal Protection v. Bruning*, 455 F.3d 859, 867 (8th Cir. 2006); Lee Epstein and Jack Knight, *The Choices Justices Make* (1998) (explaining and documenting strategic voting within the Supreme Court, especially on decisions about when to grant review). Our discussion of Chief Justice Roberts's possible reasoning is based on off-the-record conversations with members of the Supreme Court's bar.

53. *Moser v. Marie*, 135 S. Ct. 511 (Nov. 12, 2014) (denying stay to Kansas); *Haley v. Condon*, 135 S. Ct. 702 (Nov. 20, 2014) (denying stay to South Carolina; Scalia and Thomas published a dissenting opinion).

54. *Latta v. Otter*, 771 F.3d 456, mandate stayed 135 S. Ct. 344 (Oct. 8) (Justice Kennedy, referring the application to the full court), stay vacated, 135 S. Ct. 345 (Oct. 10, 2014, after examination by the full court), cert. denied, 135 S. Ct. 2931 (June 30, 2015) (Idaho) and 136 S. Ct. 13 (July 24, 2015) (Nevada).

21. Self-Determination

1. Debbie Cenziper and Jim Obergefell, *Love Wins: The Lovers and Lawyers Who Fought the Landmark Case for Marriage Equality*, 128 (2016) (quotation in text). The account that follows draws from Jim Obergefell's memoir as well as from personal conversations Christopher Riano had with Obergefell.

2. Cenziper and Obergefell, *Love Wins*, 38 (quotation in text).

3. Sheryl Gay Stolberg, *Gay Rights Case Caps Transition for Cincinnati*, New York Times, April 26, 2015 (quotation in text); Christopher Riano telephone interview and email exchanges with Alphonse Gerhardstein (Sept. 2018).

4. Cenziper and Obergefell, *Love Wins*, 128–135, 133 (quotation in text).

5. Riano exchanges with Gerhardstein; Cenziper and Obergefell, *Love Wins*, 53–66.

6. *Obergefell v. Wymsylo*, 962 F. Supp. 2d 968, 978 (S.D. Ohio Dec. 23, 2013) (quotation in text). See Cenziper and Obergefell, *Love Wins*, 141–148, 161–169 (arguments and strategies of Obergefell's lawyers).

7. *Bourke v. Beshear*, 996 F. Supp. 2d 542 (W.D. Ky. Feb. 12, 2014). See Complaint, *Bourke v. Beshear*, No. 3-13-CV-750-H (W.D. Ky., filed July 26, 2013), 2013 WL 3859038; second amended complaint, *Bourke* (filed Nov. 15, 2013), 2013 WL 6162946 (additional plaintiff couples); Lance Poston interview of Michael DeLeon (Dec. 11, 2017), OutSouth LGBTQ+ Oral History Project.

8. *Bourke v. Beshear*, 996 F. Supp. 2d 542 (W.D. Ky. Feb. 12, 2014); Cenziper and Obergefell, *Love Wins*, 169–172.

9. *Tanco v. Haslam*, 7 F. Supp. 3d 759 (M.D. Tenn. March 14, 2014).

10. Complaint, *Henry v. Wymsylo*, No. 1:14CV000129 (S.D. Ohio, filed Feb. 2, 2014), 2014 WL 505174; *Henry v. Himes*, 14 F. Supp. 3d 1036 (S.D. Ohio April 14, 2014). See Cenziper and Obergefell, *Love Wins*, 173–177; Amber Hunt, *What's at Stake for Married Gay Couples*, Cincinnati Enquirer, April 20, 2015; Mark Sherman, *Stories of Love, Life, Death in the High Court's Marriage Cases*, Associated Press, April 26, 2015.

11. *Love v. Beshear*, 989 F. Supp. 2d 536 (W.D. Ky. July 1, 2014).

12. Cenziper and Obergefell, *Love Wins*, 209 (quotation in text).

13. *DeBoer v. Snyder*, 772 F.3d 388 (6th Cir. Nov. 6, 2014). Cf. *Thomas More Law Center v. Obama*, 651 F.3d 549, 565–566 (6th Cir. 2011) (Sutton's deferring to the political process that produced Obamacare).

14. The quotations in the immediate text and in the five paragraphs that follow are taken from the audio recordings of the oral arguments in *DeBoer v. Snyder* (Michigan), *Obergefell v. Hodges* (Ohio), *Bourke v. Beshear* (Kentucky), and *Tanco v. Haslam* (Tennessee), http://player.piksel.com/p/w70z36r9.

15. For leading cases applying a deferential rational basis approach, see *Johnson v. Robison*, 415 U.S. 361, 383 (1974); *Williamson v. Lee Optical, Inc.*, 348 U.S. 483 (1955); *Royster Guano Co. v. Virginia*, 253 U.S. 412, 415 (1920).

16. *DeBoer*, pp. 434–435 (Daughtrey's dissenting opinion), pp. 422–425 (Sutton's discussion of the DeBoer-Rowse family).

17. *DeBoer*, pp. 396–399 (majority opinion); *Loving v. Virginia*, 388 U.S. 1 (1967).

18. *DeBoer*, p. 403 (quotation in text, from the majority opinion). On *Loving* and "original understanding," compare Alexander Bickel, *The Original Understanding and the Segregation Decision*, 69 Harv. L. Rev. 1, 58 (1955), with Michael McConnell, *The Originalist Case for* Brown v. Board of Education, 19 Harv. J.L. & Pub. Policy 457 (1995).

19. Ohio Const., 1851, art. I, § 1–2 (first quotation in text); Iowa Const., 1857, art. I, § 6 (second quotation); *Wally's Heirs v. Kennedy*, 10 Tenn. (2 Yer.) 554, 555–557 (1831) (third quotation). See Jonathan Entin, *An Ohio Dilemma: Race, Equal Protection, and the Unfulfilled Promise of a State Bill of Rights*, 51 Clev. St. L. Rev. 395, 396–397 (2004); Melissa Lamb Saunders, *Equal Protection, Class Legislation, and Colorblindness*, 96 Mich. L. Rev. 245, 251–268 (1997) (collecting cases). On original meaning, not original understanding, see Antonin Scalia and Bryan Garner, *Reading Law* (2012).

20. Charles Sumner, *Equality Before the Law; Unconstitutionality of Separate Colored Schools in Massachusetts: Argument of Charles Sumner, Esq., Before the Supreme Court of Massachusetts in the Case of* Sarah C. Roberts v. City of Boston, 10–11 (Boston: B. F. Roberts, 1849) (first quotation in text, with our emphasis); Cong. Globe, 39th Cong., 1st Sess. 2766 (1866) (remaining quotations from Senator Howard). See Cong. Globe, 39th Cong., p. 2961 (Senator Poland) (similar), p. 2459 (Speaker Stevens); Joseph Story, *Commentaries on the Constitution of the United States*, vol. 2, 676–677 (Thomas Cooley 4th ed. 1873). See also William Nelson, *The Fourteenth Amendment: From Political Principle to Judicial Doctrine*, 67, 73, 79 (1988); Steven Calabresi and Julia Rickert, *Originalism and Sex Discrimination*, 90 Tex. L. Rev. 1, 36–41 (2011); William Eskridge Jr., *Original Meaning and Marriage Equality*, 52 Hous. L. Rev. 1067 (2015).

21. *Hall v. Hall*, 95 Mich. App. 614, 615 (1980) (per curiam); Mich. Const., art. I, § 25 (quotation in text, with our emphasis added); Michigan House Fiscal Agency, *Legislative Analysis: Prohibit Same-Sex Marriages and Similar Unions*, 4 (Oct. 15, 2004); *National Pride at Work, Inc. v. Governor of Mich.*, 748 N.W.2d 524 (Mich. 2008); Glen Staszewski, *The Bait-and-Switch in Direct Democracy*, 2006 Wis. L. Rev. 17. Cf. *Bassett v. Snyder*, 59 F. Supp. 3d 837 (E.D. Mich. Nov. 12, 2014) (invalidating as class legislation a statute seeking to entrench the *Pride at Work* discrimination).

22. John Hurd, *Topics of Jurisprudence Connected with Conditions of Freedom and Bondage*, 44 (1856) (quotation in text); *Baker v. State*, 744 A.2d 864 (Vt. 1999). On Michigan's pervasive discrimination against lesbian and gay families, see petitioners' reply brief, pp. 5–6, *DeBoer v. Snyder*, Docket No. 14-571 (US Supreme Court, filed April 27, 2015), 2015 WL 1776078.

23. *DeBoer*, 772 F.3d, pp. 404–405 (quotations in text, from the majority opinion). See *Dandridge v. Williams*, 397 U.S. 471, 486–487 (1970) (cited as an example of ordinary rational basis review along these lines).

24. *DeBoer*, p. 436 (first quotation in text, from Daughtrey's dissenting opinion); Sumner, *Equality Before the Law*, 10–11 (second quotation); *Cruzan v. Director, Missouri Dep't of Health*, 497 U.S. 261, 300 (1990) (third quotation, from Scalia's concurring opinion). Accord, *Railway Express Agency v. New York*, 336 U.S. 106, 112–113 (1949) (Jackson's concurring opinion that inspired the Scalia quotation).

25. *Henry v. Himes*, 14 F. Supp. 3d 1036 (S.D. Ohio) (accepting Gerhardstein's full faith and credit argument for adoption decrees); Brief for [Tennessee] petitioners, pp. 23–25, *Tanco v. Haslam*, Docket No. 14-562 (US Supreme Court, filed Feb. 27, 2015), 2015 WL 860739. Gerhardstein and Landenwich also argued that Ohio's and Kentucky's novel and targeted nonrecognition rules brought their Super-DOMAs within the reasoning of *Windsor*. Brief for [Ohio] petitioners, pp. 24–25, *Obergefell v. Hodges*, Docket No. 14-556 (US Supreme Court, filed Feb. 27, 2015), 2105 WL 860738; Brief for [Kentucky] petitioners, pp. 52–58, *Bourke v. Beshear*, Docket No. 14-574 (US Supreme Court, filed Feb. 27, 2015), 2015 WL 860741.

26. U.S. Const., art. IV, § 1 (prescribe effect clause).

27. William Eskridge interview of Douglas Hallward-Driemeier, Washington, DC (June 23, 2016). On the litigation history of *Obergefell*, see Nathaniel Frank, *Awakening: How Gays and Lesbians Brought Marriage Equality to America*, 334–354 (2017).

28. *Brenner v. Scott*, 999 F. Supp. 2d 1278 (N.D. Fla. Aug. 14, 2014) (invalidating Florida's constitutional Super-DOMA), stay denied sub nom. *Armstrong v. Brenner*, 135 S. Ct. 890 (Dec. 19, 2014).

29. William Wagner, *Mr. Bursch Goes to Washington*, 2017 Michigan Super Lawyers, Sept. 2017.

30. Letter from Alphonse Gerhardstein, Douglas Hallward-Driemeier, Carole Stanyar, and Daniel Canon, counsel of record, to Scott Harris, clerk of the [Supreme] Court, March 17, 2015.

31. On the Kentucky Barbeque, see Cenziper and Obergefell, *Love Wins*, 242–244; Christopher Riano telephone interview of Alphonse Gerhardstein (2016).

32. Our description of the Ann Arbor moot is based upon off-the-record conversations with several of the people in Room 232 as well as written notes of the proceedings. For an earlier account, see Frank, *Awakening*, 338–342.

33. On the scientific consensus that first cousin (or even closer) marriages pose no genetic risks, see Carolyn Bratt, *Incest Statutes and the Fundamental Right of Marriage: Is Oedipus Free to Marry?*, 18 Fam. L.Q. 257 (1984).

34. Our quotation for April DeBoer is taken from several off-the-record accounts of the Ann Arbor ambush and was confirmed in a conversation with DeBoer.

35. Letter from Alphonse Gerhardstein, Douglas Hallward-Driemeier, Carole Stanyar, and Daniel Canon, counsel of record, to Scott Harris, clerk of the [US Supreme] Court, March 31, 2015.

36. *Cleveland Bd. of Ed. v. LaFleur*, 414 U.S. 632, 639 (1974), quoted in brief for the petitioners, p. 56, *DeBoer v. Snyder*, Docket No. 14-571 (US Supreme Court, filed Feb. 27,

2015), 2015 WL 860740 (first quotation in text); *Lawrence v. Texas*, 539 U.S. 558, 574 (2003), quoted in brief for petitioners, pp. 13–14, *Tanco v. Haslam*, Docket No. 14-562 (US Supreme Court, filed Feb. 27, 2015), 2105 WL 860739 (second quotation); *Zablocki v. Redhail*, 434 U.S. 374 (1978) (state cannot constitutionally deny fundamental right to marry to divorced spouses because they have not paid alimony or child support).

37. Brief of historians of marriage and the American Historical Association as amici curiae, *Obergefell v. Hodges*, Docket Nos. 14-556 et al. (US Supreme Court, filed March 6, 2015), 2105 WL 1022698; Brief for petitioners, *Obergefell* (filed Feb. 27, 2015), 2015 WL 860738; Brief for petitioners, *DeBoer v. Snyder*, Docket No. 14-571 (US Supreme Court, filed Feb. 27, 2015), 2015 WL 860740; Brief for petitioners, pp. 52–58, *Bourke v. Beshear*, Docket No. 14-574 (US Supreme Court, filed Feb. 27, 2015), 2015 WL 860741 (nonrecognition argument entirely sounding in equal protection); Brief for petitioners, *Tanco v. Haslam*, Docket No. 140562 (US Supreme Court, filed Feb. 27, 2015) (nonrecognition argument sounding mainly in due process). Relevant amicus briefs, all filed in support of all six appeals under the caption of *Obergefell v. Hodges* (Supreme Court Docket Nos. 14-556 et al.) included brief for amici curiae Cato Institute, William Eskridge Jr., and Steven Calabresi, *Obergefell* (filed March 5, 2015), 2015 WL 1062557; Brief for amici curiae Kenneth Mehlman et al., *Obergefell* (filed March 5, 2015), 2015 WL 981540; Brief for the United States, *Obergefell* (filed March 6, 2015), 2015 WL 1004710; William Eskridge interview of former solicitor general Donald Verrilli, Washington, DC (July 2017).

38. Brief for respondents, p. 1, *DeBoer*, 2015 WL 1384104 (first quotation in text); *Schuette v. Coalition to Defend Affirmative Action*, 572 U.S. 291, 313 (2014) (second and third quotations); respondents' brief, p. 10, *DeBoer* (final quotation).

39. Brief for Conference of Catholic Bishops, *Obergefell* (filed April 2, 2015), 2105 WL 1519042; Brief for Douglas Laycock, Thomas C. Berg, David Blankenhorn, Marie Failinger, and Edward McGlynn Gaffney as amicus curiae, *Obergefell* (filed March 6, 2015), 2015 WL 1048450; *United States v. Windsor*, 570 U.S. 744, 770 (2013) (first quotation in text); Brief of major religious organizations as amici curiae, p. 3, *Obergefell* (filed April 2, 2015), 2015 WL 1534341 (representing the Church of Jesus Christ, the National Association of Evangelicals, the Lutheran Church/Missouri Synod, the Church of God, and the Southern Baptists) (second quotation).

40. Brief for Gary Gates as amicus curiae, *Obergefell* (filed March 6, 2015), 2015 WL 1021451; Brief amicus curiae of American College of Pediatricians, Family Watch Foundation, Loren Marks, Mark Regnerus, and Donald Sullins, *Obergefell* (filed April 2, 2015), 2015 WL 1534077.

41. Brief of Massachusetts [and sixteen other marriage equality jurisdictions], p. 24, *Obergefell* (filed March 6, 2015), 2015 WL 1048440 (quotation in text), pp. 22–24 (data). Accord, Marcus Dillender, *The Death of Marriage? The Effects of New Forms of Legal Regulation on Marriage Rates in the United States*, 51 Demography 563 (2014) (large pop-

ulation survey demonstrating no correlation between marriage equality and any decline in marriage).

42. Brief of amici curiae 100 Scholars of Marriage, *Obergefell* (filed April 2, 2015), 2015 WL 1519039, app. B (technical analysis of the marriage trends in marriage equality states and countries); Mircea Trandafir, *The Effect of Same-Sex Marriage Laws on Different-Sex Marriage: Evidence from the Netherlands*, 51 Demography 317 (2014).

43. William Eskridge conversation with Mary Bonauto and Douglas Hallward-Driemeier, Washington, DC (June 23, 2016); *Searcy v. Strange*, 135 S. Ct. 940 (Feb. 9, 2015) (denying stay of injunction in Alabama marriage case), pp. 940–942 (dissenting views of Thomas and Scalia).

44. Brief for conflicts of law and family law scholars, *Obergefell* (filed March 6, 2015), 2015 WL 1022697; U.S. Const., art. IV, § 1 ("Congress may by general Laws prescribe the Manner in which such Acts, Records and Proceedings shall be proved, *and the Effect thereof*"). Cf. William Eskridge Jr., *Credit Is Due*, The New Republic, June 17, 1996 (arguing that the clause does not empower Congress to authorize discriminatory choice of law rules). On the triumph of the celebration rule after the demise of laws barring different-race marriages, see Andrew Koppelman, *Same-Sex, Different States: When Same-Sex Marriages Cross State Lines* (2006).

45. William Eskridge telephone interview of John Bursch (Aug. 17, 2018).

46. Cenziper and Obergefell, *Love Wins*, 251–253; Eskridge telephone interview of Bursch.

47. The narrative and quotations in text and in the next sixteen paragraphs are taken from the transcript of the *Obergefell* oral argument, 2015 WL 1929996 (April 28, 2015).

48. *Lawrence v. Texas*, 539 U.S. 558, 579 (2003) (quotation in text). Roberts, Scalia, and Alito erroneously believed that no society had recognized same-sex marriages until the Netherlands did so in 2001; in fact, dozens of societies have recognized same-sex unions as marriages. William Eskridge Jr., *The Case for Same-Sex Marriage: From Sexual Liberty to Civilized Commitment*, chap. 2 (1996). A classics major at Hamilton, Bonauto knew about this history but shrewdly dodged the point, lest her entire argument become bogged down in a marginally relevant anthropology of marriage.

49. The text is based upon an extended telephone conversation between John Bursch and William Eskridge. Bursch does not agree with our view that Schaerr's brief might support the Jenga theory; he responds that Schaerr's data were preliminary at best and did not prove causation.

50. *Butler v. Wilson*, 415 U.S. 953 (1974). See *Langone v. Coughlin*, 712 F. Supp. 1061 (N.D.N.Y. 1989), where the court revisited the same (but amended) New York regulation upheld in *Butler* and struck down the regulation under *Turner v. Safley*, 482 U.S. 78 (1987).

51. Our discussion of the justices' deliberations is drawn from off-the-record conversations with a variety of informed insiders. On Roberts's deference to the political

process in the Obamacare case, see Joan Biskupic, *The Chief: The Life and Turbulent Times of Chief Justice John Roberts*, 221–248 (2019).

52. *Planned Parenthood of Southeastern Pennsylvania v. Casey*, 505 U.S. 833, 851 (1992) (joint opinion) (quotation in text, reportedly written by Kennedy).

53. Lawrence Tribe and Joshua Matz, *The Constitutional Inevitability of Same-Sex Marriage*, 71 Md. L. Rev. 471 (2012). For an illustration of the "equal access" focus for marriage rights by the other four majority justices, see *Kerry v. Din*, 135 S. Ct. 2128, 2142 (2015) (dissenting opinion by Breyer, joined by Ginsburg, Sotomayor, and Kagan) (arguing that a citizen married to a noncitizen ought to have access to her husband's company unless the government can produce a factual reason to separate them). See Kerry Abrams, *The Rights of Marriage:* Obergefell, Din, *and the Future of Constitutional Family Law*, 103 Cornell L. Rev. 501 (2018) (reading *Obergefell* in light of *Din*, and vice versa).

54. *Obergefell v. Hodges*, 135 S. Ct. 2584, 2600–2601 (2015) (all the quotations in text).

55. *Obergefell*, pp. 2602–2604 (six or seven new paragraphs added to the opinion at the suggestion of others in the majority). See *Obergefell*, pp. 2602–2603 (quotations in text); *Kirchberg v. Feenstra*, 450 U.S. 455 (1981) (striking down a "lord and master" statute).

56. *Obergefell*, p. 2606 (quotation in text).

57. Eskridge telephone interview of Bursch; Email from John Bursch to William Eskridge, May 20, 2019 (quotation in text).

58. Pamela Karlan, *Equal Protection, Due Process, and the Stereoscopic Fourteenth Amendment*, 33 McGeorge L. Rev. 473 (2002) (quotation in text). Accord, Laurence Tribe, Lawrence v. Texas: *The "Fundamental Right" That Dare Not Speak Its Name*, 117 Harv. L. Rev. 1893 (2004) and *Equal Dignity: Speaking Its Name*, 129 Harv. L. Rev. Forum 16 (2015); Kenji Yoshino, *The New Equal Protection*, 124 Harv. L. Rev. 747 (2011).

59. The last three sentences of the paragraph in the text paraphrase an email from Jonathan Rauch to William Eskridge, May 30, 2019.

60. Friedrich von Hayek, *Law, Legislation, and Liberty: Rules of Order* (1973) (defending a government of rigorously enforced general rules); Friedrich von Hayek, *Law, Legislation, and Liberty: The Political Order of a Free People* (1979) (critique of top-down social engineering and defense of common law libertarian constitutionalism).

61. *Obergefell*, pp. 2629, 2630 n.22, 2640 (quotations in text from Scalia's dissenting opinion), p. 2643 (quotation from Alito's dissenting opinion).

62. *Obergefell*, p. 2612 (first quotation from Roberts's dissenting opinion), pp. 2619–2620 (right to marry precedents presume conjugality). See *Obergefell*, p. 2622 (second quotation), citing *Lochner v. New York*, 198 U.S. 45 (1906); A. Raymond Randolph, *Before* Roe v. Wade: *Judge Friendly's Draft Abortion Opinion*, 29 Harv. J.L. & Pub. Pol'y 1035, 1036–1037, 1058 (2006).

63. Jonathan Rauch, *How Can the Supreme Court Help Gay Rights? By Keeping Out Entirely*, New Republic, Dec. 12, 2012 (quotation in text).

64. *Obergefell*, pp. 2616–2617 (Roberts's dissent), citing and discussing *Dred Scott v. Sandford*, 60 U.S. 393 (1857); compare with *Dred Scott*, p. 409 (quotation in text); see pp. 413–416 (collecting post-Independence marriage laws and policies marking "negroes" as inferior, even in states like Massachusetts that abolished slavery).

65. *Obergefell*, pp. 2631–2640 (Thomas's dissenting opinion).

66. On anti-commandeering, see Jed Rubenfeld, *The Right of Privacy*, 102 Harv. L. Rev. 737 (1989); Kenji Yoshino, *A New Birth of Freedom?* Obergefell v. Hodges, 129 Harv. L. Rev. 147 (2015).

67. *Obergefell*, pp. 2640–2643 (Alito's dissenting opinion). See Gerard Bradley, *Learning to Live with Same-Sex Marriage?*, Public Discourse, May 22, 2018.

68. *Masterpiece Cakeshop, Ltd. v. Colorado Civil Rights Commission*, 138 S. Ct. 1719 (2018).

69. See Amy Gutmann and Dennis Thompson, *Why Deliberative Democracy?*, 96–99 (2004); Glen Staszewski, *Obergefell and Democracy*, 97 B.U.L. Rev. 31 (2017); William Eskridge conversation with former Justice Anthony Kennedy (May 15, 2019); *Johnson v. Texas*, 491 U.S. 397, 420 (1989) (Kennedy's concurring opinion in the flag-burning case).

70. Daily Dish, *Mildred Loving, 40 Years Later*, The Atlantic, June 18, 2007 (quotation in text).

71. The official White House video of the president's conversation with Jim Obergefell is available at https://www.cnn.com/videos/politics/2015/06/26/jim-obergefell-president-obama-phone-call-same-sex-marriage.white-house/video/playlists/same-sex-marriage-debate/.

22. From Outlaws to In-Laws

1. Bob Connelly, *50 Years After "The Homosexuals,"* The Advocate, Jan. 2, 2017 (quotations in text).

2. Donald Webster Cory [pen name for Edward Sagarin], *The Homosexual in America: A Subjective Approach* (1951) (tolerable but pathetic variation approach to homosexuality). See William Eskridge Jr., *Dishonorable Passions: Sodomy Laws in America, 1861–2003*, 109–135 (2008); Lillian Faderman, *Odd Girls and Twilight Lovers: A History of Lesbian Life in Twentieth Century America* (1991); David Johnson, *The Lavender Scare: The Cold War Persecution of Gays and Lesbians in the Federal Government* (2004).

3. William Eskridge interview of Franklin Kameny, Washington, DC (Jan. 17, 2004); Petitioner's brief, *Kameny v. Brucker*, 1960 Term, No. 676 (US Supreme Court, filed Jan. 27, 1961), see pp. 24–29 (quotations in text); William Eskridge Jr., *January 27, 1961: The Birth of Gaylegal Equality Arguments*, 58 NYU Ann. Survey Am. Law 39 (2001); Michael Long, ed., *Gay Is Good: The Life and Letters of Gay Rights Pioneer Franklin Kameny* (2014).

4. Petitioner's brief, *Kameny*, pp. 32, 34–35, 37, 49, 56 (quotations in text).

5. *Kameny v. Brucker*, 365 U.S. 843 (March 20, 1961); Justice William Brennan papers, Library of Congress (according to Brennan's marked sheets, no justice voted to take review in *Kameny v. Brucker*); Constitution of the Mattachine Society of Washington, art. II, § 1(a)–(c) (quotations in text).

6. William Eskridge Jr., *Sexual and Gender Variation in American Public Law: From Malignant to Tolerable to Benign*, 57 UCLA L. Rev. 1333 (2010) and *Channeling: Identity-Based Social Movements and Public Law*, 150 U. Pa. L. Rev. 419 (2001). For predecessors of the "outlaws to in-laws" metaphor, see King's Head Theatre, *Outlaws to In-Laws* (2017) (seven short plays); Kenneth Sherrill and Alan Yang, *From Outlaws to In-Laws*, 11 Public Perspective 20 (Cornell Univ.), Jan.–Feb. 2000 (changing attitudes).

7. The Advocates, *Should Marriages Between Homosexuals Be Permitted?*, WGBH Radio, May 2, 1974, http://openvault.wgbh.org/catalog/V_57993D38129A433AAD10C7B 04D019EF6 (quotations in text, from Kameny's commentary); *Dean v. District of Columbia*, 653 A.2d 307 (D.C. 1995) (describing and dismissing Dean and Gill's marriage lawsuit); Brett Zongker, *Gay Rights Pioneer Honored on Capitol Hill*, Associated Press, Nov. 15, 2011 (Kameny's memorial service).

8. On backlash when social movements win victories in court, see Gerald Rosenberg, *The Hollow Hope: Can Courts Bring About Social Change?*, 339–419 (2d ed. 2008) (leading analysis); John D'Emilio, *The Marriage Fight Is Setting Us Back*, Gay & Lesbian Rev. Worldwide 10–11, Nov.–Dec. 2006; Susan Faludi, *Backlash: The Undeclared War Against American Women* (2006); Michael Klarman, Brown *and* Lawrence *(and* Goodridge*)*, 104 Mich. L. Rev. 431, 459–473 (2005). Cf. Michael Klarman, *From the Closet to the Altar: Courts, Backlash, and the Struggle for Same-Sex Marriage*, 165–192 (2012) (balanced analysis, retreating from the author's 2005 backlash fears).

9. Derrick Bell Jr., Brown v. Board of Education *and the Interest-Convergence Dilemma*, 93 Harv. L. Rev. 518 (1980). See Derrick Bell, *Silent Covenants:* Brown v. Board of Education *and the Unfulfilled Hopes for Racial Reform* (2004).

10. Elisabeth Young-Bruehl, *The Anatomy of Prejudices* (1996) (theorizing prejudices as functional and mobile, with homophobia serving several different psychological needs); Jasbir Puar, *Terrorist Assemblages: Homonationalism in Queer Times* (2007) (explaining how Western anti-homophobia has been deployed to justify Islamophobia); Reva Siegel, *The Modernization of Marital Status Law: Adjudicating Wives' Rights to Earnings, 1860–1930*, 82 Geo. L.J. 2127 (1995) (providing an example of how old stereotypes bend the application of new rights).

11. William Eskridge interview of Franklin Kameny, Washington, DC (May 2010).

12. Miranda Fricker, *Epistemic Injustice: Power and the Ethics of Knowing* (2007); Trystan Goetze, *Hermeneutical Dissent and the Species of Hermeneutical Injustice*, 33 Hypatia 73 (Winter 2018).

13. George Chauncey, *Why Marriage? The History Shaping Today's Debate Over Gay Equality*, 23–86 (2005); Nan Hunter, *Varieties of Constitutional Experience: Democracy and the Marriage Equality Campaign*, 64 UCLA L. Rev. 1662 (2017).

14. Douglas NeJaime, *Winning Through Losing*, 96 Iowa L. Rev. 941 (2011) (discussing *Bowers, Baehr,* and *Dale,* and arguing that the gay rights movement used losses to generate enthusiasm and funds for future triumphs).

15. For a variety of theories about when the critical turning point for marriage equality might have occurred, compare Jo Becker, *Forcing the Spring: Inside the Fight for Marriage Equality* (2014); with Hunter, *Varieties;* and with Evan Wolfson, *Why Marriage Matters: America, Equality, and Gay People's Right to Marry* (2004).

16. Nate Silver, *Support for Gay Marriage Outweighs Opposition in Polls,* New York Times, May 9, 2012, graph updated through 2013 at https://fivethirtyeight.com/wp -content/uploads/2013/03/fivethirtyeight-0326-marriage2-blog4801.png?w=1150; Andrew Flores and Scott Barclay, Williams Institute, *Trends in Public Support for Marriage for Same-Sex Couples by State* (April 2015).

17. On the evolution of marriage, see Nancy Cott, *Public Vows: A History of Marriage and the Nation* (2000) and *No Objections: What History Tells Us About Remaking Marriage,* Bost. Rev., Jan.–Feb. 2011; Andrew Cherlin, *The Marriage-Go-Round: The State of Marriage and the Family in America Today* (2010); Stephanie Coontz, *Marriage, A History: From Obedience to Intimacy or How Love Conquered Marriage* (2005).

18. The need for grassroots organizing was clear even before the Hawai'i campaign foundered. See Mary Bonauto, *The Litigation: First Judicial Victories in Vermont, Massachusetts, and Connecticut,* in Kevin Cathcart and Leslie Gabel-Brett, eds., *Love Unites Us: Winning the Freedom to Marry in America,* 73 (2016); Joseph Watson, producer, Vermont Freedom to Marry Task Force, *The Freedom to Marry: A Green Mountain View* (video, 1996); Evan Wolfson, "Freedom to Marry Coalition: Communications Strategy" (1995) (strategies for using "media advocacy to create positive impressions and reverse negative public opinion regarding same-gender marriage").

19. Martha Nussbaum, *From Disgust to Humanity: Sexual Orientation and Constitutional Law* (2010); William Eskridge Jr., *Body Politics:* Lawrence v. Texas *and the Constitution of Disgust and Contagion,* 57 Fla. L. Rev. 1011 (2005).

20. The Advocates, *Should Marriages Between Homosexuals Be Permitted?* (quotation in text, from Noble's "testimony"); Marc Solomon, *Winning Marriage: The Inside Story of How Same-Sex Couples Took on the Politicians and Pundits—and Won* (2014).

21. William Eskridge Jr. and Darren Spedale, *Gay Marriage: For Better or for Worse? What We've Learned from the Evidence* (2006), updated in appendix 2 of this volume. See also William Eskridge Jr., *Equality Practice: Civil Unions and the Future of Gay Rights* (2002); Kees Waaldijk, *Small Change: How the Road to Same-sex Marriage Got Paved in the Netherlands,* in Robert Wintemute and Mads Andenaes, eds., *Legal Recognition of Same-Sex Partnerships: A Study of National, European and International Law,* 437–464 (2001).

22. PFLAG policy statement on marriage (Jan. 17, 2000); Brief of PFLAG as amicus curiae in support of petitioners, *Obergefell v. Hodges,* Docket Nos. 14-556 et al. (US Supreme Court, filed March 6, 2015).

23. Jane O'Reilly, *The Night Phyllis Schlafly Went Over the Rainbow*, The Baffler, Sept. 9, 2016. After Mrs. Schlafly's death, a pro-Trump faction led by John and Andy Schlafly formed the Schlafly Eagles; Anne Schlafly Cori retained control of the Eagle Forum.

24. William Eskridge Jr., *Backlash Politics: How Constitutional Litigation Has Advanced Marriage Equality in the United States*, 93 B.U.L. Rev. 275 (2013); Andrew Flores and Scott Barclay, *Backlash, Consensus, Legitimacy, or Polarization? The Effect of Same-Sex Marriage Policy on Mass Attitudes*, 69 Pol. Res. Q. 43–56 (2016); Thomas Keck, *Beyond Backlash: Assessing the Impact of Judicial Decisions on LGBT Rights*, 43 Law & Soc'y Rev. 151 (2009).

25. Gwendolyn Leachman, *Institutionalizing Essentialism: Mechanisms of Intersectional Subordination Within the LGBT Movement*, 2016 Wis. L. Rev. 655; William Eskridge telephone interview of Phyllis Watts (July 2018) (quotation in text). See Rhonda Gibson, *Coverage of Gay Males, Lesbians in Newspaper Lifestyle Sections*, 25 Newspaper Research Journal 90, 90 (2004) (*Goodridge* was the turning point in newspaper coverage of the marriage issue).

26. Ellen Ann Andersen, *Out of the Closet and into the Courts: Legal Opportunity Structure and Gay Rights Litigation*, 183–184, 197–198 (2005); Michael Mello, *Legalizing Gay Marriage* (2004) (Vermont); Daniel Pinello, *America's Struggle for Same-Sex Marriage*, 190–193 (2006); Keck, *Beyond Backlash*, 157–158.

27. Mae Kuykendall, *Resistance to Same-Sex Marriage as a Story About Language: Linguistic Failure and the Priority of a Living Language*, 34 Harv. CR-CL L. Rev. 385 (1999); *Obergefell v. Hodges*, 135 S. Ct. 2584 (2015) (Kennedy's majority opinion), p. 2612 (quotation in text, from Roberts's dissenting opinion), pp. 2626–2627 (Scalia's dissenting opinion).

28. Gary Blasi and John Jost, *System Justification Theory and Research: Implications for Law, Legal Advocacy, and Social Justice*, 94 Calif. L. Rev. 1119 (2006).

29. Richard Albert, *American Exceptionalism in Constitutional Amendment*, 69 Ark. L.R. 217, 221 (2016); Mila Versteeg and Emily Zackin, *American Constitutional Exceptionalism Revisited*, 81 U. Chi. L. Rev. 1641, 1669 (2014).

30. Richard Wolf, *From Massachusetts, Lessons on Gay Marriage—and Divorce*, USA Today, May 17, 2015; William Eskridge telephone interview of Avery Nortonsmith (Aug. 21, 2018) (quotations in text).

31. Angela Simon, *The Relationship Between Stereotypes of and Attitudes Toward Lesbians and Gays*, in Gregory Herek, ed., *Stigma and Sexual Orientation: Understanding Prejudice Against Lesbians, Gay Men, and Bisexuals*, 62–63 (1998) (quotation in text).

32. 120 Cong. Rec. H7487 (July 12, 1996) (quotation in text, from Barr); Representative Jared Polis press release, *Landmark Legislation to Repeal the Discriminatory Defense of Marriage Act (DOMA) Is Introduced* (March 11, 2011) (Barr's supporting DOMA's repeal); Bill Clinton, *It's Time to Overturn DOMA*, Washington Post, March 7, 2013; Email from Richard Socarides to William Eskridge, June 9, 2019.

33. *Bowers v. Hardwick,* 478 U.S. 186, 191 (1986) (first quotation in text), p. 197 (second quotation, from Burger's concurring opinion); Powell papers, Washington & Lee University School of Law, case files (*Bowers*) (third quotation, from an early draft of Powell's concurring opinion).

34. *Lawrence v. Texas,* 539 U.S. 558, 567 (2003); Dale Carpenter, *Flagrant Conduct: The Story of* Lawrence v. Texas (2012); Evan Thomas, *First: Sandra Day O'Connor,* chap. 14 (2019); William Eskridge interview of Stuart Delery, Washington, DC (March 29, 2019).

35. Steven Calabresi and Hannah Begley, *Originalism and Same-Sex Marriage,* 70 U. Miami L. Rev. 648 (2016); Dale Carpenter, *A Conservative Defense of* Romer v. Evans, 76 Ind. L.J. 403 (2001). Cf. John Yoo, *Does the Constitution Protect Against Sex Discrimination?,* Nat'l Rev., Jan. 5, 2011. For Judge Posner's odyssey on the marriage issue, compare Richard Posner, *Sex and Reason,* 309–311 (1992) (opposing same-sex marriage because it would "promote homosexuality") and *Should There Be Homosexual Marriage? If so, Who Should Decide?,* 95 Mich. L. Rev. 1578 (1997) (skeptically reviewing Eskridge, *The Case for Same-Sex Marriage: From Sexual Liberty to Civilized Commitment* [1996]) with *Baskin v. Bogan,* 766 F.3d 648 (7th Cir. 2014) (arguments against same-sex marriage are "so full of holes" that they "cannot be taken seriously"), and Posner, *Eighteen Years On: A Re-Review,* 125 Yale L.J. 533 (2015) (oops, Eskridge had it right in 1996).

36. *Should Marriages Between Homosexuals Be Permitted?* (quotation in text, from Kameny); William Eskridge Jr., *Some Effects of Identity-Based Social Movements on Constitutional Law in the Twentieth Century,* 100 Mich. L. Rev. 2062 (2002).

37. Clifford Rosky, *Anti-Gay Curriculum Laws,* 117 Colum. L. Rev. 1461, 1487–1494 (2017) (sex education laws responding to AIDS), 1498–1501 (sex education emphasizing abstinence until marriage); GLSEN, *The 2015 National School Climate Survey: The Experiences of Lesbian, Gay, Bisexual, Transgender, and Queer Youth in Our Nation's Schools* (2015).

38. Personal Responsibility and Work Opportunity Reconciliation Act of 1996, Pub. L. No. 104-193, 110 Stat. 2105, codified at 42 U.S.C. § 710 (2012); Rosky, *Anti-Gay Curriculum Laws,* 1472, n.66 (listing states with abstinence-until-marriage laws); Amanda Harmon Cooley, *Constitutional Representations of the Family in Public Schools: Ensuring Equal Protection for All Students Regardless of Parental Sexual Orientation or Gender Identity,* 76 Ohio St. L.J. 1007 (2015).

39. *Obergefell,* p. 2605 (quotation in text), p. 2601, quoted and followed in *Pavan v. Smith,* 137 S. Ct. 2075 (June 26, 2017) (per curiam).

40. *Pavan,* p. 2079 (quotation in text, from Gorsuch's dissenting opinion); *Henry v. Himes,* 14 F. Supp. 3d 1036 (S.D. Ohio 2014) (affirmed in *Obergefell*).

41. Michael Gerhardt, *Super Precedent,* 90 Minn. L. Rev. 1204 (2006); *Richmond Med. Ctr. for Women v. Gilmore,* 219 F.3d 376, 376–377 (4th Cir. 2000); William Eskridge Jr. and John Ferejohn, *Super Statutes,* 50 Duke L.J. 1215 (2001) (analogous concept that

was an inspiration for Senator Arlen Specter's 2005 reference to "super-duper precedents" like *Roe v. Wade*).

42. 1992 Ala. Acts No. 92-590, codified at Ala. Code § 16-40A-2(c)(8) (quotation in text). Similar statutes in Utah, 2001 Utah Laws 442, and Arizona, 1991 Ariz. Laws ch. 269 (S.B. 1346), were repealed in 2017 and 2019, respectively. See also William Eskridge Jr., *No Promo Homo: The Sedimentation of Antigay Discourse and the Channeling Effect of Judicial Review*, 75 NYU L. Rev. 1327 (2000); Leora Hoshall, *Afraid of Who You Are: No Promo Homo Laws in Public School Sex Education*, 22 Tex. J. Women & L. 219, 222 (2013); Rosky, *Anti-Gay Curriculum Laws*, 1470–1472 (breaking up such laws into "no promo homo" and "anti-homo" laws).

43. CDC, *HIV/AIDS Among Women Who Have Sex with Women* (June 2006) (no confirmed cases of female-to-female sexual transmission of HIV); Bethany Everett, *Sexual Orientation Disparities in Sexually Transmitted Infections: Examining the Intersection Between Sexual Identity and Sexual Behavior*, 42 Archives Sexual Behav. 225 (2013) (fewer STDs in lesbian relationships than straight ones); George Lemp et al., *HIV Seroprevalence and Risk Behaviors Among Lesbians and Bisexual Women in San Francisco and Berkeley, California*, 85 Am. J. Pub. Health 1549 (1995).

44. Charles Sumner, *Equality Before the Law: Unconstitutionality of Separate Colored Schools in Massachusetts. Argument of Charles Sumner, Esq., Before the Supreme Court of Massachusetts in the Case of* Sarah C. Roberts v. City of Boston, 11 (Boston: B. F. Roberts, 1849) (quotation in text); CDC, "LGBT Youth," https://www.cdc.gov/lgbthealth/youth.htm.

45. *Hazelwood Sch. Dist. v. Kuhlmeier*, 484 U.S. 260 (1988). Accord, *Bethel Sch. Dist. v. Fraser*, 478 U.S. 675 (1986).

46. *Romer v. Evans*, 517 U.S. 620, 633 (1996) (quotation in text). See *United States v. Windsor*, 570 U.S. 744 (2013); Dale Carpenter, Windsor *Products: Equal Protection from Animus*, 2013 Sup. Ct. Rev. 183, 217–218.

47. *Frontiero v. Richardson*, 411 U.S. 677, 686 (1973) (quotations in text, from plurality opinion); *City of Cleburne v. Cleburne Living Ctr.*, 473 U.S. 432, 441 (1985); *Lyng v. Castillo*, 477 U.S. 635, 638 (1986); Serena Mayeri, *Reasoning from Race: Feminism, Law, and the Civil Rights Revolution* (2011). On heightened scrutiny for sexual orientation classifications, see *United States v. Windsor*, 699 F.3d 169 (2d Cir. 2012); *SmithKline Beecham v. Abbott Laboratories*, 740 F.3d 471 (9th Cir. 2014); *In re Marriage Cases*, 183 P.3d 384 (Cal. 2008); *Kerrigan v. Comm'r of Pub. Health*, 957 A.2d 407 (Conn. 2008). On the virtue of state constitutional protection of rights not supported by Supreme Court decisions, see William Brennan Jr., *State Constitutions and the Protection of Individual Rights*, 90 Harv. L. Rev. 489, 502–504 (1980); Jeffrey Sutton, *51 Imperfect Solutions: States and the Making of American Constitutional Law* (2018).

48. *Obergefell*, p. 2596 (first quotation in text), p. 2600 (second quotation), p. 2596 (third quotation).

49. *McLaughlin v. Florida*, 379 U.S. 184 (1964) (race is a suspect classification); *Loving v. Virginia*, 388 U.S. 1 (1967) (same); *Craig v. Boren*, 429 U.S. 190 (1976) (sex is quasi-suspect); William Eskridge Jr. and Philip Frickey, *The Supreme Court, 1993 Term—Foreword: Law as Equilibrium*, 108 Harv. L. Rev. 26, 53–56 (1994) (Supreme Court has "inverted" the political powerlessness criterion, namely, by recognizing suspect classifications at the very point when the disadvantaged group was securing some political cogency).

50. Paula Ettelbrick, *Since When Is Marriage a Path to Liberation?*, OUT/LOOK, Fall 1989, 9, 14; Nancy Polikoff, *Beyond (Straight and Gay) Marriage: Valuing All Families Under the Law* (2008).

51. Eric Adam and Betsy Cooper, *Equal Rights vs. Special Rights: Rights Discourse, Framing, and Lesbian and Gay Antidiscrimination Policy in Washington State*, 42 Law & Soc. Inquiry 830, 846–850 (2017); Equality Act, H.R. 5, 116th Cong. (2019). On the Title VII debate, see *Zarda v. Altitude Express, Inc.*, 883 F.3d 100 (2d Cir., en banc, Feb. 26, 2018), cert. granted, 139 S. Ct. 1599 (April 22, 2019) (Supreme Court will review decision finding gay employees covered by sex discrimination bar); *R.G. & H.G. Harris Funeral Homes v. EEOC*, 884 F.3d 560 (6th Cir. 2018), cert. granted, 139 S. Ct. 1599 (April 22, 2019) (Supreme Court will review decision finding trans employees covered by sex discrimination bar); William Eskridge Jr., *Title VII's Statutory History and the Sex Discrimination Argument for LGBT Workplace Protections*, 127 Yale L.J. 322 (2017).

52. Bell, *Interest-Convergence Dilemma*, 523 (quotation in text). See Justin Driver, *Rethinking the Interest-Convergence Thesis*, 105 Nw. U.L. Rev. 149 (2011).

53. Hunter, *Varieties*; Anthony Michael Kreis, *Gay Gentrification: Whitewashed Fictions of LGBT Privilege and the New Interest-Convergence Dilemma*, 31 Law & Inequality 117 (2013); Neo Khuu, Comment, Obergefell v. Hodges: *Kinship Formation, Interest Convergence, and the Future of LGBTQ Rights*, 64 UCLA L. Rev. 184 (2017).

54. Martha Davis, *Brutal Need: Lawyers and the Welfare Rights Movement, 1960–1973* (1995) (detailed account of the welfare rights social movement).

55. Brett McDonnell, *Is Incest Next?*, 10 Cardozo Women's L.J. 337 (2004).

56. Darren Lenard Hutchinson, *"Gay Rights" for "Gay Whites"? Race, Sexual Identity, and Equal Protection Discourse*, 85 Cornell L. Rev. 1358 (2000); Leachman, *Institutionalizing Essentialism*. See Ralph Richard Banks, *Is Marriage for White People? How the African American Marriage Decline Affects Everyone* (2011); R. Kelly Raley, Megan Sweeney, and Danielle Wondra, *The Growing Racial and Ethnic Divide in U.S. Marriage Patterns*, 25 Future Children 89–109 (2015).

57. Gary Gates, Williams Institute, *Same-Sex Couples in Census 2010: Race and Ethnicity* (April 26, 2013).

58. William Eskridge Jr. and Nan Hunter, *Sexuality, Gender, and the Law* (1997) (casebook featuring rights for transgender persons as central to the gay rights movement).

59. Email from Sean Lund to William Eskridge, May 14, 2019. The 2016 *Restaurant* ad is available at http://www.lgbtmap.org/restaurant-ad.

60. The Freedom for All Massachusetts ad campaign is available at https://www.freedommassachusetts.org/videos/ (quotation in text).

61. Joan Nestle et al., eds., *GenderQueer: Voices from Beyond the Gender Binary* (2002); Kimberly Yuracko, *Gender Nonconformity and the Law* (2016); Jessica Clarke, *They, Them, and Theirs*, 132 Harv. L. Rev. 894 (2019); Kate Bornstein, *Gender Outlaw: On Men, Women, and the Rest of Us* (1994).

62. Sonia Katyal, *The Numerus Clausus of Sex*, 84 U. Chi. L. Rev. 389 (2017); Heath Fogg Davis, *Beyond Trans: Does Gender Matter?* (2017); Dean Spade, *Documenting Gender*, 59 Hastings L.J. 731 (2008); Clarke, *They, Them, and Theirs*, 936–945; *Zzyym v. Kerry*, 220 F. Supp. 3d 1106 (Colo. 2016) (arbitrary for State Department to insist on sex-binary passport identification).

63. Jonathan Rauch, *It's Time to Drop the "LGBT" from "LGBTQ,"* The Atlantic, Jan.–Feb. 2019.

64. Judith Butler, *Gender Trouble* (1990); Michel Foucault, *The History of Sexuality: Volume 1: An Introduction* (1978). See Eskridge and Hunter, *Sexuality* (early compilation of Butler, Foucault, and other "queer theory" scholars for law students).

65. "Beyond Same-Sex Marriage: A New Strategic Vision for All Our Families and Relationships" (Aug. 8, 2006), https://mronline.org/2006/08/08/beyond-same-sex-marriage-a-new-strategic-vision-for-all-our-families-relationships/.

66. On the marriage equality–freedom to marry movement as an ongoing campaign, see Hunter, *Varieties*, 1687–1707. On polycentric constitutionalism, see William Eskridge Jr. and John Ferejohn, *A Republic of Statutes: The New American Constitution*, chap. 1 (2010); Robert Post and Reva Siegel, *Legislative Constitutionalism and Section Five Power: Policentric Interpretation of the Family and Medical Leave Act*, 112 Yale L.J. 1943 (2003); Barry Friedman, *Dialogue and Judicial Review*, 91 Mich. L. Rev. 577, 581 (1993).

67. *ERA and Homosexual "Marriages,"* Phyllis Schlafly Report, vol. 8, no. 2, Sept. 1974 (quotation in text).

68. Craig Osten and Alan Sears, *The Homosexual Agenda: Exposing the Principal Threat to Religious Liberty Today*, 12 (2003) (quotation in text). Throughout their book, Osten and Sears referred to homosexuality as "disordered," a vice curable through conversion therapy, "wicked," and diseased.

69. Margaret Sanger, *An Autobiography* (1971 ed.). See Ellen Chesler, *Woman of Valor: Margaret Sanger and the Birth Control Movement in America* (1992); David Garrow, *Liberty and Sexuality: The Right to Privacy and the Making of Roe v. Wade* (1994); Linda Gordon, *Woman's Body, Woman's Right: Birth Control in America* (1976).

70. Sarah Kliff, *We Polled 1,060 Americans About Abortion. This Is What They Got Wrong*, Vox, Feb. 26, 2016, https://www.vox.com/a/abortion-statistics-opinions-2016

/poll; Carolyn Davis, *Look for Politics to Shift as Young People Increasingly Support Abortion Rights*, USA Today, May 1, 2018.

71. Sarah McCammon, *Americans' Support for Abortion Rights Wanes as Pregnancy Progresses*, National Public Radio, June 13, 2018.

72. Violence Against Women Act of 1994, P.L. 103-322 (1994); Conversations with Professor Victoria Nourse, 2003–2019 (Nourse was Biden's counsel who worked on VAWA).

73. Katha Pollitt, *There's a Reason Gay Marriage Is Winning, While Abortion Rights Are Losing*, The Nation, April 22, 2015; Katha Pollitt, *A Man's Guide to Abortion*, The Nation, June 3, 2019 (quotations in text).

74. Katha Pollitt, *Pro: Reclaiming Abortion Rights* (2014).

75. *The Immigration Closet*, Back Story, National Public Radio, Dec. 2015, https://soundcloud.com/backstory/the-immigration-closet-1 (interview with Tony Sullivan); William Eskridge Jr., *Law and the Production of Deceit*, in Austin Sarat, ed., *Law and Lies: Deception and Truth-Telling in the American Legal System*, 254–312 (2015) (linking the immigration closet with the closet for sexual minorities). See Cecilia Menjívar and Leisy Abrego, *Legal Violence in the Lives of Immigrants: How Immigration Enforcement Affects Families, Schools, and Workplaces* (Center for American Progress, Dec. 2012); Cong. Budget Office, *The Impact of Unauthorized Immigrants on the Budgets of State and Local Governments* (2007) (tax revenues much greater than benefit payments to undocumented immigrants).

76. For example, Miriam Jordan, *Making President Trump's Bed: A Housekeeper Without Papers*, New York Times, Dec. 6, 2018.

77. Petitioner's brief, *Kameny*, pp. 24–29 (libertarian objections to the government's discharge because of homosexual advances).

23. The Golden Rule

1. James Davison Hunter, *Culture Wars: The Struggle to Control the Family, Art, Education, Law, and Politics in America* (1992); Robert Cochran Jr. and Michael Helfand, *The Competing Claims of Law and Religion: Who Should Influence Whom?*, 39 Pepperdine L. Rev. 1051, 1056 (2013).

2. Statement of faith, St. Paul's Lutheran Church (2015) (quotations in text); Commission on Theology and Church Relations of the Lutheran Church—Missouri Synod, *Human Sexuality: A Theological Perspective* (Sept. 1981) (traditionalist understanding of sexual morality, grounded in conjugal marriage).

3. US Commission on Civil Rights, *Peaceful Coexistence: Reconciling Nondiscrimination Principles with Civil Liberties*, 29 (2016) (quotation in text, from chairman Martin Castro).

4. See Netta Barak-Corren, *The War Within* (draft 2018) (rejecting the "culture war" paradigm and analyzing the response of religious leaders to liberty-equality conflicts in schools).

5. Evangelical Lutheran Church of America, *Human Sexuality: Gift and Trust* (2009); Letter from Elizabeth Eaton, presiding bishop, Evangelical Lutheran Church, June 30, 2015; Pew Research Center, *Views About Homosexuality Among Members of the Lutheran Church—Missouri Synod,* http://www.pewforum.org/religious-landscape -study/religious-denomination/lutheran-church-missouri-synod/views-about-homo sexuality/. See Judith Areen, *Uncovering the Reformation Roots of American Marriage and Divorce Law,* 26 Yale J.L. & Feminism 29 (2014).

6. Elder Dallin Oaks, "Principles to Govern Possible Public Statement on Legislation Affecting Rights of Homosexuals" (Aug. 7, 1984), Prince Archives; William Eskridge Jr. and Robin Fretwell Wilson, *Religious Freedom, LGBT Rights, and the Prospects for Common Ground,* 441–459 (2019).

7. Elliott-Larsen Civil Rights Act, 1976 Mich. Pub. Acts No. 453.

8. Endorsing the nondiscrimination norm for sexual and gender minorities are United Church of Christ (Congregationalists), "Council on Social Action Resolution on Homosexuality" (1969); Unitarian Universalist, "General Assembly Resolution on Homosexuality" (1970); Central Conference of American Rabbis, "Convention Resolution on Homosexuality" (1977) (Reform Judaism); Presbyterian Church USA, General Assembly, "The Church and Homosexuality" (1978); Episcopal Church, General Convention, "Human Sexuality" (1980); US Conference of Catholic Bishops, "Ministry to Persons with a Homosexual Inclination" (2006); Committee on Jewish Laws and Standards, "On Homosexuality" (1992) (Conservative Judaism); United Methodist Church, Resolution, "Opposition to Homophobia and Heterosexism" (2008); Islamic Society of North America, "Statement Endorsing ENDA" (2013). Encouraging discrimination are Southern Baptist Convention, "Resolution on Homosexuality" (1977, updated periodically); Russian Orthodox Church, "Basis of the Social Concept" (2016).

9. For "love the sinner, hate the sin" expressions, see Congregation for the Doctrine of the Faith, "On the Pastoral Care of Homosexual Persons" (1986); Rabbinical Council of America, "Declaration on the Torah Approach to Homosexuality" (2011); United Methodist Church, "Book of Discipline (Social Principles)" (2016); Assemblies of God, General Presbytery, "Official Statement on Homosexuality, Marriage, and Sexual Identity" (2014); First Presidency, Church of Jesus Christ, *General Handbook* (as of 2019); National Baptist Convention, "Baptist Denominations & Doctrines Frequently Asked Questions" (as of 2019). See also Southern Baptist Convention, "Resolution on 'Same-Sex Marriage' and Civil Rights Rhetoric" (2012) (milder disapproval than in previous years); Russian Orthodox Church, "Basis of the Social Concept" (2016) (similar).

10. Mark Achtemeier, *The Bible's Yes to Same-Sex Marriage: An Evangelical's Change of Heart,* 1–5 (2014) (quotation in text); Presbyterian Church USA, 221st General Assembly, "Resolution to Change the Book of Order to Allow Same-Sex Marriages" (June 14, 2014) (taking effect in March 2015 after ratification by a majority of presbyteries).

11. Letter from Katherine Morton Achtemeier to William Eskridge, March 7, 2016; William Eskridge Jr., *The Case for Same-Sex Marriage: From Sexual Liberty to Civilized Commitment* (1996) (appendix collecting a few dozen letters from religious leaders supporting marriage equality in the District of Columbia marriage equality litigation).

12. Stephen Haynes, *Noah's Curse: The Biblical Justification of American Slavery* (2002); William Eskridge Jr., *Noah's Curse: How Religion Often Conflates Status, Belief, and Conduct to Resist Antidiscrimination Norms*, 45 Ga. L. Rev. 657 (2011).

13. Frances FitzGerald, *The Evangelicals: The Struggle to Shape America*, 2–3 (2017) (identifying which faith traditions are considered Evangelical); William Martin, *With God on Our Side: The Rise of the Religious Right in America* (1996).

14. *Pastor Steven Anderson's Genocide of Homosexuals*, https://www.youtube.com/watch?v=gVseLfwfCMA (quotations in text).

15. SBC, Kansas City, "Resolution on Homosexuality" (June 14–16, 1977) (first quotation in text); SBC, New Orleans, "Resolution on Homosexual Marriages" (June 1996) (subsequent quotations). SBC resolutions against gay marriage, domestic partnerships, and civil unions are available at http://www.sbc.net/resolutions/about/gay%20marriage. See Oran Smith, *The Rise of Baptist Republicanism* (1997).

16. SBC, "Resolution on 'Same-Sex Marriage' and Civil Rights Rhetoric" (2012) (quotations in text); Sarah Posner, *Amazing Disgrace: How Did Donald Trump—a Thrice-Married, Biblically Illiterate Sexual Predator—Hijack the Religious Right?*, New Republic, March 20, 2017 (Land's ouster because of racially divisive jibes and plagiarism).

17. Our discussion of the 2014 conference is based upon videotapes available on YouTube.

18. Rev. J.D. Greear, "Preaching Like Jesus to the LGBT Community and Its Supporters," National Conference on the Gospel, Homosexuality, and the Future of Marriage, Oct. 30, 2014; Jim Daly, Focus on the Family, "Reconcilable Differences: Building Bridges with Those Who Disagree About Marriage," Conference on the Gospel, Homosexuality, Oct. 30, 2014. See Glenn Stanton, Focus on the Family, "Loving My (LGBT) Neighbor," Conference on the Gospel, Homosexuality, Oct. 28, 2014.

19. Rev. Ronnie Floyd, *The Gay Agenda: It's Dividing the Family, the Church, and a Nation* (2004); Rev. Frank Page, SBC president, *Southern Baptists and Homosexuality*, SBC Life: Journal of the Southern Baptist Convention, Dec. 2014; SBC, "Position Statement on Sexuality" (as of 2019); Focus on the Family, "Counseling for Sexual Identity Concerns" (2018).

20. David Gushee, *Changing Our Mind*, 64–72 (rev. ed. 2015) (analysis of Levitical abominations); William Eskridge telephone interview of David Gushee (Sept. 10, 2018).

21. Gushee, *Changing Our Mind*, 103–104 (quotation in text).

22. Gushee, *Changing Our Mind*, 91–98, 98 (quotation in text); Dietrich Bonhoeffer, "Creation and Fall: A Theological Exposition of Genesis 1–3" (lectures, University of Berlin, 1932–1933).

23. Willow Creek Community Church, Elder statements, "Marriage, Singleness, and Sexual Practice" (updated as of Jan. 2016); Andy Stanley, *Deep and Wide: Creating Churches Unchurched People Love to Attend* (2012); John Blake, *Two Preaching Giants and the "Betrayal" That Tore Them Apart*, CNN, Nov. 19, 2012.

24. Elizabeth Dias, *Inside the Evangelical Fight Over Gay Marriage*, Time, Jan. 15, 2015; Madeleine Buckley, *Notable Christians Who've Had a Change of Heart on LGBT Issues*, Religion News Service, July 12, 2017.

25. National Association of Evangelicals, executive committee, "Fairness for All" motion (approved Oct. 2, 2018); Rev. J.D. Greear, "How the Fall Affects Us All" (Jan. 27, 2019), with response by Rev. Jonathan Shelley, Stedfast Baptist Church, Fort Worth, TX, March 2019 (quotation in text), excerpts from both available at https://www.youtube.com/watch?v=KDwaH7dZrho.

26. Pope Paul VI, "Pastoral Constitution of the Church in the Modern World (*Gaudium et spes*)" (Dec. 7, 1965) (first quotation in text); Congregation for the Doctrine of the Faith, *Persona humana*, chap. 11 (Dec. 29, 1975) (second quotation), chap. 8 (remaining quotations, citing New Testament verses). See Vincent Genovesi, *In Pursuit of Love*, 187–191 (1996). The Congregation later opined: such persons "must be accepted with respect, compassion and sensitivity. Every sign of unjust discrimination in their regard should be avoided." *Catechism of the Catholic Church*, nos. 2358, 2396 (1994).

27. John McNeill, SJ, *The Church and the Homosexual* (1976); John McNeill, SJ, *Address to First National Dignity Conference*, National Catholic Reporter, Oct. 5, 1973; Barbara Rick, director, *In Good Conscience: Sister Jeannine Gramick's Journey of Faith* (Out of the Blue Films, 2009) (quotations in text).

28. Father Charles Curran, *Transition and Tradition in Moral Theology* (1979); Thomas Thurston, *Homosexuality and Roman Catholic Ethics* (1995); *Catechism of the Catholic Church*, nos. 2358, 2396 (1994). But see Congregation for the Doctrine of the Faith, "Letter to the Bishops of the Catholic Church on the Pastoral Care of Homosexual Persons," ¶ 3 (Oct. 1, 1986) (quotation in text); Congregation for the Doctrine of the Faith, "Considerations Regarding Proposals to Give Legal Recognitions to Unions between Homosexual Persons" (June 3, 2003).

29. Robert Shine, *"There Is No Place for Homophobia," Pope Francis Told Gay Former Student*, New Ways Ministry, Nov. 1, 2016 (quoting Pope Francis's letter to gay friend); William Eskridge telephone interview of James Martin, SJ (April 20, 2019); William Eskridge interview of Sr. Jeannine Gramick, New Haven, CT (Jan. 2017).

30. For an insider's informal account of the Extraordinary Synod, see the postings for October 2014 in Rocco Palmo's blog, *Whispers in the Loggia*, http://whispersintheloggia.blogspot.com/2014/10/.

31. Jonathan Capehart, *Synod Draft Furthers "Welcoming" Tone Towards Gay People from Pope Francis*, Washington Post, Oct. 14, 2014 (quotations in text, from ¶¶ 50, 52 of the draft report).

32. Synod of Bishops, "Final Report of the Synod of Bishops to the Holy Father, Pope Francis" (Oct. 24, 2015) (initial quotations in text); James Martin, SJ, *Five Important Things the Synod on the Family Accomplished*, America, Oct. 25, 2015 (last quotation).

33. The quotations in the text are all taken from "Post-Synodal Apostolic Exhortation *Amoris Laetitia* by the Holy Father Francis to Bishops, Priests and Deacons, Consecrated Persons, Christian Married Couples, and All the Lay Faithful," ¶¶ 11–19 (March 19, 2016) (Genesis assumption of conjugal marriage), ¶¶ 52, 301–302, 308 (pastoral discretion for "irregular" unions that are not marriages), ¶¶ 250–251 (no gay marriage but affirming pastoral support for gay people).

34. James Martin, SJ, *How Parishes Can Welcome L.G.B.T. Catholics*, America, Aug. 23, 2018 (quotation in text); Martin, *Building a Bridge: How the Catholic Church and the LGBT Community Can Enter into a Relationship of Respect, Compassion, and Sensitivity* (2017, rev. ed. 2018).

35. Lance Poston interview of Michael DeLeon (Dec. 11, 2017), OutSouth LGBTQ+ Oral History Project (quotation in text); *Our Persons of the Year for 2015*, Editorial, National Catholic Reporter, Dec. 28, 2015.

36. Poston interview of DeLeon (quotation in text); Amanda Terkel, *Catholic Cemetery Rejects Supreme Court Plaintiffs' Headstone Design Celebrating Marriage Equality*, HuffPost, May 17, 2016; William Eskridge conversation with Newt and Callista Gingrich, Basilica of the National Shrine of the Immaculate Conception, Washington, DC (April 26, 2019).

37. Martha Elson, *Clergy Weighs Kim Davis's Legal, Moral Rights*, Cincinnati Enquirer, Sept. 13, 2015.

38. First Presidency and Council of the Twelve Apostles of the Church of Jesus Christ of Latter-day Saints, "The Family: A Proclamation to the World," ¶ 2 (Sept. 23, 1995) (all the quotations in text). On the centrality of gender in the Mormon cosmology, see Church of Jesus Christ, "Mother in Heaven" (2015); Terryl Givens, *Wrestling the Angel: The Foundations of Mormon Thought: Cosmos, God, Humanity*, 106–112, 274–279 (2014); David Paulsen and Martin Pulido, *"A Mother There": A Survey of Historical Teachings About Mother in Heaven*, 50 BYU Studies 70–97 (2011).

39. President Spencer Kimball et al., *The Church and the Proposed Equal Rights Amendment: A Moral Issue*, Ensign 11 (1980). On opposition to the ERA, see William Eskridge Jr., *Latter-day Constitutionalism: Sexuality, Gender, and Mormons*, 2016 U. Ill. L. Rev. 1227, 1234–1238; D. Michael Quinn, *The LDS Church's Campaign Against the Equal Rights Amendment*, 20 J. Mormon Hist. 85–155 (1994); Neil Young, *"The ERA Is a Moral Issue": The Mormon Church, LDS Women, and the Defeat of the Equal Rights Amendment*, 59 Am. Q. 623 (2007).

40. Courage Campaign Issues Committee, *Home Invasion* (Oct. 31, 2008), https://www.youtube.com/watch?v=q28UwAyzUkE (quotations in text).

41. Jessica Garrison and Joanna Lin, *Prop 8 Protesters Target Mormon Temple in Westwood*, Los Angeles Times, Nov. 7, 2008; Gregory Prince, *Gay Rights and the Mormon Church: Intended Actions, Unintended Consequences*, 161 (2019) (quotation in text).

42. Prince, *Gay Rights and the Mormon Church*, 164–167 (quotations in text; detailed insider account of the anti–Proposition 8 backlash within the Church).

43. Stephanie Mencimer, *Mormon Church Abandons Its Crusade Against Gay Marriage*, Mother Jones, April 12, 2013. Our discussion in this and following paragraphs is based upon Prince, *Gay Rights and the Mormon Church*, 175–218, and off-the-record conversations in Salt Lake City.

44. Maria La Ganga, *An Embrace That Swayed the Mormon Church on Gay Rights*, Los Angeles Times, Jan. 31, 2015; Scott Taylor, *LDS Church Defends Actions in Plaza "Kissing" Incident*, Deseret News, July 18, 2009 (Church's side of the story); Colbert Report, *Nailed 'Em—Mormon Church Trespassing* (Nov. 3, 2009), http://www.cc.com/video-clips/olb2ep/the-colbert-report-nailed—em—mormon-church-trespassing.

45. La Ganga, *Embrace*.

46. Prince, *Gay Rights and the Mormon Church*, 184–186.

47. William Eskridge telephone interview of Clifford Rosky, legal counsel, Equality Utah (Oct. 1, 2015); Off-the-record conversations.

48. Peggy Fletcher Stack, *New Mormon Church Website Has Softer Tone on Gays*, Salt Lake Tribune, Dec. 7, 2012. Dallin Oaks's video is available at https://mormonandgay.lds.org/videos?id=7254846371177561723&lang=eng.

49. Jennifer Dobner, *New Mormon Policy Makes Apostates of Married Same-Sex Couples, Bars Children from Rites*, Salt Lake Tribune, Nov. 6, 2015 (quotations in text).

50. Church of Jesus Christ of Latter-day Saints, "Single-Parent Families" (2006) (quotation in text); LDS Family Services, *Adoption and the Unwed Mother*, Ensign (Feb. 2002); Jane Edwards, *Has the LDS Church Changed Its Policies on Adoption?*, First Mother Forum (Sept. 29, 2013).

51. Brady McCombs, *Mormon Support for Gay Marriage Gradually Grows*, Associated Press, May 4, 2018; Edward Kimball, *Spencer W. Kimball and the Revelation on Priesthood*, 47 BYU Studies Quarterly, Iss. 2, pp. 43–44 (quotation in text); Elizabeth Dias, *Mormon Church to Allow Children of LGBT Parents to Be Baptized*, New York Times, April 4, 2019. Cf. Lester Bush Jr., *Mormonism's Negro Doctrine: A Historical Overview*, 8 Dialogue 54 (Spring 1973).

52. *Fulton v. City of Philadelphia*, 922 F.3d 140 (3d Cir. April 22, 2019) (upholding termination of municipal contracts with Catholic foster care service); US Conference of Catholic Bishops, "Discrimination Against Catholic Adoption Services" (2018); Kayla Mullen, *Same-Sex Couples to Receive Benefits*, Observer [Notre Dame, IN], Oct. 16, 2014 (controversy at Notre Dame over its extension of spousal benefits to same-sex married couples).

53. *Masterpiece Cakeshop, Ltd. v. Colorado Civil Rights Comm'n*, 138 S. Ct. 1712 (2018); J. Stuart Adams, *Cultivating Common Ground: Lessons from Utah for Living with Our Differences,* in Eskridge and Wilson, *Prospects for Common Ground,* 441–459.

54. *Hosanna-Tabor Evangelical Lutheran Church & School v. EEOC,* 565 U.S. 171 (2012) (first quotation in text), p. 199 (second quotation, from Alito's concurring opinion); *Obergefell v. Hodges,* 135 S. Ct. 2584, 2607 (2015) (third quotation).

55. I.R.C. § 501(c)(3), 26 U.S.C. § 501(c)(3) (quotation in text); William Eskridge interview of Donald Verrilli, Washington, DC (July 2018).

56. *Bob Jones Univ. v. United States,* 461 U.S. 574 (1983), upholding Revenue Ruling 71–447, 1971–2 Cum. Bull. 230; *Obergefell,* p. 2626 (Roberts's dissenting opinion).

57. Mark Lehman and David Dorn, *Obtaining Tax Exempt Status for Religious Institutions,* 7 Colum. J. Tax Law 7–8 (2016) (IRS statement responding to *Obergefell*); Nicholas Mirkay, *Globalism, Public Policy, and Tax-Exempt Status: Are U.S. Charities Adrift at Sea?,* 91 N.C.L. Rev. 851, 871 (2013) (IRS will deny tax-exempt status for charitable institutions that engage in "certain illegal activity"); Marcus Owens, Bob Jones, Obergefell, *and the IRS,* AHLA Connections, March 2016 (quotation in text).

58. Samuel Brunson and David Herzig, *A Diachronic Approach to* Bob Jones: *Religious Tax Exemptions After* Obergefell, 92 Ind. L.J. 1175, 1203–1204 (2017) (quotation in text).

59. Religious Freedom Restoration Act of 1993, P.L. 103-141, 107 Stat. 1488 (1993) (quotations in text); *Boy Scouts of America v. Dale,* 530 U.S. 640, 659 (2000); Douglas NeJaime and Reva Siegel, *Religious Exemptions and Anti-Discrimination Law in* Masterpiece Cakeshop, 128 Yale L.J. Forum 201, 205–210 (Sept. 14, 2018).

60. *Employment Division v. Smith,* 494 U.S. 872, 883–886 (1990); *City of Boerne v. Flores,* 521 U.S. 507, 537 (1997) (Stevens's concurring opinion, opposing a constitutional rule that would require government to prefer a religious point of view); *Wallace v. Jaffree,* 472 U.S. 38, 52–55 (1985) (similar).

61. *Masterpiece,* pp. 1727–1729 (facts of the case, including the parallel complaints), pp. 1728–1731 (court's holding); Brief for petitioners, *Masterpiece,* Docket No. 16-111 (US Supreme Court, filed Aug. 31, 2017), 2017 WL 3913762. Compare *Masterpiece,* pp. 1748–1752 (Ginsburg's dissenting opinion) and pp. 1733–1734 (Kagan's concurring opinion, agreeing with most of Ginsburg's analysis) with pp. 1734–1740 (Gorsuch's concurring opinion, responding to Ginsburg). Compare also *Trump v. Hawaii,* 138 S. Ct. 2392 (2018) (upholding the Trump travel ban) with pp. 2433–2448 (Sotomayor's dissenting opinion, demonstrating anti-Muslim justifications for travel ban).

62. Brief for petitioners, pp. 16–38, *Masterpiece;* Brief for the United States as amicus curiae, *Masterpiece,* Docket No. 16-111 (US Supreme Court, filed Sept. 7, 2017), 2017 WL 4004530; *Masterpiece,* pp. 1740–1745 (Thomas's concurring opinion, joined by Gorsuch); *Hurley v. Irish-American Gay, Lesbian and Bisexual Group of Boston,* 515 U.S. 567 (1995).

63. *Masterpiece*, pp. 1727–1729 (quotations from court's opinion, approved in Ginsburg's dissent, p. 1748); *Newman v. Piggie Park Enterprises*, 256 F. Supp. 941 (D.S.C. 1966), aff'd, 390 U.S. 400 (1968). On the religious view that Scripture forbids "mixing" of the races, see Eskridge, *Noah's Curse*, 672–677.

64. NeJaime and Siegel, *Religious Exemptions*, 201–205; Joseph William Singer, *We Don't Serve Your Kind Here: Public Accommodations and the Mark of Sodom*, 95 B.U.L. Rev. 929, 946–947 (2015). *Hurley* was a harder case than its 9-0 disposition indicates, because counsel conceded that the parade excluded the openly gay marching unit because of *both* their sexual orientation *and* their expression. Oral argument, p. 49, *Hurley* (April 25, 1995), 1995 WL 301703.

65. *Rumsfeld v. Forum for Academic & Institutional Rights, Inc.*, 547 U.S. 47, 62 (2006) (quotations in text). See *Hurley*, pp. 568, 572–573; *Christian Legal Society v. Martinez*, 561 U.S. 661 (2010).

66. Robin Fretwell Wilson, *Bathrooms and Bakers: How Sharing the Public Square Is the Key to a Truce in the Culture Wars*, in Eskridge and Wilson, *Prospects for Common Ground*, 402–420.

67. Douglas Laycock, *Liberty and Justice for All*, in Eskridge and Wilson, *Prospects for Common Ground*, 24–37; Kent Greenawalt, *Mutual Tolerance and Sensible Exemptions*, in Eskridge and Wilson, 102–110; Michael McConnell, *Dressmakers, Bakers, and the Equality of Rights*, in Eskridge and Wilson, 378–384; Douglas NeJaime and Reva Siegel, *Conscience Wars: Complicity-Based Conscience Claims in Religion and Politics*, 124 Yale L.J. 2516 (2015). See *State v. Arlene's Flowers, Inc.*, 389 P.3d 543 (Wash. 2017), vacated and remanded, 138 S. Ct. 2671 (2018), on remand, 193 Wash. 2d 469 (June 6, 2019) (petition for Supreme Court review, filed Sept. 11, 2019); *Elane Photography, LLC v. Willock*, 309 P.3d 53 (N.M. 2013), cert. denied, 572 U.S. 1046 (2014).

68. Lance Wickman, "Promoting Religious Freedom in a Secular Age: Fundamental Principles, Practical Priorities, and Fairness for All," https://www.mormonnewsroom .org/article/promoting-religious-freedom-secular-age-fundamental-principles -practical-priorities-fairness-for-all (quotations in text).

69. Robin Fretwell Wilson, *When Governments Insulate Dissenters from Social Change: What* Hobby Lobby *and Abortion Conscience Clauses Teach About Specific Exemptions*, 48 U.C. Davis L. Rev. 703 (2104); *Burwell v. Hobby Lobby Stores, Inc.*, 573 U.S. 672 (2014).

70. Our account of S.B. 1062 is based upon coverage from the Arizona News Service; our interviews with some of the participants (including former general counsel of the Arizona Chamber of Commerce Kory Langhofer, New Haven, CT [March 8, 2018]; Chamber chief of staff Brittany Kaufman, Phoenix [May 3, 2018]; former Mesa, AZ, mayor Scott Smith [telephone interview May 3, 2018]; former executive director of the Arizona Republican Party Chad Heywood [telephone interview May 1, 2018]); and a few off-the-record conversations.

71. Bob Moser, *Why the Religious Right Is Terrified of Pete Buttigieg*, New Republic, April 10, 2019.

72. *Kitchen v. Herbert*, 961 F. Supp. 2d 1181, 1193–1194 (D. Utah, Dec. 20, 2013), aff'd, 755 F.3d 1193 (10th Cir. June 25, 2014), cert. denied, 135 S. Ct. 265 (Oct. 6, 2014); Prince, *Gay Rights and the Mormon Church*, 219–230.

73. Prince, *Gay Rights and the Mormon Church*, 230–235; William Eskridge interviews of Utah senator Stuart Adams, Champaign, IL (Sept. 10–11, 2015); Peggy Fletcher Stack, *In Major Move, Mormon Apostles Call for Statewide LGBT Protections*, Salt Lake Tribune, Jan. 27, 2015.

74. William Eskridge telephone interview of Robin Wilson (Sept. 18, 2015).

75. S.B. 296, § 1, codified at Utah Code § 34A-5-102(1)(h)(ii) (restrictive definition of "employer," including an exemption for the Boy Scouts), § 5, codified at Utah Code § 34A-5-106(3)(a)(ii) (limited exemption for religious schools), §§ 7–8, codified at Utah Code §§ 34A-5-109–34A-5-110 (dress code and bathroom provisions), § 14, codified at Utah Code § 57-21-3(2), (7) (limited exemptions in housing law for nonprofits and educational institutions, including BYU).

76. S.B. 296, § 10(1), codified at Utah Code § 34A-5-112(1) (quotation in text).

77. The original draft of S.B. 297, with the religious exemptions quoted in the text, is available at https://le.utah.gov/~2015/bills/static/sb0297.html.

78. Jennifer Dobner and Robert Gehrke, *LGBT Leaders Concerned About Adams' Religious-Protection Bill*, Salt Lake Tribune, March 6, 2015.

79. William Eskridge Jr. and Robin Fretwell Wilson, *Introduction*, in Eskridge and Wilson, *Prospects for Common Ground*.

80. Wilson, *Bathrooms and Bakers*, 405 (quotation in text).

81. Fairness for All Act, H.R. 5331, 116th Cong. (introduced Dec. 6, 2019); proposed Civil Rights Act of 1964, tit. II, § 201(b)(11)(C), 42 U.S.C. § 2000a(b)(11)(C) (excepting claims of race, color, and national origin discrimination from the broad carve-out of religious and affiliated institutions from the amended Civil Rights Act).

82. Lucas Acosta, HRC, "Civil Rights Groups: The 'Fairness for All' Act Is an Affront to Existing Civil Rights" (Dec. 6, 2019), https://www.hrc.org/blog/civil-rights-groups-the-fairness-for-all-act-is-an-affront-to-existing-civi (first quotation in text); Daniel Silliman, *LGBT Rights-Religious Liberty Bill Proposed in Congress*, Christianity Today, Dec. 6, 2019; Shane Vander Hart, *Is the Fairness for All Act Really Fair to All?*, Caffeinated Thoughts, Dec. 9, 2019 (second quotation).

83. See Jonathan Rauch, *Nondiscrimination for All*, National Affairs, Summer 2017.

24. Families We Choose

1. Jane Eisner interview of Justice Ruth Bader Ginsburg (Feb. 5, 2018), https://forward.com/opinion/393687/jane-eisner-interviews-ruth-bader-ginsburg-transcript/ (quotation in text). See also Ruth Bader Ginsburg, with Mary Hartnett and Wendy Webster Williams, *My Own Words* (2016); Betsy West and Julie Cohen, directors, *RBG* (Magnolia Pictures, 2018) (award-winning documentary). In the account that follows, we

have also drawn from William Eskridge's conversations with Marty, Ruth, and Jane Ginsburg over the years.

2. Eisner interview of Ginsburg (quotation in text and story of her experience at Paul, Weiss).

3. Kathryn Shulz, *The Many Lives of Pauli Murray*, The New Yorker, April 17, 2017 (quotations in text). See Pauli Murray, *Song in a Weary Throat: An American Pilgrimage* (1987) (autobiography); Sarah Azaransky, *The Dream Is Freedom: Pauli Murray and American Democratic Faith* (2011).

4. Rosalind Rosenberg, *Jane Crow: The Life of Pauli Murray*, 58–59, 138 (2017) (quotations in text); Patricia Bell-Scott, *The Firebrand and the First Lady*, 21–33 (2016) (Murray's theory of democratic legitimacy).

5. Pauli Murray, "A Proposal to Reexamine the Applicability of the Fourteenth Amendment to State Laws and Practices Which Discriminate on the Basis of Sex Per Se" (Dec. 1962), in President's Commission on the Status of Women papers, Schlesinger Library, Box 8, Folder 62; Pauli Murray and Mary Eastwood, *Jane Crow and the Law: Sex Discrimination and Title VII*, 34 Geo. Wash. L. Rev. 232, 233 (1965) (quotations in text).

6. Eskridge's off-the-record exchange with a Columbia faculty member (quotation in text).

7. West and Cohen, *RBG* (quotation in text).

8. Brief for the appellant, *Reed v. Reed*, Docket No. 70-4 (US Supreme Court, filed June 25, 1971), 1971 WL 133596 (Ginsburg-Murray brief for the ACLU); Serena Mayeri, *Reasoning from Race: Feminism, Law, and the Civil Rights Movement*, 34–38, 61–63 (2011); William Eskridge Jr., *Some Effects of Identity-Based Social Movements on Constitutional Law in the Twentieth Century*, 100 Mich. L. Rev. 2062, 2124–2133 (2002). See ACLU, *Tribute: The Legacy of Ruth Bader Ginsburg and WRP Staff*, https://www.aclu.org/other /tribute-legacy-ruth-bader-ginsburg-and-wrp-staff.

9. *Reed v. Reed*, 404 U.S. 71 (1971) (loosely following the analysis of the ACLU brief for the petitioner); *Moritz v. Commissioner*, 469 F.2d 466 (10th Cir. 1972).

10. *Frontiero v. Richardson*, 411 U.S. 677 (1973) (Brennan's plurality opinion adopted the ACLU's reasoning to support strict scrutiny of sex-based classifications; four other justices concurred based on *Reed*); *Craig v. Boren*, 429 U.S. 190 (1976) (Brennan's opinion for the court follows the ACLU's brief to invalidate a sex-based classification, but under a "heightened scrutiny" standard); *Kirchberg v. Feenstra*, 450 U.S. 455 (1981) (closely following the amicus brief for ACLU to strike down state lord-and-master law).

11. *Weinberger v. Wiesenfeld*, 420 U.S. 636 (1975), see p. 655 (Rehnquist's concurring opinion).

12. William Eskridge Jr., *Dishonorable Passions: Sodomy Law in America, 1861–2003*, chap. 5 (2008) (ACLU-inspired reform, reordering the criminal sanction away from morals-enforcement toward harm prevention); National Coalition of Gay Rights Organizations, 1972 Gay Rights Platform, State Level Proposals ¶¶ 5, 7–8 (radical proposals for state deregulation of family).

13. Hiroki Kimiko Keavney, "Christian, Queer and Interracial: The Story of Pauli Murray and Irene Barlow" (master's thesis, San Francisco State University, Sept. 2016).

14. *Obergefell v. Hodges*, 135 S. Ct. 2584, 2594, 2600 (2015) (quotations in text); Luncheon conversation about *Obergefell*, June 26, 2015, at AALS Workshop on Next Generation Issues on Sex, Gender and the Law, Orlando, FL (June 26, 2015); Deborah Widiss, *Nonmarital Families and (or After?) Marriage Equality*, 42 Fla. St. U.L. Rev. 547 (2015). For feminist theories decentering family law from marriage, see Martha Fineman, *The Neutered Mother, the Sexual Family, and Other Twentieth-Century Tragedies* (1995); Nancy Polikoff, *Beyond (Straight and Gay) Marriage: Valuing All Families Under the Law* (2008).

15. Serena Mayeri, *Marriage (In)equality and the Historical Legacies of Feminism*, 126 Calif. L. Rev. Cir. 126, 135 (2015) (first quotation in text); Melissa Murray, Obergefell v. Hodges *and Nonmarriage Inequality*, 104 Calif. L. Rev. 1207 (2016) (second quotation); Katherine Franke, *Wedlocked: The Perils of Marriage Equality* (2105). Accord, Clare Huntington, Obergefell's *Conservatism: Reifying Familial Fronts*, 84 Fordham L. Rev. 23, 31 (2015); Anthony Infanti, *Victims of Our Own Success: The Perils of* Obergefell *and* Windsor, 76 Ohio St. L.J. 79 (2015); Catherine Powell, *Up from Marriage: Freedom, Solitude, and Individual Autonomy in the Shadow of Marriage Equality*, 84 Fordham L. Rev. 69, 69–70 (2015); Widiss, *Nonmarital Families*, 552–553.

16. On anti-commandeering, see Jed Rubenfeld, *The Right of Privacy*, 102 Harv. L. Rev. 737 (1989). On equal liberty, see Kenji Yoshino, *The New Equal Protection*, 124 Harv. L. Rev. 747 (2011) and *A New Birth of Freedom?* Obergefell v. Hodges, 129 Harv. L. Rev. 147 (2015); Pamela Karlan, *Equal Protection, Due Process, and the Stereoscopic Fourteenth Amendment*, 33 McGeorge L. Rev. 473 (2002). On the earlier equal-access approach to marriage articulated by four of the five *Obergefell* justices, see *Kerry v. Din*, 135 S. Ct. 2128, 2142 (2015) (Breyer's dissenting opinion, joined by Ginsburg, Sotomayor, Kagan); Kerry Abrams, *The Rights of Marriage:* Obergefell, Din, *and the Future of Constitutional Family Law*, 103 Cornell L. Rev. 501 (2018).

17. Kath Weston, *Families We Choose: Lesbians, Gays, Kinship* (1991).

18. Cynthia Grant Bowman, *Unmarried Couples, Law, and Public Policy* (2010); Marsha Garrison, *Nonmarital Cohabitation: Social Revolution and Legal Regulation*, 42 Fam. L.Q. 309 (2008); Serena Mayeri, *Marital Supremacy and the Constitution of the Nonmarital Family*, 52 Calif. L. Rev. 1277 (2015).

19. Carole Shammas, *A History of Household Government in America*, 186–187 (2002) (appendix, revealing dramatic fall in fertility and child-bearing rates over American history); Carl Degler, *At Odds: Women and the Family in America from the Revolution to the Present* (1980) (key role played by women's increasing independence); Herma Hill Kay, *From the Second Sex to the Joint Venture: An Overview of Women's Rights and Family Law in the United States During the Twentieth Century*, 88 Calif. L. Rev. 2017, 2019–2020 (2000) (similar); June Carbone and Margaret Brinig, *Rethinking Marriage: Feminist Ideology, Economic Change, and Divorce Reform*, 65 Tul. L. Rev. 953 (1991) (key role played by economic transformations).

20. Nancy Cott, *Public Vows: A History of Marriage and the Nation*, 9–23, 132–179 (2000) (quotation in text); Nancy Cott, *Divorce and the Changing Status of Women in Eighteenth Century Massachusetts*, 33 Wm. & Mary Q. 586 (1976); Carbone and Brinig, *Rethinking Marriage*, 961–963.

21. Thus, in state high court marriage decisions between 1993 and 2010, no fewer than twenty-one female justices voted to invalidate state exclusions of lesbian and gay couples from marriage rights: Nakayama (Hawai'i), Johnson and Skoglund (Vermont), Marshall and Cowin (Massachusetts), Fairhurst, Bridge, and Owens (Washington), Kaye and Ciparick (New York), Poritz, Long, and LaVecchia (New Jersey), Raker and Battaglia (Maryland), Kennard and Werdegar (California), Katz (Connecticut), Ternus (Iowa), and Jimenez Maes and Vigil (New Mexico). Only five female justices voted to sustain exclusions: Sosman (Massachusetts), Madsen (Washington), Graffeo (New York), Corrigan (California), and Vertefeuille (Connecticut).

Among federal female circuit judges, only Cook (Sixth Circuit) voted against marriage equality (*DeBoer*). Lynch (First Circuit), Daughtrey (Sixth Circuit), Berzon (Ninth Circuit), and Williams (Seventh Circuit) voted for marriage equality, as did Justices Ginsburg, Sotomayor, and Kagan (each twice in formal opinions and more than a dozen times in procedural dispositions). A handful of female federal district judges delivered decisions in these cases, and they all decided for marriage equality: Jones (New York), Wright Allen (Virginia), Trager (Tennessee), and Grande (Alabama).

22. Andrew Cherlin, *The Marriage-Go-Round: The State of Marriage and the Family in America Today*, 29–32 (2009) (the high value Americans place on "expressive individualism" reveals itself in a pro-choice philosophy for family relations); James Q. Wilson, *The Marriage Problem: How Our Culture Has Weakened Families*, 84–88, 96 (2002) (lamenting the same trend); Andrew Cherlin, *The De-institutionalization of American Marriage*, 66 J. Marriage & Family 848 (2004); Carl Schneider, *Moral Discourse and the Transformation of American Family Law*, 83 Mich. L. Rev. 1803, 1847 (1985). See Naomi Cahn and June Carbone, *Red Families v. Blue Families: Legal Polarization and the Creation of Culture* (2010) (tracing the contested ascendancy of "blue [state] marriage" reflecting the individualist assumptions of the liberal approach); Mark Regnerus and Jeremy Uecker, *Premarital Sex in America: How Young Americans Meet, Mate, and Think About Marrying*, chap. 6 (2011) (in both red states and blue states, youth value sexual experience based on mutual pleasure).

23. Margaret Sanger, *Happiness in Marriage*, 6, 20–23, 137–146 (1926); *Griswold v. Connecticut*, 381 U.S. 479 (1965); *Eisenstadt v. Baird*, 405 U.S. 438, 453 (1972) (quotation in text). See Beth Bailey, *From Front Porch to Back Seat: Courtship in Twentieth-Century America* (1988); Robert Bellah et al., *Habits of the Heart: Individualism and Commitment in American Life* (1996) (decline of communitarian social norms, replaced by personal choice); Richard Posner, *Sex and Reason* (1992) (liberal account grounded on sexual freedom). On the entrenchment of a sex-for-pleasure norm, see Catherine Chilman, US Department of Health, Education, and Welfare, Pub. No. 79-1426, *Ado-*

lescent Sexuality in a Changing American Society: Social and Psychological Perspectives, 67–90, 103–180 (1978); David Allyn, Make Love, Not War—The Sexual Revolution: An Unfettered History, 3–40 (2000).

24. Gary McDowell, Congress and the Courts, Pub. Int. 89, 100, Summer 1990 (first quotation in text, in turn quoting West Va. State Bd. of Educ. v. Barnette, 319 U.S. 624, 642 (1943)); Casey v. Planned Parenthood of Southeastern Pa., 505 U.S. 833, 851 (1992) (second quotation, from the joint opinion); Obergefell, p. 2630, n.22 (Scalia's "hide my head in a bag" crack). See Eskridge, Effects of Identity-Based Social Movements on Constitutional Law, 2236–2250; Glenn Reynolds, Sex, Lies, and Jurisprudence: Robert Bork, Griswold, and the Philosophy of Original Understanding, 24 Ga. L. Rev. 1045, 1105 (1990).

25. Weston, Families We Choose; Anne Fullerton, The Families We Choose, Kinfolk, Iss. 17, https://kinfolk.com/the-families-we-choose/. For a critical evaluation, see George Dent, Families We Choose? Visions of a World Without Blood Ties, 2 Int'l J. Jurisp. Fam. 13 (2011).

26. William Eskridge Jr., Family Law Pluralism: The Guided-Choice Regime of Menus, Default Rules, and Override Rules, 100 Geo. L.J. 1881 (2012); Jana Singer, The Privatization of Family Law, 1992 Wis. L. Rev. 443; Carl Schneider, The Channeling Function in Family Law, 20 Hofstra L. Rev. 495 (1992); Katharine Bartlett, Feminism and Family Law, 33 Fam. L.Q. 475 (1999).

27. Lawrence v. Texas, 539 U.S. 558, 562 (2003) (quotation in text); Martin v. Ziherl, 607 S.E.2d 367 (Va. 2005) (applying Lawrence to invalidate a fornication law). See Eskridge, Dishonorable Passions, 387–407; Martha Mahoney, Forces Shaping the Law of Cohabitation for Opposite-Sex Couples, 7 J.L. & Fam. Stud. 135 (2005).

28. Brief amicus curiae Family Research Council, Inc., and Focus on the Family in support of the respondents, Lawrence v. Texas, Docket No. 02-102 (US Supreme Court, filed Feb. 18, 2003), 2003 WL 470066 (Bradley and George brief).

29. Marvin v. Marvin, 557 P.2d 106, 110 (Cal. 1976) (applying normal contract principles to a cohabiting couple). See Martha Ertman, Love's Promises: How Formal and Informal Contracts Shape All Families (2015); William Eskridge Jr., Nan Hunter, and Courtney Joslin, Sexuality, Gender, and the Law, 792–796 (4th ed. 2018) (surveying different state practices); Cynthia Grant Bowman, Legal Treatment of Cohabitation in the United States, 26 L. & Pol'y 119 (2004).

30. Cynthia Grant Bowman, Unmarried Couples, Law, and Public Policy (2010); Grace Ganz Blumberg, Cohabitation Without Marriage: A Different Perspective, 28 UCLA L. Rev. 1125 (1981). Accord, William Reppy Jr., Property and Support Rights of Unmarried Cohabitants: A Proposal for Creating a New Legal Status, 44 La. L. Rev. 1677 (1984).

31. Levy v. Louisiana, 391 U.S. 68, 70 (1968) (quotation in text); Glona v. American Guar. & Liability Ins. Co., 391 U.S. 73, 75–76 (1968); Stanley v. Illinois, 405 U.S. 645 (1972); Serena Mayeri, Marital Supremacy and the Constitution of the Nonmarital Family, 52 Calif. L. Rev. 1277, 1284–1310 (2015) (detailed analysis of the early nonmarital children cases).

32. Uniform Parentage Act (UPA) § 2 (1973) (quotation in text); Mayeri, *Marital Supremacy*, 1310–1340; Brief for respondents, *Drew Mun. Separate Sch. Dist. v. Andrews*, Docket No. 74-1318 (US Supreme Court, filed Jan. 5, 1976), 1976 WL 181168 (Rhonda Copelan and Nancy Stearns); Brief for Equal Rights Advocates and ACLU as amici curiae, *Drew*, 1974 WL 175944 (Ruth Ginsburg and Wendy Williams). See Martha Zingo and Kevin Early, *Nameless Persons: Legal Discrimination Against Nonmarital Children in the United States* (1994).

33. *In re Jacob*, 660 N.E.2d 397 (N.Y. 1995). See Daniel Winunwe Rivers, *Radical Relations: Lesbian Mothers, Gay Fathers, and Their Children in the United States Since World War II*, 193–195 (2013); Nancy Polikoff, *This Child Does Have Two Mothers: Redefining Parenthood to Meet the Needs of Children in Lesbian-Mother and Other Nontraditional Families*, 78 Geo. L.J. 459 (1990); Paula Ettelbrick, *Who Is a Parent? The Need to Develop a Lesbian Conscious Family Law*, 10 N.Y.L. Sch. J. Hum. Rts. 513 (1993).

34. *In re Custody of H.S.H.-K.*, 533 N.W.2d 419, 436 (Wis. 1995) (first quotation in text); *V.C. v. M.J.B.*, 748 A.2d 549, 550 (N.J. 2000) (second quotation); Eskridge, Hunter, and Joslin, *Sexuality, Gender, and the Law*, 938–952; Nancy Polikoff, *From Third Parties to Parents: The Case of Lesbian Couples and Their Children*, 77 Law & Contemp. Probs. 195, 208 (2014).

35. Naomi Cahn, *The New Kinship* (2013); Douglas NeJaime, *The Nature of Parenthood*, 126 Yale L.J. 2260 (2017) (detailed analysis of state parental recognition rules, demonstrating that gender-nonconforming persons have the hardest time establishing parental rights).

36. UPA § 204(a) (2017) (gender-neutral marital presumption of parenthood and "holding out" as a basis for parental recognition), § 301 ("voluntary acknowledgment of parentage"), § 609 (recognizing de facto parental rights), §§ 703, 809, and 815 (recognizing "intended parents" based on ART agreements). See Courtney Joslin, *Nurturing Parenthood Through the UPA (2017)*, 127 Yale L.J. Forum 589 (2018).

37. *Obergefell*, p. 2605 (quotation in text).

38. Tex. Fam. Code § 6.204(b) (first quotation in text); *Pidgeon v. Turner*, 538 S.W.3d 73, 87 (Tex. June 30, 2017), cert. denied, 138 S. Ct. 505 (Dec. 4, 2017) (second quotation). See plaintiffs' motion for summary judgment, *Pidgeon v. Turner*, Cause No. 2014-61812 (Dist. Ct. Harris Cnty., filed July 18, 2018).

39. Charles Sumner, *Equality Before the Law; Unconstitutionality of Separate Colored Schools in Massachusetts: Argument of Charles Sumner, Esq., Before the Supreme Court of Massachusetts in the Case of Sarah C. Roberts v. City of Boston*, 10–11 (Boston: B. F. Roberts, 1849) (first quotation in text); *Obergefell*, pp. 2601–2602 (remaining quotations).

40. Tamara Metz, *Untying the Knot: Marriage, the State, and the Case for Their Divorce* (2010); Polikoff, *Beyond (Straight and Gay) Marriage*; Robin West, *Marriage, Sexuality, and Gender* (2007); David Boaz, *Privatize Marriage*, Slate, April 25, 1997 (quotation in text); Alice Ristroph and Melissa Murray, *Disestablishing the Family*, 119 Yale L.J. 1236, 1240 (2010); 2019 Ala. Laws S.B. 69 (May 2019) (replacing civil mar-

riage licensing with filing marriage contracts). On earlier demands by Radicalesbians for the abolition of civil marriage, see Alice Echols, *Daring to Be Bad: Radical Feminism in America, 1967–1975* (1990).

41. Robin Fisher et al., Tax Policy Center, Urban Institute & Brookings Institution, *Same-Sex Marriage Tax Filers After* Windsor *and* Obergefell (Feb. 28, 2018).

42. Jeffrey Jones, Gallup, *In U.S., 10.2% of LGBT Adults Now Married to Same-Sex Spouse* (June 22, 2017) (data in text).

43. CDC, *Provisional Number of Marriages and Marriage Rate: United States, 2000–2017*, https://www.cdc.gov/nchs/data/dvs/national-marriage-divorce-rates-00-17.pdf.

44. CDC, *Marriage Rates by State: 1990, 1995, and 1999–2017*, https://www.cdc.gov/nchs/data/dvs/state-marriage-rates-90-95-99-17.pdf.

45. Deirdre Bowen, *All That Heaven Will Allow: A Statistical Analysis of the Co-Existence of Same-Sex Marriage and Gay Matrimonial Bans*, 91 Denver U.L. Rev. 277, 302–303 (2014).

46. Brief of amici curiae 100 Scholars of Marriage in support of respondents, *Obergefell v. Hodges*, Docket Nos. 14-556 et al. (US Supreme Court, filed April 2, 2015), 2015 WL 1519039.

47. David Orr, Cook county clerk, *Opposite-Sex Civil Unions: Motives for Not Marrying* (Dec. 21, 2011); John Culhane, *No to Nuptials: Will Opposite-Sex Civil Unions Spell the End of Traditional Marriage?*, Slate, Jan. 3, 2012; Cara Buckley, *Gay Couples, Choosing to Say "I Don't,"* New York Times, Oct. 25, 2013; Patricia Cain, *Taxation of Same-Sex Couples After* United States v. Windsor: *Did the IRS Get It Right in Revenue Ruling 2013-17?*, 6 Elon L. Rev. 269 (2014).

48. June Carbone and Naomi Cahn, *Marriage Markets: How Inequality Is Remaking the American Family* (2014); June Carbone and Naomi Cahn, *The Triple System of Family Law*, 2013 Mich. St. L. Rev. 1185, 1190 (quotation in text); Kathryn Edin and Joanna M. Reed, *Why Don't They Just Get Married? Barriers to Marriage Among the Disadvantaged*, 15 Future Children 117, 118 (2005). For marriage-encouraging policy proposals, see David Blankenhorn, *Time for a New Pro-Family Coalition in America*, Deseret News, March 14, 2015; Eskridge, *Family Law Pluralism*, 1960–1961.

49. *Beyond Same-Sex Marriage: A New Strategic Vision for All Our Families and Relationships* (July 26, 2006), https://mronline.org/2006/08/08/beyond-same-sex-marriage-a-new-strategic-vision-for-all-our-families-relationships/.

50. Murray, *Nonmarriage Inequality*, 1244, n.233 (concern that twenty state Super-DOMA bars to civil unions will be hard to challenge after *Obergefell*); *Obergefell*, p. 2605 (quotation in text).

51. Murray, *Nonmarriage Inequality*, 1248 (concern that states will be reluctant to protect unmarried partners after *Obergefell*); *Blumenthal v. Brewer*, 69 N.E.3d 834, 852–858 (Ill. 2016) (quotation in text), reaffirming *Hewitt v. Hewitt*, 394 N.E.2d 1204 (Ill. 1979) (precluding cohabiting couples from *Marvin* claims, based upon the statutory abolition of common-law marriages).

52. Cf. Courtney Joslin, *The Gay Rights Canon and the Right to NonMarriage*, 97 B.U.L. Rev. 425, 481–482 (2017) (similar critique of *Blumenthal v. Brewer*).

53. Elizabeth Brake, *Minimizing Marriage: Marriage, Morality, and the Law* (2012) (quotation in text).

54. *Diaz v. Brewer*, 656 F.3d 1008, 1014 (9th Cir. 2011); Kaiponanea Matsumura, *A Right Not to Marry*, 84 Fordham 1509, 1511 (2016) (quotation in text, from letters to Arizona state employees); 2012 Wash. Sess. Laws 203 (converting same-sex domestic partnerships to marriages on July 1, 2014); Implementing the Guarantee of Equal Protection, 2009 Conn. Acts No. 9-13 § 12(a) (converting existing civil unions to marriages after Oct. 1, 2010); N.H. Rev. Stat. § 457:46 (similar); Civil Marriage Equality and Religious Freedom Act of 2013, 79 Del. Laws ch. 19, § 6 (2013) (similar).

55. See appendix 1 for citations to the state laws referenced. For the new California law, see Adam Baum, *California Governor Signs Domestic Partnership Law: Heterosexual Couples Now Have an Alternative to Marriage in California*, Associated Press, July 30, 2019.

56. Dolores Chandler, *Black Revolutionaries You Need to Know: Pauli Murray*, Scalawag Magazine, May 26, 2016 (quotation in text), https://www.scalawagmagazine.org /2016/05/black-revolutionaries-you-need/.

57. International Foundation of Employee Benefit Plans, *Employers Drop Domestic Partnership Benefits* (Aug. 1, 2017); International Foundation of Employee Benefit Plans, *Employee Benefits Survey: 2018 Results*, 31 (2018); HRC, *Corporate Equality Index 2019: Rating Work Places on Lesbian, Gay, Bisexual, Transgender and Queer Equality*, 6 (2019). See Rita Pyrillis, *More Employers Are Dropping Domestic Partner Benefits*, Workforce, Nov. 9, 2017.

58. *DeBoer v. Snyder*, 973 F. Supp. 2d 757 (S.D. Mich. 2014), rev'd, 772 F.3d 388 (6th Cir. 2014), rev'd sub nom. *Obergefell v. Hodges*, 135 S. Ct. 2584 (2015); *Sessions v. Morales-Santana*, 137 S. Ct. 1678, 1689 (2017) (quotation in text, in turn quoting *Califano v. Westcott*, 443 U.S. 76, 84 (1979)).

59. Joslin, *Nurturing Parenthood Through the UPA* (2017); Douglas NeJaime, *Marriage Equality and the New Parenthood*, 129 Harv. L. Rev. 1185 (2016).

60. *Obergefell*, p. 2601, quoted and followed in *Pavan v. Smith*, 137 S. Ct. 2075 (June 26, 2017) (per curiam). But see *Pavan*, pp. 2079–2080 (Gorsuch's dissenting opinion, joined by Thomas and Alito, reading *Obergefell* more narrowly).

61. *McLaughlin v. Jones*, 401 P.3d 492, 498 (Ariz. 2017) (first quotation in text); UPA § 204(a)(1)(A) (2017) (second quotation); NeJaime, *Nature of Parenthood*, 2363–2366 (listing states with gender-neutral marital presumptions). See Eskridge, Hunter, and Joslin, *Sexuality, Gender, and the Law*, 905–911.

62. *Brooke S.B. v. Elizabeth A.C.C.*, 61 N.E.3d 488, 498 (N.Y. 2016) (first quotation in text), overruling *Alison D. v. Virginia M.*, 572 N.E.2d 27 (N.Y. 1991); UPA, prefatory note, pp. 1–2 (2017) (second quotation); UPA § 809 (2017) (VAPs extended to nonbiological parents).

63. Khiara Bridges, Windsor, *Surrogacy, and Race,* 89 Wash. L. Rev. 1125 (2016); June Carbone and Naomi Cahn, *Marriage and the Marital Presumption Post-*Obergefell, 84 UMKC L. Rev. 663, 670 (2016) (estimate for "surrogay-cy").

64. 2012 Calif. Stats. ch. 466 (A.B. 1217), codified at Calif. Family Code §§ 7960–7962; Calif. Family Code § 7613.5 (nonmandatory forms to assure the rights of intended parents); Ark. Code § 9-10-201(b)-(c). See Courtney Joslin, Shannon Minter, and Catherine Sakimura, *Lesbian, Gay, Bisexual, and Transgender Family Law* § 4.1 (2017) (half the states have no clear law on surrogacy); NeJaime, *Nature of Parenthood,* 2376–2379 (survey of state statutes and judicial decisions regulating gestational surrogacy).

65. *In re Baby M.,* 537 A.2d 1227 (N.J. 1988) (surrogacy contracts contrary to public policy); *A.G.R. v. D.H.R. & S.H.,* No. FD-09-0018-07 (N.J. Super. Dec. 23, 2009); Eskridge, Hunter, and Joslin, *Sexuality, Gender, and the Law,* 915–916 (applying *Baby M.* to a gestational "surrogay-cy" contract).

66. *Sharon S. v. Superior Court,* 31 Cal. 4th 417 (2003); *In re Hart,* 806 A.2d 1179 (Del. 2001); *In re M.M.D.,* 662 A.2d 837 (D.C. 1995); *Petition of K.M.,* 653 N.E.2d 888 (Ill. 1995); *Adoption of K.S.P.,* 804 N.E.2d 1253 (Ind. 2004); *Adoption of M.A.,* 930 A.2d 1088 (Maine 2007); *In re Tammy,* N.E.2d (Mass. 1995); *Adoption by H.N.R.,* 666 A.2d 535 (N.J. 1995); *In re Jacob,* 660 N.E.2d 397 (N.Y. 1995); *Adoption of R.B.F.,* 803 A.2d 1195 (Pa. 2002); *In re B.L.V.B.,* 628 A.2d 1271 (Vt. 1993). See also *Wheeler v. Wheeler,* 642 S.E.2d 103 (Ga. 2007) (denying review to a lower court judgment granting second-parent adoption).

67. *In re Adoption of Baby Z.,* 724 A.2d 1035 (Ct. 1999); *S.J.L.S. v. T.L.S.,* 265 S.W.3d 804 (Ky. 2008); *Adoption of Luke,* 263 Neb. 365 (Neb. 2002); *Boseman v. Jarrell,* No. 416PA08-2 (N.C. 2010); *Adoption of Jane Doe,* 719 N.E.2d 1071 (Ohio 1998); *In re Angel Lace M.,* 516 N.W.2d 578 (Wis. 1994). On Michigan's post-2002 reluctance to allow second-parent adoptions, see Wyatt Fore, DeBoer v. Snyder: *A Case Study of Litigation and Social Reform,* 12 Mich. J. Gender & Law 169, 172–174 (2015). Cf. *Usitalo v. Landon,* 829 N.W.2d 359, 364 (Mich. App. 2012) (refusing to accept a collateral attack on earlier second-parent adoptions).

68. *V.L. v. E.L.,* 136 S. Ct. 1017, 1020 (2016) (per curiam), following *Baker v. General Motors Corp.,* 522 U.S. 222, 233 (1998) (quotation in text). Cf. *Weinberger v. Wiesenfeld,* 420 U.S. 636, 655 (1975) (Rehnquist's concurring opinion, emphasizing the needs of children with paternal caregivers).

69. Murray, *Nonmarriage Inequality,* 1254–1256; *Brooke S.B.,* p. 498 (quotation in text); Courtney Joslin, *De Facto Parentage and the Modern Family,* 40 Fam. Adv. 31 (2018).

70. *Conover v. Conover,* 146 A.3d 433, 448–451 (Md. 2016) (quotation in text).

71. *Brooke S.B.,* p. 498 (quotation in text); Douglas NeJaime, *The Story of* Brooke S.B. v. Elizabeth A.C.C.: *Parental Recognition in the Age of LGBT Equality,* in Melissa Murray, Katherine Shaw, and Reva Siegel, eds., *Reproductive Rights and Justice Stories,* 245 (2019). Accord, *A.A. v. B.B.,* 384 P.3d 878 (Haw. 2016).

72. *Eldredge v. Taylor,* 339 P.3d 888, 893–894 (Okla. Nov. 12, 2014); *Ramey v. Sutton,* 362 P.3d 217, 221 (Okla. Nov. 17, 2015). Accord, *Russell v. Pasik,* 178 So. 3d 55 (Fla. App. 2015); *Brooke S.B.,* p. 504 (Pigott's concurring opinion); *Hawkins v. Grese,* 809 S.E.2d 441 (Va. App. 2018).

73. Douglas NeJaime, *The Constitution of Parenthood,* 72 Stan. L. Rev. 261 (2020); *Stanley v. Illinois,* 405 U.S. 645 (1972).

74. *Smith v. Organization of Foster Families for Equality and Reform,* 431 U.S. 816 (1977) (denying liberty interest for foster parents); *Troxel v. Granville,* 530 U.S. 57 (2000) (protecting liberty interest of legal parent against intrusive visitation rights statutory vested in grandparents).

75. On attachment theory, see Ayelet Blecher–Prigat, *Rethinking Visitation: From a Parental to a Relational Right,* 16 Duke J. Gender L. & Pol'y 1, 7 (2009); Suzanne Goldberg, *Family Law Cases as Law Reform Litigation: Unrecognized Parents and the Story of Alison D. v. Virginia M.,* 17 Colum. J. Gender & L. 307 (2008).

76. UPA § 201 (2017) (listing various legal mechanisms for recognizing or establishing legal parenthood).

77. *Conover,* p. 455 (first quotation in text, from Watts's concurring opinion); William Eskridge Jr., *Gaylaw: Challenging the Apartheid of the Closet,* 291–292 (1999) (coining the term *polyparenting*); Eskridge, Hunter, and Joslin, *Sexuality, Gender, and the Law,* 957–970 (polyparenting cases and laws); June Carbone and Naomi Cahn, *Parents, Babies, and More Parents,* 92 Chi.-Kent L. Rev. 9, 13 (2017) (second quotation in text).

78. 2013 Cal. Stats. ch. 564 (S.B. 274), overriding *In re M.C.,* 195 Cal.App.4th 197 (2011), codified at Cal. Family Code § 7612(c) (quotations in text). For other legislative recognitions for polyparenting, see Del. Code § 8-201(a)(4), (b)(6), (c); D.C. Code § 16-831(1)(A)(iii); Maine Rev. Stat. tit. 19-A, § 1853(2); Wash. Code § 26.26A.460(3); UPA § 613 (2017) (choice between a cap on two parents or an allowance of three parents under the conditions laid out in the California law).

79. *Thomas S. v. Robin Y.,* 618 N.Y.S.2d 386 (App. Div. 1994); *S.M. v. E.C.,* 2014 WL 2921905 (Cal. App. 2014): Eskridge, Hunter, and Joslin, *Sexuality, Gender, and the Law,* 927–936 (criticisms of *Thomas S.*), 963–970 (appraisal of *S.M.* and the new California law).

80. Cf. *Troxel,* pp. 68–72 (O'Connor's plurality opinion, restricting a statute granting unrestricted visitation to a grandparent but suggesting that access could be required if the child would suffer harm otherwise), 78–79 (Souter's opinion concurring in the judgment, with similar reasoning).

81. Ronald Den Otter, *In Defense of Plural Marriage* (2015). See Sanford Levinson, *The Meaning of Marriage: Thinking About Polygamy,* 42 San Diego L. Rev. 1049 (2005).

82. Rose McDermott, *The Evils of Polygyny: Evidence of Its Harm to Women, Men, and Society* (Kristen Renwick Moore, ed., 2018); Rose McDermott, *Expert Report Prepared for the Attorney General of Canada* (July 15, 2010) (early presentation of McDermott's comparative-culture analysis of polygyny's effects on women).

83. Ertman, *Love's Promises.*

84. E. J. Graff, *What Is Marriage For?* (1999); David Chambers, *What If? The Legal Consequences of Marriage and the Legal Needs of Lesbian and Gay Male Couples,* 45 Mich. L. Rev. 447 (1996).

85. Our description of the SFI program and the quotations are drawn from its website, www.supportingfatherinvolvementsfi.com. See Marsha Kline Pruett et al., *Enhancing Father Involvement in Low-Income Families: A Couples Group Approach to Preventive Intervention,* 88 Child Dev. 398–407 (March/April 2017). For a summary of the empirical support for SFI, see Pruett et al., *Enhancing Paternal Engagement in a Coparenting Paradigm,* 2017 Child Dev. Persps. 1–6.

Postscript

1. Our account of the wedding comes from William Eskridge and Christopher Riano interviews of April DeBoer, Jayne Rowse, Wendy DeBoer, Bernard Friedman, Dana Nessel, Carole Stanyar, and Mary Bonauto. See also the homemade video at https://www.youtube.com/watch?v=9kQVXmHz3NU.

2. *McConnell v. Blue Earth County,* No. 07-CV-16-4559 (Minn. Dist. Court, Blue Earth Cnty. Sept. 18, 2018) (Judge Anderson's order); Blue Earth Marriage Certificate No. 434960 (Sept. 3, 1971, recorded Oct. 3, 2018); Email from Jack Baker aka Pat Lyn McConnell [Jack's married name] to Gail Karwoski, cc to William Eskridge, "Blue Earth County Recorded the Marriage!," Oct. 5, 2018 (quotation in text).

ACKNOWLEDGMENTS

We could not have completed this volume without the invaluable research and production assistance of Don Patron and Patricia Page, as well as that contributed by many Yale law students, especially Eric Baudry (Yale Law School, Class of 2019), Matthew Butler (Class of 2018), D. H. Dilbeck (Class of 2021), Jonathan Green (Class of 2020), Ezra Husney (Class of 2021), William Kamin (Class of 2020), Yena Lee (Class of 2019), Alexandra Lichtenstein (Class of 2020), Brennon Mendez (Class of 2021), Nicole Ng (Class of 2022), Kathryn Pogin (Class of 2021), Father Patrick Reidy (Class of 2021), Charlotte Schwartz (Class of 2019), Daniel Strunk (Class of 2019), Todd Venook (Class of 2019), as well as Samantha Godwin, a fellow at the Yale Law School. We appreciate the assistance of Paul Cotler (Class of 2020) at the University of Pennsylvania Law School.

Deans Robert Post and Heather Gerken of the Yale Law School supported this army of research associates and financed a Yale Law School conference seeking "Common Ground" between religious traditionalists and LGBTQ+ persons in the wake of nationwide marriage equality. The Oscar M. Reubhausen Fund at the Yale Law School generously financed the research trips all across the country, from Portland, Maine, to Phoenix to Atlanta to San Francisco and Los Angeles to Detroit to Honolulu. The Yale Law Library, under the leadership of associate deans Blair Kaufman and Teresa Miguel-Stearns, assisted our research and secured many books and thousands of pages of archival materials we needed for the project.

Dean Theodore Ruger of the University of Pennsylvania Law School provided us with an office, research support, and excellent colleagues who helped us finalize the first draft of this volume. Artist Don Patron created or formalized the pictures that grace several of the chapters. Patricia Page and William Nelson created the marriage maps found in several chapters.

Several intellectuals read and improved the entire volume, and we are particularly indebted to William Frucht, Matthew Krumholtz, Gregory Prince, and anonymous readers solicited by Yale University Press. Dozens of other readers corrected and improved particular chapters, some requesting anonymity. Each coauthor blames the other for any remaining mistakes.

The prelude and postscript to this volume focus the reader's attention on the family of April DeBoer and Jayne Rowse, the Michigan couple who were among the plaintiffs in *Obergefell v. Hodges* (2015). We were tangentially involved in the trial sustaining their claims and came to know the family through April's mother, Wendy Brown DeBoer. We got to know the family and their primary lawyers, Carole Stanyar, Dana Nessel, and Ken Magill. In our view, the heart and soul of marriage equality find no better representatives than Jayne Rowse, April DeBoer, and their five children: Nolan, Ryanne, Jacob, Rylee, and Kennedy.

For chapter 1, the marriage cases of the 1970s, we are indebted to comments and corrections from Michael McConnell, Jack Baker, and Catherine Fosl. The Reverend Troy Perry, the founder of the Metropolitan Churches of Christ, gave us an invaluable account of the earliest public marriages as well as comments on the chapter. Patricia Page and Alexandra Lichtenstein tracked down information about Jason (formerly Neva) Heckman. Julie Krishnaswami secured the appellate briefs in the Washington marriage case from the Washington State Law Library in the Temple of Justice, Olympia.

Our account of the 1975 Colorado marriage licenses in chapter 2 could not have been accomplished without the cooperation of Clela Rorex, the clerk who issued the six marriage licenses, as well as the leads generated by D. H. Dilbeck, Shawn Fettig, Jonathan Green, and William Kamin. Patricia Page tracked down most of the twelve persons who received Colorado marriage licenses, including Annice Joan Ritchie and Susan Furtney, who generously shared their recollections, and David McCord, who filled in some personal details in letters from prison in Arizona.

Our treatment of AIDS and domestic partnerships in chapter 3 owes much to Suzanne Goldberg and Walter Rieman, surviving partners of Paula Ettelbrick and Tom Stoddard, who inspired the chapter. Matt Coles, Jack Quinn, and Charles McIlhenny gave us insights into the politics of San Francisco's domestic partnership campaigns. For the internal marriage politics of Lambda, we learned a lot from talking with Richard Socarides, John Duran, and one other member of the Lambda board during that period, as well as Evan Wolfson. We are also grateful to Lisa Rosen-Metsch for her keen eye and insights into early HIV/AIDS research.

Chapter 4 (Hawai'i) benefited from interviews over twenty years with Genora Dancel and Ninia Baehr, as well as more recent interviews of and editorial comments from Dan Foley, Antoinette Pregil and Tammy Rodrigues, Richard Eichor, Duke Aoina, Evan Wolfson, Kyle Pruett, and David Smith. Julie Krishnaswami worked with the Hawai'i Supreme Court to secure dozens of briefs and other litigation documents for that state's marriage litigation. Gregory Prince gave us access to his archives on the Latter-day

Saints' involvement in the Hawai'i marriage litigation, legislation, and constitutional amendment.

Interviews and comments on drafts of chapter 5 by Phil Burress, Vickie Burress, and Stephanie McCloud (Burress's daughter), augmented with research by Daniel Strunk, enriched our account of DOMA and its political context. Generous interviewees and readers also included Mark Agrast, Elizabeth Birch, Mike McCurry, Steven Gunderson, K.Z. Smith, Richard Socarides, and several congressional staff members speaking off the record. Alexandra Lichtenstein mined the Clinton presidential papers more thoroughly than anyone had previously attempted and helped us understand the president's complicated relationship to DOMA. Phyllis Frye provided us with a detailed account of the first DOMA decision, involving Christie Littleton, and commented on a draft of the chapter.

Carole Migden explained the details of California's legislative process and the complexities of domestic partnership legislation, the foundation for chapter 6. Geoff Kors helped us understand the equal benefits ordinance adopted by San Francisco in 1996. Sheila Kuehl, Jackie Goldberg, Jon Davidson, Jenny Pizer, Doreena Wong, and Al Lo-Faso provided valuable insights into the California partnership statutes. Hans Johnson and Luis Lopez connected us with sources and helped us understand the political topography of California. The California legislature made available to us thousands of pages of documents considered during committee and chamber consideration of domestic partnership bills.

Our education about the Vermont marriage case and the civil unions law, the focus of chapter 7, began with conversations and interviews with Susan Murray and Beth Robinson spanning two decades, complemented by an interview with and comments from Craig and Deborah Bensen, reflecting a different point of view. Valuable interviews and editorial comments from Nina Beck and Stacy Jolles, Holly Puterbaugh and Lois Farnham, Tom Little, and Richard Sears were tremendously helpful. The Vermont legislature sent us tapes of the committee and chamber deliberations.

Our examination in chapters 8 and 9 of the advance of marriage equality in Massachusetts owes a great deal to critical comments from GLAD's lawyers and documents from GLAD's archives, which will ultimately be housed at Yale University. Invaluable background conversations and interviews with Mary Bonauto, Josh Friedes, Arline Isaacson, Kris Mineau, and Marc Solomon helped us understand the marriage litigation and the constitutional conventions. Jonathan Green and Matthew Butler enabled us to appreciate the nuances of Governor Romney's dynamic stance toward LGBTQ+ rights issues.

Very generously, Maggie Gallagher spoke with us about her life and her involvement in the campaign to reaffirm one-man, one-woman marriage that was transformed by the April 2003 conference at Osprey Point, the centerpiece of chapter 10. Our account also reflects our conversations, interviews, and emails with David Blankenhorn and

Katherine Spaht. Gerry Bradley filled in the details of the drafting process for the Federal Marriage Amendment. The discussion of *Lawrence v. Texas* (2003) is based on research and interviews Eskridge conducted for *Dishonorable Passions* (2008), updated by conversations with former clerks for Justice O'Connor. Off-the-record conversations with congressional and White House staff inform our discussion of President Bush's support for and the Senate's rejection of the FMA in 2004. Ken Mehlman, President Bush's campaign manager, gave us useful background context.

Our account of the Winter of Love, examined in chapter 11, draws from personal interviews of and/or comments on earlier chapter drafts from Kate Kendell, Terry Stewart, Shannon Minter, Jon Davidson, Steve Yawa, and Dennis Herrera. Our understanding of the *Marriage Cases* is richly informed by Chief Justice George's memoirs as well as by off-the-record conversations with California Supreme Court insiders.

Chapter 12's analysis draws heavily from our conversations and interviews with the Latter-day constitutionalists themselves—Lynn Wardle, Bill Duncan, and Monte Neil Stewart. We are grateful to these generous lawyers, and to conversations with other participants and church leaders we met at a BYU forum on religious freedom held in July 2018. Our discussion of the developments in Colorado benefited from telephone interviews with Ted Trimpa, Pat Steadman, and Jim Pfaff.

The story of the "Winning Marriage" meetings in 2005 (the starting point for chapter 13) is based on an interview with former Gill Fund official Katherine Peck as well as conversations and emails with Rea Carey, Matt Coles, and Nan Hunter over the years. Anne Stanback and Charlotte Kinlock led us through the long history of Connecticut's pathbreaking Love Makes a Family organization. Ben Klein and Mary Bonauto were important sources for our discussion of the Connecticut marriage case. As with our accounts of the other state supreme court decisions in this volume, we read all the briefs filed on appeal, read a transcript of or listened to the oral argument, and spoke with court insiders off the record. GLAD's archives gave us detailed records of the Connecticut legislature's deliberations over almost a decade; former governor Rell provided helpful background from the state's top GOP official.

Continuing with acknowledgments for chapter 13, we are grateful to several participants for our account of the 2009 Vermont marriage law: Beth Robinson, Craig Bensen, Shap Smith, Richard Sears, Claire Ayer, and a few off-the-record informants. Robin Wilson and Doug Laycock provided documents and insights into the religious exemptions contained in the 2009–2011 marriage statutes. Camilla Taylor not only talked with us but provided useful documents and leads for Iowa. Senator Doug Shull gave personal insight into the 2006 defeat of the marriage amendment in the Iowa Senate. In addition to the briefs and an audio recording of the oral argument, we learned a lot about *Varnum* through off-the-record conversations with Iowa Supreme Court insiders.

Key sources for California's Proposition 8 campaign in chapter 14 were David Fleischer's important retrospective on the campaign and interviews and/or comments on earlier chapter drafts from Frank Schubert, Maggie Gallagher, Dustin Lance Black, Kate Kendell, Geoff Kors, Sean Lund, Ineke Mushovic, Jenny Pizer, Doreena Wong, and Thalia Zepatos. We appreciate Gregory Prince making available his archive of those documents from the Church of Jesus Christ of Latter-day Saints relevant to its role in the campaign.

For the Proposition 8 trial, examined in chapter 15, we talked on the record with most of the primary legal actors, namely, Vaughn Walker, Ted Olson, Chuck Cooper, Dennis Herrera, Terry Stewart, Jeremy Goldman, Jon Davidson, and Jenny Pizer; we talked with others off the record. We appreciate their cooperation, but we learned a lot from talking with a variety of nonlawyers, especially Dustin Lance Black, David Blankenhorn, Maggie Gallagher, Katherine Young, and Loren Marks. The AFER Archives of trial documents were of course invaluable, and we read and reread the trial transcript with admiration and fascination.

Our tale of three men in a room in chapter 16 could not have been possible without numerous interviews of and insights from Alphonso David, Daniel O'Donnell, and Tom Duane; the help of their exceedingly talented staffers; and numerous off-the-record insights and comments from elected and appointed officials within New York State. We also benefited from interviews and conversations with Brian Silva, Marty Rouse, and Marc Solomon. Former chief judge Judith Kaye gave us an incredibly candid interview during her last days, and to her we are deeply and forever indebted.

Chapter 17, featuring the Obama administration's contribution to LGBT rights and the marriage debate, benefited from interviews and conversations with Valerie Jarrett, Brian Bond, Greg Craig, Bob Bauer, Tony West, Stuart Delery, and Don Verrilli, as well as off-the-record comments from a number of Department of Justice and White House officials. Sophia Lee and other participants in the University of Pennsylvania's symposium on administrative constitutionalism provided comments and insights that reshaped this chapter. Associates of then–vice president Joe Biden provided us with many insights into Biden's May 2012 surprise and the White House's reaction.

Giving generously of their time in several interviews and with helpful comments on drafts of chapter 18 (the 2012 ballot initiatives) were Frank Schubert, Marc Solomon, Thalia Zepatos, Phyllis Watts, and Evan Wolfson. We also gained insights from our interviews of Delman Coates, Josh Friedes, Phil Lloyd, Sean Lund, Ineke Mushovic, and Marty Rouse. Wolfson and Zepatos made available contemporaneous internal Freedom to Marry documents relevant to the November 2012 ballot campaigns. We benefited from in-depth research into, and critique of, the Minnesota campaign by Yale law student Irina Vaynerman.

Our treatment of Edie Windsor's case in chapter 19 owes a great deal to the sharp editorial eye of her widow, Judith Kasen-Windsor. We appreciate comments on earlier drafts of the chapter from Mary Bonauto, Stuart Delery, James Esseks, Vicki Jackson, Don Verrilli, and federal district and appellate court insiders. On the Supreme Court's decision in Edie Windsor's successful challenge to DOMA, Paul Clement, as well as Verrilli and Bonauto, gave us valuable insights, as did Supreme Court insiders.

Our understanding of the Michigan marriage trial, the centerpiece of chapter 20, was enriched by repeated interviews and conversations with Carole Stanyar, Dana Nessel, and Bob Mogill (all lawyers for the plaintiffs) and with Mark Regnerus and Loren Marks (the state's star witnesses). Judge Bernard Friedman and his staff, as well as his former clerk, Judge Judith Levy, made themselves available for consultation and reviewed a draft of our chapter.

We interviewed most of the key lawyers involved in the Supreme Court litigation in *Obergefell v. Hodges* (2015), and they gave us valuable insights that were the basis of much analysis in chapter 21: Mary Bonauto, John Bursch, Stuart Delery, Douglas Hallward-Driemeier, Gene Schaerr, and Donald Verrilli. Al Gerhardstein, Dana Nessel, Carole Stanyar, and Jeff Sutton (in several public programs we attended) provided insights into the Sixth Circuit litigation. More than a dozen people attending the "secret Ann Arbor Ambush" gave us off-the-record accounts of the moot that determined who would be the principal advocate for marriage equality in the Supreme Court proceedings.

Our decades-long acquaintance with the late Frank Kameny inspired chapter 22's treatment of marriage equality as a social movement campaign, and this entire volume is part of Frank's legacy. We completely revised this chapter in response to comments by Georgetown law professors Nan Hunter, Victoria Nourse, and Larry Solum and by the students in the Nourse-Solum public law seminar, especially Casey Chalback, Max Crema, Courtney Daukas, George Dobbins, Stephanie Goldberg, Alex Petros, Sara Rothman, Lauren Simenauer, George Tomlinson, and Caroline Williamson. Kathryn Pogin pointed us toward important feminist literature (such as the work of Miranda Fricker) that helped us theorize this chapter. Sean Lund and Ineke Mushovic gave us invaluable feedback on appropriate use of terminology.

Chapter 23's analysis of religion and religious liberty in the wake of *Obergefell* owes much to detailed comments on earlier versions of this chapter from Alexander Dushku, Sister Jeannine Gramick, Father James Martin, Douglas NeJaime, Father Patrick Reidy, and Robin Wilson. We also learned a great deal from the conference on religious liberty and LGBT equality hosted by Robin Wilson and one of us at the Yale Law School in January 2017. Conversations with Jenny Pizer, William Lori, Michael McConnell, Kent Greenawalt, Douglas NeJaime, Reva Siegel, Michael Leavitt, and Louise Melling enriched our thinking on these issues. We are grateful to Greg Prince, the late Von Keetch, Alexander Dushku, and other Latter-day Saints for general comments and archival documents.

A workshop at the University of Pennsylvania generated ideas and improvements in chapter 24, on families and family law after *Obergefell*. Particularly useful comments came from Serena Mayeri, Steve Burbank, Ted Ruger, and Amanda Shanor. Our colleague Douglas NeJaime has educated us through his important scholarship on LGBTQ+ families and through detailed comments on an earlier version of this chapter. Critically important to this chapter have been conversations with Ruth, Marty, and Jane Ginsburg, a family that has inspired our work as law professors, our enthusiasm for public law, and our decision to write a detailed treatment of the marriage debate.

William Kamin cite-checked and added new materials that are the basis for appendix 1, the fifty-state survey.

The state marriage data assembled in appendix 3 reflects excellent legwork by Julie Krishnaswami at the Yale Law School Library and by Eric Baudry, who did county-by-county research for Colorado. Data were provided either electronically or by mail from the Connecticut, Hawai'i, Iowa, and New York Departments of Public Health; Maine's Division of Public Health Systems; the Massachusetts Department of Social Services; the Oregon Health Authority; Vermont's Department of Health; and Washington's Office of the Secretary of State.

We are indebted to Ninia Baehr, John Banta, Phil Burress, Genora Dancel, Paula Ettelbrick, Maggie Gallagher, Danny O'Donnell, Don Patron, and Frank Schubert for the photographs that they have provided, and to Patricia Page and Bill Nelson for the maps they created for this volume.

Index of Names

Cross-references to subjects refer to the Index of Subjects.

Gabbard, Mike (cont.)
  launching the National Campaign
  to Protect Marriage (Feb. 1996), 120.
  See also Alliance for Traditional
  Marriage—Hawaiʻi (ATM)
Gallagher, Maggie (NOM, now Archdiocese of San Francisco), family
  and youth, 248–250, 254, 270–271,
  278–279, 320, 322–323, 368–369,
  380, 392, 394, 403, 411–412, 423,
  427, 555, 558, 570, 724, 728, 745;
  her intellectual flourishing at
  Yale College, 249; her unexpected
  pregnancy, 249–250; her critique
  of liberal feminism, 250; her theory
  of marriage, family, and the welfare
  of children, 262, 320, 322–323, 724,
  728, 745; her marriage to Raman
  Srivastav, 250; her beloved sons,
  Patrick and Bair, 250, 254, 281;
  her leadership in lobbying and
  congressional deliberation for
  Federal Marriage Amendment
  (2004–2006), 270–271, 278–279;
  founding NOM (2007), 368–369;
  her key role in securing funds for
  collecting signatures for Proposition
  8 to go on ballot (2008), 380, 392,
  394, 403, 411–412, 423, 427; her
  involvement in California's federal marriage equality litigation
  (2009–2010), 555, 558, 570
Gallo, Betty (Love Makes a Family),
  340–341, 343
Garcia, Violet, and Annice Joan
  Ritchie, 39, 53
Gardner, Harlan, 498–499, 647
Garlow, [Reverend] James (Jim), 379,
  384, 389
Garry, Joan (GLAAD), 457
Gates, Dr. Gary (Williams Institute),
  testimony in Michigan's marriage

equality trial (Feb. 2014), 557, 564,
  566; amicus brief in *Obergefell v.
  Hodges* (2015), 600
Gates, [Secretary of Defense] Robert,
  459
George, Robert (Princeton), and Cindy
  Schrom, 254–256, 258, 264–265,
  267, 278, 280, 368, 403–404,
  411–412, 428, 490–91, 567, 681,
  699, 717–718, 723; his theory
  of pluralist perfection, 255; his
  natural law justification for one-
  man, one-woman marriage as an
  "intrinsic good," 255–256, 264;
  his co-authorship of the Federal
  Marriage Amendment (1999–2001),
  258–259, 718; his role in creating the
  National Organization for Marriage
  (NOM), 280, 368; his participation
  in the California federal marriage
  litigation (2009–2010), 404, 411–412,
  428; his authorship and sponsorship of the ecumenical *Manhattan
  Declaration* (2008), 490–491; his
  pervasive role in the political as well
  as intellectual campaign against
  marriage equality, 255–256, 258,
  264–265, 278, 280, 490–491, 699
George, [California chief justice]
  Ronald (Ron), 153; decision halting
  Winter of Love (2004), 293–296,
  299; decision in *California Marriage Cases* (2008), 304, 306–307,
  411, 646
Gerhardstein, Alphonse (Al) and Mimi,
  133, 581–585, 592–596, 609; his
  challenge to Cincinnati's initiative
  repealing its anti-discrimination
  ordinance (1994–1997), 133, 581–582;
  his challenge to Ohio's refusal to
  include same-sex spouses on death
  certificates (Obergefell's case),

582–585, 593; his challenge to Ohio's refusal to include same-sex spouses on birth certificates, 583–585; his briefing and oral argument in the Sixth Circuit for *Obergefell v. Hodges* (2014), 585; his being the first to file a petition for Supreme Court review, 593; his participation in the Kentucky moot to determine who would argue question two in *Obergefell v. Hodges* (2015), 595–596

Gill, Nancy, and Marcelle LaTourneau, 523–526

Gill, Patrick, and Craig Dean, 77, 625. See also *Dean v. District of Columbia* (1995)

Gill, Thomas, 95–96

Gill, Tim, 230, 280, 327–331, 337, 361–362, 399, 439; the organizer and funder for resetting marriage equality strategy after disastrous 2004 elections, 230, 280, 327–331, 361–362, 439; his rebuke to Dustin Lance Black at Outgiving (2009), 399

Gingrich, Candace, 110

Gingrich, [House Speaker] Newt and Callista (now Ambassador to the Holy See), 110, 118, 122, 135, 246, 549, 677; his role in passing DOMA (1996), 135, 549

Ginsburg, [Justice] Ruth Bader, and Martin (Marty) Ginsburg, 131, 267–268, 429, 531–541, 576–577, 593, 604–613, 688, 702–715, 722, 734, 738, 744, 746; her early family life, with daughter Jane, 702–703, 707; professional discrimination against her by law schools and law firms, 703–706; her appointments at Rutgers Law and Columbia Law, 704–706; her work for the ACLU's Women's Rights Project (1971–1979),

708; her pioneering advocacy for heightened equal protection scrutiny for sex-based classifications, 707–709; her participation in *Romer v. Evans* (1996), 131; her participation in *Lawrence v. Texas* (2003), 267–268; her strong skepticism regarding DOMA in *United States v. Windsor* (2013), 538–539; her persuading Justice Kennedy to add significant equal protection analysis to his majority opinion in *Obergefell v. Hodges* (2015), 611–613, 744; consequences of her liberal feminist stance for family law, 709, 722

Girgis, Sherif (Yale Law), 567

Giske, Emily, 437–438, 442, 445

Glendon, Mary Ann (Harvard Law), 233, 258, 262, 271; as drafter of the Federal Marriage Amendment, 258, 262

Glick, [New York assembly member] Deborah, 431–442; successful co-sponsor of New York's Sexual Orientation Non-Discrimination Act (2002), 432–433; co-sponsor of marriage equality bills in New York Assembly (2007–2011), 435–436, 441–442

Goldberg, [California assembly member] Jackie, and Sharon Stricker, 147–148, 163–170, 283, 288; as host for dinners by the California Legislature's Lesbian and Gay Caucus (2000–2004), 147; as primary sponsor of Comprehensive Domestic Partnership Act (2003), 166–170; her marriage during the Winter of Love (2004), 288

Goldberg, Suzanne (Lambda Legal, now Columbia Law), 78, 126; as partner with Paula Ettelbrick, 78; co-counsel in *Romer v. Evans* (1996), 126

Kagan, [Solicitor General, then Justice]
Elena, 458, 461, 464, 531, 537–541,
576, 593, 606–607, 612; her
participation in oral argument
and conference in *United States v.
Windsor* (2013), 429; her participation in oral argument and conference in *Obergefell v. Hodges* (2015),
593; her performance of a same-sex
marriage before *Obergefell*, 612
Kameny, Dr. Franklin (Mattachine
Society of Washington), 9, 11, 29,
623–625–630, 640–642, 646, 649,
658–659, 709; his early life, military
service, and higher education, 623;
his loss of federal employment
because of his homosexuality, 623;
his landmark litigation and Supreme
Court petition, demanding an end
to gay people's "second-class citizenship" (1960), 623, 640; his insistence
that gay is good, 9, 624, 628–629; his
counsel to Jack Baker and Mike
McConnell, 9, 29; his support for
marriage equality, 29, 624; his
sacrifices for the gay rights movement, 658; his aversion to "odious
conformity," 626
Kane, [Pennsylvania attorney general]
Kathleen, 560
Kane, Stanley, 15
Kaplan, David, 17, 527
Karger, Fred, 393
Karlan, Pamela (Stanford Law), 532, 614
Kasper, [Archbishop] Walter, 674
Katulski, Davina (MECA), 160, 285
Katyal, [Acting Solicitor General] Neal,
471, 473; his adherence to the
executive branch's duty to defend
federal statutes, 473
Katyal, Sonia (Berkeley Law), 651

Katz, Herman, 42
Katz, [Connecticut justice] Joette, 347
Katz, [California assembly member]
Richard, 154
Kawa, Steve, and Dan Henkle, 284,
287–288
Kaye, [New York chief judge] Judith, 72,
316, 325, 411, 431–432, 450–452, 721;
her role in *Braschi* (1989), 72–73, 433;
her landmark opinion for *In re Jacob*
(1995), 721; her famous dissenting
opinion in *Hernandez v. Robles*
(2006), 325, 431–433, 452; her delight
with the New York marriage law, 452
Keeley, [California assembly member]
Fred, 166; sponsor of California civil
unions bill in 2002 (AB 2216), 166
Kehoe, [California assembly member]
Christine, 148, 168
Keisling, Mara (National Center for
Transgender Equality), 426
Kelly, [Minnesota justice] L. Fallon, 16
Kelly, [Judge] Paul, 572
Kendell, Kate (NCLR), and Sandy
Holmes, 76, 148, 163, 170, 282,
284–285, 295, 297, 304, 310, 372–373,
429, 630; originally a marriage
skeptic, 76; her role in the Proposi-
tion 22 campaign (2000), 163, 170;
adviser to Mayor Newsom during
Winter of Love (2004), 284–285;
participation in the California
marriage litigation (2004–2008),
295, 297; her central role in the
Proposition 8 campaign (2008),
372–373
Kennard, [California justice] Joyce,
294–295, 304, 306–307
Kennedy, [Justice] Anthony (Tony) and
Mary, 52, 129–131, 266–268, 396,
399, 405, 421, 429, 514, 521, 523,

Hawai'i marriage equality case (1993–1999), 77–78, 90, 97, 100–101, 103, 108; primary organizer of the National Freedom to Marry Coalition (1995), 111–112; his claim that the full faith and credit clause would require all states to recognize valid same-sex marriages (1994–1996), 117–119, 125, 135; founder of Freedom to Marry (2003), 336; participant in the "Winning Marriage" meetings (2005), 337–338, 342–344; role of Freedom to Marry 2.0 in the New York marriage law (2011), 487; in President Obama's coming out of the closet in favor of marriage equality (2012), 456; and in the 2012 ballot campaigns, 493, 512; "losing forward" as a strategy for a despised minority, 629–630. *See also* Freedom to Marry

Wood, James, 21

Woodall, Jim (CWA), 110, 119

Woods, Bill, 83, 96

Woodward, Virginia, and Sheila Sernovitz (now Sheila and Virginia Burgos-Law), 52

Yanta, Kalley King: *Minnesota Marriage Minutes*, 502

Yogman, Judith (Office of Massachusetts Attorney General), 221–222

Yorksmith, Pam and Nicole, 584–585

Yoshino, Kenji (NYU Law), 410

Young, Barbara and Steve, 383, 390, 679; internal critics of the role of the Church of Jesus Christ in the Proposition 8 campaign (2008–2009), 383, 390; supporters of Affirmation (organization for Latter-gay Saints), 679

Young, [Vermont representative] Jeff, 352–353

Young, Katherine (Magill University), 408–410; brutal deposition examination by David Boies (2009), 408, 410, 423; her reasons for declining to testify at the 8 trial (2010), 409–410

Ysunza, Larry, and Timothy (Tim) Love, 584

Zablocki, [Milwaukee county clerk] Thomas, 21–22

Zamora, David, and Dave McCord, 35, 37, 53–54

Zarella, [Connecticut justice] Peter, 347–348

Zarrillo, Jeff, and Paul Katami, 400, 413

Zepatos, Thalia (Task Force, then Freedom to Marry), 482–486, 488, 492–494, 496–498, 500, 512

Zuckerman, [Vermont representative] David, 351, 353

INDEX OF SUBJECTS

Cross-references to names refer to the Index of Names.

tion as a primary argument against marriage equality, 99–100, 251–253, 261–262, 271, 323–324. *See also* Women's social status and economic opportunities

Democratic legitimacy, 606–608, 613, 616–617, 619–620, 704; justification for strong judicial deference to legislative and popular line-drawing in statutes and initiatives, 619; less applicable when statutes and initiatives rely on "suspect" classifications such as race and sex or exclude minorities from "fundamental" rights such as voting and marriage, 617, 620; as the central argument made by counsel for the states in *Obergefell v. Hodges* (2015), 606–608, 613, 616

"Democrats: Say I Do" (2012), 478

Demographic history of the American family, 44–45, 57–59, 60–62, 71–72, 99–100; long-term decline in marriage rates, rise in age of marriage, and decline in the size of marital households, 99, 261–262, 713–715; and effects of women's greater social and economic power, 99, 713–715

Department of Justice, 124–125, 133, 460–461, 463–467, 470–475, 526–527, 545–546; its evaluation of proposed defense of marriage legislation (1996), 124–125, 133; its ever-narrowing arguments in support of DOMA (2009–2011), 460–461, 463–465, 471–472; its internal debate whether to continue defending DOMA (2009–2011), 461, 463, 464–467, 470–474; its conclusion that DOMA was uncon-

stitutional (2011), 474–475, 526–527. *See also* Civil Division; Civil Rights Division; Office of Legal Counsel; Office of the Solicitor General

Designated beneficiaries, 71, 196, 326–333, 719–720, 731–733, 745–746, 776–777; as an example of responsible partnering apart from marriage, 326–333; annual numbers for registrants (2009–2017), 732–733, 776–777; as an item on the menu of relationship options in Colorado, 719, 731–732. *See also* Colorado's Designated Beneficiaries Agreements Act

Dewey Square, 372, 377, 484; its flawed strategy for defeating California's Proposition 8 (2008), 372, 377

Dignity, 46, 130, 181, 186, 197, 223, 268, 362, 464, 507, 542–543, 586, 611–614, 617–618, 624, 674, 676, 690–691, 746; relevance to Kennedy's majority opinions in *Lawrence* (2003), 265–266; *Windsor* (2013), 542–543; and *Obergefell* (2015), 611–614; and pushback from Justice Thomas, 617–618

Direct democracy. *See* Initiatives; Referenda

District of Columbia's early marriage bill (1975), and fears raised by churches that bill would allow same-sex marriages, 40–41; sponsor's amendment to clarify marriage bill as leaving traditional definition intact, 41

District of Columbia's Health Benefits Expansion Act (1992), recognizing domestic partnerships, 70, 118; amended to expand domestic partnerships, including different-sex

of statewide domestic partnerships in Maryland (2012) and New Jersey (2007, 2013) and their post-marriage equality expansion in California (2019), 732

Domestic partnership statewide statutes, with comprehensive coverage similar to civil unions, 304; California (2003), 304; expanded to include all couples (2019), 732; Washington (2009), 334; Nevada (2009), 546

Domestic partnership status, as an alternative to marriage, 68, 157, 309; or an item in the menu of relationship options offered by some states, 718–720; and religion-based objections, 152, 170, 185–186

"Domestic unit," 189, 197

Don't Ask, Don't Tell, an updated version of the traditional exclusion of lesbian, gay, and bisexual persons from the armed forces, 109, 461; its statutory codification (1993), 550; the process for its repeal (2009–2011), 469, 476, 503

Don't Ask, Don't Tell Repeal Act of 2010, P.L. 111–321, 124 Stat. 3515 (Dec. 22, 2010), 469

Don't Defend, Do Enforce, where the executive continues to apply a statutory exclusion that it declines to defend in court, 466, 541; Dawn Johnsen's proposed application to statutory HIV exclusion (1995), 466; revival of Johnsen idea by OLC and White House Counsel during the DOMA deliberations (2010–2011), 473; Department of Justice's decision not to defend DOMA in *Windsor* and other cases (2011), 474

Doyle v. Secretary of the Commonwealth, 858 N.E.2d 1090 (Mass. 2006), 242

Drake Law School, 311–312. See also *Changing Perspectives of the Family* (1994)

"Dream Team" for marriage equality in California, 2004–2008 (Allred, Codell, Coles, Davidson, Minter, Stewart, Pizer), 296

Dred Scott v. Sandford, 60 U.S. 393, 409 (1957), 29, 229, 415–416, 610, 617; example of judicial activism allegedly similar to judicially-imposed marriage equality, 229, 610, 617; close connection between citizenship and the right to marry, 415–416; and duty to serve in the armed forces, 470; early exemplar of "originalist" jurisprudence, 610, 617

Dudgeon v. United Kingdom, No. 7525/76 (Eur. Ct. Hum. Rts. Oct. 22, 1981), 266

Duty to defend statutory policies even when an administration believes them misguided, 465–467, 471–473; as applied to title III of the Voting Rights Act (1969–1970), 465–467; as applied to DOMA (2010–2011), 466–467; exception for statutes that attack executive authority, 466; exception for statutes for which there is no plausible constitutional defense, 472; "John Roberts" exception for statutory affirmative action, 466; "Dawn Johnsen" exception for exclusionary statutes motivated by animus or denial of citizenship for a minority, 466

Eagle Forum, 120, 695
East Lake Church, 667, 671
Ebell theatre, Los Angeles, 427

Hollingsworth v. Perry, 570 U.S. 693
(2013), 531, 535–537; narrow conference vote to take the case for review
(only four votes were needed), 429;
Dellinger-Gornstein-Lederman
amicus brief, 536–538; oral argument and conference among the
justices (March 2013), 535–537;
Supreme Court's opinion, dismissing the appeal for lack of standing,
536; dissenting opinion, 537; missed
opportunity to address the merits of
the Fourteenth Amendment
marriage equality claim, 549
Home Invasion (campaign ad, 2008),
679
"Homosexual agenda," 269
"Homosexual and Lesbian Marriage"
(HLM), an older Latter-day Saints'
term for same-sex marriage (1980s,
1990s), 92, 94, 313
"The Homosexual Couple," *Look*
(Jan. 26, 1971), by Jack Star, 16
Homosexuality, negative references:
as an abomination contrary to the
Word of the Lord and/or to nature,
40, 48, 117, 164, 189; as a reversion
to animalistic state, e.g., homosexuals as "wolves" and "baboons," 50;
as morally depraved, 147; and
"perverted," 20, 384; as selfish
and anti-family, 50, 392; as a mental
illness, 28, 50; as psychopathic,
622; as contagious, 56, 639; as an
objective moral disorder, 45; as
"weird," 107; as similar to alcoholism, 110; as virtually normal, 109;
as an unfortunate condition that
might be tolerated but not encouraged, 622
Homosexuality, positive references: as
a natural variation in human

sexuality, 252; as good, 9, 214, 624;
as pro-family, 59, 179, 214, 711–713
*Hosanna-Tabor Evangelical Lutheran
Church & School v. EEOC*, 565 U.S.
171 (2012), 685
Howard Law School, 704
*How Different Are the Adult Children of
Parents Who Have Same-Sex
Relationships? Findings from the New
Family Structures Study*, 41 Soc. Sci.
Res. 752–770 (July 2012), by Mark
Regnerus, with responses and
Rengerus's reply in Nov. 2012,
556–558. *See also* New Family
Structures Study
*(How) Does the Sexual Orientation of
Parents Matter?*, 66 Am. Soc. Rev.
159 (2001), by Judith Stacey and
Timothy Biblarz, 319
Human Rights Campaign (HRC), 90,
118, 273, 337, 366, 378, 435, 437,
444–445, 464, 488, 492–497, 507,
521, 681, 699; its leadership in
Hawai'i marriage referendum, 90;
its opposition to DOMA (1996), 118;
support for San Francisco's implementation of its Equal Benefits
Ordinance, 152–153; proliferation of
corporate domestic partnership
benefits, 153; Work Net plus Workplace Equality Scores, 153; opposition
to Federal Marriage Amendment,
276; its involvement in "Winning
Marriage" deliberations (2005), 338;
its grassroots campaign for marriage
equality bills in New York's legislature (2009 and 2011), 435, 437; its
support for heightened scrutiny for
sexual orientation exclusions during
Obama Administration, 464;
its participation in 2012 ballot
campaigns, especially Washington,

Sliding scale scrutiny under state and federal equal protection clauses and considering (1) the fishiness of the exclusionary classification, (2) the importance of the rights denied the excluded class, and (3) the weightiness of the state's interest in exclusion, 183, 217; Chief Justice Amestoy's majority opinion in *Baker v. State* (1999), 183; Chief Justice Marshall's plurality opinion in *Goodridge v. Department of Social Services* (2003), 224; Justice Kennedy's majority opinions in *Lawrence v. Texas* (2003), 267–268; and *United States v. Windsor* (2013), 542

"Smeltdown" (June 2009), ferocious reaction by gay bloggers and lawyers to the Obama administration's initial motion to dismiss, 460; as a turning point in the Obama Administration's attention to the marriage equality issue (summer 2009), 460

Smelt v. United States, Case No. SACV 09–00286 DOC (MLGx) (C.D. Cal. Aug. 24, 2009), 2009 WL 10674308, 460; government's motion to dismiss and the firestorm resulting from it, 460; Roosevelt Room meeting to reset the administration's DOMA defense, 462; government's reply brief and court's order dismissing complaint, 463

Social movements and what they might learn from the success of marriage equality: role played by good fortune, 626; convergence with the social movement's goal and the drift of society, 626; the beneficiaries as a dispersed minority coming out and self-identifying, 625; demonstration that rights and benefits of the minority will not hurt third parties or the common good, 625–626; the need for massive funding deployed in support of a well-organized campaign, 626

Social science evidence that sexual orientation of parents generates "no differences" in life outcomes for their children, 218, 222, 317, 554; accepted by leading associations of experts, 317; criticized for lack of random samples, 316, 555, 570; for relying on small volunteer subjects, for relying on subjective criteria and self-reporting by parents, 316–317; defended against foregoing criticisms, 317, 554; accepted after full trial on the merits in *DeBoer v. Snyder* (2014), 571

Social Security Act of 1935 (as amended), 517, 642

Sodom and Gomorrah (Genesis 19:1–29), 43

SOGI (Sexual Orientation, Gender Identity) anti-discrimination laws, 646, 693; Utah SOGI law (2015), 694

Solicitor General of the United States, and issues raised by constitutional marriage equality federal and state constitutional litigation, 464–466, 605; "Sarah Palin" argument against abandoning the department's defense of DOMA, (2010–2011), 466–471; briefing and oral argument in *United States v. Windsor* (2013), 537; and *Hollingsworth* (2013), 534; "eight-state solution" offered